Edition 5

Essentials of Entrepreneurship and Small Business Management

Thomas W. Zimmerer
St. Leo University

Norman M. Scarborough
Presbyterian College

with Doug Wilson
University of Oregon

PEARSON
Prentice
Hall

Upper Saddle River, New Jersey 07458

Library of Congress Cataloging-in-Publication Data

Zimmerer, Thomas.
    Essentials of entrepreneurship and small business management / Thomas W. Zimmerer,
Norman M. Scarborough, Doug Wilson.— 5th ed.
        p. cm.
    Includes bibliographical references and index.
    ISBN-13: 978-0-13-229438-6
    ISBN-10: 0-13-229438-9
    1. Small business—Management. 2. New business enterprises—Management.
    I. Scarborough, Norman M. II. Wilson, Doug. III. Title.
    HD62.7.Z55 2007
    658.02′2—dc22   2006102375

Acquisitions Editor: Jon Axelrod
Editor-in-Chief: David Parker
VP/Editorial Director: Jeff Shelstad
Product Development Manager:
Ashley Santora
Project Manager: Claudia Fernandes
Editorial Assistant: Kristen Varina
Media Project Manager: Ashley Lulling
Marketing Manager: Anne Howard
Marketing Assistant: Susan Osterlitz
Associate Director, Production Editorial:
Judy Leale
Managing Editor: Renata Butera
Production Editor: Kelly Warsak
Permissions Coordinator: Charles Morris
Associate Director, Manufacturing:
Vinnie Scelta
Manufacturing Buyer: Michelle Klein
Design/Composition Manager:
Christy Mahon
Composition Liaison: Suzanne Duda

Art Director: Janet Slowik
Interior Design: Karen Quigley
Cover Design: Karen Quigley
Cover Photo: Ingram Publishing/Getty
Images
Illustration (Interior): ElectraGraphics, Inc.
Director, Image Resource Center:
Melinda Patelli
Manager, Rights and Permissions: Zina Arabia
Manager, Visual Research: Beth Brenzel
Manager, Cover Visual Research &
Permissions: Karen Sanatar
Image Permission Coordinator:
Kathy Gavilanes
Photo Researcher: Sheila Norman
Composition: Techbooks
Full-Service Project Management:
Penny Walker/Techbooks
Printer/Binder: Courier/Kendallville
Cover Printer: Phoenix Color Corp.
Typeface: 10/12 Times

Credits and acknowledgments borrowed from other sources and reproduced, with permission, in this textbook appear on appropriate page within text.

Pearson Education LTD.
Pearson Education Singapore, Pte. Ltd
Pearson Education, Canada, Ltd
Pearson Education–Japan

Pearson Education Australia PTY, Limited
Pearson Education North Asia Ltd
Pearson Educación de Mexico, S.A. de C.V.
Pearson Education Malaysia, Pte. Ltd.

10 9 8 7 6 5 4 3
ISBN-13: 978-0-13-229438-6
ISBN-10: 0-13-229438-9

To Cindy, whose patience is always tested during a writing project of this magnitude. Your love, support, and understanding are a vital part of every book.
You are the love of my life.

—NM

To Linda, whose unconditional love motivates me to strive daily to earn her respect. Her commitment to our life makes all things possible.

—TW

To Judy, whose love and support was an essential part of this work. I am so thankful to be on life's journey with you.

—DL

"May your own dreams be your only boundaries."
—The Reverend Purlie Victorious Judson, in "Purlie,"
Broadway Theater, 1970

Brief Contents

Contents

SECTION IV   Putting the Business Plan to Work: Sources of Funds   462

Chapter 13   Sources of Financing: Debt and Equity   462

Chapter 14   Choosing the Right Location and Layout   514

Chapter 15   Global Aspects of Entrepreneurship   559

Chapter 16   Building a New Venture Team and Planning for the Next Generation   596

Preface

Entrepreneurship has become a major force in the global economy. Policy makers across the world are discovering that economic growth and prosperity lie in the hands of entrepreneurs—those dynamic, driven men and women who are committed to achieving success by creating and marketing innovative, customer-focused new products and services. Not only are these entrepreneurs creating economic prosperity, but many of them are also striving to make the world a better place in which to live. Those who possess this spirit of entrepreneurial leadership will continue to lead the economic revolution that has proved time and again its ability to raise the standard of living for people everywhere. We hope that you will join this economic revolution to bring about lasting, positive changes in your community and around the world. If you are interested in launching a business of your own, *Essentials of Entrepreneurship and Small Business Management* is the book for you.

This fifth edition of *Essentials of Entrepreneurship and Small Business Management* introduces you to the process of creating a new venture and provides you with the knowledge you need to launch your business so that it has the greatest chance for success. One of the hallmarks of every edition of this book has been a very practical, "hands-on" approach to entrepreneurship. We strive to equip you with the tools you will need for entrepreneurial success. With the help of this textbook and your instructor, we hope that you will follow your dream of becoming a successful entrepreneur.

Key Text Features

- To emphasize the practical nature of this book, we have added a new feature, "Hands on…How to," which selects a concept from each chapter and explains how students can put it to practice in their own companies. These features include such topics as how to "Transform Your Great Business Idea into Reality," "Create a Culture of Innovation," "Provide Superior Customer Service," "Calculate Your Company's Pocket Price Band," and many others.
- We have included in this edition 11 brief cases that cover a variety of topics (see the Case Matrix that appears on the inside cover). All of the cases are about small companies, and most are companies that students can research online. These cases challenge students to think critically about a variety of topics that are covered in the text—from developing a business strategy and building a brand to protecting intellectual property and financing a business—and are ideal for either individual or group assignments.
- This edition features an updated, attractive, full-color design and a layout that includes an in-margin glossary and learning objectives and is designed to be user-friendly. Each chapter begins with learning objectives, which are repeated as in-margin markers within the chapter to guide students as they study.
- This edition once again emphasizes the importance of creating a business plan for a successful new venture. Sections II and III of this edition focus on "Building the Business Plan" and Section IV covers "Putting the Business Plan to Work."
- Chapter 2, "Inside the Entrepreneurial Mind: From Ideas to Reality," explains the creative process entrepreneurs use to generate business ideas and to recognize entrepreneurial opportunities. Students learn to think like entrepreneurs.
- Chapter 4, "Conducting a Feasibility Analysis and Crafting a Winning Business Plan," now includes a section on screening entrepreneurs' potential ideas using a feasibility analysis. Instructors also can choose to bundle Prentice Hall's Business Feasibility Analysis Pro or Palo Alto's Business Plan Pro software with this edition of *Essentials of Entrepreneurship and Small Business Management* at a special package price.
- This edition includes separate chapters on "Forms of Business Ownership" (Chapter 5) and "Franchising and the Entrepreneur" (Chapter 6).

- Chapter 9, "E-Commerce and the Entrepreneur," serves as a practical guide to using the Web to conduct business in the twenty-first century.
- Several "You Be the Consultant" features appear in every chapter. These popular features challenge students to apply what they've learned in the course. Each chapter contains at least two of these boxed illustrations, which are based on actual companies. Each one poses a problem or an opportunity and includes questions that focus students' attention on key issues and helps them to hone their analytical and critical thinking skills. These "You Be the Consultant" illustrations are ideal for short individual or group assignments or for launching lively class discussions. Featured companies include Under Armour (Chapter 3), Cirque du Soleil (Chapter 4), NetFlix (Chapter 8), Magnetech Industrial Services (Chapter 16), and many others.
- We have added several "Ethics and Entrepreneurship" features that give students the opportunity to wrestle with some of the ethical dilemmas that entrepreneurs face in business. Encouraging them to think about and discuss these issues now will prepare them for making the right decisions later.
- Many real-world examples are presented that are easy to spot because they are set off in italics with in-margin markers. These examples allow students to see how entrepreneurs are putting into practice the concepts that they are learning about in the book and in class. These examples help students to remember key concepts in the course.
- A sample business plan for a fictitious business named Total Health and Fitness, a full-service health club and restaurant, is included both in the text and on the Companion Web site. Students also have access to other sample business plans at Palo Alto's Business Plan Pro Web site, http://www.paloalto.com/ps/bp/samples.cfm. Many courses in entrepreneurship and small business management require students to write business plans. Students of entrepreneurship find it helpful to have a model that guides them as they build their plans. This sample plan, created by a student, serves as one model.
- Business Plan Pro, the best-selling business planning software package from Palo Alto Software, is a valuable tool that helps students to build winning business plans for their entrepreneurial ideas. Every chapter contains an updated Business Plan Pro exercise that enables students to apply the knowledge they have gained from studying this book to build a business plan with Business Plan Pro. A brief user guide is available in the instructor's manual. (Business Plan Pro, ISBN 0-13-187484-5) Instructors also can choose to have Business Plan Pro bundled with the textbook at a special value price. They should contact their local Prentice Hall sales representative for more information.

Supplements

- A useful companion Web site, http://www.prenhall.com/scarborough, offers free access to learning resources including multiple-choice quizzes, Web essays, and links to relevant small business sites.
- There is a series of videos selected by one of the authors that is designed to illustrate the principles of entrepreneurship discussed in this book. These short videos are ideal for helping students to master the concepts in the textbook and for launching meaningful class discussions. The videos are available on DVD (ISBN 0-13-229442-7)
- There is a printed Instructor's Manual and Test Item File (ISBN 0-13-229439-7)
- The Instructor's Resource CD-ROM contains the Instructor's Manual, Test Item File, TestGen test-generating software, and PowerPoint slides (ISBN 0-13-229440-0)
- The Business Disc is a sophisticated experiential learning simulation that leads students through the steps of planning and managing a small business. Using video vignettes, students interact with scores of real people as they build and operate various kinds of business: service, retail, or manufacturing. The "Business Disc Exercises" in the Instructor's Manual enable students to link the chapter content to the Business Disc experience. (ISBN 0-13-229445-1)

- Instructor's resources are available at Prentice Hall's Instructor's Resource Center for *Essentials of Entrepreneurship and Small Business Management, 5/e,* which is found at http://www.prenhall.com/irc. Here instructors can access print, media, and presentation resources available with this book in downloadable, digital format. The Instructor's Resource Center Web site contains detailed descriptions of all of the foregoing supplements.
- SafariX eTextbooks Online, the largest eTextbook store on the Internet, offers students flexibility in their choice of textbook format. Developed for students seeking to save money on required or recommended textbooks, SafariX eTextbooks Online saves students up to 50% off the suggested list price of the print text. Students simply select their eText by title or author and purchase immediate access to the content for the duration of the course using any major credit card. With a SafariX eText, students can search for specific keywords or page numbers, make notes online, print out reading assignments that incorporate lecture notes, and bookmark important passages for later review. For more information, or to purchase a SafariX eTextbook, visit http://www.safarix.com.

Beyond the Textbook

The authors have used their combined 75 years of teaching experience (and their combined 57 years of experience writing textbooks) to produce a book that contains a multitude of both student- and instructor-friendly features. We trust that this edition of *Essentials of Entrepreneurship and Small Business Management* will help the next generation of entrepreneurs to reach their full potential and achieve their dreams of success as independent business owners. It is their dedication, perseverance, and creativity that keep the world's economy moving forward.

Acknowledgments

Working with every author team is a staff of professionals who work extremely hard to bring a book to life. They handle the thousands of details involved in transforming a rough manuscript into the finished product you see before you. Their contributions are immeasurable, and we appreciate all they do to make this book successful. We have been blessed to work with the following outstanding publishing professionals:

David Parker, editor-in-chief, whose wisdom and guidance throughout this project were invaluable. In many years in the publishing business, we have worked with many editors, and David is the best we have had the privilege to work with. We appreciate his creativity, integrity, honesty, and leadership.

Claudia Fernandes, our exceptionally capable project manager, who was always just an e-mail away when we needed her help with a seemingly endless number of details. She did a masterful job of coordinating the many aspects of this project.

Kelly Warsak, production editor, who skillfully guided the book through the long and sometimes difficult production process with a smile and a "can-do" attitude. She is always a pleasure to work with.

Sheila Norman, photo researcher, who took our ideas for photos and transformed them into meaningful images.

Philip Koplin, copy editor, whose linguistic polishing made the content of this edition flow smoothly.

Anne Howard, marketing manager, whose input helped focus this edition at an evolving market.

We also extend a big "Thank You" to the corps of Prentice Hall sales representatives, who work so hard to get our books into customers' hands and who represent the front line in our effort to serve out customers' needs. They are the unsung heroes of the publishing industry.

Special thanks to the following academic reviewers, whose ideas, suggestions, and thought-provoking input have helped to shape this and past editions of our two books *Essentials of Entrepreneurship and Small Business Management* and *Effective Small Business Management.* We always welcome feedback from our customers!

Bernard Zannini, Northern Essex Community College

Bruce Bachenheimer, Pace University

Thomas Schramko, University of Toledo

Ina Kay Van Loo, WVU Institute of Technology

Caroline E. W. Glackin, Delaware State University

Michael L. Menefee, Purdue University

Stephen O. Handley, University of Washington—Bothell

Terry J. Schindler, University of Indianapolis

Ethné Swartz, Fairleigh Dickinson University

Nancy Bowman, Baylor University

John deYoung, Cumberland Community College

Art Elkins, University of Massachusetts

W. Bruce Erickson, University of Minnesota

Gregory Worosz, Schoolcraft College

Annamary Allen, Broome Community College

Tom Bergman, Northeastern State University

Charles Hubbard, University of Arkansas

E. L. (Betty) Kinarski, Seattle University

Michael S. Broida, Miami University

Richard Cuba, University of Baltimore

Kathy J. Daruty, L.A. Pierce College

Stuart Devlin, New Mexico State University

George J. Foegen, Metropolitan State College of Denver

Martin K. Marsh, California State University–Bakersfield

Charles H. Matthews, University of Cincinnati

Louis D. Ponthieu, University of North Texas

Nick Sarantakes, Austin Community College

Barry L. Van Hook, Arizona State University

Bernard W. Weinrich, St. Louis Community College

Dick LaBarre, Ferris State University

Deborah Streeter, Cornell University

Jim Walker, Moorhead State University

Bill Snider, Cuesta College

Fred Hughes, Faulkner University

William Meyer, TRICOMP

Michael Dickson, Columbus State Community College

Kevin Banning, University of Florida

Paul Lamberson, Riverton, WY

R.D. Butler, Trenton State College

David O'Dell, McPherson State College

Donald Wilkinson, East Tennessee State University

Joseph Salamone, State University of New York at Buffalo

Milton Miller, Carteret Community College

Professor M. Ala, California State University–Los Angeles

Sol Ahiarah, Buffalo State College

John E. Butler, University of Washington

Mary Lou Lockerby, College of DuPage

Jan Feldbauer, Austin Community College

Gita DeSouza, Pennsylvania State University

Pamela Clark, Angelo State University

John Todd, University of Arkansas

Peter Mark Shaw, Tidewater Community College

John Phillips, University of San Francisco

Ralph Jagodka, Mt. San Antonio College

Marcella Norwood, University of Houston

Khaled Sartawi, Fort Valley State University

Lon Addams, Weber State University

John Moonen, Daytona Beach Community College

Jack Sheeks, Broward Community College

Linda Newell, Saddleback College

James Browne, University of Southern Colorado

John McMahon, Mississippi County Community College

Charles Toftoy, George Washington University

Ben Powell, University of Alabama

Kyoung-Nan Kwon, Michigan State University

Judy Dietert, Southwest Texas State University

Many thanks to Josh Sudbury for allowing us to use the plan he created for Total Health and Fitness as the sample business plan in this edition. Josh has what it takes to be a successful entrepreneur, and we appreciate his willingness to allow his plan to serve as a model for other entrepreneurs as they build their plans.

We also are grateful to our colleagues who support us in the sometimes grueling process of writing a book: Foard Tarbert, Sam Howell, Jerry Slice, Meredith Holder, Suzanne Smith, Jody Lipford, Rickey Madden, and Kristy Hill of Presbyterian College.

Finally, we thank Cindy Scarborough, Linda Zimmerer, and Judy Wilson for their love, support, and understanding while we worked many long hours to complete this book. For them, this project represents a labor of love.

Norman M. Scarborough
William H. Scott III Associate Professor of Information Science
Presbyterian College
Clinton, South Carolina
e-mail: nmscarb@presby.edu

Thomas W. Zimmerer
Professor of Management
Saint Leo University
St. Leo, Florida

Doug Wilson
Lundquist College of Business
University of Oregon
Eugene, Oregon
e-mail: douglw@uoregon.edu

The Challenge of
Entrepreneurship

1 | The Foundations of Entrepreneurship

Small opportunities are often
the beginning of great
enterprises. —Demosthenes

Pain is temporary; quitting
lasts forever. —Lance Howard

Learning Objectives

On completion of this chapter, you will be able to:

1 Define the role of the entrepreneur in business in the United States and across the world.
2 Describe the entrepreneurial profile and evaluate your potential as an entrepreneur.
3 Describe (A) the benefits and (B) the drawbacks of entrepreneurship.
4 Explain the forces that are driving the growth of entrepreneurship.
5 Explain the cultural diversity of entrepreneurship.
6 Describe the important role small businesses play in our nation's economy.
7 Describe the 10 deadly mistakes of entrepreneurship and how to avoid them.
8 Put failure into proper perspective.
9 Explain how an entrepreneur can avoid becoming another failure statistic.

LEARNING OBJECTIVES
1. Define the role of the entrepreneur in business in the United States and across the world.

The World of the Entrepreneur

Welcome to the world of the entrepreneur! Across the globe, growing numbers of people are realizing their dreams of owning and operating their own businesses. Although the level of entrepreneurial activity in the United States is down from record levels a few years ago, entrepreneurship continues to thrive in our nation. Every year, American entrepreneurs launch more than 850,000 new businesses, and the level of interest in pursuing entrepreneurship as a career remains high among people in all age groups.[1] Eighty-four percent of those who launch businesses are doing so for the first time.[2] This entrepreneurial spirit is the most significant economic development in recent business history. Around the globe, these heroes of the new economy are reshaping the business environment, creating a world in which their companies play an important role in the vitality of the global economy. With amazing vigor, their businesses have introduced innovative products and services, pushed back technological frontiers, created new jobs, opened foreign markets, and, in the process, provided their founders with the opportunity to do what they enjoy most.

Interest in entrepreneurship has never been higher. The future of entrepreneurial activity looks incredibly bright, given that the last two decades have seen record numbers of entrepreneurs launching businesses. Many of the world's largest companies continue to engage in massive downsizing campaigns, dramatically cutting the number of employees on their payrolls. This flurry of "pink slips" has spawned a new population of entrepreneurs: "castoffs" from large corporations (in which many of these individuals thought they would be lifetime ladder-climbers) with solid management experience and many productive years left before retirement. Small business researcher David Birch reports that over a recent five-year period, the largest companies in the United States shed 2 million jobs; during the same period, small businesses created 10 million jobs![3]

One casualty of this downsizing has been the long-standing notion of job security in large corporations. As a result, members of Generation X (people born between 1965 and 1981) and Generation Y (people born between 1982 and 1995) no longer see launching a business as being a risky career path. Having watched large companies lay off their parents after many years of service, these young people see entrepreneurship as the ideal way to create their own job security and success. They are eager to control their own destinies.

The downsizing trend among large companies has created a more significant philosophical change. It has ushered in an age in which "small is beautiful." Twenty-five years ago, competitive conditions favored large companies with their hierarchies and layers of management; today, with the pace of change constantly accelerating, fleet-footed, agile, small companies have the competitive advantage. These nimble competitors can dart into and out of niche markets as they emerge and recede; they can move faster to exploit market opportunities; and they can use modern technology to create within a matter of weeks or months products and services that once took years and all of the resources a giant corporation could muster. The balance has tipped in favor of small, entrepreneurial companies. Howard Stevenson, Harvard's chaired professor of entrepreneurship, says, "Why is it so easy [for small companies] to compete against giant corporations? Because while they [the giants] are studying the consequences, [entrepreneurs] are changing the world."[4]

One of the most comprehensive studies of global entrepreneurship, conducted by the Global Entrepreneurship Monitor (GEM), shows significant variation in the rate of new business formation among the nations of the world when measured by total entrepreneurial activity, or TEA (see Figure 1.1). The study found that 11.3 percent of the adult population in the United States—roughly one in nine people—is working to start a business. Nations in the Americas—North, South, and Latin—led the world in entrepreneurial activity, with Asian countries posting the lowest levels of entrepreneurship. The study also concluded that these different rates of entrepreneurial activity may account for as much as one-third of the variation in the rates of economic growth among these nations.[5] The GEM study also reports that globally men are twice as likely to start a business as women (although that trend is exactly the *opposite* in the United States), that the majority of

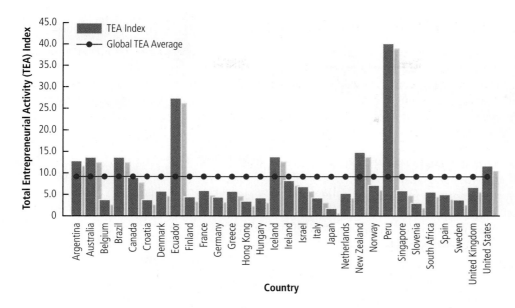

FIGURE 1.1

Entrepreneurial Activity across the Globe: Persons per 100 Adults Aged 18 to 64 Years Old Engaged in Entrepreneurial Activity

Source: 2004 Global Entrepreneurship Monitor Executive Report, http://www.gemconsortium.org/download/1123522826468/GEM_2004_Exec_Report.pdf. p.17.

entrepreneurs turn to family members and informal investors for external capital, and that nearly one-third of global entrepreneurs are between the ages of 25 and 44 years.[6]

The United States and many other nations are benefiting from this surge in global entrepreneurial activity. Eastern European countries, China, Vietnam, and many other nations whose economies were state controlled and centrally planned are now fertile ground for growing small businesses. Even in Japan, where the total entrepreneurial activity index is a meager 1.5, entrepreneurs are hard at work.

Risa Koyanagi

For instance, Risa Koyanagi convinced the president of a clothing company in Harajuku, Tokyo, one of Japan's most important fashion centers, to invest $25,000 so she could launch her own clothing line, which specializes in sporty, somewhat revealing garments for petite women. (Koyanagi is 5 feet, 1 inch tall and weighs 92 pounds.) To create buzz for her new company, Koyanagi convinced some well-connected friends to give some of her designs to Japanese pop stars such as Ayumi Hamazaki, and soon Koyanagi's clothes, which range in price from $35 to $400, were adorning celebrities appearing in newspapers and on television. Koyanagi's company, which she says is growing at "well over 100 percent a year," generates annual sales of more than $6 million and is quite profitable. Perhaps the most significant indication of her company's success is the fact that other design companies, including a few large ones, have begun knocking off some of Koyanagi's designs. She says her next move will be to expand her designs into accessories such as shoes and jewelry, and she plans to begin selling her line in the United States.[7]

Wherever they may choose to launch their companies, these business builders continue to embark on one of the most exhilarating—and one of the most frightening—adventures ever known: launching a business. It's never easy, but it can be incredibly rewarding, both financially and emotionally. It can be both thrilling and dangerous, like living life without a safety net. Still, true entrepreneurs see owning a business as the real measure of success. Indeed, entrepreneurship often provides the only avenue for success to those who otherwise might have been denied the opportunity.

Who are these entrepreneurs, and what drives them to work so hard with no guarantee of success? What forces lead them to risk so much and to make so many sacrifices in an attempt to achieve an ideal? Why are they willing to give up the security of a steady paycheck working for someone else to become the last person to be paid in their own companies? This chapter will examine the entrepreneur, the driving force behind the American economy.

From Entrepreneur to Celebrity and from Celebrity to Entrepreneur

Pimp My Ride

At age 14, Ryan Friedlinghaus became enamored with the custom car show circuit and was soon customizing cars that were so good that they appeared on numerous magazine covers. To achieve the custom looks he wanted in the cars he worked on, however, he had to deal with a multitude of specialty shops for parts and services. One day, he vowed, he would start his own total-service customizing shop that offered all components in-house. In 1994, Friedlinghaus, just 20 years old, borrowed $5,000 from his grandfather to start West Coast Customs (WCC), a groundbreaking company in the customizing business. WCC's creative designs often are a pleasant surprise for car owners, who range from young adults with modest budgets to high-end clients that include a who's who list of athletes and movie stars. Friedlinghaus and WCC are stars in their own right, best known as the magicians behind MTV's hit show *Pimp My Ride*, which transforms clunker cars into one-of-a-kind show-stoppers. Because of the celebrity status the show has given Friedlinghaus and his company of automotive artists, WCC's calendar is booked months in advance. "There are no limits to what we can do," he says. "We like challenges."

P. Did It

Sean Combs was born in Harlem and was raised by his mother after his father was murdered when Sean was just two years old. Better known by his nickname, P. Diddy, Combs went on to become a successful rap star and actor. Today, Combs is an entrepreneur who heads Bad Boy Worldwide, a conglomerate that generates $300 million a year in sales from a record label, restaurants, a marketing company, and the Sean John clothing line, for which he recently won the Best Menswear Designer Award (the fashion industry's equivalent of an Oscar). Not just another star who licensed his name for a line of clothing, Combs recently opened a Sean John boutique on toney Fifth Avenue in New York City. Combs is very much a "hands-on" business owner, even spending some time teaching Bad Boy's summer interns himself. Combs also makes sure his company lives up to its social responsibility. He has given generous gifts to his alma mater, Howard University, and to numerous charities, including one he established called Daddy's House Social Programs. Recently, Combs ran in the New York City Marathon to raise $4 million for New York City public schools.

From Sit-Com to Entrepreneur

Many people remember Suzanne Somers as Chrissy, the ditzy blonde on the 1980's sit-com *Three's Company*, but there is much more to this former television star, who now manages her own company, ELO Somers Licensing (ELO stands for her business philosophy: Extraordinarily Low Overhead). From ELO's headquarters in Calabasas, California, Somers sells clothing, jewelry, skin-care products, diet food, fitness equipment, and others—300 different products in all—mostly through the Home Shopping Network (HSN). In fact, Somers' has sold more than $30 million of her Trilliant bracelet, making it the best-selling piece of jewelry in the history of the HSN. In the last three years, ELO's revenues have grown 100 percent a year thanks to Somers' sincerity and openness as she talks about the challenges she has faced in life and how she uses the products she sells. "She's able to talk to people about how life isn't perfect," says Marty Mealon, president of HSN US. One of her company's most successful products is the Thighmaster, which Somers created as a way to keep her legs in shape. "Ten million Thighmasters later," she quips, "mine turned out to be a good idea." These days, Somers stays busy writing books (11 so far with contracts for 7 more), but she is always looking for new ideas. She is trying to sell her husband and business partner, Alan Hamel, on the concept of Somersize Cafés, a chain of restaurants that will serve healthy meals. "My husband rolls his eyes," she laughs, "but I've got to make this happen."

Newman's Own

In 1982, movie star Paul Newman and writer A. E. Hotchner decided to launch a business and donate 100 percent of its after-tax profits to charities. The result was Newman's Own, a business that began by selling salad dressings and has expanded into steak sauces, beverages, salsa, pasta sauces, and popcorn. (The popcorn took two years and 70 different blends to perfect.) Not only have Newman and Hotchner had a great deal of fun running the company, but they also have made a difference in the lives of many people. Since the company's beginning, Newman's Own has donated more than $150 million to thousands of worthy charities that operate on low overhead.

From Supermodel to Entrepreneur

Former supermodel Kathy Ireland once made her living by selling her good looks. Her photo appeared in 13 issues of the famous *Sports Illustrated* swimsuit edition. The typical supermodel's career is quite short, however. What's a supermodel to do when the cameras stop clicking? For Ireland, the answer was "launch my own business," Kathy Ireland Worldwide, a company that brings in more than $1 billion in sales of clothing and home furnishings, much of it for K-Mart. "When I was modeling," says Ireland, "I would always look at the client and think, 'That's what I want to do.' I wanted to be the client." She started realizing that dream in 1993 when she put her name on a line of socks. K-Mart decided to market them and eventually sold 1 million

pairs! Today, Ireland is the CEO and chief designer of her 37-person company, yet she devotes time to raising her three children, helping several charities, teaching Sunday school, and writing books, including *Powerful Inspirations*, now in its third printing. Because she is a busy working mother, many of Ireland's designs are aimed at other busy moms, and the products have proved to be very successful. Building a brand "requires infrastructure, leadership, and a strong, committed sales and distribution force," she says. "We've built our brand from the ground up."

1. In addition to the normal obstacles of starting a business, what barriers do celebrity entrepreneurs face?
2. What advantages do celebrity entrepreneurs have when launching a business?
3. Use the Internet to research other celebrities who have become entrepreneurs or entrepreneurs who have become celebrities and prepare a one-page report on his or her entrepreneurial story.

Sources: April Y. Pennington, "Custom Made," *Entrepreneur*, July 2005, p. 37; Elyssa Lee and Rob Turner, "Celebrity Entrepreneurs," *Inc.*, December 2004, pp. 70–81; Julia Boorstin, "For Suzanne Somers, the Thigh's Not the Limit," *Fortune*, June 14, 2004, p. 44; Kiri Blakeley, "The Model Mogul," *Forbes*, July 5, 2004, p. 116.

What Is an Entrepreneur?

LEARNING OBJECTIVES
2. Describe the entrepreneurial profile and evaluate your potential as an entrepreneur.

An **entrepreneur** is one who creates a new business in the face of risk and uncertainty for the purpose of achieving profit and growth by identifying significant opportunities and assembling the necessary resources to capitalize on them. Although many people come up with great business ideas, most of them never act on their ideas. Entrepreneurs do. The process of creative destruction, in which entrepreneurs create new ideas and new businesses that make existing ones obsolete, is a sign of a vibrant economy. Although this constant churn of businesses—some rising, others sinking, and many failing—concerns some people, in reality it is an indication of a healthy, growing, economic system that is creating new and better ways of serving people's needs and improving their quality of life and standard of living.

entrepreneur
one who creates a new business in the face of risk and uncertainty for the purpose of achieving profit and growth by identifying significant opportunities and assembling the necessary resources to capitalize on them.

Researchers have invested a great deal of time and effort over the last few decades trying to paint a clear picture of "the entrepreneurial personality." Although these studies have identified several characteristics entrepreneurs tend to exhibit, none of them has isolated a set of traits required for success. We now turn to a brief summary of the entrepreneurial profile.[8]

1. ***Desire for responsibility.*** Entrepreneurs feel a deep sense of personal responsibility for the outcome of ventures they start. They prefer to be in control of their resources, and they use those resources to achieve self-determined goals.
2. ***Preference for moderate risk.*** Entrepreneurs are not wild risk takers but are instead calculating risk takers. A study of the founders of the businesses listed as *Inc.* magazine's fastest-growing companies found no correlation between risk tolerance and entrepreneurship. "The belief that entrepreneurs are big risk takers just isn't true,"

says researcher and former *Inc.* 500 CEO Keith McFarland.[9] Unlike "high-rolling, riverboat" gamblers, entrepreneurs rarely gamble. Their goals may appear to be high—even impossible—in others' eyes, but entrepreneurs see the situation from a different perspective and believe that their goals are realistic and attainable. They usually spot opportunities in areas that reflect their knowledge, backgrounds, and experiences, which increases their probability of success. One writer observes

> Entrepreneurship is not the same thing as throwing darts and hoping for the best. It is about planning and taking calculated risks based upon knowledge of the market, the available resources or products, and a predetermined measure of the potential for success.[10]

In other words, successful entrepreneurs are not as much risk takers as they are risk eliminators, removing as many obstacles to the successful launch of their ventures as possible. One of the most successful ways of eliminating risks is to build a solid business plan for a venture.

3. ***Confidence in their ability to succeed.*** Entrepreneurs typically have an abundance of confidence in their ability to succeed. They tend to be optimistic about their chances for success. In a recent National Small Business Poll, the National Federation of Independent Businesses (NFIB) found that business owners rated the success of their companies quite high—an average of 7.3 on a scale of 1 (a total failure) to 10 (an extreme success).[11] This high level of optimism may explain why some of the most successful entrepreneurs have failed in business—often more than once—before finally succeeding. "I don't believe in luck," says Kerri Evans, owner of a mobile pet grooming business. "I believe in myself."[12]

4. ***Desire for immediate feedback.*** Entrepreneurs enjoy the challenge of running a business, and they like to know how they are doing and are constantly looking for feedback. "I love being an entrepreneur," says Nick Gleason, co-founder of CitySoft Inc., a Web-page design firm based in Cambridge, Massachusetts. "There's something about the sheer creativity and challenge of it that I like."[13]

5. ***High level of energy.*** Entrepreneurs are more energetic than the average person. That energy may be a critical factor, given the incredible effort required to launch a start-up company. Long hours and hard work are the rule rather than the exception, and the pace can be grueling.

COMPANY Profile

iRobot

When Colin Angle and Helen Greiner, MIT graduates whose joint interest in robotics brought them together, formed a business venture, iRobot, they and their six employees routinely spent 18 hours a day creating software and assembling prototype robots. Their hard work paid off; their company has become the leader in the field of robotics. iRobot has developed a multitude of robots for a wide variety of market segments, ranging from My Real Baby ("an interactive, robotic, artificially-intelligent, emotionally-responsive baby doll") for kids and Roomba (an automatic vacuum cleaner) for busy homeowners to the MicroRig (a device that takes sensors to the bottom of oil wells) for industry and Ariel (a robot capable of removing obstacles on land and underwater) for the military.[14]

6. ***Future orientation.*** Entrepreneurs have a well-defined sense of searching for opportunities. They look ahead and are less concerned with what they did yesterday than with what they might do tomorrow. Not satisfied to sit back and revel in their success, real entrepreneurs stay focused on the future. Tom Stemberg, founder of the Staples office supply chain, went on to start Zoots, a 54-store dry cleaning chain (he came up with the idea after a dry cleaners lost one of his Brooks Brothers dress shirts), and Olly Shoes, a small chain of children's shoe stores (he came up with the idea after a frustrating experience shopping for shoes for his four boys).

Entrepreneurs see potential where most people see only problems or nothing at all, a characteristic that often makes them the objects of ridicule (at least until their ideas become huge successes). Whereas traditional managers are concerned with managing available *resources*, entrepreneurs are more interested in spotting and capitalizing on *opportunities*. The United States leads the world in the percentage of opportunity entrepreneurs, those who start businesses because they spot an opportunity in the marketplace, compared to necessity entrepreneurs, those who start businesses because they cannot find work any other way.[15]

Serial entrepreneurs, those who repeatedly start businesses and grow them to a sustainable size before striking out again, push this characteristic to the maximum. The majority of serial entrepreneurs are leapfroggers, people who start a company, manage its growth until they get bored, and then sell it to start another. A few are jugglers (or parallel entrepreneurs), people who start and manage several companies at once.

serial entrepreneurs entrepreneurs who repeatedly start businesses and grow them to a sustainable size before striking out again.

Ron Berger is a classic leapfrogging serial entrepreneur, having started five companies, one right after the other. Berger's business ventures include a camera retailer that grew to 54 stores before it folded, a company that managed the system by which video stores pay fees to movie studios, and his current business, Figaro's, a take-and-bake pizza restaurant that generates more than $24 million a year in sales.[16]

Ron Berger

It's almost as if serial entrepreneurs are addicted to launching businesses. "Starting a company is a very imaginative, innovative, energy-driven, fun process," says Dick Kouri, who has started 12 companies in his career and now teaches entrepreneurship at the University of North Carolina. "Serial entrepreneurs can't wait to do it again."[17]

7. *Skill at organizing.* Building a company "from scratch" is much like piecing together a giant jigsaw puzzle. Entrepreneurs know how to put the right people together to accomplish a task. Effectively combining people and jobs enables entrepreneurs to transform their visions into reality.

8. *Value of achievement over money.* One of the most common misconceptions about entrepreneurs is that they are driven wholly by the desire to make money. To the contrary, *achievement* seems to be entrepreneurs' primary motivating force; money is simply a way of "keeping score" of accomplishments—a symbol of achievement. One business researcher says, "What keeps the entrepreneur moving forward is more complex—and more profound—than mere cash. It's about running your own show. It's about doing what is virtually impossible."[18]

Other characteristics frequently exhibited by entrepreneurs include the following:

High degree of commitment. Entrepreneurship is hard work, and launching a company successfully requires total commitment from an entrepreneur. Business founders often immerse themselves completely in their companies. Most entrepreneurs have to overcome seemingly insurmountable barriers to launch a company and to keep it growing. That requires commitment.

Tolerance for ambiguity. Entrepreneurs tend to have a high tolerance for ambiguous, ever-changing situations, the environment in which they most often operate. This ability to handle uncertainty is critical because these business builders constantly make decisions using new, sometimes conflicting information gleaned from a variety of unfamiliar sources. Based on his research, entrepreneurial expert Amar Bhidé says that entrepreneurs exhibit "a willingness to jump into things when it's hard to even imagine what the possible set of outcomes will be."[19]

Flexibility. One hallmark of true entrepreneurs is their ability to adapt to the changing demands of their customers and their businesses. In this rapidly changing global economy, rigidity often leads to failure. As our society, its people, and their tastes change, entrepreneurs also must be willing to adapt their businesses to meet those changes. When their ideas fail to live up to their expectations, successful entrepreneurs change them!

S.O.S. Pads

In 1917, Ed Cox invented a pre-soaped steel-wool scouring pad that was ideal for cleaning pots and used it as a "calling card" in his sales calls. Although his efforts at selling pots proved futile, Cox noticed how often his prospects asked for the soap pads. He quickly forgot about selling pots and shifted his focus to selling the scouring pads, which his wife had named S.O.S. ("Save Our Saucepans"), and went on to start a business that still thrives.[20]

Tenacity. Obstacles, obstructions, and defeat typically do not dissuade entrepreneurs from doggedly pursuing their visions. They simply keep trying.

Snocap

Shawn Fanning, who unleashed the downloaded digital music wars when he created Napster, a program that allowed users to download songs over the Internet without paying for them, lost the legal battle to keep his company going in 2002 over copyright infringement. One week after Napster closed, Fanning began planning his next entrepreneurial venture, a company called Snocap that works with major companies in the recording industry to operate a music file-sharing database that allows authorized users to download legally the songs for which they have paid.[21]

What conclusion can we draw from the volumes of research conducted on the entrepreneurial personality? Entrepreneurs are not of one mold; no one set of characteristics can predict who will become entrepreneurs and whether or not they will succeed. Indeed, *diversity* seems to be a central characteristic of entrepreneurs. One researcher of the entrepreneurial personality explains, "Entrepreneurs don't fit any statistical norm . . . . Most are aberrant or a bit odd by nature."[22] Entrepreneurs tend to be nonconformists, a characteristic that seems to be central to their views of the world and to their success.

As you can see from the examples in this chapter, *anyone*, regardless of age, race, gender, color, national origin, or any other characteristic, can become an entrepreneur (although not everyone should). There are no limitations on this form of economic expression. Entrepreneurship is not a mystery; it is a practical discipline. Entrepreneurship is not a genetic trait; it is a skill that most people can learn. The editors of *Inc.* magazine claim, "Entrepreneurship is more mundane than it's sometimes portrayed. . . . You don't need to be a person of mythical proportions to be very, very successful in building a company."[23]

The Benefits of Entrepreneurship

Surveys show that owners of small businesses believe they work harder, earn more money, and are more satisfied than if they worked for someone else. Indeed, a study by the Gallup Organization found that 86 percent of small business owners would choose to own their own companies if they had it to do all over.[24] Before launching any business venture, every potential entrepreneur should consider the benefits of small business ownership.

Opportunity to Create Your Own Destiny

Owning a business provides entrepreneurs the independence and the opportunity to achieve what is important to them. Entrepreneurs want to "call the shots" in their lives, and they use their businesses to make that desire a reality.

Doug Danforth

After spending years in the construction business, Doug Danforth decided to pursue his dream of opening a flower shop in his hometown of Green Bay, Wisconsin. "I had managed two floral shops years before I went into the construction business, and I liked it a lot," he says. Danforth scraped together $900 of his own money, convinced family members to put up a small amount of cash, and launched his shop, which he has built into a thriving business. "I wanted to control my own destiny," he says. "I knew I wanted to be my own boss."[25]

Like Doug Danforth, entrepreneurs reap the intrinsic rewards of knowing they are the driving forces behind their businesses.

Opportunity to Make a Difference

Increasingly, entrepreneurs are starting businesses because they see an opportunity to make a difference in a cause that is important to them. Whether it is providing low-cost, sturdy housing for families in developing countries or establishing a recycling program to preserve Earth's limited resources, entrepreneurs are finding ways to combine their concerns for social issues and their desire to earn a good living.

Concerned about protecting the environment, gardening enthusiast Lars Hundley launched a Web-based company, CleanAirGardening.com, which sells environmentally friendly lawn care and gardening products, from a spare room in his apartment. Hundley, who now operates his business from an office in his three-bedroom home, is constantly adding new products to the Web site, which also includes a comprehensive list of links that teach visitors about environmentally safe gardening and lawn care. Based on the responses from his growing list of customers, "I think I am certainly making a difference," says Hundley.[26]

CleanAirGardening.com

Opportunity to Reach Your Full Potential

Too many people find their work boring, unchallenging, and unexciting. But not entrepreneurs! To them, there is little difference between work and play; the two are synonymous. Entrepreneurs' businesses become their instruments for self-expression and self-actualization. They know that the only boundaries on their success are those imposed by their own creativity, enthusiasm, and vision. Owning a business gives them a sense of empowerment. Barbie Dallman, who left the security (and the hassles) of corporate life at age 30 to start a résumé service, says, "Starting my own business was a spiritual awakening. I found out what was important to me—being able to follow my own interests."[27]

Opportunity to Reap Impressive Profits

Although money is not the primary force driving most entrepreneurs, the profits their businesses can earn are an important motivating factor in their decisions to launch companies. Most entrepreneurs never become super-rich, but many of them do become quite wealthy. In fact, nearly 75 percent of those on the *Forbes* list of the 400 richest Americans are first-generation entrepreneurs![28] According to research by Thomas Stanley and William Danko, self-employed business owners make up two-thirds of American millionaires. "Self-employed people are four times more likely to be millionaires than people who work for others," says Danko.[29] The typical millionaire's business is not a glamorous, high-tech enterprise; more often, it is something much less glamorous—scrap metal, welding, auctioneering, garbage collection, and the like.

When Sam Walton launched Wal-Mart near his hometown of Bentonville, Arkansas, reaching the list of the wealthiest people in the United States wasn't even imaginable to him. Walton died in 1992, and his family business has grown into the largest company in the world; the 39 percent of Wal-Mart stock that the Walton family controls is worth $90 billion (an amount equivalent to the Gross Domestic Product of Singapore!), making them the richest family in the United States.[30]

Sam Walton

Table 1.1 offers a brief profile of some of the wealthiest Americans in history.

Opportunity to Contribute to Society and Be Recognized for Your Efforts

Often, small business owners are among the most respected and most trusted members of their communities. Business deals based on trust and mutual respect are the hallmark of many established small companies. These owners enjoy the trust and recognition they receive from the customers they have served faithfully over the years. A study by the National Federation of Independent Businesses found that 78 percent of Americans believe that small business exerts a positive influence on the country's direction, a ranking exceeded only by science and technology.[31]

TABLE 1.1 Wealthiest Americans in History

Who	Comment	Business	Wealth as a Percentage of the U.S. Economy*
John D. Rockefeller (1839–1937)	America's first billionaire. Created America's most powerful monopoly, the Standard Oil Company.	Oil	1.53%
Sam Walton (1918–1992)	Launched Wal-Mart near his hometown of Bentonville, Arkansas, and built it into the largest company in the world.	Retail	1.30%
Cornelius Vanderbilt (1794–1877)	Known as the "Commodore." Borrowed $100 from his mother at age 12 to start what became the Staten Island Ferry.	Railroad and shipping	1.15%
John Jacob Astor (1763–1848)	A German-born immigrant who began as a fur trader	New York real estate	0.93%
Stephen Girard (1750–1831)	Largest investor in the First Bank of the United States. Loaned the U.S. Treasury $8 million to finance the War of 1812.	Shipping and banking	0.67%
Andrew Carnegie (1835–1919)	A "rags to riches" story. Started as a bobbin boy and went on to found U.S. Steel.	Steel	0.60%
Alexander Turney Stewart (1803–1876)	Founded the first department store in the United States.	Retail	0.56%
Frederick Weyerhauser (1834–1914)	Made his fortune as American's demand for lumber exploded.	Timber	0.55%
Bill Gates (1955–)	Dropped out of Harvard and launched Microsoft Corporation with Paul Allen. Wealthiest man in the world today.	Computer software	0.43%
Larry Ellison (1944–)	Started Oracle Corporation with $2,000 of his own money. Now the second-largest maker of computer software behind Microsoft.	Computer software	0.15%
Michael Dell (1965–)	Started Dell Computer from his dormitory room at the University of Texas. Sales now exceed $56 billion a year.	Computers	0.11%

*Calculated by dividing person's total wealth by the U.S. GDP at the time of death, or if person is still living, by 2001 GDP.
Source: Adapted from "The World's Richest People," Forbes, February 26, 2003, http://www.forbes.com/lists/2003/02/26/billionaireland.html; "Richest Americans in History," Forbes ASAP, August 24, 1998, p. 32; Rachel Emma Silverman, "Rich & Richer: Fifty of the Wealthiest People of the Past 1,000 Years," Wall Street Journal Reports: The Millenium, January 11, 1999, pp. R6–R10.

Playing a vital role in their local business systems and knowing that their work has a significant impact on how smoothly our nation's economy functions is yet another reward for small business managers. One survey reports that 72 percent of business owners say that what they enjoy most about being a business owner is contributing to the local community.[32]

Opportunity to Do What You Enjoy and Have Fun at It

A common sentiment among small business owners is that their work really isn't work. Most successful entrepreneurs choose to enter their particular business fields because they have an interest in them and enjoy those lines of work. They have made their avocations (hobbies) their vocations (work) and are glad they did. These entrepreneurs are living Harvey McKay's advice: "Find a job doing what you love, and you'll never have to work a day in your life." The journey rather than the destination is the entrepreneur's greatest reward.

CHAPTER 1 • THE FOUNDATIONS OF ENTREPRENEURSHIP

"Starting a company is very hard to do," says entrepreneur and small business researcher David Birch. "The risks are enormous; the anxiety is enormous. The only business you should start is one in which you have a huge interest, or else you won't have the persistence to stick with it. Get into [a business] because you're fanatically interested in it."[33]

In 1996, twins Izzy and Coco Tihanyi decided to quit their desk jobs to transform their passion for surfing into a business venture. The Tihanyi sisters took $328 in savings and Izzy's surfboard collection and launched Surf Diva, a school that teaches women to surf. Since then, thousands of women, including the actress Minnie Driver, have learned the finer points of surfing at one of Surf Diva's three locations in California. In addition to the surfing school, the Tihanyis also sell surf boards and apparel under the Surf Diva brand through a company-owned boutique and 50 retailers in the United States, Japan, and England. Company headquarters in La Jolla is less than a block away from the beach, but the sisters' work seems more like play to them. "A big problem is keeping the office chairs dry," says Izzy. "We just put towels on them, but maybe we should buy vinyl chairs or something."[34]

COMPANY
Profile

Surf Diva

Sisters Izzy and Coco Tihany, founders of Surf Diva, a company that teaches women the joys of surfing and sells casual clothing, have transformed their lifelong passion for surfing into a successful business. The only problem: Their office chairs are always wet!

Not only have the Tihanyi twins found a way to make a living, but what is more important, they are doing something they love!

You
Be the Consultant

These Boots Are Made for Riding

In the late 1980s, Beth Cross was a management consultant for Bain and Company, where she worked with rising athletic shoe companies such as Reebok to incorporate the latest materials and technology such as gel padding, air pockets, and carbon fiber. Cross, who had grown up on a horse farm outside Swarthmore, Pennsylvania, soon recognized a market opportunity that she could capitalize on using her equestrian background and business experience: riding boots. At the time, the market for leather riding boots was dominated by two brands that had been around since the days of Wyatt Earp and were owned by business tycoon Warren Buffett: Justin Boots and Tony Lama.

Cross's market research confirmed that the riding boot market had substantial purchasing power; some 20 million riders participated in equestrian sports worldwide. She also discovered that the market had seen no real innovations in a century and that a common customer complaint was that existing models of riding boots, whether Western or English, were not well

Beth Cross left her job as a management consultant and with her friend Pam Parker launched Ariat, a company that provides the most technologically advanced boots in the market to the world's top equestrians. Ariat's ability to integrate athletic shoe technology and comfort into riding boots is a key ingredient in its rapid growth.

designed and were very uncomfortable, at least until the rider was able to break them in, a process that could mean months of aching feet and blisters. In 1992, Cross quit her consulting job, and working from her home with her friend Pam Parker, created a business plan so that the two could take on the established companies in the riding boot market with a new boot that was as ranch-ready as any cowboy boot but was as comfortable as an athletic shoe. They launched their company, Ariat International, with $250,000 Cross assembled from her own pockets and from family and friends and with the help of Reebok's head of business development, Angel Martinez, whose daughter is an equestrian. (The company's name is derived from the Italian "aria," a perfect solo performance.) Ariat introduced riding boots that featured patented technology designed to deliver stability, durability, and comfort. Cross and Parker assembled a team of footwear engineers and designers and turned them loose to create an innovative performance riding boot. They started by redesigning the outsole, developing a new arch support system, and transforming the shape and fit of the boot to emulate modern athletic shoes. Indeed, Ariat is known as the pioneer of integrating athletic shoe technology into equestrian footwear. Throughout the process, Cross, Parker, and their team of footwear engineers included the opinions and feedback from hundreds of riders who field-tested their designs. The result was a boot that combined the comfort, fit, and performance of athletic shoes with the stylish look of a classic riding boot.

Cross convinced Reebok's Martinez to join the Ariat board of directors, which gave the young company credibility in the industry and helped it to land a $9 million investment from a venture capital firm in 1996. Ariat keeps its operations lean, operating with just 100 employees, most of whom are in sales and service. Cross has forged relationships with suppliers of high-quality leather in Europe and with contract manufacturers in China experienced in making shoes and boots.

Ariat has won patents on a variety of boot features, including gel and carbon fiber components that reduce weight and lower costs.

Ariat shipped its first pair of boots in 1993, and serious equestrians recognized the difference in fit and performance almost immediately. With only a small marketing budget, Cross had to be creative. She hauled Ariat boots to horse shows in her car. Although the company could not afford to sponsor professional riders, she decided to give away Ariat boots to up-and-coming riders for publicity. Seeding the market this way paid off as growing numbers of customers began requesting the brand at tack stores, from catalogs, and from online retail outlets, all of which began to carry the Ariat brand. Today the company offers a full range of Western and English riding boots, work boots, casual footwear, and riding apparel. Ariat International, a privately held company, generates sales of more than $80 million a year and controls about 17 percent of the U.S. market for Western wear. With revenues climbing at an impressive 25 percent a year, the company leads the industry in sales growth. Ariat's international sales are climbing even faster—at a rate of 75 percent a year. Cross sees a bright future for her company and has set ambitious goals for it over the next decade. "I believe we are well positioned to achieve our goal of becoming the number one equestrian brand in the world," she says.

1. Explain how Beth Cross exhibits the entrepreneurial spirit.
2. How did Cross discover the business opportunity around which she built Ariat International? Do you think this process is typical of entrepreneurs? Explain.

Sources: Adapted from Michael V. Copeland, "These Boots Really Were Made for Walking," *Business 2.0,* October 2004, pp. 72–74; "A Sure Thing: Ariat International," Ariat International Press Kit, http://www.ariat.com/about_media_presskit.aspx; "The History of Ariat," Ariat International, http://www.ariat.com/about_history.aspx.

LEARNING OBJECTIVES
3B. Describe the drawbacks of entrepreneurship.

The Potential Drawbacks of Entrepreneurship

Although owning a business has many benefits and provides many opportunities, anyone planning to enter the world of entrepreneurship should be aware of its potential drawbacks. Individuals who prefer the security of a steady paycheck, a comprehensive benefits package, a two-week paid vacation, and the support of a corporate staff probably should not go into business for themselves. Some of the disadvantages of entrepreneurship include the following:

Uncertainty of Income

Opening and running a business provides no guarantee that an entrepreneur will earn enough money to survive. Some small businesses barely earn enough to provide the owner-manager with an adequate income. In a business's early days the owner often has trouble meeting financial obligations and may have to live on savings. The steady income that comes with working for someone else is absent. The owner is always the last one to be paid. One California couple left their corporate jobs that together brought in $120,000 a year to start a small vineyard; their combined income in their first year of business: $30,000.

Risk of Losing Your Entire Investment

The small business failure rate is relatively high. According to recent research, 35 percent of new businesses fail within two years, and 54 percent shut down within four years. Within six years, 64 percent of new businesses will have folded. Studies also show that when a company creates at least one job in its early years, the probability of failure after six years plummets to 35 percent![35]

Before "reaching for the golden ring," entrepreneurs should ask themselves if they can cope psychologically with the consequences of failure:

- What is the worst that could happen if I open my business and it fails?
- How likely is the worst to happen? (Am I truly prepared to launch my business?)
- What can I do to lower the risk of my business failing?
- If my business were to fail, what is my contingency plan for coping?

Long Hours and Hard Work

Business start-ups often demand that owners keep nightmarish schedules. According to a recent Dun & Bradstreet survey, 65 percent of entrepreneurs devote more than 40 hours per week to their companies (see Figure 1.2). In many start-ups, six- or seven-day workweeks with no paid vacations are the norm. In fact, one study by American Express found that 29 percent of small business owners had no plans to take a summer vacation. The primary reason? "Too busy."[36] These owners feel the pressure because they know that when the business closes, the revenue stops coming in, and customers go elsewhere. "You must have stamina to see it through," says Chantelle Ludski, founder of London-based fresh!, an organic food company. "I put in many 16-hour workdays. Holidays and time off are things that go out the window!"[37]

Lower Quality of Life until the Business Gets Established

The long hours and hard work needed to launch a company can take their toll on the other aspects of the entrepreneur's life. Business owners often find that their roles as husbands or wives and fathers or mothers take a back seat to their roles as company founders. Holly Dunlap, a 32-year-old designer of women's shoes, handbags, and party dresses that she

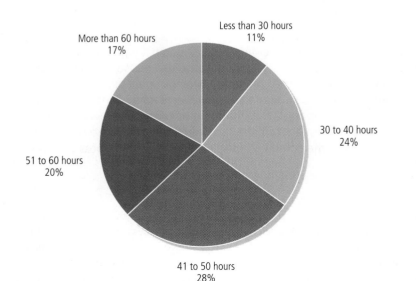

Less than 30 hours
11%

More than 60 hours
17%

30 to 40 hours
24%

51 to 60 hours
20%

41 to 50 hours
28%

FIGURE 1.2

Number of Hours per Week Entrepreneurs Devote to Their Businesses.

Source: Adapted from Dun & Bradstreet, *21st Annual Small Business Survey Summary Report*, 2002, p. 35.

FIGURE 1.3

Entrepreneur Age When Business Was Formed

Source: Global Entrepreneurship Monitor, 2004.

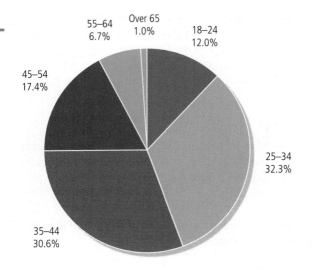

sells through Hollywould, the boutique she founded with locations in New York City and Palm Beach, Florida, admits that she is married to her business. Her 14-hour workdays leave little time for lunch most days or for a quiet evening with friends. "As my mother has pointed out," she says, "businesses do not produce grandchildren."[38] Part of the problem is that half of all entrepreneurs launch their businesses between the ages of 25 and 39 years, just when they start their families (see Figure 1.3). As a result, marriages, families, and friendships are too often casualties of small business ownership. "The traits that make you a successful entrepreneur are not the things you can turn off when you walk in the door at home," says one entrepreneurial researcher, describing how owning a business often conflicts with one's family and social life.[39]

High Levels of Stress

Starting and managing a business can be an incredibly rewarding experience, but it also can be a highly stressful one. Entrepreneurs often have made significant investments in their companies, have left behind the safety and security of a steady paycheck, and have mortgaged everything they own to get into business. Failure may mean total financial ruin, and that creates intense levels of stress and anxiety. Sometimes entrepreneurs unnecessarily bear the burden of managing alone because they cannot bring themselves to delegate authority and responsibility to others in the company, even though their employees are capable.

DeMars and Associates

Jo DeMars, founder of DeMars and Associates, a company that manages warranty disputes and arbitration for automakers, guided her company's growth for 13 years by micromanaging every aspect of it. Both DeMars and the company paid a price, however. "I was burned out and exhausted," she says. Because she was so focused on day-to-day issues, DeMars was neglecting the company's strategic management. Her solution was to take a four-month sabbatical and to allow her management team (and a trusted consultant) to run the company, which thrived in her absence. Now back at the helm, DeMars encourages employees to make daily decisions while she focuses on broader issues, such as writing the company's first comprehensive business plan and creating a new division.[40]

Complete Responsibility

It's great to be the boss, but many entrepreneurs find that they must make decisions on issues about which they are not really knowledgeable. Many business owners have difficulty finding advisors. A recent national small business poll conducted by the National Federation of Independent Businesses found that 34 percent of business owners have no one person to turn to for help when making a critical business decision.[41] When there is no one to ask, the pressure can build quickly. The realization that the decisions they make are the cause of success or failure has a devastating effect on some people. Small business owners discover quickly that *they* are the business.

Discouragement

Launching a business is a substantial undertaking that requires a great deal of dedication, discipline, and tenacity. Along the way to building a successful business, entrepreneurs will run headlong into many different obstacles, some of which appear to be insurmountable. In the face of such difficulties, discouragement and disillusionment are common emotions. Successful entrepreneurs know that every business encounters rough spots along the way, and they wade through difficult times with lots of hard work and an abundant reserve of optimism.

Behind the Boom: What's Feeding the Entrepreneurial Fire

LEARNING OBJECTIVES
4. Explain the forces that are driving the growth of entrepreneurship.

What forces are driving this entrepreneurial trend in our economy? Which factors have led to this age of entrepreneurship? Some of the most significant ones include the following:

Entrepreneurs as heroes. An intangible but very important factor is the attitude that Americans have toward entrepreneurs. As a nation we have raised them to hero status and have held out their accomplishments as models to follow. Business founders such as Bill Gates (Microsoft Corporation), Mary Kay Ash (Mary Kay Cosmetics), Jeff Bezos (Amazon.com), Michael Dell (Dell Computer Corporation), and Ben Cohen and Jerry Greenfield (Ben & Jerry's Homemade Inc.) are to entrepreneurship what Tiger Woods and Kevin Garnett are to sports.

Entrepreneurial education. Colleges and universities have discovered that entrepreneurship is an extremely popular course of study. Disillusioned with corporate America's downsized job offerings and less promising career paths, a rapidly growing number of students sees owning a business as an attractive career option. Today more than 2,100 colleges and universities offer courses in entrepreneurship and small business to some 200,000 students. Many colleges and universities have difficulty meeting the demand for courses in entrepreneurship and small business.

Demographic and economic factors. Nearly two-thirds of entrepreneurs start their businesses between the ages of 25 and 44 years, and much of our nation's population falls into that age range. In addition, the economic growth that spanned most of the 1980s and 1990s created a significant amount of wealth among people of this age group and many business opportunities on which they can capitalize.

Shift to a service economy. The service sector produces 80 percent of the jobs and 64 percent of the Gross Domestic Product (GDP) in the United States, which represents a sharp rise from just a decade ago. Because of their relatively low start-up costs, service businesses have become very popular among entrepreneurs. The booming service sector continues to provide many business opportunities, and not all of them are in high-tech fields.

Nathan McKelvey used his experience as a pilot and a manager of private jets for another company to launch CharterAuction.com, a business that locates private jets for clients through an online auction format. Before taking the entrepreneurial plunge, McKelvey conducted extensive research on the private jet industry and made a thorough analysis of his competition. "This was a $2 billion industry that was underserved," says McKelvey. His research proved to be accurate; McKelvey's company, which he started in 1999, now has 25 employees and generates $15 million in annual sales.[42]

CharterAuction.com

FIGURE 1.4

U.S. Retail e-Commerce Sales (excluding travel), 2004–2009 (billions and % increase vs. prior year)

Note: eMarketer benchmarks its retail e-commerce sales figures against US Department of Commerce data, for which the last full year measured was 2005
Source: eMarketer, April 2006.

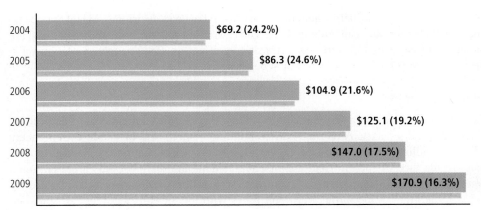

2004	$69.2 (24.2%)
2005	$86.3 (24.6%)
2006	$104.9 (21.6%)
2007	$125.1 (19.2%)
2008	$147.0 (17.5%)
2009	$170.9 (16.3%)

World Wide Web
the vast network that links computers around the globe via the Internet and opens up oceans of information to its users and a major business opportunity for entrepreneurs.

Technological advances. With the help of modern business machines such as personal computers, laptop computers, fax machines, copiers, color printers, answering machines, and voice mail, even one person working at home can look like a big business. At one time, the high cost of such technological wizardry made it impossible for small businesses to compete with larger companies that could afford the hardware. Today, however, powerful computers and communication equipment are priced within the budgets of even the smallest businesses. Although entrepreneurs may not be able to manufacture heavy equipment in their spare bedrooms, they can run a service- or information-based company from their homes very effectively and look like any Fortune 500 company to customers and clients.

Independent lifestyle. Entrepreneurship fits the way Americans want to live—independent and self-sustaining. People want the freedom to choose where they live, the hours they work, and what they do. Although financial security remains an important goal for most entrepreneurs, many place top priority on lifestyle issues such as more time with family and friends, more leisure time, and more control over work-related stress.

e-Commerce and the World Wide Web. The proliferation of the **World Wide Web,** the vast network that links computers around the globe via the Internet and opens up oceans of information to its users, has spawned thousands of entrepreneurial ventures since its beginning in 1993. Online commerce is growing rapidly (see Figure 1.4), creating many opportunities for Web-savvy entrepreneurs. Travel services, computer hardware and software, books, music, videos, and consumer electronics are among the best-selling items on the Web, but entrepreneurs are learning that they can use this powerful tool to sell just about anything! Approximately 57 percent of small businesses use the Internet for business-related purposes, and 70 percent have Web sites. Those that do have Web sites reap benefits quickly. The most commonly cited benefit of launching a Web site is additional customers; in fact, after launching a site, 41 percent of small companies reported an increase in sales. Fifty-five percent- of small companies with Web sites report that their sites are either breaking even or are earning a profit.[43] These "netpreneurs" are using their Web sites to connect with their existing customers and, ultimately, to attract new ones. "Small businesses that use the Web to market their products and services outperform those that don't," says an executive at Verizon, which sponsors an annual small business Internet survey. "The promise of the Internet is starting to pay off."[44]

ShavingCream.com

After spending more than 30 years in sales and marketing for a variety of companies, Mark Williams took a leap of faith and went into business for himself, launching ShavingCream.com after spending several months researching the concept and preparing a business plan. "The chance to work for myself, to put my ideas into play, to answer only to myself are what drove me to start my own business," says Williams. As its name suggests, Williams' company sells a wide selection of shaving creams as well as skin and hair care products online. Williams decided to create an e-commerce company because he realized that the Web was the "new sales frontier" and that it offered a much lower cost of entry for a retail operation than establishing a brick-and-mortar store. Williams launched his company in time to capitalize on the busy Christmas season, and the company's customer base—and its sales, thanks to repeat customers—have grown rapidly since its opening. Shaving Cream.com "has created a very healthy lifestyle for me and my family," says Williams. "I can work from home if I want, enjoy flexible working hours, spend quality time with my family and friends, exercise, and work with my wife."[45]

International opportunities. No longer are small businesses limited to pursuing customers within their own national borders. The shift to a global economy has opened the door to tremendous business opportunities for entrepreneurs willing to reach across the globe. Although the United States is an attractive market for entrepreneurs, approximately 95 percent of the world's population lives outside its borders. World-altering changes such as the crumbling of the Berlin Wall, the collapse of Communism, and the breaking down of trade barriers through trade agreements have changed the world order and have opened more of the world market to entrepreneurs. Today, small businesses can have a global scope from their inception. Small companies comprise 97 percent of all businesses engaged in exporting, yet they account for only 30 percent of the nation's export sales.[46] Most small companies do not take advantage of export opportunities, often because their owners don't know how or where to start an export initiative. Although terrorism and global recessions have slowed the growth of international trade somewhat, global opportunities for small businesses have a long-term positive outlook.

Although going global can be fraught with dangers and problems, many entrepreneurs are discovering that selling their products and services in foreign markets is really not so difficult. Small companies that have expanded successfully into foreign markets tend to rely on the following strategies:

- Researching foreign markets thoroughly.
- Focusing on a single country initially.
- Utilizing government resources designed to help small companies establish an international presence.
- Forging alliances with local partners.

For nearly all of the nearly five decades it has existed, Hibco Plastics, a small maker of foam packaging based in Yadkinville, New York, sold its products strictly in the United States. In 1993, however, the company lost its largest customer, IBM, and sales immediately dropped 30 percent. Just as the company was beginning to recover, it was hit by an economic recession, and once again sales fell precipitously from $13.3 million to $10 million, forcing its owners, the Pavlanskey brothers Mark, Jon, and Keith, to lay off 40 percent of its workforce. Hibco's management team was forced to be creative, weighing options they had never before considered, including developing new products and exporting. In 2003, the Pavlanskeys took a crash course in global business, and Hibco began exporting to Mexico foam packaging and a synthetic soil ("rubber dirt") used for shipping plants. Building on its early exporting success, Hibco is entering export markets for foam roofing and insulation material and specialty packaging for the medical industry. Sales have recovered to $14 million, and the workforce is back to 100 employees. The Pavlanskeys say that exporting has transformed Hibco's entire culture from a once-complacent operation into a thriving, dynamic business. Exporting "keeps us on our toes in our core business," says Mark.[47]

Hibco Plastics

Collegiate Entrepreneurs

For growing numbers of students, college is not just a time of learning, partying, and growing into young adulthood; it is fast becoming a place for building a business. More than 2,100 colleges and universities offer courses in entrepreneurship and small business management, and many of them have trouble keeping up with demand for these classes. "Students used to come to college and assume that five to ten years down the road, they'd start a business," says Gerry Hills, co-founder of the Collegiate Entrepreneurs Organization (CEO). Today, "they come in preparing to get ideas and launch."

Many of these collegiate entrepreneurs' ideas come from their college experiences. As a freshman enrolling in Santa Clara University in California, Ryan Garman faced the stereotypical moving day woes, struggling to pack and haul his belongings from his parents' home in Las Vegas to his dorm room in Santa Clara. Hoping to get an early start, he arrived on campus at 5 a.m., only to end up waiting in line with 2,400 other students who also were moving in. "It was miserable," he recalls. "I thought, 'There has to be a better way.'" What if college students could buy furnishings designed for small dorm spaces and then have the items shipped directly to their dorms so that they are waiting there when the students arrive? Garman began developing a business plan for his idea and discovered that students and their parents spend $2.6 billion a year on college dorm and apartment furnishings. By his sophomore year, Garman had convinced three friends—Kevon Saber, Chad Arimura, and Ivan Dwyer—to join in launching the business venture, which Garman named AllDorm Inc.

Although they were still in college when they launched AllDorm.com, Garman, Saber, Arimura, and Dwyer knew that they needed input from students in other parts of the country. They developed a network of contacts at other colleges and universities and asked them for input on various types of dorm furnishings and decorations. Now several years past graduation, the AllDorm founders recognize the need to stay in close contact with the ever-changing tastes of the college market. They always have two student interns on their staff whose input they find to be extremely valuable.

The interns also get to test new product ideas and offer feedback on them. Early on, the entrepreneurs also made the wise decision to recruit several experienced business owners and experts to serve on the AllDorm advisory board. The network of contacts that advisory board members have provided the company has proved to be another important resource.

AllDorm offers customers more than 6,000 items, ranging from beanbag chairs and mini-refrigerators to shower sandals and shelving, but the company keeps costs low by stocking no inventory. Instead, it uses proprietary e-commerce software to link to its suppliers, who then ship the items ordered directly to AllDorm's customers. The company also coordinates delivery dates with each college and university to make sure shipments don't arrive too early and are returned. "When you're in college," says Garman, "you can study, you can party, or you can start a company. We chose to start a company."

Jeffrey Betz, Cecilia Domingos, and Michael Lobsinger, MBA students at Rensselaer Polytechnic Institute, also started their company, Orca Gear Inc., while in college. However, their idea came from a different source of inspiration: a class assignment. They recognized the market potential of a product that resulted from a year-long assignment in one of their entrepreneurship classes and decided to build a company around it: a stylish inflatable life jacket that looks like a regular jacket "that people will want to wear," says Betz, unlike the standard bulky orange life jackets that have been around for years. The company's mission is to revolutionize the life-jacket market with its cutting-edge, Float Tech™ life jacket.

The entrepreneurs earned most of their seed capital to launch the business by winning business plan competitions, tapping their professors for free consulting advice, and convincing local companies to help them perfect the product design—for free. "For the first two years, no one really charged us anything," recalls Betz. Sales for their company, now called Float Tech, have passed the $1 million mark, and the co-founders, who say their success is proof that entrepreneurship can be taught, are aiming for annual sales of $15 to $20 million within five years.

Budding entrepreneurs at a growing number of colleges can take advantage of special programs designed to create a culture for entrepreneurship. For instance, the University of Maryland's Hinman Campus Entrepreneurship Opportunities program provides space in a specially outfitted dormitory for 100 students who want to build their own companies. Students not only share living space with like-minded entrepreneurial types—an ideal setting for encouraging start-ups—but they also have access to amenities such as a professionally appointed conference room, wireless Internet access, smart whiteboards, ample computer facilities, video-conferencing equipment, copiers, and a phone system that simultaneously rings home and cellular phones so that no one misses an important business call. Weekly presentations from entrepreneurs, venture capitalists, attorneys, and others help students to define their business ideas and develop their business plans. Two hundred students recently applied for the 100 available spots in the dorm with its incubator-like business environment. The program, which won the Price Institute Innovative Entrepreneurship Educators Award, is working. Twenty of the students already have launched companies, including a medical software company and a textbook sales business. "It's often over those late-night pizzas where the best ideas are born," says one official. One student entrepreneur in the program agrees, "A lot of it is the community. Being around people in the program inspires one to think about other opportunities out there. What I've learned here is how to plan, how to make a business actually work."

1. In addition to the normal obstacles of starting a business, what other barriers do collegiate entrepreneurs face?
2. What advantages do collegiate entrepreneurs have when launching a business?
3. What advice would you offer a fellow college student about to start a business?
4. Work with a team of your classmates to develop ideas about what your college or university could do to create a culture of entrepreneurship on your campus or in your community.

Sources: Mark Henricks, "Honor Roll," *Entrepreneur*, April 2005, pp. 68–73; Nichole L. Torres, "Big Biz on Campus," *Entrepreneur B.Y.O.B.*, December 2004, p. 130; Nichole L. Torres, "Hit the Floor," *Entrepreneur*, May 2005, p. 122; Nichole L. Torres, "Inside Job," *Entrepreneur*, March 2005, p. 132; Michael Myser, "Giving College Kids a Smoother Move," *Business 2.0*, June 2004, p. 82; Nichole L. Torres, "Class Acts," *Entrepreneur*, June 2003, http://www.entrepreneur.com/article/print/0,2361,309005,00.html; Ellen McCarthy, "A Dorm for Dreamers," *Washington Post*, October 30, 2002, p. E1; "Hinman CEOs Living-Learning Entrepreneurship Program," http://www.hinmanceos.umd.edu/.

The Cultural Diversity of Entrepreneurship

LEARNING OBJECTIVES
5. Explain the cultural diversity of entrepreneurship.

As we have seen, virtually anyone has the potential to become an entrepreneur. Indeed, diversity is a hallmark of entrepreneurship. We now explore the diverse mix of people who make up the rich fabric of entrepreneurship.

Young Entrepreneurs

Young people are setting the pace in starting businesses. Disenchanted with their prospects in corporate America and willing to take a chance at controlling their own destinies, scores of young people are choosing entrepreneurship as their primary career path. A study by Babson College found that members of Generation X (people born between 1965 and 1981) are three times more likely than those in other age groups to launch businesses. Members of this generation are responsible for about 80 percent of all business start-ups, making Generation X the most entrepreneurial generation in history![48] There is no slow-down in sight as this generation flexes its entrepreneurial muscle. "Generation X" might be more appropriately called "Generation E."

Even teenagers and those in their early 20s (the Millennium Generation, born after 1982), show high levels of interest in entrepreneurship. Young entrepreneur camps are popping up all around the country to teach youthful business-building "wannabes" how to launch and run a business, and many of them are fulfilling their dreams. When she was just a sophomore in high school, Natalie Morris created a line of custom-made purses and handbags. Morris, who sells her stylish purses and bags at salons and boutiques across upstate South Carolina, recently received the South Carolina Young Entrepreneur of the

FIGURE 1.5

Reasons Women Give for Starting Businesses

Source: Center for Women's Business Research.

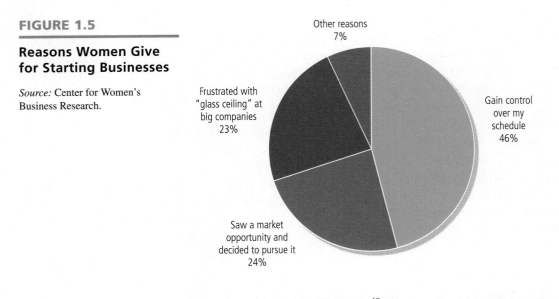

Other reasons
7%

Frustrated with "glass ceiling" at big companies
23%

Gain control over my schedule
46%

Saw a market opportunity and decided to pursue it
24%

Year Award from Merrill Lynch.[49] Because of young people such as Morris, the future of entrepreneurship looks very bright.

Women Entrepreneurs

Despite years of legislative effort, women still face discrimination in the work force. However, small business has been a leader in offering women opportunities for economic expression through employment and entrepreneurship. Increasing numbers of women are discovering that the best way to break the "glass ceiling" that prevents them from rising to the top of many organizations is to start their own companies. In fact, women are opening businesses at a rate about twice that of the national average.[50] Women entrepreneurs have even broken through the comic strip barrier. Blondie Bumstead, long a typical suburban housewife married to Dagwood, now owns her own catering business with her best friend and neighbor Tootsie Woodley. Although about 69 percent of women-owned businesses are concentrated in retailing and services (as are most businesses), female entrepreneurs are branching out rapidly into previously male-dominated industries. According to the Center for Women's Business Research, the fastest-growing industries for women-owned companies are construction, transportation, communications, utilities, and agribusiness.[51] Figure 1.5 shows the reasons women give for starting businesses.

Although the businesses women start tend to be smaller than and require half as much start-up capital as those men start, their impact is anything but small. The nearly 11 million women-owned companies in the United States employ more than 19.1 million workers and generate sales of more than $2.5 trillion a year! Women now own about 48% of all privately-held businesses in the United States.[52] Although their businesses tend to grow more slowly than those owned by men, women-owned businesses have a higher survival rate than U.S. businesses overall. Female entrepreneurs today are more likely than ever to be highly educated and to have managerial experience in the industries in which they start their companies.[53]

COMPANY Profile

Tennessee Bun Company

Cordia Harrington, a former real estate agent, wanted more control over her work hours and decided to open a McDonald's franchise. This single mother of three children was very successful and went on to own three McDonald's restaurants. While serving on a supplier audit committee for McDonald's, Harrington saw a business opportunity when she realized that the franchiser's two suppliers of hamburger buns could not keep up with demand. She sold her McDonald's franchises and built the world's most automated bakery, the Tennessee Bun Company (TBC), which is capable of turning out 60,000 buns an hour. Four years and 30 interviews later, Harrington finally convinced McDonald's to become a customer. Today, McDonald's is her largest customer, and TBC supplies buns and muffins to more than 600 McDonald's restaurants in the southeastern United States. As TBC's customer list expanded to include other large restaurant chains, Harrington saw the chance to launch a trucking business called Bun Lady Transport to speed the delivery of her baked products.[54]

Minority Entrepreneurs

Another rapidly growing segment of the small business population is minority-owned businesses. Hispanics, Asians, and African-Americans, are the minority groups most likely to become entrepreneurs, and minority entrepreneurs are launching businesses at a rate that is 1.5 times the national average.[55] Like women, minorities cite discrimination as a principal reason for their limited access to the world of entrepreneurship. Minority-owned businesses have come a long way in the last decade, however, and their success rate is climbing.

After launching Roc-A-Fella Records with rapper Jay-Z and Kareem "Biggs" Burke, entrepreneur Damon Dash launched several other business ventures including film making, an urban lifestyle magazine, watches, a line of MP3 players, and a clothing line called Rocawear, which alone generates $350 million in annual sales for Dash Ventures. "Don't accept 'no' for an answer," Dash advises other entrepreneurs. "No one wanted to give me an opportunity, so I had to do it my own way."[56]

Dash Ventures

A study by the Small Business Administration reported that minorities now own 15 percent of all businesses.[57] Minority-owned businesses generate $591 billion in annual revenues and employ more than 4.51 million workers with a payroll of more than $96 billion.[58] The future is promising for this new generation of minority entrepreneurs, who are better educated, have more business experience, and are better prepared for business ownership than their predecessors.

Immigrant Entrepreneurs

The United States has always been a melting pot of diverse cultures, and many immigrants have been drawn to this nation by its promise of economic freedom. Unlike the unskilled "huddled masses" of the past, today's immigrants arrive with more education and experience. Although many of them come to the United States with few assets, their dedication and desire to succeed enable them to achieve their entrepreneurial dreams.

After emigrating from Ukraine, Dr. Alexander Krilov became the business manager for Los Angeles Lakers basketball star Stanislav Medvedenko. That experience gave Krilov and his wife, Julia Butler, the idea to take traditional Russian nested dolls and put the images of famous National Basketball Association (NBA) players on them. Getting approval from the NBA took time, but Krilov and Butler persevered and won the rights to create nested dolls with portrait-quality images of many NBA stars. Since then, their company, Newcrafters Nesting Dolls, has forged similar deals with Major League Baseball and the National Hockey League as well as Elvis Presley and I Love Lucy properties and generates more than $1 million in annual sales.[59]

Newcrafters Nesting Dolls

Part-Time Entrepreneurs

Starting a part-time business is a popular gateway to entrepreneurship. Part-time entrepreneurs have the best of both worlds: They can ease into business for themselves without sacrificing the security of a steady paycheck and benefits. Approximately 15 million Americans are self-employed part-time. A major advantage of going into business part-time is the lower risk in case the venture flops. Many part-timers are "testing the entrepreneurial waters" to see whether their business ideas will work, whether there is sufficient demand for their products and services, and whether they enjoy being self-employed. As they grow, many part-time enterprises absorb more of the entrepreneur's time until they become full-time businesses.

Joe Carmen decided to keep his job at a technology firm when he started his online guitar string company, String This! Inc. Carmen created a Web site and filled customer orders in the evenings and on weekends. Two years after start-up, however, Carmen transformed his business into a full-time venture when his company downsized and he was laid off.

StringThis! Inc.

Carmen rewrote his business plan and made a few adjustments in the way he ran the business. Within a year, he received a lucrative offer to sell the business, and he accepted it. He is now planning the launch of his next business, which will be a full-time venture.[60]

Home-Based Businesses

Home-based businesses are booming! Fifty-three percent of all businesses are home-based, but about 91 percent of them are very small with no employees other than the principal.[61] Several factors make the home the first-choice location for many entrepreneurs:

- Operating a business from home keeps start-up and operating costs to a minimum.
- Home-based companies allow owners to maintain a flexible lifestyle and workstyle. Many home-based entrepreneurs relish being part of the "open-collar workforce."
- Technology, which is transforming many ordinary homes into "electronic cottages," allows entrepreneurs to run a wide variety of businesses from their homes.
- Many entrepreneurs use the Internet to operate e-commerce businesses from their homes that literally span the globe.

In the past, home-based businesses tended to be rather unexciting cottage industries such as crafts or sewing. Today's home-based businesses are more diverse; modern home-based entrepreneurs are more likely to be running high-tech or service companies with millions of dollars in sales. The average home-based entrepreneur works 61 hours a week and earns an income of $63,000.[62] Studies by Link Resources Corporation, a research and consulting firm, suggest that the success rate for home-based businesses is high: 85 percent of such businesses are still in operation after three years.[63]

COMPANY Profile

MusicStack

Dave Stack operates a Web site from his home for his company, MusicStack, which combines the inventory of more than 3,000 music and record stores that compete on price and selection. MusicStack, which generates more than $5 million in annual sales, allows the 3,000 individual stores to manage their own inventories and prices and offers customers more than 15 million items ranging from CDs, mini-discs, vinyl records, and eight-track tapes—more than online giants eBay and Amazon.com. "Fresh inventory is not a problem," says Stack. "The sheer volume of the site makes [MusicStack] different."[64]

Table 1.2 offers 18 "rules" home-based entrepreneurs should follow to be successful.

TABLE 1.2 Follow These Rules for a Successful Home-Based Business

Rule 1. Do your homework. Much of a home-based business's potential for success depends on how much preparation an entrepreneur makes *before* ever opening for business. The public library is an excellent source for research on customers, industries, competitors, and the like.

Rule 2. Find out what your zoning restrictions are. In some areas local zoning laws make running a business from home illegal. Avoid headaches by checking these laws first. You can always request a variance.

Rule 3. Choose the most efficient location for your office. About half of all home-based entrepreneurs operate out of spare bedrooms. The best way to determine the ideal office location is to examine the nature of your business and your clients. Avoid locating your business in your bedroom or your family room.

Rule 4. Focus your home-based business idea. Avoid the tendency to be "all things to all people." Most successful home-based businesses focus on a particular customer group or on some specialty.

Rule 5. Discuss your business rules with your family. Running a business from your home means you can spend more time with your family . . . and that your family can spend more time with you. Establish the rules for interruptions up front.

Rule 6. Select an appropriate business name. Your first marketing decision is your company's name, so make it a good one! Using your own name is convenient, but it's not likely to help you sell your product or service.

TABLE 1.2 *Continued*

Rule 7. Buy the right equipment. Modern technology allows a home-based entrepreneur to give the appearance of any *Fortune* 500 company, but only if you buy the right equipment. A well-equipped home office should have a separate telephone line, a computer, a laser or inkjet printer, a fax machine (or board), a copier, a scanner, and an answering machine (or voice mail), but realize that you don't have to have everything from Day One.

Rule 8. Dress appropriately. Being an "open-collar worker" is one of the joys of working at home. But when you need to dress up (to meet a client, make a sale, meet your banker, close a deal), do it! Avoid the tendency to lounge around in your bathrobe all day.

Rule 9. Learn to deal with distractions. The best way to fend off the distractions of working at home is to create a business that truly interests you. Budget your time wisely. Your productivity determines your company's success.

Rule 10. Realize that your phone can be your best friend . . . or your worst enemy. As a home-based entrepreneur, you'll spend lots of time on the phone. Be sure you use it productively.

Rule 11. Be firm with friends and neighbors. Sometimes friends and neighbors get the mistaken impression that because you're at home, you're not working. If one drops by to chat while you're working, tactfully ask them to come back "after work."

Rule 12. Take advantage of tax breaks. Although a 1993 Supreme Court decision tightened considerably the standards for business deductions for an office at home, many home-based entrepreneurs still qualify for special tax deductions on everything from computers to cars. Check with your accountant.

Rule 13. Make sure you have adequate insurance coverage. Some homeowner's policies provide adequate coverage for business-related equipment, but many home-based entrepreneurs have inadequate coverage on their business assets. Ask your agent about a business owner's policy (BOP), which may cost as little as $300 to $500 per year.

Rule 14. Understand the special circumstances under which you can hire outside employees. Sometimes zoning laws allow in-home businesses but they prohibit hiring employees. Check zoning laws carefully.

Rule 15. Be prepared if your business requires clients to come to your home. Dress appropriately (no pajamas!). Make sure your office presents a professional image.

Rule 16. Get a post office box. With burglaries and robberies on the rise, you're better off using a "P.O. Box" address rather than your specific home address. Otherwise you may be inviting crime.

Rule 17. Network, network, network. Isolation can be a problem for home-based entrepreneurs, and one of the best ways to combat it is to network. It's also a great way to market your business.

Rule 18. Be proud of your home-based business. Merely a decade ago there was a stigma attached to working from home. Today, home-based entrepreneurs and their businesses command respect. Be proud of your company!

Sources: Lynn Beresford, Janean Chun, Cynthia E. Griffin, Heather Page, and Debra Phillips, "Homeward Bound," *Entrepreneur*, September 1995, pp. 116–118; Jenean Huber, "House Rules," *Entrepreneur*, March 1993, pp. 89–95; Hal Morris, "Home-Based Businesses Need Extra Insurance," *AARP Bulletin*, November 1994, p. 16; Stephanie N. Mehta, "What You Need," *Wall Street Journal*, October 14, 1994, p. R10; Jeffery Zbar, "Home Free," *Business Start-Ups*, June 1999, pp. 31–37.

Family Businesses

A **family-owned business** is one that includes two or more members of a family with financial control of the company. Family businesses are an integral part of our economy. Of the 25 million businesses in the United States, 90 percent are family-owned and managed. These companies account for 60 percent of total U.S. employment and 78 percent of all new jobs, pay 65 percent of all wages, and generate 50 percent of the nation's GDP. Not all of them are small; 37 percent of the *Fortune* 500 companies are family businesses.[65]

"When it works right," says one writer, "nothing succeeds like a family firm. The roots run deep, embedded in family values. The flash of the fast buck is replaced with long-term plans. Tradition counts."[66] Despite their magnitude, family businesses face a major threat, a threat from within: management succession. Only 30 percent of family businesses

family-owned business
one that includes two or more members of a family with financial control of the company.

survive to the second generation, just 12 percent make it to the third generation, and only 3 percent survive into the fourth generation and beyond. Business periodicals are full of stories describing bitter disputes among family members that have crippled or destroyed once-thriving businesses.

To avoid such senseless destruction of valuable assets, founders of family businesses should develop plans for management succession long before retirement looms before them.

After he underwent quadruple heart bypass surgery at age 42, George Davenport, second-generation owner of D&D Motors, a successful auto dealership in Greer, South Carolina, established by Davenport's father in 1937, decided it was time to develop a management succession plan for the family business. "I've spent my whole life building this business," he says. "I'd roll over in my grave if they shut it down after I die." With the help of a family business consultant, the family created a comprehensive succession plan that addressed management as well as estate planning issues. Today, all three of Davenport's children hold offices in the company, each in charge of the area that best suits his or her skills.[67]

Copreneurs

copreneurs

entrepreneurial couples who work together as co-owners of their businesses.

"Copreneurs" are entrepreneurial couples who work together as co-owners of their businesses. Unlike the traditional "Mom and Pop" team (Pop as "boss" and Mom as "subordinate"), copreneurs "are creating a division of labor that is based on expertise as opposed to gender," says one expert.[68] Studies show that companies co-owned by spouses represent one of the fastest-growing business sectors.

Managing a small business with a spouse may appear to be a recipe for divorce, but most copreneurs say otherwise. "There is nothing more exciting than nurturing a business and watching it grow with someone you love," says Marcia Sherrill, who, with her husband, William Kleinberg, runs Kleinberg Sherrill, a leather goods and accessories business.[69] Successful copreneurs learn to build the foundation for a successful working relationship before they ever launch their companies. Some of the characteristics they rely on include the following:

- An assessment of whether their personalities will mesh—or conflict—in a business setting.
- Mutual respect for each other and one another's talents.
- Compatible business and life goals—a common vision.
- A view that they are full and equal partners, not a superior and a subordinate.
- Complementary business skills that each acknowledges and appreciates and that lead to a unique business identity for each spouse.
- The ability to keep lines of communication open, talking and listening to each other about personal as well as business issues.
- A clear division of roles and authority, ideally based on each partner's skills and abilities, to minimize conflict and power struggles.
- The ability to encourage each other and to lift up a disillusioned partner.
- Separate workspaces that allow them to escape when the need arises.
- Boundaries between their business life and their personal life so that one doesn't consume the other.
- A sense of humor.
- The realization that not every couple can work together.

Although copreneuring isn't for everyone, it works extremely well for many couples and often leads to successful businesses. "Both spouses are working for a common purpose but also focusing on their unique talents," says a family business counselor. "With all these skills put together, one plus one equals more than two."[70]

In 1995, Dennis and Susie Thompson left the security of their well-paying corporate jobs to operate a Great Harvest bakery franchise. Their jobs kept them so busy that they "never saw each other," says Susie, so they decided to run the bakery together. Early on, while the Thompsons were defining their roles and settling in to them, disagreements were common. Their business succeeded, partly because the copreneurs established a clear division of responsibilities and stuck to it. Dennis handles production and operations; Susie is responsible for marketing and management. The couple has since opened a second franchise, and they credit their joint efforts for their success. "A lot of husbands and wives can't work together," says Dennis, "but for us it worked out great."[71]

Corporate Castoffs

Concentrating on shedding the excess bulk that took away their flexibility and speed, many large American corporations have been downsizing in an attempt to regain their competitive edge. For decades, one major corporation after another has announced layoffs, and not just among blue-collar workers. Companies are cutting back their executive ranks as well. Millions of people have lost their jobs, and these corporate castoffs have become an important source of entrepreneurial activity. Some 20 percent of these discharged corporate managers have become entrepreneurs, and many of those left behind in corporate America would like to join them.

Many corporate castoffs are deciding that the best defense against future job insecurity is an entrepreneurial offense.

Barry Brinker was in his mid-30s when the large company in which he served as director of new product development was bought by an even larger business. Brinker was one of hundreds of employees whose jobs were eliminated. Rather than risk becoming the victim of another layoff at a large company, Brinker decided to start his own business. Today, Brinker operates BB International, a million-dollar-a-year business that designs and sells jewelry to upscale retailers across the United States ranging from small boutiques to Saks Fifth Avenue and Neiman Marcus. "Being fired was the best thing that ever happened to me," says Brinker, who claims that he would not have accomplished all he has without the push from the corporate nest.[72]

BB International

Corporate Dropouts

The dramatic downsizing of corporate America has created another effect among the employees left after restructuring: a trust gap. The result of this trust gap is a growing number of dropouts from the corporate structure who then become entrepreneurs. Although their workdays may grow longer and their incomes may shrink, those who strike out on their own often find their work more rewarding and more satisfying because they are doing what they enjoy. Other entrepreneurs are inspired to launch their companies after being treated unfairly by large, impersonal corporate entities.

In the 1950s, Marion Kauffman was so successful as a salesman for a pharmaceutical company that his pay exceeded that of the company president, who promptly cut Kauffman's sales territory. Kauffman managed to rebuild sales so that he once again earned more than the boss, who then cut Kauffman's commission rate. Outraged, Kauffman left to start his own business, Marion Laboratories, which he sold to Dow Chemical Company in 1989 for $5.2 billion! Before his death in 1993, Kauffman established the Ewing Marion Kauffman Foundation in Kansas City, Missouri, to promote entrepreneurship.[73]

Marion Laboratories

Because they have college degrees, a working knowledge of business, and years of management experience, both corporate dropouts and castoffs may ultimately increase the small business survival rate. A recent survey by Richard O'Sullivan found that 64 percent of people starting businesses have at least some college education, and 14 percent have advanced degrees.[74] Better-trained, more experienced entrepreneurs are less likely to fail.

Social Entrepreneurs

Social entrepreneurs use their skills not only to create profitable business ventures, but also to achieve social and environmental goals for the common good. Their businesses often have a triple bottom line that encompasses economic, social, and environmental

social entrepreneurs
entrepreneurs who use their skills not only to create profitable businesses, but also to achieve social and environmental goals for the common good.

objectives. These entrepreneurs see their businesses as mechanisms for achieving social goals that are important to them as individuals.

Charlie Trotter, owner of the award-winning Chicago restaurant that bears his name, draws crowds of patrons willing to pay $135 or more per person for a world-class dining experience and to wait three months for a reservation. In addition to achieving his goal of operating a profitable restaurant, Trotter also works hard to make sure his business makes a difference to the people of Chicago. Every weeknight, Trotter devotes one of his restaurant's magnificent eight-course seatings to local high school students as part of his Excellence Initiative, which is designed not only to allow students to enjoy a stellar meal, but also to tour the restaurant and hear staff members talk about their passion for their work and their commitment to excellence. "This is about showing them what intensity is and what exuberance is," says Trotter. In addition to the Excellence Initiative, Trotter donates some of the company's profits to local charities. He also has raised $450,000 to fund scholarships for worthy students at culinary schools. "Anyone can raise money and give it away," says Trotter. "What's most interesting to me is having the young folks here in the restaurant and spreading the idea that you get what you give."[75]

LEARNING OBJECTIVES
6. Describe the important role small businesses play in our nation's economy.

small business

one that employs fewer than 100 people.

The Power of "Small" Business

Of the 25 million businesses in the United States, approximately 24.92 million, or 99.7 percent, are considered "small." Although there is no universal definition of a small business (the U.S. Small Business Administration has more than 800 definitions of a small business based on industry categories), a common delineation of a **small business** is one that employs fewer than 100 people. They thrive in virtually every industry, although the majority of small companies are concentrated in the service and retail industries (see Figure 1.6). Although they may be small businesses, their contributions to the economy are anything but small. For example, small companies employ 51 percent of the nation's private sector work force, even though they possess less than one-fourth of total business assets. Almost 90 percent of small businesses employ fewer than 20 workers. Because they are primarily labor intensive, small businesses actually create more jobs than do big businesses. In fact, small companies have created two-thirds to three-fourths of the net new jobs in the U.S. economy.[76]

David Birch, president of the research firm Arc Analytics, says, however, that the ability to create jobs is not distributed evenly across the small business sector. His research shows that just 3 percent of these small companies created 70 percent of the net new jobs in the economy, and they did so across all industry sectors, not just in "hot" industries.

FIGURE 1.6

Small Businesses by Industry

Source: U.S. Small Business Administration, 2005.

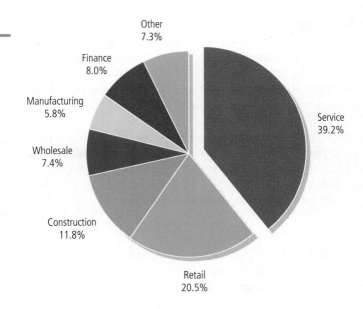

Birch calls these job-creating small companies "**gazelles**," those growing at 20 percent or more per year for four years with at least $100,000 in annual sales. His research also identified "mice," small companies that never grow much and don't create many jobs. The majority of small companies are "mice." Birch tabbed the country's largest businesses "elephants," which have continued to shed jobs for several years.[77]

Not only do small companies lead the way in creating jobs, but they also bear the brunt of training workers for them. One study by the Small Business Administration concluded that small businesses are the leaders in offering training and advancement opportunities to workers. Small companies offer more general skills instruction and training than large ones, and their employees receive more benefits from the training than do those in larger firms. Although their training programs tend to be informal, in-house, and on-the-job, small companies teach employees valuable skills, from written communication to computer literacy.[78]

Small businesses also produce 51 percent of the country's private GDP and account for 47 percent of business sales.[79] In fact, the U.S. small business sector is the world's third-largest "economy," trailing only the entire U.S. economy and China![80] Small companies also are incubators of new ideas, products, and services. Small firms actually create 13 to 14 times more innovations per research employee than large companies.[81] Traditionally, small businesses have played a vital role in innovation, and they continue to do so today. Many important inventions trace their roots to an entrepreneur, including the zipper, FM radio, the laser, air conditioning, the escalator, the light bulb, the personal computer, and the automatic transmission.

gazelles
small companies that are growing at 20 percent or more per year with at least $100,000 in annual sales; they create 70 percent of net new jobs in the economy.

Hands on ... How to

Transform Your Great Business Idea into Reality

It happens thousands of times every day: Someone comes up with a great idea for a new product, a modification of an existing product, or a new service. He or she is absolutely certain that the idea is going to be "the next big thing." Indeed, the U.S. Patent and Trademark Office (USPTO) receives more than 366,000 patent applications a year (but issues only about 187,000 patents a year). Technological advances, the Internet, faster communication tools, increased global interconnectivity, and computer-aided-design tools that allow inventors to go from the idea stage to creating a prototype faster than ever have made transforming a great idea into reality much easier than at any point in the past.

Does a "great idea" necessarily transfer into a successful business? Not always. So . . . what can a creative genius with a great idea do to put it to the test of business viability?

Step 1: Put your vision down on paper. You can draw a sketch of your concept by hand, use one of the many computer programs such as Adobe Illustrator to help you, or hire a freelance artist (perhaps from a local college or university) to help you. Getting a sketch and a description of your idea forces you to think about the total concept as well as the features of the product or service. It also makes it easier for you to explain your idea to others and to move on to Step 2.

Step 2: Test it to see if it really is a good idea. The reality is that transforming an idea into a successful business concept is much like the television show *American Idol*. For every person who really is a great singer, there are 99 people who can't stay on key but who *think* they are great singers. (Remember how bad a singer William Hung was, despite the fact that he actually made it onto television?) This step involves getting a reality check from other people—and not just friends and relatives who may not tell you what they really think about your idea because they don't want to hurt your feelings. One key is to involve potential customers and people who are knowledgeable about the particular industry into which your idea fits in evaluating your idea.

This step requires potential entrepreneurs to maintain a delicate balance between getting valuable feedback on their idea and protecting it from those who might steal it. Before they reveal their ideas to other people, some would-be entrepreneurs rely on nondisclosure agreements, contracts in which the other party promises not to use the idea for his or her own gain or to reveal it to others. Typically, the feedback, input, and advice entrepreneurs get at this phase far outweigh the risks of disclosing their ideas to others. "If you are on a mission, your first concern shouldn't be what someone takes from you but to be aggressive in refining [your idea]," says Rich Sloan, co-host with his brother Jeff of StartupNation.com and a nationally syndicated radio show designed to offer advice to entrepreneurs and inventors.

Sometimes entrepreneurs discover that Step 2 is as far as they should go; otherwise, they would be wasting time, talent, and resources. For instance, one venture capital investor recalls listening as an inventor excitedly described how he had figured out a creative way to speed the signal that passed from the keyboard of a computer to the processor so that text would appear on the screen faster. The only problem: Text already appears on a computer screen much faster than the human eye can blink! Who would notice the difference? "He'd created an elegant technical solution to a problem that didn't exist," says the venture capitalist.

Other entrepreneurs receive confirmation that they really are on to something in Step 2. While driving a long stretch of Western highway, truck driver Jeremiah Hutchins was listening to news reports and talk shows about a missing California girl. "All [of] the shows kept saying, 'If only they'd had better information about her,'" he recalls. Hutchins, together with a friend who was a security guard for the same trucking firm, had been toying with the idea of producing business cards on mini-CDs. He thought, "Why not apply the same concept to children's identification information?"

The next morning, Hutchins contacted a police investigator whom his wife knew to get feedback on his idea from a potential user of his idea. The police officer expressed a great deal of interest in the idea and encouraged Hutchins to pursue it. His next stop was the Internet, on which he conducted searches on "children identification." When his searches turned up very few leads, Hutchins concluded that there was very little competition in this market niche. Hutchins then went back to the police investigator to ask about the types of information police would need in a missing child case and then figured out how to put it on a mini-CD that parents could keep.

Using the information from the police investigator, Hutchins and his partner began developing a prototype mini-CD, testing everything from different types of digital cameras, CD burners, and ink to see which ones resisted smudges. Within 10 days, with prototype in hand, they made a presentation to Hutchins' police contact, who was so impressed that she invited the entrepreneurs to a local safety fair, where they had the chance to interact with real paying customers. Just three weeks after his initial brainstorm, Safe Kids Card Inc. sold 150 IDs to parents for $20 each. More important, the safety fair gave the entrepreneurs a solid gauge of the potential their idea had in the marketplace. Today, Safe Kids Card Inc. generates more than $1 million in revenue and has 44 franchises across the United States and three international operations selling children's ID cards for $13 each.

Step 3: Decide how serious you are about pursuing your idea and turning it into a business venture. As you have seen in this chapter, building a business is not for the faint-hearted. It requires a serious commitment of time, talent, energy, and resources. Taking the time to evaluate honestly the advantages and the disadvantages of owning your own business will help you to decide whether you should take the first step toward entrepreneurship.

Sources: Adapted from "U.S. Patent Statistics Chart," U.S. Patent and Trademark Office, http://www.uspto.gov/web/offices/ac/ido/oeip/taf/us_stat.htm; Gwendolyn Bounds, "You Have a Great Idea. Now What?" *Wall Street Journal*, May 9, 2005, pp. R1, R3; Michael V. Copeland and Andrew Tilin, "The New Instant Companies," *Business 2.0*, June 2005, pp. 82–94; Daniel Roth, "The Amazing Rise of the Do-It-Yourself Economy," *Fortune*, May 30, 2005, pp. 45–46.

The Ten Deadly Mistakes of Entrepreneurship

Because of their limited resources, inexperienced management, and lack of financial stability, small businesses suffer a mortality rate significantly higher than that of larger, established businesses. Figure 1.7 illustrates the small business survival rate over a 10-year period. Exploring the circumstances surrounding business failure may help you to avoid it.

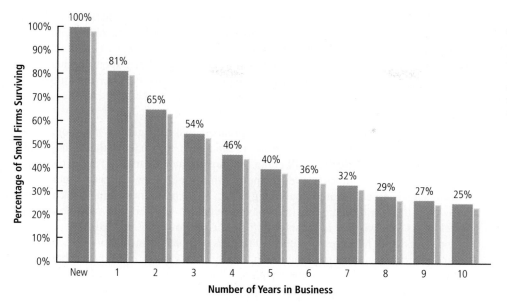

FIGURE 1.7

Small Business Survival Rate

Source: *NFIB Small-Business Policy Guide,* 2003, http://www.nfib.com/object/2753115.html, p. 16.

1. ***Management mistakes.*** In most small businesses, poor management is the primary cause of business failure. Sometimes the manager of a small business does not have the capacity to operate it successfully. The owner lacks the leadership ability, sound judgment, and knowledge necessary to make the business work. Many managers simply do not have what it takes to run a small enterprise. "What kills companies usually has less to do with insufficient money, talent, or information than with something more basic: a shortage of good judgment and understanding at the very top," says one business researcher.[82]

2. ***Lack of experience.*** Small business managers need to have experience in the field they want to enter. For example, if an entrepreneur wants to open a retail clothing business, he or she should first work in a retail clothing store. This will provide practical experience as well as knowledge about the nature of the business, which can spell the difference between failure and success. One aspiring entrepreneur who wanted to launch a restaurant went to work for a national chain known for its high-quality management training program after he graduated from college. After completing the training program, he took on a variety of tasks, from cook to manager, in one of the chain's restaurants. He took advantage of every subsequent training opportunity the company offered and asked lots of questions. He began developing a business plan based on his idea for a restaurant, and after nearly five years, he left to start his own restaurant. He credits the knowledge and experience he gained during that time for much of his success in the business.

   Ideally, a prospective entrepreneur should have adequate technical ability (a working knowledge of the physical operations of the business and sufficient conceptual ability); the power to visualize, coordinate, and integrate the various operations of the business into a synergistic whole; and the skill to manage the people in the organization and motivate them to higher levels of performance.

3. ***Poor financial control.*** Sound management is the key to a small company's success, and effective managers realize that any successful business venture requires proper financial control. Business success also requires having a sufficient amount of capital on hand at start-up. Undercapitalization is a common cause of business failure because companies run out of capital before they are able to generate positive cash flow. Many small business owners make the mistake of beginning their businesses on a "shoestring," which can be a fatal error. Entrepreneurs tend to be overly optimistic and often misjudge the financial requirements of going into business. As a result, they start off undercapitalized and can never seem to catch up financially as their companies consume increasing amounts of cash to fuel their growth.

   Another aspect of adequate financial control is implementing proper cash management techniques. Many entrepreneurs believe that profit is what matters most in a new venture, but cash is the most important financial resource a company owns.

Maintaining adequate cash flow to pay bills on time is a constant challenge for entrepreneurs, especially those in the turbulent start-up phase or for established companies experiencing rapid growth. Fast-growing companies devour cash fast! Poor credit screening, sloppy debt collection practices, and undisciplined spending habits are common factors in many business bankruptcies. One Internet company that ultimately went bust spent valuable cash on frivolous items such as a $40,000 conference table and a huge office aquarium that cost $4,000 a month to maintain.[83]

4. *Weak marketing efforts.* Sometimes entrepreneurs make the classic "*Field of Dreams* mistake." Like Kevin Costner's character in the movie, they believe that if they "build it," customers automatically "will come." Although the idea makes for a great movie plot, in business, it almost never happens. Building a growing base of customers requires a sustained, creative marketing effort. Keeping them coming back requires providing them with value, quality, convenience, service, and fun—and doing it all quickly. As you will see in Chapter 8, "Building a Powerful Marketing Plan," small companies do not have to spend enormous sums of money to sustain a successful marketing effort. Creative entrepreneurs find innovative ways to market their businesses effectively to their target customers without breaking the bank.

5. *Failure to develop a strategic plan.* Too many small business managers neglect the process of strategic planning because they think that it is something that benefits only large companies. "I don't have the time" or "We're too small to develop a strategic plan," they rationalize. Failure to plan, however, usually results in failure to survive. Without a clearly defined strategy, a business has no sustainable basis for creating and maintaining a competitive edge in the marketplace. Building a strategic plan forces an entrepreneur to assess *realistically* a proposed business's potential. Is it something customers are willing and able to purchase? Who is the target customer? How will the business attract and keep those customers? What is the company's basis for serving customers' needs better than existing companies? How will the business gain a sustainable edge over its rivals? We will explore these and other vital issues in Chapter 3, "Designing a Competitive Business Model and Building a Solid Strategic Plan."

6. *Uncontrolled growth.* Growth is a natural, healthy, and desirable part of any business enterprise, but it must be planned and controlled. Management expert Peter Drucker says that start-up companies can expect to outgrow their capital bases each time sales increase 40 to 50 percent.[84] Ideally, expansion should be financed by the profits they generate ("retained earnings") or by capital contributions from the owners, but most businesses wind up borrowing at least a portion of the capital investment.

Expansion usually requires major changes in organizational structure, business practices such as inventory and financial control procedures, personnel assignments, and other areas. The most important change, however, occurs in managerial expertise. As the business increases in size and complexity, problems increase in magnitude, and the entrepreneur must learn to deal with them. Sometimes entrepreneurs encourage rapid growth, only to have the business outstrip their ability to manage it.

Avico and Prizm

Robert Schell, whose e-commerce consulting company, Avico, was growing fast enough to make *Inc.* magazine's list of the 500 fastest-growing companies in the United States, discovered too late the perils of rapid growth. Expanding too rapidly stretched the company's resources beyond their capacity and Schell's ability to control the business, and he was forced to lay off all of his employees and close the company. Schell, who now owns another company, Prizm, that also has made it to the *Inc.* 500 list, has used what he learned from his previous failure to avoid making the same mistakes again. "If a company doesn't have the right foundation, it can fall apart like a house of cards," he says.[85]

7. *Poor location.* For any business, choosing the right location is partly an art and partly a science. Too often, business locations are selected without proper study, investigation, and planning. Some beginning owners choose a particular location just because they noticed a vacant building. The location question is much too critical to leave to chance. Especially for retailers, the lifeblood of the business—sales—is influenced heavily by choice of location.

Before Dylan and Elise Fager bought their Mailboxes, Etc. (MBE) franchise, they invested a great deal of time researching the ideal site. Their final choice was a site across the street from a major shopping mall, which generated lots of customer traffic every day. The Fagers' research also showed them that the site was within five miles of 2 to 3 million square feet of office space, providing prime access to large numbers of potential customers. The Fagers' franchise was so successful that they quickly opened a second MBE franchise in the downtown district. A major advantage of that site was a complete lack of nearby competition.[86]

COMPANY
Profile

Mailboxes, Etc.

8. ***Improper inventory control.*** Normally, the largest investment a small business owner makes is in inventory, yet inventory control is one of the most neglected managerial responsibilities. Insufficient inventory levels result in shortages and stockouts, causing customers to become disillusioned and leave. A more common situation is that the manager has not only too much inventory, but also too much of the *wrong type* of inventory. Many small firms have an excessive amount of cash tied up in an accumulation of useless inventory. Computerized point-of-sale systems are now priced low enough to be affordable for small businesses, and they can track items as they come in and go out, allowing business owners to avoid inventory problems.

9. ***Incorrect pricing.*** Establishing prices that will generate the necessary profits means that business owners must understand how much it costs to make, market, and deliver their products and services. Too often, entrepreneurs simply charge what competitors charge or base their prices on some vague idea of "selling the best product at the lowest price," both of which approaches are dangerous. Small business owners usually underprice their products and services. The first step in establishing accurate prices is to know what a product or service costs to make or to provide. Then, business owners can establish prices that reflect the image they want to create for their companies, always, of course, with an eye on the competition.

10. ***Inability to make the "Entrepreneurial Transition."*** Making it over the "entrepreneurial start-up hump" is no guarantee of business success. After the start-up, growth usually requires a radically different style of management, one that entrepreneurs are not necessarily good at. The very abilities that make an entrepreneur successful often lead to managerial ineffectiveness. Growth requires entrepreneurs to delegate authority and to relinquish hands-on control of daily operations, something many entrepreneurs simply cannot do. Growth pushes them into areas where they are not capable, yet they continue to make decisions rather than involve others.

Table 1.3 explains some of the symptoms of these 10 deadly mistakes.

TABLE 1.3 Symptoms of the 10 Deadly Mistakes of Entrepreneurship

Entrepreneurs whose businesses fail usually can look back on their experiences and see what they did wrong, vowing never to make the same mistake again. If you find yourself making any of the following statements as you launch your business, look out! You may become a victim of one of the 10 deadly mistakes of entrepreneurship.

"We've got a great product (or service)! It will sell itself." Don't get so caught up in your product or service that you forget to evaluate whether real, live customers are willing and able to pay for it. Oh ... and no product or service has ever "sold itself."

"With a market this big, we only need a tiny share of it to become rich." Entrepreneurs tend to be overly optimistic in their sales, profits, and cash flow estimates, especially in the beginning. Most don't realize until they get into business how tough it really is to capture even a tiny share of the market.

"Strategic plan?! We don't need a strategic plan. That's only for big corporations." One of the quickest and surest paths to failure is neglecting to build a strategic plan that defines some point of distinction for your company. A plan helps you focus on what you can do for your customers that your competitors cannot.

"What a great business idea! It's cheap, easy to start, and it's the current rage," Because a business idea is so cheap and easy to start does not necessarily make it attractive. Too many entrepreneurs get clobbered in such businesses once the market matures and the competition gets stiff or the fad passes.

TABLE 1.3 *Continued*

"We may not know what we're doing yet, but we've got enough capital to last us until we do. We'll figure it out as we go" Everything—especially launching a business—takes longer and costs more than you think. Experienced entrepreneurs call it "the rule of two and three," Start-ups take either twice as long or need three times as much money (or both) to get off the ground as the founders forecast. Plan accordingly.

"Our forecast shows that we'll be making profits within three months; and that's very conservative ... really," Everyone expects entrepreneurs to be optimistic about their ventures' future, but you have to temper your optimism with reality. Launching a business on the basis of one set of forecasts is asking for trouble. Make sure you develop at least three sets of forecasts—pessimistic, most likely, and optimistic—and have contingency plans for all three.

"It's a good thing that we've got enough capital to last us the few months until we hit our break-even point." Attracting adequate start-up financing is essential to launching your business, but you also have to have access to *continuing* sources of funding. Growing businesses consume cash, and fast-growing businesses consume cash even faster. Don't become a victim of your own success; make sure you establish reliable sources of capital once your business is up and running.

"We'll make it easy for customers to buy from us. We'll extend credit to almost anyone to make a sale. One of the shortest routes to cash flow problems is failing to manage customer credit. It's easy to make a sale, but remember: Sales don't count unless you actually collect the payments for them. Watch for slow-paying customers.

"We're in the big time now. Our largest customer is [insert name of large customer here]." Landing a big customer is great, but it's dangerous to become overly dependent on a single customer for most of your sales. What happens if they decide to squeeze you for price concessions or to go to a competitor?

"Let's have our annual meeting in the Cayman Islands. We're the only 'stockholders,' and, besides, we deserve it. We've worked hard." Avoid the tendency to drain cash out of your business unnecessarily. A good rule of thumb: Don't start your business unless you have enough savings to support yourself (without taking cash from it) until the business breaks even.

"Let's go with this location. I know it's 'off the beaten path,' but it's so much cheaper!" For some businesses, choice of location is not a crucial issue. However, if your company relies on customers coming into your place of business to make sales, do not settle for the cheapest location. There's a reason such places are cheap! It's better to pay a higher price for a location that produces adequate sales volume.

"We're so small here. Everybody knows what our goals and objectives are." Just because a business is small doesn't necessarily mean that everyone who works there understands where you are trying to take the company. Do not assume that people will read your mind concerning your company's mission, goals, and objectives. You must communicate your vision for the business to everyone involved in it.

"This business is so easy it can run itself." Don't fool yourself. The only place a business will run itself is downhill! You must manage your company, and one of the most important jobs you have as leader is to prioritize your business's objectives.

"Of course our customers are satisfied! I never hear them complain." Most customers never complain about poor service or bad quality. They simply refuse to do business with you again. More often than not, the service and level of "personal treatment" that customers receive is what allows many small businesses to gain an edge over their larger rivals. Unfortunately, it's also one of the most overlooked aspects of a business. Set up a system to get regular feedback from your customers.

"What do you mean we're out of cash? We've been making a profit for months now, and sales are growing." Don't confuse cash and profits. You cannot spend profits—just cash. Many businesses fail because their founders mistakenly assume that if profits are rising, so is the company's cash balance. To be successful, you must manage both profits and cash!

Sources: Adapted from Ram Charan and Jerry Useem, "Why Companies Fail," *Fortune,* May 27, 2002, pp. 50–62; Frederick J. Beste III, "Avoiding the Traps Set for Small Firms," *Nation's Business,* January 1999, p. 10; Mel Mandell, "Fifteen Start-Up Mistakes," *Business Start-Ups,* December 1995, p. 22; Kenneth Labich, "Why Companies Fail," *Fortune,* November 14, 1994, pp. 52–68; Sharon Nelton, "Ten Key Threats to Success," *"Nation's Business,* June 1992, pp. 22–30; Robert J. Cook, "Famous Last Words," *Entrepreneur,* June 1994, pp. 122–128; David M. Anderson, "Deadly Sins," *Entrepreneur B.Y.O.B.,* August 2001, pp. 107–109; Geoff Williams, "109 Million Dollars Baked in a Pie," *Entrepreneur, B.Y.O.B.,* September 2001, pp. 107–109.

The first time Jerry Seinfeld walked onto the stage as a professional comedian, he looked at the audience and froze. He managed to stumble through a minute-and-a-half of his material before being booed off the stage. Like true entrepreneurs, however, Seinfeld refused to give up in the face of failure and went on to create one of the most successful television series of all time based on his standup comedy routines.

Putting Failure into Perspective

LEARNING OBJECTIVES
8. Put failure into the proper perspective.

Because they are building businesses in an environment filled with uncertainty and shaped by rapid change, entrepreneurs recognize that failure is likely to be part of their lives, but they are not paralyzed by that fear. "The excitement of building a new business from scratch is greater than the fear of failure," says one entrepreneur who failed in business several times before finally succeeding.[87] Entrepreneurs use their failures as a rallying point and as a means of refocusing their business ventures for success. They see failure for what it really is: an opportunity to learn what does not work. Successful entrepreneurs have the attitude that failures are simply stepping stones along the path to success

Failure is a natural part of the creative process. The only people who never fail are those who never do anything or never attempt anything new. Baseball fans know that Babe Ruth held the record for career home runs (714) for many years, but how many know that he also held the record for strikeouts (1,330)? Successful entrepreneurs know that hitting an entrepreneurial home run requires a few strikeouts along the way, and they are willing to accept them. Failure is an inevitable part of being an entrepreneur, and true entrepreneurs don't quit when they fail. One entrepreneur whose business burned through $800 million of investors' money before folding says, "If you're an entrepreneur, you don't give up when times get tough."[88]

One hallmark of successful entrepreneurs is the ability to fail *intelligently*, learning why they failed so that they can avoid making the same mistake again. They know that business success does not depend on their ability to avoid making mistakes but on their ability to be open to the lessons each mistake teaches. They learn from their failures and use them as fuel to push themselves closer to their ultimate target. Entrepreneurs are less worried about what they might lose if they try something and fail than about what they might lose if they fail to try.

Entrepreneurial success requires both persistence and resilience, the ability to bounce back from failure. Thomas Edison discovered about 1,800 ways not to build a light bulb before hitting on a design that worked. Walt Disney was fired from a newspaper job because, according to his boss, he "lacked imagination and had no good ideas." Disney also went bankrupt several times before he created Disneyland. R. H. Macy failed in business seven times before his retail store in New York City became a success. In the spirit of true entrepreneurship, these visionary business leaders refused to give up in the face of failure; they simply kept trying until they achieved success.

If at First You Don't Succeed, So What!?

"Would you like for me to give you a formula for success? It's quite simple, really: Double your rate of failure. You are thinking of failure as the enemy of success. But it isn't at all. You can be discouraged by failure, or you can learn from it. So go ahead and make mistakes. Make all you can. Because remember, that's where you will find success."

—**Thomas J. Watson**
Founder, IBM

Thomas Watson understood what true entrepreneurs know: that failure is a necessary and important part of the entrepreneurial process and that it does not have to be permanent. Some of the world's greatest entrepreneurs failed (some of them many times) before they finally succeeded. Henry Ford's first business, the Detroit Automobile Company, failed less than two years after Ford and his partners started it. Ford's second auto company also failed, but his third attempt in the then-new auto manufacturing business was, of course, a huge success. The Ford Motor Company, which is still controlled by the Ford family, is a major player in the automotive industry and is one of the largest companies in the world. Milton Hershey launched his first candy shop at age 18 in Philadelphia; it failed after six years. Four more attempts at building a candy business also failed before Hershey finally hit on success with the Lancaster Caramel Company, the business that was the parent of the famous Hershey Foods Corporation. Today, Hershey is the leading manufacturer of chocolate products in the United States and exports to more than 90 countries.

In post–World War II Japan, Masaru Ibuka and Akio Morita formed a partnership to produce an automatic rice cooker. Unfortunately, their machine burned the rice and was a flop. Their company sold just 100 cookers. Ibuka and Morita refused to give up, however, and created another company to build an inexpensive tape recorder that they sold to schools. Their tape recorder proved to be successful, and the company eventually became the consumer electronics giant Sony Corporation.

Rick Rosenfield and Larry Flax wrote a screenplay that never sold, started an Italian restaurant that went bankrupt, and developed a mobile skateboard park that quickly flopped. Then, in 1984, they tried the restaurant business again, launched the California Pizza Kitchen, and struck pay dirt. The California Pizza Kitchen is now a successful and well-recognized chain.

Over the course of his career, Dick Enrico has launched 20 companies that have either failed or been sold at fire sale prices, but Enrico took the lessons learned from his many failures and used them to build an exercise equipment business into a highly successful chain of 33 stores that generates more than $50 million in annual sales. Dick's brother, Roger, who achieved success in the corporate world by working his way to the top spot at soft drink giant Pepsico, admires Dick's business acumen. "He is the quintessential man of perseverance," says Roger. "It is that ability to persevere and to stay with it that makes really good business leaders."

Gail Borden (1801–1874) also knew about failure because he had a great deal of experience with it. One of his first inventions, the Terraqueous Wagon, a combination of wagon and sailboat that was designed to travel on both land and water, sank on its first trial run. Several years later, after returning to the United States from London where he had been promoting another invention, the condensed meat biscuit (a concoction of dehydrated meat and flour), Borden saw four babies die from tainted milk. He dropped the meat biscuit to focus on making milk safer for human consumption. He knew that the key was to remove the water from the milk, but the challenge was to do so without affecting its taste. For two years, he worked without success, always ending up with scorched milk. Ultimately Borden developed a vacuum condensation process that successfully removed the water from milk without adversely affecting its flavor. After three unsuccessful attempts, Borden finally won a patent for his process in 1856 and set up a manufacturing plant. It failed. A second attempt to produce condensed milk also failed. Undaunted, Borden convinced New York financier Jeremiah Milbank to invest in a new milk-processing venture, and this one succeeded. The New York Condensed Milk Company supplied much-needed nourishment to troops during the Civil War before becoming a staple in American households. Today, Borden Inc. is a multibillion-dollar conglomerate that still manufactures condensed milk using the same process that Borden developed 150 years ago. When he died in 1874, Gail Borden was buried beneath a tombstone that read, "I tried and failed; I tried again and succeeded."

1. Do the entrepreneurs described above exhibit the true entrepreneurial spirit? If so, how?
2. How do these entrepreneurs view failure? Is their view typical of most entrepreneurs?

3. James Joyce said, "Mistakes are the portals of discovery." What did he mean? Do you agree? Why is Joyce's idea important to entrepreneurs?

Sources: Adapted from Janet Adamy, "Try, Try Again," *Wall Street Journal*, July 12, 2004, p. R9; "Gail Borden," http://www.famoustexans.com/GailBorden.htm; Jeffrey Shuman and David Rottenberg, "Famous Failures," *Business Start-Ups*, February 1999, pp. 32–33; Francis Huffman, "A Dairy Tail," *Entrepreneur*, August 1993, p. 182; Bob Gatty, "Building on Failure," *Nation's Business*, April 1987, pp. 50–51.

Frank Giotto operates three successful businesses, including Fiber Instrument Sales, a fiber-optic cable business, but Giotto would not be a successful entrepreneur today if he had let failure stop him. Giotto started five other companies that failed before he achieved his current success. One business delivered pickles and olives to grocery stores, another sold pizza to supermarket deli counters, and one offered guided tours of Utica, New York. Despite his failures, Giotto kept trying. When it comes to failure, entrepreneurs' motto seems to be: Failure is temporary; quitting is permanent.[89]

Frank Giotto

How to Avoid the Pitfalls

We have seen the most common reasons behind many small business failures. Now we must examine the ways to avoid becoming another failure statistic and gain insight into what makes a successful business. The suggestions for success follow naturally from the causes of business failure.

LEARNING OBJECTIVES
9. Explain how an entrepreneur can avoid becoming another failure statistic.

Know Your Business in Depth

We have already emphasized the need for the right type of experience in the business you plan to start. Get the best education in your business area you possibly can *before* you set out on your own. Become a serious student of your industry. Read everything you can that relates to your industry—trade journals, business periodicals, books, research reports—and learn what it takes to succeed in it. Personal contact with suppliers, customers, trade associations, and others in the same industry is another excellent way to get that knowledge. Smart entrepreneurs join industry trade associations and attend trade shows to pick up valuable information and to make key contacts before they open their doors for business.

Before she launched Executive Temporaries, Suzanne Clifton contacted other entrepreneurs in the temporary personnel services business (far enough away from her home base to avoid competitors) to find out "what it takes to operate this kind of business." She picked up many valuable tips and identified the key factors required for success. Today her company is a highly respected leader in the industry.[90]

Executive Temporaries

Successful entrepreneurs are like sponges, soaking up as much knowledge as they can from a variety of sources.

Develop a Solid Business Plan

For any entrepreneur, a well-written business plan is a crucial ingredient in preparing for business success. Without a sound business plan, a firm merely drifts along without any real direction. Yet entrepreneurs, who tend to be people of action, too often jump right into a business venture without taking time to prepare a written plan outlining the essence of the business. Unfortunately, most entrepreneurs never take the time to develop a solid business plan. Not only does a plan provide a pathway to success, but it also creates a benchmark against which an entrepreneur can measure actual company performance. Resources to create a business plan, including software such as Business Plan Pro™, which may accompany this book, are available to help aspiring and current business owners create their business plans. Building a successful business begins with implementing a sound business plan with laser-like focus.

A business plan allows entrepreneurs to replace sometimes-faulty assumptions with facts before making the decision to go into business. The planning process forces entrepreneurs to ask and then answer some difficult, challenging, and crucial questions.

TerraCycle International

In his freshman year at Princeton, Tom Szaky created a business plan that helped him to launch TerraCycle International, a company that uses red worms to compost food waste into nutrient-rich soil. Szaky's ingenious plan was to sell waste disposal services to restaurants, schools, penitentiaries, and other institutions; the worms transform the waste into organic soil, which the company sells at premium prices to garden centers, nurseries, supermarkets, and other retail outlets. Because many of its key "employees" are worms and because the company can sell the organic soil they produce at premium prices, TerraCycle offers waste disposal fees that are 25 percent below those of traditional waste-disposal companies. Szaky's research told him that the organic segment of the potting soil industry is a multi-billion-dollar business and has been growing at double-digit rates for the last several years. TerraCycle recently signed a contract with clients across northern New Jersey to process 130 tons of food waste a day. Szaky's plans include expansion into the global market, and the company already has inquiries from potential partners in four countries.[91]

We will discuss the process of developing a business plan in Chapter 4, "Conducting a Feasibility Analysis and Crafting a Winning Business Plan."

Manage Financial Resources

The best defense against financial problems is to develop a practical information system and then use this information to make business decisions. No entrepreneur can maintain control over a business unless he or she is able to judge its financial health.

The first step in managing financial resources effectively is to have adequate start-up capital. Too many entrepreneurs begin their businesses with too little capital. One experienced business owner advises, "Estimate how much capital you need to get the business going and then double that figure." His point is well taken; it almost always costs more to launch a business than any entrepreneur expects.

The most valuable financial resource to any small business is *cash*. Although earning a profit is essential to its long-term survival, a business must have an adequate supply of cash to pay its bills and obligations. Some entrepreneurs count on growing sales to supply their company's cash needs, but this almost never happens. Growing companies usually consume more cash than they generate, and the faster they grow, the more cash they gobble up! Business history is littered with failed companies whose founders had no idea how much cash their businesses were generating and were spending cash as if they were certain there was "plenty more where that came from." We will discuss cash management techniques in Chapter 12, "Managing Cash Flow."

Understand Financial Statements

Every business owner must depend on records and financial statements to know the condition of her or his business. All too often entrepreneurs use these only for tax purposes and not as vital management control devices. Truly to understand what is going on in the business, an owner must have at least a basic understanding of accounting and finance.

When analyzed and interpreted properly, these financial statements are reliable indicators of a small firm's health. They can be quite helpful in signaling potential problems. For example, declining sales, slipping profits, rising debt, and deteriorating working capital are all symptoms of potentially lethal problems that require immediate attention. We will discuss financial statement analysis in Chapter 11, "Creating a Successful Financial Plan."

Learn to Manage People Effectively

No matter what kind of business you launch, you must learn to manage people. Every business depends on a foundation of well-trained, motivated employees. No business owner can do everything alone. The people an entrepreneur hires ultimately determine the heights to which the company can climb—or the depths to which it can plunge. Attracting and retaining a corps of quality employees is no easy task, however. It remains a challenge for every small business owner. "In the end, your most dominant sustainable resource is the quality of the people you have," says one small business expert.[92] We will discuss the techniques of managing and motivating people effectively in Chapter 16, "Building a New Venture Team and Planning for the Next Generation."

Keep in Tune with Yourself

"Starting a business is like running a marathon. If you're not physically and mentally in shape, you'd better do something else," says one business consultant.[93] The success of your business will depend on your constant presence and attention, so it is critical to monitor your health closely. Stress is a primary problem, especially if it is not kept in check.

Successful entrepreneurs recognize that their most valuable asset is their time, and they learn to manage it effectively to make themselves and their companies more productive. None of this, of course, is possible without passion—passion for their businesses, their products or services, their customers, their communities. Passion is what enables a failed entrepreneur to get back up, try again, and make it to the top.

Chapter Summary by Learning Objectives

1. Define the role of the entrepreneur in business in the United States and around the world.

Entrepreneurship is thriving in the United States, but the current wave of entrepreneurship is not limited to this country; many nations across the globe are seeing similar growth in their small business sectors. A variety of competitive, economic, and demographic shifts have created a world in which "small is beautiful."

Capitalist societies depend on entrepreneurs to provide the drive and risk taking necessary for the system to supply people with the goods and services they need.

2. Describe the entrepreneurial profile and evaluate your potential as an entrepreneur.

Entrepreneurs have some common characteristics, including a desire for responsibility, a preference for moderate risk, confidence in their ability to succeed, desire for immediate feedback, a high energy level, a future-directed orientation, skill at organizing, and a valuing of achievement over money. In a phrase, they are tenacious high achievers.

3A. Describe the benefits of entrepreneurship.

Driven by these personal characteristics, entrepreneurs establish and manage small businesses to gain control over their lives, make a difference in the world, become self-fulfilled, reap unlimited profits, contribute to society, and do what they enjoy doing.

3B. Describe the drawbacks of entrepreneurship.

Entrepreneurs also face certain disadvantages, including uncertainty of income, the risk of losing their investments (and more), long hours and hard work, a lower quality of life until the business gets established, high stress levels, and complete decision-making responsibility.

4. Explain the forces that are driving the growth of entrepreneurship.

Several factors are driving the boom in entrepreneurship, including the portrayal of entrepreneurs as heroes, better entrepreneurial education, economic and demographic factors, a shift to a service economy, technological advances, more independent lifestyles, and increased international opportunities.

5. Explain the cultural diversity of entrepreneurship.

Several groups are leading the nation's drive toward entrepreneurship: women, minorities, immigrants, part-timers, home-based business owners, family business owners, copreneurs, corporate castoffs, and corporate dropouts.

6. Describe the important role small businesses play in our nation's economy.

The small business sector's contributions are many. They make up 99 percent of all businesses, employ 51 percent of the private sector workforce, have created two-thirds to three-fourths of the net new jobs in the economy, produce 51 percent of the country's private gross domestic product, and account for 47 percent of all business sales.

7. Describe the 10 deadly mistakes of entrepreneurship.

There are no guarantees that the business will make a profit or even survive. Small Business Administration statistics show that 64 percent of new businesses will fail within six years. The 10 deadly mistakes of entrepreneurship include management mistakes, lack of experience, poor financial control, weak marketing efforts, failure to develop a strategic plan, uncontrolled growth, poor location, lack of inventory control, incorrect pricing, and inability to make the "entrepreneurial transition."

8. Put failure into the proper perspective.

Entrepreneurs recognize that failure is a natural part of the creative process. Successful entrepreneurs have the attitude that failures are simply stepping stones along the path to success, and they refuse to be paralyzed by a fear of failure.

9. Explain how an entrepreneur can avoid becoming another business failure statistic.

Entrepreneurs can employ several general tactics to avoid these pitfalls. They should know their businesses in depth, prepare a solid business plan, manage financial resources effectively, understand financial statements, learn to manage people, and try to stay healthy.

Discussion Questions

1. What forces have led to the boom in entrepreneurship in the United States and across the globe?
2. What is an entrepreneur? Give a brief description of the entrepreneurial profile.
3. *Inc.* magazine claims, "Entrepreneurship is more mundane than it's sometimes portrayed . . . you don't need to be a person of mythical proportions to be very, very successful in building a company." Do you agree? Explain.
4. What are the major benefits of business ownership?
5. Which of the potential drawbacks to business ownership are most critical?
6. Briefly describe the role of the following groups in entrepreneurship: women, minorities, immigrants, "part-timers," home-based business owners, family business owners, copreneurs, corporate castoffs, and corporate dropouts.
7. What is a small business? What contributions do they make to our economy?
8. Describe the small business failure rate.
9. Outline the causes of business failure. Which problems cause most business failures?
10. How does the typical entrepreneur view the possibility of business failure?
11. How can the small business owner avoid the common pitfalls that often lead to business failures?
12. Why is it important to study the small business failure rate and the causes of business failures?
13. Explain the typical entrepreneur's attitude toward risk.
14. Are you interested in someday launching a small business? If so, when? What kind of business? Describe it. What can you do to ensure its success?

Business Plan Pro

This book may include the best-selling business planning software Business Plan Pro™ by Palo Alto Software, Inc. This software can assist you in four ways as you begin to build your business plan.

1. *Structure.* Business Plan Pro provides a structure for the process of creating a business plan. There are general business plan standards and expectations, and Business Plan Pro has a recognized and well-received format that lends credibility to your plan. A comprehensive plan that follows a generally recognized outline adds credibility and, if it is a part of the plan's purpose, of being funded.

2. *Efficiency.* Business Plan Pro will save you time. Once you become familiar with the interface, Business Plan Pro creates all of the essential financial statements for you based on the information the software prompts you to enter. The income statement, balance sheet, and your profit and loss statement are formatted for you once the data are there.

3. *Examples.* Business Plan Pro includes dozens of example business plans. Seeing examples of other plans can be a helpful learning tool as you create a plan that is unique based on *your* product or service and *your* market.

4. *Appearance.* Business Plan Pro automatically incorporates relevant tables and graphs into your text. The result is a cohesive business plan that combines text, tables, and charts and enhances the impact of your document.

Writing a business plan is more than just creating a document. The process can be the most valuable benefit of all. A business plan requires you to "tell your story" about your business. It addresses why your business concept is viable, who your market is, what you offer that market, why you believe your offer represents a unique value, how you are going to reach your market, and how your business is going to be funded and, based on your projections, financially successful.

Creating a business plan is a learning process. For the start-up business, completing a business plan allows you better to understand what to do before you start writing checks and seek funding to open the doors of your business. The current business owner can benefit from writing a business plan to better address challenges and optimize opportunities. Business Plan Pro is a tool that assists you with this process. The software guides you through the process by asking a series of questions with software "wizards" to help you to build your business plan as you bring the vision of your business to paper.

At the end of each chapter in this book you will find a Business Plan Pro activity that applies the concepts discussed. These activities will enable you to build your plan one step at a time in manageable components. You will be able to assemble your plan in a way that captures the information you know about your business and also raise key questions that will push you to learn more in areas you may not have considered. Business Plan Pro will guide you through each step to complete your plan as you progress through this book. This combination of learning concepts and then applying them in your business plan can be powerful. It represents a critical step toward launching a business or establishing a better understanding of the business you now own.

The following exercises will lead you through the process of creating your own business plan. If you or your group does not have a business concept in mind, select a business idea and work through these steps. Future chapters will ask you to validate and change this concept as needed.

The EasyPlan Wizard™ within Business Plan Pro is another optional resource that will guide you through the process of creating your business plan, and, just as you follow the guidance each chapter offers, this will not proceed chronologically through the outline. Instead, it will skip from section to section as you build concepts about your business, the products and services you offer, the markets you will serve, and your financial information. You can use the wizard or follow the sections of the outline based on the guidance from each chapter. Both options will lead you through the entire process and help you to create a comprehensive business plan.

Business Plan Exercises
On the Web

First, visit the Web site designed for this book at www.prenhall.com/scarborough. Look for the Business Plan Resource tab at the top along with the chapters, and review the information that is provided in that section. The information and links here will be a resource for you as you progress through each chapter and as you develop your business plan.

In the Software

Follow the instructions included on the CD to install Business Plan Pro. After you first open Business Plan Pro—preferably on a PC with an Internet connection—open the Sample Plan Browser. The Sample Plan Browser allows you to preview a library of sample business plans. You will find numerous business plan examples ranging from restaurants to accounting firms to non-profit organizations. A tool will help you to sort through these plans based on a specific industry or key words. Don't be concerned about finding a plan that is identical to your business concept. Instead, look for plans that contain parallel characteristics, such as a product or service plan, or one that is targeted to consumers versus business customers. Review several of these plans to get a better idea of the outline and content. This may give you a clearer vision of what *your* finished business plan will look like.

Sample Plans

Click on the Sample Plan Browser within the software and review these two plans: The Daily Perc and Corporate Fitness.

1. Compare the table of contents of each plan. What differences do you notice?
2. Review the executive summary of each plan. What is the key difference in these two business concepts?
3. What similarities do the plans share regarding the reasons they were written?
4. As you look through the plans, what are some common tables and charts you find embedded into the text? What value do these tables and charts offer the reader?

Building Your Business Plan

Open Business Plan Pro and select the choice that allows you to start a new plan. You may want to view the movie, which will give you an animated and audio overview of the software. Then allow the EasyPlan Wizard to "ask" you about your start date, the title of your plan, and other basic information including the following:

1. Do you sell products or services?
2. Is your business a profit or a nonprofit organization?
3. Is your business a start-up operation or an ongoing business?

4. What kind of business plan do you want to create? Choose "complete business plan" here.

5. Do you want to include the SWOT (strengths, weaknesses, opportunities, and threats) analysis—check this box—and will you have a Web site?

6. A series of financial questions to structure the financial aspects of your plan with assistance throughout.

7. Do you want to prepare a plan for three years (a standard plan) or a longer-term plan of five years, both with a one-year monthly breakdown?

Save these decisions by using the drop-down menu under File and clicking on Save or by clicking on the Save icon at the top right of the menu bar. You can change your response to these decisions at any time as you build your plan.

Review the outline of your plan by clicking on the Preview icon on the top of your screen or by clicking on File, Print, and then Preview within the Print window. Based on your responses to the Wizard questions, you will now see the outline of your business plan. The software will enable you to change and modify the plan outline in any way you choose at any time. Business Plan Pro will help you to build your plan one step at a time as you progress through each chapter.

Beyond the Classroom . . .

1. Choose an entrepreneur in your community and interview him or her. What's the "story" behind the business? How well does the entrepreneur fit the entrepreneurial profile described in this chapter? What advantages and disadvantages does the owner see in owning a business? What advice would he or she offer to someone considering launching a business?

2. Select one of the categories under the section "The Cultural Diversity of Entrepreneurship" in this chapter and research it in more detail. Find examples of business owners in that category. Prepare a brief report for your class.

3. Search through recent business publications (especially those focusing on small companies) and find an example of an entrepreneur, past or present, who exhibits the entrepreneurial spirit of striving for success in the face of failure. Prepare a brief report for your class.

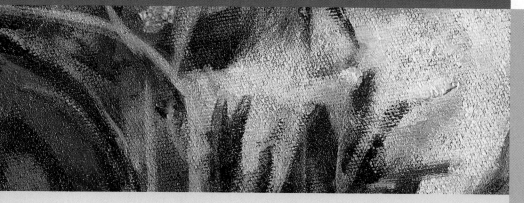

2 | Inside the Entrepreneurial Mind: From Ideas to Reality

Imagination is the highest kite one can fly. —Lauren Bacall

Think left and think right and think low and think high. Oh, the thinks you can come up with if only you try. —Theodor Geisel (Dr. Suess)

Learning Objectives

On completion of this chapter, you will be able to:

1 Explain the differences among creativity, innovation, and entrepreneurship.
2 Describe why creativity and innovation are such integral parts of entrepreneurship.
3 Understand how the two hemispheres of the human brain function and what role they play in creativity.
4 Explain the 10 "mental locks" that limit individual creativity.
5 Understand how entrepreneurs can enhance their own creativity and that of their employees as well.
6 Describe the steps in the creative process
7 Discuss techniques for improving the creative process.
8 Describe the protection of intellectual property through patents, trademarks, and copyrights.

One of the tenets of entrepreneurship is the ability to create new and useful ideas that solve the problems and challenges people face every day. Entrepreneurs achieve success by creating value in the marketplace when they combine resources in new and different ways to gain a competitive edge over rivals. From Alexander Fleming's pioneering work that resulted in a treatment for infections (penicillin) and the founders of the Rocket Chemical Company's fortieth try to create an industrial lubricant (WD-40) to Jeff Bezos' innovative use of the World Wide Web in retailing (Amazon.com) and Ted Turner's unique approach to the availability of television news (CNN), entrepreneurs' ideas have transformed the world.

As you learned in Chapter 1, entrepreneurs can create value in a number of ways—inventing new products and services, developing new technology, discovering new knowledge, improving existing products or services, finding different ways of providing more goods and services with fewer resources, and many others. Indeed, finding new ways of satisfying customers' needs, inventing new products and services, putting together existing ideas in new and different ways, and creating new twists on existing products and services are hallmarks of the entrepreneur!

Freitag Bags

Needing a waterproof bag to transport his art to class, Markus Freitag invited his brother Daniel to help design one. Using recycled truck tarpaulins, seatbelts, bicycle inner tubes, and airbags, the Freitags came up with a sturdy, creative product, one that has won numerous design awards and is sold worldwide.

Twenty-two-year-old Markus Freitag, who was studying in Zurich, Switzerland, rode his bike to art class every day. Because Zurich averages 127 rainy days a year, Freitag's sketches often got soaked on the trip. He searched for a messenger bag like the ones bicycle messengers in New York City use but could not find one. Recognizing a business opportunity, Markus and his brother Daniel, a graphic designer, sat down one evening to brainstorm ideas for a new waterproof messenger bag made from recycled materials. They decided to use seat belts as straps and bicycle inner tubes to insulate the bag's seams. "But we had no idea what to use for the bag itself," recalls Markus. As they talked, Markus looked out the kitchen window that overlooked autobahn A3 and saw trucks carrying cargo from Germany to Italy tucked safely underneath waterproof vinyl tarpaulins imprinted with bright logos. "How about those?" he asked, pointing to a passing truck. A short time later, Markus rode his bike to a Zurich truck depot, where he convinced the manager to let him have 30 square feet of discarded tarps, which he took home and soaked in the bathtub to remove the grime. He stitched together a bag on an industrial sewing machine he borrowed and sent the prototype to Daniel, who had moved to San Francisco. Daniel soon returned to Zurich, and the brothers transformed their apartment into a factory and warehouse for their bags. When their roommates began to complain, they decided to rent an actual warehouse. Demand for their bags took off when a Swiss newspaper printed a story on the Freitags and named their bags the cool product of the week. Today, the Freitags sell their messenger bags from their Web site and in 250 stores worldwide at prices ranging from $70 to $220. In addition to the satisfaction of building a successful business, the Freitags take pride in knowing that their first bag, the Top Cat, is on display in New York's Museum of Modern Art with the Apple iPod and other design classics.[1] Like many innovators, the Freitags created a successful business by taking several everyday items that had existed for many years and combining them in a different way.

Creativity, Innovation, and Entrepreneurship

LEARNING OBJECTIVES
1. Explain the differences among creativity, innovation, and entrepreneurship.

A recent study by the Small Business Administration found that small firms produce more economically and technically important innovations than larger firms.[2] What is the entrepreneurial "secret" for creating value in the marketplace? In reality, the "secret" is no secret at all: it is applying creativity and innovation to solve problems and to exploit opportunities that people face every day. **Creativity** is the ability to develop new ideas and to discover new ways of looking at problems and opportunities. **Innovation** is the ability to *apply* creative solutions to those problems and opportunities to enhance or to enrich people's lives. Harvard's Ted Levitt says that creativity is *thinking* new things, and innovation is *doing* new things. In short, entrepreneurs succeed by *thinking and doing* new things or old things in new ways. Simply having a great new idea is not enough; transforming the idea into a tangible product, service, or business venture is the essential next step. Management legend Peter Drucker says, "Innovation is the specific instrument of entrepreneurs, the means by which they exploit change as an opportunity for a different business or a different service."[3]

Successful entrepreneurs come up with ideas and then find ways to make them work to solve a problem or to fill a need. In a world that is changing faster than most of us ever could have imagined, creativity and innovation are vital to a company's success—and survival. That is true for businesses in every industry—from automakers to tea growers—and for companies of all sizes. However, creativity and innovation are the signatures of small, entrepreneurial businesses. Creative thinking has become a core business skill, and entrepreneurs lead the way in developing and applying that skill. In fact, creativity and innovation often lie at the heart of small companies' ability to compete successfully with their larger rivals. Even though they cannot outspend their larger rivals, small companies can create powerful, effective competitive advantages over big companies by "out-creating" and "out-innovating" them! If they fail to do so, entrepreneurs don't stay in business very long. Leadership expert Warren Bennis says, "Today's successful companies live and die according to the quality of their ideas."[4]

Sometimes innovation involves generating something from nothing. However, innovation is more likely to result from elaborating on the present, from putting old things together in new ways, or from taking something away to create something simpler or better. An experiment designed to improve the adhesive on tape resulted in a glue that hardly stuck at all. Although most researchers might have considered the experiment a total failure and scrapped it, this researcher asked a simple, creative question: What can you do with a glue when you take away most of its stickiness? The answer led to the invention of one of the most popular office products of all time: 3M's Post-it note™.

In many cases, creative ideas spring up from the most unexpected places. Edwin Land, one of America's most prolific inventors, credits his three-year-old daughter with the idea of the Polaroid camera. On a vacation trip in 1943, she asked why she couldn't see the photograph Land had just taken of her. During the next hour, as he walked around with his family, Land's mind was at work on his daughter's question. Before long, he had worked out the concept of building the camera that launched the era of instant photography, "The camera and the film became clear to me," Land recalls. "In my mind they were so real that I spent several hours describing them." Land's invention—instant photography—was so outlandish that only a child could conceive of it![5]

More often, creative ideas arise when entrepreneurs look at something old and think of something new or different. Legendary Notre Dame football coach Knute Rockne, whose teams dominated college football in the 1920s, got the idea for his constantly shifting backfields while watching a burlesque chorus routine! Rockne's innovations in the backfield (which included the legendary "Four Horsemen") and his emphasis on the forward pass (a legal but largely unused tactic in his era) so befuddled opposing defenses that his teams compiled an impressive 105-12-5 record. Similarly, military tacticians, needing better camouflage designs to protect troops and equipment in World War I, borrowed ideas from the "cubist" art of Picasso and Braque. Their improved camouflage patterns helped the Allies win the war.[6] More recently, one entrepreneur helped solve a problem that plagued U.S. troops in the deserts of Saudi Arabia and Kuwait during Desert Storm. U.S. military experts discovered that enemy aircraft were able to detect the location of troops and equipment by looking for the repeating patterns in the camouflage used to hide them. The entrepreneur began selling the military a special

creativity
the ability to develop new ideas and to discover new ways of looking at problems and opportunities.

innovation
the ability to apply creative solutions to problems and opportunities to enhance or to enrich people's lives.

camouflage whose pattern never repeated. He developed it using technology he was already employing to produce multicolored, multipatterned area rugs (each one unique) for the home market.

Entrepreneurs also create innovations to solve problems they observe, often problems they face themselves.

Accentra

Running late for an important meeting with a venture capital firm where he was to make a pitch for $5 million for a chain of restaurants, Todd Moses picked up a stapler to staple the copies of his 19-page plan. On the first copy, the staple went only halfway through, and then it jammed completely, tearing the pages of the second copy. Trying to pull out the staple, Moses cut his finger and bled on the several other copies. Furious, he threw the stapler against the wall and went to his meeting where he apologized not only for being late, but also for being short of copies. That night, Moses thought back to the stapler. Because he once had worked for a hardware manufacturer, he recalled a reliable, easy-to-use, heavy-duty staple gun used in construction. Unable to sleep, he searched the Internet to see if anyone had invented a similar office stapler but found nothing. In the world of desktop staplers, "there wasn't much innovation," he says. The next morning, Moses tracked down Joel Marks, the designer of the spring-loaded mechanism used in the heavy-duty construction stapler, and convinced him to collaborate with Moses on an office version. Before long, they had designed a compact model that used less than one-fourth the force that a traditional office stapler required and was more reliable. Moses and Marks found a Taiwanese manufacturer to produce the new stapler and formed a company called Accentra to market the device, which they named the PaperPro. In just 40 days, Moses met with 120 distributors and convinced 119 of them, including industry giant Staples, to carry the PaperPro. Accentra now sells the PaperPro in more than 60 countries worldwide, generates $50 million in annual sales, and is preparing to introduce a new and improved hole puncher.[7]

Entrepreneurship is the result of a disciplined, systematic process of applying creativity and innovation to needs and opportunities in the marketplace. It involves applying focused strategies to new ideas and new insights to create a product or a service that satisfies customers' needs or solves their problems. It is much more than random, disjointed tinkering with a new gadget. Millions of people come up with creative ideas for new or different products and services; most of them, however, never do anything with them. Entrepreneurs are people who connect their creative ideas with the purposeful action and structure of a business. Thus, successful entrepreneurship is a constant process that relies on creativity, innovation, and application in the marketplace.

Innovation must be a constant process because most ideas don't work and most innovations fail. One writer explains, "Trial—and lots of error—is embedded in entrepreneurship."[8] Karen Anne Zien, co-founder of Polaroid Corporation's Creativity and Innovation Lab, estimates that for every 3,000 new product ideas, 4 make it to the development stage, 2 are actually launched, and only 1 becomes a success in the market. These new products are crucial to companies' success, however. According to Robert Cooper, a researcher who has analyzed thousands of new product launches, new products on average account for a whopping 40 percent of companies' sales.[9] Still, successful entrepreneurs recognize that many failures will accompany innovations, and they are willing to accept their share of failures because they know that failure is merely part of the creative process. Entrepreneurship requires business owners to be bold enough to try their new ideas, flexible enough to throw aside those that do not work, and wise enough to learn about what will work based on their observations of what did not. We now turn our attention to creativity, the creative process, and methods of enhancing creativity.

Creativity—A Necessity for Survival

LEARNING OBJECTIVES
2. Describe why creativity and innovation are such integral parts of entrepreneurship.

In this fiercely competitive, fast-faced, global economy, creativity is not only an important source for building a competitive advantage, but it also is a necessity for survival. When developing creative solutions to modern problems, entrepreneurs must go beyond merely relying on what has worked in the past. "A company that's doing all the things that used to guarantee success—providing quality products backed by great service, marketing with flair, holding down costs, and managing cash flow—is at risk of being flattened if it fails to become an engine of innovation," says one business writer.[10] Transforming their organizations into engines of innovation requires entrepreneurs to cast off the limiting assumptions, beliefs, and behaviors and to develop new insights into the relationship among resources, needs, and value. In other words, they must change their perspectives, looking at the world in new and different ways.

Entrepreneurs must always be on guard against traditional assumptions and perspectives about how things out to be because they are certain killers of creativity. Such self-imposed mental constraints and other paradigms that people tend to build over time push creativity right out the door. A **paradigm** is a preconceived idea of what the world is, what it should be like, and how it should operate. These ideas become so deeply rooted in our minds that they become immovable blocks to creative thinking, even though they may be outdated, obsolete, and no longer relevant. In short, they act as logjams to creativity. Look, for example, at the following illustrations and read the text aloud:

paradigm
a preconceived idea of what the world is, what it should be like, and how it should operate.

Paris	Once	A Bird
in the	in a	in the
the Spring time	a Lifetime	the Hand

If you're like most people, you didn't notice the extra word in each phrase ("Paris in the the spring time"). Why? Part of the reason is that we see what we expect to see! Past experiences shape the ways in which we perceive the world around us ("We've always done it this way"). That is why children are so creative and curious about new possibilities; society has not yet brainwashed them into an attitude of conformity, nor have they learned to accept *traditional* solutions as the *only* solutions. Retaining their creative "inner child," entrepreneurs are able to throw off the shackles on creativity and see opportunities for creating viable businesses where most people see what they've always seen (or, worse yet, see nothing).

Source: © 2002 Randy Glasbergen. www.glasbergen.com

Many years ago, during an international chess competition, Frank Marshall made what has become known as one of the most beautiful—and one of the most creative—moves ever made on a chess board. In a crucial game in which he was evenly matched with a Russian master player, Marshall found his queen under serious attack. Marshall had several avenues of escape for his queen available. Knowing that the queen is one of the most important offensive players on the chessboard, spectators assumed that Marshall would make a conventional move and push his queen to safety.

Using all the time available to him to consider his options, Marshall picked up his queen—and paused—and put it down on the most *illogical* square of all, a square from which the queen could easily be captured by any one of three hostile pieces. Marshall had done the unthinkable! He had sacrificed his queen, a move typically made only under the most desperate of circumstances. All the spectators—even Marshall's opponent—groaned in dismay. Then, the Russian, and finally the crowd, realized that Marshall's move was, in reality, a brilliant one. No matter how the Russian opponent took the queen, he would eventually be in a losing position. Seeing the inevitable outcome, the Russian conceded the game. Marshall had won the match in a rare and daring fashion: he had won by sacrificing his queen![11]

What lesson does this story hold for entrepreneurs? By suspending conventional thinking long enough to even consider the possibility of such a move, Marshall was able to throw off the usual paradigms constraining most chess players. He had looked beyond the traditional and orthodox strategies of the game and was willing to take the risk of trying an unusual tactic to win. The result: he won. Although not every creative business opportunity that entrepreneurs take will be successful, many who, like Frank Marshall, are willing to go beyond conventional wisdom will be rewarded for their efforts. Successful entrepreneurs, those who are constantly pushing technological and economic boundaries forward, constantly ask, "Is it time to sacrifice the queen?"

Merely generating one successful creative solution to address a problem or a need, however, usually is not good enough to keep an entrepreneurial enterprise successful in the long run. Success—even survival—in this fiercely competitive, global environment requires entrepreneurs to tap their creativity (and that of their employees) constantly. Entrepreneurs can be sure that if they have developed a unique, creative solution to solve a problem or to fill a need, a competitor (perhaps one six times zones away) is hard at work developing an even more creative solution to render theirs obsolete. This extremely rapid and accelerating rate of change has created an environment in which staying in a leadership position requires constant creativity, innovation, and entrepreneurship. A company that has achieved a leadership position in an industry but then stands still creatively is soon toppled from its perch as number one.

Can Creativity Be Taught?

For many years, conventional wisdom held that a person was either creative—imaginative, free-spirited, and entrepreneurial—or he or she was not. Therefore, some people were considered to be at the other end of the spectrum and were restrictively logical, narrow-minded, and rigid. Today, we know better. Research shows that *anyone* can learn to be creative. "Every person can be taught techniques and behaviors that help them generate more ideas," says Joyce Wycoff, author of several books on creativity.[12] The problem is that in most organizations, employees have never been expected to be creative. In addition, many businesses fail to foster an environment that encourages creativity among employees. Restricted by their traditional thinking patterns, most people never tap into their pools of innate creativity, and the company becomes stagnant. Creative exercises such as the one illustrated in Figure 2.1 can help adults to reconnect with the natural creativity they exhibited so willingly as children.

Not only can entrepreneurs and the people who work for them learn to think creatively, but they must for their companies' sake! "Innovation and creativity are not just for artists," says Wycoff. "These are skills with a direct, bottom-line payoff."[13]

Capitol Concierge

For instance, Mary Naylor, owner of Capitol Concierge, a company that provides concierge services in office building lobbies, looks to an unusual source for new ideas about how to promote her business: junk mail. "I collect junk mail and keep it in a box I call 'Mary's Ideas,'" says Naylor. "I get inspiration from things most people throw away. When I want to kick start my creative processes, I go to my box and see what's new."[14]

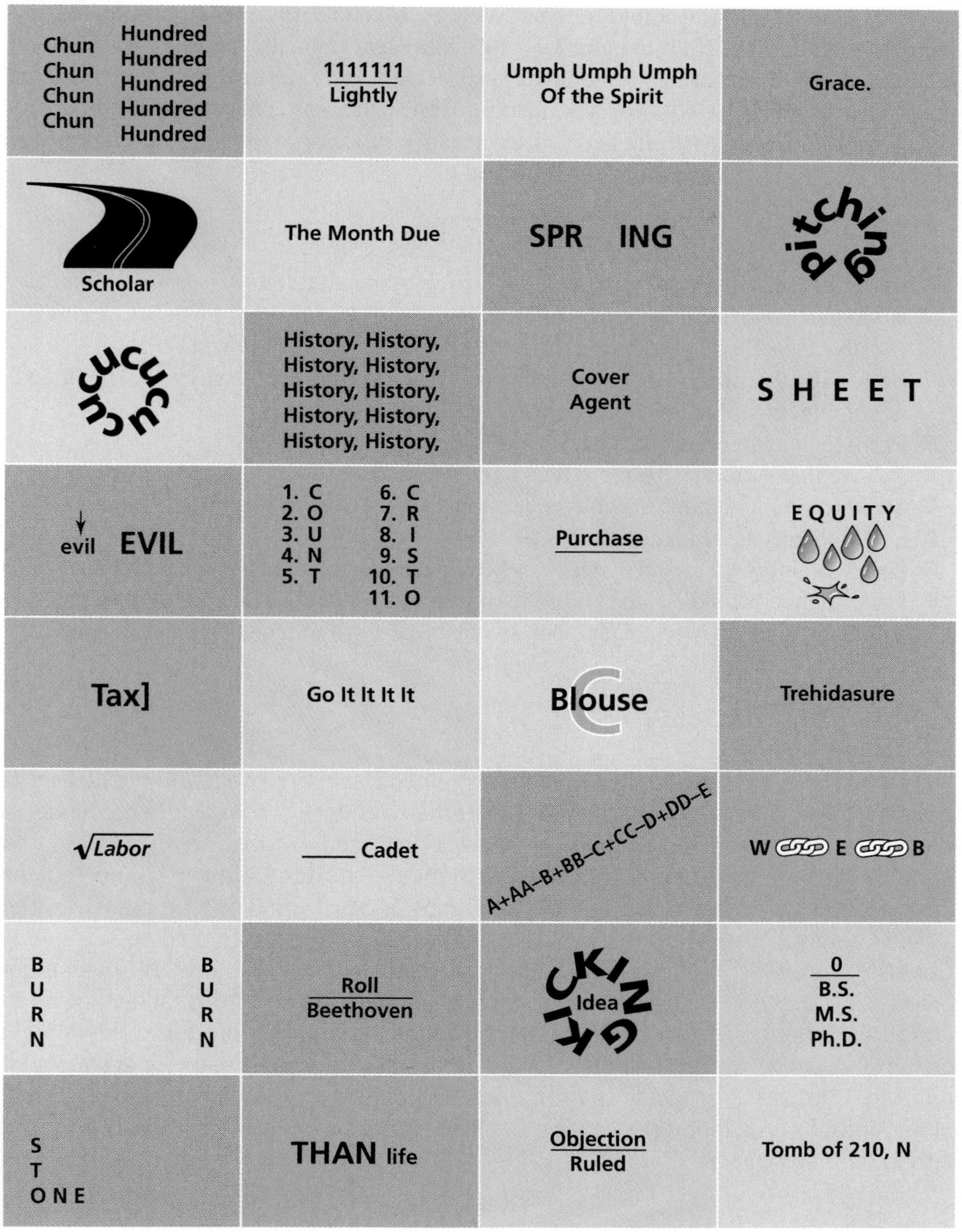

FIGURE 2.1

How Creative Are You? Can You Recognize the Well-Known Phrases These Symbols Represent?

Chun Hundred Chun Hundred Chun Hundred Chun Hundred Hundred	<u>1111111</u> Lightly	Umph Umph Umph Of the Spirit	Grace.
(road) Scholar	The Month Due	SPR ING	pitching *(circular)*
cucucuc *(circular)*	History, History, History, History, History, History, History, History, History, History,	Cover Agent	S H E E T
↓ evil EVIL	1. C 6. C 2. O 7. R 3. U 8. I 4. N 9. S 5. T 10. T 11. O	Purchase	E Q U I T Y 💧💧💧 😭
Tax]	Go It It It It	Blouse	Trehidasure
√Labor	_____ Cadet	A+AA–B+BB–C+CC–D+DD–E	W ⟨chain⟩ E ⟨chain⟩ B
B B U U R R N N	<u>Roll</u> Beethoven	KICKING Idea	0 B.S. M.S. Ph.D.
S T O N E	THAN life	<u>Objection</u> Ruled	Tomb of 210, N

Before entrepreneurs can draw on their own creative capacity or stimulate creativity in their own organizations, they need to understand creative thinking.

Creative Thinking

LEARNING OBJECTIVES
3. Understand how the two hemispheres of the human brain function and what role they play in creativity.

Research into the operation of the human brain shows that each hemisphere of the brain processes information differently and that one side of the brain tends to be dominant over the other. The human brain develops asymmetrically, and each hemisphere tends to specialize in certain functions. The left-brain is guided by linear, vertical thinking (from one logical conclusion to the next), whereas the right-brain relies on kaleidoscopic, lateral thinking (considering a problem from all sides and jumping into it at different points). The left-brain handles language, logic, and symbols; the right-brain takes care of the body's emotional, intuitive, and spatial functions. The left-brain processes information in a step-by-step fashion, but the right-brain processes it intuitively—all at once, relying heavily on images.

Left-brained, vertical thinking is narrowly focused and systematic, proceeding in a highly logical fashion from one point to the next. Right-brained, lateral thinking, on the other hand, is somewhat unconventional, unsystematic, and unstructured, much like the image of a kaleidoscope whirling around to form one pattern after another. Right-brain driven, lateral thinking lies at the heart of the creative process. Those who have learned to develop their right-brained thinking skills tend to:

- Always ask the question, "Is there a better way?"
- Challenge custom, routine, and tradition.
- Be reflective, often staring out windows, deep in thought. (*How many traditional managers would stifle creativity by snapping these people out of their "daydreams," chastise them for "loafing," and admonish them to "get back to work?"*)
- Be prolific thinkers. They know that generating lots of ideas increases the likelihood of coming up with a few highly creative ideas.
- Play mental games, trying to see an issue from different perspectives.
- Realize that there may be more than one "right answer."
- See mistakes and failures as mere "pit stops" on the way to success.
- See problems as springboards for new ideas.
- Relate seemingly unrelated ideas to a problem to generate innovative solutions.
- Have "helicopter skills," the ability to rise above the daily routine to see an issue from a broader perspective and then swoop back down to focus on an area in need of change.

COMPANY Profile

Energy Conversion Devices

Stanford Ovshinsky, now 80, has used right-brained thinking to generate the ideas that have led him to earn an amazing 274 patents. Ovshinsky, who skipped college to become a tool-maker and machinist, used his first-hand knowledge of machinery to earn his first patent in the 1940s for a high-speed, automated machine tool he designed. His curiosity led him to study neurophysiology, from which he branched into a field known as disordered materials physics. In 1960, he founded a company, Energy Conversion Devices, that has produced low-cost solar-powered batteries, a rechargeable battery that powers hybrid-electric cars, rewritable CDs and DVDs, and many other important inventions. Most of his patents and his company's products derive from Ovshinsky's ability to translate his knowledge of unstructured elements and superconductivity into useful products that produce clean energy. "Most people think in two dimensions," says a long-time colleague. "Stan thinks not only in three dimensions but also in different colors."[15]

Although each hemisphere of the brain tends to dominate in its particular functions, the two halves normally cooperate, with each part contributing its special abilities to accomplish those tasks best suited to its mode of information processing. Sometimes, however, the two hemispheres may even compete with each other, or one half may choose not to participate. Some researchers have suggested that each half of the brain has the capacity to keep information from the other! The result, literally, is that "the left hand doesn't know what the right hand is doing." Perhaps the most important characteristic of this split-brain phenomenon is that an individual can learn to control which side of the brain is dominant in a given situation. In other words, a person can learn to "turn down" the dominant left hemisphere (focusing on logic and linear thinking) and "turn up" the right hemisphere (focusing on intuition and unstructured thinking) when a situation requiring creativity arises.[16] To get a little practice at this "shift," try the visual exercises presented in Figure 2.2. When viewed from one perspective, the picture in the middle portrays an attractive young lady with a feather in her hair and a boa around her shoulders. Once you shift your perspective, however, you will see an old woman with a large nose wearing a scarf on her head! This change in the image seen is the result of a shift from one hemisphere in the viewer's brain to the

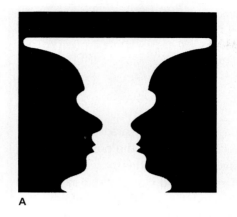

A

B

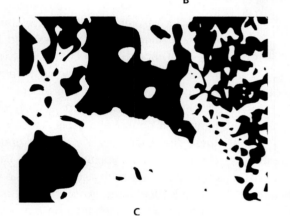

C

FIGURE 2.2

What Do You See?

Source: Thomas W. Zimmerer and Norman M. Scarborough, *Entrepreneurship and New Venture Formation*, © 1995. Reprinted by permission of Prentice Hall, Inc., Upper Saddle River, NJ.

other. With practice, a person can learn to control this mental shift, tapping the pool of creativity that lies hidden within the right side of the brain. This ability has tremendous power to unleash the creative capacity of entrepreneurs. The need to develop this creative ability means that exploring inner space (the space within our brains)—not outer space—becomes the challenge of the century.

Successful entrepreneurship requires both left- and right-brained thinking. Right-brained thinking draws on the power of divergent reasoning, which is the ability to create a multitude of original, diverse ideas. Left-brain thinking counts on convergent reasoning, the ability to evaluate multiple ideas and choose the best solution to a given problem. Entrepreneurs need to rely on right-brain thinking to generate innovative product, service, or business ideas. Then, they must use left-brain thinking to judge the market potential of the ideas they generate. Successful entrepreneurs have learned to coordinate the complementary functions of each hemisphere of the brain, using their brain's full creative power to produce pragmatic innovation. Otherwise, entrepreneurs, who rarely can be accused of being "half-hearted" about their business ideas, run the risk of becoming "half-headed."

How can entrepreneurs learn to tap their innate creativity more readily? The first step is to break down the barriers to creativity that most of us have erected over the years. We now turn our attention to these barriers and some suggested techniques for tearing them down.

You
Be the Consultant

The Spirit of Entrepreneurship in the Olympics

With his innovative high jumping technique that became known as the Fosbury Flop, Dick Fosbury won an Olympic gold medal, set a new world record, and invented a new style of high jumping that athletes still use today.

Entrepreneurs aren't the only ones who use creativity to create competitive advantages for themselves. Throughout history, Olympic athletes have pushed back the frontiers of their sports by developing new techniques, improved training methods, and innovative solutions to existing problems. Two of the best examples of applying creativity to their sports are figure skater Sonja Henie and high jumper Dick Fosbury. Although their sports are at different extremes of the Olympic spectrum, both of these athletes relied on the creative process to throw off the paradigms that bound the other athletes competing in these sports.

Before Sonja Henie came along, figure skating routines were exactly that—routine. In competitions, skaters performed a series of precise moves that emphasized accuracy and control. But when the young Norwegian glided onto the ice, skating changed forever. Bringing the beauty and movement of ballet to the skating rink, Henie transformed the sport into the graceful combination of motion, music, and muscle that it remains today. From 1927 to 1936, Henie dominated ice skating by creatively blending her graceful ballet skills with her strength on the ice. She won 10 straight world championships, eight European titles, and a record three Olympic gold medals. Trained in both dance and ballet as

a child, Henie cast aside the existing paradigms of what ice skating was as she recognized the possibilities of transferring dance movements onto the ice.

After winning her last world championship in 1936, Henie used her dance and skating skills to get into show business. She became an international star in movies and in traveling ice shows that gave her the freedom to use her creative genius on the ice. Even her glamorous and daring (for the 1930s) costumes proved to be an exciting innovation in ice skating as they emphasized the grace and flow of her movements. Later generations of ice skaters would push the sport even farther. Tenley Albright (1956 Olympics) and Peggy Fleming (1968 Olympics) introduced spins, twirls, and leaps. More recently, Tara Lipinsky, Kristi Yamaguchi, Nancy Kerrigan, Katarina Witt, and others have injected an element of gymnastics to ice skating, performing triple jumps and double and triple Axels. Yet every one of these champions owes a debt of gratitude to Sonja Henie, the daring young skater who had the creativity and the courage to make innovations on the ice.

Until 1968, much like ice skating, the sport of high jumping had changed little since its origins in ancient Greece. Athletes sprinted toward the bar and then leaped forward and upward, rolling over the bar face down. In the 1968 Olympics in Mexico City, Dick Fosbury revolutionized the sport with his innovative style of high jumping. He approached the bar at a different angle and then curved his body over the bar face *up*, kicking his legs over the end of the jump. Based on the principles of biomechanics, the "Fosbury Flop," as the style became known, transfers the weight of the jumper over the bar in stages. It also requires less energy and is more efficient. The result of Fosbury's innovation? An Olympic gold medal, a new world high jump record (Fosbury broke the old record by 6 cm), and the satisfaction of creating a new style of high jumping used by athletes across the world even today.

Sonja Henie and Dick Fosbury became champions by applying creativity and innovation to the sports they loved so much. Similarly, entrepreneurs can become "champions" in their industries by using their creative spirits to come up with new ideas, better products and services, and innovative techniques. Successful entrepreneurs rely on their ability to see the same things everyone else sees and to dream what no one else dreams.

1. What is a paradigm? How does a paradigm stifle creativity?
2. Work with a small group of your classmates to identify a local business that is bound by a paradigm. What impact is this paradigm having on the busi-

ness? Identify the paradigm and then generate as many creative suggestions as you can in 20 minutes that would change this paradigm.
3. What can entrepreneurs do to throw off existing paradigms?

Source: "Innovations of the Olympic Games," *Fortune,* January 27, 1992, pp. 28–29.

Barriers to Creativity

The number of potential barriers to creativity is virtually limitless—time pressures, unsupportive management, pessimistic co-workers, overly rigid company policies, and countless others. Perhaps the most difficult hurdles to overcome, however, are those that individuals impose on themselves. In his book *A Whack on the Side of the Head*, Roger von Oech identifies 10 "mental locks" that limit individual creativity[17]:

1. *Searching for the one "right" answer.* Deeply ingrained in most educational systems is the assumption that there is one "right" answer to a problem. The average student who has completed four years of college has taken more than 2,600 tests; therefore, it is not unusual for this one-correct-answer syndrome to become an inherent part of our thinking. In reality, however, most problems are ambiguous. Depending on the questions one asks, there may be (and usually are) several "right" answers.

When representatives from Jacksonville, Florida, made a proposal to the National Football League (NFL) to host the 2005 Super Bowl, they knew that they had to overcome one major disadvantage: a lack of high-end hotel space, always a key factor in the NFL's bid requirements. The team's approach was based on the assumption that there was more than one right answer to providing upscale hotel space, and they came up with an innovative solution: they would dock cruise ships along the St. Johns River that would serve as floating hotels, putting guests within easy walking distance of the football stadium! Shortly after the meeting, NFL officials named Jacksonville the host city for the 2005 Super Bowl, making it the smallest city ever to host the big game.[18]

COMPANY Profile

Jacksonville, Florida
When Jacksonville, Florida, city officials bid to host Super Bowl XXXIX, they knew that they had to overcome a huge obstacle: a lack of high-end hotel rooms. Their creative solution was to dock cruise ships along the St. Johns River to serve as floating hotels. The result of their creative thinking? Jacksonville became the smallest city ever to host a Super Bowl game.

2. *Focusing on "being logical."* Logic is a valuable part of the creative process, especially when evaluating ideas and implementing them. However, in the early imaginative phases of the process, logical thinking can restrict creativity. Focusing too much effort on being logical also discourages the use of one of the mind's most powerful creations: intuition. Von Oech advises us to "think something different" and to use nonlogical thinking freely, especially in the imaginative phase of the creative process. Intuition, which is based on the accumulated knowledge and experiences a person encounters over the course of a lifetime and resides in the subconscious, can be unlocked. It is a crucial part of the creative process because using it often requires one to tear down long-standing assumptions that limit creativity and innovation.

Charles Arntzen is an entrepreneur who challenges traditional assumptions, and his efforts may revolutionize the concept of immunization and save millions of lives around the world. Arntzen, who grew up on a farm before earning his Ph.D. in molecular biology at Purdue University and working at DuPont and the U.S. Department of Agriculture, traveled to Bangkok, Thailand, where he was touring the city's famous floating market. As he watched

ENTREPRENEURIAL Profile

Charles Arntzen

hundreds of farmers selling their harvest from wooden boats in the Klong canals, he noticed a mother feeding her infant a banana. From his travels, Arntzen knew that worldwide 30 million infants go without basic immunizations each year and that 3 million of those children die from preventable diseases. As he watched the infant eat the banana, Arntzen thought: What if that banana could immunize the infant against disease? When he returned home, Arntzen began to work on his idea of incorporating vaccines into food. If he could engineer plants to produce specific proteins that would cause the human body to produce protective antibodies, he could eliminate the need to acquire, refrigerate, and transport fragile vaccines, an especially critical problem for poor nations. Within weeks, Arntzen had uncovered enough supporting research to prove that his idea could work. "I was looking for a way to combine my agricultural expertise with human medicine," he says. Arntzen has invested $5 million to develop potatoes and tomatoes that can serve as vaccines and is searching for the $20 million more he needs to finance the clinical trials required by the Food and Drug Administration. "We're trying to create a new paradigm [that] could save millions of lives," he says.[19]

3. ***Blindly following the rules.*** We learn at a very early age not to "color outside the lines," and we spend the rest of our lives blindly obeying such rules. Sometimes, creativity depends on our ability to break the existing rules so that we can see new ways of doing things. Consider, for example, the top row of letters on a standard typewriter or computer keyboard:

Qwertyuiop

In the 1870s, Sholes & Company, a leading manufacturer of typewriters, began receiving numerous customer complains about its typewriter keys sticking together when typists' fingers were practiced enough to go really fast. Company engineers came up with an incredibly creative solution to eliminate the problem of sticking keys. They designed a less efficient keyboard configuration, placing the letters O and I (the third- and sixth-most-commonly used letters of the alphabet) so that the weakest fingers (the ring and little fingers) would strike them. By slowing down typists with this inefficient keyboard, the engineers solved the sticking-keys problem. Today, despite the fact that computer technology has eliminated all danger of sticking keys, this same inefficient keyboard configuration remains the industry standard!

4. ***Constantly being practical.*** Imagining impractical answers to "what if" questions can be powerful stepping stones to creative ideas. Suspending practicality for a while frees the mind to consider creative solutions that otherwise might never arise. Whenever Thomas Edison hired an assistant to work in his creative laboratory, he would tell the new employee, "Walk through town and list 20 things that interest you." When the worker returned, Edison would ask him to split the list into two columns. Then he would say, "Randomly combine objects from column A and column B and come up with as many inventions as you can." Edison's methods for stimulating creativity in his lab proved to be successful; he holds the distinction of being the only person to have earned a patent every year for 65 consecutive years![20]

Periodically setting aside practicality allows entrepreneurs to consider taking a product or a concept from one area and placing it in a totally different application.

Richard Rawls

Richard Rawls, who once owned a company that sold firefighting foam, recognized that fire-retardant foams sometimes failed to work because they evaporated or slid off the vertical surfaces of the buildings they were designed to protect from flames. He began exploring the possibility of using fire-retardant gels to solve the problem, eventually settling on a gel made from a superabsorbent plastic called polyacrylate. He got the idea from a disposable diaper! The fibrous material in those diapers, which can hold as much as 1,000 times its weight in water, turns into a thick goo when it gets wet—the perfect way to protect a structure from fire. Experimenting in his backyard, Rawls modified the mixture to come up with the right gel consistency. Fire departments across the country have added the fire-retardant gel to their arsenal of fire-fighting weapons.[21]

5. *Viewing play as frivolous.* A playful attitude is fundamental to creative thinking. There is a close relationship between the "haha" of humor and the "aha" of discovery. Play gives us the opportunity to reinvent reality and to reformulate established ways of doing things. Children learn when they play, and so can entrepreneurs. Watch children playing and you will see them invent new games, create new ways of looking at old things, and learn what works (and what doesn't) in their games.

    Entrepreneurs can benefit from playing in the same way that children do. They, too, can learn to try new approaches and discover what works and what doesn't. Creativity results when entrepreneurs take what they have learned at play, evaluate it, corroborate it with other knowledge, and put it into practice. Encourage employees to have fun when solving problems; they are more likely to push the boundaries and come up with a genuinely creative solution if they do. What kind of invention would Wile E. Coyote, who seems to have an inexhaustible supply of ideas for catching Road Runner in those cartoons, create in this situation? How might the Three Stooges approach this problem? What would Seinfeld's Kramer suggest? A group of fundraisers was discussing the plans for an upcoming annual fund-raising banquet, which had been the organization's primary source of income for many years. Lamenting the declining turnout over the last several years and the multitude of other organizations that were using banquets as a source of revenue, one officer jokingly said, "Maybe we should have a 'nonbanquet,' where people pay not to tie up several hours, eat rubber chicken, and listen to some dull speaker talk about a topic they'd rather not hear about." The other officers laughed at the idea initially and then began throwing in humorous ideas of their own. The group mustered the courage to try out their creative solution, and their "nonbanquet" was a tremendous success. It raised more money than the organization had ever generated before, and no one had to attend!

6. *Becoming overly specialized.* Defining a problem as one of "marketing" or "production" or some other area of specialty limits the ability to see how it might be related to other issues. Creative thinkers tend to be "explorers," searching for ideas outside their areas of specialty. The idea for the roll-on deodorant stick came from the ballpoint pen. The famous Mr. Potato Head toy was invented by a father sitting with his family at the dinner table who noted how much fun his children had playing with their food. Velcro was invented by a man who, while hiking one day to take a break from work, had to stop to peel sticky cockleburs from his clothing. As he picked them off, he noticed how their hooked spines caught on and held tightly to the cloth. When he resumed his hike, he began to think about the possibilities of using a similar design to fasten objects together. Thus was born Velcro!

Betty Nesmith Graham wanted to become an artist, but after a divorce left her with her young son to raise alone, Graham took a job as an executive secretary shortly after World War II. A dedicated employee, Graham began searching for a way to correct her typing mistakes. (Remember that this was before computers were commonplace, and typewriters were the only "word processors.") Recalling how artists often paint over their mistakes, Graham thought that typists might be able to paint over their errors as well. At home, she mixed up a batch of tempera water-based paint to match the stationery her company used and used it to paint over her typing mistakes. Her boss never noticed, but another secretary did and asked for a bottle of the mixture. Graham found a green bottle at home, put some of the correcting fluid in it, and labeled it "Mistake Out." Soon other secretaries were clamoring for the product, and from her north Dallas home, Graham started the Mistake Out Company (later changing the name to the Liquid Paper Company). She turned her kitchen into a small factory, where her son Michael (who went on to be a star in the 1960s music group, The Monkees) helped her pour the concoction into small bottles. When her boss fired her, Graham turned her part-time, home-based business into a full-time venture, eventually selling it in 1980 for $47.5 million.[22]

Liquid Paper Company

7. *Avoiding ambiguity.* Ambiguity can be a powerful creative stimulus; it encourages us to "think something different." Being excessively detailed in an imaginative situation tends to stifle creativity. Ambiguity, however, requires us to consider at least two different, often contradictory notions at the same time, which is a direct channel to creativity. Ambiguous situations force us to stretch our minds beyond their normal boundaries and to consider creative options we might otherwise ignore. Although ambiguity is not a desired element when entrepreneurs are evaluating and implementing ideas, it is a valuable tool when they are searching for creative ideas and solutions. Entrepreneurs are famous for asking a question and then going beyond the first answer to explore other possible answers. The result is that they often find business opportunities by creating ambiguous situations.

Tom and Sally's Handmade Chocolates

Copreneurs Tom and Sally Fegley, owners of Tom and Sally's Handmade Chocolates, considered the possibility of other answers to the question, "What uses exist for chocolate sauce?" Although most people see chocolate sauce merely as a topping for ice cream or other desserts, their friend Larry (whom they have nicknamed "Dirty Larry") came up with a different idea. The Fegleys were trying to come up with an innovative recipe that would keep going their string of awards at a local fund-raising event devoted to celebrating chocolate, the Brown-Out. Their fun-loving friend suggested they shoot for the Most Decadent Award. "I'll go naked," he said. "You paint melted chocolate all over my body, and you'll win!" Although the Fegleys declined Larry's offer, his suggestion got them thinking. Before long, Tom had whipped up a batch of chocolate dessert topping, labeled it "Chocolate Body Paint," and included the following directions on the bottle: "Heat to 98.6 degrees, apply liberally, and let your imagination run wild." Today, Chocolate Body Paint is the Fegley's best-selling product, and it has won awards and has been featured in publications ranging from the *Wall Street Journal* to *Playboy* magazine. "Never judge an idea by its source," advises Sally.[23]

8. *Fearing looking foolish.* Creative thinking is no place for conformity! New ideas rarely are born in a conforming environment. People tend toward conformity because they don't want to look foolish. The fool's job is to whack at the habits and rules that keep us thinking in the same old ways. In that sense, entrepreneurs are top-notch "fools." They are constantly questioning and challenging accepted ways of doing things and the assumptions that go with them. The noted entrepreneurship theorist Joseph Schumpeter wrote that entrepreneurs perform a vital function—"creative destruction"— in which they rethink conventional assumptions and discard those that are no longer useful. According to Schumpeter, "The function of entrepreneurs is to reform or revolutionize the pattern of production by exploiting an invention or, more generally, an untried technological possibility for producing a new commodity or producing an old one in a new way, by opening up a new source of supply of materials or a new outlet for products, by reorganizing an industry or so on."[24] In short, entrepreneurs look at old ways of doing things and ask, "Is there a better way?" By destroying the old, they create the new.

One way in which entrepreneurs often engage in creative destruction is by reversing their thinking. For example, one agricultural entrepreneur had been trying to solve a common problem that automatic picking machines have when picking the fruit from apple trees. The machines, which are quite efficient at picking apples growing on the outer limbs of the trees, often miss or damage the fruit growing on the inner limbs. For years, he worked to develop a machine with the dexterity to pick apples in both locations but to no avail. Finally, this entrepreneur reversed his thinking and began to focus his efforts, not on the picking machine, but *on the apple tree*! Working with horticulturists, he was able to develop a new breed of tree whose fruit grew only on the outer limbs, where standard picking machines could easily get to it! By reversing his thinking, he solved the problem and created a new business opportunity.

9. *Fearing mistakes and failure.* Creative people realize that trying something new often leads to failure; however, they do not see failure as an end. It represents a learning experience on the way to success. As you learned in Chapter 1, failure is an important part of the creative process; it signals entrepreneurs when to change their course of action. Entrepreneurship is all about the opportunity to fail! Many entrepreneurs failed numerous times before they succeeded. Despite their initial setbacks, they were able to set aside the fear of failure and kept trying.

   The key, of course, is to see failure for what it really is: a chance to learn how to succeed. Entrepreneurs who willingly risk failure and learn from it when it occurs have the best chance of succeeding at whatever they try. Charles F. Kettering, a famous inventor (he invented the lighting and ignition systems in automobiles, among other things), explains, "You fail because your ideas aren't right, but you should learn to fail intelligently. When you fail, find out *why* you failed and each time it will bring you nearer to the goal."[25] Successful entrepreneurs equate failure with innovation rather than with defeat.

10. *Believing that "I'm not creative."* Some people limit themselves because they believe creativity belongs only to the Einsteins, Beethovens, and da Vincis of the world. Unfortunately, this belief often becomes a self-fulfilling prophecy. A person who believes he or she is not creative will, in all likelihood, behave that way and will make that belief come true. Many people who are considered geniuses, visionaries, and inventors actually are no smarter and have no more innate creative ability than the average person; however, they have learned how to think creatively and are persistent enough to keep trying until they succeed.

    Successful entrepreneurs recognize that "I'm not creative" is merely an excuse for inaction. *Everyone* has within him or her the potential to be creative; not everyone will tap that potential, however. Successful entrepreneurs find a way to unleash their creative powers on problems and opportunities.

    By avoiding these 10 mental locks, entrepreneurs can unleash their own creativity and the creativity of those around them as well. Successful entrepreneurs are willing to take some risks, explore new ideas, play a little, ask "What if?" and learn to appreciate ambiguity. By doing so, they develop the skills, attitudes, and motivation that make them much more creative—one of the keys to entrepreneurial success. Table 2.1 lists some questions designed to spur imagination.

How to Enhance Creativity

Enhancing Organizational Creativity

LEARNING OBJECTIVES
5. Understand how entrepreneurs can enhance their own creativity and that of their employees as well.

Creativity doesn't just happen in organizations; entrepreneurs must establish an environment in which creativity can flourish for themselves and for their workers. New ideas are fragile creations, but the right company culture can encourage people to develop and cultivate them. Ensuring that workers have the freedom and the incentive to be creative is one of the best ways to achieve innovation. "Developing a corporate culture that both fosters and rewards creativity . . . is critical because companies must be able to churn out innovations at a fast pace since technology has shortened product life cycles," says Geoff Yang, successful entrepreneur and venture capitalist.[26] Entrepreneurs can stimulate their own creativity and encourage it among workers by following these suggestions, which are designed to create a culture of innovation.

Include Creativity as a Core Company Value Entrepreneurs have the responsibility of establishing an innovative culture in their companies, and setting a creative tone in an organization begins with the company's mission statement. Entrepreneurs should incorporate creativity and innovation into their companies' mission statements and affirm their commitment to them in internal communications. If creativity and innovation are vital to a company's success (and they usually are!), they should be a natural part of the performance appraisal process.

TABLE 2.1 Questions to Spur the Imagination

People learn at an early age to pursue answers to questions. Creative people, however, understand that good *questions* are extremely valuable in the quest for creativity. Some of the greatest breakthroughs in history came as a result of creative people asking thought-provoking questions. Bill Bowerman, contemplating a design for the soles of running shoes over a breakfast of waffles, asked, "What would happen if I poured rubber into my waffle iron?" He did, and that's how Nike shoes came to be. (The Bowerman's rubber-coated waffle iron is on display in the Nike Town superstore and museum in Chicago.) Albert Einstein, creator of the theory of relativity, asked, "What would a light wave look like to someone keeping pace with it?" Masura Ibuka, who created the Sony Walkman, asked, "Why can't we remove the recording function and speaker and put headphones on the recorder?" William Riblich, CEO of Foster-Miller Inc., a company that develops production equipment for businesses, says his company routinely asks, "In what other ways can we use this particular technology?" Answering that question enabled Foster-Miller to adapt a metallurgical heat-treating technology for use in a candy manufacturing process.

The following questions can help spur your imagination:

1. Is there a new way to do it?
2. Can you borrow or adapt it?
3. Can you give it a new twist?
4. Do you merely need more of the same?
5. Less of the same?
6. Is there a substitute?
7. Can you rearrange the parts?
8. What if you do just the opposite?
9. Can you combine ideas?
10. Can you put it to other uses?
11. What else could we make from this?
12. Are there other markets for it?
13. Can you reverse it?
14. Can you rearrange it?
15. Can you put it to another use?
16. What idea seems impossible but, if executed, would revolutionize your business?

Sources: Adapted from: David Lidsky, "Brain Calisthenics," *Fast Company,* December 2004, p. 95; Thea Singer, Christopher Caggiano, Ilan Mochari, and Tahl Raz "If You Come, They Will Build It," *Inc.,* August 2002, p. 70; Creativity Web, "Question Summary," http://www.ozemail.com/au/~caveman/Creative/Techniques/ost_quest.html; *Bits & Pieces,* February 1990, p. 20; *Bits & Pieces,* April 29, 1993, "Creativity Quiz," *In Business,* November/December 1991, p. 18, Doug Hall, *Jump Start Your Brain* (New York: Warner Books, 1995), pp. 86–87; Christine Canabou, "Imagine That," *Fast Company,* January 2001, p. 56.

Embracing Diversity One of the best ways to cultivate a culture of creativity is to hire a diverse workforce. When people solve problems or come up with ideas, they do so within the framework of their own experience. Hiring people from different backgrounds, cultural experiences, hobbies, and interests provides a company with a crucial raw material needed for creativity. Smart entrepreneurs enhance organizational creativity by hiring beyond their own comfort zones.

Expecting Creativity Employees tend to rise—or fall—to the level of expectations entrepreneurs have of them. One of the best ways to communicate the expectation of creativity is to give employees permission to be creative. At one small company that manufactures industrial equipment, the owner put a "brainstorming board" in a break area. Anyone facing a sticky problem simply posts it on a brightly colored piece of paper on the board. Other workers are invited to share ideas and suggestions by writing them on white pieces of paper and posting them around the problem. The board has generated many creative solutions that otherwise would not have come up.

Expecting and Tolerating Failure Creative ideas will produce failures as well as successes. People who never fail are not being creative. Creativity requires taking chances, and managers must remove employees' fear of failure. The surest way to quash creativity throughout an organization is to punish employees who try something new and fail.

Encouraging Curiosity Entrepreneurs and their employees constantly should ask "what if . . ." questions and to take a "maybe we could . . ." attitude. Doing so allows them to break out of assumptions that limit creativity.

Creating a Change of Scenery Periodically The physical environment in which people work has an impact on their level of creativity. The cubicles made so famous in the *Dilbert* cartoon strip can suck the creativity right out of a workspace. Transforming a typical office space—even one with cubicles—into a haven of creativity does not have to be difficult or expensive. Covering bland walls with funny posters, photographs, murals, or other artwork, adding splashes of color and incorporating live plants can enliven a workspace and enhance creativity. When Michael Sachs, founder of Sg2, a health care consulting company, conducts routine business meetings, he assembles the group in the company's boardroom in the company's Evanston, Illinois, headquarters. However, when he needs a creative solution or wants to stimulate innovation, he takes his team offsite to the Catalyst Ranch, a unique meeting space in downtown Chicago. The room's walls are decorated in bright colors, rich fabrics, and paper cuttings. Brightly colored furnishings abound, and mixed in with the plentiful supply of whiteboards and markers are toys—from Hula-Hoops and Play-Doh to Slinkies and sailboats. Natural light floods the space, where teams of workers can escape the pressures of the office and feel free to relax and let their creativity flow freely.[27] Even if going to an offsite location is not practical, entrepreneurs can still stimulate creativity by starting meetings with some type of short, fun exercise designed to encourage participants to think creatively.

Viewing Problems as Challenges Every problem offers the opportunity for innovation. Entrepreneurs who allow employees to dump all of their problems on their desks to be "fixed" do nothing to develop creativity within those employees.

Providing Creativity Training Almost everyone has the capacity to be creative, but developing that capacity requires training. One writer claims, "What separates the average person from Edison, Picasso, or even Shakespeare isn't creative capacity—it's the ability to tap that capacity by encouraging creative impulses and then acting upon them."[28] Training accomplished through books, seminars, workshops, and professional meetings can help everyone learn to tap their creative capacity.

Providing Support Entrepreneurs must give employees the tools and the resources they need to be creative. One of the most valuable resources is time. Cambridge Consultants, a company that creates products for clients in five industries, allows employees to spend a portion of their time working on "pet projects" that they find exciting and believe have potential. In addition, Cambridge sets aside 10 percent of its annual revenue to provide seed capital for spin-off companies based on employees' most promising ideas. If the spin-off succeeds, the employee gets to operate it and enjoy the profits, in which Cambridge shares. If it fails, the employee gets his or her old job back, and Cambridge simply writes off the investment as a loss.[29] Entrepreneurs should remember that creativity often requires nonwork phases, and allowing employees the time to "daydream" is an important part of the creative process.

Developing a Procedure for Capturing Ideas Workers in every organization come up with creative ideas; however, not every organization is prepared to capture those ideas. The unfortunate result is that ideas that might have vaulted a company ahead or made people's lives better simply evaporate. Without a structured approach for collecting of employees' creative concepts, a business leaves its future to chance. Clever entrepreneurs establish processes within their companies that are designed to harvest the results of employees' creativity. George Calhoun, Chairman of Isco International, a company that makes wireless communications products, routinely sends employees to work with customers all over the globe, knowing that they will come back with insights and ideas they otherwise might never have had. The company captures those ideas in "trip reports" that employees make on their return.[30]

Talking with Customers Innovative companies take the time to get feedback about how they use the companies' products or services, listening for new ideas. CLAAS KGaA, a German manufacturer of agricultural equipment, operates practice centers in each of its principal markets. These centers serve as model farms where farmers can test new equipment and company officials can observe farmers first hand as they use CLAAS products, sometimes in ingenious ways that company employees never could have imagined.[31]

Looking for Uses for Your Company's Products or Services in Other Markets Focusing on the "traditional" uses of a product or service limits creativity—and a company's sales. Entrepreneurs can boost sales by finding new applications, often in unexpected places, for their products and services.

QuVIS

QuVIS, a small company based in Topeka, Kansas, had developed a technique for transmitting digital pictures faster and without the distortion and blurring that typically plagues high-resolution images when they are compressed. The company had established customers in the film-making industry, in which editors used the system to touch up video images, and at theme parks, where animators created special effects for high-tech rides. After watching the space shuttle Columbia disaster in 2003, in which a piece of falling foam breached the integrity of the spaceship and caused it to break up on reentry, a creative group of workers realized that the small company's high-definition digital imaging system could help NASA monitor the safety of the launch of the space shuttle Discovery on its "Return to Flight" mission, the first since the Columbia disaster. After many months of testing, NASA installed more than 100 cameras equipped with QuVIS's Acuity system, which allowed engineers to beam launch photos with much less distortion to labs for analysis much faster. When another piece of foam broke loose during the Discovery launch, NASA engineers were able to use the photos from QuVIS's Acuity system to determine that the astronauts could return to earth safely.[32]

Rewarding Creativity Entrepreneurs can encourage creativity by rewarding it when it occurs. Financial rewards can be effective motivators of creative behavior, but nonmonetary rewards such as praise, recognition, and celebration, usually offer more powerful incentives for creativity.

Digital Communications Corporation

Digital Communications Corporation, a small company that develops advanced wireless technologies, recognizes employees who develop patentable inventions with stock options, cash awards, and honors at an Inventors' Dinner. The reward system works; within two years after implementing it, the number of patent applications Digital Communications filed increased by a factor of five![33]

Modeling Creative Behavior Creativity is "caught" as much as it is "taught." Companies that excel at innovation find that the passion for creativity starts at the top. Entrepreneurs who set examples of creative behavior, taking chances, and challenging the status quo will soon find their employees doing the same.

Lush Cosmetics

At Lush Cosmetics, a fast-growing maker of soaps, shampoos, lotions, and moisturizers, founder Mark Constantine understands that a constant stream of innovative new products is one key to his company's success. That's why he holds annual "Mafia meetings," at which Constantine and his staff mark one-third of the company's products for elimination. Although dropping one-third of Lush's product line every year is risky and means that the product development team must come up with at least 100 new products annually, it gives team members incredible freedom and fearlessness to dream. CEO Constantine himself works on new product development for Lush, and most of his ideas, like those of other team members, never make into finished products. By modeling creative behavior, Constantine encourages creativity among his staff.[34]

TABLE 2.2 Ten "Secrets" for Leading Creativity

Leaders at innovative companies know that their roles in stimulating creativity and establishing a culture that embraces and encourages creativity are vital. Katherine Catlin, founder of a consulting firm specializing in leadership and innovation, has identified the following characteristics exhibited by leaders of innovation.

1. *They think.* These leaders invest time in thinking because they recognize the power of their own creativity and the ideas it generates.

2. *They are visionaries.* These people are totally focused on the values, vision, and mission of their companies and express them through their companies' products and services as well as through its culture. They are able to communicate to others exactly what they want to accomplish.

3. *They listen to customers.* They recognize that customers or potential customers can be a valuable source of new ideas for product or service development and improvement, sales techniques, and market positioning.

4. *They understand how to manage ideas.* As they search for new ideas and creative solutions, these managers look to a variety of sources—customers, employees, the board of directors, and even their own dreams.

5. *They are people-centered.* These leaders hire people for their creative abilities and then place them in a setting that enables that creativity to blossom. They see their employees and their employees' ideas as an important part of their companies' competitive edge.

6. *They maintain a culture of "change."* These leaders do not simply manage change; they embrace it. They seek out change, recognizing that there is a constant need to improve.

7. *They maximize team synergy, balance, and focus.* Realizing that teamwork fosters creativity and innovation, these leaders bring together people from diverse backgrounds into teams to maximize their companies' creative output.

8. *They hold themselves and others accountable for extremely high standards of performance.* These leaders demand results of the highest quality from themselves and their employees and are unwilling to settle for anything less.

9. *They refuse to take "no" for an answer.* These leaders persist in the face of adversity even when others say it cannot be done.

10. *They love what they do and have fun doing it.* These leaders' passion for their work is contagious, empowering everyone in the organization to accomplish everything they possibly can.

Source: Katherine Catlin, "10 Secrets to Leading Innovation, "*Entrepreneur,* September 2002, p. 72.

Table 2.2 describes 10 "secrets" for leading innovation in an organization.

Building a creative environment takes time, but the payoffs can be phenomenal. 3M, a company that is famous for cultivating a creative environment, estimates that 70 percent of its annual sales comes from creative ideas that originated from its workforce. As one creativity consultant explains, "For your employees to be more creative, you have to create an environment that values their creativity."[35]

Enhancing Individual Creativity

Just as entrepreneurs can cultivate an environment of creativity in their organizations by using the techniques described above, they can enhance their own creativity by using the following techniques:

Allow yourself to be creative. As we have seen, one of the biggest obstacles to creativity occurs when a person believes that he or she is not creative. Giving yourself the permission to be creative is the first step toward establishing a pattern of creative thinking. Refuse to give in to the temptation to ignore ideas simply because you fear that someone else may consider them "stupid." When it comes to creativity, there are no stupid ideas!

Give your mind fresh input every day. To be creative, your mind needs stimulation. Do something different each day—listen to a new radio station, take a walk through a park or a shopping center, pick up a magazine you never read.

Agenda Dynamics Inc.

When Janet Harris-Lange, founder of Agenda Dynamics Inc., a meeting and event management company, needs a fresh idea for an upcoming event, she makes an effort to expose her mind to new stimuli. In the past, she has walked through a second-hand thrift shop, shopped in a dime store, talked with children, and put on funny hats to generate creative ideas for her clients' events, something that is vital to her company's success. "To be better than the competition, I have to employ creative thinking," she says.[36]

Observe the products and services of others companies, especially those in completely different markets. Creative entrepreneurs often borrow ideas from companies that are in businesses totally unrelated to their own. In the 1950s, Ruth and Elliott Handler, co-founders of Mattel Inc., drew the inspiration for the best-selling doll of all time, Barbie (named after the Handler's daughter), from a doll called Lilli that was based on a shapely character in a German comic strip and then borrowed the idea of dressing her in stylish outfits from cardboard cut-out games that were popular in that era. Another example of borrowing an idea occurred when Jean Nidetech made Weight Watchers a major force in the weight loss industry by applying the support group technique from Alcoholics Anonymous to the diet plan she had developed.[37]

Recognize the creative power of mistakes. Innovations sometimes are the result of serendipity, finding something while looking for something else, and sometimes they arise as a result of mistakes. Creative people recognize that even their errors may lead to new ideas, products, and services. Charles Goodyear worked for five years trying to combine rubber with a variety of chemicals to prevent it from being too soft in hot weather and too brittle in cold weather. One cold night in 1839, Goodyear was combining rubber, sulfur, and white lead when he accidentally spilled some of the mixture on a work stove. The substances melted together to form a new compound that had just the properties Goodyear was looking for! Goodyear named the process he discovered accidentally "vulcanization," and today practically every product made from rubber depends on it.[38]

Keep a journal handy to record your thoughts and ideas. Creative ideas are too valuable to waste, so always keep a journal nearby to record them as soon as you get them. Leonardo Da Vinci was famous for writing down ideas as they struck him. Patrick McNaughton invented the neon blackboards restaurants use to advertise their specials, as well as more than 30 other products, many of which are sold through the company that he and his sister, Jamie, own. McNaughton credits much of his creative success to the fact that he writes down every idea he gets and keeps it in a special folder. "There's no such thing as a crazy idea," he insists.[39]

Listen to other people. No rule of creativity says that an idea has to be your own! Sometimes the best business ideas come from someone else, but entrepreneurs are the ones to act on them.

Ranchmark

While celebrating his friend Robert Lewis' birthday, Thomas Perlmutter presented Lewis with a gift, a Montblanc fountain pen packaged in a hard plastic case known as a "clamshell." Unable to pry open the clamshell, Lewis simply gave up and began teasing Perlmutter, whose company designed inserts for those obnoxious clamshells. Half-jokingly, his wife said, "You should invent something to open those things." Before their dinner was finished, Perlmutter and Lewis had sketched a design of a safe, easy-to-use tool that would crack open even the toughest clamshell. Within two months, they had forged a prototype, which they named the OpenX. The entrepreneurs worked with a factory in Taiwan to produce the OpenX and launched a company called Ranchmark to market the device. Ranchmark sells the OpenX from its Web site and through retailers across the United States for $9.95. The day after the popular blog Gizmodo said that the OpenX was "a great solution to an infuriating problem," Ranchmark sold 1,110 units. "I was part of the problem," laughs Perlmutter, "and now I have created the solution."[40]

Listen to customers. Some of the best ideas for new products and services or new applications of an existing product or service come from a company's customers. Entrepreneurs who take the time to listen to their customers often receive ideas they may never have come up with on their own. At Lush Cosmetics, founder Mark Constantine routinely draws ideas for new products or product names from the company's loyal customers (affectionately known as "Lushies") in the company's chat room.[41]

Talk to a child. As we grow older, we learn to conform to society's expectations about many things, including creative solutions to problems. Children place very few limitations on their thinking; as a result, their creativity is practically boundless. (Remember all of the games you and your friends invented when you were young?) Frustrated at not being able to use the small pieces of broken crayons, 11-year-old Cassidy Goldstein invented a plastic crayon holder now sold in stores across the United States. Inspired by the plastic tubes that keep roses fresh in transport, Goldstein developed a plastic device capable of holding a crayon, no matter how small it is.[42]

Keep a toy box in your office. Your box might include silly objects such as wax lips, a yo-yo, a Slinky, fortune cookie sayings, feathers, a top, a compass, or a host of other items. When you are stumped, pick an item at random from the toy box and think about how it relates to your problem.

Read books on stimulating creativity or take a class on creativity. Creative thinking is a technique that anyone can learn. Understanding and applying the principles of creativity can improve dramatically the ability to develop new and innovative ideas.

Take some time off. Relaxation is vital to the creative process. Getting away from a problem gives the mind time to reflect on it. It is often during this time, while the subconscious works on a problem, that the mind generates many creative solutions. One creativity expert claims that fishing is the ideal activity for stimulating creativity. "Your brain is on high alert in case a fish is around," he says, "but your brain is completely relaxed. This combination is the time when you have the 'Aha!' moment."[43]

You Be the Consultant

The Creative Side of Entrepreneurship

When St. Petersburg, one of the most splendid, harmonious cities in Europe, was being laid out early in the eighteenth century, many large boulders brought by a glacier from Finland had to be removed. One particularly large rock was in the path of one of the principal avenues that had been planned, and bids were solicited for its removal. The bids submitted were very high. This was understandable because at that time modern equipment did not exist and there were no high-powered explosives. As officials pondered what to do, a peasant presented himself and offered to get rid of the boulder for a much lower price than those submitted by other bidders. Since they had nothing to lose, officials gave the job to the peasant.

The next morning he showed up with a crowd of other peasants carrying shovels. They began digging a huge hole next to the rock. They propped up the rock with timbers to prevent it from rolling into the hole. When the hole was deep enough, the timber props were removed and the rock dropped into the hole below the street level. Then they covered it with dirt and carted the excess dirt away.

This is an early example of what creative thinking can do to solve a problem. The unsuccessful bidders only thought about moving the rock from one place to another on the city's surface. The peasant looked at the problem from another angle. He considered another dimension—up and down. He couldn't lift it up, so he put it underground!

Managers at the Cleveland Museum used a similar kind of creative thinking to ensure the success of a dazzling exhibit of ancient Egyptian treasures. Taking a different marketing approach, museum managers held a free private showing for the city's taxi drivers. Some of the museum's snooty, blue-blood patrons scoffed at the idea and dismissed it as an exercise in foolishness. After all, they said, taxi drivers aren't known for their polish or their culture. But the museum managers persisted. Impress the cab drivers, they reasoned, and the "cabbies" would be more likely to recommend the new exhibit to their customers, who would, in turn, flock to the museum. That's exactly what happened. During the exhibit's run in Cleveland, the museum enjoyed shoulder-to-shoulder attendance, thanks to talkative cab drivers and creative museum managers!

The principal at one Oregon middle school used creativity to solve a maintenance problem. Girls would put on lipstick in the bathrooms and then press their lips to the mirror, leaving dozens of sticky lip prints that the maintenance crew had to scrub off. The principal invited all of the girls to the bathroom, where she explained the problem and the time and cost associated with cleaning the mirrors every day. She then asked the maintenance man to demonstrate how difficult it was to scrub off the lipstick. He took out a long-handled squeegee, dipped it in a toilet, and proceeded to clean the mirror with it. Since then, no lip prints have appeared on the mirrors in the girls' bathrooms!

1. Contact a local small business owner and ask him or her about a problem his or her company is facing. Work with a small team of your classmates and use the type of creative thinking described above to generate potential solutions to the problem. Remember to think creatively!

Sources: Bernard Percy and Marina Leight, "Side by Side," *Converge,* April–May 2002, p. 11; Charles R. Davey, "Oddball Ideas Aren't So Odd," *Industry Week,* August 3, 1992, p. 7; *Bits & Pieces,* October 15, 1992, pp. 8–10.

LEARNING OBJECTIVES
6. Describe the steps in the creative process.

The Creative Process

Although creative ideas may appear to strike as suddenly as a bolt of lightning, they are actually the result of the creative process, which involves seven steps:

1. Preparation

2. Investigation

3. Transformation

4. Incubation

5. Illumination

6. Verification

7. Implementation

Step 1. Preparation This step involves getting the mind ready for creative thinking. Preparation might include a formal education, on-the-job training, work experience, and taking advantage of other learning opportunities. This training provides a foundation on which to build creativity and innovation. As one writer explains, "Creativity favors the prepared mind."[44] For example, Dr. Hamel Navia, a scientist at tiny Vertex Pharmaceuticals, recently developed a promising new drug to fight the AIDS virus. His preparation included earning an advanced degree in the field of medicine and learning to use computers to create three-dimensional images of the protein molecules he was studying.[45] How can you prepare your mind for creative thinking?

■ Adopt the attitude of a lifelong student. Realize that educating yourself is a never-ending process. Look at every situation you encounter as an opportunity to learn.

Ravi Vaidyanathan, a research scientist at Orbital Research Inc., a small high-tech firm based in Cleveland, began studying the reflexes of the cockroach after observing its uncanny ability to escape an approaching shoe. Vaidyanathan used what he learned from the insect to create a neural network called BioAVERT based on a mathematical algorithm for the company that promises to improve the navigation systems in cars, ships, airplanes, and other methods of transportation. "By mimicking a cockroach," he says, "we're able to come up with a neural network for very fast responses."[46]

Orbital Research Inc.

- Read . . . a lot . . . and not just in your field of expertise. Many innovations come from blending ideas and concepts from different fields in science, engineering, business, and the arts. Reading books, magazines, and papers covering a variety of subject matter is a great way to stimulate your creativity.
- Clip articles of interest to you and create a file for them. Over time, you will build a customized encyclopedia of information from which to draw ideas and inspiration.
- Take time to discuss your ideas with other people, including those who know little about it, as well as experts in the field. Sometimes, the apparently simple questions an "unknowledgeable" person asks lead to new discoveries and to new approaches to an old problem.

Dave Wiggins, president of American Wilderness Experience, Inc., an adventure travel company, gets valuable ideas from his wife, Carol, a network of business advisors, and his employees. The idea for the company's most popular trip, snowmobiling in Yellowstone National Park, came from one of the company's guides. "I find it extremely helpful to get different perspectives from people I respect and trust," says Wiggins.[47]

American Wilderness Experience Inc.

- Join professional or trade associations and attend their meetings. There you have the chance to brainstorm with others who have similar interests. Learning how other people have solved a particular problem may give you fresh insight into solving it.
- Invest time in studying other countries and their cultures; then travel there. Our global economy offers incredible business opportunities for entrepreneurs with the necessary knowledge and experience to recognize them. One entrepreneur began a lucrative business exporting a variety of consumer products to Latvia after he accompanied his daughter there on a missionary trip. He claims that he never would have seen the opportunity had he not traveled to Latvia with his daughter.
- Develop listening skills. It's amazing what you can learn if you take the time to listen to other people, especially those who are older and have more experience. Try to learn something from everyone you meet.
- Eliminate creative distractions. Interruptions from telephone calls, e-mails, and visitors can crush creativity. Allowing employees to escape to a quiet, interruption-free environment enhances their ability to be creative.

Step 2. Investigation This step requires one to develop a solid understanding of the problem, situation, or decision at hand. To create new ideas and concepts in a particular field, an individual first must study the problem and understand its basic components. Creative thinking comes about when people make careful observations of the world around them and then investigate the way things work (or fail to work). For example, Dr. Navia and another scientist at Vertex had spent several years conducting research on viruses and on a protein that blocks a type of virus enzyme called a protease. His exploration of the various ways to block this enzyme paved the way for his discovery.

After earning his Ph.D. in chemistry, Christopher Leamon began researching targeted anticancer therapy using molecules that tumors absorb as "Trojan horses" to deliver drugs that are lethal to them. Initially, Leamon had focused on the vitamin biotin, but after nine months of research and hard work, "it was a total failure," he says. One morning while sitting at the breakfast table with his wife, Leamon, a long-time cereal lover, was reading the ingredients on the nutrition panel of his box of Kellogg's Frosted Flakes. One of the

Endocyte

items, folic acid, caught his attention. Leamon dashed off to the library and found a research paper on how folic acid enters a human cell. "I knew this was it," he recalls. Before long, Leamon had developed a technique for attaching cancer drugs to folic acid so that they would be absorbed and enable the cells to fight the disease in much the same way they battle infections. Leamon has licensed the promising therapy to a company called Endocyte, which plans to have drugs on the market within a few years. "There are lots of 'Eureka' moments in the lab," says Leamon. "None as great as the one with the folic acid though. That breakfast redefined my career and my life."[48]

convergent thinking
the ability to see similarities and the connections among various data and events.

Step 3. Transformation Transformation involves viewing the similarities and the differences among the information collected. This phase requires two types of thinking: convergent and divergent. **Convergent thinking** is the ability to see the *similarities* and the connections among various and often diverse data and events.

Profile

SBI Enterprises

Physicist Bruce Middleton used convergent thinking to develop the idea for the award-winning Flybar, the highest flying pogo stick in the world.

While pedaling his daughters to school on a bicycle, physicist Bruce Middleton was annoyed by a stop sign at the bottom of a hill. "You lose your momentum," he explains. Middleton began to ponder a bike's ability to store kinetic energy, thinking how a steel spring could capture the energy released during braking and release it later. His calculations, however, showed that the spring would have to weigh 150 pounds. One day while in a hardware store, Middleton noticed a display rack of slingshots and his mind returned to the kinetic energy problem. He calculated that rubber's energy-storing capacity is 10 to 20 times greater than steel's. "That was the real breakthrough," he says. Thinking back to his childhood days, Middleton had the idea of replacing the steel springs in a pogo stick with rubber. To test his idea, he bought surgical tubing from a medical supply store but quickly realized that it was too bulky. Later, while walking through a thrift store, Middleton noticed a pair of "moon boots," shoes fitted with rubber bands that allow the wearer to bounce as if on a trampoline. Inspired, he purchased industrial-strength rubber bands and used the planks from his IKEA couch to build a pogo stick prototype. Eureka! The prototype bounced four feet off the ground. "The limiting factor was courage rather than mechanics," he recalls. Middleton then worked with SBI Enterprises, the world's oldest pogo stick manufacturer, to create the Flybar pogo stick. Eight-time World Cup skateboarding champion Andy MacDonald is working with SBI and Middleton to market the world's highest-flying pogo stick.[49]

divergent thinking
the ability to see the differences among various data and events.

Divergent thinking is the ability to see the *differences* among various data and events. While developing his AIDS-fighting drug, Dr. Navia studied the work of other scientists whose attempts at developing an enzyme-blocking drug had failed. He was able to see the similarities and the differences in his research and theirs and to build on their successes while avoiding their failures.

How can you increase your ability to transform the information collected into a purposeful idea?

- Evaluate the parts of the situation several times, trying to grasp the "big picture." Getting bogged down in the details of a situation too early in the creative process can diminish creativity. Look for patterns that emerge.
- Rearrange the elements of the situation. By looking at the components of an issue in a different order or from a different perspective, you may be able to see the similarities and the differences among them more readily. Rearranging them also may help uncover a familiar pattern that had been masked by an unfamiliar structure.
- Try using synectics (a term derived from the Greek words for "to bring together" and "diversity"), taking two seemingly nonsensical ideas and combining them. For instance, why not launch a bookstore with no physical storefront and no books—an

accurate description of what Jeff Bezos did when he came up with the idea for Amazon.com.[50]

- Before locking into one particular approach to a situation, remember that several approaches might be successful. If one approach produces a dead end, don't hesitate to jump quickly to another. Considering several approaches to a problem or opportunity simultaneously would be like rolling a bowling ball down each of several lanes in quick succession. The more balls you roll down the lanes, the greater is the probability of hitting at least one strike. Resist the temptation to make snap judgments on how to tackle a problem or opportunity. The first approach may not be the best one.

Step 4. Incubation The subconscious needs time to reflect on the information collected. To an observer, this phase of the creative process would be quite boring; it looks as though nothing is happening! In fact, during this phase, it may appear that the creative person is *loafing*. Incubation occurs while the individual is away from the problem, often engaging in some totally unrelated activity. Dr. Navia's creative powers were working at a subconscious level even when he was away from his work, not even thinking about his research on AIDS-fighting drugs.

How can you enhance the incubation phase of the creative process, letting ideas marinate in your mind?

- Walk away from the situation. Time away from a problem is vital to enhancing creativity. A study by Wilson Brill, an expert on creativity, of how 350 great ideas became successful products shows that two-thirds of the ideas came to people while they were *away* from work—in the shower, in their cars, in bed, on a walk, and other nonwork situations.[51] Doing something totally unrelated to the problem gives your subconscious mind the chance to work on the problem or opportunity. Indeed, the "three b's"—bath, bed, and bus—are conducive to creativity. "I do some of my best thinking in my hot tub at home," says American Wilderness Experience's Dave Wiggins. "I sit there, look at the stars, and come up with some pretty good ideas."[52]
- Take the time to daydream. Although it may *look* as if you're doing nothing, daydreaming is an important part of the creative process. That's when your mind is most free from paradigms and other self-imposed restrictions on creativity. Feel free to let your mind wander, and it may just stumble onto a creative solution.
- Relax —and play—regularly. Perhaps the worst thing you can do for creativity is to work on a problem or opportunity constantly. Soon enough, fatigue walks in, and creativity walks out! Great ideas often are incubated on the golf course, on the basketball court, in the garden, or in the hammock.
- Dream about the problem or opportunity. Although you may not be able to dream on command, thinking about an issue just before you drift off to sleep can be an effective way to encourage your mind to work on it while you sleep, a process called lucid dreaming. When he gets in bed, prolific inventor, serial entrepreneur, and author Ray Kurzweil focuses on a particular problem, sometimes imagining that he is giving a speech about his success at solving it. "This has the purpose of seeding your subconscious to influence your dreams," he explains. Often, while he is asleep, ideas and potential solutions to the problem drift into his dreams. When he begins to awaken but is still in that nether land of semi-sleep, Kurzweil merges the logic of conscious thought with the content of his dreams. The process often produces astonishing insights that Kurzweil says he otherwise might have missed.[53]

Patrick Dori came up with the idea for his business from an intense dream in which he was floating in midair over a beach watching a contraption made of iron roll across the sand. "You could put advertising on that machine," he remembers dreaming. Today, Dori is the owner of Beach'N Billboard, a New Jersey company that imprints beach sand with advertisements for products including Snapple and Skippy Peanut Butter![54]

Beach'N Billboard

- Work on the problem or opportunity in a different environment—somewhere other than the office. Take your work outside on a beautiful fall day or sit on a bench in a mall. The change of scenery will likely stimulate your creativity.

Step 5. Illumination This phase of the creative process occurs at some point during the incubation stage when a spontaneous breakthrough causes "the light bulb to go on." It may take place after five minutes—or five years. In the illumination stage, all of the previous stages come together to produce the "Eureka factor"—the creation of the innovative idea. In one study of 200 scientists, 80 percent said that at least once a solution to a problem had "just popped into their heads"—usually when they were away from the problem.[55] For Dr. Navia, the illumination stage occurred one day while he was reading a scientific journal. As he read, Dr. Navia says he was struck with a "hallucination" of a novel way to block proteases.

Although the creative process itself may last for months or even years, the suddenness with which the illumination step occurs can be deceiving. For example, one night, Kent Murphy, an electrical engineer, began dreaming about what it would be like to be a photon of light. "I was riding a ray of light moving through the fiber," he recalls about his dream. Murphy, who holds 30 patents, used the insight from his dream to invent a fiber-optic gauge that monitors on a real-time basis the structural wear in airplanes.[56] Barry Kemp says that the idea for the TV series *Coach* popped into his head—characters, plotline, and all—at 3 o'clock in the morning. He got up and scribbled seven pages of notes that became the foundation for the successful sit-com. A professor of mathematical sciences came up with an important new theory to explain how gravity works in the rotation of spiral galaxies, a problem that has perplexed physicists and astronomers for decades, while gazing at a ceiling fan in a restaurant. Like a point on the blade of a ceiling fan, he thought (he was daydreaming at the time), the speed of a star in a spinning galaxy is slower if it lies closer to the axis. He developed an equation to test his theory and then compared its results to various measurements of galactic rotation. The results were consistent with reality, and the theory worked![57]

Step 6. Verification For entrepreneurs, validating an idea as accurate and useful may include conducting experiments, running simulations, test marketing a product or service, establishing small-scale pilot programs, building prototypes, and engaging in many other activities designed to verify that the new idea will work and is practical to implement. The goal is to subject the innovative idea to the test of cold, hard reality. At this phase, appropriate questions to ask include the following:

- Is it *really* a better solution to a particular problem or opportunity? Sometimes an idea that appears to have a bright future in the lab or on paper dims considerably when put to the test of reality.
- Will it work?
- Is there a need for it?
- If so, what is the best application of this idea in the marketplace?
- Does this product or service idea fit into our core competencies?
- How much will it cost to produce or to provide?
- Can we sell it at a reasonable price that will produce adequate sales, profit, and return on investment for our business?

Ramtron International Corporation, a maker of memory chips, uses a "product justification form" to collect information from the idea generator as well as from other departments in the company so it can verify the potential of each idea.[58] To test the value of his new drug formulation, Dr. Navia used powerful computers at Vertex Pharmaceuticals to build three-dimensional Tinkertoy-like models of the HIV virus and then simulated his new drug's ability to block the protease enzyme. Subsequent testing of the drug verified its safety. "I was convinced that I had an insight that no one else had," he recalls.[59]

Step 7. Implementation The focus of this step is to transform the idea into reality. Plenty of people come up with creative idea for promising new products or services, but most never take them beyond the idea stage. What sets entrepreneurs apart is that they *act* on their ideas. An entrepreneur's philosophy is "Ready, aim, fire," not "Ready, aim, aim, aim, aim, ..."

NCT Group, a small company, had developed a system that sent mirror images of sound waves through ceramic tiles to cancel out noise. One day, an engineer wondered what would happen if he sent music instead of "anti-noise" through the tiles. He connected a radio to the unit, and from the flat tiles came the sound of the Beatles! The company took the engineer's discovery and developed two-inch-thick wall-mounted speakers that produce high-quality audio for the consumer market! Another small business, Cygnus Inc., had created a patch that was designed to deliver drugs through the wearer's skin. While taking apart a patch one day, a researcher realized that not only did it deliver drugs, but it also absorbed material from the body. Cygnus transformed the discovery into a line of watch-like devices that monitor the glucose levels of diabetic patients.[60]

The key to both companies' success was their ability to take a creative idea for a useful new product and turn it into a reality. As one creativity expert explains, "Becoming more creative is really just a matter of paying attention to that endless flow of ideas you generate, and learning to capture and act upon the new that's within you."[61]

For Dr. Navia and Vertex Pharmaceuticals, the implementation phase required testing the drug's ability to fight the deadly virus in humans. If it proved to be effective, Vertex would complete the process by bringing the drug to market. In this final phase of testing, Navia was so certain that he was on the verge of a major breakthrough in fighting AIDS that he couldn't sleep at night. Unfortunately the final critical series of tests proved that Dr. Navia's flash of creativity was, as he now says, "completely, totally, and absolutely incorrect." Although his intuition proved to be wrong this time, Dr. Navia's research into fighting AIDS continues. Much of the current work at Vertex is based on Dr. Navia's original idea. Although it proved to be incorrect, his idea has served a valuable purpose: generating new ideas. "We are now applying a powerful technology in HIV research that wasn't used before, one inspired by a hunch," he says.[62]

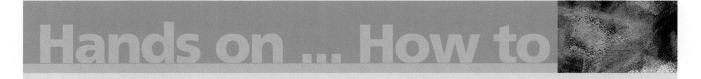

Hands on ... How to

Create a Culture of Innovation

Creating a culture in which creativity and innovation thrive is no easy task for an entrepreneur and requires a well-balanced management approach. A heavy-handed management style stifles creativity and invites high turnover rates among creative types. An approach that is too laissez-faire can lead to lapses in productivity and chaos. "The workplace of today isn't set up to manage creative people," says Richard Florida, author of *The Rise of the Creative Class*. "It's a recipe for competitive disaster to manage creative people like they're industrial workers." What can entrepreneurs do to build a culture of innovation that encourages and supports daily creativity among employees?

Step 1. Recognize that creativity comes from everywhere in your company. A common misconception is that only certain types of people have

creative ability and that most people lack it. Research shows that *anyone* with normal intelligence has the capacity to be creative; it's up to business owners to unleash employees' creativity for the benefit of the company and society as a whole. The goal is to get everyone in the organization—from the factory floor to the finance department—involved in generating creative solutions.

Step 2. Don't count on money as the primary motivator of creativity. Money can be an important motivator for some employees, but research suggests that it is not the primary motivator of creative behavior. Far more important as motivators are recognition and appreciation of creativity and the freedom and the autonomy to pursue creative solutions. In fact, when it comes to creativity, pay-for-performance systems may not be the best solutions because they encourage employees to avoid taking chances to develop creative solutions. (Remember that failure is a natural part of the creative process.) To encourage creativity among employees, entrepreneurs must create a work environment that supports, values, recognizes, and encourages creative behavior. In addition, assigning people projects based not only on their experience and education but also on their interests can stimulate creativity. People tend to be more creative when they genuinely care about their work and are learning new skills. That's why Google allows employees to spend up to 20 percent of their time working on "Googlettes," projects in which the employees are interested and see potential for business development.

Step 3. Let employees know that taking chances—and the failure that sometimes results—are acceptable outcomes. For creativity to blossom, employees have to know that it is safe to take chances that might result in failure. They have to know that they won't be punished for an innovative solution that fails, even if it costs the company money. The fastest way to snuff out creativity is to punish those who dare to take creative chances and fail.

Step 4. Provide the necessary resources, especially time, for employees to be creative. To be productive in their "regular" work, employees must have the proper resources. The same is true for their creative work. Creativity-training programs, a work environment that allows employees to interact freely (as opposed to staying locked up in their offices or, worse, cubicles), a diverse group of co-workers, and physical surroundings that are comfortable, relaxed, and pleasant are just some to the factors that can enhance creativity.

Step 5. Protect them from creativity killers. Protecting employees from creativity killers such as interruptions allows them to focus on the task at hand and to be more creative. Perhaps the most important resource entrepreneurs can give employees is *time*. Research shows that people are least creative when they are under intense pressure to meet a short deadline. Time pressure short-circuits the creative process you learned about in this chapter. Although emergencies will pop up in business periodically, a business owner who plans and schedules work in advance can remove much of the time pressure that erodes creativity.

Step 6. Allow time for dreaming and creative thinking. Although employees must stay focused on the problem at hand to produce results, creativity demands that they have time to step away from it so that the incubation process can take place. Just because a worker is staring out of a window does not meant that he or she is loafing. Sometimes the most creative ideas come about when, to a casual observer, employees look as if they are daydreaming.

Step 7. Eliminate bureaucratic procedures that add no value. There is no room for punch clocks in businesses that count on creative genius for survival. Where possible, smart entrepreneurs allow employees to establish policies and procedures within certain boundaries. Jobs designed around flextime, job sharing, telecommuting, and other techniques that accommodate the busy lifestyles of modern workers go a long way toward enhancing creativity.

Step 8. Encourage collaboration rather than competition for the best creative results. Many managers believe that the best way to stimulate creativity is to use the "*Survivor*" approach, establishing competition among teams of workers. It's just not true! Although competition may result in a hit reality television show, research shows that creativity actually *suffers* when competition is introduced. When it comes to creativity, competition shuts off information and idea sharing, both essential parts of the creative process.

Step 9. Let employees have fun! Creativity thrives where employees are having fun. That doesn't mean that employees should spend most of their time playing games, but they should be able to enjoy their work and their work environment. Smart entrepreneurs know that the Nerf basketball hoop can be just as important a business tool as a fax machine. Providing a physical workspace that includes light (natural, if possible), offbeat, inspiring artwork, plants, goofy toys, the occasional office pizza, and whiteboards are excellent ways to create an environment primed for creativity.

Sources: Adapted from Linda Tischler, "The Care and Feeding of the Creative Class," *Fast Company*, December 2004, pp. 93–95; Chris Pentilla, "An Art in Itself," *Entrepreneur*, December 2003, pp. 96–97; Juanita Weaver, "Under Pressure," *Entrepreneur*, August 2003, pp. 68–69; Bill Breen, "The 6 Myths of Creativity," *Fast Company*, December 2004, pp. 75–78; Anne Fisher, "How to Encourage Bright Ideas," *Fortune*, May 3, 2004, p. 70.

Techniques for Improving the Creative Process

LEARNING OBJECTIVES
7. Discuss techniques for improving the creative process.

Teams of people working together usually can generate more and more-creative ideas. Four techniques that are especially useful for improving the quality of creative ideas from teams are brainstorming, mind-mapping, TRIZ, and rapid prototyping.

Brainstorming

A creative process in which a small group of people interact with very little structure with the goal of producing a large *quantity* of novel and imaginative ideas is called **brainstorming.** The goal is to create an open, uninhibited atmosphere that allows members of the group to "free-wheel" ideas. Participants should suggest any ideas that come to mind *without evaluating or criticizing them.* As group members interact, each idea sparks the thinking of others, and the spawning of ideas becomes contagious. For a brainstorming session to be successful, entrepreneurs should use the following guidelines:

brainstorming
a process in which a small group of people interact with very little structure with the goal of producing a large quantity of novel and imaginative ideas.

- Keep the group small—just five to eight members. Amazon founder Jeff Bezos uses the "two-pizza rule"—if a brainstorming group can eat two pizzas, it's too big.[63]
- Make the group as diverse as possible. Include people with different backgrounds, disciplines, and perspectives. At Joe Design Inc., a successful design firm, every employee in the small firm takes part in brainstorming sessions. "We bring in everybody from the bookkeeper to the office manager because they see things completely differently than we do," says co-founder Joe Rai.[64]
- Company rank and department affiliation are irrelevant. Every member of the brainstorming team is on equal ground.
- Have a well-defined problem for the group to address but don't reveal it ahead of time. Otherwise, participants will discuss their ideas, criticize them, and engage in other creativity-limiting activities. Stating the problem in the form of a "Why," "How," or "What" question often helps.
- Limit the session to 40 to 60 minutes. Beyond that, participants grow weary, and creativity flags because brainstorming is an intense activity.
- Take a field trip. Visit the scene of the problem, if possible. Research shows that brainstorming teams that go "onsite" actually come up with more and better ideas.[65]
- Appoint someone (preferably not a brainstorming participant) the job of recorder. The recorder should write every idea on a flip chart or board so that everyone can see it.
- Use a seating pattern that encourages communication and interaction (e.g., circular or U-shaped arrangements).
- Throw logic out the window. The best brainstorming sessions are playful and anything but logical.
- Encourage *all* ideas from the team, even wild and extreme ones. Discourage participants from editing their ideas. Not only can ideas that initially seem crazy get the group's creative juices flowing, but they also can spread creativity like wildfire. In addition, the group often can polish some of these wild ideas into practical, creative solutions!
- Establish a goal of *quantity* of ideas over *quality* of ideas. There will be plenty of time later to evaluate the ideas generated. At Ideo Inc., a Silicon Valley design firm, brainstorming teams shoot for at least 150 ideas in a 30- to 45-minute session.[66] When chemist Linus Pauling received his second Nobel Prize, someone asked him how he came up with so many great ideas. Pauling replied simply, "I come up with lots of ideas."[67]
- *Forbid* evaluation or criticism of any idea during the brainstorming session. No idea is a bad idea. Criticism slams the brakes on the creative process instantly!
- Encourage participants to use "idea hitch-hiking," building new ideas on those already suggested. Often, some of the best solutions are those that are piggybacked on others.
- Dare to imagine the unreasonable. Creative ideas often arise when people suspend conventional thinking to consider far-fetched solutions.

Digital River is a company based in Eden Prairie, Minnesota, that provides e-commerce solutions for businesses and counts on a fresh supply of ideas to maintain a competitive edge. Every Friday morning at 8 a.m., CEO Joel Ronning assembles the 45 members of the company's "entrepreneurial council" to brainstorm ways to enhance customer service, boost revenues, or cut costs. In just three years, the team has generated ideas for everything from better ways to train new employees to more effective sales techniques, and, according to Ronning, has saved or made Digital River hundreds of thousands of dollars. As an added incentive for creativity, Ronning awards $2,500 every quarter for the best idea generated.[68]

COMPANY
Profile

Digital River

Mind-Mapping

Another useful tool for jump-starting creativity is mind-mapping, an extension of brain-storming. One strength of mind-mapping is that it reflects the way the brain actually works. Rather than throwing out ideas in a linear fashion, the brain jumps from one idea to another. In many creative sessions ideas are rushing out so fast that many are lost if a person attempts to shove them into a linear outline. Creativity suffers. **Mind-mapping** is a graphical technique that encourages thinking on both sides of the brain, visually displays the various relationships among ideas, and improves the ability to view a problem from many sides.

The mind-mapping process works in the following way:

mind-mapping
a graphical technique that encourages thinking on both sides of the brain, visually displays the various relationships among ideas, and improves the ability to view a problem from many sides.

■ Start by writing down or sketching a picture symbolizing the problem or area of focus in the center of a large blank page. Tony Buzan, originator of the mind-mapping technique, suggests using ledger paper or covering an entire wall with butcher paper to establish a wide open attitude toward creativity.

■ Write down *every* idea that comes into your mind, connecting each idea to the central picture or words with a line. Use key words and symbols to record ideas in short-hand. Work as quickly as possible for no more than 20 minutes, doing your best to capture the tide of ideas that flows from your brain. Just as in brainstorming, do not judge the quality of your ideas; just get them onto the paper. Build new ideas on the backs of existing ones. If you see a connection between a new idea and one already on the paper, connect them with a line. If not, simply connect the idea to the center symbol. You will organize your ideas later in the process.

■ When the flow of ideas slows to a trickle, stop! Don't try to force creativity.

■ Allow your mind to rest for a few minutes and then begin to integrate the ideas on the page into a mind map. Use colored pens and markers to connect ideas with similar themes or to group ideas into related clusters. As you organize your thoughts, look for new connections among your ideas. Sometimes the brain needs time to process the ideas in a mind map. (Recall the incubation stage of the creative process.) Walking away from the mind map and the problem for a few minutes or a few hours may lead to several new ideas or to new relationships among ideas. One entrepreneur created the format for his company's business plan with a mind map rather than with a traditional linear outline. When he finished, he not only knew what he should include in his plan, but he also had a clear picture of the order in which to sequence the elements.

Source: Copyright 2002 by Randy Glasbergen. www.glasbergen.com

"My boss sent me to a mind mapping workshop and now I can't refold my brain!"

TRIZ

In 1946, Genrich Altshuller, a 22-year-old naval officer in the former Soviet Union, developed a process with a name derived from the acronym for the Russian phrase that translates as "theory of inventive problem solving" or TRIZ (pronounced "trees"). TRIZ is a systematic approach designed to help solve any technical problem, whatever its source. Unlike brainstorming and mind-mapping, which are right-brained activities, TRIZ is a left-brained, scientific, step-by-step process that is based on the study of hundreds of the most innovative patents across the globe. Altshuller claimed that these innovations followed a particular set of patterns. Unlocking the principles behind those patterns allows one not only to solve seemingly insurmountable problems, but also to predict where the next challenges would arise.

Altshuller and his colleagues developed 40 principles underlying these innovative patents and then developed the "TRIZ contradiction matrix," a tool that combines these principles to solve a problem. They recognized that innovations come about when someone is able to overcome the inherent contradictions in a process. For instance, in the packaging industry, a contradiction exists between the effectiveness of child-proof safety caps for medicine containers and making those containers easy for authorized users to open. Manufacturers of mattresses face the contradiction of making mattresses that are both hard and soft. Too often, companies rely on a very unimaginative solution to contradictions such as these; they compromise. Rather than settle for a mediocre compromise, the TRIZ contradiction matrix is designed to *resolve* these conflicts using the 40 principles Altshuller developed. One axis of the matrix displays the characteristic of the process to be improved, and the other axis displays the conflicting characteristic that is becoming worse.

For example, suppose that a candy maker wants to make syrup-filled, bottle-shaped chocolates by molding the chocolate bottles and then pouring syrup into the mold. To speed production of the finished product to meet demand, the business owner tries heating the syrup to allow for faster pouring, but the heated syrup melts the molded chocolate bottles and distorts their shape (the contradiction; see Figure 2.3). Using the TRIZ contradiction matrix, the candy maker recognizes the problem as a conflict between speed and shape. Speed is the characteristic to be improved, and shape is the characteristic that is getting worse. The principles that the matrix suggests for solving this problem include the following:

1. Changing the dynamics of the object or the environment (e.g., making a rigid part flexible).
2. Discarding or recovering parts of an object (e.g., dissolving a protective case when it is no longer needed).
3. Causing an object to vibrate or oscillate (e.g., transforming a standard knife into an electric knife by introducing oscillating blades).
4. Changing the properties of the object (e.g., freezing the chocolate syrup and then molding the bottles around the syrup).

Choosing principle number 4, the candy maker decides to change the properties of the chocolate syrup by adding a compound that causes it to solidify when exposed to air, making it easier and faster to coat with chocolate. Once enclosed inside the chocolate, the syrup once again becomes a liquid. Problem solved![69]

Rapid Prototyping

Generating creative ideas is a critical step in the process of taking an idea for a product or a service successfully to the market. However, entrepreneurs find that most of their ideas won't work, and that is where rapid prototyping plays an important part in the creative process. The premise behind **rapid prototyping** is that transforming an idea into an actual model will point out flaws in the original idea and will lead to improvements in its design. "If a picture is worth a thousand words, a prototype is worth ten thousand," says Steve Vassallo of Ideo Inc.[70]

The three principles of rapid prototyping are the three R's: rough, rapid, and right. Models do not have to be perfect; in fact, in the early phases of developing an idea, perfecting a model usually is a waste of time. The key is to make the model good enough to

rapid prototyping
the process of creating a model of an idea, enabling an entrepreneur to discover flaws in the idea and to make improvements in the design.

FIGURE 2.3

TRIZ Contradiction Matrix

		Characteristic that is getting worse					
		Volume of stationary object	Speed	Force	Stress or pressure	Shape	Stability of the object
Characteristic to be improved	**Volume of stationary object**	—	*	Taking out Mechanical vibration Thermal expansion	Intermediary Parameter changes	Nested doll Taking out Parameter changes	Discarding and recovering Mechanics substitution Parameter changes Composite materials
	Speed	*	—	The other way round Mechanics substitution Dynamics Periodic action	Universality Mechanical vibration Strong oxidants Composite materials	Dynamics Discarding and recovering Mechanical vibration Parameter changes	Mechanics substitution Homogeneity Segmentation Mechanical vibration
	Force	Taking out Phase transitions Mechanical vibration Thermal expansion	The other way round Mechanics substitution Dynamics Equipotentiality	—	Mechanical vibration Skipping Beforehand cushioning	Preliminary action Parameter changes Composite materials Discarding and recovering	Parameter changes Preliminary action Skipping
	Stress or pressure	Parameter changes Intermediary	Universality Parameter changes Phase transitions	Phase transitions Parameter changes Skipping	—	Parameter changes Asymmetry Dynamics Preliminary action	Parameter changes Homogeneity Taking out Composite materials
	Shape	Nested doll Taking out Parameter changes	Parameter changes Discarding and recovering Mechanical vibration	Parameter changes Preliminary action Thermal expansion Composite materials	Discarding and recovering Dynamics Preliminary action Spheroidality and curvature	—	Homogeneity Segmentation Mechanical vibration Asymmetry

Source: TRIZ 40, http://www.triz40.com/aff_Matrix.htm.

determine what works and what does not. Doing so allows an entrepreneur to develop prototypes rapidly, moving closer to a successful design with each iteration. The final R, right, means building lots of small models that focus on solving particular problems with an idea. "You're not trying to build a complete model," says Vassallo. "You're just focusing on a small section of it."[71]

Be the Consultant

Evaluating Ideas for Their Market Potential

Legend has it that in 1899, Charles H. Duell, U.S. Commissioner of Patents, advised President McKinley to close the U.S. Patent Office because "Everything that can be invented has been invented." Duell was way off the mark, of course; the U.S. Patent and Trademark Office has issued more than 7 million patents since

1899. However, does a great idea that earns a patent mean that the inventor has the foundation for a successful business?

Not necessarily. Alden McMurtry, a Connecticut tinkerer, in 1911 rushed to the U.S. Patent Office with his immortal design for the bubble-hat. It used a hidden gas canister to send soap bubbles out of a hat—perfect, Mr. McMurtry thought, for show-stopping chorus numbers. It never became a commercial success. Other patents that demonstrate Americans' creative if not always marketable ideas include the underwater airplane, protective glasses for chickens, a 12-foot-long TV remote control, bird diapers, and a dog-shaped vacuum cleaner.

How can an entrepreneur evaluate the market potential of a new product or service idea? The following questions can help any entrepreneur or inventor assess the profit potential of a creative idea:

- What benefits does the product or service offer customers? Is there a real need for it?
- Have you pinpointed the exact problems or difficulties your idea aims to solve? Have you considered the problems or difficulties it might create?
- On a scale of 1 to 10, how difficult will it be to execute the idea and sell it commercially?
- Does the product or service have natural sales appeal? Can customers afford it? Will they buy it? Why?
- What existing products or services would compete with your idea? Is your product or service superior to these competing products or services? If so, in what way?
- On a scale of 1 to 10, how easily can potential customers understand the benefits of your new product or service idea? Are they obvious?
- On a scale of 1 to 10, how complex is the product or service? If it is a product, can you make a prototype of it yourself?
- On a scale of 1 to 10, how complex is the distribution or delivery system necessary to get the product or service into customers' hands?
- How unique is your product or service? How easily can other companies imitate your idea?
- How much will it cost to produce or provide the product or service? To distribute it?

To evaluate creative ideas for their commercial potential, Mail Boxes Etc. relies on a set of 20 criteria, each weighted to reflect its importance, and a scoring scale of minus 2 to plus 2. By multiplying an idea's score on each criterion by the criterion's weight, managers cal-

culate a total score that gives them a sense of an idea's market potential. Michael Michalko, author of *Cracking Creativity: The Secrets of Creative Geniuses*, suggests using the PMI (Plus, Minus, Interesting) technique. "First, list all of the positive (plus) aspects of the idea," he says. "Then list all of the negative (minus) aspects of the idea. Last, list everything that's interesting [about it], but you're not sure if it's a plus or a minus." Evaluating an idea in this way will lead to one of three results. "You'll decide it's a bad idea, you'll decide it's a good idea, or you'll recycle it into something else," says Michalko.

Try your hand at this process. Assume the role of consultant and help Randi Altschul evaluate the market potential of her business idea. One day, Randi was trying to use her malfunctioning cellular phone in her car when she became so frustrated that she was tempted to throw the expensive phone out the window. That's when the idea of a disposable cellular phone came to her. Using her background in inventing board games, Randi worked with engineers to design an ultrathin (the equivalent in size to three credit cards), inexpensive phone whose circuitry is printed in with conductive ink. The two-inch by three-inch phone gives users 60 minutes of calling time (outgoing calls only) and a hands-free attachment, all for an estimated average price of $20 (and a $2 to $3 rebate for returning the phone instead of tossing it). Randi and partner Lee Volte are working through their company, Dieceland Technologies, to apply the same technology used in the cell phone to create a paper laptop computer that they expect to serve as an Internet access device that will sell for $20.

1. Use the resources on the World Wide Web and your library to explore the prospects for Randi Altschul's cell phone.
2. Use the information you collect to answer as many of the questions listed above as possible. Conduct a PMI (plus, minus, interesting) analysis for Randi's idea.

Sources: Adapted from Mary Bellis, "Disposable Cell Phone–Phone Card Phone," *Inventors*, http://inventors.about.com/library/weekly/aa22801b.htm; Joshua Hyatt, "Inside an Inventive Mind," *FSB*, March 2002, p. 26; Jane Bahls, "Got a Winner?" *Business Start-Ups*, March 1999, pp. 6–7; Patricia L. Fry, "Inventor's Workshop," *Business Start-Ups*, August 1997, pp. 34–37; Peter Carbonara, "What Do You Do with a Great Idea?" *Business Start-Ups*, August/September, pp. 28–58; Michael W. Miller, "It Seemed Like a Good Idea," *Wall Street Journal*, May 24, 1993, p. R24; Don Debelak, "Ready or Not?" *Business Start-Ups*, January 1998, pp. 62–65; Karen Axelton, "Imagine That!" *Business Start-Ups*, April 1998, p. 96; Susan Greco, "Where Great Ideas Come From," *Inc.*, April 1998, pp. 76–86; Ross McDonald, "Patent Office Gold," *Kiplinger's Personal Finance Magazine*, June 2002, p. 124; Michael S. Malone, "The Smother of Invention," *Forbes ASAP*, June 24, 2002, pp. 32–40.

Intellectual Property: Protecting Your Ideas

Once entrepreneurs come up with innovative ideas for a product or service that has market potential, their immediate concern should be to protect it from unauthorized use. The U.S. Chamber of Commerce estimates that intellectual property theft and piracy and counterfeiting of goods cost businesses $250 billion a year.[72] Entrepreneurs must understand how to put patents, trademarks, and copyrights to work for them.

Patents

patent

a grant from the federal government's Patent and Trademark Office to the inventor of a product, giving the exclusive right to make, use, or sell the invention in this country for 20 years from the date of filing the patent application.

A **patent** is a grant from the United States Patent and Trademark Office (PTO) to the inventor of a product, giving the exclusive right to make, use, or sell the invention in this country for 20 years from the date of filing the patent application. The purpose of giving an inventor a 20-year monopoly over a product is to stimulate creativity and innovation. After 20 years, the patent expires and cannot be renewed. Most patents are granted for new product inventions (called utility patents), but *design patents*, extending for 14 years beyond the date the patent is issued, are given to inventors who make new, original, and ornamental changes in the design of existing products that enhance their sales. Inventors who develop a new plant can obtain a *plant patent*, provided they can reproduce the plant asexually (e.g., by grafting or cross-breeding rather than planting seeds). To be patented, a device must be new (but not necessarily better!), not obvious to a person of ordinary skill or knowledge in the related field, and useful. A device *cannot* be patented if it has been publicized in print anywhere in the world or if it has been used or offered for sale in this country prior to the date of the patent application. A U.S. patent is granted only to the true inventor, not a person who discovers another's invention, and is effective only in the United States and its territories. Inventors who want to sell their inventions abroad must file for patents in each country in which they plan to do business. Once a product is patented, no one can copy or sell it without getting a license from its creator. A patent does not give one the right to make, use, or sell an invention, but the right to exclude others from making, using, or selling it.

Although inventors are never assured of getting a patent, they can enhance their chances considerably by following the basic steps suggested by the PTO. Before beginning the often lengthy and involved procedure, inventors should obtain professional assistance from a patent practitioner—a patent attorney or a patent agent—who is registered with the PTO. Only those attorneys and agents who are officially registered may represent an inventor seeking a patent. A list of registered attorneys and agents is available at the PTO's Web site. Approximately 98 percent of all inventors rely on these patent experts to steer them through the convoluted process. Legal fees for filing a patent application range from $5,000 to $20,000, depending on the complexity of the product.[73] One study reports that for the typical small business, obtaining a patent and maintaining it for 20 years cost about $10,000.[74]

The Patent Process Since George Washington signed the first patent law in 1790, the U.S. Patent and Trademark Office (http://www.uspto.gov) has issued patents on everything imaginable (and some unimaginable items, too), including mouse traps (of course!), Robert Fulton's steamboat, animals (genetically engineered mice), Thomas Edison's light bulb, golf tees (764 different patents), games, and various fishing devices. The J. M. Smucker Company even holds a patent issued in 1999 on a "sealed, crustless sandwich," a peanut butter and jelly sandwich it markets very successfully under the name "Uncrustables."[75] The PTO also has issued patents on business processes—methods of doing business—including Amazon.com's controversial patent on its "1-Click" technology, which allows users to store their customer information in a file and then recall it with one mouse click at checkout. To date the PTO has issued more than 7 million patents, and it receives more than 360,000 new applications each year (see Figure 2.4)![76] To receive a patent, an inventor must follow these steps:

Establish the invention's novelty. An invention is not patentable if it is known or has been used in the United States or has been described in a printed publication in this or a foreign country.

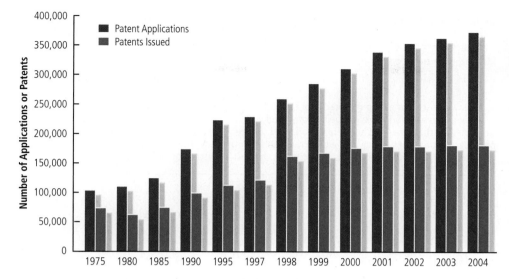

FIGURE 2.4

Number of Patent Applications and Patents Issued

Source: U.S. Patent and Trademark Office, 2005.

Document the device. To protect their patent claims, inventors should be able to verify the date on which they first conceived the idea for their inventions. Inventors can document a device by keeping dated records (including drawings) of their progress on the invention and by having knowledgeable friends witness these records. Inventors also can file a disclosure document with the PTO, a process that includes writing a letter describing the invention and sending a check for $10 to the PTO. A disclosure document is *not* a patent application, but it does provide evidence of the date an inventor conceived an invention.

Search existing patents. To verify that the invention truly is new, not obvious, and useful, an inventor must conduct a search of existing patents on similar products. The purpose of the search is to determine whether the inventor has a chance of getting a patent. Most inventors hire professionals trained in conducting patent searches to perform the research. Inventors themselves can conduct an online search of all patents granted by the PTO since 1976 from the office's Web site. An online search of these patents does not include sketches; however, subscribers to Delphion's Research Intellectual Property Network can access patents, including sketches, as far back as 1971 at http://www.delphion.com/.

Study search result. Once the patent search is finished, inventors must study the results to determine their chances of getting a patent. To be patentable, a device must be sufficiently different from what has been used or described before and must not be obvious to a person having ordinary skill in the area of technology related to the invention.

Submit the patent application. If an inventor decides to seek a patent, he or she must file an application describing the invention with the PTO. The typical patent application runs 20 to 40 pages, although some, especially those for biotech or high-tech products are tens of thousands of pages long. The longest patent application to date is one for a gene patent that was 6 million pages long![77] Most inventors hire patent attorneys or agents to help them complete their patent applications. Figure 2.5 shows a portion of the application for a rather unusual patent, number 5,971,829.

Prosecute the patent application. Before the PTO will issue a patent, one of its examiners studies the application to determine whether the invention warrants a patent. Approval of a patent normally takes about two and one-half years from the date of filing. If the PTO rejects the application, the inventor can amend the application and resubmit it to the PTO.

Defending a patent against "copycat producers" can be expensive and time-consuming but often is necessary to protect an entrepreneur's interest. The median cost of a patent infringement lawsuit seeking less than $1 million is about $500,000 if the case goes to trial (about half that if the parties settle before going to trial), but the odds of winning are

FIGURE 2.5

Patent Number 5,971,829

United States Patent
Hartman

5,971,829
October 26, 1999

Motorized ice cream cone

Abstract

A novelty amusement eating receptacle for supporting, rotating and sculpting a portion of ice cream or similarly malleable food while it is being consumed comprising: a hand-held housing, a cup rotatably supported by the hand-held housing and adapted to receive and contain a portion of ice cream or food product of similar consistency, and a drive mechanism in the hand-held housing for imparting rotation upon the cup and rotationally feeding its contents against a person's outstretched tongue.

Inventors: **Hartman; Richard B.** (P.O. Box 228, Issaquah, WA 98027)
Appl. No.: **036398**
Filed: **March 6, 1998**

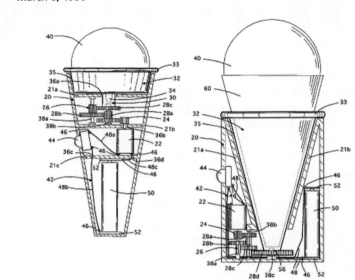

in the patent holder's favor. More than 60 percent of those holding patents win their infringement suits.[78]

Knockoffs of its famous "Big Bertha" golf club have kept Callaway Golf Company busy defending its patents against counterfeiters. The company once discovered a competitor making a look-alike driver it called the "Big Bursa." Experts estimate that in some cases, the knockoffs, with their steeply discounted prices, actually outsell the original clubs![79]

With its global reach and speedy convenience, the World Wide Web has only compounded the problem of counterfeit sales, especially among luxury items such as Luis Vuitton and Coach bags, Cartier jewelry, and Chanel perfumes.

Trademarks

A **trademark** is any distinctive word, phrase, symbol, design, name, logo, slogan, or trade dress that a company uses to identify the origin of a product or to distinguish it from other goods on the market. (A **service mark** is the same as a trademark except that it identifies and distinguishes the source of a service rather than a product.) A trademark serves as a company's "signature" in the marketplace. A trademark can be more than just a company's logo, slogan, or brand name; it can also include symbols, shapes, colors, smells, or sounds. For instance, Coca Cola holds a trademark on the shape of its bottle, and NBC owns a trademark on its three-toned chime. Motorcycle maker Harley-Davidson has applied for trademark protection for the shape of its oil tanks and the throaty rumbling sound its engines make![80]

While they were vacationing in Hawaii, Lauren Gartner and Edna Bayliff craved a cheese-burger but had trouble finding one, so they decided to open a restaurant that specialized in burgers. The name they chose for a burger restaurant located in Maui was, of course, "Cheeseburger in Paradise"—a phrase borrowed from Jimmy Buffet's song of the same name. They hired an attorney to acquire the service mark for the name. The restaurant thrived, and Buffet filed a lawsuit claiming that he owned the rights to the song title for all commercial uses. Gartner and Bayliff defended their right to use the name, pointing to their service mark. As the lawsuit dragged on, the entrepreneurs opened a second Cheeseburger in Paradise location in Waikiki. Several years after the legal battle began, Gartner and Bayliff conceded the rights to the name—excluding their two existing locations—to Buffet, who launched his own chain of restaurants called "Margaritaville" after another one of his songs. Gartner and Bayliff have since opened several more restaurants in Hawaii and on the West Coast under the name "Cheeseburgers, Mai Tais, and Rock-n-roll."[81]

Cheeseburger in Paradise

Components of a product's identity such as these are part of its **trade dress,** the unique combination of elements that a company uses to create a product's image and to promote it. For instance, a Mexican restaurant chain's particular décor, color schemes, design, and overall "look and feel" would be its trade dress. To be eligible for trademark protection, trade dress must be inherently unique and distinctive to a company, and another company's use of that trade dress must be likely to confuse customers.

trade dress
the unique combination of elements that a company uses to create a product's image and to promote it.

The Zippo Manufacturing Company, which has been making its distinctive metal ciga-rette lighter since 1932, has trademarked the shape of its classic lighter with the PTO to protect it from an onslaught of cheap imitations. Every year, the company sells more than 12 million lighters with their gently curved metal case, beveled edges, and distinctive flip-top. Zippo estimates that look-a-like knockoffs, many of which are made in China, have been skimming off as much 30 percent of the company's sales by infringing on its trade dress.[82]

Zippo Manufacturing Company

There are 1.5 million trademarks registered in the United States, 900,000 of which are in actual use (see Figure 2.6). Federal law permits a manufacturer to register a trade-mark, which prevents other companies from employing a similar mark to identify their goods. Before 1989, a business could not reserve a trademark in advance of use. Today, the first party who either uses a trademark in commerce or files an application with the PTO has the ultimate right to register that trademark. Unlike patents and copyrights,

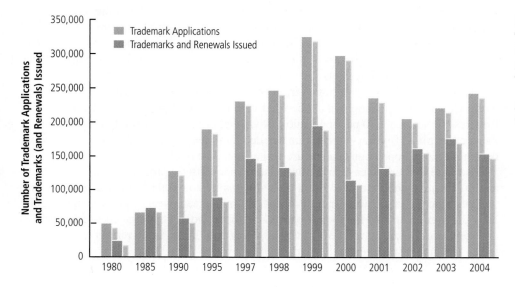

FIGURE 2.6

Number of Trademark Applications and Trademarks Issued

Source: U.S. Patent and Trademark Office, 2005.

which are issued for limited amounts of time, trademarks last indefinitely as long as the holder continues to use it. (Five years after a trademark's registration date, the entrepreneur must file an affidavit of use with the PTO.) However, a trademark cannot keep competitors from producing the same product and selling it under a different name. It merely prevents others from using the same or confusingly similar trademark for the same or similar products.

Many business owners are confused by the use of the symbols "™" and "®." Anyone who claims the right to a particular trademark (or service mark) can use the "™" (or "ˢᴹ") symbols without having to register the mark with the PTO. The claim to that trademark or service mark may or may not be valid, however. Only those businesses that have registered their marks with the PTO can use the "®" symbol. Entrepreneurs do not have to register trademarks or service marks to establish their rights to those marks; however, registering a mark with the PTO does give entrepreneurs greater power to protect their marks. Filing an application to register a trademark or service mark is relatively easy, but it does require a search of existing names.

Cosmic Debris, Etc.

Cosmic Debris, Etc., a 25-employee company based in Oakland, California, created a popular character known as Emily the Strange, a girl who dresses in black and whose favorite phrase is "Get lost!." The company generates $5 million in annual sales marketing a variety of products such as T-shirts and backpacks bearing the image of Emily the Strange. Unfortunately, knock-off artists around the world have been stealing the company's trademarked images and putting them on unlicensed garments. To cope with the threat of millions in lost sales, Cosmic Debris managers hired a private investigator, tracked some of the worst perpetrators to Taiwan, and worked with police there to confiscate cartons of counterfeit product.[83]

An entrepreneur may lose the exclusive right to a trademark if it loses its unique character and becomes a generic name. Aspirin, escalator, thermos, brassiere, super glue, yo-yo, and cellophane all were once enforceable trademarks that have become common words in the English language. Such generic terms can no longer be licensed as trademarks.

Copyrights

copyright

an exclusive right that protects the creators of original works of authorship such as literary, dramatic, musical, and artistic works.

A **copyright** is an exclusive right that protects the creators of original works of authorship such as literary, dramatic, musical, and artistic works (e.g., art, sculptures, literature, software, music, videos, video games, choreography, motion pictures, recordings, and others). The internationally recognized symbol "©" denotes a copyrighted work. A copyright protects only the form in which an idea is expressed, not the idea itself. A copyright on a creative work comes into existence the moment its creator puts that work into a tangible form. Just as with a trademark, obtaining basic copyright protection does *not* require registering the creative work with the U.S. Copyright Office (http://lcweb.loc.gov/copyright).

Registering a copyright, however, does give creators greater protection over their work. Copyright applications must be filed with the Copyright Office in the Library of Congress for a fee of $30 per application. A valid copyright on a work lasts for the life of the creator plus 70 years after his or her death. When a copyright expires, the work becomes public property and can be used by anyone free of charge.

Because they are so easy to duplicate, computer software programs, videotapes, CDs, and DVDs are among the most-often pirated items by copyright infringers. Experts estimate that the global software industry loses $12 billion each year to pirates who illegally copy programs and that Hollywood loses $2 billion to those who forge counterfeit movies and sell them. Because they are so adept at plying their trade, video pirates often manage to beat genuine distributors to the market with movies![84]

TABLE 2.3 Characteristics of Patents, Trademarks, and Copyrights

Type of Protection	What It Covers	Time Required	Cost
Copyright	Works of original authorship such as books or software	About two weeks	About $30
Trademark	Logos, names, phrases	Six months to one year	$900 to $1,500
Design patent	The look of an original product	Up to two years	$5,000 to $20,000
Utility patent	How an original product works	Two to five years	$5,000 to $20,000
Business method patent	A business process or procedure	Two to five years	$5,000 to $20,000

Source: Anne Field, "How to Knock Out Knock Offs," *Business Week,* March 14, 2005, http://www.businessweek.com/@@7oPzclQQnlwLqxsA/magazine/content/05_11/b3924446.htm.

Thimbleberries, a small company that sells designs and fabrics to quilters and generates $2 million in annual sales, copyrights every one of its designs, and the company's name is a registered trademark. When CEO Lynette Jensen discovered that 20 eBay sellers were listing what they claimed were Thimbleberries quilting kits—a product the company has never made—she took immediate action, sending letters to the offenders threatening legal action if they did not stop immediately. The Thimbleberries name quickly disappeared from the products listed on the eBay auction site.[85]

Thimbleberries

Table 2.3 provides a summary of the characteristics of patents, trademarks, and copyrights.

Protecting Intellectual Property

Acquiring the protection of patents, trademarks, and copyrights is useless unless an entrepreneur takes action to protect those rights in the marketplace. Unfortunately, not every businessperson respects others' rights of ownership to products, processes, names, and works, and some infringe deliberately on those rights with impunity. In other cases, the infringing behavior simply is the result of a lack of knowledge about others' rights of ownership. After acquiring the proper legal protection through patents, copyrights, or trademarks, entrepreneurs must monitor the market (and the World Wide Web in particular) for unauthorized, copycat users. If an entrepreneur has a valid patent, trademark, or copyright, stopping an infringer usually requires nothing more than a stern "cease and desist" letter from an attorney. Often, offenders do not want to get into expensive legal battles and agree to stop their illegal behavior. If that tactic fails, the entrepreneur may have no choice but to bring an infringement lawsuit, many of which end up being settled out of court.

The primary weapon an entrepreneur has to protect patents, trademarks, and copyrights is the legal system. The major problem with relying on the legal system to enforce ownership rights, however, is the cost and time of infringement lawsuits, which can quickly exceed the budget of most small businesses and occupy huge blocks of managers' time. Lawsuits always involve costs. Before pursuing what could become an expensive and drawn-out legal battle, an entrepreneur must consider the following issues:

- Can your opponent afford to pay if you win?
- Do you expect to get enough from the suit to cover the costs of hiring an attorney and preparing a case?
- Can you afford the loss of time, money, and privacy from the ensuing lawsuit?

Chapter Summary by Learning Objectives

1. Explain the differences among creativity, innovation, and entrepreneurship.

The entrepreneur's "secret" for creating value in the marketplace is applying creativity and innovation to solve problems and to exploit opportunities that people face every day. Creativity is the ability to develop new ideas and to discover new ways of looking at problems and opportunities. Innovation is the ability to apply creative solutions to those problems and opportunities to enhance or to enrich people's lives. Entrepreneurship is the result of a disciplined, systematic process of applying creativity and innovation to needs and opportunities in the marketplace.

2. Describe why creativity and innovation are such integral parts of entrepreneurship.

Entrepreneurs must always be on guard against paradigms—preconceived ideas of what the world is, what it should be like, and how it should operate—because they are logjams to creativity. Successful entrepreneurs often go beyond conventional wisdom as they ask "Why not . . .?"

Success—even survival—in this fiercely competitive, global environment requires entrepreneurs to tap their creativity (and that of their employees) constantly.

3. Understand how the two hemispheres of the human brain function and what role they play in creativity.

For years, people assumed that creativity was an inherent trait. Today, however, we know better. Research shows that almost anyone can learn to be creative. The left hemisphere of the brain controls language, logic, and symbols, processing information in a step-by-step fashion. The right hemisphere handles emotional, intuitive, and spatial functions, processing information intuitively. The right side of the brain is the source of creativity and innovation. People can learn to control which side of the brain is dominant in a given situation.

4. Explain the 10 "mental locks" that limit individual creativity.

The number of potential barriers to creativity is limitless, but entrepreneurs commonly face 10 "mental locks" on creativity: Searching for the one "right" answer; focusing on "being logical;" blindly following the rules; constantly being practical; viewing play as frivolous; becoming overly specialized; avoiding ambiguity; fearing looking foolish; fearing mistakes and failure; and believing that "I'm not creative."

5. Understand how entrepreneurs can enhance their own creativity and that of their employees as well.

Entrepreneurs can stimulate creativity in their companies by expecting creativity; expecting and tolerating failure; encouraging curiosity; viewing problems as challenges; providing creativity training; providing support; rewarding creativity; and modeling creativity. Entrepreneurs can enhance their own creativity by using the following techniques: allowing themselves to be creative; giving their minds fresh input every day; keeping a journal handy to record their thoughts and ideas; reading books on stimulating creativity or taking a class on creativity; taking some time off to relax.

6. Describe the steps in the creative process.

The creative process consists of seven steps: Step 1. Preparation—involves getting the mind ready for creative thinking; Step 2. Investigation—requires the individual to develop a solid understanding of the problem or decision; Step 3. Transformation—involves viewing the similarities and the differences among the information collected; Step 4. Incubation—allows the subconscious mind to reflect on the information collected; Step 5. Illumination—occurs at some point during the incubation stage when a spontaneous breakthrough causes "the light bulb to go on;" Step 6. Verification—involves validating the idea as accurate and useful; and Step 7. Implementation—involves transforming the idea into a business reality.

7. Discuss techniques for improving the creative process.

Four techniques that are especially useful for improving the creative process are as follows:

- Brainstorming is a process in which a small group of people interact with very little structure with the goal of producing a large *quantity* of novel and imaginative ideas.
- Mind-mapping is a graphical technique that encourages thinking on both sides of the brain, visually displays the various relationships among ideas, and improves the ability to view a problem from many sides.
- TRIZ is a systematic approach designed to help solve any technical problem, whatever its source. Unlike brainstorming and mind-mapping, which are right-brained activities, TRIZ is a left-brained, scientific, step-by-step process that is based on the study of hundreds of the most innovative patents across the globe.
- Rapid prototyping is based on the premise that transforming an idea into an actual model will point out flaws in the original idea and will lead to improvements in its design.

8. Describe the protection of intellectual property through patents, trademarks, and copyrights.

A patent is a grant from the federal government that gives an inventor exclusive rights to an invention for 20 years.

A trademark is any distinctive word, symbol, or trade dress that a company uses to identify its product and to distinguish it from other goods. It serves as a company's "signature" in the marketplace.

A copyright protects original works of authorship. It covers only the form in which an idea is expressed and not the idea itself and lasts for 70 years beyond the creator's death.

Discussion Questions

1. Explain the differences among creativity, innovation, and entrepreneurship.
2. How are creativity, innovation, and entrepreneurship related?
3. Why are creativity and innovation so important to the survival and success of a business?
4. One entrepreneur claims, "Creativity unrelated to a business plan has no value." What does he mean? Do you agree?
5. What is a paradigm? What impact do paradigms have on creativity?
6. Can creativity be taught or is it an inherent trait? Explain.
7. How does the human brain function? What operations does each hemisphere specialize in? Which hemisphere is the "seat" of creativity?

8. Briefly outline the 10 "mental locks" that can limit individual creativity. Give an example of a situation in which you subjected yourself to one of these mental locks.
9. What can entrepreneurs do to stimulate their own creativity and to encourage it among workers?
10. Explain the steps of the creative process. What can an entrepreneur do to enhance each step?
11. Explain the differences among a patent, a trademark, and a copyright. What form of intellectual property does each protect?

Business Plan Pro

 The creative process can help you to develop your business concept and add dimension to an existing business venture. The process of creating your business plan will enable you to refine and test your creative ideas.

Business Plan Exercises

Select one of the creative processes mentioned in this chapter. You may want to consider mind-mapping, TRIX, or brainstorming if you are in a group. Apply this technique to your business concept. If your business idea is in the embryonic stage, use this exercise to bring focus to the business. If you have a solid grasp on your business concept, use one of these creative techniques to address a specific business challenge or to explore a potential opportunity for your business.

On the Web

Identify at least three key words or phrases that you associate with your business concept. For example, if your business is a specialty retail and online store selling wakeboards, you may consider the terms "wakeboards," "water sports," and "boards." Enter terms relevant to your business in your favorite search engine and see what information appears.

1. What companies advertise under those terms?
2. What are the top three listings?
3. How is your business unique from those businesses listed, including the fact that your business may offer a local presence?
4. What other attributes set your business apart from what you see on the Web?

Make note of anything that you learned or observed from what you saw online.

In the Software

Open Business Plan Pro and the business plan you began in Chapter 1. If this exercise has changed any of your initial concepts or produced an entirely different business concept, think about why the exercise led you down a different path. If that venture is different, select the Create a new business plan option and work through the wizards as you did before. Once again, you can view the outline created based on those responses by clicking on the Preview icon or going to File, Print, and then Print Preview.

Sample Plans

Open the Sample Plan Browser in Business Plan Pro; it will be helpful to have an Internet connection when you do. Enter one or more of the search terms you selected in the exercise in the search window of the Sample Plan Browser. Do any sample plans appear based on the term you entered? If so, review those plans. Will one of those plans be a potential resource for you as create your business plan? Remember, the sample plan does not have to be identical to your business concept. With even distant similarities, sample plans may be a resource for you based on its general content or layout.

Building Your Business Plan

Open your business plan and go to the section titled "Product and Service Description." You can do that by clicking on the Plan Outline icon at the top of your screen or clicking on View and selecting Outline from the drop-down menu. Within that section, begin to describe the products or services your business will offer. Notice that you have the option to view that section of a sample plan by clicking on Examples in the upper right hand section of the screen. Now, go to the "Market Needs" section of the plan. Make a few notes here regarding the needs that your products and services satisfy. We will revisit these sections, so just make comments that will help you develop your thoughts as you progress through the chapters.

Beyond the Classroom . . .

1. Your dinner guests are to arrive in five minutes, and you've just discovered that you forgot to chill the wine! Wanting to maintain your reputation as the perfect host/hostess, you must tackle this problem with maximum creativity. What could you do? Generate as many solutions as you can in five minutes working alone. Then, work with two or three students in a small group to brainstorm the problem.

2. Work with a group of your classmates to think of as many alternative uses for the commercial lubricant WD-40 as you can. Remember to think *fluidly* (generating a quantity of ideas) and *flexibly* (generating unconventional ideas).

3. Review the following list of household appliances. Working with a small group of your classmates, select one and use the brainstorming technique to develop as many alternative uses for the appliance as you can in 15 minutes. Remember to abide by the rules of brainstorming! The appliances: dishwasher, clothes dryer, curling iron, toaster oven, iron, microwave oven, coffeemaker, and any others you want to use.

4. A major maker of breakfast cereals was about to introduce a new multigrain cereal. Its principal selling point is that it features "three great tastes" in every bowl: corn, rice, and wheat. Because a cereal's name is an integral part of its marketing campaign, the company hired a very costly consulting firm to come up with the right name for the new product. The consulting firm tackled the job using "a combination of structural linguistics and personal creativity." One year and many dollars later, the consulting firm gave its recommendation.

   Take 20 minutes to list names that you think would be appropriate for this cereal. Make brief notes about why you think each name is appropriate.

   Your professor may choose to prepare a list of names from all of the members of your class and may take a vote to determine the "winner."

5. Each hemisphere of the brain processes information differently, and one hemisphere tends to dominate the other. Consider the following lists of words and decide which one best describes the way you make decisions and solve problems:

Metaphor	Logic
Dream	Reason
Humor	Precision
Ambiguity	Consistency
Play	Work
Approximate	Exact
Fantasy	Reality
Paradox	Direct
Diffuse	Focused
Hunch	Analysis
Generalization	Specific
Child	Adult

   If you chose the list on the left, you tend to engage in "soft" thinking, which suggests a right-brain orientation. If you chose the list on the right, you tend to engage in "hard" thinking, which suggests a left-brain orientation.

   Creativity relies on both "soft" and "hard" thinking. Each plays an important role in the creative process but at different phases.

   A. Identify which type of thinking—"soft" or "hard"—would be most useful in each of the seven stages of the creative process.

   B. List five things you can do to develop your thinking skills in the area ("soft" or "hard") that least describes your decision-making style.

6. Interview at least two entrepreneurs about their experiences as business owners. Where did their business ideas originate? How important are creativity and innovation to their success? How do they encourage an environment of creativity in their businesses?

3 | Designing a Competitive Business Model and Building a Solid Strategic Plan

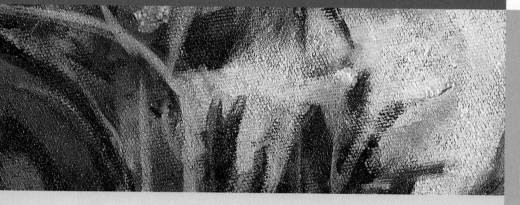

If you aim at nothing, you'll hit it every time. —Zig Ziglar

The best way to predict the future is to invent it. —Alan Kay

Learning Objectives

On completion of this chapter, you will be able to:

1 Understand the importance of strategic management to a small business.
2 Explain why and how a small business must create a competitive advantage in the market.
3 Develop a strategic plan for a business using the nine steps in the strategic planning process.
4 Discuss the characteristics of three basic strategies—low cost, differentiation, and focus—and know when and how to employ them.
5 Understand the importance of controls such as the balanced scorecard in the planning process.

Few activities in the life of a business are as vital—or as overlooked—as that of developing a strategy for success. Too often, entrepreneurs brimming with optimism and enthusiasm launch businesses destined for failure because their founders never stop to define a workable strategy that sets them apart from their competition. Because they tend to be people of action, entrepreneurs often find the process of developing a strategy dull and unnecessary. Their tendency is to start a business, try several approaches, and see what works. Without a cohesive plan of action, however, these entrepreneurs have as much chance of building a successful business as a defense contractor attempting to build a jet fighter without blueprints. Companies lacking clear strategies may achieve some success in the short run, but as soon as competitive conditions stiffen or an unanticipated threat arises, they usually "hit the wall" and fold. Without a basis for differentiating itself from a pack of similar competitors, the best a company can hope for is mediocrity in the marketplace.

In today's global competitive environment, any business, large or small, that is not thinking and acting strategically is extremely vulnerable. Every business is exposed to the forces of a rapidly changing competitive environment, and in the future small business executives can expect even greater change and uncertainty. From sweeping political changes around the planet and rapid technological advances to more intense competition and newly emerging global markets, the business environment has become more turbulent and challenging to business owners. Although this market turbulence creates many challenges for small businesses, it also creates opportunities for those companies that have in place strategies to capitalize on them. Historically important, entrepreneurs' willingness to adapt, to create change, to experiment with new business models, and to break traditional rules has become more important than ever. "It's not the strongest or the most intelligent [companies that] survive," says American Express CEO Ken Chenault, "but those most adaptive to change."[1]

Perhaps the biggest change business owners face is unfolding now: the shift in the world's economy from a base of *financial* to *intellectual* capital. "Knowledge is no longer just a factor of production," says futurist Alvin Toffler. "It is the *critical* factor of production."[2] Today, a company's intellectual capital is likely to be the source of its competitive advantage in the marketplace. **Intellectual capital** comprises three components:[3]

intellectual capital
a key source of a company's competitive advantage that comprises (1) human capital, (2) structural capital, and (3) customer capital.

1. *Human capital*, the talents, creativity, skills, and abilities of a company's workforce, shows up in the innovative strategies, plans, and processes that the people in an organization develop and then passionately pursue.
2. *Structural capital*, the accumulated knowledge and experience that a company possesses, can take many forms including processes, software, patents, copyrights, and, perhaps most important, the knowledge and experience of the people in a company.
3. *Customer capital* is the established customer base, positive reputation, ongoing relationships, and goodwill that a company builds up over time with its customers.

Increasingly, entrepreneurs are recognizing that the capital stored in these three areas forms the foundation of their ability to compete effectively and that they must manage this intangible capital base carefully. Every business uses all three components in its strategy, but the emphasis they place on each one varies.

Whole Foods

Whole Foods, a highly successful retailer of natural and organic foods with 172 stores in North America and the United Kingdom, relies heavily on human capital as the basis for its competitive advantage in the marketplace. The company subjects all job applicants to a thorough screening process, carefully selecting only those who demonstrate a passion for what lies at the heart of its competitive edge: a love of food and dedication to customer service. Unlike most of its competitors in the supermarket industry, Whole Foods invests heavily in training its workers (called Team Members inside the company) so that they can demonstrate and explain to customers the features and the benefits of the company's natural foods. In addition, managers recognize that food preferences vary from one region of a nation to another, and they give Team Members at the local level a great deal of autonomy in the selection of foods they stock. Because of its recognition of the role Team

Members play in the company's success and its employee-friendly policies, Whole Foods is consistently listed on *Fortune's* "100 Best Companies to Work For" list. Even though its cost structure is not the lowest in the industry, the company is growing rapidly because owners know that its loyal customers do not shop there searching for the lowest prices.[4]

This knowledge shift will create as much change in the world's business systems as the Industrial Revolution did in the agriculture-based economies of the 1800s. The Knowledge Revolution will spell disaster for those companies who are not prepared for it, but it will spawn tremendous opportunities for those entrepreneurs equipped with the strategies to exploit these opportunities. Management legend Jack Welch, who masterfully guided General Electric for many years, says, "Intellectual capital is what it's all about. Releasing the ideas of people is what we've got to do if we are going to win."[5] However, in practice, releasing people's ideas is much more difficult than it appears. The key is to encourage employees to generate a large volume of ideas, recognizing that only a few (the best) will survive. According to Gary Hamel, author of *Inside the Revolution*, "If you want to find a few ideas with the power to enthrall customers, foil competitors, and thrill investors, you must first generate hundreds and potentially thousands of unconventional strategic ideas. Put simply, you have to crush a lot of rock to find a diamond."[6] In other words, small companies must use the creative techniques discussed in Chapter 2 as one source of competitive advantage over their rivals.

The rules of the competitive game of business are constantly changing. To be successful, entrepreneurs can no longer do things in the way they've always done them. Fortunately, successful entrepreneurs have at their disposal a powerful weapon to cope with a hostile, ever-changing environment: the process of strategic management. **Strategic management** involves developing a game plan to guide a company as it strives to accomplish its vision, mission, goals, and objectives and to keep it from straying off its desired course. The idea is to give an entrepreneur a blueprint for matching the company's strengths and weaknesses to the opportunities and threats in the environment.

Building a Competitive Advantage

The goal of developing a strategic plan is to create for the small company a **competitive advantage**—the aggregation of factors that sets a small business apart from its competitors and gives it a unique position in the market that is superior to its competition. From a strategic perspective, the key to business success is to develop a unique competitive advantage, one that creates value for customers and is difficult for competitors to duplicate. A company that gains a competitive advantage becomes a leader in its market and can achieve above-average profits.

Early in its existence, the Blockbuster Video chain gained a significant advantage over rival video rental stores when it negotiated a deal with the major movie studios to purchase videos for just $6 each, plus a revenue sharing agreement of 40 percent of the rental fees. The agreement meant that Blockbuster could lower the cost of its inventory to less than one-tenth of that of its competitors, who were still paying an average of $65 per video! Blockbuster's significantly lower costs meant that it could stock thousands more video titles than any of its rivals, enabling the company to offer customers a tangible benefit (greater selection and in-stock guarantees) while creating a sizeable competitive advantage in the market.[7]

Building a competitive advantage alone is not enough; the key to success over time is building a *sustainable* competitive advantage. In the long run, a company gains a sustainable competitive advantage through its ability to develop a set of core competencies that enable it to serve its selected target customers better than its rivals. **Core competencies** are a unique set of capabilities that a company develops in key areas, such as superior quality,

strategic management
the process of developing a game plan to guide a company as it strives to accomplish its vision, mission, goals, and objectives and to keep it from straying off course.

LEARNING OBJECTIVES
2. Explain why and how a small business must create a competitive advantage in the market.

competitive advantage
the aggregation of factors that sets a small business apart from its competitors and gives it a unique position in the market superior to its competition.

COMPANY **Profile**

Blockbuster Video

core competencies
a unique set of capabilities that a company develops in key operational areas that allow it to vault past competitors.

FIGURE 3.1

Building a Sustainable Competitive Advantage

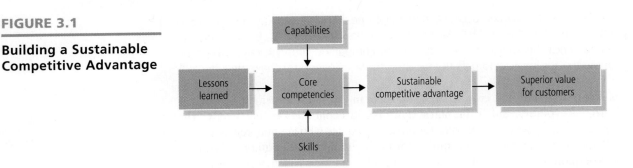

customer service, innovation, team-building, flexibility, responsiveness, and others, that allow it to vault past competitors. As the phrase suggests, they are central to a company's ability to compete successfully and are usually the result of important skills and lessons a business has learned over time. Two of the Disney Company's core competencies are animation and the ability to create magical experiences for guests at its theme parks through superior customer service. After company founder Walt Disney died, however, the company lost its focus, moved away from these core competencies, and struggled as its competitive edge in animated films slipped away to smaller competitors such as Pixar.

Typically, a company develops core competencies in no more than five or six (often fewer) areas. These core competencies become the nucleus of a company's competitive advantage and are usually quite enduring over time. Markets, customers, and competitors may change, but a company's core competencies are more durable, forming the building blocks for everything a company does. To be effective strategically, these competencies should be difficult for competitors to duplicate, and they must provide customers with an important perceived benefit. Small companies' core competencies often have to do with the advantages of their size—such as agility, speed, closeness to their customers, superior service, or the ability to innovate. In short, their small size is an advantage, allowing them to do things that their larger rivals cannot. The key to success is building the company's strategy on these core competences and concentrating them on providing superior service and value for its target customers (see Figure 3.1).

Netflix

Reed Hastings, founder of Netflix, transformed the video rental industry when he created a Web-based model that allows customers to make their video selections online and to avoid having to pay late fees. Hastings' next innovation is to deliver movies over the Internet without having to ship DVDs through its distribution centers.

Blockbuster Video's early market dominance in the video rental business did not go unchallenged, and its competitive advantage proved to be unsustainable over time. The most serious challenge comes from Netflix, a small company that has created a unique online DVD rental service. Software entrepreneur Reed Hastings saw the Web as a way to revolutionize the delivery of videos to consumers and launched the company in 1997 by investing his own money and raising $120 million in equity capital. For a monthly subscription fee, customers log onto the Netflix Web site and pick the movies they want to rent and the order in which they want to receive them. The order goes to one of the 35 Netflix regional distribution centers that is closest to the customer, where employees fill the order. Customers can keep a DVD as long as they want without incurring any late fees, and shipping (both ways) is free. When a customer returns a DVD, a computer scans it, looks up the next video on the customer's order, and sends it out. About 90 percent of DVDs come in and go out on the same day. Netflix is building its competitive advantage on several core competencies. Hastings created the business system that drives Netflix using his extensive knowledge of computer software. One venture capitalist says Netflix's "film recommendation software, its merchandising, and the inventory control systems are so sophisticated. It isn't that they couldn't be replicated, but they're hard to do, and it'll take a lot of money, time, and commitment to get it right as Netflix has." CineMatch, the company's proprietary film suggestion software (29,000 lines of code), uses customers' ratings from past films they have rented to suggest new ones. The CineMatch system works so well that its recommendations account for 70 percent of the movies Netflix customers rent! Netflix also has entered into revenue-sharing deals with 50 film distributors, including most of the major studios, giving it an inventory of more than 50,000 titles, including lesser-known, niche films as well as box office hits. The largest Blockbuster Video stores have 7,000 to 8,000 titles. Netflix's strategy of offering customers maximum convenience—free in-home delivery, no due dates, no late fees, and no return shipping charges—has enabled it to increase its customer base to 3 million people. Once the industry leader, Blockbuster is now relentlessly pursuing Netflix with an online DVD rental service of its own and has attracted 1 million customers. Amazon, which has launched a similar service in England as a test run for entering the U.S. market, also promises to be a formidable competitor. Hastings, however, is not standing still; his goal is to have 20 million subscribers by 2010. How? His next innovation involves working in a strategic alliance with TiVo to allow customers of both services to download movies over the Internet. In fact, Hastings projects that by 2010, Netflix will deliver most of its movies over the Internet rather than shipping DVDs through its distribution centers.[8]

No business can be everything to everyone. In fact, one of the biggest pitfalls many entrepreneurs stumble into is failing to differentiate their companies from the crowd of competitors. Entrepreneurs often face the challenge of setting their companies apart from their larger, more powerful competitors (who can easily outspend them) by using their creativity and the special abilities their businesses offer customers. Developing core competencies does *not* necessarily require a company to spend a great deal of money. It does, however, require an entrepreneur to use creativity, imagination, and vision to identify those things that it does best and that are most important to its target customers. Businesses have a huge number of ways to create a competitive edge, but building strategy around a company's core competencies allows it to gain a sustainable competitive edge based on what it does best.

Tom's of Maine

Tom's of Maine has built its reputation over the last 35 years as a back-to-nature company that sells a line of more than 90 all-natural personal care products with environmentally friendly packaging and donates 10 percent of its pre-tax profits to charity. Founder Tom Chappell's company competes in the same industry as giants such as Unilever, Colgate-Palmolive, and Procter & Gamble by focusing on its base of environmentally conscious customers and by promoting itself as a company "working with nature to make a difference." Gearing up for growth, Tom's of Maine has introduced a line of herbal remedy products as well as a line of toothpastes for adults and children. Like all of its other products, the new toothpastes contain no artificial flavors, dyes, sweeteners, or preservatives, nor are they tested on animals. Tom's of Maine is the only company to have a complete line of all-natural fluoride toothpastes that are approved by the American Dental Association. The toothpastes and all of the company's product extensions are based on its core competency of developing and manufacturing all-natural, environmentally friendly products that meet the highest standards of quality and safety, something that enables Tom's products to sell at a premium. Another core competency is the company's stellar reputation among a loyal customer base as a business with a deep sense of ethics and environmental and social responsibility. (Chappell is the only CEO to have earned a master's degree at the Harvard Divinity School.) Explaining the company's enduring success, Gwynne Rogers of the Natural Marketing Institute says, "Lots of companies foster sustainable business practices, but they don't make them relevant to consumers. Tom's has positioned its mission right at the point of sale."[9]

When it comes to developing a strategy for establishing a competitive advantage, small companies such as Tom's of Maine have a variety of natural advantages over their larger competitors. Small businesses often have narrower product lines, more clearly defined customer bases, a special connection with their customers, and specific geographic market areas. Entrepreneurs usually are in close contact with their markets, giving them valuable knowledge on how to best serve their customers' needs and wants. Because of the simplicity of their organization structures, small business owners are in touch with employees daily, often working side by side with them, allowing them to communicate strategic moves first-hand. Consequently, small businesses find that strategic management comes more naturally to them than to larger companies with their layers of bureaucracy and far-flung operations.

Strategic management can increase a small company's effectiveness, but entrepreneurs first must have a process designed to meet their needs and their business's special characteristics. It is a mistake to attempt to apply a big business's strategic development techniques to a small business because a small business is not merely "a little big business." Because of their size and their particular characteristics—small resource base, flexible managerial style, informal organizational structure, and adaptability to change—small businesses need a different approach to the strategic management process. The strategic management procedure for a small business should include the following features:

LEARNING OBJECTIVES
3. Develop a strategic plan for a business using the nine steps in the strategic planning process.

- Use a relatively short planning horizon—two years or less for most small companies.
- Be informal and not overly structured; a shirtsleeve approach is ideal.
- Encourage the participation of employees and outside parties to improve the reliability and creativity of the resulting plan.
- Do not begin with setting objectives because extensive objective setting early on may interfere with the creative process of strategic management.
- Maintain flexibility; competitive conditions change too rapidly for any plan to be considered permanent.
- Focus on strategic *thinking*, not just planning, by linking long-range goals to day-to-day operations.
- Let planning be an ongoing process because businesses and the competitive environment in which they operate constantly change.

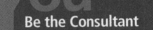

You Be the Consultant

Who Says Shopping for Groceries Can't Be Fun?

In an industry famous for razor-thin profit margins, high levels of employee turnover, and intense competition usually based on price, Wegmans, a family-owned chain of 67 supermarkets in New York, New Jersey, Pennsylvania, and Virginia, is quite unique. It has to be. Traditional grocers are under attack on many fronts. Mass merchandisers such as Wal-Mart with its superstore concept are taking customers, sales, and market share from traditional grocers. Mass merchandisers' now control one-third of the grocery market, and experts predict that their market share will continue to rise, hitting about 40 percent in 2008. Customers say they are bored with the shopping experience at most traditional grocers. One recent study reports that 84 percent of shoppers say that traditional grocery stores are all alike. Over the past several years, several chains have struggled to survive, and some have declared bankruptcy or were bought out by competitors.

How does this relatively small chain of grocery stores founded in 1930 by brothers John and Walter Wegman manage not only to survive, but also to claim a spot near the top of the industry? Although the answer to that question involves as many components as the number of brands on the cereal aisle in one of the Wegmans stores, much of the credit goes to the company's clever retail strategy and the way it treats employees. That strategy took root early in the company's existence when its founding brothers built a 300-seat café in their first store in Rochester, New York, a concept that was unheard of in 1930. When Robert Wegman, son of one of the founders, took over the company in 1950, he instituted a host of employee-friendly benefits such as profit-sharing and full medical coverage long before benefits of this type were popular. When asked why he made such a bold move, Robert, now chairman of the company, says simply, "I was no different from them."

Wegmans' annual salaries for full-time workers and hourly wages for part-time workers are among the highest in the industry. Not only do the higher wages discourage labor unions from setting up shop, but they also keep the employee turnover rate—and the resulting costs of constantly having to hire and train new workers—well below the industry average. Wegmans' generous pay scale and its consistent listing as one of the 100 best companies to work for also attracts quality workers. In fact, the sous chef at its Pittsford, New York, store previously worked at the French Laundry, the famous Napa Valley restaurant that is consistently voted as the best in the United States.

In addition to excellent pay, Wegmans also offers college scholarships for both its full- and part-time employees. Over the last two decades, the company has awarded more than $54 million in scholarships to some 17,500 workers. Wegmans also sends many of its employees to locations around the world to learn about or to locate new and unique sources of foods—from wine and cheese to mushrooms and sushi. After all, reasons Robert's son, Danny, who now manages Wegmans, what good is it to offer 500 varieties of cheese if employees can't explain to customers the best way to serve them, which types of crackers to serve them on, and which wines go best with them?

Although Wegmans approach to managing people pushes its labor cost to 15 to 17 percent of sales (compared with 12 percent of sales for the average supermarket), its annual turnover rate for full-time employees is just 6 percent, less than one-third the industry average of 19 percent. More than 20 percent of Wegmans' employees have 10 years or more of service, and this shows up in the wealth of knowledge about the company's products that they enthusiastically share with customers. "It's our [employees'] knowledge that can help the customer," says Danny. "So the first pump we have to prime is our own people."

Almost everyone Wegmans hires has a keen interest in food, but the real acid test for new hires is a passion for taking care of customers. Indeed, Wegmans' focus on customer service is another component of its strategy for success. Every employee in the store has the power to do whatever it takes to keep customers happy without having to involve a manager higher up the chain of command. One worker even cooked a customer's Thanksgiving turkey for her in the store when the bird proved to be too big to fit in her oven. Why does Wegmans go to such lengths for its customers? Because it pays big dividends! The Wegmans know that satisfied customers keep coming back and that they spend more when they do. However, Wegmans' wants to do more than satisfy customers; the goal is to build an emotional connection with them. One Gallup survey finds that shoppers who were emotionally connected to a supermarket spent 46 percent more than shoppers who were satisfied but lacked an emotional bond with the store.

Wegmans' retail strategy involves offering customers superior service and the convenience of one-stop shopping. Each store—the new ones are 130,000 square feet, three times the size of the typical supermarket—provides shoppers with a huge selection of top-quality products ranging from national brands such as Cocoa Puffs to upscale organic produce, all displayed with the flair and style of an upscale retail boutique. Each store also boasts a bookstore, child play centers, a dry cleaner, a photo processing lab, a video rental center, a wine shop, a pharmacy, a florist, international newspapers, and an $850 espresso maker. "Going there is not just shopping," says one industry consultant. "It's an event." The result is that Wegmans' sales per square foot of store space is 50 percent higher than the industry average of $9.29.

The Wegman family intentionally follows a methodical growth strategy, opening only two new stores a year. To make sure each new store is a success, the company puts some of the best and brightest workers from its existing stores to work in its new ones. After earning an undergraduate degree in mechanical engineering and an MBA, Heather Pawlowski decided to enter Wegmans management training program, in which she learned all of the aspects of store operations first-hand. When asked about the company's consistent track record of success, Pawlowski, now one of the company's vice presidents, says, "We're taking customers to a place they have not been before."

1. Explain the core competencies that Wegmans has built. What is the source of its core competencies?
2. Identify Wegmans' strengths, weaknesses, opportunities, and threats. (You may want to use the Web or your library to read more about this interesting company.)
3. How has Wegmans' strategy created a competitive edge for the company in its markets? How does the company sustain its competitive edge? What suggestions can you offer for ensuring that Wegmans maintains its competitive edge?

Sources: Matthew Boyle, "The Wegmans Way," *Fortune,* January 24, 2005, pp. 62–68; "About Us," Wegmans, http://www.wegmans.com/about.

The Strategic Management Process

Strategic management is a continuous process that consists of nine steps:

Step 1   Develop a clear vision and translate it into a meaningful mission statement.

Step 2   Assess the company's strengths and weaknesses.

Step 3   Scan the environment for significant opportunities and threats facing the business.

Step 4   Identify the key factors for success in the business.

Step 5   Analyze the competition.

Step 6   Create company goals and objectives.

Step 7   Formulate strategic options and select the appropriate strategies.

Step 8   Translate strategic plans into action plans.

Step 9   Establish accurate controls.

Step 1. Develop a Clear Vision and Translate It into a Meaningful Mission Statement

Vision   Throughout history, the greatest political and business leaders have been visionaries. Whether the vision is as grand as Martin Luther King Jr.'s "I have a dream" speech or as simple as Ray Kroc's devotion to quality, service, cleanliness, and value at McDonald's, the purpose is the same: to focus everyone's attention on the same target and to inspire them to reach it. The vision is future-oriented and touches everyone associated with the company—employees, investors, lenders, customers, and the community. It is an expression of what an entrepreneur stands for and believes in. Highly successful entrepreneurs are able to communicate their vision and their enthusiasm about that vision to those around them.

A vision is the result of an entrepreneur's dream of something that does not exist yet and the ability to paint a compelling picture of that dream for everyone to see. It answers the question "Where are we going?" A clearly defined vision helps a company in three ways:

1. *Vision provides direction.* Entrepreneurs who spell out the vision for their company focus everyone's attention on the future and determine the path the business will take to get there.
2. *Vision determines decisions.* The vision influences the decisions, no matter how big or how small, that owners, managers, and employees make every day in a business. This influence can be positive or negative, depending on how well defined the vision is.
3. *Vision motivates people.* A clear vision excites and ignites people to action. People want to work for a company that sets its sights high.

Vision is based on an entrepreneur's values. Explaining how an entrepreneur's values are the nucleus around which a company grows, author and consultant Ken Blanchard says, "Winning companies first emphasize values—the beliefs that you, as the business owner, have about your employees, customers, quality, ethics, integrity, social responsibility, growth, stability, innovation, and flexibility. Managing by values—not by profits—is a powerful process."[10] Successful entrepreneurs build their businesses around a set of three to six core values, which might range from respect for the individual and innovation to creating satisfied customers and making the world a better place.

Hewlett Packard

In 1957, 18 years after they had launched the company bearing their names, Bill Hewlett and Dave Packard were pleased with their company's rapid growth but were concerned that the business might lose its "small company atmosphere." The cofounders took 20 of their best employees to an upscale resort in California's wine country (on one of the first recorded corporate retreats) to define the type of culture Hewlett Packard would foster. By the end of the retreat, the team had drafted a set of values that ultimately became the basis of "the HP Way," the highly admired culture the company retained long after the death of its founders.[11]

Indeed, truly visionary entrepreneurs see their companies' primary purpose as more than just "making money." One writer explains, "Almost all workers are making decisions, not just filling out weekly sales reports or tightening screws. They will do what they think best. If you want them to do as the company thinks best too, then you must [see to it that] that have an inner gyroscope aligned with the corporate compass."[12] That gyroscope's alignment depends on the entrepreneur's values and how well he or she transmits them throughout the company.

The best way to put values into action is to create a written mission statement that communicates those values to everyone the company touches.

Mission Statement The **mission statement** addresses another basic question of any business venture: "What business are we in?" Establishing the purpose of the business in writing must come first in order to give the company a sense of direction. "If you don't reduce [your company's purpose] to paper, it just doesn't stick," says the owner of an architecture firm. "Reducing it to paper really forces you to think about what you are doing."[13] As an enduring declaration of a company's purpose, a mission statement is the mechanism for making it clear to everyone the company touches "why we are here" and "where we are going."

> **mission statement**
> an enduring declaration of a company's purpose that addresses the first question of any business venture: What business am I in?

Chick-fil-A

Truett Cathy, founder of the highly successful restaurant chain Chick-fil-A, recalls a time when his business was struggling because of intensifying competition from big hamburger chains. The company, with 200 outlets at the time, was struggling to keep operating costs under control as inflation threatened to push them ever higher. Cathy scheduled an executive retreat at a lake outside of Atlanta, where managers could relax and talk about their concerns and ideas for the company. His oldest son, Dan, director of operations, asked, "Why are we in business? Why are we here?" Cathy was about to tell his son that this retreat was no time to dwell on philosophical issues because there were bigger problems to solve. "Then," recalls Cathy, "I realized he was serious. His question both challenged and inspired us." In the ensuing brainstorming session, the group defined values that became Chick-fil-A's mission statement: "To glorify God by being faithful stewards of all that is entrusted to us. To have a positive influence on all who come in contact with Chick-fil-A." With their purpose clearly defined, the management team went on to lead the company in a growth spurt in which sales climbed 30 percent a year. Today, the company has more than 1,000 restaurants across the country (none of which are open on Sundays).[14]

Without a concise, meaningful mission statement, a small business risks wandering aimlessly in the marketplace, with no idea of where to go or how to get there. The mission statement sets the tone for the entire company and focuses its attention on the right direction.

Elements of a Mission Statement A sound mission statement need not be lengthy to be effective. Three key issues entrepreneurs and their employees should address as they develop a mission statement for their businesses include the following:

- The *purpose* of the company: What are we in business to accomplish?
- The *business* we are in: How are we going to accomplish that purpose?
- The *values* of the company: What principles and beliefs form the foundation of the way we do business?

A company's mission statement may be the most essential and basic communications that it puts forward. If the people on the plant, shop, retail, or warehouse floor don't know what a company's mission is, then, for all practical purposes, it does not have one! The mission statement expresses a company's character, identity, and scope of operations, but writing it is only half the battle, at best. The most difficult part is *living* that mission every day. *That's* how employees decide what really matters. To be effective, a mission statement must become a natural part of the organization, embodied in the minds, habits, attitudes, and decisions of everyone in the company every day. According to the Workplace 2000

Source: Copyright 2004 by Randy Glasbergen. www.glasbergen.com

"It's not a great mission statement, but we'll revise it if things get better."

Employee Insight Survey, 89 percent of employees say their companies have mission statements. Unfortunately, only 23 percent of workers believe their company's mission statement has become a way of doing business![15] One business writer claims, "If what you say about your firm's values and mission isn't true, you're in worse trouble than if you'd never articulated it in the first place."[16] Five years after founding Field Trip Factory Inc., a business that organizes life skill educational field trips for students, Susan Singer saw the need to update the company's mission statement. At a company retreat, she and her employees decided that their existing mission statement no longer reflected what the company actually stood for and did. A brainstorming session yielded a new mission statement that Singer says is helping her company improve its bottom line. "It became so clear what we do vs. what we want to be," she says.[17]

Starbucks

A well-used mission statement serves as a strategic compass for a small company. In its mission statement, Starbucks commits not only to building a successful coffee business, but also to strengthening the communities in which the company operates and to protecting the environment. Consider the message that Starbucks' two-part mission statement sends to company stakeholders:

Starbucks Mission: Establish Starbucks as the premier purveyor of the finest coffee in the world while maintaining our uncompromising principles while we grow. The following six guiding principles will help us measure the appropriateness of our decisions:

- Provide a great work environment and treat each other with respect and dignity.
- Embrace diversity as an essential component of the way we do business.
- Apply the highest standards of excellence to the purchasing, roasting, and fresh delivery of our coffee.
- Develop enthusiastically satisfied customers all of the time.
- Contribute positively to our communities and our environment.
- Recognize that profitability is essential to our future success.

Environmental Mission Statement: Starbucks is committed to a role of environmental leadership in all facets of our business.

We fulfill this mission by a commitment to:

- Understanding of environmental issues and sharing information with our partners.
- Developing innovative and flexible solutions to bring about change.
- Striving to buy, sell and use environmentally friendly products.
- Recognizing that fiscal responsibility is essential to our environmental future.
- Instilling environmental responsibility as a corporate value.[18]

A company may have a powerful competitive advantage, but it is wasted unless (1) the owner communicates that advantage to workers, who, in turn, work hard to communicate it to customers and potential customers and (2) customers recommend the company to their friends because they understand the benefits they are getting from it that they cannot get elsewhere. *That's* the real power of a mission statement. Table 3.1 offers some useful tips on writing a mission statement.

Step 2. Assess the Company's Strengths and Weaknesses

Having defined the vision that he or she has for the company and translated that vision into a meaningful mission statement, an entrepreneur can turn his or her attention to assessing company strengths and weaknesses. Building a successful competitive strategy requires a business to magnify its strengths and overcome or compensate for its weaknesses. **Strengths** are positive internal factors that a company can draw on to accomplish its mission, goals, and objectives. They might include special skills or knowledge, a positive public image, an experienced sales force, an established base of loyal customers, and many other factors. **Weaknesses** are negative internal factors that inhibit a company's ability to accomplish its mission, goals, and objectives. A lack of capital, a shortage of skilled workers, the inability to master technology, and an inferior location are examples of weaknesses.

Identifying strengths and weaknesses helps owners to understand their businesses as they exist (or, for start-ups, will exist). An organization's strengths should originate in the core competencies that are essential to gaining an edge in each of the market segments in which the firm competes. The key to building a successful strategy is using the company's underlying strengths as its foundation and matching those strengths against competitors' weaknesses.

One effective technique for taking this strategic inventory is to prepare a balance sheet of the company's strengths and weaknesses (see Table 3.2). The positive side should reflect important skills, knowledge, or resources that contribute to the firm's success. The negative side should record honestly any limitations that detract from the company's ability to compete. This balance sheet should analyze all key performance areas of the business—human resources, finance, production, marketing, product development, organization, and others. This analysis should give owners a more realistic perspective of their businesses, pointing out foundations on which they can build future strengths and obstacles that they must remove for the business to progress. This exercise can help entrepreneurs move from their current position to future actions.

Step 3. Scan the Environment for Significant Opportunities and Threats Facing the Business

Opportunities Once entrepreneurs have taken an internal inventory of company strengths and weaknesses, they must turn to the external environment to identify any opportunities and threats that might have a significant impact on the business. **Opportunities** are positive external options that a firm can exploit to accomplish its mission, goals, and objectives. The number of potential opportunities is limitless, so entrepreneurs need to analyze only those factors that are most significant to the business

strengths
positive internal factors that a company can use to accomplish its mission, goals, and objectives.

weaknesses
negative internal factors that inhibit the accomplishment of a company's mission, goals, and objectives.

opportunities
positive external options that a firm can exploit to accomplish its mission, goals, and objectives.

TABLE 3.1 Tips for Writing a Powerful Mission Statement

A mission statement is a useful tool for getting everyone fired up and heading in the same direction, but writing one is not as easy as it may first appear. Here are some tips for writing a powerful mission statement:

- *Keep it short.* The best mission statements are just a few sentences long. If they are short, people will tend to remember them better.

- *Keep it simple.* Avoid using fancy jargon just to impress outsiders such as customers or suppliers. The first and most important use of a mission statement is inside a company.

- *Take a broad view, but not too broad.* If it is too specific, a mission statement can limit a company's potential. Similarly, a mission statement is too broad if it applies to any company in the industry. When asked what business his company was in, Rob Carter, a top manager at FedEx, did not mention shipping packages quickly; instead, his response was, "We're in the business of engineering time."

- *Get everyone involved.* If the boss writes the company mission statement, who is going to criticize it? Although the entrepreneur has to be the driving force behind the mission statement, everyone in the company needs the opportunity to have a voice in creating it. Expect to write several drafts before you arrive at a finished product.

- *Keep it current.* Mission statements can get stale over time. As business and competitive conditions change, so should your mission statement. Make a habit of evaluating your mission periodically so that it stays fresh.

- *Make sure that your mission statement reflects the values and beliefs you hold dear.* They are the foundation on which your company is built.

- *Make sure your mission includes values that are worthy of your employees' best efforts.* One entrepreneur says that a mission statement should "send a message to employees, suppliers, and customers as to what the purpose of the company is aside from just making profits."

- *Make sure your statement reflects a concern for the future.* Business owners can get so focused on the present that they forget about the future. A mission statement should be the first link to the company's future.

- *Keep the tone of the statement positive and upbeat.* No one wants to work for a business with a pessimistic outlook of the world.

- *Consider using your mission statement to lay an ethical foundation for your company.* This is the ideal time to let employees know what you company stands for—and what it won't stand for.

- *Look at other companies' mission statements to generate ideas for your own.* Two books, *Say It and Live It: The 50 Corporate Mission Statements That Hit the Mark,* by Patricia Jones and Larry Kahaner (New York: Currency/Doubleday, 1995), and *Mission Statements: A Guide to the Corporate and Nonprofit Sectors,* by John W. Graham and Wendy C. Havlick (New York: Garland, 1994), are useful resources.

- *Make sure that your mission statement is appropriate for your company's culture.* Although you should look at other companies' missions, do not make the mistake of trying to copy them. Your company's mission is unique to you and your company.

- *Use it.* Don't go to all of the trouble of writing a mission statement just to let it collect dust. Post it on bulletin boards, print it on buttons and business cards, stuff it into employees' pay envelopes. Talk about your mission often, and use it to develop your company's strategic plan. That's what it's for!

Sources: Adapted from Ken Blanchard, "The New Bottom Line," *Entrepreneur,* February 1998, pp. 127–131; Alan Farnham, Brushing Up Your Vision Thing," *Fortune,* May 1, 1995, p. 129; Sharon Nelton, "Put Your Purpose in Writing," *Nation's Business,* February 1994, pp. 61–64; Jacquelyn Lynn, "Single-Minded," *Entrepreneur,* January 1996, p. 97.

(probably two or three at most). The key is to focus on the most promising opportunities that fit most closely with the company's strengths and core competencies.

When identifying opportunities, an entrepreneur must pay close attention to new potential markets. Are competitors overlooking a niche in the market? Is there a better way to reach customers? Can we develop new products that offer customers better value? What opportunities are trends in the industry creating?

TABLE 3.2 **Identifying Company Strengths and Weaknesses**

Strengths (Positive Internal Factors)	Weaknesses (Negative Internal Factors)

Aviation Partners

Rising fuel prices have created problems for many businesses, but few have felt the impact as directly as those in the airline industry. Yet rising energy prices have produced a significant opportunity for Aviation Partners, a small company founded by a group of retired aeronautic engineers. Noting that birds' wings turn up at the tips to provide more lift and less drag (hence requiring birds to use less energy), the founders of Aviation Partners developed "winglets," small fins attached to the ends of wings that extend upward, for use on commercial jets. Tests indicated that jets using the winglets were far more fuel-efficient than those without them. In the late 1990s, however, the small company found it difficult to market the winglets because jet fuel prices were just 50 cents a gallon. As jet fuel prices climbed significantly over the next several years, Aviation Partners, now partnering with Boeing Company, found airlines much more interested in their product. Although the cost to install the winglets can run as high as $700,000 per plane, the savings in fuel costs add up to the millions over the life of a jet. Aviation Partners is capitalizing on this opportunity and counts among its customers virtually every airline in operation today.[19]

As Aviation Partners' experience illustrates, opportunities arise as a result of factors that are beyond entrepreneurs' control. Constantly scanning for those opportunities that best match their companies' strengths and core competencies and then pouncing on them ahead of competitors is the key to success.

M Cubed

When demand for the composite materials manufactured by Steve Warshaw's company M Cubed declined as the semiconductor market slumped, he began searching for opportunities to apply the company's expertise in other industries. As the United States stepped up its efforts in the war of terrorism, Warshaw spotted an opportunity to produce the ceramic plates used in bulletproof vests. Although the finished product was quite different from semiconductors, M Cubed found it quite easy to adapt its techniques and technology to produce strong yet lightweight panels capable of stopping even armor-piercing bullets. Shifting to this new market has accelerated M Cube's sales, and Warshaw sees tremendous potential for future growth as both law enforcement and military officials increase their purchases of bulletproof vests.[20]

Threats Negative external forces that inhibit a company's ability to achieve its mission, goals, and objectives are referred to as **threats.** Threats to the business can take a variety of forms, such as competitors entering the local market, a government mandate regulating a business activity, an economic recession, rising interest rates, technological advances making a company's product obsolete, and many others. For instance, video on demand and digital downloading pose a serious threat to both retailers of DVDs and to companies that rent them from storefronts (Blockbuster) or online (Netflix).

Many small retailers face a threat from "big box" retailers such as Wal-Mart, Home Depot, Circuit City, and others offering lower prices because of their high-volume purchasing power, huge advertising budgets, and mega-stores that attract customers for miles around.

threats
negative external forces that inhibit a company's ability to achieve it mission, goals, and objectives.

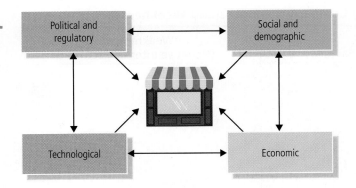

Kenneth Stone, a professor at Iowa State University and a leading researcher on Wal-Mart's impact on small companies, says that after Wal-Mart entered Iowa in 1983, 23 percent of drugstores and 45 percent of hardware stores disappeared.[21] However, small businesses with the proper strategies in place do *not* have to fold in the face of intense competition.

*Dobson's Gifts and
General Hardware*

After Wal-Mart, Home Depot, Tractor Supply Company, and Lowe's opened next to their second-generation small hardware store in Greenville, South Carolina, Terry and Debbie Dobson changed their competitive strategy and refocused their business, Dobson's Gifts and General Hardware, more on gifts and less on the standard hardware items their larger rivals sold. The Dobsons now rely on a focus strategy that emphasizes unique gifts and home décor items with a distinctively local flavor and specialty hardware items such as loose nuts and bolts, pocket knives, and Radio Flyer wagons that their big box competitors overlook. The Dobsons continue to set their business apart by offering a high level of personal service, including knowledgeable, long-time employees and a home delivery service that customers love. "I'm within a rock's throw of my two major competitors," says Terry, "and actually we're glad they're here now. They bring in traffic, and we draw off that traffic."[22]

Although they cannot control the threats themselves, entrepreneurs such as the Dobsons must prepare a plan for shielding their businesses from these threats.

Figure 3.2 illustrates that opportunities and threats are products of the interactions of forces, trends, and events outside the direct control of the business. These external forces have direct impact on the behavior of the markets in which the business operates, the behavior of competitors, and the behavior of customers. Table 3.3 provides a form that allows business owners to take a strategic inventory of the opportunities and threats facing their companies.

The interactions of strengths and weaknesses and opportunities and threats can be the most revealing aspects of using a SWOT analysis as part of a strategic plan. This analysis also requires entrepreneurs to take an objective look at their businesses and the environment in which they operate as they address many issues fundamental to their companies' success in the future.

TABLE 3.3 Identifying Opportunities and Threats

Opportunities (Positive External Factors)	Threats (Negative External Factors)

Ethics and Entrepreneurship

Tunes for the Taking

Before music downloading became so popular, music lovers often bought a single CD for just one song. Given the attitude, "Who wants to pay nearly $20 for one song?" it is little wonder that customers embraced "free" music download services such as Napster (the original), KaZaA, and Grokster. Still, those downloading music without paying for it had to feel a twinge of guilt about the ethics of their actions. Then there were all of those lawsuits that the Recording Industry Association of America (RIAA) was filing against heavy downloaders, many of them college students. Who wants to be sued for downloading music, especially when damages can range from $750 to $150,000 per copyright violation? Representing the five major music companies, the RIAA filed 261 lawsuits against individuals it claimed had illegally used file-sharing software to distribute vast numbers of copyrighted songs. The suits claim that illegal file sharing is responsible for falling sales of recorded music and for robbing artists of their royalties. In addition, modern technology makes it quite easy for computer users to "rip and burn" tracks from CDs to create their own favorites or to store on their MP3 players. Indeed, shipments of recorded music have fallen 26 percent since 1999, and sales of blank CDs now exceed those of prerecorded CDs. "Our industry is being ravaged by piracy," says a top executive at one music company.

To combat declining sales, the recording industry is attempting to create new business models that incorporate the legitimate sale of recorded music online. All of the major music companies are cooperating with Apple Computer Inc.'s industry-leading iTunes Music Store, which allows users to download songs *legally* for just 99 cents each. (Music companies receive roughly 65 cents for every downloaded song.) Users can listen to a 30-second preview of any song and, if they like it, can purchase a high-quality legal download with just one mouse-click. There is no subscription fee, and the iTunes library contains more than 1.5 million songs from the major music companies and more than 1,000 independent record companies as well as 10,000 audiobooks. Shoppers can browse titles by artist, song title, or genre. Because of the many benefits it offers, industry analysts predict that by 2010, digitally downloaded music will comprise between one-fourth to one-third of the recording industry's sales. "It pained us to see the music companies and the technology companies threatening to take each other to court," says Apple founder Steve Jobs. "We thought that rather than sit around and throw stones, we'd actually do something about this."

Throughout its history, the music industry has benefited from introducing new musical formats, from 78 rpm singles to the 33 rpm vinyl LP album to the eight-track tape to the Compact Disc. The transformation to digitally downloaded music, however, may be the most significant change of all. Not only would it be more convenient for customers, but the switch also would cut costs for all of the music companies by virtually eliminating manufacturing and distribution costs.

Music artists themselves see downloading as a double-edged sword. One survey reports that only three percent of music artists say that the Internet has hurt their ability to protect their creative work. Forty-seven percent agreed that peer-to-peer networks prevented them from earning royalties from their songs, but 43 percent said that those same networks helped artists promote and distribute their material. Two-thirds of the survey's respondents said that file-sharing posed little threat to them.

It's ironic that the music industry is struggling in an era when people are listening to music more than ever before. They simply aren't paying for the privilege of listening the way they used to. Downloading, file sharing, and ripping and burning also pose a serious threat to music retailers, most of which are stuck selling music in a format (CDs) customers seem to dislike. Many music retail chains have either filed for Chapter 11 bankruptcy protection (Wherehouse and Tower Records) or have simply closed (National Record Mart).

Entrepreneur Bob French thinks he may have discovered one way to preserve retail music outlets with his

Mix and Burn machine, a device that allows users to scroll through a database of songs, listen to the ones they choose, create a personal playlist, and then burn the songs to a CD. French's company, Mix and Burn, currently provides a library of 320,000 songs but offers additions weekly. French has established relationships with all five of the major music companies but has had difficulty signing independent record labels onto the company's service. "We really focused on getting those major labels done to make this a viable business," explains French. "Next year at this time, there will be more content from independent producers."

Jack Dennis, owner of the Earshot Music store in downtown Greenville, South Carolina, was one of the early adopters of the Mix and Burn technology. Still a traditional music store, Earshot has transformed itself with the addition of 12 Mix and Burn stations grouped together in an area of the store called "The Blender" that in just a short time has become one of the most popular spots in the store. There customers can download five songs for $9.99 and 99 cents for each subsequent song. "We wanted to be able to offer digital technology in a retail environment," says Dennis. You buy songs just like you would off the Internet, except you are here at our store."

1. One analyst says, "Many music listeners have shown little regard for the idea that downloading a song from a file-sharing service such as KaZaA is tantamount to shoplifting from Tower Records." Comment.
2. What strategic recommendations can you make to the music industry concerning the future of digital downloading?
3. What strategic recommendations can you make to music retailers concerning the future of digital downloading?

Sources: "Survey: Net File-Sharing Doesn't Hurt Most Musicians," CNN.com, December 6, 2004; Bruce Orwall, Martin Peers, and Ethan Smith, "Music Industry Presses 'Play' on Plan to Save Its Business," *Wall Street Journal*, September 9, 20003, pp. A1–A14; "Apple Kicks Off iTunes Music Store Countdown to Half a Billion Songs," http://www.Apple.com/pr/library/2005/jul/05itms_live.html; Devin Leonard, "Songs in the Key of Steve," *Fortune*, May 12, 2003, pp. 53–62; Alex Veiga, "Students Still Go for Hot Music, Despite Available Legal Options," *Greenville News*, August 20, 2005, p. 12A; Paul Keegan, "Is the Music Store Over?" *Business 2.0*, March 2004, pp. 115–119; Lilla Callum-Penso, "Technology Offers New Ways to Mix It Up," *Greenville News*, August 8, 2005, pp. 1D, 3D.

Step 4. Identify the Key Factors for Success in the Business

Key Success Factors Every business is characterized by controllable variables that determine the relative success of market participants. Identifying and manipulating these variables is how a small business gains a competitive advantage. By focusing efforts to maximize their companies' performance on these key success factors, entrepreneurs can achieve dramatic market advantages over their competitors. Companies that understand these key success factors tend to be leaders of the pack, whereas those that fail to recognize them become also-rans.

key success factors
the factors that determine a company's ability to compete successfully in an industry.

Key success factors (KSFs) come in a variety of different patterns depending on the industry. Simply stated, they are the factors that determine a company's ability to compete successfully in an industry. Every company in an industry must understand the key success factors driving the industry; otherwise, they are likely to become industry "also-rans" like the horses trailing the pack in the Kentucky Derby. Many of these sources of competitive advantages are based on cost factors such as manufacturing cost per unit, distribution cost per unit, or development cost per unit. Some are less tangible and less obvious but are just as important, such as superior product quality, solid relationships with dependable suppliers, superior customer service, a highly trained and knowledgeable sales force, prime store locations, readily available customer credit, and many others. For example, one restaurant owner identified the following key success factors:

- Tight cost control (labor costs, 15 to 18 percent of sales and food costs, 35 to 40 percent of sales)
- Trained, dependable, honest in-store managers
- Close monitoring of waste
- Careful site selection (the right location)

TABLE 3.4 Identifying Key Success Factors

Key Success Factor	How Your Company Rates
1	Low 1 2 3 4 5 6 7 8 9 10 High
2	Low 1 2 3 4 5 6 7 8 9 10 High
3	Low 1 2 3 4 5 6 7 8 9 10 High
4	Low 1 2 3 4 5 6 7 8 9 10 High
5	Low 1 2 3 4 5 6 7 8 9 10 High

Conclusions:

List the specific skills, characteristics, and core competencies that your business must possess if it is to be successful in its market segment.

- High food quality
- Consistency
- Cleanliness
- Friendly and attentive service from a well-trained wait staff

These controllable variables determine the ability of any restaurant in his market segment to compete. Restaurants lacking these KSFs are not likely to survive, but those that build their strategies with these factors in mind will prosper. However, before entrepreneurs can build a strategy around the industry's KSFs, they must identify them. Table 3.4 presents a form to help owners identify the most important success factors in the industry and their implications for their companies.

Identifying the KSFs in an industry allows entrepreneurs to determine where they should focus their companies' resources strategically. It is unlikely that a company, even a large one, can excel on every KSF it identifies. Therefore, as they begin to develop their strategies, most entrepreneurs focus on surpassing their rivals on one or two KSFs to build a sustainable competitive edge. As a result, KSFs become the cornerstones of a company's strategy.

John H. Daniel Company, a custom tailor of high-end men's suits in Knoxville, Tennessee, understands that attracting and retaining skilled master tailors is crucial to its success. The company, founded in 1928, produces 75,000 to 80,000 made-to-measure suits a year that retail at prices ranging from $800 to $3,000, and sells them under a variety of labels. Unfortunately, the number of master tailors in the United States is negligible, and the family-owned business dedicates a significant portion of its budget to searching them out in foreign countries such as Turkey, Italy, and Vietnam. Owners Richard and Benton Bryant send scouts on recruiting trips to these countries and then pay to relocate the master tailors they hire along with their families to Tennessee. The company provides low-interest loans to help families get settled, and a company attorney handles all of the paperwork necessary to get visas for the tailors and their families.[23]

John H. Daniel Company

Step 5. Analyze the Competition

Ask most small business owners to identify the greatest challenge their companies face and the most common response is *competition*. One study of small business owners by the National Federation of Independent Businesses (NFIB) reports that small business owners believe they operate in a highly competitive environment and that the level of competition is increasing.[24] The World Wide Web and e-commerce have increased the ferocity and the scope of the competition entrepreneurs face as well and have forced

FIGURE 3.3

How Small Businesses Compete

Source: William J. Dennis, Jr.,
National Small Business Poll:
Competition (Washington, DC:
National Federation of Independent
Businesses, 2003), Vol. 3,
Issue 8, p. 1.

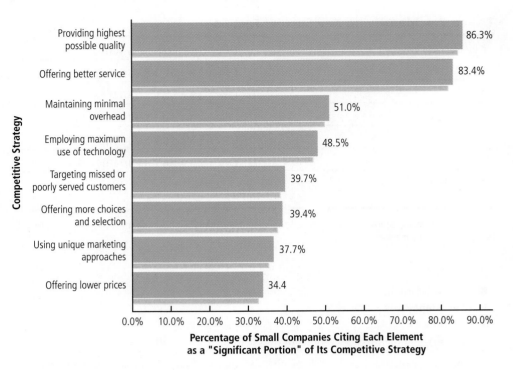

many business owners to reshape completely the ways in which they do business. Figure 3.3 shows the competitive strategies that small business owners rely on most heavily to compete with their rivals.

Joseph-Beth Booksellers

Neil Van Uum, owner of Joseph-Beth Booksellers, a small chain of six bookstores, faces intense competition from larger, more powerful rivals in an industry that has seen thousands of small booksellers close within the last decade. Yet, Joseph-Beth Booksellers manages not only to survive, but also to thrive in an industry where giants such as Barnes and Noble and Borders Books saturate local markets with retail outlets and Amazon blankets the market from its perch high atop the online food chain. "Either you have to be very niche[-oriented], or you need a physical presence that says you're significant," says Michael Powell, owner of Powell's Books, a legendary 70,000-square-foot bookstore in downtown Portland, Oregon. Like Powell, Van Uum has chosen to create a significant physical presence. His stores average 30,000 square feet, about 5,000 square feet larger than a typical Barnes and Noble store. Like most successful independent bookstores, Joseph-Beth emphasizes superior customer service, sponsors unique, in-store events (wine tastings, book signings, appearances by the Berenstain Bears for kids), and specializes in books that reflect local tastes. For instance, the Lexington, Kentucky, store located in the Mall at Lexington Green stocks more than 1,000 books by local authors, something national chain stores don't do. Going one better than Barnes and Noble's coffee bar and pastry shop, each Joseph-Beth store contains a full-service restaurant, each offering entrees inspired by cookbooks the company sells. Every store also includes a stationery department, a board game section, and a "health and well-being section" selling lotions, soaps, scented candles, and quilted tote bags. A store décor that includes cherry bookcases, comfortable couches, and fireplaces encourages shoppers to linger, and, of course, buy more. Dan Burstin, author of the popular *Secrets of the Code,* recently appeared in two Joseph-Beth stores to discuss his work. "What they've done," he says, "is turn these stores into cultural centers."[25]

Keeping tabs on rivals' movements through competitive intelligence programs is a vital strategic activity. "Business is like any battlefield. If you want to win the war, you have to know who you're up against," says one small business consultant.[26] Unfortunately, most businesses are not very good at competitive intelligence; 97 percent of U.S. businesses do not systematically track the progress of their key competitors.[27] The primary goals of a competitive intelligence program include the following:

- Avoiding surprises from existing competitors' new strategies and tactics.
- Identifying potential new competitors.
- Improving reaction time to competitors' actions.
- Anticipating rivals' next strategic moves.

Competitor Analysis Sizing up the competition gives a business owner a more realistic view of the market and his or her company's position in it. Yet not every competitor warrants the same level of attention in the strategic plan. *Direct competitors* offer the same products and services, and customers often compare prices, features, and deals from these competitors as they shop. *Significant competitors* offer some of the same products and services. Although their product or service lines may be somewhat different, there is competition with them in several key areas. *Indirect competitors* offer the same or similar products or services only in a small number of areas, but their target customers seldom overlap yours. Entrepreneurs should monitor closely the actions of their direct competitors, maintain a solid grasp of where their significant competitors are heading, and spend only minimal resources tracking their indirect competitors.

A competitive intelligence exercise enables entrepreneurs to update their knowledge of competitors by answering the following questions:

- Who are your primary competitors? Where are they located? (The *Yellow Pages* is a great place to start.)
- What distinctive competencies have they developed?
- How do their cost structures compare to yours? Their financial resources?
- How do they market their products and services?
- What do customers say about them? How do customers describe their products or services; their way of doing business; the additional services they might supply?
- What are their key strategies?
- What are their strengths? How can your company surpass them?
- What are their major weaknesses? How can your company capitalize on them?
- Are new competitors entering the business?

According to the Society of Competitive Intelligence, 95 percent of the competitive intelligence information is available from public sources that anyone can access—if they know how.[28] Gathering information on competitors does not require entrepreneurs to engage in activities that are unethical, illegal, or unsavory (such as dumpster diving). One expert says that competitive intelligence (CI) involves "taking information from the public domain, adding it to what you know about your company and your industry, and looking for patterns."[29] Entrepreneurs using the following low-cost competitive intelligence methods can collect a great deal of information about their rivals:

- Read industry trade publications for announcements and news stories about competitors.
- Ask questions of customers and suppliers on what they hear competitors may be doing. In many cases, this information is easy to gather because some people love to gossip.
- Regularly debrief employees, especially sales representatives and purchasing agents. Experts estimate that 70 to 90 percent of the competitive information a company needs already resides with employees who collect it in their routine dealings with suppliers, customers, and other industry contacts.[30]
- Attend trade shows and collect competitors' sales literature.
- Watch for employment ads and job postings from competitors; knowing what types of workers they are hiring can tell you a great deal about their future plans.
- Conduct patent searches (see Chapter 2) for patents that competitors have filed. This gives important clues about new products they are developing.
- Environmental Protection Agency reports can provide important information about the factories of manufacturing companies, including the amounts and the kinds of

emissions released. A private group, Environmental Protection, also reports emissions for specific plants.[31]

- Learn about the kinds and amounts of equipment and raw materials competitors are importing by studying the *Journal of Commerce* Port Import Export Reporting Service (PIERS) database. These clues can alert an entrepreneur to new products a competitor is about to launch.

- If appropriate, buy competitors' products and assess their quality and features. Benchmark their products against yours. The owner of a mail-order gourmet brownie business periodically places orders from her primary rivals and compares their packaging, pricing, service, and quality to her own.[32]

- Obtain credit reports on each of your major competitors to evaluate their financial condition. For as little as $122, Dun & Bradstreet and other research firms provide detailed credit reports of competitors that can be helpful in a strategic analysis.

- Publicly held companies must file periodic reports with the Securities and Exchange Commission (SEC), including quarterly 10-Q and annual 10-K reports. Information on publicly held companies is available at the Securities and Exchange Commission Web site (http://www.sec.gov).

- Investigate Uniform Commercial Code reports. Banks file these with the state whenever they make loans to businesses. These reports often include the amount of the loan and what it is for.

- Check out the resources of your local library, including articles, computerized databases, and online searches. Press releases, which often announce important company news, can be an important source of competitive intelligence. Many companies supply press releases through the PR Newswire. For local competitors, review back issues of the area newspaper for articles on and advertisements by competitors.

- Use the vast resources of the World Wide Web to learn more about your competitors. Visit their Web sites periodically to see what news is contained there. The Web enables small companies to uncover valuable competitive information at little or no cost. (Refer to our Web site at http://www.prenhall.com/scarborough for an extensive listing of more than 1,200 useful small business Web sites.)

- Visit competing businesses periodically to observe their operations. Tom Stemberg, CEO of Staples, a chain of office supply superstores, says, "I've never visited a store where I didn't learn something."[33]

competitive profile matrix
a tool that allows a business owner to evaluate their companies against major competitors using the key success factors for that market.

Entrepreneurs can use the results of their competitive intelligence efforts to construct a competitive profile matrix for its most important competitors. A **competitive profile matrix** allows owners to evaluate their firms against the major competitor using the key success factors for that market segment. The first step is to list the key success factors identified in Step 4 of the strategic planning process (refer to Table 3.4) and to attach weights to them reflecting their relative importance. (For simplicity, the weights in this matrix sum add up to 1.00.) In this example, notice that product quality is weighted twice as heavily (twice as important) as is price competitiveness.

The next step is to identify the company's major competitors and to rate each one (and your company) on each of the key success factors:

If factor is a:	Rating is:
Major weakness	1
Minor weakness	2
Minor strength	3
Major strength	4

Once the rating is completed, the owner simply multiplies the weight by the rating for each factor to get a weighted score, and then adds up each competitor's weighted scores to get a total weighted score. Table 3.5 shows a sample competitive profile matrix for a small company. The results should show which company is strongest, which is weakest, and

TABLE 3.5 Sample Competitive Profile Matrix

Key Success Factor (from Step 4)	Weight	My Company Score	My Company Weighted Score	Competitor 1 Score	Competitor 1 Weighted Score	Competitor 2 Score	Competitor 2 Weighted Score
Quality	0.25	4	1.00	2	0.50	2	0.50
Customer Retention	0.20	3	0.60	2	0.40	3	0.60
Location	0.16	4	0.60	3	0.45	4	0.60
Perception of Value	0.20	4	0.80	2	0.40	3	0.60
Cost Control	0.20	3	0.60	1	0.20	4	0.80
Total	100%		3.60		1.95		3.10

which of the key success factors each one is best and worst at meeting. By carefully studying and interpreting the results, an entrepreneur can begin to envision the ideal strategy for building a competitive edge in her or his market segment.

Knowledge Management Unfortunately, many small companies fail to gather competitive intelligence because their owners mistakenly assume that it is too costly or simply unnecessary. In reality, the cost of collecting information about competitors and the competitive environment typically is minimal, but it does require discipline. Thanks in large part to the Internet, "all companies, large and small, have virtually the same access to information," says competitive intelligence consultant Leonard Fuld.[34] Identifying and organizing the information a company possesses and then getting it efficiently to those who need it when they need it is the real challenge. In an age in which knowledge is the primary source of a company's competitive edge, the key is learning how to *manage* the knowledge and information a company accumulates. A study by software firm Business Objects found that 90 percent of managers admit they make most of their decisions using instinct because they lack the right information when they need it![35]

Knowledge management is the practice of gathering, organizing, and disseminating the collective wisdom and experience of a company's employees for the purpose of strengthening its competitive position. "Knowledge management allows you to determine the explicit knowledge that is somewhere in your organization and that you can leverage rather than having to reinvent the wheel," says Dorothy Leonard-Barton, author of *Wellsprings of Knowledge*.[36] Unfortunately, a study by Accenture reports that nearly half of businesses have no formal process for capturing workers' knowledge so that it can be passed on to others.[37] As growing numbers of baby boomers retire and take their accumulated knowledge with them, these companies face the threat of a serious "brain drain" that could hurt their ability to compete. Business owners who do practice knowledge management realize that knowledge is power and that managing it can produce huge benefits. Because of their size and simplicity, small businesses have an advantage over large companies when it comes to managing employees' collective knowledge.

The first step in creating a knowledge management program is to take an inventory of the special knowledge a company possesses that gives it a competitive advantage. This involves assessing the knowledge bank that employees at all levels of the organization have compiled over time. The second step is to organize the essential knowledge and disseminate it throughout the company to those who need it. High-tech solutions such as e-mail, computerized databases, document sharing, and special knowledge management software that allows many different employees to work on a project simultaneously are important tools, but low-tech methods such as whiteboards, Post-it notes, and face-to-face meetings can be just as effective in small companies. "To understand and respond to the kaleidoscopic patterns of new opportunities and potential dangers to its mission, an organization must mobilize the distributed intelligence of its members and listen to the collective knowledge of the whole," says one expert.[38]

knowledge management the practice of gathering, organizing, and disseminating the collective wisdom and experience of a company's employees for the purpose of strengthening its competitive position.

eBay

As eBay, provider of the popular online marketplace, expanded its operations globally, managers began to assemble the collective knowledge from employees about what works—and what doesn't—and make it available to everyone in the company. The resulting playbooks—one for every function within the company, from product management to Web development—give managers and employees in every country how-to manuals for establishing the eBay model and expanding their divisions. They teach managers how to create the ideal conditions for electronic trading on eBay to flourish in a particular country. For instance, Gregory Boutte, country manager for France, learned from an eBay playbook that it doesn't make sense to spend money on television ads until the number of customers using the site reaches a critical mass. As new ideas arise throughout the company, managers make a concerted effort to capture them and incorporate them into each playbook.[39]

You Be the Consultant

Protect This Business!

Kevin Plank may not have been a star when he played college football at the University of Maryland, but he has become an entrepreneurial superstar because the success of Under Armour, the company he founded during his senior year in college. As a special teams captain, Plank grew weary of wearing a heavy, sweat-soaked cotton T-shirt under his football pads. He began to research the properties of various fabrics, and he produced sample shirts made with a polyester blend base layer that fit as snugly as Spiderman's suit and were extremely lightweight, durable, and capable of wicking away perspiration so that they stayed dry. He tested early prototypes himself, and, at first, his teammates laughed at him because the fabric resembled lingerie. Before long, however, those teammates were asking for shirts of their own!

After graduating, Plank received a trademark for the name Under Armour and launched a business from the basement of his grandmother's townhouse in Washington, D.C., which served as the company's first office, warehouse, distribution center—and bedroom. He started the company with $20,000 of his own money and $40,000 in credit card debt he ran up on five cards before landing a $250,000 loan guaranteed by the U.S. Small Business Administration. Plank used a network of contacts he had developed during his years of playing football to get Under Armour shirts into the hands of top college and professional football players such as Eddie George and Frank Wychek.

Sales for Plank's company started slowly, but he managed to land accounts with the football teams at the University of Arizona and Georgia Institute of Technology. Under Armour's first big break came in 1999, when its shirts appeared in the film *Any Given Sunday*. Before the film aired, Plank took out a $25,000 ad in *ESPN* magazine, counting on the movie to attract attention for the small company's products. It worked. Today, thousands of athletes in a variety of sports wear Under Armour clothing, generating more than $200 million in annual sales for the company. Under Armour has since developed distinct product lines for six different sports under every playing condition and every season. Athletes from little league to the pros are dedicated to their Under Armour clothing. Although Plank's company pays a few star athletes to wear Under Armour; most of its endorsements are unofficial. Yet the company gets tremendous amounts of publicity when Barry Bonds, Roger Clemens, Allen Iverson, LaVar Arrington, and other pros display Under Armour garments on national television.

The market for performance apparel, which Plank created almost single-handedly, is the fastest-growing segment of the athletic equipment market. Under Armour has extended its product line to include sports bras, batting gloves, loose-fitting shirts, sweat suits, boxers, and many others—for a total of 300 products. Succeeding against the odds, Plank's bold entrepreneurial moves, aggressive advertising and public relations campaign, and superior product quality have enabled Under Armour to capture about 75 percent of the market for compression performance apparel, far surpassing the "big three" industry giants, Nike, Reebok, and Adidas. Although Under Armour may have caught the industry giants napping, they have awakened and are fighting back. All three companies have introduced products similar to Under Armour and are promoting them aggressively. "We're not taking this lying down," declares Ken Barker, director of apparel at Adidas America. "It's a war." Nike, whose Nike Pro brand is second to Under Armour, launched an ad campaign aimed squarely at Under Armour. Its "For Warriors" campaign was one of the largest in the history of the company, whose $13 billion in annual sales dwarfs Under Armour's annual revenues.

Small companies such as Under Armour that surprise the established players in a market with an innovative approach soon find themselves facing what some experts call the "disrupter's dilemma." Although Under Armour took the lead when it jolted the industry with its innovative new products, Plank's small company has become the hunted in a high-stakes game of cat and mouse. The dilemma Plank's company faces is, "What do we do next?" With competition intensifying, Under Armour cannot bask in the glow of its past successes. "Most people are saying [that] we're going to trip up at some point—it's just a matter of when," says Plank. "Our job is to prove them wrong."

One of Under Armour's most recent moves was to aim its products at women, which also poses a challenge. Most of the company's early ads (which proved to be hugely successful) were testosterone-laden spots featuring his former teammate Eric Ogbogu from the National Football League with the tag line "Protect this house," a reference to sports teams winning on their home fields. The challenge the company faces is appealing to women without alienating its core customer base, which consists primarily of young male athletes. Ads featuring soccer star Heather Mitts wearing Under Armour garments made for women are designed to introduce the brand to women athletes, to many of whom the brand is new. Under Armour also has received exposure in some 50 movies, including the hit *Million Dollar Baby*, and on a dozen TV shows, including *The Apprentice*. After the ads and television and movie placements, Under Armour has seen sales to women climb from 13 percent of revenue to 19 percent.

Plank knows that his company is in a battle and that his competitors are much bigger and stronger. Yet he remains confident that his company's future is bright because he has been both a fierce competitor and an entrepreneur since he was a child. Ignored as a scholarship player in college, Plank made the team as a walk-on and then went on to become a starter and a team captain thanks to his persistence and dogged determination. Once, when he was assigned to block his friend, 6-foot, 4-inch, 269-pound Eric Ogbogu, the much smaller Planck undertook the task with such enthusiasm that Ogbogu ended up on his back with a mild concussion. Can he do the same to Nike, Reebok, and Adidas?

1. What strategic challenges does the "disrupter's dilemma" pose for Under Armour?
2. What strategic recommendations can you make for Under Armour as the competition in the performance apparel heats up?
3. Work with a group of your classmates to develop a list of lessons you can learn from Kevin Plank and Under Armour about how small companies can compete successfully with much larger firms that have more resources.

Sources: Chuck Salter, "Protect This House," *Fast Company*, August 2005, pp. 70–75; Karen E. Spaeder, "Beyond Their Years: Kevin Plank," *Entrepreneur*, November 2003, p. 76; Kevin Plank and Mark Hyman, "How I Did It," *Inc.*, December 2003, pp. 102–104; "Company Overview," Under Armour, http://www.underarmour.com/ua2/biz/pages/company_overview.asp.

Step 6. Create Company Goals and Objectives

Before entrepreneurs can build a comprehensive set of strategies, they must first establish business goals and objectives, which give them targets to aim for and provide a basis for evaluating their companies' performance. Without them, it is impossible to know where a business is going or how well it is performing. The following conversation between Alice and the Cheshire Cat, taken from Lewis Carroll's *Alice in Wonderland*, illustrates the importance of creating meaningful goals and objectives as part of the strategic management process:[40]

"Would you tell me please, which way I ought to go from here?" asked Alice.

"That depends a good deal on where you want to get to," said the Cat.

"I don't much care where . . . ," said Alice.

"Then it doesn't matter which way you go," said the Cat.

A small business that "doesn't much care where" it wants to go (i.e., one that has no goals and objectives) will find that "it really doesn't matter which way" it chooses to go (i.e., its strategy is irrelevant).

goals
the broad, long-range attributes a business seeks to accomplish; they tend to be general and sometimes even abstract.

Goals Business **goals** are the broad, long-range attributes that a business seeks to accomplish; they tend to be general and sometimes even abstract. Goals are not intended to be specific enough for a manager to act on, but simply state the general level of accomplishment sought. Do you want to boost your market share? Does your cash balance need strengthening? Would you like to enter a new market or increase sales in a current one? Do you want to develop new products or services? Researchers Jim Collins and Jerry Porras studied a large group of businesses and determined that one of the factors that set apart successful companies from unsuccessful ones was the formulation of very ambitious, clear, and inspiring long-term goals. Collins and Porras call them BHAGs ("Big Hairy Audacious Goals," pronounced "bee-hags") and say that their main benefit is to inspire and focus a company on important actions that are consistent with its overall mission.[41]

Addressing these broad issues will help you focus on the next phase—developing specific, realistic objectives.

objectives
more specific targets of performance, commonly addressing areas such as profitability, productivity, growth, and other key aspects of a business.

Objectives Business **objectives** are more specific targets of performance. Common objectives concern profitability, productivity, growth, efficiency, markets, financial resources, physical facilities, organizational structure, employee welfare, and social responsibility. Because some of these objectives might conflict with one another, it is important to establish priorities. Which objectives are most important? Which are least important? Arranging objectives in a hierarchy according to their priority can help an entrepreneur resolve conflicts when they arise. Well-written objectives have the following characteristics:

They are specific. Objectives should be quantifiable and precise. For example, "to achieve a healthy growth in sales" is not a meaningful objective; however, "to increase retail sales by 12 percent and wholesale sales by 10 percent in the next fiscal year" is precise and spells out exactly what management wants to accomplish.

They are measurable. Managers should be able to plot the organization's progress toward its objectives; this requires a well-defined reference point from which to start and a scale for measuring progress.

They are assignable. Unless an entrepreneur assigns responsibility for an objective to an individual, it is unlikely that the company will ever achieve it. Creating objectives without giving someone responsibility for accomplishing it is futile.

They are realistic, yet challenging. Objectives must be within the reach of the organization or motivation will disappear. In any case, managerial expectations must remain high. In other words, the more challenging an objective is (within realistic limits), the higher the performance will be. Set objectives that will challenge your business and its employees.

They are timely. Objectives must specify not only what is to be accomplished, but also when it is to be accomplished. A time frame for achievement is important.

They are written down. This writing process does not have to be complex; in fact, the manager should make the number of objectives relatively small, from 5 to 15.

The strategic planning process works best when managers and employees are actively involved in setting goals and objectives together. Developing a plan is top management's responsibility, but executing it falls to managers and employees; therefore, encouraging them to participate broadens the plan's perspective and increases the motivation to make the plan work. In addition, managers and employees know a great deal about the organization and usually are willing to share their knowledge.

Step 7. Formulate Strategic Options and Select the Appropriate Strategies

By this point in the strategic management process, entrepreneurs should have a clear picture of what their businesses do best and what their competitive advantages are. They also should understand their firms' weaknesses and limitations as well as those of its competitors. The next step is to evaluate strategic options and then prepare a game plan designed to achieve the stated mission, goals, and objectives.

Strategy A **strategy** is a road map of the actions an entrepreneur draws up to achieve a company's mission, goals, and objectives. In other words, the mission, goals, and objectives spell out the ends, and the strategy defines the means for reaching them. A strategy is the master plan that covers all of the major parts of the organization and ties them together into a unified whole. The plan must be action oriented; it should breathe life into the entire planning process. An entrepreneur must build a sound strategy based on the preceding steps that uses the company's core competencies and strengths as the springboard to success. Joseph Picken and Gregory Dess, authors of *Mission Critical: The 7 Strategic Traps that Derail Even the Smartest Companies,* write, "A flawed strategy—no matter how brilliant the leadership, no matter how effective the implementation—is doomed to fail. A sound strategy, implemented without error, wins every time."[42]

strategy
a road map of the actions an entrepreneur draws up to fulfill a company's mission, goals, and objectives.

An avid bicyclist, Grant Petersen, quit his job at the bicycle division of Japanese conglomerate Bridgestone in 1994 to start his own specialty bicycle manufacturing business, Rivendell Bicycle Works. In an industry dominated by giant companies, Petersen and his eight workers, including his bookkeeper wife, succeed by implementing a well-planned niche strategy, selling "retro-bikes" that are made of old-fashioned steel rather than the latest carbon fiber composites and use manual derailleurs rather than modern sophisticated electronic gear shifters. "Our whole business is based on selling things that are unpopular," says Petersen. Rivendell sells just 600 bicycles a year, but they are all hand-built with exquisite attention to detail and sell for $1,700 to $4,000. To promote his business, Petersen sells subscriptions to a quarterly publication called the *Rivendell Reader* for $20 a year ($200 for 99 years) in which bicycle enthusiasts can read articles covering everything from "Bicycling 101" to "Comparing Centerpulls and Cantilevers." Of course, a catalog featuring the company's products accompanies every issue of the reader. Petersen says that the 6,200 subscribers purchase an average of $260 of merchandise through the catalog each year. Demand for Rivendell bicycles is so strong that customers wanting to purchase one of the high-end custom models are on a waiting list of 18 months. To fuel the company's growth, Petersen has introduced two new lower-priced models and has expanded his base of dealers. Moderate growth is fine with Petersen, but he still wants his company to remain small. He seems to enjoy the fact that he makes the beeswax lubricant for bolt threads in his kitchen and sells it in Dixie cups![43]

Grant Petersen

A successful strategy is comprehensive and well integrated, focusing on establishing the key success factors that the manager identified in Step 4. For instance, if maximum shelf space is a key success factor for a small manufacturer's product, the strategy must identify techniques for gaining more in-store shelf space (e.g., offering higher margins to distributors and brokers than competitors do, assisting retailers with in-store displays, or redesigning a wider, more attractive package).

Three Strategic Options Obviously, the number of strategies from which the small business owner can choose is enormous. When all the glitter is stripped away, however, three basic strategies remain. In his classic book *Competitive Strategy,* Michael Porter defines these strategies: (1) cost leadership, (2) differentiation, and (3) focus (see Figure 3.4).[44]

COST LEADERSHIP A company pursuing a **cost leadership strategy** strives to be the lowest-cost producer relative to its competitors in the industry. Low-cost leaders have a competitive advantage in reaching buyers whose primary purchase criterion is price, and they have the power to set the industry's price floor. This strategy works well when buyers are sensitive to price changes, when competing firms sell the same commodity products and compete on the basis of price, and when companies can benefit from economies of

cost leadership strategy
a strategy in which a company strives to be the lowest-cost producer relative to its competitors in the industry.

FIGURE 3.4

Three Strategic Options

Competitive Advantage

	Uniqueness perceived by the customer	Low cost position
Industry	Differentiation	Low cost
Niche	Differentiation focus	Cost focus

Target Market

scale. Not only is a low-cost leader in the best position to defend itself in a price war, but it also can use its power to attack competitors with the lowest price in the industry.

There are many ways to build a low-cost strategy, but the most successful cost leaders know where they have cost advantages over their competitors, and they use these as the foundation for their strategies. They also are committed to squeezing unnecessary costs out of their operations.

COMPANY Profile

JetBlue Airways

Because its workforce is not unionized, JetBlue Airlines has a significant advantage over its rivals in labor costs, and it has more flexibility in job assignments for its cross-trained workers. Pilots even pitch in to help flight attendants clean cabins, which keeps flight turnaround times short. Reservation-takers work from their homes, creating significant cost savings for themselves and for the company. Because the company offers stock options to its workers, employees often are willing to work for lower salaries. The result is that JetBlue's labor cost is just 25 percent of revenues compared to 33 to 44 percent of revenues for its competitors, and the company uses this to deploy its fleet of planes more efficiently and more profitably than its competition. JetBlue also flies just two types of planes—Airbus A320s and Embraer 190s—to keep maintenance and training costs low. Every JetBlue seat is upholstered in leather, a luxury that costs $15,000 more per plane but sends an important signal to passengers. In addition, the leather surfaces are easier to maintain and last much longer, lowering JetBlue's costs. The net effect of this cost-leadership strategy is that JetBlue's operating cost is the lowest in the industry—just six cents per seat-mile compared with eight to twelve cents per seat-mile for older, "legacy" carriers. JetBlue and other low-cost carriers use their lower cost structures to put pressure on legacy carriers (many of which have declared bankruptcy), who find it increasingly difficult to raise fares in markets where they compete directly. "The low-cost airlines are now dictating pricing in our business," says a top manager at one legacy airline. "Every time the [legacy airlines] match the fares of the discounters, they lose money."[45]

Of course, there are dangers in following a cost leadership strategy. Sometimes, a company focuses exclusively on lower manufacturing costs, without considering the impact of purchasing, distribution, or overhead costs. Another danger is incorrectly identifying the company's true cost drivers. Although their approach to managing is characterized by frugality, companies that understand cost leadership are willing to invest in those activities that drive costs out of doing business, whether it is technology, preventive maintenance, or some other factor. Finally, a firm may pursue a low-cost leadership strategy so zealously that in its drive to push costs downward, it eliminates product or service features that customers consider to be essential.

Under the right conditions, a cost leadership strategy executed properly can be an incredibly powerful strategic weapon. Small discount retailers that live in the shadows of Wal-Mart and thrive even when the economy slows succeed by relentlessly pursuing low-cost strategies. Small chains such as Fred's, Dollar General, Family Dollar, and 99 Cents Only cater to low- and middle-income customers who live in inner cities or rural areas. They offer inexpensive products such as food, health and beauty products, cleaning supplies, clothing, and seasonal merchandise, and many of the items they stock are closeout buys (purchases made as low as 10 cents on the dollar) on brand name merchandise. These companies also strive to keep their overhead costs as low as possible. For instance, 99 Cents

Only, whose name describes its merchandising strategy, is housed in a no-frills warehouse in an older section of City of Commerce, California.[46] The success of these stores proves that companies pursuing a cost leadership strategy must emphasize cost containment in *every* decision, from where to locate the company headquarters to which items to stock.

DIFFERENTIATION A company following a **differentiation strategy** seeks to build customer loyalty by positioning its goods or services in a unique or different fashion. That, in turn, enables the business to command a higher price for its products or services than competitors. There are many ways to create a differentiation strategy, but the key is to be special at something that is important to the customer. In other words, a business strives to be better than its competitors at something customers value.

differentiation strategy
a strategy in which a company seeks to build customer loyalty by positioning its goods or services in a unique or different fashion.

Urban Outfitters, a 75-store chain selling clothing for young people, has achieved success by implementing a contrarian strategy to distinguish itself from the cookie-cutter stores on which many of its national retail competitors rely. "Shopping here should be like a treasure hunt," says the company's general merchandising manager. Indeed, the company engages customers' sense of adventure by displaying one-of-a-kind vintage garments next to new fashions and unique, funky home décor items such as beaded curtains and cocktail shakers. Founder Richard Hayne encourages customers to return to Urban Outfitters outlets by stocking small batches of new merchandise and employing a visual arts staff to redesign its stores every two weeks. "Rather than relying on identical stores," says one industry analyst, "Urban creates an experience that's intellectually stimulating." Customers seem to enjoy the "organized clutter" layout because they shop for an average of 45 minutes per visit, twice as long as shoppers spend in a typical clothing store. In another clever move, every Urban Outfitters store places Xboxes and vintage video games in the men's section to keep bored boyfriends from pressuring female shoppers into leaving! To ensure that it sells the latest fashions, the company sends teams of buyers and designers on globe-hopping trips, where they look for design inspirations. The teams have come back with ideas for tunics from Stockholm and art deco jewelry from a Prague art museum. Urban Outfitters' differentiation strategy works well; its stores generate $596 in annual sales per square foot of space, 80 percent higher than its competitors.[47]

Urban Outfitters

If a small company can improve a product's (or service's) performance, reduce the customer's cost and risk of purchasing it, or provide intangible benefits that customers value (such as status, prestige, a sense of safety, among others), it has the potential to be a successful differentiator. Companies that execute a differentiation strategy successfully can charge premium prices for their products and services, increase their market share, and reap the benefits of customer loyalty and retention. To be successful, a business must make its product or service truly different, at least in the eyes of its customers.

Entrepreneur Yngve Bergqvist has no trouble setting his hotel in Jukkasjärvi, Sweden, apart from others. Located 125 miles above the Arctic Circle, the aptly named Ice Hotel offers travelers a unique experience. *Everything* in the hotel—walls, beds, night tables, chairs, cinema, bars—is made from 30,000 tons of snow and 10,000 tons of crystal clear ice harvested from the Torne River! Each of the 60 rooms is unique, designed by a different artist from around the world. Guests sleep in insulated sleeping bags on ice beds covered with thin mattresses and plenty of reindeer blankets. Because temperatures inside the hotel typically hover at 5 degrees below zero (centigrade), guests cannot take their luggage to their ice rooms; it will freeze! Amenities include an ice bar, an ice chapel, an ice cinema, and an ice art exhibition. The

Ice Hotel

A stay at the Ice Hotel in Jukkasjärvi, Sweden, is like an evening in no other hotel in the world. *Everything* in the hotel—the walls, the beds, the bar, the glasses—is made of ice! Rebuilt every year from ice from the Torne River, the Ice Hotel is the ultimate example of a differentiation strategy.

30,000-square-foot Ice Hotel is open from December through April (it melts in the spring), but during its brief existence, it will accommodate some 5,000 guests at rates ranging from $200 to $500 per night! Countless rock groups, including Van Halen, have shot music videos at the Ice Hotel. It's not about comfort," says co-owner Arne Bergh. "It's a journey, an adventure."[48]

Although few businesses are innately as unique as the Ice Hotel, the goal for a company pursuing a differentiation strategy is to create that kind of uniqueness in the minds of its customers. The key to a successful differentiation strategy is to build it on a core competency, something a small company is uniquely good at doing in comparison to its competitors. Common bases for differentiation include superior customer service, special product features, complete product lines, instantaneous parts availability, absolute product reliability, supreme product quality, and extensive product knowledge. To be successful, a differentiation strategy must create the perception of value in the customer's eyes. No customer will purchase a good or service that fails to produce its perceived value, no matter how real that value may be. One business consultant advises, "Make sure you tell your customers and prospects what it is about your business that makes you different. Make sure that difference is on the form of a true benefit to the customer."[49]

Other small companies that are deploying a differentiation strategy successfully include the following:

- Woodentoys-and-more.com is an online store that sells upscale children's toys. Shoshana Bailey started the company when she had difficulty finding creative, educational toys for her grandchildren at mass merchandisers such as Wal-Mart and Toys-R-Us. Some of her company's best-selling items include a $147 hand-made wooden train set and a $420 cherry wood rocking horse made by a Tennessee craftsman. "Mass-market retailers can't stock all of these unique toys," explains one industry analyst. "Their job is to stock the most in-demand toys."[50]
- PrarieStone Pharmacy is using technology to offer fast service and individual attention to customers getting drug prescriptions filled. At locations inside Lund Food Holdings, a chain of upscale supermarkets in the Minneapolis-St. Paul area, PrarieStone stores drugs in a high-tech vertical container that saves space, dispenses the most often prescribed drugs automatically, and allows pharmacists to have more face-to-face time with customers. A system of bar-code scanners verifies the accuracy of every order and protects customers from medication errors. PrarieStone also was the first pharmacy in the nation to offer automated multidose packaging for customers taking multiple medications. A specialized machine organizes the various drugs and then packages them in a sealed sleeve marked with the time of day the patient should take the medication. Not only does the technology provide cost savings for PrarieStone, but it also speeds up transaction times, enhances safety for customers, and gives pharmacists more time to spend working with customers rather than counting pills manually.[51]

Small companies encounter risks when pursuing a differentiation strategy. One danger is trying to differentiate a product or service on the basis of something that does not boost its performance or lower its cost to customers. Another pitfall is trying to differentiate on the basis of something that customers do not see as important. Business owners also must consider how long they can sustain a product's or service's differentiation; changing customer tastes make the basis for differentiation temporary at best. Imitations and "knock-offs" from competitors also pose a threat to a successful differentiation strategy. For instance, entrepreneurs in Finland have built an ice hotel to compete with the original ice hotel in Sweden. Designers of high-priced original clothing see much cheaper knock-off products on the market shortly after their designs hit the market. Another pitfall is overdifferentiating and charging so much that the company prices its products out of the market. The final risk is focusing only on the physical characteristics of a product or service and ignoring important psychological factors such as status, prestige, and image, which can be powerful sources of differentiation.

FOCUS A **focus strategy** recognizes that not all markets are homogeneous. In fact, in any given market, there are many different customer segments, each having different needs, wants, and characteristics. The principal idea of this strategy is to select one or more market segments, identify customers' special needs, wants, and interests, and approach them with a good or service designed to excel in meeting these needs, wants, and interests. Focus strategies build on *differences* among market segments. For instance, most markets contains a population of customers who are willing and able to pay for premium goods and services, giving small companies the opportunity to follow a focus strategy aimed at the premium segment of the market.

A successful focus strategy depends on a small company's ability to identify the changing needs of its targeted customer group and to develop the skills required to serve them. That means an entrepreneur and everyone in the organization must have a clear understanding of how to add value to the product or service for the customer. How does the product or service meet the customer's needs at each stage—from raw material to final sale?

Rather than attempting to serve the total market, the focusing firm specializes in serving a specific target segment or niche. A focus strategy is ideally suited to many small businesses, which often lack the resources to reach the overall market. Their goal is to serve their narrow target markets more effectively and efficiently than do competitors that pound away at the broad market. Common bases for building a focus strategy include zeroing in on a small geographic area, targeting a group of customers with similar needs or interests (e.g., left-handed people), specializing in a specific product or service (e.g., Batteries Plus, a store that sells and services every kind of battery imaginable), or selling specialized knowledge (e.g., restoring valuable works of art).

focus strategy

a strategy in which a company selects one or more market segments, identifies customers' special needs, wants, and interests, and approaches them with a good or service designed to excel in meeting those needs, wants, and interests.

After researching the $6.2 billion-a-year breakfast cereal industry, David Roth and Rick Bacher decided to start a restaurant dedicated to the popular breakfast food. (One of the factors that prompted Roth, a former marketing consultant, to come up with the idea was a meeting with an executive who kept a stash of Cocoa Puffs hidden in his briefcase.) Initially targeting college students ("They basically live on cereal," jokes Roth), the two friends launched Cereality in the Arizona State University food court in 2003. The pilot store was so successful that Roth and Bacher have opened stores in Philadelphia and Chicago and are planning to set up Cereality outlets in hospitals, airports, train stations, office buildings, and other college campuses. For about $4, customers can fill up their Cereality Chinese-food-like bucket with two scoops of any of the more than 30 brands of cereal on the menu (from Fruit Loops to Corn Chex), add one of more than 40 toppings, ranging from bananas or dried cherries to chocolate malt balls, and top it off with milk (several varieties here as well). "Cerealogists" dressed in pajama tops also sell cereal bars, Cereality Bites™ snack mixes and "Slurrealities®" (smoothies made with cereal) that account for one-third of a Cereality outlet's sales. "The idea is to become the Starbucks of cereal," says Roth.[52]

The most successful focusers build a competitive edge by concentrating on specific market niches and serving them better than any other competitor can. Essentially, this strategy depends on creating value for the customer either by being the lowest-cost producer or by differentiating the product or service in a unique fashion, but doing it in a narrow target segment. To be worth targeting, a niche must be large enough to be profitable, reasonably reachable through advertising media, and capable of sustaining a business over time (i.e.,

not a passing fad). Consider the following examples of companies that operate quite successfully in small, yet profitable, niches:

■ The Flutter Fetti Fun Factory specializes in making—and dropping—confetti. The small company has dropped its patented product, Flutter Fetti ("The only party confetti that Flutters, Flies, and Floats"™), at a variety of high-profile events, including the Republican and Democratic national conventions, the Olympics, Mardi Gras, presidential inaugural balls, the Macy's Thanksgiving Day Parade, and music concerts by Shania Twain, Britney Spears, and Paul McCartney.[53]

■ After his father, Joe, moved into his new Beverly Hills, California, home, Jeff Smith, a wine connoisseur, organized Joe's 5,000-bottle wine collection. When a family friend saw the result, he offered the younger Smith $500 to organize his wine cellar. "That's when the light bulb went off," says Smith, who then started his company, Carte du Vin, from a spare bedroom in his Hollywood Hills, California, home. A customized software package categorizes his clients' wine collections by type, vintage, critics' ratings, peak drinking date, and price. The database that he uses contains information on more than 10,000 wines, but Smith and his two part-time employees are constantly updating and expanding it. Once he organizes a client's wine cellar, Smith provides a leather-bound printout and a password-protected Web site customers can access anytime. Smith also performs monthly wine cellar maintenance for many of his clients after initially organizing their collections.[54]

Although it can be a highly profitable strategy, pursuing a focus strategy is not without risks. Companies sometimes must struggle to capture a large enough share of a small market to be profitable. If a small company is successful in a niche, there is also the danger of larger competitors entering the market and eroding it. Entrepreneurs following this strategy often face a constant struggle to keep costs down; the small volume of business that some niches support pushes production costs upward, making a company vulnerable to lower-cost competitors as their prices spiral higher. Sometimes a company with a successful niche strategy gets distracted by its success and tries to branch out into other areas. As it drifts farther away from its core strategy, it loses its competitive edge and runs the risk of confusing or alienating its customers. Muddying its image with customers puts a company in danger of losing its identity.

Strategy in Action   The strategies a small business pursues depend on its competitive advantages in the market segments in which it competes. In some cases, the business will implement multiple strategies across several segments. When a business has a well-defined strategic advantage, it may pursue highly aggressive growth strategies in an attempt to increase its market share. This is especially true when a business achieves a "first-mover" advantage in a market with little direct competition. By being the first in the market, it establishes name recognition and a loyal customer base. Starbucks Coffee continues to reap the benefits of being the first company to establish a chain of upscale retail coffee houses in major markets after Howard Shultz traveled to Milan, Italy, and noticed the tremendous popularity of espresso bars. A year later, in 1984, Schultz launched his coffee bar concept as a test in Seattle, Washington. Today, the chain has nearly 6,000 locations around the globe! Aggressive strategies sometimes can backfire if larger competitors decide to fight back. In many cases, the old adage of being the "big frog in a small pond" allows a small business to earn a handsome profit in a market niche without attracting the attention of larger competitors.
Small companies must develop strategies that exploit all of the competitive advantages of their size by:

■ Responding quickly to customers' needs.
■ Remaining flexible and willing to change.
■ Constantly searching for new, emerging market segments.
■ Building and defending market niches.
■ Erecting "switching costs," the costs a customer incurs by switching to a competitor's product or service, through personal service and loyalty.
■ Remaining entrepreneurial and willing to take risks and act with lightning speed.
■ Constantly innovating.

Hands on ... How to

Beat Big-Box Competitors

It's the news that sends shivers down the spines of small business owners everywhere: Wal-Mart (or any other "big-box" retailer) is coming to town. "How can my small business compete against the largest company in the world?" they wonder. "Can my business survive?"

Although no business owner welcomes a threat of this magnitude from a giant competitor with greater buying power, more name recognition, and a reputation for driving small companies out of business, it is no reason to fold up the tent and go home. Smart entrepreneurs know that, by formulating and executing the proper strategy, they not only can survive in the face of big box competitors, but they also can thrive in their presence.

Rule 1. Don't play their game. A fundamental concept in strategy is to avoid matching your company's weaknesses against a competitor's strengths. For instance, because Wal-Mart buys in such huge volume from its supplier, it can extract the lowest prices from them. Small companies purchasing from those same suppliers cannot; therefore, it makes little sense for small companies to try to compete with Wal-Mart and other giant retailers on the basis of price. Unless your small company has another, more significant cost advantage, competing on the basis of price is a recipe for disaster.

Rule 2. Hit 'em where they ain't. Jeff Brotman, founder of Costco, a discount warehouse that goes up against Wal-Mart's Sam's Club discount warehouses, has been competing in competition with the industry giant for two decades. "When [Wal-Mart] comes to town," he says, "it usually means death and destruction." By pursuing a niche, however, Costco has managed to grow despite Wal-Mart's power. Even though Costco has 218 fewer locations than Sam's Club, Costco manages to generate more sales and higher profits than its rival. Brotman's strategy is to target small business owners with more upscale products than Sam's Club typically offers. When he first launched the company, Brotman's research showed that small business owners were among the wealthiest people in a typical community, but, because of their business experience, they were always looking for a good bargain. "They want high-end merchandise that reflects their status, but they'd prefer it cheap," he says. That's just what Costco delivers. A Costco store carries only half as many items as a Sam's Club outlet, but the selection is quite different and is designed to appeal to upscale shoppers—Godiva chocolates, Coach handbags, Waterford crystal, Dom Perignon champagne, J. A. Henckels International cutlery, and others. Like Wal-Mart, Costco has developed a highly effective supply chain system to keep stores stocked with the best-selling items. "This business is a game of inches," says Brotman, "so we'll get a little better every year."

Rule 3. Hire the best . . . and train them. Costco pays its workers at rates well above the industry average, which keeps turnover rates low (in fact, the lowest in the industry) and productivity high, giving it another edge over Wal-Mart. Small companies cannot always afford to pay the highest wages in an area; however, because their companies are small, entrepreneurs have the opportunity to create a work environment in which employees can thrive. For instance, one small company attracts and retains quality workers by allowing them to use flexible work schedules that make it easier for them to manage their busy lives. The owner also invests heavily in training workers so that they can move up the organization—and the pay scale—faster. The training pays off, however, in the form of greater productivity, lower turnover, increased customer satisfaction, and higher sales per employee. Paying attention to seemingly small details such as more communication, frequent recognition for jobs well done, less bureaucracy, and flexible benefits enables small companies to build a loyal, motivated workforce that can outperform those at larger companies.

Rule 4. Bring back what the big boys have eliminated. Many companies in the supermarket industry have taken a beating as discount mass retailers have expanded their superstore concepts into more markets across the United States. Yet, many small supermarket chains have thrived by taking a completely different strategic approach, building small stores that allow shoppers to make their purchases quickly and conveniently. A Wal-Mart supercenter, for instance, adds about 40,000 grocery items to the already mind-boggling 116,000 items in its outlets. Customers have a wide selection of products at low prices, but many have grown weary of the time they have to invest to navigate these cavernous stores just to find the items they need. That's exactly what small grocers such as Save-a-Lot are counting on. Going back to the days of the old corner grocer, the St. Louis-based chain keeps its 1,250 stores small—operated by no more than 25 employees—and sells no more than 1,250 grocery items in each one. To keep its costs and prices low, Save-a-Lot carefully selects neighborhood locations and emphasizes private label items (in fact, private label items make up 75 percent of the company's inventory).

Rule 5. Beat them at the service game. In tennis, the serve is one of the most important parts of the game; so it is in the retail game. Small companies can differentiate themselves from their larger, more powerful rivals by emphasizing superior, friendly, personal service, something their size makes them uniquely capable of doing. For instance, Dick's Sporting Goods, a chain of 240 sporting goods stores, relentlessly trains its workers so they can share their knowledge of the company's products and how best to use them with customers. Despite the low prices they offer customers, giant chain stores are famous for failing to provide even basic customer service and product information, once again giving small companies the opportunity to outperform their giant rivals. "Customers today want information," says Dick's CEO, Ed Stack, whose father founded the company in 1948. "They're not going to go somewhere where they are ignored." At Dick's, customers in the golf

shop are likely to work with a PGA golf pro, and hunters and fishermen can talk with sales people who are enthusiasts of those sports. The store layout encourages customers to test products—from bicycles and running shoes to golf clubs and tennis rackets—before they purchase them. Dick's stores also offer a wider selection of sporting goods than Wal-Mart does. When it comes to managing inventory and supplier relationships, the company has taken a page from Wal-Mart's playbook. The automated system keeps inventory very lean and operates on a just-in-time basis, enabling Dick's to boast an inventory turnover ratio of 3.7 times a year, far above the industry average of 2.7.

1. Why do many small businesses fail when a big discount retailer such as Wal-Mart becomes a competitor?

2. Work with a team of your classmates to identify a local small business that competes with a big discounter. Which of these strategies has the small company employed to become a stronger competitor? What other strategies would you recommend to the owner of this business?

3. Based on your work in Question 2, develop a one-page report summarizing your strategic suggestions.

Sources: Matthew Maier, "How to Beat Wal-Mart," *Business 2.0,* pp. 108–114; Rhonda Abrams, "Small Businesses Can Compete with the Big Guys," *Business,* September 26, 2004, p. 8; Ann Zimmerman, "Behind the Dollar-Store Boom: A Nation of Bargain Hunters," *Wall Street Journal,* December 13, 2004, pp. A1, A10; Barry Cotton, and Jean-Charles Cachon, "Resisting the Giants: Small Retail Entrepreneurs Against Mega-Retailers—An Empirical Study," Presented at the International Council for Small Business 2005 World Conference, June 2005; Amy Merrick, Gary McWilliams, Ellen Byron, and Kortney Stringer, "Targeting Wal-Mart," *Wall Street Journal,* December 1, 2004, pp. B1, B2.

Step 8. Translate Strategic Plans into Action Plans

No strategic plan is complete until it is put into action; planning a company's strategy and implementing it go hand in hand. Entrepreneurs must convert strategic plans into operating plans that guide their companies on a daily basis and become a visible, active part of the business. No small business can benefit from a strategic plan sitting on a shelf collecting dust. Unfortunately, failure to implement a strategy effectively is a common problem. In a recent survey conducted by Marakon Associates and the Economist Intelligence Unit, senior executives reported that their companies had achieved only 63 percent of the results expected in their strategic plans.[55] The lesson is that even sound strategies, unless properly implemented, will fail.

Implementing the Strategy Implementing a strategy successfully requires both a process that fits a company's culture and the right people committed to making that process work. Getting the right people in place starts with the selection process but includes every other aspect of the human resources function, from job design and training to motivational methods and compensation. To make their strategic plans workable, entrepreneurs should divide them into projects, carefully defining each one by the following:

Purpose. What is the project designed to accomplish?

Scope. Which areas of the company will be involved in the project?

Contribution. How does the project relate to other projects and to the overall strategic plan?

Resource requirements. What human and financial resources are needed to complete the project successfully?

Timing. Which schedules and deadlines will ensure project completion?

Once entrepreneurs assign priorities to projects, they can begin to implement the strategic plan. Involving employees and delegating adequate authority to them is essential because these projects affect them most directly. If an organization's people have been involved in the strategic management process to this point, they will have a better grasp of the steps they must take to achieve the organization's goals as well as their own professional goals. Early involvement of the work force in the strategic management process is a luxury that larger businesses cannot achieve. Commitment to reaching the company's objectives is a powerful force, but involvement is a prerequisite for achieving total employee commitment. The greater the level of involvement of those who will implement a company's strategy (often those at the lower levels of an organization) in the process of creating the strategy (often the realm of those at the top of an organization), the more likely it is that the strategy will be successful. Without a team of committed, dedicated employees, a company's strategy, no matter how precisely planned, usually fails.

Step 9. Establish Accurate Controls

So far, the planning process has created company objectives and has developed a strategy for reaching them, but rarely, if ever, will the company's actual performance match stated objectives. Entrepreneurs quickly realize the need to control actual results that deviate from plans.

Controlling the Strategy Planning without control has little operational value; therefore, a sound planning program requires a practical control process. The plans created in the strategic planning process become the standards against which actual performance is measured. It is important for everyone in the organization to understand—and to be involved in—the planning and controlling process.

Controlling plans and projects and keeping them on schedule means that an entrepreneur must identify and track key performance indicators. The source of these indicators is the operating data from the company's normal business activity; they are the guideposts for detecting deviations from established standards. Financial, production, sales, inventory, quality, customer service and satisfaction, and other operating records are primary sources of data managers can use to control activities. For example, on a customer service project, performance indicators might include the number of customer complaints, the number of orders returned, the percentage of on-time shipments, and a measure of order accuracy.

The most commonly used indicators of a company's performance are financial measures; however, judging a company's performance solely on the basis of financial measures can lead to strategic myopia. To judge the effectiveness of their strategies, many companies are developing a **balanced scorecard,** a set of multidimensional measurements that are unique to a company and that incorporate both financial and operational measures to give managers a quick yet comprehensive picture of the company's overall performance. One writer says that a balanced scorecard

is a sophisticated business model that helps a company understand what's really driving its success. It acts a bit like the control panel on a spaceship—the business equivalent of a flight speedometer, odometer, and temperature gauge all rolled into

LEARNING OBJECTIVES
5. Understand the importance of controls such as the balanced scorecard in the planning process.

balanced scorecard
a set of multidimensional measurements that are unique to a company and that incorporate both financial and operational measures to give managers a quick yet comprehensive picture of a company's overall performance.

one. It keeps track of many things, including financial progress and softer measurements—everything from customer satisfaction to return on investment—that need to be managed to reach the final destination: profitable growth.[56]

Rather than sticking solely to the traditional financial measures of a company's performance, the balanced scorecard gives managers a comprehensive view from *both* a financial and an operational perspective. The premise behind such a scorecard is that relying on any single measure of company performance is dangerous. Just as a pilot in command of a jet cannot fly safely by focusing on a single instrument, an entrepreneur cannot manage a company by concentrating on a single measurement. The complexity of managing a business demands that an entrepreneur be able to see performance measures in several areas simultaneously. "Knowing whether an enterprise is viable or not doesn't mean looking at just the bottom line," says one manager.[57] Scoreboards that combine relevant results from all aspects of the operation allow everyone in the organization to see how their job performance connects to a company's mission, goals, and objectives.

When creating a balanced scorecard for a company, an entrepreneur should establish goals for each critical indicator of company performance and then create meaningful measures for each one.

Certifiedmail.com

Court Coursey, founder of Certifiedmail.com, a company that delivers certified mail electronically, has developed a scorecard that encompasses measures on everything from financial performance to employee satisfaction. Every quarter, Coursey presents Certifiedmail.com's one-page scorecard to his 10 employees for review. "It's a good way to get a grasp on the company and how it's performing," he says. The scorecard gives Coursey important feedback that allows him to adjust his management style and the company's direction when necessary. The scorecard already has improved Certifiedmail.com's performance. One of Coursey's top priorities is cost control, and the scorecard recently pointed out a wasteful practice that he halted. The scorecard "showed me a way to save money," he says. "And it was something I may not have seen without this feedback."[58]

Ideally, a balanced scorecard looks at a business from four important perspectives (see Figure 3.5)[59]:

Customer Perspective: How do customers see us? Customers judge companies by at least four standards: time (how long it takes the company to deliver a good or service), quality (how well a company's product or service performs in terms of reliability, durability, and accuracy), performance (the extent to which a good or service performs as expected), and service (how well a company meets or exceeds customers' expectations of value). Because customer-related goals are external, managers must translate them into measures of what the company must do to meet customers' expectations.

Internal Business Perspective: At what must we excel? The internal factors on which managers should focus are those that have the greatest impact on customer satisfaction and retention and on company effectiveness and efficiency. Developing goals and measures for factors such as quality, cycle time, productivity, costs, and others that employees directly influence is essential.

Innovation and Learning Perspective: Can we continue to improve and create value? This view of a company recognizes that the targets required for success are never static; they are constantly changing. If a company wants to continue its pattern of success, it cannot stand still; it must continuously improve. A company's ability to innovate, learn, and improve determines its future. These goals and measures emphasize the importance of continuous improvement in customer satisfaction and internal business operations.

Financial Perspective: How do we look to shareholders? The most traditional performance measures, financial standards tell how much the company's overall strategy and its execution are contributing to its bottom line. These measures focus on such

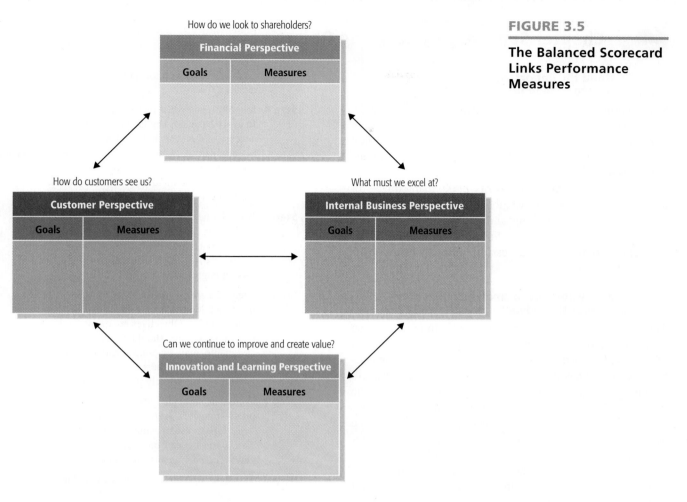

FIGURE 3.5

The Balanced Scorecard Links Performance Measures

factors as profitability, growth, and shareholder value. On balanced scorecards, companies often break their financial goals into three categories: survival, success, and growth.

Although the balanced scorecard is a vital tool that helps managers keep their companies on track, it is also an important tool for changing behavior in an organization and for keeping everyone focused on what really matters. Used properly, balanced scorecards allow managers to see how actions in each of the four dimensions of performance influence actions in the others. As competitive conditions and results change, managers can use the balanced scorecard to make corrections in plans, policies, strategies, and objectives to get performance back on track. A practical control system is also economical to operate. Most small businesses have no need for a sophisticated, expensive control system. The system should be so practical that it becomes a natural part of the management process.

Conclusion

The strategic planning process does *not* end with the nine steps outlined here; it is an ongoing procedure that entrepreneurs must repeat. With each round, managers and employees gain experience, and the steps become easier. The planning process outlined here is designed to be as simple as possible. No small business should be burdened with an elaborate, detailed formal planning process that it cannot easily use. Such processes require excessive amounts of time to operate, and they generate a sea of paperwork. Entrepreneurs need neither.

What does this strategic planning process lead to? It teaches business owners a degree of discipline that is important to business survival. It helps them to learn about their businesses, their core competencies, their competitors, and, most important, their customers. Although strategic planning cannot guarantee success, it does dramatically increase a small company's chances of survival in a hostile business environment.

Chapter Summary by Learning Objectives

1. Understand the importance of strategic management to a small business.

Small companies that lack clear strategies may achieve some success in the short run, but as soon as competitive conditions stiffen or an unanticipated threat arises, they usually "hit the wall" and fold. Without a basis for differentiating itself from a pack of similar competitors, the best a company can hope for is mediocrity in the marketplace. In today's intensely competitive global environment, entrepreneurs who are not thinking and acting strategically are putting their businesses at risk. Strategic management is the mechanism for operating successfully in a chaotic competitive environment.

2. Explain why and how a small business must create a competitive advantage in the market.

The goal of developing a strategic plan is to create for the small company a competitive advantage—the aggregation of factors that sets the small business apart from its competitors and gives it a unique position in the market. Every small firm must establish a plan for creating a unique image in the minds of its potential customers. A company builds a competitive edge on its core competencies, which are a unique set of capabilities that a company develops in key operational areas, such as quality, service, innovation, team building, flexibility, responsiveness, and others, that allow it to vault past competitors. They are what the company does best and are the focal point of the strategy. This step must identify target market segments and determine how to position the firm in those markets. Entrepreneurs must identify some way to differentiate their companies from competitors.

3. Develop a strategic plan for a business using the nine steps in the strategic planning process.

Small businesses need a strategic planning process designed to suit their particular needs. It should be relatively short, be informal and not structured, encourage the participation of employees, and not begin with extensive objective setting. Linking the purposeful action of strategic planning to an entrepreneur's ideas can produce results that shape the future.

Step 1 Develop a clear vision and translate it into a meaningful mission statement. Highly successful entrepreneurs are able to communicate their vision to those around them. The firm's mission statement answers the first question of any venture: What business am I in? The mission statement sets the tone for the entire company.

Step 2 Assess the company's strengths and weaknesses. Strengths are positive internal factors; weaknesses are negative internal factors.

Step 3 Scan the environment for significant opportunities and threats facing the business. Opportunities are

positive external options; threats are negative external forces.

Step 4 Identify the key factors for success in the business. In every business, key factors that determine the success of the firms in it, and so they must be an integral part of a company's strategy. Key success factors are relationships between a controllable variable and a critical factor influencing the firm's ability to compete in the market.

Step 5 Analyze the competition. Business owners should know their competitors' business almost as well as they know their own business. A competitive profile matrix is a helpful tool for analyzing competitors' strengths and weaknesses.

Step 6 Create company goals and objectives. Goals are the broad, long-range attributes that the firm seeks to accomplish. Objectives are quantifiable and more precise; they should be specific, measurable, assignable, realistic, timely, and written down. The process works best when managers and employees are actively involved.

Step 7 Formulate strategic options and select the appropriate strategies. A strategy is the game plan the firm plans to use to achieve its objectives and mission. It must center on establishing for the firm the key success factors identified earlier.

Step 8 Translate strategic plans into action plans. No strategic plan is complete until the owner puts it into action.

Step 9 Establish accurate controls. Actual performance rarely, if ever, matches plans exactly. Operating data from the business assembled into a comprehensive scorecard serve as an important guidepost for determining how effective a company's strategy is. This information is especially helpful when plotting future strategies.

The strategic planning process does not end with these nine steps; rather, it is an ongoing process that an entrepreneur will repeat.

4. Discuss the characteristics of three basic strategies—low cost, differentiation, and focus—and know when and how to employ them.

Three basic strategic options are cost leadership, differentiation, and focus. A company pursuing a cost leadership strategy strives to be the lowest-cost producer relative to its competitors in the industry. A company following a differentiation strategy seeks to build customer loyalty by positioning its goods or services in a unique or different fashion. In other words, the firm strives to be better than its competitors at something that customers value. A focus strategy recognizes that not all markets are homogeneous. The principal idea of this strategy is to select one or more segments, identify customers' special needs, wants, and interests, and approach them with a good or service designed to excel in meeting these needs, wants, and interests. Focus strategies build on *differences* among market segments.

5. Understand the importance of controls such as the balanced scorecard in the planning process.

Just as a pilot in command of a jet cannot fly safely by focusing on a single instrument, a entrepreneur cannot manage a company by concentrating on a single measurement. The balanced scorecard is a set of measurements unique to a company that includes both financial and a balanced scorecard of financial and operational measures gives managers a quick yet comprehensive picture of the company's total performance.

Discussion Questions

1. Why is strategic planning important to a small company?
2. What is a competitive advantage? Why is it important for a small business to establish one?
3. What are the steps in the strategic management process?
4. "Our customers don't just like our ice cream," write Ben Cohen and Jerry Greenfield, co-founders of Ben and Jerry's Homemade Inc. "They like what our company stands for. They like how doing business with us makes them feel." What do they mean?
5. What are strengths, weaknesses, opportunities, and threats? Give an example of each.
6. Explain the characteristics of effective objectives. Why is setting objectives important?
7. What are business strategies?
8. Describe the three basic strategies available to small companies. Under what conditions is each most successful?
9. "It's better to be a company with a great strategy in a crummy business than to be a company with a crummy strategy in a great business," says one business expert. Do you agree? Explain.
10. Explain how a company can gain a competitive advantage using each of the three strategies described in this chapter: cost leadership, differentiation, and focus. Give an example of a company that is using each strategy.
11. How is the controlling process related to the planning process?
12. What is a balanced scorecard? What value does it offer entrepreneurs who are evaluating the success of their current strategies?

Business Plan Pro

 We are now going to think about your business from a strategic perspective. This will involve first describing your business objectives, drafting your mission statement, identifying "keys to success," conducting a SWOT analysis, and making initial comments about your strategy and your competitive advantage.

Business Plan Exercises

On the Web

Visit http://www.prenhall.com/scarborough and click on the Business Plan Resources tab. Scroll down and find the information with the heading Standard Industry Classification Codes. Step through the process to find the Standard Industry Classification code associated with your industry. Then, review the information associated with the Competitor Analysis section. This information may provide insight into learning more about your industry competitors on a global, national, or even on a local basis.

In the Software

Open your business plan in Business Plan Pro. You are now going to add text to the strategic areas mentioned in this chapter. Don't worry about perfecting this information. You will want to capture your thoughts and ideas so you can come back to these topics, add detail, and make certain the sections are congruent with your entire plan. Before we do that, let's look at some examples of each of these sections in one or more of the sample plans that you had selected earlier.

Sample Plans

Review the following sections, as they appear, of one or more of the sample plans that you identified earlier:

- Mission Statement
- Objectives
- SWOT Analysis
- Keys to Success
- Competition, Buying Patterns, and Main Competitors
- Value Proposition
- Competitive Edge
- Strategy and Implementation Summary

Note the information captured in these sections of the plans. Some areas may be quite elaborate, whereas others might be brief and contain only bullet points. As you look at each plan, determine whether it provides the needed information under each topic and think about the type of information you will include in your plan.

Building Your Business Plan

Here are some tips you may want to consider as you tackle each of these sections:

Mission statement. Use your mission statement to establish your fundamental goals for the quality of your business offering. The mission statement represents the opportunity to answer the questions "What business are you in?" and "Why does your business exist?" This may include the value you offer and the role customers, employees and owners play in providing and benefiting from that value. A good mission statement can be a critical element in defining your business and communicating this definition to key stakeholders including investors, partners, employees, and customers.

Objectives. Objectives should be specific goals that are quantifiable and measurable. Setting measurable objectives will enable you to track your progress and measure your results.

SWOT analysis. What are the internal strengths and weaknesses of your business? As you look outside the organization, what are the external opportunities and threats? List these and then assess what this tells you about your business. How can you leverage your strengths to take advantage of the opportunities ahead? How can you further develop or minimize the areas of weaknesses?

Keys to success. Virtually every business has critical aspects that make the difference between success and failure. These may be brief bullet point comments that capture key elements that will make a difference in accomplishing your stated objectives and realizing you mission.

Competition, buying patterns, and main competitors. Discuss your ideal position in the market. Think about specific kinds of features and benefits your business offers and how that is unique compared to what is available to your market today. Why do people buy your ser-

vices instead of other services your competitor offer? Discuss your primary competitor's strengths and weaknesses. Consider their service offering, pricing, reputation, management, financial position, brand awareness, business development, technology, and any other factors that may be important. What market segments do they occupy? What strategy to they appear to pursue? How much of a competitive threat do the present?

Value proposition. A value proposition is a clear and concise statement that describes the tangible value-based result a customer receives from using your product or service. The more specific and meaningful this statement is from a customer's perspective, the better. Once you have your value proposition, look at your organization—and your business plan—in terms of how well you communicate the service proposition and fulfill your promise to your customers or clients.

Your competitive edge. A competitive edge may build on your value proposition and seeks to capture the unique value—in whatever terms the customer defines that value—that your business offers. Your competitive edge may be through your product, customer service, method of distribution, pricing, or promotional methods. It describes how your business is uniquely different from all others in a way that is sustainable over time.

Strategy and implementation. This is a section that you will build on and, for now, make comments that capture your plans for the business. This describes the game plan and provides focus to realize your venture's objectives and mission. Based on your initial strategic analysis, which of the three business strategies—low cost, differentiation, or focus—will you use to give your company a competitive advantage? How will this strategy capitalize on your company's strengths and appeal to your customer's need? You will later build on this information as you formulate action plans to bring this strategic plan to life.

Capture your ideas in each of these sections and continually ask yourself about the relevance of this information. If it does not add value to your business plan, there is no need to include this information.

 ## Beyond the Classroom . . .

1. Contact the owner of a small business that competes directly with an industry giant (such as Home Depot, Wal-Mart, Barnes & Noble, or others). What does the owner see as his or her competitive advantage? How does the business communicate this advantage to its customers? What competitive strategy is the owner using? How successful is it? What changes would you suggest the owner make?

2. In his book *The HP Way,* Dave Packard, co-founder of Hewlett Packard, describes the seven commitments of the HP Way:

   ■ Profit—the ultimate source of corporate strength.
   ■ Customers—constant improvement in the value of the products and services the company offers them.

- Field of interest—seeking new opportunities but limiting them to complementary products and services based on company core competences.
- Growth—a measure of strength and a requirement for survival.
- Employees—provide opportunities for advancement, share in their success, and offer job security based on performance.
- Organization—foster individual motivation, initiative, and creativity by giving employees the freedom to work toward established goals and objectives.
- Citizenship—contribute in a positive way toward the community and society at large.

In what ways do these values help HP to define its vision? Its competitive edge? How important is it for entrepreneurs to define a system of values to guide their companies?

3. Contact a local entrepreneur and help him or her devise a balanced scorecard for his or her company. What goals did you and the owner establish in each of the four perspectives? What measures did you use to judge progress toward those goals?

4. Use the strategic tools provided in this chapter to help a local small business owner discover his or her firm's strengths, weaknesses, opportunities, and threats; identify the relevant key success factors; and analyze its competitors. Help the owner devise a strategy for success for his or her business.

5. Choose an entrepreneur in your community and interview him or her. Does the company have a strategic plan? A mission statement? Why or why not? What does the owner consider the company's strengths and weaknesses to be? What opportunities and threats does the owner perceive? What image is the owner trying to create for the business? Has the effort been successful? (Do you agree?) Which of the generic competitive strategies is the company following? Who are the company's primary competitors? How does the owner rate his or her chances for success in the future (use a low [1] to high [10] scale). When you have completed the interview, use the evaluation questionnaire (1 = low to 10 = high) to rate the company's strategic orientation. Compare your evaluation with other classmates. What, if any, generalizations can you draw from the interview?

4 | Conducting a Feasibility Analysis and Crafting a Winning Business Plan

A good beginning makes a good end. —Proverb

In preparing for battle, I have always found that plans are useless, but planning is indispensable.
—Dwight Eisenhower

Learning Objectives

On completion of this chapter, you will be able to:

1 Discuss the steps involved in subjecting a business idea to a feasibility analysis.
2 Explain why every entrepreneur should create a business plan, as well as the benefits of developing a plan.
3 Describe the elements of a solid business plan.
4 Explain the "five Cs of credit" and why they are important to potential lenders and investors reading business plans.
5 Describe the keys to making an effective business plan presentation.

For many entrepreneurs, the easiest part of launching a business is coming up with an idea for a new business concept or approach. As you learned in Chapter 2, entrepreneurs do not lack creativity and are responsible for some of the world's most important innovations. Business success, however, requires much more than just a great new idea. Once entrepreneurs develop an idea for a business, the next step is to subject it to a feasibility analysis to determine whether they can transform the idea into a viable business. A **feasibility analysis** is the process of determining whether an entrepreneur's idea is a viable foundation for creating a successful business. Its purpose is to determine whether a business idea is worth pursuing. If the idea passes the feasibility analysis, the entrepreneur's next step is to build a solid business plan for capitalizing on the idea. If the idea fails to pass muster, the entrepreneur drops it and moves on to the next opportunity. He or she has not wasted valuable time, money, energy, and other resources creating a full-blown business plan, or worse, launching a business that is destined to fail because it is based on a flawed concept. Although it is impossible for a feasibility study to guarantee an idea's success, conducting a study reduces the likelihood that entrepreneurs will spend too much of their time pursuing fruitless business ventures.

A feasibility study is *not* the same as a business plan; both play important, but separate, roles in the start-up process. A feasibility study answers the question, "Should we proceed with this business idea?" Its role is to serve as a filter, screening out ideas that lack the potential for building a successful business, *before* an entrepreneur commits the necessary resources to building a business plan. A feasibility study primarily is an investigative tool. It is designed to give an entrepreneur a picture of the market, sales, and profit potential of a particular business idea. Will a ski resort located here attract enough customers to be successful? Will customers in this community support a sandwich shop with a retro rock-n-roll theme? Can we build the product at a reasonable cost and sell it at a price customers are willing and able to pay? Does this entrepreneurial team have the ability to implement the idea successfully?

A business plan, on the other hand, is a planning tool for transforming an idea into reality. It builds on the foundation of the feasibility study but provides a more comprehensive analysis than a feasibility study. It functions primarily as a planning tool, taking an idea that has passed the feasibility analysis and describing how to turn it into a successful business. Its primary goals are to guide entrepreneurs as they launch and operate their businesses and to help them acquire the necessary financing to launch.

Feasibility studies are particularly useful when entrepreneurs have generated multiple ideas for business concepts and must winnow their options down to the best choice. They enable entrepreneurs quickly to explore the practicality of each of several potential paths for transforming an idea into a successful business venture. Sometimes the result of a feasibility study is the realization that an idea simply won't produce a viable business, no matter how it is organized. In other cases, a study shows an entrepreneur that the business idea is a sound one but must be organized in a different fashion to be profitable.

feasibility analysis
the process of determining whether an entrepreneur's idea is a viable foundation for creating a successful business.

Conducting a Feasibility Analysis

A feasibility analysis consists of three interrelated components: an industry and market feasibility analysis, a product or service feasibility analysis, and a financial feasibility analysis (see Figure 4.1).

Industry and Market Feasibility Analysis

When evaluating the feasibility of a business idea, entrepreneurs find a basic analysis of the industry and targeted market segments a good starting point. The focus in this phase is twofold: (1) to determine how attractive an industry is overall as a "home" for a new business, and (2) to identify possible niches a small business can occupy profitably.

The first step in assessing industry attractiveness is to paint a picture of the industry with broad strokes, assessing it from a "macro" level. Answering the following questions will help:

- How large is the industry?
- How fast is it growing?

LEARNING OBJECTIVES
1. Discuss the steps involved in subjecting a business idea to a feasibility analysis.

FIGURE 4.1

Elements of a Feasibility Analysis

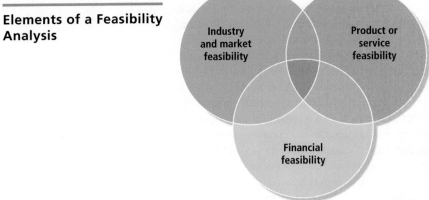

- Is the industry as a whole profitable?
- Is the industry characterized by high profit margins or razor-thin margins?
- How essential are its products or services to customers?
- What trends are shaping the industry's future?
- What threats does the industry face?
- What opportunities does the industry face?
- How crowded is the industry?
- How intense is the level of competition in the industry?
- Is the industry young, mature, or somewhere in between?

Addressing these questions helps entrepreneurs to determine whether the potential exists for sufficient demand for their products and services.

A useful tool for analyzing an industry's attractiveness is the **five forces model** developed by Michael Porter of the Harvard Business School (see Figure 4.2). Five forces interact with one another to determine the setting in which companies compete and hence the attractiveness of the industry: (1) The rivalry among the companies competing in the industry, (2) the bargaining power of suppliers to the industry, (3) the bargaining power of buyers, (4) the threat of new entrants to the industry, and (5) the threat of substitute products or services.

Rivalry Among Companies Competing in the Industry The strongest of the five forces in most industries is the rivalry that exists among the businesses competing in a particular market. Much like the horses running in the Kentucky Derby, businesses in a market are jockeying for position in an attempt to gain a competitive advantage. When a company

five forces model
a model that recognizes the power of five forces—rivalry among competing firms, bargaining power of suppliers, bargaining power of buyers, threat of new entrants, and threat of substitute products or services—on an industry.

FIGURE 4.2

The Five Forces Model of Competition

Source: Adapted from Michael E. Porter, "How Competitive Forces Shape Strategy," *Harvard Business Review*, Vol. 57, No. 2, March–April 1979, pp. 137–145.

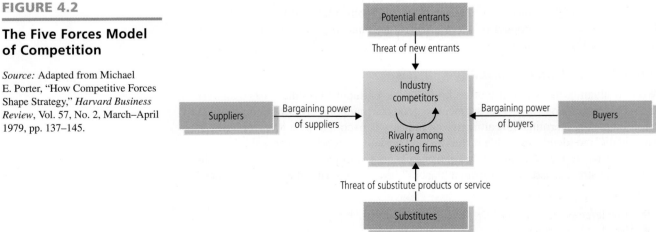

creates an innovation or develops a unique strategy that transforms the market, competing companies must adapt or run the risk of being forced out of business. This force makes markets a dynamic and highly competitive place. Generally, an industry is more attractive when the following conditions hold:

- The number of competitors is large or, at the other extreme, quite small (fewer than five).
- Competitors are not similar in size or capability.
- The industry is growing at a fast pace.
- The opportunity to sell a differentiated product or service is present.

Bargaining Power of Suppliers to the Industry The greater the leverage that suppliers of key raw materials or components have, the less attractive is the industry. For instance, because they supply the chips that serve as the "brains" of PCs and because those chips make up a sizeable portion of the cost of a computer, chip makers such as Intel and Advanced Micro Devices (AMD) exert a great deal of power over computer manufacturers such as Dell, Hewlett-Packard, and Gateway. Generally, an industry is more attractive when the following conditions hold:

- Many suppliers sell a commodity product to the companies in it.
- Substitute products are available for the items suppliers provide.
- Companies in the industry find it easy to switch from one supplier to another or to substitute products (i.e., "switching costs" are low).
- The items suppliers provide the industry account for a relatively small portion of the cost of the industry's finished products.

Bargaining Power of Buyers Just as suppliers to an industry can be a source of pressure, buyers also have the potential to can exert significant power over a business, making it less attractive. When the number of customers is small and the cost of switching to competitors' products is low, buyers' influence on companies is high. Famous for offering its customers low prices, Wal-Mart, the largest company in the world, is also well known for applying relentless pressure to its 21,000 suppliers for price concessions, which it almost always manages to get.[1] Generally, an industry is more attractive when the following conditions hold:

- Industry customers' "switching costs" to competitors' products or to substitutes are relatively high.
- The number of buyers in the industry is large.
- Customers demand products that are differentiated rather than purchase commodity products that they can obtain from any supplier (and subsequently can pit one company against another to drive down price).
- Customers find it difficult to gather information on suppliers' costs, prices, and product features—something that is becoming much easier for customers in many industries to do by using the World Wide Web.
- The items companies sell to the industry account for a relatively small portion of the cost of their customers' finished products.

Threat of New Entrants to the Industry The larger the pool of potential new entrants to an industry, the greater is the threat to existing companies in it. This is particularly true in industries in which the barriers to entry, such as capital requirements, specialized knowledge, access to distribution channels, and others, are low. Generally, an industry is more attractive to new entrants when the follow conditions hold:

- The advantages of economies of scale are absent. Economies of scale exist when companies in an industry achieve low average costs by producing huge volumes of items (e.g., computer chips).
- Capital requirements to enter the industry are low.
- Cost advantages are not related to company size.

- Buyers are not extremely brand-loyal, making it easier for new entrants to the industry to draw customers away from existing businesses.
- Governments, through their regulatory and international trade policies, do not restrict new companies from entering the industry.

Threat of Substitute Products or Services Substitute products or services can turn an entire industry on its head. For instance, many makers of glass bottles have closed their doors in recent years as their customers—from soft drink bottlers to ketchup makers—have switched to plastic containers, which are lighter, less expensive to ship, and less subject to breakage. Printed newspapers have seen their readership rates decline as new generations of potential readers turn to online sources of news that are constantly updated. Generally, an industry is more attractive when the following conditions hold:

- Quality substitute products are not readily available.
- The prices of substitute products are not significantly lower than those of the industry's products.
- Buyers' cost of switching to substitute products is high.

After surveying the power these five forces exert on an industry, entrepreneurs can evaluate the potential for their companies to generate reasonable sales and profits in a particular industry. In other words, they can answer the question, "Is this industry a good home for my business?" Table 4.1 provides a matrix that allows entrepreneurs to assign quantitative scores to the five forces influencing industry attractiveness. Note that the lower the score for an industry, the more attractive it is.

The next step in assessing an industry is to identify potentially attractive niches that exist in it. As you learned in Chapter 2, many small businesses prosper by sticking to niches in a market that are too small to attract the attention of large competitors. Occupying an industry niche enables a business to shield itself to some extent from the power of the five forces. The key questions entrepreneurs address here are, "Can we identify a niche that is large enough to produce a profit? Or can we position our company uniquely in the market to differentiate it from the competition in a meaningful way?"

TABLE 4.1 Five Forces Matrix

Assign a value to rate the importance of each of the five forces to the industry on a 1 (not important) to 5 (very important) scale. Then assign a value to reflect the threat that each force poses to the industry. Multiply the importance rating in column 2 by the threat rating in column 3 to produce a weighted score. Add the weighted scores in column 3 to get a total weighted score. This score measures the industry's attractiveness. The matrix is a useful tool for comparing the attractiveness of different industries.

Minimum Score = 5 (Very attractive)
Maximum Score = 125 (Very unattractive)

Force	Importance (1 to 5)*	Threat to Industry (1 to 5)**	Weighted Score Col 2 × Col 3
Rivalry among companies competing in the industry	5	5	25
Bargaining power of suppliers in the industry	2	2	4
Bargaining power of buyers	2	4	8
Threat of new entrants to the industry	3	4	12
Threat of substitute products or services	4	3	12
		Total	61

*Scale of importance from 1 = not important to 5 = very important. **Scale of threat to the industry from 1 = low, 3 = medium, to 5 = high.

Entrepreneurs who have designed successful focus or differentiation strategies for their companies can exploit these niches to their advantage.

Questions entrepreneurs should address in this portion of the feasibility analysis include the following:

- ■ Which niche in the market will we occupy?
- ■ How large is this market segment, and how fast is it growing?
- ■ What is the basis for differentiating our product or service from competitors?
- ■ Do we have a superior business model that will be difficult for competitors to reproduce?

In 1984, Michael Dell, founder of Dell Inc., created a superior business model that revolutionized the retail computer industry and toppled the industry leader, IBM, a company that many industry experts thought was invincible when it came to selling personal computers. Dell transformed the industry by designing a business model based on selling customized PCs directly to consumers without using retail outlets. The impact on the company's fortunes was significant; higher inventory turnover rates, increased customer satisfaction levels, and higher profit margins than the industry average were just some of the benefits Dell experienced. Dell's model really showed its muscle with the advent of the Web; today, Dell, the industry leader with nearly 35 percent market share in PCs, sells an average of $135 million worth of computers online each day![2]

COMPANY Profile

Dell Inc.

One technique for gauging the quality of a company's business model involves **business prototyping,** in which entrepreneurs test their business models on a small scale before committing serious resources to launch a business that might not work. Business prototyping recognizes that every business idea is a hypothesis that needs to be tested before an entrepreneur takes it to full scale. If the test supports the hypothesis and its accompanying assumptions, it is time to launch a company. If the prototype flops, the entrepreneur scraps the business idea with only minimal losses and turns to the next idea.

business prototyping
a process in which entrepreneurs test their business models on a small scale before committing serious resources to launch a business that might not work.

Before they launched Little Earth Productions, Inc., a company that makes distinctive fashion accessories such as belts, handbags, and wallets from recycled bottle caps, license plates, tires, hubcaps, and other items, entrepreneurs Ava DeMarco and Robert Brandegee used business prototyping to test their unique concept. "We had a gut feeling about recycled fashion accessories, and the research we did confirmed our instincts," says DeMarco. "Before we invested a lot of time and money, we took a look at the market to make certain we were targeting the right buyers and offering products they wanted and could afford." Their first move was to set up booths displaying their unique products at various arts and crafts festivals in their local community, Pittsburgh,

COMPANY Profile

Little Earth Productions Inc.

Before entrepreneurs Ava DeMarco and Robert Brandegee launched Little Earth Productions, Inc., a company that makes fashion accessories (such as this purse) from recycled license plates, bottle caps, hubcaps, and other material, they used business

prototyping to test their concept. The lessons they learned selling their products at arts and crafts festivals allowed them to hone their idea into a successful business.

Pennsylvania. They were able to get face to face with buyers, learn what appealed to them, and find out what they were like—all important steps to building a successful business. They learned, for instance, that their primary customers were people in their teens to mid-30s who appreciated the recycling aspect of the company's products but were more interested in its distinctive fashion-forward accessories. "It was a good way to watch people use our products," says DeMarco. "We also got a lot of good feedback on price and comments on how our products worked or didn't work for them." Using the information they had gathered from the festivals, DeMarco and Brandegee refined their business concept and rented a booth at a big industry trade show in Miami, where they came away with more than $24,000 worth of orders.[3]

The World Wide Web makes business prototyping practical, fast, and easy. Entrepreneurs can test their ideas by selling their products on established sites such as eBay or by setting up their own Web sites to gauge customers' response. Frank Ross, a home-based entrepreneur who dropped out of corporate America, operates three successful online businesses. Before launching them, however, he tested his business concepts on eBay. Ross explains:

> If you're considering selling a product line online as your home-based business, there is really no better place to test a market than eBay. It's considerable trouble to set up a Web site, and it can be expensive if your product fails. (I've made that mistake.) If you want to be sure you have a viable, salable product line prior to going to the trouble and expense of setting up a Web site, try selling on eBay. For the price of a few listings, you will be able to tell very quickly what kind of market you have for your potential Web store, and it may also help you weed out any problems you had not thought of.[4]

You Be the Consultant

A Circus Strategy

With its innovative, off-the-wall acts, dramatic staging, and talented staff of performers and engineers, Cirque du Soleil (French for "Circus of the Sun") has built a successful strategy that gives it a unique position in the entertainment market.

When visitors arrive at the company headquarters of Cirque du Soleil (French for "Circus of the Sun") in Montreal, Quebec, the 27-foot-long clown shoe is the first hint that the company it houses is quite unique. Indeed, Cirque du Soleil is one of the most successful entertainment companies in the world, and its success is due to the differentiation strategy that the company executes with the same precision that its world-class acrobats demonstrate in their performances. All 15 of the productions the company has created since its founding in 1984 have been huge successes, a particularly impressive record when considering the fact that 9 of 10 Broadway shows fail to earn back the money originally invested in them. Five Cirque shows tour the globe accompanied by their own custom-designed 2,500-seat tents; four others play in permanent locations in Las Vegas and Orlando. Even though ticket prices range from $45 to $150, Cirque manages to sell 97 percent of available seats for its shows. Although it uses the word "circus" in its name, Cirque is a far cry from the traditional traveling circus with its ringmaster, clowns, tightrope walkers, and daredevils. Cirque shows feature the same types of performers as traditional circuses, but it combines them in innovative, off-the-wall acts with New Age music, surreal costumes, and dazzling staging to create some of the most memorable and entertaining shows on the planet. For example, in its show called *O*, trapeze artists swing high above the stage before diving into a huge, 25-foot-deep on-stage lake that disappears in seconds with the help of a hydraulically powered pump designed by the company's team of talented engineers. Cirque du Soleil's strategy incorporates five key components that enable it to hold a unique position in the entertainment market:

1. ***Meticulous brand management.*** Cirque is a hotbed of creativity, and managers guard the brand carefully. Shows have a long gestation period (about three years) to ensure quality and distinctiveness. "Each show is a new member of the family, and we never want twins," says Daniel Gauthier, co-founder of Cirque.

2. ***Acquisition of world-class talent.*** At the heart of every show are the performers, and Cirque constantly patrols the world in search of the best. The company has 12 full-time talent scouts who travel the globe searching out performers whom they add to the company's database (the largest of its kind in the world) of 20,000 potential recruits. The scouts have recruited performers from such far-flung places as the Olympic games, the Moscow Circus school, a Mongolian elementary school, and the Imperial Orgy erotic arts festival in New York City.

3. ***Stringent cost control.*** Top managers meet with creative directors to set a budget and an opening date for each new show and then step back and let the directors work their creative magic. The directors can spend the budget—typically $10 to $25 million—in any way they choose, and company president Daniel Lamarre says that no director has ever come back to ask for more money. "Cirque allows you to approach shows with the artistic priority first," explains Franco Dragone, who led the creative teams for six of Cirque's nine current productions.

4. ***Investment in research and development (R&D).*** To make certain that its shows are different from those of other entertainment companies and stimulating to its target audience (which is very upscale, college-educated, and heavily populated by women), Cirque invests heavily in R&D. As a percentage of sales, the company spends on R&D twice what the average U.S. corporation spends, and it shows on stage—from the unusual props performers use and waterproof makeup invented by Cirque cosmetologists to the evaporating indoor lake and an elaborate on-stage blizzard. The technology keeps audiences mesmerized, wondering what is coming next.

5. ***Concerted efforts in opportunity recognition and strategic planning.*** Cirque managers intentionally have kept the company growing at a controlled pace. Building on the company's ability to transform itself in each of its unique shows, managers are considering expanding Cirque's circle of influence. "We define ourselves as a creative content provider," explains Lamarre. In the future, managers are planning to take Cirque's creative approach into new industries such as television, hotels, restaurants, and nightclubs. "Whether you are an innkeeper or a restaurateur, you are entertaining on some level," says Lyn Heward, president of the creative content division (and a former competitive gymnastics coach). Ideas being batted around for a Cirque resort include a Las Vegas resort that would feature New Age music, brightly colored furniture, and theatrical lighting throughout the building. Lamarre envisions jugglers serving as waiters. "We want to challenge our creative people to work in new mediums," he says.

Questions

1. How has Cirque du Soleil redefined the industry in which it competes with its differentiation strategy? What benefits does the company reap from having done so?

2. Use the Web to learn more about Cirque du Soleil's unique approach to the entertainment industry. Select one of the projects the company is considering as part of its strategy for the future (television show, hotel, restaurants, and nightclubs). Work with a team of your classmates to brainstorm ideas for applying Cirque's unique approach to entertainment to the project you selected.

3. How would you define the company's core competencies? Given these core competencies, can you spot other opportunities Cirque might be able to exploit?

4. What threats does the company's strategies pose?

Source: Adapted from Geoff Keighley, "The Phantasmagoria Factory," *Business 2.0*, January/February 2004, pp. 103–107.

Product or Service Feasibility Analysis

Once entrepreneurs discover that sufficient market potential for their product or service idea actually exists, they sometimes rush in with their exuberant enthusiasm ready to launch a business without actually considering whether they can actually produce the product or provide the service at a reasonable cost. A **product or service feasibility analysis** determines the degree to which a product or service idea appeals to potential customers and identifies the resources necessary to produce the product or provide the service. This portion of the feasibility analysis addresses two questions:

- Are customers willing to purchase our goods and services?
- Can we provide the product or service to customers at a profit?

To answer these questions, entrepreneurs need feedback from potential customers. Getting that feedback might involve engaging in primary research such as customer surveys and focus groups, gathering secondary customer research, building prototypes, and conducting in-home trials.

Conducting **primary research** involves collecting data first-hand and analyzing it; **secondary research** involves gathering data that have already been compiled and are available, often at a very reasonable cost or sometimes even free. In both types of research, gathering both quantitative and qualitative information is important to drawing accurate conclusions about a product's or service's market potential. Primary research techniques include the following:

Customer surveys and questionnaires. Keep them short. Word your questions carefully so that you do not bias the results, and use a simple ranking system (e.g., a 1-to-5 scale, with 1 representing "definitely would not buy" and 5 representing "definitely would buy"). Test your survey for problems on a small number of people before putting it to use. Web surveys are inexpensive, easy to conduct, and provide feedback fast. Monster.com, the online job search company, recently conducted an online survey of 30,000 customers and integrated the results from the survey into every aspect of the company's operation. "The survey results impact policy, process, product development and marketing efforts," says Chip Henry, Monster.com's, vice president, voice of the customer (note the unique job title). "There's nothing in the company that isn't touched as a result of the surveys."[5]

Focus groups. A **focus group** involves enlisting a small number of potential customers (usually 8 to 12) to give feedback on specific issues about a product or service (or the business idea itself). Listen carefully for what focus group members like and don't like about your product or service as they tell you what is on their minds. The founders of one small snack food company that produced apple chips conducted several focus groups to gauge customers' acceptance of the product and to guide many key business decisions, ranging from the product's name to its packaging. Once again, consider creating virtual focus groups on the Web; one small bicycle retailer conducts 10 online focus groups each year at virtually no cost and gains valuable marketing information from them. Feedback from online customers is fast, convenient, and real-time.

Secondary research, which is usually less expensive to collect than primary data, includes the following sources:

Trade associations and business directories. To locate a trade association, use *Business Information Sources* (University of California Press) or the *Encyclopedia of Associations* (Gale Research). To find suppliers, use *The Thomas Register of American Manufacturers* (Thomas Publishing Company) or *Standard and Poor's Register of Corporations, Executives, and Industries* (Standard and Poor Corporation). *The American Wholesalers and Distributors Directory* includes details on more than 18,000 wholesalers and distributors.

Direct mail lists. You can buy mailing lists for practically any type of business. *The Standard Rates and Data Service (SRDS) Directory of Mailing Lists* (Standard Rates and Data) is a good place to start looking.

product or service feasibility analysis
an analysis that determines the degree to which a product or service idea appeals to potential customers and indentifies the resources necessary to produce the product or provide the service.

primary research
information that an entrepreneur collects first-hand and analyzes.

secondary research
information that has already been compiled and is available for use, often at a very reasonable cost or sometimes even free.

focus group
a market research technique that involves enlisting a small number of potential customers (usually 8 to 12) to give feedback on specific issues about a product or service (or the business idea itself).

Demographic data. To learn more about the demographic characteristics of customers in general, use *The Statistical Abstract of the United States* (Government Printing Office). Profiles of more specific regions are available in *The State and Metropolitan Data Book* (Government Printing Office). *The Sourcebook of Zip Code Demographics* (CACI, Inc.) provides detailed breakdowns of the population in every zip code in the country. *Sales and Marketing Management's Survey of Buying Power* (Bill Communications) has statistics on consumer, retail, and industrial buying. *Demographics USA* provides users with one of the most extensive collections of demographic and marketing data available. It contains more than 1,700 pages of useful reports, which range from business characteristics and retail sales by merchandise line to buying power indices and detailed demographics by county and by zip code.

Census data. The Bureau of the Census publishes a wide variety of reports that summarize the wealth of data found in its census database, which is available at most libraries and at the Census Bureau's Web site (http://www.census.gov).

Forecasts. The *U.S. Global Outlook* traces the growth of 200 industries and gives a five-year forecast for each one. Many government agencies, including the Department of Commerce, offer forecasts on everything from interest rates to the number of housing starts. A government librarian can help you to find what you need.

Market research. Someone may already have compiled the market research you need. *The FINDex Worldwide Directory of Market Research Reports, Studies, and Surveys* (Cambridge Information Group) lists more than 10,600 studies available for purchase. Other directories of business research include *Simmons Study of Media and Markets* (Simmons Market Research Bureau Inc.) and the *A.C. Neilsen Retail Index* (A.C. Neilsen Company).

Articles. Magazine and journal articles pertinent to your business are a great source of information. Use the *Reader's Guide to Periodical Literature*, the *Business Periodicals Index* (similar to the *Reader's Guide* but focuses on business periodicals), and *Ulrich's Guide to International Periodicals* to locate the ones you need.

Local data. Your state department of commerce and your local chamber of commerce will very likely have useful data on the local market of interest to you. Call to find out what is available.

World Wide Web. Most entrepreneurs are astounded at the marketing information that is available on the World Wide Web (WWW). Using one of the search engines, you can gain access to a world of information—literally!

Prototypes One of the most effective ways to gauge the viability of a product is to build a prototype of it. A **prototype** is an original, functional model of a new product that entrepreneurs can put into the hands of potential customers so that they can see it, test it, and use it. Prototypes usually point out potential problems in a product's design, giving inventors the opportunity to fix them even before they put the prototype into customers' hands. The feedback customers give entrepreneurs based on prototypes often leads to design improvements and new features, some of which the entrepreneurs might never have discovered on their own. Makers of computer software frequently put prototypes of new products into customers' hands as they develop new products or improve existing ones. Known as *beta tests*, these trials result in an iterative design process in which software designers collect feedback from users and then incorporate their ideas into the product for the next round of tests.

prototype
an original, functional model of a new product that entrepreneurs can put into the hands of potential customers so they can see it, test it, and use it.

Entrepreneur Shawn Donegan teamed up with inventor Mike Puczkowski to launch Trac Tool Inc., a Cleveland, Ohio–based business that markets Speed Rollers, a paint application system aimed at professional paint contractors. Puczkowski's invention features an airless paint pump that feeds paint onto one of two rollers, eliminating the need to dip the rollers into a paint tray and making the system four to five times faster than using traditional rollers. Donegan and Puczkowski built several models of the system before they had a prototype that worked. Early prototypes pointed out several problems the

COMPANY
Profile

Trac Tool Inc.

entrepreneurs had to fix, including a valve that could handle only a fraction of the pressure that a typical airless system delivers and coupling joints that leaked paint. "Once we redesigned the components, we tested them thoroughly," says Donegan. "We wanted to ensure worker safety and product quality before proceeding." They used the prototype to conduct focus groups with paint contractors, industry experts, and property managers to get feedback on the product and its features. The response from the focus groups was very positive, leading Donegan and Puczkowski to launch Trac Tool Inc., which now generates more than $3 million in sales of the Speed Rollers system.[6]

Existing companies can benefit from creating prototypes as well. As their business grew, Ava DeMarco and Robert Brandegee, founders of Little Earth Productions, changed their approach to developing new products. "When we first started out, we designed new products two weeks before a trade show and hoped people would buy them," says DeMarco. Today, the company creates a small number of prototypes, places them in half a dozen or so retail stores, and tests customers' responses to them. "The feedback lets us know if we're on the right track with a new product before we invest time and money," explains DeMarco.[7]

In-Home Trials One technique that reveals some of the most insightful information into how customers actually use a product or service is also the most challenging to coordinate: in-home trials. An **in-home trial** involves sending researchers into customers' homes to observe them as they use the company's product or service.

in-home trial
a research technique that involves sending researchers into customers' homes to observe them as they use the company's product or service.

Intuit, the software company that produces popular programs such as Quicken, QuickBooks, and TurboTax, was one of the first companies to adopt in-home trials as part of its product development process in 1989. In the company's follow-me-home program, software engineers hang around a retail store, waiting for customers to buy an Intuit product. They then ask to go into customers' homes, where they watch how customers install and use the software and listen to their suggestions in a natural setting. Intuit has adapted the program to its call centers, where customers call with questions about Intuit software. Software managers and product engineers periodically sit at call center employees' desks, looking for ways to improve the employees' ability to serve customers more effectively. The company also combs through blogs and Intuit online communities, looking for comments and feedback about its software products. The process works; the latest version of Quicken included 121 customer-recommended improvements.[8]

Financial Feasibility Analysis

The final component of a feasibility analysis involves assessing the financial feasibility of a proposed business venture. At this stage of the process, a broad financial analysis is sufficient. If the business concept passes the overall feasibility analysis, an entrepreneur should conduct a more thorough financial analysis when creating a full-blown business plan. The major elements to be included in a financial feasibility analysis include the initial capital requirement, estimated earnings, and the resulting return on investment.

Capital Requirements Just as a Boy Scout needs fuel to start a fire, an entrepreneur needs capital to start a business. Some businesses require large amounts of capital, but others do not. Typically, service businesses require less capital to launch than manufacturing or retail businesses. Start-up companies often need capital to purchase equipment, buildings, technology, and other tangible assets as well as to hire and train employees, promote their products and services, and establish a presence in the market. A good feasibility analysis will provide an estimate of the amount of start-up capital an entrepreneur will need to get the business up and running. For instance, Shawn Donegan and Mike Puczkowski needed $150,000 to launch Trac Tool Inc. and bring the Speed Rollers paint system to market. They spent most of that start-up capital to develop and test the prototype and to introduce the product at the Painting and Decorating Contractors of America trade show.[9]

You will learn more about finding sources of business funding, both debt and equity, in Chapter 13, "Sources of Financing: Debt and Equity."

Estimated Earnings In addition to producing an estimate of the start-up company's capital requirements, an entrepreneur also should forecast the earning potential of the proposed business. Industry trade associations and publications such as the *RMA Annual Statement Studies* offer guidelines on preparing sales and earnings estimates. From these, entrepreneurs can estimate the financial results they and their investors can expect to see from the business venture.

Return on Investment The final aspect of the financial feasibility analysis combines the estimated earnings and the capital requirements to determine the rate of return the venture is expected to produce. One simple measure is the rate of return on the capital invested, which is calculated by dividing the estimated earnings the business yields by the amount of capital invested in the business. Although financial estimates at the feasibility analysis stage typically are rough, they are an important part of the entrepreneur's ultimate "go/no go" decision about the business ventures. A venture must produce an attractive rate of return relative to the level of risk it requires. This risk–return tradeoff means that the higher the level of risk a prospective business involves, the higher the rate of return it must provide to the entrepreneur and investors. Why should an entrepreneur take on all of the risks of starting and running a business that produces a mere three or four percent rate of return when he or she could earn that much in a risk-free investment at a bank or other financial institution? You will learn more about developing detailed financial forecasts for a business start-up in Chapter 11, "Creating a Successful Financial Plan."

Wise entrepreneurs take the time to subject their ideas to a feasibility analysis like the one described here, whatever outcome it produces. If the study suggests that transforming the idea into a viable business is not feasible, the entrepreneur can move on to the next idea, confident that he or she has not wasted valuable resources launching a business destined to fail. If the analysis shows that the idea has real potential as a profitable business, the entrepreneur can pursue it, using the information gathered during the feasibility analysis as the foundation for building a sound business plan. We now turn our attention to that process.

You Be the Consultant

How a Ruined Shirt Launched a Successful Venture

A simple trip to the dry cleaners changed Robert Byerley's career path. When the Dallas businessman picked up his clothes, he discovered that the cleaner had ruined one of his $100 dress shirts. He would have been satisfied if the owner of the cleaner had offered to replace his shirt, but he did not. He didn't even apologize to Byerley, and that's when Byerley decided to do something about it.

Although the Dallas market was crowded with dry cleaning establishments, Byerley left his corporate job to launch Bibbentuckers, a dry cleaning operation that offers Dallas residents better quality and better service at higher prices than other dry cleaning establishments. He suspected that a segment of the market would be willing to pay premium prices for a cleaner that offered convenient locations, superior quality and service, and extra amenities. Byerley didn't rely on his instincts alone, however. Before starting Bibbentuckers, Byerley did plenty of research and put together a business plan to guide his entrepreneurial venture.

He started with the vision he had for his business. One night when he couldn't sleep, Byerley began listing the characteristics he wanted his dry cleaners to exhibit. Based on his negative experience with his former dry cleaner, Byerley listed "standing behind our work" first. He listed nine other items, including a drive-up service with curbside delivery, a computerized system that would track clothes through the entire process and would use bar code scanners to read customers' cleaning preferences, and a cleaning process that used the most current, environmentally friendly equipment and materials.

The one item that was not on his list: low prices. "The things I wanted in a perfect dry cleaner were incompatible with a discount operation," he explains.

Byerley's next step was to research the industry and the market potential for his venture. He spent a solid week in the library, where he learned all about the dry cleaning industry, a $16 billion-a-year business dominated by small independent operators who competed primarily on the basis of price. He also discovered that dry cleaning establishments accounted for a large number of customer complaints with the Better Business Bureau. The number one complaint? "Cleaners didn't stand behind what they did," says Byerley with a smile. He also learned about legislation that was about to take effect that would change the way cleaners handled their cleaning solvents.

As he assembled his plan, Byerley realized he could use his environmentally friendly approach to cleaning as a marketing tool, something that very few operators were doing. He researched the existing competition in Dallas and discovered that several dry cleaners were taking a premium approach to the market. Realizing that he had to differentiate his business from his competitors, Byerley gave his outlets a unique and appealing design. The free-standing stores' professionally appointed décor included attractive awnings and drive-through lanes as well as television screens and free refreshments. "I wanted a place that people would feel comfortable leaving their best clothes, a place that paired five-star service with an establishment that didn't look like a dry cleaner," he says.

One key question to be answered, of course, was "Would customers be willing to pay for quality, service, and convenience?" To find out, Byerley hired a marketing firm and conducted focus groups of potential customers who discussed everything from the look of the company's buildings to its name. Byerley even took clothes to the 15 best cleaners in town and let the members of the focus groups critique them to learn exactly what customers' expectations were. His goal was to exceed their expectations.

After synthesizing all of his research into a plan, Byerley launched Bibbentuckers in the Dallas suburb of Plano. From his research, he knew that the typical dry cleaner generates $250,000 in revenue a year. Byerley knew his research and planning had paid off when his first store was on track to surpass $1 million in sales in its first year and began earning a profit after just four months. He opened two more stores before stepping out of the daily operation of the company to serve as chairman of the board. He is now involved in another business start-up, and he and his co-founders are taking the same fastidious approach to researching the industry and the business before they are ready to launch. In fact, a team of 13 people has already spent a year researching the venture to be sure they get it right the first time.

1. Why is it important for entrepreneurs to research their industry and markets before launching a business? Why do so many fail to do so?

2. Suppose that a close friend is considering launching a new restaurant (or some other type of business you choose). What type of research would you advise your friend to conduct? Where would you suggest your friend look for the information he or she needs?

3. Refer to Question 2. How would you advise your friend to get feedback from potential customers about his or her business concept?

Source: Adapted from Ann Zimmerman, "Do the Research," *Wall Street Journal*, May 9, 2005, pp. R3–R4.

Why Develop a Business Plan?

LEARNING OBJECTIVES
2. Explain why every entrepreneur should create a business plan, as well as the benefits of developing a plan.

business plan
a written summary of an entrepreneur's proposed business venture, its operational and financial details, its marketing opportunities and strategy, and its managers' skills and abilities.

Any entrepreneur who is in business or is about to launch a business needs a well-conceived and factually based business plan to increase the likelihood of success. For decades, research has proven that companies that engage in business planning outperform those that do not. Unfortunately, studies also show that small companies are especially lackadaisical in their approach to developing business plans. Many entrepreneurs never take the time to develop plans for their businesses; unfortunately, the implications of the lack of planning are all too evident in the high failure rates that small companies experience.

A **business plan** is a written summary of an entrepreneur's proposed business venture, its operational and financial details, its marketing opportunities and strategy, and its managers' skills and abilities. There is no substitute for a well-prepared business plan, and there are no shortcuts to creating one. The plan serves as an entrepreneur's road map on the journey toward building a successful business. It describes the direction the company is taking, what its goals are, where it wants to be, and how it's going to get there. The plan is written proof that an entrepreneur has performed the necessary research, has studied the business opportunity adequately, and is prepared to capitalize on it with a sound business model. In short, a business plan is an entrepreneur's best insurance against launching a business destined to fail or mismanaging a potentially successful company.

A business plan serves three essential functions. First and most important, it guides an entrepreneur by charting the company's future course of action and devising a strategy for success. The plan provides a battery of tools—a mission statement, goals, objectives, market analysis, budgets, financial forecasts, target markets, and strategies—to help entrepreneurs lead a company successfully. It gives managers and employees a sense of direction, but only if everyone is involved in creating, updating, or altering it. As more team members become committed to making the plan work, the plan takes on special meaning. It gives everyone targets to shoot for, and it provides a yardstick for measuring actual performance against those targets, especially in the crucial and chaotic start-up phase. Creating a plan also forces entrepreneurs to subject their ideas to the test of reality. Can this business idea actually produce a profit?

The second function of the business plan is to attract lenders and investors. Too often small business owners approach potential lenders and investors without having prepared to sell themselves and their business concept. Simply scribbling a few rough figures on a note pad to support a loan application is not enough. Applying for loans or attempting to attract investors without a solid business plan rarely attracts needed capital. Rather, the best way to secure the necessary capital is to prepare a sound business plan, which enables an entrepreneur to communicate to potential lenders and investors the potential the business opportunity offers. Entrepreneurs must pay attention to details because they are germane to their sales presentations to potential lenders and investors. The quality of the firm's business plan weighs heavily in the decision to lend or invest funds. It is also potential lenders' and investors' first impression of the company and its managers. Therefore, the finished product should be highly polished and professional in both form and content.

A business plan must prove to potential lenders and investors that a venture will be able to repay loans and produce an attractive rate of return. Entrepreneur and author Neal Stephenson, who started several high-tech companies before focusing on a writing career, explains his experience writing a business plan:

> As I was trying to write my plan, something came into focus for me that should have been obvious from the very beginning. I was proposing to borrow a lot of money from strangers and gamble it on doing something. If it didn't work, these people would lose their money, which is a very sobering prospect. It really shakes you up and makes you think very hard about what it is you are doing . . . . We're using other people's real money, and those people could get hurt.[10]

Building a plan forces a potential entrepreneur to look at his or her business idea in the harsh light of reality. It also requires the entrepreneur to assess the venture's chances of success more objectively. A well-assembled plan helps prove to outsiders that a business idea can be successful. To get external financing, an entrepreneur's plan must pass three tests with potential lenders and investors: (1) the reality test, (2) the competitive test, and (3) the value test. The first two tests have both an external and an internal component:

Reality test. The external component of the reality test revolves around proving that a market for the product or service really does exist. It focuses on industry attractiveness, market niches, potential customers, market size, degree of competition, and similar factors. Entrepreneurs who pass this part of the reality test prove in the marketing portion of their business plan that there is strong demand for their business idea.

The internal component of the reality test focuses on the product or service itself. Can the company *really* build it for the cost estimates in the business plan? Is it truly different from what competitors are already selling? Does it offer customers something of value?

Competitive test. The external part of the competitive test evaluates the company's relative position to its key competitors. How do the company's strengths and weaknesses match up with those of the competition? Do these reactions threaten the new company's success and survival?

The internal competitive test focuses on management's ability to create a company that will gain an edge over existing rivals. To pass this part of the competitive test, a plan must prove the quality, skill, and experience of the venture's management team. What other resources does the company have that can give it a competitive edge in the market?

Value test. To convince lenders and investors to put their money into the venture, a business plan must prove to them that it offers a high probability of repayment or an attractive rate of return. Entrepreneurs usually see their businesses as good investments because they consider the intangibles of owning a business—gaining control over their own destinies, freedom to do what they enjoy, and other factors; lenders and investors, however, look at a venture in colder terms: dollar-for-dollar returns. A plan must convince lenders and investors that they will earn an attractive return on their money.

The same business basics that investors have employed for decades to evaluate the financial potential of a new venture are still valid today, although during the dot-com craze in the late 1990s, many entrepreneurs and investors lost site of the importance of practical, profitable business models. The collapse of many of those dot-com companies at the beginning of the twenty-first century proved that unrealistic "smoke and mirror" assumptions are no substitute for sound business basics. "Those businesses had full tech staffs and fat marketing budgets," says one business writer, "but a lot of them went belly up because their business plans were no better than the Titanic's plans for dealing with icebergs."[11]

Today what matters most are realistic financial projections based on research and reasonable assumptions. A new venture must have both a long-term strategic vision and a practical focus on operations. In their business plans, entrepreneurs must be able to communicate clearly an understanding of the following issues:

- Cost of raw materials and supplies
- Unit labor costs
- Market-determined selling prices and gross profit margins
- Break-even point for their businesses[12]

Sometimes the greatest service a business plan provides an entrepreneur is the realization that "it just won't work." The time to find out a potential business idea won't succeed is in the planning stages *before* an entrepreneur commits significant resources to a venture. In other cases it reveals important problems to overcome before launching a company.

The real value in preparing a business plan is not so much in the plan itself as it is in the *process* an entrepreneur goes through to create the plan. Although the finished product is useful, the process of building a plan requires an entrepreneur to subject his or her idea to an objective, critical eva
her company, its target market, its
essential to making the venture a su
replace "I think's" with more "I know
cheaper than making them in reality.
risk and uncertainty in launching a c
right way!

Third, a business plan is a reflec
entrepreneur has thought seriously a
Preparing a solid plan demonstrates tl
the idea to paper. Building a plan also
tive and the negative aspects of the bu
ness plan makes a positive first impre:
lenders and investors read a business

behind it. Sophisticated investors will not take the time to meet with an entrepreneur whose business plan fails to reflect a serious investment of time and energy. They know that an entrepreneur who lacks this discipline to develop a good business plan likely lacks the discipline to run a business.

The business plan should reflect the fire and passion an entrepreneur has for the venture. For this reason an entrepreneur cannot allow others to prepare the business plan for him or her because outsiders cannot understand the business nor envision the proposed company as well as the entrepreneur can. The entrepreneur is the driving force behind the business idea and is the one who can best convey the vision and the enthusiasm he or she has for transforming that idea into a successful business. In addition, because the entrepreneur will make the presentation to potential lenders and investors, he or she must understand every detail of the business plan. Otherwise, an entrepreneur cannot present it convincingly, and in most cases the financial institution or investor will reject it. Investors want to feel confident that an entrepreneur has realistically evaluated the risk involved in the new venture and has a strategy for addressing it. Furthermore, as you can expect, they also want to see proof that a business will be profitable and produce a reasonable return on their investment.

Perhaps the best way to understand the need for a business plan is to recognize the validity of the "two-thirds rule," which says that only two-thirds of the entrepreneurs with a sound and viable new business venture will find financial backing. Those who do find financial backing will only get two-thirds of what they initially requested, and it will take them two-thirds longer to get the financing than they anticipated. The most effective strategy for avoiding the two-thirds rule is to build a business plan!

The Elements of a Business Plan

LEARNING OBJECTIVES
3. Describe the elements of a solid business plan.

Smart entrepreneurs recognize that every business plan is unique and must be tailor-made. They avoid the off-the-shelf, "cookie-cutter" approach that produces look-alike plans. The elements of a business plan may be standard, but the way entrepreneurs tell their stories should be unique and reflect their enthusiasm for the new venture. If this is a first attempt at writing a business plan, it may be very helpful to seek the advice of individuals with experience in this process. Accountants, business professors, attorneys, and consultants with Small Business Development Centers can be excellent sources of advice in creating and refining a plan. (For a list of Small Business Development Center locations, see the Small Business Administration's Web SBDC Web page at http://www.sba.gov/SBDC/.) Entrepreneurs also can use business planning software available from several companies to create their plans. Some of the most popular programs include Business Plan Pro (Palo Alto Software), BizPlan Builder (Jian Tools), PlanMaker (Power Solutions for Business), and Plan Write (Business Resources Software). These planning packages help entrepreneurs to organize the material they have researched and gathered, and they provide helpful tips on plan writing and templates for creating financial statements. These planning packages produce professional-looking business plans, but entrepreneurs who use them face one drawback: the plans they produce often look the same, as if they came from the same mold. That can be a turn-off for professional investors, who see hundreds of business plans each year.

Initially, the prospect of writing a business plan may appear to be overwhelming. Many entrepreneurs would rather launch their companies and "see what happens" than invest the necessary time and energy defining and researching their target markets, defining their strategies, and mapping out their finances. After all, building a plan is hard work! However, it is hard work that pays many dividends, not all of which are immediately apparent. Entrepreneurs who invest their time and energy in building plans are better prepared to face the hostile environment in which their companies will compete than those who do not. Earlier, we said that a business plan is like a road map that guides an entrepreneur on the journey to building a successful business. If you were making a journey to a particular destination through unfamiliar, harsh, and dangerous territory, would you rather ride with someone equipped with a road map and a trip itinerary or with someone who didn't believe in road maps or in planning trips, destinations, and layovers? Although building a business plan does not *guarantee* success, it *does* raise an entrepreneur's chances of succeeding in business.

A business plan typically ranges from 25 to 40 pages in length. Shorter plans usually are too sketchy to be of any value, and those much longer than this run the risk of never getting used or read! This section explains the most common elements of a business plan. However, entrepreneurs must recognize that, like every business venture, every business plan is unique. An entrepreneur should view the following elements as a starting point for building a plan and should modify them as needed to better tell the story of his or her new venture.

Title Page and Table of Contents

A business plan is a professional document and should contain a title page with the company's name, logo, and address as well as the names and contact information of the company founders. Many entrepreneurs also include on the title page the copy number of the plan and the date on which it was issued.

Business plan readers appreciate a table of contents that includes page numbers so that they can locate the particular sections of the plan in which they are most interested.

Executive Summary

To summarize the presentation to each potential financial institution or investors, the entrepreneur should write an executive summary. It should be concise—a maximum of two pages—and should summarize all of the relevant points of the business venture. The executive summary is a synopsis of the entire plan, capturing its essence in a capsulized form. It should briefly describe the following:

- The company's business model and the basis for its competitive edge.
- The company's target market(s) and the benefits its products or services will provide customers.
- The qualifications of the founders and key employees.
- The key financial highlights (e.g., sales and earnings projections, capital required, rates of return on the investment, and when any loans will be repaid).

The executive summary is a written version of what is known as "the elevator pitch." Imagine yourself on an elevator with a potential lender or investor. Only the two of you are on the elevator, and you have that person's undivided attention for the duration of the ride, but the building is not very tall! To convince the investor that your business is a great investment, you must boil your message down to its essence—key points that you can communicate in just a matter of one or two minutes.

The executive summary *must* capture the reader's attention. If it misses the mark, the chances of the remainder of the plan being read are minimal. A well-developed, coherent summary introducing the financial proposal establishes a favorable first impression of the entrepreneur and the business and can go a long way toward obtaining financing. Although the executive summary is the first part of the business plan, it should be the last section written.

Vision and Mission Statement

As you learned in Chapter 3, a mission statement expresses in words an entrepreneur's vision for what his or her company is and what it is to become. It is the broadest expression of a company's purpose and defines the direction in which it will move. It anchors a company in reality and serves as the thesis statement for the entire business plan. Every good plan captures an entrepreneur's passion and vision for the business, and the mission statement is the ideal place to express them.

Company History

The owner of an existing small business who is creating a business plan should prepare a brief history of the operation, highlighting the significant financial and operational events in the company's life. This section should describe when and why the company was formed, how it has evolved over time, and what the owner envisions for the future. It should highlight the successful accomplishment of past objectives such as developing prototypes, earning patents, achieving market-share targets, or securing long-term customer contracts. This section also should describe the company's current image in the marketplace.

Business and Industry Profile

To acquaint lenders and investors with the industry in which a company competes, an entrepreneur should describe it in the business plan. This section should provide the reader with an overview of the industry or market segment in which the new venture will operate. Industry data such as market size, growth trends, and the relative economic and competitive strength of the major firms in the industry all set the stage for a better understanding of the viability of the new product or service. Strategic issues such as ease of market entry and exit, the ability to achieve economies of scale or scope, and the existence of cyclical or seasonal economic trends further help readers to evaluate the new venture. This part of the plan also should describe significant industry trends and key success factors as well as an overall outlook for its future. Information about the evolution of the industry helps the reader to comprehend its competitive dynamics. The *U.S. Industrial Outlook Handbook* is an excellent reference that profiles a variety of industries and offers projections for future trends in them. Another useful resource of industry and economic information is the *Summary of Commentary on Current Economic Conditions*, more commonly known as the Beige Book. Published eight times a year by the Federal Reserve, the Beige Book provides detailed statistics and trends in key business sectors and in the overall economy. It offers valuable information on topics ranging from tourism and housing starts to consumer spending and wage rates. Entrepreneurs can find this wealth of information at their fingertips on the Web at http://www.federalreserve.gov/FOMC/BeigeBook/2005/.

This portion of the plan also should describe the existing and anticipated profitability of the industry. Any significant entry or exit of firms or consolidations and mergers should be discussed in terms of their impact on the competitive behavior of the market. The entrepreneur also should mention any events that have significantly affected the industry in the last 10 years.

This section should contain a statement of the company's general business goals and then work down to a narrower definition of its immediate objectives. Together they should spell out what the business plans to accomplish and how, when, and who will do it. **Goals** are broad, long-range statements of what a company plans to achieve in the future that guide its overall direction. In other words, they address the question, "What do I want my company to look like in three to five years?"

Objectives, on the other hand, are short-term, specific performance targets that are attainable, measurable, and controllable. Every objective should reflect some general business goal and should include a technique for measuring progress toward its accomplishment. To be meaningful, an objective must have a time frame for achievement. Both goals and objectives should relate to the company's basic mission (see Figure 4.3).

Business Strategy

Another important part of a business plan is the owner's view of the strategy needed to meet—and beat—the competition. In the previous section, the entrepreneur defined *where* to take the business by establishing goals and objectives. This section addresses the question of *how* to get there—business strategy. Here an entrepreneur must explain how he or she plans to gain a competitive edge in the market and what sets the business apart from the competition. The entrepreneur should comment on how he or she plans to achieve business goals and objectives in the face of competition and government regulation and should identify the image that the business will try to project. An important theme in this section is what makes the company unique in the eyes of its customers. One of the quickest routes to business failure is trying to sell "me-too" products or services that offer customers nothing new, better, bigger, faster, more convenient, or different from existing products or services.

goals
broad, long-range statements of what a company plans to achieve in the future that guide its overall direction.

objectives
short-term specific performance targets that are attainable, measurable, and controllable.

FIGURE 4.3

The Relationships among Mission, Goal, and Objectives

COMPANY Profile

First Penthouse

After moving to London, entrepreneurs Annika and Håkan Olsson came up with the idea of adding modular penthouses to existing flat-roof buildings. Building a business plan convinced the couple that a market existed for their unique product, one that adds value for both landlords and tenants.

While renovating their top-floor apartment in Stockholm, Sweden, civil engineers Håkan and Annika Olsson came up with a unique idea for creating high-quality modular penthouses that could be manufactured in factories and installed atop existing flat-roof buildings. When the couple moved to London, they purchased aerial photographs of the city and marked all of the flat-roof buildings in red ink. "We knew we had a good business idea when the whole picture was red," says Håkan. After conducting more research and building a business plan, the Olssons launched First Penthouse, a company specializing in rooftop development. Their business model adds value both for tenants, who get ritzy penthouse living quarters where none existed before, and for landlords, whose property values are enhanced by the addition of the modular penthouses. First Penthouse offers the convenience of one-day installation of its penthouses and guarantees no disturbances to existing residents. Like most entrepreneurs, the Olssons had to overcome obstacles, including banks that were hesitant to extend credit "because the idea was so new," says Håkan. (To get the capital they needed, the Olssons used angel financing, a topic you will learn more about in Chapter 13, when they convinced a wealthy friend to put up most of the $400,000 they needed to create and install the first penthouse.) To convince balking regulators, the Olssons agreed to use special "quiet" tools and to place soundproof mats over the roofs on which they worked. Sales of the company's penthouses are growing, and the Olssons are planning to take their concept into other large urban markets around the world, including New York City.[13]

The strategy section of the business plan should outline the methods the company can use to satisfy the key success factors required to thrive in the industry. If, for example, a strong, well-trained sales force is considered critical to success, the owner must devise a plan of action for assembling one. The foundation for this part of the business plan comes from the material in Chapter 3, "Designing a Competitive Business Model and Building a Solid Strategic Plan."

Description of the Firm's Product or Service

An entrepreneur should describe the company's overall product line, giving an overview of how customers use its goods or services. Drawings, diagrams, and illustrations may be required if the product is highly technical. It is best to write product and service descriptions in a jargon-free style so that laypeople can understand them. A statement of a product's position in the product life cycle might also be helpful. An entrepreneur should include a summary of any patents, trademarks, or copyrights protecting the product or service from infringement by competitors. Finally, it is helpful provide an honest comparison the company's product or service with those of competitors, citing specific advantages or improvements that make the company's goods or services unique and indicating plans for creating the next generation of goods and services that will evolve from the present product line.

The emphasis of this section should be on defining the unique characteristics of the company's products or services and the *benefits* customers get by purchasing them, rather than on just a "nuts and bolts" description of the *features* of those products or services. A **feature** is a descriptive fact about a product or service ("An ergonomically designed, more comfortable handle"). A **benefit** is what a customer gains from the product or service feature ("Fewer problems with carpal tunnel syndrome and increased productivity"). Advertising legend Leo Burnett once said, "Don't tell the people how good you make the goods; tell them how good your goods make them." This part of the plan must describe how a business will transform tangible product or service *features* into important, but often intangible, customer *benefits*—for example, lower energy bills, faster access to the Internet, less time writing checks to pay monthly bills, greater flexibility in building floating structures, shorter time required to learn a foreign language, or others. Remember: Customers buy benefits, *not* product or service features.

feature
a descriptive fact about a product or service.

benefit
what a customer gains from the product or service.

Manufacturers should describe their production process, strategic raw materials required, sources of supply they will use, and their costs. They should also summarize the production method and illustrate the plant layout. If the product is based on a patented or proprietary process, a description (including diagrams, if necessary) of its unique market advantages is helpful. It is also helpful to explain the company's environmental impact and how the entrepreneur plans to mitigate any negative environmental consequences the process may produce.

As the value of the automobiles Americans drive has increased, so has their desire to maintain the value of their cars by keeping them showroom clean. Some 75,000 car washes operate across the United States, but they vary drastically in terms of service and quality. Matthew Lieb and Chris Jones saw the opportunity to offer a superior car wash service and created Swash, a state-of-the art, no-muss, no-fuss car wash in which customers select the services they want to purchase at an ATM-like machine and remain in their comfort of their vehicles. Cleaning services are delivered by software-controlled equipment that never lays a brush on the car and the process is environmentally friendly from start to finish—all in just five minutes.[14]

COMPANY
Profile

Swash

Stressing unique features such as these to investors can help to differentiate a product or process from those of competitors.

Marketing Strategy

One crucial concern of entrepreneurs and the potential lenders and investors who finance their companies is whether there is a real market for the proposed good or service. Every entrepreneur must therefore describe the company's target market and its characteristics. Defining the target market and its potential is one of the most important—and most challenging—parts of building a business plan. Creating a successful business depends on an entrepreneur's ability to attract real customers who are willing and able to spend real money to buy its products or services. Perhaps the worst marketing error an entrepreneur can commit is failing to define his or her target market and trying to make the business "everything to everybody." Small companies usually are much more successful when focusing on a specific market niche where they can excel at meeting customers' special needs or wants.

One technique for identifying potential target markets is to list all of the features your company's product or service provides and then translate those features into a list of benefits (refer to the previous section). The next step is to develop a list of the types of people who need or could use those benefits. Be creative, and let your mind roam free. Once you have identified potential target markets, you can begin to research them to narrow the list down to the most promising one or two. Those are the markets your company should pursue.

One growing and evolving target market for small businesses is teenagers. By 2010, the number of teens will grow to 35 million (that's nearly 12 percent of the U.S. population), but even more important than their numbers is this group's purchasing power. According to Teenage Research Unlimited, teens spend $170 billion a year, an amount larger than the gross domestic products of Finland, Portugal, and Greece![15] Because they are not tied down with mortgage and car payments, most of teenagers' spending is discretionary, an appealing fact for many savvy entrepreneurs looking to connect with this target market. The teen market also is important to businesses because teenagers exert strong influence over family purchases and tend to be early adopters of products and services that set societal trends. (Who were the early adopters of iPods? Teens.) "Young consumers are a very important market," explains Mike Gatti, a top manager at the Retail Advertising and Marketing Association. "Young people have their own money and make their own buying decisions, and they are growing more important as society changes. Parents are getting more time starved, and they treat their children more like adults than previous generations of parents did."[16]

Firefly Mobile, a cell phone company based in Lincolnshire, Illinois, markets its Firefly cell phone squarely at kids, billing it as "the mobile phone for mobile kids." Recognizing that kids today could use cell phones to keep in touch with the important people in their lives, company founder Don Deubler came up with the idea for a cell phone tailored specifically for kids, one that is easier to use than a cell phone designed for adults and would give parents more control over its use. Working directly with kids, Deubler came up with a clever design. For instance, the Firefly has no keypad like a traditional cell phone. Instead, it has just five simple buttons, and parents can program the phone to make and accept calls for up to 20 numbers of their choice (avoiding teenage pranks such as calling Australia to see what the temperature is). The Firefly is proving to be popular with dual-career couples with hectic schedules and with parents who are concerned about their children's safety. To make the phone appealing to the kids using it, Firefly has incorporated cool colors, lights, sounds, and animations (with input from customers) into its design.[17]

Defining a company's target market involves using the techniques described in more detail in Chapter 8, "Building a Powerful Marketing Plan," but a business plan should address the following questions:

- Who are my target customers (age, gender, income level, and other demographic characteristics)?
- Where do they live, work, and shop?
- How many potential customers are in my company's trading area?
- Why do they buy? What needs and wants drive their purchase decisions?
- What can my business do to meet those needs and wants better than my competitors?
- Knowing my customers needs, wants, and habits, what should be the basis for differentiating my business in their minds?

Proving that a profitable market exists involves two steps: showing customer interest and documenting market claims.

Showing Customer Interest An entrepreneur must be able to prove that his or her target customers need or want his or her good or service and are willing to pay for it. Two of the most reliable techniques involve building a working prototype of a product so that customers can see how it works and producing a small number of products so that customers can actually use them. An entrepreneur might offer a prototype or an actual product to several potential customers to get written testimonials and evaluations to show investors. Another way to get useful feedback is to sell the product to several customers at a discount. This would prove that there are potential customers for the product and would allow demonstrations of the product in operation. Getting a product into customers' hands early in the process is also an excellent way to get valuable feedback that can lead to significant design improvements and increased sales down the road.

Documenting Market Claims Too many business plans rely on vague generalizations such as, "This market is so huge that if we get just 1 percent of it, we will break even in 8 months." Statements such as this are not backed by facts and usually reflect an entrepreneur's unbridled optimism. In most cases, they are also unrealistic! Market share determination is not obtained by a "shoot from the hip" generalization; on the contrary, sophisticated investors expect to see research that supports the claims an entrepreneur makes about the market potential of a product or service.

Providing facts about the sales potential of a product or service requires market research. Results of market surveys, customer questionnaires, and demographic studies lend credibility to an entrepreneur's frequently optimistic sales projections. (You will learn more about market research techniques and resources in Chapter 8, "Building a Powerful Marketing Plan.")

To gather data for their business plan, Joe Robertson and Dave Dudley decided to put their invention, the Spin Clean, a device that uses water pressure to clean swimming pool filters quickly and easily, into customers' hands and get their responses. After refining the design with several prototypes, Robertson and Dudley built a small number of the products and convinced seven nearby pool supply stores to carry them. The Spin Clean sold out quickly, and the entrepreneurs had the facts to prove that their product had real sales potential.[18]

One of the goals of this section of the business plan is to lay the foundation for the financial forecasts that come later in the plan. A start-up company's financial forecasts must be based on more than just wishful thinking. As much as possible, they should be built on research and facts. Many entrepreneurs build financial models for their potential business by applying information collected from trade or professional associations, local chambers of commerce, articles in magazines and newspapers, market studies conducted by themselves or others, government agencies, and, of course, the Web. With the availability of this volume of information, the sales, cost, and net income projections in a business plan should be a great deal more accurate than sketchy estimates scribbled on the backs of napkins.

This section of the business plan should address the following topics:

Advertising. Once an entrepreneur defines her or his company's target market, she or he can design a promotion and advertising campaign to reach those customers most effectively and efficiently. Which media are most effective in reaching the target market? How will they be used? How much will the promotional campaign cost? How can the company benefit from publicity?

Market size and trend. How large is the potential market? Is it growing or shrinking? Why? Are the customer's needs changing? Are sales seasonal? Is demand tied to another product or service?

Location. For many businesses, choosing the right location is a key success factor. For retailers, wholesalers, and service companies, the best location usually is one that is most convenient to their target customers. By combining census data and other market research with digital mapping software, entrepreneurs can locate sites with the greatest concentrations of their customers and the least interference from competitors. Which specific sites put the company in the path of its target customers? Do zoning regulations restrict the use of the site? For manufacturers, the location issue often centers on finding a site near its key raw materials or near its major customers. Using demographic reports and market research to screen potential sites takes the guesswork out of choosing the ideal location for a business.

Pricing. What does the product or service cost to produce or deliver? What is the company's overall pricing strategy? What image is the company trying to create in the market? Will the planned price support the company's strategy and desired image? (See Figure 4.4.) Can it produce a profit? How does the planned price compare to those of similar products or services? Are customers willing to pay it? What price tiers

FIGURE 4.4

The Links among Pricing, Perceived Quality, and Company Image

exist in the market? How sensitive are customers to price changes? Will the business sell to customers on credit? Will it accept credit cards?

Distribution. How will the product or service be distributed? What is the average sale? How many sales calls does it take to close a sale? What are the incentives for salespeople? What can the company do to make it as easy as possible for customers to buy?

This portion of the plan also should describe the channels of distribution that the business will use (mail, in-house sales force, sales agent, retailers). The owner should summarize the firm's overall pricing and promotion strategies, including the advertising budget, media used, and publicity efforts. The company's warranties and guarantees for its products and services should be addressed as well.

Competitor Analysis

An entrepreneur should discuss the new venture's competition. Failing to assess competitors realistically makes entrepreneurs appear to be poorly prepared, naive, or dishonest, especially to potential lenders and investors. An analysis of each significant competitor should be presented. Entrepreneurs who believe they have no competitors are only fooling themselves and are raising a huge red flag to potential lenders and investors. Gathering information on competitors' market shares, products, and strategies is usually not difficult. Trade associations, customers, industry journals, marketing representatives, and sales literature are valuable sources of data. This section of the plan should focus on demonstrating that the entrepreneur's company has an advantage over its competitors. Who are the company's key competitors? What are their strengths and weaknesses? What are their strategies? What images do they have in the marketplace? How successful are they? What distinguishes the entrepreneur's product or service from others already on the market, and how will these differences produce a competitive edge? This section of the plan should demonstrate that the firm's strategies are customer focused.

Paper Mojo

Frustrated with her job as a Web-site designer, Shelly Gardner-Alley decided to launch an e-commerce business with her husband. The couple did not have a particular product in mind, so they invested considerable time in researching markets that would be most suitable for e-commerce and would allow them to differentiate their business from the competition. They finally settled on an online business selling high-end, decorative paper from all over the world—ranging from silk paper from Japan to translucent vellum from France—at prices ranging from $2 to $16 per sheet. Before launching their business, Paper Mojo, one of their first tasks was to study their competition. Gardner-Alley discovered that most companies lacked extensive product lines, and she decided to use that as one differentiating point for her business. As a former Web-site designer, Gardner-Alley also noted that the few companies that did have broad product lines suffered from poorly designed Web sites that made shopping a chore for customers. A well-designed Web site that would be easy to navigate became another basis for differentiating her company from the competition. Paper Mojo's sales took off after Gardner-Alley submitted the site to search engine Yahoo!, which featured the new business in a newsletter. Gardner-Alley's extensive research and the decision to build her business model on a platform of outperforming the competition in ways that directly benefit customers are paying off.[19]

Description of the Management Team

The most important factor in the success of a business venture is the quality of its management, and financial officers and investors weigh heavily the ability and experience of the company's managers in their financing decisions. Thus, a plan should describe the qualifications of business officers, key directors, and any person with at least 20 percent ownership in the company. *Remember: Lenders and investors prefer experienced managers.*

A management team with industry experience and a proven record of success goes a long way in adding credibility to the new venture.

When Jason Henry, Anil Nair, and Heath Seymour wrote the business plan for their company, Inkwell Fine Arts, LLC, a company that sells customized, high-quality art prints to interior designers over the Web, they emphasized the diverse and complementary backgrounds of their management team as well as their business experience. Seymour, an artist, manages the artistic and creative aspects of the business, Henry handles daily operations, and Nair oversees the Web site and the information technology components. With the three founders working in tandem, Inkwell Fine Arts is able to offer interior designers prints made to their specifications—the exact size, colors, and medium they need to decorate a client's living or work space.[20]

Inkwell Fine Arts, LLC

Résumés in a plan should summarize each key person's education, work history (emphasizing managerial responsibilities and duties), and relevant business experience. When compiling a personal profile, an entrepreneur should review the primary reasons for small business failure (refer to Chapter 1) and show how the management team will use its skills and experience to avoid them. Entrepreneurs should not cover up previous business failure, however. Failing in business no longer has a terrible stigma attached to it. In fact, many investors are suspicious of entrepreneurs who have never experienced a business failure.

When considering investing in a business, lenders and investors look for the experience, talent, and integrity of the people who will breathe life into the plan. This portion of the plan should show that the company has the right people organized in the right fashion for success. One experienced private investor advises entrepreneurs to remember the following:

- Ideas and products don't succeed; people do. Show the strength of your management team. A top-notch management team with variety of proven skills is crucial.
- Show the strength of key employees and how you will retain them. Most small companies cannot pay salaries that match those at large businesses, but stock options and other incentives can improve employee retention.
- A board of directors or advisers consisting of industry experts lends credibility and can enhance the value of the management team.[21]

Plan of Operation

To complete the description of the business, the owner should construct an organizational chart identifying the business's key jobs and the qualifications of the people occupying them. Assembling a management team with the right stuff is difficult, but keeping it together until the company is established may be harder. Thus, the entrepreneur should describe briefly the steps taken to encourage important officers to remain with the company. Employment contracts, shares of ownership, and perks are commonly used to keep and motivate such employees.

Finally, a description of the form of ownership (partnership, joint venture, S Corporation, LLC) and of any leases, contracts, and other relevant agreements pertaining to the business is helpful. (You will learn more about this topic in Chapter 5, "Forms of Business Ownership.")

Pro Forma (Projected) Financial Statements

One of the most important sections of the business plan is an outline of the proposed company's financial statements—the "dollars and cents" of the proposed venture. In fact, one survey found that 74 percent of bankers say that financial documentation is the most important aspect of a business plan for entrepreneurs seeking loans.[22] For an existing business, lenders and investors use past financial statements to judge the health of the company and its ability to repay loans or generate adequate returns; therefore, an owner should supply copies of the firm's financial statements from the last three years. Ideally, these statements should be audited by a certified public accountant because most financial institutions prefer that extra reliability, although a financial review of the statements by an accountant sometimes may be acceptable.

Whether assembling a plan for an existing business or for a start-up, an entrepreneur should carefully prepare monthly projected (or pro forma) financial statements for the operation for the next year (and for two more years by quarter) using past operating data, published statistics, and research to derive three sets of forecasts of the income statement, balance sheet, cash forecast (always!), and a schedule of planned capital expenditures. (You will learn more about creating projected financial statements in Chapter 11, "Creating a Successful Financial Plan.") The forecasts should cover pessimistic, most likely, and optimistic conditions to reflect the uncertainty of the future. When in doubt, be up front and include some contingencies for any costs that you are unsure about.

It is essential that all three sets of forecasts be realistic. Entrepreneurs must avoid the tendency to "fudge the numbers" just to make their businesses look good. Lenders and investors compare these projections against published industry standards and can detect unrealistic forecasts. In fact, some venture capitalists automatically discount an entrepreneur's financial projections by as much as 50 percent. After completing these forecasts, an entrepreneur should perform a break-even analysis and a ratio analysis on the projected figures.

It is also important to include a statement of the *assumptions* on which these financial projections are based. Potential lenders and investors want to know how an entrepreneur derived forecasts for sales, cost of goods sold, operating expenses, accounts receivable, collections, accounts payable, inventory, taxes, and other items. Spelling out realistic assumptions gives a plan more credibility and reduces the tendency to include overly optimistic estimates of sales growth and profit margins. Greg Martin, a partner in the venture capital company Redpoint Ventures, says, "I have problems with start-ups making unrealistic assumptions—how much money they need or how quickly they can ramp up revenue. Those can really kill a deal for me."[23]

In addition to providing valuable information to potential lenders and investors, projected financial statements help entrepreneurs to run their businesses more effectively and more efficiently after the start-up. They establish important targets for financial performance and make it easier for an entrepreneur to maintain control over routine expenses and capital expenditures.

The Loan or Investment Proposal

The loan or investment proposal section of the business plan should state the purpose of the financing, the amount requested, and the plans for repayment or, in the case of investors, an attractive exit strategy. When describing the purpose of the loan or investment, an entrepreneur must specify the planned use of the funds. General requests for funds using terms such as "for modernization," "working capital," or "expansion" are unlikely to win approval. Instead, entrepreneurs should use more detailed descriptions such as "to modernize production facilities by purchasing five new, more efficient looms that will boost productivity by 12 percent" or "to rebuild merchandise inventory for fall sales peak, beginning in early summer." Entrepreneurs should state the precise amount requested and include relevant backup data, such as vendor estimates of costs or past production levels. Entrepreneurs should not hesitate to request the amount of money needed but should not inflate the amount, anticipating the financial officer to "talk them down." Remember: Lenders and investors are normally very familiar with industry cost structures.

Another important element of the loan or investment proposal is the repayment schedule and exit strategy. A lender's main consideration in granting a loan is the reassurance that the applicant will repay, whereas an investor's major concern is earning a satisfactory rate of return. Financial projections must reflect a company's ability to repay loans and produce adequate returns. Without this proof, a request for funding stands little chance of being approved. It is necessary for the entrepreneur to produce tangible evidence showing the ability to repay loans or to generate attractive returns. "Plan an exit for the investor," advises the owner of a financial consulting company. "Generally, the equity investor's objective with early stage funding is to earn a 30% to 50% annual return over the life of the investment. To enhance the investor's interest in your enterprise, show how they can 'cash out' perhaps through a public offering or acquisition."[24]

Finally, an entrepreneur should have a timetable for implementing the proposed plan. He or she should present a schedule showing the estimated start-up date for the project and noting any significant milestones along the way. Entrepreneurs tend to be optimistic, so document how and why the timetable of events is realistic.

It is beneficial to include an evaluation of the risks of a new venture. Evaluating risk in a business plan requires an entrepreneur to walk a fine line, however. Dwelling too much on everything that can go wrong will discourage potential lenders and investors from financing the venture. Ignoring the project's risks makes those who evaluate the plan tend to believe an entrepreneur to be naïve, dishonest, or unprepared. The best strategy is to identify the most significant risks the venture faces and then to describe the plans the entrepreneur has developed to avoid them altogether or to overcome the negative outcome if the event does occur.

There is a difference between a *working* business plan—the one the entrepreneur is using to guide the business—and the *presentation* business plan—the one he or she is using to attract capital. Although coffee rings and penciled-in changes in a working plan don't matter (in fact, they're a good sign that the entrepreneur is actually using the plan), they have no place on a plan going to someone outside the company. A plan is usually the tool that an entrepreneur uses to make a first impression on potential lenders and investors. To make sure that impression is a favorable one, an entrepreneur should follow these tips:

- Realize that first impressions are crucial. Make sure the plan has an attractive (not necessarily expensive) cover.
- Make sure the plan is free of spelling and grammatical errors and "typos." It is a professional document and should look like one.
- Make it visually appealing. Use color charts, figures, and diagrams to illustrate key points. Don't get carried away, however, and end up with a "comic book" plan.
- Include a table of contents with page numbers to allow readers to navigate the plan easily. Reviewers should be able to look through a plan and quickly locate the sections they want to see.
- Make it interesting. Boring plans seldom get read.
- A plan must prove that the business will make money. In one survey of lenders, investors, and financial advisors, 81 percent said that, first and foremost, a plan should prove that a venture will earn a profit.[25] Start-ups do not necessarily have to be profitable immediately, but sooner or later (preferably sooner), they must make money.
- Use computer spreadsheets to generate financial forecasts. They allow entrepreneurs to perform valuable "what if" (sensitivity) analysis in just seconds.
- *Always* include cash flow projections. Entrepreneurs sometimes focus excessively on their proposed venture's profit forecasts and ignore cash flow projections. Although profitability is important, lenders and investors are much more interested in cash flow because they know that's where the money to pay them back or to cash them out comes from.
- The ideal plan is "crisp," long enough to say what it should but not so long that it is a chore to read.
- Tell the truth. Absolute honesty is always critical when preparing a business plan.

Write a Plan That Will Win You Money

At first, writing a business plan may seem like a daunting task, but like most big projects, the key to success is to take one step at a time. Often the toughest part is getting started! Entrepreneurs who take the time to research and write a business plan discover that, even though the plan itself is extremely useful for launching and managing their businesses and for raising capital, the real value lies in the *process* they go through to create the plan. Preparing a plan gives them a solid foundation from which to run their companies.

Another important use for a business plan is in raising the capital entrepreneurs need to launch their companies, a task that often proves to be quite challenging. How can you write a plan that will attract the capital you need to launch your business? The following tips will help.

Tip #1. Know your audience. As you write your plan, keep in mind your audience. Remember that potential lenders, private investors, venture capitalists, and other potential sources of funds receive hundreds of business plans a year. Most of them fail in two key areas: capturing the reader's attention in a compelling way and spelling out how the business offers customers a product or service that is different or better in some way. Writing a business plan requires entrepreneurs to walk a fine line between being optimistic about the business's market potential and realistically laying out the challenges and the risks involved. None of this matters, of course, if your executive summary fails to hook the reader in the first place. Be sure to invest plenty of time in honing the executive summary so that it communicates the basic business concept and its benefits in just a few sentences or paragraphs.

Tip #2. Know the elements of a business plan. The business plan outline and discussion in this chapter provide you with all of the elements a sound plan should contain. However, the way in which you organize and present them is up to you. Remember that because each entrepreneur and each business idea are unique, each business plan also should be unique. Don't fall into the "cookie-cutter" trap. Cover the topics potential lenders and investors expect to see, but do it in your own style and in a way that is appropriate for your business.

Tip #3. Recognize the importance of strategy to your business success. Experienced lenders and investors know that the real key to building a successful company lies in creating and then executing a sound business strategy. Don't give short shrift to explaining your company's strategy for gaining a competitive edge in the plan. Experienced lenders and investors know that's how a company achieves a sustainable record of success. Too often, entrepreneurs focus on creating financial forecasts without describing the strategies that will enable them to achieve those numbers.

Tip #4. Be thorough but not excessive. Potential lenders and investors want proof that entrepreneurs have done their homework—analyzing the industry, researching their target markets, studying the competition, and covering other important elements of a plan. However, they don't want to wade through a lengthy tome to understand the essence of your business idea. Stay focused as you write, and limit your plan to no more than 40 pages if possible.

Tip #5. Be sure your financial forecasts are realistic. Experienced lenders and investors know that entrepreneurs tend to be optimists and that the financial projections they produce for their business plans also are optimistic. One of the fastest paths to having your business plan rejected is to include financial forecasts that are so optimistic that they are unreasonable. You may want to ask an accountant, a banker, or some other financial expert to review your financial forecasts before presenting your plan to potential lenders and investors.

Tip #6. Explain the exit strategy. Investors, in particular, are in the business of investing in start-up businesses for one reason: to make money when they cash out their ownership in the business. Any plan aimed at potential investors should explain how the company intends for investors to get their money back—preferably with a big return on their investments. Will the company make an initial public offering? Will it look to be bought out by a larger business? Potential lenders want to see evidence that the company will generate sufficient cash flow to be able to repay loans on time.

What Lenders and Investors Look for in a Business Plan

Banks usually are not a new venture's sole source of capital because a bank's return is limited by the interest rate it negotiates, but its risk could be the entire amount of the loan if the new business fails. Once a business is operational and has established a financial track record, however, banks become a regular source of financing. For this reason the small business owner needs to be aware of the criteria lenders and investors use when evaluating the creditworthiness of entrepreneurs seeking financing. Lenders and investors refer to these criteria as the **five Cs of credit**: capital, capacity, collateral, character, and conditions.

LEARNING OBJECTIVES
4. Explain the "five Cs of credit" and why they are important to potential lenders and investors reading business plans.

five Cs of credit
criteria lenders and investors use to evaluate the creditworthiness of entrepreneurs seeking financing: capital, capacity, collateral, character, and conditions.

Capital

A small business must have a stable capital base before any lender is willing to grant a loan. Otherwise the lender would be making, in effect, a capital investment in the business. Most banks refuse to make loans that are capital investments because the potential for return on the investment is limited strictly to the interest on the loan, and the potential loss would probably exceed the reward. In fact, the most common reasons that banks give for rejecting small business loan applications are undercapitalization and too much debt. Banks expect a small company to have an equity base of investment by the owner(s) that will help to support the venture during times of financial strain, which are common during the start-up and growth phases of a business. Lenders and investors see capital as a risk-sharing strategy with entrepreneurs.

Capacity

A synonym for capacity is cash flow. Lenders and investors must be convinced of the firm's ability to meet its regular financial obligations and to repay loans, and that takes cash. In Chapter 9, we will see that more small businesses fail from lack of cash than from lack of profit. It is possible for a company to be showing a profit and still have no cash—that is, to be technically bankrupt. Lenders expect small businesses to pass the test of liquidity, especially for short-term loans. Potential lenders and investors examine closely a small company's cash flow position to decide whether it has the capacity necessary to survive until it can sustain itself.

Collateral

Collateral includes any assets an entrepreneur pledges to a lender as security for repayment of a loan. If the company defaults on the loan, the lender has the right to sell the collateral and use the proceeds to satisfy the loan. Typically, banks make very few unsecured loans (those not backed by collateral) to business start-ups. Bankers view the entrepreneurs' willingness to pledge collateral (personal or business assets) as an indication of their dedication to making the venture a success. A sound business plan can improve a banker's attitude toward a venture.

Character

Before extending a loan to or making an investment in a small business, lenders and investors must be satisfied with an entrepreneur's character. The evaluation of character frequently is based on intangible factors such as honesty, integrity, competence, polish, determination, intelligence, and ability. Although the qualities judged are abstract, this evaluation plays a critical role in the decision to put money into a business or not.

Lenders and investors know that most small businesses fail because of incompetent management, and they try to avoid extending loans to high-risk entrepreneurs. A solid business plan and a polished presentation by the entrepreneur can go far in convincing the banker of the owner's capability.

Conditions

The conditions surrounding a funding request also affect an entrepreneur's chances of receiving financing. Lenders and investors consider factors relating to a business's operation such as potential growth in the market, competition, location, strengths, weaknesses, opportunities, and threats. Again, the best way to provide this relevant information is in a business plan. Another important condition influencing the banker's decision is the shape of the overall economy, including interest rate levels, inflation rate, and demand for money. Although these factors are beyond an entrepreneur's control, they still are an important component in a banker's decision.

The higher a small business scores on these five Cs, the greater its chance will be of receiving a loan. The wise entrepreneur keeps this in mind when preparing a business plan and presentation.

LEARNING OBJECTIVES
5. Describe the keys to making an effective business plan presentation.

Making the Business Plan Presentation

Lenders and investors are favorably impressed by entrepreneurs who are informed and prepared when requesting a loan or investment. When attempting to secure funds from professional venture capitalist or private investors, the written business plan almost always precedes the opportunity to meet face to face. Typically, an entrepreneur's time for presenting her or his business opportunity will be quite limited. (When presenting a plan to a venture capital forum, the allotted time is usually no more than 15 to 20 minutes, and at some forums, the time limit is a mere 5 or 6 minutes.). When the opportunity arises, an entrepreneur must be well prepared. It is important to rehearse, rehearse, and then rehearse more. It is a mistake to begin by leading the audience into a long-winded explanation about the technology on which the product or service is based. Within minutes most of the audience will be lost; and so is any chance the entrepreneur has of obtaining the necessary financing for her or his new venture.

You Be the Consultant

The Presentation

Dick Bardow sat quietly in his car, pondering why he had failed to convince Pat Guinn, managing partner of Next Century Venture Capital, to provide the start-up capital he needed to launch the business that would present his new high-tech medical invention. Bardow had spent the past three-and-a-half years researching and developing the concept, and now that he had a product in hand, he was ready to take it to the market. The idea for Bardow's new venture had been simmering for many years during his stints as a researcher for a major medical lab and as a technical advisor for a medical products company. Bardow had learned a great deal about use of the end product in his technical job, which he took after earning a Master's degree

in Biomedical Engineering. But it was during his tenure at the medical lab that Bardow saw the importance of staying on the cutting edge of technology in the field of medicine. He also saw the tremendous profit potential of successful medical products.

Driving home, Bardow replayed his meeting with Guinn in his mind. "How could those venture capitalists have missed the tremendous opportunity right in front of them?" he mused. During his 45-minute meeting with Guinn and her staff, Bardow had spent 30 minutes explaining how the technology had evolved over time, how he had developed the product, and why it was technologically superior to anything on the market. "I've got them where I want then, now," he remembers thinking. "They can't help but see the incredible power of this technology." Throughout his corporate career, Bardow had earned a reputation for his ability to explain abstract ideas and highly technical concepts to his fellow scientists. Over the years, he had made dozens of presentations at scientific professional meeting, all of which were well received.

Bardow had to admit, however, that he was puzzled by all of the questions Guinn had asked him toward the end of their meeting. They weren't at all what he was expecting! "She never asked a single question about my product, its design, the technology behind it, or the patent I have pending," he muttered. He remembered her questioning him about a "market analysis" and how and to whom he planned to market his product. "How foolish!" he thought. "You can't forecast exact sales for a new product. Once this product is on the market and the medical industry sees what it can do, we'll have all the sales we'll need—and more." Bardow was convinced that Guinn simply didn't understand that new, innovative products create their own markets. "I've seen it dozens of times," he said. Dick was beginning to believe that venture capital firms were too focused on revenues, profits, and return on investment. "Don't they know that those things are outcomes?" he thought. "They come . . . in time."

1. Identify the possible problems with Dick Bardow's presentation of his business plan to Pat Guinn and the other venture capitalists.
2. Should potential lenders and investors evaluate new ventures that are based on cutting-edge technology differently from other business ventures? Explain.
3. List at least five suggestions you would make to Dick Bardow to improve his business plan and his presentation of it.

Helpful tips for making a business plan presentation to potential lenders and investors include the following:

- Demonstrate enthusiasm about the venture, but don't be overemotional.
- Know your audience thoroughly, and work to establish a rapport with them.
- "Hook" investors quickly with an up-front explanation of the new venture, its opportunities, and the anticipated benefits to them.
- Hit the highlights; specific questions will bring out the details later. Don't get caught up in too much detail in early meetings with lenders and investors.
- Keep your presentation simple by limiting it to the two or three (no more) major points you must get across to your audience.
- Avoid the use of technological terms that will likely be above most of the audience. Do at least one rehearsal before someone who has no special technical training. Tell that person to stop you anytime he or she does not understand what you are talking about. When this occurs (and it likely will) rewrite that portion of your presentation.
- Use visual aids. They make it easier for people to follow your presentation, but do not make the visual aids the "star" of the presentation. They should merely support and enhance your message.
- Close by reinforcing the nature of the opportunity. Be sure you have sold the benefits the investors will realize when the business is a success.
- Be prepared for questions. In many cases, there is seldom time for a long "Q&A" session, but interested investors may want to get you aside to discuss the details of the plan.
- Follow up with every investor to whom you make a presentation. Don't sit back and wait; be proactive. They have what you need—investment capital. Demonstrate that you have confidence in your plan and have the initiative necessary to run a business successfully.

Battle of the Plans

In 1984, two MBA students at the University of Texas thought that an experience to teach entrepreneurship in the same comprehensive way that "moot court" competitions taught law would be a good idea. They approached some of their professors and soon launched Moot Corp., the country's first business plan competition in which students competed not only for pride but also for start-up capital to launch their businesses. In 1989, the Massachusetts Institute of Technology started the MIT $10K (now $50K) Entrepreneurship Competition, and many other colleges and universities have followed suit with business plan competitions of their own. "In the 1980s and even in the 1990s, putting on a competition like this was a radical concept," says Randy Swangard, director of the New Venture Championship, a business plan competition started in 1991 at Lundquist College.

Today dozens of colleges and universities across the United States sponsor business plan competitions, and it is not uncommon for the winners to attract impressive amounts of venture capital from judges. "I have been amazed at the quality of the plans and the companies coming out of these competitions," says Steve Kaplan of the University of Chicago. One student team that recently won the $20,000 first prize at the University of Pennsylvania's Wharton Business Plan Competition spotted an opportunity in the health care industry based on the research of team leader Dhavel Gosalia, a doctoral student in bioengineering. The team's plan for FibrinX is based on the fact that fish blood clots more readily than mammalian blood. FibrinX plans to market a tissue sealant derived from the blood plasma of the Atlantic salmon that stimulates and enhances the human body's natural blood-clotting process for treating patients with serious injuries or those undergoing surgery. Because fish show no tendencies for transmitting blood-borne diseases such as AIDS and hepatitis, FibrinX's product offers another key advantage: safety.

One winning team at Harvard's business plan competition also went on to launch the company for which they created the plan, Chemdex, an e-commerce site that buys and sells life science products. The young entrepreneurs raised $13 million from one of the nation's best-known venture capital firms and later made a public stock offering . . . and it was only a *runner-up* in the competition! The winning company was an Internet consulting company named Zefer that attracted $100 million in start-up capital, the largest private funding ever for an Internet start-up.

Faculty and students alike find the idea of business plan competitions appealing because they provide an all-encompassing educational experience. As they prepare their plans, students learn a comprehensive set of business skills, ranging from conducting industry and market research and assembling a new venture team to developing realistic financial forecasts and writing mission statements. They also learn valuable skills as they present their plans to panels of judges that often comprise successful entrepreneurs, bankers, venture capitalists, and other business heavyhitters. "If you want to launch an entrepreneurship program at your business school," advises Gary Cadenhead, director of Moot Corp., "it makes sense to start a business plan competition because students learn topics such as intellectual property and trademarks, venture capital, and guerrilla marketing." Two valuable lessons that often come from business plan competitions are that it takes more than just a good idea to build a successful business venture and that building a business is hard work.

One of the largest business plan competitions is the Venture Bowl, founded by entrepreneur and venture capitalist David Geliebter. Open to any start-up team with a member who is a part-time or full-time student at any college or university in North America, Venture Bowl offers big prize money: $500,000 for first place, $250,000 for second place, and $125,000 each for two third-place finishers. In one recent Venture Bowl competition, Harvard University students Michelle Crames and Jeff Norton beat out hundreds of challengers to take the first-place prize with their business plan for Lean Forward Media, an interactive media company that holds the exclusive home entertainment rights to the Choose Your Own Adventure® series of children's books. "Venture Bowl has been an extraordinary experience for us," says Norton. "It gave us the opportunity to showcase ourselves and our company to a stellar group of judges who provided invaluable advice." Since winning the competition, Crames and Norton have launched Lean Forward with the goal of adapting to DVD the popular books' idea of allowing readers to determine the ending by making decisions for the main character ("you") along the way. "Lean Forward Media is a wonderful example of the entrepreneurial spirits that exists on America's campuses," says Geliebter.

According to one business writer, "Business plan competitions remind would-be entrepreneurs that success requires a solid business plan even more than a bountiful bank balance. Once students have truly learned that business basic, they're not only better prepared to play the entrepreneurial game, they're more likely to end up as winners."

1. If your school does not already have a business plan competition, work with a team of your classmates in a brainstorming session to develop ideas for creating one. What would you offer as a prize? How would you finance the competition? Whom

would you invite to judge it? How would you structure the competition?

2. Use the World Wide Web to research business plan competitions at other colleges and universities across the nation. Using the competitions at these schools as benchmarks and the ideas you generated in Question 1, develop a format for a business plan competition at your school.

3. Assume that you are a member of a team of entrepreneurial students competing in a prestigious business plan competition. Outline your team's strategy for winning the competition.

Sources: Adapted from Tricia Bisoux, "Winning Ways," *BizEd*, September/October 2004, pp. 26–32; Suzanne Isack, "Search for Next Google on America's College Campuses," The National Institute for Entrepreneurship, May 12, 2004, pp.1–2; Nichole L. Torres, "Planning for Gold," *Entrepreneur B.Y.O.B.*, November 2004, pp. 112–118; Marc Ballon, "MIT Springboard Sends Internet Company Aloft," *Inc.*, December 1998, pp. 23–25; MIT $50K Entrepreneurship Competition, http://www.50k.mit.edu/; Alex Frankel, "Battle of the Business Plans," *Forbes ASAP*, August 23, 1999, pp. 22–24; Michael Warshaw, "The Best Business Plan on the Planet," *Inc.*, August 1999, pp. 80–90; "Eight Great Business Plans, But Only One Is the Winner," Knowledge@Wharton, May 5, 2005, http://www.knowledge.wharton.upenn.edu/index.cfm?fa=printArticle&ID=1190.

Conclusion

Although there is no guarantee of success when launching a business, the best way to insure against failure is create a business plan. A good plan serves as an entrepreneurial strategic compass that keeps a business on course as it travels into an uncertain future. In addition, a solid plan is essential to raising the capital needed to start a business; lenders and investors demand it. It is absolutely essential for the business plan to be built on facts and realistic assumptions. Nothing destroys an entrepreneur's credibility faster than a document or presentation that lacks substance and is viewed by potential investors as a complete fabrication or an exercise in wishful thinking.

Business Plan Format

Although every company's business plan will be unique, reflecting its individual circumstances, certain elements are universal. The following outline summarizes these components:

I. Executive Summary (not to exceed two pages)
- **A.** Company name, address, and phone number
- **B.** Name, address, and phone number of all key people
- **C.** Brief description of the business, its products and services, and the customer problems they solve
- **D.** Brief overview of the market for your products and services
- **E.** Brief overview of the strategies that will make your firm a success
- **F.** Brief description of the managerial and technical experience of key people
- **G.** Brief statement of the financial request and how the money will be used
- **H.** Charts or tables showing highlights of financial forecasts

II. Vision and Mission Statement
    A. Entrepreneur's vision for the company
    B. "What business are we in?"
    C. Values and principles on which the business stands
    D. What makes the business unique? What is the source of its competitive advantage?

III. Company History (for existing businesses only)
    A. Company founding
    B. Financial and operational highlights
    C. Significant achievements

IV. Business and Industry Profile
    A. Industry analysis
        1. Industry background and overview
        2. Significant trends
        3. Growth rate
        4. Key success factors in the industry
    B. Outlook for the future stages of growth (start-up, growth, maturity)
    C. Company goals and objectives
        1. Operational
        2. Financial
        3. Other

V. Business Strategy
    A. Desired image and position in market
    B. SWOT analysis
        1. Strengths
        2. Weaknesses
        3. Opportunities
        4. Threats
    C. Competitive strategy
        1. Cost leadership
        2. Differentiation
        3. Focus

VI. Company Products and Services
    A. Description
        1. Product or service features
        2. Customer benefits
        3. Warranties and guarantees
        4. Uniqueness
    B. Patent or trademark protection
    C. Description of production process (if applicable)
        1. Raw materials
        2. Costs
        3. Key suppliers
    D. Future product or service offerings

VII. Marketing Strategy
    A. Target market
        1. Complete demographic profile
        2. Other significant customer characteristics
    B. Customers' motivation to buy
    C. Market size and trends
        1. How large is the market?
        2. Is it growing or shrinking? How fast?

    D. Advertising and promotion
       1. Media used—reader, viewer, listener profiles
       2. Media costs
       3. Frequency of usage
       4. Plans for generating publicity
    E. Pricing
       1. Cost structure
          a. Fixed
          b. Variable
       2. Desired image in market
       3. Comparison against competitors' prices
    F. Distribution strategy
       1. Channels of distribution used
       2. Sales techniques and incentives

VIII. Location and Layout
    A. Location
       1. Demographic analysis of location versus target customer profile
       2. Traffic count
       3. Lease/rental rates
       4. Labor needs and supply
       5. Wage rates
    B. Layout
       1. Size requirements
       2. Americans with Disabilities Act compliance
       3. Ergonomic issues
       4. Layout plan (suitable for an Appendix)

IX. Competitor Analysis
    A. Existing competitors
       1. Who are they? Create a competitive profile matrix.
       2. Strengths
       3. Weaknesses
    B. Potential competitors: companies that might enter the market
       1. Who are they?
       2. Impact on your business if they enter

X. Description of Management Team
    A. Key managers and employees
       1. Their backgrounds
       2. Experience, skills, and know-how they bring to the company
    B. Résumés of key managers and employees (suitable for an Appendix)

XI. Plan of Operation
    A. Form of ownership chosen and reasoning
    B. Company structure (organization chart)
    C. Decision-making authority
    D. Compensation and benefits packages

XII. Financial Forecasts (suitable for an Appendix)
    A. Financial statements
       1. Income statement
       2. Balance sheet
       3. Cash flow statement
    B. Break-even analysis
    C. Ratio analysis with comparison to industry standards (most applicable to existing businesses)

XIII. Loan or Investment Proposal
   A. Amount requested
   B. Purpose and uses of funds
   C. Repayment or "cash-out" schedule (exit strategy)
   D. Timetable for implementing plan and launching the business

XIV. Appendices—Supporting documentation, including market research, financial statements, organization charts, resumes, and other items.

Chapter Summary by Learning Objectives

1. Discuss the steps involved in subjecting a business idea to a feasibility analysis.

A feasibility analysis consists of three interrelated components: an industry and market feasibility analysis, a product or service feasibility analysis, and a financial feasibility analysis. The goal of the feasibility analysis is to determine whether an entrepreneur's idea is a viable foundation for creating a successful business.

2. Explain why every entrepreneur should create a business plan, as well as the benefits of developing a plan.

A business plan serves two essential functions. First and most important, it guides the company's operations by charting its future course and devising a strategy for following it. The second function of the business plan is to attract lenders and investors. Applying for loans or attempting to attract investors without a solid business plan rarely attracts needed capital

Preparing a sound business plan clearly requires time and effort, but the benefits greatly exceed the costs. Building the plan forces a potential entrepreneur to look at her or his business idea in the harsh light of reality. It also requires the owner to assess the venture's chances of success more objectively. A well-assembled plan helps prove to outsiders that a business idea can be successful.

The *real* value in preparing a business plan is not so much in the plan itself as it is in the process the entrepreneur goes through to create the plan. Although the finished product is useful, the process of building a plan requires an entrepreneur to subject her or his idea to an objective, critical evaluation. What the entrepreneur learns about the company, its target market, its financial requirements, and other factors can be essential to making the venture a success.

3. Describe the elements of a solid business plan.

Although a business plan should be unique and tailor-made to suit the particular needs of a small company, it should cover these basic elements: an executive summary, a mission statement, a company history, a business and industry profile, a description of the company's business strategy, a profile of its products or services, a statement explaining its marketing strategy, a competitor analysis, owners' and officers' résumés, a plan of operation, financial data, and the loan or investment proposal.

4. Explain the "five Cs of credit" and why they are important to potential lenders and investors reading business plans.

Small business owners needs to be aware of the criteria bankers use in evaluating the credit-worthiness of loan applicants—the five Cs of credit: capital, capacity, collateral, character, and conditions.

Capital—Lenders expect small businesses to have an equity base of investment by the owner(s) that will help to support the venture during times of financial strain.

Capacity—A synonym for capacity is cash flow. The bank must be convinced of the firm's ability to meet its regular financial obligations and to repay the bank loan, and that takes cash.

Collateral—Collateral includes any assets the owner pledges to the bank as security for repayment of the loan.

Character—Before approving a loan to a small business, the banker must be satisfied with the owner's character.

Conditions—The conditions—interest rates, the health of the nation's economy, industry growth rates, and so on—surrounding a loan request also affect the owner's chance of receiving funds.

5. Describe the keys to making an effective business plan presentation.

Lenders and investors are favorably impressed by entrepreneurs who are informed and prepared when requesting a loan or investment.

Tips include: Demonstrate enthusiasm about the venture, but don't be overemotional; "hook" investors quickly with an up-front explanation of the new venture, its opportunities, and the anticipated benefits to them; use visual aids; hit the highlights of your venture; don't get caught up in too much detail in early meetings with lenders and investors; avoid the use of technological terms that will likely be above most of the audience; rehearse your presentation before giving it; close by reinforcing the nature of the opportunity; and be prepared for questions.

Discussion Questions

1. Explain the steps involved in conducting a feasibility analysis.
2. Why should an entrepreneur develop a business plan?
3. Describe the major components of a business plan.
4. How can an entrepreneur seeking funds to launch a business convince potential lenders and investors that a market for the product or service really does exist?
5. How would you prepare to make a formal presentation of your business plan to a venture capital forum?
6. What are the 5 Cs of credit? How does a potential lender use them to evaluate a loan request?

Business Plan Pro

This chapter on the creation of a successful business plan is designed to test your business concept. The following exercises will assist you in validating or challenging your business concept. You will also begin to work through the situation analysis part of your plan to better understand your market. Be as objective as possible as you work through these exercises. Rely on your ability to gather information and make realistic assessments and projections as the exercises require.

Business Plan Exercises

On the Web

Go to http://www.prenhall.com/scarborough to the Business Plan Resource tab. If you have not done this yet, find the Standard Industry Classification (SIC) Code associated with your industry. You will find a link in the SIC Code information that will connect you to a resource to help you do that. Explore the information and links that are available to you on that site to learn more about the size of the industry and its growth, trends, and issues. Based on the industry you have selected and the associated SIC code, apply Porter's five forces model. Consider the five forces—the bargaining power of buyers, the power of suppliers, the threat of new entrants, the threat of substitute products, and the level of rivalry. Again, you will find additional information on Porter's five forces model in the "Strategy" section of this same site. Look for information on the Web that may assist you with this analysis. Based on this information, how attractive do you consider this industry? How would you assess the opportunity this industry presents? Does this information encourage you to become involved in this industry, or does it highlight significant challenges?

In the Software

Your text may have come with Business Feasibility Analysis Pro. This software is designed to take you through the essential steps of assessing the feasibility of your business concept. It addresses the overall feasibility of your product or service, helps you to conduct an industry assessment, reviews your management skills, and steps through a preliminary financial analysis. The software provides "feedback" based on your input through four components of the feasibility analysis with a numerical assessment. You can then export this information directly into Business Plan Pro.

Business Plan Pro will also be a good resource to help you assess the feasibility of your business concept in the areas of product, service, market organization, and financial feasibility. For example, you can enter the initial capital requirements for the business in the start-up and expenses section. Your sales forecast will help to predict the revenue that may be generated, and this will help to determine your return on investment. If you have these estimates available, enter those into your plan. Based on that information, refer to the Profit and Loss statement. At what point, if any, does that statement indicate that your venture will begin generating a profit based on those forecasts and expenses. In what year does that occur? Do you find that amount of time acceptable? If you are seeking investors, will they find that timeframe acceptable? Is the return on investment promising, and does this venture merit taking on the associated level of risk? We will talk more about these sections of your plan as you progress through the chapters.

Sample Plans

Review the start-up sample plans called "IntelliChild.com" and "Fantastic Florals."

1. What was the total amount of the start-up investment for each of these plans?
2. At one point—in months or years—did the plan indicate that it would begin making a profit?
3. What was the total profit that was projected in the year following this point?
4. Based on the break-even point, which of these ventures do you find most attractive?
5. Based the projections by year three, which plan appears to offer the greatest financial potential?
6. How does the scale and potential of these two opportunities compare to those in your plan?

Building Your Business Plan

Review the information in Market Analysis section. Continue to build your information in this section based on the outline. Now, go to Sales Strategy section and you will find information to help you to project your expenses. You may enter your numbers in the table itself or use the Wizard that will pop up to assist you with this process. You can manipulate the visual graph to build that forecast based on a visual growth curve or enter the actual data. If your business is a start-up venture, your expenses will include those figures along with your ongoing expense projections. At this point, don't worry about the accuracy of your projection. Enter data into the software; you can change those numbers at any time. Look at the Profit and Loss statement. Do you find that acceptable? At what point in time will your business begin making a profit?

As you build your plan, you will want to check to see that the outline and structure of your plan are a good fit to tell your story. Although the outline in Business Plan Pro is not identical to the outline presented in the chapter, by "right clicking" on the outline, you can move, add, and delete any topic you choose to modify the plan you create.

Beyond the Classroom . . .

1. Contact a local entrepreneur who recently launched a business. Did he or she prepare a business plan before starting the company? Why or why not? If the entrepreneur did not create a plan, is he or she considering doing so now? If the entrepreneur did create a plan, what benefits did he or she gain from the process? How long did it take to complete the plan? How did he or she put the plan to use during the start-up phase? Does he or she intend to keep the business plan updated? What advice does he or she have to offer another entrepreneur about to begin writing a business plan?

2. Interview a local banker who has experience in making loans to small businesses. Ask him or her the following questions.
   A. How important is a well-prepared business plan?
   B. How important is a smooth presentation?
   C. How does the banker evaluate the owner's character?
   D. How heavily does the bank weigh the five Cs of credit?
   E. What percentage of small business owners are well prepared to request a bank loan?
   F. What are the most common reasons the bank rejects small business loan applications?

3. Interview a small business owner who has requested a bank loan or an equity investment from external sources. Ask him or her these questions:
   A. Did you prepare a written business plan before approaching the financial officer?
   B. If the answer is "yes," did you have outside or professional help preparing it?
   C. How many times have your requests for additional funds been rejected? What reasons were given for the rejection?

5 | Forms of Business Ownership

> A friendship founded on business is a good deal better than a business founded on friendship. —John D. Rockefeller

> It's just paper. All I own is a pickup truck and a little Wal-Mart stock. —Sam Walton

Learning Objectives

On completion of this chapter, you will be able to:

1 Explain the advantages and the disadvantages of the three major forms of ownership: (A) the sole proprietorship, (B) the partnership, and (C) the corporation.

2 Discuss the advantages and the disadvantages of the S corporation, the limited liability company, the professional corporation, and the joint venture.

Once an entrepreneur makes the decision to launch a business, one of the first issues he or she faces is choosing a form of ownership. Too often entrepreneurs invest insufficient time and effort in evaluating the impact that the various forms of ownership would have on them and their businesses. They simply select a form of ownership by default or choose the form that appears to be most popular at the time. Choosing a form of ownership is important because it is a decision that has far-reaching effects for both the entrepreneur and the business. Although the decision is not irreversible, changing from one ownership form to another can be difficult, time consuming, complicated, and expensive. In many instances, switching an existing business from one form of ownership to another can trigger onerous tax consequences for the owners. Therefore, it is important for entrepreneurs to get it right the first time.

There is no one "best" form of ownership. The form of ownership that is best for one entrepreneur may not be suitable at all for another. Choosing the "right" form of ownership means that entrepreneurs must understand the characteristics of each form and how well those characteristics match their business and personal circumstances. Only then can an entrepreneur make an informed decision about a form of ownership. The following are some of the most important issues entrepreneurs should consider when they are evaluating the various forms of ownership:

Tax considerations. The amount of net income an entrepreneur expects the business to generate and the tax bill the owner must pay are important factors when choosing a form of ownership. The graduated tax rates that apply to each form of ownership, the government's constant tinkering with the tax code, and the year-to-year fluctuations in a company's income make some forms of ownership more attractive than others.

Liability exposure. Certain forms of ownership offer business owners greater protection from personal liability that might result from financial problems, faulty products, and a host of other difficulties. Entrepreneurs must decide the extent to which they are willing to assume personal responsibility for their companies' financial obligations.

Start-up and future capital requirements. Forms of ownership differ in their ability to raise start-up capital. Depending on how much capital an entrepreneur needs and where he or she plans to get it, some forms are superior to others. In addition, as a business grows, so does its appetite for capital, and some forms of ownership make it easier to attract external growth capital than others.

Control. By choosing certain forms of ownership, an entrepreneur automatically gives up some control over the company. Entrepreneurs must decide early on how much control they are willing to sacrifice in exchange for help from other people to build a successful business.

Managerial ability. Entrepreneurs must assess their skills and abilities to manage a business effectively. If they lack ability or experience in key areas, they may need to choose a form of ownership that allows them to bring in other owners who can provide the necessary skills for the company to succeed.

Business goals. How big and how profitable an entrepreneur plans for the business to become will influence the form of ownership chosen. Businesses often switch forms of ownership as they grow, but moving from some formats to others can be extremely complex and expensive.

Management succession plans. When choosing a form of ownership, business owners must look ahead to the day when they will pass their companies on to the next generation or to a buyer. Some forms of ownership make this transition much smoother than others.

Cost of formation. Some forms of ownership are much more costly and involved to create. Entrepreneurs must weigh carefully the benefits and the costs of the particular form they choose.

When it comes to organizing their businesses, entrepreneurs have a wide choice of forms of ownership, including a sole proprietorship, a general partnership, a limited partnership, a corporation, an S-corporation, and a limited liability company. Figure 5.1

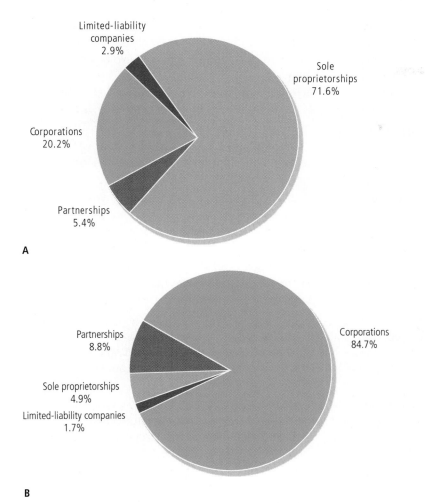

FIGURE 5.1

**Forms of Business Ownership.
(A) Percentage of Businesses;
(B) Percentage of Sales**

Source: BizStats.com, "Total Number of U.S. Businesses," http//:www.bizstats.com/ businesses.htm

provides a breakdown of these forms of ownership. Notice that sole proprietorships account for the greatest percentage of businesses, but corporations generate the largest proportion of business sales. This chapter discusses the key features of these various forms of ownership, beginning with the three most basic forms: the sole proprietorship, the partnership, and the corporation.

Come up with the Perfect Moniker for Your Business

When Mike Rohan started a financial software company in 2002, he came up with what he thought was a clever business name: Aucent. Within two years, Rohan realized that the company's name had become a liability. It failed to suggest to potential customers exactly what Aucent could do for them, it was hard to spell, its pronunciation was unclear, and it was not particularly memorable. Rohan decided to hire a San Francisco naming company, Igor International, to help him come up with a better name for his company. After much research and analysis, Rohan settled on Rivet. Because it is reminiscent of the sound that a frog makes ("ribbet"), the name has a friendly tone and is easy to remember. Before adopting the new name, the Rohan tested it on existing customers and others; almost all were enthusiastic about it.

For another company in Stamford, Connecticut, the choice of a business name became the company's worst enemy. GHB Marketing Communications started getting numerous e-mails and phone calls requesting a certain product. Sounds harmless, right? Wrong! The product that many of those customers were seeking was GHB, an illegal drug also known as ecstasy. "Imagine having a 30-year-old company named LSD, Inc. in the late 60s," explains company President Mark Bruce. "Then you can begin to understand what we went through." The new name (HiTechPR) costs the owners $20,000.

Choosing a memorable name can be one of the most enjoyable—and most challenging—aspects of starting a business. It also is an extremely important task because it has long-term implications and is the single most visible attribute of a company. The business name is the first connection that many customers will have with a company, and it should create an appropriate image in their minds. "A name is a cornerstone for branding," says the president of one small design firm specializing in branding. If done properly, a company's name will portray the business's personality, will stand out in a crowd, and will stick in the minds of consumers. Large companies may spend hundreds of thousands of dollars in their search for just the right name. Although entrepreneurs don't have the resources to enable them to spend that kind of money to find the ideal name, they can use the following process to come up with the perfect name for their businesses:

1. Decide on the image you want your company to project to customers, suppliers, bankers, the press, the community, and others. Do you want to create an air of sophistication, the suggestion of a bargain, a sense of adventure, the implication of trustworthiness and dependability, or a spirit of fun and whimsy? The right name can go a long way toward communicating the right image for a company.
2. Make a list of your competitors' business names. The idea is *not* to borrow from their ideas but to try to come up with a name that is unique. Do you notice any trends among competitors' names? What are the similarities? What are the differences?
3. Work with a group of the most creative people you know to brainstorm (refer to Chapter 2 for details on the brainstorming process) potential names for your business. Don't worry about quality at this point; the goal is to generate a large quantity of names. The idea is to come up with at least 100 potential names. Having a dictionary, a

thesaurus, and samples (or graphics) of your company's products and services will help to stimulate creativity.

4. After allowing them to percolate for a few days, evaluate the names generated in the brainstorming session. Narrow the list of choices to 10 or so names with the greatest potential. Print each name in large font on a single page and look at them. Which ones are visually appealing? Which ones lend themselves to being paired with a clever logo?
5. Reassemble your creative group, present each name you have printed, and discuss its merits and challenges. It helps to have a designated person to record the group's comments. The group may come to a consensus on a preferred name; if not, you can use a round-by-round voting process to move the group toward a consensus.
6. Conduct a search at the U.S. Patent and Trademark Office Web site (http://www.uspto.gov) to see whether the leading names on your list are already registered trademarks for existing businesses. Remember, however, that the same name can be registered as a trademark as long as the product, service, or company's business does not overlap. If your company conducts e-commerce, you will need to check with one of the name registration services to see whether a dot-com version of the name is available.
7. Make your choice. Including input from others is useful when selecting a business name, but the final choice is yours.
8. Register your company name with the U.S. Patent and Trademark Office. Doing so gives you maximum protection from others using the name you worked so hard to create.

Other helpful tips for creating the ideal business name include the following:

■ Look at your name from your potential customer's perspective. Do customers need reassurance (Gentle Dentistry), or do they prefer a bit of humor (Barking Lot Dog Grooming)? Other options include using a name that conveys an image to your customers that expresses your business strategy. For example: Discount Hair Products, Quality Muffler, or Pay-Less Auto Detailing. In addition, most of us are familiar with the really upscale practice of including foreign phrases (especially French) to convey an exclusive image.

La Petite Day care sounds more up scale than the Small Day Care.

- Decide the most appropriate single quality of the business that you want to convey and incorporate it into your business name. Avoid sending a mixed or inappropriate message. Avoid business names that might leave potential customers confused about what your business does. Remember: The company name will be displayed on all of your advertising and printed material.

- Avoid names that are hard to spell, pronounce, or remember. This is especially true if your business is an Internet company or if you plan to have a Web site. Try typing in "posiesbythedozenandthensome-fromrosie.com" a few times before you decide this is the name for your online flower store!

- Select a name that is short, fun, attention getting, and memorable. Not only is Google fun to say, it is also quite memorable (and quite successful, too; how many times do you hear people using this company name as a verb? "I googled myself and found 27 hits!") The name can be your initial marketing tool for attracting new customers. Rosiesposies.com may be a better choice in the example directly above. Naming experts say that a great name has "emotional hang time," a football metaphor to describe a name that stays in your mind.

- Be creative but maintain good taste! Lisa Rothstein found the perfect name for her business, which sells fresh-baked gourmet brownies as corporate gifts: Brownie Points. Rothstein's company name recently won the "Name to Fame" contest sponsored by *Entrepreneur* magazine and the Small Business Television Network. Rothstein and a college roommate came up with Brownie Points long before Rothstein ever decided to launch the business.

- Make sure the name you choose won't get dated quickly. Big Stiff Hair Salon might have been a great name in the 50s, but it would have died a horrible death in the 60s as long, straight locks became the norm.

- Be careful that the name, while catchy and cute, doesn't create a negative image. Ask yourself: Does Rent-a-Wreck attract you because you think you'll save money on a car rental or does the name put you off because you question the reliability of their cars?

- Once you have selected a suitable name, practice using it for a few days. Try it out on friends and family. "Hello, I am the CEO of FlubberDuds" may get on your nerves after the first few times.

- Finally, after all is said and done and you are comfortable with your choice, conduct a name search to make sure that no one else in your jurisdiction has already claimed the name. This is an especially tedious chore if you are starting an Internet company. Registering a domain name sometimes can be daunting because you will find that your brilliant idea is already registered.

There are millions of names in the marketplace. Coming up with the one that is just right for your business can help greatly in creating a brand image for your business. Choosing a name that is distinctive, memorable, and positive can go a long way toward helping you achieve success in your business venture. What's in a name? Everything!

Sources: Alex Frankel, "The New Science of Naming," *Business 2.0*, December 2004, pp. 53–55; Rhonda Abrams, "Sometimes Business Success Is All in the Name," *Business*, July 23, 2000, p. 3; Paul Tulenko, "Choose Name Carefully for Start-up Business," *Business*, February 6, 2000, p. 3; Jerry Fisher, "You Name It," *Entrepreneur B.Y.O.B.*, December 2001, pp. 112–116; Elizabeth Weinstein, "GHB Marketing Finds Its Name Is One Thing It Doesn't Want To Plug," *Wall Street Journal*, June 7, 2001, p. B1; Andrew Raskin, "The Name of the Game," *Inc.*, February 2000, pp. 31–32; Rhonda Adams "Sometimes Business Success Is All in the Name," *Business*, July 23, 2000, p. 3; Tomima Edmark, "What's in a Name?" *Entrepreneur*, October 1999, pp. 163–165; Jeff Wuorio, "'Oedipus Wrecks' and Other Business Names to Avoid," *bCentral*, www.bCentral.com/articles/wuorio/153.asp.

The Sole Proprietorship

The simplest and most popular form of ownership remains the **sole proprietorship.** The sole proprietorship, as its name implies, is a business owned and managed by one individual. Sole proprietorships make up nearly 72 percent of all businesses in the United States.

LEARNING OBJECTIVES

1A. Explain the advantages and disadvantages of the sole proprietorship.

sole proprietorship
a business owned and managed by one individual; the business and the owner are one and the same in the eyes of the law.

The Advantages of a Proprietorship

Simple to Create One of the most attractive features of a proprietorship is how fast and simple it is to begin. If an entrepreneur wants to operate a business under his own name (e.g., Strossner's Bakery), he simply obtains the necessary licenses from state, county, and/or local governments and begins operation! For most entrepreneurs, it is possible to start a proprietorship in a single day.

Least Costly Form of Ownership to Begin In addition to being easy to begin, the proprietorship is generally the least expensive form of ownership to establish. There is no need to create and file legal documents that are recommended for partnerships and required for corporations. An entrepreneur simply goes to the city or county government, states the nature of the business he or she will start, and pays the appropriate fees and license costs. Paying these fees and license costs gives the entrepreneur the right to conduct business in that particular jurisdiction.

Someone planning to conduct business under a trade name should acquire a Certificate of Doing Business under an Assumed Name from the secretary of state. The fee for filing this certificate usually is nominal. Acquiring this certificate involves conducting a legal search to ensure that the name chosen is not already registered as a trademark or a service mark with the secretary of state. Filing this certificate also notifies the state who owns the business. In a proprietorship, the owner *is* the business.

Profit Incentive One major advantage of proprietorships is that once owners pay all of their companies' expenses, they can keep the remaining profits (less taxes, of course). The profit incentive is a powerful one, and profits represent an excellent way of "keeping score" in the game of the business. Sole proprietors report the net income of their businesses on Schedule C of IRS Form 1040, and the amount is taxed at the entrepreneur's personal tax rate. Because they are self-employed, sole proprietors' income from their business activities also is subject to the self-employment tax, which currently stands at 15.3 percent (an amount equal to the 7.65 percent employers pay plus the 7.65 percent employees contribute toward the Social Security and Medicare programs) of the proprietor's income. A ceiling on the Social Security portion of the self-employment tax does apply.

Total Decision-Making Authority Because the sole proprietor is in total control of operations, he or she can respond quickly to changes, which is an asset in a rapidly shifting market. The freedom to set the company's course of action is a major motivational force. For those who thrive on the enjoyment of seeking new opportunities in business, the freedom of fast, flexible decision making is vital. Many sole proprietors thrive on the feeling of control they have over their personal financial futures and the recognition they earn as the owners of their businesses.

No Special Legal Restrictions The proprietorship is the least regulated form of business ownership. In a time when government requests for information seem never ending, this feature has much merit.

Easy to Discontinue If an entrepreneur decides to discontinue operations, he or she can terminate the business quickly even though he or she will still be personally liable for any outstanding debts and obligations that the business cannot pay.

Entrepreneurs considering the sole proprietorship as a form of ownership also must be aware of its disadvantages.

The Disadvantages of a Proprietorship

unlimited personal liability
a situation in which the sole proprietor is personally liable for all of the business's debts.

Unlimited Personal Liability Probably the greatest disadvantage of a sole proprietorship is the **unlimited personal liability** of the owner, which means that the sole proprietor is personally liable for all of the business's debts. Remember: In a proprietorship, the owner *is* the business. He or she owns all of the business's assets, and if the business fails, creditors can force the sale of these assets to cover its debts. If unpaid business debts remain, creditors can also force the sale of the proprietor's *personal* assets to recover payment. In short, the company's debts are the owner's debts. Laws vary from one state to another, but most states require creditors to leave the failed business owner a minimum amount of equity in a home, a car, and some personal items. The reality is that failure of a business can ruin a sole proprietor financially.

When Max Baer started a production studio in Memphis, Tennessee, he chose to operate as a sole proprietor. Then, a former employee sued Baer. Although he negotiated a modest out-of-court settlement in the case, Baer realized that a sole proprietorship left all of his personal assets at risk and converted his company into a corporation to gain the benefit of limited personal liability.[1]

Max Baer

Limited Skills and Capabilities A sole proprietor has total decision-making authority, but that does not mean that he or she has the range of skills that running a successful business requires. Each of us has areas in which our education, training, and work experiences have taught us a great deal; yet there are other areas in which our decision-making ability is weak. Many business failures occur because owners lack the skills, knowledge, and experience in areas that are vital to business success. Owners tend to push aside problems they don't understand or don't feel comfortable with in favor of those they can solve more easily. Unfortunately, the problems they set aside seldom solve themselves. By the time an owner decides to ask for help in addressing these problems, it may be too late to save the company.

Feelings of Isolation Running a business alone allows an entrepreneur maximum flexibility, but it also creates feelings of isolation; there is no one else to turn to for help when solving problems or getting feedback on a new idea. Most sole proprietors will admit that there are times when they feel the pressure of being alone and fully and completely responsible for every major business decision. It's a challenge to learn what you need to know about aspects of the business about which you may have had little, or no, previous experience.

Limited Access to Capital If a business is to grow and expand, a sole proprietor often needs additional financial resources. However, many proprietors have already put all they have into their businesses and have used their personal resources as collateral to acquire loans, making it difficult to borrow additional funds. A sole proprietorship is limited to whatever capital the owner can contribute and whatever money he or she can borrow. In short, unless they have great personal wealth, proprietors find it difficult to raise additional money while maintaining sole ownership. Most banks and other lending institutions have well-defined formulas for determining borrowers' eligibility. Unfortunately, many sole proprietorships cannot meet those borrowing requirements, especially in the early days of business.

Lack of Continuity of the Business Lack of continuity is inherent in a sole proprietorship. If the proprietor dies, retires, or becomes incapacitated, the business automatically terminates. Unless a family member or employee can take over (which means that person is now a sole proprietor), the business could be in jeopardy. Because people look for secure employment and an opportunity for advancement, proprietorships often have trouble recruiting and retaining good employees. If no one is willing to step in to run the business in the founder's absence, creditors can petition the courts to liquidate the assets of the dissolved business to pay outstanding debts.

Some entrepreneurs find that forming partnerships is one way to overcome the disadvantages of the sole proprietorship. For instance, when one person lacks specific managerial skills or has insufficient access to needed capital, he or she can compensate for these weaknesses by forming a partnership with someone with complementary management skills or money to invest.

partnership
an association of two or more people who co-own a business for the purpose of making a profit.

partnership agreement
a document that states in writing the terms under which the partners agree to operate the partnership and protects each partner's interest in the business.

ENTREPRENEURIAL
Profile

Ken Clansky

The Partnership

A **partnership** is an association of two or more people who co-own a business for the purpose of making a profit. In a partnership the co-owners (partners) share the business's assets, liabilities, and profits according to the terms of a previously established partnership agreement (if one exists).

The law does not require a partnership agreement (also known as the articles of partnership), but it is wise to work with an attorney to develop one that spells out the exact status and responsibility of each partner. All too often the parties think they know what they are agreeing to, only to find later that no real meeting of the minds took place. A **partnership agreement** is a document that states in writing the terms under which the partners agree to operate the partnership and protects each partner's interest in the business. Every partnership should be based on a written agreement. "When two entrepreneurial personalities are combined, there is a tremendous amount of strength and energy, but it must be focused in the same direction, or it will tear the relationship apart," explains one business writer. "A good partnership agreement will guide you through the good times, provide you with a method for handling problems, and serve as the infrastructure for a successful operation."[2]

After several years of running his own business that specialized in creating government databases, Ken Clansky decided to enter into a partnership with the owner of a company whose services complemented those Clansky's business offered. The two agreed to be equal partners in the combined venture, but they neglected to create a partnership agreement. They soon discovered that their business goals and their managerial styles differed significantly, and conflicts surfaced. In retrospect, "We were both trying to run the show," says Clansky, who left the partnership and made a career change. "A business partnership is much more complex than it seems," he says.[3]

When no partnership agreement exists, the Uniform Partnership Act (UPA) governs a partnership, but its provisions may not be as favorable as a specific agreement hammered out among the partners. Creating a partnership agreement is not costly. In most cases the partners can discuss their preferences for each of the provisions in advance. Once they have reached an agreement, an attorney can draft the formal document. Banks will often want to see a copy of the partnership agreement before lending money to a partnership. Probably the most important feature of the partnership agreement is that it resolves potential sources of conflict that, if not addressed in advance, could later result in partnership battles and the dissolution of an otherwise successful business. Spelling out details—in particular, sticky ones such as profit splits, contributions, workloads, decision-making authority, dispute resolution, dissolution, and others—in a written agreement at outset will help to avoid damaging tension in a partnership that could lead to a business "divorce." Business divorces, like marital ones, are almost always costly and unpleasant for everyone involved.

Generally, a partnership agreement can include any terms the partners want (unless they are illegal). The standard partnership agreement will likely include the following:

1. *Name of the partnership.*
2. *Purpose of the business.* What is the reason the business was brought into being?
3. *Domicile of the business.* Where will the principal business be located?
4. *Duration of the partnership.* How long will the partnership last?
5. *Names of the partners and their legal addresses.*
6. *Contributions of each partner to the business at the creation of the partnership and later.* This includes each partner's investment in the business. In some situations a partner may contribute assets that are not likely to appear on a balance sheet. Experience, sales contacts, and a good reputation in the community may be reasons for asking a person to join in partnership.
7. *Agreement on how the profits or losses will be distributed.*

8. *Procedure for expansion through the addition of new partners.*
9. *Agreement on distribution of assets if the partners voluntarily dissolve the partnership.*
10. *Sale of partnership interest.* The articles of partnership should include terms defining how a partner can sell his or her interest in the business.
11. *Salaries, draws, and expense accounts for the partners.* How much money will each partner draw from the business? Under what circumstances? How often?
12. *Absence or disability of one of the partners.* If a partner is absent or disabled for an extended period of time, should the partnership continue? Will the absent or disabled partner receive the same share of profits as he or she did prior to the absence or disability? Should the absent or disabled partner be held responsible for debts incurred while unable to participate?
13. *Dissolution of the partnership.* Under what circumstances will the partnership dissolve? How will the assets of the business be valued for dissolution?
14. *Alternations or modifications of the partnership agreement.* No document is written to last forever. Partnership agreements should contain provisions for alternations or modifications.

The Uniform Partnership Act The Uniform Partnership Act (UPA) codifies the body of law dealing with partnerships in the United States (except in Louisiana, which has not adopted the UPA and where state law governs in the absence of a partnership agreement). Under the UPA, the three key elements of any partnership are common ownership interest in a business, sharing the business's profits and losses, and the right to participate in managing the operation of the partnership. Under the act each partner has the *right* to:

1. Share in the management and operations of the business.
2. Share in any profits the business might earn from operations.
3. Receive interest on additional advances made to the business.
4. Be compensated for expenses incurred in the name of the partnership.
5. Have access to the business's books and records.
6. Receive a formal accounting of the partnership's business affairs.

The UPA also sets forth the partners' general obligations. Each partner is *obligated* to:

1. Share in any losses sustained by the business.
2. Work for the partnership without salary.
3. Submit differences that may arise in the conduct of the business to majority vote or arbitration.
4. Give the other partner complete information about all business affairs.
5. Give a formal accounting of the partnership's business affairs.

David Gage, a partnership mediator, suggests that partners also create a "partnership charter," a document that "serves as a guide for running the business and dealing with one another." Whereas a partnership agreement addresses the legal and business issues of running a business, a partnership charter covers the interpersonal aspects of the partners' relationships and serves as a helpful tool for managing the complexity of partnership relations.[4] Even with a partnership charter and a partnership agreement, a partnership must have two more essential elements above all others: mutual trust and respect. Any partnership missing these elements is destined to fail.

The Advantages of the Partnership

Easy to Establish Like a proprietorship, a partnership is easy and inexpensive to establish. The owner must obtain the necessary business licenses and submit a minimal number of forms. In most states, partners must file a Certificate for Conducting Business as Partners if the business is run under a trade name.

Complementary Skills In a sole proprietorship, the owner must wear many different hats, and not all of them will fit well. In successful partnerships, the parties' skills and abilities usually complement one another, strengthening the company's managerial foundation.

Chilly Willy's

While developing a business plan for a competition in their sophomore year at Colgate University, friends and fraternity brothers Chris Nordsiek, Preston Burnes, and Matt Brown came up with the idea for a restaurant in Hamilton, New York. The trio realized that each person had different skills and strengths that complemented those of the others, that they shared a common business vision, and that they enjoyed working together. It was only natural that after graduating Nordsiek, Burnes, and Brown launched Chilly Willy's, a fast-service restaurant with a Mexican theme. "If two of us are disagreeing about something," says Nordsiek, "we'll bring in the third guy, and he'll make the call or arbitrate. We put the success of the restaurant before everything else."[5]

Division of Profits There are no restrictions on how partners distribute the company's profits as long as they are consistent with the partnership agreement and do not violate the rights of any partner. The partnership agreement should articulate the nature of each partner's contribution and proportional share of the profits. If the partners fail to create an agreement, the UPA says that the partners share equally in the partnership's profits, even if their original capital contributions were unequal.

Larger Pool of Capital The partnership form of ownership can significantly broaden the pool of capital available to a business. Each partner's asset base enhances the business's pool of capital and improves its ability to borrow needed funds; together, partners' personal assets support greater borrowing capacity.

Ability to Attract Limited Partners When partners share in owning, operating, and managing a business, they are **general partners.** General partners have unlimited liability for the partnership's debts and usually take an active role in managing the business. Every partnership must have at least one general partner, although there is no limit on the number of general partners a business can have.

  Limited partners cannot participate in the day-to-day management of a company, and they have limited liability for the partnership's debts. If the business fails, they lose only what they have invested in it and no more. A limited partnership can attract investors by offering them limited liability and the potential to realize a substantial return on their investments if the business is successful. Many individuals find it very profitable to invest in high-potential small businesses, but only if they avoid the disadvantages of unlimited liability while doing so.

  Essentially, limited partners usually are financial investors who do not want to participate in the day-to-day operation of the business. If limited partners are "materially and actively" engaged in a business (defined as spending more than 500 hours per year in the company) or if they hold themselves out as general partners, they will be treated as general partners and will lose their limited liability protection. Two types of limited partners are silent partners and dormant partners. **Silent partners** are not active in a business but generally are known to be members of the partnership. **Dormant partners** are neither active nor generally known to be associated with the business. We will discuss limited partnerships in the next section of this chapter.

Little Governmental Regulation Like the sole proprietorship, partnerships are not burdened with red tape.

Flexibility Although not as flexible as sole ownership, a partnership can generally react quickly to changing market conditions because the partners can respond quickly and

---

general partners
partners who share in owning, operating, and managing a business and who have unlimited personal liability for the partnership's debts.

limited partners
partners who do not take an active role in managing a business and whose liability for the partnership's debts is limited to the amount they have invested.

silent partners
limited partners who are not active in a business but generally are known to be members of the partnership.

dormant partners
limited partners who are neither active in a business nor generally known to be associated with the business.

creatively to new opportunities. In large partnerships, however, getting partners' approval can slow a company's strategic actions.

Taxation The partnership itself is not subject to federal taxation. It serves as a conduit for the profits or losses it earns or incurs; its net income or losses are passed along to the partners as personal income, and the partners pay income tax on their distributive shares based on their personal tax rates. The partnership files an informational return, Form 1065, with the IRS that reports its net income for the tax year and the percentages of the business that each partner owns. The partnership provides each partner with a Schedule K-1 that shows his or her share of partnership's net income (or loss). Partners must pay taxes on their respective shares of the partnership's net income, even if none of that income actually is distributed to them. A partnership, like a sole proprietorship, avoids the "double taxation" disadvantage associated with the corporate form of ownership.

The Disadvantages of the Partnership

Unlimited Liability of at Least One Partner At least one member of every partnership must be a general partner. A general partner has unlimited personal liability for any debts that remain after the partnership's assets are exhausted. In addition, general partners' liability is *joint and several*, which means that creditors can hold all partners equally responsible for the partnership's debts or they can collect the entire debt from just one partner.

Capital Accumulation Although the partnership form of ownership is superior to the proprietorship in its ability to attract capital, it is generally not as effective as the corporate form of ownership, which can raise capital by selling shares of ownership to outside investors.

Difficulty in Disposing of Partnership Interest without Dissolving the Partnership Most partnership agreements restrict how partners can dispose of their shares of the business. Often, an agreement requires a partner to sell his or her interest to the remaining partner(s). Even if the original agreement contains such a requirement and clearly delineates how the value of each partner's ownership will be determined, there is no guarantee that the other partner(s) will have the financial resources to buy the seller's interest. When the money is not available to purchase a partner's interest, the other partner(s) may be forced either to accept a new partner or to dissolve the partnership, distribute the remaining assets, and begin again.

Unless the partnership agreement states otherwise, a partner may sell his or her interest in the business to another person without the consent of the remaining partners. However, that person does *not* automatically become a partner in the business. The transferee has the right to receive the former partner's share of the company's net income (or loss), but he or she does not have the right to take an active role in managing the business, gain access to the business's books, or demand a formal accounting of the partnership's business affairs.

When a partner withdraws from the partnership, the partnership ceases to exist unless there are specific provisions in the partnership agreement for a smooth transition. When a general partner dies, becomes incompetent, or withdraws from the business, the partnership automatically dissolves, although it may not terminate. Even when there are numerous partners, if one chooses to disassociate from the business, the remaining partners will probably form a new partnership.

Lack of Continuity If one partner dies, complications arise. Partnership interest is often nontransferable through inheritance because the remaining partner(s) may not want to be in a partnership with the person who inherits the deceased partner's interest. Partners can make provisions in the partnership agreement to avoid dissolution due to death if all parties agree to accept as partners those who inherit the deceased's interest.

Potential for Personality and Authority Conflicts Being in a partnership is much like being in a marriage. Making sure partners' work habits, goals, ethics, and general business philosophy are compatible is an important step in avoiding a nasty business divorce. Engaging in serious discussions with potential partners before launching a business together is a valuable and revealing exercise. Never assume that you know how a potential partner will behave in a business setting. One way to "test drive" a potential partnership is to work with a prospective partner on a joint project to get a sense of how compatible your work styles, business philosophies, and personalities really are.

One entrepreneur launched a telecommunications company with three friends but quickly came to regret his choice of partners. "I was naïve," he says. "I didn't screen our business goals. They wanted the company to pay for their cars and to conduct business meetings in the Bahamas. I wanted to plow the money back into the business." Because his partners voted as a block, this entrepreneur finally realized he was fighting a losing battle. His partners kept draining the company's cash to pay for executive perks until the business collapsed. The entrepreneur and his former friends and partners do not even speak to one another now.[6]

No matter how compatible partners are, friction among them is inevitable. They key is to have a mechanism such as a partnership agreement and open lines of communication for managing conflict. The demise of many partnerships can be traced to interpersonal conflicts and the lack of a procedure to resolve those conflicts.

Partners Are Bound by the Law of Agency A partner is like a spouse in that decisions made by one in the name of the partnership bind all. Each partner is an agent for the business and can legally bind the partnership and, hence, the other partners to contracts, even without the remaining partners' knowledge or consent. Because of this agency power, all partners must exercise good faith and reasonable care when performing their responsibilities. Consider the case of a partner who signs a three-year lease for a business jet, a move that only worsens the small company's cash flow struggles. Although the remaining partners may not have been not in favor of the decision, they are obligated to the contract by their partner's actions.

Some partnerships survive a lifetime, while others suffer from many of the preceding problems. In a general partnership, the continued exposure to unlimited personal liability for partners' actions can wear an entrepreneur down. An entrepreneur knowing that he or she could lose his or her personal assets because of a partner's bad business decision is a fact of life in partnerships. Conflicts between or among partners can force an otherwise thriving business to close. Few partnerships ever put into place a mutually agreed on means for conflict resolution. Without such a mechanism, disagreements can escalate to the point at which the partnership is dissolved and the business ceases to operate.

Keeping a Partnership Thriving

Forming a partnership offers entrepreneurs many advantages but can create many business problems as well. What steps can partners take to avoid the pitfalls of partnerships?

Paul and Jim were great friends who decided to go into business together. They launched their courier business on a handshake and a pledge to share and share alike. Trouble soon loomed over the partnership, however, the result of Jim's gambling habit. Jim assumed that, as co-founder of the company, he was entitled to help himself to cash whenever he was running low. Because of his gambling habit, Jim's cash often ran low. Paul managed to cope with Jim's "withdrawals" until two large thugs camped out in the foyer of the business and refused to leave until they collected $2,500 for Jim's losing Super Bowl bet with a bookie. Paul locked the

company safe and hid the key. When Jim discovered that he could no longer raid the company's cash, he brought a guard dog to work, put it in the cab of Paul's truck, and had the receptionist ask Paul to move his truck.

Three middle managers at a plastics fabricator purchased the company in a leveraged buyout. The business took off, and profits climbed much higher than they had expected. Unfortunately, two of the partners began plotting to keep most of the largesse for themselves by subtly pressuring the third partner out of the business. They scheduled important business meetings and "forgot" to tell him about them. They took key customers to lunch and did not invite him. They awarded themselves big raises and gave him an extra week of vacation. "They threw every humiliation at me they could think of," says the third partner, looking back on the situation. "I was so absorbed with building the company that I didn't dream *they* weren't." He was shocked when his partners walked into his office one afternoon and announced, "John, when you go home tonight, don't bother coming back." John *did* come back—with an exit agreement the three had signed when they created their partnership. Unfazed, his former partners used that contract against him as well, enforcing the noncompete clause the agreement contained against him.

These partnership horror stories (and there are *many* more out there) are enough to discourage any entrepreneur from entering into a partnership. Structured properly, however, a partnership can be very successful and quite rewarding for its founders. For instance, Marty Ambuehl and Neil Clark formed their first business partnership as college friends when they co-founded a piano moving company on little more than a handshake and a slap on the back. Years later, when they launched ATM Express, a Billings, Montana, company that distributes automated teller machines, they took a much more formal approach. When their principal investor asked, "What happens if the two of you get to the point where you don't want to be partners anymore," they created employment contracts that locked them into the partnership for five years. They also created a buy-sell agreement that gives one partner the right of first refusal if the other partner decides he wants out.

Ambuehl and Clark also drew up documents that addressed the ways in which they agreed to handle big decisions and difficult problems that they knew would eventually arise. That document alone proved to be quite valuable when they had the opportunity to purchase a related business. Ambuehl saw the purchase as a major opportunity for their business to grow, but Clark saw it as a huge risk and was reluctant to take such a big step. To resolve the stalemate, the partners turned to their agreement: They would make a major move such as an acquisition only if both of them agreed on it. "If there's no agreement, there's no deal," says Clark. "That's the solution." Ambuehl agrees. "You're fooling yourself if you think there's never going to be a disagreement," he says. "Neil and I don't try to back one another into a corner. We know we have to bend."

Avoiding ugly and costly business divorces that too often bring an end to businesses requires an ongoing and active effort. Experts suggest that partners follow these guidelines to keep their partnerships going strong:

- Ask yourself, "Do I really need a partner?" A potential partner should bring to the business skills, contacts, financing, knowledge, or something else that you don't have. The ideal partner is one whose skills, talents, and abilities *complement* yours rather than *mirror* them.
- Take a close look at what you're getting. How well do you really know your potential partner? One of the best ways to test your compatibility is to work on projects together before you decide to go into business with one another.
- Invest in the relationship, not just the deal making. Partners must constantly work to strengthen their relationships. You cannot delegate or ignore this role; otherwise, the partnership is destined to fail.
- Respect your differences but expect to work out conflicts. When potential sources of conflict exist, address them immediately. Festering wounds seldom heal themselves.
- Divide business responsibilities and duties according to each partner's skills, interests, and abilities.
- Be prepared to change. Be open to new opportunities, and share with your partners what you see. Partnerships must evolve to survive.
- Help your partners to succeed. Work hard to see that every partner plays a role in the business that affords him or her the opportunity to be successful.
- Make sure your partners are people you admire, respect, and enjoy being around.

1. Research relationships between partners and add at least three guidelines to those listed above.
2. Develop a list of the types of behavior that is almost certain to destroy a partnership.
3. Suppose that two of your friends are about to launch a business together with nothing but a handshake. "We've been best friends since grammar school," they say. What advice would you give them?

Sources: Dimitra Kessenides, "Happy Together," *Inc.*, November 2004, pp. 54–56; Robert A. Mamis, "Partner Wars," *Inc.*, June 1994, http://pf.inc.com/magazine/19940601/2956.html; Rosabeth Moss Kanter, "Six Rules for a Happy Marriage . . . Uh, Partnership", *Business 2.0*, April 2002 p. 114; Paulette Thomas, "Networking Provides Partnership's Funding," *Wall Street Journal*, October 14, 2003, p. B4; Nichole L. Torres, "A Week in Review," *Entrepreneur*, October 2005, pp. 92–94.

Limited Partnerships

limited partnership
a partnership composed of at least one general partner and at least one limited partner.

A **limited partnership** is composed of at least one general partner and at least one limited partner. In a limited partnership the general partner is treated, under the law, exactly as in a general partnership. Limited partners are treated as investors in the business venture, and they have limited liability for the partnership's debts. They can lose only the amount they have invested in the business. Because of this advantage, limited partnerships own many professional sports teams.

Most states have ratified the Revised Uniform Limited Partnership Act. When forming a limited partnership, its founders are required to file a Certificate of Limited Partnership with the secretary of state's office. Although the requirements vary from one state to another, the Certificate of Limited Partnership typically includes the following information:

1. The name of the limited partnership.
2. The general character of its business.
3. The address of the office of the firm's agent authorized to receive summonses or other legal notices.

4. The name and business address of each partner, specifying which ones are general partners and which are limited partners.
5. The amount of cash contributions actually made, and agreed to be made in the future, by each partner.
6. A description of the value of noncash contributions made or to be made by each partner.
7. The times at which additional contributions are to be made by any of the partners.
8. Whether and under what conditions a limited partner has the right to grant limited partner status to an assignee of his or her interest in the partnership.
9. If agreed on, the time or the circumstances when a partner may withdraw from the firm (unlike the withdrawal of a general partner, the withdrawal of a limited partner does *not* automatically dissolve a limited partnership).
10. If agreed on, the amount of, or the method of determining, the funds to be received by a withdrawing partner.
11. Any right of a partner to receive distributions of cash or other property from the firm, and the times and circumstances for such distributions.
12. The time or circumstances when the limited partnership is to be dissolved.
13. The rights of the remaining general partners to continue the business after withdrawal of a general partner.
14. Any other matters the partners want to include.

Every limited partnership must have at least one general partner, but there is no limit to the number of general or limited partners allowed. The general partner has the same rights and duties as under a general partnership: the right to make decisions for the business, to act as an agent for the partnership, to use the property of the partnership for normal business, and to share in the business's profits. The limited partner does not have the right to engage actively in managing the business. In fact, if a limited partner takes an active part in managing the business (more than 500 hours per year), he or she forfeits the limited liability status and is treated just like a general partner. Limited partners can, however, make management suggestions to the general partners, inspect the business, and make copies of business records. A limited partner is, of course, entitled to a share of the business's profits as specified in the Certificate of Limited Partnership. The primary disadvantage of limited partnerships is the complexity and the cost of establishing and maintaining them.

Wolfgang Puck, the Austrian-born chef who has won national acclaim for his unique food combinations such as scrambled egg pizza with smoked salmon and banana chocolate chip soufflé, and his wife, Barbara Lazaroff, operate three dozen upscale restaurants across the United States. The largest division of their business, the Food Company, is a corporation, but Puck and Lazaroff rely on limited partnerships to operate the restaurants in their Fine Dining Group. For instance, each of the company's various Spago's (Beverly Hills, Palo Alto, Maui, and Las Vegas) has a distinct collection of owners as do the other restaurants in the group such as Postrio and Chinois.[7]

Wolfgang Puck

World-famous chef Wolfgang Puck and his wife Barbara Lazaroff operate the restaurants in their company's Fine Dining Group–Spago, Postrio, and others-through limited partnerships.

Limited Liability Partnerships

Many states now recognize a **limited liability partnership (LLP)** in which *all* partners in a business are limited partners, which gives them the advantage of limited liability for the debts of the partnership. Most states restrict LLPs to certain types of professionals such as attorneys, physicians, dentists, accountants, and others. However, many states restrict the limited liability advantage of LLPs to the results of actions taken by other partners. For instance, if an LLP sells a defective product that injures a customer, the injured customer could sue the business *and* the partners as individuals. The partners' unlimited personal liability exposure means that their personal assets would be at risk.

limited liability partnership (LLP)
a special type of limited partnership in which *all* partners, who in many states must be professionals, are limited partners.

Just as with any limited partnership, the partners must file a Certificate of Limited Partnership in the state in which the partnership will conduct business, and the partnership must identify itself as an LLP to those with whom it does business. In addition, like every partnership, an LLP does not pay taxes; its income is passed through to the limited partners, who pay taxes on their shares of the company's income.

Master Limited Partnership

master limited partnership (MLP)
a partnership whose shares are traded on stock exchanges, just like a corporation's.

A relatively new form of business structure, the **master limited partnership (MLP)** is just like a regular limited partnership, except that its shares are traded just like shares of common stock. They provide most of the same advantages to investors as a corporation—including limited liability. Operationally, a master limited partnership behaves like a corporation, and some even trade on major stock exchanges. In 1987, congressional legislation provided that any MLP not involved in natural resources such as oil, natural gas, or real estate would be taxed as a corporation and consequently eliminated their ability to avoid the disadvantage of double taxation that corporations experience.

Sunoco Logistics

Sunoco Logistics, a company that refines and stores crude oil and refined oil products, formed a master limited partnership to take advantage of the "pass through" treatment of its net income. Because the MLP simply passes its net income through to its owners, Sunoco Logistics avoids the double taxation that it would incur if it were a corporation.[8]

LEARNING OBJECTIVES
1C. Explain the advantages and disadvantages of the corporation.

corporation
a separate legal entity apart from its owners which receives the right to exist from the state in which it is incorporated.

domestic corporation
a corporation doing business in the state in which it is incorporated.

foreign corporation
a corporation doing business in a state other than the one in which it is incorporated.

alien corporation
a corporation formed in another country but doing business in the United States.

publicly held corporation
a corporation that has a large number of shareholders and whose stock usually is traded on one of the large stock exchanges.

closely held corporation
a corporation whose shares are controlled by a relatively small number of people, often family members, relatives, friends, or employees.

Corporations

The corporation is the most complex of the three major forms of business ownership. It is a separate entity apart from its owners, and may engage in business, make contracts, sue and be sued, own property, and pay taxes. The Supreme Court has defined the **corporation** as "an artificial being, invisible, intangible, and existing only in contemplation of the law."[9] Because the life of the corporation is independent of its owners, the shareholders can sell their interests in the business without affecting its continuation.

Corporations (also known as "C Corporations") are creations of the states. When a corporation is founded, it accepts the regulations and restrictions of the state in which it is incorporated and any other state in which it chooses to do business. A corporation doing business in the state in which it is incorporated is a **domestic corporation.** When a corporation conducts business in another state, that state considers it to be a **foreign corporation.** A corporation that is formed in another country but does business in the United States is called an **alien corporation.**

Corporations have the power to raise large amounts of capital by selling shares of ownership to outside investors, but many corporations have only a handful of shareholders. A **publicly held corporation** has a large number of shareholders, and its stock usually is traded on one of the large stock exchanges. A **closely held corporation** has shares that are controlled by a relatively small number of people, often family members, relatives, friends, or employees. Its stock is not traded on any stock exchange but instead is passed from one generation to the next. Many small corporations are closely held.

A corporation must report annually its financial operations to its home state's secretary of state. These financial reports become public record. If a corporation's stock is sold in more than one state, the corporation must comply with federal regulations governing the sale of corporate securities. There are substantially more reporting requirements for a corporation than for the other forms of ownership.

How to Incorporate

Most states allow entrepreneurs to incorporate without the assistance of an attorney. Some states even provide incorporation kits to help in the incorporation process. Although it is cheaper for entrepreneurs to complete the process themselves, it is not always the best idea. In some states, the application process is complex, and the required forms are confusing. The price for filing incorrectly can be high. If an entrepreneur completes the incorporation process improperly, it is generally invalid.

Once the owners decide to form a corporation, they must choose a state in which to incorporate. If the business will operate within a single state, it is probably most logical to incorporate in that state. States differ—sometimes rather dramatically—in the requirements they place on the corporations they charter and how they treat the corporations created within their borders. They also differ in the tax rates they impose on corporations, the restrictions they place on corporations' activities, the capital they require for a company to incorporate, and the fees or organization taxes they charge to incorporate. Delaware, for instance, offers low incorporation fees, favorable laws, and minimal legal requirements, and many corporations are chartered there.

To create a corporation, every state requires a Certificate of Incorporation or charter to be filed with the secretary of state. The following information is generally required to be in the Certificate of Incorporation:

The corporation's name. The corporation must choose a name that is not so similar to that of another firm in that state that it causes confusion or lends itself to deception. It must also include a term such as "corporation," "incorporated," "company," or "limited" to notify the public that they are dealing with a corporation.

The corporation's statement of purpose. The incorporators must state in general terms the intended nature of the business. The purpose must, of course, be lawful. An illustration might be "to engage in the sale of office furniture and fixtures." The purpose should be broad enough to allow for some expansion in the activities of the business as it develops.

The corporation's time horizon. Most corporations are formed with no specific termination date; they are formed "for perpetuity." However, it is possible to incorporate for a specific duration (e.g., 50 years).

Names and addresses of the incorporators. The incorporators must be identified in the articles of incorporation and are liable under the law to attest that all information in the articles of incorporation is correct. Some states require one or more of the incorporators to reside in the state in which the corporation is being created.

Place of business. The street and mailing addresses of the corporation's principal office must be listed. For a domestic corporation, this address must be in the state in which incorporation takes place.

Capital stock authorization. The articles of incorporation must include the amount and class (or type) of capital stock the corporation wants to be authorized to issue. This is *not* the number of shares it must issue; a corporation can issue any number of shares up to the total number authorized. This section must also define the different classification of stock and any special rights, preferences, or limits each class has.

Capital required at the time of incorporation. Some states require a newly formed corporation to deposit in a bank a specific percentage of the stock's par value prior to incorporating.

Provisions for preemptive rights, if any, that are granted to stockholders. If a corporation later issues more shares of the stock it is authorized to issue, its original investors' shares of ownership would be diluted. To prevent this dilution, some corporations grant **preemptive rights** to shareholders, which give them the ability to purchase enough shares to maintain their original percentage of ownership in the company.

Restrictions on transferring shares. Many closely held corporations—those owned by a few shareholders, often family members—require shareholders interested in selling their stock to offer it first to the corporation. (Shares the corporation itself owns are called **treasury stock**.) To maintain control over their ownership, many closely held corporations exercise their right, known as the **right of first refusal.**

preemptive rights
the rights of a corporation's original investors to purchase enough shares of future stock issues to maintain their original percentage of ownership in the company.

treasury stock
the shares of its own stock that a corporation owns.

right of first refusal
a provision requiring shareholders who want to sell their stock to offer it first to the corporation.

bylaws

the rules and regulations the officers and directors establish for a corporation's internal management and operation.

Names and addresses of the officers and directors of the corporation.

Rules under which the corporation will operate. **Bylaws** are the rules and regulations the officers and directors establish for the corporation's internal management and operation.

Once the secretary of state of the incorporating state has approved a request for incorporation and the corporation pays its fees, the approved articles of incorporation become its charter. With the charter in hand, the next order of business is to hold an organizational meeting for the stockholders to formally elect directors who, in turn, will appoint the corporate officers.

The Advantages of the Corporation

Limited Liability of Stockholders Because it is a separate legal entity, a corporation allows investors to limit their liability to the total amount of their investment in the business. In other words, creditors of the corporation cannot lay claim to shareholders' personal assets to satisfy the company's unpaid debts. The legal protection of personal assets from business creditors is of critical concern to many potential investors.

This shield of limited liability may not be impenetrable, however. Because start-up companies are so risky, lenders and other creditors often require the founders of corporations to personally guarantee loans made to the business. Experts estimate that 95 percent of small business owners have to sign personal guarantees to get the financing they need. By making these guarantees, owners are putting their personal assets at risk (just as in a proprietorship) despite choosing the corporate form of ownership.

The corporate form of ownership does not protect its owners from being held personally liable for fraudulent or illegal acts, however. Court decisions have extended the personal liability of the owners of small corporations beyond the financial guarantees that banks and other lenders require, "piercing the corporate veil" much more than ever before. Courts increasingly are holding entrepreneurs *personally* liable for environmental, pension, and legal claims against their corporations. Courts will pierce the corporate veil and hold entrepreneurs liable for the company's debts and obligations if the owners deliberately commit criminal or negligent acts when handling corporate business. Courts ignore the limited liability shield the corporate form of ownership provides when an entrepreneur:

1. Uses corporate assets for personal reasons or commingles them with his or her personal assets.
2. Fails to act in a responsible manner and creates an unwarranted level of financial risk for the stockholders.
3. Makes financial misrepresentations, such as operating with more than one set of books.
4. Takes actions in the name of the corporation that were not authorized by the board of directors.

Liability problems associated with piercing the corporate veil almost always originate from actions and decisions that fail to maintain the integrity of a corporation. The most common cause of these problems, especially in closely held corporations, is corporate owners and officers failing to keep their personal funds and assets separate from those of the corporation.

Table 5.1 offers some useful suggestions for avoiding legal tangles in a corporation.

Ability to Attract Capital Because of the limited liability they offer their investors, corporations have proved to be the most effective form of ownership for accumulating large amounts of capital. Limited only by the number of shares authorized in its charter (which can be amended), a corporation can raise money to begin business and expand by selling shares of its stock to investors. A corporation can sell its stock to a limited number of private investors in a private placement or to the public through an initial public offering (or IPO).

TABLE 5.1 Avoiding Legal Tangles in a Corporation

Steps that entrepreneurs should take to avoid legal problems if they own a corporation include the following:

- *Identify the company as a corporation by using "Inc." or "Corporation" in the business name.* This alerts all who do business with a company that it is a corporation.

- *File all reports and pay all necessary fees required by the state in a timely manner.* Most states require corporations to file reports with the secretary of state on an annual basis. Failing to do so will jeopardize the validity of your corporation and will open the door for personal liability problems for its shareholders.

- *Hold annual meetings to elect officers and directors.* In a closely held corporation, the officers elected may *be* the shareholders, but that does not matter. Corporations formed by an individual are not required to hold meetings, but the sole shareholder must file a written consent form.

- *Keep minutes of every meeting of the officers and directors, even if it takes place in the living room of the founders.* It is a good idea to elect a secretary who is responsible for recording the minutes.

- *Make sure that the corporation's board of directors makes all major decisions.* Problems arise in closely held corporations when one owner makes key decisions alone without consulting the elected board.

- *Make it clear that the business is a corporation by having all officers sign contracts, loan agreements, purchase orders, and other legal documents in the corporation's name rather than their own names.* Failing to designate their status as agents of the corporation can result in the officers being held personally liable for agreements they think they are signing on the corporation's behalf.

- *Keep corporate assets and the personal assets of the owners separate.* Few things make courts more willing to hold shareholders personally liable for a corporation's debts than commingling corporate and personal assets. In some closely held corporations, owners have been known to use corporate assets to pay their personal expenses (or vice versa) or to mix their personal funds with corporate funds into a single bank account. Protect the corporation's identity by keeping it completely separate from the owners' personal identities.

One of the most successful initial public offerings in recent years was Google's IPO. When founders Sergey Brin and Larry Page, who founded the company in their college dorm room, took their company public, they sold 19.6 million shares at $85 per share, raising $1.67 billion to fund Google's growth and expansion.[10]

Google

You will learn more about IPOs in Chapter 13, "Sources of Financing: Debt and Equity."

Ability to Continue Indefinitely Unless a corporation fails to pay its taxes or is limited to a specific length of life by its charter, it can continue indefinitely. The corporation's existence does not depend on the fate of any single individual. Unlike a proprietorship or partnership, in which the death of a founder ends the business, a corporation lives beyond the lives of those who gave it life. This perpetual life gives rise to the next major advantage—transferable ownership.

Transferable Ownership Unlike an investment in a partnership, shares of ownership in a corporation are easily transferable. If stockholders want to liquidate their shares of ownership in a corporation, they can sell their shares to someone else. Billions of shares of stock representing ownership in companies are traded daily on the world's stock exchanges. Shareholders can also transfer their stock through inheritance to a new generation of owners. During all of these transfers of ownership, the corporation continues to conduct business as usual.

The Disadvantages of the Corporation

Cost and Time Involved in the Incorporation Process Corporations can be costly and time consuming to establish and to maintain. The owners are giving birth to an artificial legal entity, and the gestation period can be prolonged, especially for a novice. In some states an attorney must handle the incorporation process, but in most states entrepreneurs can complete all of the required forms alone. However, entrepreneurs must exercise great caution when incorporating without the help of an attorney. In addition, incorporating a business requires a variety of fees that are not applicable to proprietorships or partnerships. The average cost to create a corporation is around $1,000, but, depending on the complexity of the organization, fees can range from $500 and $2,500. In addition, a corporation must have a board of directors, and the board must conduct an annual meeting and maintain written records of that meeting.

double taxation
a disadvantage of the corporate form of ownership in which a corporation's profits are taxed twice: at the corporate rate and at the individual rate (on the portion of profits distributed as dividends).

Double Taxation Because a corporation is a separate legal entity, it must pay taxes on its net income at the federal level, in most states, and to some local governments as well. Before stockholders receive a penny of its net income as dividends, a corporation must pay these taxes at the *corporate* tax rate, a graduated tax on corporate profits. Then, stockholders must pay taxes on the dividends they receive from these same profits at the *individual* tax rate. Thus, a corporation's profits are taxed twice. This **double taxation** is a distinct disadvantage of the corporate form of ownership. Under current tax rates (which are progressive for both the corporation and the individual), the magnitude of the double tax ranges from 23.1 percent to 57.1 percent, depending on the corporation's earnings.[11]

Potential for Diminished Managerial Incentives As corporations grow, they often require additional managerial expertise beyond what the founder can provide. Because they have most of their personal wealth tied up in their companies, entrepreneurs have an intense interest in making them successful and are willing to make sacrifices for them. Professional managers the entrepreneur brings in to help run the business as it grows do not always have the same degree of interest in or loyalty to the company. As a result, the business may suffer without the founder's energy, care, and devotion. One way to minimize this potential problem is to link managers' (and even employees') compensation to the company's financial performance through a profit-sharing or bonus plan. Corporations can also stimulate managers' and employees' incentive on the job by creating an employee stock ownership plan (ESOP) in which managers and employees become part or whole owners in the company.

Legal Requirements and Regulatory Red Tape Corporations are subject to more legal, reporting, and financial requirements than other forms of ownership. Corporate officers must meet more stringent requirements for recording and reporting management decisions and actions. They must also hold annual meetings and consult the board of directors about major decisions that are beyond day-to-day operations. Managers may be required to submit some major decisions to the stockholders for approval. Corporations that are publicly held must file quarterly (10-Q) and annual (10-K) reports with the Securities and Exchange Commission (SEC). These reports are available to the public, and anyone, including competitors, can access them.

Potential Loss of Control by the Founder(s) When entrepreneurs sell shares of ownership in their companies, they relinquish some control. Especially when they need large capital infusions for start-up or growth, entrepreneurs may have to give up *significant* amounts of control, so much, in fact, that the founder becomes a minority shareholder. Losing majority ownership—and therefore control—in a company leaves the founder in a precarious position. He or she no longer has the power to determine the company's direction; "outsiders" do. In some cases, founders' shares have been so diluted that majority shareholders actually vote them out of their jobs!

In 1975, Bill Gates and Paul Allen founded Microsoft as a partnership. At that time, Bill Gates owned 50% of the business. As the entrepreneurs needed additional capital, they made an initial public offering. Later, to fund the business's rapid growth, Gates sold additional shares of common stock. The result has been a dilution of co-founder Bill Gate's percentage of ownership to 18.5%. However, there is no reason to feel sorry for Gates; the value of his Microsoft stock has pushed his net worth to $51 billion, making him the wealthiest person in the United States![12]

Other Forms of Ownership

In addition to the sole proprietorship, the partnership, and the corporation, entrepreneurs can choose from other forms of ownership, including the S corporation, the limited liability company, the professional corporation, and the joint venture.

The S Corporation

In 1954 the Internal Revenue Service Code created the Sub-chapter S corporation. In recent years the IRS has shortened the title to S corporation and has made a few modifications in its qualifications. An **S corporation** is a distinction that is made only for federal income tax purposes, and is, in terms of its legal characteristics, no different from any other corporation. Although Congress has simplified some of the rules and requirements for S corporations, a business seeking "S" status still must meet the following criteria:

S corporation
a corporation that retains the legal characteristics of a regular (C) corporation but has the advantage of being taxed as a partnership if it meets certain criteria.

1. It must be a domestic (U.S.) corporation.
2. It cannot have a nonresident alien as a shareholder.
3. It can issue only one class of common stock, which means that all shares must carry the same rights (e.g., the right to dividends or liquidation rights). The exception is voting rights, which may differ. In other words, an S corporation can issue voting and nonvoting common stock.
4. It must limit its shareholders to individuals, estates, and certain trusts, although tax-exempt creations such as employee stock ownership plans (ESOPs) and pension plans can now be shareholders.
5. It cannot have more than 100 shareholders (increased from 75), which is an important benefit for family businesses making the transition from one generation of owners to another.
6. Less than 25 percent of the corporation's gross revenues during three successive tax years must be from passive sources.

If a corporation meets the criteria of an S corporation, its shareholders must actually elect to be treated as one. An S corporation election may be filed at any time during the 12 months that precede the taxable year for which the election is to be effective. (The corporation must have been eligible for S status for the entire year.) To make the election of S status effective for the current tax year, entrepreneurs must file Form 2553 with the IRS within the first 75 days of the corporation's fiscal year. *All* shareholders must consent to have the corporation treated as an S corporation.

The Advantages of an S Corporation An S corporation retains all of the advantages of a regular corporation, such as continuity of existence, transferability of ownership, and limited personal liability for its owners. The most notable provision of the S corporation is that it serves as a conduit for its net income, passing all of its profits or losses through to the individual shareholders, which means that its income is taxed only once at the individual tax rate. Thus, electing S corporation status avoids a primary disadvantage of the regular (or "C") corporation—double taxation. In essence, the tax treatment of an S corporation is exactly like that of a partnership. The corporation files an informational return (1120-S) with the IRS and provides its shareholders with Schedule K-1, which reports their proportional shares of the company's profits. The shareholders report their portions of the S corporation's earnings on their individual income tax returns (Form 1040) and pay taxes on those profits at the individual tax rates (even if they never take the money out of the business). This tax treatment can cause problems for individual shareholders, however. If an S corporation earns a profit but managers choose to plow that income back into the business in the form of retained earnings to fuel its growth and expansion, shareholders still must pay taxes on their share of the company's net income. In that case, shareholders will end up paying taxes on "phantom income" they never actually received.

Another advantage the S corporation offers is avoiding the tax C corporations pay on assets that have appreciated in value and are sold. S corporations also are not subject to the self-employment tax that sole proprietors and general partners must pay; however, they are responsible for payroll taxes (for Social Security and Medicare) on the wages the S corporation pays its employees. Therefore, owners of S corporations must be sure that the salaries they draw are reasonable; salaries that are too low or too high draw scrutiny from the IRS.

One significant change to the laws governing S corporations that benefits entrepreneurs involves subsidiary companies. Before 1998, if an entrepreneur owned separate but affiliated companies, he or she had to maintain each one as a distinct S corporation with its own accounting records and tax return. Under current law, business owners can set up all of these affiliated companies as qualified S corporation subsidiaries ("Q Subs") under the umbrella of a single company, each with its own separate legal identity, and still file a single tax return for the parent company. For entrepreneurs with several lines of businesses, this change means greatly simplified tax filing. Owners also can use losses from one subsidiary company to offset profits from another to minimize their tax bills.

Disadvantages of an S Corporation When the Tax Reform Act (TRA) of 1986 restructured individual and corporate tax rates, many business owners switched to S corporations to lower their tax bills. For the first time since Congress enacted the federal income tax in 1913, the maximum individual rate was lower than the maximum corporate rate. However, in 1993 Congress realigned the tax structure by raising the maximum personal tax rate to 39.6 percent from 31 percent. This new rate was 4.6 percent *higher* than the maximum corporate tax rate of 35 percent, making S corporation status less attractive than before. Today, however, the maximum tax rate for individuals is 35 percent, and for corporations, it is 39 percent. Entrepreneurs considering both C corporation and S corporation status must consider the total impact of the decision on their companies, especially the tax implications (including the impact of the C corporation's double taxation penalty on the portion of its net income distributed as dividends).

Another disadvantage of the S corporation is that the costs of many benefits—insurance, meals, lodging, and others—paid to shareholders with 2 percent or more of stock cannot be deducted as business expenses for tax purposes; these benefits are then considered to be taxable income. In addition, S corporations offer shareholders only a limited range of retirement benefits, while regular corporations make a wide range of retirement plans available.

When Is an S Corporation a Wise Choice? Choosing S corporation status is usually beneficial to start-up companies anticipating net losses. In this case, an entrepreneur can use the loss to offset other income, thus saving money in the long run. Companies that plan to reinvest most of their earnings to finance growth also find S corporation status favorable. Small business owners who intend to sell their companies in the near future will prefer "S" over "C" status because the taxable gains on the sale of an S corporation are generally lower than those of a C corporation.

On the other hand, small companies with the following characteristics are *not* likely to benefit from S corporation status:

- Highly profitable personal service companies with large numbers of shareholders, in which most of the profits are passed on to shareholders as compensation or retirement benefits.

- Fast-growing companies that must retain most of their earnings to finance growth and capital spending.
- Corporations in which the loss of benefits to shareholders exceeds tax savings.
- Corporations in which the income before any compensation to shareholders is less than $100,000 per year.
- Corporations with sizable net operating losses that cannot be used against S corporation earnings.

Liquidating an S Corporation

Even though an S corporation has perpetual life just like a C corporation, the time may come when the stockholders want to dissolve the company. Liquidating an S corporation requires an entrepreneur to take the following actions:

- Pay all taxes and debts.
- Obtain the written approval of shareholders to dissolve the company.
- File a statement of intent to dissolve with the secretary of state's office in which the S corporation resides.
- Distribute all remaining assets of the corporation to shareholders.

The Limited Liability Company (LLC)

A relatively new creation, the **limited liability company (LLC)** is, like an S corporation, a cross between a partnership and a corporation. Like S corporations, LLCs offer their owners limited personal liability for the debts of the business, providing a significant advantage over sole proprietorships and partnerships. LLCs, however, are not subject to many of the restrictions currently imposed on S corporations and offer more flexibility than S corporations. For example, S corporations cannot have more than 100 shareholders, none of whom can be a foreigner or a corporation. S corporations are also limited to only one class of stock. LLCs eliminate those restrictions. In most states an LLC can have just one owner, but a few states require LLC to have at least two owners (called "members"). LLCs offer their owners limited liability without imposing any requirements on their characteristics or any ceiling on their numbers. LLC members can include non-U.S. citizens, partnerships, and corporations. Unlike a limited partnership, which prohibits limited partners from participating in the day-to-day management of the business, an LLC does not restrict its members' ability to become involved in managing the company.

In addition to offering its members the advantage of limited liability, LLCs also avoid the double taxation imposed on C corporations. Like an S corporation, an LLC does not pay income taxes; its income flows through to the members, who are responsible for paying income taxes on their shares of the LLC's net income. Because they are not subject to the many restrictions imposed on other forms of ownership, LLCs offer entrepreneurs another significant advantage: flexibility. An LLC permits its members to divide income (and thus tax liability) as they see fit, including allocations that differ from their percentages of ownership. Like an S corporation, the members' share of an LLC's earnings is not subject to the self-employment tax. However, the managing member's share of the LLC's earnings is subject to the self-employment tax just as a sole proprietor's or a general partner's earned income is.

These advantages make the LLC an ideal form of ownership for many small companies across many industries—retail, wholesale, manufacturing, real estate, or service. Because they offer the tax advantage of a partnership, the legal protection of a corporation, and maximum operating flexibility, LLCs have become an extremely popular form of ownership among entrepreneurs.

limited liability company (LLC)
a relatively new form of ownership that, like an S corporation, is a cross between a partnership and a corporation; it is not subject to many of the restrictions imposed on S corporations.

Marian Fletcher launched a profitable party planning and catering service in 1995 as a sole proprietorship. Her company, Let's Go Party, grew quickly, and Fletcher wanted to bring her daughter into the business as an owner. Reviewing the advantages and disadvantages of each form of ownership led Fletcher to create an LLC. "We decided this was the best way to go for us," she says. "In case anything happens, my daughter and I won't

Let's Go Party

As the owner of this pastry shop knows, operating a sole proprietorship offers many advantages, but entrepreneurs considering this form of ownership must be aware of its disadvantages as well.

be liable for anything more than what we have invested in the company already." Fletcher, who set up her LLC without the help of an attorney for just $50, also found the LLC's tax treatment to be a major advantage for her and her daughter.[6]

articles of organization
the document that creates an LLC by establishing its name, its method of management, its duration, and other details.

Creating an LLC is much like creating a corporation. Forming an LLC requires an entrepreneur to create two documents: the articles of organization (which must be filed with the secretary of state) and the operating agreement. The LLC's **articles of organization,** similar to the corporation's articles of incorporation, actually creates the LLC by establishing its name and address, its method of management (board managed or member managed), its duration, and the names and addresses of each organizer. In most states the company's name must contain the words "limited liability company," "limited company," or the letters "L.L.C." or "L.C." Unlike a corporation, an LLC does not have perpetual life; in most states an LLC's charter may not exceed 30 years. However, the same factors that would cause a partnership to dissolve would also cause the dissolution of an LLC before its charter expires.

operating agreement
the document that establishes for an LLC the provisions governing the way it will conduct business.

The **operating agreement,** similar to a corporation's bylaws, outlines the provisions governing the way the LLC will conduct business, such as members' capital contributions to the LLC, the admission or withdrawal of members, distributions from the business, and how the LLC will be managed. To ensure that their LLCs are classified as a partnership for tax purposes, entrepreneurs must draft the operating agreement carefully. The operating agreement must create an LLC that has more characteristics of a partnership than of a corporation to maintain this favorable tax treatment. Specifically, an LLC cannot have any more than *two* of the following four corporate characteristics:

1. *Limited liability.* Limited liability exists if no member of the LLC is personally liable for the debts or claims against the company. Because entrepreneurs choosing this form of ownership usually do so to get limited liability protection, the operating agreement almost always has this characteristic.
2. *Continuity of life.* Continuity of life exists if the company continues to exist in spite of changes in stock ownership. To avoid continuity of life, any LLC member must have the power to dissolve the company. Most entrepreneurs choose to omit this characteristic from their LLC's operating agreements.
3. *Free transferability of interest.* Free transferability of interest exists if each LLC member has the power to transfer her or his ownership to another person freely and without the consent of other members. To avoid this characteristic, the operating agreement must state that a recipient of a member's LLC stock cannot become a substitute member without the consent of the remaining members.
4. *Centralized management.* Centralized management exists if a group that does not include all LLC members has the authority to make management decisions and to conduct company business. To avoid this characteristic, the operating agreement must state that the company elects to be "member managed."

Despite their universal appeal to entrepreneurs, LLCs suffer some disadvantages. They can be expensive to create, often costing between $1,500 and $5,000. Unlike corporations, which can operate "for perpetuity," LLCs have limited life spans. Because there is no stock involved, this form of ownership also is not suitable for companies whose owners plan to raise money through an initial public offering or who want to use stock options or an employee stock ownership plan as incentives for employees.

Entrepreneurs who want to provide attractive benefits to themselves and their employees will not find this form of ownership appealing because the cost of those benefits is not tax deductible in an LLC.

Although an LLC may be ideally suited for an entrepreneur launching a new company, it may pose problems for business owners considering converting an existing business to an LLC. Switching to an LLC from a general partnership, a limited partnership, or a sole proprietorship reorganizing to bring in new owners is usually not a problem. However, owners of corporations and S corporations would incur large tax obligations if they converted their companies to LLCs.

To date, the biggest disadvantage of the LLC stems from its newness. No uniform legislation for LLCs exists (although a Uniform Limited Liability Act is pending at the federal level). Every state now recognizes the LLC as a legal form of ownership.

You

Be the Consultant

Which Form Is Best?

Watoma Kinsey and her daughter Katrina are about to launch a business that specializes in children's parties. Their target audience is upscale families who want to throw unique, memorable parties to celebrate special occasions for their children between the ages of 5 and 15 years. They have leased a large building and have renovated it to include many features designed to appeal to kids, including special gym equipment, a skating rink, an obstacle course, a mockup of a pirate ship, a ball crawl, and even a moveable haunted house. They can offer simple birthday parties (cake and ice cream included) or special theme parties as elaborate as the customer wants. Their company will provide magicians, clowns, comedians, jugglers, tumblers, and a variety of other entertainers.

Watoma and Katrina have each invested $45,000 to get the business ready to launch. Based on the quality of their business plan and their preparation, they have negotiated a $40,000 bank loan. Because they both have families and own their own homes, they want to minimize their exposure to potential legal and financial problems. A significant portion of their start-up costs went to purchase a liability insurance policy to cover the Kinseys in case a child is injured at a party. If their business plan is accurate, they will earn a small profit in their first year (about $1,500) and a more attractive profit of $16,000 in their second year of operation. Within five years, they expect their company to generate as much as $50,000 in profits. They have agreed to split the profits—and the workload—equally.

If the business is as successful as they think it will be, the Kinseys eventually want to franchise their company. That, however, is part of their long-range plan. For now, they want to perfect their business system and prove that it can be profitable before they try to duplicate it in the form of franchises.

As they move closer to the launch date for their business, the Kinseys are reviewing the different forms of ownership. They know that their decision has long-term implications for themselves and for their business, but they aren't sure which form of ownership is best for them.

1. Which form(s) of ownership would you recommend to the Kinseys? Explain.
2. Which form(s) of ownership would you recommend the Kinseys *avoid*? Explain.
3. What factors should the Kinseys consider as they evaluate the various forms of ownership?

The Professional Corporation

Professional corporations are designed to offer professionals—lawyers, doctors, dentists, accountants, and others—the advantages of the corporate form of ownership. They are ideally suited for professionals, who must always be concerned about malpractice lawsuits, because they offer limited liability. For example, if three doctors formed a professional corporation, none of them would be liable for the others' malpractice. (Of course, each would be liable for his or her own actions.) Creating a professional corporation is no different from creating a regular corporation. Professional corporations are often identified by the abbreviations P.C. (professional corporation), P.A. (professional association), or S.C. (service corporation). A professional corporation has the following additional limitations beyond the standard corporation:

- All shares of stock of the corporation must be owned and held by individuals licensed in the profession of the corporation.
- At least one of the incorporators must be licensed in the profession.
- At least one director and one officer must be licensed in the profession.
- The articles of incorporation, in addition to all other requirements, must designate the personal services to be provided by the corporation.
- The professional corporation must obtain from the appropriate licensing board a certification that declares the shares of stock are owned by individuals who are duly licensed in the profession.

The Joint Venture

A joint venture is very much like a partnership, except that it is formed for a specific purpose. For instance, suppose that you own a 500-acre tract of land 60 miles from Chicago that has been cleared and is normally used in agricultural production. You have a friend who has solid contacts among major musical groups and would like to put on a concert. You expect prices for your agricultural products to be low this summer, so you and your friend form a joint venture for the specific purpose of staging a three-day concert. Your contribution will be the exclusive use of the land for one month, and your friend will provide all the performers as well as technicians, facilities, and equipment. All costs will be paid out of receipts, and the net profits will be split, with you receiving 20 percent for the use of your land. When the concert is over, the facilities removed, and the accounting for all costs completed, you and your friend split the profits 20:80, and the joint venture terminates.

In any endeavor in which neither party can effectively achieve the purpose alone, a joint venture becomes a common form of ownership. The "partners" form a new joint venture for each new project they undertake. The income derived from a joint venture is taxed as if it arose from a partnership.

Table 5.2 provides a summary of the key features of the major forms of ownership discussed in this chapter.

TABLE 5.2 Characteristics of the Major Forms of Ownership

Characteristic	Sole Propristorship	General Partnership	Limited Partnership	C Corporation	S Corporation
Definition	A for-profit business owned and operated by one person	A for profit-business jointly owned and operated by two or more people	One general partner and one or more partners with limited liability and no rights of management	An artificial legal entity separate from its owners and formed under state laws	An artificial legal entity that is structured like a C corporation but taxed by the federal government like a partnership
Ease of formation	Easiest form of business to set up; if necessary, acquire licenses and permits, register fictitious name, and obtain taxpayer identification	Easy to set up and operate; a written partnership agreement is highly recommended; must acquire an employer ID number; if necessary, register fictitious name	File a Certificate of Limited Partnership with the secretary of state; name must show that business is a limited partnership; must have written agreement, and must keep certain records	File articles of incorporation and other required reports with the secretary of state; prepare bylaws and follow corporate formalities	Must meet all criteria to file as an S corporation; must file timely election with the IRS (within $2\frac{1}{2}$ months of first taxable year)
Owner's personal liability	Unlimited	Unlimited for general partners, limited for limited partners	Limited	Limited	Limited
Number of owners	One	Two or more	At least, one general partner and any number of limited partners	Any number	Maximum of 100 with restrictions as to who they are
Tax liability	Single tax: personal tax rate	Single tax: partners pay on their proportional shares at their individual rate	Same as general partnership	Double tax: corporation pays tax and shareholders pay tax on dividends distributed	Single tax: owners pay on their proportional shares at individual rate
Maximum tax rate	35%	35%	35%	39% corporate plus 35% individual	35%
Transferability of ownership	Fully transferable through sale or transfer of company assets	May require consent of all partners	Same as general partnership	Fully transferable	Transferable (but transfer may affect S status)
Continuity of the business	Ends on death or insanity of proprietor or on termination by proprietor	Dissolves on death, insanity, or retirement of a general partner (business may continue)	Same as general partnership	Perpetual life	Perpetual life
Cost of Formation	Low	Moderate	Moderate	High	High
Liquidity of the owner's investment in the business	Poor to average	Poor to average	Poor to average	High	High
Ability to raise capital	Low	Moderate	Moderate to high	Very high	High
Formation procedure	No special steps required other than buying necessary licenses	No written partnership agreement required (but highly advisable)	Must comply with state laws regarding limited partnership	Must meet formal requirements specified by state law	Must follow same procedures as C corporation, then elect S status with IRS

Chapter Summary by Learning Objectives

1A. Explain the advantages and the disadvantages of the sole proprietorship.

A sole proprietorship is a business owned and managed by one individual and is the most popular form of ownership.

Sole proprietorships offer these *advantages*: They are simple to create; they are the least costly form to begin; the owner has total decision-making authority; there are no special legal restrictions; and they are easy to discontinue.

They also suffer from these *disadvantages*: unlimited personal liability of the owner; limited managerial skills and capabilities; limited access to capital; lack of continuity.

1B. Explain the advantages and the disadvantages of the partnership.

A partnership is an association of two or more people who co-own a business for the purpose of making a profit. Partnerships offer these *advantages*: ease of establishing; complementary skills of partners; division of profits; larger pool of capital available; ability to attract limited partners; little government regulation flexibility; and tax advantages.

Partnerships suffer from these *disadvantages*: unlimited liability of at least one partner; difficulty in disposing of partnership interest; lack of continuity; potential for personality and authority conflicts; and partners bound by the law of agency.

1C. Explain the advantages and the disadvantages of the corporation.

A corporation, the most complex of the three basic forms of ownership, is a separate legal entity. To form a corporation, an entrepreneur must file the articles of incorporation with the state in which the company will incorporate. Corporations offer these *advantages*: limited liability of stockholders; ability to attract capital; ability to continue indefinitely; and transferable ownership.

Corporations suffer from these *disadvantages*: cost and time involved in incorporating; double taxation; potential for diminished managerial incentives; legal requirements and regulatory red tape; and potential loss of control by the founder(s).

2. Discuss the advantages and the disadvantages of the S corporation, the limited liability company, the professional corporation, and the joint venture.

Entrepreneurs can also choose from several other forms of ownership, including S corporations and limited liability companies. An S corporation offers its owners limited liability protection but avoids the double taxation of C Corporations.

A limited liability company, like an S corporation, is a cross between a partnership and a corporation, yet it operates without the restrictions imposed on an S corporation. To create an LLC, an entrepreneur must file the articles of organization and the operating agreement with the secretary of state.

A professional corporation offers professionals the benefits of the corporate form of ownership.

A joint venture is like a partnership, except that it is formed for a specific purpose.

Discussion Questions

1. What factors should an entrepreneur consider before choosing a form of ownership?
2. Why are sole proprietorships so popular as a form of ownership?
3. How can personal conflict affect a partnership?
4. What issues should the articles of partnership address? Why are the articles important to a successful partnership?
5. Can one partner commit another to a business deal without the other's consent? Why?
6. What issues should the Certificate of Incorporation cover?
7. How does an S corporation differ from a regular corporation?
8. What role do limited partners play in a partnership? What happens if a limited partner takes an active role in managing the business?
9. What advantages does a limited liability company offer over an S corporation? A partnership?
10. How is an LLC created? What criteria must an LLC meet to avoid double taxation?
11. Briefly outline the advantages and disadvantages of the major forms of ownership.

Business Plan Pro

Selecting the form of your business is an important decision. As this chapter discussed, this decision will affect the number of business owners, tax obligations, the time and cost to form the entity, the ability to raise capital, and options for transferring ownership.

Business Plan Exercises

On the Web

Go to http://www.prenhall.com/scarborough and review the business entity links associated with Chapter 5. This may provide additional information and resources to assist with your form of business. Enter the search term "business entity" in your favorite search engine and note the resources and information that this term generates.

Sample Plans

Go to the Sample Plan Browser in Business Plan Pro and look at these three business plans: Calico Computer Consulting is a sole proprietorship, Lansing Aviation is a limited liability company, and Southeast Health Plans, Inc. is a corporation. After reviewing the executive summaries of each of these plans, why do you think the owners selected this form of ownership? Considering their respective industries, what are the advantages and disadvantages that each of these business entities offer the owners? Why are these choices a good match for the business relating to ease of starting, liability, control, ability to raise capital, and transfer of ownership?

In the Software

Go to the section of Business Plan Pro called "Company Ownership." Look at the comparison matrix of the "Characteristics of Major Forms of Ownership," Table 5.2 on page 185, and consider the ramifications of your choice.

- If the business is a sole proprietorship or a partnership and the business is sued, you may be person-ally liable. Is the nature of your business one that may present this type of risk? Is this an appropriate business entity based on that potential outcome?
- Once your business becomes profitable, what is the potential tax ramifications compared to your current situation?
- What is your ideal situation regarding the long-term ownership, and what are the possible choices based on that preference.
- What should you budget for legal fees and other expenditures to form the business?
- How much time do you estimate you will need to invest to establish this business entity?
- Will you need to raise capital? How much capital will the venture require? Is this form of ownership optimal for accomplishing that objective?

As you review the instructions provided within Business Plan Pro, refer to the "Characteristics of Major Forms of Ownership" matrix to help you select the form of ownership that is best for you and your venture

Building Your Business Plan

Review the work that you have completed on your business plan. Does your chosen form of ownership "fit" your vision and the scope of the business? Will this choice of business entity offer the type of protection flexibility you desire for your business? You may also want to include comments in your plan regarding changing factors that may require you to reexamine your form of ownership in the future.

Beyond the Classroom . . .

1. Interview five local small business owners. What form of ownership did each choose? Why? Prepare a brief report summarizing your findings, and explain advantages and disadvantages those owners face because of their choices. Do you think that these business owners chose the form of ownership that is best for their particular situations? Explain.

2. Invite entrepreneurs who operate as partners to your classroom. Do they have a written partnership agreement? Are their skills complementary? How do they divide responsibility for running their company? How do they handle decision making? What do they do when disputes and disagreements arise?

6 | Franchising and the Entrepreneur

Where else [but franchising] can we find a job creator, an economic stimulator, and a personal wealth creator that gives [people] the opportunity to realize their dreams and financial security for their families beyond their wildest expectations? —Don DeBolt

Learning Objectives

On completion of this chapter, you will be able to:

1 Describe the three types of franchising: trade name, product distribution, and pure.
2 Explain (A) the benefits and (B) the drawbacks of buying a franchise.
3 Explain the laws covering franchise purchases.
4 Discuss the right way to buy a franchise.
5 Outline the major trends shaping franchising.

When Shep Bostin decided to leave his job as a top executive at a small technology firm, he knew that he wanted to run his own business. He also understood the risks and the challenges facing start-up companies, and at his stage of life, he was not willing to face those risks and challenges. Rather than launch his own independent business, Bostin chose to get into business by purchasing a franchise. After seeing a news story about Geeks on Call, a new franchise that provides on-site technical assistance for computers by dispatching a cadre of computer techies in black Chrysler PT Cruisers, Bostin thought that the franchise might be the ideal match for his skills, abilities, and interests. After checking out the franchise, Bostin decided to invest and has since expanded his franchise territory to cover three territories in Maryland.[1]

Today approximately 3,000 franchisers operate nearly 350,000 franchise outlets in the United States, and more are opening at an incredible pace both in the United States and around the world (see Figure 6.1). In fact, a new franchise opens somewhere in the world every eight minutes! Franchises account for 44 percent of all retail sales, totaling more than *$1 trillion*, and they employ 1 in every 16 workers in the United States in more than 100 major industries.[2] A recent study concludes that the economic impact of franchising on the U.S. economy is an impressive $1.5 trillion.[3] Much of the popularity of franchising stems from its ability to offer those who lack business experience the chance to own and operate a business with a high probability of success. This booming industry has moved far beyond the traditional boundaries of fast food and dry cleaning into fields as diverse as automotive air bag replacement, used clothing, dating services, and pet-sitting.

In **franchising,** semi-independent business owners (franchisees) pay fees and royalties to a parent company (franchiser) in return for the right to become identified with its trademark, to sell its products or services, and often to use its business format and system. Franchisees do not establish their own autonomous businesses; instead, they buy a "success package" from the franchiser, who shows them how to use it. Franchisees, unlike independent business owners, don't have the freedom to change the way they run their businesses—for example, shifting advertising strategies or adjusting product lines—but they do have access to a formula for success that the franchiser has worked out. Fundamentally, when they buy their franchises, franchisees are purchasing a successful business model. Many successful franchisers claim that neglecting to follow the formula is one of the chief reasons that franchisees fail. "If you are overly entrepreneurial and you want to invent you own wheel, or if you are not comfortable with following a system, then don't go down [the franchise] path," says Don DeBolt, head of the International Franchise Association.[4]

franchising
a system of distribution in which semi-independent business owners (franchisees) pay fees and royalties to a parent company (franchiser) in return for the right to become identified with its trademark, to sell its products or services, and often to use its business format and system.

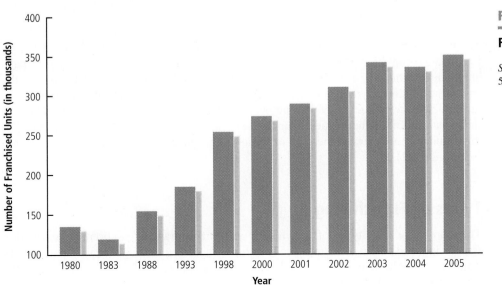

FIGURE 6.1

Franchising Growth

Source: Entrepreneur's Franchise 500 database.

FIGURE 6.2

The Franchising Relationship

Source: Adapted from National Economic Consulting Practice of PricewaterhouseCoopers, *Economic Impact of Franchised Businesses: A Study for the International Franchise Association* (New York: IFA Education Foundation, 2004), pp. 3, 5.

Element	The Franchiser	The Franchisee
Site selection	Oversees and approves; may choose site.	Chooses site with franchiser's approval.
Design	Provides prototype design.	Pays for and implements design.
Employees	Makes general recommendations and training suggestions.	Hires, manages, and fires employees.
Products and services	Determines product or service line.	Modifies only with franchiser's approval.
Prices	Can only recommend prices.	Sets final prices.
Purchasing	Establishes quality standards; provides list of approved suppliers; may require franchisees to purchase from the franchiser.	Must meet quality standards; must purchase only from approved suppliers; must purchase from supplier if required.
Advertising	Develops and coordinates national ad campaign; may require minimum level of spending on local advertising.	Pays for national ad campaign; complies with local advertising requirements; gets franchiser approval on local ads.
Quality control	Sets quality standards and enforces them with inspections; trains franchisees.	Maintains quality standards; trains employees to implement quality systems.
Support	Provides support through an established business system.	Operates business on a day-to-day basis with franchiser's support.

COMPANY
Profile

Schlachter's MAACO Auto Painting and Bodyworks

Anita Schlachter, co-owner of a highly successful MAACO (automotive services) franchise with her husband and her son, is convinced that the system the franchiser taught them is the key to their company's progress and growth. The Schlachters follow the franchiser's plan, using it as a road map to success. "If you listen to what your franchiser says and follow its policies and procedures, you'll be successful," she says. "Those who think they know more [than the franchiser] should not go into franchising."[5]

Franchising is built on an ongoing relationship between a franchiser and a franchisee. The franchiser provides valuable services such as market research, a proven business system, name recognition, and many other forms of assistance; in return, the franchisee pays an initial franchise fee as well as an on-going percentage of his or her outlet's sales to the franchiser as a royalty and agrees to operate the outlet according to the franchiser's system. Because franchisers develop the business systems their franchisees use and direct their distribution methods, they maintain substantial control over their franchisees. Yet this standardization lies at the core of franchising's success as a method of distribution (see Figure 6.2).

LEARNING OBJECTIVES
1. Describe the three types of franchising: trade name, product distribution, and pure.

trade name franchising
a system of franchising in which a franchisee purchases the right to use the franchiser's trade name without distributing particular products exclusively under the franchiser's name.

Types of Franchising

There are three basic types of franchising: trade name franchising, product distribution franchising, and pure franchising. **Trade name franchising** involves a brand name such as True Value Hardware or Western Auto. Here, the franchisee purchases the right to use the franchiser's trade name without distributing particular products exclusively under the franchiser's name. **Product distribution franchising** involves a franchiser licensing a franchisee to sell specific products under the franchiser's brand name and trademark through a selective, limited distribution network. This system is commonly used to market automobiles (Chevrolet, Lincoln, Chrysler), gasoline products (Exxon, Sunoco, Texaco), soft drinks (Pepsi Cola, Coca Cola), bicycles (Schwinn), appliances, cosmetics, and other products. These two methods of franchising allow franchisees to acquire some of the parent company's identity.

Pure franchising (or **comprehensive** or **business format franchising**) involves providing the franchisee with a complete business format, including a license for a trade name, the products or services to be sold, the physical plant, the methods of operation, a marketing plan, a quality control process, a two-way communications system, and the necessary business support services. In short, the franchisee purchases the right to use all of the elements of a fully integrated business operation. Business format franchising is the most common and the fastest growing of the three types of franchising, with four times as many outlets as trade name and product distribution franchises.[6] It is common among fast food restaurants, hotels, business service firms, car rental agencies, educational institutions, beauty aid retailers, and many other types of businesses.

> **product distribution franchising**
> a system of franchising in which a franchiser licenses a franchisee to sell its products under the franchiser's brand name and trademark through a selective, limited distribution network.
>
> **pure franchising**
> a system of franchising in which a franchiser sells a franchisee a complete business format and system.

The Benefits of Buying a Franchise

A franchisee gets the opportunity to own a small business relatively quickly, and, because of the identification with an established product and brand name, a franchise often reaches the break-even point faster than an independent business would. Still, most new franchise outlets don't break even for at least 6 to 18 months.

> **LEARNING OBJECTIVES**
> 2A. Explain the benefits of buying a franchise.

Franchisees also benefit from the franchiser's business experience. In fact, experience is the essence of what a franchisee is buying from a franchiser. Many entrepreneurs go into business by themselves and make many costly mistakes. Given the thin margin for error in the typical start-up, a new business owner cannot afford to make many mistakes. In a franchising arrangement, the franchiser already has worked out the kinks in the system by trial and error, and franchisees benefit from that experience. A franchiser has climbed up the learning curve and can share with franchisees the secrets of success that he or she has discovered in the industry.

For many first-time entrepreneurs, access to a business model with a proven track record is the safest way to own a business. Still, every potential franchisee must consider the answer to one important question: "What can a franchise do for me that I cannot do for myself?" The answer to this question will depend on one's particular situation and requires a systematic evaluation of a franchise opportunity. After careful deliberation, one person may conclude that the franchise offers nothing that he or she could not do independently, and another may decide that a franchise is the key to success as a business owner. Franchisees often cite the following advantages.

Management Training and Support

Recall from Chapter 1 that one of the leading causes of business failure is incompetent management. Franchisers are well aware of this, and, in an attempt to reduce the number of franchise casualties, they offer managerial training programs to franchisees prior to opening a new outlet. Many franchisers, especially the well-established ones, also provide follow-up training and counseling services. This service is vital because most franchisers do not require a franchisee to have experience in the business. These programs teach franchisees the details they need to know for day-to-day operations as well as the nuances of running their businesses successfully. When Floyd Sims, who had worked for a large company in the bottling and canning business for 18 years, decided to go into business for himself, he chose to purchase a McDonald's franchise mainly because of the support the franchiser offers. "I found McDonald's very supportive through the initial start-up, and that took my fear away," says Sims.[7]

Training programs often involve both classroom and on-site instruction to teach franchisees the basic operations of the business. Before beginning operations, McDonald's franchisees spend 14 days in Illinois at Hamburger University, where they learn everything from how to scrape the grill correctly to the essential elements of managing a business with high community visibility and great profit potential. MAACO franchisees spend four weeks at the company's headquarters delving into a five-volume set of operations manuals and learning to run an auto services shop. H&R Block trains its franchisees to unravel the mysteries of tax preparation, and Ben & Jerry's franchisees study at Scoop University at the company's headquarters in Burlington, Vermont. To ensure franchisees' continued success, many franchisers supplement their start-up training programs with ongoing instruction and support. For instance, Ben & Jerry's sends regional trainers to new franchisees' locations for additional training before they open their stores. Once they are up and running, franchisees also benefit from ongoing training programs from Ben & Jerry's field-based support team.[8] Franchisers offer these training programs because they realize that their ultimate success depends on their franchisees' success.

Despite the positive features of training, inherent dangers exist in the trainer–trainee relationship. Every would-be franchisee should be aware that, in some cases, "assistance" from the franchiser tends to drift into "control" over the franchisee's business. In addition, some franchisers charge fees for their training services, so franchisees should know exactly what they are agreeing to and what it costs.

Brand Name Appeal

A licensed franchisee purchases the right to use a nationally known and advertised brand name for a product or service. Thus, the franchisee has the advantage of identifying his or her business with a widely recognized trademark, which provides a great deal of drawing power, particularly for franchisees of established systems. Customers recognize the identifying trademark, the standard symbols, the store design, and the products of an established franchise. Because of the franchise's name recognition, franchisees who have just opened their outlets often discover a ready supply of customers eager to purchase their products or services. Entrepreneurs who launch independent businesses may have to work for years and spend many thousands of dollars in advertising to build a customer base of equivalent size.

One of the basic tenets of franchising is cloning the franchiser's success. For example, nearly everyone is familiar with the golden arches of McDonald's or the red roof of the Holiday Inn and the standard products and quality offered at each. A customer can be confident that the quality and content of a meal at McDonald's in Fort Lauderdale will be consistent with a meal at a San Francisco McDonald's. However, franchisees must be equally aware that negative actions by the franchiser or other franchisees can undermine the value of the brand name and have a negative impact on other stores in the chain. For instance, one of the worst cases of food poisoning ever recorded in this country hit Washington when customers of a fast food franchise ate contaminated food at several of its outlets. More than 600 people were treated at local hospitals for *Escherichia coli* poisoning, and three children died after eating the undercooked, contaminated beef served at the stores. This tragic event not only required the company to pay millions of dollars in legal settlements, but it also led to a drop in sales throughout the entire chain of restaurants for a period of time. Fortunately, the company has since rebounded from the crisis and now is one of the industry leaders in food safety procedures.

Standardized Quality of Goods and Services

Because a franchisee purchases a license to sell the franchiser's product or service and the privilege of using the associated brand name, the quality of the goods or service sold determines the franchiser's reputation. Building a sound reputation in business is not achieved quickly, although destroying a good reputation takes no time at all. If some franchisees were allowed to operate at substandard levels, the image of the entire chain would suffer irreparable damage; therefore, franchisers normally demand compliance with uniform standards of quality and service throughout the entire chain. In many cases, the franchiser conducts periodic inspections of local facilities to assist in maintaining acceptable levels of performance.

John Schnatter, founder of Papa John's, a fast-growing pizza franchise with nearly 3,000 outlets in 49 states and 20 global markets, makes personal visits to some of his franchisees' stores four to five times each week to make sure they are performing up to the company's high quality standards. Franchisees say that Schnatter, known for his attention to detail, often checks pizzas for air bubbles in the crust or tomato sauce for freshness. "Pizza is Schnatter's life, and he takes it very seriously," says one industry analyst.[9]

Maintaining quality is so important that most franchisers retain the right to terminate the franchise contract and to repurchase the outlet if the franchisee fails to comply with established standards.

National Advertising Programs

An effective advertising program is essential to the success of virtually all franchise operations. Marketing a brand name product or service over a wide geographic area requires a far-reaching advertising campaign. A regional or national advertising program benefits all franchisees, and most franchisers have one. Typically, these advertising campaigns are organized and controlled by the franchiser, but franchisees actually pay for the campaigns. In fact, they are financed by each franchisee's contribution of a percentage of monthly sales, usually 1 to 5 percent, or a flat monthly fee. For example, Subway franchisees pay 3.5 percent of gross revenues to the Subway national advertising program. These funds are pooled and used for a cooperative advertising program, which has more impact than if the franchisees spent the same amount of money separately.

Many franchisers also require franchisees to spend a minimum amount on local advertising. To supplement their national advertising efforts, both Wendy's and Burger King require franchisees to spend at least 3 percent of gross sales on local advertising. Some franchisers assist each franchisee in designing and producing its local ads. Many companies help franchisees create promotional plans and provide press releases and advertisements for grand openings.

Financial Assistance

Because they rely on their franchisees' money to grow their businesses, franchisers typically do not provide any extensive financial help for franchisees. In fact, one study reports that one-third of franchisers offer financing to their franchisees.[10] Franchisers rarely make loans to enable franchisees to pay the initial franchise fee. However, once a franchiser locates a suitable prospective franchisee, it may offer the qualified candidate direct financial assistance in specific areas, such as purchasing equipment, inventory, or even the franchise fee. Because the start-up costs of some franchises are already at breathtaking levels, some franchisers find that they must offer direct financial assistance.

For example, US Franchise Systems, franchiser of Microtel Inn and Hawthorn Suites hotels, has set up a subsidiary, US Funding Corporation, which makes available to its franchisees $200 million in construction and mortgage financing. Not only has the in-house financing program cut the time required to open a new hotel franchise, but it also has accelerated the franchise's growth rate.[11]

US Franchise Systems

In most instances, financial assistance from franchisers takes a form other than direct loans, leases, or short-term credit. Franchisers usually are willing to assist qualified franchisees in establishing relationships with banks, nonbank lenders, and other sources of funds. The support and connections from the franchiser enhance a franchisee's credit standing because lenders recognize the lower failure rate among established franchises. For instance, Papa John's, the pizza franchise, has established relationships with 10 different lenders to whom it refers franchisees in search of financing.[12]

The Small Business Administration (SBA) has created a program called the Franchise Registry that is designed to provide financing for franchisees through its loan guarantee programs (more on these in Chapter 13, "Sources of Financing: Debt and Equity"). The Franchise Registry streamlines the loan application process for franchisees that pass the screening tests at franchises that are members of the Registry. More than 600 franchises ranging from AAMCO Transmissions (automotive repair) to Zaxby's (fast food chicken restaurants) participate in the Franchise Registry program. Since 1993, the SBA has approved loan guarantees for more than 12,000 franchisees. Franchisees interested in the Franchise Registry program should visit its Web site at http://www.franchiseregistry.com.

Proven Products and Business Formats

As we have seen, franchisees essentially purchase a franchiser's experience in the form of a business system. A franchise owner does not have to build the business from scratch. Instead of being forced to rely solely on personal ability to establish a business and attract a clientele, a franchisee can depend on the methods and techniques of an established business. These standardized procedures and operations greatly enhance the franchisee's chances of success and avoid the most inefficient type of learning—trial and error. In addition, a franchisee does not have to struggle for recognition in the local marketplace as much as an independent owner might.

Z Pizza

After a brief career in professional baseball following college, Mike Harms knew that he wanted to operate a business of his own. He and his wife Erin decided that a franchise would be best for them, and they spent months engaged in extensive research and self-evaluation before settling on Z Pizza, a gourmet pizza restaurant offering toppings ranging from lime chicken and soy cheese to pine nuts and sun-dried tomatoes. The features that drew the Harms to Z Pizza are the company's high-quality product line and proven business system. "I'd never seen such a variety of toppings," says Harm, who chose Reno, Nevada, as the location for their franchise. Very much a hands-on manager, Harm has learned to rely on the Z Pizza system to make his restaurant successful. "Letting go and trusting the system that Z Pizza has put into effect was the hardest part," he admits. But, he adds, "I'm very happy. It's been more than I could ever dream of." Business has been so good that the Harms are now opening a second location in Reno.[13]

Centralized Buying Power

A significant advantage a franchisee has over an independent small business owner is participation in the franchiser's centralized and large-volume buying power. If franchisers sell goods and supplies to franchisees (not all do), they may pass on to franchisees any cost savings from quantity discounts they earn by buying in volume. For example, it is unlikely that a small, independent ice cream parlor could match the buying power of Baskin-Robbins with its 5,000-plus retail ice cream stores. In many instances, economies of scale simply preclude an independent business owner from competing head to head with a franchise operation.

Site Selection and Territorial Protection

A proper location is critical to the success of any small business, and franchises are no exception. In fact, franchise experts consider the three most important factors in franchising to be *location*, *location*, and *location*. For instance, one franchise of the Rainforest Café, a restaurant chain with a jungle theme and an in-store "retail village," located in the Mall at the Source in Westbury, New York, recently closed. The primary problem was that the existing customer base in the location did not match the company's target audience. The successful stores in the chain tend to count on visitors to popular tourist destinations, something Westbury lacked.[14]

Sometimes, entrepreneurs discover that becoming affiliated with a franchiser is the best way to get into prime locations. Many franchisers conduct an extensive location analysis for each new outlet, including researching traffic patterns, zoning ordinances, accessibility, and population density. McDonald's, for example, is well known for its ability to obtain prime locations in high-traffic areas. Although choosing a location usually is the franchisee's responsibility, the franchiser reserves the right to approve the final site. Choosing a suitable location requires a thorough location analysis, including studies of traffic patterns, zoning ordinances, accessibility, population density, and demographics. Experienced franchisers know that selecting a location in a high-traffic area but on the "wrong" side of the street can doom a unit from the outset and do everything they can to help franchisees avoid bad locations.

Some franchisers offer franchisees territorial protection, which gives existing franchisees the right to exclusive distribution of brand name goods or services within a particular geographic area. A clause establishing such a protective zone that bars other outlets from the same franchise gives franchisees significant protection and security. The size of a franchisee's territory varies from industry to industry. For example, one national fast food restaurant agrees not to license another franchisee within a mile and one-half of existing locations. A soft-serve ice cream franchiser defines its franchisees' territories on the basis of Zip Code designations. The purpose of such protection is to prevent an invasion of the existing franchisee's territory and the accompanying dilution of sales. As existing markets have become increasingly saturated with franchise outlets, the placement of new outlets has become a source of friction between franchisers and franchisees. Existing franchisees complain that franchisers are encroaching on their territories by granting new franchises so close to them that their sales are diluted. Before signing a franchise contract, every prospective franchisee must know exactly what kind of territorial protection, if any, the franchiser guarantees. Why invest years building a successful franchise in a particular location only to have the franchiser allow another franchisee to open nearby, siphoning off sales of your existing outlet?

Greater Chance for Success

Investing in a franchise is not risk free. Between 200 and 300 new franchise companies enter the market each year, and not all of them survive. However, statistics suggest that franchising is less risky than building a business from the ground up. The Department of Commerce estimates that after five years, 95 percent of franchises are still in business, compared to just 47 percent of independent businesses (see Figure 6.3). This success rate for franchises is attributed to the broad range of services, assistance, and guidelines and the comprehensive business system the franchiser provides. Statistics regarding the success of a given franchise must be interpreted carefully, however. For example, sometimes when a franchise is in danger of failing, the franchiser often repurchases or relocates the outlet and does not report it as a failure.* As a result, some franchisers boast of never experiencing a failure.

The risk involved in purchasing a franchise is two-pronged: success—or failure—depends on the franchisee's managerial skills and motivation and on the franchiser's business experience and system. Many franchisees are convinced that franchising has been the key to their success in business. "It's the opportunity to be in business for yourself but not by yourself," says one franchiser.[15]

---

*As long as an outlet's doors never close, most franchisers do not count it as a failure even if the outlet has struggled for survival and has been through a series of owners who have tried unsuccessfully to turn around its performance.

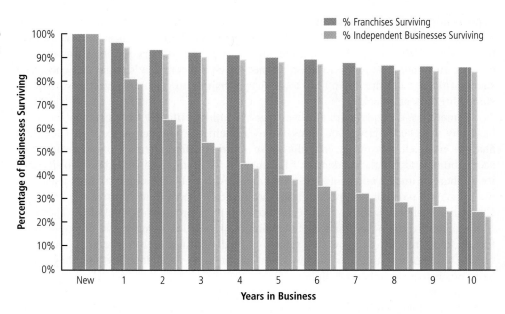

The Drawbacks of Buying a Franchise

Obviously, the benefits of franchising can mean the difference between success and failure for a small business. However, the franchisee must sacrifice some freedom to the franchiser. The prospective franchisee must explore other limitations of franchising before choosing this method of doing business.

Franchise Fees and Ongoing Royalties

Virtually every franchiser imposes some type of fees and demands a share of franchisees' sales revenue in return for the use of the franchiser's name, products or services, and business system. The fees and the initial capital requirements vary among the different franchisers. The total investment required for a franchise varies from around $1,000 for some home-based service franchises to $10 million or more for hotel and motel franchises. For example, Jazzercise, an aerobics exercise franchise, requires a capital investment that ranges from just $3,000 to $33,100, and Quiznos, the Italian-style submarine sandwich and salad chain, estimates that the total cost of opening a franchise ranges from $208,400 to $243,800. Culver's, a fast-growing regional chain that sells sandwiches (including the delicious ButterBurger®), salads, dinners, and frozen custard, requires an investment of $340,400 to $2,923,000, depending on land acquisition and building construction costs. According to a study by FRANDATA Corporation and the International Franchise Association, the average initial investment for a franchise (excluding real estate) is $318,975. Omitting the hotel and motel industry (which typically require the highest initial investments) produces an average initial franchise investment of $228,580.[16]

Start-up costs for franchises often include a variety of fees. Most franchises impose a franchise fee up front for the right to use the company name. Culver's charges a franchise fee that ranges from $30,000 to $50,000, depending on the franchisee's territory. Other franchise start-up costs might include a location analysis, site purchase and preparation, construction, signs, fixtures, equipment, management assistance, and training. Some franchise fees include these costs, but others do not. For example, Closets by Design, a company that designs and installs closet and garage organizers, entertainment centers, and home office systems, charges a franchise fee ranging from $24,500 to $39,900, which includes both a license for an exclusive territory and management training and support. Before signing any contract, a prospective franchisee should determine the total cost of a franchise, something every franchiser is required to disclose in item 10 of its Uniform Franchising Offering Circular (see the "Franchising and the Law" section later in this chapter).

Franchisers also impose continuing royalty fees as revenue-sharing devices. The royalty usually involves a percentage of gross sales with a required minimum, or a flat fee levied on the franchise. (In fact, 82 percent of franchisers charge a royalty based on a percentage of franchisees' sales.[17]) Royalty fees range from 1 percent to 11 percent, although most franchises assess a rate between 3 percent and 7 percent. The Atlanta Bread Company, for example, charges franchisees a royalty of 5 percent of gross sales, which is payable weekly. These ongoing royalties can increase a franchisee's overhead expenses significantly. Because the franchiser's royalties and fees are calculated as a percentage of a franchisee's sales, the franchiser gets paid even if the franchisee fails to earn a profit. Sometimes unprepared franchisees discover (too late) that a franchiser's royalties and fees are the equivalent of the normal profit margin for a franchise. To avoid this problem, prospective franchisees should determine exactly how much fees will be and then weigh the benefits of the services and benefits the fees cover. One of the best ways to do this is to itemize what you are getting for your money and then determine whether the cost is worth the benefits provided. Be sure to get the details on all expenses—the amount, the timing of payments, and financing arrangements; find out which items, if any, are included in the initial franchise fee and which ones are "extra."

Strict Adherence to Standardized Operations

Although franchisees own their businesses, they do not have the autonomy that independent owners have. To protect its public image, the franchiser requires that the franchisee maintain certain operating standards. For instance, the McDonald's franchisees must operate their businesses by the franchise manual, which specifies nearly every detail of running a franchise, including how many hamburger patties per pound of beef (10), how long to toast a bun (17 seconds), and how much sanitizer to use when cleaning the milkshake machine (1 packet for 2.5 gallons of water).

If a franchise constantly fails to meet the minimum standards established for the business, the franchiser may terminate its license. Many franchisers determine compliance with standards with periodic inspections and mystery shoppers. Mystery shoppers work for a survey company and, although they look like any other customer, are trained to observe and then later record on a checklist a franchise's performance on key standards such as cleanliness, speed of service, employees' appearances and attitudes, and others. McDonald's, a long-time user of mystery shoppers, even posts franchisees' mystery shoppers scores on an internal Web site so that owners can compare their scores with regional averages.[18] At times, strict adherence to franchise standards may become a burden to some franchisees. A franchisee may believe that the written reports the franchiser demands require an excessive amount of time or that enforcing specific rules that he or she thinks are unfair is not in the best interest of his or her business.

Restrictions on Purchasing

In the interest of maintaining quality standards, franchisers may require franchisees to purchase products, special equipment, or other items from the franchiser or from a list of "approved" suppliers. For example, KFC requires that franchisees use only seasonings blended by a particular company because a poor image could result from franchisees using inferior products to cut costs. Under some conditions, such purchase arrangements may be challenged in court as a violation of antitrust laws, but generally franchisers have a legal right to ensure that franchisees maintain acceptable quality standards. A franchiser may legally set the prices paid for the products it sells to franchisees but may not establish the retail prices to be charged on products sold by the franchisee. A franchiser can suggest retail prices for franchisee's products and services but cannot force the franchisee to abide by them. To do so would be a violation of the Robinson-Patman Act.

Limited Product Line

In most cases, the franchise agreement stipulates that the franchise can sell only those products approved by the franchiser. Unless they are willing to risk the cancellation of their licenses, franchisees must avoid selling any unapproved products through the franchise.

A franchise may be required to carry an unpopular product or be prevented from introducing a desirable one by the franchise agreement. A franchisee's freedom to adapt a product line to local market conditions is restricted. Some franchisers, however, actively solicit innovations and product suggestions from their franchisees. David Brandon, CEO of Domino's Pizza, says that the company's franchise system is "like working with 1,350 entrepreneurs." One franchisee invented the Heatwave bag that Domino's delivery workers use to keep pizzas piping hot, and another came up with the Spoodle, a combination spoon and ladle that measures the exact amount of pizza sauce and spreads it quickly and evenly.[19]

McDonald's

One of the advantages of owning a franchise is the management training and support the franchiser offers franchisees. These franchisees are learning how to operate a McDonald's restaurant at Hamburger University, the company's training facility in Oak Brook, Illinois. Founded in 1961, Hamburger University includes 19 full-time faculty members, classroom space, an auditorium, kitchen labs, service training labs, and more.

A McDonald's franchisee, Herb Peterson, created the highly successful Egg McMuffin while experimenting with a Teflon-coated egg ring that gave fried eggs rounded corners and a poached appearance. Peterson put his round eggs on English muffins, adorned them with Canadian bacon and melted cheese, and showed his creation to McDonald's chief Ray Kroc. Kroc devoured two of them and was sold on the idea when Peterson's wife suggested the catchy name. In 1975, McDonald's became the first fast food franchise to open its doors for breakfast, and the Egg McMuffin became a staple on the breakfast menu."[20]

Contract Terms and Renewal

Because they are written by the franchiser's attorneys, franchise contracts are always written in favor of the franchiser. Some franchisers are willing to negotiate the terms of their contracts, but many of the well-established franchisers are not because they know that they don't have to. The franchise contract is extremely important because it governs the franchiser–franchisee relationship over its life, which may last as long as 20 years. In fact, the average length of a franchise contract is 10.3 years.[21] Yet one study conducted by the Federal Trade Commission found that 40 percent of new franchisees signed their contracts without reading them![22]

Franchisees also should understand the terms and conditions under which they may renew their franchise contracts at the expiration of the original agreement. In most cases, franchisees are required to pay a renewal fee and to repair any deficiencies in their outlets or to modernize and upgrade them.

Unsatisfactory Training Programs

A major benefit of purchasing a franchise is the training that the franchiser provides franchisees so that they are able to run successful operations. The quality of franchise training programs can vary dramatically, however. "Many franchisees think they will get a lot of training but find out it's a one-week crash course," says Marko Grunhagen, a franchising expert at Southern Illinois University.[23] Before signing on with a franchise, it is wise to find out the details of the training program the franchiser provides to avoid unpleasant surprises.

Would-be franchisees must be wary of unscrupulous franchisers who promise extensive services, advice, and assistance but deliver nothing. For example, one owner relied on the franchiser to provide what had been described as an "extensive, rigorous training program" after paying a handsome technical assistance fee. The program was nothing but a set of pamphlets and do-it-yourself study guides. Other examples include impatient entrepreneurs who paid initial franchise fees without investigating the franchise and never heard from the franchiser again. Although disclosure rules have reduced the severity of the problem, dishonest characters still thrive on unprepared prospective franchisees.

Market Saturation

Franchisees in fast-growing systems reap the benefits of the franchiser's expanding reach, but they also may encounter the downside of a franchiser's aggressive growth strategy: market saturation. As the owners of many fast food and yogurt and ice cream franchises have discovered, market saturation is a very real danger. Subway, for example, grew from just 166 outlets in 1981 to nearly 25,000 outlets today (and plans to have 30,000 locations by 2010)![24] Any franchise growing that rapidly runs the risk of having outlets so close together that they cannibalize sales from one another. Although some franchisers offer franchisees territorial protection, others do not. Territorial encroachment has become a hotly contested issue in franchising as growth-seeking franchisers have exhausted most of the prime locations and are now setting up new franchises in close proximity to existing ones. In some areas of the country, franchisees are upset, claiming that their markets are oversaturated and their sales are suffering.

Less Freedom

When franchisees sign a contract, they agree to sell the franchiser's product or service by following its prescribed formula. This feature of franchising is the source of the system's success, but it also gives many franchisees the feeling that they are reporting to a "boss." Franchisers want to ensure franchisees' success, and most monitor their franchisees' performances closely to make sure franchisees follow the system's specifications. "Everything you do in a franchise will be dictated [by the franchiser] from the moment you turn the key in the door in the morning," warns Eric Karp, a Boston attorney who teaches franchising at Babson College.[25]

Strict uniformity is the rule rather than the exception. "There is no independence," says one writer. "Successful franchisees are happy prisoners."[26] As a result, highly independent, "go-my-own-way" entrepreneurs often are frustrated with the basic "go-by-the-rules" philosophy of franchising. Table 6.1 describes 10 myths of franchising.

TABLE 6.1 Ten Myths of Franchising

Myth #1. Franchising is the safest way to go into business because franchises never fail.

Although the failure rate for franchises is lower than that of independent businesses, there are no guarantees of success. Franchises can—and do—fail. Potential franchisees must exercise the same degree of caution in judging the risk of a franchise as they would any other business.

Myth #2. I'll be able to open my franchise for less money than the franchiser estimates.

Launching a business, including a franchise, normally takes more money and more time than entrepreneurs estimate. Be prepared. One franchisee of a retail computer store advises, "If a franchiser tells you you'll need $100,000 to get started, you better have $150,000."

Myth #3. The bigger the franchise organization, the more successful I'll be.

Bigger is not always better in the franchise business. Some of the largest franchise operations are struggling to maintain their growth rates because the best locations are already taken and their markets have become saturated. Market saturation is a significant problem for many large franchises, and smaller franchises are accounting for much of the growth in the industry. Early franchisees in new franchise systems often can negotiate better deals and receive more individual attention from the franchiser than those who purchase units in well-established systems.

Myth #4. I'll use 80 percent of the franchiser's business system, but I'll improve on it by substituting my experience and know-how.

When franchisees buy a franchise, they are buying, in essence, the franchiser's experience and knowledge. Why pay all of that money to a franchiser if you aren't willing to use their system? When franchisers screen potential franchisees, they look for people who are willing to fit into their systems rather than fiercely independent entrepreneurs. "[Franchisers] have spent years building the company," says Jeff Elgin, founder of FranChoice, a franchise referral consulting firm. "They don't want someone who will come in and try to innovate because that produces chaos." Ideally, franchisers look for franchisees who exhibit a balance between the free-wheeling entrepreneurial spirit and a system-focused approach.

Myth #5. All franchises are basically the same.

Each franchise has its own unique personality, requirements, procedures, and culture. Naturally, some will suit you better than others. Avoid the tendency to select the franchise that offers the lowest cost. If the franchise does not fit your needs, it is not a bargain, no matter how inexpensive it is. Ask the franchiser and existing franchisees lots of questions to determine how well

TABLE 6.1 *Continued*

you will fit into the system. One of the best ways to get a feel for a franchise's personality is to work in a unit for a time.

Myth #6. I don't have to be a hands-on manager. I can be an absentee owner and still be very successful.

Most franchisers shy away from absentee owners, and some simply do not allow them in their systems at all. They know that franchise success requires lots of hands-on attention, and the franchise owner is the best person to provide that.

Myth #7. Anyone can be a satisfied, successful franchise owner.

With more than 3,000 franchises to choose from, the odds of finding a franchise that appeals to your tastes is high. However, not everyone is cut out to be a franchisee. Those "free spirits" who insist on doing things their way most likely will be miserable in a franchise.

Myth #8. Franchising is the cheapest way to get into business for yourself.

Although bargains do exist in franchising, the price tag for buying into some well-established systems is breathtaking, sometimes running more than $1 million. Franchisers look for candidates who are on solid financial footing.

Myth #9. The franchiser will solve my business problems for me; after all, that's why I pay an ongoing royalty.

Although franchisers offer franchisees start-up and ongoing training programs, they will not run their franchisees' businesses for them. As a franchisee, your job is to take the formula that the franchiser has developed and make it work in your location. Expect to solve many of your own problems.

Myth #10. Once I open my franchise, I'll be able to run things the way I want to.

Franchisees are not free to run their businesses as they see fit. Every franchisee signs a contract that requires him or her to run the business according to the franchiser's requirements. Franchisees who violate the terms of that agreement run the risk of having their franchise relationship terminated.

Sources: Adapted from April Y. Pennington, "The Right Stuff," *Entrepreneur B.Y.O.B.,* September 2004, pp. 90–100; Andrew A. Caffey, "There's More to a Franchise Than Meets the Eye," *Entrepreneur,* May 1998, http://www.entrepreneur.com/article/0,4621,228443,00.html; Andrew A. Caffey, "Myth vs. Reality," *Entrepreneur,* October 1998, http://www.entrepreneur.com/mag/article/0,1539,229435. 00.html; Chieh Chieng, "Do You Want to Know a Secret?" *Entrepreneur,* January 1999, pp. 174–178; "Ten Most Common Mistakes Made by Franchise Buyers," Franchise Doctor, www.franchisedoc.com/mistakes.html; Devlin Smith, "The Sure Thing," *Entrepreneur B.Y.O.B.,* May 2004, p. 100.

You Be the Consultant

A Cautionary Tale

For 29 years, Jan Lee had thrived in the corporate environment at international giant IBM. When she decided that it was time for a career change, she knew she wanted to work in something completely different from the computer industry. She also knew that she had grown accustomed to having the support and guidance of a management team throughout her career and wanted that assistance to continue. That's why a franchise seemed to be the ideal solution for her second career. After evaluating several franchise opportunities, Lee decided to open a Slender Lady diet and exercise outlet near her home in Hawthorn Woods, Illinois, a Chicago suburb. "I was attracted to this business because it was about helping people, especially women, be healthier," she says.

Lee paid a $30,000 franchise fee and began getting her business ready to open. The franchiser also convinced Lee to reserve five other franchise territories in the surrounding area at a cost of $5,000 *each* so that she could open franchises there once she was able to get her initial location established. Lee soon discovered that the $30,000 franchise fee she paid for her first outlet was just the tip of the iceberg. She paid $40,000 to land a storefront location in an upscale mall that attracted many of her target customers. Signs and décor cost Lee another $9,000, and other expenses that she had not expected constantly cropped up. "Even the music you're supposed to play had to be downloaded from a certain source, and that cost extra," she says. "There was one expense after another that wasn't mentioned in the initial estimates—$10,000 in advertising, then payroll taxes—or payroll period. To get new customers, I had to hire a salesperson, who cost me $2,500 a month. That wasn't mentioned anywhere."

Lee was expecting to get lots of support from the franchiser, but she says that the company provided her with very little management and marketing assistance. She says the franchiser's idea of marketing was to use drop boxes located in nearby businesses, into which prospective customers could deposit information cards. Lee found the boxes to be of little value to her franchise's marketing efforts. "They'd be full of gum wrappers," she says. When she contacted the franchiser about the problems she was encountering, she says their response was, "Keep using the drop boxes."

As time went on and expenses mounted, Lee ran through the entire $100,000 she had saved from working at IBM. She took out a home equity loan to keep her franchise afloat, but by then a new Curves franchise had opened nearby, and new customers were increasingly more difficult to come by. Just as she did in her corporate career when things got tough, Lee responded by working harder and longer. She was spending 12 hours per day on the phone contacting people who had signed up as customers and then dropped out. "Nothing in my corporate life prepared me for this," she says. "I was exhausted and depressed all the time."

Lee soon hit the cap on her home equity line of credit, but because her franchise was operating at a loss, she could not afford to repay the loan. She was about to lose her home, and her marriage was failing. A few months later, Lee signed the franchise over to one of her employees for $1. "I just wanted out," she says.

When Lee called the Slender Lady headquarters to ask about getting a refund on the $25,000 she had put up to reserve the right to develop the other five territories, the franchiser declined. She learned that her options had expired and that the franchiser already had sold two of the territories to other franchisees. Bruce Sharpe, CEO of Slender Lady, says, "There is a time limit clearly stated in the contract. If you don't use the territory within 12 months, you lose it, and you don't get a refund because you have tied up that territory for that time."

Lee admits that she learned a valuable—and expensive—lesson. Those who have succeeded at franchising emphasize the importance of researching the franchise opportunity and the potential for the market you are considering entering before taking the plunge. Before Terry Tryon, a 30-year veteran of the insurance industry, purchased a Tutor Time daycare franchise in Wyomissing, Pennsylvania, he investigated the franchiser and the local market thoroughly. "I looked at statistics on the rising need for child care in two-income families, and then I looked at this part of Pennsylvania to see what demand was and who my competitors were likely to be," says Tryon. "A gut feeling is fine, but the more knowledge you have, the better off you are. I also talked to lots of other franchisees, some of whom had succeeded and some of whom had failed. I got more insights from the ones who failed."

1. What should Jan Lee have done differently before purchasing her Slender Lady franchise?
2. Suppose that a friend tells you that he is considering purchasing a franchise and asks for your advice about the steps he should take to ensure that he makes the right decision. What would you tell him?
3. Summarize the advantages and disadvantages your friend is likely to experience if he buys a franchise.

Source: Adapted from Anne Fisher, "Risk Reward," *FSB*, December 2005/January 2006, pp. 45–61

Franchising and the Law

LEARNING OBJECTIVES
3. Explain the laws covering franchise purchases.

The franchising boom spearheaded by McDonald's and others in the late 1950s brought with it many prime investment opportunities. However, the explosion of legitimate franchises also ushered in with it numerous fly-by-night franchisers who defrauded their franchisees. By the 1970s, franchising was rife with fraudulent practitioners. Thousands of

Uniform Franchise Offering Circular (UFOC)

a document that every franchiser is required by law to give prospective franchisees before any offer or sale of a franchise; it outlines 23 important pieces of information.

people lost millions of dollars to criminals and unscrupulous operators who sold flawed business concepts and phantom franchises to unsuspecting investors. In an effort to control the rampant fraud in the industry and the potential for deception inherent in a franchise relationship, California in 1971 enacted the first Franchise Investment Law. The law (and those of 16 other states that have since passed similar laws) requires franchisers to register a **Uniform Franchise Offering Circular (UFOC)** and deliver a copy to prospective franchisees before any offer or sale of a franchise. The UFOC establishes full disclosure guidelines for any company selling franchises.

In October 1979, the Federal Trade Commission (FTC) enacted the Trade Regulation Rule, requiring all franchisers to disclose detailed information on their operations at the first personal meeting, at least 10 days before a franchise contract is signed, or before any money is paid. The FTC rule covers *all* franchisers, even those in the 33 states lacking franchise disclosure laws. The purpose of the regulation is to assist the potential franchisee's investigation of the franchise deal and to introduce consistency into the franchiser's disclosure statements. In 1994, the FTC modified the requirements for the UFOC, making more information available to prospective franchisees and making the document shorter and easier to read and understand. The FTC's philosophy is not so much to prosecute abusers as to provide information to prospective franchisees and help them to make intelligent decisions. Although the FTC requires each franchiser to provide a potential franchisee with this information, it does not verify its accuracy. Prospective franchisees should use these data only as a starting point for the investigation. The Trade Regulation Rule requires a franchiser to include 23 major topics in its disclosure statement:

1. Information identifying the franchiser and its affiliates and describing their business experience and the franchises being sold.
2. Information identifying and describing the business experience of each of the franchiser's officers, directors, and managers responsible for the franchise program.
3. A description of the lawsuits in which the franchiser and its officers, directors, and managers have been involved. Although most franchisers will have been involved in some type of litigation, an excessive number of lawsuits, particularly if they relate to the same problem, is alarming. Another red flag is an excessive number of lawsuits brought against the franchiser by franchisees. "The history of the litigation will tell you the future of your relationship" with the franchiser, says the founder of a maid-service franchise.[27]
4. Information about any bankruptcies in which the franchiser and its officers, directors, and managers have been involved.
5. Information about the initial franchise fee and other payments required to obtain the franchise, the intended use of the fees, and the conditions under which the fees are refundable.
6. A description of any continuing payments franchisees are required to make after start-up, including royalties, service fees, training fees, lease payments, advertising or marketing charges, and others.
7. A detailed description of the typical total initial investment a franchisee must make and how and to whom these payments are made. The categories covered are the initial franchise fee, equipment, opening inventory, initial advertising fee, signs, training, real estate, working capital, legal, accounting, and utilities. These estimates, usually stated in the form of a range of numbers, give prospective franchisees an idea of how much their total start-up costs will be.
8. Information about quality requirements of goods, services, equipment, supplies, inventory, and other items used in the franchise and where franchisees may purchase them, including required purchases from the franchiser.
9. A statement (in tabular form) of the franchisee's obligations under the franchise contract, including items such as site selecting a site, paying fees, maintaining quality standards, keeping records, transferring or renewing the franchise relationship, and others.

10. A description of any financial assistance available from the franchiser in the purchase of the franchise. Although many franchisers do not offer direct financial assistance to franchisees, they may have special arrangements with lenders who help franchisees find financing.

11. A description of all obligations the franchiser must fulfill in helping a franchisee prepare to open and operate a unit. Typically the longest section in the document, this segment includes information covering location selection methods and the training program that the franchiser offers franchisees. In addition to the training that they provide new franchisees, many franchisers offer help with a grand opening for each outlet and on-site management assistance for a short time to get franchisees started.

12. A description of any territorial protection that the franchise receives and a statement as to whether the franchiser may locate a company-owned store or other franchised outlet in that territory. Given the controversy in many franchises over market saturation, franchisees should pay close attention to this section.

13. All relevant information about the franchiser's trademarks, service marks, trade names, logos, and commercial symbols, including where they are registered. Prospective franchisees should look for a strong trade or service mark that is registered with the U.S. Patent and Trademark Office.

14. Similar information on any patents, copyrights, and proprietary processes the franchiser owns and the rights franchisees have to use them.

15. A description of the extent to which franchisees must participate personally in the operation of the franchise. Many franchisers look for "hands-on" franchisees and discourage or even prohibit "absentee owners."

16. A description of any restrictions placed on the goods or services that franchises are permitted to sell and with whom franchisees may deal. The agreement usually restricts franchisees to selling only those items approved by the franchiser.

17. A description of the conditions under which the franchise may be repurchased or refused renewal by the franchiser, transferred to a third party by the franchisee, and terminated or modified by either party. This section also addresses the method established for resolving disputes.

18. A description of the involvement of celebrities and public figures in the franchise.

19. A complete statement of the basis for any earnings claims made to the franchisee, including the percentage of existing franchises that have actually achieved the results that are claimed. New rules put two requirements on franchisers making earnings claims: (1) Any earnings claim must be included in the UFOC, and (2) the claim must "have a reasonable basis at the time it is made." However, franchisers are *not* required to make any earnings claims at all; in fact, most franchisers do not, primarily because of liability concerns about committing such numbers to paper.

20. System-wide statistical information about the present number of franchises; the number of franchises projected for the future; the number of franchises terminated; the number the franchiser has not renewed; the number repurchased in the past; and a list of the names and addresses (organized by state) of other franchisees in the system and of those who have left the system within the last year. Contacting some of the franchisees who have left the system can alert would-be franchisees to potential problems with the franchise.

21. The franchiser's financial statements.

22. A copy of all franchise and other contracts (leases, purchase agreements, etc.) that the franchisee will be required to sign.

23. A standardized, detachable "receipt" to prove that the prospective franchisee received a copy of the UFOC.

The information contained in the UFOC does not fully protect a potential franchise from deception, nor does it guarantee success. It does, however, provide enough information to begin a thorough investigation of the franchiser and the franchise deal, and prospective franchisees should use it to their advantage.

The Opportunity of a Lifetime

"Honey, I think I've found it!" said Joe Willingham to his wife, Allie, as he rushed through the door. "This is just what I've been looking for, and just in time, too. My severance package from the company runs out next month. The man said that if we invested in this franchise now, we could be bringing in good money by then. It's that easy!"

Allie knew that Joe had been working hard at finding another job since he had become a victim of his company's latest downsizing, but that jobs were scarce even for someone with his managerial experience and background in manufacturing. "Nobody wants to hire a 51-year-old man with experience when they can hire 23-year-old college graduates at less than half the salary and teach them what they need to know," Joe told her after months of fruitless job hunting. That's when Joe got the idea of setting up his own business. Rather than start an independent business from scratch, Joe felt more comfortable, given his 26-year corporate career, opening a franchise. "A franchiser can give me the support I need," he told Allie.

"Tell me about this franchise," Allie said.

"It's a phenomenal opportunity for us," Joe said, barely able to contain his excitement. "I saw this booth for American Speedy Print at the Business Expo this morning. There were all kinds of franchises represented there, but this one really caught my eye," Joe said as he pulled a rather plain-looking photocopy of a brochure from his briefcase.

"Is that their brochure?" asked Allie.

"Well, the company is growing so fast that they have temporarily run out of their normal literature. This is just temporary."

"Oh . . . You would think that a printing franchise could print flashier brochures even on short notice, but I guess . . . ," said Allie.

"The main thing is the profit potential this business has," said Joe. "I met one of their franchisees. I tell you the guy was wearing a $2,000 suit if ever there was one, and he had expensive jewelry dripping from his fingers. He's making a mint with this franchise, and he said we could too!"

Joe continued, "With the severance package I have from the company, we could pay the $10,000 franchise fee and lease most of the equipment we need to get started. It'll take every penny of my package, but, hey, it's an investment in our future. The representative said the company would help us with our grand opening, and would help us compile a list of potential customers."

"What would you print?" asked Allie.

"Anything!" said Joe. "The franchisee I talked to does fliers, posters, booklets, newsletters, advertising pieces . . . you name it!"

"Oh my! It seems like you'd need lots of specialized equipment to do all of that." How much does the total franchise package cost?" asked Allie.

"Well, I'm not exactly sure. He never gave me an exact figure, but we can lease all the equipment we need from the franchiser!"

"Is this all of the material they gave you? I thought franchisers were supposed to have some kind of information packet to give to people." said Allie.

"Yeah, I asked him about that," said Joe. "He said that American Speedy Print is just a small franchise. They'd rather put their money into building a business and helping their franchisees succeed than into useless paperwork that nobody reads anyway. It makes sense to me."

"I guess so . . . ," Allie said reluctantly.

"I think we need to take this opportunity, Hon," Joe said, with a look that spoke of determination and enthusiasm. "Besides, he said that there was another couple in this county that is already looking at this franchise, and that the company will license only one franchisee in this area. They don't want to saturate the market. He thinks they may take it. I think we have to move on this now, or we'll lose the opportunity of a lifetime."

Allie had not seen Joe exhibit this much enthusiasm and excitement for anything since he had lost his job at the plant. Piles of rejection letters from his job search had sapped Joe's zest for life. Allie was glad to see "the old Joe" return, but she still had her doubts about the franchise opportunity Joe was describing.

"It might just be the opportunity of a lifetime, Joe," she said. "But don't you think we need to find out a little more about this franchise before we invest that much money? I mean . . . "

"Hon, I'd love to do that, but like the man said, we may miss out on the opportunity of a lifetime if we don't sign today. I think we've got to move on this thing now!"

1. What advice would you offer Joe about investing in this franchise? Explain.
2. Map out a plan for Joe to use in finding the right franchise for him. What can Joe do to protect himself from making a bad franchise investment?
3. Summarize the advantages and disadvantages Joe can expect if he buys a franchise.

The *Right* Way to Buy a Franchise

LEARNING OBJECTIVES
4. Discuss the right way to buy a franchise.

The UFOC is a powerful tool designed to help would-be franchisees select the franchise that is right for them and to avoid being duped by dishonest franchisers. The best defenses a prospective entrepreneur has against unscrupulous franchisers are preparation, common sense, and patience. By investigating thoroughly before investing in a franchise, a potential franchisee minimizes the risk of being hoodwinked into a nonexistent business. Asking the right questions and resisting the urge to rush into an investment decision helps a potential franchisee avoid being taken by unscrupulous operators.

Despite the protection the UFOC offers, potential franchisees must beware because franchise fraud still exists in this rapidly growing field. Dishonest franchisers tend to follow certain patterns, and well-prepared franchisees who know what to look for can avoid trouble. The following clues should arouse the suspicion of an entrepreneur about to invest in a franchise:

- Claims that the franchise contract is a standard one and that "you don't need to read it."
- A franchiser who fails to give you a copy of the required disclosure document at your first face-to-face meeting.
- A marginally successful prototype store or no prototype at all.
- A poorly prepared operations manual outlining the franchise system or no manual (or system) at all.
- Oral promises of future earnings without written documentation.
- A high franchisee turnover rate or a high termination rate.
- An unusual amount of litigation brought against the franchiser.
- Attempts to discourage you from allowing an attorney to evaluate the franchise contract before you sign it.
- No written documentation to support claims and promises.
- A high-pressure sale—sign the contract now or lose the opportunity.
- Claiming to be exempt from federal laws requiring complete disclosure of franchise details.
- "Get-rich-quick schemes," promises of huge profits with only minimum effort.
- Reluctance to provide a list of present franchisees for you to interview.
- Evasive, vague answers to your questions about the franchise and its operation.

The New York Attorney General's office recently prosecuted the perpetrators of a franchise scam that cost unsuspecting franchisees more than $900,000 and caused two franchisees to declare bankruptcy. The owners of Westcool Snacks and Beverages failed to register their franchise offering with the state and to provide copies of the franchise offering circular to prospective franchisees. They also made unsupported claims that franchisees would earn up to $780,000 a year selling the company's exclusive line of snacks and beverages (which never materialized). The franchisees, who paid between $20,000 and $50,000 each, lost all of their money when the franchiser failed to deliver on its promises.[28]

COMPANY
Profile

Westcool Snacks and Beverages

TABLE 6.2 Evaluate Yourself before Buying a Franchise

Your Abilities

- Does the franchise require technical experience or relevant education, such as auto repair, home and office decorating, or tax preperation?
- What skills do you have? Do you have computer, bookkeeping, or other technical skills?
- What specialized knowledge or talents can you bring to a business?
- Have you ever owned or managed a business?

Year Goals

- What are your goals?
- Do you require a specific level of annual income?
- Are you interested in pursuing a particular field?
- Are you interested in retail sales or performing a service?
- How many hours are you willing to work?
- Do you want to operate the business yourself or hire a manager?
- Will franchise ownership be your primary source of income or will it supplement your current income?
- Would you be happy operating the business for the next 20 years?
- Would you like to own several outlets or only one?

Your Investment

- How much money do you have to invest?
- How much money can you afford to lose?
- Will you purchase the franchise by yourself or with partners?
- Will you need financing and, if so, where can you obtain it?
- Do you have a favorable credit rating?
- Do you have savings or additional income to live on while starting your franchise?

Sources: Consumer Guide to Buying a Franchise, Federal Trade Commission, Washington, DC, http://www.business.gov/phases/launching/buy_franchise/consumer_guide.html.

Not every franchise "horror story" is the result of dishonest franchisers. More often than not, the problems that arise in franchising have more to do with franchisees who buy legitimate franchises without proper research and analysis. They end up in businesses they don't enjoy and that they are not well suited to operate. How can you avoid this mistake? The following steps will help you to make the right choice:

Evaluate Yourself

Before looking at any franchise, entrepreneurs should study their own traits, goals, experience, likes, dislikes, risk orientation, income requirements, time and family commitments, and other characteristics. Will you be comfortable working in a structured environment? What kinds of franchises fit your desired lifestyle? In what region of the country or world do you want to live and work? What is your ideal job description? Knowing what you enjoy doing (and what you don't want to do) will help you to narrow your search. The goal is to find the franchise that is right—for *you*! One characteristic successful franchisees have in common is that they genuinely enjoy their work. Table 6.2 provides a checklist for prospective franchisees to help them to evaluate their franchise potential.

Research Your Market

Before shopping for a franchise, research the market in the area you plan to serve. How fast is the overall area growing? In which areas is that growth occurring fastest? Investing some time at the library developing a profile of the customers in your target area is essential; otherwise, you will be flying blind. Who are your potential customers? What are their characteristics? What are their income and education levels? What kinds of products and services do they buy? What gaps exist in the market? These gaps represent potential franchise opportunities for you. Market research also should confirm that a franchise is not merely part of a fad that will quickly fade. Steering clear of fads and into long-term trends is one way to sustain the success of a franchise. Before Papa John's Pizza allows franchisees to open a franchise, the company requires them to spend six months to a year evaluating the market potential of the local area. "We don't just move into an area and open up 200 stores," says one manager. "We do it one store at a time."[29]

Consider Your Franchise Options

Small business magazines (and their Web sites) such as *Entrepreneur, Inc., FSB*, and others devote at least one issue to franchising, in which they often list hundreds of franchises. These guides can help you to find a suitable franchise within your price range. The Web is another valuable tool for gathering information on franchises. The Web site of organizations such as the International Franchise Association, the American Association of Franchisees and Dealers, the Canadian Franchise Association, and others offer valuable resources and advice for prospective franchisees. In addition, many cities host franchise trade shows throughout the year where hundreds of franchisers gather to sell their franchises. Attending one of these franchise showcases is a convenient, efficient way to collect information about a variety of available opportunities.

Get a Copy of the Franchiser's UFOC

Once you narrow down your franchise choices, you should contact each franchise and get a copy of its UFOC. Then read it! This document is an important tool in your search for the right franchise, and you should make the most of it. When evaluating a franchise opportunity, what should a potential franchisee look for? Although there is never a guarantee of success, the following characteristics make a franchise stand out:

- A unique concept or marketing approach. "Me-too" franchises are no more successful than "me-too" independent businesses. Pizza franchiser Papa John's has achieved an impressive growth rate by emphasizing the quality of its ingredients, while Domino's is known for its fast delivery.
- Profitability. A franchiser should have a track record of profitability and so should its franchisees. If a franchiser is not profitable, its franchisees are not likely to be either. Franchisees who follow the business format should expect to earn a reasonable rate of return.
- A registered trademark. Name recognition is difficult to achieve without a well-known and protected trademark.
- A business system that works. A franchiser should have in place a system that is efficient and is well documented in its manuals.
- A solid training program. One of the most valuable components of a franchise system is the training that it offers franchisees. The system should be relatively easy to teach.
- Affordability. A franchisee should not have to take on an excessive amount of debt to purchase a franchise. Being forced to borrow too much money to open a franchise outlet can doom a business from the outset. Respectable franchisers verify prospective franchisees' financial qualifications as part of the screening process.
- A positive relationship with franchisees. The most successful franchises are those that see their franchisees as partners . . . and treat them accordingly.

The UFOC covers the 23 items discussed in the previous section and includes a copy of the company's franchise agreement and any contracts accompanying it. Although the law requires a UFOC to be written in plain English rather than "legalese," it is best to have an attorney experienced in franchising to review the UFOC and discuss its provisions with you. Watch for clauses that give the franchiser absolute control and discretion. The franchise contract summarizes the details that will govern the franchiser–franchisee

franchisee turnover rate
the rate at which franchisees leave
a franchise system.

relationship over its life. It outlines *exactly* the rights and the obligations of each party and sets the guidelines that govern the franchise relationship. Because franchise contracts typically are long term (50 percent run for 15 years or more), it is extremely important for prospective franchisees to understand their terms *before* they sign them.

One of the most revealing items in the UFOC is the **franchisee turnover rate,** the rate at which franchisees leave the system. If the turnover rate is less than 5 percent, the franchise is probably sound. However, a franchise turnover rate approaching 20 percent is a sign of serious, underlying problems in a franchise. Satisfied franchisees are not inclined to leave a successful system.

Another important aspect of investigating a potential franchise is judging how well you fit into the company culture. Unfortunately, the UFOC isn't much help here. The best way to determine this is to actually work for a unit for a time (even if it's without pay). Doing so not only gives prospective franchisees valuable insight into the company culture, but it also enables them to determine how much they enjoy the daily activities involved in operating the franchise. "Many people don't do enough research, digging into what a company is about, what they believe in, what they're trying to accomplish, and whether they will fit into the culture," says Kevin Hogan, a consultant who works with the Whataburger franchise.[30]

Talk to Existing Franchisees

One of the best ways to evaluate the reputation of a franchiser is to interview (in person, if possible) several franchise owners who have been in business at least one year about the positive and the negative features of the agreement and whether the franchiser delivered what was promised. Did the franchise estimate their start-up costs accurately? Do they get the support the franchiser promised them? Was the training the franchiser provided helpful? How long did it take to reach the break-even point? Have they incurred any unexpected expenses? What risks are involved in purchasing a franchise? Has the franchise met their expectations concerning sales, profitability, and return on investment? What is involved in operating the franchise on a typical day? Knowing what they know now, would they buy the franchise again?

Ranch 1

Bob Phillips, a CPA looking to make a career change, wanted to make sure that he purchased the right franchise, so he invested time poring over the UFOCs he had collected from the dozen franchises that interested him. Rather than rely on the documents alone to judge the franchises, Phillips made calls to franchisees that he randomly selected from the lists included in the UFOCs (item 20). His conversations with franchisees convinced him that Ranch 1, a chain of fast food grilled chicken stores, was the best choice for him. "Almost every one wanted a second location," he says. "That's indicative of a healthy franchise system." Phillips is convinced that his thorough research led him to the right franchise. Today he owns two Ranch 1 franchises that generate more than $2 million in sales, and he plans to open eight more outlets within three years.[31]

Interviewing past franchisees to get their perspectives on the franchiser–franchisee relationship is also helpful. Why did they leave? Franchisees of some companies have formed associations, which might provide prospective franchisees with valuable information. Other sources of information include the American Association of Franchisees and Dealers, the American Franchise Association, and the International Franchise Association.

Ask the Franchiser Some Tough Questions

Take the time to ask the franchiser questions about the company and its relationship with its franchisees. You will be in this relationship a long time, and you need to know as much about it as you possibly can beforehand. What is its philosophy concerning the relationship? What is the company culture like? How much input do franchisees have into the system? What are the franchise's future expansion plans? How will they affect your franchise? Are you entitled to an exclusive territory? Under what circumstances can either party terminate the franchise agreement? What happens if you decide to sell your franchise in the future? Under what circumstances would you not be entitled to renew the agreement? What kind of earnings can you expect? (If the franchiser made no earnings claims in item 19 of the UFOC, why not?) Does the franchiser have a well-formulated strategic plan? How many franchisees own multiple outlets? (A significant percentage of multiple-unit franchisees is a good sign that a franchise's brand name and business system are strong.) Has the franchiser terminated any franchisee's contracts? If so, why? Have any franchisees failed? If so, why? How are disputes between the franchiser and franchisees settled?

Make Your Choice

The first lesson in franchising is, "Do your homework *before* you get out your checkbook." Once you have done your research, you can make an informed choice about which franchise is right for you. Then it is time to put together a solid business plan that will serve as your road map to success in the franchise you have selected. The plan is also a valuable tool to use as you arrange the financing for your franchise.

Appendix A at the end of this chapter offers a checklist of questions a potential franchisee should ask before entering into any franchise agreement.

Hands on ... How to

Select the Ideal Franchise— *For You!*

After working extra hours and many weekends as a buyer in the retail industry, Gina Frerich began to think that she should be the beneficiary of her hard work rather than some corporate giant. She was confident that her work ethic and business experience would help her succeed in business, but because she did not know how to launch a business from scratch, Frerich began looking at franchises as the gateway to business ownership. Franchises "already have the proven product, they do marketing, and, [sometimes] they provide a lot of training and support," she says. Following is a chronicle of how Frerich made her franchise selection and lessons that every prospective franchisee can learn from her experience.

> **Lesson 1. Don't be in a rush; start with a self-evaluation and then research the most suitable franchise opportunities thoroughly.** After examining the activities and work that she enjoyed most, Frerich decided that she did not want a franchise in the clothing or fashion business. Over the course of a year, she and her husband, Kevin, considered their franchise

Gina Frerich evaluated many franchise options before deciding to purchase a Cold Stone Creamery francise. What steps should entrepreneurs who are considering buying a franchise take to make sure their choice is the right one?

options. Frerich did not rush into a decision; she and Kevin spent more than two years studying and researching before narrowing their choice down to an ice cream franchise.

> **Lesson 2. Use the power of the internet in your research.** From their New Jersey home, the Frerichs used the Internet to research several franchise operations in the retail ice cream industry. Based on the research, Gina was intrigued by the

Cold Stone Creamery franchise, a retail ice cream shop that features freshly made ice cream to which customers can add a multitude of toppings. Because the chain had not yet established any outlets in the New Jersey area, Frerich did almost all of her preliminary research online. It wasn't until she was visiting family in San Diego that she actually went into a Cold Stone Creamery franchise and tasted the product. That visit confirmed all of her research about the franchise, clinching the decision. "I called my husband and said, 'You know that Cold Stone [concept] we were looking at? I just had it, and it's amazing super-premium ice cream.' It was so good."

Lesson 3. Review the Uniform Franchise Offering Circular (UFOC) with the help of an experienced attorney. Frerich found the franchiser's UFOC to be an extremely useful, comprehensive document. Poring over the document alone can be frustrating, however, because it covers so much. "The typical UFOC is about the size of a telephone book," says Eric Karp, an attorney who teaches franchising courses at Babson College. "It is enormously complex because it is so multifaceted." Karp says that some franchisees are so overwhelmed by the size of the UFOC that they make the mistake of not reading it at all.

Lesson 4. Don't be shy about asking LOTS of questions. When Frerich returned from San Diego, she contacted the Cold Stone Creamery headquarters in Scottsdale, Arizona, and asked plenty of questions. She was excited to hear that the company was about to open a flagship store in New York City's Times Square. Frerich thought that opening this high-profile store would increase the awareness of the Cold Stone Creamery brand name in the Northeast, benefiting any stores that she might open in nearby New Jersey. She submitted her official application to become a Cold Stone Creamery franchisee.

In the meantime, of course, the franchiser was evaluating Frerich to make sure that she met the company's criteria for its franchisees. "The Creamery is very selective [to] whom they award franchises," she explains. "They had to make sure it was the right fit."

Lesson 5. Talk to existing franchisees about what it's like to operate a franchise. Frerich was able to attend the Cold Stone Creamery annual franchise convention, a gathering of franchisees from all across the country. The convention was a prime opportunity for Frerich to spend a week talking to lots of veteran franchisees about the advantages and the disadvantages of owning and operating a Cold Stone Creamery franchise. "It was one of the greatest experiences throughout this adventure," she says.

Lesson 6. Take an active role in the training program. After attending the convention, Frerich enrolled in the franchiser's Ice Cream University in Scottsdale, where she spent two weeks immersed in the details of making ice cream and running a successful franchise. The course involved both classroom instruction and hands-on experience operating a real store. Most evenings she spent studying for the final exam, which paid off when Frerich made the highest score on the exam, garnering her "Scoopa Cum Laude" status. Franchisees must recognize that they are paying the franchiser to train them to operate their outlets successfully and it is their responsibility to make the most of the opportunity to learn.

Lesson 7. Utilize the franchiser's experience and support. Smart franchisees use their franchiser's experience to their benefit. For instance, Stone Cold Creamery helped Frerich with one of the most important tasks in retail operations: finding an ideal location for her store. She also drew on the franchiser's support when it came to hiring and training her staff.

Despite Frerich's thorough analysis, research, and preparation, opening day for her franchise brought unexpected challenges. A walk-in freezer went into defrost mode and refused to come out, posing a huge threat to the store's inventory of freshly made ice cream. Despite the glitch, Frerich's grand opening was a success, as is her store, whose sales exceeded the chain's average unit volume of $375,000 within two years. Although some days are stressful, Frerich believes that franchising was the right choice for her. In fact, she already has opened two more Stone Cold Creamery franchises, one in Madison and the other in Summit, New Jersey.

Sources: Adapted from *Franchisee Profiles*, Cold Stone Creamery, http://www.coldstonecreamery.com/images/news/Franchisee_Profiles_737.pdf; Anne Fisher, "Risk Reward," *FSB*, December 2005/January 2006, pp. 45–61; Nichole L. Torres, "The Inside Scoop," *Entrepreneur*, January 2005, pp. 96–102.

Trends Shaping Franchising

Franchising has experienced three major growth waves since its beginning. The first wave occurred in the early 1970s when fast food restaurants used the concept to grow rapidly. The fast food industry was one of the first to discover the power of franchising, but other businesses soon took notice and adapted the franchising concept to their industries. The second wave took place in the mid-1980s as the U.S. economy shifted heavily toward the service sector. Franchises followed suit, springing up in every service business imaginable—from maid services and copy centers to mailing services and real estate. The third wave began in the early 1990s and continues today. It is characterized by new, low-cost franchises that focus on specific market niches. In the wake of major corporate downsizing and the burgeoning costs of traditional franchises, these new franchises allow would-be entrepreneurs to get into proven businesses faster and at lower costs. These companies feature start-up costs in the $2,000 to $250,000 range and span a variety of industries—from leak detection in homes and auto detailing to daycare and tile glazing.

Other significant trends affecting franchising include the following.

Changing Face of Franchisees

Franchisees today are better educated, are more sophisticated, have more business acumen, and are more financially secure than those of just 20 years ago. Franchising is attracting skilled, experienced businesspeople whose goal is to own multiple outlets that cover entire states or regions. Many of them are former corporate managers—either corporate castoffs or corporate dropouts—looking for a new start on a more meaningful and rewarding career. They have the financial resources, management skills and experience, and motivation to operate their franchises successfully.

Bevinco

After spending 23 years with a large financial services company, Marc Weinberg's job was eliminated in a corporate restructuring move. Rather than view the layoff as a devastating blow, however, Weinberg saw it as an opportunity to fulfill his dream of operating a franchise. "I didn't want to start a new business from scratch," Weinberg says. After researching his options, Weinberg settled on a Bevinco franchise, a business that helps restaurants and bars maintain control over their beverage inventories and the cash generated from beverage sales. After eight years, Weinberg's franchise has become so successful that the Bevinco has enlisted him to help other franchisees operate their businesses. "Owning a franchise is terrific," he says. "I get to reap the rewards of my own work instead of having to contribute them all to the company."[32]

Multiple-Unit Franchising

Twenty years ago, the typical franchisee operated a single outlet. Today, however, modern franchisees increasingly have as a goal operating multiple franchise units. In **multiple-unit franchising (MUF)**, a franchisee opens more than one unit in a broad territory within a specific time period. It is no longer unusual for a single franchisee to own 25, 75, or even 100 units. According to FRANDATA, about 11 percent of franchisees operate multiple units, and that number is expected to grow rapidly over the next several years.[33] Franchisers are finding that it is far more efficient in the long run to have one well-trained franchisee operate a number of units than to train many franchises to operate that same number of outlets. A multiple-unit strategy also accelerates a franchise's growth rate. For instance, to reach its goal of adding 5,000 new outlets within five years, Allied Domecq Quick Service Restaurants, the company that sells Baskin-Robbins, Dunkin' Donuts, and Togo's franchises, began recruiting multiple-unit franchisees in 17 major markets in the United States. Many of the franchisees the company selected were existing franchisees looking to expand their businesses, but others were newcomers to the chain.[34]

The popularity of multiple-unit franchising has paralleled the trend toward increasingly experienced, sophisticated franchisees, who set high performance goals that a single outlet cannot meet. The typical multiple-unit franchisee owns between three and six units, but some franchisees own many more.

multiple-unit franchising (MUF)

a method of franchising in which a franchisee opens more than one unit in a broad territory within a specific time period.

LEARNING OBJECTIVES

5. Outline the major trends shaping franchising.

Buffalo Wild Wings

After working as executive vice-president of marketing for Wendy's and then operating his own advertising agency for 18 years, Bill Welter moved to Las Vegas, Nevada. When he arrived, he noticed the absence of his favorite restaurant back East, Buffalo Wild Wings, a franchise with which he had become familiar while working at Wendy's. Sensing an opportunity, Welter investigated the franchise and the local market thoroughly and, at age 52, decided to launch a new career as a Buffalo Wild Wings franchisee. Welter purchased the license for the entire Las Vegas area and has already opened six franchises in the area with plans to open four more within the next few years. "The most satisfying thing to me," says Welter, "is to wear a Buffalo Wild Wings shirt anywhere in this town, and people come up and say, "'That's my favorite place.' That means more to me than anything."[35]

Although operating multiple units offers advantages for both franchisers and franchisees, there are dangers. Operating multiple units requires franchisers to focus more carefully on selecting the right franchisees—those who are capable of handling the additional requirements of multiple units. The impact of selecting the wrong franchise owners is magnified when they operate multiple units and can create huge headaches for the entire chain. Franchisees must be aware of the dangers of losing their focus and becoming distracted if they take on too many units. In addition, operating multiple units means more complexity because the number of business problems franchisees face also is multiplied.

International Opportunities

One of the major trends in franchising is the internationalization of American franchise systems. Increasingly, franchising is becoming a major export industry for the United States. "Franchising is strong overseas," says an executive at the International Franchise Association. "The number of U.S. franchise companies expanding outside the U.S. border is growing steadily."[36] U.S. franchises are moving into international markets to boost sales and profits as the domestic market becomes saturated. More than 500 U.S.-based franchisers now have an international presence, and more domestic franchisers are looking to expand abroad. The International Franchise Association reports that over the last decade, nearly half of all units established by U.S.-based franchisers were opened outside of the United States.[37] For example, in 1980, McDonald's had restaurants in 28 countries; today, the company operates more than 10,000 outlets in 119 nations. Canada is the primary market for U.S. franchisers, with Mexico, Japan, and Europe following. These markets are most attractive to franchisers because they are similar to the U.S. market—rising personal incomes, strong demand for consumer goods, growing service economies, and spreading urbanization.

As they venture into foreign markets, franchisers have learned that adaptation is one key to success. Although a franchise's overall business format may not change in foreign markets, some of the details of operating its local outlets must. For instance, fast-food chains in other countries often must make adjustments to their menus to please locals' palates. In Japan, McDonald's (known as "Makudonarudo") outlets sell teriyaki burgers, rice burgers, and katsu burgers (cheese wrapped in a roast pork cutlet topped with katsu sauce and shredded cabbage) in addition to their traditional American fare. In the Philippines, the McDonald's menu includes a spicy Filipino-style burger, spaghetti, and chicken with rice. In China, KFC quickly learned that residents were not interested in cole slaw, so the company dropped the item from its menu and added local delicacies such as shredded carrots, fungus, and bamboo shoots.[38]

As China's economy continues to grow and its capital markets expand, increasing numbers of franchisers are opening locations there. Currently, more than 1,900 franchise systems operate some 82,000 outlets in China, an average of 43 units per chain (still far below the average of 540 units per chain in the United States).[39] Fast-growing Subway is the third largest U.S.-based fast food chain in China behind McDonald's and KFC. Known as Sai Bei Wei (which translates as "tastes better than others" in Mandarin), Subway has learned the importance of patience in building a franchise presence in challenging international markets. When the company opened its first outlet in China, managers had to print signs explaining how to order a sandwich. Sales of tuna salad were dismal because residents, accustomed to seeing their fish whole, did not believe the salad was made from fish at all. In addition, because Chinese diners do not like to touch their food, many of them held their sandwiches vertically, peeled the paper wrapper away gradually, and ate the contents as they would eat a banana![40]

Countries that only recently began welcoming the free market system are turning to franchising to help them move toward a market economy. Some countries of Eastern Europe, including Hungary, Poland, and Yugoslavia, are attracting franchises. Even Russia is fertile ground for franchising. McDonald's has scored a hit with its 700-seat restaurant in Moscow. Despite being one of the largest McDonald's outlets in the world, it is not uncommon to see a line of hungry customers winding along busy Pushkin Square, waiting to get in to purchase a Big Mac. Establishing franchises in these countries requires patience, however. Lack of capital, archaic infrastructure, and a shortage of hard currencies mean that profits are slow in coming. Most franchisers recognize the difficulties involved in developing franchises in foreign markets and start slowly.

You Be the Consultant

Franchisers Forge New Ground in China

Since its beginning in the United States more than 125 years ago, franchising has become an important part of the both the U.S. and the global economy. As franchisers have found it increasingly difficult to continue to wring impressive growth rates from the domestic market, they have begun to export their franchises to international markets, including those with developing economies. Indeed, franchising is ideally suited for developing economies because it allows people with limited business experience and financial resources to become part of an established business. China, with a population of 1.3 billion people and what is potentially the largest consumer market in the world, is becoming a target for many franchisers. Because the Chinese retail sector is predicted to grow consistently at 8 to 10 percent a year through 2010, many experts are calling China the most important consumer market of the twenty-first century.

Franchising is relatively new to China, but fast food franchisers see a bright future there because the fast-food industry is in its infancy and is growing very fast. KFC (formerly Kentucky Fried Chicken) established the first outlet in 1987, but it was a company-owned store rather than a true franchise. The first franchised KFC store opened in the city of Xi'an in 1993. Yum! Brands, the owner of KFC, Pizza Hut, and other franchises, has

more than 1,200 KFC and 120 Pizza Hut restaurants in China. "We're the number one brand in China," says Yum! Brands CEO David Novak. "KFC makes almost as much money in China today as it makes in the U.S."

McDonald's entered China in 1992 when it opened a store in Beijing as part of a joint venture with a local Chinese company. Working with this local partner, McDonald's has expanded to more than 600 locations across China. Meng Sun, a Chinese national who took a part-time job at a McDonald's while working on her MBA at the University of Calgary in Canada, opened McDonald's first franchised store in 2004 in Tianjin, a city of 10 million people about 70 miles southeast of Beijing. Meng Sun used $360,000 (about three million yuan) she had saved from working as a financial consultant to open her franchised store. "I thought it was a very good start for an aspiring entrepreneur," she says of her busy mall-based restaurant.

Both Yum! Brands and McDonald's have expanded their franchising operations in China slowly, as have most other successful franchisers. Jim Bryant, an international development manager for Subway, the sandwich franchise, says that when he started developing franchises in China in 1995, there was no word in the Chinese language for "franchise." (Today, there is a Chinese word for "franchise"—"jia meng," which roughly translates into "person joins group of other people.") U.S. franchisers are anxious to tap into the knowledge of the nuances of doing business in the diverse market segments that native Chinese franchisees have developed. They understand that intimate knowledge of local markets is key to their operations' success in China. Many U.S.-based franchisers say that they receive inquiries daily from people interested in opening franchises in China.

Some aspects of establishing franchises in China are no different from selling them in the United States. Finding the right businesspeople to become franchisees is a top priority, as is selecting the best locations. For instance, both KFC and McDonald's require prospective franchisees to spend at least one year working at every position in an existing restaurant. McDonald's sends its Chinese franchisees to a Hong Kong branch of its famous Hamburger University, where students learn all of the aspects of running successful outlets. Hamburger University resembles a business school; students sit in high-tech classrooms and analyze case studies in break-out groups. Unlike a business school, however, this university includes a mock restaurant, where students get

hands-on training. Instructors focus on teaching prospective franchisees to think creatively and analytically and to smile and be cheerful, skills they don't normally learn in Chinese universities and companies. U.S. franchisers operating in China know that it will take time for their investments to come to fruition, but they believe the payoffs will be worth the wait. "We are planting the seeds for a bigger future," says Sam Su, president of Yum Restaurants China.

1. Describe the opportunities and the challenges franchisers face when entering emerging markets such as China.
2. Use the Web as a resource to develop a list of at least five suggestions that will help new franchisers looking to establish outlets in China.

Sources: Adapted from Steven Gray and Geoffrey A. Fowler, "China's New Entrepreneurs," Wall Street Journal, January 25, 2003, pp. B1, B4; Stat-USA, U.S. Foreign Commercial Service, "Franchising Industry in China," http://www.buyusainfo.net/docs/x_5566195.pdf; Carlye Adler, "How China Eats a Sandwich," *Fortune*, March 21, 2005, pp. 210[B]–210[D]; Julia Boorstin, "Yum Isn't Chicken of China—or Atkins," *Fortune*, March 8, 2004, p. 50.

Smaller, Nontraditional Locations

As the high cost of building full-scale locations continues to climb, more franchisers are searching out nontraditional locations in which to build smaller, less expensive outlets. Based on the principle of **intercept marketing,** the idea is to put a franchise's products or services directly in the paths of potential customers, wherever that may be. Locations within locations have become popular. Franchises are putting scaled-down outlets on college campuses, in high school cafeterias, in sports arenas, in hospitals, on airline flights, and in zoos. St. Louis-based Pizzas of Eight already has outlets inside convenience stores, supermarkets, and bowling alleys and plans to open others in video stores.[41] Many franchisees have discovered that smaller outlets in these nontraditional locations generate nearly the same sales volume as full-sized outlets at just a fraction of the cost!

intercept marketing
the principle of putting a franchise's products or services directly in the paths of potential customers, wherever they may be.

Dunkin' Donuts

Steve Siegel, owner of 35 Dunkin' Donuts shops in the Boston area, recently began branching out into small, nontraditional locations where pedestrian traffic counts are high. One of his most profitable spots measures just 64 square feet, but because it is in a business district filled with office workers, it generates a high volume of sales. Dunkin' Donuts also has an agreement with Wal-Mart to open outlets inside some of the giant retailer's stores.[42]

Locations that emphasize convenience by being close to their customers will be a key to continued franchise growth in the domestic market.

conversion franchising
a franchising trend in which owners of independent businesses become franchisees to gain the advantage of name recognition.

Conversion Franchising

The recent trend toward **conversion franchising**, in which owners of independent businesses become franchisees to gain the advantage of name recognition, will continue. One study reports that 72 percent of franchisers in North America use conversion franchising as a growth strategy.[43] In a franchise conversion, the franchiser gets immediate entry into new markets and experienced operators; franchisees get increased visibility and often a big sales boost. It is not unusual for entrepreneurs who convert their independent stores into franchises to experience an increase of 20 percent or more in sales because of the instant name recognition the franchise offers. The biggest force in conversion franchising has been Century 21, the real estate sales company.

Master Franchising

A **master franchise** (or **subfranchise**) gives a franchisee the right to create a semi-independent organization in a particular territory to recruit, sell, and support other franchisees. A master franchisee buys the right to develop subfranchises within a broad geographic area or, sometimes, an entire country. Subfranchising "turbocharges" a franchiser's growth. Many franchisers use it to open outlets in international markets more quickly and efficiently because the master franchisees understand local laws and the nuances of selling in local markets. For instance, a master franchisee with TCBY International, a yogurt franchise, has opened 21 stores in China and Hong Kong. Based on his success in these markets, the company has sold him the master franchise in India.[44]

master franchise
a franchise that gives a franchisee the right to create a semi-independent organization in a particular territory to recruit, sell, and support other franchisees.

Piggybacking (or Combination or Multibranded Franchising)

Some franchisers also are discovering new ways to reach customers by teaming up with other franchisers selling complementary products or services. A growing number of companies are **piggybacking** outlets—combining two or more distinct franchises under one roof. This "buddy system" approach works best when the two franchise ideas are compatible and appeal to similar customers. For example, Yum! Brands, whose stable of franchises includes Taco Bell, KFC, Pizza Hut, A&W, and Long John Silver, is building hundreds of combination outlets, a concept that has proved to be highly successful. About 15 percent of the company's restaurants involve multibranding, with two or more concepts in the same location. "We find customers prefer a double-branded concept to a single brand six to one," says Yum! Brands CEO David Novak.[45]

piggybacking
a method of franchising in which two or more franchises team up to sell complementary products or services under one roof.

Properly planned, piggybacked franchises can magnify many times over the sales and profits of individual, self-standing outlets. One Baskin Robbins franchisee saw his sales climb 25 percent when he added a Blimpie Subs and Salads franchise to his existing ice cream shop. Another enterprising franchisee who combined Shell Oil (gas station), Charley's Steakery (sandwich shop), and TCBY (frozen yogurt) franchises under one roof in Columbus, Ohio, says that sales are running 10 percent more than the three outlets would generate in separate locations.[46]

Serving Dual-Career Couples and Aging Baby Boomers

Now that dual-career couples have become the norm, especially among baby boomers, the market for franchises offering convenience and time-saving devices is booming. Customers are willing to pay for products and services that will save them time or trouble, and franchises are ready to provide them. Franchisees of Around Your Neck go into the homes and offices of busy male executives to sell men's apparel and accessories ranging from shirts and ties to custom–made suits. Other areas in which franchising is experiencing rapid growth include home delivery of meals, house cleaning services, continuing education and training (especially computer and business training), leisure activities (such as hobbies, health spas, and travel-related activities), products and services aimed at home-based businesses, and health care.

Conclusion

Franchising has proved its viability in the U.S. economy and has become a key part of the small business sector because it offers many would-be entrepreneurs the opportunity to own and operate a business with a greater chance for success. Despite its impressive growth rate, the franchising industry still has a great deal of room to grow. "Franchising is really small business at its best," says Don DeBolt, president of the International Franchise Association.

Chapter Summary by Learning Objectives

1. Describe the three types of franchising: trade name, product distribution, and pure.

Trade name franchising involves a franchisee purchasing the right to become affiliated with a franchiser's trade name without distributing its products exclusively. Product distribution franchising involves licensing a franchisee to sell products or services under the franchiser's brand name through a selective, limited distribution network. Pure franchising involves a selling a franchisee a complete business format.

2. Explain (A) the benefits and (B) the drawbacks of buying a franchise.

Franchises offer many benefits: management training and support; brand name appeal; standardized quality of goods and services; national advertising programs; financial assistance; proven products and business formats; centralized buying power; territorial protection; and a greater chance of success.

Franchising also suffers from certain drawbacks: franchise fees and profit sharing; strict adherence to standardized operations; restrictions on purchasing; limited product lines; unsatisfactory training programs; market saturation; and less freedom.

3. Explain the laws covering franchise purchases.

The Federal Trade Commission (FTC) enacted the Trade Regulation Rule in 1979, which requires all franchisers to disclose detailed information on their operations at the first personal meeting or at least 10 days before a franchise contract is signed, or before any money is paid. The FTC rule covers *all* franchisers. The Trade Regulation Rule requires franchisers to provide information on 23 topics in their disclosure statements. Seventeen states have passed their own franchise laws requiring franchisers to provide prospective franchisees a Uniform Franchise Offering Circular (UFOC).

4. Discuss the right way to buy a franchise.

The following steps will help you make the right franchise choice: Evaluate yourself; research your market; consider your franchise options; get a copy of the franchiser's UFOC; talk to existing franchisees; ask the franchiser some tough questions; make your choice.

5. Outline the major trends shaping franchising.

Key trends shaping franchising today include the changing face of franchisees, international franchise opportunities, smaller, nontraditional locations, conversion franchising, multiple-unit franchising, master franchising, and piggybacking (or combination franchising).

Discussion Questions

1. What is franchising?
2. Describe the three types of franchising and give an example of each.
3. Discuss the advantages and the limitations of franchising for the franchisee.
4. Why might an independent entrepreneur be dissatisfied with a franchising arrangement?
5. What kinds of clues should tip off a prospective franchisee that he or she is dealing with a disreputable franchiser?
6. What steps should a potential franchisee take before investing in a franchise?
7. What is the function of the FTC's Trade Regulation Rule? Outline the protection the Trade Regulation Rule gives all prospective franchisees.
8. Describe the current trends in franchising.
9. One franchisee says, "Franchising is helpful because it gives you somebody [the franchiser] to get you going, nurture you, and shove you along a little. But, the franchiser won't make you successful. That depends on what you bring to the business, how hard you are prepared to work, and how committed you are to finding the right franchise for you." Do you agree? Explain.
10. What comments would you make to a highly creative and innovative person who was considering purchasing a franchise?

Business Plan Pro

BusinessPlanPro Most franchise systems will require you to submit a business plan with the application process. In many cases, the franchiser will specify what the business plan should include and may even require you follow an established business plan outline. If you are planning to purchase a franchise, investigate all of the application requirements. Determine the expectations regarding the content and structure of the business plan that you are to submit. Find out whether the franchiser has outlines or example plans or whether a plan from another franchisee is available in any form for your review.

Each year, *Entrepreneur* magazine ranks the top 500 franchise systems. *Entrepreneur* determines this ranking based on financial strength and stability, growth rate and size of the system, the number of years in business and length of time franchising, start-up costs, litigation, percentage of terminations, and whether the company provides financing.[47] The most recent ranking of the top 20 franchises is as follows.

Rank	Franchise Name	Business Description	Potential Start-up Cost
1	Subway	Sandwiches and salads	$70,000–$220,000
2	Quiznos Sub	Sandwiches and salads	$71,700–$251,100
3	Curves	Women's fitness and weight loss center	$38,400–$53,500
4	The UPS Store	Postal, business, communication	$153,900–$268,800
5	Jackson Hewitt Tax Service	Tax preparation services	$49,800–$94,000
6	Dunkin' Donuts	Donuts and baked goods	$179,000–$1,600,000
7	Jani-King	Commercial cleaning	$11,300–$34,100
8	RE/MAX International, Inc.	Real estate	$20,000–$200,000
9	7-Eleven Inc.	Convenience store	Varies
10	Liberty Tax Service	Income tax preparation services	$42,300–$52,400
11	Domino's Pizza LLC	Pizza, breadsticks, buffalo wings	$141,400–$415,100
12	Pizza Hut Inc.	Pizza	$1,100,000–$1,700,000
13	Sonic Drive In Restaurants	Drive-in restaurant	$710,000–$2,300,000
14	Century 21 Real Estate LLC	Real estate	$11,700–$522,500
15	Jan-Pro Franchising Intl Inc.	Commercial cleaning	$3,300–$49,900
16	McDonald's	Hamburgers, chicken, salads	$506,000–$1,600,000
17	ServiceMaster Clean	Cleaning and disaster restoration	$26,000–$102,300
18	Kumon Math & Reading	Supplemental education	$10,000–$30,000
19	Coldwell Banker Real Estate	Real estate	$23,500–$490,500
20	Jiffy Lube International Inc.	Fast oil change	$214,000–$273,000

Note the business category that dominates this list. Why do you think this phenomenon occurs? Note the start-up costs associated with each franchise. How do the start-up costs of service companies compare to those of the other franchises? Why does this only represent a portion of the revenue that the franchise system will require from the franchisee?

Business Plan Exercises
On the Web

Go to http://www.prenhall.com/scarborough and click on the Chapter 6 tab. Review the online franchise resources that are available. One of those links is to "The World Franchise Directory." Click on that link and enter the first letter of a familiar franchise, the letter "S," for example.

The number of franchise systems, many of them with an international presence, is staggering. Now, click on the Sample Plan tab and review the sample franchise plan included in this section. What unique characteristic do you notice about this business plan compared to others you have seen?

If you plan to purchase a franchise, visit the franchise system's Web site and request information. In most cases, you will respond to some initial questions to receive detailed franchise information. As you proceed through the process, note the specific questions regarding your sources of capital. Your access to capital will be a major qualification in determining whether you are "franchise worthy" in addition to other criteria.

In the Software

If you plan to own a franchise and that franchise system has specific business plan guidelines, modify the outline in Business Plan Pro outline to match the franchise's recommendation. To view the outline in the left-hand navigation, click on the Plan Outline icon or go to the View menu and click on Outline. Then, right-click on each of those topics that you need to change, move, or delete to meet the franchise's requirement. You may move topics up or down the outline with the corresponding arrows. To change topics from headings to subheadings, you "Demote" the topic. When you "Promote" a topic, you move a subheading to the left to a more dominant position.

Building Your Business Plan

Continue building your franchise business plan based on that outline. Use the information and verbiage that is familiar to the franchise system whenever possible. Your plan may be one of dozens received that week, and you want to demonstrate your knowledge, competence, and credibility. Your franchise business plan can be a sales tool to position you as an informed and attractive franchise owner.

Beyond the Classroom . . .

1. Visit a local franchise operation. Is it a trade name, product distribution, or pure franchise? To what extent did the franchisee investigate before investing? What assistance does the franchiser provide? How does the franchisee feel about the franchise contract he or she signed? What would he or she do differently now?

2. Use the Web to locate several franchises that interest you. Contact the franchisers and ask for their franchise packages. Write a report comparing their treatment of the topics covered by the Trade Regulation Rule. Analyze the terms of their franchise contracts. What are the major differences?

Are some terms more favorable than others? If you were about to invest in the franchise, which terms would you want to change?

3. Ask a local franchisee to approach his or her regional franchise representative about leading a class discussion on franchising.

4. Contact the International Franchise Association (1350 New York Avenue, N.W., Suite 900, Washington, D.C., 20005-4709; phone number 202 628-8000) for a copy of *Investigate Before Investing*. Prepare a report outlining what a prospective franchisee should do before buying a franchise.

APPENDIX A. A FRANCHISE EVALUATION CHECKLIST

You

1. Are you qualified to operate a franchise successfully? Do you have adequate drive, skills, experience, education, patience, and financial capacity? Are you prepared to work hard?

2. Are you willing to sacrifice some autonomy in operating a business to own a franchise?

3. Can you tolerate the financial risk? Would business failure wipe you out financially?

4. Can you juggle multiple tasks simultaneously and prioritize various projects so that you can accomplish those that are most important?

5. Are you genuinely interested in the product or service you will be selling? Do you enjoy this kind of business? Do you like to sell?

6. Do you enjoy working with and managing people? Are you a team player?

7. Will the business generate enough profit to suit you?

8. Has the franchiser investigated your background thoroughly enough to decide whether you are qualified to operate the franchise?

9. What can this franchiser do for you that you cannot do for yourself?

The Franchiser and the Franchise

1. Is the potential market for the product or service adequate to support your franchise? Will the prices you charge be in line with the market?

2. Is the market's population growing, remaining static, or shrinking? Is the demand for your product or service growing, remaining static, or shrinking?

3. Is the product or service safe and reputable?

4. Is the product or service a passing "fad," or is it a durable business idea?

5. What will the competition, direct or indirect, be in your sales territory? Do any other franchisees operate in this general area?

6. Is the franchise international, national, regional, or local in scope? Does it involve full- or part-time involvement?

7. How many years has the franchiser been in operation? Does it have a sound reputation for honest dealings with franchisees?

8. How many franchise outlets now exist? How many will there be a year from now? How many outlets are company-owned?

9. How many franchises have failed? Why?

10. How many franchisees have left the system within the last year? What were their reasons for leaving?
11. What service and assistance will the franchiser provide? What kind of training program does the franchiser offer? How long does it last? What topics does it cover? Does the franchiser offer ongoing assistance and training?
12. Will the franchise perform a location analysis to help you find a suitable site? If so, is there an extra charge for doing so?
13. Will the franchiser offer you exclusive distribution rights for the length of the agreement, or may it sell to other franchises in this area?
14. What facilities and equipment are required for the franchise? Who pays for construction? Is there a lease agreement?
15. What is the total cost of the franchise? What are the initial capital requirements? Will the franchiser provide financial assistance? Of what nature? What is the interest rate? Is the franchiser financially sound enough to fulfill all its promises?
16. How much is the franchise fee? Exactly what does it cover? Are there any ongoing fees? What additional fees are there?
17. Does the franchiser provide an estimate of expenses and income? Are they reasonable for your particular area? Are they sufficiently documented?
18. How risky is the franchise opportunity? Is the return on the investment consistent with the risks?
19. Does the franchiser offer a written contract that covers all the details of the agreement? Have your attorney and your accountant studied its terms and approved it? Do you understand the implications of the contract?
20. What is the length of the franchise agreement? Under what circumstances can it be terminated? If you terminate the contract, what are the costs to you? What are the terms and costs of renewal?
21. Are you allowed to sell your franchise to a third party? Does the franchiser reserve the right to approve the buyer?
22. Is there a national advertising program? How is it financed? What media are used? What help is provided for local advertising?
23. Once you open for business, *exactly* what support will the franchiser offer you?
24. How does the franchise handle complaints from and disputes with franchisees? How well has the system worked?

The Franchisees

1. Are you pleased with your investment in this franchise?
2. Has the franchiser lived up to its promises?
3. What was your greatest disappointment after getting into this business?
4. How effective was the training you received in helping you to run the franchise?
5. What are your biggest challenges and problems?
6. What is your franchise's cash flow like?
7. How much money are you making on your investment?
8. What do you like most about being a franchisee? Least?
9. Is there a franchisee advisory council that represents franchisees?
10. Knowing what you know now, would you buy this franchise again?

7 | Buying an Existing Business

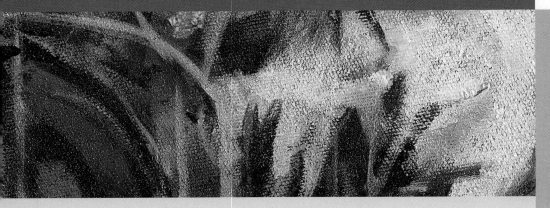

> Goodwill, like a good name, is gotten by many actions, and lost by one. —Lord Jeffrey

> There is nothing so easy to learn as experience and nothing so hard to apply. —Josh Billings

Learning Objectives

On completion of this chapter, you will be able to:

1 Understand (A) the advantages and (B) the disadvantages of buying an existing business.
2 Define the steps involved in the right way to buy a business.
3 Explain the process of evaluating an existing business.
4 Describe the various techniques for determining the value of a business.
5 Understand the seller's side of the buyout decision and how to structure the deal.
6 Understand how the negotiation process works and identify the factors that affect it.

Rather than launch their own businesses or purchase a franchise, some entrepreneurs opt for a more direct route to business ownership: They buy an existing business. In fact, in a typical year, more than 500,000 businesses are bought and sold. Each circumstance is unique, but the process of evaluating a potential business acquisition is not. The "due diligence" process that involves analyzing and evaluating an existing business for possible purchase is no less time consuming than developing a comprehensive business plan for a start-up. Done correctly, this due diligence process will reveal both the negative and the positive aspects of an existing business. Skipping or glossing over the due diligence process is a huge mistake because a business that looks good on the surface may have serious flaws at its core. Investigating a business to discover its real condition and value requires time, dedication, and, as the name implies, diligence, but the process is worthwhile because it can prevent an entrepreneur from purchasing a business destined for failure. When considering purchasing a business, the first rule is, "Do not rush into a deal." Taking shortcuts when investigating a potential business acquisition almost always leads to nasty—and expensive—surprises. Prospective buyers must be sure that they discover the answers to the following fundamental questions:

- Is the right type of business for sale in a market in which you want to operate?
- What experience do you have in this particular business and the industry in which it operates? How critical to your ultimate success is experience in the business?
- What is the company's potential for success?
- What changes will you have to make—and how extensive will they be—to realize the business's full potential?
- What price and payment method are reasonable for you and acceptable to the seller?
- Will the company generate sufficient cash to pay for itself and leave you with a suitable rate of return on your investment?
- Should you be starting a business and building it from the ground up rather than buying an existing one?

Buying an Existing Business

The Advantages of Buying an Existing Business

LEARNING OBJECTIVES
1A. Understand the advantages of buying an existing business.

Over the next decade, entrepreneurs looking to buy existing businesses will have ample opportunities to consider. A recent study by PricewaterhouseCoopers reports that 50 percent of existing company owners plan to sell their businesses within the next decade.[1] Those who purchase an existing business may reap the following benefits.

A Successful Existing Business May Continue to Be Successful Purchasing a thriving business at an acceptable price increases the likelihood of success. The previous management team already has established a customer base, built supplier relationships, and set up a business system. The customer base inherited in a business purchase can carry an entrepreneur while he or she studies how the business has become successful and how to build on that success. Time spent learning about the business and its customers before introducing changes will increase the probability that any changes made will be successful. The new owner's objective should be to make those modifications that will attract new customers while retaining the company's existing customers. Maintaining the proper balance of old and new is not an easy task, however.

An Existing Business May Already Have the Best Location When the location of the business is critical to its success (as is often the case in retailing), it may be wise to purchase a business that is already in the right place. Opening in a second-choice location and hoping to draw customers may prove fruitless. In fact, an existing business's biggest asset may be its prime location. If this advantage cannot be matched by other locations, an entrepreneur may have little choice but to buy a business instead of launching one. As part of its expansion plans, one fast food chain recently purchased a smaller chain, not so much for its customer base or other assets as for its prime store locations.

Employees and Suppliers Are Established An existing business already has experienced employees who can help the new owner through the transition phase. Experienced employees enable a company to continue to earn money while a new owner learns the business. Many new owners find it valuable to solicit ideas from employees about methods for increasing sales or reducing costs. In many cases, the previous owner may not have involved employees in this fashion and never gained the advantages found in the wisdom of employees. Few people know a job better than the people who are performing it.

In addition, an existing business has an established set of suppliers with a history of business dealings. Those vendors can continue to supply the business while the new owner investigates the products and services of other suppliers. However, suppliers may want to ensure that the new owners are capable of running the business successfully.

Cole-Kramer Imports

When Reid Chase and Scott Semel purchased Cole-Kramer Imports, a high-end candy company that imported and distributed Swiss mint candies, they invested $100,000 of their own money and borrowed the remaining $500,000. The new owners soon discovered that the previous owners had no written contracts with its key suppliers. When Chase and Semel attempted to negotiate a formal supply contract, their suppliers refused, insisting that the new owners first prove their ability to operate the candy company successfully. Chase and Semel expanded their product line beyond mints and landed several major retail accounts in the process. Convinced that the new owners could manage the business, the Swiss suppliers forged long-term contracts with Cole-Kramer Imports, whose sales climbed from $600,000 to more than $40 million in just seven years.[2]

Equipment Is Installed and Productive Capacity Is Known Acquiring and installing new equipment exerts a tremendous strain on a fledgling company's financial resources. In an existing business, a potential buyer can determine the condition of the plant and equipment and its capacity before buying. The previous owner may have established an efficient production operation through trial and error, although the new owner may need to make modifications to improve it. In many cases, entrepreneurs can purchase physical facilities and equipment at prices significantly below their replacement costs.

Inventory Is in Place and Trade Credit Is Established The proper amount of inventory is essential to both controlling costs and generating adequate sales volume. If a business has too little inventory, it will not have the quantity and variety of products it needs to satisfy customer demand. However, if a business has too much inventory, it is tying up excessive capital unnecessarily, thereby increasing costs and reducing profitability. Owners of successful established businesses have learned the proper balance between these extremes. In addition, previous owners have established trade credit relationships with vendors that can benefit the new owner. No supplier wants to lose a good customer.

The New Business Owner Hits the Ground Running Entrepreneurs who purchase existing businesses avoid the time, costs, and energy required to launch a new business. The day they take over an ongoing business is the day their revenues begin. Entrepreneurs who buy existing successful businesses do not have to invest a lifetime building a company to enjoy its success.

Mannequin Service Company

Lania D'Agostino, a sculptor who moved from Michigan to Baltimore, Maryland, to attend the Maryland Institute College of Art, began working at Mannequin Service Company, a business that specializes in designing and creating custom mannequins for museums, special events, and entertainment companies. D'Agostino spent three years learning the business before buying it from the founder, who had built the business by making display mannequins for retail stores such as Sears. After buying the business,

D'Agostino shifted the strategy to focus on highly specialized, artistic projects. A big break came for the company when D'Agostino landed a contract with Lucasfilm Inc., the company that produced the Star Wars trilogies, to provide mannequins depicting the characters from the films, from Obi-Won Kenobi and Princess Leia to Padme and Chewbacca, the Wookiee. Requiring as many as 80 hours to create, the company's character mannequins sell for $7,500 and up.[3]

The New Owner Can Use the Experience of the Previous Owner Even if the previous owner is not around after the sale, the new owner will have access to all of the business's records to guide him or her until he or she becomes acclimated to the business and the local market. The new owner can trace the impact on costs and revenues of the major decisions that the previous owner made and can learn from his or her mistakes and profit from his or her achievements. In many cases, the previous owner spends time with the new owner during the transition period, giving the new manager the opportunity to learn about the policies and procedures in place and the reasons for them. Previous owners also can be extremely helpful in unmasking the unwritten rules of business in the area, including critically important intangibles such as how to keep customers happy and whom one can trust and cannot trust. After all, most owners who sell out want to see the buyer succeed in carrying on their businesses.

Easier Financing Attracting financing to purchase an existing business often is easier than finding the money to launch a company from scratch. Many existing businesses already have established relationships with lenders, which may open the door to financing through traditional sources such as banks. As we will see later in this chapter, many business buyers also have access to another important source of financing: the seller.

It's a Bargain Some existing businesses may be real bargains. The current owners may need to sell on short notice, which may lead them to sell the business at a low price. Many small companies operate in profitable but tiny niches, making it easy for potential buyers to overlook them. The more specialized a business is, the greater the likelihood is that a buyer can find a bargain. If special skill or training is required to operate a business, the number of potential buyers will be significantly smaller. If the seller wants a substantial down payment or the entire selling price in cash, few buyers may qualify; however, those who do may be able to negotiate a good deal.

Disadvantages of Buying an Existing Business

It's a "Loser" A business may be for sale because it is struggling and the owner wants out. In these situations, a prospective buyer must be wary. Business owners sometimes attempt to disguise the facts and employ creative accounting techniques to make the company's financial picture appear much brighter than it really is. Few business sellers honestly state "It's losing money" as the reason for putting their companies up for sale. If there is one area of business where the maxim "let the buyer beware" still prevails, it is in the purchase of an existing business. Any buyer unprepared to do a complete and thorough analysis of a business may be stuck with a real loser.

Although buying a money-losing business is risky, it is not necessarily taboo. If an analysis of a company shows that it is poorly managed or suffering from neglect, a new owner may be able to turn it around. However, a prospective buyer who does not have well-defined plan for improving a struggling business should *not* consider buying it.

Andrew Taitz spent three years searching for the right business to buy. After screening many options, Taitz and a group of investors purchased Union City Body Company in Union City, Indiana, a bankrupt division of General Motors that made bodies for delivery trucks. Renamed Workhorse Custom Chassis, the company has expanded its product line to make the frames that support the wheels, engine, fuel systems, brakes, and suspension for motor homes and delivery trucks. "I saw an excellent opportunity to

Workhorse Custom Chassis

turn a low-tech, nuts-and-bolts product into a growth market," says Taitz. Taitz and his investors spent $100 million, including the initial purchase price, revamping the entire plant to make it more flexible, efficient, and ergonomically sound. Today, Workhorse builds customized frames from more than 3,500 parts one right after another on the same assembly line. Taitz also implemented a host of changes in the company's management style, cutting the workweek to four 10-hour days (from five 8-hour days) and allowing employees to work in small teams and to practice job rotation. Taitz also set up a Web site that allows customers to design their own chassis online, and the company's FasTrack program delivers a chassis to a customer in just four weeks. The result is that Workhorse's revenues exceed $300 million per year, and the company is now profitable.[4]

The Previous Owner May Have Created Ill Will   Just as ethical, socially responsible business dealings create goodwill for a company, improper business behavior creates ill will. The due diligence process may reveal that customers, suppliers, creditors, or employees may have extremely negative feelings about a company's reputation because of the unethical actions of its current owner. Business relationships may have begun to deteriorate, but their long-term effects may not yet appear in the business's financial statements. Ill will can permeate a business for years.

Employees Inherited with the Business May Not Be Suitable   Previous managers may have kept marginal employees because they were close friends or because they started with the company. A new owner, therefore, may have to make some very unpopular termination decisions. For this reason, employees often do not welcome a new owner because they feel threatened by change. Some employees may not be able to adapt to the new owner's management style, and a culture clash may result. If the due diligence efforts reveals that existing employees are a significant cause of the problems a business faces, the new owner will have no choice but to terminate them and make new hires.

The Business Location May Have Become Unsatisfactory   What was once an ideal location may have become obsolete as market and demographic trends change. Large shopping malls, new competitors, or highway re-routings can spell disaster for small retail shops. Prospective buyers should always evaluate the existing market in the area surrounding an existing business as well as its potential for expansion. Buyers must remember that they are buying the future of a business, not merely its past. A location in decline may never recover. If business success is closely linked to a good location, acquiring a business in a declining area or where demographic trends are moving downward is not a good idea. The value of the business will erode faster than the neighborhood surrounding it.

Equipment and Facilities May Be Obsolete or Inefficient   Potential buyers sometimes neglect to have an expert evaluate a company's facilities and equipment before they purchase it. Only later do they discover that the equipment is obsolete and inefficient and that the business may suffer losses from excessively high operating costs. The equipment may have been well suited to the business they purchased, but not to the business they want to build. Modernizing equipment and facilities is seldom inexpensive.

Change and Innovation Are Difficult to Implement   It is easier to plan for change than it is to implement it. Methods, policies, and procedures the previous owner used in a business may have established precedents that a new owner finds difficult to modify. Customers may resist changes the new owner wants to make to the business.

When Charles Usry purchased the landmark Esso Club in Clemson, South Carolina, he quickly discovered that the bar's regulars were skeptical of the changes he had planned to implement. Originally begun as a gas station/ grocery store in 1935, the Esso Club eventually was converted into a bar and became a legendary destination for sports fans when *ESPN the Magazine* named it one of the top must-visit locations for sports fans. When Usry announced his plans to upgrade the décor of the no-frills, cinder-block building and to transform the club into a sports bar, long-time customers and loyal visitors

howled in protest. "It's the ambiance of the place that really does it for us," says David Ford, an Esso Club regular, only half-joking. "The closest thing [to the Esso Club] is Cheers," says another long-time customer.[5]

Esso Club

When Charles Usry purchased the Esso Club a legendary destination for sports fans in Clemson, South Carolina, he began making plans to upgrade the décor of the old cinderblock building. Usry changed his plans when loyal customers resisted the changes to their beloved Esso Club.

Reversing a downward slide in an existing company's sales can be just as difficult as implementing change. Making changes that bring in new business and convince former clients to return can be an expensive, time-consuming, and laborious process. A business buyer must be aware of the effort, time, and expense it takes to change the negative momentum of a business in trouble. Before a business can go forward, it must stop going backward.

Inventory May Be Outdated or Obsolete Inventory is valuable only if it is salable. Smart buyers know better than to trust the inventory valuation on a firm's balance sheet. Some of it may actually appreciate in value in periods of rapid inflation, but inventory is more likely to depreciate. A prospective buyer must judge inventory by its market value, *not* by its book value.

Accounts Receivable May Be Worth Less Than Face Value Like inventory, accounts receivable rarely are worth their face value. The prospective buyer should age the company's accounts receivable (a breakdown of accounts 30, 60, 90, and 120 days old and beyond) to determine their collectibility. The older the receivables are, the less likely they are to be collected, and, consequently, the lower their value is. Table 7.1 shows a simple but effective method of evaluating accounts receivable once they have been aged, using the estimated probabilities of collecting the accounts.

TABLE 7.1 Valuing Accounts Receivable

A prospective buyer asked the current owner of a business about the value of her accounts receivable. The owner's business records showed $101,000 in receivables. But when the prospective buyer aged the accounts and multiplied them by his estimated collection probabilities, he discovered their real value:

Age of Accounts (days)	Amount ($)	Collection Probability (%)	Value ($)
0–30	40,000	95	38,000
31–60	25,000	88	22,000
61–90	14,000	70	9,800
91–120	10,000	40	4,000
121–150	7,000	25	1,750
151–plus	5,000	10	500
Total	101,000		78,050

Had he blindly accepted the seller's book value of these accounts receivable, this prospective buyer would have overpaid nearly $25,000 for them!

When one buyer was considering purchasing an existing business, his research showed that a substantial volume of accounts receivable were well past due. Further investigation revealed that the company and its largest customer were locked in a nasty dispute over outstanding account balances. The buyer decided to withdraw his preliminary offer.

The Business May Be Overpriced Each year, many people purchase businesses at prices far in excess of their value, which can impair the companies' ability to earn a profit and generate a positive cash flow. If a buyer accurately values a business's accounts receivable, inventories, and other assets, he or she will be in a better position to negotiate a price that will allow the business to be profitable. Making payments on a business that was overpriced is a millstone around the new owner's neck, making it difficult to keep the business afloat.

Although most buyers do not realize it, the price they pay for a company typically is not as crucial to its continued success as the terms on which they make the purchase. Of course, wise business buyers will try to negotiate a fair and reasonable price, but they are often equally interested in the more specific terms of the deal. For instance, how much cash they must pay out and when, how much of the price the seller is willing to finance and for how long, the interest rate at which the deal is financed, and other such terms can make or break a deal from the buyer's perspective. A buyer's primary concern is making sure that the terms of the deal do not endanger the company's future financial health and that they preserves the company's cash flow.

LEARNING OBJECTIVES
2. Define the steps involved in the right way to buy a business.

The Steps in Acquiring a Business

Buying an existing business can be risky if approached haphazardly. Studies show that more than 50 percent of all business acquisitions fail to meet the buyer's expectations. To avoid costly mistakes, an entrepreneur-to-be should follow a logical, methodical approach:

- Analyze your skills, abilities, and interests to determine what kind(s) of businesses you should consider.
- Prepare a list of potential candidates.
- Investigate those candidates and evaluate the best one(s).
- Explore financing options.
- Ensure a smooth transition.

Analyze Your Skills, Abilities, and Interests

The first step in buying a business is *not* searching out potential acquisition candidates. Every entrepreneur considering buying a business should begin by conducting a self-audit to determine the ideal business for him or her. The primary focus is to identify the type of business *you* will be happiest and most successful owning. Consider, for example, the following questions:

- What business activities do you enjoy most? Least? Why?
- Which industries or markets offer the greatest potential for growth?
- Which industries interest you most? Least? Why?
- What kind of business do you want to buy?
- What kinds of businesses do you want to *avoid*?
- What do you expect to get out of the business?
- How much time, energy, and money can you put into the business?
- What business skills and experience do you have? What skills and experience do you lack?
- How easily can you transfer your skills and experience to other types of businesses? In what kinds of businesses would that transfer be easiest?
- How much risk are you willing to take?

- Are you willing and able to turn around a struggling business?
- What size company do you want to buy?
- Is there a particular geographic location you desire?

Answering these and other questions beforehand will allow you to develop a list of criteria a company must meet to become a purchase candidate. Addressing these issues early in the process will also save a great deal of time, trouble, and confusion as you wade through a multitude of business opportunities. The better you know yourself and your skills, competencies, and interests, the more likely you will be to find and manage a successful business.

Prepare a List of Potential Candidates

Once you know what your goals are for acquiring a business, you can begin your search. Do *not* limit yourself to only those businesses that are advertised as being "for sale." In fact, the **hidden market** of companies that might be for sale but are not advertised as such is one of the richest sources of top-quality businesses. Many businesses that can be purchased are not publicly advertised but are available either through the owners or through business brokers and other professionals. Although they maintain a low profile, these hidden businesses represent some of the most attractive purchase targets a prospective buyer may find.

hidden market
Low-profile companies that might be for sale but are not advertised as such.

When brothers Art and Allan McCraw, two enterprising college graduates, returned to their hometown, they approached the owners of B.W. Burdette and Sons, a local hardware store that had been founded by the current owners' father 80 years earlier, about buying the business. The company was not listed for sale, but because they were familiar with the business, the McCraws knew that the current owners might be interested in selling. After several months of due diligence and negotiations, the young entrepreneurs closed the deal. They have since expanded the business to include two more locations, expanded its market reach, and increased its profitability many times over.

B.W. Burdette and Sons

How can you tap into this hidden market of potential acquisitions? Typical sources include the following:

- Business brokers
- Bankers
- Accountants
- Investment bankers
- Industry contacts—suppliers, distributors, customers, insurance brokers, and others
- "Networking"—social and business contact with friends and relatives
- Knocking on the doors of businesses you would like to buy (even if they're not advertised as being "for sale")
- Trade associations
- Newspapers and trade journals listing businesses for sale

In recent years, the World Wide Web also has become an important tool for entrepreneurs looking to buy businesses. In the past, the market for businesses was highly fragmented and unstructured, making it difficult for entrepreneurs to conduct an organized, thorough search for companies that might meet their purchase criteria. Today, hundreds of business brokers have established Web sites that list thousands of companies for sale in practically every industry imaginable, enabling entrepreneurs to search the entire country for that perfect business from the comfort of their own homes. Using the Web, potential buyers can eliminate the companies that do not suit them and can conduct preliminary research on those that look most promising. The more opportunities an entrepreneur has to find and evaluate potential acquisitions, the greater the likelihood of finding a match that meets his or her criteria.

Investigate and Evaluate Candidate Businesses and Evaluate the Best One

Finding the right company requires patience. Although some buyers find a company after only a few months of looking, the typical search takes much longer, sometimes as much as two or three years. Once you have a list of prospective candidates, it is time to do your homework. The next step is to investigate the candidates in more detail:

- What are the company's strengths? Weaknesses?
- Is the company profitable? What is its overall financial condition?
- What is its cash flow cycle? How much cash will the company generate?
- Who are its major competitors?
- How large is the customer base? Is it growing or shrinking?
- Are the current employees suitable? Will they stay?
- What is the physical condition of the business, its equipment, and its inventory?
- What new skills must you learn to be able to manage this business successfully?

Determining the answers to these and other questions addressed in this chapter will allow a prospective buyer to develop a list of the most attractive prospects and to prioritize them in descending order of attractiveness. This process also will make the task of valuing the business much easier.

Company Profile

A.M.E.'s Uniforms

When Mark Forst and his father decided to leave the corporate life and go into business for themselves, they knew that they wanted to buy an existing business rather than start their own. "We wanted a company that could use better marketing and service, one that we could take from the local to the national level," says Forst. Forst spent weeks poring over the business listings in Fort Lauderdale newspapers and hired a business broker to help uncover potential purchase candidates. One day he noticed a listing in the newspaper for a business called Rip's Uniforms that specialized in providing uniforms for postal workers. Forst and his father thought the asking price of $100,000 was reasonable, and they began researching the industry. Their research was encouraging. They discovered that the uniform supply industry had solid growth rates and that although a number of local uniform distributors were scattered across the United States, only five operated on a national level. Forst and his father began the due diligence process, talking with the small company's owners, studying the industry, and interviewing the company's vendors and its sole employee. They even conducted market research, talking with postal workers to glean ideas about how they could win them as customers and integrating what they learned into their business plan for the company. Their research of the company revealed that Rip's Uniforms had much more debt and far less inventory than the current owners believed, but the Forsts still believed in the company's potential. Using the information they had gathered, the Forsts purchased Rip's Uniforms after they were able to whittle the purchase price down to just $10,000. They renamed the company A.M.E.'s Uniforms, and sales, which now top $3 million annually, are growing so fast that the company has made *Inc.* magazine's list of the 500 fastest-growing small companies twice.[6]

Explore Financing Options

Placing a value on an existing business (a topic you will learn more about later in this chapter) represents a major hurdle for many would-be entrepreneurs. The next challenging task in closing a successful deal is financing the purchase. Although financing the purchase of an existing business usually is easier than financing a new one, some traditional lenders shy away from deals involving the purchase of an existing business. Those that are willing to finance business purchases normally lend only a portion of the value of the assets, and buyers often find themselves searching for alternative sources of funds. Fortunately, most business buyers have access to a ready source of financing: the seller.

Seller financing often is more flexible, faster, and easier to obtain than loans from traditional lenders.

Once a seller finds a suitable buyer, he or she typically will agree to finance anywhere from 25 to 80 percent of the purchase price. Usually, a deal is structured so that the buyer makes a sizeable down payment to the seller, who then finances a note for the balance. The buyer makes regular principal and interest payments over 5 to 10 years—perhaps with a larger balloon payment at the end—until the note is paid off. The terms and conditions of such a loan are a vital concern to both buyer and seller. They cannot be so burdensome that they threaten the company's continued existence; that is, the buyer must be able to make the payments to the seller out of the company's cash flow. At the same time, the deal must give the seller the financial security he or she is seeking from the sale. Defining reasonable terms is the result of the negotiation process between the buyer and the seller.

Anywhere Shoe Company

Tim Johnstone's experience in conducting due diligence for his former employer gave him an advantage when he was considering buying Anywhere Shoe Company, a Seattle-based maker and distributor of professional footwear. Johnstone's thorough analysis of the company revealed several factors that caused him concern, including a wrongful termination lawsuit filed by a former employee. Consequently, these discoveries caused him to assign a lower value to the business than the seller's asking price. Johnstone's offer included a "holdback" clause that allowed him to deduct from the purchase price the value of any undisclosed claims against Anywhere. To avoid paying off the seller at the expense of the security of the company's financial future, he also stipulated that the payout the seller was to receive would be based on the company's financial performance. Finally, Johnstone's terms required the seller to finance 55 percent of the purchase price. Initially, the owner balked at the terms but agreed to them rather than risk losing a viable buyer. "If we had not used seller financing, the deal probably wouldn't have come together," says Johnstone. His foresight paid off when, 14 months after the purchase, he discovered that a customer had filed a lawsuit against the company before he had signed the contract to buy the business. "Having seller financing gives you some protection that you otherwise might not have," says Johnstone. "It turned out to be the smartest thing I ever did."[7]

Ensure a Smooth Transition

Once the parties strike a deal, the challenge of making a smooth transition immediately arises. No matter how well planned the sale is, there are *always* surprises. For instance, the new owner may have ideas for changing the business—sometimes radically—that cause a great deal of stress and anxiety among employees and the previous owner. Charged with such emotion and uncertainty, the transition phase is always difficult and frustrating—and sometimes painful. To avoid a bumpy transition, a business buyer should do the following:

- Concentrate on communicating with employees. Business sales are fraught with uncertainty and anxiety, and employees need reassurance.
- Be honest with employees. Avoid telling them only what they want to hear. Share with the employees your vision for the business in the hope of generating a heightened level of motivation and support.
- Listen to employees. They have first-hand knowledge of the business and its strengths and weaknesses and usually can offer valuable suggestions for improving it.
- Consider asking the seller to serve as a consultant until the transition is complete. The previous owner can be a valuable resource, especially to an inexperienced buyer.

Table 7.2 describes 15 steps potential buyers should take to increase the probability that the businesses they buy are the right ones for them.

TABLE 7.2 Fifteen Steps to Buying the Company That's Right for You

1. *Make sure you shouldn't be starting a company instead.* You should have solid reasons for buying a company rather than starting one—and you should know what they are.

2. *Determine the kind of business you want—and whether you're capable of running it.* This requires an unflinching assessment of your strengths, weaknesses, personality, and goals.

3. *Consider the lifestyle you want.* What are you expecting from the business? Money? Freedom? Flexibility?

4. *Consider the location you want.* What part of the country (or world) do you want to live in?

5. *Reconsider lifestyle again.* You may own this business for a long, long time; it had better be one you enjoy.

6. *Cozy up to lenders in advance.* Visit potential lenders long before you need to borrow any money. Develop a rapport with them.

7. *Prepare to sell yourself to the seller.* You're buying their "baby," and they'll want to make sure you're the right person.

8. *Once you've defined the kind of business you're after, find the right company.* Three major sources of potential candidates are (1) the network of business people and advisers in the area, (2) business brokers specializing in companies of the size or type you want to buy, and (3) businesses that technically are not for sale but are very attractive.

9. *Choose the right seller.* Is he or she honest? What's the *real* reason he or she is selling the business?

10. *Do your research before agreeing to a price.* Ask lots of questions and get the facts to help you estimate the company's value.

11. *Make sure your letter of intent is specific.* It should establish deadlines, escape clauses, payment terms, confidentiality, and many other key issues.

12. *Don't skimp on due diligence.* Don't believe everything you see and hear; a relentless investigation will show whether the seller is telling the truth. Not all of them are.

13. *Be skeptical.* Don't fall in love with the deal; look for reasons *not* to buy the company.

14. *Don't forget to assess the employees.* You're not just buying a company; you're also buying the people who go with it.

15. *Make sure the final price reflects the company's real value.* Don't lower your chances of success by paying too much for the business.

Source: Adapted from Jay Finegan, "The Insider's Guide," *Inc.*, October 1991, pp 26–36.

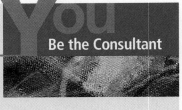

You Be the Consultant

Buying Dad's Business

Brian Schraff's father started an advertising agency for technology companies in 1976, and Brian joined the company after graduating from college in 1982. In 1996, Brian and a co-worker, Rick Roelofs, approached the elder Schraff with an offer to buy the company. "We have a completely different management philosophy in terms of the way we want to fund and capitalize the business and grow it," they told him. Their idea for increasing the company's revenue was to create a variety of services—from public relations to Internet services—around each client, which would require an investment in technology and in

staff. The approach was a far cry from the business philosophy Schraff's father employed: keep costs low.

Because Schraff's father really had not wanted to sell the business, the young men knew they had to work hard if they were going to close the deal. Their proposal included seller financing; they would make an initial down payment and then pay Schraff's father the balance of the purchase price over several years out of the company's cash flow. The elder Schraff wanted to be sure that the company would remain financially sound enough to make all of the future payments. In addition, says Brian, "my Dad was like any other entrepreneur.

He's got a lot of pride, and he had built something really great. So it was difficult for him to let go of that."

As the parties began negotiating the sale of the business, it became apparent that one of the biggest stumbling blocks was the value of the business. "For us, it wasn't an emotional issue," recalls Brian. "It was 'What would it cost us to start this thing up ourselves?' As founder, my father had a lot of blood, sweat, and tears in the agency. He [believed] that the market price should be much more—at least 100 percent more—than we thought it should be."

Brian, his father, and Roelofs went on a retreat to try to come to an agreement over the sale of the company. Brian had received some shares of ownership in the company, and that was the key to making a deal that was acceptable to everyone. "It came down to my saying, 'I want out of the company. I want to sell my shares back to you for the price you want me to buy your shares for.' Once my father said, 'There's no way I would pay you that for your shares,' we were able to come back with, 'What would you pay me, and why wouldn't that be a good price for me to pay you?'"

With buyers and seller having come to an agreement on price, the deal moved forward. Brian and Roelofs made Brian's father chief financial officer of the new company and began to make the changes they had envisioned for the agency. "It really became a team effort to make sure that the transition was working," says Brian. Today, Brian's father serves as a high-level account manager for the company's technology clients, but he no longer is involved in the management of the company on a daily basis. Brian and Roelofs have increased the agency's annual billings to more than $5 million since buying it.

In hindsight, Brian realizes that he should have conducted the deal to buy the agency from his father differently, in particular, taking steps to remove some of the emotion from the process. Buying a business is difficult enough, but the difficulty is compounded when a father–son relationship is involved.

1. Evaluate the way in which Brian Schraff went about buying his father's business. What did he do right? What did he do wrong?
2. Work with a team of your classmates to develop a list of recommendations that would have made the process go faster and more smoothly. Write a brief report (no more than one page) summarizing your recommendations and the logic behind them.

Source: Adapted from Brian Schraff, "Buyout," *Inc.*, June 2001, pp. 52–53.

Evaluating an Existing Business—The Due Diligence Process

When evaluating an existing business, a buyer can quickly feel overwhelmed by the tremendous number and complexity of the issues involved. Therefore, a smart buyer will assemble a team of specialists to help investigate a potential business opportunity. This team is usually composed of a banker, an accountant familiar with the particular industry, an attorney, and perhaps a small business consultant or a business broker. The cost of assembling a team can range from $3,000 to $20,000, but most buyers agree that using a team significantly lowers the likelihood of making a bad purchase. Because making a bad purchase will cost many times the cost of a team of experts, most buyers see it as a wise investment. It is important for a buyer to trust the members of the business evaluation team. With this team assembled, the potential buyer is ready to explore the business opportunity by examining five critical areas:

1. Why does the owner want to sell?
2. What is the physical condition of the business?
3. What is the potential for the company's products or services?
4. What legal aspects should be considered?
5. Is the business financially sound?

Evaluating these five areas of a business is known as performing **due diligence**. A prospective buyer should never consider purchasing a business without conducting the necessary due diligence to learn about the strengths, weaknesses, opportunities, and threats facing the company. "There are so many ugly stories," explains Robert Strang, president of Strang Hayes Consulting, a firm that specializes in helping prospective buyers through the due diligence process. Strang Hayes discovered that the CEO of a company that one of its

due diligence
the process of investigating the details of a company that is for sale to determine the strengths, weaknesses, opportunities, and threats facing it.

clients was considering purchasing had hidden five sexual harassment lawsuits that had been filed against him. Another search revealed that the business another buyer was considering purchasing had been banned from doing business in Florida, which was a major market for the prospective buyer.[8] The message is clear: Those buyers who neglect thorough due diligence do so at their own peril.

Why Is The Business for Sale?

Every prospective business buyer should investigate the *real* reason the business owner wants to sell. A study by DAK Group and Rutgers University found that the most common reason that owners of small businesses cite for selling their companies is to reduce the risk of having most of their personal assets tied up in their businesses (see Figure 7.1).[9] Their goal is to cash out their business investments and diversify into other types of assets. Many owners tell buyers that they have become bored or burned out and want to move on to other business ventures, but is that really the case? Note that market competition and external pressures are the next-most-common reasons owners give for selling their companies.

Smart business buyers know that the biggest and most unpleasant surprises can crop up outside the company's financial records and may never appear on the spreadsheets designed to analyze a company's financial position. For instance, a business owner might be looking to sell his or her business because a powerful new competitor is about to move into the market, a major highway rerouting will cause customer traffic to evaporate, the lease agreement on the ideal location is about to expire, or the primary customer base is declining. Every prospective buyer should investigate thoroughly any reason a seller gives for wanting to sell a business.

Businesses do not last forever, and smart entrepreneurs know when the time has come to sell. Some owners consider their behavior ethical only if they do not make false or misleading statements. Buyers should not expect to get a full disclose of the whole story behind the reasons for a business being offered for sale. In most business sales, the buyer bears the responsibility of determining whether the business is a good value. The best way to do that is to get out into the local community, talk to people, and ask a lot of questions. Visiting local business owners may reveal general patterns about the area and its overall vitality. The local Chamber of Commerce also may have useful information. Suppliers, customers, and even competitors may be able to shed light on why a business is up for sale. By combining this information with an analysis of the company's financial records, a potential buyer should be able to develop a clear picture of the business and its real value.

FIGURE 7.1

Reasons Business Owners Plan to Sell Their Companies

Source: DAK Group and Whitcomb Center for Research and Financial Services at Rutgers University.

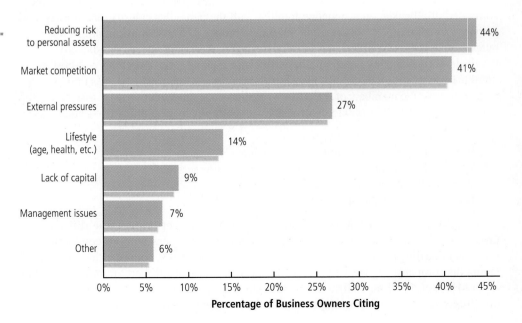

The Condition of the Business

What Is the Physical Condition of the Business? A prospective buyer should evaluate the business's assets to determine their value. Are they reasonably priced? Are they obsolete? Will they need to be replaced soon? Do they operate efficiently? The potential buyer should check the condition of both the equipment and the building. It may be necessary to hire a professional to evaluate the major components of the building—its structure and its plumbing, its electrical, and heating, and cooling systems, and other elements. Unexpected renovations are rarely inexpensive or simple and can punch a gaping hole in a buyer's financial plans.

How fresh is the company's inventory? Is it consistent with the image the new owner wants to project? How much of it would the buyer have to sell at a loss? A potential buyer may need to get an independent appraisal to determine the value of the company's inventory and other assets because the current owner may have priced them far above their actual value. These items typically comprise the largest portion of a business's value, and a potential buyer should not accept the seller's asking price blindly. Remember: *Book value is not the same as market value.* Usually, a buyer can purchase equipment and fixtures at substantially lower prices than book value. Value is determined in the marketplace, not on a balance sheet.

Other important factors that the potential buyer should investigate include the following:

Accounts receivable. If the sale includes accounts receivable, the buyer should check their quality before purchasing them. How creditworthy are the accounts? What portion of them is past due? How likely is it they can be collected? By aging the accounts receivable, a buyer can judge their quality and determine their value. (Refer to Table 7.1).

Lease arrangements. Is the lease included in the sale? When does it expire? What restrictions does it have on renovation or expansion? The buyer should determine *beforehand* what restrictions the landlord has placed on the lease and negotiate any change prior to purchasing the business.

Business records. Well-kept business records can be a valuable source of information and can tell a prospective buyer a lot about the company's pattern of success (or lack of it). Typically, buyers should expect to see financial statements documenting revenues and net income, operating budgets, and cash flow statements for at least five years. Sales and earnings forecasts from the seller for at least three years also can be helpful when trying to determine the value of a business.

Unfortunately, many business owners are sloppy record keepers. Consequently, the potential buyer and his or her team may have to reconstruct some critical records. It is important to verify as much information about the business as possible. For instance, does the owner have customer mailing lists? These lists can be a valuable marketing tool for a new business owner. Has the owner created an operations manual outlining the company's policies and procedures?

Intangible assets. Does the sale include any intangible assets such as trademarks, patents, copyrights, or goodwill? How long do patents have left to run? Is the trademark threatened by lawsuits for infringement? Does the company have logos or slogans that are unique or widely recognized? Determining the value of such intangibles is much more difficult than computing the value of the tangible assets.

Location and appearance. The location and the overall appearance of a business are important factors for a prospective buyer to consider. What had been an outstanding location in the past may be totally unacceptable today. Even if the building and equipment are in good condition and are fairly priced, the business may be located in a declining area. What other businesses operate in the surrounding area? Every buyer should consider the location's suitability not only for the present but also for several years into the future.

Table 7.3 offers a checklist of items every business buyer should investigate before closing a deal.

TABLE 7.3 A Business Buyer's Checklist

Buildings, Furnishings, and Fixtures

Every buyer should get a list of all of the fixed assets included in the purchase and then determine their condition, their age, their usefulness, and their value.

Inventory

Inventory may be the biggest part of a business sale, and it can be one of the trickiest parts of the deal. What inventory is on hand? What is its condition? How salable is it? What is its value? (Remember not to confuse *book* value with *market* value.) What is the company's merchandise return policy? How high is its return rate?

Financial Statements

Although small business owners are notoriously poor record keepers, a business buyer must have access to a company's financial statements for the last five years. This is the only way a buyer can judge the earning power of a company. The most reliable financial statements are those that have been audited by a certified public accountant. Comparing financial ratios against industry standards found in reports from RMA and Dun & Bradstreet can reveal important patterns.

Tax Returns

A good accountant should be able to reconcile the owner's or company's tax returns with its financial statements.

Sales Records

A prospective buyer should determine sales patterns by getting a monthly breakdown by product categories, sales representatives, cash versus credit, and any other significant factor for the company for three years. It is also a good idea to identify the company's top 10 customers and review their purchases over the last three years. What percentage of total sales did these 10 customers account for?

Accounts Receivable

Age the company's accounts receivable to see how many are current and how many are past due. Identify the top 10 accounts and check their credit ratings.

Accounts Payable

Conduct an analysis similar to the one for accounts receivable for the company's accounts payable. Past-due accounts are an indication that a business is experiencing cash flow difficulties.

Legal Documents

A prospective buyer should investigate all significant contracts (especially long-term ones) a company has with vendors, suppliers, distributors, lenders, employees, unions, customers, landlords, and others. Can the current owner assign the rights and obligations of these existing contracts to the buyer? If the company is incorporated, it is wise to check the articles of incorporation (or its articles of organization and operating agreement if it is a limited liability company.)

Patents, Trademarks, and Copyrights

Reviewing the documentation for any patents, trademarks, and copyrights the company holds is vital.

Lawsuits

Is the company facing any lawsuits, either current or pending?

Liabilities

It is essential that the seller provide the buyer with a complete list of liabilities that are outstanding against the company, including accounts and notes payable, loans, liens by creditors against business assets, lawsuits, and others.

Advertising and Sales Literature

A business buyer should study the company's advertising and sales literature to get an idea of the image it is projecting to its customers and the community. Talking to customers, suppliers, bankers, attorneys, and other local business owners will provide clues about the company's reputation.

TABLE 7.3 *Continued*

Organization Chart

Current employees can be a vital asset to a business buyer if they are willing to stay after the sale. Ask the seller to develop an organization chart showing the company's chain of command, and get copies of employees' job descriptions so you can understand who is responsible for which duties.

Insurance Coverage

Evaluate the types and amounts of insurance coverage the company currently has, including Workers' Compensation. Is it sufficient? If not, will you be able to obtain the necessary coverage at a reasonable price?

Sources: Adapted from "Look Before You Buy," Business Resale Network, http://www.br-network.com/features/bybl.html; "Making an In-Depth Evaluation," Business Resale Network, http://www.br-network.com/features/bybl.html; Norm Brodsky, "Caveat Emptor," *Inc.,* August 1998, pp. 31–32; "Basics of Buying a Business," American Express Small Business Exchange, http://home3.americanexpress.com/smallbusiness/resources/starting/buybiz.html.

Products and Services

What Is the Potential for the Company's Products or Services? No one wants to buy a business with a shrinking customer base. A thorough market analysis helps a buyer to develop his or her own sales forecast for an existing business (in addition to the one he or she should ask the seller to prepare). This research will tell a prospective buyer whether to consider buying a particular business and may reveal important trends in the business's sales and customer base.

Customer Characteristics and Composition Before purchasing an existing business, a buyer should analyze both existing and potential customers. Discovering why customers buy from the business and developing a profile of the company's existing customer base can help the buyer to identify a company's strengths and weaknesses and discover how to market more effectively to them. A potential buyer should determine the answers to the following questions:

- Who are the company's customers? What are their race, age, gender, and income levels? What is their demographic profile?
- Why do they buy?
- What do customers want the business to do for them? What needs are they satisfying when they make a purchase?
- How often do customers buy? Do they buy in seasonal patterns?
- How loyal are present customers?
- Is it practical to attract new customers at a reasonable cost?
- Does the business have a well-defined customer base? Is it growing? Do these customers come from a large geographic area or do they all live near the business?

Analyzing the answers to these questions can help a potential buyer to create and implement a more powerful marketing plan. Most likely he or she will try to keep the business attractive to existing customers while changing some features of its marketing plan to attract new ones.

Competitor Analysis A potential buyer must identify the company's direct competition—those businesses in the immediate area that sell the same or similar products or services. The potential profitability and survival of the business may well depend on the behavior of these competitors. Important factors to consider are the number of competitors and the intensity of the competition. How many competitors have opened in recent years? How many have closed in the last five years? What caused them to fail? Has the market already reached the saturation point? Being a latecomer in an already saturated market is not the pathway to long-term success.

When evaluating the competitive environment, a prospective buyer should address other questions:

- Which competitors have survived and what characteristics have led to their success?
- How do competitors' sales volumes compare with those of the business under consideration?
- What unique services do competitors offer?
- How well organized and coordinated are competitors' marketing efforts?
- What are the competitors' reputations?
- What are the strengths and weaknesses of the company's primary competitors? Which competitor is strongest?
- What competitive edge does each rival have?
- How can you gain market share in this competitive environment?

Legal Aspects

What Legal Aspects Should You Consider? Business buyers must be careful to avoid several legal pitfalls as they negotiate the final deal. The biggest potential legal traps include liens, bulk transfers, contract assignments, covenants not to compete, and ongoing legal liabilities.

Liens. The key legal issue in the sale of any asset is typically the proper transfer of good title from seller to buyer. However, because most business sales involve a collection of assorted assets, the transfer of a good title is more complex. Some business assets may have a **lien** (creditors' claim) against them, and unless the lien is satisfied before the sale, the buyer must assume it and is financially responsible for it. One way to reduce this potential problem is to include a clause in the sales contract stating that any liability not shown on the balance sheet at the time of sale remains the responsibility of the seller. A prospective buyer should have an attorney thoroughly investigate all of the assets for sale and their lien status before buying any business.

lien
a creditor's claim against an asset.

Bulk transfers. To protect against surprise claims from the seller's creditors after purchasing a business, the buyer should meet the requirements of a **bulk transfer** under Article 6 of the Uniform Commercial Code. Suppose that an owner owing many creditors sells his business to a buyer. The seller, however, does not use the proceeds of the sale to pay his debts to business creditors. Instead, he pockets them to use for his own benefit. Without the protection of a bulk transfer, those creditors could make claim to the assets that the buyer purchased in order to satisfy the previous owner's debts (within six months). To be effective, a bulk transfer must meet the following criteria:

bulk transfer
protects the buyer of a business's assets from the claims unpaid creditors might have against those assets.

- The seller must give the buyer a signed, sworn list of existing creditors.
- The buyer and the seller must prepare a list of the property included in the sale.
- The buyer must keep the list of creditors and the list of property for six months.
- The buyer must give written notice of the sale to each creditor at least 10 days before he or she takes possession of the goods or pays for them (whichever is first).

By meeting these criteria, a buyer acquires free and clear title to the assets purchased, which are not subject to prior claims from the seller's creditors. Because Article 6 can create quite a burden on a business buyer, 16 states have repealed it, and more may follow. About a half-dozen states have revised Article 6 to make it easier for buyers to notify creditors. Under the revised rule, if a business has more than 200 creditors, the buyer may notify them by public notice rather than by contacting them individually.

Contract assignments. Buyers must investigate the rights and the obligations they would assume under existing contracts with suppliers, customers, employees, lessors, and others. To continue the smooth operation of the business, the buyer must assume the rights of the seller under many existing contracts. Assuming these rights and obligations requires the seller to assign existing contracts to the new owner. For example, the current owner may have 4 years left on a 10-year lease and will need to assign this contract to the buyer. To protect her or his interest, the buyer (who is the assignee) should notify the other party involved in the contract of the assignment. In the previous example, the business buyer should notify the landlord promptly of the lease assignment from the previous owner.

Generally, the seller can assign any contractual right to the buyer, unless the contract specifically prohibits the assignment or the contract is personal in nature. For instance, loan contracts sometimes prohibit assignments with a **due-on-sale clause**. These clauses require the buyer to pay the full amount of the remaining loan balance or to finance the balance at prevailing interest rates. Thus, the buyer cannot assume the seller's loan (which may be at a lower interest rate than the prevailing rate on a loan). In addition, a seller usually cannot assign her or his credit arrangements with suppliers to the buyer because they are based on the seller's business reputation and are personal in nature. If such contracts are crucial to the business operation and cannot be assigned, the buyer must renegotiate new contracts. A prospective buyer also should evaluate the terms of any other unique contracts the seller has, including exclusive agent or distributor contracts, real estate leases, financing and loan arrangements, and union contracts.

Covenants not to compete. One of the most important and most often overlooked legal considerations for a prospective buyer is negotiating a **covenant not to compete** (or a **restrictive covenant** or a **noncompete agreement**) with the seller. Under a restrictive covenant, the seller agrees not to open a new, competing store within a specific time period and geographic area of the existing one. (The covenant should be negotiated with the *owner*, not with the corporation, because if the corporation signs the agreement, the owner may not be bound.) However, the covenant must be a part of a business sale and must be reasonable in scope in order to be enforceable. Although some states place limitations on the enforceability of restrictive covenants, business buyers should insist on the seller signing one. Without this protection, a buyer may find his or her new business eroding beneath his or her feet. For instance, suppose that Bob purchases a tire business from Alexandra, whose reputation in town for selling tires in unequaled. If Bob fails to negotiate a restrictive covenant, nothing can stop Alexandra from opening a new shop next to his old one and keeping all of his customers, thereby driving Bob out of business. A reasonable covenant in this case might restrict Alexandra from opening a tire store within a three-mile radius for three years. Every business buyer should negotiate a covenant not to compete with the seller.

To be enforceable, a restrictive covenant must be reasonable in geographic scope and in duration, must protect a legitimate business interest (such as a company's goodwill), and must be tied to a contract for the sale of an existing business (i.e., no "freestanding" restrictive covenants that restrain trade).

After launching Wild Oats Markets as a single store in Boulder, Colorado, Mike Gilliland turned the company into a national chain with $1 billion in annual sales. After selling out, Gilliland launched Sunflower Natural Markets, a seven-store discount natural food chain located in the Southwest. Gilliland's former company filed a lawsuit against him, claiming that launching the business was a violation of the restrictive covenant he had signed. A court enforced the noncompete agreement, forcing Gilliland to sell his shares in Sunflower Natural Markets to his former partners. Once the time limit on the restrictive covenant expired, Gilliland rejoined Sunflower Natural Markets and opened other stores.[10]

Ongoing legal liabilities. Finally, a potential buyer must look for any potential legal liabilities the purchase might expose. These typically arise from three sources: (1) physical premises, (2) product liability claims, and (3) labor relations. First, the buyer must examine the physical premises for safety. Are employees at risk because of asbestos or some other hazardous material? If the business is a manufacturing

due-on-sale clause
loan contract provision that prohibits a seller from assigning a loan arrangement to the buyer. Instead, the buyer is required to finance the remaining loan balance at prevailing interest rates.

covenant not to compete
an agreement between a buyer and a seller in which the seller agrees not to compete with the buyer within a specific time and geographic area.

Wild Oats Markets

operation, does it meet Occupational Safety and Health Administration (OSHA) and other regulatory agency requirements? One entrepreneur who purchased a retail business located in a building that once housed a gasoline service station was quite surprised when the Environmental Protection Agency informed him that he would have to pay for cleaning up the results of an old, leaking gas tank that still sat beneath the property. Even though he had no part in running the old gas station and did not know the leaking tank was there, he was responsible for the cost of the cleanup. Removing the tank and cleaning up the site cost him several thousand dollars that he had not budgeted.

Second, the buyer must consider whether existing products contain defects that could result in **product liability lawsuits,** which claim that a company is liable for damages and injuries caused by the products or services they make or sell. Existing lawsuits might be an omen of more to follow. In addition, the buyer must explore products that the company has discontinued because he or she might be liable for them if they prove to be defective. The final bargain between the parties should require the seller to guarantee that the company is not involved in any product liability lawsuits.

Third, what is the relationship between management to employees? Does a union contract exist? The time to discover sour management–labor relations is before the purchase, not after.

If the buyer's investigation reveals potential legal liabilities, it does not necessarily eliminate the business from consideration. Insurance coverage can shift such risks from the potential buyer, but the buyer should check to see whether the insurance will cover lawsuits resulting from actions predating the purchase.

product liability lawsuits
lawsuits that claim a company is liable for damages and injuries caused by the products it makes or sells.

Financial Soundness of the Business

A prospective buyer must analyze the financial records of a target business to determine its condition. He or she shouldn't be afraid to ask an accountant for help. Accounting systems and methods can vary tremendously from one type of business to another and can be quite confusing to a novice. Current profits can be inflated by changes in the accounting procedure or in the method for recording sales. For the buyer, the most dependable financial records are audited statements, those prepared by a CPA firm in accordance with generally accepted accounting principles (GAAP). Unfortunately, audited records do not exist in many small companies that are for sale. In some cases, a potential buyer has to hire an accountant to construct reliable financial statements because the owner's accounting and record keeping is so sloppy.

When evaluating the financial status of any business prospect, buyers must remember that any investment in a company should produce a reasonable salary for themselves, an attractive return on the money they invest, and enough to cover the amount they must borrow make the purchase. Otherwise, it makes no sense to purchase the business. Because most investors know that they can earn at least eight percent per year by investing wisely in the stock market, they expect any business they buy to earn at least that amount plus an extra return that reflects the additional risk of buying a business. Many owners expect to earn a return of at least 15 percent to 30 percent on the amount invested in their businesses.

Buyers also must remember that they are purchasing the future profit potential of an existing business. To evaluate the firm's profit potential, they should review past sales, operating expenses, and profits as well as the assets used to generate those profits. They must compare current balance sheets, income statements, and statements of cash flow with previous ones and then develop a set of projected statements for the next two to five years. Sales tax records, income tax returns, and financial statements are valuable sources of information.

Are profits consistent over the years, or are they erratic? Is this pattern typical in the industry, or is it a result of unique circumstances or poor management? Can the business survive with serious fluctuations in revenues, costs, and profits? If these fluctuations are the result of poor management, can a new owner turn the business around?

Some of the financial records that a potential buyer should examine include the following:

Income statements and balance sheets for the past three to five years. It is important to review data from several years because creative accounting techniques can distort financial data in any single year. Even though buyers are purchasing the future profits of a business, they must remember that many businesses intentionally keep net income low to minimize the owners' tax bills. Low earnings should prompt a buyer to investigate their causes.

Income tax returns for the past three to five years. Comparing basic financial statements with tax returns can reveal discrepancies of which the buyer should be aware. Some small business owners engage in **skimming** from their businesses—taking money from sales without reporting it as income. Owners who skim will claim their businesses are more profitable than their tax returns show. Although such under-reporting is illegal and unethical, it is surprisingly common. Buyers should *not* pay for undocumented, "phantom" earnings a seller claims exist. In fact, buyers should consider whether they want to buy a business from someone who admits to doing business unethically.

skimming
taking money from sales without reporting it as income.

Owner's compensation (and that of relatives). The owner's compensation is especially important in small companies; and the smaller the company is, the more important it will be. Although many companies do not pay their owners what they are worth, others compensate their owners lavishly. The buyer must consider the impact of fringe benefits—company cars, insurance contracts, country club memberships, and the like. It is important to adjust the company's income statements for the salary and fringe benefits that the seller has paid himself or herself and others.

Cash flow. Most buyers understand the importance of evaluating a company's profitability, but fewer recognize the necessity of analyzing its cash flow. They assume that if earnings are adequate, there will be sufficient cash to pay all of the bills and to fund an attractive salary for them. *That is not necessarily the case!* Before agreeing to a deal, prospective buyers should sit down with an accountant and convert the target company's financial statements into a cash flow forecast. This forecast must take into account not only existing debts and obligations, but also any modifications the buyer would make in the business, including necessary capital expenditures. It must also reflect the repayment of any financing the buyer arranges to purchase the company, whether it is through the seller or a traditional lender. Will the company generate enough cash to be self-supporting? How much cash will it generate for you?

A potential buyer must look for suspicious deviations from normal (in either direction) for sales, expenses, profits, cash flow, assets, and liabilities. Have sales been increasing or decreasing? Is the equipment really as valuable as it is listed on the balance sheet? Are advertising expenses unusually high or low? How is depreciation reflected in the financial statements?

This financial information gives a buyer the opportunity to verify the seller's claims about a company's performance. Sometimes, however, an owner will take short-term actions that produce a healthy financial statement but weaken the company's long-term health and profit potential. For example, a seller might lower expenses and increase earnings by gradually eliminating equipment maintenance or boost sales by selling to marginal businesses that will never pay their bills. Techniques such as these artificially inflate earnings, but a well-prepared buyer should be able to see through them.

Finally, a potential buyer should walk away from a deal—no matter how good it may appear on the surface—if the present owner refuses to disclose the company's financial records or any other operating information the buyer needs to make an informed decision. If that is the case, says Marc Kramer, author of *Small Business Turnaround*, "don't walk—run—away."[11]

Buying an existing business is a process filled with potential missteps along the way. The expression "Let the buyer beware" should be the prospective buyer's mantra

FIGURE 7.2

The Acquisition Process

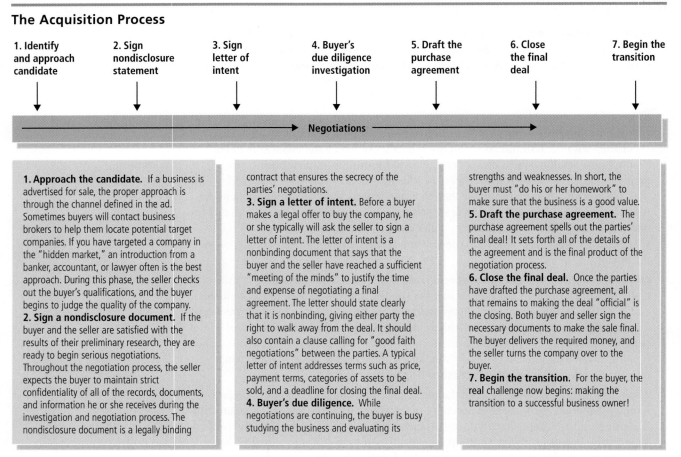

1. Identify and approach candidate
2. Sign nondisclosure statement
3. Sign letter of intent
4. Buyer's due diligence investigation
5. Draft the purchase agreement
6. Close the final deal
7. Begin the transition

Negotiations

1. Approach the candidate. If a business is advertised for sale, the proper approach is through the channel defined in the ad. Sometimes buyers will contact business brokers to help them locate potential target companies. If you have targeted a company in the "hidden market," an introduction from a banker, accountant, or lawyer often is the best approach. During this phase, the seller checks out the buyer's qualifications, and the buyer begins to judge the quality of the company. **2. Sign a nondisclosure document.** If the buyer and the seller are satisfied with the results of their preliminary research, they are ready to begin serious negotiations. Throughout the negotiation process, the seller expects the buyer to maintain strict confidentiality of all of the records, documents, and information he or she receives during the investigation and negotiation process. The nondisclosure document is a legally binding contract that ensures the secrecy of the parties' negotiations.

3. Sign a letter of intent. Before a buyer makes a legal offer to buy the company, he or she typically will ask the seller to sign a letter of intent. The letter of intent is a nonbinding document that says that the buyer and the seller have reached a sufficient "meeting of the minds" to justify the time and expense of negotiating a final agreement. The letter should state clearly that it is nonbinding, giving either party the right to walk away from the deal. It should also contain a clause calling for "good faith negotiations" between the parties. A typical letter of intent addresses terms such as price, payment terms, categories of assets to be sold, and a deadline for closing the final deal.

4. Buyer's due diligence. While negotiations are continuing, the buyer is busy studying the business and evaluating its strengths and weaknesses. In short, the buyer must "do his or her homework" to make sure that the business is a good value. **5. Draft the purchase agreement.** The purchase agreement spells out the parties' final deal! It sets forth all of the details of the agreement and is the final product of the negotiation process. **6. Close the final deal.** Once the parties have drafted the purchase agreement, all that remains to making the deal "official" is the closing. Both buyer and seller sign the necessary documents to make the sale final. The buyer delivers the required money, and the seller turns the company over to the buyer. **7. Begin the transition.** For the buyer, the **real** challenge now begins: making the transition to a successful business owner!

Source: Adapted from Price Waterhouse, *Buying and Selling: A Company Handbook* (New York: Author, 1993), pp. 38–42; Charles F. Claeys, "The Intent to Buy," *Small Business Reports*, May 1994, pp. 44–47.

throughout the entire process. However, by following the due diligence procedure described in this section, buyers can lower dramatically the probability of getting "burned" with a business that does not suit their personalities or one that is in on the verge of failure. Figure 7.2 illustrates the sequence of events leading up to a successful negotiation with a seller.

Methods for Determining the Value of a Business

Business valuation is partly an art and partly a science. Part of what makes establishing a reasonable price for a privately held business so difficult is the wide variety of factors that influence its value: the nature of the business, its position in the market or industry, the outlook for the market or industry, the company's financial status, its earning capacity, any intangible assets it may own (e.g., patents, trademarks, or copyrights), the value of other similar publicly held companies, and many other factors.

Computing the value of the company's tangible assets normally poses no major problem, but assigning a price to the intangibles, such as goodwill, almost always creates controversy. **Goodwill** represents the difference in the value of an established business and one that has not yet built a solid reputation for itself. The buyer is willing to pay extra only for those intangible assets that produce additional income. The seller, however, believes that goodwill is a measure of the hard work, sacrifice, and long hours invested in building the business, something for which he or she expects to be paid—often quite handsomely.

goodwill
the difference in the value of an established business and one that has not yet built a solid reputation for itself.

Potential buyers also must recognize the role that the seller's ego can play in the business valuation process. Norm Brodsky, who owns a successful document storage business, explains:

> As a group, we [entrepreneurs] tend to have fairly large egos, which isn't entirely bad. You need one to make a business grow . . . But our egos can get us into trouble when it comes to putting a dollar value on something we've created. We generally take the highest valuation we've heard for a company somewhat like ours—and multiply it.[12]

So, how can the buyer and the seller arrive at a fair price? There are few hard and fast rules in establishing the value of a business, but the following guidelines are helpful:

- The wisest approach is to compute a company's value using several techniques and then to choose the one that makes the most sense.
- The deal must be financially feasible for both parties. The seller must be satisfied with the price received for the business, but the buyer cannot pay an excessively high price that would require heavy borrowing and would strain his or her cash flows from the outset.
- The potential buyer must have access to the business records.
- Valuations should be based on facts, not fiction.
- No surprise is the best surprise. Both parties should commit to dealing with one another honestly and in good faith.

The main reason that buyers purchase existing businesses is to get their future earning potential. The second-most-common reason is to obtain an established asset base; it is much easier to buy assets than to build them. Although evaluation methods should take these characteristics into consideration, too many business sellers and buyers depend on rules of thumb that ignore the unique features of small companies. Often, these rules of thumb are based on multiples of a company's net earnings or sales and vary by industry.

The next section describes three basic techniques and several variations on them for determining the value of a hypothetical business, Lewis Electronics.

Balance Sheet Techniques: Net Worth = Assets − Liabilities

Balance Sheet Technique The **balance sheet technique** is one of the most commonly used methods of evaluating a business, although it is not highly recommended because it oversimplifies the valuation process. This method computes the company's net worth or owner's equity (Net worth = Total assets − Total liabilities) and uses this figure as the value. The problem with this technique is that it fails to recognize reality: Most small businesses have market values that exceed their reported book values.

The first step is to determine which assets are included in the sale. In most cases, the owner has some personal assets that he or she does not want to sell. Professional business brokers can help the buyer and the seller arrive at a reasonable value for the collection of assets included in the deal. Remember that net worth on a financial statement will likely differ significantly from actual net worth determined in the marketplace. Figure 7.3 shows the balance sheet for Lewis Electronics. Based on this balance sheet, the company's net worth is $266,091 − $114,325 = $151,766.

Variation: Adjusted Balance Sheet Technique A more realistic method for determining a company's value is to adjust the book value of net worth to reflect *actual* market value—the so-called **adjusted balance sheet technique.** The values reported on a company's books may either overstate or understate the true value of assets and liabilities. Typical assets in a business sale include notes and accounts receivable, inventories, supplies, and fixtures. If a buyer purchases accounts receivable, he or she should estimate the likelihood of their collection and adjust their value accordingly (refer to Table 7.1).

balance sheet technique
a method of valuing a business based on the value of the company's net worth (net worth = total assets − total liabilities).

adjusted balance sheet technique
a method of valuing a business based on the *market value* of the company's net worth (net worth = total assets − total liabilities).

FIGURE 7.3

Balance Sheet for Lewis Electronics

Lewis Electronics
Balance Sheet
June 30, 200X

Assets

Current Assets:

Cash	$ 11,655	
Accounts Receivable	15,876	
Inventory	56,523	
Supplies	8,574	
Prepaid Insurance	5,587	
Total Current Assets		$ 98,215

Fixed Assets:

Land		$ 24,000	
Buildings	$ 141,000		
Less Accumulated Depreciation	51,500	89,500	
Office Equipment	$ 12,760		
Less Accumulated Depreciation	7,159	5,601	
Factory Equipment	$ 59,085		
Less Accumulated Depreciation	27,850	31,235	
Trucks and Autos	$ 28,730		
Less Accumulated Depreciation	11,190	17,540	
Total Fixed Assets			$ 167,876
Total Assets:			$ 266,091

Liabilities

Current Liabilities:

Accounts Payable	$ 19,497	
Mortgage Payable (current portion)	5,215	
Salaries Payable	3,671	
Note Payable	10,000	
Total Current Liabilities		$ 38,383

Long-Term Liabilities:		
Mortgage Payable	$ 54,542	
Note Payable	21,400	
Total Long-Term Liabilities		$ 75,942
Total Liabilities		$ 114,325

Owners' Equity

Owners' Equity	$ 151,766
Total Liabilities and Owners' Equity	$ 266,091

In manufacturing, wholesale, and retail businesses, inventory is usually the largest asset in the sale. Taking a physical inventory count is the best way to determine accurately the quantity of goods to be transferred. The sale may include three types of inventory, each having its own method of valuation: raw materials, work-in-process, and finished goods. The buyer and the seller must arrive at a method for evaluating the inventory.

First in, first out (FIFO), last in, first out (LIFO), and average costing are three frequently used techniques, but the most common methods use the cost of last purchase and the replacement value of the inventory. Before accepting any inventory value, the buyer should evaluate the condition of the goods. One young couple purchased a lumberyard without sufficiently examining the inventory. After completing the sale, they discovered that most of the lumber in a warehouse they had neglected to inspect was warped and was of little value as building material. The bargain price they paid for the business turned out not to be the good deal they had expected.

To avoid problems, some buyers insist on having a knowledgeable representative on an inventory team count the inventory and check its condition. Nearly every sale involves merchandise that cannot be sold, but by taking this precaution, a buyer minimizes the chance of being stuck with worthless inventory. Fixed assets transferred in a sale might include land, buildings, equipment, and fixtures. Business owners frequently carry real estate and buildings at values well below their actual market value. Equipment and fixtures, depending on their condition and usefulness, may increase or decrease the true value of the business. Appraisals of these assets on insurance policies are helpful guidelines for establishing market value. In addition, business brokers can be useful in determining the current market value of fixed assets. Some brokers use an estimate of what it would cost to replace a company's physical assets (less a reasonable allowance for depreciation) to determine value. For Lewis Electronics, the adjusted net worth is $274,638 − $114,325 = $160,313 (see the adjusted balance sheet in Figure 7.4), indicating that some of the entries in its books did not accurately reflect true market value.

Business evaluations based on balance sheet methods suffer one major drawback: they do not consider the future earning potential of the business. These techniques value assets at current prices and do not consider them as tools for creating future profits. The next method for computing the value of a business is based on its expected future earnings.

Earnings Approach

The buyer of an existing business is essentially purchasing its future income. The **earnings approach** focuses on the future income potential of a business and assumes that a company's value depends on its ability to generate consistent earnings over time. In other words, the earnings approach recognizes that assets derive their *real* value from the income they produce in the future. There are three variations of the earnings approach.

earnings approach
a method of valuing a business that recognizes that a buyer is purchasing the future income (earning) potential of a business.

Variation 1: Excess Earnings Method This method combines the value of a business's existing assets (minus its liabilities) and an estimate of its future earnings potential to determine its selling price. One advantage of this technique is that it offers an estimate of goodwill. Goodwill is an intangible asset that often creates problems in a business sale. In fact, the most common method of valuing a business is to compute its tangible net worth and then to add an often arbitrary adjustment for goodwill. In essence, goodwill is the difference between an established, successful business and one that has yet to prove itself. It is based on the company's reputation and its ability to attract customers. A buyer should not accept blindly the seller's arbitrary adjustment for goodwill because it is likely to be inflated. The *real* value of a company's goodwill lies in its financial value to the buyer, not in its emotional value to the seller.

The excess earnings method provides a consistent and realistic approach for determining the value of goodwill. It measures goodwill by the amount of profit the business earns above that of the average firm in the same industry (its "extra earning power"). It also assumes that the owner is entitled to a reasonable return on the company's adjusted tangible net worth.

Step 1 **Compute adjusted tangible net worth.** Using the adjusted balance sheet method of valuation, the buyer should compute the firm's adjusted tangible net worth. Total tangible assets (adjusted for market value) minus total liabilities yields adjusted tangible net worth. In the Lewis Electronics example, adjusted tangible net worth is $274,638 − $114,325 = $160,313 (refer to Figure 7.4).

FIGURE 7.4

Balance Sheet for Lewis Electronics, Adjusted to Reflect Market Value

Lewis Electronics
Adjusted Balance Sheet
June 30, 200X

Assets

Current Assets:

Cash	$ 11,655	
Accounts Receivable	10,051	
Inventory	39,261	
Supplies	7,492	
Prepaid Insurance	5,587	
Total Current Assets		$ 74,046

Fixed Assets:

Land		$ 36,900	
Buildings	$ 177,000		
Less Accumulated Depreciation	51,500	125,500	
Office Equipment	$ 11,645		
Less Accumulated Depreciation	7,159	4,486	
Factory Equipment	$ 50,196		
Less Accumulated Depreciation	27,850	22,346	
Trucks and Autos	$ 22,550		
Less Accumulated Depreciation	11,190	11,360	
Total Fixed Assets			$ 200,592
Total Assets			$ 274,638

Liabilities

Current Liabilities:

Accounts Payable	$ 19,497	
Mortgage Payable (current portion)	5,215	
Salaries Payable	3,671	
Note Payable	10,000	
Total Current Liabilities		$ 38,383

Long-Term Liabilities:

Mortgage Payable	$ 54,542	
Note Payable	21,400	
Total Long-Term Liabilities		$ 75,942
Total Liabilities		$ 114,325

Owners' Equity

Owners' Equity	$ 160,313
Total Liabilities and Owners' Equity	$ 274,638

opportunity cost
the cost of the next best alternative choice; the cost of giving up one alternative to get another.

Step 2   Calculate the opportunity costs of investing in the business.
Opportunity cost represents the cost of forgoing a choice. If a buyer chooses to purchase the assets of a business, he or she cannot invest that money elsewhere. Therefore, the opportunity cost of the purchase would be the amount that the buyer could earn by investing the same amount *in a similar-risk investment*.

There are three components in the rate of return used to value a business: (1) the basic, risk-free return, (2) an inflation premium, and (3) the risk allowance for investing in the particular business. The basic, risk-free return and the inflation premium are reflected in investments such as U.S. Treasury bonds. To determine the appropriate rate of return for investing in a business, a buyer must add to this base rate a factor reflecting the risk of purchasing the company. The greater the risk, the higher will be the rate of return. A normal-risk business typically translates into a rate of return in the 20 to 25 percent range. In the Lewis Electronics example, the opportunity cost of the investment is $160,313 \times 25\% = $40,078.

The second part of the buyer's opportunity cost is the salary that he or she could earn working for someone else. For the Lewis Electronics example, if the buyer purchases the business, he or she must forgo the $25,000 salary that could be earned working elsewhere. Adding these amounts together yields a total opportunity cost of $65,078.

Step 3 **Project net earnings.** The buyer must estimate the company's net earnings for the upcoming year before subtracting the owner's salary. Averages can be misleading, so the buyer must be sure to investigate the trend of net earnings. Have they risen steadily over the last five years, dropped significantly, remained relatively constant, or fluctuated wildly? As you learned earlier in this chapter, past income statements provide useful guidelines for estimating earnings. In the Lewis Electronics example, the prospective buyer and the buyer's accountant project net earnings for the upcoming year to be $74,000.

Step 4 **Compute extra earning power.** A company's extra earning power is the difference between forecasted earnings (Step 3) and total opportunity costs (Step 2). Many small businesses that are for sale do not have extra earning power (i.e., excess earnings), and they show marginal or no profits. The extra earning power of Lewis Electronics is $74,000 − $65,000 = $8,922.

Step 5 **Estimate the value of intangibles.** The owner can use the business's extra earning power of the business to estimate the value of its intangible assets—that is, its goodwill. Multiplying the extra earning power by a years-of-profit figure yields an estimate of the intangible assets' value. The years-of-profit figure for a normal-risk business ranges from three to four. A very high risk business may have a years-of-profit figure of just one, whereas a well-established firm might warrant a years-of-profit figure of seven. For Lewis Electronics, the value of intangibles (assuming normal risk) would be $8,922 \times 3 = $26,766.

Step 6 **Determine the value of the business.** To determine the value of the business, the buyer simply adds together the adjusted tangible net worth (Step 1) and the value of the intangibles (Step 5). Using this method, we find that the value of Lewis Electronics is $160,313 + $26,766 = $187,079.

The buyer and the seller should consider the tax implications of including in the purchase the value of goodwill and the value of a covenant not to compete. Because the *buyer* can amortize both the cost of goodwill and a restrictive covenant over 15 years, the tax treatment of either would be the same for him or her. However, the *seller* would prefer to have the amount of the purchase price in excess of the value of the assets allocated to goodwill, which is a capital asset. The gain on the capital asset would be taxed at the lower capital gains rates. If that same amount were allocated to a restrictive covenant (which is negotiated with the seller personally, not the business), the seller must treat it as ordinary income, which would be taxed at regular rates that are higher than the capital gains rates.

Variation 2: Capitalized Earnings Approach A variation of the earnings approach capitalizes expected net earnings to determine the value of a business. As you learned earlier in this chapter, buyers should prepare their own pro forma income statements and should ask the seller to prepare one also. Many appraisers use a five-year weighted average of past sales (with the greatest weights assigned to the most recent years) to estimate sales for the upcoming year.

Once again, a buyer must evaluate the risk of purchasing the business to determine the appropriate rate of return on the investment. The greater the perceived risk, the higher is

capitalized earnings approach

a method of valuing a business that divides estimated earnings by the rate of return the buyer could earn on a similar-risk investment.

the return that the buyer requires. Risk determination is always somewhat subjective, but it is necessary for proper evaluation.

The **capitalized earnings approach** divides estimated net earnings (*after* subtracting the owner's reasonable salary) by the rate of return that reflects the risk level. For Lewis Electronics, the capitalized value (assuming a reasonable salary of $25,000) is

$$\frac{\text{Net earnings (after deducting owner's salary)}}{\text{Rate of return}} = \frac{\$74,000 - \$25,000}{25\%} = \$196,000$$

Clearly, firms with lower risk factors are more valuable (a 10 percent rate of return would yield a value of $499,000 for Lewis Electronics) than are those with higher risk factors (a 50 percent rate of return would yield a value of $99,800). Most normal-risk businesses use a rate-of-return factor ranging from 20 to 25 percent. The lowest risk factor that most buyers would accept for any business is around 15 percent.

Variation 3: Discounted Future Earnings Approach This variation of the earnings approach assumes that a dollar earned in the future is worth less than that same dollar today. Therefore, using this approach, the buyer estimates the company's net income for several years into the future and then discounts these future earnings back to their present value. The resulting present value is an estimate of the company's worth because it reflects the company's future earning potential stated in today's dollars.

The reduced value of future dollars represents the cost of the buyers' giving up the opportunity to earn a reasonable rate of return by receiving income in the future instead of today, a concept known as the time value of money. To illustrate the importance of the time value of money, consider two $1 million sweepstake winners. Rob wins $1 million in a sweepstakes, but he receives it in $50,000 installments over 20 years. If Rob invested every installment at 15 percent interest, he would have accumulated $5,890,505.98 at the end of 20 years. Lisa wins $1 million in another sweepstakes, but she collects her winnings in one lump sum. If Lisa invested her $1 million today at 15 percent, she would have accumulated $16,366,537.39 at the end of 20 years. The difference in their wealth is the result of the time value of money.

discounted future earnings approach

a method of valuing a business that forecasts a company's earnings several years into the future and then discounts them back to their present value.

The **discounted future earnings approach** includes five steps:

STEP 1. PROJECT FUTURE EARNINGS FOR FIVE YEARS INTO THE FUTURE One way is to assume that earnings will grow by a constant amount over the next five years. Perhaps a better method is to develop three forecasts—an optimistic, a pessimistic, and a most likely— for each year and then find a weighted average using the following formula, which weights the most likely forecast four times as heavily as either the optimistic or pessimistic forecasts:

Forecasted earnings for year *i*

$$= \frac{\text{Optimistic earnings for year } i + 4(\text{Most likely forecast for year } i) + (\text{Pessimistic forecast for year } i)}{6}$$

For Lewis Electronics, the buyer's forecasts (in dollars) are as follows:

Year	Pessimistic	Most Likely	Optimistic	Weighted Average
XXX1	65,000	74,000	92,000	75,500
XXX2	74,000	90,000	101,000	89,167
XXX3	82,000	100,000	112,000	99,000
XXX4	88,000	109,000	120,000	107,333
XXX5	88,000	115,000	122,000	111,667

Buyers must remember that the farther into the future they forecast, the less reliable their estimates will be.

STEP 2. DISCOUNT THESE FUTURE EARNINGS AT THE APPROPRIATE PRESENT VALUE RATE The rate that the buyer selects should reflect the rate he or she could earn on a similar-risk investment. Because Lewis Electronics is a normal-risk business, the buyer chooses a present value rate of 25 percent.

Year	Income Forecast (Weighted Average) ($)	Present Value Factor (at 25%)*	Net Present Value ($)
XXX1	75,500	0.8000	60,400
XXX2	89,167	0.6400	57,067
XXX3	99,000	0.5120	50,688
XXX4	107,333	0.4096	43,964
XXX5	111,667	0.3277	36,593
Total			248,712

*The appropriate present value factor can be found by looking in published present value tables, by using a calculator or computer, or by solving the formula

$$\text{Present value factor} = \frac{1}{(1 + k)^t}$$

where k is the rate of return and t is the year ($t = 1, 2, 3, \ldots, n$).

STEP 3. ESTIMATE THE INCOME STREAM BEYOND FIVE YEARS One technique suggests multiplying the fifth year income by $1 \div$ rate of return. For Lewis Electronics, the estimate is

$$\text{Income beyond year 5} = \$111,667 \times \frac{1}{25\%} = \$446,668$$

STEP 4. DISCOUNT THE INCOME ESTIMATE BEYOND FIVE YEARS USING THE PRESENT VALUE FACTOR FOR THE SIXTH YEAR For Lewis Electronics

$$\text{Present value of income beyond year 5} = \$446,668 \times 0.2622 = \$117,116$$

STEP 5. COMPUTE THE TOTAL VALUE OF THE BUSINESS Add the present value of the company's estimated earnings for years 1 through 5 (Step 2) and the present value of its earnings from year 6 on (Step 4):

$$\text{Total value} = \$248,712 + \$117,116 = \$365,828$$

The primary advantage of this technique is that it evaluates a business solely on the basis of its future earning potential, but its reliability depends on making forecasts of future earnings and on choosing a realistic present value rate. In other words, a company's present value is tied to its future performance, which is not always easy to project. The discounted cash flow technique is especially well suited for valuing service businesses (whose asset bases are often very thin) and for companies experiencing high growth rates.

Market Approach

The **market approach (or price/earnings approach)** uses the price/earnings (P/E) ratios of similar businesses listed on a stock exchange to establish the value of a company. A buyer must use businesses in the same industry whose stocks are publicly traded to get a meaningful comparison. A company's price/earnings ratio is the price of one share of its common stock in the market divided by its earnings per share (after deducting preferred stock dividends). To get a representative P/E ratio, a buyer should average the P/Es of as many similar businesses as possible.

To compute the company's value, the buyer multiplies the average price/earnings ratio by the private company's estimated earnings. For example, suppose that the buyer found

market approach
a method of valuing a business that uses the price/earnings (P/E) ratio of similar, publicly held companies to determine value.

four companies comparable to Lewis Electronics but whose stock is publicly traded. Their price/earnings ratios are

Company 1	3.3
Company 2	3.8
Company 3	4.7
Company 4	4.1
Average P/E ratio	3.975

Using this average P/E ratio produces a value of $294,150:

Value = Average PE ratio × Estimated net earnings = 3.975 × $74,000 = $294,150

The biggest advantage of the market approach is its simplicity. However, this method does have several disadvantages, including the following:

Necessary comparisons between publicly traded and privately owned companies. Because the stock of privately owned companies is not as liquid as that of publicly held companies, the P/E ratio used is often subjective and lower than that of publicly held companies.

Unrepresentative earnings estimates. A private company's net earnings may not realistically reflect its true earning potential. To minimize taxes, owners usually attempt to keep earnings low and rely on fringe benefits and bonuses to make up the difference.

Finding similar companies for comparison. Often, it is extremely difficult for a buyer to find comparable publicly held companies when estimating the appropriate P/E ratio.

Applying the after-tax earnings of a private company to determine its value. If a prospective buyer is using an after-tax P/E ratio from a public company, he or she also must use the after-tax earnings from the private company.

Despite its drawbacks, the market approach is useful as a general guide to establishing a company's value.

Which of these methods is best for determining the value of a small business? Simply stated, there is no single best method. Valuing a business is partly an art and partly a science. Use of these techniques will yield a range of values. Buyers should look for values that might cluster together and then use their best judgment to determine a reasonable offering price. Table 7.4 summarizes the valuation techniques covered in this chapter.

TABLE 7.4 What's It Worth? A Summary of Business Valuation Techniques

Balance Sheet Technique

Book value of net worth = Total assets − Total liabilities
= $266,091 − $114,325 = $151,766

Variation: Adjusted Balance Sheet Technique

Net worth adjusted to reflect market value = $274,638 − $114,325 = $160,313

Earnings Approach

Variation 1: Excess Earnings Method

Step 1: Adjusted tangible net worth = $274,638 − $114,325 = $160,313

Step 2: Opportunity costs = Opportunity cost of investing + salary forgone
= $160,313 × 25% + 25,000 = $65,078

Step 3: Estimated net earnings = $74,000

TABLE 7.4 *Continued*

Step 4: Extra earning power = Estimated net earnings − Total opportunity costs
= $74,000 − $65,078 = $8,922

Step 5: Value of intangibles (goodwill) = Extra earning power × Years of profit figure
= $8,922 × 3 = $26,766

Step 6: Value of business = Tangible net worth + Value of intangibles
= $160,313 + 26,766 = $187,079

Variation 2: Capitalized Earnings Approach

$$Value = \frac{Net\ Earnings\ (after\ deducting\ owner's\ salary)}{Rate\ of\ return\ on\ a\ similar\text{-}risk\ investment}$$

$$= \frac{\$74,000 - \$25,000}{25\%} = \$196,000$$

Variation 3: Discounted Future Earnings Approach

Step 1: Project future earnings:

Year	Pessimistic	Most Likely	Optimistic	Weighted Average*
XXX1	$65,000	$ 74,000	$ 94,000	$ 75,500
XXX2	$74,000	$ 90,000	$101,000	$ 89,167
XXX3	$82,000	$100,000	$112,000	$ 99,000
XXX4	$88,000	$109,000	$120,000	$107,333
XXX5	$88,000	$115,000	$122,000	$111,667

$$*Weighted\ average = \frac{Pessimistic + 4(Most\ likely) + Optimistic}{6}.$$

Step 2: Discount future earnings using the appropriate present value factor:

Year	Forecasted Earnings	Present Value Factor	Net Present Value
XXX1	$ 75,500	0.8000	$ 60,400
XXX2	$ 89,167	0.6400	$ 57,067
XXX3	$ 99,000	0.5120	$ 50,688
XXX4	$107,333	0.4096	$ 43,964
XXX5	$111,667	0.3277	$ 36,593
Total			$248,712

Step 3: Estimate income stream beyond 5 Years:

$$Income\ stream = Fifth\text{-}year\ forecasted\ income \times \frac{1}{Rate\ of\ return}$$

$$= \$111,667 \times \frac{1}{25\%}$$

$$= \$446,668$$

Step 4: Discount income stream beyond 5 years using sixth-year present value factor:
Present value of income stream = $446,668 × 0.2622 = $117,116

Step 5: Compute total value:
Total value = $248,712 + $117,116 = $365,828

Market Approach

Value = Estimated earnings × Average price/earnings ratio of representative companies
= $74,000 × 3.975 = $294,150

Which value is correct? *Remember:* There is no best method of valuing a business. These techniques provide only estimates of a company's worth. The particular method used depends on the unique qualities of the business and the special circumstances surrounding the sale.

Understanding the Seller's Side

A recent study by DAK Group and Columbia University's Lang Center for Entrepreneurship reports that 64 percent of the owners of closely held companies expect to sell their businesses within three years.[13] For entrepreneurs, few events are more anticipated—and more emotional—than selling their businesses. Selling their companies often produces vast personal wealth and a completely new lifestyle, and this newly gained wealth offers freedom and the opportunity to catch up on all the things the owners missed out on while building their businesses. Yet, many entrepreneurs who sell out experience a tremendous void in their lives, a "separation anxiety" that is the result of their lives having revolved around the businesses they created and nurtured for so many years. For these business owners, their companies were the focal point of their lives in their communities and were an essential part of their identities. When they sell their companies, a primary concern for many entrepreneurs is preserving the reputation, culture, and principles on which they built and operated the company. Will the new owner display the same values in managing the business? Can the company founder cope with the inevitable changes the new owner will make to the business?

California Pizza Kitchen

Seven years after founding the California Pizza Kitchen, Rick Rosenfield and Larry Flax were surprised when Pepsico offered to buy a majority stake in their company for $100 million. The soft drink giant kept Rosenfield and Flax on as co-chairmen but relieved them of any daily operating and decision-making duties and replaced them with a more experienced CEO, Fred Hipp. Hipp's strategy for the company was quite different from that of the founders, who had built the company on the basics: quality ingredients, upscale locations, and steady growth. When Hipp's decisions pushed the company toward financial ruin, Pepsico brought Rosenfield and Flax back in to save it. They closed underperforming outlets, upgraded the remaining ones, and introduced interesting new menu items designed to appeal to California Pizza Kitchen's core customers.[14]

Some business brokers differentiate between "financial buyers" and "strategic buyers." Financial buyers, usually individuals, see buying a business as a way to generate income for themselves and their families. Their primary concern is the company's ability to generate profits and positive cash flow in the future. Strategic buyers, often other businesses or even competitors, view buying a company as part of a larger picture, a piece in a strategic puzzle that gives them an advantage such as access to a new, fast-growing market, a unique product, or a new technological innovation. "Financial buyers typically will pay a lower price because they have a 'fire sale' mentality," says Andy Agrawal, a partner in an investment banking firm. "You need to find strategic buyers and paint a picture for them," he advises. "Show the strategic buyer how one plus one equals three."[15]

La Brea Bakery
Nancy Silverton sold 80 percent of LaBrea Bakery to the Irish food company IAWS Group but managed to maintain "artistic integrity" over the breads the company sells.

Nancy Silverton, who in 1989 co-founded a restaurant, Campanille, and a bakery, La Brea Bakery, with her husband in Los Angeles, managed to find a strategic buyer for La Brea bakery in the Irish food giant IAWS Group, which recently purchased 80 percent of the company for $68.5 million. When Silverton decided to sell, La Brea was generating annual profits of $9.4 million on sales of more than $50 million, primarily because the company had developed a unique flash-freezing process that allowed it to ship its breads almost anywhere without damaging its flavor and texture. (Celebrity chef Wolfgang Puck, who serves Silverton's bread at his star-studded Spago restaurant in Los Angeles, says, "Nobody's bread is as good as hers.") IAWS Group already had a par-baked operation in Europe and wanted to gain access to the premium bread market in the United States.

La Brea Bakery's established network of customers and its unique flash-freezing process were a perfect match for this strategic buyer's needs. As part of the deal, Silverton even managed to maintain "artistic integrity" over the breads the company sells.[16]

Selling a business involves developing a plan that maximizes the value of the business. Before selling her business, an entrepreneur must ask himself or herself some important questions: Do you want to walk away from the business completely, or do you plan to stay on after the sale? If you decide to stay on, how involved do you want to be in running the company? How much can you realistically expect to get for the business? Is this amount of money sufficient to maintain your desired lifestyle? Rather than sell the business to an outsider, should you be transferring ownership to your kids or to your employees? Who are the professionals—business brokers, accountants, attorneys, tax advisers—you will need to help you to close the sale successfully? How do you expect the buyer to pay for the company? Are you willing to finance at least some of the purchase price?

Sellers who have answered these fundamental questions are prepared to move forward with the sale of their companies.

You Be the Consultant

Seller's Remorse

In 1961, Larry Freeman went into his family's business, Freeman Sales Agency, like his father and his grandfather before him. The company served as a manufacturer's representative for makers of shampoos, lotions, and creams. Larry's father died in 1967, leaving Larry and his younger brother, Richard, both in their 20s, in charge of the family business. By the early 1970s, the ambitious, hard-working brothers had moved the company from just selling other manufacturers' cosmetics to producing and marketing their own line of products, some of which proved to be cutting edge at the time. For instance, the brothers launched one of the first shampoos made with all organic ingredients.

By 1984, Freeman Cosmetics, as the company was now known, was generating sales of $5 million but was losing money. Richard decided to leave the company, and Larry brought in his son, Mark, to help him run the business. The father–son team began to rebuild the company, introducing a string of new products made with oatmeal, avocadoes, and apples packaged in colorful bottles that appealed to young buyers. In 1991, Larry's sister, Jill, joined the business and found her niche in marketing. Mark had a knack for developing international markets and was busy building the Freeman's international division. Larry focused on building long-term relationships with the company's customers and guiding its social responsibility efforts. "A business is more than a business," he says. "It's a platform to do other things." For instance, in 1994, Freeman Cosmetics opened a 165,000-square-foot factory that created jobs for 300 people in South Central Los Angeles.

Since its beginning, Freeman's growth has been steady and methodical, funded solely by the company's cash flow. Larry never had brought in a dime of outside financing. By 1998, however, Freeman's sales, which had climbed to $70 million, were growing so fast that the company could no longer generate sufficient cash to fuel the growth. Larry contacted an investment banker to explore external financing options for the company and included a very explicit edict: "Do not bring me a buyer. I do not want to sell this [company]."

Ignoring Larry's decree, the investment banker brought a handful of enticing offers to Larry and the other family members involved in the business. Several family members had serious doubts about selling the company, but they all changed their minds when they began to see the offers. Dial, Inc., the consumer products giant, was offering the family $80 million for Freeman Cosmetics—far more than any of them had ever imagined they could get for their family business.

Everyone except Larry was ready to sell. He didn't need the money, and he wanted his grandchildren to have a chance to run the family business one day. Not wanting to stand in the way of his children, however, Larry reluctantly agreed to sell Freeman Cosmetics to Dial. After the closing, the family members escaped to a bathroom, where they hugged one another and cried.

The deal called for Larry to be president of Dial's personal care division, which included the newly acquired Freeman's Cosmetics. Just six weeks after closing the deal, however, Dial's chairman called Larry and told him, "Stay home; collect your checks." Larry and the rest of the Freeman clan could only stand by and watch Dial run their business. Unfortunately, the decisions Dial executives were making were running the once successful company straight into the ground. For instance, Dial managers cut Freeman's product line by one-third, closed the factory in South Central Los Angeles, and cut R&D expenditures. Sales began to slide, and the Freemans walked away in disgust from employment contracts with Dial valued at $2.5 million. "I was watching Dial destroy what it took me 25 years to build," Larry recalls.

After three years, Dial sold its personal care division, including Freeman Cosmetics, for $12 million to the Hathi Group, which was no better at running the business than Dial was. When Hathi declared bankruptcy in September 2003, the Freemans bought back their business for $10 million. Larry, Mark, and Jill are back at their same desks handling much the same areas they managed before the sale. Yet the new Freeman Cosmetics is quite different from the company they sold years ago. Instead of the vertically integrated business with 400 employees, the company is a lean, 25-person

sales and marketing company that outsources all of its manufacturing to other factories. That does not concern Mark, however, who says that manufacturing never was one of the family's strengths.

The Freemans are focusing on their company's growth, knowing that if they did it once before, they can do it again. What happens down the road once they reach their goals? "It may be that ten years from now someone makes us an offer so big that we have to take it again," says Larry with a big smile, sounding as if he already is trying to convince himself that it would be the right thing to do.

1. Why do many entrepreneurs who sell their businesses suffer from seller's remorse? Use the Web to research entrepreneurs who have sold their businesses. What emotional issues do they face after the sale?
2. Referring to entrepreneurs who sell their companies, Eugene Muscat, director of the Gellert Foundation Family Business Center at the University of San Francisco, says, "If you were a business owner and then all of a sudden all you are is just a rich person, that's a big fall from grace." What does he mean? Do you agree? How does this tendency affect entrepreneurs?
3. Could the Freemans have done anything differently to avoid the problems they encountered when they sold their family business? Write a brief report (no more than one page) summarizing your recommendations and the logic behind them.

Source: Adapted from David Whitford, "Buying Back Their Name," *Inc.*, February 2004, pp. 57–60.

Structuring the Deal

Next to picking the right buyer, planning the structure of the deal is one of the most important decisions a seller can make. Entrepreneurs who sell their companies without considering the tax implications of the deal may wind up paying the IRS as much as 70% of the proceeds in the form of capital gains and other taxes. A skilled tax adviser or financial planner can help business sellers to legally minimize the bite various taxes take out of the proceeds of the sale. When it comes to exit strategies, entrepreneurs have the following options available to them.

Exit Strategies

Straight Business Sale A straight business sale often is best for those entrepreneurs who want to step down and turn over the reins of the company to someone else.

After graduating from a community college, Paul Hanlon, then 22, took a job earning minimum wage plus commissions for a company selling portable pop-up displays for use in trade shows. Five years later, Hanlon borrowed $47,000 to buy the company for just the cost of its inventory. Over the next decade, Hanlon, who renamed the company Folio Inc., expanded its product line and landed big-name clients such as Reebok, Oracle, and GE. When he was 39, Hanlon decided to sell Folio and retire and become an author and a motivational speaker when he received an offer for $20 million.[17]

Folio Inc.

In straight business sales, owners must decide whether to sell the assets of the business or transfer ownership to the buyer through a sale of company stock. Which choice is best for the seller and the buyer depends on the form of ownership. In an S corporation, the seller does not care if it the transaction is through stock or assets because the tax considerations are the same. Owners of C corporations are far better off selling stock rather than selling assets. Buyers will generally prefer to acquire the "hard" assets of the business, thus, avoiding any potential hidden liabilities. Despite these concerns, more than 90 percent of business sales involve a sale of shares of stock.[18]

Business Sale with an Agreement from the Founder to Stay On Sometimes business owners want to sell their companies but stay on to operate them. Doing so enables an entrepreneur to avoid concentrating his or her personal wealth in a single asset—the business—and to stay involved in managing the company he or she founded.

Kevin McDonald co-founder of Compendit Inc., a consulting business specializing in enterprise resource planning, recently sold his firm to a larger company in the consulting business, Inforte Corporation, for $6 million and stayed on as executive vice-president and general manager. Inforte simply integrated Compendit into its corporate structure as a division, allowing McDonald's company to stay intact. Most of the company's 54 employees also stayed on. Although now subject to a corporate hierarchy, McDonald takes a philosophical view. "As an entrepreneur, I have always worked for my team, my customers, my wife, the bank . . . What's one more boss?"[19]

Compendit Inc.

Although this scenario sounds like the ideal solution for entrepreneurs who are seeking more free time without stepping away entirely from the companies they built, it does not always prove to be. Accustomed to being in control, making the key decisions, and calling all of the shots, entrepreneurs who sell out with an agreement to stay on often have great difficulty relinquishing control of the company to the new owner. The situation is particularly difficult when the new owner makes decisions that jeopardize the company's future, forcing the founder to stand by and watch the business spiral slowly downward toward failure.

That's exactly what happened to John Diebel, who, in 1972 founded Meade Instruments as a small telescope maker and distributor while working as an engineer at Hughes Aircraft. In 1986, having built Meade into a successful company with annual sales of nearly $14 million, Diebel sold out to Harbor Group, a St. Louis-based leveraged buyout firm, but agreed to stay on as president to manage the company. It was a move he began to regret almost immediately. The new owners cut R&D spending and new product development efforts, imposed a rigid structure on the previously nimble company, and demanded endless reports from Diebel. "John was used to reporting to himself," says Meade's former chief operating officer. "If he had a good idea, he wanted to do it. He didn't want to make a plan." Within five years of the sale, the new owner had pushed the once successful company to the brink of bankruptcy. That's when Diebel stepped in and repurchased the company for just $1,000 and the assumption of $2.4 million in existing debt. Diebel has since rebuilt Meade and restored it to profitability, making his ownership stake worth more than $30 million.[20]

Meade Instruments

Form a Family Limited Partnership Entrepreneurs also can transfer their businesses to their children but still maintain control over them by forming a family limited partnership. The entrepreneur takes the role of the general partner, and the children become limited partners in the business. The general partner keeps just 1% of the company, but the partnership agreement gives him or her total control over the business. The children own 99% of the company but have little or no say over how to run the business. Until the founder decides to step down and turn over the reins of the company to the next generation, he or she continues to run the business and, with proper planning, can set up significant tax savings when the ultimate transfer of power takes place.

Sell a Controlling Interest Sometimes business owners sell a majority interest in their companies to investors, competitors, suppliers, or large companies, retain a portion of the ownership themselves, and agree to stay on after the sale as managers or consultants.

Happp Controls

That's just the kind of deal Frank Happ, who worked his way up the ranks at a company that made coin-operated games before purchasing the business, was able to negotiate with Pfingsten Partners, a private equity firm in Deerfield, Illinois. After purchasing the business in 1986, Happ bought out several competitors, expanded into the business of distributing games, and brought his two children into the business. When Happ reached his late 50s, he decided to sell the company, which had reached annual sales of $68 million. He considered a straight business sale but instead decided to sell a controlling interest in Happ Controls to Pfingsten Partners for eight times the company's earnings and retain 8.2 percent of the business. Happ now works just 30 days a year for the company (where he reports to his son, whom Pfingsten Partners named president), leaving him plenty of time to play golf and watch his grandchildren grow up.[21]

Restructure the Company Another way for business owners to cash out gradually is to replace the existing corporation with a new one formed with other investors. The owner essentially is performing a leveraged buyout of his or her own company. For example, assume that you own a company worth $15 million. You form a new corporation with $12 million borrowed from a bank and $3 million in equity: $1.5 million of your own equity and $1.5 million in equity from an investor who wants you to stay on with the business. The new company buys your company for $15 million. You net $13.5 in cash ($15 million minus your $1.5 million equity investment) and still own 50 percent of the new leveraged business (see Figure 7.5).[22]

Sell to an International Buyer In an increasingly global marketplace, small U.S. businesses have become attractive buyout targets for foreign companies. Foreign buyers—mostly European—buy more than 1,000 U.S. businesses each year. England leads the list of nations acquiring U.S. companies, but China is coming on strong.

FIGURE 7.5

Restructuring a Business for Sale

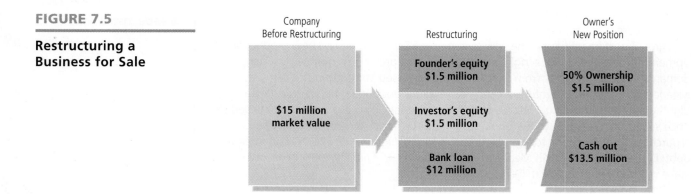

Robert Parker, owner of Adams Pressed Metals, a small, family-owned company in Galesburg, Illinois, that makes stamped metal parts, saw his company struggle when John Deere, his largest customer, began buying parts from Tri-Star International, a Chinese manufacturer. Transforming a significant threat into a substantial opportunity, Parker negotiated a deal with Tri-Star to sell a majority interest in the family-run business for $1 million. Tri-Star recognized that Adams Pressed Metals had a solid reputation among its customer base, access to important distribution channels, and a skilled workforce. "Adams will provide Tri-Star with a U.S. platform to expand its global operations," says Parker. "We saved 40 jobs, and [Tri Star] got American know-how in sales."[23]

Adams Pressed Metals

As Robert Parker's experience shows, it is not unusual in today's global economy to find companies across the globe with substantial financial resources looking to acquire small businesses in the United States. In many instances, foreign companies buy U.S.-based companies to gain access to a lucrative, growing market. They look for a team of capable managers, whom they typically retain for a given time period. They also want companies that are profitable, stable, and growing. Selling to foreign buyers can have disadvantages, however. They typically purchase 100 percent of a company, thereby making the previous owner merely an employee. Relationships with foreign owners also can be difficult to manage due to cultural and philosophical differences.

Use a Two-Step Sale For owners wanting the security of a sales contract now but not wanting to step down from the company's helm for several years, a two-step sale may be ideal. The buyer purchases the business in two phases—getting 20 to 70 percent today and agreeing to buy the remainder within a specific time period. Until the final transaction takes place, the entrepreneur retains at least partial control of the company.

Establish an Employee Stock Ownership Plan (ESOP) Some owners cash out by selling to their employees through an **employee stock ownership plan (ESOP).** An ESOP is a form of employee benefit plan in which a trust created for employees purchases their employer's stock. Here's how an ESOP works: The company transfers shares of its stock to the ESOP trust, and the trust uses the stock as collateral to borrow enough money to purchase the shares from the company. The company guarantees payment of the loan principal and interest and makes tax-deductible contributions to the trust to repay the loan (see Figure 7.6). The company then distributes the stock to employees' accounts based using a predetermined formula. In addition to the tax benefits an ESOP offers, the plan permits the owner to transfer all or part of the company to employees as gradually or as suddenly as preferred.

employee stock ownership plan (ESOP)
an employee benefit plan in which a trust created for employees purchases stock in their employer's company.

To use an ESOP successfully, a small business should be profitable (with pre-tax profits exceeding $100,000) and should have a payroll of more than $500,000 a year. Generally, companies with fewer than 15 to 20 employees do not find ESOPs beneficial. For companies that prepare properly, however, ESOPs offer significant financial and managerial benefits. Owners get great flexibility in determining their retirement schedules. An ESOP allows all parties involved to benefit, and the transfer of ownership can be timed to meet the entrepreneur's personal and financial goals.

Table 7.5 offers tips to help business sellers prepare their companies for sale to get maximum value from them.

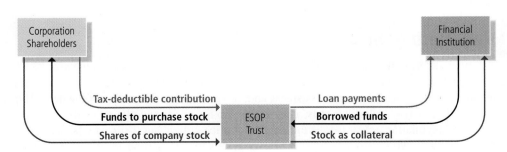

FIGURE 7.6

A Typical Employee Stock Ownership Plan (ESOP)

Source: Corey Rosen, "Sharing Ownership with Employees," *Small Business Reports*, December 1990, p. 63. © 1990 Corey Rosen. Used with permission.

TABLE 7.5 Preparing Your Company for Sale: How to Maximize Its Value

David Lobel, managing partner in a private equity firm that has purchased dozens of small companies, says that getting a company into shape to sell "can't be done overnight, but it can be done." What steps can business sellers take to prepare their companies for sale so that they can get maximum value from them? The following tips will help.

1. *Clean up the company's financial records.* Too many business owners are careless about keeping their books in pristine condition. A common excuse is "I'm too busy running my business to worry about keeping up with all of those financial records." However, a company's financial records are the raw materials from which potential buyers will establish the price they are willing to pay for a company. Make your company's financial records as tidy and as transparent as possible.

2. *Catch up on basic housekeeping.* People who are selling their houses know that cleaning and organizing their homes and eliminating clutter can add to the appeal—and to the price—of their houses. The same is true for businesses. Clean up all of the clutter that tends to build up over time, spruce up the physical appearance of the place, and put things in their proper places.

3. *Stop running personal expenses through the company.* Some business owners seek to minimize their company's tax bills by running personal expenses—for instance, gas for the family car—through the company. Tricks such as these make buyers nervous.

4. *Prepare a customer list for prospective buyers.* Buyers want to know that a company's sales will continue after they close the deal. Providing a list of important customers, including details such as how long each one has been buying from the company, how much each one has spent, key contacts (if business customers are involved), and the quality of the relationship, will add value to your business.

5. *Prepare a list of your company's key suppliers.* Which ones are most reliable? What kinds of contracts does your company have with them?

6. *Be prepared to show prospective buyers how much it costs to deliver your product or service to a customer.* Buyers want to know that the company's cost estimates are realistic.

7. *Prepare an employee policy manual.* The manual should include a job analysis for each position in the company, complete with a job description and job specifications. What rules of expected behavior does the company have?

8. *Prepare a document that describes how all of the machinery and equipment in the business works.* A list of service and repair contacts also is important.

9. *Consider removing from the payroll family members who are not essential to the operation of the business.* Many small businesses include family members whose contributions to the company are minimal.

10. *Take the time to conduct a business valuation at least every two years.* In many cases, when prospective buyers approach business owners with unsolicited offers for their companies, the entrepreneurs have no basis for making a deal because they have never taken the time to determine the value of their businesses. Seeing what makes up the real value in your business might enable you to operate it more effectively.

11. *Be prepared to stay on after the sale to help the new owner through the transition period.* In many instances, the business founder and his or her knowledge is the most important asset a company has.

12. *Take the steps listed here at least three years before you plan to sell your company.* Remember: It takes time to prepare a company for sale.

Sources: Adapted from Jim Melloan, "Sales Tips," *Inc.,* August 2004, p. 72; Laura Rich, "Seller's Market," *Inc.,* May 2005, pp. 39–42.

Negotiating the Deal

Although determining the value of a business for sale is an important step in the process of buying a business, it is not the final one. The buyer must sit down with the seller to negotiate the actual selling price for the business and, more important, the terms of the deal. The final deal the buyer strikes depends, in large part, on his or her negotiating skills. The first "rule" of negotiating a deal is to avoid confusing price with value. *Value* is what the business is actually worth; *price* is what the buyer agrees to pay. In a business sale, the party who is the better bargainer usually comes out on top. The buyer seeks to:

- Get the business at the lowest possible price.
- Negotiate favorable payment terms, preferably over time.
- Get assurances that he or she is buying the business that he or she thinks he or she is getting.
- Avoid putting the seller in a position to open a competing business.
- Minimize the amount of cash paid up front.

The seller is looking to:

- Get the highest price possible for the business.
- Sever all responsibility for the company's liabilities.
- Avoid unreasonable contract terms that might limit his or her future opportunities.
- Maximize the cash he or she gets from the deal.
- Minimize the tax burden from the sale.
- Make sure the buyer will be able to make all future payments.

One factor that makes the process of negotiating the purchase of a business challenging is that many business founders overestimate the value of their companies because of all of the "sweat equity" they have poured into their businesses over the years. One entrepreneur recalls a negotiation he was involved in for the potential purchase of a rival's business. The company had $4 million in sales but had incurred losses of more than $1 million in the previous two years, owed more than $2.5 million in unpaid bills, and had no machinery that was less than 30 years old. Much to the prospective buyer's amazement, the owner was asking $4 million for the business![24] To deal with this reality, buyers must understand the negotiation process.

Factors Affecting the Negotiation Process

Before beginning negotiations, a buyer should take stock of some basic issues. How strong is the seller's desire to sell? Is the seller willing to finance part of the purchase price? What terms does the buyer suggest? Which ones are most important to him or her? Is it urgent that the seller close the deal quickly? What deal structure best suits your needs? What are the tax consequences for both parties? Will the seller sign a restrictive covenant? Is the seller willing to stay on with the company for a time as a consultant? What general economic conditions exist in the industry at the time of the sale? Sellers tend to have the upper hand in good economic times, and buyers will have an advantage during recessionary periods in an industry.

The Negotiation Process

On the surface, the negotiation process appears to be strictly adversarial. Although each party may be trying to accomplish objectives that are at odds with those of the opposing

Copyright 2001 by Randy Glasbergen.

"To be a successful negotiator, you'll need courage, cunning, and stamina. If that doesn't work, try rock, paper, scissors."

party, the negotiation process does not have to turn into a nasty battle of wits with overtones of "If you win, then I lose." The negotiation process will go much more smoothly and much faster if both parties work to establish a cooperative relationship based on honesty and trust from the outset. A successful deal requires both parties to examine and articulate their respective positions while trying to understand the other party's position. Recognizing that neither of them will benefit without a deal, both parties must work to achieve their objectives while making certain concessions to keep the negotiations alive.

To avoid a stalled deal, a buyer should go into the negotiation with a list of objectives ranked in order of priority. Once you have developed your list of priorities, it is useful to develop what you perceive to be the seller's list of priorities. That requires learning as much as possible about the seller. Knowing which terms are most important (and which are least important) to you and to the seller enables you to make concessions without "giving away the farm" and without getting bogged down in "nit-picking," which often leads to a stalemate. If, for instance, the seller insists on a term that the you cannot agree to, you can explain why and then offer to give up something in exchange. You also should identify the one concrete objective that sits at the top of that list, the one thing you absolutely must come away from the negotiations with. The final stage of preparing for the actual negotiation is to study your list and the one you developed based on your perceptions of the seller to determine where the two mesh and where they conflict. The key to a successful negotiation is to use this analysis to look for areas of mutual benefit and to use them as the foundation for the negotiation.

Hands on ... How to

Become a Successful Negotiator

Buying or selling a business always involves a negotiation, and so do many other business activities, whether an entrepreneur is dealing with a bank, a customer, or a vendor. "Everyone negotiates something everyday," says Roger Fisher and William Ury in their book, *Getting to Yes*. "All of us negotiate many times a day." That's why negotiating skills are among the most important skills that entrepreneurs can learn. How can you become a more successful negotiator? The following advice will help.

1. *Prepare.* Good negotiators know that the formula for a successful negotiation is 90 percent preparation and 10 percent bargaining. What you do—or don't do—before the actual negotiation ever begins is a primary determinant of how successful your negotiation will be. The key is to learn as much as possible about the party with whom you will be negotiating, the issues that are most important to him or her, and his or her likely positions on those issues. Leo Riley, president of a training and consult-

Negotiating the purchase of a business can test the will, patience, and stamina of any entrepreneur. What steps can entrepreneurs take to "get to yes?"

ing firm, says, "Knowledge of their hobbies, families, dietary habits, religious beliefs, and [other traits] can be used as ice breakers or to avoid making embarrassing mistakes."

Your preparation for a negotiation also should include a statement of the outcome you desire from the negotiation. "Write down exactly what your goals are and then edit this description furiously until it is laser-focused and precise," advises John Patrick Nolan, a negotiation specialist. Then you should write down what you think your *counterpart's* goals from the negotiation are. This encourages you to look at the negotiation from a different perspective and can be a valuable and revealing exercise.

2. *Remember the difference between a "position" and an "interest."* The outcome a person wants from a negotiation is his or her position. What is much more important, however, is his or her interest, the reason behind the position he or she hopes to achieve. Focusing strictly on their positions usually leads two parties into a win–lose mentality in a negotiation, in which they try to pound one another into submission. When the parties involved in a negotiation focus on their *interests* rather than on their *positions*, however, they usually discover that there are several different solutions that both will consider acceptable and reasonable.

The Parable of the Orange provides an excellent lesson on the difference between the two. Two parties each want an orange, but there is only one orange. After much intense negotiating, the two agree to cut the orange in half. As it turns out, however, one party wanted only the rind of the orange to make cookies, and the other party wanted the orange to make orange juice. If the parties involved in the negotiation had focused on their interests and taken a problem-solving approach, they each could have gotten exactly what they wanted from the negotiation!

3. *Develop the right mindset.* Inexperienced negotiators see a negotiation as a zero-sum, win–lose game. "If you win, then I lose." Entrepreneurs who want or need to maintain ongoing relationships with the other party (e.g., buying a business from the company founder, whom you want to convince to stay on through a transition period to help you learn the business) must see negotiations in a different light. Their goal is to work toward a mutually beneficial agreement that both parties consider to be fair and reasonable.

Successful negotiations almost always involve compromise on both sides, which means that *neither* party gets *everything* that he or she wanted. "Sometimes the best deal you are going to get won't leave you jumping with joy," says Mike Staver, a negotiation consultant. In other words, successful negotiators see a negotiation not just as deal making but also as problem solving.

4. *Always leave yourself an escape hatch.* In any negotiation, you should be prepared to walk away without making a deal. Doing so, however, requires you to define what negotiation experts call a best alternative to a negotiated agreement (BATNA), which is the next-best alternative to a negotiated agreement. You cannot determine whether a negotiated agreement is suitable unless you know what your alternatives are, and one alternative (although not always the best one) is to walk away from the negotiation without an agreement—your BATNA. One writer explains, "You may never need [your BATNA], but just knowing it's in your back pocket gives you peace of mind. Without one, you can become anxious, appear desperate, and settle for a less-than-ideal solution."

Having a BATNA increases your power in a negotiation, but you should use that power judiciously. Do not use your BATNA as a threat to coerce an agreement. In addition, don't kill the deal just because you can. Instead, use your BATNA as the baseline against which you measure your negotiated alternatives.

5. *Keep your emotions in check.* Negotiations can become emotionally charged, especially if those involved allow their egos to enter into the process. It is always best to abide by the Golden Rule of Negotiating: Treat others the way you want to be treated in the negotiation. Be fair but firm. If the other party forgets the Golden Rule of Negotiating, remember that you can always walk away from the negotiation and fall back on your BATNA.

6. *Sometimes it's best to remain silent.* A common mistake many people make in the negotiation process is talking too much. Not only does remaining silent allow you to listen to the other party, but it also encourages the other party to make the first offer. Some people are disconcerted

by prolonged periods of silence and begin talking, only to erode the strength of their negotiation base.

Sources: Adapted from Rhonda Abrams, "Know What You Need before Starting to Negotiate a Deal," *Greenville News Business,* May

29, 2005, p. 8; "Negotiating to Resolve Conflict," Fed Ex Small Business Center, January 22, 2003, www.mysmallbizcenter.com/rawdoc.asp?docID=7169&temp=6378; Scott Smith, "Negotiate from Strength," *Success,* July/August 2000, pp. 74–75; Susan St. John, "Five Steps to Better Negotiating," *E-Merging Business,* Fall–Winter 2000, pp. 212–214; Rob Walker, "Take It or Leave It: The *Only* Guide to Negotiating You Will *Ever* Need, *Inc.,* August 2003, pp. 75–82.

Chapter Summary by Learning Objectives

1. Understand (A) the advantages and (B) the disadvantages of buying an existing business.

The *advantages* of buying an existing business include the following: A successful business may continue to be successful; the business may already have the best location; employees and suppliers are already established; equipment is installed and its productive capacity known; inventory is in place and trade credit established; the owner hits the ground running; the buyer can use the expertise of the previous owner; and the business may be a bargain.

The disadvantages of buying an existing business include the following: An existing business may be for sale because it is deteriorating; the previous owner may have created ill will; employees inherited with the business may not be suitable; its location may have become unsuitable; equipment and facilities may be obsolete; change and innovation are hard to implement; inventory may be outdated; accounts receivable may be worth less than face value; and the business may be overpriced.

2. Define the steps involved in the right way to buy a business.

Buying a business can be a treacherous experience unless the buyer is well prepared. The right way to buy a business is to analyze your skills, abilities, and interests to determine the ideal business for you; prepare a list of potential candidates, including those that might be in the "hidden market"; investigate and evaluate candidate businesses and evaluate the best one; explore financing options before you actually need the money; and, finally, ensure a smooth transition.

3. Explain the process of evaluating an existing business.

Rushing into a deal can be the biggest mistake a business buyer can make. Before closing a deal, every business buyer should investigate five critical areas: (1) Why does

the owner wish to sell? Look for the *real* reason. (2) Determine the physical condition of the business. Consider both the building and its location. (3) Conduct a thorough analysis of the market for your products or services. Who are the present and potential customers? Conduct an equally thorough analysis of competitors, both direct and indirect. How do they operate and why do customers prefer them? (4) Consider all of the legal aspects that might constrain the expansion and growth of the business: Did you comply with the provisions of a bulk transfer? Negotiate a restrictive covenant? Consider ongoing legal liabilities? (5) Analyze the financial condition of the business, looking at financial statements, income tax returns, and especially cash flow.

4. Describe the various techniques for determining the value of a business.

Placing a value on a business is partly an art and partly a science. There is no single "best" method for determining the value of a business. The following techniques (with several variations) are useful: the balance sheet technique (adjusted balance sheet technique); the earnings approach (excess earnings method, capitalized earnings approach, and discounted future savings approach); and the market approach.

5. Understand the seller's side of the buyout decision and how to structure the deal.

Selling a business takes time, patience, and preparation to locate a suitable buyer, strike a deal, and make the transition. Sellers must always structure the deal with tax consequences in mind. Common exit strategies include a straight business sale, a business sale with an agreement for the founder to stay on, forming a family limited partnership, selling a controlling interest in the business, restructuring the company, selling to an international buyer, using a two-step sale, and establishing an employee stock ownership plan (ESOP).

6. Understand how the negotiation process works and identify the factors that affect it.

The first rule of negotiating is to never confuse price with value. In a business sale, the party who is the better negotiator usually comes out on top. Before beginning negotia-

tions, a buyer should identify the factors that are affecting the negotiations and then develop a negotiating strategy. The best deals are the result of a cooperative relationship between the parties based on trust.

Discussion Questions

1. What advantages can an entrepreneur who buys a business gain over one who starts a business from scratch?

2. How would you go about determining the value of the assets of a business if you were unfamiliar with them?

3. Why do so many entrepreneurs run into trouble when they buy an existing business? Outline the steps involved in the *right* way to buy a business.

4. When evaluating an existing business that is for sale, what areas should an entrepreneur consider? Briefly summarize the key elements of each area.

5. What is goodwill? How should a buyer evaluate a business's goodwill?

6. What is a restrictive covenant? Is it fair to ask the seller of a travel agency located in a small town to sign a restrictive covenant for one year covering a 20-square-mile area? Explain.

7. How much negative information can you expect the seller to give you about the business? How can a prospective buyer find out such information?

8. Why is it so difficult for buyers and sellers to agree on a price for a business?

9. Which method of valuing a business is best? Why? What advice would you offer to someone who is negotiating to buy a business about determining its value?

10. Outline the different exit strategy options available to a seller.

11. One entrepreneur who recently purchased a business advises buyers to expect some surprises in the deal no matter how well prepared they may be. He says that potential buyers must build some "wiggle room" into their plans to buy a company. What steps can a buyer take to ensure that he or she has sufficient "wiggle room"?

Business Plan Pro

 This chapter has addressed acquiring an existing business. If this is your situation, determine whether the company has a business plan. If so, how recent is that plan? Is it representative of the current state of the organization? Do you have access to other historical information including the financial statements such as the profit and loss, balance sheet and cash flow statements? These documents may be a valuable resource to help you to better understand the business you may purchase.

Business Plan Exercises
On the Web

If the business has a Web site, review that site to assess the "online personality" of the business and to gather as much information as you can about the business. Does it match what you have learned about the business through the owner and other documents you have reviewed? Do a search for the business name and the owners' names on the Web. You may find that Google.com offers the most robust results. Note what you find and, again, determine if this information correlates with information from other sources.

Sample Plans

Review the executive summaries of these ongoing business plans through the Sample Plan Browser in Business Plan Pro:
- Machine Tooling
- Salvador's Sauces
- Sample Software Company
- Take Five Sports Bar
- Web Solutions, Inc.

Scan the table of contents and find the section of the plan with information on the company's past performance. What might this historical information tell you about the future potential of the venture? Which of these businesses would you expect to present the greatest profit potential based on their past performance? Which business represents the greatest risk based on these same criteria? How might this impact its purchase price?

In the Software

If the company that you are considering to buy has a business plan, enter this information into Business Plan Pro. First, select the "Existing" business plan option in the opening window. If you have access to an electronic version of company's plan you are considering purchasing, you can copy and paste text from a word processing document directly into Business Plan Pro by using the "Paste Special" option and then selecting the option "Without Formatting." This step will help to keep your formatting in order. Go to the "Company Summary" section and include the results of the due diligence process. The financial statements of the business, including the balance sheet, profit and loss, and cash flow statements for the last three years will be valuable historical data. This will set a baseline for you as you enter sales and expense scenarios into this plan. This process may help you to better assess the business's future earning potential and its current value.

Building Your Business Plan

One of advantages of using Business Plan Pro is the ease of creating different financial scenarios for your business. This can be an excellent way to explore multiple "what if" options. Once your business is in motion, updating the plan during the fiscal year and on an annual basis can be a quick and easy process. This will be an efficient way to keep your plan current and, by saving each of these files based on the date, for example, offer an excellent historical perspective of your business.

Beyond the Classroom . . .

1. Ask several new owners who purchased existing businesses the following questions:
   A. How did you determine the value of the business?
   B. How close was the price paid for the business to the value assessed prior to purchase?
   C. What percentage of the accounts receivable was collectible?
   D. How accurate were their projections concerning customers (sales volume and number of customers, especially)?

2. Visit a business broker and ask him or her how he or she brings a buyer and seller together. What does he or she do to facilitate the sale? What methods does he or she use to determine the value of a business?

3. Invite an attorney to speak to your class about the legal aspects of buying a business. How does he or she recommend a business buyer protect himself or herself legally in a business purchase?

8 | Building a Powerful Marketing Plan

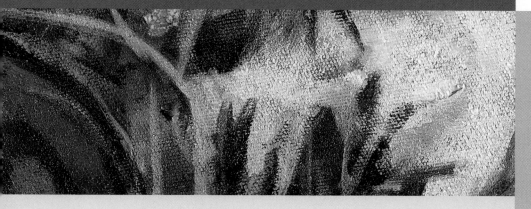

> This fishing lure manufacturer I
> know had all these flashy
> green and purple lures. I
> asked, "Do fish take these?"
> "Charlie," he said, "I don't sell
> these lures to fish."
> —Charles Munger

Learning
Objectives

On completion of this chapter, you will be able to:

1 Describe the principles of building a guerrilla marketing plan and explain the benefits of preparing one.

2 Explain how small businesses can pinpoint their target markets.

3 Discuss the role of market research in building a guerrilla marketing plan and outline the market research process.

4 Describe how a small business can build a competitive edge in the marketplace using guerrilla marketing strategies: customer focus, quality, convenience, innovation, service, and speed.

5 Discuss the marketing opportunities the World Wide Web offers entrepreneurs and how to best take advantage of them.

6 Discuss the "four P's" of marketing—product, place, price, and promotion—and their role in building a successful marketing strategy.

As you learned in Chapter 4, creating a solid business plan improves an entrepreneur's odds of building a successful company. A business plan is a valuable document that defines *what* an entrepreneur plans to accomplish in both quantitative and qualitative terms and *how* he or she plans to accomplish it. The plan consolidates many of the topics we have discussed in preceding chapters with those in this section to produce a concise statement of how an entrepreneur plans to achieve success in the marketplace. This section focuses on building two major components of every business plan: the marketing plan and the financial plan.

Too often, business plans describe in great detail what the entrepreneur intends to accomplish (e.g., "the financials") and pay little, if any, attention to the strategies proposed to achieve those targets. Too many entrepreneurs squander enormous effort pulling together capital, people, and other resources to sell their products and services because they fail to determine what it will take to attract and keep a profitable customer base. Sometimes they fail to determine whether a profitable customer base even exists! To be effective, a solid business plan must contain both a financial plan *and* a marketing plan. Like the financial plan, an effective marketing plan projects numbers and analyzes them, but from a different perspective. Rather than focus on cash flow, net income, and owner's equity, a marketing plan concentrates on the *customer*.

This chapter is devoted to creating an effective marketing plan, which is a subset of a total business plan. Before producing reams of computer-generated spreadsheets of financial projections, an entrepreneur must determine what to sell, to whom and how, on what terms and at what price, and how to get the product or service to the customer. In short, a marketing plan identifies a company's target customers and describes how that business will attract and keep them. Its primary focus is capturing and maintaining a competitive edge for a small business.

Building a Guerrilla Marketing Plan

Marketing is the process of creating and delivering desired goods and services to customers and involves all of the activities associated with winning and retaining loyal customers. The "secret" to successful marketing is to understand what your target customers' needs, demands, and wants are before your competitors can; offer them the products and services that will satisfy those needs, demands, and wants; and, provide customers service, convenience, and value so that they will keep coming back. Unfortunately, there appears to be a sizeable gap between sound marketing principles and actual marketing practices among small businesses. One study of small company marketing practices by Dun & Bradstreet revealed many serious weaknesses. For instance, the study found that just one in five small business owners creates a strategic marketing plan and that the most common sales approach is to react to customer orders rather than to proactively seek them out. (Efforts are so passive that walk-in traffic was cited as the most popular sales method.) The study also revealed that word-of-mouth promotion and referrals comprise the typical small company's marketing efforts.[1]

In a small business, the marketing function cuts across the entire company, affecting every aspect of its operation—from finance and production to hiring and purchasing—as well as the company's ultimate success. As competition for customers becomes more intense, small business owners must understand the importance of developing creative marketing strategies; their success and survival depend on it. A marketing plan is *not* just for megacorporations competing in international markets. Although they may be small and cannot match their larger rivals' marketing budgets, entrepreneurial companies are not powerless when it comes to developing effective marketing strategies. By using **guerrilla marketing strategies**—unconventional, low-cost, creative techniques—small companies can wring as much or more "bang" from their marketing bucks. For instance, facing the power of discount giants such as Wal-Mart, Target, and "category killer" superstores such as Best Buy and Circuit City determined to increase their market shares, small retail shops are turning to guerrilla marketing tactics to lure new customers and to keep existing ones. One small retailer explains, "If the chains are the steamships plowing through the ocean, then we have to be the cigarette [racing] boats zipping around and through them, changing direction on a dime. That must be our advantage when going up against the tremendous cash and resources of the biggies."[2]

LEARNING OBJECTIVES

1. Describe the principles of building a guerrilla marketing plan and explain the benefits of preparing one.

marketing
the process of creating and delivering desired goods and services to customers; involves all of the activities associated with winning and retaining loyal customers

guerrilla marketing strategies
unconventional, low-cost, creative marketing strategies designed to give small companies an edge over their larger, richer, more powerful rivals.

An effective marketing campaign does *not* require an entrepreneur to spend large amounts of money, but it does demand creativity, ingenuity, and an understanding of customers' buying habits.

Borsheim's

Borsheim's, a jewelry store in Omaha, Nebraska, has developed an effective guerrilla marketing strategy designed to attract a target audience known for its disdain of shopping: men. Every year before Christmas, Borsheim's sponsors men's night at its store, offering men a party-like atmosphere with free pizza and beer in an attempt to reduce the intimidation factor of buying jewelry for their wives and girlfriends. (The week before men's night, the store also sponsors women's night, on which the ladies are invited to come in, drink wine and Perrier, snack on hors d'ouvrès, and make out their jewelry wish lists.) Men who attend sit in leather recliners, watch "guy movies," eat pizza, drink wine, and win prizes, including a Monopoly set autographed by business legend Warren Buffett. On men's night, the store sees as much as a tenfold increase in sales, proving what some smart retailers already know: that, under the right circumstances, men can be freer with their spending than women. "This is my idea of shopping," says one contented customer from his leather lounge chair, "watching TV, drinking beer, and eating pizza."[3]

A sound guerrilla marketing plan reflects a company's understanding of its *customers* and recognizes that satisfying them is the foundation of every business. Its purpose is to build a strategy of success for a business—but *from the customer's point of view.* Indeed, the customer is the central player in the cast of every business venture. According to marketing expert Ted Levitt, the primary purpose of a business is not to earn a profit; instead, it is "to create and keep a customer. The rest, given reasonable good sense, will take care of itself."[4] Every area of the business must practice putting the customer first in planning and actions.

A guerrilla marketing plan should accomplish four objectives:

1. It should pinpoint the specific target markets the small company will serve.
2. It should determine customer needs and wants through market research.
3. It should analyze the firm's competitive advantages and build a guerrilla marketing strategy around them.
4. It should help to create a marketing mix that meets customer needs and wants.

The rest of this chapter focuses on building a customer orientation into these four objectives of the small company's marketing plan.

Pinpointing the Target Market

target market
the specific group of customers at whom a company aims its goods or services.

One of the first steps in building a guerrilla marketing plan is to identify a small company's **target market**—the specific group of customers at whom the company aims its goods or services. The more a business knows about its local markets, its customers, and their buying habits and preferences, the more precisely it can focus its marketing efforts on the group(s) of prospective and existing customers who are most likely to buy its products or services. Most marketing experts contend that the greatest marketing mistake small businesses make is failing to define clearly the target market to be served. These entrepreneurs develop new products that do not sell because they are not targeted at a specific audience's needs; they broadcast ads that attempt to reach everyone and end up reaching no one; they spend precious time and money trying to reach customers who are not the most profitable; and many of the customers they attract leave because they do not know what the company stands for. Why, then, do so many small companies make this mistake? Because it is easy and does not require market research or a marketing plan! The problem is that this is a sales-driven approach rather than a customer-driven strategy. Smart entrepreneurs know that they do not have the luxury of wasting resources; they must follow a more focused, laser-like approach to marketing.

To be customer driven, an effective marketing strategy must be based on a clear, comprehensive definition of a company's target customers. For entrepreneurs, pinpointing target customers has become more important than ever before as markets in the United States

"You don't get it, Daddy, because they're not targeting you."

have become increasingly fragmented and diverse. Mass marketing techniques no longer reach customers the way they did 30 years ago because of the influence now exerted on the nation's purchasing patterns by what were once minority groups such as Hispanics and Asian- and African-Americans. Companies using Chinese-born basketball players as spokesmen, television commercials spoken entirely in Spanish (some with no English subtitles), Hip-Hop clothing and music appearing in mainstream stores, and college cafés offering sushi and other specialty dishes are symbols of the tremendous multicultural shift that continues to take place in the United States.

Failing to pinpoint their target markets is especially ironic because small firms are far better suited to reach small, often more concentrated market segments that their larger rivals overlook or consider too small to be profitable. A customer-driven marketing strategy is a powerful strategic weapon for any company that lacks the financial and physical resources of its competitors. Customers respond when companies take the time to learn about their unique needs and offer products and services designed to satisfy them.

Zondervan Inc.

Zondervan has become the largest seller of Bibles in the world by creating a variety of different versions, each aimed at a different market segment. With its cover that mimics a basketball and comments from famous athletes, the Sports Devotional Bible is aimed at young athletes.

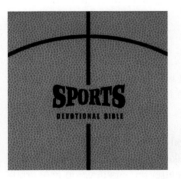

Zondervan Inc. has become the largest seller of bibles in the world by offering a variety of versions aimed at different target markets, each of which the 75-year-old company has researched thoroughly. Because women purchase more bibles than men, Zondervan created *True Identity,* a bible aimed at women that includes an "Ask Me Anything" section, a question-and-answer interview format with biblical women who speak to modern readers about life issues they faced. *True Identity* also includes "Conversations" notes, penetrating questions designed for self-reflection or for stimulating conversation with a friend or mentor. The company's *Sports Devotional Bible* is aimed at young athletes and features comments about scripture and insights from professional athletes, coaches, and other sports figures. One version of the *Sports Devotional Bible* even comes with a leather cover whose texture is the same as a football or basketball. Special "Time Out" articles explain Biblical principles and verses, often using sports illustrations. Aimed at young people, Zondervan's unorthodox *The Story* is a 30-chapter version of Scripture that reads more like a novel than a typical religious text. "Young people have so many choices," says Paul Caminiti, a Zondervan vice-president, "that we need to keep things fresh to keep them interested." The company recently introduced a downloadable MP3 bible read by people of different ages, genders, and nationalities. Zondervan's marketing strategy is working; the company has captured 27 percent of the $1 billion Christian book market.[5]

Like Zondervan's, the most successful businesses have well-defined portraits of the customers they are seeking to attract. From market research, they know their customers' income levels, lifestyles, buying patterns, likes and dislikes, and even their psychological profiles—why they buy. These companies establish prices appropriate to their target customers' buying power, product lines that appeal to their tastes, and service they expect. The payoff comes in the form of higher sales, profits, and customer loyalty.

Lucien Orza, owner of Briarcliff Bike Works, recently decided to shift his company's focus from selling relatively inexpensive recreational bikes that are sold at major discount stores to targeting cycling enthusiasts with high-end bicycles that can cost as much as $8,000 each. The cycling enthusiasts that Orza is targeting make up just five percent of the bicycle market, but their spending on their bicycles and the accessories that go with them is far above the industry average. Although Orza is selling about the same number of bicycles as he was before shifting to the new target market, his company's sales profit margins are running 10 percent higher, and he is able to spend more time with his wife and children.[6]

Briarcliff Bike Works

When companies follow a customer-driven marketing strategy, they find that their target customers permeate the entire business—from the merchandise sold and the music played on the sound system to the location, layout, and decor of the store. These business owners have an advantage over their larger rivals because the images they have created for their companies appeal to their target customers, and that's why they prosper. Without a clear picture of its target market and the image it must create to attract those customers, a small company will try to reach almost everyone and usually will end up appealing to almost no one.

The nation's increasingly diverse population offers businesses of all sizes tremendous marketing opportunities if they target specific customers, learn how to reach them, and offer goods and services designed specifically for them. Because of this diversity, a "one-size-fits-all" approach to marketing no longer works. Analysis of U.S. census data shows that Hispanics are now the nation's largest minority, followed by African-Americans and Asian-Americans. Between 2000 and 2050, growth in the populations of Hispanics and Asian- and African-Americans will far outpace the population growth of white Americans (see Figure 8.1). Greater than 13 percent of the U.S. population is of Hispanic origin (and this will grow to 24 percent of the U.S. population by 2050), but because they hail from more than 20 countries, this diverse market also requires a targeted marketing approach.[7] In addition, the population of Asian-Americans now boasts the highest rate of education of any segment and has an average household income that exceeds that of white households by $10,000. Recognizing the potential of this demographic trend, Lubna Khalid, a former model of Pakistani descent, launched Real Cosmetics, a company that produces a line of cosmetics aimed specifically at Asian women.[8]

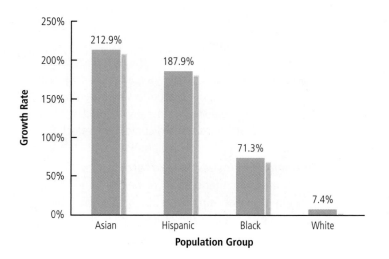

FIGURE 8.1

U.S. Population Growth Rate for Selected Groups (2000–2050)

Source: U.S. Census Bureau, 2006, http://www.census.gov.

Sometimes new target markets emerge on their own, much to the surprise of a small business owner.

W.J. Brookes

When Steve Pateman took over W.J. Brookes, the shoe manufacturing company his grandfather had founded in North Hampton, England, the 110-year-old family business was struggling as a result of intense global competition and rising costs in its core market—high-quality, traditional men's shoes. Pateman was forced to cut the company's workforce from 77 to 22 employees. Then Pateman received a phone call from a shop with an unusual request: Could he manufacture women's shoes for cross-dressing men? Pateman's company began manufacturing women's shoes in men's sizes and soon developed a complete product line under the Divine label that includes faux-leopard thigh boots with seven-and-a-half–inch heels! The business (now dubbed "the kinky boot factory") has rehired many workers, takes orders from all across the globe, and generates 50 percent of its sales from the transvestite market.[9]

Hands on ... How to

Provide Superior Customer Service: From the Blue Carpet to the Mouse

One advantage that small companies often have over their larger rivals lies in providing superior customer service. Stellar customer service does not happen on its own, however; entrepreneurs must create a strategy for providing it and then build an environment in which to implement that strategy. What steps can you take to make sure your business provides superior customer service?

Hire for attitude; train for skills. Experienced entrepreneurs know that hiring the right people is where the formula for superior customer service begins. They also know that it's best to hire people who already have good customer service skills— friendly, empathetic people who exhibit caring attitudes toward others—and then teach them the technical skills they need to perform the job well. Hiring someone who is technically capable but who lacks a customer service attitude almost always is a mistake. Small companies must create a thorough screening process so that they hire only those candidates who exhibit a customer service attitude.

Train employees to provide excellent customer service. An employee's first day on the job is the perfect time to introduce him or her to the essential role that customer service plays in your company. Rather than conduct a traditional orientation that

bores employees (filling out multiple forms in triplicate, learning where the restrooms are, learning who reports to whom), smart entrepreneurs take advantage of new employees' enthusiasm to get them focused on providing top-notch customer service. At Ritz-Carlton, a company that operates a chain of 57 award-winning hotels around the world and prides itself on "rolling out the blue carpet," new employees attend a two-day course that introduces them to the company's core values (service, of course, is one key value), its credo (which emphasizes that "the genuine care and comfort of our guests is our highest mission"), and the 20 Ritz Carlton "basics" (principle number 13 is "Never lose a guest"). New hires then attend a three-week course that teaches them the skills necessary to perform their jobs to Ritz-Carlton's high exacting standards.

Treat employees the way you want them to treat your customers. Managers who are disrespectful of their employees and treat them poorly should not be surprised when those employees are disrespectful of the company's customers and treat them poorly. It doesn't matter how focused on customer service a small company's motto is; employees' attitudes toward customers reflects managers' attitudes toward employees.

Empower employees to take care of your customers. To offer customers the ultimate in customer service, employees must have the freedom to sometimes bend or even break the rules, especially in those situations in which a customer has a complaint or is unhappy. Rather than force employees to stick to the rules (and, in the process, risk losing a customer forever), smart entrepreneurs give employees the authority to take whatever steps are necessary to fix the problem and make the customer happy. For instance, at Ritz-Carlton, every staff member has the authority to spend as much as $2,000 without a manager's approval to resolve any guest's problem.

"Wow" your customers with service. Another key to stellar customer service is *exceeding*, not just meeting, customers' expectations. Providing service that makes customers say "Wow!" will keep them coming back time after time. When an administrative assistant at a Ritz-Carlton hotel overheard a guest lamenting that he had forgotten his dress shoes and would have to wear hiking boots to an important meeting the next day, she saw an opportunity to offer "wow" service. Early the next morning, she delivered to the awestruck guest a pair of dress shoes in his size and favorite color. Another loyal Ritz-Carlton customer? You bet!

Listen . . . and learn from your customers. If companies are willing to listen, their customers will tell them how to provide excellent customer service.

Pay attention to the details. Customer service usually boils down to taking care of the details, and few companies are better at details than Disney. Disney's view is that "everything speaks" either positively or negatively to customers. Disney makes sure its theme parks are spotless because litter speaks of poor quality and service (and, in company lingo, is "a bad Mickey.") Disney knows that its park sweepers have the greatest number of guest encounters of any of its employees; that's why they get extensive customer service training, including how to read guests' body language so they can offer help before guests even ask for it. One researcher who studied the role of the sweepers at Disney concludes that Disney's hiring and training of its sweepers

gives it a competitive advantage. "One of the things that struck me about the sweepers is that in other [theme parks], they are not all treated with the importance Disney attaches to them," he says.

Instill a service attitude into the company culture. Talking about customer service is not sufficient. Employees look to company owners and managers as role models of customer service behavior. Business owners who fail to set a positive customer service example should not expect their employees to demonstrate an attitude of customer service either. That's one reason Disney executives spend time working the "front lines" in the park during peak holiday seasons. They are sending a clear message to cast members (Disney's term for its employees) that every job is important and that customer service really does matter. For instance, George Aguel, a senior vice-president for Disney, has donned a costume and worked a shift at the Haunted Mansion and has worked behind the counter in a Disney restaurant. The practice also keeps managers in touch with customers by giving them a dose of reality.

Use technology (where appropriate) to improve customer service. At Ritz-Carlton, employees have access to an in-house database called the Customer Loyalty Anticipation Satisfaction System (CLASS). CLASS stores the knowledge that the company has gathered about its customers in the past so that employees can offer them "wow" service. For example, when a customer checks in, the system might remind an employee that she prefers a foam pillow rather than one made of feathers and wants a copy of the *Wall Street Journal* with a glass of orange juice in the morning. Employees can provide these extras without having to ask the guest about her preferences every time she visits.

Sources: Duff McDonald, "Roll out the Blue Carpet," *Business 2.0*, May 2004, pp. 53–54; Alan M. Webber, "How You Can Help Them," *Fast Company*, November 1997, p. 128; Douglas P. Shuit, "Magic for Sale," *Workforce Management*, September 2004, pp. 35–40; *Be Our Guest: Perfecting the Art of Customer Service* (New York: Disney Institute, 2001).

Determining Customer Needs and Wants through Market Research

LEARNING OBJECTIVES
3. Discuss the role of market research in building a guerrilla marketing plan and outline the market research process.

The changing nature of the U.S. population is a potent force altering the landscape of business. Shifting patterns in age, income, education, race, and other population characteristics (which are the subject of **demographics**) will have a major impact on companies, their customers, and the way companies do business with those customers. Businesses that

demographics
the study of important population characteristics such as age, income, education, race, and others.

ignore demographic trends and fail to adjust their strategies accordingly run the risk of becoming competitively obsolete.

A demographic trend is like a train; a business owner must find out early on where it's going and decide whether or not to get on board. Waiting until the train is roaring down the tracks and gaining speed means it's too late to get on board. However, by checking the schedule early and planning ahead, an entrepreneur may find himself or herself at the train's controls wearing the engineer's hat. Similarly, small companies that spot demographic trends early and act on them can gain a distinctive edge in the market. An entrepreneur's goal is to make sure his or her company's marketing plan is on track with the most significant trends that are shaping the industry. For instance, companies are increasingly aiming their products at women because of their growing purchasing power and the influence they exert on family buying decisions. Targeting women successfully, however, requires more than introducing a product in pink (which, according to research, is exactly the *wrong* thing to do to attract women buyers).

COMPANY Profile

Beringer Blass Wine Estates

After discovering that women make 80 percent of all wine purchases, Beringer Blass Wine Estates, a Napa Valley winery, introduced White Lie, the first wine aimed specifically at women. The winery's market research showed that women preferred wines with lower alcohol content and fewer calories but were not interested in a "diet wine" that compromised on taste. By harvesting grapes earlier in the season, the company was able to create a wine with 32 percent less alcohol and 25 percent fewer calories than regular Chardonnay without sacrificing taste. As part of its marketing strategy, Beringer will distribute White Lie primarily through grocery stores, where women are most likely to purchase wine, and will advertise the label on radio and billboards as well as on Web sites that women visit most often.[10]

Trends are powerful forces and can be an entrepreneur's greatest friend or greatest enemy. In the restaurant industry, traditional fast food chains are struggling to sustain mediocre growth rates, while restaurants based on the "fast casual" concept, a hybrid of fast food and traditional full-service restaurants, make up the hottest sector. In fact, fast food giants McDonald's and Wendy's have purchased promising companies in the fast casual sector such as Boston Market, Panera Bread, Chipotle, and Baja Fresh. Diners want the speed and convenience of a fast food restaurant as well as the higher-quality, healthier fare of full-service restaurants. Several factors are driving this trend: diners who are "burned out" on burgers and concerned about the health considerations of fast food diets, the growing population of empty-nest baby-boomers who are tired of cooking, the increasing purchasing power of members of Generation X, who never enjoyed cooking at home, and customers whose busy lives lead them to spend more on dining out than on food prepared in their homes. In fact, half of all food dollars spent by U.S. households goes to food purchased outside the home.[11] For entrepreneurs who are observant and position their companies to intercept them, trends can be to their companies what the perfect wave is to a surfer. For entrepreneurs who ignore them or discount their importance, trends can leave their companies stranded like a boat stuck in the mud at low tide.

The Value of Market Research

market research
the vehicle for gathering the information that serves as the foundation for the marketing plan; it involves systematically collecting, analyzing, and interpreting data pertaining to a company's market, customers, and competitors.

By performing some basic market research, small business owners can detect key demographic and market trends. Indeed, *every* business can benefit from a better understanding of its market, customers, and competitors. "Market information is just as much a business asset and just as important as your inventory or the machine you have in the back room," says one marketing consultant.[12] **Market research** is the vehicle for gathering the information that serves as the foundation for the marketing plan. It involves systematically collecting, analyzing, and interpreting data pertaining to a company's market, customers, and competitors. The objective of market research is to learn how to improve the level of satisfaction for existing customers and to find ways to attract new customers. Get specific by asking and answering questions such as the following:

- Who are my customers and potential customers?
- What are they looking for?
- What kind of people are they?
- How old are they?
- Are they male or female?
- What kinds of jobs do they hold?
- What is their household income?
- Where do they live?
- How often do they buy these products or services?
- What models, styles, colors, or flavors do they prefer?
- Why do—or don't—they buy from my business?
- How well do my products or services fit their needs and wants?
- What hours do they prefer to shop?
- How do they perceive my business?
- Which advertising media are likely to reach them?
- How do customers perceive my business versus competitors?

This type of information is an integral part of developing a marketing plan that produces results.

When marketing their goods and services, small companies must avoid mistakes because there is no margin for error when funds are scarce and budgets are tight. Small businesses simply cannot afford to miss their target markets, and market research can help them zero in on the bull's eye.

Pulte Homes

Bill Pulte, founder of Pulte Homes, which has become the largest homebuilder in the United States, credits sophisticated market research for much of his company's success. Pulte marketers scour a database of more than 500,000 consumers, which they have divided into 11 target groups, ranging from "starters" (first-time buyers, typically young couples in their 20s and early 30s looking to break out of the rental cycle by purchasing a basic house averaging just over 2,500 square feet) to "active adult retirees" (baby boomers from ages 55 and up who are easing into retirement and are looking for homes averaging just over 2,800 square feet with lots of luxurious features and with access to golf and health clubs). "Toyota sells Corollas to entry-level buyers, Camrys to the middle market, and Lexuses to the top," explains CEO Richard Dugas. "Why can't we do the same thing in homebuilding?" Using their 11 profiles as a guide, Pulte managers scout out states, cities, and even neighborhoods that match the profile of their target customers. "We buy land where customer demand most exceeds supply," says Dugas. Pulte managers also found ways to use their market research to lower costs. The company had been offering customers a wide array of choices on everything from countertops and windows to toilets and doorknobs, requiring it to purchase small batches of items from 17 different suppliers. However, research showed that 80 percent of the company's homebuyers selected the same carpet, countertops, siding, and other features, enabling Pulte to whittle its list of suppliers, buy in greater volume, and negotiate lower prices with the remaining vendors.[13]

One of the worst—and most common—mistakes entrepreneurs make is assuming that a market exists for their product or service. The time to find out whether customers will buy your product or service is *before* you invest thousands of dollars to launch it! Market research can tell entrepreneurs whether a sufficient customer base exists and how likely those customers are to purchase their products or services. In addition to collecting and analyzing demographic data about the people in a particular geographic area and comparing the results to the profile of a typical customer, entrepreneurs can learn much by actually observing, mingling with, and interviewing customers as they shop. The founder of one snack-food company says that he learns a great deal about packaging and design and product placement by hanging around the aisles of grocery stores and watching shoppers' buying behavior. Other companies videotape customers while they are shopping to get a clear picture of their buying habits. Hands-on market research techniques such as these allow entrepreneurs to get past the barriers that consumers often put up and to uncover their true preferences and hidden thoughts.

Market research does *not* have to be time-consuming, complex, or expensive to be useful. By applying the same type of creativity to market research that they display when creating their businesses, entrepreneurs can perform effective market research "on the cheap." Consider the following examples:

- When Dov Charney founded American Apparel in Los Angeles in1997, his focus was on manufacturing simple, high-quality T-shirts made from superior cotton with no logos and no ornamentation. Although the company has extended its product line to include socks, underwear, tank tops, polo shirts, swimwear, baby clothes, and even dog clothes, T-shirts still account for a significant portion of its sales. Because American Apparel's target customer is young people ranging from 15 to 25 years old, the company now offers brightly colored T-shirts but continues to set itself apart from competitors with shirts featuring slim cuts that enhance the wearer's muscles and curves. In fact, to learn about the proper fit for women's T-shirts, Charney went to clubs featuring exotic dancers, knowing he could find women of all body shapes there. He gave away lots of T-shirts and asked the women for feedback on how to improve their fit so that the shirts would flatter women's bodies.[14]

- Inexpensive market research is one key to success for the Southern California retail chain Hot Topic. No one could confuse one of the chain's 346 stores with the Gap or American Eagle, who sell jeans, crop-tops, and khaki pants to athletic-looking young people. Since Orv Madden founded the first Hot Topic store in Montclair, California, in 1989, market research has led the company to target "alternative" teens, who make up 17 percent of all high school students. At Hot Topic, angst-filled teens browse among displays of fishnet stockings, blue hair dye, glow-in-the-dark tongue rings, black gothic patent leather platform boots with four-and-a-half–inch heels, red feather "blood angel" wings, and pink fur pants. To stay on the cutting edge of the ever-changing fashion tastes of its customers, Hot Topic sends its buyers to rock concerts and raves its "alternative" customers frequent to see and to photograph what performers and fashion-forward fans are wearing. The company also surveys teens who come into its stores about their favorite bands, clothing preferences, and ideas.[15]

As these examples prove, meaningful market research for a small business can be informal; it does not have to be highly sophisticated or expensive to be valuable.

Many entrepreneurs are discovering the power, the speed, the convenience, and the low cost of conducting market research over the World Wide Web. Online surveys, customer opinion polls, and other research projects are easy to conduct, cost virtually nothing, and help companies to connect with their customers. With Web-based surveys, businesses can get real-time feedback from customers, often using surveys they have designed themselves.

Faith Popcorn, a marketing consultant, encourages small business owners to be their own "trend-tracking sleuths." Merely by observing their customers' attitudes and actions, small business owners can shift their product lines and services to meet changing tastes in the market. To spot significant trends, Popcorn suggests the following[16]:

- Read as many current publications as possible, especially ones you normally would not read.
- Watch the top 10 TV shows because they are indicators of consumers' attitudes and values and what they're going to be buying.
- See the top 10 movies. They also influence consumer behavior, from language to fashions. In the 1930s, Hollywood star Clark Gable took off his shirt in *It Happened One Night* and revealed a bare chest; undershirt sales soon took a dive. After Will

Smith and Tommy Lee Jones donned Ray-Ban sunglasses in *Men in Black*, sales of the sunglasses tripled.[17]

- Talk to at least 150 customers a year about what they're buying and why. Make a conscious effort to spend time with some of your target customers, preferably in an informal setting, to find out what they are thinking.
- Talk with the 10 smartest people you know. They can offer valuable insights and fresh perspectives that you may not have considered.
- Listen to your children. ("They can be tremendous guides for you," says Popcorn.)

Next, entrepreneurs should make a list of the major trends they spot and should briefly describe how well their products or services match these trends. Companies whose products or services are diverging from major social, demographic, and economic trends rather than converging with them must change their course or run the risk of failing because their markets can evaporate before their eyes. How can entrepreneurs find the right match among trends, their products or services, and the appropriate target markets? Market research!

How To Conduct Market Research

The goal of market research is to reduce the risks associated with making business decisions. It can replace misinformation and assumptions with facts. Opinion and hearsay are not viable foundations on which to build a solid marketing strategy. Successful market research consists of four steps: define the objective, collect the data, analyze and interpret the data, and draw conclusions.

Step 1. Define the Objective The first, and most crucial, step in market research is to define the research objective clearly and concisely. A common error at this stage is to confuse a symptom with the true problem. For example, dwindling sales is not a problem; it is a symptom. To get to the heart of the matter, entrepreneurs must list all the possible factors that could have caused it. Do we face new competition? Are our sales representatives impolite or unknowledgeable? Have customer tastes changed? Is our product line too narrow? Do customers have trouble finding what they want? Is our Web site giving customers what they want? Is it easy to navigate? One entrepreneur wanting to discover the possible causes of his company's poorly performing Web site videotaped customers as they used it and then interviewed them. After studying the videos and listening to their comments, he redesigned the site to make it easier for users to maneuver through its pages and refocused its content.

In some cases, business owners may be interested in researching a specific type of question. What are the characteristics of my customers? What are their income levels? What radio stations do they listen to? Why do they shop here? What factors are most important in their buying decisions?

Step 2. Collect the Data The marketing approach that dominates today is **individualized (or one-to-one) marketing**, which gathers data on individual customers and then develops a marketing program designed specifically to appeal to their needs, tastes, and preferences. In a society in which people feel so isolated and interactions are so impersonal, one-to-one marketing gives a business a competitive edge. Companies following this approach know their customers, understand how to give them the value they want, and, perhaps most important, know how to make them feel special and important. The idea is to treat each customer as an individual, and the goal is to transform a company's best and most profitable customers into loyal, lifetime customers.

Individualized marketing requires business owners to gather and assimilate detailed information about their customers. Fortunately, owners of even the smallest companies now have access to affordable technology that creates and manages computerized databases, allowing them to develop close, one-to-one relationships with their customers. Much like gold nuggets waiting to be discovered, significant amounts of valuable information about customers and their buying habits is hidden *inside* many small businesses,

individualized (one-to-one marketing)
a system based on gathering data on individual customers and developing a marketing program designed to appeal specifically to their needs, tastes, and preferences.

tucked away in computerized databases. For most business owners, collecting useful information about their customers and potential new products and markets is simply a matter of sorting and organizing data that are already floating around somewhere in their companies. One marketing research expert explains the situation this way[18]:

> You know a lot about your customers. You know who they are, where they live, what their buying habits are. And if you're like most companies, you've done absolutely nothing with that pile of market intelligence. It just sits there, earning you no money and creating zero shareholder value.

The key is to mine the data that most companies have at their disposal and turn them into useful information that allows the company to court its customers with special products, services, ads, and offers that appeal most to them.

Silverman's

At Silverman's, a men's clothing in chain in the Dakotas, owner Stephen Silverman and a salesperson recently were reviewing a customer's purchasing history on a computer that doubles as a cash register. The flowchart revealed that he had spent more than $2,000 and had shopped four times in the previous six months. Looking at the average time between his visits, they noted that he should be coming in soon. Examining the profile more closely, they saw that this customer prefers double-breasted suits, likes Perry Ellis and Christian Dior suits in gray or blue, and has one shoulder slightly lower than the other. He also was among the customers who received a direct-mail ad featuring the upcoming season's new suits. Then, as if on cue, the customer walked in the door! The salesperson greeted him enthusiastically, personally, and knowledgeably. Within 15 minutes, he completed the sale, and the customer raved about how much he enjoys shopping at Silverman's because they know just what he likes and make it so easy to buy. Silverman's chalked up another sale to a satisfied, loyal customer thanks to its "segment of one" marketing strategy.[19]

Figure 8.2 shows how to develop a successful one-to-one marketing strategy.

How can entrepreneurs collect such valuable market and customer information? Two basic methods are available: conducting *primary research*, data you collect and analyze yourself, and gathering *secondary research*, data that have already been compiled and are available, often at a very reasonable cost (even free). Primary research techniques include the following:

FIGURE 8.2

How to Become an Effective One-to-One Marketer

Source: Adapted from Susan Greco, "The Road to One-to-One Marketing," *Inc.*, October 1995, pp. 56–66.

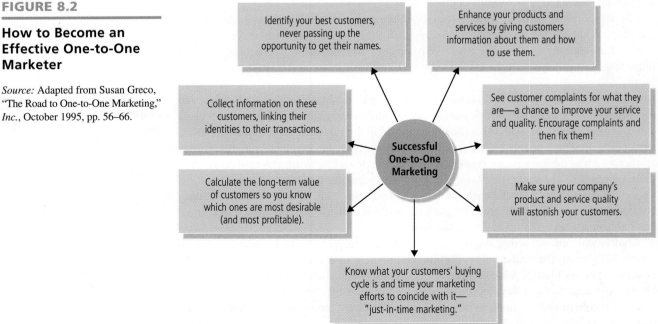

Identify your best customers, never passing up the opportunity to get their names.

Enhance your products and services by giving customers information about them and how to use them.

Collect information on these customers, linking their identities to their transactions.

See customer complaints for what they are—a chance to improve your service and quality. Encourage complaints and then fix them!

Successful One-to-One Marketing

Calculate the long-term value of customers so you know which ones are most desirable (and most profitable).

Make sure your company's product and service quality will astonish your customers.

Know what your customers' buying cycle is and time your marketing efforts to coincide with it—"just-in-time marketing."

■ *Customer surveys and questionnaires.* Keep them short. Word your questions carefully so that you do not bias the results, and use a simple ranking system (e.g., a 1-to-5 scale, with 1 representing "unacceptable" and 5 representing "excellent"). Test your survey for problems on a small number of people before putting it to use. Web surveys are inexpensive, easy to conduct, and provide feedback fast. Femail Creations, a mail-order company that sells clothing, accessories, and gifts to women, uses Web surveys to gather basic demographic data about its customers and to solicit new product ideas as well. Customer responses have led to profitable new product lines for the small company.[20]

■ *Focus groups.* Enlist a small number of customers to give you feedback on specific issues in your business—quality, convenience, hours of operation, service, and so on. Listen carefully for new marketing opportunities as customers or potential customers tell you what is on their minds. Once again, consider using the Web; one small bicycle company conducts 10 online focus groups each year at virtually no cost and gains valuable marketing information from them.

■ *Daily transactions.* Sift as much data as possible from existing company records and daily transactions—customer warranty cards, personal checks, frequent-buyer clubs, credit applications, and others.

■ *Other ideas.* Set up a suggestion system (for customers and employees) and use it. Establish a customer advisory panel to determine how well your company is meeting needs. Talk with suppliers about trends they have spotted in the industry. Contact customers who have not bought anything in a long time and find out why. Contact people who are not customers and find out why. Teach employees to be good listeners and then ask them what they hear.

One consumer research company, ShopperTrak RCT, employs "video mining," strategically located video cameras that record shoppers' behavior, to give its retail clients important marketing information. The information captured by the tiny cameras provides data on everything from the density of shopping traffic in a particular store aisle and how long shoppers linger at a display to the reactions of customers watching the latest high-definition televisions on display and an estimate of a store's conversion ratio, the percentage of people entering the store who actually make a purchase.[21]

Secondary research, which is usually less expensive to collect than primary data, includes the following sources:

■ *Business directories.* To locate a trade association, use *Business Information Sources* (University of California Press) or the *Encyclopedia of Associations* (Gale Research). To find suppliers, use *The Thomas Register of American Manufacturers* (Thomas Publishing Company) or *Standard and Poor's Register of Corporations, Executives, and Industries* (Standard and Poor Corporation). *The American Wholesalers and Distributors Directory* includes details on more than 18,000 wholesalers and distributors.

■ *Direct mail lists.* You can buy mailing lists for practically any type of business. *The Standard Rates and Data Service (SRDS) Directory of Mailing Lists* (Standard Rates and Data) is a good place to start looking.

■ *Demographic data.* To learn more about the demographic characteristics of customers in general, use *The Statistical Abstract of the United States* (Government Printing Office). Profiles of more specific regions are available in *The State and Metropolitan Data Book* (Government Printing Office). *The Sourcebook of Zip Code Demographics* (CACI, Inc.) provides detailed breakdowns of the population in every Zip Code in the country. *Sales and Marketing Management's Survey of Buying Power* (Bill Communications) has statistics on consumer, retail, and industrial buying.

■ *Census data.* The Bureau of the Census publishes a wide variety of reports that summarize the wealth of data found in its census database, which is available at most libraries and at the Census Bureau's Web site (http://www.census.gov).

■ *Forecasts.* The *U.S. Global Outlook* tracks the growth of 200 industries and gives a five-year forecast for each one. Many government agencies, including the U.S.

Department of Commerce, offer forecasts on everything from interest rates to the number of housing starts. A government librarian can help you find what you need.

■ *Market research.* Someone may already have compiled the market research you need. *The FINDex Worldwide Directory of Market Research Reports, Studies, and Surveys* (Cambridge Information Group) lists more than 10,600 studies available for purchase. Other directories of business research include *Simmons Study of Media and Markets* (Simmons Market Research Bureau Inc.) and the *A.C. Neilsen Retail Index* (A.C. Neilsen Company).

■ *Articles.* Magazine and journal articles pertinent to your business are a great source of information. Use the *Reader's Guide to Periodical Literature*, the *Business Periodicals Index* (similar to the *Reader's Guide* but focuses on business periodicals), and *Ulrich's Guide to International Periodicals* to locate the ones you need.

■ *Local data.* Your state department of commerce and your local chamber of commerce will very likely have useful data on the local market of interest to you. Call to find out what is available.

■ *World Wide Web.* Most entrepreneurs are astounded at the marketing information that is available on the World Wide Web (WWW). Using one of the search engines, you can gain access to a world of information—literally! The Web Destinations section of the Web site for this book provides links to hundreds of useful Web sites for entrepreneurs.

data mining

a process in which computer software that uses statistical analysis, database technology, and artificial intelligence finds hidden patterns, trends, and connections in data so that business owners can make better marketing decisions and predictions about customers' behavior.

Thanks to advances in computer hardware and software, data mining, once available only to large companies with vast computer power and large market research budgets, is now possible for even very small businesses. **Data mining** is a process in which computer software that uses statistical analysis, database technology, and artificial intelligence finds hidden patterns, trends, and connections in data so that business owners can make better marketing decisions and predictions about customer's behavior. By finding relationships among the many components of a data set, identifying clusters of customers with similar buying habits, and predicting customers' buying patterns, data mining gives entrepreneurs incredible marketing power.

For an effective individualized marketing campaign to be successful, business owners must collect three types of information:

1. *Geographic.* Where are my customers located? Do they tend to be concentrated in one geographic region?
2. *Demographic.* What are the characteristics of my customers (age, education levels, income, gender, marital status, and many other features).
3. *Psychographic.* What drives my customers' buying behavior? Are they receptive to new products or are they among the last to accept them? What values are most important to them?

Step 3. Analyze and Interpret the Data The results of market research alone do not provide a solution to the problem; business owners must attach some meaning to them. What do the facts mean? Is there a common thread running through the responses? Do the results suggest any changes needed in the way the business operates? Are there new opportunities the owner can take advantage of? There are no hard-and-fast rules for interpreting market research results; entrepreneurs must use judgment and common sense to determine what the results of their research mean.

Step 4. Draw Conclusions and Act The market research process is not complete until the business owner acts on the information collected. In many cases, the conclusion is obvious once a small business owner interprets the results of the market research. Based on an understanding of what the facts really mean, the owner must then decide how to use the information in the business. For example, the owner of a retail shop discovered from a survey that her customers preferred evening shopping hours over early morning hours. She made the schedule adjustment, and sales began to climb.

Data Mining: A Sure Bet for Harrah's

More than 25 million customers of Harrah's Entertainment, the parent company of 28 gambling casinos in 13 states, use personalized frequent-gambler cards (just like the ones shoppers use in grocery stores) called Total Rewards to earn free trips, meals, hotel rooms, and other perks from Harrah's. As good a deal as that is for the company's loyal customers, it's an even better deal for Harrah's. Harrah's uses the data it collects to refine its customer base, which is now divided into 90 distinct demographic and psychographic segments, and to customize its marketing efforts to individual customers' preferences. For instance, the company's research shows that those who comprise the "Upsides" group have the potential to double their gambling with Harrah's. The "Past Dues" are previous customers who have not visited a Harrah's casino recently but are likely to if given the proper incentive (which Harrah's does). When customers swipe their cards, the company knows which games they played, how many machines they played, how many wagers they made, the amount of their average wager, the total amount wagered, as well as the history of their gambling behavior at every Harrah's casino across the country. "By the time someone has made a third visit to us," says Tim Stanley, Harrah's Chief Information Officer (CIO), "we can predict where and how long they'll stay and how they'll play in the casino and spend money." The system also can tell managers how a visitor's bets are going in real time. When the system detects a gambler on a losing streak, it dispatches a "luck ambassador" with a small gift to boost gambler's ego. (Harrah's has learned that giving small gifts to losing gamblers encourages them to continue playing and increases the probability that they will return to a Harrah's casino.)

Harrah's collects all of this data about its customers' gambling tendencies in its information technology center in Memphis, Tennessee, and then uses data mining software to extract meaningful information about how best to market to them. Unlike most of its casino competitors, Harrah's does not target "high rollers," wealthy patrons who are capable of gambling hundreds of thousands of dollars at a time. Known to insiders as "whales," these big-stakes gamblers wager (and often

lose) huge sums of money, but casinos must court them with expensive, palatial suites, free shopping trips, free chartered flights, and other pricey "comps." Competition for this small, jet-set group is intense. Instead, Harrah's takes an approach used by the best retailers: targeting its best and most profitable customers, known inside the company as AEPs, "avid experienced players," who are low rollers with modest incomes and who spend between $100 and $499 per trip, and then working hard to keep them coming back. Harrah's still offers "comps"—free trips, dinners, tickets to a show, or hotel rooms—to its best customers, but they are much less expensive than those the high rollers expect. As a result, Harrah's casinos emphasize the games that will attract its target customers, slot machines and video poker machines, rather than the baccarat that the billionaire players prefer.

Analysis shows that 30 percent of Harrah's avid experienced players account for 80 percent of its revenues and nearly 100 percent of its profits. Why? Most of them are locals who visit Harrah's casinos regularly. Harrah's, of course, knows this, and markets to them accordingly. Using the information it has collected, the company separates its customers into three tiers based on their "customer value," a calculation of the total revenue they theoretically can generate for the company. The more they spend at Harrah's, the farther up the chain customers move, progressing from the gold level to platinum and finally diamond. Those with the highest customer value get special perks, ranging from cheaper hotel rates to deep discounts on a chartered jet headed for (where else?) a Harrah's casino.

Harrah's CEO, Gary Loveman, gets much of the credit for Harrah's creative marketing approach. "He has a lot of very unconventional ways to look at the gaming business—looking at it as a retailer, looking at the distribution points, taking a very macro point of view," says an industry analyst. "He's really brought a new and different perspective to anything [the industry] has seen in the past." Perhaps that's because Loveman was once a Harvard University Business School professor who had done consulting work with Harrah's after it had invested in a $17 million computer system to harvest data from its customers across all of its casinos, which at the time was a revolutionary idea in the industry. The company hired Loveman in 1998 as chief operating officer to orchestrate a plan for analyzing and using the data it collected as a potent marketing force. Loveman says that the entire data mining system is all about getting to know Harrah's customers so well through data profiling that the company can offer them the perfect reason to wager at Harrah's rather than at a competing casino. "All we used to know was how much money we made on each machine, but we couldn't connect what kind of customer used them," he says. "This is the replacement of intuition and hunch with science." The model uses neural networks and other sophisticated techniques of analysis to compare how much customers are capable of spending on gaming, how much they are actually spending, and how best to close that gap.

The payoff has been exceptional; Harrah's sales, profits, market share, and customer response rate to promotions have climbed dramatically. When Loveman started work, Harrah's was getting 36 cents of the total gaming dollars its customers spent. "We realized that if we could just get to 40 cents, that would be monstrous," he says. As a result of its more targeted marketing efforts, Harrah's "wallet share" currently stands at 45 cents! Harrah's is the most profitable company in the gaming industry. In addition, the company, once considered an "also-ran" in the industry, is now the largest casino operator in the United States after making several key acquisitions, including the famed Binion's Horseshoe Casino.

"We see 250,000 to 350,000 customers each day," says CIO Stanley, "and it's been very profitable for us to offer the best service to the biggest spenders. We have the data and can respond to customers individually in real time."

1. Work with a group of your classmates in a brainstorming session to identify other businesses (for example, a local small company) that could benefit from a data collection and mining system like the one Harrah's uses so effectively. In what ways could these businesses use data to become more effective marketers?
2. Discuss the ethical issues that Harrah's faces as a result of its data collection and data mining efforts.
3. What benefits does Harrah's gain from its data mining efforts and the resulting marketing strategy? What benefits do Harrah's customers gain?

Sources: Julie Schlosser, "Teacher's Bet," *Fortune*, March 8, 2004, pp. 158–164; Christina Binkley, "Taking Retailers' Cues, Harrah's Taps into Science of Gambling," *Wall Street Journal*, November 22, 2004, pp. A1, A8; Carol Pogash, "From Harvard Yard to Vegas Strip," *Forbes ASAP*, October 7, 2001, pp. 48–52; Joe Ashbrook Nickell, "Welcome to Harrah's," *Business 2.0*, April 2002, pp. 49–54; "About Us," Harrah's Entertainment, http://www.harrahs.com/about_us/index.html; Stephane Fitch, "Stacking the Deck," *Forbes*, July 5, 2004, pp. 132–134; Carol Hymowitz, "CEOs Use Technology to Gather Information, Build Customer Loyalty," *Wall Street Journal*, October 26, 2004, p. B1.

LEARNING OBJECTIVES
4. Describe how a small business can build a competitive edge in the marketplace using guerrilla marketing strategies: customer focus, quality, convenience, innovation, service, and speed.

Plotting a Guerrilla Marketing Strategy: How to Build a Competitive Edge

A competitive edge is crucial for business success. A small company has a competitive edge when customers perceive that its products or services are superior to those of its competitors. A business owner can create this perception in a variety of ways. Small companies sometimes try to create a competitive edge by offering the lowest prices. This approach may work for many products and services—especially those that customers see as being commodities—but price can be a dangerous criterion upon which to build a competitive edge. Independent hardware stores have discovered that large chains can use their buying power to get volume discounts and undercut the independents' prices. Entrepreneurs are using customer-focused techniques such as personal service and advice, individual attention, charge accounts, and convenience to differentiate themselves and to retain customer loyalty. Although they face fierce competition from large "category killers," these small companies are thriving by providing the services and products that their larger competitors cannot because they are too big and impersonal.

Successful entrepreneurs often use the special advantages that flow from their companies' smallness to build a competitive edge over their larger rivals. Their close contact with their customers, personal attention, focus on service, and organizational and managerial flexibility provide a solid foundation from which to build a towering competitive edge in the market. Small companies can exploit their size to become more effective than their

FIGURE 8.3

The Relationship Marketing Process

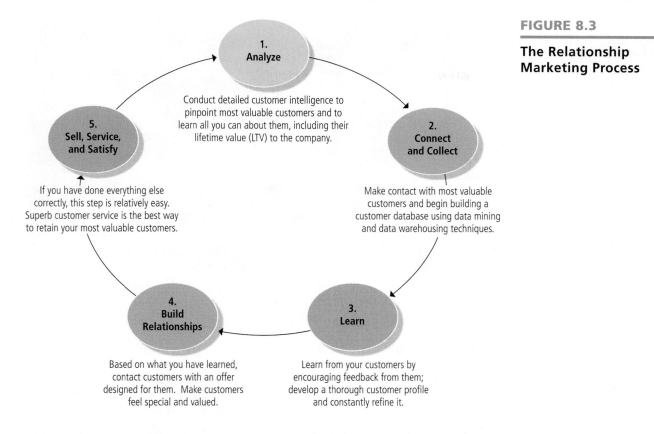

1. Analyze

Conduct detailed customer intelligence to pinpoint most valuable customers and to learn all you can about them, including their lifetime value (LTV) to the company.

5. Sell, Service, and Satisfy

If you have done everything else correctly, this step is relatively easy. Superb customer service is the best way to retain your most valuable customers.

2. Connect and Collect

Make contact with most valuable customers and begin building a customer database using data mining and data warehousing techniques.

4. Build Relationships

Based on what you have learned, contact customers with an offer designed for them. Make customers feel special and valued.

3. Learn

Learn from your customers by encouraging feedback from them; develop a thorough customer profile and constantly refine it.

larger rivals at **relationship marketing (customer relationship management) (CRM)**—developing, maintaining, and managing long-term relationships with customers so that they will want to keep coming back to make repeat purchases (see Figure 8.3). This concept recognizes that customers have a lifetime value to a business and that keeping the best customers over time may be a company's greatest sustainable advantage. CRM puts the customer at the center of a company's thinking, planning, and action and shifts the focus away from a product or service to customers and their needs and wants. CRM requires business owners to take the following steps:

- Collect meaningful information about existing customers and compile it in a database. Robert Ferrand, owner of SaddleTech, a small company that makes measurement tools and custom-fit orthotics for saddles, devotes time and energy to collecting information about his customers. "My first step in new customer relationships is to gather as much information about [my customers] and their needs as possible," he says.[22]
- Mine the database to identify the company's best and most profitable customers, their needs, and their buying habits. In most companies, a small percentage of customers account for the majority of sales and profits. These are the customers on whom a business should focus its attention and efforts.
- Use the mined information to develop lasting relationships with these best customers, the ones that offer the most attractive lifetime values to the company, and to serve them better. This often requires entrepreneurs to "fire" some customers that require more attention, time, and expense than they generate in revenue for the business. Failure to do so, however, reduces a company's return on its CRM effort.

relationship marketing (customer relationship management)
the process of developing, maintaining, and managing long-term relationships with customers so they will keep coming back to make repeat purchases.

Rachel Weingarten, owner of GTK Marketing Group, recalls a celebrity client whose arrogance and ever-escalating demands made life for Weingarten and her staff miserable. When the celebrity began ignoring the company's invoices, Weingarten decided to fire her as a client, even though the account represented a significant amount of the company's billings. The company quickly replaced the lost business, and sales climbed higher. Looking back, Weingarten says, "Not only had we done the right thing by banishing such a negative influence [on our company], but we opened ourselves up to attracting the right kind of client.[23]

GTK Marketing Group

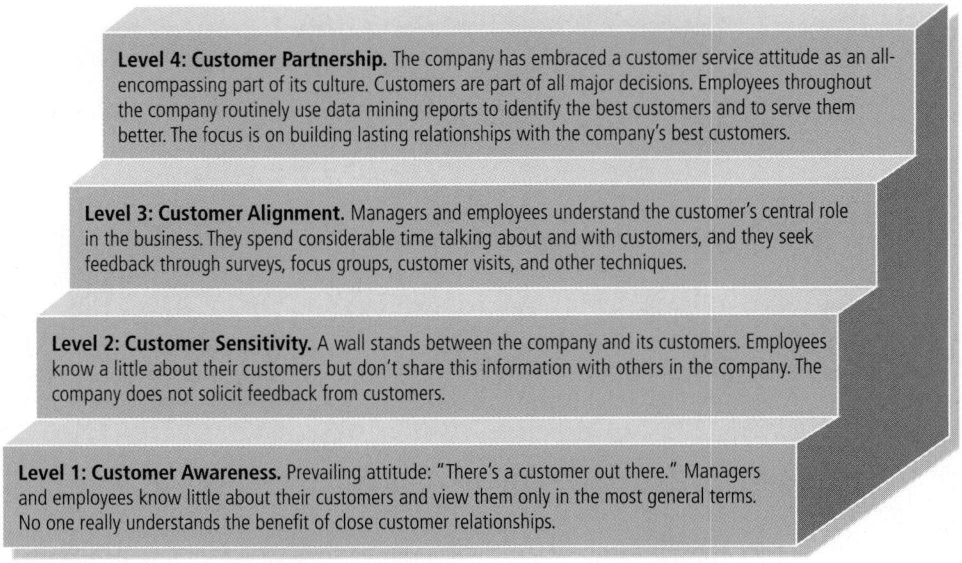

FIGURE 8.4

Four Levels of Customer Sensitivity

Level 4: Customer Partnership. The company has embraced a customer service attitude as an all-encompassing part of its culture. Customers are part of all major decisions. Employees throughout the company routinely use data mining reports to identify the best customers and to serve them better. The focus is on building lasting relationships with the company's best customers.

Level 3: Customer Alignment. Managers and employees understand the customer's central role in the business. They spend considerable time talking about and with customers, and they seek feedback through surveys, focus groups, customer visits, and other techniques.

Level 2: Customer Sensitivity. A wall stands between the company and its customers. Employees know a little about their customers but don't share this information with others in the company. The company does not solicit feedback from customers.

Level 1: Customer Awareness. Prevailing attitude: "There's a customer out there." Managers and employees know little about their customers and view them only in the most general terms. No one really understands the benefit of close customer relationships.

- Attract more customers that fit the profile of the company's best customers.
- Stay in contact with the company's customers between sales. For instance, e-mail or print newsletters that offer customers useful information or valuable tips not only create goodwill for a small business, but they also serve as important reminders, maintaining customers' interests in the company and keeping its name in front of its best customers.

revenue at risk
a measure that calculates the sales revenue a company would lose by measuring the percentage of customers that would leave because of poor service.

Businesses that provide poor customer service are in grave danger. Their owners discover that unless they provide their customers with satisfactory service and value, customers do not remain loyal, choosing instead to buy from other companies. Hepworth, a consulting firm that specializes in customer retention, measures its clients' **revenue at risk,** which calculates the sales revenue a company would lose by measuring the percentage of customers that would leave because of poor service. According to Hepworth's research, for companies that score in the top 25 percent on customer loyalty, revenue at risk averages just 3 percent. However, for companies that have loyalty scores in the bottom 25 percent, poor customer service puts at risk an average of more than 12 percent of company revenue.[24] Today, earning customers' loyalty requires businesses to take customer focus and service to unprecedented levels, and that requires building long-term relationships with customers. Research shows that customers who are satisfied with a company's products and level of customer service are more likely to be repeat customers and are less sensitive to price increases.[25] To make customer relationship management work, a small business must achieve the highest of the four levels of customer involvement illustrated in Figure 8.4.

Guerrilla Marketing Principles

To be successful guerrilla marketers, entrepreneurs must be as innovative in creating their marketing strategies as they are in developing new product and service ideas. Table 8.1 describes several low-cost, creative, and highly effective guerrilla marketing tactics small businesses have used to outperform their larger rivals.

From a broader perspective, the following 12 principles can help business owners to create powerful, effective guerrilla marketing strategies.

Find a Niche and Fill it As you learned in Chapter 3, "Designing a Competitive Business Model and Building a Solid Strategic Plan," many successful small companies choose their niches carefully and defend them fiercely rather than compete head to head with larger rivals. A niche strategy allows a small company to maximize the advantages of its size and to compete effectively even in industries dominated by giants by serving its target customers better than do its competitors. Focusing on niches that are too small to be

TABLE 8.1 Guerrilla Marketing Tactics

Help organize and sponsor a service- or community-oriented project.

Sponsor offbeat, memorable events. Build a giant banana split; rent a theater for a morning and invite kids for a free viewing.

Always be on the lookout for new niches to enter. Try to develop multiple niches.

Offer to speak about your business, industry, product, or service to local organizations.

Ask present customers for referrals.

Sell at every opportunity. One brewery includes a minicatalog advertising T-shirts and mugs in every six-pack it sells. Orders for catalog items are climbing fast.

Develop a sales "script" that asks customers a series of questions to hone in on what they are looking for and that will lead them to the conclusion that your product or service is IT!!

Offer customers gift certificates. They really boost your cash flow.

Create samples of your product and give them to customers. You'll increase sales later.

Offer a 100 percent, money-back, no-hassles guarantee. By removing the customer's risk of buying, you increase your product's attractiveness.

Create a "Frequent Buyer" program. Remember how valuable existing customers are. Work hard to keep the customers you have! One coffee shop kept its customers coming back with a punch-card promotion that gave a free pound of coffee after a customer purchased nine pounds.

Clip articles that feature your business and send reprints to customers and potential customers. Keep reminding them of who you are and why you're valuable to them.

Test how well your ads "pull" with coded coupons that customers bring in. Focus your ad expenditures on those media that produce the best results for you.

Create "tip sheets" to pass out to customers and potential customers—for example, landscape tips on lawn maintenance.

Find ways to make your product or service irresistible to your customers. One furniture company mails a Polaroid photo of big-ticket items customers are considering, and sales closing rates have climbed 25 percent.

Create an award for your community—for example, a landscape company presented a "best yard" award each season.

Conduct a contest in the community—for example, a photographer sponsored a juried photo contest for different age groups.

Collect testimonials from satisfied customers and use them in ads, brochures, and so on. Testimonials are one of the most effective forms of advertising.

Get a journalist to help you write a story "pitch" for local media.

Show an interest in your customers' needs. If you spot a seminar that would be of interest to them, tell them. Become a valuable resource for them.

Find unique ways to thank customers (especially first-time buyers) for their business—a note, a lunch, a gift basket, and so on.

Give loyal customers a "freebie" occasionally. You might be surprised at how long they will remember it.

Create a newsletter that features your customers or clients and their businesses—for example, a photo of a client using your product in his or her business.

Cooperate with other businesses selling complementary products and services in marketing efforts and campaigns, a process called fusion marketing. Share mailing lists and advertising time or space, or work together on a special promotion.

Use major competitors' coupons against them. The owner of an independent sandwich shop routinely pulled business from a nearby national chain by advertising that he would accept its coupons.

Market your company's uniqueness. Many customers enjoy buying from small companies that are different and unique. The owners of the only tea plantation in the United States used that fact to their advantage in establishing a customer base.

Sources: Adapted from Jay Conrad Levinson, "Attention Getters," *Entrepreneur,* March 1998, p. 88; Lynn Beresford, Janean Chun, Cynthia E. Griffin, Heather Page, and Debra Phillips, "Marketing 101," *Entrepreneur,* May 1996, pp. 104–114; Guen Sublette, "Marketing 101," *Entrepreneur,* May 1995, pp. 86–98; Denise Osburn, "Bringing Them Back for More," *Nation's Business,* August 1995, p. 31R; Jay Conrad Levinson, "Survival Tactics," *Entrepreneur,* March 1996, p. 84; Tom Stein, "Outselling the Giants," *Success,* May 1996, pp. 38–41.

attractive to large companies is a common recipe for success among thriving small companies. "Finding unserved niches is an excellent way to begin 'whupping' the big guys, if not in their own back yard, at least on the same street," says one marketing expert.[26]

Scottevest LLC

Scott Jordan, founder of Scottevest (pronounced "Scotty-vest") LLC, invented a stylish, lightweight jacket that doubles as a carry-on bag for frequent travelers, who always seem to have more electronic gear and other stuff than they have pockets to put it in. The Scottevest jacket has 22 adjustable pockets, all connected by electronic conduits woven into its seams that are designed to hold personal digital assistants (PDAs), cell phones, modems, portable computers, iPods, a host of other personal electronic devices, and a water bottle. With a portable power supply in a pocket, the wearer can power up all of his or her electronic gadgets through the jacket's "personal area network." Jordan's company received a publicity boost when a lead character on a cable television series donned one of the jackets. Scottevest was profitable in its first year of operation after ringing up sales of more than $3 million.[27]

Niche markets such as the one Jordan is targeting are ideally suited for small businesses. "If a small business follows the principles of targeting, segmenting, and differentiating, it doesn't have to collapse to larger companies," says marketing expert Phil Kotler.[28]

Don't Just Sell; Entertain Numerous surveys have shown that consumers are bored with shopping and that they are less inclined to spend their scarce leisure time shopping than ever before. Winning customers today requires more than low prices and wide merchandise selection; increasingly, businesses are adopting strategies based on **entertailing**—the notion of drawing customers into a store by creating a kaleidoscope of sights, sounds, smells, and activities, all designed to entertain—and, of course, sell (think Disney). The primary goal of entertailing is to catch customers' attention and engage them in some kind of entertaining experience so that they shop longer and buy more goods or services. Entertailing involves "making [shopping] more fun, more educational, more interactive," says one retail consultant.[29] To better serve its customers, Butterfly Studio, a New York City hair salon, now offers appointments well into the evening hours as well as upbeat music booming from an upgraded sound system and complimentary cocktails. Every month, the salon also sponsors a "Social Butterfly" event, at which customers enjoy mini-makeovers, drinks, and music and preview the latest product lines from jewelry designers. In just six months, the salon's owner says the approach increased sales by $50,000.[30]

Research supports the benefits of entertailing's hands-on, interactive, educational approach to selling; one study found that, when making a purchase, 34 percent of consumers are driven more by emotional factors such as fun and excitement than by logical factors such as price and convenience.[31] Entertailing's goal, of course, is not only to entertain but also to boost sales.

entertailing
a marketing concept designed to draw customers into a store by creating a kaleidoscope of sights, sounds, smells, and activities, all designed to entertain—and, of course, sell.

Cabela's

Few retailers practice entertailing as well as Cabela's, an innovative company that sells a wide selection of outdoor gear, mostly to hunters and fishermen. The company generates impressive sales through its catalog operations, its Web site, and its 22 stores, all of which are located in small towns in rural America. (Sydney, Nebraska, is host to one store and company headquarters.) What is even more amazing is that Cabela's has achieved its position as one of the hottest retailers in the industry by targeting an unusual customer: men who typically hate to shop. Men (and often their families) routinely drive hundreds of miles to visit a Cabela's store, where they spend hours shopping for everything from guns and decoys to fishing rods and tents. The stores' immense drawing power is due in part to the breadth and depth of the company's product lines. (Cabela's product lines run 6 to 10 times deeper than a typical discounter selling outdoor equipment.) Brothers Jim and Dick Cabela know that entertaining customers encourages them to shop longer and spend more. They spend lavishly on each store they build, including glass ceilings that let in natural light and aquariums containing 8,000 gallons of freshwater and game fish in natural settings. A major component of their entertailing strategy is the 45 percent of the floor space taken up by nature scenes situated throughout the stores. One store contains 237,000 square feet of space, the equivalent of five football fields, and another features a waterfall spilling into a stream stocked with trout. Others show off museum-quality taxidermy work. Shoppers stop to marvel at a mountain populated by a grizzly bear, caribou, and big-horn sheep or a display of an African savannah with two lions attacking a zebra. Each store contains about 400 displays, some of which cost more than $10,000. Cabela's may be the only company in the world to have an executive whose title is taxidermy purchasing specialist! Obviously, a hit with its prime target audience—men who enjoy the outdoors—Cabela's also is popular with their wives and children because of the expanded line of gifts and clothing it offers.[32]

Strive to Be Unique One of the most effective guerrilla marketing tactics is to create an image of uniqueness for your business. As you learned in Chapter 3, "Designing a Competitive Business Model and Building a Solid Strategic Plan, entrepreneurs can achieve a unique place in the market in a variety of ways, including through the products and services they offer, the marketing and promotional campaigns they use, the store layouts they design, and the business strategies they employ. The goal is to stand out from the crowd; few things are as uninspiring to customers as a "me-too" business that offers nothing unique.

In an industry dominated by giant companies such as Hallmark and Gibson, entrepreneur Bridget Hobson, founder of Quiplip Inc., has found a way to stand out in the greeting card business. Rather than create the standard sentimental cards decorated with flowers or pictures of serene mountain streams, Hobson sells a line of cards with sharp, sometimes caustic, but always funny messages (see Figure 8.5). Quiplip's Graphitude series uses charts and graphs to convey messages. One card shows a pie chart with "food," "sleep," "shelter," and "you" sectors; the biggest wedge, of course, is "you." A birthday card from Quiplip's Blunt line asks, "Did I at least get the month right? Happy Birthday." The message on a get well card is, "Can I try some of your painkillers? Get well soon." After experiencing difficulty finding cards that suited her personality, Hobson launched Quiplip and sales, which are growing rapidly, have surpassed $400,000. "There are so many warm and fuzzy cards out there," she says. "I [thought] there had to be a niche for these drier sarcastic cards."[33]

Quiplip Inc.

FIGURE 8.5

Samples from Quiplip Inc.'s Unique Line of Greeting Cards

Source: © Quiplip/Bridget Hobson, 2006. Quiplip Inc., http://www.quiplip.com.

Connect with Customers on an Emotional Level Closely linked to creating for a business an identity that resonates with customers is the strategy of creating an emotional attachment with customers. Companies that establish a deeper relationship with their customers than one based merely on making a sale have the capacity to be exceptional guerrilla marketers. These businesses win because customers receive an emotional boost every time they buy these companies' products or services. They connect with their customers emotionally by supporting causes that are important to their customer base, taking exceptional care of their customers, surpassing customers' expectations in quality and service, or making doing business with them an enjoyable experience. Building and nurturing an ongoing relationship with customers establishes a relationship of trust, a vital component of every marketing effort. One recent study found that 82 percent of customers stop using products from companies they believe have betrayed their trust.[34]

Another important aspect of connecting with customers is defining the company's **unique selling proposition (USP),** a key customer benefit of a product or service that sets it apart from its competition. To be effective, a USP must actually *be* unique, something the competition does not (or cannot) provide, as well as compelling enough to encourage customers to buy. Unfortunately, many business owners never define their companies' USP, and the result is an uninspiring "me-too" message that cries out "buy from us" without offering customers any compelling reason to do so.

A successful USP answers the critical question every customer asks: "What's in it for me?" A successful USP should express in no more than 10 words what a business can do for its customers. Can your product or service save your customers time or money, make their lives easier or more convenient, improve their self-esteem, or make them feel better? If so, you have the foundation for building a USP. For instance, the owner of a quaint New England bed and breakfast came up with a four-word USP that captures the essence of the escape her business offers guests from their busy lives: "Delicious beds, delicious breakfasts." Shmuel Gniwisch, CEO of Ice.com, an online jewelry store, expresses his company's USP quite simply: "We are a candy store for women." Sheila Paterson, co-founder of Marco International, a marketing consulting firm, says her company's USP is "Creative solutions for impossible marketing problems."[35]

The best way to identify a meaningful USP that connects a company to its target customers is to describe the primary benefit(s) its product or service offers customers and then to list other, secondary benefits it provides. A business is unlikely to have more than three top benefits. When describing the top benefits the company offers its customers, entrepreneurs must look beyond just the physical characteristics of the product or service. Sometimes the most powerful USP is the *intangible or psychological* benefit a product or service offers customers—for example, safety, security, acceptance, status, and others. Entrepreneurs must be careful, however, to avoid stressing minuscule differences that are irrelevant to customers. It is also important to develop a brief list of the facts that support your company's USP—for example, 24-hour service, a fully trained staff, awards won, and so on. By focusing the message on these top benefits and the facts supporting them, business owners can communicate their USPs to their target audiences in meaningful, attention-getting ways. Building a firm's marketing message around its core USP spells out for customers the specific benefit they get if they buy that product or service and why they should do business with your company rather than with the competition. Finally, once a small company begins communicating its USP to customers, it has to fulfill the promise. Nothing erodes a company's credibility as quickly as promising customers a benefit and then failing to deliver on that promise.

Many small companies are finding common ground with their customers on an issue that is becoming increasingly important to many people: the environment. Small companies selling everything from jeans to toothpicks are emphasizing their environmentally friendly products and are making an emotional connection with their customers in the process.

unique selling proposition (USP)

a key customer benefit of a product or service that sets it apart from the competition; it answers the critical question every customer asks: "What's in it for me?"

Rogan NYC and Recycline Inc.

Rogan NYC sells its Loomstate jeans, which are made of cotton grown without the use of pesticides and chemical fertilizers, at prices that range from $159 to $182. Eric Hudson, CEO of Recycline Inc., finds that customers are snapping up the personal care items his company makes from recycled products ranging from plastic soda bottles to grocery carts. Although the prices of many of the company's products, which include toothbrushes, shaving razors, toothbrushes, and more, are higher than those for standard products that are not made from recycled materials, demand remains strong among the company's target customers. "More and more people consider the environment, along with price and color, when they make a purchase," explains Hudson.[36]

Customers feel good about doing business with companies that support environmental causes, donate a portion of their pre-tax earnings to philanthropic organizations, and operate with a clear sense of fulfilling their social responsibility.

Create an Identity for Your Business through Branding One of the most effective ways for entrepreneurs to differentiate their businesses from the competition is to create a unique identity for it through branding. Although they may not have the resources to build a brand name as well known as Coca-Cola, entrepreneurs can be successful in building a brand identity for their companies on a smaller scale in the markets they serve. **Branding** involves communicating a company's unique selling proposition to its target customers in a consistent and integrated manner. A brand is a company's "face" in the marketplace, and it is built on a company's promise of providing quality goods or services to satisfy multiple customer needs. Companies that build brands successfully benefit from increased customer loyalty, the ability to command higher prices, greater visibility, and increased name recognition. "A brand is the most valuable piece of real estate in the world," says one marketing expert, calling it "a corner of the customer's mind."[37]

branding
communicating a company's unique selling proposition to its target customers in a consistent and integrated manner.

A California-based hamburger chain called In-N-Out Burger is thriving because its owners have built a meaningful brand methodically over time. Started in 1948 by Harry and Esther Snyder as a single drive-through stand in Baldwin Park, a Los Angeles suburb, In-N-Out has grown to 175 locations in three western states by sticking to its basic formula for success: top-quality, freshly ground beef on buns baked daily, with side orders of hand-cut potatoes served quickly. (The outlets have no freezers and no microwave ovens.) In other words, simplicity reigns—no chicken, no salads, no desserts, no kiddie toys—just really good basic burgers, fries, soft drinks, and milk shakes. In-N-Out does not compete by offering low prices and relying on 99-cent items to generate customer traffic like so many of its larger rivals; the company simply delivers what it promises. Devoted In-N-Out customers happily wait in line to pay full price for a double-double combo (two beef patties and two slices of cheese on a fresh-baked bun with an order of fries and a soft drink). The multiple components of the Snyder family's marketing strategy combine to make In-N-Out a huge success in a very competitive industry.[38]

In-N-Out Burger

Figure 8.6 shows a grid designed to help entrepreneurs to determine the attributes of their products and services that offer the greatest potential for building a brand.

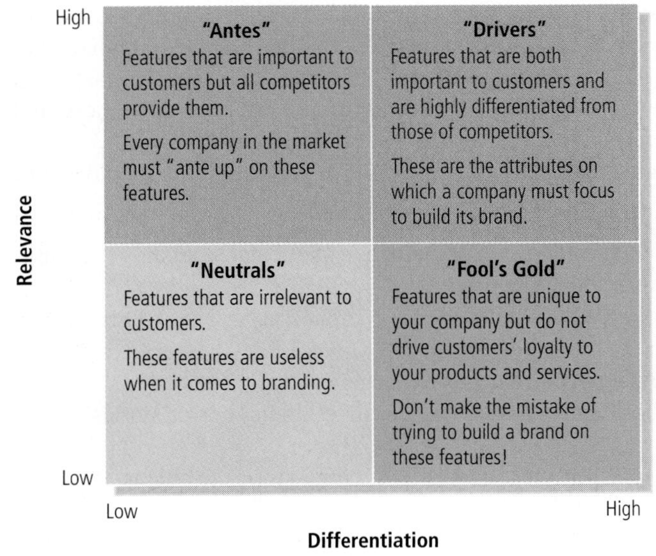

High		
"Antes"	**"Drivers"**	
Features that are important to customers but all competitors provide them.	Features that are both important to customers and are highly differentiated from those of competitors.	
Every company in the market must "ante up" on these features.	These are the attributes on which a company must focus to build its brand.	
"Neutrals"	**"Fool's Gold"**	
Features that are irrelevant to customers.	Features that are unique to your company but do not drive customers' loyalty to your products and services.	
These features are useless when it comes to branding.	Don't make the mistake of trying to build a brand on these features!	

Relevance (vertical axis, Low to High)

Low — Differentiation — High

FIGURE 8.6

Building a Brand

Source: Adapted from "What Really Matters in Building a Brand," The *McKinsey Quarterly*, May 2004, http://www.mckinseyquarterly.com/newsletters/chartfocus/2004_htm.

Start a Blog A Web log ("blog") is a frequently updated online personal journal that contains a writer's ideas on a multitude of topics and links to related sites. The proliferation of blogs has been stupendous; everyone from teenagers to giant corporations has created a blog. Technorati, a company that tracks blogs, estimates that 14 million blogs exist online, with 80,000 more being added daily.[39] Business blogging can be an effective part of a guerrilla marketing strategy, enabling an entrepreneur to communicate with large numbers of customers very economically. Blogs that attract the attention of existing and potential customers boost a company's visibility and its sales. Companies post their blogs, promote them on their Web sites and on other blogs, and then watch as the viral nature of the Web takes over with visitors posting comments and e-mailing their friends about the blog. In fact, many small companies allow customers to contribute to their blogs, offering the potential for one of the most valuable marketing tools: unsolicited endorsements from satisfied users. Blogging's informal dialogue is an ideal match for small companies whose culture and style also are casual.

Blogs can serve many business purposes, including keeping customers updated on new products, enhancing customer service, and promoting the company. Increasingly, they are becoming mainstream features on business Web sites. For example, Macromedia, a publisher of software, uses a blog to keep customers informed about product updates. If monitored regularly, blogs also can give entrepreneurs keen insight into their customers' viewpoints and preferences. One business writer says that blogs are "like a never-ending focus group."[40] Creating a blog is not risk-free, however. Companies must be prepared to deal with negative feedback from some visitors.

Denali Flavors

One company that has had tremendous success with blogs is Denali Flavors, a small business that creates specialty flavors for the ice cream industry, including the popular Moose Tracks® flavor. Even though Moose Tracks is one of the industry's best-selling flavors, managers at Denali Flavors realized that a significant percentage of the population had never heard of it. They decided to create four blogs aimed at different target audiences to promote their product. For instance, the Moosetopia blog is strictly an entertainment blog "written" by the Moose Tracks mascot (a moose, of course), who travels the globe and posts pictures of himself at famous tourist spots. The Denali Flavors blog provides an inside look at events inside the small company and asks for feedback from customers on a wide range of topics. The company's most popular blog is its Free Money Finance blog, which offers useful advice on personal finance issues and is "sponsored by" Denali. Since implementing its blogging marketing strategy, Denali reports that its Web site visits are up 25.7 percent, and that the time visitors spend on the site is up 23.4 percent—impressive results for an investment of just $700.[41]

Focus on the Customer Too many businesses have lost sight of the important component of every business: the customer. Wooing disillusioned customers back will require businesses to focus on them as never before. Businesses must realize that everything in the business—even the business itself—depends on creating a satisfied customer. One entrepreneur says, "If you're not taking care of your customers and nurturing that relationship, you can bet there's someone else out there who will."[42]

Businesses are just beginning to discover the true costs of poor customer relations. For instance:

- Sixty-seven percent of customers who stop patronizing a particular store do so because an indifferent employee treated them poorly.[43]
- Ninety-six percent of dissatisfied customers never complain about rude or discourteous service, but . . .
- Ninety-one percent will not buy from the business again.
- One hundred percent of those unhappy customers will tell their "horror stories" to at least 9 other people.
- Thirteen percent of those unhappy customers will tell their stories to at least 20 other people.[44]

According to the authors of *Keeping Customers for Life*, "The nasty result of this customer indifference costs the average company from 15 to 30 percent of gross sales."[45] Because 70 percent of the average company's sales come from present customers, few can afford to alienate any shoppers. In fact, the typical business loses 20 percent of its customers each year. However, a study by the consulting firm Bain & Co. shows that companies that retain just 5 percent more customers experience profit increases of at least 25 percent and, in some cases, as much as 95 percent.[46] Other studies show that high levels of customer retention result in above-average profits and superior growth in market share.[47] Powell's Books, a Portland, Oregon, landmark known as the "City of Books" for its huge inventory, has built a solid base of loyal customers in its 30-plus-year history, enabling the company to compete successfully against industry giants Barnes and Noble and Books-a-Million. Powell's Books has hosted several weddings for customers who met there, and one customer's ashes are interred (at his request) in one of the columns that is made to look like a stack of books at the northwest entrance to the store. Now *that's* customer loyalty![48]

Because about 20 percent of a typical company's customers account for about 80 percent of its sales, it makes more sense to focus resources on keeping the best (and most profitable) customers than to spend them chasing "fair weather" customers who will defect to any better deal that comes along. Suppose that a company increases its customer base by 20 percent each year, but it retains only 85 percent of its existing customers. Its effective growth rate is just 5 percent per year [20% − (100% − 85%) = 5%]. If this same company can raise its customer retention rate to 95 percent, its net growth rate *triples* to 15 percent [20% − (100% − 5%) = 15%].[49]

Although winning new customers keeps a company growing, keeping existing ones is essential to success. Research shows that repeat customers spend 67 percent more than new customers. In addition, attracting a new customer actually costs the typical business *seven to nine times* as much as keeping an existing one.[50] Therefore, small business owners would be better off asking "How can we improve customer value and service to encourage our existing customers to do more business with us?" than "How can we increase our market share by 10 percent?" The *real* key to marketing success lies in a company's existing customer base.

COMPANY
Profile

Chico's

At Chico's, a clothing store targeting women of the baby-boomer generation, customers who purchase $500 in merchandise become members of Chico's Passport Club, which gives them a variety of perks, including a five percent discount on all purchases. The Club already has more than 435,000 members, and another 2 million are working toward the $500 goal. Chico's management is well aware of the benefits of retaining these loyal customers. Club members "spend 40 percent more than the usual customer and come in six times as often," says chief financial officer Charles Klemen.[51]

The most successful small businesses have developed a customer focus and have instilled a customer satisfaction attitude *throughout* the company. They understand that winning customers for life requires practicing **customer experience management (CEM),** systematically creating the optimum experience for their customers every time they interact with the company (see Figure 8.7). Companies with world-class CEM attitudes set themselves apart by paying attention to little things such as responding to questions or complaints promptly, remembering a customer's unique product or service preferences, or sending a customer a copy of an article of interest to him or her. Taking care of the small interactions a company has with its customers over time adds up to a positive service experience. For example, a small flower shop offers a special service for customers who forget that special event. The shop will insert a card reading, "Please forgive us! Being short-handed this week, we were unable to deliver this gift on time. We hope the sender's thoughtfulness will not be less appreciated because of our error. Again, we apologize."[52] Avis, the car rental company that "tries harder," breaks down the entire care rental process into more than 100 incremental steps and analyzes each one in meticulous detail from the customer's perspective to improve its customers' experiences. The company

customer experience management (CEM)
the process of systematically creating the optimum experience for their customers every time they interact with the company.

FIGURE 8.7

Principles of Customer Experience Management (CEM)

Source: Adapted from "Wake-up Call: To Fix CRM, Fix the Customer Experience Now!," BearingPoint White Paper, Fall 2005, p. 5, http://www.bearingpoint.com.

Every customer interaction includes:

- Intimate understanding of each customer's needs, wants, preferences, and peculiarities.
- Personal, customized messages in marketing, sales, service, and advertising.
- Consistent, courteous, and professional treatment by everyone in the company.
- Responsive, rapid handling of requests, questions, problems, and complaints.
- Helpful information and advice delivered proactively, where appropriate.
- Involvement of caring, well-trained people rather than strict reliance on technology for service delivery.
- Long-term view of the company/customer relationship rather than a focus on "making a sale."
- Emphasis on sustaining an ongoing relationship built on trust and respect.
- Frequent and visible demonstrations of commitment to nurturing the company/customer relationship.

Satisfied, loyal, repeat (and profitable) customers

frequently surveys customers to determine the factors that are most important to them (convenience, speed, safety, customer service, and price often top the list) and then sets out to find ways to incorporate those into every transaction. The Avis Preferred service program, which makes rental car pickup a snap and shaves 10 minutes off the average pickup time, is just one example of Avis' customer-focused efforts.[53]

How do these companies manage their customer relationships and stay focused so intently on their customers? They constantly ask customers four basic questions and then act on what they hear:

1. What are we doing right?
2. How can we do that even better?
3. What have we done wrong?
4. What can we do in the future?

Build-A-Bear Workshops

Maxine Clark, founder of Build-A-Bear Workshops, a company that lets kids of all ages build their own stuffed animals in an upbeat, interactive experience, visits two or three of her company's 200-plus stores every week so that she can spend face-to-face time with customers. She hands out thousands of business cards (her title is listed as "chief executive bear"), which results in thousands of e-mails from her customers. What does she get from all of this customer interaction? "Ideas," she says. "I used to feel like I had to come up with all the ideas myself, but it's so much easier relying on my customers [for help]." Many customers' ideas have made it to Build-A-Bear's shelves. To test ideas, Clark submits them to her "virtual cub advisory council," a community of children on her e-mail list that also helps her spot trends on which the company can capitalize. Clark says one secret to running a successful business is "never forgetting what it's like to be a customer."[54]

Table 8.2 offers some basic strategies for developing and retaining loyal customers.

Devotion to Quality   In this intensely competitive global business environment, quality goods and services are a prerequisite for success—and even survival. According to one marketing axiom, the worst of all marketing catastrophes is to have great advertising and a poor-quality product. Customers have come to expect and demand quality goods and services, and those businesses that provide them consistently have a distinct competitive advantage. Research by Josh Gordon, author of *Selling 2.0*, shows that almost 60 percent

TABLE 8.2 Strategies for Developing and Retaining Loyal Customers

Identify your best customers and give them incentives to return. Focus resources on the 20 percent of customers that account for 80 percent of sales.

When you create a dissatisfied customer, fix the problem fast. One study found that, given the chance to complain, 95 percent of customers will buy again *if* a business handles their complaints promptly and effectively. The worst way to handle a complaint is to ignore it, to pass it off to a subordinate, or to let a lot of time slip by before dealing with it.

Make sure your business system makes it easy for customers to buy from you. Eliminate unnecessary procedures that challenge customers' patience.

Encourage customer complaints. You can't fix something if you don't know it's broken. Find out what solution the customer wants and try to come as close to that as possible.

Contact lost customers to find out why they left. You may uncover a problem you never knew existed.

Ask employees for feedback on improving customer service. A study by Technical Assistance Research Programs (TARP), a customer service research firm, found that front-line service workers can predict nearly 90 percent of the cases that produce customer complaints. Emphasize that *everyone* is part of the customer satisfaction team.

Get total commitment to superior customer service from top managers—and allocate resources appropriately.

Allow managers to wait on customers occasionally. It's a great dose of reality. The founder of a small robot manufacturer credits such a strategy with saving his company. "We now require every officer of this company—including myself—to meet with customers at least four times a month," he says.

Carefully select and train *everyone* who will deal with customers. Never let rude employees work with customers.

Develop a service theme that communicates your attitude toward customers. Customers want to feel they are getting something special.

Reward employees "caught" providing exceptional service to the customer.

Get in the habit of calling customers by name. It's one of the most meaningful ways of connecting with your customers.

Remember: The customer pays the bills. Special treatment wins customers and keeps them coming back.

Sources: Adapted from Jerry Fisher, "The Secret's Out," *Entrepreneur,* May 1998, pp. 112–119; Laura M. Litvan, "Increasing Revenue with Repeat Sales," *Nation's Business,* January 1996, pp. 36–37; "Encourage Customers to Complain," *Small Business Reports,* June 1990, p. 7; Dave Zielinski, "Improving Service Doesn't Require a Big Investment," *Small Business Reports,* February 1991, p. 20; John H. Sheridan, "Out of the Isolation Booth," *Industry Week,* June 19, 1989, pp. 18–19; Lin Grensing-Pophal, "At Your Service," *Business Start-Ups,* May 1995, pp. 72–74.

of customers who change suppliers say they switched because of problems with a company's products or services.[55]

Today, quality is more than just a slogan posted on the company bulletin board; world-class companies treat quality as a strategic objective—an integral part of a company's strategy and culture. This philosophy is called **total quality management (TQM)**—quality not just in the product or service itself, but also in *every* aspect of the business and its relationship with the customer and *continuous improvement* in the quality delivered to customers.

Companies on the cutting edge of the quality movement are developing new ways to measure quality. Manufacturers were the first to apply TQM techniques, but retail, wholesale, and service organizations have seen the benefits of becoming champions of quality. They are tracking customer complaints, contacting "lost" customers, and finding new ways to track the cost of quality (COQ) and their return on quality (ROQ). ROQ recognizes that, although any improvement in quality may improve a company's competitive ability, only those improvements that produce a reasonable rate of return are worthwhile. In essence,

total quality management (TQM)

the philosophy of producing a high-quality product or service and achieving quality in every aspect of the business and its relationship with the customer; the focus is on continuous improvement in the quality delivered to customers.

ROQ requires managers to ensure that the quality improvements they implement will more than pay for themselves.

The key to developing a successful TQM philosophy is seeing the world from the customer's point of view. In other words, quality must reflect the needs and wants of the customer. How do customers define quality? According to one survey, Americans rank the quality of a product in this order: reliability (average time between failures), durability (how long it lasts), ease of use, a known or trusted brand name, and, last, low price.[56]

PediSedate

After using traditional anesthesiology equipment (masks that cover the entire face) to sedate young children for medical procedures and seeing the fear and trauma it caused his young patients, anesthesiologist Geoffrey Hart set out to design a new, less-intimidating device and came up with the PediSedate, a high-quality medical device that looks—and acts, at least in part—like a toy. PediSedate is a brightly colored headset that connects to a CD player or a Gameboy. One earpiece delivers music or the sounds of the video game, and the other earpiece uses sophisticated equipment to monitor oxygenation of the blood. Once the child is comfortable with the headset, a swiveling snorkel that swings down in front of the child's mouth delivers the sedative gas and monitors the young patient's respiration. Hart's focus on creating a quality product that delivers ease of use for both young patients and the physicians using PediSedate has led to a successful business. Hart says that many of the children on whom his invention was first used liked it so much that they asked if they could take it home![57]

When buying services, customers look for similar characteristics: tangibles (equipment, facilities, and people), reliability (doing what you say you will do), responsiveness (promptness in helping customers and in solving problems), and assurance and empathy (conveying a caring attitude). For example, the owner of a very successful pest-control company offers his customers a unique, unconditional guarantee: If the company fails to eliminate all insect and rodent breeding and nesting areas on a client's premises, it will refund the customer's last 12 monthly payments and will pay for one year's service by another exterminator. The company has had to honor its guarantee only once in 17 years.

Companies that excel at providing quality products and services discover tangible benefits in the form of increased sales, more repeat customers, higher customer retention, and lower costs. Small businesses that have succeeded in building a reputation for top-quality products and services rely on the following guidelines to "get it right the first time":

- Build quality into the process; don't rely on inspection to obtain quality.
- Foster teamwork and dismantle the barriers that divide departments.
- Establish long-term ties with select suppliers; don't award contracts on low price alone.
- Provide managers and employees the training needed to participate fully in the quality improvement program.
- Empower workers at all levels of the organization; give them authority and responsibility for making decisions that determine quality.
- Get managers' commitment to the quality philosophy. Otherwise, the program is doomed. Describing his leadership role in his company's TQM philosophy, one CEO says, "People look to see if you just talk about it or actually do it."[58]
- Rethink the processes the company uses to get its products or services to its customers. In its early years, Cirrus Design, a maker of small, four-seat airplanes, was plagued by poor quality in its avionic devices and frames that vibrated excessively. By listening to customer complaints and suggestions, employees at the small company redesigned the production process and improved the quality of its airplanes enough to make them the fastest-selling small planes in the world today.[59]
- Be willing to make changes in processes wherever they may be necessary.
- Reward employees for quality work. Ideally, workers' compensation is linked clearly and directly to key measures of quality and customer satisfaction.
- Develop a company-wide strategy for constant improvement of product and service quality.

Attention to Convenience Ask customers what they want from the businesses they deal with and one of the most common responses is "convenience." In this busy, fast-paced world of dual-career couples and lengthy commutes to and from work, customers increasingly are looking for convenience. Convenience is the driving force behind the boom in home cleaning services. The U.S. Department of Commerce reports that 80 percent of two-income families now use such services.[60] Several studies also have found that customers rank easy access to goods and services at the top of their purchase criteria. Unfortunately, too few businesses deliver adequate levels of convenience, and they fail to attract and retain customers. One print and framing shop, for instance, alienated many potential customers with its abbreviated business hours—9 to 5 daily, except for Wednesday afternoons, Saturdays, and Sundays, when the shop was closed! Other companies make it a chore to do business with them. In an effort to defend themselves against unscrupulous customers, these businesses have created elaborate procedures for exchanges, refunds, writing checks, and other basic transactions. One researcher claims, "What they're doing is treating the 98% of honest customers like crooks to catch the 2% who are crooks."[61]

Successful companies go out of their way to make sure that it is easy for customers to do business with them. The HomeBased Warehouse in San Bernadino, California, has borrowed an idea from fast food restaurants to make buying lumber more convenient for its customers: drive-in windows. More than 200 cars a day pull in and load up with lumber before driving to the cashier's booth to pay. The drive-through "has increased [sales] volume and enhanced contractor business. They like the time-saving [convenience] of being able to drive in, load up, and cash out at the outside register," says one manager.[62] In Las Vegas, a couple can pull up into the Tunnel of Vows at the famous Little White Chapel, and an ordained minister at the drive-through window will marry them! Business has been so brisk that the owner of the chapel recently expanded the tunnel to include "a romantic ceiling with cherubs and starlights."[63]

How can entrepreneurs boost the convenience level of their businesses? By conducting a "convenience audit" from the customer's point of view to get an idea of its ETDBW ("Easy-to-Do-Business-With") index:

- Is your business located near your customers? Does it provide easy access?
- Are your business hours suitable to your customers? Should you be open evenings and weekends to serve them better?
- Would customers appreciate pickup and delivery service? The owner of a restaurant located near a major office complex installed a Web site and a fax machine to receive orders from busy office workers; a crew of employees delivers lunches to the workers at their desks.
- Does your company make it easy for customers to make purchases on credit or with credit cards?
- Are your employees trained to handle business transactions quickly, efficiently, and politely? Waiting while rude, poorly trained employees fumble through routine transactions destroys customer goodwill.
- Does your company offer "extras" that make customers' lives easier? With a phone call to one small gift store, a customer in need of a special gift simply tells how much she wants to spend, and the owner takes care of the rest—selecting the gift, wrapping it, and shipping it. All the customer has to do is pay the invoice when it arrives in the mail.
- Can you "bundle" some of your existing products or services to make it easier for customers to use them? Whether it involves gardening tools or a spa treatment, assembling products and services into ready-made, all-in-one kits appeals to busy customers and can boost sales.
- Can you adapt existing products to make them more convenient for customers? When J.M. Smucker Company began test marketing a pre-made, frozen peanut butter and jelly sandwich, CEO Tim Smucker was amazed at the results. The sandwiches, called Uncrustables, generated $20 million in sales, and Smucker now sells them nationwide.[64]

■ Does your company handle telephone calls quickly and efficiently? Long waits "on hold," transfers from one office to another, and too many rings before answering signal to customers that they are not important. Jerre Stead, CEO of Ingram Micro Inc., a distributor of computer products, expects every telephone call to the company to be answered within three seconds![65]

An entire industry of small companies dedicated to convenience has emerged to help busy customers to decorate their homes during the hectic holiday season. Landscapers, florists, interior decorators, and other owners of seasonal businesses looking to boost cash flow during their slowest time of the year are charging fees ranging from just a few hundred dollars to tens of thousands of dollars to deck homeowners' halls with festive lights and decorations, saving them the time and the trouble of decorating. "We live in a society where we hire people to do everything [for us]—walk our dogs, feed our fish, do our windows," says Mark Martin, who focuses on his plant maintenance company 11 months of the year. "Why not hire someone to decorate our homes for the holidays?" asks Martin, whose clients call him "Mr. Christmas."[66]

Concentration on Innovation Innovation is the key to future success. Markets change too quickly and competitors move too fast for a small company to stand still and remain competitive. Because they cannot outspend their larger rivals, small companies often turn to superior innovation as the way to gain a competitive edge. "Never stop innovating or taking risks," says Michael Dell, founder of Dell Computer. "Keep raising the bar, not just for the industry but for yourself."[67]

Thanks to their organizational and managerial flexibility, small businesses often can detect and act on new opportunities faster than large companies. Innovation is one of the hallmarks of entrepreneurs, and it shows up in the new products, unique techniques, and unusual marketing approaches they introduce. Despite their limited resources, small businesses frequently are leaders in innovation. For instance, in the hotly competitive pharmaceutical industry, the dominant drugs in many markets were discovered by small companies rather than the industry giants such as GlaxoSmithKline or Upjohn with their multi-million-dollar R&D budgets.

Obviously, there is more to innovation than spending megadollars on research and development. "It takes money to fund a business," says one small business advisor, "but it's continuous creativity that keeps the venture running smoothly and profitably."[68] How do small businesses manage to maintain their leadership role in innovating new products and services? They use their size to their advantage, maintaining their speed and flexibility much like a martial arts expert does against a larger opponent. Their closeness to their customers enables them to read subtle shifts in the market and to anticipate trends as they unfold. Their ability to concentrate their efforts and attention in one area also gives small businesses an edge in innovation. One venture capitalist explains, "Small companies have an advantage: a dedicated management team totally focused on a new product or market."[69]

Tiaki International

Entrepreneur Chris Anderson is the founder of New Zealand-based Tiaki International, the world's first gold-farming company. Anderson, 31 years old, worked for 8 years refining a chemical process that causes certain plants to "hyperaccumulate" gold particles that exist in soil. Planting canola, corn, or mustard plants treated with the company's special chemical solution on abandoned mining sites enables them to absorb gold particles from the soil and store them in their roots and leaves. The plants detoxify the soil and, when harvested and incinerated at 92°F, the plants yield the gold they have stored. "The value of the 'crop' should provide a cash incentive for miners to clean their land," says one industry analyst.[70]

Dedication to Service and Customer Satisfaction Customer service has become a lost art in our society. A recent survey by the Pew Charitable Trusts found that 46 percent of customers had walked out of a store within the last year because of poor service.[71] The penalties associated with providing poor customer service can be severe. One study by Amdocs, a company specializing in CRM products, found that customers are willing to withstand just two negative customer service experiences before taking their business elsewhere.[72] Smart companies are rediscovering that unexpected innovative, customized service can be a powerful strategic weapon. Providing incomparable service—not necessarily a low price—is one of the most effective ways to attract and maintain a growing customer base. In fact, one study of consumer behavior reported that 73 percent of customers buy for reasons other than price.[73] "If you want to be a great marketer," says Pat Croce, entrepreneur and former owner of the Philadelphia 76ers professional basketball team, "you have to fulfill what you are selling with customer service, with exceeding expectations, with giving a little extra, with surprising the customer."[74]

Although more companies than ever before are preaching customer service to employees, the reality is that most Americans still rate U.S. companies low on customer service. In one survey of 200 companies, 57 percent of the managers said that "customer service" is their top priority. However, 73 percent said that the only way to survive is with "price competition."[75] This short-run philosophy short-circuits real progress toward superior customer service. "Sales starts a customer relationship," says one customer service expert. "Service turns it into a profitable or unprofitable relationship."[76]

Successful businesses recognize that superior customer service is only an intermediate step toward the goal of customer *satisfaction*. These companies seek to go beyond customer satisfaction, striving for *customer astonishment*. They concentrate on providing customers with quality, convenience, and service *as their customers define those terms.*

After 26 years in the retail boat business, William McGill, owner of MarineMax, an association of luxury boat retailers, recognized that his industry was characterized by extremely poor service. McGill saw an opportunity to differentiate MarineMax by offering customers unparalleled service and "no-haggle" prices. For inexperienced customers or those who are just plain nervous about taking a new boat out by themselves for the first time, MarineMax will provide a captain at no extra charge. The captain will keep coming back until the customer learns to handle the boat alone. The company also has a staff of repair technicians who are on call 24 hours per day. Every MarineMax boat over 20 feet in length carries a full two-year warranty from bow to stern, twice as long as the typical warranty in the industry. Because McGill has learned that his customers' families influence how often they upgrade to bigger (and more expensive) boats, he sponsors regular seminars and fun events to teach spouses and kids how to get the most out of their boats—and to look at new, larger models. MarineMax also perpetuates customer loyalty through its "getaways," trips that range from one-day outings on a Minnesota lake to two-week trips to the Bahamas. The company services all boats before a trip and sends along a crew of technicians to fix any problems that crop up. All of this superior service costs MarineMax money, and McGill's prices reflect the extra costs. The company figures that 2.5 percent to 6 percent of a boat's price goes to cover the extra service it provides. Customers do not seem to mind slightly higher prices, however; MarineMax's profit margin is more than twice the industry average, and sales are climbing.[77]

COMPANY Profile

MarineMax

Certainly the least expensive—and the most effective—way to achieve customer satisfaction is through friendly, personal service. Numerous surveys of customers in a wide diversity of industries, from manufacturing and services to banking and high tech, conclude that the most important element of service is "the personal touch." Calling customers by name, making attentive, friendly contact, and truly caring about their needs and wants is much more essential than any other factor—even convenience, quality, and speed. In our society, business transactions have become so automated that the typical customer is starved for personal attention. Genuine customer service requires that the business bridge that service gap, treat each customer as an individual, and transform "high-tech" applications into a "high-touch" attitude.

© RHYMES WITH ORANGE
Hilary B. Price. King Features
Syndicate.

How can a company achieve stellar customer service and satisfaction?

Listen to customers. The best companies constantly listen to their customers and respond to what they hear. This allows them to keep up with customers' changing needs and expectations. The best way to find out what customers really want and value is to ask them. Businesses rely on a number of techniques including surveys, focus groups, telephone interviews, comment cards, suggestion boxes, toll-free hotlines, and regular one-on-one conversations (perhaps the best technique). The Internet is another useful tool for getting feedback from customers; many companies solicit complaints, suggestions, and ideas through their Web sites.

JetBlue

David Neeleman, founder of JetBlue, a highly successful low-cost airline, boards at least one flight each month for the sole purpose of spending time with customers and listening to their ideas and comments. What does he get out of the experience? Ideas. "I get most of my ideas on flights," Neeleman says. "Customers tell me what they want." In addition, staying in close contact with his customers enables Neeleman to spot trends and shifts in the market, both of which are valuable as he makes strategic decisions for the company. He also sends a clear and important message to the company's employees and shapes its culture. On the flights, Neeleman not only talks with customers, but he also dons an apron and works with the flight attendants on board to serve drinks and snacks. Employees "know that Neeleman isn't sitting behind a desk somewhere counting his stock options," says one businessman who encountered Neeleman on a recent flight. "He's putting in overtime, and he's doing it with them. He's on their team."[78]

It is important for entrepreneurs to keep customer feedback in its proper perspective, however. Although listening to customers does produce valuable feedback for business owners in many areas, it is *not* a substitute for an innovative company culture, solid market research, and a well-devised marketing plan. Companies that rely solely on their customers to guide their marketing efforts often find themselves lagging the competition. Customers rarely have the foresight to anticipate market trends and do not always have a clear view of how new products or services could satisfy their needs.

Define superior service. Based on what customers say, managers and employees must decide exactly what "superior service" means in the company. Such a statement should (1) be a strong statement of intent, (2) differentiate the company from others, and (3) have value to customers. Deluxe Corporation, a printer of personal checks, defines superior service quite simply: "Forty-eight hour turnaround; zero defects."[79]

Set standards and measure performance. To be able to deliver on its promise of superior service, a business must establish specific standards and measure overall performance against them. Satisfied customers should exhibit at least one of three behaviors: loyalty (increased customer retention rate), increased purchases (climbing sales and sales per customer), and resistance to rivals' attempts to lure them away with lower prices (market share and price tolerance).[80] Companies must track their performance on these and other service standards and reward employees accordingly.

Examine your company's service cycle. What steps must a customer go through to get your product or service? Business owners often are surprised at the complexity that has seeped into their customer service systems as they have evolved over time. One of the most effective techniques is to work with employees to flowchart each component in the company's service cycle, including *everything* a customer has to do to get your product or service. The goal is to look for steps, policies, and procedures that are unnecessary, redundant, or unreasonable and then to eliminate them.

Hire the right employees. The key ingredient in the superior service equation is *people*. There is no substitute for friendly, courteous sales/service representatives. "You can't create world-class customer care if you hire run-of-the-mill employees," says customer service expert Ron Zemke.[81] Business owners must always be on the lookout for employees who are empathetic, flexible, articulate, creative, and able to think for themselves.

Train employees to deliver superior service. Successful businesses train *every* employee who deals directly with customers; they don't leave customer service to chance. Superior service companies devote one to five percent of their employees' work hours to training, concentrating on how to meet, greet, and serve customers. Leading mail-order companies such as Lands' End and L.L. Bean spend *many* hours training the employees who handle telephone orders before they deal with their first customer.

Founded as an apothecary in New York's East Village in 1851, Kiehl's has become a highly successful seller of cosmetics and skin-care products by emphasizing superior customer service and product quality. The company's employees take the time to educate customers about the product line and then let them test it themselves by giving away more than 12 million sample packets and tubes of product samples each year. Kiehl's understands the importance of a highly trained staff to its strategy and invests heavily in upgrading their skills. The company dedicates 10 percent of its compensation budget to send new hires to four-week training programs in New York, Miami, or San Francisco.[82]

Kiehl's

Empower employees to offer superior service. One of the most important variables that determine whether employees deliver superior service is the degree to which they perceive they have permission to do so. The goal is to push decision making down the organization to the employees who have contact with customers. This includes giving them the latitude to circumvent "company policy" if it means improving customer satisfaction. If frontline workers don't have this power to solve disgruntled customers' problems, they fear being punished for overstepping their boundaries and become frustrated, and the superior service cycle breaks down. To be empowered, employees need knowledge and information, adequate resources, and managerial support.

Treat employees with respect and show them how valuable they are. Satisfied employees tend to create satisfied customers. "There's a definite proven connection between employee happiness and customer happiness," says JoAnna Brandi, a customer service consultant. In fact, one study reports that a one percent change in employee morale results in a two percent change in customer satisfaction.[83]

Don Slivensky, CEO of MicroTek Computer Labs, a computer training company, understands the connection well and works hard to keep his employees happy. In the past, Slivensky has paid for employees' honeymoons, provided down payments for employees to purchase homes, and sent $500 gift cards to workers expecting babies. "If people are happy," he says, "they enjoy taking care of customers."[84]

MicroTek Computer Labs

Use technology to provide improved service. The role of technology is not to create a rigid bureaucracy but to free employees from routine clerical tasks, giving them more time and better tools to serve customers more effectively. Ideally, technology gives workers the information they need to help their customers and the time to serve them.

To use technology effectively, entrepreneurs must ask, "What is the best technology for our strategy?" This question that leads to four key service issues: (1) What is our primary service strategy? (i.e., What do we want customers to think of when they hear our name?) (2) What barriers are preventing our company from fully implementing this strategy now? (3) What, if anything, can technology do to overcome these barriers? (4) What is our strategy for encouraging our customers to adopt the new technology?[85]

Waldorf-Astoria Hotel

At the Hilton's Waldorf-Astoria Hotel in New York City, guest service agents equipped with wireless tablet PCs and portable printers greet road-weary travelers who want to bypass the front desk and go to their rooms. Hotel employees take the front desk to the customers, enabling them to check in as they exit their cabs or to check out as they step off the elevator. Hilton uses the wireless computer system in several of its upscale hotels across the world, saving guests time and making their hotel stays more convenient. "We've checked in groups of guests on the beach in Hawaii," says Thomas Spitler, Hilton's vice-president of operations.[86]

Reward superior service. What gets rewarded gets done. Companies that want employees to provide stellar service must offer rewards for doing so. A study by the National Science Foundation concluded that when pay is linked to performance, employees' motivation and productivity climb by as much as 63 percent.[87]

Get top managers' support. The drive toward superior customer service will fall far short of its target unless top managers support it fully. Success requires more than just a verbal commitment; it calls for managers' involvement and dedication to making service a core company value. Achieving customer satisfaction must become part of the strategic planning process and work its way into every nook and cranny of the organization. Once it does, employees will be able to provide stellar customer service with or without a checklist of "do's and don'ts."

View customer service as an investment, not an expense. The companies that lead the way when it comes to retaining their customers view the money they spend on customer service as an investment rather than an expense. One of the most effective ways for entrepreneurs to learn this lesson is to calculate the cost of poor customer service to their companies. Once they calculate it, the cost of lost customers due to poor service is so astonishing to most business owners that they quickly become customer service zealots. For instance, the owner of a small restaurant calculated that if every day he lost to poor service one customer who spent just $5 per week, his business was losing $94,900 in revenue per year! The restaurateur immediately changed his approach to customer service.

Emphasis on Speed Technology, particularly the Internet, has changed the pace of business so dramatically that speed has become a major competitive weapon. Today's customers expect businesses to serve them at the speed of light. Providing a quality product at a reasonable price once was sufficient to keep customers happy, but that is not enough for modern customers, who can find dozens of comparable products with a just few mouse clicks. Speed reigns. World-class companies recognize that reducing the time it takes to develop, design, manufacture, and deliver a product reduces costs, increases quality, improves customer satisfaction, and boosts market share. A study by McKinsey and Company found that high-tech products that come to market on budget but six months late earn 33 percent less profit over five years. Bringing the product out on time but 50 percent over budget cuts profits just 4 percent![88] Service companies also know that they must build speed into their business system if they are to satisfy their impatient, time-pressured customers.

Victory in this time-obsessed economy goes to the company that can deliver goods and services the fastest, not necessarily those that are the biggest and most powerful. Business is moving so rapidly today that companies "need to accomplish in 90 days what traditionally took a year," explains one entrepreneur.[89] Businesses that can satisfy their customers' insatiable appetites for speed have a distinct advantage.

Super Fast Pizza

After deciding not to order a delivery pizza one cold January night because of the typical extended wait, Scott Matthew woke the next morning with an idea for a pizza delivery business with a competitive advantage based on speed. "I woke up thinking about vans with ovens in them where you cook the pizza on the way to the [customer]," says Matthew. "You'd be able to deliver it in about 20 minutes." Within a year, Matthew had launched Super Fast Pizza in Fond Du Lac, Wisconsin, using specially customized software and Sprinter vans converted into licensed mobile kitchens. The software enables employees to take orders by telephone and e-mail even if they are en route to another delivery. Not only do customers get their pizzas faster, but the pizzas themselves are fresher and hotter than those from standard pizza delivery services because they truly are straight out of the oven. Super Fast Pizzas rang up sales of $300,000 in its first year of operation, and Matthew has plans to take the concept nationwide within 10 years.[90]

This philosophy of speed is based on **time compression management (TCM),** which involves three principles:

1. Speeding new products to market.
2. Shortening customer response time in manufacturing and delivery.
3. Reducing the administrative time required to fill an order.

time compression management (TCM)
a marketing strategy that relies on three principles: (1) speeding products to market, (2) shortening customer response time in manufacturing and delivery, and (3) reducing the administrative time required to fill an order.

Studies show plenty of room for improvement; most businesses waste 85 to 99 percent of the time it takes to produce products or services without ever realizing it.[91] Speeding up their businesses process and service delivery times can give a small company a competitive edge.

Ping

Ping, a maker of golf clubs and golf accessories, has built a sophisticated design, manufacturing, and order fulfillment system that enables it to ship custom-made clubs ordered from one of 2,500 pro shops in the United States to its customers within 48 hours. The process originates with a Web-based ordering system and includes a computer system that schedules production runs in the most efficient manner. Applying the same techniques to its regular product line, Ping can turn out 13 new product lines a year, a fivefold increase from 2001. Computer-aided design software and programs allow engineers to test various designs virtually and shave months off the time required for traditional design and testing methods. "We're a small, family-owned business competing with Nike, Callaway, and TaylorMade Adidas," says John Solheim, son of founder Karsten Solheim. "Our business model has evolved. Not only do we pay attention to detail, but we also have custom-fitting, assembly-to-order, and rapid delivery."[92]

Although speeding up the manufacturing process is a common goal, companies using TCM have learned that manufacturing takes only 5 to 10 percent of the total time between an order and getting the product into the customer's hands. The rest is consumed by clerical and administrative tasks. "The primary opportunity for TCM lies in its application to the administrative process," says one manager.

Companies relying on TCM to help them turn speed into a competitive edge should apply the following guidelines:

- "Re-engineer" the entire process rather than attempt to do the same things in the same way, only faster. Peter Schultz, founder of Symyx, a small technology company in Santa Clara, California, applied the principles of rapid drug development used in the pharmaceutical industry to the field of materials science and changed the way new chemical compounds are created. Symyx's technology allows its employees to test small amounts of chemicals and metals in parallel—up to 1,000 combinations per day—to create new materials. Processes that not so long ago required two years of intense work now produce marketable results in less than that. "If you have speed advantage, you win," explains a manager at Dow Chemical Company, one of Symyx's customers.[93]
- Create cross-functional teams of workers and give them the power to attack and solve problems. In world-class companies, product teams include engineers, manufacturing workers, sales people, quality experts—even customers.
- Set aggressive goals for time reduction and stick to the schedule. Some companies using TCM have been able to reduce cycle time from several weeks to just a few hours!
- Rethink the supply chain. Can you electronically link with your suppliers or your customers to speed up orders and deliveries?
- Instill speed in the culture. At Domino's Pizza, kitchen workers watch videos of the fastest pizza makers in the country.
- Use technology to find shortcuts wherever possible. Properly integrated into a company's strategy for speed, technology can restructure a company's operating timetable. Rather than build costly, time-consuming prototypes, many time-sensitive businesses use computer-aided design and computer-assisted manufacturing (CAD/CAM) to speed product design and testing.
- Put the Internet to work for you. Perhaps nothing symbolizes speed better than the Internet, and companies that harness its lightning-fast power can become leaders in TCM.

Be the Consultant

Netflix: Keeping Customers Happy

When he launched Netflix, Reed Hastings transformed the video rental business by introducing a new business model based on the convenience the Internet offers and by creating the world's largest online DVD rental service. Rather than visit video rental stores with limited inventories (between 7,000 and 8,000 titles on average) and contend with return deadlines and possible late fees, customers subscribe to Netflix for a monthly fee and gain access to an inventory of more than 55,000 titles, including box office hits as well as niche films and foreign films, that they can keep as long as they like without having to worry about paying late fees. Subscribers simply go to the Netflix Web site and create a list of films they want to see, and the Netflix customer service system takes over. Invisible to the customer, the system processes the orders from the customer's viewing list and mails the DVDs (no additional shipping charges) from one of its 37 distribution centers. When the customer returns a DVD (free return shipping) to Netflix, the system ships the next video on the customer's list.

Although the process appears on the surface to be quite simple, it actually is the result of a complex software system containing more than one million lines of code that Hastings, a former software entrepreneur, master-minded. One of the system's most ingenious and most popular features is Cinematch, another sophisticated program that Hastings created to recommend movies that are most likely to appeal to Netflix customers using the videos they have selected in the past. The more movies a customer rates, the more accurate are Cinematch's recommendations. For instance, one cus-tomer who gives *Pride and Prejudice* a high rating might find that Cinematch recommends *Shakespeare in Love*. Another customer who enjoys *O' Brother, Where Art Thou?* would see *Second Hand Lions* appear as a rec-ommendation. "It's like having your own personal box office," says Kelly Mooney, president of a customer ser-vice consulting firm. Cinematch has a database of more than half-a-billion movie ratings, and Netflix customers add a million new ones each day.

Cinematch is an important part of Netflix's strategy because it uses the principles of mass customization to deliver a one-to-one customer service experience, something that is vital to companies operating online, where customer interactions are either nonexistent or highly impersonal. "Our warehouse employees never interact with the customer," explains Hastings, "so what we focus on instead is having the Web site be the most personalized Web site in the world. If the Starbucks secret is a smile when you get your latte, ours is that the Web site adapts to the individual's taste." The Cinematch system works so well that its recommenda-tions account for 70 percent of the movies Netflix cus-tomers rent.

To offer customers more value for their monthly membership fees, Netflix recently launched its "Friends" service. Members who sign up can see which movies their friends are watching, which ones they liked and did not like, and what they say in their reviews about the movies they have watched. Not only does the service engage customers, but it also allows Netflix to identify a spike in the demand for a particu-lar film so it can avoid stockouts of that film. Netflix also has upgraded its customer service software so that single accounts can create multiple profiles—for instance, one profile for each member of a family or for each roommate in an apartment. Each person in the account can create his or her own video queue, giving movies as diverse as *Amadeus, March of the Penguins*, and *The Wedding Crashers* equal play time in the living room.

Hastings' goal for Netflix is to have 20 million sub-scribers by 2010. How? Hastings recognizes that video-on-demand will be the next "big thing" in the industry and could make Netflix's existing business model obso-lete. His strategy is to build strategic alliances with other companies such as TiVo to allow customers of both ser-vices to download movies over the Internet. In fact, Hastings projects that by 2010, Netflix will deliver most of its movies over the Internet rather than shipping DVDs through its distribution centers. Cable television companies, which currently offer their own versions of video-on-demand, and other download services will offer Netflix stiff competition. Hastings, however, believes that his company's emphasis on providing superior customer service will make the difference. "The best companies continue to innovate, listen to their cus-tomers, and come up with things they'll like," says one industry analyst, who sees Netflix as the industry leader. "That's how Netflix operates."

Hastings understands the importance of customer retention and does everything in his power to hold on to Netflix customers, who can cancel their subscriptions at any time without penalty. "Once you subscribe," says Hastings, "our interest is purely your happiness."

1. Identify the key components of Netflix's guerrilla marketing strategy and evaluate the effectiveness of each one on a 10-point scale: 1 (very ineffec-tive) to 10 (very effective). Explain the reasons for your rankings.
2. Identify the opportunities and threats facing Netflix. How can Netflix use its existing marketing strategy to ensure that it retains its competitive advantage in the face of these opportunities and threats?
3. Form a small team with some of your classmates, visit the Netflix Web site (http://www.netflix.com), and engage in a brainstorming session to develop a unique selling proposition (USP) for the company.

Sources: Jena McGregor, "At Netflix, the Secret Sauce Is the Software," *Fast Company*, October 2005, pp. 47–51; John Heilemann, "Showtime for Netflix," *Business 2.0*, March 2005, pp. 36–38; "Netflix Makes It Big in Hollywood," *Fortune*, June 13, 2005, p. 34; "About Netflix," Netflix, http://www.netflix.com/PressRoom?id=1005; "Netflix," *Wikipedia*, http://en.wikipedia.org/wiki/Netflix; Alan Cohen, "The Great Race," *FSB*, December 2002/January 2003, pp. 42–48; Brad Stone, "I Want a Movie! Now!" *Newsweek*, September 13, 2005, www.msnbc.com/id/5915470/site/newsweek; Jeffrey M. O'Brien, "The Netflix Effect," *Wired*, Issue 10.12, December 2002; "Wal-Mart, Netflix Agree on DVD Deal," *ZDNet*, http://news.zdnet.com/2100-9595_22-5713298.html.

World Wide Web (WWW)
the vast network that links computers around the globe via the Internet and opens up endless oceans of information to its users.

Marketing on the World Wide Web

Much like the telephone and the fax machine, the World Wide Web has become an essential business tool for entrepreneurs. Online retail sales now exceed $145 billion annually, far above the $8 billion generated in 1998, and are growing at a rate of 12 to 18 percent a year.[94] Experts estimate that in 2008, 10 percent of all retail sales will occur online.[95] Recognizing the potential for boosting sales for their businesses, growing numbers of entrepreneurs are integrating the Web into their guerrilla marketing strategies. A survey by Harris Interactive reports that 35 percent of small business owners say that having a Web site is the most important tool available to them for expanding their businesses.[96]

Although 70 percent of small business owners in the United States have a presence on the **World Wide Web** (double the percentage of small businesses that were operating online in 2002), the vast network that links computers around the globe via the Internet and opens up endless oceans of information to its users, many of them are still struggling to understand how to make the Web work for them and how they can establish a meaningful presence on it.[97] The Web gives small businesses the power to broaden their marketing scope to unbelievable proportions. By building a creative, attractive Web site, even the smallest companies can market their products and services to customers around the globe. Indeed, one of greatest benefits to small business owners of launching a Web site is providing customers with another convenient shopping channel. A study of small business owners in the United States, Germany, and the United Kingdom reports that more than 75 percent of respondents say their Web sites offer major benefits to their marketing efforts, overall customer communication, and their ability to attract new customers.[98]

With its ability to display colorful graphics, sound, animation, and video as well as text, the Web allows small companies to equal—even surpass—their larger rivals' Web presence. Although small companies cannot match the marketing efforts of their larger competitors dollar for dollar, a creative Web page can be the great equalizer in a small company's marketing program, giving it the ability to conduct global business at very low cost. Because Web-based businesses are open around the clock seven days per week, they can reach customers anywhere in the world. In addition, the Web gives entrepreneurs the flexibility to operate their companies from virtually anywhere in the world.

Small companies that have established well-designed Web sites and understand the Web's power as a marketing tool are reaping the benefits of e-commerce. If a business has the proper marketing strategy in place, it can use the Web to magnify its ability to provide superior customer service at minimal cost. A customer-oriented Web site allows customers to gather information about a product or service, have their questions answered, download diagrams and photographs, place orders easily, and track the progress of their orders. As a marketing tool, the Web allows entrepreneurs to provide both existing and potential customers with meaningful information in an *interactive* rather than a passive setting. Well-designed Web sites often include interactive features that allow customers to access information about a company and its history, three-dimensional views or videos of its products and services in use, and other features such as question-and-answer sessions with experts or the ability to conduct e-mail conversations with company officials.

Small companies that have had the greatest success selling on the Web have marketing strategies that emphasize their existing strengths and core competencies. Their Web marketing strategies reflect their "brick-and-mortar" marketing strategies, often focusing on building relationships with their customers rather than merely scouting for a sale. These companies understand their target customers and know how to reach them using the Web. They create Web sites that provide meaningful information to their customers, that customize themselves based on each customer's interests, and that make it easy for customers to find what they want. In short, their Web sites create the same sense of trust and personal attention customers get when dealing with a local small business.

That's exactly what Jeremy Shepherd, founder of PearlParadise.com, has accomplished with his company's Web site. While working as a flight attendant for Northwest Airlines in 1996, Shepherd had a layover in Beijing, where he purchased a complete set of freshwater pearls for just $20 as a Christmas gift for his girlfriend. When she had them appraised, they both were surprised that the pearls were valued at $600—30 times what he had paid for them! Shepherd, then just 22 years old, saw a prime business opportunity and launched PearlParadise.com (and opened a retail store in Santa

PearlParadise.com

Entrepreneur Jeremy Shepherd regularly travels to China, where he purchases the pearls that he sells on his company's Web site, pearlparadise.com. Shepherd has discovered that selling online upscale items such as pearls requires an integrated marketing strategy.

Monica, California). Over the next eight years, he traveled to China more than 200 times, learning everything he could about pearls and buying millions of them. In 1997, PearlParadise.com's online sales were just $8,000. Within eight years, they had climbed to more than $5 million. The key to Shepherd's online success has been his marketing strategy. To encourage customers to make high-dollar purchases online, he blankets the PearlParadise.com Web site with educational materials ranging from information on how pearls are produced and harvested to how the various types of pearls differ from one another. Other key components of the marketing strategy are the company's 90-day money-back guarantee and its second-appraisal guarantee: If an independent appraisal fails to produce a value that is at least five times the price the customer paid, the customer is entitled to a full refund. Shepherd also makes sure that when customers call or e-mail with questions, one of his highly trained employees, all of whom have earned pearl certificates from the Gemological Institute of America, responds promptly. Word-of-mouth advertising from satisfied customers is important in the high-end jewelry business, and Shepherd does everything he can to encourage it. The Web site features a customer feedback section, and twice a year (before Christmas and Mother's Day), Shepherd invites customers to a special Web site designed just for them where they can purchase featured items at significant discounts. One recent Christmas sale featuring Tahitian pearls generated $100,000 in sales. Shepherd also donated some of his company's pearls and gift certificates to be included in the stars' gift baskets at recent Oscar Awards ceremonies, resulting in visits from many celebrities, including Emmy Rossum (*Phantom of the Opera*) and Alan Rickman (the Harry Potter films). Another tactic that Shepherd uses to cultivate customer loyalty and trust is sending customers a documentary on pearling, a video filmed at one of the company's pearl suppliers and narrated by Shepherd. Online sales now account for half of PearlParadise.com's annual revenues.[99]

Using the Web as a marketing tool requires more than establishing a Web site and waiting for customers to come calling. Just as in any marketing venture, the key to successful marketing on the World Wide Web is selling the right product or service at the right price to the right target audience. Entrepreneurs on the Web, however, also have two additional challenges: attracting Web users to their Web sites and converting them into paying customers. That requires setting up an electronic storefront that is inviting, easy to navigate, interactive, and offers more than a monotonous laundry list of standard items. It also requires promoting the Web site in all of a company's marketing material, from print ads and radio spots to business cards and company letterhead. With a solid marketing strategy as a guide, small companies can—and are—selling everything from wine and vacations to jewelry and electronics successfully on the Web. You will learn more about e-commerce in the next chapter.

The Marketing Mix

The major elements of a marketing strategy are the four P's of marketing—**p**roduct, **p**lace, **p**rice, and **p**romotion. These four elements are interconnected, and, when properly coordinated with a solid marketing plan, increase the sales appeal of a product or service. Small

LEARNING OBJECTIVES
6. Discuss the "four P's" of marketing—product, place, price, and promotion—and their role in building a successful marketing strategy.

FIGURE 8.8

The Product Life Cycle

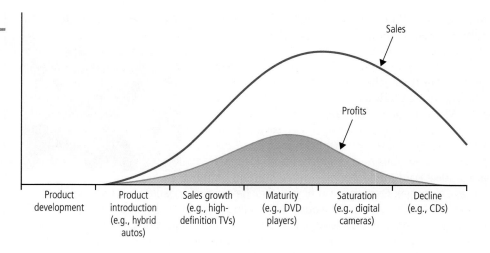

business managers must integrate these elements to maximize the impact of their product or service on the consumer. All four P's must reinforce the image of the product or service the company presents to the potential customer. One long-time retailer claims, "None of the modern marvels of computerized inventory control and point-of-sale telecommunications have replaced the need for the entrepreneur who understands the customer and can translate that into the appropriate merchandise mix."[100]

Product

The product itself is an essential element in marketing. A product is any item or service that satisfies the need of a customer. Products can have form and shape, or they can be services with no physical form. Products travel through various stages of development. The **product life cycle** (see Figure 8.8) describe these stages of growth; knowing which stage of the life cycle a product is in allows managers to make decisions about whether to continue selling the product, when to introduce new follow-up products, and when to introduce changes to an existing product.

product life cycle
the stages of development, growth, and decline in a product's life.

Storm Products

Bill Chrisman, founder of Storm Products, has stimulated sales in an otherwise flat market by introducing scented bowling balls. Scents range from chocolate and piña colada to grape and cherry.

Storm Products, a small maker of bowling balls, has generated a small growth spurt in an otherwise flat market with the introduction of its scented bowling balls. Company founder Bill Chrisman, an avid bowler and owner of a small chemical company, thought that existing bowling balls were far too plain and decided to manufacture a ball infused with pleasant scents, including grape, amaretto, cherry, cranberry, plum, chocolate, and piña colada. Many professional bowlers on the Pro Bowling Tour use Storm's scented balls, and sales at the small company are climbing.[101]

introductory stage
the stage in which a product or service must break into the market and overcome customer inertia.

In the **introductory stage,** marketers present their product to potential consumers. Initial high levels of acceptance are rare. Generally, new products must break into existing markets and compete with established products. Advertising and promotion help the new product to become recognized more quickly. Potential customers must get information about the product, how to use it, and the needs it can satisfy. The cost of marketing a product at this level of the life cycle is usually high because a company must overcome customer resistance and inertia. Thus, profits are generally low, or even negative, in the introductory stage.

After the introductory stage, the product enters the **growth and acceptance stage.** In the growth stage, customers begin to purchase the product in large enough numbers for sales to rise and profits to materialize. Products that reach this stage, however, do not necessarily become successful. If in the introductory or the growth stage the product fails to meet consumer needs, it does not sell and eventually disappears from the marketplace. According to Greg Stevens, president of a new-product research company, an average of just 2 new products are launched out of every 3,000 ideas generated; of the 2 actually launched, only 1 succeeds.[102] For successful products, sales and profit margins continue to rise through the growth stage.

In the **maturity and competition stage,** sales volume continues to rise, but profit margins peak and then begin to fall as competitors enter the market. Normally, this causes reduction in the product's selling price to meet competition and to hold its share of the market.

Sales peak in the **market saturation stage** of the product life cycle and give the marketer fair warning that it is time to introduce the next-generation product.

The final stage of the product life cycle is the **product decline stage.** Sales continue to drop, and profit margins fall drastically. However, when a product reaches this stage of the cycle, it does not mean that it is doomed to failure. Products that have remained popular are always being revised. No firm can maintain its sales position without product innovation and change. Binney & Smith, the maker of Silly Putty, which was first introduced at the 1950 International Toy Fair and has had lifetime sales of more than 300 million "eggs," the equivalent of 4,500 tons of silly putty, has introduced new gold, Day-Glo, and glow-in-the-dark colors. These innovations have caused the classic toy's sales to rebound, appealing to new generations of children.[103]

The time span of the stages in the product life cycle depends on the type of products involved. High-fashion and fad clothing have a short product life cycle, lasting for only four to six weeks. Products that are more stable may take years to complete a life cycle. Research conducted by MIT suggests that the typical product's life cycle lasts 10 to 14 years, but the length of that life cycle appears to be shrinking.[104]

Thomas Venable, owner of Spectrum Control, Inc., a maker of control systems for the electronics industry, uses the concept of the product life cycle to plan the introduction of new products to his company's product line. Too often, companies wait too late into the life cycle of one product to introduce another. The result is that they are totally unprepared when a competitor produces "a better mousetrap" and their sales decline. "If you are not developing something new early in the current product's life cycle, you're living on borrowed time," says Venable. "If you wait until your line is mature, you're dead."[105]

In Venable's industry, a 12-year life cycle is common. His company's strategy is to begin turning out prototypes of sequel products 2 to 3 years before the maturity phase of the original product (see Figure 8.9). "The whole idea behind the process is to avoid crises," Venable says. "You want to be ready to go with the second product, just as the first one is about to die off."[106]

growth and acceptance stage

the stage in which customers begin to purchase a product in large enough numbers for sales to rise and profits to materialize.

maturity and competition stage

the stage in which sales rise, but profits peak and then fall as competitors enter the market.

market saturation stage

stage in which sales peak, indicating the time to introduce the next-generation product.

product decline stage

the stage in which sales continue to fall and profit margins decline drastically.

FIGURE 8.9

Time between Introduction of Products

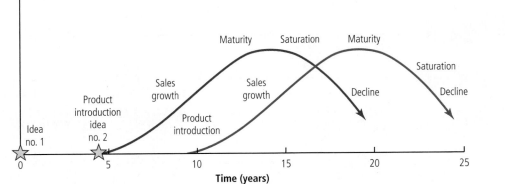

Place

Place (or method of distribution) has grown in importance as customers expect greater service and more convenience from businesses. This trend is one of the forces driving the rapid growth of the Web as a shopping tool; customers simply place their orders with a few mouse clicks, and within a few days, the merchandise appears on their doorsteps! Entrepreneurs have come up with other clever ways to distribute their products and services and offer their customers more convenience. For instance, many traditionally stationary businesses have added wheels, becoming mobile animal clinics, computer shops, dentist offices, and windshield repair services. Others build on the model popularized by Tupperware in the 1950s, distributing their products through home-based parties. For instance, Susan Handley, who started Beijo Bags LLC in 2002, uses home-based parties as the primary distribution method for the stylish, functional handbags her company produces. Handley, who started in business by selling her first 300 handbags at a holiday fair, says that the company's home-based "showcase parties" generate annual sales of $10 million.[107]

Any activity involving movement of goods to the point of consumer purchase provides place utility. Place utility is directly affected by the marketing channels of distribution, the path that goods or services and their titles take in moving from producer to consumer. Channels typically involve a number of middlemen who perform specialized functions that add valuable utility to the goods or service. These middlemen provide time utility (making the product available when customers want to buy it) and place utility (making the product available where customers want to buy it).

In 1995, after observing the success of a classical music CD sold by lingerie retailer Victoria's Secret, New York producer and recording engineer Billy Straus launched Rock River Communications, a company that produces branded music compilations. He convinced buyers at Pottery Barn to test market 15,000 copies of a jazz compilation titled *A Cool Christmas*. The retailer sold the entire order in just three weeks, opening the door to Rock River as the music supplier to other major retail outlets such as J.Crew, Eddie Bauer, Lane Bryant, Banana Republic, Old Navy, and, somewhat surprisingly, Jiffy Lube and Chef Boyardee. Rock River's sells more than $8 million worth of music compilations annually, making it the equivalent of a midsize record label.[108]

For consumer goods, there are four common channels of distribution (see Figure 8.10).

1. ***Manufacturer to consumer.*** In some markets, producers sell their goods or services directly to consumers. Services, by nature, follow this channel of distribution. Dental care and haircuts, for example, go directly from creator to consumer.
2. ***Manufacturer to retailer to consumer.*** Another common channel involves a retailer as a middleman. Many clothing items, books, shoes, and other consumer products are distributed in this manner.
3. ***Manufacturer to wholesaler to retailer to consumer.*** This is the most common channel of distribution. Prepackaged food products, hardware, toys, and other items are commonly distributed through this channel.

FIGURE 8.10

**Channels of Distribution:
Consumer Goods**

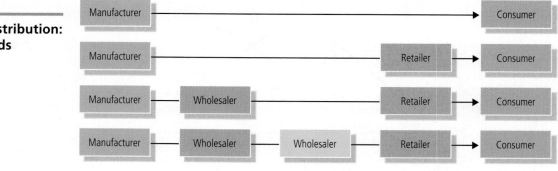

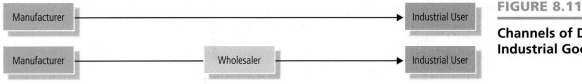

FIGURE 8.11

Channels of Distribution: Industrial Goods

4. *Manufacturer to wholesaler to wholesaler to consumer.* Some consumer goods (e.g., agricultural goods and electrical components) follow this pattern of distribution.

Two channels of distribution are common for industrial goods (see Figure 8.11):

1. *Manufacturer to industrial user.* The majority of industrial goods are distributed directly from manufacturers to users. In some cases, the goods or services are designed to meet the user's specifications.
2. *Manufacturer to wholesaler to industrial user.* Most low-expense items (paper clips, paper, rubber bands, cleaning fluids) that firms commonly use are distributed through wholesalers. For most small manufacturers, distributing goods through established wholesalers and agents is often the most effective route.

Price

Almost everyone agrees that the price of the product or service is a key factor in the decision to buy. Price affects both sales volume and profits, and without the right price, both sales and profits will suffer. The right price for a product or service depends on three factors: (1) a company's cost structure, (2) an assessment of what the market will bear, and (3) the desired image the company wants to create in its customers' minds.

For small businesses, nonprice competition, that is, focusing on factors other than price, often is a more effective strategy than trying to beat larger competitors in a price war. Nonprice competition, such as free trial offers, free delivery, lengthy warranties, and money-back guarantees, intends to play down the product's price and stress its durability, quality, reputation, or special features. We discuss pricing in more detail in Chapter 10, "Pricing Strategies."

Promotion

Promotion involves both advertising and personal selling. Its goal is to inform and persuade consumers. Advertising communicates to potential customers through some mass medium the benefits of a good or service. Personal selling involves the art of persuasive sales on a one-to-one basis. A small company's promotional program can play a significant role in creating a specific image in its customers' minds—whether it is upscale, discount, or somewhere in between. "Marketing is not a battle of products; it's a battle of perceptions," says one marketing expert.[109]

Chapter Summary by Learning Objectives

1. Describe the principles of building a guerrilla marketing plan and explain the benefits of preparing one.

A major part of the entrepreneur's business plan is the marketing plan, which focuses on a company's target customers and how best to satisfy their needs and wants. A solid marketing plan should do the following:

- Determine customer needs and wants through market research.
- Pinpoint the specific target markets the company will serve.
- Analyze the firm's competitive advantages and build a marketing strategy around them.
- Create a marketing mix that meets customer needs and wants.

2. Explain how small businesses can pinpoint their target markets.

Sound market research helps the owner to pinpoint his or her target market. The most successful businesses have well-defined portraits of the customers they are seeking to attract.

3. Discuss the role of market research in building a guerrilla marketing plan and outline the market research process.

Market research is the vehicle for gathering the information that serves as the foundation of the marketing plan. Good research does *not* have to be complex and expensive to be useful. The steps in conducting market research include the following:

- Defining the objective: "What do you want to know?"
- Collecting the data from either primary or secondary sources.
- Analyzing and interpreting the data.
- Drawing conclusions and acting on them.

4. Describe how a small business can build a competitive edge in the marketplace using guerrilla marketing strategies: customer focus, quality, convenience, innovation, service, and speed.

When plotting a marketing strategy, owners must strive to achieve a competitive advantage—some way to make their companies different from and better than the competition. Successful small businesses rely on 10 ways to develop a competitive edge:

- Find a niche and fill it
- Don't just sell; entertain
- Strive to be unique
- Connect with the customer on an emotional level
- Focus on the customer
- Be devoted to quality
- Give attention to convenience
- Concentrate on innovation
- Be dedicated to service
- Emphasize speed

5. Discuss the marketing opportunities the World Wide Web offers entrepreneurs and how to best take advantage of them.

The Web offers small business owners tremendous marketing potential on par with their larger rivals. Entrepreneurs are just beginning to uncover the Web's profit potential, which is growing rapidly. Establishing a presence on the Web is important for companies targeting educated, wealthy, young customers. Successful Web sites are attractive, inviting, easy to navigate, and interactive and offer users something of value.

6. Discuss the "four P's" of marketing—product, place, price, and promotion—and their role in building a successful marketing strategy.

The marketing mix consists of the "4 P's":

- *Product.* Entrepreneurs should understand where in the product life cycle their products are.
- *Place.* The focus here is on choosing the appropriate channel of distribution and using it most efficiently.
- *Price.* Setting the right price for a product or service is partly an art and partly a science.
- *Promotion.* Promotion involves both advertising and personal selling.

Discussion Questions

1. Define the marketing plan. What lies at its center?
2. What objectives should a marketing plan accomplish?
3. How can market research benefit a small business owner? List some possible sources of market information.
4. Does market research have to be expensive and sophisticated to be valuable? Explain.
5. Describe several market trends that are driving markets into the next millennium and their impact on small businesses.
6. Why is it important for small business owners to define their target markets as part of their marketing strategies?
7. What is a competitive advantage? Why is it important for a small business owner to create a plan for establishing one?

8. Describe how a small business owner could use the following sources of a competitive advantage:
   - Focusing on a niche
   - Entertailing
   - Striving to be unique
   - Start a blog
   - Connecting with customers on an emotional level
   - Creating an identity for the business through branding
   - Focusing on the customer
   - Being devoted to quality
   - Paying attention to convenience
   - Concentrating on innovation
   - Being dedicated to service
   - Emphasizing speed
9. One manager says, "When a company provides great service, its reputation benefits from a stronger

emotional connection with its customers, as well as from increased confidence that it will stand behind its products." Do you agree? Explain. If so, describe a positive service experience you have had with a company and your impressions of that business. What are the implications of a company providing poor customer service? Describe a negative service experience you have had with a company and your impressions of that business. How likely are you to do business with that company again?

10. Consumer behavior expert and retail consultant Paco Underhill says, "A [retail] store is a 3-D brand. Everything that's there has to be there for a reason."

    A. Do you agree? Explain.

    B. Find two retail stores in the local area, one that offers a good example of a three-dimensional brand and one that does not. Prepare a one-page summary explaining you reasoning for selecting these two stores.

11. What marketing potential does the World Wide Web offer small businesses? What does it take for a company to market successfully using the Web?

12. Explain the concept of the marketing mix. What are the four P's?

13. List and explain the stages in the product life cycle. How can a small firm extend its product's life?

14. With a 70 percent customer retention rate (average for most U.S. firms, according to the American Management Association), every $1 million of business will grow to more than $4 million within 10 years. If you retain 80 percent of your customers, the $1 million will grow to a little over $6 million. If you can keep 90 percent of your customers, that $1 million will grow to more than $9.5 million. What can the typical small business do to increase its customer retention rate?

Business Plan Pro

 You will use the marketing concepts in this chapter along with those from previous chapters to continue to build your business plan. The marketing section of your plan will add greater depth to your situation analysis and offer additional insight for your business strategy. For most business plans, 25 to 35 percent of the plan is devoted to the marketing plan. Your business plan will seek to describe how you determined that a market exists for the products or services of your business, identify the market segments you are targeting, establish the unique selling proposition to differentiate your products and services, and describe how you will reach the market and motivate customers to purchase.

Business Plan Exercises

On the Web

The Internet is a highly efficient tool for conducting market research. Your market research should provide specific information about your target market and the key factors that influence their buying decisions. Your business plan will benefit from even the most elementary market research, and, if it does not provide new information, that research may validate what you do know. Market research is often associated with elaborate processes conducted by third parties that demand a tremendous amount of time and money. However, casual and efficient market research can be valuable and the degree of fit with your plan may be based on the quality, cost, or the amount of time to acquire the information. The Web can help you to determine what form of market research is going to work best for your plan. Make that

determination based on the value you will receive versus the time and other resources you need to invest to gain access to that information.

The Internet can help you to identify associations by industry. Once you have identified your industry, determine the industry's associations, comprised of stakeholders for that industry. Assess what information is on their Web site. Does the industry association have publications available? What benefits do they provide to their members? What does it cost to join the association? Industry associations may be a valuable source of market research.

Excellent data are also available through U.S. Government resources and is available on the Web in the following areas:

- Small Business Administration (SBA): http://www.sba.gov
- Small Business Development Center (SBDC): http://www.sba.gov/sbdc
- U.S. Census Bureau: http://www.census.gov/
- U.S. Department of Commerce: http://www.trade.gov
- U.S. Chamber of Commerce: http://www.uschamber.com

For example, the information through the U.S. Census Bureau at its Web site provides a menu of available demographic reports that include reports on various manufacturing industries, county-specific economic surveys, business patterns for a specific Zip Code, and others. Additional online information is available through educational resources on community college, college, and university Web sites.

Private market research sources are plentiful on the Web. Although most provide this information for a fee, many sites offer preliminary information at no cost. One example is geocluster data called PRIZM, an acronym for "Potential Rating Index by Zip Markets." These market data, available through Claritas Inc., offer descriptions of consumers by ZipCode beyond that of traditional demographic data. PRIZM data classifies US neighborhoods into 66 distinct lifestyle groups based on education, affluence, family life cycle, urbanization, mobility, race, and ethnicity. You can look up PRIZM information by going to http://www.claritas.com/MyBestSegments and click on the "Zip Code Look-Up" tab at the top. Enter your Zip Code into the search window for your results and you may be impressed by what you find—all at no cost. Other market research information is available through sites such as Zap Data at http://www.zapdata.com. Here, you will find industry data reports with preliminary information, also at no charge. This information, sorted by Standard Industrial Classification code, tracks how many companies are in the industry, their average sales, the number of employees, the company size, and their locations.

The Web can also be helpful in finding publications that focus on your topic and geographic business area. Looking at online magazine, newspaper, and other publications may be an efficient way to search for related articles and other information. Many industry-specific magazines publish statistical editions and market reviews at regular intervals. Search the indexes to identify published information that might help the marketing section of your business plan. You may find an index listing for an article that forecasts your industry or addresses industry economics or trends. You can also contact their editorial departments using their Web site or phone number for additional information.

In the Software

Review some of the sample business plans that you felt were the most helpful. Review the marketing plan section of these plans and note the type and depth of market information they include. This information is essential to establish a solid understanding of the market your business will serve and to use as the basis for developing and validating your strategy. Now, go to each of the following sections in your business plan.

Your Company. Review the work that you began in the "Your Company" section of your business plan. As you review that information, does it capture a marketing focus? Does this section place the necessary emphasis on valuing the customer relationship? Add to and edit your work to reflect this critical perspective.

What You Are Selling? Make certain this section presents what you are selling to your customer. It must concisely communicate this in a way that represents your customers and the value they will realize from choosing to do business with you and benefit from your products and services.

Service Summary. Think about the unique nature of the services your business provides. How will your services offer greater benefit than those of your competitors? How will your services be superior and provide meaningful value to your customers in a way that will enhance their loyalty? Address these questions in this section of your plan.

Your Market. Add information that you have gleaned from your marketing research to describe your market in as much detail as possible.

Target Market Segment. Review the concepts in "Pinpointing the Target Market" on page 265. Use those concepts to help you to develop a clear picture of your target customers. Use the Web to research how electronics retailer Best Buy created profiles of its target customers (Buzz, the Techie, Barry, the Wealthy Professional, and others). Use the same technique to develop profiles of your company's target customers. You may want to incorporate these profiles into this section to describe your target market segment.

Competition. A detailed and thorough discussion and analysis of each of the current and potential competitor is critical. There is no substitute for this depth of analysis. The business plan must demonstrate that you have evaluated this critical factor and can identify, in realistic and practical terms, how your business will successfully compete. Demonstrate your knowledge of why customers make purchasing decisions and how your proposed venture can gain their business. Be honest and objective as you describe your competitors' strengths and weaknesses. Discuss the customer appeal, pricing strategies, advertising campaigns, and the products and services that competitors offer.

Competitive Edge. Based on the foregoing information, review the "Competitive Edge" section of your plan. What unique attributes does your business offer that will provide real or perceived benefits for your customers? Make sure that you capture those thoughts in this section. Be as detailed as possible, and specifically explain your strategies for creating this advantage. Incorporate material from your marketing and sales plan that will show how these strategic advantages will support your sales forecast.

The Sales Forecast. Review the sales forecast that you entered in the previous chapters. Does that forecast look realistic? Does the cost of goods seem accurate? Go to the narrative section of the sales forecast and explain the numbers in the sales forecast. Include any assumptions on which you have developed your sales forecast. Explain why your sales are projected to change over time. Include any key events that may affect your sales and how and why they will influence the sales forecast. Finally, as you evaluate your numbers and the assumptions that support them, ask yourself if they are realistic. Developing financial forecasts using published statistics from sources such as RMA Annual Statement Studies (http://www.rmahq.org), market research, industry studies, and other sources lends credibility to your plan. Once again, you will find information and links at http://www.prenhall/scarborough.com that may be helpful.

Marketing Plan Summary. A marketing strategy should present a clear link to generating sales revenue. Use a detailed analysis and explanation of all assumptions on which the analysis rests. Your company's pricing, product distribution, and promotion plans combined should produce a unified marketing strategy.

Building Your Business Plan

Continue to build your business plan with the new information you have acquired. Step back to assess whether you have a solid understanding of your market and whether your business plan effectively communicates that knowledge.

Beyond the Classroom . . .

1. Interview the owner of a local restaurant about its marketing strategy. From how large a geographic region does the restaurant draw its clientele? What is the firm's target market? What are its characteristics? Does the restaurant have a competitive edge?

2. Select a local small manufacturing operation and evaluate its primary product. What stage of the product life cycle is it in? What channels of distribution does the product follow as it leaves the manufacturer?

3. Visit the Web site for the Small Business Administration's "Marketing Mall" at http://www.onlinewbc.gov/docs/market/. Interview a local business owner, using the resources there as a guide. What sources for developing a competitive edge did you find? What weaknesses do you see? How do you recommend overcoming them? What recommendations can you make to help the owner make better use of its marketing techniques? Evaluate the business's approach to the four P's of

marketing. What guerrilla marketing strategies can you suggest to enhance current marketing efforts?

4. Contact three local small business owners and ask them about their marketing strategies. How have they achieved a competitive edge? Develop a series of questions to judge the sources of their competitive edge—a focus on the customer; devotion to quality; attention to convenience; concentration on innovation; dedication to service; and emphasis on speed. How do the businesses compare?

5. Select three local businesses (one large and two small) and play the role of "mystery shopper." How easy was it to do business with each company? How would you rate their service, quality, and convenience? Were sales people helpful and friendly? Did they handle transactions professionally and courteously? How would rate the business's appearance? How would you describe each company's competitive advantage? What future would you predict for each company? Prepare a brief report for your class on your findings and conclusions.

9 | E-Commerce and the Entrepreneur

The Internet remains a place where you can start with nothing and soon challenge the gods. —Mark DiMassimo

Learning Objectives

On completion of this chapter, you will be able to:

1. Describe the benefits of selling on the World Wide Web.
2. Understand the factors an entrepreneur should consider before launching into e-commerce.
3. Explain the 12 myths of e-commerce and how to avoid falling victim to them.
4. Explain the basic strategies entrepreneurs should follow to achieve success in their e-commerce efforts.
5. Learn the techniques of designing a killer Web site.
6. Explain how companies track the results from their Web sites.
7. Describe how e-businesses ensure the privacy and security of the information they collect and store from the Web.

As a student of business, you are fortunate to be witnessing the early stages of growth of a tool that is reshaping the way companies of all sizes operate: E-commerce. E-commerce is creating a new way of doing business, one that is connecting producers, sellers, and customers via technology in ways that have never been possible before. The result is a whole new set of companies built on business models that are turning traditional methods of commerce and industry on their heads. Companies that ignore the impact of the Internet on their markets run the risk of becoming as relevant to customers as a rotary-dial telephone. The most successful companies are embracing the Internet, not as merely another advertising medium or marketing tool, but as a mechanism for transforming their companies and changing *everything* about the way they do business. As these companies discover new, innovative ways to use the Internet, computers, and communications technology to connect with their suppliers and to serve their customers better, they are creating a new industrial order. In short, e-commerce has launched a revolution. Just as in previous revolutions in the business world, some older, established players are being ousted, and new leaders are emerging. The winners are discovering new business opportunities, new ways of designing work, and new ways of organizing and operating their businesses. Yet one lesson that entrepreneurs engaged in e-commerce have learned is that business basics still apply, whether a company is on the Web or not. Companies engaging in e-commerce still have to take care of their customers and earn a profit to stay in business.

Perhaps the most visible changes are occurring in the world of retailing. Although e-commerce will not replace traditional retailing, no retailer, from the smallest corner store to industry giant Wal-Mart, can afford to ignore the impact of the World Wide Web on its business model. Companies can take orders at the speed of light from anywhere in the world and at any time of day. The Internet enables companies to collect more information on customers' shopping and buying habits than any other medium in history. This ability means that companies can focus their marketing efforts like never before—for instance, selling garden supplies to customers who are most likely to buy them and not wasting resources trying to sell to those who have no interest in gardening. The capacity to track customers' Web-based shopping habits allows companies to personalize their approaches to marketing and to realize the benefits of individualized (or one-to-one) marketing (refer to Chapter 8). Ironically, the same Web-based marketing approach that allows companies to get so personal with their customers also can make shopping extremely impersonal.

www.CartoonStock.com

"Good afternoon, gentlemen, and welcome to multi.global.industries.com... otherwise known as my basement."

Entrepreneurs who set up shop on the Web most likely will never meet their customers face to face or even talk to them. Yet those customers, who can live anywhere in the world, will visit the online store at all hours of the day or night and expect to receive individual attention. Making a Web-based marketing approach succeed requires that a business strike a balance, creating an e-commerce strategy that capitalizes on the strengths of the Web while meeting customers' expectations of convenience and service.

In the world of e-commerce, the new business models recognize the power the Internet gives customers. Pricing, for example, is no longer as simple as it once was for companies. The Web's global reach means that entrepreneurs can no longer be content to take into account only local competitors when setting their prices. With a few mouse clicks, customers can compare the prices of the same or similar products and services from companies across the globe. In the new wired and connected economy, the balance of power is shifting to customers, and new business models recognize this fact. Whatever products they may sell—from digital cameras and high-definition televisions to cars and flowers—retailers are dealing with customers who are more informed and aware of the price and feature comparisons of the items for which they are shopping. One study by JupiterResearch reports that 85 percent of Internet users research products and services online before buying them in stores or by telephone.[1] These informed shoppers are taking price out of the buying equation, causing retailers to emphasize other factors such as service or convenience to build long-term relationships. This trend also points to the need for retailers marketing their products and services to take a multichannel selling approach that includes the Web as one option.

In the fast-paced world of e-commerce, size no longer matters as much as speed and flexibility. One of the Web's greatest strengths is its ability to provide companies with instantaneous customer feedback, giving them the opportunity to learn and to make necessary adjustments. Businesses, whatever their size, that are willing to experiment with different approaches to reaching customers and are quick to learn and adapt will grow and prosper; those that cannot will fall by the wayside. The Internet is creating a new industrial order, and companies that fail to adapt to it will soon become extinct. E-commerce is transforming the way businesses in almost every industry operate. For instance, Web-based companies are changing the grocery business, which has been anchored in brick-and-mortar stores for generations. Companies such as FreshDirect, SimonDelivers, Peapod, and others allow their customers to shop for groceries at any time of the day without having to walk the aisles of a store picking over peppers and poring over pomegranates. Instead, customers log on to these companies' Web sites, place their orders (up to two weeks in advance, in some cases) with a few mouse clicks, and then sit back while workers fill their requests and deliver their groceries to their doorsteps. Not only do customers save valuable time, but many also say that the items they receive from online grocers are fresher and of higher quality than those they used to purchase in stores. Although online grocers account for less than one percent of grocery sales in the United States, their sales are growing much faster than the sales of the industry as a whole. By creating innovative, easy-to-use Web sites that maximize customer convenience, these online supermarkets are changing the way traditional companies in the industry must compete. Already, traditional grocers such as Albertsons, Safeway, and others are experimenting with their own versions of online shopping.

Experts estimate that nearly 10 percent of the world's population, some 627 million people, has shopped online at least once.[2] The items purchased most often online are books, music (which is shifting rapidly away from CDs to digital downloads of songs), DVDs, travel services, clothing, tickets for entertainment events, electronics, and toys.[3] However, companies can—and do—sell practically anything over the Web, from antiques and pharmaceuticals to groceries and drug-free urine. Forrester Research estimates that 12 percent of total retail sales in the United States will occur online in 2010, totaling $316 billion.[4]

Companies of all sizes are busy establishing a presence on the Web because that's where their customers are. The Pew Internet and American Life Project reports that, on a typical day, 70 million Americans go online, a 37 percent increase from 2000.[5] Consumers have adopted the Internet much more quickly than they did any other major past innovation. It reached 50 percent penetration in the United States in just seven years, compared to 30 years for the computer, 40 years for electricity, and more than 100 years for steam power.[6] A study by JupiterResearch predicts that by 2010, the Internet will influence one-half of all retail sales, either by people making purchases online or by those who will shop, compare, and gather information online about products and services before making a purchase offline.[7]

Benefits of Selling on the Web

LEARNING OBJECTIVES
1. Describe the benefits of selling on the World Wide Web.

The first e-commerce transaction took place on August 11, 1994, when NetMarket, a small company founded by recent college graduate Daniel Kohn, sold a CD by Sting, *Ten Summoner's Tales*, to a student at Swarthmore College for $12.48 plus shipping.[8] From these humble beginnings grew a distribution channel that now accounts for $145 billion in annual retail sales. Small businesses that are doing business on the Web experience many benefits (see Figure 9.1). We now examine some of these benefits more closely.

- ■ ***The opportunity to increase revenues and profits.*** For many small businesses, launching a Web site is the equivalent of opening a new sales channel. Companies that launch e-commerce efforts soon discover that their sites are generating additional sales from new audiences of customers. A recent survey by IPSOS and PayPal reports that 72 percent of small companies selling online say that the Web has increased their sales. In the same study, 65 percent of the companies report that e-commerce had boosted their profits as well.[9]

- ■ ***The ability to expand their reach into global markets.*** The Web is the most efficient way for small businesses to sell their products to the millions of potential customers who live outside the United States. Tapping into these global markets through more traditional methods would be too complex and too costly for the typical small business. Yet with the Web, a small company can sell its products efficiently to customers anywhere in the world at any time of day.

- ■ ***The ability to remain open 24 hours a day, seven days a week.*** More than half of all retail sales occur after 6 p.m., when many traditional stores close. Extending the hours a brick-and-mortar store remains open can increase sales, but it also takes a toll on the business owner and the employees. With a Web site up and running, however, a small company can sell around the clock without having to incur additional staffing expenses. Customers never have to worry about whether an online store is open for business.

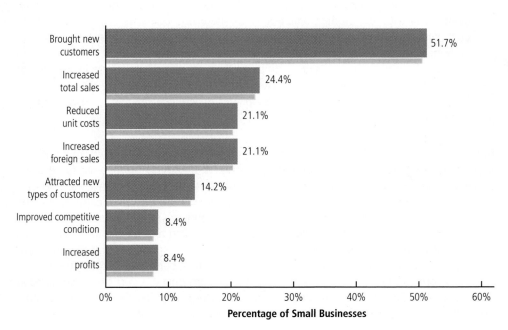

FIGURE 9.1

Benefits to Small Businesses of Web Sites

Source: National Federation of Independent Businesses, 2002.

Brought new customers — 51.7%
Increased total sales — 24.4%
Reduced unit costs — 21.1%
Increased foreign sales — 21.1%
Attracted new types of customers — 14.2%
Improved competitive condition — 8.4%
Increased profits — 8.4%

Percentage of Small Businesses

■ *The capacity to use the Web's interactive nature to enhance customer service.* Although selling on the Web can be highly impersonal because of the lack of human interaction, companies that design their sites properly can create an exciting, interactive experience for their online visitors. Customers can contact a company at any time of the day, control the flow of information they get, and in some cases interact with company representatives in real time. In addition, technology allows companies to "personalize" their sites to suit the tastes and preferences of individual customers. Drawing on a database containing information customers have provided in the past, Web sites can customize themselves, displaying content that appeals to an individual visitor.

Lillian Vernon

Lillian Vernon, an online and catalog retailer selling housewares and gift items, recently launched a redesigned Web site capable of customizing itself based on individual customers' past buying behavior. "If I know that all you ever buy on my site are kids' products, I want to make sure that a good portion of what you see are kids products," says Peter Shapiro, the company's senior vice-president of e-commerce. By tracking customers' purchasing patterns, the site also makes personalized product recommendations to repeat shoppers.[10]

■ *The power to educate and to inform.* Far more than most marketing media, the Web gives entrepreneurs the power to educate and to inform customers. Women and members of Generation Y, especially, crave product information before they make purchases. The Web allows business owners to provide more detailed information to visitors than practically any other medium. For instance, a travel company advertising an Alaskan tour in a newspaper or magazine might include a brief description of the tour, a list of the destinations, a telephone number, the price, and perhaps a photo or two. A Web-based promotion for the same tour could include all of the this information as well as a detailed itinerary with dozens of breath-taking outdoor photographs; descriptions and photographs of all accommodations; advice on what to pack; airline schedules, seating configurations, and availability; information on optional side trips; comments from customers who have taken this tour before; and links to other Web sites about Alaska, the weather, and fun things to do in the region.[11]

■ *The ability to lower the cost of doing business.* The Web is one of the most efficient ways of reaching both new and existing customers. Properly promoted, a Web site can reduce a company's cost of generating sales leads, providing customer support, and distributing marketing materials. For instance, car dealers must spend $500 on average to get a potential customer into their showrooms; for a $40 listing fee, those same dealers can list a car on the popular auction site eBay, where they get an average of eight customers bidding to buy.[12] By integrating its Web site with its inventory control system, a company also can reduce its inventory costs by shortening the sales cycle. In addition, linking their Web sales activity to their suppliers enables businesses to cut their purchasing and administrative costs. The IPSOS/PayPal survey mentioned earlier reports that 73 percent of small companies experience savings by lowering their administrative costs.[13]

Brady Corporation

Brady Corporation, an 87-year-old company that makes all types of signs, from identification tags to stop signs, faced a multitude of problems stemming from its outdated order processing, accounts receivable, and quality control systems. Managers saw the opportunity the Web offered to correct errors, lower costs, and improve customer satisfaction. The company created Web-to-Workbench, a system that sends customer orders directly to the factory floor. Because the system allows customers to design and pay for their own signs online, Brady's accounts receivable problems have all but disappeared, and its order processing costs fell 88 percent from $16 per order to just $2 per order. Because the system allows customers to preview the final design of their signs online, errors that used to result in millions of dollars of returned signs have been reduced dramatically. Customer satisfaction is higher because Brady now ships most orders within 24 hours of receiving them.[14]

- *The ability to spot new business opportunities and to capitalize on them.* E-commerce companies are poised to give customers just what they want when they want it. As the number of dual-career couples rises and the amount of available leisure time shrinks, consumers are looking for ways to increase the convenience of shopping, and the Web is fast becoming the solution they seek. Increasingly, customers view shopping as an unpleasant chore that cuts into already scarce leisure time, and they are embracing anything that reduces the amount of time they must spend shopping. "Given the time pressures of balancing work, household duties, child care, and social activities it's not hard to see why the Internet, with its convenience advantage, will increasingly become the smart way to shop," says Geoffrey Ramsey, an expert on e-commerce. Entrepreneurs who tap into customers' need to buy goods more conveniently and with less hassle are winning the battle for market share. New opportunities to serve customers' changing needs and wants are constantly arising, and the Web is the birthplace of many of them.

- *The ability to grow faster.* The Web has the power to accelerate a small company's growth. A recent study by AllBusiness.com reports that the owners of small and medium-sized businesses say that the Internet is the primary driver of their companies' growth.[15]

- *The power to track sales results.* The Web gives businesses the power to track virtually any kind of activity on their Web sites, from the number of visitors to the click-through rates on their banner ads. Because of the Web's ability to monitor traffic continuously, entrepreneurs can judge the value their sites are generating for their companies.

When Steven McKean, founder of BuyTelco Inc., a company that helps individuals and businesses to select the best high-speed Internet plans from cable and DSL providers, analyzed the performance of his company's Web site, he realized that the conversion rate was a meager 0.7 percent. (A Web site's **conversion rate** is the percentage of visitors to a Web site who actually make a purchase.) "Not even one out of 100 people would buy," recalls McKean. The Web analytics software McKean used allowed him to see exactly how customers were navigating and using the site and where they were abandoning it. He saw that the biggest problem was that BuyTelco's checkout process required customers to wade through five Web pages, each requiring customers to enter information—an onerous task that many simply refused to complete. "We were collecting a lot of redundant and unnecessary information," says Mckean. "It was a very heavy, arduous task." McKean streamlined the information the site collected from customers, shortening the checkout process from five Web pages to just one. The changes resulted in an immediate improvement in BuyTelco's conversion rate, from 0.7 percent to 3 percent.[16]

BuyTelco Inc.

conversion rate
the percentage of visitors to a Web site who actually make a purchase.

In essence, the Web allows small businesses to match the efficiencies of big companies by increasing their reach and the scope of their operations, by connecting with suppliers and customers to lower costs, and by measuring the results of their e-commerce efforts.

Michael Bornstein, who had been running three successful skateboard stores in Southern California, wanted to expand his business and shift its focus to sell more profitable skateboard equipment and accessories. He decided that the Web was the key to success for his expansion strategy. First, he consolidated his three stores into two, and used the third as the Internet and mail order center for Skate America. After spending a year developing a business plan and a Web site, Bornstein launched the company. It took a few months before his site was picked up by search engines such as Yahoo, but then sales took off. Within two years, Bornstein closed his two retail stores to focus on Web sales. Bornstein has redesigned Skate America's Web site over the years, and today it is one of the most sophisticated in the industry, yet it remains one of the simplest for customers to use. Shoppers can create custom-designed skateboards or buy prebuilt models and order parts or accessories with ease. Bornstein has linked his company's just-in-time inventory system

Skate America

to his Web site, which gives him an advantage over competitors because he avoids the problems of excess inventory. Because of Bornstein's successful e-commerce strategy, Skate America's sales have climbed from $1 million in its first year to more than $7 million today.[17]

LEARNING OBJECTIVES
2. Understand the factors an entrepreneur should consider before launching into e-commerce.

Factors to Consider before Launching into E-Commerce

Despite the many benefits the Web offers, not every small business owner is ready to embrace e-commerce. Approximately 70 percent of small business owners in the United States have a presence on the Web, double the percentage that were operating online in 2002.[18] Of those small business owners who have not taken their businesses online, 77 percent say their products and services are not suitable for sale on the Web. Another 37 percent say that they do not see any benefits to selling online.[19] Why are these small companies hesitant to embrace the Web as a business tool? For many entrepreneurs, the key barrier is not knowing where or how to start an e-commerce effort, while for others cost and time concerns are major issues. Other roadblocks include the fear that customers will not use the Web site and the problems associated with ensuring online security.

Whatever their size, traditional companies must realize that selling their products and services on the Web is no longer an option. Entrepreneurs who ignore the strategic implications of establishing a Web presence for their companies are putting their businesses at risk. "Any company that wants to make it in the years ahead must make the technology and the processes of the Internet part of its core competence," says one experienced venture capitalist.[20] However, before launching an e-commerce effort, business owners should consider the following important issues:

- How a company exploits the Web's interconnectivity and the opportunities it creates to transform relationships with its suppliers and vendors, its customers, and other external stakeholders is crucial to its success.
- Web success requires a company to develop a plan for integrating the Web into its overall strategy. The plan should address issues such as site design and maintenance, creating and managing a brand name, marketing and promotional strategies, sales, and customer service.
- Developing deep, lasting relationships with customers takes on even greater importance on the Web. Attracting customers on the Web costs money, and companies must be able to retain their online customers to make their Web sites profitable.
- Creating a meaningful presence on the Web requires an ongoing investment of resources—time, money, energy, and talent. Establishing an attractive Web site brimming with catchy photographs of products is only the beginning.
- Measuring the success of its Web-based sales effort is essential if a company is to remain relevant to customers whose tastes, needs, and preferences are always changing.

Doing business on the Web takes more time and energy than many entrepreneurs expect. Answering the following questions will help entrepreneurs to make sure they are ready to do business on the Web and avoid unpleasant surprises in their e-commerce efforts:

- What exactly do you expect a Web site to do for your company? Will it provide information only, reach new customers, increase sales to existing customers, improve communication with customers, enhance customer service, or reduce your company's cost of operation? Will customers be able to place orders from the site, or must they call your company to buy?
- How much can you afford to invest in an e-commerce effort?
- What rate of return do you expect to earn on that investment?
- How long can you afford to wait for that return?
- How well suited are your products and services for selling on the Web?

TABLE 9.1 Assessing Your Company's Web Potential

Considering launching an online company or transforming a brick-and-mortar business into one with an online presence? The following questions will help you to assess your company's Web potential.

1. Does your product have broad appeal to customers everywhere?
2. Do you want to sell your product to customers outside of your immediate geographic area?
3. Can the product you sell be delivered conveniently and economically?
4. Can your company realize significant cost advantages, such as lower rent, labor, inventory, and printing expenses, by going online?
5. Can you draw customers to your company's Web site with a reasonable investment?

- How will the "back office" of your Web site work? Will your site be tied into your company's inventory control system?
- How will you handle order fulfillment? Can your fulfillment system handle the increase in volume you are expecting?
- What impact, if any, will your Web site have on your company's traditional channels of distribution?
- What mechanism will your site use to ensure secure customer transactions?
- How will your company handle customer service for the site? What provisions will you make for returned items?
- How do you plan to promote the site to draw traffic to it?
- What information will you collect from the visitors to your site? How will you use it? Will you tell visitors how you intend to use this information?
- Have you developed a privacy policy? Have you posted that policy on your company's Web site for customers?
- Have you tested your site with real, live customers to make sure that it is easy to navigate and easy to order from?
- How will you measure the success of your company's Web site? What objectives have you set for the site?

Table 9.1 provides a set of questions designed to help entrepreneurs assess their companies' potential to become an online success.

Twelve Myths of E-Commerce

LEARNING OBJECTIVES
3. Explain the 12 myths of e-commerce and how to avoid falling victim to them.

Although many entrepreneurs have made their fortunes through e-commerce, setting up shop on the Web is no guarantee of success. Scores of entrepreneurs have plunged unprepared into the world of e-commerce only to discover that there is more to it than merely setting up a Web site and waiting for the orders to start pouring in. Make sure that you do not fall victim to one of the following e-commerce myths.

Myth 1. Setting up a Business on the Web Is Easy and Inexpensive

A common misconception is that setting up an effective Web site for an online business is easy and inexpensive. Although practically anyone with the right software can post a static page in just a few minutes, creating an effective, professional, and polished Web site can be an expensive, time-consuming project. The good news is that setting up a business online is getting easier and less expensive. Most small businesses set up their Web pages as simple "electronic flyers," pages that post product information, a few photographs, prices, and telephone and fax numbers. Although these simple sites lack the capacity for true electronic commerce, they do provide a company with another way of reaching both new and existing customers.

In fact, many small businesses outsource most (sometimes all) of the activities associated with conducting business online to companies that specialize in e-commerce services.

These companies prefer to focus on their core competencies—product design, marketing, extending a brand, manufacturing, and others—and hire other companies whose core competencies reside in e-commerce to handle Web site design, hosting, order processing, and order fulfillment ("pick, pack, and ship"). Rather than make constant investments in technology that may not produce a reasonable return, these small companies preserve their capital and their energy and focus them on the aspects of business that they do best.

Linens 'n Things

When Linens 'n Things, traditionally a brick-and-mortar retailer of bed and bath furnishings, launched into e-commerce in 2000, the company handled order processing and fulfillment in-house, even creating its own customer support call center. After several years, managers decided that e-commerce was not one of the company's core competencies and began to consider outsourcing some of its Web-based operations. In the end, they decided to focus on operating Linens 'n Things retail stores and to outsource the entire e-commerce effort to GSI Commerce, a company that specializes in e-commerce services for business. In addition to Linens 'n Things, GSI Commerce's list of clients includes Timberland, Reebok, Major League Baseball, and Public Broadcasting Service, among others.[21]

The Finish Line

Another retailer, The Finish Line, a company that sells athletic wear and accessories, took a different approach from Linens 'n Things to its e-commerce business. It, too, initially launched its own Web site and the order processing and fulfillment activities associated with it. Over time, The Finish Line developed expertise in order fulfillment, customer service, and inventory management, areas managers decided to keep in-house. Having outgrown its initial Web site and recognizing that Web site design and maintenance was not a core competency, the company hired Art Technology Group, a company that specializes in Web sites, to develop an upgraded, more functional Web site. The new site gives managers important insight into Web shoppers' behavior and preferences using sophisticated Web analytics. Almost immediately on launching the new site, the company's online cart abandonment rate dropped and sales climbed. "We're starting to embrace the site as a research tool to drive more traffic to our stores, rather than as just another retail channel," says Kent Zimmerman, The Finish Line's director of e-commerce.[22]

Companies that decide to operate their own e-commerce businesses quickly learn that setting up a site is only the first investment required. Sooner or later, most companies encounter follow-up investments, including updating and revising the Web site, buying more hardware to support the Web site, automating or expanding their warehouses to meet customer demand, integrating their inventory control system into the Web site, and increasing customer call-center capacity. When it comes to e-commerce, the lesson for entrepreneurs is this: Focus your efforts on the core competencies that your company has developed, whether they reside in "traditional" business practices or online, and outsource all of the other aspects of doing business online to companies that have the expertise to make your e-commerce business successful.

Myth 2. If I Launch a Site, Customers Will Flock to It

Some entrepreneurs think that once they set up their Web sites, their expenses end there. Not true! Without promotional support, no Web site will draw enough traffic to support a business. With more than three billion Web pages in existence and the number growing daily, getting a site noticed in the crowd has become increasingly difficult. Even listing a site with popular Web search engines cannot guarantee that customers surfing the Web will find your company's site. Just like traditional retail stores seeking to attract customers, virtual companies have discovered that drawing sufficient traffic to a Web site requires constant promotion—and lots of it! Setting up a Web site and then failing to drive customers to it with adequate promotional support is like setting up a physical store in a back alley; you may be in business, but nobody knows you're there!

Entrepreneurs with both physical and virtual stores must promote their Web sites at every opportunity by printing their URL (universal resource locator, address on the Internet) on everything related to their physical stores—on signs, in print and broadcast ads, on shopping bags, on merchandise labels, and anywhere else their customers will see. Issuing a press release that announces a company's new or revised Web site will drive traffic to the site. Virtual shop owners should consider buying ads in traditional advertising media as well as using banner ads, banner exchange programs, and cross-marketing arrangements with companies selling complementary products on their on Web sites. The key to promoting a Web site is networking, building relationships with other companies, customers, trade associations, online directories, and other Web sites your company's customers visit. "You need to create relationships with the businesses and people with whom you share common customers," says Barbara Ling, author of a book on e-commerce. "Then you need to create links between sites to help customers find what they are looking for."[23]

Convincing other online sites to establish links to your company's site will boost your Web site's rankings among major search engines. Some entrepreneurs have boosted traffic to their Web sites by selling their products on eBay and then drawing those customers to their companies' Web sites. Other techniques for promoting a site include creating some type of interactivity with customers such as a Web-based newsletter, writing articles that link to the company's site, hosting a chat room that allows customers to interact with one another and with company personnel, sponsoring an online contest, or establishing a Web log (or "blog," a regularly updated online journal).

Web logs are easy and inexpensive to create (blog templates are available for free online), but they require regular updating to attract and retain visitors. Web logs with fresh, entertaining content can be an effective way to promote a small company and to draw potential customers to its Web site. In addition, because they are updated frequently and include links to other sites, blogs can lead to higher rankings in search engine results for small companies that use them.

Dennis Woo, founder of GreenCine, an online DVD rental company, was skeptical in 2002 when one of his 10 employees, David Hudson, asked if he could start a blog about film festivals, independent films, and alternative cinemas. Woo agreed, and Hudson began blogging about news from the world of independent and alternative films. The results were far beyond what Woo and Hudson could have imagined. Today, the blog (http://www.daily.greencine.com/) draws more than 80,000 visitors each month, and Woo credits the traffic from the blog with doubling his company's sales. "When we started off, I was skeptical about whether it would be successful, but it is core to our strategy," says Woo.[24]

COMPANY
Profile

GreenCine

Myth 3. Making Money on the Web Is Easy

Promoters who hawk "get-rich-quick" schemes on the Web lure many entrepreneurs with the promise that making money on the Web is easy. It isn't. Making money on the Web is possible, but it takes time, effort, and a solid plan and requires an investment up front. As hundreds of new sites spring up every day, getting a company's site noticed requires more effort and marketing muscle than ever before. Attracting customers to a Web site is really no different from attracting customers to a brick-and-mortar store; entrepreneurs have to define their target customers, devise a marketing plan to reach them, and offer them good value and superior customer service to keep them coming back. Getting noticed online requires a solid marketing effort. One study by the management consulting firm Boston Consulting Group and shop.org, an Internet retailing trade association, found that Web retailers invested 65 percent of their revenues in marketing and advertising, compared to their offline counterparts, who invested just 4 percent.[25]

Myth 4. Privacy Is Not an Important Issue on the Web

The Web allows companies to gain access to almost unbelievable amounts of information about their customers. Many sites offer visitors "freebies" in exchange for information about themselves. Companies then use this information to learn more about their target customers and how to market to them most effectively. Companies that collect information from their online customers have the responsibility of keeping it secure, however. A survey by Ponemon Institute and Watchfire found that 80 percent of Internet users said that privacy of their personal information was either important or very important.[26] Protecting online customers' privacy has become a topic of debate among many interested parties, including government agencies, consumer watchdog groups, customers, and industry trade associations. Jupiter Media Metrix estimates that if online companies adequately addressed privacy and security issues and alleviated customers' fear of breaches, online retail sales would be 24 percent higher.[27]

Companies that collect information from their online customers must safeguard their customers' privacy, protect the information they collect from unauthorized use, and use it responsibly. That means that businesses should post a privacy policy on their Web sites, explaining to customers how they intend to use the information they collect. Then, they must be sure to follow it! One of the surest ways to alienate online customers is to abuse the information collected from them by selling it to third parties or by spamming customers with unwanted solicitations. BBBOnLine offers a useful resource center designed to help small business owners wanting to establish or upgrade their Web site's privacy policies (http://www.bbbonline.org/understandingprivacy/).

Many online customers don't trust the Web sites they visit. Businesses that publish privacy policies and then adhere to them build trust among their customers, an important facet of doing business on the Web. According to John Briggs, director of e-commerce for the Yahoo Network, customers "need to trust the brand they are buying and believe that their online purchases will be safe transactions. They need to feel comfortable that [their] personal data will not be sold and that they won't get spammed by giving their e-mail address. They need to know about shipping costs, product availability, and return policies up front."[28] Privacy *does* matter on the Web, and businesses that respect and protect their customers' privacy will win their customers' trust. Trust is the foundation on which the long-term customer relationships that are so crucial to Web success are built.

Myth 5. The Most Important Part of Any E-Commerce Effort Is Technology

Although understanding the technology of e-commerce is an important part of the formula for success, it is *not* the most crucial ingredient. What matters most is the ability to understand the underlying business and to develop a workable business model that offers customers something of value at a reasonable price while producing a reasonable return for the company. The entrepreneurs who are proving to be most successful in e-commerce are those who know how their industries work inside and out and then build an e-business around their expertise. They know that they can hire webmasters, database experts, and fulfillment companies to design the technical aspects of their businesses, but that nothing can substitute for a solid understanding of their industry, their target market, and the strategy needed to pull the various parts together. The key is seeing the Web for what it really is: a way to transform in a positive fashion the way they do business by serving their customers more efficiently and effectively through another channel.

Edmunds Publications

Founded in 1966 to publish printed guides for buyers of new and used cars, Edmunds Publications changed very little over the next two decades about the way it operated, selling its manuals to bookstores, libraries, financial institutions, and individuals. In 1988, however, Peter Steinlauf bought the small company and began making changes to realize the potential he saw in it. After moving the company to car-crazy California, Steinlauf began exploring other ways to publish the auto cost and pricing information customers found so valuable. A computer CD proved to be a short-lived innovation, but in 1994 when Steinlauf offered the information on a pre-Web, text-only "gopher site" called the Electronic Newsstand, Edmunds became the first company to offer consumer automotive information (including dealer invoice prices) on the Internet. As word spread about the information Edmunds was posting, the volume of traffic on the Electronic Newsstand overwhelmed the site's capacity, and 1995, Edmunds launched its own Web site, becoming the first automotive information site on the then-new Web. Initially, Edmunds managers saw the Web site as a tool for marketing the company's print products, but they soon saw the power of the Web for transforming their entire business. Today, the

Edmunds Web site contains more than 800,000 pages of information (which, unlike printed manuals, the company can update constantly) on a vast array of automotive topics, and more than 200,000 people a day visit it. The company still sells its information in print, but manuals account for less than one percent of its revenues. The immense volume of traffic the Edmunds site generates enables the company to provide automotive information free to users; Edmunds produces most of its $50 million in annual revenues by selling ads on its site to a wide variety of businesses targeting customers looking for automotive information.[29]

The real key to Edmunds.com's success on the Web is the knowledge that its managers and employees built over the years on how to collect and publish automotive information, to which they then applied the technology of the Web. Unfortunately, too many entrepreneurs tackle e-commerce by focusing on technology first and then determine how that technology fits their business idea. "If you start with technology, you're likely to be going to buy a solution in search of a problem," says Kip Martin, Program Director of META Group's Electronic Business Strategies. Instead, he suggests, "Start with the business and ask yourself what you want to happen and how you'll measure it. *Then* ask how the technology will help you achieve your goals. Remember: Business first, technology second."[30]

Myth 6. "Strategy? I Don't Need a Strategy to Sell on the Web! Just Give Me a Web Site, and the Rest Will Take Care of Itself"

Building a successful e-business is no different than building a successful brick-and-mortar business, and that requires a well-thought-out strategy. Building a strategy means that an entrepreneur must first develop a clear definition of the company's target audience and a thorough understanding of those customers' needs, wants, likes, and dislikes. To be successful, a Web site must be appealing to the customers it seeks to attract just as a traditional store's design and décor must draw foot traffic. If a Web site is to become the foundation for a successful e-business, an entrepreneur must create it with the target audience in mind.

Recall from Chapter 3 that one goal of developing a strategy is to set a business apart from its competitors. The same is true for creating a strategy for conducting business online. It is just as important, if not more important, for an online business to differentiate itself from the competition if it is to be successful. Unlike customers in a retail store, who must exert the effort to go to a competitor's store if they cannot find what they want, online customers only have to make a mouse click or two to go to a rival Web site. Therefore, competition online is fierce, and to succeed, a company must have a sound strategy.

In 1997, Jake Jacobs and his brother Michael decided to launch a company to sell used "retro" office furniture (their father had been in the used furniture business) and opened for business in the funky Williamsburg section of Brooklyn, New York. Within a matter of months, their store, Two Jakes Furniture, was attracting designers and architects looking for unique furnishings and accent pieces for their clients. As e-commerce accelerated in 2000, the two Jakes decided to launch a Web site designed by one of their employees. The site was little more than an electronic flyer for Two Jakes, but it launched the small company into the world of e-commerce. When the Jacobs' decided to add new furniture to their product line in 2003, they knew that integrating a fully transactional Web site capable of handling e-commerce would be essential to their success. They hired a part-time employee who also happened to be a Web designer to create the front-end of the site and then hired a friend of that worker as a consultant to create the back-office portion of the Web site. The Jacobs built the site so that customers could see photos of the company's inventory and know which items are in stock. Online sales now make up more than seven percent of Two Jakes' sales, and the Jacobs' are planning a redesign of their Web site that will add more customer-friendly features such as customer wish lists, product recommendations, customer reviews, and others. Promoting their site is a constant challenge because of the small company's limited budget. The brothers use print advertising and search engine

Two Jakes Furniture

marketing on Google, but their biggest break came when the stars of the cable television series *Queer Eye for the Straight Guy* showed up one day to shop at Two Jakes. The national exposure boosted sales in the store and the volume of traffic online, and Jake says that every week the company continues to get customers who saw the show.[31]

Myth 7. On the Web, Customer Service Is Not As Important As It Is in a Traditional Retail Store

Many Web sites treat customer service as an afterthought, and it shows. Sites that are difficult to navigate, slow to load, or confusing will turn customers away quickly, never to return. The fact is that customer service is just as important (if not more so) on the Web as it is in traditional brick-and-mortar stores. As shoppers become more accustomed to shopping online, they have higher expectations of the sites on which they shop. One recent study by Harris Interactive reports that more than 80 percent of online shoppers said that they were unwilling to accept lower levels of customer service than they would in offline, traditional stores.[32]

There is plenty of room for improvement in customer service on the Web. Research shows that 57 percent of Web shoppers who fill their online shopping carts abandon them without checking out. The result is that for every $1 customers spend online, they leave behind $4.51 in merchandise in abandoned shopping carts.[33] The most common reasons for leaving a site without purchasing include the following: (1) shipping and handling charges were too high, (2) delivery times were too long, (3) the checkout process required too much information and too much time to make a purchase, and (4) insufficient product information was available.[34]

In an attempt to improve the level of service they offer, many sites provide e-mail links to encourage customer interaction. Unfortunately, when responding to e-mail takes a very low priority at some e-businesses, customers take it as a clear sign of poor service. A recent Mystery Shopper Survey by the E-Tailing Group found that the average e-mail response time was 29 hours, and some companies failed to respond to e-mails at all.[35] The lesson for e-commerce entrepreneurs is simple: Devote time, energy, and money to developing an effective method for providing superior customer service. Those who do will build a sizeable base of loyal customers who will keep coming back. Perhaps the most significant actions online companies can take to bolster their customer service efforts are to create a well-staffed and well-trained customer response team, offer a simple return process, and provide an easy order-tracking process so customers can check the status of their orders at any time. Establishing a policy of responding to all customer e-mails within 24 hours and sending customers order and shipping confirmations and "thank you for your order" e-mails can go a long way to enhancing online customer service. Amazon.com's 500-plus service representatives have access to a database that contains a customer's complete history with the company so that they can serve customers faster and better. The database also keeps track of customers' purchase preferences and is the source of the site's ability to make customized product recommendations to shoppers.

Myth 8. Flash Makes a Web Site Better

Businesses that fall into this trap pour most of their e-commerce budgets into designing flashy Web sites with all of the "bells and whistles." The logic is that to stand out on the Web, a site really has to sparkle. That logic leads to a "more is better" mentality when designing a site. On the Web, however, "more" does *not* necessarily equate to "better."

Edler Group

Rick Edler, owner of the Edler Group, a California real estate company, learned this lesson the hard way. Edler's first foray onto the Web was a simple site, one that followed the "electronic flyer" approach and cost just $285. A confessed gadget freak, Edler soon decided to revamp his company's site to incorporate lots of features and lots of flash. "We were going to dazzle everyone with all of the technology," he recalls. The site, which cost $7,000 to design, literally pulsed with color and motion as spinning graphics moved around the screen. It even included movie listings. But the site was a failure, never drawing much traffic at all. The busy design with all of its features meant that the site was very slow to download. "You just stared at it like you were watching a commercial," says Edler. "We were scaring people away." Edler quickly scrapped the site and for $2,000 built a much simpler one that allows buyers to get the details on a listing and take a video tour of a house. The site also includes links to other useful real estate pages. Customer response to the newly designed site (http://www.edlergroup.com) has been positive, and more important, the site is now helping realtors to close sales.[36]

Keep the design of your site simple. Although fancy graphics, bright colors, playful music, and spinning icons can attract attention, they also can be quite distracting, and, as Rick Edler learned, very slow to download. One study reports that 48 percent of Internet users have terminated an online purchase because of slow-loading Web pages.[37]

Myth 9. It's What's up Front That Counts

Designing an attractive Web site is important to building a successful e-business. However, designing the back office, the systems that take over once a customer places an order on a Web site, is just as important as designing the site itself. If the behind-the-scenes support is not in place or cannot handle the traffic from the Web site, a company's entire e-commerce effort will come crashing down. The potentially large number of orders that a Web site can generate can overwhelm a small company that has failed to establish the infrastructure needed to support the site. Although e-commerce can lower many costs of doing business, it still requires a basic infrastructure in the channel of distribution to process orders, maintain inventory, fill orders, and handle customer service. Many entrepreneurs hoping to launch virtual businesses are discovering the need for a "clicks-and-mortar" approach to provide the necessary infrastructure to serve their customers. "The companies with warehouses, supply-chain management, and solid customer service are going to be the ones that survive," says Daryl Plummer, head of the Gartner Group's Internet and new media division.[38]

To customers, a business is only as good as its last order, and many e-companies are not measuring up. Many small e-tailers' Web sites do not offer real-time inventory lookup, which gives online shoppers the ability to see whether an item they want to purchase is actually in stock. In addition, many have not yet linked their Web sites to an automated back office, which means that processing orders takes longer and that errors are more likely. As software to integrate Web sites with the back office becomes easier to use and more affordable, more businesses will offer these features, but in the meantime some customers will have to endure late shipments, incorrect orders, and poor service.

Web-based entrepreneurs often discover that the greatest challenge their businesses face is not necessarily attracting customers on the Web but creating a workable order fulfillment strategy. Order fulfillment involves everything required to get goods from a warehouse into a customer's hands and includes order processing, warehousing, picking and packing, shipping, and billing. In a study of the connection between online companies' order fulfillment processes and their ultimate success or failure, researchers Sergui Netessine, Taylor Randall, and Nels Rudi found an important link. They concluded, "if an Internet company chooses its supply chain type logically—if it's aligned with its strategy, products, and operating environment—it's highly correlated with success."[39]

The busiest online shopping day of the year, Cyber Monday, takes place on the Monday after Thanksgiving, when workers return to their jobs and begin their online Christmas shopping.

Red Envelope, an online retailer that sells more than 1,000 different items ranging from cashmere robes and leather-bound journals to baby quilts and jewelry—generates half of its annual sales between October and December and understands the importance of Cyber Monday. Managing the back office of its e-commerce efforts is crucial to filling the flood of customer orders on time. After Red Envelope experienced problems filling orders during one holiday season, CEO Allison May reworked the company's entire order fulfillment strategy—from Web site to warehouse. A redesigned Web site made it easier for customers to find the items they were looking for, and an expanded customer call center

Red Envelope

was able to improve customer service. A warehouse renovation and a technology upgrade enabled employees to "pick and pack" customers' orders more quickly and more accurately. The majority of the upgrade was completed by the summer, Red Envelope's slowest season, and the new system paid off that fall when Red Envelope saw sales and customer service levels climb.[40]

Some entrepreneurs choose to handle order fulfillment in-house with their own employees, while others find it more economical to hire specialized fulfillment houses to handle these functions. Virtual order fulfillment (or drop-shipping) suits many e-tailers perfectly. When a customer orders a product from its Web site, the company forwards the order to its wholesaler or distributor, who then ships the product to the customer with the online merchant's label on it.

Spun.com

Spun.com, an online CD retailer, has managed to generate a profit without incurring the expense of an estimated $8 million investment in inventory by using wholesale distributor Alliance Entertainment as its virtual order fulfillment source. Founded in 1998 by brothers Andrew and Steven Gundy, Spun.com also operates a music exchange, in which customers can trade used CDs, DVDs, and video games for online credit toward the purchase of new or used items.[41]

Although e-tailers avoid the major investments in inventory and the problems associated with managing it, they lose control over delivery times and service quality. In addition, finding a fulfillment house willing to handle a relatively small volume of orders at a reasonable price can be difficult for some small businesses. Major fulfillment providers include FedEx, UPS, NewRoads, and NFI Interactive, and many others.

Myth 10. E-Commerce Will Cause Brick-and-Mortar Retail Stores to Disappear

The rapid growth of e-commerce does pose a serious threat to traditional retailers, especially those who fail to find ways to capitalize on the opportunities the Web offers them. However, it is unlikely that Web-based shopping will replace customers' need and desire to visit real stores selling real merchandise that they can see, touch, and try on. Some products simply lend themselves to selling in real stores more naturally than in online shops, but with the right strategies, entrepreneurs are finding success selling online almost every product imaginable. Virtual stores have, and will, continue to drive out of existence some traditional companies that resist creating new business models or are too slow to change. To remain competitive, traditional bricks-and-mortar stores must find ways to blend their operations with an online presence to become clicks-and-mortar businesses that can make the convenience, the reach, and the low transaction costs of the Web work for them.

TopBulb

Originally launched in 1930 as an industrial supply business called Gray Supply Company, TopBulb has grown into an e-tailer of specialty and hard-to-find light bulbs. With an inventory of more than one million bulbs of more than 5,000 different types and styles, TopBulb sells light bulbs that range in price from 37 cents to more than $800. When CEO Phil Bonello took over the company in 1999, he transformed it from a brick-and-mortar, catalog-based business into one built on e-commerce. Initially, TopBulb retained its focus on its base of industrial customers and builders, but in 2001, Bonello used the Web to begin marketing to retail customers as well. Selling to retail customers required the company to upgrade its Web site so that shoppers can search for bulbs by lighting application. The addition of a "Light Menu" keeps track of customers' past purchases to make shopping easier. "The Web site allows us to market in markets that otherwise we could not address," says Bonello. "We get customers from all over the world. That would never have happened in the old business." Today 40 percent of TopBulb's sales come from the Web.[42]

Myth 11. The Greatest Opportunities for E-Commerce Lie in the Retail Sector

As impressive as the growth rate and total volume for online retail sales are, they are dwarfed by those in the online business-to-business (B2B) sector, in which businesses sell to one another rather than to retail customers. eMarketer estimates that global business-to-business e-commerce sales now exceed $2.5 trillion a year.[43] That volume of sales is nearly 17 times the amount of business-to-consumer e-commerce! Entrepreneurs who are looking to sell goods to other businesses on the Web will find plenty of opportunities available in a multitude of industries.

B2B e-commerce is growing so rapidly because of its potential to boost productivity, slash costs, and increase profits. This brand of e-commerce is transforming the way companies purchase parts, supplies, and materials as well as the way they manage inventory and process transactions. The Web's power to increase the speed and the efficiency of the purchasing function represents a fundamental departure from the past. Experts estimate that transferring purchasing to the Web can cut total procurement costs by 10 percent and transaction costs by as much as 90 percent, saving companies billions of dollars a year.[44] For instance, Chris Cogan, CEO of an Internet purchasing site for hotels, restaurants, and health care companies, explains, "We estimate [that] the average cost of executing a paper purchase order is $115." Businesses using his company's Web-based purchasing system "get that cost down to $10," he says.[45]

Business-to-business e-commerce is growing because of the natural link that exists with B2B e-commerce. As we have seen, one of the greatest challenges Web-based retailers face is obtaining and delivering the goods their customers order fast enough to satisfy customers' expectations. Increasingly, Web-based companies are connecting their front office sales systems and their back office purchasing and order fulfillment systems with those of their suppliers. The result is a faster, more efficient method of filling customer orders. So far the most successful online B2B companies are those that have discovered ways of tying their front offices, their back offices, their suppliers, and their customers together into a single, smoothly functioning, Web-based network.

Myth 12. It's Too Late to Get on the Web

A common myth, especially among small companies, is that those businesses that have not yet moved onto the Web have missed a golden opportunity. E-commerce is still in its childhood. Companies are still figuring out how to succeed on the Web, learning which techniques work and which ones don't. For every e-commerce site that exists, a trio of others has failed. An abundance of business opportunities exists for those entrepreneurs insightful enough to spot them and clever enough to capitalize on them.

One fact of e-commerce that has emerged is the importance of speed. Companies doing business on the Web have discovered that those who reach customers first often have a significant advantage over their slower rivals. "The lesson of the Web is not how the big eat the small, but how the fast eat the slow," says a manager at a venture capital firm specializing in Web-based companies.[46]

Succumbing to this myth often leads entrepreneurs to make a fundamental mistake once they finally decide to go online: They believe they have to have a "perfect" site before they can launch it. Few businesses get their sites "right" the first time. In fact, the most successful e-commerce sites are constantly changing, removing what does not work and adding new features to see what does. Successful Web sites are much like a well-designed flower garden, constantly growing and improving, yet changing to reflect the climate of each season. Their creators worry less about creating the perfect site at the outset than about getting a site online and then fixing it, tweaking it, and updating it to meet changing customer demands. "The person trying to create the perfect [online] store will fail," says Gerry Goldsholle, founder of two Web sites aimed at small companies. "Part of the Internet process is 'try it, learn from it, and fix it.' Delay is your biggest enemy. If you delay, someone else will do it."[47]

E-Commerce the Right Way

A key component of Earth Treks' rapid growth is its Web-based marketing strategy. The company not only seeks to attract visitors to its site with live reports from expeditions, but it also strives to build a sense of community among its customers and to cultivate the next generation of customers.

From the Top of the World . . .

Earth Treks, a small company offering professional guide services and experiences for mountain and ice climbs, has found a way to keep customers returning frequently to its Web site (http://www.earthtreksclimbing.com): It takes them on virtual climbs to exotic locations such as Ecuador's Cotopaxi volcano or to the most challenging summit in the world, the 29,035-foot peak of Mt. Everest. Company guides on these semiannual expeditions use laptop computers and satellite connections to post daily to the Web e-mail journals, digital photographs, and streaming video of their climbs, and climbing enthusiasts from all over the world log on to get the latest updates. Someone who has never been on a climb, especially one as difficult as ascending Mt. Everest, cannot really imagine what it is like, but Earth Treks does everything it can to make the experience real. On a recent excursion he led to Everest, company founder Chris Warner posted the following accounts:

May 23
I pulled myself up the last of this rock pitch and there, a rise or two above me, was the summit.

100 feet away, an undulating crest . . . I made it to the top just past 10 am, and searched for a place to sit down. Naoki handed me his camera and I snapped some photos of him. Clouds were hiding much of the view, but Lhotse looked incredible, with the Lhotse Coulior rising straight up the black face. Makalu was capped by clouds as was Cho Oyu.

May 26
Hey guys. Yes we did have a near disaster on our hands, and I did find myself in the unusual situation of spending two long days at 27,400 ft crying and weakening and hoping and working hard to find a way to keep hope and progress alive. I will write about it soon, but right now, my body and mind are not quite in the same place.

Fifty thousand visitors logged onto the company's Web site the day Warner reached the summit of Mt. Everest.

Web Treks' Web-based marketing strategy has much to do with the fact that its revenues have doubled in just two years and continue to grow rapidly. Devoted climbers are fascinated by the online journals and pictures posted there and often book a climb with Earth Treks, but the site sends a clear message to visitors: If you are into climbing, whether as a hobby or as a serious obsession, this site is for you! The unique online experience creates a sense of community among Earth Treks' customers that many other companies find so elusive. The company is receiving record numbers of requests from serious climbers who want to scale the world's most challenging summits.

Earth Treks also is using its Web site to cultivate its next generation of customers. With the help of two local teachers, Warner started Shared Summits, a program in which students from ages 6 to 18 can follow climbers' adventures and learn about different countries, climates, geography, and cultures as well as about leadership and teamwork, and earn school credit. Due to the success of the program, the company now hosts kids' birthday parties and has record enrollment in its Youth Rox program, which trains youngsters the basics of climbing on its indoor climbing walls.

The Earth Treks' Web site has returned many times over the original $3,000 Warner spent to create it and the $7,200 a year spent to maintain it.

. . . To the Gourmet's Kitchen

Spencer Chesman, founder of one of the first gourmet food sites on the Web, has built a highly successful, multi-million-dollar business aimed at gourmands everywhere. Launched in 1997 from Yorktown Heights, New York, iGourmet is more than a one-stop shop for exotic foods; it has become a gourmet food *authority*. On its Web site (http://www.igourmet.com), customers can see large color pictures of every product and read complete descriptions as they shop. A recipe section and a "related items" button help customers find everything they need and boost sales of complementary products. Shoppers can browse the wine and cheese tastings iGourmet sponsors across the country, can sign up for a regularly published e-newsletter, get tips for hosting a party, and even read selections from the *Encyclopedia of Cheese*.

Those searching for just the right gift can use the iGourmet Gift Finder, which allows them to select a price range; then the site pops up a few pages of gift suggestions in that range. Because many of the items it ships around the world are perishable, iGourmet developed a special foam-lined shipping chest that keeps items cool for up to 48 hours. Just in case, the company offers a 100 percent guaranteed return policy. If a customer is dissatisfied with any product from iGourmet, the company will refund the full purchase price within five business days. It's no wonder that *Forbes* magazine has named iGourmet the best gourmet food Web site three years in a row and that 75 percent of the company's customers return to make repeat purchases.

1. Which of the strategies for e-success described in this chapter are these two companies using? Explain.
2. Although Earth Treks and iGourmet are in very different businesses, what similarities do you see in their approaches to e-commerce?
3. Visit the Web sites for these two companies and note the design elements and online marketing strategies they employ. Then go to the Web site for a local business with which you are familiar and, in a brainstorming session with several of your classmates, develop a set of strategies for e-success based on what you have learned

Sources: Constance Loizos, "Traffic Magnets," *Inc. Technology*, November 2001, pp. 140–142; Earth Treks, http://www.earthtreks. com; Melissa Campanelli, "Dot.common Sense," *Entrepreneur*, May 2002, pp. 34–36; "About iGourmet," iGourmet, http://www.igourmet. com.

Strategies for E-Success

The typical Internet user is online for an average of 14 hours a week, an amount that equals the amount of time the average person spends each week watching television. By comparison, the typical person spends an average of two hours per week reading newspapers, one hour per week reading magazines, and five hours per week listening to radio.[48] In other words, people now spend more time online than ever before. However, converting these Web surfers into online customers requires a business to do more than merely set up a Web site and wait for the hits to start rolling up. You may be ready to sell, but no one knows you are there! Building sufficient volume for a site takes energy, time, money, creativity, and, perhaps most important, a well-defined marketing and promotional strategy. One business writer explains that success in e-commerce "isn't glamorous at all," and explains, "The difference between Web success and Web failure often hinges on how carefully people sift through details and fine-tune niggling plans. E businesses that actually get it . . . understand how to use the Web to push the envelope, to create new tools and business models."[49]

Although the Web is a unique medium for creating a company, launching an e-business is not much different from launching a traditional offline company. The basic drivers of a successful business remain in place on the Web on Main Street. To be successful, both offline and online companies require solid planning and a well-formulated strategy that emphasizes customer service. The goals of e-commerce are no different from those of traditional offline businesses—to increase sales, improve efficiency, and boost profits by serving customers better.

LEARNING OBJECTIVES
4. Explain the basic strategies entrepreneurs should follow to achieve success in their e-commerce efforts.

Altrec.com

When long-time friends Mike Morford, Blaine Donnelson, and Shannon Stowell launched Altrec.com (pronounced "all trek") in 1999, they saw an opportunity to create "an outdoor lifestyle destination Web site that brings together everything necessary for individuals to satisfy their passion for the outdoors." The online retailer sells outdoor gear from more than 300 of the world's top makers of clothing and accessories on a Web site built around "passion points" ranging from camping and fly fishing to snowboarding and mountain climbing. The site makes shopping extremely easy for customers with detailed product information, product comparison and sizing charts, 360-degree product views that offer a zoom option, customer product reviews, and many other features. Not only can customers buy equipment at altrec.com, but they also can book trips to exotic locations, peruse photo galleries and diaries from traveling journalists, and even find locations for getting their outdoor equipment repaired. Customer service representatives provide around-the-clock assistance, answer questions, and can even guide customers (by taking long-distance control of their Web browsers) to the correct pages on the site. Altrec's combination of product selection, superb customer service, and convenience have produced dramatic growth rates for the company; more than 600,000 guests visit its Web site each month.[50]

How a company integrates the Web into its overall business strategy determines how successful it ultimately will become. Following are some guidelines for building a successful Web strategy for a small e-company.

Focus on a Niche in the Market

Rather than try to compete head to head with the dominant players on the Web who have the resources and the recognition to squash smaller competitors, entrepreneurs should consider focusing on serving a market niche. Smaller companies' limited resources usually are better spent serving niche markets than trying to be everything to everyone (recall the discussion of the focus strategy in Chapter 3). The idea is to concentrate on serving a small corner of the market the giants have overlooked. Niches exist in every industry and can be highly profitable, given the right strategy for serving them. A niche can be defined in many ways, including by geography, customer profile, product, product usage, and many others.

The Web provides an ideal mechanism for reaching niche customers, as the following examples illustrate:

Dogbooties.com

Many small companies have discovered that the Web is the ideal medium for implementing a focus strategy. Companies that sell highly specialized products such as Dogbooties.com can reach customers around the world very inexpensively with their Web sites.

Dogbooties.com reaches around the globe to find customers who own sled dogs, hunting dogs, or dogs with tender feet, or who simply want their dogs to be on the cutting edge of fashion. In addition to dog booties, the company, founded in 1995 by copreneurs Louise and Greg Russell, sells other dog-related accessories. "The Internet allows us to reach all over the world inexpensively," says Greg.[51]

SaltWorks Inc.

Mark Zoske and Naomi Novotny co-founded SaltWorks Inc. in 2005 and say that their company is the world's leading business that focuses exclusively on sea salt. With 10,000 customers in its database, SaltWorks racks up more than $4 million in annual sales, and its product line includes everything from shakers of gourmet Salish Alderwood Smoked Salt to the 44,000-pound containers of salt it acquires for its customers in the spice business. The Saltworks Web site attracts more than 3,000 visitors each day, and, according to Novotny, "E-commerce is our main advantage. We are really the only salt company that specializes in sea salt. We are out on the Web, and our competitors just aren't there."[52]

Chris Gwynn also focuses on a niche market with his company, Fridgedoor.com, which he bills as "the Web's magnet store." From Quincy, Massachusetts, Gwynn sells novelty and custom-designed refrigerator magnets. Customers looking for refrigerator magnets can find designs ranging from Betty Boop to the Virgin Mary.[53]

Fridgedoor.com

As these small companies prove, the Web, due to its broad reach, is the ideal mechanism for implementing a focus strategy because small companies can reach large numbers of customers with a common interest.

Develop a Community

On the Web, competitors are just a mouse click away. To attract customers and keep them coming back, e-companies have discovered the need to offer more than just quality products and excellent customer service. Many seek to develop a community of customers with similar interests, the nucleus of which is their Web site. The idea is to increase customer loyalty by giving customers the chance to interact with other like-minded visitors or with experts to discuss and learn more about topics they are passionate about. "It's not going to be a direct revenue source," says Howard Rheingold, author of *The Virtual Community*, "but it may offer you insight for creating new products. It may help you establish better relationships and more loyalty with your customers."[54]

E-mail lists, chat rooms, customer polls ("What is your favorite sports drink?"), blogs, guest books, and message boards are powerful tools for building a community of visitors at a site because they give visitors the opportunity to have conversations about products, services, and topics that interest them.

Anne Kelly, founder of Junonia, a company that specializes in selling clothing to the 40 percent of women in the United States who wear a size 14 and up, launched her business in the mid-1990s as a catalog business. The idea came to her when she realized that plus-sized women had great difficulty finding attractive, high-quality sportswear. In 1999, Kelly took her company online, and although Junonia still sends out six million catalogs a year, it generates half of its sales from the Web site, which recently was named one of the top 50 Best of the Web retail sites by *Internet Retailer Magazine*. Much of the site's success comes from the sense of community Kelly has created for her online customers as they interact with the company. For instance, the Junonia site includes a "notebook" section that contains articles ("Fashion and Function"), interviews with interesting Junonia customers, and, of course, feedback and testimonials from satisfied customers. "Our initial focus was to create an efficient and reliable shopping experience," says the company's e-commerce director, Tom Lindmeier. "We are now offering our customers something more—a feeling of connection to our brand—one that resonates with their aspirations and lifestyle." Anne Kelly also posts her e-mail address and her telephone number on the site so that customers can contact her directly. "I love to hear from customers," she says.[55]

Junonia

Like Junonia, companies that successfully create a community around their Web sites turn mere customers into loyal fans who keep coming back and, better yet, invite others to join them.

Attract Visitors by Giving Away "Freebies"

One of the most important words on the Internet is "free." Many successful e-merchants have discovered the ability to attract visitors to their site by giving away something free and then selling them something else. One e-commerce consultant calls this cycle of giving something away and then selling something "the rhythm of the Web."[56] The "freebie" must be something customers value, but it does *not* have to be expensive nor does it have to be a product. In fact, one of the most common giveaways on the Web is *information*. (After all, that's what most people on the Web are after!) Creating a free online or e-mail newsletter with links to your company's site, of course, and to others of interest is one of the most effective ways of driving potential customers to a site. Meaningful content presented in a clear, professional fashion is a must. Experts advise keeping online newsletters short—no more than about 600 words. *Poor Richard's E-Mail Publishing* by Chris Pirillo (Top Floor Publishing) offers much useful advice on creating online newsletters.

Lonely Planet

To attract customers to its travel Web site, Lonely Planet, a publisher of travel books sold in more than 200 countries, offers customers travel tips and advice, articles filled with useful information, travel blogs by the authors of the books it publishes, and a free newsletter. The site's main section is "Worldguide," a handy hub that allows visitors to select a country and access an exhaustive compendium of information about it, from how to get there and the currency used to its history and culture. The "Postcard" section provides travel updates and travel warnings as well as actual messages from postcards sent in by Lonely Planet travelers. Lonely Planet recognizes that offering customers a great deal of useful travel information for free on its Web site increases the likelihood that they will purchase the company's travel books. The Lonely Planet Web site, which recently won a Webby Award (the Web equivalent of an Emmy Award, which recognizes excellence in Web design, creativity, usability, and functionality), has been a key reason that the company sells more than 6.5 million books per year.[57]

Make Creative Use of E-mail, but Avoid Becoming a Spammer

Used properly and creatively, e-mail can be an effective, low-cost way to build traffic on a Web site, and small business owners recognize this. According to the Interland Business Barometer, 70 percent of the owners of small and medium-sized businesses say that e-mail is critical to their success.[58] Just as with a newsletter, an e-mail's content should offer something of value to recipients. Supported by online newsletters or chat rooms, customers welcome well-constructed permission e-mail that directs them to a company's site for information or special deals, unlike unsolicited and universally despised e-mails known as "spam." Spam is a growing problem on the Internet; Symantec, a company that specializes in information security, estimates that 67 percent of e-mails sent is spam![59]

To avoid having their marketing messages become part of that electronic clutter, companies should rely on permission e-mails, collecting visitors' e-mail addresses (and their permission to send them e-mail messages) when they register on a site to receive a "freebie." To be successful at collecting a sufficient number of e-mail addresses, a company must make it clear to customers that they will receive messages that are meaningful to them and that the company will not sell e-mail addresses to others (which should be part of its posted privacy policy). Once a business has a customer's permission to send information in additional e-mail messages, it has a meaningful marketing opportunity to create a long-term customer relationship and to build customer loyalty. Junonia, the company that sells plus-size clothing for women, relies on permission e-mail more heavily than it has in the past. "We were doing four to five e-mailings a month," says Tom Lindmeier Junonia's e-commerce director. "Now we do two a week." As its success with e-mail grows, the company hopes to be able to reduce the number of catalogs it sends customers—currently eighteen 56-page catalogs each year. "Catalogs are very expensive to send out, but e-mail costs almost nothing," says Lindmeier.[60]

Figure 9.2 shows e-mail read and click-through rates by day of the week.

Make Sure Your Web Site Says "Credibility"

Online shoppers are wary, and with the prevalence of online fraud, they have every right to be. In essence, many shoppers simply do not trust Web sites. Unless a company can build visitors' trust in its Web site, selling to them is virtually impossible. Visitors begin to evaluate the credibility of a site as soon as they arrive. Does the site look professional? Are there misspelled words and typographical errors? If the site provides information, does it note the sources of that information? If so, are those sources legitimate? Are they trustworthy? Is the presentation of the information fair and objective, or is it biased? Are there dead links on the site? Does the company have its privacy and merchandise return policies posted in a prominent place?

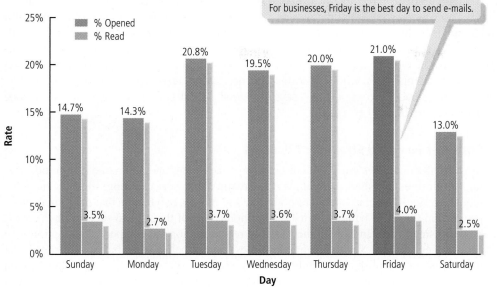

FIGURE 9.2

E-Mail and Click-Through Rates by Day of the Week

Source: eROI, January 2006.

One of the simplest ways to establish credibility with customers is to use brand names they know and trust. Whether a company sells nationally recognized brands or its own well-known private brand, using those names on its site creates a sense of legitimacy. People buy brand names they trust, and online companies can use that to their advantage. Businesses selling lesser-known brands should use customer testimonials and endorsements (with their permission, of course) about a product or service.

Another effective way to build customer confidence is by joining an online seal program such as TRUSTe or BBBOnLine. The online equivalent of the Underwriter Laboratories stamp or the *Good Housekeeping* Seal of Approval, these seals mean that a company meets certain standards concerning the privacy of customers' information and the resolution of customer complaints. TopBulb.com, the company that sells every kind of light bulb imaginable, has won the BBBOnLine reliability seal of approval and displays it prominently on its Web site. Providing a street address, an e-mail address, and a toll-free telephone number also send a subtle message to shoppers that a legitimate business is behind a Web site. Another effective technique is to include an "About Us" page on the Web site so that customers can read about the company's story—its founders, how they started the business, the challenges they have overcome, and other details. Customers enjoy supporting small businesses with which they feel a connection, and this is a perfect opportunity for a small company to establish that connection. Many small companies include photographs of their brick-and-mortar stores and of their employees to combat the Web's anonymity and to give shoppers the feeling that they are supporting a friendly small business. One small online retailer includes on his Web site short anecdotes about his dog, Cody, the official company mascot, and Cody's "views" on featured products. The response to the technique has been so strong that Cody has become a celebrity among the company's customers and even has her own e-mail address.

Steve Blackwell, who in 1997 co-founded e-weddingbands.com, an online company that sells all types of wedding bands, loose diamonds, and bridal gifts, knew that to be successful he had to design a Web site that communicated to customers a message of trust, confidence, and credibility. Blackwell has achieved that goal by using several techniques. The company's site includes a prominent link to customer testimonials—currently 10 pages of them. In addition, e-weddingbands.com posts on its home page a certificate from GeoTrust ensuring that the company's online transactions are secured with SSL technology as well as its BBBOnLine reliability certificate. Customers can click on the BBBOnLine link to get a background report on e-weddingbands.com. The site's front page also has a

e-weddingbands.com

prominent link to the company's guarantee policy: Customers can return a ring within 30 days for any reason. E-weddingbands.com also offers customers a price guarantee: If a customer finds the same ring online for a lower price, e-weddingbands.com will beat it. The FAQ (frequently asked questions) section of the site repeats these guarantees as well. Finally, when a customer makes a purchase, the order is assigned to one of the company's employees, who sends the customer a personal e-mail. "If you have problems, you can go back to that person," says Blackwell. "It's that one-on-one customer service that really helps."

Consider Forming Strategic Alliances

Most small companies engaged in e-commerce lack the brand and name recognition that larger, more established companies do. Creating that sort of recognition on the Web requires a significant investment of both time and money, two factors that most small companies find scarce. If building name recognition is one of the keys to success on the Web, how can small companies with their limited resources hope to compete? One option is to form strategic alliances with bigger companies that can help a small business achieve what it could not accomplish alone. Entrepreneurs also should consider forming alliances with nonprofit organizations such as civic or community groups, hobby clubs, and others as a way of promoting their online businesses. Describing the need for small companies to consider forming strategic alliances, Philip Anderson of Dartmouth's Tuck School of Business says, "You need to build [market] share fast, and that means you have to have more resources than you can get your mitts on by yourself."[61]

Before plunging into a strategic alliance with a partner, however, entrepreneurs must understand their dark side. Research shows that 55 percent of strategic alliances unravel within three and one-half years.[62] The most common reasons for splitting up? One study found the following causes: incompatible corporate cultures (75 percent), incompatible management personalities (63 percent), and differences in strategic priorities (58 percent).[63]

Table 9.2 offers seven questions every entrepreneur should ask before entering into a strategic alliance with a partner.

Make the Most of the Web's Global Reach

Despite the Web's reputation as an international marketplace, many Web entrepreneurs fail to utilize fully its global reach. More than 1.02 billion people around the world use the Internet, and more than 77 percent of them live outside the United States.[64] Only 27.6 percent of Web users throughout the world speak English, and that percentage is declining.[65]

TABLE 9.2 Questions to Ask *before* Entering a Strategic Alliance

Unfortunately, most strategic alliances fail. In his book, *Partnering Intelligence: Creating Value for Your Business by Building Strong Alliances* (Davies-Black Publishing), Stephen M. Dent offers seven questions every entrepreneur should ask *before* forging an alliance:

1. What is your potential partner's business vision?

2. What are its strategies for achieving its vision?

3. Where does it want to go as a company?

4. What are its values and ethics?

5. What kind of corporate culture does it have?

6. What types of relationships and partnerships does it already have and how well are they working out?

7. Has it conducted an internal assessment of its strengths, weaknesses, and culture?

Based on the answers to these seven questions, entrepreneurs can assess how compatible potential partners are with their own business vision and goals.

Source: Robert McGarvey, "Made for Each Other?" *Entrepreneur,* February 2000, p. 79.

Limiting a global market to only a small portion of its potential by ignoring foreign customers makes little sense.

COMPANY
Profile

BackWoods Grocery Inc.

When Lisa and Paul Beckham launched BackWoods Grocery, an online food and outdoor cookware site, they had no intentions of taking international orders because they thought dealing with tariffs, duties, and customs issues would be too complicated. An order from an English-speaking customer in Switzerland soon changed their minds, however. Lisa Beckham visited the U.S. Postal Service Web site to learn about shipping details and then let the customer (who paid the shipping charges) decide which method to use. To avoid the risks of currency fluctuations, Beckham accepted credit card payment in U.S. dollars only, and the customer's credit card issuer made the conversion. Today, BackWoods Grocery encourages foreign orders from Web customers; foreign sales account for just two percent of revenues but are growing fast.[66]

E-companies wanting to draw significant sales from foreign markets must design their sites with these foreign customers in mind. A common mechanism is to include several "language buttons" on the opening page of a site that take customers to pages in the language of their choice. Experienced e-commerce companies have learned that offering a localized page for every country or region they target pays off in increased sales.

Virtual companies trying to establish a foothold in foreign markets by setting up Web sites dedicated to them run the same risk that actual companies do: offending international visitors by using the business conventions and standards the companies are accustomed to using in the United States. Business practices, even those used on the Web, that are acceptable, even expected, in the United States may be taboo in other countries. Color schemes can be important, too. Selecting the "wrong" colors and symbols on a site targeting people in a particular country can hurt sales and offend visitors. For example, in the United States and Asia, the "thumbs-up" gesture indicates a positive result, but in Europe and Latin America, it is obscene! A little research into the subtleties of a target country's culture and business practices can save a great deal of embarrassment and money. Creating secure, simple, and reliable payment methods for foreign customers also will boost sales.

When translating the content of their Web pages into other languages, e-companies must use extreme caution. This is *not* the time to pull out their notes from an introductory Spanish course and begin their own translations. Hiring professional translation and localization services to convert a company's Web content into other languages minimizes the likelihood of a company unintentionally offending foreign customers.

Figure 9.3 shows the e-readiness rankings, a measure of an area's readiness to support and nurture e-commerce businesses, of the world's major regions.

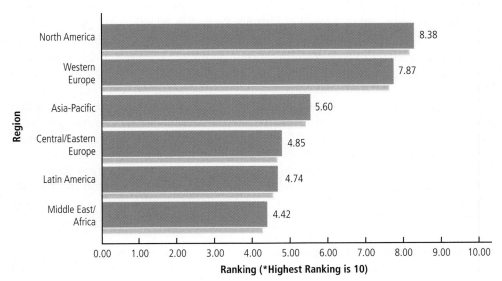

FIGURE 9.3

E-Readiness Ranking

Source: The Economist Intelligence Unit in cooperation with the IBM Institute for Business Value, *The 2005 E-Readiness Rankings* (London: Author, 2005), http://graphics.eiu.com/files/ad_pdfs/2005Ereadiness_Ranking_WP.pdf#search=%22"The%202005%20E-Readiness%20Rankings"%20%22.

Promote Your Web Site Online and Offline

E-commerce entrepreneurs must use every means available—both online and offline—to promote their Web sites and to drive traffic to it. In addition to using traditional online techniques such as registering with search engines, using pay-per-click techniques, and creating blogs, Web entrepreneurs must promote their sites offline as well. Ads in other media such as direct mail or newspapers that mention a site's URL will bring customers to it. As noted earlier, it is also a good idea to put the company's Web address on *everything* a company publishes, from its advertisements and letterhead to shopping bags, business cards—even employees' uniforms! The techniques for generating publicity for an offline business covered in Chapter 8 can be just as effective for online businesses needing to make their domain names better known without breaking their budgets. A passive approach to generating Web site traffic is a recipe for failure; entrepreneurs who are as innovative at promoting their e-businesses as they are at creating them can attract impressive numbers of visitors to their sites.

Develop an Effective Search Engine Optimization (SEO) Strategy

Because of the growing popularity of search engines among Internet shoppers, Web search strategies have become an essential part of online companies' promotion strategies. A recent survey by Plunkett Research Ltd. reports that 84 percent of online shoppers use search engines to find information on the Internet.[67] Given that the sheer volume of Web pages, which number well into the billions, is overwhelming, it is no surprise that Internet shoppers use search engines extensively. Studies by Jupiter Media Metrix show that 77 percent of Internet shoppers go straight to a search engine to find the products and services they want. Unfortunately, business owners invest less than one percent of their marketing budget in landing highly placed spots on popular search engines.[68] For a company engaged in e-commerce, a well-defined search marketing strategy is a vital part of its overall marketing plan.

One of the biggest challenges facing e-commerce entrepreneurs is maintaining the effectiveness of their search engine marketing strategies. Because the most popular search engines are constantly updating and refining their algorithms—the secretive formulas and methodology search engines use to find and rank the results of Web searches—Web entrepreneurs also must evaluate and constantly refine their search strategies. A company's Web search strategy must recognize the three basic types of search engine results: natural or organic listings, paid or sponsored listings, and paid inclusion. **Natural (or organic) listings** arise as a result of "spiders," powerful programs that search engines use to crawl around the Web and analyze sites for keywords, links, and other data. Based on what they find, spiders use complex algorithms to index Web sites so that a search engine can display a listing of relevant Web sites when a person enters a keyword in the engine to start a search. Some search engines use people-powered searches rather than spider-powered ones to assemble their indexes. With natural listings, an entrepreneur's goal is to get his or her Web site displayed at or near the top of the list of search results, a technique known as search engine optimization. Table 9.3 offers tips for improving search placement results.

natural (or organic) listings search engine listings that are the result of "spiders," powerful programs that crawl around the Web and analyze sites for keywords, links, and other data.

MyWeddingFavors.com

Brad Fallon, founder of MyWeddingFavors.com, an online business that sells small wedding-related products such as candles and place-card holders, credits a clever search engine strategy with helping his company reach more than $1 million in sales in its first year. Fallon, a former search engine optimization specialist, used his knowledge of search engines to build his e-commerce company. "We can track our revenue results right to our results on the search engine listing," he says. Starting with a Yahoo! Store–based site, Fallon made sure the pages on his site included all of the right keywords, meta descriptions, and title tags. He also made sure that the site's links were the type that search engine spiders would detect easily, and he used a reciprocal exchange program to create a Web of links from other wedding sites to MyWeddingFavors.com, a move that increases the site's link popularity rating and boosts its search engine ranking.[69]

paid (or sponsored) listings short text advertisements with links to the sponsoring company's Web site that appear on the results page of a search engine when the user types in a keyword or phrase.

Paid (or sponsored) listings are short text advertisements with links to the sponsoring company's Web site that appear on the results pages of a search engine when a user types in a keyword or phrase. Entrepreneurs should use paid search listings to accomplish what natural

TABLE 9.3 Techniques for Optimizing Search Engine Use

Because of their widespread use among Web users, search engines are one of the most effective ways to drive traffic to your Web site. What can business owners do to optimize their use of search engines? The following tips will help:

- Conduct brainstorming sessions to develop a list of keywords and phrases that searchers are likely to use when using a search engine to locate a company's products and services and then use those words and phrases on your Web pages. Usually, simple terms are better than industry jargon.

- Visit competitors' sites for keyword ideas, but avoid using the exact phrases. Simply right-clicking on a competitor's Web page and choosing "View Source" will display the keywords used on the site.

- Ask customers which words and phrases they use when searching for the products and services the company sells.

- Consider using less obvious keywords and brand names in your pay-per-click search engine strategy. For instance, rather than use just "bicycles," a small bicycle retailer should consider keywords such as "racing bikes" or "LeMond."

- Use data analysis tools to review Web logs to find which words and phrases (and which search engines) brought visitors to your company's Web site.

- Submit your Web site to multiple search engines. Spending time listing your site with every search engine is wasteful. The "must-have" search engines include Google, Yahoo!, MSN, AlltheWeb, AltaVista, Ask Jeeves, Inktomi, and Open Directory Project. They account for about 99 percent of all searches conducted online.

- Pay for preferred placement in key search engines by bidding on keywords, but be sure you know how much you can afford to bid for keywords. Fees are usually set on a pay-per-click basis, which means you pay for search engine placement only when it works.

- Place as title tags, meta tags, and the text on your Web pages keywords that Web users are likely to use in their searches. Do *not,* however, list these keywords dozens or hundreds of times in an attempt to boost your search ranking. This technique is known as keyword stuffing, and Web spiders look for it. If they find it, they penalize the guilty site with lower search rankings, and some even ban the site from listings.

- Find out which words users enter into search engines to find your products or services. Techniques include visiting competitors' Web sites and right-clicking to "View Source" to see which keywords they use, asking customers, using services such as Wordtracker that monitor popular search phrases, and relying on analytics software that tracks how users arrived at your site.

- Add links to other sites. Many "spider-based" search engines such as Google and AltaVista look for them, and the greater the number of valid links your site has, the higher is its search ranking. Do not use "link farms," however, sites that artificially inflate the number of links that a site uses, a technique called "spamdexing." Web spiders are wise to link farms too, and they penalize or ban sites that use them from their search rankings.

- List your products or services separately. The more specific your Web site is, the more likely it will show up in keyword searches.

- Be patient, especially if you use free search engine placement. It often takes four to eight weeks before a site shows up in major search engines.

- Monitor search engine listing results using analytics software that tracks many important statistics such as the total number of visitors, which search engines they used, the keywords they typed in, and many others. These statistics can be valuable tools, helping business owners to refine their search engine marketing techniques over time.

- Monitor search engine performance and productivity regularly. It changes constantly, and what worked three months ago may not be producing results today. Landing a Top 10 spot on a search engine is a dynamic and ongoing process. "Analyze, optimize, submit, monitor, and then repeat the process," says Shari Thurow, a search engine optimization expert.

listings cannot. Google, the most popular search engine, displays paid listings as "sponsored links" at the top and down the side of each results page, and Yahoo! shows "sponsored results" at the top and the bottom of its results pages. With this pay-for-placement method, advertisers bid on keywords to determine their placement on a search engine's results page. The highest bidder for a keyword gets the most prominent placement (at the top) on the search engine's results page when a user types in that keyword on the search engine. The advertiser pays only when a shopper clicks through to its Web site from the search engine. For this reason, paid listings also are called pay-for-placement, pay-per-click, and pay-for-performance ads. At one popular search engine, the average bid for keywords in its paid listings is 40 cents, but some words can bring as little as 5 cents or as much as $100.* Although it can be expensive, one advantage of paid listings is the ability of the advertiser to evaluate the effectiveness of the each listing. "You can track down to the individual keyword exactly what it's worth all the way to the conversion rate, says Brad Fallon of MyWeddingFavors.com, who uses paid listings to supplement his natural search listings efforts. "It's crazy not to do it."[70]

MFW Vacation Rentals

Cheryl Quist, owner of MFW Vacation Rentals, manages six luxury rental houses near Mendocino, California, that rent for about $2,500 per week. Recognizing that the market for her rental houses is small, Quist turned to the Web to reach potential customers. She began by advertising the properties on a few vacation Web sites such as VacationRentals.com before she decided to test paid listings on the Overture search engine. Although she still advertises on the vacation Web sites, Quist puts most of her marketing budget into buying keywords on Overture, which costs about $3,000 a year. Between 60 and 70 percent of her customer leads come from her company's Overture listings. "The keywords that people use when searching for vacation rentals allow you to carefully target your audience," Quist says. Entrepreneurs must be careful, however, because paid listings can strain a small company's marketing budget. Quist says that her top keyword— "Mendocino vacation rentals"—"started off at about two dollars a click, and now it's up to over three dollars [per click]." With Overture, Quist can activate and de-activate her keyword campaign at any time—for example, when all of her houses are booked or during seasonal peaks and troughs, allowing her to minimize costs.[71]

The accompanying "Hands on . . . How to" feature explains how to determine the value of a keyword using a diagnostic known as the cost of acquisition.

Determine How Much You Can Afford to Bid on That Keyword

Creating a Web site for a company without a strategy for driving traffic to it is fruitless and an incredible waste of resources. A strategy to maximize your e-company's natural listing on search engines is important, but even the best search engine strategy cannot produce top search engine rankings every time. That's why it is imperative for entrepreneurs to supplement their companies' natural listings with paid listings. With paid listings, companies pay for top-tier search results by bidding on keywords and paying for them on a per-click basis. The high-

est bidder for a keyword gets the most prominent placement (at the top) on the search engine's results page when a user types in that keyword on the search engine. The company pays only when a shopper clicks through to its Web site from the search engine. This cost of this technique can add up quickly, and search engines allow entrepreneurs to set spending caps on their accounts so they don't overspend. "When people don't know what they're doing [with paid listings], it's very easy for them to get hurt," says Jeff Binder, an e-commerce expert.

So how much should you bid on a keyword? You have to do the math to see how much you can afford to spend. It all begins with calculating your e-company's conversion rate, the percentage of visitors to your company's Web site who actually make a purchase. Conversion rates vary

---

*An online merchant's cost per sale = cost per click ÷ merchant's conversion rate. For example, a merchant with a one percent conversion rate who submits a keyword bid of 10 cents per click is paying $10 per sale ($0.10 ÷ 0.01 = $10).

from one online industry to another, but the average conversion rate is about 2.3 percent. That means that for every 1,000 visitors to a company's site, 23 of them actually make a purchase. For this example, let's assume that your company's conversion rate is 2.5 percent.

The next step is to calculate your company's profit per online sale. Like conversion rates, the profit a company earns per sale varies dramatically from one industry to another. A company that sells upscale jewelry online may generate a profit per sale of several hundreds of dollars, but a company that sells books or DVDs may make a profit of a just few dollars—or just a few pennies—per sale. For our example, let's assume that your company's profit per sale is $9.00.

To calculate the maximum amount your company could afford to bid on a key word, use the following formula:

Maximum keyword bid = Conversion rate × Profit per sale

For your company, the result is

Maximum keyword bid = 2.5% × $9.00 = $0.225 or 22.5 cent per click

This is the *maximum* amount you should be willing to bid for a keyword search term.

Suppose you bid 18 cents per click for a keyword on a popular search engine. If 1,000 shoppers click through to your Web site, your total cost of the paid listing would be $180 (1,000 shoppers clicking through × $0.18 per click = $180). With a conversion rate of 2.5 percent, you can expect 25 sales (1,000 shoppers × 2.5% conversion rate = 25 customers). If your normal profit is $9.00 per sale, these 25 sales will generate $225 in profit. Subtracting the $180 cost of acquiring these customers leaves your company with a net profit of $45. As long as your company's profit per sale is greater than its cost of acquisition, your company will make money on its paid listing. Notice that the maximum bid you can afford on a keyword is sensitive to your company's conversion rate. In this example, if the company's conversion rate were 4 percent (rather than 2.5 percent), the maximum bid for a keyword would be 36 cents (4% × $9.00 = $0.36) rather than 22.5 cents. Similarly, if a company's profit per sale increases, the amount it can afford to bid on a keyword also goes up. In this example, a company with a 4 percent conversion rate and a profit per sale of $20 would have a maximum bid of 80 cents (4% × $20 = $0.80).

The next issue, of course, is which keywords to bid on. One way to determine the words that are most likely to drive customers to your company's Web site is to use the keyword tool on the major search engines. Simply enter a keyword, and the tool produces a report showing how many times shoppers typed in that keyword as well as other keywords related to it. For instance, a recent search for "wedding ring" on Overture's Key Word Tool revealed that shoppers typed in the phrase "wedding ring" 165,277 times. Other related terms included "titanium wedding ring," (65,992 times), "platinum wedding ring" (30,469 times), and even "cheap diamond wedding ring" (254 times). The most popular terms in the resulting lists offer clues about the ones you will want to consider bidding on. You also will want to build these words into the meta tags, text, and titles of the pages of your company's Web site to boost its ranking in natural and organic sites.

Bidding on general keywords such as "clothing" not only can cost a small company lots of money, but it also tends to bring to a Web site shoppers who are not the company's best prospects for becoming paying customers. (Imagine a small company bidding $0.18 per click on the phrase "wedding ring" and getting the 165,277 "hits" mentioned in the previous example. If all 165,277 shoppers clicked through to its site, the cost to the company would be $29,750!) A better keyword strategy is to use more-specific terms such as "Western clothing" or "baby clothes" that are far less expensive per click and are more likely to attract the particular customers a company is targeting.

A common mistake entrepreneurs make is failing to bid on a sufficient number of keywords. "A lot of people bid on just the basic terms," says Brad Fallon, a search engine optimization specialist and owner of a successful e-commerce business. "They don't drill down far enough to words that might get only one search a day. If you have lots of key words that have only a few searches [each] and add them all together, they can produce a significant amount of business." In addition, these less popular keywords cost almost nothing but still generate sales. "You want to bid on thousands of terms," advises Fallon.

Finally, you must use Web analytics software to track the results of your paid listing campaign. Which search engines are customers using most often to enter your company's Web site? Which keywords are most successful at driving customers to your site? What impact are paid listings having on your company's conversion rate? Learning the answers to these and other related questions will help you to get the greatest return for the least investment in a paid listings strategy.

Sources: Adapted from James Maguire, "Starting Your Own E-Business, Part 4: Marketing on a Shoestring," *E-Commerce Guide*, October 24, 2005, www.ecommerce-guide.com/solutions/advertising/article.php/3558651; James Maguire, "MyWeddingFavors Shares Search Success Secrets," *E-Commerce Guide*, October 8, 2004, www.ecommerce-guide.com/solutions/advertising/article.php/3419121; Catherine Seda, "In the Click," *Entrepreneur*, August 2004, pp. 61–63.

paid inclusion
a search engine strategy in which a company pays a search engine for the right to submit either selected pages or the content of its entire Web site.

Another popular alternative to paid listings for increasing a site's visibility is a tool known as paid inclusion. In **paid inclusion,** a company pays a search engine for the right to submit either selected pages or the content of its entire Web site. (Google does not offer paid inclusion.) To keep their natural listings current, search engines regularly crawl through the Internet in the hunt for new and updated Web sites and material to include in their databases, but searching through the huge volume of pages on the Web means that it may take weeks or even months to locate a company's Web site. Because a company pays to submit its Web content into the search engine's database, a paid inclusion eliminates the necessity of waiting for a search engine to find its site. Not every search engine accepts paid inclusions, however.

Lippincott Williams & Wilkins

Lippincott Williams & Wilkins, a Philadelphia publisher of medical information, offered such a wide variety of products that describing them with a reasonable number of key-words was impractical. Heather Walls, the company's Internet content specialist, decided to try paid inclusions instead, which allowed the search engines to draw on the entire content of the company's site. Since Walls began using paid inclusions, traffic to the publisher's Web site has risen 15 percent. In addition, she discovered that visitors who come to the site by way of the search engines are twice as likely to make a purchase as those the company reaches through other media.[72]

LEARNING OBJECTIVES
5. Learn the techniques of designing a killer Web site.

Designing a Killer Web Site

World Wide Web users are not a patient lot. They sit before their computers, surfing the Internet, their fingers poised on their mouse buttons, daring any Web site to delay them with files that take a long time (to many, that's anything more than about 8 seconds) to load. Slow-loading sites or sites that don't deliver on their promises will cause a Web user to move on faster than a bolt of lightning can strike. Research shows that 59 percent of online customers buy from just a handful of sites that they consider safe and reliable and with which they are familiar.[73] With literally millions of Web sites online, how can entrepreneurs design a Web site that will capture and hold potential customers' attention long enough to make a sale? What can they do to keep customers coming back on a regular basis? There is no sure-fire formula for stopping surfers in their tracks, but the following suggestions will help.

Understand Your Target Customer

Before launching into the design of their Web sites, entrepreneurs must develop a clear picture of their target customers. Only then will they be ready to design a site that will appeal to their customers. The goal is create a design in which customers see themselves when they visit. Creating a site in which customers find a comfortable fit requires a careful blend of market research, sales know-how, and aesthetics. The challenge for a business on the Web is to create the same image, style, and ambiance in its online presence as in its offline stores. For example, a Web site that sells discount baby clothing will have an entirely different look and feel than one that sells upscale outdoor gear.

Give Customers What They Want

Although Web shoppers are price-conscious, they rank fast delivery as the most important criterion in their purchase decisions. Studies also show that surfers look for a large selection of merchandise available to them immediately. Remember that the essence of the selling on the Web is providing *convenience* to customers. Sites that allow them to shop whenever they want, choose from a wide selection of products, find what they are looking for quickly and easily, and pay for it conveniently and securely will keep customers coming back.

Select an Intuitive Domain Name

Decide on a domain name that is consistent with the image you want to create for your company and register it. Entrepreneurs should never underestimate the power of the right domain name or URL, which is a company's address on the Internet. It not only tells Web surfers where to find a company, but it also should suggest something about the company and what it does. Even the casual Web surfer could guess that the "toys.com" name belongs to a company selling children's toys. (It does; it belongs to eToys Inc., which also owns "etoys.com," "e-toys.com," and several other variations of its name.) Entrepreneurs must recognize that a domain name is part of the brand they are creating and should create the proper image for the company.

The ideal domain name should be:

- ■ *Short.* Short names are easy for people to remember, so the shorter a company's URL is, the more likely it is that potential customers will recall it.
- ■ *Memorable.* Not every short domain name is necessarily memorable. Some business owners use their companies' initials as their domain name (for example, http://www.sbfo.com for Stanley Brothers Furniture Outlet). The problem with using initials for a domain name is that customers rarely associate the two, which makes a company virtually invisible on the Web.
- ■ *Indicative of a company's business or business name.* Perhaps the best domain name for a company is one that customers can guess easily if they know the company's name. For instance, mail order catalog company J.Crew's URL is http://www.jcrew.com, and New Pig, a maker of absorbent materials for a variety of industrial applications, uses http://www.newpig.com as its domain name. (The company carries this concept over to its toll-free number, which is 1-800-HOT-HOGS.)
- ■ *Easy to spell.* Even though a company's domain name may be easy to spell, it is usually wise to buy several variations of the correct spelling simply because some customers are not likely to be good spellers.

Just because you come up with the perfect URL for your company's Web site does not necessarily mean that you can use it. Domain names are given on a first-come, first-serve basis. Before business owners can use a domain name, they must ensure that someone else has not already taken it. The simplest way to do that is to go to a domain name registration service such as Network Solutions' Internic at http://www.networksolutions.com/ or Netnames at http://www.netnames.com to conduct a name search. Entrepreneurs who find the domain name they have selected already registered to someone else have two choices: they can select another name, or they can try to buy the name from the original registrant. After Becca Williams, founder of Wallnutz, a small company that sells paint-by-number wall murals for children's rooms, came up with the ideal name for her business, she discovered that someone else had already registered the domain name wallnutz.com. She contacted the original registrant and purchased the rights to the name.[74] Some businesses are able to buy the rights to their company names relatively cheaply, but not every online business is as fortunate. Business incubator eCompanies purchased the rights to the domain name "business.com" from an individual for $7.5 million![75]

Finding unregistered domain names is becoming more difficult; 98 percent of the words in *Webster's English Dictionary* have been registered as Internet domain names![76] Once entrepreneurs find an unused name that is suitable, they should register it (plus any variations of it)—and the sooner, the better! Registering is quite easy: simply use one of the registration services cited previously to fill out a form and pay $98, which registers the name for two years. The registration renewal fee is $49 per year, but discounts for multiple-year registrations apply. The next step is to register the domain name with the U.S. Patent and Trademark Office (USPTO) at a cost of $245. The USPTO's Web site (http://www.uspto.gov/) not only allows users to register a trademark online, but it also offers useful information on trademarks and the protection they offer.

Make Your Web Site Easy to Navigate

Research shows that the leading factor in convincing online shoppers to make a purchase from a Web site is its ease of navigation. The starting point for evaluating a site's navigability is to conduct a user test. Find several willing shoppers, sit them down in front of a computer, and watch them as they cruise through the company's Web site to make a purchase. It is one of the best ways to get meaningful, immediate feedback on the navigability of a site. Watching these test customers as they navigate the site also is useful. Where do they pause? Do they get lost in the site? Are they confused by the choices the site gives them? Is the checkout process too complex? Are the navigation buttons from one page of the site to another clearly marked, and do they make sense? (One popular Web site critic says that sites with vague navigation tools are guilty of "mystery meat navigation.") "Eighty percent of visitors will leave [a Web site] if they can't find what they are looking for after three pages," says Bryan Eisenberg, an e-commerce consultant.[77]

Successful Web sites recognize that shoppers employ different strategies to make a purchase. Some shoppers want to use a search tool, others want to browse through product categories, and still others prefer a company to make product recommendations. Effective sites accommodate all three strategies in their design. Two important Web site design features that online companies often get wrong involve the mechanisms by which customers locate products and then get information about them.

Locating Products Customers won't buy what they cannot find. Products should be easy for customers to find, no matter how many pages a Web site includes. Too often, online companies do a poor job of product categorization, listing their product lines in ways that may make sense to them but that befuddle the typical shopper. User tests can be extremely helpful in revealing product categorization problems. In addition to establishing simple product categories that reflect the way customers actually shop (for example, including categories such as business dress, business casual, sportswear, outerwear, formal wear, shoes, and accessories for a clothing store), one simple solution is to use an on-site search tool. An easy-to-use on-site search tool, which can cost anywhere from less than $1,000 to more than $30,000, can pay for itself many times over in increased sales and higher conversion rates. In addition, an on-site search tool will reveal volumes of information about which items shoppers are looking for and how they search for them, information online merchants can use in their keyword strategies for paid listings.

TapeInfo.com

TapeInfo.com, an online company that targets industrial customers with a complete line of adhesive tapes and foams, makes it easy for customers to find exactly what they need among the 7,084 types of adhesives the company stocks. The site's Build-a-Tape option allows customers to find the tape they need by selecting from drop-down boxes specific product attributes such as type of adhesive, backing, function, color, and others. Customers who are not certain about the type of tape they need and are not able to provide specifications can use the site's Solve-a-Tape feature, which acts like an online customer service representative and asks a series of questions before making an adhesive recommendation. The Compare-a-Tape option allows users to enter a particular brand and type of tape and then compare it to other, similar types of tape. TapeInfo.com, which recently won an award from Crain's BtoB as one of the "Top 10 Great Web Sites," is reaping the benefits of its easy-to-navigate site. The Web site accounts for more than 25 percent of TapeInfo.com's sales, and more than 50 percent of its sales leads originate with the site.[78]

Getting Product Information Once a site is designed to enable shoppers to find products easily, the next task online merchants face is to provide enough product information to convince shoppers to buy. Unlike at brick-and-mortar stores, customers cannot pick up an item, try it on, or engage a sales person in a face-to-face conversation about its features and merits. Online merchants must walk a fine line because providing too little information may fail to answer the questions customers have, causing them to abandon their shopping carts. On the other hand, providing too much information can overwhelm customers, who aren't willing to wade through reams of text just to find the answer to some basic questions. The solution is to provide basic product information in easy-to-understand terms (always including a picture of the item) and also to provide a link to more detailed information (which should be only one click away) that customers can click to if they choose. Where appropriate, photos that provide a 360-degree product view can boost conversion rates as well. Giving customers the option of enlarging a photo also helps, but the enlarged photo must be much bigger. Many Web sites make the mistake of enlarging photos by only 20 percent; a better choice is to fill the screen with a *much* bigger photo.

Create a Gift Idea Center

Online retailers have discovered that one of the most successful tools for improving their conversion rates is to offer a gift idea center. A gift idea center is a section of a Web site that includes a variety of gift ideas that shoppers can browse through for ideas based on price, gender, or category. Gift centers can provide a huge boost for e-tailers, particularly around holidays, because they offer creative suggestions for shoppers looking for the perfect gift.

Francoise and John Shirley, who in 1999 co-founded Sleepyheads.com, an online company that sells a variety of sleepwear and accessories, recently added a gift idea center to their company's Web site and found that their average order size increased from $75 to $125. Shoppers can access the gift center easily from a link on the home page and can find gift suggestions organized into creative categories such as "Good Luck," "New Mom and Mom-to-Be," "Boyfriend Breakup," and "Gifts for Me." Every month, the Shirleys update the gift selection and rotate some of the categories, depending on the season.[79]

Sleepyheads.com
When Francoise and John Shirley, co-founders of Sleepyheads.com, an online company that sells sleepwear and accessories, added a gift idea center to the company's Web site, sales increased.

Other variations of this approach that have proved to be successful for e-commerce entrepreneurs include suggested-items pages, bargain basement pages, and featured sale pages.

Build Loyalty by Giving Online Customers a Reason to Return to Your Web Site

The typical e-commerce site experiences a 60 percent turnover rate among its customers every six weeks.[80] Just as with brick-and-mortar retailers, e-tailers that constantly have to incur the expense of attracting new customers find it difficult to remain profitable because of the extra cost required to acquire customers. One of the most effective ways to encourage customers to return to a site is to establish an incentive program that rewards them for repeat purchases. "Frequent-buyer" programs that offer discounts or points toward future purchases, give-aways such as T-shirts emblazoned with a company's logo, or special services are common components of incentive programs. Incentive programs that are properly designed with a company's target customer in mind really work. A study by market research firm NFO Interactive found that 53 percent of online customers say they would return to a particular site to shop if it offered an incentive program.[81]

Establish Hyperlinks with Other Businesses, Preferably Those Selling Products or Services That Complement Yours

Listing the Web addresses of complementary businesses on a company's site and having them list your address on their sites offers customers more value and can bring traffic to your site that you otherwise would have missed. For instance, the owner of a site selling upscale kitchen gadgets should consider a cross-listing arrangement with sites that feature gourmet recipes, wines, and kitchen appliances.

Include an E-mail Option and a Telephone Number in Your Site

Customers will appreciate the opportunity to communicate with your company. When you include e-mail access on your site, be sure to respond to it promptly. Nothing alienates cybercustomers faster than a company that is slow to respond or fails to respond to their e-mail messages. Also be sure to include a toll-free telephone number for customers who prefer to call with their questions. Unfortunately, many companies either fail to include their telephone numbers on their site or bury them so deeply within the site's pages that customers never find them. Smart Web entrepreneurs put a toll-free number on every page of their Web site.

Give Shoppers the Ability to Track Their Orders Online

Many customers who order items online want to track the progress of their orders. One of the most effective ways to keep a customer happy is to send an e-mail confirmation that your company received the order and another e-mail notification when you ship the order. The shipment notice should include the shipper's tracking number and instructions on how to track the order from the shipper's site. Order and shipping confirmations instill confidence in even the most Web-wary shoppers.

Offer Web Shoppers a Special All Their Own

Give Web customers a special deal that you don't offer in any other advertising piece. Change your specials often (weekly, if possible) and use clever "teasers" to draw attention to the offer. Regular special offers available only on the Web give customers an incentive to keep visiting a company's site.

Follow a Simple Design

Catchy graphics and photographs are important to snaring customers, but designers must choose them carefully. Designs that are overly complex take a long time to download, and customers are likely to move on before they appear.

Following are some specific design tips:

■ Avoid clutter. The best designs are simple and elegant with a balance of text and graphics.

■ Avoid huge graphic headers that must download first, prohibiting customers from seeing anything else on your site as they wait (or more likely, *don't* wait). Use graphics judiciously so that the site loads quickly. Zona Research reports that if a sight fails to load within 8 seconds, one-third of potential visitors will leave; a site failing to load within 12 seconds produces a 70 percent abandonment rate.[82]

■ Include a menu bar at the top of the page that makes it easy for customers to find their way around the site.

■ Make the site easy to navigate by including navigation buttons at the bottom of pages that enable customers to return to the top of the page or to the menu bar. This avoids what one expert calls "the pogo effect," by which visitors bounce from page to page in a Web site looking for what they need. Without navigation buttons or a site map page, a company runs the risk of customers getting lost in its site and leaving.

■ Regularly look for broken links on your site and purge them.

■ Incorporate meaningful content in the site that is useful to visitors, well organized, easy to read, and current. The content should be consistent with the message a company sends in the other advertising media it uses. Although a Web site should be designed to sell, providing useful, current information attracts visitors, keeps them coming back, and establishes a company's reputation as an expert in the field.

■ Include a "frequently asked questions"(FAQ) section. Adding this section to a page can reduce dramatically the number of telephone calls and e-mails customer service representatives must handle. FAQ sections typically span a wide range of issues—from how to place an order to how to return merchandise—and cover whatever topics customers most often want to know about.

■ Be sure to post prominently privacy and return policies as well as product guarantees the company offers.

■ If your site is heavy on content, say, 100 or more pages, or has more than 100 products for sale, include a search tool that allows visitors to find the product or information they want. Smaller, simpler sites can get by without a search tool if they are organized properly. Setting up a search tool is easy with either a remote search service (available for a monthly fee) or off-the-shelf software.

- Avoid fancy typefaces and small fonts because they are too hard to read. Limit font and color choices to two or three to avoid a circus look.
- Be vigilant for misspelled words, typographical errors, and formatting mistakes; they destroy a site's credibility in no time.
- Avoid using small fonts on "busy" backgrounds; no one will read them!
- Use contrasting colors of text and graphics. For instance, blue text on a green background is nearly impossible to read.
- Be careful with frames. Using frames that are so thick that they crowd out text makes for a poor design.
- Test the site on different Web browsers and on different-size monitors. A Web site may look exactly the way it was designed to look on one Web browser and be a garbled mess on another. Sites designed to display correctly on large monitors may not view well on small ones.
- Use your Web site to collect information from visitors, but don't tie up visitors immediately with a tedious registration process. Most will simply leave the site never to return. Offers for a free e-mail newsletter or a contest giveaway can give visitors enough incentive to register with a site.
- Avoid automated music that plays continuously and cannot be cut off.
- Make sure the overall look of the page is appealing. "When a site is poorly designed, lacks information, or cannot support customer needs, that [company's] reputation is seriously jeopardized," says one expert.[83]
- Remember: Simpler usually is better.

Create a Fast, Simple Checkout Process

One sure-fire way to destroy an online company's conversion rate is to impose a lengthy, convoluted checkout process that requires customers to wade through pages of forms to fill out just to complete a purchase. When faced with a lengthy checkout process, customers simply abandon a site and make their purchases elsewhere. One recent study of online retailers by the E-Tailing Group reports that the average number of clicks required from product selection to final checkout was 5.2. E-commerce experts suggest that the top-performing sites require a maximum of five clicks to check out, but the fewer the steps required to check out, the more successful will be the site at generating sales.[84]

Once customers put items into a shopping cart, they should be able to see a complete list and photographs of the products they have selected and should be able to access more information about them with one click. The cart should allow customers to change product quantities (and, believe it or not, to remove items from the cart). Every cart must have a "return to shopping" link in it as well.

Assure Customers That Their Online Transactions Are Secure

If you are serious about doing business on the Web, make sure that your site includes the proper security software and encryption devices. Computer-savvy customers are not willing to divulge their credit card numbers on sites that are not secure.

Post Shipping and Handling Charges up Front

A common gripe among online shoppers is that some e-tailers fail to reveal their shipping and handling charges early in the checkout process. JupiterResearch reports that 63 percent of online buyers have abandoned an online shopping cart because they thought the shipping and handling charges were too high.[85] Responsible online merchants keep shipping and handling charges reasonable and display them early on in the buying process.

Confirm Transactions

Order-confirmation e-mails, which a company can generate automatically, let a customer know that the company received the online order and can be an important first line of defense against online fraud. If the customer claims not to have placed the order, the company can cancel it and report the credit card information as suspicious. Confirmation e-mails can contain ads or coupons for future purchases, but they should be short.

Keep Your Site Updated

Customers want to see something new when they visit stores, and they expect the same when they visit virtual stores as well. Delete any hyperlinks that have disappeared, and keep the information on your Web site current. One sure way to run off customers on the Web is to continue to advertise your company's "Christmas Special" in August! On the other hand, fresh information and new specials keep customers coming back.

Test Your Site Often

Smart e-commerce entrepreneurs check their sites frequently to make sure they are running smoothly and are not causing customers unexpected problems. A good rule of thumb is to check your site at least monthly—or weekly if its content changes frequently.

Consider Hiring a Professional to Design Your Site

Pros can do it a lot faster and better than you can. However, don't give designers free rein to do whatever they want to with your site. Make sure it meets your criteria for an effective site that can sell.

Entrepreneurs must remember that on the World Wide Web every company, no matter how big or small it is, has the exact same screen size for its site. What matters most is not the size of your company but how you put that screen size to use.

You Be the Consultant

E-Commerce Fulfillment Strategies: Your Choice

Once they have their Web sites up and running and orders are coming in, online entrepreneurs must fill those orders, ship them, and manage any customer service issues that might arise after the sale. The way in which small e-commerce handle order fulfillment varies dramatically, however, as the following examples demonstrate. Some companies choose to outsource order fulfillment, letting specialized companies handle all of the activities behind the "Buy" button on their Web site, and others choose to keep the entire operation in-house and handle it themselves.

Outsource and Keep Your Focus

In 1997, when Brad Chase launched Progressive Health Nutraceuticals, an online business that sells all-natural

remedies, he handled his own order fulfillment but was soon spending two to three hours a day packing and shipping customer orders. He decided that it was time to shift to a virtual inventory strategy and outsource his company's order fulfillment tasks to a professional specializing in that area, iFulfill, an Ohio-based order fulfillment company. The company that manufactures Chase's product line of herbal remedies (Chase outsources production as well as order fulfillment) ships inventory already tagged with appropriate labels and barcodes directly to iFulfill's warehouse, where it is checked into the company's system. When a customer order comes in to Progressive Health Nutraceuticals, it is automatically sent to iFulfill, where employees pick, pack, and fill the order before shipping it out to the customer in a Progressive Health Nutraceuticals box with an invoice imprinted with Chase's company's name. iFulfill even sends customers order confirmation e-mails, telling them that the order has shipped and when they can expect delivery.

Chase admits that outsourcing most of the aspects of his business reduces his profit margin, but it also keeps his costs low and allows him to focus on marketing and growing his business. "They definitely charge a premium, but you have to realize that I'm not paying [inventory] storage costs," says Chase. "I don't have to worry about insurance. I don't have to worry about all the headaches that come with employees. It's all under one roof [at iFulfill], which makes good sense to me." Relying on an order fulfillment house does not mean that an online entrepreneur is abandoning responsibility for managing the business, however. "It's still the business owner's responsibility to buy the merchandise, make sure it's in stock, present the information on the Web site, market the Web site, market to consumers, and maintain that relationship with the consumers," says one e-commerce expert.

Manage the Process In-House

When Keith Spear, a former professional bowler, began selling bowling balls on the Internet in 1996 even before the World Wide Web emerged as a business tool, he discovered that filling customer orders was a time-consuming, error-prone activity. In those days, employees transcribed orders from the Internet, took them to the company warehouse, selected the product, and filled out a shipping order—all by hand. "It took a tremendous amount of time," recalls Spear. In addition, the process was error-prone. "It's amazing how many mistakes you're going to make doing it manually like that," he says. Soon Spear graduated to selling bowling balls around the world on Bowlingball.com, a Web site he designed and built himself. At the time, there were no reliable off-the-shelf e-commerce software packages, no ready-made online shopping carts, and no order fulfillment houses, so out of necessity, Spear learned programming and eventually developed his own tools for conducting business online.

Building on the distinctive competences Spear built over time, Bowlingball.com's e-commerce system is now totally automated. The software tools the company now relies on to manage its online operations, however, are no longer in-house; instead, Bowlingball.com uses

automated systems from its shipper, UPS, to handle its shipping, customer notification, and supply chain management. With UPS WorldShip, Bowlingball.com's online orders are automatically transmitted to its shipping department, where the system directs an employee to the proper location for filling the order. The computer system prints out the customer's shipping label, and the package is ready for the next UPS pickup. The system then sends a confirmation e-mail to the customer that includes a package tracking number. The WorldShip system also generates all of the export documents required for international orders. Processing an order for shipment now takes the company just seconds, and the system's on-time delivery record is 99 percent.

Although Bowlingball.com stocks a huge inventory of $8 million worth of bowling balls in its 15,000-square-foot warehouse, the company sometimes relies on drop shipping to fill orders for unusual or hard-to-find items. When an order arrives for an item that the company does not stock, the WorldShip system automatically generates an e-mail request to one of the Bowlingball.com's regular suppliers (who also use WorldShip), who ships the order directly to Bowlingball.com's customer. To the customer, the transaction is transparent—as if the order came directly from Bowlingball.com itself.

Bowlingball.com's annual sales have climbed from $1.2 million to more than $10 million in just three years. "There's no way we could do the volume of business we're doing today if we didn't have these tools," says Spear.

1. What benefits does a company gain by outsourcing its order fulfillment activities? What are the risks of this virtual inventory strategy?
2. What benefits does a company gain by maintaining in-house its order fulfillment activities? What are the risks of this strategy?
3. What advice would you offer a business owner who has just launched an e-commerce company about driving traffic to the company's Web site?

Sources: Jennifer Schiff, "Outsourcing Your Fulfillment: What You Need to Know," *Small Business Computing*, May 26, 2005, www.smallbusinesscomputing.com/emarketing/article.php/3507976; Devin Comisky, "From the Forums: Drop Shipping Confusion," *E-Commerce Guide*, April 13, 2005, www.ecommerce-guide.com/news/trends/article.php/3497491; Gerry Blackwell, "UPS Throws a Strike for Small Business," *Small Business Computing*, September 21, 2005, http://www.smallbusinesscomputing.com/biztools/article.php/3550411.

Tracking Web Results

Software Solutions

As they develop their Web sites, entrepreneurs seek to create sites that generate sales by converting visitors into customers, improve customer relationships, or lower costs. How can entrepreneurs determine the effectiveness of their sites? **Web analytics,** tools that measure a Web site's ability to attract customers, generate sales, and keep customers coming back, help entrepreneurs to know what works—and what doesn't—on their sites. Unfortunately, only about 40 percent of e-businesses use Web analytics strategically to refashion their Web sites and improve their performance.[86] Online companies that use Web analytics have an advantage over those that do not. Their owners can review the data collected from their customers' Web site activity, analyze them, make adjustments to the Web site, and then start the monitoring process over again to see whether the changes improve the site's performance. In other words, Web analytics give entrepreneurs the ability to apply the principles of continuous improvement to their sites. In addition, the changes these e-business owners make are based on facts (the data from the Web analytics) rather than on mere guesses about how customers interact with a site. There are many Web analytics software packages, but effective ones offer the following types of information:

Web analytics

tools that measure a Web site's ability to attract customers, generate sales, and keep customers coming back.

- *Commerce metrics.* These are basic analytics such as sales revenue generated, number of items sold, which products are selling best (and which are not), and others.
- *Visitor segmentation measurements.* These measurements provide entrepreneurs valuable information about online shoppers and customers, including whether they are return customers or new customers, how they arrived at the site (for example, via a search engine or a pay-per-click ad), which search terms they used (if they used a search engine), and others.
- *Content reports.* This information tells entrepreneurs which products customers are looking for and which pages they view most often (and least often), how they navigate through the site, how long they stay, which pages they are on when they exit, and more. Using this information, an entrepreneur can get an idea of how effective the site's design is.
- *Process measurements.* These metrics help entrepreneurs to understand how their Web sites attract visitors and convert them into customers. Does the checkout process work smoothly? How often do shoppers abandon their carts? At what point in the process do they abandon them? These measures can lead to higher conversion rates for an online business.

In the early days of e-commerce, entrepreneurs strived to create sites that were both "sticky" and "viral." A **sticky site** is one that acts like electronic flypaper, capturing visitors' attention and offering them useful, interesting information that makes them stay at the site. The premise of stickiness is that the longer customers stay in a site, the more likely they are to actually purchase something and to come back to it. A **viral site** is one that visitors are willing to share with their friends. This "word-of-mouse" advertising is one of the most effective ways of generating traffic to a company's site. As the Web has matured as a marketing channel, however, the shortcomings of these simple measures have become apparent, and other e-metrics continue to emerge. E-businesses now focus on other measures of online performance, including **recency,** the length of time between a customer's visits to a Web site. The more frequently customers visit a site, the more likely they are to become loyal customers. Other common measures of Web site performance include the following:

sticky site

one that acts like electronic flypaper, capturing visitors' attention and offering them useful, meaningful information that makes them stay at the site.

viral site

one that visitors are willing to share with their friends.

recency

the length of time between a customer's visit to a Web site.

click-through rate

the proportion of people who see a small company's online ad and actually click on it to reach the company's Web site.

- The **click-through rate (CTR)** is the proportion of people who see a company's online ad and actually click on it to reach the company's Web site. Each time an ad is displayed is called an impression; therefore,

$$CTR = \frac{Number\ of\ clicks}{Number\ of\ impressions}$$

For instance, if a company's ad is displayed 500 times in one day and 12 people clicked on it, the CTR is $12 \div 500 = 0.024 = 2.4\%$.

- The **cost per acquistion (CPA)** is the cost a company incurs to generate each purchase (or customer registration):

$$CPA = \frac{\text{Total cost of acquiring a new customer}}{\text{Number of new customers}}$$

For example, if a company purchases an advertisement in an e-magazine for $200 and it yields 15 new customers, then the cost of acquistion is $200 ÷ 15 = $13.33.

- The **conversion (or browse-to-buy) ratio** is the proportion of visitors to a site who actually make a purchase. It is one of the most important measures of Web success, and is calculated as follows:

$$\text{Conversion rate} = \frac{\text{Number of customers who made a purchase}}{\text{Number of visitors to the site}}$$

Although conversion rates vary dramatically across industries, the average conversion rate is 2.3 percent. In other words, of every 1,000 people who visit a Web site, 23 of them actually make a purchase. Table 9.4 offers practical advice to entrepreneurs seeking to boost their conversion rates.

Gathering Performance Indicators

How can online entrepreneurs gather the information to make these calculations to determine whether their sites are producing a reasonable return on investment? Answering that question means that entrepreneurs must track visitors to their sites, the paths they follow within the site, and the activity they generate while there. A variety of methods for tracking Web results is available, but the most commonly used ones include counters and log-analysis software. The simplest technique is to use a **counter,** which records the number of "hits" a Web site receives. Although counters measure activity on a site, they do so only at the broadest level. If a counter records 10 hits, for instance, there is no way to know whether those hits came as a result of 10 different visitors or as a result of just one person making 10 visits. In addition, counters cannot tell Web entrepreneurs where visitors to their sites come from or which pages they look at on the site.

A more meaningful way to track activity on a Web site is through **log-analysis software.** Server logs record every page, graphic, audio clip, or photograph that visitors to a site access, and log-analysis software analyzes these logs and generates reports describing how visitors behave when they get to a site. With this software, entrepreneurs can determine how many unique visitors come to their site and how many times repeat visitors come back. Owners of e-stores can discover which FAQ customers click on most often, which part of a site they stayed in the longest, which site they came from, and how the volume of traffic at the site affected the server's speed of operation. **Click-stream analysis software** allows entrepreneurs to determine the paths visitors take while on a site and to pinpoint the areas in which they spend the most—and the least—time. These tools give entrepreneurs the ability to infer what visitors think about a Web site, its products, its content, its design, and other features. Feedback from log-analysis software helps entrepreneurs to redesign their sites to eliminate confusing navigation, unnecessary graphics, meaningless content, incomplete information, and other problems that can cause visitors to leave.

cost per acquisition (CPA)
the cost a company incurs to generate each purchase (or customer registration).

conversion (or browse-to-buy) ratio
the proportion of visitors to a site who actually make a purchase.

counter
the simplest mechanism for tracking activity on a Web site by counting the number of "hits" the site receives.

log-analysis software
programs that analyze server logs that record visitors' actions on a Web site and then generate meaningful reports for managers.

click-stream analysis software
software that allows entrepreneurs to determine the paths visitors take while on a site and to pinpoint the areas in which they spend the most—and the least—time.

When Don Becklin opened Motorcycle-Superstore.com in 1998, he quickly realized the need for reliable information from Web analytics software. "We had a tough time deciphering [the site's] traffic and sales patterns," says Becklin. The Web analytics software revealed that Motorcycle-Superstore.com was losing lots of customers during the checkout process. Customers would add items to their shopping carts, begin checking out, and then abandon the cart and the site. Becklin and his employees redesigned the entire checkout process with the goal of increasing the site's conversion rate. The changes "have made a huge difference," says Becklin. "With Web Analytics, we've been able to identify what is working and what is not."[87]

COMPANY
Profile

Motorcycle-Superstore.com

TABLE 9.4 Tips for Boosting Your Conversion Rate

Looking for ways to boost your online company's conversion rate? Try these techniques:

■ Include an on-site search tool that makes it easy for shoppers to find the items they are seeking. Any shopper's search should turn up the requested item as well as sales "boosters" such as special offers and cross-sells (products that complement the requested item).

■ Streamline the checkout process. Making checkout as simple and fast as possible increases the probability of closing an online sale.

■ Organize your site so that navigating it is as simple and as intuitive as possible. Online shoppers are frustrated easily by confusing sites. "Eighty percent of shoppers will leave after three pages" if they cannot find what they want, says one conversion rate expert.

■ Offer an attractive display of products for customers. The most successful online retailers engage in visual merchandising just like their brick-and-mortar counterparts. Set the stage properly to encourage shoppers to buy.

■ Offer something free. Whether it is a "buy two, get one free" deal or an offer for free shipping, the word "free" gets attention online.

■ Do everything you can to win shoppers' trust. Anything that causes shoppers to doubt the legitimacy of your Web site or your business will lower your company's conversion rate.

■ Encourage repeat customers to keep repeating. One of the easiest ways to increase conversion rates is to romance your existing customers. The possibilities are endless but might include timely e-mails and special offers or discounts just for existing customers.

■ Let customers know whether the items they have selected are in stock and when they will be shipped. Lack of information about product availability and delivery dates can destroy a company's conversion rate.

■ Include a prominently displayed "Buy" button at every opportunity. A study by Jakob Nielsen, a Web design expert, found that six percent of all online "sales catastrophes" (a failure to make a sale) were the result of customers who had already decided to make a purchase but had difficulty getting the item into a shopping cart! Locating at the top of Web pages a "Buy" button that is set off in a different color makes it easy for customers to find their way to a shopping cart.

Sources: Jennifer Schiff, "Getting More out of Your Web Site," *E-Commerce Guide,* November 29, 2005, www.ecommerce-guide.com/solutions/building/article.php/3567091; James Maguire, "E-Commerce Design: The Product Page Is King," *Small Business Computing,* February 3, 2006, www.smallbusinesscomputing. com/emarketing/article.php/3582696; James Maguire, "E-Commerce Design: Category Pages," *E-Commerce Guide,* January 30, 2006, www.ecommerce-guide.com/ solutions/design/article.php/3581446; James Maguire, "Merchant Secrets for Driving Conversion: Part 1," *Small Business Computing,* November 22, 2005, www.smallbusinesscomputing.com/emarketing/article.php/3566026; James Maguire, "Merchant Secrets for Driving Conversion: Part 2," *Small Business Computing,* November 14, 2005, www.smallbusinesscomputing.com/emarketing/article.php/3563956. Christopher Saunders, "How Do I: Attract and Keep Customers?" *E-Commerce,* June 8, 2004, www.ecommerce.internet.com/how/ customers/article/0..10363_3365551.00.html.

Other tracking methods available to owners of e-businesses include the following:

■ *Clustering.* This software observes visitors to a Web site, analyzes their behavior, and then groups them into narrow categories. Companies then target each category of shoppers with products, specials, and offers designed to appeal to them.

■ *Collaborative filtering.* This software uses sophisticated algorithms to determine visitors' interests by comparing them to other shoppers with similar tastes. Companies then use this information to suggest products in which an individual customer would most likely be interested, given his or her profile.

■ *Profiling systems.* These programs tag individual customers on a site and note their responses to the various pages in the site. Based on the areas a customer visits most, the software develops a psychographic profile of the shopper. For instance, a visitor who reads an article on massage techniques might receive an offer for a book on alternative medicine or a magazine focusing on environmental issues.

■ *Artificial Intelligence (AI).* This software, sometimes called neural networking, is the most sophisticated of the group because it actually learns from users' behavior. The more these programs interact with customers, the "smarter" they become. Over time, they can help online marketers to know which special offers work best with which customers, when customers are most likely to respond, and how to present the offer.

Ensuring Web Privacy and Security

Privacy

LEARNING OBJECTIVES
7. Describe how e-businesses ensure the privacy and security of the information they collect and store from the Web.

The Web's ability to track customers' every move naturally raises concerns over the privacy of the information companies collect. E-commerce gives businesses access to tremendous volumes of information about their customers, creating a responsibility to protect that information and to use it wisely. According to the Pew Internet & American Life Project, 86 percent of Internet users say they worry about online privacy.[88] To make sure they are using the information they collect from visitors to their Web sites legally and ethically, companies should take the following steps:

Take an Inventory of the Customer Data Collected The first step to ensuring proper data handling is to assess exactly the type of data the company is collecting and storing. How are you collecting them? Why are you collecting them? How are you using them? Do visitors know how you are using the data? Do you need to get their permission to use them in this way? Do you use all of the data you are collecting?

Develop a Company Privacy Policy for the Information You Collect A **privacy policy** is a statement explaining the nature of the information a company collects online, what it does with that information, and the recourse customers have if they believe the company is misusing the information. Several online privacy firms, such as TRUSTe (http://www.truste.org), BBBOnLine (http://www.bbbonline.com), and BetterWeb (http://www.betterWeb.com), offer Web "seal programs," the equivalent of a *Good Housekeeping* seal of privacy approval. To earn a privacy seal of approval, a company must adopt a privacy policy, implement it, and monitor its effectiveness. Many of these privacy sites also provide online policy wizards, automated questionnaires that help e-business owners create comprehensive privacy statements.

privacy policy
a statement explaining the nature of the information a company collects online, what it does with that information, and the recourse customers have if they believe the company is misusing the information.

Post Your Company's Privacy Policy Prominently on Your Web Site and Follow It Creating a privacy policy is not sufficient; posting it in a prominent place on the Web site (it should be accessible from *every* page on the Web site) and then abiding by it make a policy meaningful. One of the worst mistakes a company can make is to publish its privacy policy online and then to fail to follow it. Not only is this unethical, but it also can lead to serious damage awards if customers take legal action against the company.

Security

A company doing business on the Web faces two conflicting goals: (1) to establish a presence on the Web so that customers from across the globe can have access to its site and (2) to maintain a high level of security so that the business, its site, and the information it collects is safe from hackers and intruders intent on doing harm. Companies have a number of safeguards available to them, but hackers with enough time, talent, and determination usually can beat even the most sophisticated safety measures. If hackers manage to break into a system, they can do irreparable damage, stealing programs and sensitive customer data, modifying or deleting valuable information, changing the look and content of sites, or crashing sites altogether. A study by the Federal Bureau of Investigation and the Computer Security Institute found that 40 percent of all companies experience an attempted theft of data.[89] For instance, hackers using stolen passwords recently gained unauthorized access to a database at information broker LexisNexis, where they stole the personal information of more than 310,000 people.[90] Identity theft is now the fastest-growing white-collar crime in the United States. The Federal Trade Commission estimates that 10 million Americans have been victims of identity theft (although about 70 percent of it is committed offline), which has resulted in $48 billion in damages to businesses.[91]

To minimize the likelihood of invasion by hackers, e-companies rely on a several tools, including virus detection software, intrusion detection software, and firewalls. At the most basic level of protection is **virus detection software,** which scans computer drives for viruses, nasty programs written by devious hackers and designed to harm computers and the information they contain. ICSA Lab's Virus Prevalence Survey reports that both the frequency and the cost of virus attacks on business continue to climb.[92] The severity of viruses ranges widely, from relatively harmless programs that put humorous messages on a user's screen to those that erase a computer's hard drive or cause the entire system to crash. Because hackers are *always* writing new viruses to attack computer systems, entrepreneurs must keep their virus detection software up to date and must run it often. An attack by one virus can bring a company's entire e-commerce platform to a screeching halt in no time.

Intrusion detection software is essential for any company doing business on the Web. These packages constantly monitor the activity on a company's network server and sound an alert if they detect someone breaking into the company's computer system or if they detect unusual network activity. Intrusion detection software not only can detect attempts by unauthorized users to break into a computer system while they are happening, but it also can trace the hacker's location. Most packages also have the ability to preserve a record of the attempted break-in that will stand up in court so that companies can take legal action against cyber-intruders. Web security companies such as ScanAlert provide software that scans a small business's Web site daily to certify that it is "Hacker Safe." Online companies using the software are able to post a certification mark signifying that their sites are protected from unauthorized access.

A **firewall** is a combination of hardware and software operating between the Internet and a company's computer network that allows employees to have access to the Internet but keeps unauthorized users from entering a company's network and the programs and data it contains. Establishing a firewall is essential to operating a company on the Web, but entrepreneurs must make sure that their firewalls are set up properly. Otherwise, they are useless. One study of more than 2,000 Web sites by ISCA.net, a security consulting firm, found that even though every site had a firewall in place, more than 80 percent were vulnerable to attack with commonly available software because they were not properly designed.[93] Even with all of these security measures in place, it is best for a company to run its Web page on a separate server from the network that runs the business. If hackers break into the Web site, they still do not have access to the company's sensitive data and programs.

Perhaps the most effective security strategy is to build layers of security using all three of these tools and to encrypt sensitive data so that if a breach does occur, the hacker cannot read the data. In addition, business owners should require employees who are authorized to access sensitive data to use passwords.

The Computer Security Institute (http://www.gocsi.com/) offers articles, information, and seminars to help business owners maintain computer security. The *Business Security e-Journal* (http://www.lubrinco.com) is a free monthly newsletter on computer security, and *Information Security Magazine* (http://www.infosecuritymag.com/), published by the International Computer Security Association (CSA; http://www.icsa.net/), also offers helpful advice on maintaining computer security. For entrepreneurs who want to test their sites' security, the ICSA offers its Security Snapshot system (free of charge) that runs various security tests on a site and then e-mails a "Risk Index" score in six different categories, including the site's risk of hacker intrusion.

In e-commerce just as in traditional retail, sales do not matter unless a company gets paid! On the Web customers demand transactions they can complete with ease and convenience, and the simplest way to allow customers to pay for e-commerce transactions is with credit cards. From a Web customer's perspective, however, one of the most important security issues is the security of their credit card information.

virus detection software
programs that scan computer drives for viruses, nasty programs written by devious hackers and designed to harm computers and the information they contain.

intrusion detection software
programs that constantly monitor the activity on a company's network server and sound an alert if they detect someone breaking into the system or if they detect unusual network activity.

firewall
a combination of hardware and software that allows employees to have access to the Internet but keeps unauthorized users from entering a company's network and the programs and data it contains.

Processing credit card transactions requires a company to obtain an Internet merchant account from a bank or financial intermediary. Setup fees for an Internet merchant account typically range from $500 to $1,000, but companies also pay monthly access and statement fees of between $40 and $80 plus a transaction fee of 10 to 60 cents per transaction. Once an online company has a merchant account, it can accept credit cards from online customers. To ensure the security of their customers' credit card numbers, online retailers typically use secure sockets layer (SSL) technology to encrypt customers' transaction information as it travels across the Internet. By using secure shopping cart features from storefront-building services or Internet service providers, even the smallest e-commerce stores can offer their customers secure online transactions.

Online credit card transactions also pose a risk for merchants; online companies lose an estimated $2.8 billion to online payment fraud each year.[94] The most common problem is **chargebacks,** online transactions that customers dispute. Unlike credit card transactions in a retail store, those made online involve no signatures, so Internet merchants incur the loss when a customer disputes an online credit card transaction. The research firm Yankee Group estimates that between one and two percent of all e-commerce transactions are attempts at fraud.[95] A thief in Romania recently tried to use a stolen credit card to purchase eight handbags from Velma Handbags, a small company founded by Margaret Cobbs, but the company that handles her credit card transactions discovered the attempt and stopped the $380 transaction.[96]

chargebacks
online transactions that customers dispute.

One way to prevent fraud is to ask customers for their card verification value (CVV or CVV2), the three-digit number above the signature panel on the back of the credit card, as well as their card number and expiration date. Online merchants also can subscribe to a real-time credit card processing service that authorizes credit card transactions, but the fees can be high. In addition, using a shipper that provides the ability to track shipments enables online merchants to prove that the customer actually received the merchandise and can help to minimize the threat of payment fraud.

Chapter Summary by Learning Objectives

E-commerce is creating a new economy, one that is connecting producers, sellers, and customers via technology in ways that have never been possible before. In this fast-paced world of e-commerce, size no longer matters as much as speed and flexibility. The Internet is creating a new industrial order, and companies that fail to adapt to it will soon become extinct.

1. Describe the benefits of selling on the World Wide Web.

Although a Web-based sales strategy does not guarantee success, the companies that have pioneered Web-based selling have realized many benefits, including the following:

- The opportunity to increase revenues.
- The ability to expand their reach into global markets.
- The ability to remain open 24 hours a day, seven days a week
- The capacity to use the Web's interactive nature to enhance customer service.
- The power to educate and to inform
- The ability to lower the cost of doing business.
- The ability to spot new business opportunities and to capitalize on them.
- The power to track sales results.

2. Understand the factors an entrepreneur should consider before launching into e-commerce.

Before launching an e-commerce effort, business owners should consider the following important issues:

- How a company exploits the Web's interconnectivity and the opportunities it creates to transform relationships with its suppliers and vendors, its customers, and other external stakeholders is crucial to its success.
- Web success requires a company to develop a plan for integrating the Web into its overall strategy. The plan should address issues such as site design and maintenance, creating and managing a brand name, marketing and promotional strategies, sales, and customer service.
- Developing deep, lasting relationships with customers takes on even greater importance on the Web. Attracting customers on the Web costs money, and companies must be able to retain their online customers to make their Web sites profitable.
- Creating a meaningful presence on the Web requires an ongoing investment of resources—time, money, energy, and talent. Establishing an attractive Web site

brimming with catchy photographs of products is only the beginning.

■ Measuring the success of its Web-based sales effort is essential for a company to remain relevant to customers whose tastes, needs, and preferences are always changing.

3. Explain the 12 myths of e-commerce and how to avoid falling victim to them.

The 12 myths of e-commerce are as follows:

1. Setting up a business on the Web is easy and inexpensive.
2. If I launch a site, customers will flock to it.
3. Making money on the Web is easy.
4. Privacy is not an important issue on the Web.
5. The most important part of any e-commerce effort is technology.
6. "Strategy? I don't need a strategy to sell on the Web! Just give me a Web site, and the rest will take care of itself."
7. On the Web, customer service is not as important as it is in a traditional retail store.
8. Flash makes a Web site better.
9. It's what's up front that counts.
10. E-commerce will cause brick-and-mortar retail stores to disappear.
11. The greatest opportunities for e-commerce lie in the retail sector.
12. It's too late to get on the Web.

4. Explain the basic strategies entrepreneurs should follow to achieve success in their e-commerce efforts.

Following are some guidelines for building a successful Web strategy for a small e-company:

■ Focus on a niche in the market.
■ Develop a community of online customers.
■ Attract visitors by giving away "freebies."
■ Make creative use of e-mail but avoid becoming a "spammer."
■ Make sure your Web site says "credibility."
■ Consider forming strategic alliances with larger, more established companies and not-for-profit organizations.
■ Make the most of the Web's global reach.
■ Promote your Web site online and offline.
■ Develop an effective search engine optimization strategy.

5. Learn the techniques of designing a killer Web site.

There is no sure-fire formula for stopping Web surfers in their tracks, but the following suggestions will help:

■ Understand your target customer.
■ Give customers want they want.

■ Select a domain name that is consistent with the image you want to create for your company and register it.
■ Make your Web site easy to navigate.
■ Create a gift idea center.
■ Build loyalty by giving online customers a reason to return to your Web site.
■ Establish hyperlinks with other businesses, preferably those selling products or services that complement yours.
■ Include an e-mail option and a telephone number in your site.
■ Give shoppers the ability to track their orders online.
■ Offer Web shoppers a special all their own.
■ Follow a simple design for your Web page.
■ Create a fast, simple checkout process.
■ Assure customers that their online transactions are secure.
■ Post shipping and handling charges up front.
■ Confirm transactions.
■ Keep your site updated.
■ Test your site often.
■ Consider hiring a professional to design your site.

6. Explain how companies track the results from their Web sites.

The simplest technique for tracking the results of a Web site is the use of a counter, which records the number of "hits" a Web site receives. Another option for tracking Web activity is through log-analysis software. Server logs record every page, graphic, audio clip, or photograph that visitors to a site access, and log-analysis software analyzes these logs and generates reports describing how visitors behave when they get to a site. Key metrics for measuring the effectiveness of a site's performance include the click-through rate, the cost per acquisition, and the conversion rate.

7. Describe how e-businesses ensure the privacy and security of the information they collect and store from the Web.

To make sure they are using the information they collect from visitors to their Web sites legally and ethically, companies should take the following steps:

■ Take an inventory of the customer data collected.
■ Develop a company privacy policy for the information collected.
■ Post the company's privacy policy prominently on the Web site and follow it.

To ensure the security of the information they collect and store from Web transactions, companies should rely on virus and intrusion detection software and firewalls to ward off attacks from hackers.

Discussion Questions

1. In what ways have the Internet and e-commerce changed the ways companies do business?
2. Explain the benefits to a company of selling on the Web.
3. Discuss the factors entrepreneurs should consider before launching an e-commerce site.
4. What are the 12 myths of e-commerce? What can an entrepreneur do to avoid them?
5. Explain the basic approaches available to entrepreneurs for launching an e-commerce effort. What are the advantages, the disadvantages, and the costs associated with each one?
6. What strategic advice would you offer to an entrepreneur about to start an e-company?
7. What design characteristics make for a successful Web page?
8. Explain the characteristics of an ideal domain name.
9. Describe the techniques that are available to e-companies for tracking results from their Web sites. What advantages does each offer?
10. What steps should e-businesses take to ensure the privacy of the information they collect and store from the Web?
11. What techniques can e-companies use to protect their banks of information and their customers' transaction data from hackers?
12. Why does evaluating the effectiveness of a Web site pose a problem for online entrepreneurs?

Business Plan Pro

One of the initial questions asked in the initial Business Plan Pro wizard relates to your business Web site. What was your response to that question, yes or no? Use the contents of this chapter to review your decision. Think about the presence you would like your business to have on the Web. Is your Web site going to be an "information-only" site, or do you plan to have a robust online store? As you look through the list of the 12 myths mentioned in this chapter, ask yourself whether you have fallen prey to any of these myths.

Business Plan Exercises

On the Web

If you are planning on a Web site that is for information-only purposes, go to sites that accomplish that goal. For example, you may want to visit http://www.epinions.com. Note the layout and navigation of the site and how it presents this information. If you plan to have a dynamic online store, Amazon.com's site was a pioneer in the evolution of online shopping. Go to http://www.amazon.com and take a fresh look at the attributes of the site. What of the site that makes it simple, efficient and "safe" to new and returning buyers?

Now locate three Web sites that you find to have attractive parallels with the look and feel of your future Web site. These sites may be from entirely different industries but possess attributes that you find appealing. Identify those qualities and explore how your site might also benefit from those attributes.

In the Software

Open your business plan in Business Plan Pro and go to the "Web Summary" section. If you have changed your mind about having a Web site, click on "View" and "Wizard"

and change that decision. The outline of your business plan will then reflect that change and bring the "Web Summary" section into your outline. Read the instructions within the software and click on the sample plan link in the upper right-hand section of the instructions. Add content to this section. These questions may help you to consider the following:

- Do you have a URL registered for your business? If not, how will you begin that process to secure and register that Web address?
- How would you assess the general level of comfort that your target market has with the Web? For example, are they a technologically savvy group that uses the Web as a part of their daily life, or is this group an older audience that is learning how to leverage the power of the Web?
- List the objectives you hope to realize through your Web site.
- Is your site going to have an online store? If so, explore how to implement credit card or other online payment options.
- Who will design and launch the site? Will you or someone in your organization, or will you outsource that work?
- How will you measure, track, and assess the performance of your site, and how often that will occur?
- Are you going to incorporate Web analytics tools and resources that may help you to measure your Web site's performance?
- Does your business plan demonstrate that you have planned and budgeted for your Web site based on the required resources to design, launch, and maintain your site?

Building Your Business Plan

The additions you have made regarding your Web site may be significant or minimal. Step back and review what you have captured in your plan to date. With these additions, does your plan continue to tell a consistent and coherent story about your business? Review and edit other sections that may be impacted by your additions to the Web section. Some of those sections may include areas that relate to marketing promotions, communications, expenses, and revenues.

Beyond the Classroom . . .

1. Work with a team of your classmates to come up with an Internet business you would be interested in launching. Come up with several suitable domain names for your hypothetical e-company. Once you have chosen a few names, go to a domain name registration service such as Network Solutions' Internic at http://www.networksolutions.com/ or Netnames at http://www.netnames.com to conduct a name search. How many of the names that your team came up with were already registered to someone? If an entrepreneur's top choice for a domain name is already registered to someone else, what options does he or she have?

2. Select several online companies with which you are familiar and visit their Web sites. What percentage of them have privacy policies posted on their sites? How comprehensive are these policies? What percentage of the sites that you visited belong to a privacy watchdog agency such as TRUSTe or BBBOnLine? How important is a posted privacy policy for e-companies? Explain.

3. Visit five e-commerce sites on the Web and evaluate them on the basis of the Web site design principles described in this chapter. How well do they measure up? What suggestions can you offer for improving the design of each site? If you were a customer trying to make a purchase from each site, how would you respond to the design?

4. Visit the "Understanding Privacy" Web site at BBBOnLine (http://www.bbbonline.org/ understandingprivacy/). Contact the owner of a Web-based business in your town and use the assessment tool "How's Your Privacy Quotient" from the BBBOnLine Web site to evaluate the company's privacy policy. How does the company score on the PQ assessment tool? Use the resources on this site and others to develop a list of suggestions for improving the company's score.

10 | Pricing Strategies

Learning Objectives

On completion of this chapter, you will be able to:

1 Discuss the relationships among pricing, image, competition, and value.
2 Describe effective pricing techniques for introducing new products or services and for existing ones.
3 Explain the pricing methods and strategies for (A) retailers, (B) manufacturers, and (C) service firms.
4 Describe the impact of credit on pricing.

Setting prices is a business decision governed by both art and science—with a measure of instinct thrown in for good measure. Setting prices for their products and services requires entrepreneurs to balance a multitude of complex forces, many of them working in opposite directions. Entrepreneurs must determine prices for their goods and services that will draw customers and produce a profit. Unfortunately, many small business owners set prices without enough information about their cost of operations and the nature of their customers. Price is an important factor in building long-term relationships with customers, and haphazard pricing techniques can confuse and alienate customers and endanger a small company's profitability. Setting prices is not only one of the toughest decisions small business owners face, but it also is one of the most important. Research by the consulting firm McKinsey and Company shows that proper pricing strategies have far greater impact on a company's profits than corresponding reductions in fixed or variable costs.[1] Improper pricing has destroyed countless businesses whose owners mistakenly thought their prices were high enough to generate a profit when, in fact, they were not.

Timeless Message

After working with a consultant, Jeff Trott, founder of Timeless Message, a company that sells bottles with greeting messages inside them, raised its prices from an average of $30 per bottle to $60 per bottle. The company had underestimated both its costs and the market value of its products. The price increase resulted in a brief sales dip, but, according to Trott, "We started making a profit for the first time in four years. It was like we had been shipping a ten-dollar bill out the door with each order."[2]

Pricing decisions cut across every aspect of a small company, influencing everything from its marketing and sales efforts to its operations and strategy. Price is the monetary value of a product or service in the marketplace; it is a measure of what the customer must give up to obtain various goods and services. Price also is a signal of a product's or service's value to an individual, and different customers assign different values to the same goods and services. From an entrepreneur's viewpoint, price must be compatible with customers' perceptions of value. "Pricing is not just a math problem," says one business writer. "It's a psychology test."[3] The psychology of pricing is an art much more than it is a science. It focuses on creating value in the customer's mind but recognizes that value is what the customer perceives it to be. In many cases, customers look to a product's or service's price for clues about value. Consider the following examples, which illustrate the sometimes puzzling connection between price and perceived value:

- In the ultra-premium segment of the watch industry, Rolex, Cartier, Patek Philippe, Chopard, Toric, Blancpain, and Corum are legendary brands of handmade watches that sell at prices ranging from $10,000 to $50,000. To some people, owning one of these watches is a hallmark of financial success, even though they are less accurate at keeping time than a $10 quartz-driven Timex.[4]

- To establish a niche in the beer market, microbrewers in the United States began producing small batches of high-quality beer in the European style, focusing on ales, porters, and stouts rather than the lagers the giant brewers were selling. Moving even farther upscale in the beer market (which has seen relatively flat sales compared to a 63 percent increase in wine sales since 1991), small brewers are marketing premium craft beers with all of the cachet of wine—at premium prices, of course. In addition to its 18.5 percent alcohol content and $16 per bottle price, Dogfish Head Brewery's Fort Beer has a raspberry flavor, and the company suggests that connoisseurs drink it from a champagne flute. Microbrewer Samuel Adams makes the world's most expensive beer. Its Utopia, made from special malts and yeast, sells for $100 per bottle. Because the company produces just 8,000 bottles a year, some bottles of Utopia have fetched as much as $200 on eBay![5]

- The Renaissance Pen Company markets fountain pens made from gold and platinum and encrusted with diamonds selling for as much as $230,000. It also sells a pen that contains the crystallized DNA of Abraham Lincoln for only $1,650.[6]

As you can see, setting higher prices sometimes can *increase* appeal of a product or service ("If you charge more, you must be worth it"). Value for these products is not found in their superior technical performance but in their scarcity and uniqueness and the resulting image they create for the buyer. Although an entrepreneur must recognize the shallow depth of the market for such ultra-luxury items, the ego-satisfying ownership of limited-edition watches, pens, cars, jewelry, and other items is the psychological force supporting the premium price strategy.

Three Potent Forces: Image, Competition, and Value

Price Conveys Image

A company's pricing policies communicate important information about its overall image to customers. For example, the prices charged by a posh men's clothing store reflect a completely different image from those charged by a factory outlet. Customers look at prices to determine what type of store they are dealing with. High prices frequently convey the idea of quality, prestige, and uniqueness to customers. "People bring a whole set of equations with them when they make a purchase, and one of the values for most people is that high price equals quality," says Rob Docters, a pricing expert.[7] Accordingly, when developing a marketing approach to pricing, entrepreneurs must establish prices that are compatible with what customers expect and are willing to pay. Too often, small business owners *underprice* their goods and services, believing that low prices are the only way they can achieve a competitive advantage. A study by the Copernicus consulting firm found that only 15 to 35 percent of customers consider price to be the chief criterion when selecting a product or service.[8]

A common pricing mistake small business owners make is failing to recognize the extra value, convenience, service, and quality they give their customers—all things many customers are willing to pay for. These companies fall into the trap of trying to compete solely on the basis of price when they lack the sales volume—and, hence, the lower cost structures—of their larger rivals. It is a recipe for failure. "People want quality," says one merchant selling upscale goods at upscale prices. "They want value. But if you lower prices, they think that you are lowering the value and lowering the quality."[9] Lowering prices may be a dangerous cycle that can destroy a business. A study of businesses in multiple industries by Rafi Mohammed, author of *The Art of Pricing*, found that those companies that raised prices by 1 percent saw their profits increase 11 percent. Those that raised their prices by 10 percent realized profit increases of 100 percent![10] The study does not imply that businesses have free rein to raise prices to any level, but it does suggest that many companies could raise their prices enough to improve their financial results significantly if they can convince customers that their products offer superior value.

In the crowded soft drink market, the battle for market share often boils down to price competition among the industry giants Coca-Cola and Pepsi. However, some small companies have managed to carve out niches in the soft drink market with higher-priced specialty products that are made with all-natural ingredients, offer exotic flavors, or provide some other appealing twist.

In 2002, Eric Schnell and Steven Kessler introduced the Steaz Green Tea Soda line as part of their new business, the Healthy Beverage Company, as a nutritious alternative to regular carbonated soft drinks. Their lightly carbonated beverage contains green tea (touted by many health care professionals for its antioxidant properties) and sugar cane juice and is certified as "organic" by the U.S. Department of Agriculture. Marketing their tea-soda combination as a healthy beverage alternative to conventional soft drinks allows the company to charge $1.50 for a 12-ounce bottle, a healthy price premium over standard carbonated drinks.[11]

Healthy Beverage Company

By emphasizing the uniqueness of their organic green tea-soda combination drink, Eric Schnell and Steven Kessler, co-founders of Steaz Green Tea Soda, are able to charge a premium price over regular carbonated drinks.

One key to setting prices properly is based on understanding a company's target market, the customer groups at which the small company is aiming its goods or services. Target market, business image, and pricing strategy are closely related.

Sway and Cake and TBC

When Tamara Donaghy-Bates launched Sway & Cake, a Seattle, Washington, retail store selling women's clothing, her target audience was young professional women in their late 20s to late 30s who are looking for something other than traditional styles. Donaghy-Bates describes the clothing she sells in Sway & Cake as "funky" and "flirty"—trendy, fashion-forward styles that are common in metropolitan areas such as New York or Los Angeles but are hard to find in conservative towns such as Seattle. Her upscale pricing strategy is geared toward her target audience, and it works; her company's first-year sales exceeded $800,000. Working with customers every day in the shop provided Donaghy-Bates with clear insight into her customers' fashion preferences, and she soon saw an opportunity to tap into another target audience with a different pricing strategy: students and young women in their early to mid 20s. To reach this group of customers, Donaghy-Bates opened TBC (To Be Continued) in Seattle as a lower-cost outlet for similar styles of clothing that she sells in Sway & Cake. In fact, nearly half of the merchandise sold in TBC is clothing that did not sell in Sway & Cake and has been marked down at a significant discount, sometimes as much as 50 or 60 percent off the normal retail price. TBC's remaining merchandise is new, lower priced, and aimed at a younger audience. Customers have responded to both stores' pricing strategies and merchandise mix, and combined sales for the two stores have grown well beyond the $1 million mark.[12]

Competition and Pricing

When setting prices, entrepreneurs should take into account their competitors' prices, but they should *not* automatically match or beat them. Although price is an important factor in the purchase decision, it is not the only consideration for shoppers. Two factors are vital to studying the effects of competition on the small company's pricing policies: the location of the competitors and the nature of the competing goods and services. In most cases, unless a company can differentiate the quality and the quantity of extras it provides, it must match the prices charged by nearby competitors for identical items. For example, if a self-service station charges a nickel more per gallon for gasoline than does another self-service station across the street, customers will simply go across the street to buy. Without the advantage of a unique business image—quality of goods sold, value of services provided, convenient location, favorable credit terms—a small company must match local competitors' prices or lose sales. Although the prices that distant competitors charge are not nearly as critical to the small business as are those of local competitors, it can be helpful to know them and to use them as reference points. Before matching any competitor's prices, however, small business owners should consider the rival's motives. The competition may be establishing its price structure based on a unique set of criteria and a totally different strategy. Blindly matching competitors' prices can lead a company to financial ruin, and companies that set their prices this way typically do so because they perceive themselves in a position of strategic weakness.

The nature of the competitors' goods and services also influences a company's pricing policies. Entrepreneurs must monitor competitors' prices on products that are identical to or are close substitutes for those they sell and then strive to keep their prices in line with them. For example, the local sandwich shop should consider the hamburger restaurant, the taco shop, and the roast beef shop as competitors because they all serve fast foods. Although none of them offers the identical menu of the sandwich shop, they are all competing for the same quick-meal dollar. Of course, if a small business can differentiate its products by creating a distinctive image in customers' minds or by offering superior service, quality, convenience, or speed, it can charge prices higher than those of its competitors. Because competitors' prices can have a dramatic impact on a small company's prices, entrepreneurs should make it a habit to monitor their rivals' prices, especially on identical items.

When Anthony Shurman launched Yosha Enterprises in 2002, a company that markets liquid breath mints, he established a price of $1.99 for a 36-mint package. Later, in response to competitors' prices, he lowered the price to $1.79 and then to $1.69 per pack. Momints contained more mints than any of the competing brands, but customers failed to recognize that benefit, and based their purchase decisions on the package price. When Shurman recently rolled out Momints at a regional chain of grocery stores, he cut the size of the pack to the industry standard 28 mints and set a price of 99 cents. "Our sales went up 350 percent," he says. Yosha generates $3 million in annual revenue, and Shurman believes that he can sell even more mints at the lower 99-cent price.[13]

Generally, entrepreneurs should avoid head-to-head price competition with other firms that can more easily achieve lower prices through lower cost structures. For instance, most locally owned drugstores cannot compete with the prices of large national drug chains. However, many local drugstores operate successfully by using nonprice competition; these stores offer more personalized service, free delivery, credit sales, and other extras that the chains have eliminated. Nonprice competition can be an effective strategy for a small business in the face of larger, more powerful enterprises, especially because there are many dangers in experimenting with price changes. Price shifts cause fluctuations in sales volume that a small company may not be able to tolerate. In addition, frequent price changes may damage a company's image and its customer relations.

Attempting to undercut competitors' prices may lead to a price war, one of the most deadly games a small business can play. Price wars can eradicate companies' profit margins and scar an entire industry for years. "Many entrepreneurs cut prices to the point of unprofitablility just to compete," says one business writer. "In doing so, they open the door to catastrophe. Less revenue often translates into lower quality, poorer service, sloppier salesmanship, weaker customer loyalty, and financial disaster."[14] Price wars usually begin when one competitor thinks he or she can achieve higher volume instantaneously by lowering prices. Rather than sticking to their strategic guns, competitors believe they must follow suit.

Entrepreneurs usually overestimate the power of price cuts, however. Sales volume rarely increases enough to offset the lower profit margins of a lower price. A business with a 25 percent gross profit margin that cuts its price by 10 percent would have to *triple* its sales volume just to break even. In a price war, a company may cut its prices so severely that it is impossible to achieve the volume necessary to offset the lower profit margins. Even when price cuts work, their effects often are temporary. Customers lured by the lowest price usually have almost no loyalty to a business. The lesson: The best way to survive a price war is to stay out of it by emphasizing the unique features, benefits, and value your company offers its customers.

Focus on Value

Ultimately, the "right" price for a product or service depends on one factor: the value that it provides for a customer. There are two aspects of value, however. Entrepreneurs may recognize the *objective* value of their products and services, which is the price customers would be willing to pay if they understood perfectly the benefits that a product or service delivers for them. Unfortunately, few, if any, customers can see a product's or a service's true objective value; instead, they see only its *perceived* value, which determines the price they are willing to pay for it. Research into purchasing decisions has revealed a fundamental problem that adds to the complexity of a business owner's pricing decision: People faced with pricing decisions often act irrationally. In one classic study, researchers asked shoppers if they would travel an additional 20 minutes to save $5 on a calculator that costs $15; most said they would. When asked the same question about a $125 jacket, most of the shoppers said no, even though they would be saving the exact same amount of money! "People make [purchasing] decisions piecemeal, influenced by the context of the choice," says Richard Thaler, who won a Nobel Prize for his work in behavioral economics.[15]

Note that value does not necessarily correspond to low price, however. Businesses that underprice their products and services or run special discount price promotions may be short-circuiting the value proposition they are trying to build and communicate to their customers. Customers may respond to price cuts, but companies that rely on them to boost sales risk undermine the perceived value of their products and services. In addition, once customers grow accustomed to buying products and services during special promotions, the habit can be difficult to break. They simply wait for the next sale. Some companies in the auto industry have faced this problem as customers accustomed to buying autos with large rebates postpone buying new cars until automakers offer them special incentives. The result has been fluctuating sales and a diminished value of those automotive brands.

One of the most important determinants of customers' response to a price is whether they perceive the price to be a fair exchange for the value they receive from the product or service. The good news is that companies can influence through marketing and other efforts customers' perception of value. "The price you get for a product is a function of what it's truly worth—and how good a job you do communicating that value to the end user," says one entrepreneur.[16] Indeed, setting a product's or a service's price is another way a company can communicate value to its customers. For most shoppers, three reference points define a fair price: the price they have paid for the product or service in the past, the prices competitors charge for the same or similar product or service, and the costs a company incurs to provide the product or service. The price that customers have paid in the past for an item serves as a baseline reference point, but people often forget that inflation causes a company's costs to rise from year to year. Therefore, it is important for business owners to remind customers periodically that they must raise prices to offset the increased cost of doing business. "Over time, costs always go up," says Norm Brodsky, owner of a successful document storage company. "I'd rather raise prices a little every year or with every new contract than be forced to demand a big increase down the road."[17]

As we have seen already, companies often find it necessary to match competitors' prices on the same or similar items unless they can establish a distinctive image in customers' minds. One of the most successful strategies for companies facing direct competition is to differentiate their products or services by adding value for customers and then charging for it. For instance, a company might offer faster delivery, a longer product warranty, extra service, or something else that adds value to an item for its customers and allows the business to charge a higher price.

Perhaps the least understood of the three reference points is a company's cost structure. Customers often underestimate the costs businesses incur to provide products and services, whether it is a simple cotton T-shirt on a shelf in a beach-front shop or a life-saving drug that may have cost hundreds of millions of dollars and many years to develop. They forget that business owners must make or buy the products they sell, market them, pay their employees, and cover a host of other operating expenses, ranging from health care to legal fees. Entrepreneurs facing rapidly rising costs in their businesses should consider the following strategies:

- *Communicate with customers.* Rather than hide bad news from customers, let them know what is happening. When the owner of a wholesale coffee business saw coffee bean prices escalate because of bad weather in key coffee-producing countries, he included copies of news articles in a letter he sent to customers explaining his company's price increases.
- *Focus on improving efficiency in the company.* One way to lessen the impact of rising costs in one area of a business is to look for ways to cut costs in other areas. Improving operating efficiency may not offset totally the increased costs of doing business, but it will help dampen their effects.
- *Consider absorbing the cost increases.* When Norm Brodsky, owner of the document storage company mentioned earlier, saw his competitors add a fuel surcharge to their customers' bills to offset steep increases in gas prices, he decided *not* to add a fuel surcharge. Then, he used the pricing decision to attract new accounts, telling them, "We have found other ways besides a surcharge to deal with the problem. When we say the price [of our contract] is fixed for five years, we mean it, and you can count on it." Brodsky also used the fuel surcharge issue to build loyalty among his existing customers, something he is certain will pay off in the future.[18]

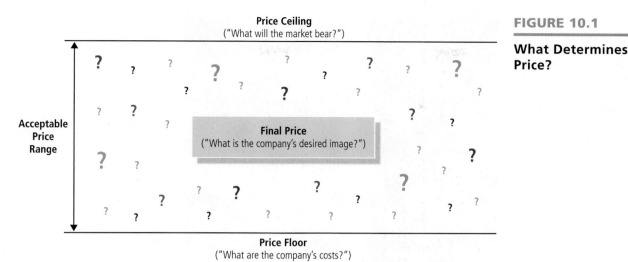

FIGURE 10.1

What Determines Price?

- *Emphasize the value your company's product or service delivers to customers.* Customers have a tendency to forget the benefits and value a business provides unless an entrepreneur periodically reminds them.
- *Anticipate rising costs and try to lock in prices early.* By tracking coffee and tea prices on commodities exchanges every day, the owner of a small coffee and tea shop was able to anticipate price increases for her raw materials and committed early on to purchase 125,000 pounds of coffee at a fixed price for one year. When coffee prices doubled, she saved more than $80,000.

Setting prices with an emphasis on value is more important than trying to choose the ideal price for a product. In fact, for most products there is an acceptable price range, not a single ideal price. This price range is the area between the price ceiling defined by customers in the market and the price floor established by the company's cost structure. An entrepreneur's goal is to position the company's prices within this acceptable price range. The final price that business owners set depends on the desired image they want to create for the business in their customers' minds—discount, middle-of-the-road, or prestige (see Figure 10.1).

Setting appropriate prices requires more than just choosing a number based solely on intuition. Rather, proper pricing policies require information, facts, and analysis. The factors that small business owners must consider when determining the final price for goods and services include the following:

- Product or service costs
- Market factors—supply and demand
- Sales volume
- Competitors' prices
- A company's competitive advantage
- Economic conditions
- Business location
- Seasonal fluctuations
- Psychological factors
- Credit terms and purchase discounts
- Customers' price sensitivity
- Desired image

Although business owners may not be able to charge the ideal price for a product or service, they should set the price high enough to cover their costs and earn a reasonable profit but low enough to attract customers and generate an adequate sales volume.

After the terrorist attacks in 2001 dampened attendance at Broadway, theaters cut their prices. As audiences returned, theaters were able to raise their ticket prices. Even though they charge more than $100 per ticket, popular shows such as *Wicked* (featuring here Idina Menzel (l) as Elpheba and Kristin Chenoweth (r) as Glinda) play to sold out houses almost every night.

Furthermore, the right price today may be completely inappropriate tomorrow because of changing market and competitive conditions. Broadway shows, which had suffered steep sales declines in the wake of the terrorist attacks in 2001, recently pushed ticket prices above the $100 level as audiences returned and shows began selling out once again. *Monty Python's Spamalot* was the first hit show to push through the psychological $100 price ceiling, but long-running *Mamma Mia!* and *Wicked* quickly followed suit. The decisions were based on the fact that all three shows were playing to sold-out houses almost every night of the week, but theater managers were quick to point out that customers could still buy standing-room-only tickets for as little as $20.[19]

For many businesses, the pricing decision has become more challenging because the World Wide Web gives customers access to incredible amounts of information about the prices of items ranging from cars to computers. Increasingly, customers are using the Web to find the lowest prices available. To maintain their profitability, companies have responded with **customized or dynamic pricing,** in which they set different prices on the same products and services for different customers using the information they have collected about their customers. For instance, a first-time customer making a purchase at an online store may pay a higher price for an item than a regular customer who shops there frequently pays for that same item. AllState Insurance Company relies on a huge database of statistical research that includes information ranging from customers' driving records and their age to their credit scores and whether they pay their bills on time to determine the prices it charges for insurance coverage. AllState's credit-derived premiums have enabled the company to go from a system that established prices using three broad-based categories to one that divides customers into nearly 400 categories, each with its own price point. Since implementing the dynamic pricing strategy, AllState's sales and profitability have climbed significantly.[20]

customized or dynamic pricing
a pricing technique that sets different prices on the same products and services for different customers using the information that a company collects about its customers.

Pricing Strategies and Tactics

LEARNING OBJECTIVES
2. Describe effective pricing techniques for introducing new products or services and for existing ones.

There is no limit to the number of variations in pricing strategies and tactics. This wide variety of options is exactly what allows the small business manager to be so creative. This section examines some of the more commonly used tactics under a variety of conditions. Pricing always plays a critical role in a firm's overall strategy; pricing policies must be compatible with a company's total marketing plan and the image it plans to create in the marketplace.

Introducing a New Product

Entrepreneurs are often apprehensive to set the price of a new product when they have no precedent on which to base their decisions. If the new product's price is excessively high, it is in danger of failing because of low sales volume. However, if its price is too low, the product's sales revenue might not cover costs. In addition, the company runs the risk of establishing the product's perceived value at a low level. The management consulting firm McKinsey and Company claims that 80 to 90 percent of the pricing problems on new products are the result of companies setting prices that are too low.[21] When pricing any new product, the owner should try to satisfy three objectives:

1. ***Getting the product accepted.*** No matter how unusual a product is, its price must be acceptable to a company's potential customers. The acceptable price range for a new product depends, in part, on the product's position:
   - Revolutionary products are so new and unique that they transform existing markets. The acceptable price range for revolutionary products tends to be rather wide, but the businesses introducing them must be prepared to make an investment in educating customers about them.
   - Evolutionary products offer upgrades and enhancements to existing products. The acceptable price range for evolutionary products is not a wide as it is for revolutionary products. Companies that introduce evolutionary products with many new features at prices that are too low may initiate a price war.
   - Me-too products, as the name suggests, offer the same basic features as existing products on the market. The acceptable price range for these products is quite narrow, and many companies introducing them find themselves left with me-too pricing strategies that are the same or similar to those of their competitors.
2. ***Maintaining market share as competition grows.*** If a new product is successful, competitors will enter the market, and the small company must work to expand or at least maintain its market share. Continuously reappraising the product's price in conjunction with special advertising and promotion techniques helps to retain a satisfactory market share.
3. ***Earning a profit.*** Obviously, a small firm must establish a price for the new product higher than its cost. Entrepreneurs should not introduce a new product at a price below cost because it is much easier to lower a price than to increase it once the product is on the market. Pricing their products too low is a common and often fatal mistake for new businesses; entrepreneurs are tempted to underprice their products and services when they enter a new market to ensure their acceptance or to gain market share quickly. Doing so, however, sets customers' value expectations at low levels as well, and that can be a difficult perception to overcome.

Linda Calder, owner of Calder & Calder Promotions, a company that produces trade shows, knows how difficult it can be to raise prices. When she launched her company, Calder decided to set her price below the average price of competing trade show production companies because she thought that would give her a competitive edge. "My fee was so low . . . I sold out but did not make a profit," she says. Realizing her mistake, Calder raised prices in her second year, but her customers balked. Her sales fell by 50 percent.[22]

Calder & Calder Promotions

Entrepreneurs have three basic strategies to choose from when establishing a new product's price: a penetration pricing strategy; a skimming pricing strategy; and a sliding-down-the-demand-curve strategy.

Market Penetration If a small business introduces a product into a highly competitive market in which a large number of similar products are competing for acceptance, the product must penetrate the market to be successful. To gain quick acceptance and extensive distribution in the mass market, entrepreneurs should consider introducing the product at a low price. In other words, it should set the price just above total unit cost to develop a wedge in the market and quickly achieve a high volume of sales. The resulting low profit margins tend to discourage competitors from entering the market with similar products.

In most cases, a penetration pricing strategy is used to introduce relatively low-priced goods into a market where no elite segment and little opportunity for differentiation exists. The introduction is usually accompanied by heavy advertising and promotional techniques, special sales, and discounts. Entrepreneurs must recognize that penetration pricing is a long-range strategy; until customers accept the product, profits are likely to be small. If the strategy works and the product achieves mass market penetration, sales volume will increase, and the company will earn adequate profits. The objectives of the penetration strategy are to break into the market quickly, generate a high sales volume as soon as possible, and build market share. Many consumer products, such as soap, shampoo, and light bulbs, are introduced through penetration pricing strategies.

Majesco

Majesco, a small company that competes against many industry giants in the video game business, uses a penetration pricing strategy for most of the games it sells. The company releases 5 to 10 new games each year, and 80 percent of them are "bargain titles," targeted for sale in retailers' discount bins, where they are priced from $9.99 to $19.99. "There's not much competition in the value-game market," explains company co-founder Jesse Sutton. Because the average cost of producing budget games is far below that of creating premium games with sophisticated graphics, Majesco can break even on sales of just 15,000 to 50,000 units for its budget games compared to 200,000 to 1 million units for premium games. One of the company's most popular titles, *Hypersonic Extreme,* has sold more than 170,000 units, earning the company a solid profit.[23]

Skimming A skimming pricing strategy often is used when a company introduces a new product into a market with little or no competition. Sometimes the firm employs this tactic when introducing a product into a competitive market that contains an elite group that is able to pay a higher price. Here a firm uses a higher-than-normal price in an effort to quickly recover the initial developmental and promotional costs of the product. Start-up costs usually are substantial due to intensive promotional expenses and high initial production costs. The idea is to set a price well above the total unit cost and to promote the product heavily to appeal to the segment of the market that is not sensitive to price. Such a pricing tactic often reinforces the unique, prestigious image of a store and projects a quality image of the product. Another advantage of this technique is that the manager can correct pricing mistakes quickly and easily. If the firm sets a price that is too low under a penetration strategy, raising the price can be very difficult. If a firm using a skimming strategy sets a price too high to generate sufficient volume, it can always lower the price. Successful skimming strategies require a company to differentiate its products or services from those of the competition, justifying the above-average price.

Sliding Down the Demand Curve One variation of the skimming price strategy is called sliding down the demand curve. Using this tactic, the small company introduces a product at a high price. Then, technological advances enable the firm to lower its costs quickly and to reduce the product's price before its competition can. By beating other businesses in a price decline, the small company discourages competitors and gradually, over time, becomes a high-volume producer. High-definition television sets are a prime

Cornered by Baldwin

Jewelry

"Too pricey? Perhaps you wish to see something in macaroni and spray paint?"

example of a product introduced at a high price that quickly cascaded downward as companies forged important technological advances and took advantage of economies of scale. When they were first introduced in 1999, high-definition TVs sold for $19,000; today, they are priced at $1,000 or less.

Sliding is a short-term pricing strategy that assumes that competition will eventually emerge. Even if no competition arises, however, the small business almost always lowers the product's price to attract a larger segment of the market. Nonetheless, the initial high price contributes to a rapid return of start-up costs and generates a pool of funds to finance expansion and technological advances.

Pricing Established Goods and Services

Each of the following pricing tactics or techniques can become part of the toolbox of pricing tactics entrepreneurs can use to set prices of established goods and services.

Odd Pricing Although studies of consumer reactions to prices are mixed and generally inconclusive, many small business managers use the technique known as **odd pricing.** These managers prefer to establish prices that end in odd numbers such as 5, 7, or 9 because they believe that merchandise selling for $12.69 appears to be much cheaper than the item priced at $13.00. Psychological techniques such as odd pricing are designed to appeal to certain customer interests, but research on their effectiveness is mixed. Some studies show no benefits from using odd pricing, but others have concluded that the technique can produce significant increases in sales.

odd pricing
a pricing technique that sets prices that end in odd numbers to create the psychological impression of low prices.

Price Lining **Price lining** is a technique that greatly simplifies the pricing function by pricing different products in a product line at different price points, depending on their quality, features, and cost. Under this system, entrepreneurs stock merchandise in several different price ranges, or price lines. Each category of merchandise contains items that are similar in appearance but that differ in quality, cost, performance, or other features. For example, most music and video stores use price lines for their CDs and DVDs to make it

price lining
a technique that greatly simplifies the pricing function by pricing different products in a product line at different price points, depending on their quality, features, and cost.

easier for customers to select items and to simplify inventory planning. Many lined products appear in sets of three—good, better, and best—at prices designed to satisfy different market segment needs and incomes. Price lining can boost a store's sales because it makes goods available to a wide range of shoppers, simplifies the purchase decision for customers, and allows them to keep their purchases within their budgets.

leader pricing
a technique that involves marking down the normal price of a popular item in an attempt to attract more customers who make incidental purchases of other items at regular prices.

Leader Pricing **Leader pricing** is a technique in which a retailer marks down the customary price (i.e., the price consumers are accustomed to paying) of a popular item in an attempt to attract more customers. The company earns a much smaller profit on each unit because the markup is lower, but purchases of other merchandise by customers seeking the leader item often boost sales and profits. In other words, the incidental purchases that consumers make when shopping for the leader item boost sales revenue enough to offset a lower profit margin on the leader. Grocery stores frequently use leader pricing. For instance, during the holiday season, stores often use turkeys as a price leader, knowing that they will earn higher margins on the other items shoppers purchase with their turkeys.

zone pricing
a technique that involves setting different prices for customers located in different territories because of different transportation costs.

Geographic Pricing Small businesses whose pricing decisions are greatly affected by the costs of shipping merchandise to customers across a wide range of geographic regions frequently employ one of the geographic pricing techniques. For these companies, freight expenses comprise a substantial portion of the cost of doing business and may cut deeply into already narrow profit margins. One type of geographic pricing is **zone pricing,** in which a small company sells its merchandise at different prices to customers located in different territories. For example, a manufacturer might sell at one price to customers east of the Mississippi and at another to those west of the Mississippi. The U.S. Postal Service's varying parcel post charges offer a good example of zone pricing. The company must be able to show a legitimate basis (e.g., differences in selling or transporting costs) for the price discrimination or risk violating Section 2 of the Clayton Act.

delivered pricing
a technique in which a firm charges all of its customers the same price regardless of their location.

Another variation of geographic pricing is uniform **delivered pricing,** a technique in which a firm charges all of its customers the same price regardless of their location, even though the cost of selling or transporting merchandise varies. The firm calculates the proper freight charges for each region and combines them into a uniform fee. The result is that local customers subsidize the company's charges for shipping merchandise to distant customers.

FOB-Factory
a pricing method in which a company sells merchandise to customers on the condition that they pay all shipping costs.

A final variation of geographic pricing is **FOB-Factory,** in which a company sells its merchandise to customers on the condition that they pay all shipping costs. In this way, the company can set a uniform price for its product and let each customer cover the freight costs.

opportunistic pricing
a pricing method that involves charging customers unreasonably high prices when goods or services are in short supply.

Opportunistic Pricing When products or services are in short supply, customers are willing to pay more for products they need. Some businesses use such circumstances to maximize short-term profits by engaging in price gouging. Many customers have little choice but to pay the higher prices. **Opportunistic pricing** may backfire, however, because customers know that unreasonably high prices mean that a company is exploiting them. For example, after a devastating Los Angeles earthquake, one convenience store jacked up prices on virtually every item, selling small bottles of water for $8 each. Neighborhood residents had no choice but to pay the higher prices. After the incident, many customers remembered the store's unfair prices and began to shop elsewhere. The convenience store's sales slipped and never recovered.

discounts or markdowns
reductions from normal list prices.

Discounts Many small business managers use **discounts or markdowns**—reductions from normal list prices—to move stale, outdated, damaged, or slow-moving merchandise. A seasonal discount is a price reduction designed to encourage shoppers to purchase merchandise before an upcoming season. For instance, many retail clothiers offer special sales on winter coats in midsummer. Some firms grant purchase discounts to special groups of customers, such as senior citizens or students, to establish a faithful clientele and to generate repeat business. For example, one small drugstore located near a state

university offered a 10 percent student discount on all purchases and was quite successful in developing a large volume of student business.

Multiple-unit pricing is a promotional technique that offers customers discounts if they purchase in quantity. Many products, especially those with relatively low unit value, are sold using multiple pricing. For example, instead of selling an item for 50 cents, a small company might offer five for $2.

multiple-unit pricing
a technique offering customers discounts if they purchase in quantity.

Bundling Many small businesses have discovered the marketing benefits of **bundling,** grouping together several products or services, or both, into a package that offers customers extra value at a special price. For instance, many software manufacturers bundle several computer programs (such as a word processor, spreadsheet, database, presentation graphics, and Web browser) into "suites" that offer customers a discount over purchasing the same packages separately. Fast food outlets often bundle items into "meal deals" that customers can purchase at lower prices than if they bought the items separately.

bundling
a pricing method that involves grouping together several products or services, or both, into a package that offers customers extra value at a special price.

Recognizing that each fall the 15 million students who set out for college spend more than $210 million to furnish and decorate their dormitory rooms and apartments, one retailer began offering a line of bundled products aimed squarely at this target audience. The company's Dorm Room line includes Kitchen in a Box, a set of between 46 and 80 starter pieces that are suitable for equipping an empty kitchen. One set that is priced at $80 includes pieces that would cost $140 if purchased separately. The company's Bath in a Box includes over-sized towels that are convenient for dorm life and a laundry bag with handy instructions for washing clothes for students who have not yet mastered the art of sorting clothes.[24]

Optional-product pricing involves selling the base product for one price but selling the options or accessories for it at a much higher markup. Automobiles are often sold at a base price with each option priced separately. In some cases, the car is sold with some of the options "bundled" together, as explained previously.

optional product pricing
a technique that involves selling the base product for one price but selling the options or accessories for it at a much higher markup.

Kettler, a German company that makes upscale tricycles, uses an optional-product pricing strategy that more closely mimics BMW than Babies "R" Us. A basic model of its most popular tricycle, The Navigator, starts at $70, but a host of options ranging from a seat belt ($15.99) to a little red bell ($5.99) quickly pushes the price to $150 or more, far above the price of an average tricycle. Despite Kettler's premium prices, parents who want only the best for their children are snapping up the company's high-quality tricycles fast enough that its sales are growing at nearly 20 percent a year.[25]

Kettler

captive-product pricing
a technique that involves selling a product for a low price and charging a higher price for the accessories that accompany it.

byproduct pricing
a technique in which the revenues from the sale of byproducts allow a company to be more competitive in its pricing of the main product.

Captive-product pricing is a pricing strategy in which the base product is not functional without the appropriate accessory. King Gillette, the founder of Gillette, taught the business world that the real money is not in selling the razor (the product) but in selling the blades (the accessory)! Most companies in the desktop printer business use this technique. They introduce a printer at a low initial price and then price replacement cartridges so that they earn high margins on them. Manufacturers of electronic games also rely on captive-product pricing, earning lower margins on the game consoles and substantially higher margins on the game cartridges.

Byproduct pricing is a technique in which the revenues from the sale of byproducts allow a company to be more competitive in its pricing of the main product. For years, sawmills thought that the bark from the trees they processed was a nuisance. Now it is packaged and sold to gardeners who use the bark chips for ground cover. Zoos across the globe offer one of the most creative examples of byproduct pricing, packaging once-worthless exotic animal droppings and marketing it as fertilizer under the clever name "Zoo Doo."

Suggested Retail Prices Many manufacturers print suggested retail prices on their products or include them on invoices or in wholesale catalogs. Small business owners frequently follow these suggested retail prices because this eliminates the need to make a pricing decision. Nonetheless, following prices established by a distant manufacturer may create problems for the small firm. For example, a haberdasher may try to create a high-quality, exclusive image through a prestige pricing policy, but manufacturers may suggest discount outlet prices that are incompatible with the small firm's image. Another danger of accepting the manufacturer's suggested price is that it does not take into consideration a small company's cost structure or competitive situation. A manufacturer cannot force a business to accept a suggested retail price or require a business to agree not to resell merchandise below a stated price because this would be a violation of the Sherman Antitrust Act and other legislation.

You Be the Consultant

Pricing for Value

After spending 15 years as an executive in the textile industry and 3 years as an elementary school teacher, Jeannette Doellgast made a major career move. With her husband and business partner, Alam El Din, she purchased the Plumbush Inn, a bed-and-breakfast (B&B) located in the scenic town of Cold Spring, New York. Shortly after taking over the inn, which had been in business for 30 years, Doellgast and El Din realized that they needed to raise the prices they charged for both the rooms they rented and the meals they served in their dining area. "It was a risk," says Doellgast. Most of their customers were regulars, so the couple took the time to explain the new pricing policy with each one. A few customers were displeased, but most accepted the price increases without complaint. The increases have put the Plumbush Inn in a much stronger financial position. Revenues have climbed to $1.25 million, and profits are up.

As they considered their pricing options, Doellgast and El Din spent time defining the image they wanted the inn to have and the target customers they wanted to attract. In the end, they defined the inn as a B&B where couples could go for a romantic escape rather than one where a family with children might stop for inexpensive lodging on their way to some vacation destination. Doellgast says that once they settled on the image they wanted to create, the price increases were essential. "A richer experience costs more money to provide," she explains. The meals in the Plumbush Inn dining room are a perfect example. "We are a slow dining experience," says Doellgast. "We don't buy anything frozen. Everything is fresh, which makes a difference in the price." The chef also uses organic products, which typically cost more, but diners appreciate the fine dining experience they get at the inn. Even the customers who initially complained about the price increases have returned and are satisfied because they now receive a higher level of service. "People bring with them a whole set of equations when they make a purchase, and one of the values for most people is that high price equals quality," explains pricing expert Rob Docters. "Pricing is not just about cost," he says. It's about value."

Before establishing their new pricing structure, Doellgast and El Din researched their competitors' prices. Their competitors' prices were a consideration in making their own pricing decisions, but the primary factors were the image they wanted to create for the Plumbush Inn and the customers they were targeting. "Pricing is an art, but it's not only about pricing," says Deollgast. It's about differentiating yourself and deciding what your niche [is] and what the value of your niche [is]. If you build your business around low price, somebody is going to come in next week and undercut you. [In that case], you really haven't established your market."

What steps can entrepreneurs take when it comes to setting prices the right way? The following tips will help:

- Know your costs, including the direct and the indirect costs, of providing your product or service.
- Don't set your price below your costs. "We lose money on every unit we sell, but we make up for it in volume" is a business philosophy that never works.
- Price increases are easier to accomplish when a company faces fewer competitors. The more

intense the competition, the more difficult it is to raise prices.

- If you need to raise prices shortly after launching your business, try to soften the blow by bundling products and services to create more value for customers.
- Assign someone in your company to track competitors' prices regularly (at least monthly) and to present the results on a timely basis.
- Do not blindly follow your competitors' pricing strategies.
- Base your pricing on the value that your product or service offers customers. Remember that sometimes the most valuable components of a product or service are intangible.
- Define the image you want to create for your business and use your pricing strategy to communicate that image to your customers and to position your company in the market.

1. Why do many entrepreneurs underprice their goods and services, especially when they first get into business? Discuss the connection between the prices a company establishes for its goods and services and the image it creates for the company.
2. What is the impact of these pricing errors on a small company? What steps can entrepreneurs take to avoid this problem?

Sources: Geoff Williams, "Name Your Price," *Entrepreneur*, September 2005, pp. 108–115; Bridget McCrea, "When Is the Price Right? Effective Pricing Is Crucial to Remain Competitive and Move Product," *Black Enterprise*, July 2004, pp. 78–79.

Pricing Strategies and Methods for Retailers

LEARNING OBJECTIVES
3A. Explain the pricing methods and strategies for retailers.

As customers have become more price-conscious, retailers have changed their pricing strategies to emphasize value. This value/price relationship allows for a wide variety of highly creative pricing and marketing practices. As discussed previously, delivering high levels of recognized value in products and services is one key to retail customer loyalty.

Markup

The basic premise of a successful business operation is selling a good or service for more than it costs. The difference between the cost of a product or service and its selling price is called **markup (or markon)**. Markup can be expressed in dollars or as a percentage of either cost or selling price:

markup (or markon)
the difference between the cost of a product or service and its selling price.

$$\text{Dollar markup} = \text{Retail price} - \text{Cost of the merchandise}$$

$$\text{Percentage (of retail price) markup} = \frac{\text{Dollar markup}}{\text{Retail price}}$$

$$\text{Percentage (of cost) markup} = \frac{\text{Dollar markup}}{\text{Cost of unit}}$$

For example, if a man's shirt costs $15 and a business owner plans to sell it for $25, the markup would be as follows:

$$\text{Dollar markup} = \$25 - \$15 = \$10$$

$$\text{Percentage (of retail price) markup} = \$10 \div \$25 = 40\%$$

$$\text{Percentage (of cost) markup} = \$10 \div \$15 = 66.67\%$$

Notice that the cost of merchandise used in computing markup includes not only the wholesale price of the merchandise, but also any incidental costs (e.g., selling or transportation charges) that the retailer incurs and a profit minus any discounts (quantity, cash) that the wholesaler offers.

Once a business owner has a financial plan, including sales estimates and anticipated expenses, he or she can compute the firm's initial markup. The initial markup is the *average* markup required on all merchandise to cover the cost of the items, all incidental expenses, and a reasonable profit:

$$\text{Initial dollar markup} = \frac{\text{Operating expenses} + \text{Reductions} + \text{Profits}}{\text{Net sales} + \text{Reductions}}$$

In this calculation, operating expenses include the cost of doing business, such as rent, utilities, and depreciation, and reductions include employee and customer discounts, markdowns, special sales, and the cost of stockouts.

For example, if a small retailer forecasts sales of $380,000, expenses of $140,000, and $24,000 in reductions, and he or she expects a profit of $38,000, the initial markup percentage is calculated as follows

$$\text{Initial markup percentage} = \frac{\$140{,}000 + \$24{,}000 + \$38{,}000}{\$380{,}000 + \$24{,}000} = 50\%$$

This retailer thus knows that an average markup of 50 percent is required to cover costs and generate an adequate profit.

Some businesses employ a standard markup on all of their merchandise. This technique, which is usually used in retail stores carrying related products, applies a standard percentage markup to all merchandise. Most stores find it much more practical to use a flexible markup, which assigns various markup percentages to different types of products. Because of the wide range of prices and types of merchandise they sell, department stores frequently rely on a flexible markup. It would be impractical for them to use a standard markup on all items because they have such a divergent cost and volume range. For instance, the markup percentage for socks is not likely to be suitable as a markup for washing machines.

Once an owner determines the desired markup percentage, he or she can compute the appropriate retail price. Knowing that the markup of a particular item represents 40 percent of the retail price gives

$$\text{Cost} = \text{retail price} - \text{markup}$$

$$= 100\% - 40\%$$

$$= 60\% \text{ of retail price}$$

Assuming that the cost of the item is $18.00, the retailer can rearrange the percentage (of retail price) markup formula:

$$\text{Retail price} = \text{Dollar cost} \div \text{Percentage of retail price}$$

The retailer computes a price as follows:

$$\text{Retail price} = \$18.00 \div 0.60 = \$30.00$$

Thus, the owner establishes a retail price of $30.00 for the item using a 40 percent markup.

Finally, retailers must verify that the retail price they have calculated is consistent with their planned initial markup percentage. Will it cover costs and generate the desired profit?

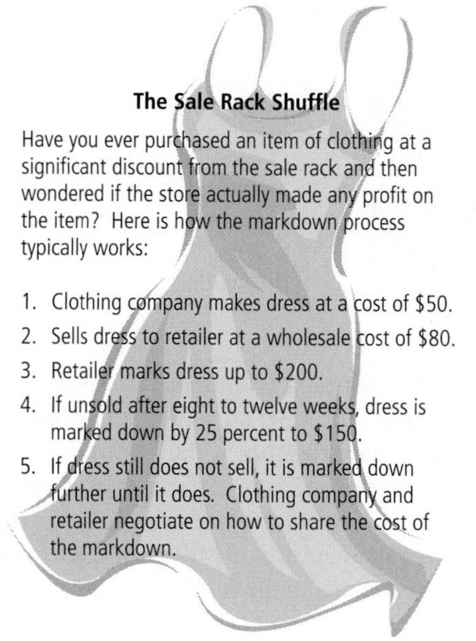

FIGURE 10.2

**The Mathematics
of Markups and
Markdowns**

The Sale Rack Shuffle

Have you ever purchased an item of clothing at a
significant discount from the sale rack and then
wondered if the store actually made any profit on
the item? Here is how the markdown process
typically works:

1. Clothing company makes dress at a cost of $50.
2. Sells dress to retailer at a wholesale cost of $80.
3. Retailer marks dress up to $200.
4. If unsold after eight to twelve weeks, dress is
   marked down by 25 percent to $150.
5. If dress still does not sell, it is marked down
   further until it does. Clothing company and
   retailer negotiate on how to share the cost of
   the markdown.

Is it congruent with the firm's overall price image? Is the final price in line with the company's strategy? Is it within an acceptable price range? How does it compare to the prices charged by competitors? And, perhaps most important, are the customers willing and able to pay this price? Figure 10.2 explains the mathematics of markups—and markdowns—at the retail level.

Follow-the-Leader Pricing

Some small companies make no effort to be price leaders in their immediate geographic areas and simply follow the prices that their competitors establish. Entrepreneurs wisely monitor their competitors' pricing policies and individual prices by reviewing their advertisements or by hiring part-time or full-time comparison shoppers. However, some retailers use this information to establish "me-too" pricing policies, which eradicate any opportunity to create a special price image for their businesses. Although many retailers must match competitors' prices on identical items, maintaining a follow-the-leader pricing policy may not be healthy for a small business because it robs the company of the opportunity to create a distinctive image in its customers' eyes.

Below-Market Pricing

Some small businesses choose to create a discount image in the market by offering goods at below-market prices. By setting prices below those of their competitors, these firms hope to attract a sufficient level of volume to offset the lower profit margins. Many retailers using a below-market pricing strategy eliminate most of the extra services that their above-market-pricing competitors offer. For instance, these businesses trim operating costs by cutting out services like delivery, installation, credit granting, and sales assistance. Below-market pricing strategies can be risky for small companies because they require them to constantly achieve high sales volume to remain competitive.

Pricing Concepts for Manufacturers

LEARNING OBJECTIVES
3B. Explain the pricing methods
and strategies for manufacturers.

For manufacturers, the pricing decision requires the support of accurate, timely accounting records. The most commonly used pricing technique for manufacturers is cost-plus pricing. Using this method, a manufacturer establishes a price that is composed of direct materials, direct labor, factory overhead, selling and administrative costs, plus the desired profit margin. Figure 10.3 illustrates the cost-plus pricing components.

FIGURE 10.3

Cost-Plus Pricing Components

The main advantage of the cost-plus pricing method is its simplicity. Given the proper cost accounting data, computing a product's final selling price is relatively easy. In addition, because they add a profit onto the top of their companies' costs, manufacturers are guaranteed the desired profit margin. This process, however, does not encourage the manufacturers to use their resources efficiently. Even if the company fails to employ its resources in the most effective manner, it will still earn a reasonable profit, and thus there is no motivation to conserve resources in the manufacturing process. Finally, because manufacturers' cost structures vary so greatly, cost-plus pricing fails to consider the competition (and market forces) sufficiently. Despite its drawbacks, the cost-plus method of establishing prices remains prominent in many industries such as construction and printing.

Direct Costing and Price Formulation

One requisite for a successful pricing policy in manufacturing is a reliable cost accounting system that can generate timely reports to determine the costs of processing raw materials into finished goods. The traditional method of product costing is called **absorption costing** because all manufacturing and overhead costs are absorbed into a finished product's total cost. Absorption costing includes direct materials, direct labor, plus a portion of fixed and variable factory overhead in each unit manufactured. Full absorption financial statements are used in published annual reports and in tax reports and are very useful in performing financial analysis. However, full absorption statements are of little help to manufacturers when determining prices or the impact of price changes.

A more useful technique for managerial decision making is **variable (or direct) costing,** in which the cost of the products manufactured includes only those costs that vary directly with the quantity produced. In other words, variable costing encompasses direct materials, direct labor, and factory overhead costs that vary with the level of the firm's output of finished goods. Those factory overhead costs that are fixed (rent, depreciation, insurance) are *not* included in the costs of finished items. Instead, they are considered to be expenses of the period.

A manufacturer's goal when establishing prices is to discover the combination of selling price and sales volume that covers the variable costs of producing a product and contributes toward covering fixed costs and earning a profit. The problem with using full-absorption costing for this is that it clouds the true relationships among price, volume, and costs by including fixed expenses in unit cost. Using a direct costing basis yields a constant unit cost for the product no matter what volume of production. The result is a clearer picture of the price/volume/costs relationship.

The starting point for establishing product prices is the direct cost income statement. As Table 10.1 indicates, the direct cost statement yields the same net income as does the full-absorption income statement. The only difference between the two statements is the format. The full-absorption statement allocates costs such as advertising, rent, and utilities according to the activity that caused them, but the direct cost income statement separates expenses into their fixed and variable components. Fixed expenses remain constant regardless of the production level, but variable expenses fluctuate according to production volume.

When variable costs are subtracted from total revenues, the result is the amount remaining that contributes to covering fixed expenses and earning a profit. Expressing this value as a percentage of total revenue yields the company's contribution margin.

absorption costing
the traditional method of product costing in which all manufacturing and overhead costs are absorbed into the product's total cost.

variable (or direct) costing
a method of product costing that includes in the product's cost only those costs that vary directly with the quantity produced.

TABLE 10.1 Full-Absorption versus Direct-Cost Income Statement

Full-Absorption Income Statement

Sales revenue		$ 790,000
Cost of goods sold		
Materials	250,500	
Direct labor	190,200	
Factory overhead	120,200	560,900
Gross profit		$ 229,100
Operating expenses		
General and administrative	66,100	
Selling	112,000	
Other	11,000	
Total operating expenses		189,100
Net income (before taxes)		$ 40,000

Direct-Cost Income Statement

Sales revenue (100%)		$ 790,000
Variable costs		
Materials	250,500	
Direct labor	190,200	
Variable factory overhead	13,200	
Variable selling expenses	48,100	
Total variable costs (63.54%)		502,000
Contribution margin (36.46%)		288,000
Fixed costs		
Fixed factory overhead	107,000	
Fixed selling expenses	63,900	
General and administrative	66,100	
Other fixed expenses	11,000	
Total fixed expenses (31.39%)		248,000
Net income (before taxes) (5.06%)		$ 40,000

Computing the contribution margin is a critical step in establishing prices through the direct costing method. This manufacturer's contribution margin is 36.5 percent.

Computing the Break-Even Selling Price

The manufacturer's contribution percentage tells what portion of total revenues remains after covering variable costs to contribute toward meeting fixed expenses and earning a profit. This manufacturer's contribution margin is 36.5 percent, which means that variable costs absorb 63.5 percent of total revenues. In other words, variable costs make up 63.5 percent $(1.00 - 0.365 = 0.635)$ of the product's selling price. Suppose that this manufacturer's variable costs include the following:

Material	$2.08/unit
Direct labor	$4.12/unit
Variable factory overhead	$0.78/unit
Total variable cost	$6.98/unit

The minimum price at which the manufacturer would sell the item for is $6.98. Any price below this would not cover variable costs. To compute the break-even selling price for this product, we find the selling price using the following equation:

Selling price
$$= \frac{\text{Profit} + (\text{Variable cost per unit} \times \text{Quantity produced}) + \text{Total fixed cost}}{\text{Quantity produced}}$$

To break even, the manufacturer assumes $0 profit. Suppose that his plans are to produce 50,000 units of the product and that fixed costs will be $110,000. The break-even selling price is as follows:

Break-even selling price
$$= \frac{\$0 + (\$6.98 \text{ per unit} \times 50,000 \text{ units}) + \$110,000}{50,000 \text{ units}}$$

$$= \frac{\$459,000}{50,000 \text{ units}}$$

$$= \$9.18 \text{ per unit}$$

Thus, $2.20 ($9.18/unit − $6.98/unit) of the $9.18 break-even price contributes to meeting fixed production costs. But suppose the manufacturer wants to earn a $50,000 profit. Then the selling price is calculated as follows:

Selling price
$$= \frac{\$50,000 + (\$6.98 \text{ per unit} \times 50,000 \text{ units}) + \$110,000}{50,000 \text{ units}}$$

$$= \frac{\$509,000}{50,000 \text{ units}}$$

$$= \$10.18 \text{ per unit}$$

Now the manufacturer must decide whether customers will purchase 50,000 units at $10.18. If not, he or she must decide either to produce a different, more profitable product or to lower the selling price. Any price above $9.18 will generate some profit, although less than that desired. In the short run, the manufacturer could sell the product for less than $9.18 if competitive factors so dictated, but not below $6.98 because this would not cover the variable cost of production.

Because the manufacturer's capacity in the short run is fixed, pricing decisions should be aimed at employing these resources most efficiently. The fixed costs of operating the plant cannot be avoided, and the variable costs can be eliminated only if the firm ceases offering the product. Therefore, the selling price must be at least equal to the variable costs (per unit) of making the product. Any price above this amount contributes to covering fixed costs and providing a reasonable profit.

Of course, over the long run, the manufacturer cannot sell below total costs and continue to survive. So, selling price must cover total product cost—both fixed and variable—and generate a reasonable profit.

Hands on ... How to

Calculate Your Company's Pocket Price Band

When entrepreneurs make pricing decisions, they usually look at the retail price or the invoice price they

charge. Doing so, however, may be misleading if the company offers significant "off-invoice" discounts such as cash discounts for paying early, quantity discounts for large purchases, special promotional discounts, and others. These invoice leakages mean that a business is getting less, sometimes far less, than the retail or

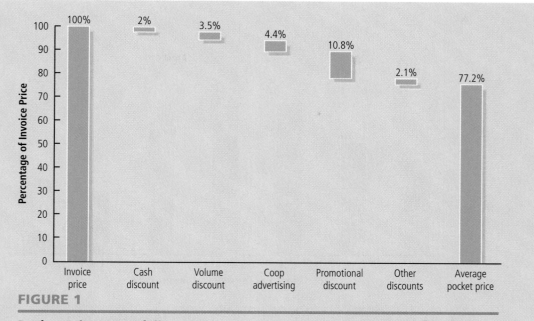

FIGURE 1

Pocket Price Waterfall?

invoice price listed. In some cases, a company's pocket price, the price it receives for a product or a service after deducting all discounts and purchase incentives, is far below the listed retail or invoice price. The impact of these discounts can be significant. Research by the consulting firm McKinsey and Company shows that a decrease of one percent in a typical company's average prices will reduce its operating profits by eight percent if all other factors remain constant.

How are discounts affecting your business? To find out, you need to estimate your company's pocket price waterfall (see Figure 1) and its pocket price band. The pocket price waterfall starts with a company's invoice or retail price on the far left of the diagram and then shows how much every discount or incentive the company offers its customers reduces that price. In the example in Figure 1, this small manufacturer offers a cash discount for early payment that shaves 2.0 percent off of the retail price, a 3.5 percent discount for companies whose purchases exceed a particular volume, a cooperative advertising program (in which it splits the cost of advertising its products with retailers) that amounts to 4.4 percent, and periodic promotional discounts to move products that average 10.8 percent. Other discounts the company offered customers further reduced its pocket price. In the end, the company's average pocket price is 77.2 percent of the listed invoice price.

Not every customer qualifies for every discount, however. The type and the amount of the discount vary from one customer to another; the pocket prices they pay can vary a good deal. Therefore, it is important to estimate the width of the company's pocket price band, which shows the percentage of sales accounted for by each pocket price (shown as a percentage of the listed invoice or retail price) (see Figure 2). In this example, pocket prices that are 90 percent or more of the company's invoice price account for just 28.3 percent of its total revenue. Conversely, pocket prices that are 80 percent or less of its invoice price make up 46.2 percent of its total revenue. The final step in the process is to identify the individual customers that make up each segment of the company's pocket price band.

A wide pocket price band is not necessarily bad. It simply shows that some customers generate much higher pocket prices than others. When a band is wide, small changes in its shape can produce big results for a company. If an entrepreneur can increase sales at the upper end of the band while reducing or even dropping those at the lower end of the band, both the company's revenues and profits will climb. If a company's price band is narrow, an entrepreneur has less room to maneuver prices, changing the shape of the band is more difficult, and any changes the entrepreneur can make tend to have less impact on the company's sales and revenues.

When one lighting company calculated its pocket price band, managers were surprised at its width. Once managers realized how big a dent discounts were putting in its revenues and profits, they worked with the sales force to realign the company's discount structure. Some of the company's smallest accounts had been getting the largest discounts, despite their small volume of purchases. Managers also focused on boosting

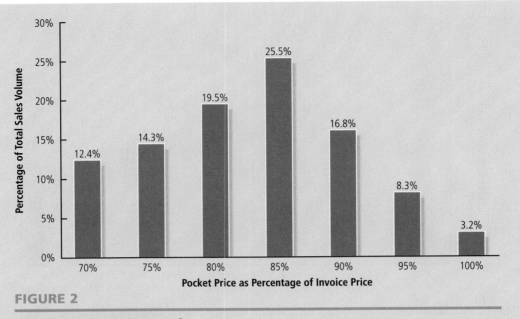

FIGURE 2

Sample Pocket Price Band

sales to those accounts that were producing the highest pocket prices. These changes resulted in the company's average pocket price rising by 3.8 percent and its profits climbing 51 percent.

Discounts tend to work their way into a company's pricing structure gradually over time, often one transaction at a time, especially if an entrepreneur gives sales representatives latitude to negotiate prices with customers. Few companies make the effort to track these discounts, and, as a result, few companies realize the impact that discounts have on their profitability. By monitoring their companies' pocket price waterfall and the resulting pocket price band, entrepreneurs can improve significantly the revenue and the profits they generate.

Sources: Michael V. Marn, Eric V. Roegner, and Craig C. Zawada, "The Power of Pricing," The McKinsey Quarterly, Number 1, 2003, www.mckinseyquarterly.com.

Pricing Strategies and Methods for Service Firms

LEARNING OBJECTIVES
3C. Explain the pricing methods and strategies for service firms.

A service firm must establish a price based on the materials used to provide the service, the labor employed, an allowance for overhead, and a profit. As in the manufacturing operation, a service business must have a reliable, accurate accounting system to keep a tally of the total costs of providing the service. Most service firms base their prices on an hourly rate, usually the actual number of hours required to perform the service. Some companies, however, base their fees on a standard number of hours, determined by the average number of hours needed to perform the service. For most firms, labor and materials comprise the largest portion of the cost of the service. To establish a reasonable, profitable price for service, the small business owner must know the cost of materials, direct labor, and overhead for each unit of service. Using these basic cost data and a desired profit margin, an owner of the small service firm can determine the appropriate price for the service.

Consider a simple example for pricing a common service—television repair. Ned's T.V. Repair Shop uses the direct costing method to prepare an income statement for exercising managerial control (see Table 10.2). Ned estimates that he and his employees spent about 12,800 hours in the actual production of television service. Therefore, total cost per productive hour for Ned's T.V. Repair Shop comes to the following:

$$\$172,000 \div 12,800 \text{ hours} = \$13.44/\text{hour}$$

TABLE 10.2 Direct-Cost Income Statement, Ned's T.V. Repair Shop

Sales revenue		$199,000
Variable expenses		
Labor	52,000	
Materials	40,500	
Variable factory overhead	11,500	
Total variable expenses		104,000
Fixed expenses		
Rent	2,500	
Salaries	38,500	
Fixed overhead	27,000	
Total fixed expenses		68,000
Net income		$ 27,000

Now Ned must add in an amount for his desired profit. He expects a net operating profit of 18 percent on sales. To compute the final price he uses the following equation:

Price per hour

$$= \text{Total cost per productive hour} \times \frac{1.00}{1.00 - \text{Net profit target as percentage of sales}}$$

$$= \$13.44 \times 1.219$$

$$= \$16.38 \text{ per hour}$$

A price of $16.38 per hour will cover Ned's costs and generate the desired profit. The wise service shop owner computes his cost per production hour at regular intervals throughout the year. Rapidly rising labor costs and material prices dictate that the service firm's price per hour be computed even more frequently. As in the case of the retailer and the manufacturer, Ned must evaluate the pricing policies of competitors, and decide whether his price is consistent with his firm's image.

Of course, the price of $16.38 per hour assumes that each job requires the same amount of materials. If this is not a valid assumption, Ned must recalculate the price per hour *without* including the cost of materials:

$$\text{Cost per productive hour} = \frac{\$172.000 - \$40,500}{12,800 \text{ hours}}$$

$$= \$10.27 \text{ per hour}$$

Adding in the desired 18 percent net operating profit on sales gives

$$\text{Price per hour} = \frac{\$10.27}{\text{hour}} \times \frac{1.00}{1.00 - 0.18}$$

$$= \frac{\$10.27}{\text{hour}} \times 1.219$$

$$= \$12.52 \text{ per hour}$$

Under these conditions, Ned would charge $12.52 per hour plus the actual cost of materials used and any markup on the cost of material. A repair job that takes four hours to complete would have the following price:

Cost of service (4 hours × $12.52/hour)	$50.08
Cost of materials	$21.00
Markup on material (20%)	$4.20
Total price	$75.28

Concepts in Success

Finding the right price for his business and event planning service was a problem facing Joshua Estrin, founder of Concepts in Success. Initially, Estrin established a reasonable annual salary for himself and then set the price for each project as a percentage of that salary. Because that system required him to spend excessive amounts of time documenting details of every expense for his clients, Estrin soon switched to an hourly rate that exceeded $100 per hour. Now that he has more experience, Estrin charges for the services that Concepts in Success offers using set price points that depend on the services his clients choose. Estrin's pricing policy is working. His company now generates $1 million in annual revenue and counts several major corporations, including American Express, Hertz, and PepsiCo, among its clients.[26]

Be the Consultant

Pricing Web Services

Kerry Pinella, a recent business graduate of a small private college, started her career working for a large multinational computer software maker as a sales representative. After two years in sales, Kerry applied for a position on a development team that was working on software applications for the World Wide Web. Kerry thrived on the team atmosphere and learned the technical aspects of the new assignment very quickly. Not only did her team bring their project in on budget, but it also completed it slightly ahead of schedule. Team members give much of the credit for the project's success to Kerry's unofficial role as team leader. Her work ethic and relentless pursuit of quality inspired other team members.

After Kerry's team completed their project, however, Kerry had a hard time recapturing the thrill and excitement of developing the World Wide Web software. Subsequent projects simply could not measure up to the "magic" of that first assignment. After talking with several of the members of that software team, Kerry discovered that they felt the same way. Before long, Kerry and two of her former team members left the company to launch their own computer consulting company, Web Consultants. Having worked on the forefront of the Web's commercialization, Kerry and her partners saw the potential it had for revolutionizing business. Their company would specialize in developing , designing, and maintaining Web sites for clients. In their first year of business, Web Consultants accepted jobs from virtually anybody who wanted a Web site. Although they experienced some growing pains, Web Consultants quickly earned a reputation for producing quality work on time and became more selective in the jobs it bid on.

Halfway into their second year of operation, the partners planned a weekend retreat at a nearby resort so they could get away, review their progress, and plan for the future. As they reviewed their latest financial statements, one of the questions that kept popping up dealt with pricing. Were Web Consultant's pricing policies appropriate? Its sales were growing twice as fast as the industry average, and the company's bid-winning ratio was well above that of practically all of its competitors. For the current year, sales were up, but Web Consultants' net profits were virtually the same as they had been in their first year.

Pulling the records from a computer database for each job they had completed since founding the company, they found that the partners and their employees had spent 22,450 hours developing projects for their clients at a total cost of $951,207. "We were shooting for a net profit of 25 percent on sales," Kerry reminded her partners, "but we so far, our net profit margin is just 7.7 percent, only one-third of our target."

"Maybe we could increase our profits if we increased our sales," offered one partner.

The partners began to wonder whether their price of $45 per hour was appropriate. Admittedly, they had been so busy completing projects for clients that they had not kept up with what their competitors were charging. Nor had they been as diligent in analyzing their financial statements as they should have been.

As Kerry closed the cover on her laptop computer, she looked at her partners and asked, "What should Web Consultant's hourly price be?"

1. Help Kerry answer the question she posed.
2. What factors should Kerry and her partners consider when determining Web Consultant's final price?
3. Is the company's current price too low? If so, what signals could have alerted Kerry and her partners?

The Impact of Credit on Pricing

Consumers crave convenience when they shop, and one of the most common conveniences they demand is the ability to purchase goods and services on credit. Small businesses that fail to offer credit to their customers lose sales to competitors who do. However, companies that do sell on credit incur additional expenses for offering this convenience. Small companies have three options for selling to customers on credit: credit cards, installment credit, and trade credit.

Credit Cards

Credit cards have become a popular method of payment among customers, who now make 30 percent of personal consumption expenditures with credit cards. Approximately 73 percent of the adult U.S. population uses credit cards to make purchases, and the average U.S. household has 17 credit cards carrying an average interest rate of 18.9 percent a year.[27] The number of credit cards in circulation in the United States exceeds 1.5 billion, an average of more than 8.5 cards per person! Customers use credit cards to make purchases of more than $2.2 trillion a year, an amount equal to about 20 percent of the total U.S. gross domestic product. The average amount a household charges to credit cards in a year now exceeds $15,000.[28] Studies have found that accepting credit cards increases the probability, speed, and magnitude of customer spending. In addition, surveys show that customers rate businesses offering credit options higher on key performance measures such as reputation, reliability, and service.[29] In short, accepting credit cards broadens a small company's customer base and closes sales that it would normally lose if customers had to pay in cash.

Increasingly, customers are using credit cards to pay for micropurchases, those costing less than $5. The research company Gartner Inc. predicts that by 2020, the average American adult will make more than 20 micropurchases per month on either debit or credit cards. To make sure that they capture their share of those small purchases, fast food restaurants now accept credit and debit cards. As a result, quick-service restaurants have seen sales climb rapidly and the average transaction time drop. For instance, average sales have risen from $5 to $7 since McDonald's began accepting debit and credit cards, and the cashless transactions have shaved seven seconds off the average service time. Customers now purchase more than $37 billion worth of fast food on their debit and credit cards a year.[30]

The convenience of credit cards is not free to business owners, however. Companies must pay to use the system, typically one to six percent of the total credit card charges, which they must factor into the prices of their products or services. They also pay a transaction fee of 5 to 25 cents per charge. Given customer expectations, small businesses cannot drop major cards, even when the big credit card companies raise the fees that merchants must pay. Fees operate on a multistep process. On a typical $100 Visa or MasterCard purchase, a processing bank buys the credit card slip from the retailer for $98.25. Then, that bank sells the slip to the bank that issued the card for about $98.49. The $1.75 discount from the purchase price is called the **interchange fee,** the fee that banks collect from retailers whenever customers use a credit or a debit card to pay for a purchase. A study by Morgan Stanley estimates that the average interchange fees for Visa and MasterCard transactions will increase from 1.75 percent to 1.86 percent in 2010.[31] Before it can accept credit cards, a business must obtain merchant status from either a bank or an independent sales organization (ISO).

interchange fee
the fee that banks collect from retailers whenever customers use a credit or a debit card to pay for a purchase.

In 2003, the first time in history, shoppers used credit and debit cards more often than cash or checks to make retail purchases.[32] As debit cards have become more widely used, many small businesses are equipping their stores to handle debit card transactions, which act as electronic checks, automatically deducting the purchase amount immediately from a customer's checking account. The equipment is easy to install and to set up, and the cost to the company is negligible. The payoff can be big, however, in the form of increased sales and decreased losses due to bad checks. "How can you possibly lose when you're offering customers another avenue for purchasing merchandise?" says Mark Knauff, who recently installed a debit card terminal in his guitar shop.[33]

Online merchants face one major challenge when customers pay by credit card. Because there is no actual signature captured during the transaction, some customers later deny that they made the purchase and dispute the charge. These chargebacks represent a significant threat to online merchants. First Data Corporation, the largest credit card processor in the United States, says that 1.25% of all Internet transactions are charged back, compared with just 0.33% of catalog transactions by telephone and mail and 0.14% of storefront retail transactions. New computer software is attempting to reduce this fraud by checking whether customers' shipping addresses match their billing addresses.

Installment Credit

Small companies that sell big-ticket consumer durables, such as major appliances, cars, and boats, frequently rely on installment credit to support their sales efforts. Because very few customers can purchase such items in a single lump-sum payment, small businesses finance them over an extended time. The time horizon may range from just a few months to 30 or more years. Most companies require customers to make an initial down payment for the merchandise and then finance the balance for the life of the loan. The customer repays the loan principal plus interest on the loan. One advantage of installment loans for a small business is that the owner retains a security interest as collateral on the loan. If a customer defaults on the loan, the owner still holds the title to the merchandise. Because installment credit absorbs a small company's cash, many rely on financial institutions such as banks and credit unions to provide installment credit. When a company has the financial strength to "carry its own paper," the interest income from the installment loan contract often yields more than the initial profit on the sale of the product. For some businesses, such as furniture stores, this traditionally has been a major source of income.

Trade Credit

Companies that sell small-ticket items frequently offer their customers trade credit, that is, they create customer charge accounts. The typical small business bills its credit customers each month. To speed collections, some offer cash discounts if customers pay their balances early; others impose penalties on late payers. Before deciding to use trade credit as a competitive weapon, the small business owner must make sure that the firm's cash position is strong enough to support the additional pressure.

Chapter Summary by Learning Objective

1. Discuss the relationships among pricing, image, competition, and value.

Setting prices for their products and services requires entrepreneurs to balance a multitude of complex forces. When it comes to setting prices, three forces are particularly important: image, competition, and value. A company's pricing policies communicate important information about its overall image to customers. A company's prices must be consistent with the image it projects to its customers. When setting prices, entrepreneurs should take into account their competitors' prices, but they should *not* automatically match or beat them. The "right" price for a product or service also depends on the value that it provides for customers.

2. Describe effective pricing techniques for introducing new products or services and for existing ones.

Pricing a new product is often difficult for the small business manager, but it should accomplish three objectives: getting the product accepted; maintaining market share as the competition grows; and earning a profit. Generally, there are three major pricing strategies used to introduce new products into the market: penetration, skimming, and sliding down the demand curve.

Pricing techniques for existing products and services include odd pricing, price lining, leader pricing, geographic pricing, opportunistic pricing, discounts, and suggested retail pricing.

3. Explain the pricing methods and strategies for (A) retailers, (B) manufacturers, and (C) service firms.

Pricing for the retailer means pricing to move merchandise. Markup is the difference between the cost of a product or service and its selling price. Most retailers compute their markup as a percentage of retail price, but some retailers put a standard markup on all their merchandise; more frequently, they use a flexible markup.

A manufacturer's pricing decision depends on the support of accurate cost accounting records. The most common technique is cost-plus pricing, in which the manufacturer charges a price that covers the cost of producing a product plus a reasonable profit. Every manufacturer should calculate a product's break-even price, the price that produces neither a profit nor a loss.

Service firms often suffer from the effects of vague, unfounded pricing procedures, and frequently charge the going rate without any idea of their costs. A service firm must set a price based on the cost of materials used, labor involved, overhead, and a profit. The proper price reflects the total cost of providing a unit of service.

4. Describe the impact of credit on pricing.

Offering consumer credit enhances a small company's reputation and increases the probability, speed, and magnitude of customers' purchases. Small firms offer three types of consumer credit: credit cards, installment credit, and trade credit (charge accounts).

Discussion Questions

1. How does pricing affect a small firm's image?
2. What competitive factors must the small firm consider when establishing prices?
3. Describe the strategies a small business could use in setting the price of a new product. What objectives should the strategy seek to achieve?
4. Define the following pricing techniques: odd pricing, price lining, leader pricing, geographic pricing, and discounts.
5. Why do many small businesses use the manufacturer's suggested retail price? What are the disadvantages of this technique?
6. What is a markup? How is it used to determine individual price?

7. What is a standard markup? A flexible markup?
8. What is cost-plus pricing? Why do so many manufacturers use it? What are the disadvantages of using it?
9. Explain the difference between full-absorption costing and direct costing. How does absorption costing help a manufacturer determine a reasonable price?
10. Explain the technique for a small service firm setting an hourly price.
11. What benefits does a small business get by offering customers credit? What costs does it incur?

Business Plan Pro

As the chapter describes, setting the price of your products and services and understanding your break-even point are major elements of your business plan. Resources and information are available within Business Plan Pro that may help you to better understand the impact that pricing will have on your business.

Business Plan Exercises

On the Web

Do some competitive pricing research on the Web. Search for products and services that are similar to what you are offering and list their price points. Check to see that you are making parallel comparisons of these products. For example, are you considering the entire price, which may include shipping, handling, complementary products, and other attributes that will influence the final price to the customer? Do you consider these businesses to be direct competitors? If not, why? What does this information tell you about your price point? Does your price point coincide with your stated business strategy?

In the Software

Open your business plan and locate the "Break Even" section under "Financial Plan." Follow the instructions and enter the information that will enable to you to determine your break-even point. This will require you to have estimated figures for your fixed costs, variable costs, and price. Once you have entered that information, look at the break-even point shown in units and revenue. Based on what you find, is this break-even point realistic? How long do you expect it would take to reach your break-even point? Is this timeframe acceptable? Now, increase your price by 10%. What does this do to your break-even point? You may want to experiment with your break-even point by entering different price points and costs to see the impact price will have on the break-even point when you will begin making a profit.

Building Your Business Plan

Go to the "Sales Forecast" table under the "Sales Strategy" section. An optional wizard will appear that you may select to help you through the process, or you can enter your information directly on the worksheet. If you have not done so yet, enter your price information in that section. Work through the rest of the table as you estimate your direct unit costs. The instructions and examples will assist you through that process.

Beyond the Classroom . . .

1. Interview a successful small retailer and ask the following questions: Do they seek a specific image through their prices? What type of outlet do you consider the retailer to be? What role do their competitors play in their pricing strategy? Do they use specific pricing techniques such as odd pricing, price lining, leader pricing, or geographic pricing?

    How are discounts calculated? What markup percentage does the firm use? How are prices derived? What are their cost structures?

2. Select an industry that has several competing small firms in your area. Contact these firms and compare their approaches to determining prices. Do prices on identical or similar items differ? Why?

11 | Creating a Successful Financial Plan

> Volume is vanity; profitability is sanity. —Brad Skelton
>
> It is better to solve problems than crises. —John Guinther

Learning Objectives

On completion of this chapter, you will be able to:

1. Understand the importance of preparing a financial plan.
2. Describe how to prepare the basic financial statements and use them to manage a small business.
3. Create projected (pro forma) financial statements.
4. Understand the basic financial statements through ratio analysis.
5. Explain how to interpret financial ratios.
6. Conduct a break-even analysis for a small company.

LEARNING OBJECTIVES
1. Understand the importance of preparing a financial plan.

financial management

a process that provides entrepreneurs with relevant financial information in an easy-to-read format on a timely basis; it allows entrepreneurs to know not only how their businesses are doing financially, but also why they are performing that way.

Fashioning a well-designed, logical financial plan as part of a comprehensive business plan is one of the most important steps to launching a new business venture. Entrepreneurs who fail to develop workable strategies for earning a profit within a reasonable time eventually will suffer the ultimate business penalty: failure. Potential lenders and investors demand a realistic financial plan before putting their money into a start-up company. More important, a financial plan is a vital tool that helps entrepreneurs to manage their businesses more effectively, steering their way around the pitfalls that cause failures. Proper **financial management** requires putting in place a system that provides entrepreneurs with relevant financial information in an easy-to-read format on a timely basis; it allows entrepreneurs to know not only *how* their businesses are doing financially, but also *why* their companies are performing that way. The information in a small company's financial records is one resource to which competitors have no access. Smart entrepreneurs recognize this and put their companies' numbers to work for them so that they can make their businesses more successful. "Salted away in your accounting records are financial alerts, ways to trim costs, and tips on where profit is hiding," explains one business writer.[1]

Unfortunately, failure to collect and analyze basic financial data is a common mistake among entrepreneurs. According to one survey, one-third of all entrepreneurs run their companies *without any kind of financial plan.*[2] Another study found that only 11 percent of small business owners analyzed their financial statements as part of the managerial planning and decision-making process.[3] To reach profit objectives, entrepreneurs must be aware of their firms' overall financial position and the changes in financial status that occur over time. Most accounting experts advise entrepreneurs to use one of the popular computerized small business accounting programs such as QuickBooks, Peachtree Accounting, Small Business Accounting, Netsuite, and others to manage routine record-keeping tasks. Working with an accountant to set up the system at the outset and then having a trained employee enter the transactions is most efficient for most businesses. These programs make analyzing a company's financial statements, preparing reports, and summarizing data a snap.

This chapter focuses on some very practical tools that will help entrepreneurs to develop a workable financial plan, keep them aware of their company's financial plan, and enable them to plan for profit. They can use these tools to help them anticipate changes and plot an appropriate profit strategy to meet them head on. These profit-planning techniques are not difficult to master, nor are they overly time consuming. We will discuss the techniques involved in preparing projected (pro forma) financial statements, conducting ratio analysis, and performing break-even analysis.

Basic Financial Statements

LEARNING OBJECTIVES
2. Describe how to prepare the basic financial statements and use them to manage a small business.

Before we begin building projected financial statements, it would be helpful to review the basic financial reports that measure a company's financial position: the balance sheet, the income statement, and the statement of cash flows. The level of financial sophistication among small business owners may not be high, but the extent of financial reporting among small businesses is. Most small businesses regularly produce summary financial information, almost all of it in the form of these traditional financial statements.

The Balance Sheet

balance sheet

a financial statement that provides a snapshot of a business's financial position, estimating its worth on a given date; it is built on the fundamental accounting equation: Assets = Liabilities + Owner's equity.

current assets

assets such as cash and other items to be converted into cash within one year or within the company's normal operating cycle.

The **balance sheet** takes a "snapshot" of a business's financial position, providing owners with an estimate of its worth on a given date. Its two major sections show the assets the business owns and the claims creditors and owners have against those assets. The balance sheet is usually prepared on the last day of the month. Figure 11.1 shows the balance sheet for Sam's Appliance Shop for the year ended December 31, 200X.

The balance sheet is built on the fundamental accounting equation: Assets = Liabilities + Owner's equity. Any increase or decrease on one side of the equation must be offset by an increase or decrease on the other side; hence the name *balance sheet.* It provides a baseline from which to measure future changes in assets, liabilities, and equity. The first section of the balance sheet lists the company's assets (valued at cost, not actual market value) and shows the total value of everything the business owns. **Current assets** consist of cash and

FIGURE 11.1

Balance Sheet, Sam's Appliance Shop

Assets		
Current Assets		
Cash		$49,855
Accounts Receivable	$179,225	
Less Allowance for Doubtful Accounts	$6,000	$173,225
Inventory		$455,455
Prepaid Expenses		$8,450
Total Current Assets		$686,985
Fixed Assets		
Land		$59,150
Buildings	$74,650	
Less Accumulated Depreciation	$7,050	$67,600
Equipment	$22,375	
Less Accumulated Depreciation	$1,250	$21,125
Furniture and Fixtures	$10,295	
Less Accumulated Depreciation	$1,000	$9,295
Total Fixed Assets		$157,170
Intangibles (Goodwill)		$3,500
Total Assets		$847,655
Liabilities		
Current Liabilities		
Accounts Payable		$152,580
Notes Payable		$83,920
Accrued Wages/Salaries Payable		$38,150
Accrued Interest Payable		$42,380
Accrued Taxes Payable		$50,820
Total Current Liabilities		$367,850
Long-Term Liabilities		
Mortgage		$127,150
Note Payable		$85,000
Total Long-Term Liabilities		$212,150
Owner's Equity		
Sam Lloyd, Capital		$267,655
Total Liabilities and Owner's Equity		$847,655

items to be converted into cash within one year or within the normal operating cycle of the company, whichever is longer, such as accounts receivable and inventory, and **fixed assets** are those acquired for long-term use in the business. Intangible assets include items such as goodwill, copyrights, and patents that, although valuable, are not tangible.

The second section shows the business's **liabilities**—the creditors' claims against the company's assets. **Current liabilities** are those debts that must be paid within one year or within the normal operating cycle of the company, whichever is longer, and **long-term liabilities** are those that come due after one year. This section of the balance sheet also shows the **owner's equity,** the value of the owner's investment in the business. It is the balancing factor on the balance sheet, representing all of the owner's capital contributions to the business plus all accumulated (or retained) earnings not distributed to the owner(s).

fixed assets
assets acquired for long-term use in a business.

liabilities
creditors' claims against a company's assets.

current liabilities
those debts that must be paid within one year or within the normal operating cycle of a company.

long-term liabilities
liabilities that come due after one year.

owner's equity
the value of the owner's investment in the business.

The Income Statement

income statement (profit and loss statement or "P&L")
a financial statement that represents a "moving picture" of a business, comparing its expenses against its revenue over a period of time to show its net profit (or loss).

cost of goods sold
the total cost, including shipping, of the merchandise sold during the accounting period.

The **income statement (profit and loss statement or "P&L")** compares expenses against revenue over a certain period of time to show the firm's net profit (or loss). The income statement is a "moving picture" of a firm's profitability over time. The annual P&L statement reports the bottom line of the business over the fiscal/calendar year. Figure 11.2 shows the income statement for Sam's Appliance Shop for the year ended December 31, 200X.

To calculate net profit or loss, an entrepreneur records sales revenues for the year, which includes all income that flows into the business from sales of goods and services. Income from other sources (rent, investments, interest) also must be included in the revenue section of the income statement. To determine net sales revenue, owners subtract the value of returned items and refunds from gross revenue. **Cost of goods sold** represents the total cost, including shipping, of the merchandise sold during the accounting period. Manufacturers, wholesalers, and retailers calculate cost of goods sold by adding purchases

FIGURE 11.2

Income Statement, Sam's Appliance Shop

Net Sales Revenue		$1,870,841
Credit Sales	$1,309,589	
Cash Sales	$561,252	
Cost of Goods Sold		
Beginning Inventory, 1/1/xx	$805,745	
+ Purchases	$939,827	
Goods Available for Sale	$1,745,572	
− Ending Inventory, 12/31/xx	$455,455	
Cost of Goods Sold		$1,290,117
Gross Profit		$580,724
Operating Expenses		
Advertising	$139,670	
Insurance	$46,125	
Depreciation		
Building	$18,700	
Equipment	$9,000	
Salaries	$224,500	
Travel	$4,000	
Entertainment	$2,500	
Total Operating Expenses		$444,495
General Expenses		
Utilities	$5,300	
Telephone	$2,500	
Postage	$1,200	
Payroll Taxes	$25,000	
Total General Expenses		$34,000
Other Expenses		
Interest Expense	$39,850	
Bad Check Expense	$1,750	
Total Other Expenses		$41,600
Total Expenses		$520,095
Net Income		$60,629

to beginning inventory and subtracting ending inventory. Service-providing companies typically have no cost of goods sold because they do not carry inventory.

Net sales revenue minus cost of goods sold results in a company's gross profit. Dividing gross profit by net sales revenue produces the **gross profit margin,** a percentage that every small business owner should watch closely. If a company's gross profit margin slips too low, it is likely that it will operate at a loss (negative net income). Many business owners whose companies are losing money mistakenly believe that the problem is inadequate sales volume; therefore, they focus on pumping up sales at any cost. In many cases, however, the losses their companies are incurring are the result of an inadequate gross profit margin, and pumping up sales only deepens their losses! Repairing a poor gross profit margin requires a company to raise prices, cut manufacturing or purchasing costs, refuse orders with low profit margins, or add new products with more attractive profit margins. Monitoring the gross profit margin over time and comparing it to those of other companies in the same industry are important steps to maintaining a company's long-term profitability.

gross profit margin
gross profit divided by net sales revenue.

After evaluating his company's gross profit margin, Brad Skelton, managing director of Skelton Tomkinson, a contract shipper based in Brisbane, Australia, decided to raise prices with the intent of driving away the company's least profitable customers so he could focus on a niche in shipping heavy machinery. Although sales dropped a significant amount initially, they have since rebounded to $20 million per year. The company's niche strategy and its focus on growing its "bottom line" (profits) rather than its "top line" (sales) have paid off handsomely in terms of profitability; Skelton Tomkinson's profits have climbed 98 percent![4]

Skelton Tomkinson

Operating expenses include those costs that contribute directly to the manufacture and distribution of goods. General expenses are indirect costs incurred in operating the business. "Other expenses" is a catch-all category covering all other expenses that do not fit into the other two categories. Total revenue minus total expenses gives the net income (or loss) for the accounting period. Comparing a company's current income statement to those of prior accounting periods often reveals valuable information about key trends and a company's progress toward its financial goals.

operating expenses
those costs that contribute directly to the manufacture and distribution of goods.

The Statement of Cash Flows

The **statement of cash flows** show the changes in the firm's working capital from the beginning of the year by listing both the sources and the uses of those funds. Many small businesses never need to prepare such a statement, but in some cases creditors, investors, new owners, or the IRS may require this information.

To prepare the statement, the owner must assemble the balance sheets and the income statements summarizing the present year's operations. The owner begins with the company's net income for the period (from the income statement), then adds the sources of the company's funds—borrowed funds, owner contributions, decreases in accounts receivable, increases in accounts payable, decreases in inventory, depreciation, and any others. Depreciation is listed as a source of funds because it is a noncash expense that has already been deducted as a cost of doing business. Because the owner has already paid for the item being depreciated, however, its depreciation is a source of funds. Next the owner subtracts the uses of these funds—plant and equipment purchases, dividends to owners, repayment of debt, increases in accounts receivable, decreases in accounts payable, increases in inventory, and so on. The difference between the total sources and the total uses is the increase or decrease in working capital. By investigating the changes in their companies' working capital and the reasons for them, owners can create a more practical financial action plan for the future of the enterprise.

statement of cash flows
a financial statement showing the changes in a company's working capital from the beginning of the year by listing both the sources and the uses of those funds.

These financial statements are more than just complex documents used only by accountants and financial officers. When used in conjunction with the analytical tools described in the following sections, they can help entrepreneurs to map a firm's financial future and actively plan for profit. Mere preparation of these statement is not enough, however; owners and employees must *understand and use* the information contained in them to make the business more effective and efficient.

CFO-of-the-Day

At 23 years old and just out of college, Maria Mantz had worked for Development Counsellors International (DCI), a New York City public relations firm, for only five months. Yet here she was shuffling spreadsheets and waiting to present the company's monthly financial report to 30 of her colleagues. As she approached the podium, her nervousness abated. "Several accounts had quite an increase in May," she began, pointing out revenue tables she had included in the handouts. She then gestured to a flip chart and asked, "Does anyone know what the five clients listed here have in common?"

"They're all performance-based accounts," said one account executive, referring to clients whose fees are based on performance.

"Right," Mantz replied. "In fact, 20 percent of our billings for May came from performance-based accounts. Is this a good thing or a bad thing?"

The group began to discuss the question, and then Mantz finished her presentation. It was exactly what Andrew Levine, DCI's president, was hoping to see. Levine's goal is to have every DCI employee—from receptionists to president—understand the company's financial statements by presenting them to their colleagues. Each month, a different employee has the responsibility of leading the company's monthly financial meeting to go over the numbers. The CFO-of-the-day provides a breakdown of revenues and expenses, points out trends, launches discussions about everything from cost cutting to energy conservation, and fields questions. At the end of the session, the CFO-of-the-day reveals DCI's bottom line, showing whether the company met its profit goal for the month. It's an important number because every time DCI's retained earnings increases by $100,000, 30 percent of it is distributed among employees in their next paychecks.

DCI, with annual revenues of nearly $4.5 million, began the CFO-of-the-day program in 1996 and has been profitable ever since. In addition to the company's outstanding financial performance, Levine says employee tenure is longer than before the program began—an average of five years, compared to just two and one-half years before. Customer retention rates also are up.

Levine introduced the concept soon after taking over the company from his father, who founded DCI in 1960. Long before the term "open-book management," which refers to business owners sharing the financial results of their companies' performances with employees, was ever coined, Levine began practicing the concept. There was only one problem with the monthly meetings: Employees were bored. "Most of our staffers were poor at math, and here I was talking about statistics and ratios," he says. At one meeting, Levine asked his employees how to calculate a company's profit, and only one worker, receptionist Sergio Barrios, knew the answer. "It was mind-boggling," recalls Levine.

That's when the idea for the CFO-of-the-day hit him. Why not require employees to present the company's financial report at the monthly meetings? To do that, each worker at least would have to learn the basics of financial management. Levine appointed Barrios, the receptionist, as the first CFO-of-the-day, and she did a terrific job of explaining the company's financial statements in a way that any layperson could understand them. Since then, the program has transformed even the most unlikely employees, including Mantz, into financial wizards.

When she first joined the company, Mantz watched her co-workers master DCI's financial statements and soon realized that she could as well. The day before the monthly financial meeting, Mantz spent an hour going over the monthly financial statements with Levine and DCI's controller, Carrie Nepo. Nepo walked Mantz through the financial statements, allowing her to ask questions along the way. The three talked about trends that would form the basis for good discussions at the meeting. Mantz then took four spreadsheets and spent another hour reviewing the company's financial statements on her own. The next morning, Mantz performed a "dress rehearsal" of her presentation before Levine and Nepo before making her presentation to her co-workers that afternoon.

"It's a good way to learn how things add up," says Mantz. "I understand things much better now that I've done it." One benefit is that employees see exactly how their daily decisions and actions have an impact on the company's financial performance—and on their own compensation. Levine sees evidence that employees care more about revenues and expenses when they understand their impact on the company's financial statements and when they have a stake in the company's profits. DCI's profit-sharing program is integrally linked to the success of its open-book management style. Levine keeps things simple, using the analogy of a bucket being filled with sand. Every time DCI's profits reach the brim, employees receive 30 percent of the bucket in their next checks.

DCI reaps other benefits as well. "I'm a new, young employee," says Mantz. "I'm being trained not only as a PR executive but also as a business executive."

1. Use the resources of the World Wide Web to research open-book management. Discuss the benefits of open-book management for the companies using it and for employees of those companies.
2. What factors are necessary to the success of an open-book management program such as the one DCI uses? What are the risks associated with open-book management?
3. Why don't more small businesses use open-book management?

Source: Adapted from Nadine Heintz, "Everyone's a CFO," *Inc.,* September 2005, pp. 42–44.

Creating Projected Financial Statements

LEARNING OBJECTIVES
3. Create projected (pro forma) financial statements.

Creating projected financial statements helps the small business owner to transform business goals into reality. Budgets answer such questions as: What profit can the business expect to earn? If the owner's profit objective is x dollars, what sales level must the company achieve? What fixed and variable expenses can be expected at that level of sales? The answers to these and other questions are critical in formulating a functional financial plan for the small business.

This section will focus on creating projected income statements and balance sheets for a small start-up. These projected (or pro forma) statements are a crucial component of every business plan because they estimate the profitability and the overall financial condition of a company in the future. They are an integral part of convincing potential lenders and investors to provide the financing needed to get the company off the ground (the topic of Chapter 13). In addition, because these statements project a company's financial position through the end of the forecasted period, they help entrepreneurs to plan the route to improved financial strength and healthy business growth. To be useful, however, these forecasts must be *realistic*! "A business plan is not complete until it contains a set of financial projections that are not only inspiring but also logical and defensible," says one business writer.

Because an established business has a history of operating data from which to construct pro forma financial statements, the task is not nearly as difficult as it is for the beginning business. When creating pro forma financial statements for a brand-new business, an entrepreneur typically relies on published statistics summarizing the operation of similar-size companies in the same industry. These statistics are available from a number of sources (described later), but this section draws on information found in the Risk Management Association's (RMA) *Annual Statement Studies*, a compilation of financial data on nearly 200,000 companies across more than 700 industries organized by Standard Industrial Classification (SIC) Code and North American Industry Classification System (NAICS).

Pro Forma Statements for the Small Business

One of the most important tasks confronting the entrepreneur launching a new enterprise is to determine the amount of funding needed to begin operation as well as the amount required to keep the company going through its initial growth period until it can generate positive cash flow. The amount of money needed to begin a business depends on the type of operation, its location, inventory requirements, sales volume, and many other factors. However, every new firm must have enough capital to cover all start-up costs, including funds to rent or buy plant, equipment, and tools, as well as pay for advertising, wages, licenses, utilities, and other expenses. In addition, entrepreneurs must maintain a reserve of capital to carry the company until it begins to generate positive cash flow. Too often entrepreneurs are overly optimistic in their financial plans and fail to recognize that expenses initially exceed income (and cash outflow exceeds cash inflow) for most small firms. This period of net losses (and negative cash flow) is normal and may last from just a few months to several years. During this time, entrepreneurs must be able to pay the company's regular bills, meet payrolls, maintain adequate levels of inventory, take advantage of cash discounts, grant customers credit, and meet their personal financial obligations.

The Pro Forma Income Statement Although they are projections, financial forecasts must be based in reality; otherwise the resulting financial plan is nothing more than a hopeless dream. When creating a projected income statement, an entrepreneur has two options: to develop a sales forecast and work down or set a profit target and work up. Developing a realistic sales forecast for a business startup is not always easy, but with creativity and research it is possible. Talking with owners of existing businesses in the industry (outside of the local trading area, of course) can provide meaningful insight into the sales levels a company can expect to generate during its early years. For a reasonable fee, entrepreneurs can access published aggregated financial statistics that industry trade associations collect on the companies in their industries. Other organizations, such as the RMA and Dun & Bradstreet, publish useful financial information for a wide range of industries. Web searches and trips to the local library will produce the desired information. Interviews with potential customers and test marketing an actual product or service also can reveal the number of customers a company can expect to attract. Multiplying the number of customers by projected prices yields a revenue estimate. One method for checking the accuracy of a sales revenue estimate is to calculate the revenue other companies in the same industry generate per employee and compare it to your own projected revenue per employee. A value that is out of line with industry standards is not likely to be realistic.

Many entrepreneurs prefer the other method of creating a projected income statement, targeting a profit figure and then "working up" to determine the sales level they must achieve to reach it. Of course, it is important to compare this sales target against the results of the marketing plan to determine whether it is realistic. The next step is to estimate the expenses that the business will incur in securing those sales. In any small business, the annual profit must be large enough to produce a return for time the owners spend operating the business plus a return on their investment in the business.

An entrepreneur who earns less in his or her own business than he or she could earn working for someone else must weigh carefully the advantages and disadvantages of choosing the path of entrepreneurship. Why be exposed to all of the risks, sacrifices, and hard work of beginning and operating a small business if the rewards are less than those of remaining in the secure employment of another? Although there are many nonfinancial benefits of owning a business, the net profit after taxes a company generates should be at least as much as an entrepreneur could earn by working for someone else.

An adequate profit must also include a reasonable return on the owner's total investment in the business. The owner's total investment is the amount contributed to the company at its inception plus any retained earnings (profits from previous years funneled back into the operation). If a would-be owner has $70,000 to invest and can invest it in securities and earn 10 percent, he or she should not consider investing it in a business venture that would yield only 3 percent.

An entrepreneur's target income is the sum of a reasonable salary for the time spent running the business and a normal return on the amount invested in the firm. Determining how much this should be is the first step in creating the pro forma income statement.

An entrepreneur then must translate this target profit into a net sales figure for the forecasted period. To calculate net sales from a target profit, the entrepreneur can use published industry statistics. Suppose an entrepreneur wants to launch a small retail bookstore and has determined that his target net income is $30,000. Statistics gathered from RMA's *Annual Statement Studies* show that the typical bookstore's net profit margin (net profit ÷ net sales) is 7.3 percent. Using this information, he can compute the sales level required to produce a net profit of $30,000:

$$\text{Net profit margin} = \frac{\text{Net profit}}{\text{Net sales (annual)}}$$

$$7.3\% = \frac{\$30,000}{\text{Net sales (annual)}}$$

$$\text{Net sales} = \frac{\$30,000}{0.073} = \$410,959$$

Now this entrepreneur knows that to make a net profit of $30,000 (before taxes), he must achieve annual sales of $410,959. To complete the projected income statement, the owner simply applies the appropriate statistics from *Annual Statement Studies* to the annual sales figure. Because the statistics for each income statement item are expressed as percentages of net sales, he merely multiplies the proper percentage by the annual sales figure to obtain the desired value. For example, cost of goods sold usually comprises 61.4 percent of net sales for the typical small bookstore. So the owner of this new bookstore expects his cost of goods sold to be the following:

$$\text{Cost of goods sold} = \$410,959 \times 0.614 = \$252,329$$

The bookstore's complete projected income statement is shown as follows:

Net sales	(100%)	$410,959
− Cost of goods sold	(61.4%)	$252,329
Gross profit margin	(38.6%)	$158,630
− Operating expenses	(31.3%)	$128,630
Net profit (before taxes)	(7.3%)	$ 30,000

At this point, the business appears to be a lucrative venture. But remember: this income statement represents a sales goal that the owner may not be able to reach. The next step is to determine whether this required sales volume is reasonable. One useful technique is to break down the required annual sales volume into *daily* sales figures. Assuming the store will be open six days per week for 50 weeks (300 days), we see that the owner must average $1,370 per day in sales:

$$\text{Average daily sales} = \$410,959/300 \text{ days}$$
$$= 1,370 \text{ day}$$

This calculation gives the owner a better perspective of the sales required to yield an annual profit of $30,000.

To determine whether the profit expected from the business will meet or exceed the target income, the entrepreneur should also create an income statement based on a realistic sales estimate. The previous analysis shows an entrepreneur the sales level needed to reach a desired profit. But what happens if sales are lower? Higher? The entrepreneur requires a reliable sales forecast using the market research techniques described in Chapter 6.

Suppose, for example, that after conducting a marketing survey of local customers and talking with nearby business owners, the prospective bookstore operator projects annual sales for the proposed business to be only $385,000. The entrepreneur must take this expected sales figure and develop a pro forma income statement:

Net Sales	(100%)	$385,000
− Cost of Goods Sold	(61.4%)	$236,390
Gross Profit Margin	(38.6%)	$148,610
− Operating Expenses	(31.3%)	$ 83,505
Net Profit (before taxes)	(7.3%)	$ 28,105

Based on sales of $385,000, this entrepreneur should expect a net income (before taxes) of $28,105. If this amount is acceptable as a return on the investment of time and money in the business, he should proceed with his planning.

At this stage in developing the financial plan, the owner should create a more detailed picture of the venture's expected operating expenses. One common method is to use the operating statistics data found in *Dun & Bradstreet's Cost of Doing Business* reports. These booklets document typical selected operating expenses (expressed as a percentage of net sales) for 190 different lines of businesses. Contacting potential vendors, suppliers, and providers to get estimates of expenses increases the accuracy of the expected expenses on a projected income statement. One entrepreneur who was preparing a business plan for the launch of an upscale women's clothing store contacted local utility companies, insurance agencies, radio and television stations, and other vendors to get estimates of her utility, insurance, advertising, and other general expenses.

To ensure that no business expenses have been overlooked in preparing the business plan, entrepreneurs should list all of the expenses they will incur and have an accountant review the list. Sometimes in their estimates of expenses entrepreneurs neglect to include salaries for themselves, which immediately raises a red flag among lenders and investors. Without drawing a salary, how will an entrepreneur pay his or her personal bills? At the other extreme, lenders and investors frown on exorbitantly high salaries for owners of business start-ups. Typically, salaries are not the best use of cash in a start-up; one guideline is to draw a salary that is about 25 to 30 percent below the market rate for a similar position (and to make adjustments from there if conditions warrant). In addition, as the company grows, executive salaries should be among the *last* expenses to be increased. Reinvesting the extra money back into the company for essentials will accelerate its growth rate even more.

Smart Furniture

When Stephen Culp created the financial plan for his company, Smart Furniture, he decided to draw no salary for the first three years in business, choosing instead to live off of his savings. He invested that money in the business, and it paid off.

Stephen Culp, who in 2001 started Smart Furniture, a Chattanooga, Tennessee-based modular furniture company, drew no salary at all for his first three years in business, choosing instead to live very frugally off of his personal savings. Culp planned his company this way from the outset, using the money he could have drawn as his salary to hire two employees who played key roles in tripling the company's sales in just three years. "It's a prioritization of cash flow," explains Culp. "If I can survive on cereal and take all that cash that I would have spent on a more extravagant lifestyle and put it back into the company, it increases my chances of success." Culp's plan called for attracting venture capital to accelerate his company's growth, and he knew that he would have to include a salary for himself before approaching venture capital firms. Culp researched the industry and talked with colleagues to determine a reasonable salary, discounted that number by 30 percent, and came up with a salary of less than $100,000. "I'm still trying to show investors that I'm in this for the long haul," he says.[5]

Figures 11.3 and 11.4 show two useful forms designed to help entrepreneurs estimate both monthly and start-up expenses. Totals derived from this list of expenses should approximate the total expense figures calculated from published statistics. Naturally, entrepreneurs should be more confident in their own list of expenses because they reflect their company's particular set of circumstances.

The Pro Forma Balance Sheet In addition to projecting a small company's net profit or loss, an entrepreneur must develop a pro forma balance sheet outlining the fledgling firm's assets and liabilities. Most entrepreneurs' primary concern is profitability because, on the surface, the importance of a business's assets is less obvious. In many cases, small companies begin their lives on weak financial footing because entrepreneurs fail to

FIGURE 11.3

Anticipated Expenses

Source: U.S. Small Business Administration, *Checklist for Going into Business.* (Small Marketers Aid No. 71) (Washington, DC, 1982), pp. 6–7.

Worksheet No. 2
Estimated Monthly Expenses

Your estimate of monthly expenses based on sales of $ _____ per year.
Your estimate of how much cash you need to start your business (see column 3).
What to put in column 2. (These figures are typical for one kind of business. You will have to decide how many months to allow for in your business.)

Item	Column 1	Column 2	Column 3
Salary of owner-manager	$	$	2 times column 1
All other salaries and wages			3 times column 1
Rent			3 times column 1
Advertising			3 times column 1
Delivery expense			3 times column 1
Supplies			3 times column 1
Telephone and telegraph			3 times column 1
Other utilities			3 times column 1
Insurance			Payment required by insurance company
Taxes, including Social Security			4 times column 1
Interest			3 times column 1
Maintenance			3 times column 1
Legal and other professional fees			3 times column 1
Miscellaneous			3 times column 1
Starting Costs You Have to Pay Only Once			Leave column 2 blank
Fixtures and equipment			Fill in worksheet 3 and put the total here
Decorating and remodeling			Talk it over with a contractor
Installation of fixtures and equipment			Talk to suppliers from whom you buy these
Starting inventory			Suppliers will probably help you estimate this
Deposits with public utilities			Find out from utilities companies
Legal and other professional fees			Lawyer, accountant, and so on
Licenses and permits			Find out from city offices what you have to have
Advertising and promotion of opening			Estimate what you'll use
Accounts receivable			What you need to buy more stock until credit customers pay
Cash			For unexpected expenses or losses, special purchases, etc.
Other			Make a separate list and enter total
Total Estimated Cash You Need To Start		$	Add up all the numbers in column 2

FIGURE 11.4

Anticipated Expenditures for Fixtures and Equipment

Source: U.S. Small Business Administration, *Checklist for Going into Business* (Small Marketers Aid No. 71) (Washington, DC: Author, 1982), pp. 6–7.

Leave out or add items to suit your business. Use separate sheets to list exactly what you need for each of the items below.	If you plan to pay cash in full, enter the full amount below and in the last column.	If you are going to pay by installments, fill out the columns below. Enter in the last column your down payment plus at least one installment.			Estimate of the cash you need for furniture, fixtures, and equipment.
		Price	Down payment	Amount of each installment	
Counters	$	$	$	$	$
Storage shelves, cabinets					
Display stands, shelves, tables					
Cash register					
Safe					
Window display fixtures					
Special lighting					
Outside sign					
Delivery equipment if needed					
Total furniture, fixtures, and equipment (Enter this figure also in worksheet 2 under "Starting Costs You Have to Pay Only Once.")					$

Worksheet No. 3
List of Furniture, Fixtures, and Equipment

determine their firms' total asset requirements. To prevent this major oversight, entrepreneurs should prepare a projected balance sheet listing every asset their businesses will need and all the claims against these assets.

Assets. Cash is one of the most useful assets the business owns; it is highly liquid and can quickly be converted into other tangible assets. But how much cash should a small business have at its inception? Obviously, there is no single dollar figure that fits the needs of every small firm. One practical rule of thumb, however, suggests that a company's cash balance should cover its operating expenses (less depreciation, a noncash expense) for at least one inventory turnover period. Using this guideline, the cash balance for the small bookstore is calculated as follows:

Operating expenses = $158,630 (from projected income statement)
Less: depreciation (1.4% of annual sales*) of $5,753

Equals: cash expenses (annual) = $152,877

Annual inventory turnover ratio* = 3.6 times per year

$$\text{Cash requirement} = \frac{\text{Cash expenses}}{\text{Average inventory turnover ratio}}$$

$$= \frac{\$152,877}{3.6}$$

$$= \$42,466$$

*From Risk Management Association, *Annual Statement Studies*.

Notice the inverse relationship between the small firm's average turnover ratio and its cash requirement. The smaller the number of inventory turns a company generates, the higher is its cash requirement.

Another decision facing the entrepreneur is how much inventory the business should carry. A rough estimate of the inventory requirement can be calculated from the information found on the projected income statement and from published statistics:

Cost of goods sold = $252,329 (from projected income statement)

$$\text{Average inventory turnover} = \frac{\text{Cost of goods sold}}{\text{Inventory level}} = 3.6 \text{ times per year}$$

Substituting, we obtain

$$3.6 \text{ times per year} = \frac{\$252,329}{\text{Inventory level}}$$

Solving for the inventory level gives

Inventory level = $70,091

Entrepreneurs can use the planning forms shown in Figures 11.3 and 11.4 to estimate fixed assets (land, building, equipment, and fixtures). Suppose the estimate of fixed assets is as follows:

Fixtures	$27,500
Office equipment	4,850
Computers/cash register	3,125
Signs	6,200
Miscellaneous	1,500
Total	**$43,175**

Liabilities. To complete the projected balance sheet, the owner must record all of the small firm's liabilities—the claims against its assets. The bookstore owner was able to finance 50 percent of the inventory and fixtures ($48,796) through suppliers and has a short-term note payable in the amount of $3,750. The only other major claim against the firm's assets is a note payable to the entrepreneur' father-in-law for $40,000. The difference between the company's assets ($157,532) and its total liabilities ($92,546) represents the owner's investment in the business (owner's equity) of $64,986.

The final step is to compile all of these items into a projected balance sheet, as shown in Figure 11.5.

FIGURE 11.5

Projected Balance Sheet for a Small Bookstore

Source: U.S. Small Business Administration, *Checklist for Going into Business* (Small Marketers Aid No. 71) (Washington, DC: Author, 1982), p. 12.

Assets		Liabilities	
Current Assets		**Current Liabilities**	
Cash	$ 42,466	Accounts Payable	$ 48,796
Inventory	70,091	Note Payable	3,750
Miscellaneous	1,800		
Total Current Assets	$114,357	Total Current Liabilities	$ 52,546
Fixed Assets		**Longs-Term Liabilities**	
Fixtures	$ 27,500	Note Payable	$ 40,000
Office Equipment	4,850		
Computer/Cash Register	3,125	Total Liabilities	$ 92,546
Signs	6,200		
Miscellaneous	1,500		
Total Fixed Assets	$ 43,175	**Owner's Equity**	$ 64,986
Total Assets	$157,532	**Total Liabilities and Owner's Equity**	$157,532

The Choice Is Yours

It's a common trap that catches many entrepreneurs: the pursuit of growth at all costs. Rather than see the many contributions their businesses make to the local community and the accomplishments they have achieved, entrepreneurs often have a nagging sense of inadequacy. No matter how successful they may appear to be, it's never quite enough. After 19 years in business, Jay Goltz, the owner of highly successful picture framing business with $7 million in sales and 75 employees, compared his business to those of Richard Branson and Michael Dell and concluded that his company was "dinky." That set him off on a drive for growth, diversification, and expansion that nearly ruined his personal life and put his successful business in peril. Then, at a retirement party for one of his employees, the guest of honor turned to Goltz in front of everyone and thanked him for all he had done for her and her co-workers over the years. It was then that Goltz realized that he did not have to build a billion-dollar company like Dell's and Branson's to be considered a success. He had made a difference in the lives of many people and in the local community. "Having calm, controlled growth is good," he says. Now approaching 50, Goltz says that rather than having a midlife crisis, "I'm having midlife contentment. For me, happiness is not about building a $110 million company."

Focusing on growing the top line (revenue) can cause small companies to make sacrifices on its bottom line (profits). "Bigger is better—that's the old Holy Grail," says Paul Schaye, a manager at an investment banking firm. "It gets you bragging rights at the bar, but those bragging rights are what drives people to do crazy things." Sharon Anderson Wright, owner of Half Price Books, has managed to avoid the siren's song of growth at whatever cost. Wright has continued the same simple formula for success with the business that her mother, Pat Anderson, followed when she opened the first Half Price Books in an abandoned laundromat in 1972. Unlike so many bookstores that offer cappuccinos and biscotti in well-lit stores that take an almost antiseptic approach to selling books, Wright's formula relies on stores that are not always well organized but have lots of "personality" and are staffed by friendly, knowledgeable employees who love books. As the company's name implies, Half Price Books also sells used books at very low prices. The combination of low prices, friendly service, and long-time, knowledgeable employees keeps customers coming back regularly. "Our cash cow is our repeat customers," says Wright. "The last thing we want to do is grow too fast and become impersonal."

Wright now has 79 stores in 11 states, and the company generates $120 million a year in revenues. Half Price Books could grow much faster, but Wright has held back on the reins of growth. The company is profitable and debt-free, and sales are climbing as demand for used books is growing rapidly. Whereas Barnes and Noble and Borders typically open 40 new stores a year, Wright chooses to open 6 or 8 new stores in carefully selected locations. The company's target customer is middle-aged with an average annual income of $50,000 and has a college degree. When Wright considers a location for a new store, she looks for sites that have high concentrations of customers that fit this profile.

Wright routinely turns down offers from other companies to buy Half Price Books, and she pays for the company's expansion out of retained earnings, refusing to borrow money to finance growth. If Half Price Books grew any faster, she reasons, she would have to borrow money and then reflect the cost of the borrowed funds in the form of higher prices for the books she sells. "We were raised as kids to do only the things that we could afford," says Wright. "Why would I run my company any differently?"

When Wright is considering opening a new store, she does so only if a long-time manager will move and set up the store. Not only does this policy cut training costs, but it also complements Wright's management philosophy. She promotes from within and provides full-time employees health insurance, regular training programs, and a profit-sharing plan. Fast growth is not an enticement to Wright and other entrepreneurs of her ilk. These visionary entrepreneurs prefer to grow steadily at their own manageable pace and to define their success in terms of satisfied customers, dedicated employees, and profitable companies.

1. Why is it so easy for entrepreneurs to fall into the high-growth trap, even when growing fast may have negative repercussions on their companies?

2. What benefits do entrepreneurs such as Jay Goltz and Sharon Anderson Wright experience by choosing to pursue profitability over sales growth? What are the costs of such a strategy?

3. Research the companies listed on the *Inc.* 500 list of the fastest-growing companies in the United States from two to five years ago. Find the most recent listing of the *Inc.* 500 list. How many of the companies from the past appear on the current list? Use *Inc.*

magazine and the resources of the World Wide Web to research some of the companies that appeared on the earlier list but that are missing from the current list. What happened to them? What lessons can entrepreneurs learn from their stories?

Source: Adapted from Bo Burlingham, "There's a Choice," *Inc.*, February 2006, pp. 80–89; Ellyn Spragins and Verne Harnish, "Size Doesn't Matter—Profits Do," *FSB*, March 2004, pp. 37–42.

Ratio Analysis

LEARNING OBJECTIVES
4. Understand the basic financial statements through ratio analysis.

Once an entrepreneur has the business up and running with the help of a solid financial plan, the next step is to keep the company moving in the right direction with the help of proper financial controls. Establishing these controls—and using them consistently—is one of the keys to keeping a business vibrant and healthy. "If you don't keep a finger on the pulse of your company's finances, you risk making bad decisions," explains one business writer. "You could be in serious financial trouble and not even realize it."[6]

A smoothly functioning system of financial controls is essential to achieving business success. Such a system can serve as an early warning device for underlying problems that could destroy a young business. According to one writer:
"A company's financial accounting and reporting systems will provide signals, through comparative analysis, of impending trouble, such as:

■ Decreasing sales and falling profit margins.
■ Increasing corporate overheads.
■ Growing inventories and accounts receivable.

These are all signals of declining cash flows from operations, the lifeblood of every business. As cash flows decrease, the squeeze begins:

■ Payments to vendors become slower.
■ Maintenance on production equipment lags.
■ Raw material shortages appear.
■ Equipment breakdowns occur.

All of these begin to have a negative impact on productivity. Now the downward spiral has begun in earnest. The key is hearing and focusing on the signals."[7]

What are these signals, and how does an entrepreneur go about hearing and focusing on them? One extremely helpful tool is ratio analysis. **Ratio analysis,** a method of expressing the relationships between any two elements on financial statements, provides a convenient technique for performing financial analysis. When analyzed properly, ratios serve as barometers of a company's financial health. "You owe it to yourself to understand each ratio and what it means to your business," says one accountant. "Ratios point out potential trouble areas so you can correct them before they multiply."[8] Ratio analysis allows entrepreneurs to determine whether their companies are carrying excessive inventory, experiencing heavy operating expenses, overextending credit, taking on too much debt, and managing to pay their bills on time and to answer other questions relating to the efficient and effective operation of the overall business. Unfortunately, few business owners actually use ratio analysis; one study discovered that only 27 percent of small business owners compute financial ratios and use them in managing their businesses.[9]

Clever business owners use financial ratio analysis to identify problems in their businesses while they are still problems and not business-threatening crises. Tracking these

ratio analysis
a method of expressing the relationship between any two accounting elements that allows business owners to analyze their companies' financial performances.

ratios over time permits an owner to spot a variety of red flags that are indications of these problem areas. This is critical to business success because business owners cannot solve problems they do not know exist!

At Atkinson-Baker & Associates, a Los Angeles court-reporting service, every one of the firm's 50 employees is responsible for tracking every day a key financial statistic relating to his or her job. CEO Alan Atkinson-Baker believes that waiting until the month's end to compile financial ratios takes away a company's ability to respond to events as they happen. "Employees have statistics for their jobs, and it helps them see how well they are producing," he says. Because the statistics are linked directly to their jobs, employees quickly learn which numbers to track and how to compile or to calculate them. "Each day everybody reports their statistics," explains Atkinson-Baker. "It all goes into a computer . . . and we keep track of it all." A spreadsheet summarizes the calculations and generates 27 graphs so managers can analyze trends in a meeting the following morning. One rule the company developed from its financial analysis is "Don't spend more today than you brought in yesterday." Atkinson-Baker explains, "You can never run into trouble as long as you stick to that rule." He also notes that effective financial planning would be impossible without timely data. "When we have had problem areas, the statistics have helped us catch them before they become a bigger problem," he says.[10]

Business owners also can use ratio analysis to increase the likelihood of obtaining loans. By analyzing their financial statements with the use of ratios, business owners can anticipate potential problems and identify important strengths in advance. And loan officers *do* use ratios to analyze the financial statements of companies applying for loans, comparing them against industry averages and looking for trends over time.

How many ratios should the small business manager monitor to maintain adequate financial control over the firm? The number of ratios that an owner could calculate is limited only by the number of accounts on a firm's financial statements. However, tracking too many ratios only creates confusion and saps the meaning from an entrepreneur's financial analysis. The secret to successful ratio analysis is *simplicity*, focusing on just enough ratios to provide a clear picture of a company's financial standing.

Twelve Key Ratios

In keeping with the idea of simplicity, we will describe 12 key ratios that will enable most business owners to monitor their companies' financial positions without becoming bogged down in financial details. This chapter presents explanations of these ratios and examples based on the balance sheet and the income statement for Sam's Appliance Shop shown in Figures 11.1 and 11.2. We will group them into four categories: liquidity ratios, leverage ratios, operating ratios, and profitability ratios.

liquidity ratios
tell whether a small business will be able to meet its short-term obligations as they come due.

Liquidity Ratios **Liquidity ratios** tell whether a small business will be able to meet its short-term financial obligations as they come due. These ratios can forewarn a business owner of impending cash flow problems. A small company with solid liquidity not only is able to pay its bills on time, but it also has enough cash to take advantage of attractive business opportunities as they arise. The primary measures of liquidity are the current ratio and the quick ratio.

current ratio
measures a small firm's solvency by indicating its ability to pay current liabilities out of current assets.

1. *Current ratio.* The **current ratio** measures a small firm's solvency by indicating its ability to pay current liabilities (debts) from current assets. It is calculated in the following manner:

$$\text{Current ratio} = \frac{\text{Current assets}}{\text{Current liabilities}}$$

$$= \frac{\$686,985}{\$367,850}$$

$$= 1.87:1$$

Sam's Appliance Shop has $1.87 in current assets for every $1 it has in current liabilities.

Current assets are those that an owner expects to convert into cash in the ordinary business cycle, and normally include cash, notes/accounts receivable, inventory, and any other short-term marketable securities. Current liabilities are those short-term obligations that come due within one year, and include notes/accounts payable, taxes payable, and accruals.

The current ratio is sometimes called the *working capital ratio* and is the most commonly used measure of short-term solvency. Typically, financial analysts suggest that a small business maintain a current ratio of at least 2:1 (i.e., two dollars of current assets for every one dollar of current liabilities) to maintain a comfortable cushion of working capital. Generally, the higher a company's current ratio, the stronger is its financial position; a high current ratio, however, does not guarantee that a company is using its assets in the most profitable manner. For example, a business may be have an abundance of accounts receivable (many of which may not even be collectible) or may be overinvesting in inventory.

With its current ratio of 1.87, Sam's Appliance Shop could liquidate its current assets at 53.5% (1 ÷ 1.87 = 0.535) of its book value and still manage to pay its current creditors in full.

2. *Quick ratio.* The current ratio sometimes can be misleading because it does not show the quality of a company's current assets. As we have already seen, a company with a large number of past-due receivables and stale inventory could boast an impressive current ratio and still be on the verge of financial collapse. The **quick ratio (acid test ratio)** is a more conservative measure of a company's liquidity because it shows the extent to which its most liquid assets cover its current liabilities. This ratio includes only a company's "quick assets," excluding the most illiquid asset of all—inventory. It is calculated as follows:

quick ratio (acid test ratio)
a conservative measure of a firm's liquidity, measuring the extent to which its most liquid assets cover its current liabilities.

$$\text{Quick ratio} = \frac{\text{Quick assets}}{\text{Current liabilities}}$$
$$= \frac{\$686,985 - \$455,455}{\$367,850}$$
$$= 0.61{:}1$$

Sam's Appliance Shop has 63 cents in quick assets for every $1 of current liabilities.

Quick assets include cash, readily marketable securities, and notes/accounts receivables, assets that can be converted into cash immediately if needed. Most small firms determine quick assets by subtracting inventory from current assets because they cannot convert inventory into cash quickly. Moreover, inventory is the asset on which losses are most likely to occur in case of liquidation.

The quick ratio is a more specific measure of a firm's ability to meet its short-term obligations and is a more rigorous test of its liquidity. It expresses capacity to pay current debts if all sales income ceased immediately. Generally, a quick ratio of 1:1 is considered satisfactory. A ratio of less than 1:1 indicates that the small firm is overly dependent on inventory and on future sales to satisfy short-term debt. A quick ratio of greater than 1:1 indicates a greater degree of financial security.

Leverage Ratios Leverage ratios measure the financing supplied by a firm's owners against that supplied by its creditors; they are a gauge of the depth of a company's debt. These ratios show the extent to which an entrepreneur relies on debt capital (rather than equity capital) to finance operating expenses, capital expenditures, and expansion costs. As such, it is a measure of the degree of financial risk in a company. Generally, small businesses with low leverage ratios are less affected by economic downturns, but the returns for these firms are lower during economic booms. Conversely, small firms with high leverage ratios are more vulnerable to economic slides because their debt loads demolish cash flow; however, they have greater potential for large profits.

leverage ratios
measure the financing supplied by a firm's owners against that supplied by its creditors; they are a gauge of the depth of a company's debt.

Over the last decade, American businesses have relied increasingly on debt financing to fuel their growth and expansion. Nonfinancial businesses in the United States have $4.97 trillion in outstanding debt, double the amount in 1995.[11]

**Ironbound Heat
Treating Company**

John Ross, owner of Ironbound Heat Treating Company, a metal heat-treating company that was profitable on sales of $4 million, experienced severe problems with his company's debt load as a result of a combination of unfortunate events. By focusing on a niche, Ross' company was growing rapidly, but the loss of a big customer caused revenue to dip. Then Ironbound had to spend $1 million to replace a steel furnace that was crucial to its operation. The company's debt ratios skyrocketed, causing it to spin out of control. Rather than declare bankruptcy, Ross worked with a business credit counseling company to renegotiate his company's payments on the debt, giving it some breathing room. To get the business back on track, Ross decided to sell it to a larger company, Metal Improvement Company, which agreed to pay off all of Ironbound's debt as part of the deal.[12]

debt ratio

measures the percentage of total assets financed by a company's creditors compared to its owners.

3. ***Debt ratio.*** A small company's **debt ratio** measures the percentage of total assets financed by its creditors compared to its owners. The debt ratio is calculated as follows:

$$\text{Debt ratio} = \frac{\text{Total debt (or liabilities)}}{\text{Total assets}}$$

$$= \frac{\$367,850 + \$212,150}{\$847,655}$$

$$= 0.68{:}1$$

Creditors have claims of 68 cents against every $1 of assets that Sam's Appliance Shop owns.

Total debt includes all current liabilities and any outstanding long-term notes and bonds. Total assets represent the sum of the firm's current assets, fixed assets, and intangible assets. A high debt ratio means that creditors provide a large percentage of a company's total financing and, therefore, bear most of its financial risk. Owners generally prefer higher leverage ratios; otherwise, business funds must come either from the owners' personal assets or from taking on new owners, which means giving up more control over the business. In addition, with a greater portion of a firm's assets financed by creditors, the owner is able to generate profits with a smaller personal investment. Creditors, however, typically prefer moderate debt ratios because a lower debt ratio indicates a smaller chance of creditor losses in case of liquidation. To lenders and creditors, high debt ratios mean a higher risk of default.

According to a senior analyst at Dun & Bradstreet's Analytical Services, "If managed properly, debt can be beneficial because it's a great way to have money working for you. You're leveraging your assets, so you're making more money than you're paying out in interest." However, excessive debt can be the downfall of a business. "As we pile up debt on our personal credit cards our lifestyles are squeezed," he says. "The same thing happens to a business. Overpowering debt sinks thousands of businesses each year."[13]

debt to net worth (debt to equity) ratio

expresses the relationship between the capital contributions from creditors and those from owners and measures how highly leveraged a company is.

4. ***Debt to net worth ratio.*** A small firm's **debt to net worth (debt to equity) ratio** also expresses the relationship between the capital contributions from creditors and those from owners and measures how highly leveraged a company is. This ratio reveals a company's capital structure by comparing what the business "owes" to "what it is worth." It is a measure of the small firm's ability to meet both its creditor and owner obligations in case of liquidation. The debt to net worth ratio is calculated as follows:

$$\text{Debt to net worth ratio} = \frac{\text{Total debt (or liabilities)}}{\text{Tangible net worth}}$$

$$= \frac{\$367,850 + \$212,150}{\$267,655 - \$3,500}$$

$$= 2.20{:}1$$

Sam's Appliance Shop owes creditors $2.20 for every $1 of equity that Sam owns.

Total debt is the sum of current liabilities and long-term liabilities, and tangible net worth represents the owners' investment in the business (capital + capital stock + earned surplus + retained earnings) less any intangible assets (e.g., goodwill) the firm owns.

The higher this ratio, the more leverage a business is using and the lower the degree of protection afforded creditors if the business should fail. A higher debt to net worth ratio also means that the firm has less capacity to borrow; lenders and creditors see the firm as being "borrowed up." Conversely, a low ratio typically is associated with a higher level of financial security, giving the business greater borrowing potential.

As a company's debt to net worth ratio approaches 1:1, the creditors' interest in the business approaches that of the owners'. If the ratio is greater than 1:1, creditors' claims exceed those of the owners', and the business may be undercapitalized. In other words, the owner has not supplied an adequate amount of capital, forcing the business to be overextended in terms of debt.

5. *Times interest earned ratio.* The **times interest earned ratio** is a measure of a small firm's ability to make the interest payments on its debt. It tells how many times a company's earnings cover the interest payments on the debt it is carrying. This ratio measures the size of the cushion a company has in covering the interest cost of its debt load. The times interest earned ratio is calculated as follows:

times interest earned ratio measures a small firm's ability to make the interest payments on its debt.

$$\text{Times interest earned ratio} = \frac{\text{Earnings before interest and taxes (EBIT)}}{\text{Total interest expense}}$$

$$= \frac{\$60,629 - \$39,850}{\$39,850}$$

$$= 2.52{:}1$$

Sam's Appliance Shop's earnings are 2.5 times greater than its interest expense.

EBIT is the firm's profit *before* deducting interest expense and taxes; the denominator measures the amount the business paid in interest over the accounting period.

A high ratio suggests that the company would have little difficulty meeting the interest payments on its loans; creditors see this as a sign of safety for future loans. Conversely, a low ratio is an indication that the company is overextended in its debts; earnings will not be able to cover its debt service if this ratio is less than one. "I look for a [times interest earned] ratio of higher than three-to-one," says one financial analyst, "which indicates that management has considerable breathing room to make its debt payments. When the ratio drops below one-to-one, it clearly indicates management is under tremendous pressure to raise cash. The risk of default or bankruptcy is very high."[14] Many creditors look for a times interest earned ratio of at least four-to-one to six-to-one before pronouncing a company a good credit risk.

Although low to moderate levels of debt can boost a company's financial performance, trouble looms on the horizon for businesses whose debt loads are so heavy that they must starve critical operations, research and development, customer service, and others just to pay interest on the debt. Because their interest payments are so large, highly leveraged companies find that they are restricted when it comes to spending cash, whether on an acquisition, normal operations, or capital spending.

Debt is a powerful financial tool, but companies must handle it carefully—just as a demolitionist handles dynamite. And, like dynamite, too much debt can be deadly. Unfortunately, some companies have pushed their debt loads beyond the safety barrier (see Figure 11.6) and are struggling to survive.

Rick Sapio, CEO of Tri-Star Industries, a hardware distributor in Chicago, put his company on the fast-growth track and took on loads of debt to pay for it. With the company solidly profitable ($2 million) on sales of $10 million, Sapio borrowed more money to acquire another company for $4 million. Within a year of the acquisition, Tri-Star's sales had climbed, but it was losing $1.4 million a year, and Sapio had to sell the business to pay off the debt the company had accumulated. "We'd be sitting on $12 to $14 million in retained earnings right now if I had been satisfied with a $10 million company," says Sapio regretfully.[15]

Tri-Star Industries

Like dynamite, debt financing can be a powerful tool, but companies must handle it carefully, or it can be deadly.

Managed carefully, debt can boost a company's performance and improve its productivity. Its treatment in the tax code also makes debt a much cheaper means of financing growth than equity. When companies with AA financial ratings borrow at, say, 8 percent, the after-tax cost is about 5.75 percent (because interest payments to lenders are tax deductible); equity financing often costs twice that.

Table 11.1 describes how lenders view liquidity and leverage.

operating ratios

help an entrepreneur evaluate a small company's overall performance and indicate how effectively the business employs its resources.

average inventory turnover ratio

measures the number of times its average inventory is sold out, or turned over, during an accounting period.

Operating Ratios   **Operating ratios** help an entrepreneur evaluate a small company's overall performance and indicate how effectively the business employs its resources. The more effectively its resources are used, the less capital a small business will require. These five operating ratios are designed to help entrepreneurs spot those areas they must improve if their business is to remain competitive.

6. *Average inventory turnover ratio.* A small firm's **average inventory turnover ratio** measures the number of times its average inventory is sold out, or turned over, during the accounting period. This ratio tells the owner whether an entrepreneur is managing inventory properly. It apprises the owner of whether the business inventory

FIGURE 11.6

The Right Amount of Debt Is a Balancing Act

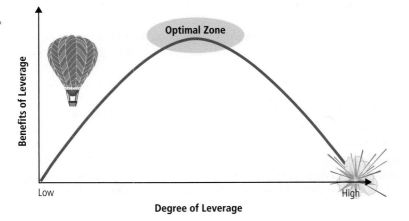

TABLE 11.1 How Lenders View Liquidity and Leverage

	Liquidity	Leverage
Low	If chronic, this is often evidence of mismanagement. It is a sign that the owner has not planned for the company's working capital needs. In most businesses characterized by low liquidity, there is usually no financial plan. This situation is often associated with last minute or "Friday night" financing.	This is a very conservative position. With this kind of leverage, lenders are likely to lend money to satisfy a company's capital needs. Owners in this position should have no trouble borrowing money.
Average	This is an indication of good management. The company is using its current assets wisely and productively. Although they may not be impressed, lenders feel comfortable making loans to companies with adequate liquidity.	If a company's leverage is comparable to that of other businesses of similar size in the same industry, lenders are comfortable making loans. The company is not overburdened with debt and is demonstrating its ability to use its resources to grow.
High	Some lenders look for this because it indicates a most conservative company. However, companies that constantly operate this way usually are forgoing growth opportunities because they are not making the most of their assets.	Businesses that carry excessive levels of debt scare most lenders off. Companies in this position normally will have a difficult time borrowing money unless they can show lenders good reasons for making loans. Owners of these companies must be prepared to sell lenders on their ability to repay.

Source: Adapted from David H. Bangs, Jr., *Financial Troubleshooting* (Dover, NH: Upstart Publishing Company, 1992), p. 124.

is understocked, overstocked, or obsolete. The average inventory turnover ratio is calculated as follows:

$$\text{Average inventory turnover ratio} = \frac{\text{Cost of goods sold}}{\text{Average inventory}}$$

$$= \frac{\$1,290,117}{(\$805,745 + \$455,455)/2}$$

$$= 2.05 \text{ times per year}$$

Sam' Appliance Shop turns its inventory about two times a year, or once every 178 days.

Average inventory is the sum of the value of the firm's inventory at the beginning of the accounting period and its value at the end of the accounting period, divided by 2.

This ratio tells an entrepreneur how fast merchandise is moving through the business and helps him or her to balance the company's inventory on the fine line between oversupply and undersupply. To determine the average number of days units remain in inventory, the owner can divide the average inventory turnover ratio into the number of days in the accounting period (e.g., 365 days ÷ average inventory turnover ratio). The result is called *days' inventory* (or *average age of inventory*). Auto dealerships often use the average age of inventory as a measure of their performance.

An above-average inventory turnover indicates that the small business has a healthy, salable, and liquid inventory and a supply of quality merchandise supported by sound pricing policies. A below-average inventory turnover suggests an illiquid inventory characterized by obsolescence, overstocking, stale merchandise, and poor purchasing procedures.

Frank Toledano, president of Tiger Imports Group, a Highpoint, North Carolina business that imports high-end Italian leathers, relies on the inventory turnover ratio to know when to discontinue one of the company's 100 different styles of leather. Toledano's suppliers require a minimum purchase of $10,000, and with sales of $5 million, Tiger Imports cannot afford to tie up valuable cash in product lines that move slowly. When the inventory turnover ratio of a particular type of leather begins to slow, Toledano does not reorder it and moves on to other, faster-selling lines.[16]

Tiger Imports Group

A healthy average inventory turnover ratio means that inventory is moving through a business at a brisk pace. If a company's average inventory turnover ratio is too low, it will experience a buildup in inventory.

Businesses that turn their inventories more rapidly require a smaller inventory investment to produce a particular sales volume. That means that these companies tie up less cash in inventory that idly sits on shelves. For instance, if Sam's could turn its inventory *four* times each year instead of just *two*, the company would require an average inventory of just $322,529 instead of the current level of $630,600 to generate sales of $1,870,841. Increasing the number of inventory turns would free up more than $308,000 in cash currently tied up in excess inventory! Sam's would benefit from improved cash flow and higher profits.

The inventory turnover ratio can be misleading, however. For example, an excessively high ratio could mean that the firm has a shortage of inventory and is experiencing stockouts. Similarly, a low ratio could be the result of planned inventory stockpiling to meet seasonal peak demand. Another problem is that the ratio is based on an inventory balance calculated from two days out of the entire accounting period. Thus, inventory fluctuations due to seasonal demand patterns are ignored, which may bias the resulting ratio. There is no universal, ideal inventory turnover ratio. Financial analysts suggest that a favorable turnover ratio depends on the type of business, its size, its profitability, its method of inventory valuation, and other relevant factors. For instance, the typical supermarket turns its inventory on average about 16 times a year, but a jewelry store averages just 1.5 to 2 inventory turns a year.

average collection period ratio (days sales outstanding, DSO)

measures the number of days it takes to collect accounts receivable.

7. *Average collection period ratio.* A small firm's **average collection period ratio (days sales outstanding, DSO)** is a measure of the average number of days it takes to collect accounts receivable. To compute the average collection period ratio, you must first calculate the firm's receivables turnover. Given that Sam's *credit* sales for the year

were $1,309,589 (out of the total sales of $1,870,841), then the company's receivables turnover ratio is as follows:

$$\text{Receivables turnover ratio} = \frac{\text{Credit sales}}{\text{Accounts receivables}}$$

$$= \frac{\$1,309,589}{\$179,225}$$

$$= 7.31 \text{ times/year}$$

Sam's Appliance Shop turns over its receivables 7.31 times per year. This ratio measures the number of times the firm's accounts receivable turn over during the accounting period. The higher the firm's receivables turnover ratio, the shorter the time lag is between the sale and the cash collection.

Use the following to calculate the firm's average collection period ratio:

$$\text{Average collection period ratio} = \frac{\text{Days in accounting period}}{\text{Receivables turnover ratio}}$$

$$= \frac{365 \text{ days}}{7.31 \text{ times/year}}$$

$$= 50.0 \text{ days}$$

The lower a company's average collection period, the faster it is collecting its receivables. Sam's Appliance Shop's accounts receivable are outstanding for an average of 50 days. Typically, the higher a firm's average collection period ratio, the greater is its chance of incurring bad debt losses.

One of the most useful applications of the collection period ratio is to compare it to the industry average and to the firm's credit terms. Such a comparison will indicate the degree of the small company's control over its credit sales and collection techniques. A healthy collection period ratio depends on the industry in which a company operates. For instance, a study by REL Consultancy Group found that the average collection period for companies selling technology hardware is 69 days; for retailers of food, it is just 10 days.[17] Perhaps the most meaningful analysis is comparing the collection period ratio to a company's credit terms. One rule of thumb suggests that a company's collection period ratio should be no more than one-third greater than its credit terms. For example, if a small company's credit terms are net 30, its average collection period ratio should be no more than 40 days. A ratio greater than 40 days indicates poor collection procedures.

Slow payers represent a great risk to many small businesses. Many entrepreneurs proudly point to rapidly rising sales only to find that they must borrow money to keep their companies going because their credit customers are paying their bills in 45, 60, or even 90 days instead of the desired 30. Slow receivables are a real danger because they usually lead to a cash crisis that threatens a company's survival. Table 11.2 shows how to calculate the savings associated with lowering a company's average collection period ratio.

8. ***Average payable period ratio.*** The converse of the average collection period, the **average payable period ratio,** is a measure of the average number of days it takes a company to pay its accounts payable. Like the average collection period, it is measured in days. To compute this ratio, we first calculate the payables turnover ratio. Sam's payables turnover ratio is as follows:

average payable period ratio
measures the number of days it takes a company to pay its accounts payable.

$$\text{Payables turnover ratio} = \frac{\text{Purchases}}{\text{Accounts payable}}$$

$$= \frac{\$939,827}{\$152,580}$$

$$= 6.16 \text{ times/year}$$

TABLE 11.2 How Lowering Your Average Collection Period Can Save You Money

Too often, entrepreneurs fail to recognize the importance of collecting their accounts receivable on time. After all, collecting accounts is not as glamorous or as much fun as generating sales. Lowering a company's average collection period ratio, however, *can* produce tangible—and often significant—savings. The following formula shows how to convert an improvement in a company's average collection period ratio into dollar savings:

$$\text{Annual savings} = \frac{\text{Credit sales} \times \text{Annual interest rate} \times \text{Number of days average collection period is lowered}}{365}$$

where
Credit sales = Company's annual credit sales in dollars
Annual interest rate = Interest rate at which the company borrows money
Number of days average collection period is lowered = Difference between the previous year's average collection period ratio and the current one

Example:
Sam's Appliance Shop's average collection period ratio is 50 days. Suppose that the previous year's average collection period ratio was 58 days, an 8-day improvement. The company's credit sales for the most recent year were $1,309,589. If Sam borrows money at 8.75%, this 8-day improvement has generated savings for Sam's Appliance Shop of

$$\text{Savings} = \frac{\$1,309,589 \times 8.75\% \times 8 \text{ days}}{365 \text{ days}} = \$2,512$$

By collecting his accounts receivable just 8 days faster on the average, Sam has saved his business more than $2,512! Of course, if a company's average collection period ratio rises, the same calculation will tell the owner how much that costs.

Source: Adapted from "Days Saved, Thousands Earned," *Inc.,* November 1995, p. 98.

To find the average payable period, we use the following computation:

$$\text{Average payable period} = \frac{\text{Days in accounting period}}{\text{Payables turnover ratio}}$$
$$= \frac{365 \text{ days}}{6.16 \text{ times/year}}$$
$$= 59.3 \text{ days}$$

Sam's Appliance Shop takes an average of 59 days to pay its accounts with suppliers.

An excessively high average payables period ratio indicates the presence of a significant amount of past-due accounts payable. Although sound cash management calls for a business owner to keep his or her cash as long as possible, slowing payables too drastically can severely damage the company's credit rating. Ideally, the average payable period would match (or exceed) the time it takes to convert inventory into sales and ultimately into cash. In this case, the company's vendors would be financing its inventory and its credit sales. Amazon.com reaps the benefits of this situation; it does not pay its vendors until after it collects from its customers.[18]

One of the most meaningful comparisons for this ratio is against the credit terms suppliers offer (or an average of the credit terms offered). If the average payable ratio slips beyond vendors' credit terms, it is an indication that the company is suffering from a sloppy accounts payable procedure or from cash shortages, and its credit rating is in danger. If this ratio is significantly lower than vendors' credit terms, it may be a sign that the firm is not using its cash most effectively.

We will see the impact that these three operating ratios—inventory turnover, accounts receivable, and accounts payable have on a small company's cash flow in the next chapter.

9. *Net sales to total assets ratio.* A small company's **net sales to total assets ratio (total asset turnover ratio)** is a general measure of its ability to generate sales in relation to its assets. It describes how productively the firm employs its assets to produce sales revenue. The total assets turnover ratio is calculated as follows:

$$\text{Total assets turnover ratio} = \frac{\text{Net sales}}{\text{Net total assets}}$$

$$= \frac{\$1,870,841}{\$847,655}$$

$$= 2.21:1$$

Sam's Appliance Shop is generating $2.21 in sales for every dollar of assets.

The denominator of this ratio, net total assets, is the sum of all of a company's assets (cash, inventory, land, buildings, equipment, tools, and everything it owns) less depreciation. This ratio is meaningful only when compared to that of similar firms in the same industry category. A total assets turnover ratio below the industry average indicates that a small firm is not generating an adequate sales volume for its asset size.

An excessively low net sales to assets ratio indicates that a small firm is not employing its assets efficiently or profitably. On the other hand, an extremely high ratio may indicate an inadequate level of assets to maintain a suitable level of sales, which puts creditors in a more vulnerable position. Monitoring this ratio over time is very helpful in maintaining a sufficient asset base as a small business grows.

Profitability Ratios **Profitability ratios** indicate how efficiently a small company is being managed. They provide the owner with information about a company's bottom line; in other words, they describe how successfully the firm is using its available resources to generate a profit.

10. *Net profit on sales ratio.* The **net profit on sales ratio (profit margin on sales or net profit margin)** measures a company's profit per dollar of sales. The computed percentage shows the portion of each sales dollar remaining after deducting all expenses. The profit margin on sales is calculated as follows:

$$\text{Net profit on sales ratio} = \frac{\text{Net profit}}{\text{Net sales}}$$

$$= \frac{\$60,629}{\$1,870,841}$$

$$= 3.24\%$$

For every dollar in sales Sam's Appliance Shop generates, Sam keeps 3.24 cents in profit.

Many small business owners believe that a high profit margin on sales is necessary for a successful business operation, but this is a myth. To evaluate this ratio properly, an entrepreneur must consider a firm's asset value, its inventory and receivables turnover ratios, and its total capitalization. For example, the typical small supermarket earns an average net profit of only one or two cents on each dollar of sales, but, as we have seen, its inventory turnover ratio is 16 times a year. If a company's profit margin on sales is below the industry average, it may be a sign that its prices are too low, that its costs are excessively high, or both.

> **net sales to total assets (total asset turnover) ratio**
> measures a company's ability to generate sales in relation to its asset base.

> **profitability ratios**
> indicate how efficiently a small company is being managed.

> **net profit on sales ratio (profit margin on sales or net profit margin)**
> measures a company's profit per dollar of sales.

James Wong, co-founder and CEO of Avidian Technologies, a software provider based in Bellevue Washington, monitors the company's net profit margin closely. Avidian Technologies' average annual growth rate has averaged 400 percent for several years, and Wong knows that such fast-paced growth can wreak havoc on a successful company's bottom line. He monitors the company's cash flow daily and never allows its net profit margin to dip below 15 percent. Wong's attentiveness has paid off for Avidian.

COMPANY

Profile

Avidian Technologies

Despite its rapid growth rate, the company has no significant debt and has taken on no outside investors. "I've learned that profitability takes conscious effort," says Wong. "If you just keep growing, for growth's sake, you won't be nearly as profitable."[19]

A natural reaction to low profitability ratios is to embark on a cost-cutting effort. Although minimizing costs can improve profitability, entrepreneurs must be judicious in their cost cutting, taking a strategic approach rather than imposing across-the-board cuts. Cutting costs in areas that are vital to operating success—such as a retail jeweler cutting its advertising expenditures—can inhibit a company's ability to succeed and can lead to failure. For instance, choosing to lay off workers, a common reaction at many companies facing financial challenges, often backfires. Not only does a company risk losing talented workers and the knowledge they have built up over time, but research also shows that repeated rounds of layoffs destroy the morale and the productivity of the remaining workers.[20] In other cases, entrepreneurs on cost-cutting vendettas alienate employees and sap worker morale by eliminating nitpicking costs that affect employees adversely and really do not save much money. The owner of one company thought he would save money by eliminating the free coffee the company provided for its workers. Employee productivity took a hit, however, when workers began taking trips several times a day to a nearby coffee shop. "What a wonderful productivity enhancer!" says one former employee sarcastically.[21]

If a company's net profit on sales ratio is excessively low, the owner first should check the gross profit margin (net sales minus cost of goods sold expressed as a percentage of net sales). Of course, a reasonable gross profit margin varies from industry to industry. For instance, a service company may have a gross profit margin of 75 percent, while a manufacturer's may be 35 percent. The key is to know what a reasonable gross profit margin is for your particular business. If this margin slips too low, it puts a company's future in immediate jeopardy. An inadequate gross profit margin cannot cover all of a company's business expenses and still be able to generate a profit.

Monitoring the net profit margin is especially important for fast-growing companies in which sales are climbing rapidly. Unbridled growth can cause expenses to rise faster than sales, eroding a company's net profit margin. Success can be deceptive: Sales are rising, but profits are shrinking. Ideally, a company reaches a point at which it achieves **operating leverage,** a situation in which increases in operating efficiency mean that expenses as a percentage of sales revenues flatten or even decline. As a result, the company's net profit margin will climb as it grows.

operating leverage
a situation in which increases in operating efficiency mean that expenses as a percentage of sales revenue flatten or even decline.

Mutuals.com

In 1994, when Rick Sapio launched Mutuals.com, a mutual fund advisory and account management service, he was able to raise $14 million in equity capital from private and institutional investors. That largess and the ease with which he raised it gave Sapio an excuse for ignoring the importance of operating leverage. "We were not accountable to being a profitable company at the beginning," he says, "and our energies weren't focused on [analyzing] expenses. We were looking only at revenue." Even though Mutuals.com's sales were growing at an average of 113% a year, the company lost money consistently. Sapio decided to get serious about controlling costs. Every day at 4:37 p.m. just after the markets close, Sapio and his top managers gather to assess the company's financial results for that day, and each person is responsible for reporting one revenue item and one expense item. "Every line item on our financial statement has a name attached to it," says Sapio. Since 1999, the company's revenues have increased 190 percent and expenses are actually dropping about 4 percent a year, producing a solid net profit margin of 15 percent.[22]

net profit to assets ratio
measures how much profit a company generates for each dollar of assets that it owns.

11. *Net profit to assets ratio.* The **net profit to assets ratio (return on assets ratio)** tells how much profit a company generates for each dollar of assets that it owns. This ratio describes how efficiently a business is putting to work all of the assets it owns to generate a profit. It tells how much net income an entrepreneur is squeezing from each dollar's worth of the company's assets. It is calculated as follows:

$$\text{Net profit to assets ratio} = \frac{\text{Net profit}}{\text{Total assets}}$$

$$= \frac{\$60,629}{\$847,655}$$

$$= 7.15\%$$

Sam's Appliance shop earns a return of 7.15 percent on its asset base. This ratio provides clues about the asset intensity of an industry. Return on assets ratios that are below 5 percent are indicative of asset-intense industries that require heavy investments in assets to stay in business (e.g., manufacturing and railroads). Return on assets ratios that exceed 20 percent tend to occur in asset-light industries such as business or personal services—for example, advertising agencies and computer services. A net profit to assets ratio that is below the industry average suggests that a company is not using its assets very efficiently to produce a profit. Another common application of this ratio is to compare it to the company's cost of borrowed capital. Ideally, a company's return on assets ratio (ROA) should exceed the cost of borrowing money to purchase those assets. Companies that experience significant swings in the value of their assets over the course of a year often use an average value of the asset base over the accounting period to get a more realistic estimate of this ratio.

12. **Net profit to equity ratio.** The **net profit to equity ratio (return on net worth ratio)** measures the owners' rate of return on investment (ROI). Because it reports the percentage of the owners' investment in the business that is being returned through profits annually, it is one of the most important indicators of a firm's profitability or a management's efficiency. The net profit to equity ratio is computed as follows:

net profit to equity ratio (return on net worth ratio) measures the owners' rate of return on investment.

$$\text{Net profit to equity ratio} = \frac{\text{Net profit}}{\text{Owner's equity (or net worth)}}$$

$$= \frac{\$60,629}{\$267,655}$$

$$= 22.65\%$$

Sam is earning 22.65 percent on the money he has invested in this business.

This ratio compares profits earned during the accounting period with the amount the owner has invested in the business during that time. If this interest rate on the owners' investment is excessively low, some of this capital might be better employed elsewhere.

Be the Consultant

All Is Not Paradise in Eden's Garden: Part 1

Joe and Kaitlin Eden, co-owners of Eden's Garden, a small nursery, lawn, and garden supply business, have just received their year-end financial statements from their accountant. At their last meeting with their accountant, Shelley Edison, three months ago, the Edens had mentioned that they seemed to be having trouble paying their bills on time. "Some of our suppliers have threatened to put us on 'credit-hold,'" said Joe.

"I think you need to sit down with me very soon and let me show you how to analyze your financial statements so you can see what's happening in your business,"

Edison told them at that meeting. Unfortunately, that was the beginning of Eden's Garden's busy season, and the Edens were so busy running the company that they never got around to setting a time to meet with Shelley.

"Now that business has slowed down a little, perhaps we should call Shelley and see what she can do to help us understand what our financial statements are trying to tell us," said Kaitlin.

"Right. Before it's too late to do anything about it," said Joe, pulling out the following financial statements.

Balance Sheet, Eden's Garden

Assets

Current Assets

Cash		$6,457
Accounts receivable		
Less allowance for	$29,152	
doubtful accounts	$3,200	$25,952
Inventory		$88,157
Supplies		$7,514
Prepaid expenses		$1,856
Total current assets		$129,936

Fixed Assets

Land		$59,150
Buildings	$51,027	
Less accumulated depreciation	$2,061	$48,966
Autos	$24,671	
Less accumulated depreciation	$12,300	$12,371
Equipment	$22,375	
Less accumulated depreciation	$1,250	$21,125
Furniture and fixtures	$10,295	
Less accumulated depreciation	$1,000	$9,295
Total fixed assets		$150,907
Intangibles (goodwill)		$0
Total assets		$280,843

Liabilities

Current Liabilities

Accounts payable	$54,258
Notes payable	$20,150
Credit line payable	$8,118
Accrued wages/salaries payable	$1,344
Accrued interest payable	$1,785
Accrued taxes payable	$1,967
Total current liabilities	$87,622

Long-Term Liabilities

Mortgage	$72,846
Note payable	$47,000
Total long-term liabilities	$119,846

Owner's equity

Sam Lloyd, capital	$73,375
Total liabilities and owner's equity	$280,843

Income Statement, Eden's Garden

Net sales revenue*		$689,247

Cost of Goods Sold

Beginning inventory, 1/1/xx	$78,271	
+ purchases	$403,569	
Goods available for sale	$481,840	
− ending inventory, 12,31/xx	$86,157	
Cost of goods sold		$395,683
Gross profit		$293,564

Operating Expenses

Advertising	$22,150	
Insurance	$9,187	
Depreciation		
Building	$26,705	
Autos	$7,895	
Equipment	$11,200	
Salaries	$116,541	
Uniforms	$4,018	
Repairs and maintenance	$9,097	
Travel	$2,658	
Entertainment	$2,798	
Total operating expenses		$212,249

General Expenses

Utilities	$7,987	
Telephone	$2,753	
Professional fees	$3,000	
Postage	$1,892	
Payroll taxes	$11,589	
Total general expenses		$27,221

Other Expenses

Interest expense	$21,978	
Bad check expense	$679	
Miscellaneous expense	$1,248	
Total other expenses		$23,905
Total expenses		$263,375
Net income		$30,189

*Credit sales represented $289,484 of this total.

1. Assume the role of Shelley Edison. Using the financial statements for Eden's Garden, calculate the 12 ratios covered in this chapter.
2. Do you see any ratios that, on the surface, look suspicious? Explain.

Interpreting Business Ratios

Ratios are useful yardsticks when measuring a small firm's performance and can point out potential problems before they develop into serious crises. But calculating these ratios is not enough to ensure proper financial control. In addition to knowing how to calculate these ratios, entrepreneurs must understand how to interpret them and apply them to managing their businesses more effectively and efficiently.

With the help of financial ratios, Linda Nespole, a top manager at Hi-Shear Technology Inc., an aerospace subcontracting company in Torrance, California, noticed the company's performance beginning to slip. Given the signals her analysis revealed, she immediately devised a strategy to restore Hi-Shear's financial position, focusing first on cost-cutting measures. Simply charting the company's major costs led Nespole to discover leaking water pipes and inefficient lighting that were driving up costs unnecessarily. Some basic repairs lowered utility costs significantly, and a new, more efficient lighting system paid for itself in just six months. Nespole's cost-saving attitude took hold throughout the entire company, and soon all 125 employees were finding ways to keep costs down—from switching long-distance carriers to cutting the cost of its 401(k) retirement plan by 30 percent.[23]

Hi-Shear Technology Inc.

Not every business measures its success with the same ratios. In fact, key performance ratios vary dramatically across industries and even within different segments of the same industry. Entrepreneurs must know and understand which ratios are most crucial to their companies' success and focus on monitoring and controlling those. Sometimes business owners develop ratios and measures that are unique to their own operations to help them achieve success. Known as **critical numbers,** these indicators measure key financial and operational aspects of a company's performance. When these critical numbers are headed in the right direction, a business is on track to achieve its objectives. The owner of a delivery company breaks his business into four categories and tracks critical numbers for each one. Every Monday morning, he gets a report comparing the previous week's critical numbers to those of the previous 28 weeks and the same week for the previous three years. "In 30 seconds, I can see what's going on in every part of my delivery business," he says. "I get another sheet for my storage business because I need to track a different set of numbers there, but the idea is the same."[24] Examples of critical numbers at other companies include the following:

critical numbers
indicators that measure key financial and operational aspects of a company's performance; when these numbers are moving in the right direction, a business is on track to reach its objectives.

- The gross profit margin of a manufacturer of pallets.
- Sales per labor hour at a supermarket.
- The number of new boxes put into storage each week in a records storage business. "Tell me how many new boxes came in during [a particular week]," says Norm Brodsky, owner of a successful records storage company, "and I can tell you our overall sales figure for [that week] within one or two percent of the actual figure."[25]
- Food costs as a percentage of sales for a restaurant. When rising cheese prices pushed food costs as a percentage of sales to 40 percent at Mark Parry's pizza restaurant, he was forced to raise prices. "We're not set to [earn] a profit when we're [operating] at 40 percent food costs," says Parry.[26]
- The utilization ratio, billable hours as a percentage of total hours worked at an Internet service provider.
- The load factor, the percentage of seats filled with passengers, at an airline.[27]

Critical numbers may be different for two companies who compete in the same industry. The key is knowing what *your* company's critical numbers are, monitoring them, and then driving them in the right direction. That requires communicating the importance of these critical numbers to employees and giving them feedback on how well the business is achieving them.

One California retail chain established the daily customer count and the average sale per customer as its critical numbers. The company organized a monthly contest with prizes and posted charts tracking each store's performance. Soon, employees were working hard to improve their stores' performances over the previous year and to outdo other stores in the chain. The healthy rivalry among stores boosted the company's performance significantly.[28]

Another valuable way to use ratios is to compare them with those of similar businesses in the same industry. By comparing the company's financial statistics to industry averages, an entrepreneur is able to locate problem areas and maintain adequate financial controls. "By themselves, these numbers are not that meaningful," says one financial expert of ratios, "but when you compare them to [those of] other businesses in your industry, they suddenly come alive because they put your operation in perspective."[29]

The principle behind calculating these ratios and comparing them to industry norms is the same as that of most medical tests in the health care profession. Just as a healthy person's blood pressure and cholesterol levels should fall within a range of normal values, so should a financially healthy company's ratios. A company cannot deviate too far from these normal values and remain successful for long. When deviations from "normal" do occur (and they will), a business owner should focus on determining the cause of the deviations (see Table 11.3). In some cases, such deviations are the result of sound business decisions, such as taking on inventory in preparation for the busy season, investing heavily in new technology, and others. In other instances, however, ratios that are out of the normal range for a particular type of business are indicators of what could become serious problems for a company. Properly used, ratio analysis can help owners to identify potential problem areas in their businesses early—*before* they become crises that threaten their very survival.

Several organizations regularly compile and publish operating statistics, including key ratios, that summarize the financial performance of many businesses across a wide range of industries. The local library should subscribe to most of these publications:

Risk Management Association. Founded in 1914, the Risk Management Association publishes its *Annual Statement Studies*, showing ratios and other financial data for more than 700 different industrial, wholesale, retail, and service categories that are organized by North American Industry Classification System (NAICS) and Standard Industrial Classification (SIC) code.

Dun & Bradstreet, Inc. Since 1932, Dun & Bradstreet has published *Key Business Ratios*, which covers 22 retail, 32 wholesale, and 71 industrial business categories. Dun & Bradstreet also publishes *Cost of Doing Business*, a series of operating ratios compiled from the IRS's *Statistics of Income*.

Vest Pocket Guide to Financial Ratios. This handy guide, published by Prentice Hall, gives key ratios and financial data for a wide variety of industries.

Industry Spotlight. Published by Schonfeld & Associates, this publication, which can be customized for any one of more than 150 industries, contains financial statement

TABLE 11.3 Putting Your Ratios to the Test

When comparing your company's ratios to your industry's standards, ask the following questions:

1. Is there a significant difference in my company's ratio and the industry average?
2. If so, is this a *meaningful* difference?
3. Is the difference good or bad?
4. What are the possible causes of this difference? What is the most likely cause?
5. Does this cause require that I take action?
6. What action should I take to correct the problem?

Source: Adapted from George M. Dawson, "Divided We Stand," *Business Start-Ups,* May 2000, p. 34.

data and key ratios from more than 95,000 tax returns. *Industry Spotlight* also provides detailed financial information for both profitable companies and those with losses.

Bank of America. Periodically, the Bank of America publishes many documents relating to small business management, including the *Small Business Reporter*, which details costs of doing business ratios.

Trade associations. Virtually every type of business is represented by a national trade association, which publishes detailed financial data compiled from its membership. For example, owners of small supermarkets could contact the National Association of Retail Grocers or check the *Progressive Grocer,* its trade publication, for financial statistics relevant to their operations.

Government agencies. Several government agencies (the Federal Trade Commission, Interstate Commerce Commission, Department of Commerce, Department of Agriculture, and Securities and Exchange Commission) offer a great deal of financial operating data on a variety of industries, although the categories are more general. In addition, the IRS annually publishes *Statistics of Income,* which includes income statement and balance sheet statistics compiled from income tax returns. The Census Bureau also publishes the *Census of Business*, which gives a limited amount of ratio information.

What Do All of These Numbers Mean?

Learning to interpret financial ratios just takes a little practice. This section will show you how it's done by comparing the ratios from the operating data already computed for Sam's to those taken from RMA's *Annual Statement Studies.* (The industry median is the ratio falling exactly in the middle when sample elements are arranged in ascending or descending order.)

Sam's Appliance Shop	Industry Median

Liquidity ratios. These tell whether a small business will be able to meet its maturing obligations as they come due.

1. Current ratio = 1.87:1   1.50:1

    Sam's Appliance Shop falls short of the rule of thumb of 2:1, but its current ratio is above the industry median by a significant amount. Sam's should have no problem meeting its short-term debts as they come due. By this measure, the company's liquidity is solid.

2. Quick ratio = 0.63:1   0.50:1

    Again, Sam's is below the rule of thumb of 1:1, but the company passes this test of liquidity when measured against industry standards. Sam's relies on selling inventory to satisfy short-term debt (as do most appliance shops). If sales slump, the result could be liquidity problems for Sam's. Sam should consider building a cash reserve as a precautionary measure.

Leverage ratios. These measure the financing supplied by a firm's owners against that supplied by its creditors and serve as a gauge of the depth of a company's debt.

3. Debt ratio = 0.68:1   0.64:1

    Creditors provide 68 percent of Sam's total assets, very close to the industry median of 64 percent. Although Sam's does not appear to be overburdened with debt, the company might have difficulty borrowing additional money, especially from conservative lenders.

4. Debt to net worth ratio = 2.20:1   1.90:1

    Sam's Appliance Shop owes creditors $2.20 for every $1.00 the owner has invested in the business (compared to $1.90 in debt to every $1.00 in equity for the typical business). Although this is not an exorbitant amount of debt, many lenders and creditors will see Sam's as "borrowed up." The company's borrowing capacity is limited because creditors' claims against the business are more than twice those of the owners. Sam should consider increasing his owner's equity in the business through retained earnings or by paying down some of the company's debt.

5. Times interest earned ratio = 2.52:1   2.0:1

   Sam's earnings are high enough to cover the interest payments on its debt by a factor of 2.52, slightly better than the typical firm in the industry, whose earnings cover its interest payments just two times. Sam's Appliance Shop has a cushion (although a small one) in meeting its interest payments.

   Operating ratios. These evaluate the firm's overall performance and show how effectively it is putting its resources to work.

6. Average inventory turnover ratio = 2.05 times/year   4.0 times/year

   Inventory is moving through Sam's at a very slow pace, *half* that of the industry median. The company has a problem with slow-moving items in its inventory and, perhaps, too much inventory. Which items are they, and why are they slow-moving? Does Sam need to drop some product lines? Sam must analyze his company's inventory and reevaluate his inventory control procedures.

7. Average collection period ratio = 50.0 days   19.3 days

   Sam's Appliance Shop collects the average account receivable after 50 days (compared with the industry median of 19 days), more than two and one-half times longer. A more meaningful comparison is against Sam's credit terms; if credit terms are net 30 (or anywhere close to that), Sam's has a dangerous collection problem, one that drains cash and profits and demands *immediate* attention! He must implement the cash management procedures you will learn about in Chapter 12.

8. Average payable period ratio = 59.3 days   43 days

   Sam's payables are nearly 40 percent slower than those of the typical firm in the industry. Stretching payables too far could seriously damage the company's credit rating, causing suppliers to cut off future trade credit. This could be a sign of cash flow problems or a sloppy accounts payable procedure. This problem also demands *immediate* attention. Once again, Sam must implement proper cash management procedures to resolve this problem.

9. Net sales to total assets ratio = 2.21:1   2.7:1

   Sam's Appliance Shop is not generating enough sales, given the size of its asset base. This could be the result of a number of factors—improper inventory, inappropriate pricing, poor location, poorly trained sales personnel, and many others. The key is to find the cause . . . *Fast!*

   Profitability ratios. These measure how efficiently a firm is operating and offer information about its bottom line.

10. Net profit on sales ratio = 3.24%   7.6%

    After deducting all expenses, 3.24 cents of each sales dollar remains as profit for Sam's—less than half the industry median. Sam should check his company's gross profit margin and investigate its operating expenses, checking them against industry standards and looking for those that are out of balance.

11. Net profit to assets ratio = 7.15%   5.5%

    Sam's generates just a return of 7.15% for every $1 in assets, which is 30 percent above the industry average. Given his asset base, Sam is squeezing an above-average return out of his company. This could be an indication that Sam's is highly profitable; however, given the previous ratio, this is unlikely. It is more likely that Sam's asset base is thinner than the industry average.

12. Net profit to equity ratio = 22.65%   12.6%

    Sam's Appliance Shop's owners are earning 22.65 percent on the money they have invested in the business. This yield is nearly twice that of the industry median,

© www.CartoonStock.com

"This one pretty much sums it up."

and, given the previous ratio, is more a result of the owners' relatively low investment in the business than an indication of its superior profitability. Sam is using O.P.M. (Other People's Money) to generate a profit in his business.

When comparing ratios for their individual businesses to published statistics, small business owners must remember that the comparison is made against averages. An entrepreneur should strive to achieve ratios that are at least as good as these average figures. The goal should be to manage the business so that its financial performance is above average. As they compare their company's financial performance to those covered in the published statistics, they inevitably will discern differences between them. They should note those items that are substantially out of line from the industry average. However, a ratio that varies from the average does not *necessarily* mean that the small business is in financial jeopardy. Instead of making drastic changes in financial policy, entrepreneurs must explore *why* the figures are out of line.

Greg Smith, CEO of Petra Group, a systems integrator with $1.5 million in annual sales, once gave little thought to comparing his company's financial performance against industry standards. Then, Petra Group's sales flattened and Smith's company faced the prospect of losing money for the first time. Smith worked with an accounting firm, using information from the Risk Management Association and a nonprofit organization that provides similar studies, to analyze his company's financial position. Comparing his numbers to industry statistics, Smith quickly saw that his payroll expenses for his 15-person company were too high to allow the company to generate a profit. He also discovered that Petra Group's debt ratio was too high. To restore his company's financial strength, Smith reduced his staff by two and began relying more on temporary employees and independent contractors. He realigned Petra Group's financing, reducing the company's line of credit from $100,000 to just $35,000. The analysis also revealed several strengths for the company. For instance, the company's average collection period was 36.5 days, compared to an industry average of 73 days. Smith continues to use ratio comparisons to make key decisions for his company, and he credits the initial financial analysis with getting his company back on the track to profitability.[30]

COMPANY
Profile

Petra Group

FIGURE 11.7

Trend Analysis of Ratios

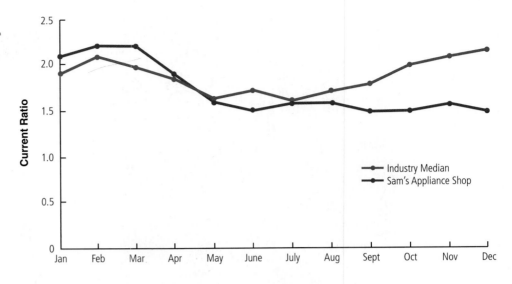

In addition to comparing ratios to industry averages, owners should analyze their firms' financial ratios over time. By themselves, these ratios are "snapshots" of a company's financial position at a single instant; but by examining these trends over time, an entrepreneur can detect gradual shifts that otherwise might go unnoticed until a financial crisis is looming (see Figure 11.7).

Be the Consultant

All Is Not Paradise in Eden's Garden: Part 2

Remember Joe and Kaitlin Eden, co-owners of Eden's Garden? Assume the role of Shelley Edison, their accountant. Tomorrow, you have scheduled a meeting with them to review their company's financial statements and to make recommendations about how they can improve their company's financial position. Use the following worksheet to summarize the ratios you calculated earlier in this chapter. Then, compare them against the industry averages from the Risk Management Association's *Annual Statement Studies.*

Ratio Comparison

Ratio	Eden's Garden	Garden Supply Industry Median*
Liquidity Ratios		
Current ratio		1.4
Quick ratio		0.5
Leverage Ratios		
Debt ratio		0.6
Debt to net worth ratio		1.8
Times interest earned ratio		2.6

Operating Ratios	
Average inventory turnover ratio	5.6
Average collection period ratio	9 days
Average payable period ratio	17 days
Net sales to total assets ratio	3.0
Profitability Ratios	
Net profit on sales ratio	7.5%
Net profit to assets ratio	9.1%
Net profit to equity ratio	15.0%

*Risk Management Association's *Annual Statement Studies.*

1. Analyze the comparisons you have made of Eden's Garden's ratios with those from the Risk Management Association. What "red flags" do you see?

2. What might be causing the deviations you have observed?

3. What recommendations can you make to the Edens to improve their company's financial performance in the future?

Break-Even Analysis

Another key component of every sound financial plan is a break-even analysis. A small company's **break-even point** is the level of operation (sales dollars or production quantity) at which it neither earns a profit nor incurs a loss. At this level of activity, sales revenue equals expenses, that is, the firm "breaks even." By analyzing costs and expenses, an entrepreneur can calculate the minimum level of activity required to keep the firm in operation. These techniques can then be refined to project the sales needed to generate the desired profit. Most potential lenders and investors will require entrepreneurs to prepare a break-even analysis to assist them in evaluating the earning potential of the new business. In addition to its being a simple, useful screening device for financial institutions, break-even analysis can also serve as a planning device for the small business owner. It occasionally will show a poorly prepared entrepreneur just how unprofitable a proposed business venture is likely to be.

Calculating the Break-Even Point

A small business owner can calculate a firm's break-even point by using a simple mathematical formula. To begin the analysis, the owner must determine fixed costs and variable costs. **Fixed expenses** are those that do not vary with changes in the volume of sales or production (e.g., rent, depreciation expense, interest payments). **Variable expenses,** on the other hand, vary directly with changes in the volume of sales or production (e.g., raw material costs, sales commissions).

Some expenses cannot be neatly categorized as fixed or variable because they contain elements of both. These semivariable expenses change, although not proportionately, with changes in the level of sales or production (electricity is one example). These costs remain constant up to a particular production or sales volume, and then climb as that volume is exceeded. To calculate the break-even point, an entrepreneur must separate these expenses into their fixed and variable components. A number of techniques can be used (which are beyond the scope of this text), but a good cost accounting system can provide the desired results.

Here are the steps an entrepreneur must take to compute the break-even point using an example of a typical small business, the Magic Shop:

Step 1 Determine the expenses the business can expect to incur. With the help of a budget, an entrepreneur can develop estimates of sales revenue, cost of goods sold, and expenses for the upcoming accounting period. The Magic Shop expects net sales of $950,000 in the upcoming year, with a cost of goods sold of $646,000 and total expenses of $236,500.

Step 2 Categorize the expenses estimated in Step 1 into fixed expenses and variable expenses. Separate semivariable expenses into their component parts. From the budget, the owner anticipates variable expenses (including the cost of goods sold) of $705,125 and fixed expenses of $177,375.

Step 3 Calculate the ratio of variable expenses to net sales. For the Magic Shop, this percentage is $705,125 ÷ $950,000 = 74 percent. So the Magic Shop uses $0.74 out of every sales dollar to cover variable expenses, leaving $0.26 as a contribution margin to cover fixed costs and make a profit.

Step 4 Compute the break-even point by inserting this information into the following formula:

$$\text{Break-even sales (\$)} = \frac{\text{Total fixed cost}}{\text{Contribution margin expressed as percentage of sales}}$$

For the Magic Shop,

$$\text{Break-even sales (\$)} = \frac{\$177,375}{0.26}$$

$$= \$682,212$$

LEARNING OBJECTIVES
6. Conduct a break-even analysis for a small company.

break-even point
the level of operation (sales dollars or production quantity) at which a company neither earns a profit nor incurs a loss.

fixed expenses
expenses that do not vary with changes in the volume of sales or production.

variable expenses
expenses that vary directly with changes in the volume of sales or production.

Thus, the Magic Shop will break even with sales of $682,212. At this point, sales revenue generated will just cover total fixed and variable expense. The Magic Shop will earn no profit and will incur no loss. We can verify this with the following calculations:

Sales at break-even point	$ 682,212
− Variable expenses (74% of sales)	−504,837
Contribution margin	177,375
− Fixed expenses	−177,375
Net profit (or net loss)	$ 0

Adding in a Profit

What if the Magic Shop's owner wants to do *better* than just break even? His analysis can be adjusted to consider such a possibility. Suppose the owner expects a reasonable profit (before taxes) of $80,000. What level of sales must the Magic Shop achieve to generate this? He can calculate this by treating the desired profit as if it were a fixed cost. In other words, he modifies the formula to include the desired net income:

$$\text{Sales (\$)} = \frac{\text{Total fixed expenses } + \text{ Desired net income}}{\text{Contribution margin expressed as a percentage of sales}}$$

$$= \frac{\$177,375 + \$80,000}{0.26}$$

$$= \$989,904$$

To achieve a net profit of $80,000 (before taxes), the Magic Shop must generate net sales of $989,904.

Break-Even Point in Units

Some small businesses may prefer to express the break-even point in units produced or sold instead of in dollars. Manufacturers often find this approach particularly useful. The following formula computes the break-even point in units:

$$\text{Break-even volume} = \frac{\text{Total fixed costs}}{\text{Sales price per unit } - \text{ Variable cost per unit}}$$

For example, suppose that Trilex Manufacturing Company estimates its fixed costs for producing its line of small appliances at $390,000. The variable costs (including materials, direct labor, and factory overhead) amount to $12.10 per unit, and the selling price per unit is $17.50. So, Trilex computes its contribution margin in the following way:

$$\text{Contribution margin} = \text{price per unit } - \text{ variable cost per unit}$$

$$= \$17.50 \text{ per unit } - \$12.10 \text{ per unit}$$

$$= \$5.40 \text{ per unit}$$

So, Trilex's break-even volume is as follows:

$$\text{Break-even volume} = \frac{\text{Total fixed costs}}{\text{Per unit contribution margin}}$$

$$= \frac{\$390,000}{\$5.40 \text{ per unit}}$$

$$= 72,222 \text{ units}$$

To convert this number of units to break-even sales dollars, Trilex simply multiplies it by the selling price per unit:

$$\text{Break-even sales} = 72,222 \text{ units} \times \$17.50 \text{ per unit} = \$1,263,889$$

Trilex could compute the sales required to produce a desired profit by treating the profit as if it were a fixed cost:

$$\text{Sales (units)} = \frac{\text{Total fixed costs} + \text{Desired net income}}{\text{Per unit contribution margin}}$$

For example, if Trilex wanted to earn a $60,000 profit, its required sales would be:

$$\text{Sales (units)} = \frac{\$390,000 + \$60,000}{\$5.40 \text{ per unit}} = 83,333 \text{ units}$$

which would require 83,333 units $\times$ $17.50 per unit = $1,458,328 in sales.

Constructing a Break-Even Chart

The following steps outline the procedure for constructing a graph that visually portrays the firm's break-even point (that point where revenues equal expenses):

Step 1 On the horizontal axis, mark a scale measuring sales volume in dollars (or in units sold or some other measure of volume). The break-even chart for the Magic Shop shown in Figure 11.8 uses sales volume in dollars because it applies to all types of businesses, departments, and products.

Step 2 On the vertical axis, mark a scale measuring income and expenses in dollars.

Step 3 Draw a fixed expense line intersecting the vertical axis at the proper dollar level parallel to the horizontal axis. The area between this line and the horizontal axis represents the firm's fixed expenses. On the break-even chart for the Magic Shop shown in Figure 11.8, the fixed expense line is drawn horizontally beginning at $177,375 (point *A*). Because this line is parallel to the horizontal axis, it indicates that fixed expenses remain constant at all levels of activity.

Step 4 Draw a total expense line that slopes upward beginning at the point where the fixed-cost line intersects the vertical axis. The precise location of the total expense line is determined by plotting the total cost incurred at a particular sales volume. The total cost for a given sales level is found by using the following formula:

Total = Fixed expenses + Variable expenses expressed as a % of sales

$\qquad \times$ Sales level expenses

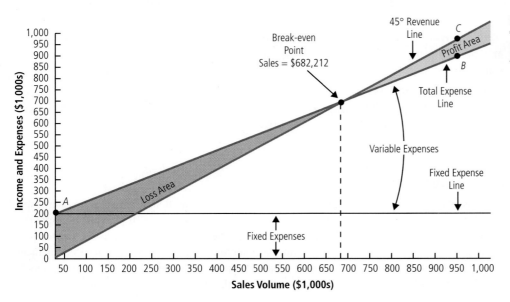

FIGURE 11.8

Break-Even Chart for the Magic Shop

At an arbitrarily chosen sales level of $950,000, the Magic Shop's total costs would be as follows:

$$\text{Total expenses} = \$177,375 + (0.74 \times \$950,000)$$
$$= \$880,375$$

Thus, the Magic Shop's total cost is $880,375 at a net sales level of $950,000 (point *B*). The variable-cost line is drawn by connecting points *A* and *B*. The area between the total cost line and the horizontal axis measures the total costs the Magic Shop incurs at various levels of sales. For example, if the Magic Shop's sales are $850,000, its total costs will be $806,375.

Step 5 Beginning at the graph's origin, draw a 45-degree revenue line showing where total sales volume equals total income. For the Magic Shop, point *C* shows that sales = income = $950,000.

Step 6 Locate the break-even point by finding the intersection of the total-expense line and the revenue line. If the Magic Shop operates at a sales volume to the left of the break-even point, it will incur a loss because the expense line is higher than the revenue line over this range. This is shown by the triangular section labeled Loss Area. On the other hand, if the firm operates at a sales volume to the right of the break-even point, it will earn a profit because the revenue line lies above the expense line over this range. This is shown by the triangular section labeled Profit Area.

Be the Consultant

Where Do We Break Even?

Anita Dawson is doing some financial planning for her music store. Based on her budget for the upcoming year, Anita is expecting net sales of $495,000. She estimates that cost of goods sold will be $337,000 and that other variable expenses will total $42,750. Using the previous year as a guide, Anita anticipates fixed expenses of $78,100.

Anita recalls an earlier meeting with her accountant, who mentioned that her store had already passed the break-even point eight and one-half months into the year. She was pleased, but really didn't know how the accountant had come up with that calculation. Anita is considering expanding her store into a vacant building next to her existing location and taking on three new product lines. The company's cost structure would change, adding another $66,000 to fixed costs and $22,400 to variable expenses. Anita believes the expansion could generate additional sales of $102,000.

She wonders what she should do.

1. Calculate Anita's break-even point without the expansion plans. Draw a break-even chart.
2. Compute the break-even point assuming that Anita decides to expand.
3. Would you recommend that Anita expand her business? Explain.

Using Break-Even Analysis

Break-even analysis is a useful planning tool for the potential small business owner, especially when approaching potential lenders and investors for funds. It provides an opportunity for integrated analysis of sales volume, expenses, income, and other relevant factors. Break-even analysis is a simple, preliminary screening device for the entrepreneur faced with the business start-up decision. It is easy to understand and use. With just a few calculations, the small business owner can determine the effects of various financial strategies on the business operation. It is a helpful tool for evaluating the impact of changes in investments and expenditures. Greg Smith, for instance, knows that Petra Group's break-even point is $23,000 per week, and he compares sales to that figure every week.[31]

Calculating the break-even point for a start-up business is important because it tells an entrepreneur the minimum volume of sales required to stay in business in the long run.

PowerNap Sleep Centers

Steve RamsDell, founder of PowerNap Sleep Centers, tested his unique business concept—providing spaces for weary travelers to catch a nap—at the Boca Raton International Airport. "We do much more than just give people a place to rest," says RamsDell. "It's like a mini-vacation." The company's DreamSuites are decorated in various themes, including Asian Mist and Tropical Isle. Amenities include aromatherapy, massage tables, recordings of nature sounds, and alarm clocks, and the price is 70 cents per minute. Before setting up a subsidiary, minneNAPolis, in the Mall of America, the largest mall in the United States, located in Bloomington, Minnesota, RamsDell calculated that he would have to sell $700 of nap time to tired shoppers to break even. Given the mall's 4.3 miles of retail stores and attractions, RamsDell thinks he will hit his break-even point quickly. "We're appealing to people who shop all day until they're tired," explains RamsDell.[32]

Break-even analysis does have certain limitations. It is too simple to use as a final screening device because it ignores the importance of cash flows. In addition, the accuracy of the analysis depends on the accuracy of the revenue and expense estimates. Finally, the assumptions pertaining to break-even analysis may not be realistic for some businesses. Break-even calculations assume the following: fixed expenses remain constant for all levels of sales volume; variable expenses change in direct proportion to changes in sales volume; and changes in sales volume have no effect on unit sales price. Relaxing these assumptions does not render this tool useless, however. For example, the owner could employ nonlinear break-even analysis using a graphical approach.

Chapter Summary by Learning Objectives

1. Understand the importance of preparing a financial plan.

Launching a successful business requires an entrepreneur to create a solid financial plan. Not only is such a plan an important tool in raising the capital needed to get a company off the ground, but it also is an essential ingredient in managing a growing business.

Earning a profit does not occur by accident; it takes planning.

2. Describe how to prepare the basic financial statements and use them to manage a small business.

Entrepreneurs rely on three basic financial statements to understand the financial conditions of their companies:

1. *The balance sheet.* Built on the accounting equation Assets = Liabilities + Owner's equity (Capital), it provides an estimate of the company's value on a particular date.
2. *The income statement.* This statement compares the firm's revenues against its expenses to determine its net profit (or loss). It provides information about the company's bottom line.

3. *The statement of cash flows.* This statement shows the change in the company's working capital over the accounting period by listing the sources and the uses of funds.

3. Create projected (pro forma) financial statements.

Projected financial statements are a basic component of a sound financial plan. They help the manager plot the company's financial future by setting operating objectives and by analyzing the reasons for variations from targeted results. In addition, the small business in search of start-up funds will need these pro forma statements to present to prospective lenders and investors. They also assist in determining the amount of cash, inventory, fixtures, and other assets the business will need to begin operation.

4. Understand the basic financial statements through ratio analysis.

The 12 key ratios described in this chapter are divided into four major categories: *liquidity ratios,* which show the small firm's ability to meet its current obligations; *leverage ratios,* which tell how much of the company's financing is provided by owners and how much by creditors; *operating ratios,* which show how effectively the firm uses its resources; *and profitability ratios,* which disclose the company's profitability.

Many agencies and organizations regularly publish such statistics. If there is a discrepancy between the small firm's ratios and those of the typical business, the owner should investigate the reason for the difference. A below-average ratio does not necessarily mean that the business is in trouble.

5. Explain how to interpret financial ratios.

To benefit from ratio analysis, the small company should compare its ratios to those of other companies in the same line of business and look for trends over time.

When business owners detect deviations in their companies' ratios from industry standards, they should determine the cause of the deviations. In some cases, such deviations are the result of sound business decisions; in other instances, however, ratios that are out of the normal range for a particular type of business are indicators of what could become serious problems for a company.

6. Conduct a break-even analysis for a small company.

Business owners should know their firm's break-even point, the level of operations at which total revenues equal total costs; it is the point at which companies neither earn a profit nor incur a loss. Although just a simple screening device, break-even analysis is a useful planning and decision-making tool.

Discussion Questions

1. Why is developing a financial plan so important to an entrepreneur about to launch a business?
2. How should a small business manager use the 12 ratios discussed in this chapter?
3. Outline the key points of the 12 ratios discussed in this chapter. What signals does each give the manager?
4. Describe the method for building a projected income statement and a projected balance sheet for a beginning business.
5. Why are pro forma financial statements important to the financial planning process?
6. How can break-even analysis help an entrepreneur planning to launch a business?

Business Plan Pro

 One of the significant advantages Business Plan Pro offers is the efficient creation of pro forma financial statements including the balance sheet, profit and loss statement, and cash flow statement. Once you enter the revenues, expenses, and other relevant figures, your financial statements are done! This can save an incredible amount of time, and the format is one that is commonly recognized and respected by bankers and investors. The simplicity of this process also enables you to create "what if" scenarios based on various levels of anticipated revenues and expenses simply by saving versions of your business plan under unique file names.

Business Plan Exercises
On the Web

Go to http://www.bplans.com/bc/# or use the link at http://www.prenhall.com/scarborough under the Business Plan Resource tab, Finance and Business Calculators. Here you will find a collection of online tools including a Break Even Calculator. Open this tool and enter the information it requests—the average per unit revenue, the average per unit cost, and the estimated monthly fixed costs you anticipate. This tool will calculate your break-even point in units and revenue. Change the data and observe the difference it makes in your break-even point. What does this tell you about the level of risk that you may experience based on the most realistic projections you can make?

In the Software

Select a sample plan that you have found to be interesting. Go to the "Financial Plan" section and look at their financial statements within the text of the business plan. Notice how the statements are organized. Month-to-month detail is provided for at least the first year with annual totals for subsequent years. Also note the associated tables and graphics that appear within the financial plan. Graphics can be excellent communication tools, particularly when you are communicating information about financial trends and comparisons.

Building Your Business Plan

Review all information that you have within the "Financial Plan" section of your business plan. Add any "Important Assumptions" to this section as you deem necessary. This is a good place to make notes and comments to test or further research any of these assumptions. If you are in the start-up stage, capture the costs that you expect will be incurred to launch your business. The "Investment Offering" may appear, based on your choice in the Plan Wizard, and you can complete that information. Review your information for your break-even analysis and then review the financial statements including your profit and loss, cash flow, and balance sheet statements.

This chapter identifies 12 key business ratios. Based on your projections, determine each of those ratios. Compare them to industry standard ratios. Most, if not all, of these ratios are available through Business Plan Pro's "ratio" section, the final topic in the "Financial Plan" section.

Ratio Analysis

	Your Projected Ratio	Industry Ratio	Variance
1. Current ratio	_____	_____	_____
2. Quick ratio	_____	_____	_____
3. Debt ratio	_____	_____	_____
4. Deb to net worth ratio	_____	_____	_____
5. Times interest earned ratio	_____	_____	_____
6. Average inventory turnover ratio	_____	_____	_____
7. Average collection period ratio	_____	_____	_____
8. Average payable period ratio	_____	_____	_____
9. Net sales to total assets ratio	_____	_____	_____
10. Net profit on sales ratio	_____	_____	_____
11. Net profit to assets ratio	_____	_____	_____
12. Net profit to equity ratio	_____	_____	_____

If you notice significant differences in these comparisons, determine why those variances exist. Might this be telling you something about the reality of your projections, or is this just due to the stage and differences of your business compared to the larger industry? These ratios can be excellent tools for helping you to question, test, and validate your assumptions and projections. Good business planning, solid projections, and a thorough analysis of these ratios can help you to launch a more viable business with greater certainty of the outcome.

Beyond the Classroom . . .

1. Ask the owner of a small business to provide your class with copies of the firm's financial statements (current or past).

   - Using these statements, compute the 12 key ratios described in this chapter.
   - Compare the company's ratios with those of the typical firm in this line of business.
   - Interpret the ratios and make suggestions for operating improvements.
   - Prepare a break-even analysis for the owner.

2. Find a publicly held company of interest to you that provides its financial statements on the Web. You can conduct a Web search using the company's name or you can find lists of companies at the Securities and Exchange Commission's EDGAR database at http://www.sec.gov/cgi-bin/srch-edgar or you can visit the Report Gallery at AnnualReports.com at http://www.reportgallery.com/. Analyze the company's financial statements by calculating the 12 ratios covered in this chapter and compare these ratios to industry averages found in RMA's *Annual Statement Studies* or Dun & Bradstreet's *The Cost of Doing Business* reports. Do you spot any problem areas? Strengths? What recommendations can you make to improve the company's financial position? What do you project the company's future to be?

12 | Managing Cash Flow

A deficit is what you have when you haven't got as much as when you had nothing.
—Gerald F. Lieberman

Cash is king, but barter is the next best thing.
—Krista Vardabash

Learning Objectives

On completion of this chapter, you will be able to:

1 Explain the importance of cash management to a small company's success.
2 Differentiate between cash and profits.
3 Understand the five steps in creating a cash budget and use them to create one.
4 Describe fundamental principles involved in managing the "big three" of cash management: accounts receivable, accounts payable, and inventory.
5 Explain the techniques for avoiding a cash crunch in a small company.

Cash—a four-letter word that has become a curse for many small businesses. Lack of this valuable asset has driven countless small companies into bankruptcy. Unfortunately, many more firms will become failure statistics because their owners have neglected the principles of cash management that can spell the difference between success and failure. "Everything is about cash," says entrepreneur turned venture capitalist Guy Kawasaki, "raising it, conserving it, collecting it."[1] Indeed, developing a cash forecast is essential for new businesses because early on companies usually do not generate sufficient cash to stay afloat. A common cause of business failures, especially in start-up and fast-growth companies, is overemphasis on increasing sales with little concern for collecting the receivables those sales create. Another problem is that owners neglect to forecast how much cash their companies will need until they reach the point of generating positive cash flow. The result is always the same: a cash crisis.

Salon.com, one of the first e-magazines, was founded in 1995 by David Talbot and several of his colleagues from the *San Francisco Examiner* and has struggled with cash flow since it began. The magazine, which has lost more than $83 million and has experienced negative cash flow since its inception, burned through the cash generated from its initial public offering in 1999. The company, which generates half of its revenue from online advertisements, saw its cash balance drop precipitously when online advertising dipped industry-wide in 2000. The balance of Salon.com's revenue comes from subscriptions to its online articles and user forums, although the number of subscribers fell to 30,000 from 140,000 when the company began charging for its content. Managers at the company say that the number of paying subscribers has since rebounded to 74,000. To have enough cash to pay its bills, Salon.com on several occasions has had to rely on eleventh-hour cash infusions from investors, including Adobe Systems founder John Arnock and William Hambrecht, founder of the underwriting firm that handled Salon.com's initial public offering. In its struggle to survive, the company has made many attempts to conserve cash, including cutting its staff from 175 people to 65, imposing 15 percent cuts in salaries, and even renegotiating rental payments on its headquarters. Its cost-cutting and revenue-enhancing efforts are paying off; after a decade, Salon.com finally has reached the break-even point.[2]

Salon.com

As you learned in the previous chapter, controlling the financial aspects of a business using the traditional analysis of basic financial statements with ratios is immensely important; however, by themselves, these techniques are insufficient for achieving business success. Entrepreneurs are prone to focus on their companies' income statements—particularly sales and profits. The income statement, of course, shows only part of a company's financial picture. It is entirely possible for a business to earn a profit and still go out of business *by running out of cash*. In other words, managing a company's total financial performance effectively requires an entrepreneur to look beyond the "bottom line" and focus on what it takes to keep a company going—cash.

Monitoring your cash flow statement "is more important than watching your income statement or balance sheet," says Scott Trenner, owner of S.T. Lube, a company that operates six Jiffy Lube franchises. Trenner knows firsthand the importance of positive cash flow. His company ran into serious cash flow problems as he focused on rapid growth. "I was building a multi-million-dollar empire," he recalls, "but my revenues never caught up with my expenses." Cash was so tight that Trenner had trouble meeting the payroll for his company's 65 employees. "I once had to get a two-week, $30,000 loan from my father when we were struggling," he recalls. The turning point came when Trenner created a statement to track and analyze his company's cash flow. "We stopped focusing only on expansion and started paying attention to day-to-day management," he says. "By keeping a close eye on our cash flow statement, we went from a negative cash flow to a positive cash flow of $1,000 a week and turned around a $140,000 deficit in three years."[3]

S.T. Lube

cash management
the process of forecasting, collecting, disbursing, investing, and planning for the cash a company needs to operate smoothly.

Cash Management

A survey by the National Federation of Independent Businesses found that 67 percent of small business owners say they have at least occasional problems managing cash flow; 19 percent of business owners report cash flow as a continuing problem.[4] The only way to avoid this potentially business-crushing predicament is by using the principles of cash management. **Cash management** involves forecasting, collecting, disbursing, investing, and planning for the cash a company needs to operate smoothly. Cash management is a vital task because cash is the most important yet least productive asset that a small business owns. A business must have enough cash to meet its obligations or it will be declared bankrupt. Creditors, employees, and lenders expect to be paid on time, and cash is the required medium of exchange. However, some firms retain an excessive amount of cash to meet any unexpected circumstances that might arise. These dormant dollars have an income-earning potential that owners are ignoring, and this restricts a firm's growth and lowers its profitability. Investing these dollars, even for a short time, can add to a company's earnings. Proper cash management permits the owner to adequately meet the cash demands of the business, avoid retaining unnecessarily large cash balances, and stretch the profit-generating power of each dollar the business owns.

Although cash flow difficulties afflict companies of all sizes and ages, young companies, especially, are cash sponges, soaking up every available dollar and always hungry for more. The reason usually is that their cash-generating "engines" are not operating at full speed yet and cannot provide enough power to generate the cash necessary to cover rapidly climbing operating expenses. Entrepreneurs must manage cash flow from the day they launch their businesses.

Entrepreneurs must manage cash flow from the day they launch their businesses. More companies fail for a lack of cash than for a lack of profit!

Shortly after he launched his new company on June 16, 1903, entrepreneur Henry Ford ran headlong into a cash crisis that nearly wiped out the Ford Motor Company. Start-up expenses (including $10,000 to the Dodge brothers for engines and other parts and $640 to the Hartford Rubber Works for 64 tires) quickly soaked up Ford's $28,000 in start-up capital he and 11 associates invested, and by July 10, the company's cash balance had fallen to a mere $223.65. Another payroll and more parts orders were just around the corner, and the 25-day-old company was already on the brink of a financial collapse. On July 11, an investor saved the day with a $5,000 contribution. Four days later the Ford Motor Company sold its first car to Dr. E. Pfennig of Chicago, pushing the company's cash balance to $6,486.44. From this shaky financial beginning grew one of the largest automakers in the world.[5]

COMPANY Profile

Ford Motor Company

Managing cash flow is also an acute problem for rapidly growing businesses. In fact, fast-track companies are most likely to suffer cash shortages. Many successful, growing, and profitable businesses fail because they become insolvent; they do not have adequate cash to meet the needs of a growing business with a booming sales volume. If a company's sales are up, its owner also must hire more employees, expand plant capacity, increase the sales force, build inventory, and incur other drains on the firm's cash supply. During rapid growth, cash collections typically fall behind, compounding the problem. Cash flows out of these high-growth companies much faster than it comes in. The head of the National Federation of Independent Businesses says that many small business owners "wake up one day to find that the price of success is no cash on hand. They don't understand that if they're successful, inventory and receivables will increase faster than profits can fund them."[6] The resulting cash crisis may force the owner to lose equity control of the business or, ultimately, declare bankruptcy and close. Table 12.1 shows how to calculate the additional cash required to support an increase in sales.

The first step in managing cash more effectively is to understand the company's **cash flow cycle**—the time lag between paying suppliers for merchandise or materials and receiving payment from customers for the product or service (see Figure 12.1). The longer this cash

cash flow cycle
the time lag between paying suppliers for merchandise or materials and receiving payment from customers.

TABLE 12.1 How Much Cash Is Required to Support an Increase in Sales?

Too often, entrepreneurs believe that increasing sales is the ideal solution to a cash crunch only to discover (often after it is too late) that it takes extra cash to support extra sales. This worksheet demonstrates how to calculate the amount of additional cash required to support an increase in sales.

To make the calculation, a business owner needs the following information:

- The increase in sales planned ($)
- The time frame for adding new sales (days)
- The company's gross profit margin, gross profit ÷ net sales (%)
- The estimated additional expenses required to generate additional sales ($)
- The company's average collection period (days)

To calculate the amount of additional cash needed, use the following formula:

Extra cash required = [(New sales − Gross profit + Extra overhead) × (Average collection period × 1.20*)] ÷ (Time frame in days for adding new sales)

*The extra 20 percent is added as a cushion.

Consider the following example:

The owner of Ardent Company wants to increase sales by $75,000 over the next year. The company's gross profit margin is 30 percent of sales (so its gross profit on these additional sales would be $75,000 × 30% = $22,500), its average collection period is 47 days, and managers estimate that generating the additional sales will require an increase in expenses of $21,300. The additional cash that Ardent will need to support this higher level of sales is

Extra cash required = [($75,000 − $22,500 + 21,300) × (47 × 1.2)] ÷ 365 = $11,404

Advent will need $11,404 in extra cash to support the additional sales of $75,000 it plans to bring in over the next year.

Source: Adapted from Norm Brodsky, "Paying for Growth: How Much Cash You Need to Carry New Sales," Inc. Online Tools & Apps: Worksheet, http://www.inc.com/tools/details/0,6152,CNT61_HOMI_LOC0_NAVhome_TOL11648,00.html.

FIGURE 12.1

The Cash Flow Cycle

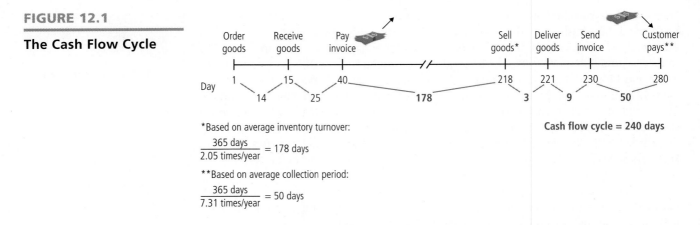

*Based on average inventory turnover:

$$\frac{365 \text{ days}}{2.05 \text{ times/year}} = 178 \text{ days}$$

Cash flow cycle = 240 days

**Based on average collection period:

$$\frac{365 \text{ days}}{7.31 \text{ times/year}} = 50 \text{ days}$$

flow cycle, the more likely it is that the business owner will encounter a cash crisis. Preparing a cash forecast that recognizes this cycle, however, will help to avoid a crisis. Understanding the cash flow patterns of a business over the course of a year is essential to creating a successful cash management strategy. Business owners should calculate their cash flow cycles whenever they prepare their financial statements (or at least quarterly). On a *daily* basis, business owners should generate a report showing the following items: total cash on hand, bank balance, summary of the day's sales, summary of the day's cash receipts, summary of the day's cash disbursements, and a summary of accounts receivable collections. Compiling these reports into monthly summaries provides the basis for making reliable cash forecasts.

The next step in effective cash management is to analyze the cash flow cycle, looking for ways to reduce its length. Reducing the cycle from 240 days to, say, 150 days would free up incredible amounts of cash that this company could use to finance growth and dramatically reduce its borrowing costs. What steps would you suggest the owner of the business whose cash flow cycle is illustrated in Figure 12.1 take to reduce its length?

Table 12.2 describes the five key cash management roles every entrepreneur must fill.

TABLE 12.2 Five Cash Management Roles of the Entrepreneur

Role 1: Cash Finder

As an entrepreneur, this is your first and foremost responsibility. You must make sure there is enough capital to pay all present (and future) bills. This is not a one-time task; it is an ongoing job.

Role 2: Cash Planner

As cash planner, you need to make sure the company's cash is used properly and efficiently. You must keep track of its cash, make sure it is available to pay bills, and plan for its future use. Planning requires you to forecast the company's cash inflows and outflows for the months ahead with the help of a cash budget (discussed elsewhere in this chapter).

Role 3: Cash Distributor

This role requires you to control the cash needed to pay the company's bills and the priority and the timing of those payments. Forecasting cash disbursements accurately and making sure the cash is available when payments come due are essential to keeping the business solvent.

Role 4: Cash Collector

As cash collector, your job is to make sure your customers pay *their* bills on time. Too often, entrepreneurs focus on pumping up sales while neglecting to collect the cash from those sales. Having someone in your company responsible for collecting accounts receivable is essential. Uncollected accounts drain a small company's pool of cash very quickly.

Role 5: Cash Conserver

This role requires you to make sure your company gets maximum value for the dollars it spends. Whether you are buying inventory to resell or computers to keep track of what you sell, it is important to get the most for your money. Avoiding unnecessary expenditures is an important part of this task. The goal is to spend cash so it will produce a return for the company.

Source: Adapted from Bruce J. Blechman, "Quick Change Artist," *Entrepreneur,* January 1994, pp. 18–21.

FIGURE 12.2

Cash Flow

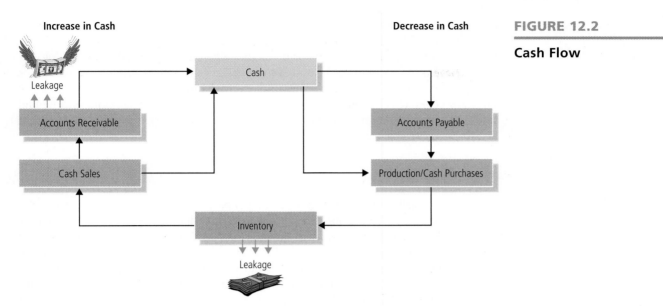

Increase in Cash   **Decrease in Cash**

Cash and Profits Are Not the Same

When analyzing cash flow, entrepreneurs must understand that cash and profits are not the same. Attempting to discern the status of a small company's cash position by analyzing its profitability is futile; profitability is not necessarily highly correlated with cash flow. Profit (or net income) is the difference between a company's total revenue and its total expenses. It measures how efficiently a business is operating. Cash is the money that is free and readily available to use in a business. **Cash flow** measures a company's liquidity and its ability to pay its bills and other financial obligations on time by tracking the flow of cash into and out of the business over a period of time. Many small business owners soon discover that profitability does not guarantee liquidity. As important as earning a profit is, no business owner can pay suppliers, creditors, employees, the government, and lenders in profits; that requires *cash*! Although profits are tied up in many forms, such as inventory, computers, or machinery, cash is the money that flows through a business in a continuous cycle without being tied up in any other asset. "Businesses fail not because they are making or losing money," warns one financial expert, "but because they simply run out of cash."[7]

Figure 12.2 shows the flow of cash through a typical small business. Cash flow is the volume of actual cash that comes into and goes out of the business during an

cash flow
a method of measuring a company's liquidity and its ability to pay its bills and other financial obligations on time by tracking the flow of cash into and out of the business over a period of time.

"Well, gentlemen, there's your problem."

accounting period. Decreases in cash occur when the business purchases, on credit or for cash, goods for inventory or materials for use in production. A business sells the resulting inventory either for cash or on credit. When a company takes in cash or collects payments on accounts receivable, its cash balance increases. Notice that purchases for inventory and production *lead* sales; that is, these bills typically must be paid *before* sales are generated. On the other hand, collection of accounts receivable *lags* behind sales; that is, customers who purchase goods on credit may not pay until the next month.

The Cash Budget

The need for a cash budget arises because in every business the cash flowing in is rarely "in sync" with the cash flowing out. This uneven flow of cash creates periodic cash surpluses and shortages, making it necessary for entrepreneurs to track the flow of cash through their businesses so they can project realistically the cash available throughout the year. Many entrepreneurs operate their businesses without knowing the pattern of their cash flows, believing that the process is too complex or time consuming. In reality, entrepreneurs simply cannot afford to disregard the process of cash management. They must ensure that their businesses have on hand an adequate but not excessive supply of cash to meet their operating needs. The goal of cash management is to have enough cash available to meet the company's cash needs at a given time.

How much cash is enough? What is suitable for one business may be totally inadequate for another, depending on each firm's size, nature, seasonal pattern of sales, and particular situation. The small business manager should prepare a **cash budget,** which is nothing more than a "cash map" showing the amount and the timing of the cash receipts and the cash disbursements day by day, week by week, or month by month. It is used to predict the amount of cash the firm will need to operate smoothly over a specific period of time, and it is a valuable tool in managing a company successfully. A cash budget can illuminate a host of approaching problems, giving entrepreneurs adequate time to handle, or better yet, avoid them. A cash budget reveals important clues about how well a company balances its accounts payable and accounts receivable, controls inventory, finances its growth, and makes use of the cash it has.

cash budget
a "cash map" showing the amount and the timing of cash receipts and cash disbursements on a daily, weekly, or monthly basis.

One consultant recalls how a cash budget helped salvage a once-successful service firm that had fallen on hard times. The five-year-old firm with $20 million in annual billings began to lose money and was having trouble paying its bills. After working with the consultant, the company began sending customer invoices much faster and implemented a much stricter collection policy. The new collection system involved employees in collecting overdue payments and took immediate action when an account became overdue. Managers set up a receivables report and reviewed it at weekly staff meetings. They also beefed up the company's financial reports, added a cash budget, and used it to make managerial decisions. Within six months, the company's cash balance had improved dramatically (a turnaround of $1.5 million), managers were able to pay down a line of credit at the bank, and the business was back on track.

Preparing a Cash Budget

LEARNING OBJECTIVES
3. Understand the five steps in creating a cash budget and use them to create one.

Typically, small business owners should prepare a projected monthly cash budget for at least one year into the future and quarterly estimates for another. The forecast must cover all seasonal sales fluctuations. The more variable a firm's sales pattern, the shorter should be its planning horizon. For example, a firm whose sales fluctuate widely over a relatively short time frame might require a weekly cash budget. The key is to track cash flows over time. The timing of a company's cash flow is as important as the amounts. "An alert cash flow manager keeps an eye not on cash receipts or on cash demands as average quantities but on cash as a function of the *calendar*," says one business owner.[8]

Regardless of the time frame selected, a cash budget must be in writing for an entrepreneur properly to visualize a company's cash position. Creating a written cash plan is not an excessively time-consuming task and can help the owner to avoid unexpected cash shortages, a situation that can cause a business to fail. One financial consultant describes "a client who won't be able to make the payroll this month. His bank agreed to meet the payroll for him—but banks don't like to be surprised like that," he adds.[9] Preparing a cash budget will help business owners to avoid such adverse surprises and will also let an owner know if he or she is keeping excessively large amounts of cash on hand. Computer spreadsheets such as those generated by Microsoft Excel and others make the job fast and easy to complete and allow entrepreneurs to update their cash flow forecasts with very little time and effort.

A cash budget is based on the cash method of accounting, which means that cash receipts and cash disbursements are recorded in the forecast *only when the cash transaction is expected to take place*. For example, credit sales to customers are not reported until the company expects to receive the cash from them. Similarly, purchases made on credit are not recorded until the owner expects to pay them. Because depreciation, bad debt expense, and other noncash items involve no cash transfers, they are omitted entirely from the cash budget.

A cash budget is nothing more than a forecast of the firm's cash inflows and outflows for a specific time period, and it will never be completely accurate. However, it does give an entrepreneur a clear picture of a company's estimated cash balance for the period, pointing out where external cash infusions may be required or where surplus cash balances may be available to invest. Also, by comparing actual cash flows with projections, an owner can revise the forecast so that future cash budgets will be more accurate.

Computer Gallery

Joseph Popper, CEO of Computer Gallery, knows how deadly running out of cash can be for a small company and does everything he can to make sure his business avoids that trap. Popper uses a computer spreadsheet to extract key sales, collection, and disbursement totals and to generate the resulting cash balance each day. Even when he is traveling, Popper keeps up with his company's daily cash balance. He has the spreadsheet results sent to an Internet service, which E-mails them to his alphanumeric pager every day he is out of the office. "We've been paranoid about cash from day one," Popper says. But his system keeps accounts receivable in control, ensures that the company's available cash is working hard, and improves his relationship with the company's banker.[10]

Formats for preparing a cash budget vary depending on the pattern of a company's cash flow. Table 12.3 shows a monthly cash budget for a small department store over a four-month period. Each monthly column should be divided into two sections—estimated and actual (not shown)—so that each succeeding cash forecast can be updated according to actual cash transactions. Comparing forecasted amounts to actual cash flows and learning the causes of any significant discrepancies allows entrepreneurs to improve the accuracy of future cash budgets. There are five basic steps in completing a cash budget:

1. Determining an adequate minimum cash balance.
2. Forecasting sales.
3. Forecasting cash receipts.
4. Forecasting cash disbursements.
5. Determining the end-of-month cash balance.

Step 1. Determining an Adequate Minimum Cash Balance

What is considered an excessive cash balance for one small business may be inadequate for another, even though the two firms are in the same industry. Some suggest that a firm's cash balance should equal at least one-fourth of its current debts, but this general rule clearly will not work for all small businesses. The most reliable method of

TABLE 12.3 Cash Budget for Small Department Store

Assumptions:

Cash balance on December 31 = $12,000

Minimum cash balance desired = $10,000

Sales are 75% credit and 25% cash.

Credit sales are collected in the following manner,

- 60% collected in the first month after the sale
- 30% collected in the second month after the sale
- 5% collected in the third month after the sale
- 5% are never collected

Sales forecasts are follows:	Pessimistic	Most Likely	Optimistic
October (actual)		$300,000	
November (actual)		350,000	
December (actual)		400,000	
January	$120,000	150,000	$175,000
February	160,000	200,000	250,000
March	160,000	200,000	250,000
April	250,000	300,000	340,000

The store pays 70% of sales price for merchandise purchased and pays for each month's anticipated sales in the preceding month.

Rent is $2,000 per month.

An interest payment of $7,500 is due in March.

A tax prepayment of $50,000 must be made in March.

A capital addition payment of $130,000 is due in February.

Utilities expenses amount to $850 per month.

Miscellaneous expenses are $70 per month.

Interest income of $200 will be received in February.

Wages and salaries are estimated to be

   January—$30,000

   February—$40,000

   March—$45,000

   April—$50,000

deciding the right minimum cash balance is based on past experience. Past operating records will indicate the cash cushion an entrepreneur needs to cover any unexpected expenses after all normal cash outlays are deducted from the month's cash receipts. For example, past records may indicate that it is desirable to maintain a cash balance equal to five days' sales. Seasonal fluctuations may cause a firm's minimum cash balance to change. For example, the desired cash balance for a retailer in December may be greater than in June.

Step 2. Forecasting Sales

The heart of the cash budget is the sales forecast. It is the central factor in creating an accurate picture of the firm's cash position because sales ultimately are transformed into cash receipts and cash disbursements. For most businesses, sales constitute the major source of the cash flowing into the business. Similarly, sales of merchandise require that cash to be used to replenish inventory. As a result, the cash budget is only as accurate as the sales forecast from which it is derived.

TABLE 12.3 *Continued*

Cash Budget—Passimistic Sales Forecast

	Oct.	Nov.	Dec.	Jan.	Feb.	Mar.	Apr.
Cash Receipts:							
Sales	$300,000	$350,000	$400,000	$120,000	$160,000	$160,000	$250,000
Credit Sales	225,000	262,500	300,000	90,000	120,000	120,000	187,500
Collections:							
60%—1st month after sale				$180,000	$54,000	$ 72,000	$ 72,000
30%—2nd month after sale				78,750	90,000	27,000	36,000
5%—3rd month after sale				11,250	13,125	15,000	4,500
Cash Sales				30,000	40,000	40,000	62,500
Interest				0	200	0	0
Total Cash Receipts				$300,000	$197,325	$154,000	$175,000
Cash Disbursements:							
Purchases				$112,000	$112,000	$175,000	$133,000
Rent				2,000	2,000	2,000	2,000
Utilities				850	850	850	850
Interest				0	0	7,500	0
Tax Prepayment				0	0	50,000	0
Capital Addition				0	130,000	0	0
Miscellaneous				70	70	70	70
Wages/Salaries				30,000	40,000	45,000	50,000
Total Cash Disbursements				$144,920	$284,920	$280,420	$185,920
End-of-Month Balance:							
Cash (beginning of month)				$ 12,000	$167,080	$ 79,485	$ 10,000
+ Cash Receipts				300,000	197,325	154,000	175,000
− Cash Disbursements				144,920	284,920	280,420	185,920
Cash (end of month)				167,080	79,485	(46,935)	(920)
Borrowing/Repayment				0	0	56,935	10,920
Cash (and of month [after borrowing])				$167,080	$ 79,485	$ 10,000	$ 10,000

(Continues)

For an established business, a sales forecast is based on past sales, but owners must be careful not to be excessively optimistic in projecting sales. Economic swings, increased competition, fluctuations in demand, normal seasonal variations, and other factors can drastically affect sales patterns and, therefore, a company's cash flow. Most businesses, from retailers and hotels to accounting firms and builders, have sales patterns that are "lumpy" and not evenly distributed throughout the year. For instance, costume makers generate almost all of their sales before Halloween but must invest in the raw materials and the labor to make the costumes in the spring and summer months, when their cash balances are at their lowest.[11] The typical wine and spirits shop makes 15 to 18 percent of its total sales volume for the entire year between December 15 and December 31.[12] For fireworks companies, the three weeks before July 4 account for the majority of annual sales, with another smaller peak occurring before New Year's Eve.[13] Forty percent of all toy sales take place in the last six weeks of the year, and companies that make fruitcakes typically generate 50 percent to 90 percent of their sales during the holiday season.[14] For companies with such highly seasonal sales patterns, proper cash management is an essential activity.

TABLE 12.3 *Continued*

Cash Budget—Most Likely Sales Forecast

	Oct.	Nov.	Dec.	Jan.	Feb.	Mar.	Apr.
Cash Receipts:							
Sales	$300,000	$350,000	$400,000	$150,000	$200,000	$200,000	$300,000
Credit Sales	225,000	262,500	300,000	112,000	150,000	150,000	225,000
Collections:							
60%—Ist month after sale				$180,000	$ 67,500	$ 90,000	$ 90,000
30%—2nd month after sale				78,750	90,000	33,750	45,000
5%—3rd month after sale				11,250	13,125	15,000	5,625
Cash Sales				37,500	50,000	50,000	75,000
Interest				0	200	0	0
Total Cash Receipts				$307,500	$220,825	$188,750	$215,625
Cash Disbursements:							
Purchases				$140,000	$140,000	$210,000	$175,000
Rent				2,000	2,000	2,000	2,000
Utilities				850	850	850	850
Interest				0	0	7,500	0
Tax Prepayment				0	0	50,000	0
Capital Addition				0	130,000	0	0
Miscellaneous				70	70	70	70
Wages/Salaries				30,000	40,000	45,000	50,000
Total Cash Disbursements				$172,920	$312,920	$315,420	$227,920
End-of-Month Balance:							
Cash (beginning of month)				$ 12,000	$146,580	$ 54,485	$ 10,000
+ Cash Receipts				307,500	220,825	188,750	215,625
− Cash Disbursements				172,920	312,920	315,420	227,920
Cash (end of month)				146,580	54,485	(72,185)	(2,295)
Borrowing/Repayment				0	0	82,185	12,295
Cash (end of month [after borrowing])				$146,580	$ 54,485	$ 10,000	$ 10,000

67 Wine and Spirits

During the holiday season, Bernie Weisner, owner of 67 Wine and Spirits in New York City, must increase his shop's inventory by more than $500,000 above normal. Because his suppliers require payment in 30 days, Weisner must manage his company's cash flow carefully and must make sure that he purchases items that will sell quickly. Still, he relies on a line of credit to ensure that 67 Wine and Spirits avoids a cash crisis. "It's good to have a friendly bank," he says.[15]

Several quantitative techniques, which are beyond the scope of this text (linear regression, multiple regression, time series analysis, exponential smoothing), are available to owners of existing businesses with an established sales pattern for forecasting sales. These methods enable the small business owner to extrapolate past and present sales trends to arrive at a fairly accurate sales forecast.

The task of forecasting sales for a new firm is more difficult but not impossible. For example, the new owner might conduct research on similar firms and their sales patterns in the first year of operation to come up with a forecast. The local chamber of commerce and trade associations in the various industries also collect such information.

TABLE 12.3 *Continued*

Cash Budget—Optimistic Sales Forecast

	Oct.	Nov.	Dec.	Jan.	Feb.	Mar.	Apr.
Cash Receipts:							
Sales	$300,000	$350,000	$400,000	$175,000	$250,000	$250,000	$340,000
Credit Sales	225,000	262,500	300,000	131,250	187,500	187,500	255,000
Collections:							
60%—1st month after sale				$180,000	$ 78,750	$112,500	$112,500
30%—2nd month after sale				78,750	90,000	39,375	56,250
5%—3rd month after sale				11,250	13,125	15,000	6,563
Cash Sales				43,750	62,500	62,500	85,000
Interest				0	200	0	0
Total Cash Receipts				$313,750	$244,575	$229,375	$260,313
Cash Disbursements:							
Purchases				$175,000	$175,000	$238,000	$217,000
Rent				2,000	2,000	2,000	2,000
Utilities				850	850	850	850
Interest				0	0	7,500	0
Tax Prepayment				0	0	50,000	0
Capital Addition				0	130,000	0	0
Miscellaneous				70	70	70	70
Wages/Salaries				30,000	40,000	45,000	50,000
Total Cash Disbursements				$207,920	$347,920	$343,420	$269,920
End-of-Month Balance:							
Cash (beginning of month)				$ 12,000	$117,830	$ 14,485	$ 10,000
+ Cash Receipts				313,750	244,575	229,375	296,125
− Cash Disbursements				207,920	317,920	343,120	269,920
Cash (end of month)				117,830	14,485	(99,560)	36,205
Borrowing/Repayment				0	0	109,560	0
Cash (end of month [after borrowing])				$117,830	$ 14,485	$ 10,000	$ 36,205

Publications such as RMA's *Annual Statement Studies*, which profiles financial statements for companies of all sizes in hundreds of industries, is also a useful tool. Market research is another source of information that may be used to estimate annual sales for the fledgling firm. Other potential sources that may help to predict sales include census reports, newspapers, radio and television customer profiles, polls and surveys, and local government statistics. Talking with owners of similar businesses (outside the local trading area, of course) can provide entrepreneurs with realistic estimates of start-up sales. Table 12.4 provides an example of how one entrepreneur used such marketing information to derive a sales forecast for his first year of operation.

No matter what techniques entrepreneurs employ, they must recognize that even the best sales estimates will be wrong. Many financial analysts suggest that the owner create *three* estimates—an optimistic, a pessimistic, and a most likely sales estimate—and then make a separate cash budget for each forecast (a very simple task with a computer spreadsheet). This dynamic forecast enables the owner to determine the range within which sales will likely be as the year progresses.

TABLE 12.4 Forecasting Sales for a Business Start-up

Robert Adler wants to open a repair shop for imported cars. The trade association for automotive garages estimates that the owner of an imported car spends an average of $485 per year on repairs and maintenance. The typical garage attracts its clientele from a trading zone (the area from which a business draws its customers) within a 20-mile radius. Census reports show that the families within a 20-mile radius of Robert's proposed location own 84,000 cars, of which 24 percent are imports. Based on a local consultant's market research, Robert believes he can capture 9.9 percent of the market this year. Robert's estimate of his company's first year's sales are as follows:

Number of cars in trading zone	84,000 autos
× Percent of imports	× 24%
= Number of imported cars in trading zone	20,160 imports
Number of imports in trading zone	20,160 imports
× Average expenditure on repairs and maintenance	× $485
= Total import repair sales potential	$9,777,600
Total import repair sales potential	$9,777,600
× Estimated share of the market	× 9.9%
= Sales estimate	$967,982

Now Robert Adler can convert this annual sales estimate of $967,982 into monthly sales estimates for use in his company's cash budget.

Be the Consultant

The Big Bang and Cash Flow Management

It is one week before the Independence Day holiday, and CEO Bruce Zoldan is monitoring the heavy rush of customer traffic at the Phantom Fireworks outlet in Youngstown, Ohio. In the three-week period leading up to July 4, the small chain of fireworks stores will face a heavy flood of customers pouring through its doors from 7 AM until midnight, all of them looking for the ingredients for a brilliant Fourth of July fireworks celebration. During this three-week burst of activity, Phantom Fireworks will sell more than 25 million pounds of fireworks, and sales at any one of its 41 stores often reach $400,000 a day.

After the peak Independence Day holiday, however, sales at many Phantom stores typically plummet to just $5,000 a day. That's when the real work for Zoldan and his staff begins. "We have 11 months of logistics for one month of sales," he says. Not only does gearing up for a one-month sales blitz require lots of advance planning, it also demands some clever cash management techniques. Even though sales are concentrated in just one month of the year, Phantom Fireworks expenses continue year-round.

The process begins shortly after the July Fourth peak season, when Alan Zoldan, the company's executive vice-president and Bruce Zoldan's brother, flies to China to place orders for the next year. On a typical 10-day trip, Alan will watch thousands of sample fireworks, busily scribbling notes while suppliers show off their latest fireworks creations. In his notes, Alan marks the most promising products with either three stars ("pretty good") or four stars ("a keeper"). He even jots down potential names that Phantom can give to the products as they come to him. "Cometary Chaos" is one name that came to him recently and ended up as the name the company used to market the fiery explosives.

The Zoldan brothers became fascinated with fireworks as children when their father, a traveling salesman, would bring them home, and many neighbors asked to buy them. When Bruce was in college, he began selling fireworks out of the trunk of his mother's car and then opened his first fireworks retail store in 1979. At the time, just 23 states allowed fireworks sales; today, 43 states permit the sale of fireworks. In the 1990s, as the Web was beginning to take off, Bruce had the foresight to register the domain name fireworks.com. Today the company's Web site gets millions of hits a year (not surprisingly, most of them occur in the weeks leading up to July 4) and is the Phantom Fireworks most important marketing tool. Bruce says that a potential buyer offered the company "seven figures" for the rights to the fireworks.com domain name, but he refuses to sell. "If they offered me $10 million, I wouldn't do it," he says.

Selling fireworks in the off-season remains a challenge, although the company does see a much smaller peak just before New Year's Eve. Phantom Fireworks conserves its advertising dollars by sending clever—and cheap—e-mail ads. During the Christmas holidays, Phantom sends out 80,000 holiday cards that include a $50 gift card. To promote the company in the fall, when Phantom places most of its product orders, the company sponsors a contest offering prizes to customers who suggest the best names for its new fireworks products. One recent winner, Bada-Bing, Bada-Boom, apparently was inspired by television show *The Sopranos*. The company offers a "no-duds, money-back guarantee" on everything it sells.

In March, fireworks shipments begin arriving from China, where most fireworks producers are located. After passing through several inspections and spot-

checks by U.S. Customs, the fireworks arrive at Phantom Firework's 12 warehouses. There, professional "shooters" test-fire samples of the shipments. After adding safety and instructional fliers to the packages, the fireworks are then sent to the individual stores. To boost sales during the peak season, Phantom mails VIP cards to its best customers, those purchasing at least $400 worth of fireworks, entitling them to discounts. (According to Zoldan, 65 percent of Phantom's customers are male.) A few customers really splurge on their personal fireworks show. Stephen Rehman, from Baltimore, recently purchased more than $4,400 worth of fireworks for a July 4 fireworks party he was planning for 400 guests.

1. What impact do highly seasonal sales such as those at Phantom Fireworks have on a small company's cash flow?
2. What advice can you offer the Zoldans about coping with the effects of Phantom Fireworks' highly irregular sales patterns? About managing cash flow in general?

Source: Adapted from Gwendolyn Bounds, "Preparing for the Big Bang," *Wall Street Journal*, June 29, 2004, pp, B1, B7.

Step 3. Forecasting Cash Receipts

As noted earlier, sales constitute the primary source of cash receipts. When a firm sells goods and services on credit, the cash budget must account for the delay between the sale and the actual collection of the proceeds. Remember: You cannot spend cash you haven't collected yet! For instance, an appliance store might not collect the cash from a refrigerator sold in February until April or May, and the cash budget must reflect this delay. To project accurately cash receipts, an entrepreneur must analyze accounts receivable to determine the company's collection pattern. For example, past records may indicate that 20 percent of sales are for cash, 50 percent are paid in the month following the sale, 20 percent are paid two months after the sale, 5 percent are paid after three months, and 5 percent are never collected. In addition to cash and credit sales, a small business may receive cash in a number of forms—interest income, rental income, dividends, and others.

Collecting accounts receivable promptly poses problems for many small companies; in fact, difficulty in collecting accounts receivable is the primary cause of cash flow problems cited by small business owners (see Figure 12.3).[16] Figure 12.4 demonstrates the

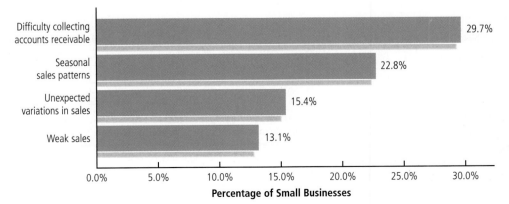

FIGURE 12.3

Causes of Cash Flow Problems in Small Business

Source: National Federation of Independent Businesses, *National Small Business Poll: The Cash Flow Problem* (Washington, DC: Author, 2002), p. 7.

FIGURE 12.4

Collecting Delinquent Accounts

Source: Commercial Collection Agency Section of the Commercial Law League of America.

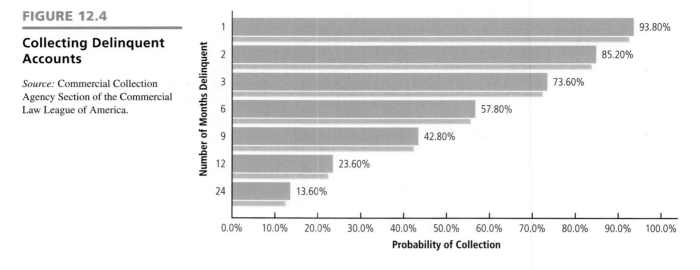

importance of acting promptly once an account becomes past due. Notice how the probability of collecting an outstanding account diminishes the longer the account is delinquent. Table 12.5 illustrates the high cost of failing to collect accounts receivable on time.

Verse Group

When Randy Ringer created the business plan for Verse Group, a two-year-old marketing consulting firm in New York City, he created cash flow forecasts on the assumption that clients would pay their invoices within 30 days. As he researched the industry further, Ringer discovered that most clients took twice as long to pay their bills, and he and his partner revised their business plan to reflect the slower accounts receivable. They decided to keep six months' worth of cash on hand, double the original amount they had planned to maintain. Before launching Verse Group, Ringer and his partner also decided to establish a policy of pre-billing certain jobs that require a substantial investment up front to bring in cash more quickly. "Slow receivables," says Ringer, "have changed the way we do business."[17]

TABLE 12.5 Managing Accounts Receivable

Are your customers who purchase on credit paying late? If so, these outstanding accounts receivable probably represent a significant leak in your company's cash flow. Slow-paying customers, in effect, are borrowing money from your business interest-free. They are using your money without penalty while you forgo opportunities to place it in interest-earning investments or must pay interest on money you must borrow to replace the missing funds. Exactly how much is poor credit control costing your company? The answer may surprise you.

The first step is to calculate your company's average collection period ratio (See "Operating Ratios" section in Chapter 11). The second step is to age your accounts receivable to determine how many accounts are current and how many are overdue. The following example shows how to use these numbers to calculate the cost of past due accounts for a company whose credit terms are "net 30":

Average collection period	65 days
− credit terms	− 30 days
Excess in accounts receivable	35 days
Average daily sales of $21,500* × 35 days	$752,500
× Normal rate of return	× 8%
Annual cost of excess	$60,200

Slow-paying customers are costing this company more than $60,000 a year! If your business is highly seasonal, quarterly or monthly figures may be more meaningful than annual ones.

---

*Average daily sales = Annual sales ÷ 365 days = $7,847,500 ÷ 365 = $21,500

Source: Adapted from "Financial Control," *Inc.* Reprinted with permission of the publisher.

Step 4. Forecasting Cash Disbursements

Most owners of established businesses have a clear picture of the firm's pattern of cash disbursements. In fact, many cash payments, such as rent, loan repayments, and interest, are fixed amounts due on specified dates. The key factor when forecasting disbursements for a cash budget is to record them in *the month in which they will be paid, not when the obligation is incurred*. Of course, the number of cash disbursements varies with each particular business, but the following disbursement categories are standard: purchase of inventory or raw materials; wages and salaries; rent, taxes, loans, and interest; selling expenses; fixed-asset purchases; overhead expenses; and miscellaneous expenses.

Usually, an owner's tendency is to underestimate cash disbursements, which can result in a cash crisis. To prevent this, wise entrepreneurs cushion their cash disbursement accounts, assuming they will be higher than expected. This is particularly important for entrepreneurs opening new businesses. In fact, some financial analysts recommend that new owners estimate cash disbursements as best they can and then add another 10 to 25 percent of the total. Whatever forecasting technique is used, entrepreneurs must avoid underestimating cash disbursements, which may lead to severe cash shortages and possible bankruptcy.

Sometimes business owners have difficulty developing initial forecasts of cash receipts and cash disbursements. One of the most effective techniques for overcoming the "I don't know where to begin" hurdle is to make a *daily* list of the items that generated cash (receipts) and those that consumed it (disbursements).

Susan Bowen, CEO of Champion Awards, a $9 million T-shirt screen printer, monitors cash flow by tracking the cash that flows into and out of her company every day. Focusing on keeping the process simple, Bowen sets aside a few minutes each morning to track updates from the previous day on four key numbers:

- Accounts Receivable:
  1. What did we bill yesterday?
  2. How much did we actually collect?
- Accounts payable:
  3. What invoices did we receive yesterday?
  4. How much in total did we pay out?

If Bowen observes the wrong trend—more new bills than new sales or more money going out than coming in—she makes immediate adjustments to protect her cash flow. The benefits produced (not the least of which is the peace of mind in knowing that no cash crisis is looming) more than outweigh the ten minutes she invests in the process every day. "I've tried to balance my books every single day since I started my company in 1970," says Bowen.[18]

COMPANY
Profile

Champion Awards

Step 5. Estimating the End-of-Month Cash Balance

To estimate a company's cash balance for each month, a business owner first must determine the cash balance at the beginning of each month. The beginning cash balance includes cash on hand as well as cash in checking and savings accounts. As development of the cash budget progresses, the cash balance at the end of a month becomes the beginning balance for the following month. Next, the owner simply adds total cash receipts and subtracts total cash disbursements to obtain the end-of-month balance before any borrowing takes place. A positive amount indicates that the firm has a cash surplus for the month, but a negative amount shows a cash shortage will occur unless the owner is able to collect or borrow additional funds.

Normally, a firm's cash balance fluctuates from month to month, reflecting seasonal sales patterns. Such fluctuations are normal, but business owners must watch closely for patterns of increases and decreases in the cash balance over time. A trend of increases indicates that the small firm has ample cash that could be placed in some income-earning investment. On the other hand, a pattern of cash decreases should alert the owner that the business is approaching a cash crisis.

A cash budget not only illustrates the flow of cash into and out of the small business, but it also allows the owner to *anticipate* cash shortages and cash surpluses. "Then," explains a small business consultant, "you can go to the bank and get a 'seasonal' line of credit for six months instead of twelve. Right there you can cut your borrowing costs in half."[19] By planning cash needs ahead of time, a small business is able to achieve the following benefits:

- Increase the amount and the speed of cash flowing into the company.
- Reduce the amount and the speed of cash flowing out of the company.
- Make the most efficient use of available cash.
- Take advantage of money-saving opportunities, such as quantity and cash discounts.
- Finance seasonal business needs.
- Develop a sound borrowing program.
- Develop a workable program of debt repayment.
- Impress lenders and investors with its ability to plan and repay financing.
- Provide funds for expansion.
- Plan for investing surplus cash.

"Cash flow spells survival for every business," claims one expert. "Manage cash flow effectively, and your business works. If your cash flow is not well managed, then sooner or later your business goes under. It's that simple."[20] Unfortunately, most small business owners forego these benefits because they fail to manage their cash properly. One recent study reported that just 32 percent of all small businesses owners used some formal technique for tracking their companies' cash flow.[21] Because cash flow problems usually sneak up on a business over time, improper cash management often proves to be a costly—and fatal—mistake.

Be the Consultant

In Search of a Cash Flow Forecast

"I'll never make that mistake again," Douglas Martinez said to himself as he got into his car. Martinez had just left a meeting with his banker, who had not been optimistic about the chances of Martinez's plumbing supply company getting the loan it needed. "I should have been better prepared for the meeting," he muttered, knowing that he could be angry only at himself. "That consultant at the Small Business Development Center was right. Bankers' primary concern when making loans is cash flow."

"At least I salvaged the meeting by telling him I wasn't ready to officially apply for a loan yet," Martinez thought. "But I've got a lot of work to do. I've got a week to figure out how to put together a cash budget to supplement my loan application. Maybe that consultant can help me."

When he returned to his office, Martinez gathered up the file folders containing all of his fast-growing company's financial reports and printed his projected revenues and expenses using his computer spreadsheet. Then he called the SBDC consultant he had worked with when he was launching his company and explained the situation. When he arrived at the consul-

tant's office that afternoon, they started organizing the information. Here is what they came up with:

Current cash balance	$8,750
Sales pattern	71% on credit and 29% in cash
Collections of credit sales	68% in the same month as the sale 19% in the first month after the sale 7% in the second month after the sale 6% never collected (bad debts)

Sales forecasts:

	Pessimistic	Most Likely	Optimistic
July (actual)	—	$18,750	—
August (actual)	—	$19,200	—
September (actual)	—	$17,840	—
October	$15,000	$17,500	$19,750
November	$14,000	$16,500	$18,500
December	$11,200	$13,000	$14,000
January	$ 9,900	$12,500	$14,900
February	$10,500	$13,800	$15,800
March	$13,500	$17,500	$19,900

Utilities expenses	$800 per month.
Rent	$1,200 per month
Truck loan	$317 per month

Estimated wages and salaries (including payroll taxes):		Computer supplies	$75 per month
October	$2,050	Advertising	$550 per month
November	$1,825	Legal and accounting fees	$250 per month
December	$1,725	Miscellaneous expenses	$60 per month
January	$1,725		
February	$1,950		
March	$2,425		

The company pays 63 percent of the sales price for the inventory it purchases, an amount that it actually pays in the following month. (Martinez has negotiated "net 30" credit terms with his suppliers.)

A tax payment of $1,400 is due in December

Martinez has established a minimum cash balance of $2,000 and can borrow money at an interest rate of 8.75 percent

Other expenses:

Insurance premiums	$1,200, payable in August and February.
Office supplies	$95 per month
Maintenance	$75 per month

"Well, what do you think?" Douglas asked the consultant.

1. Assume the role of the SBDC consultant and help Douglas to put together a cash budget for the six months beginning in October.
2. What conclusions can you draw about Douglas' business from this cash budget?
3. What suggestions can you make to help Douglas improve his company's cash flow?

The "Big Three" of Cash Management

It is unrealistic for business owners to expect to trace the flow of every dollar through their businesses. However, by concentrating on the three primary causes of cash flow problems, they can dramatically lower the likelihood of experiencing a devastating cash crisis. The "big three" of cash management are accounts receivable, accounts payable, and inventory. A firm should always try to accelerate its receivables and to stretch out its payables. A good cash management "recipe" involves collecting your company's cash as quickly as possible, economizing to keep costs low, and paying out your company's cash as slowly as possible. Business owners also must monitor inventory carefully to avoid tying up valuable cash in an excessive supply of inventory.

Accounts Receivable

Selling merchandise and services on credit is a necessary evil for most small businesses. Many customers expect to buy on credit, and business owners extend it to avoid losing customers to competitors. However, selling to customers on credit is expensive; it requires more paperwork, more staff, and more cash to service accounts receivable. In addition, because extending credit is, in essence, lending money, the risk involved is higher. Every business owner who sells on credit will encounter customers who pay late or, worst of all, who never pay at all. Figure 12.5 depicts the results of a study by American Express of small business owners who have cash flow concerns; note that the greatest cash flow problem these entrepreneurs cite is collecting accounts receivable.

Selling on credit is a common practice in business. Experts estimate that 90 percent of industrial and wholesale sales are on credit and that 40 percent of retail sales are on account.[22] One survey of small businesses across a variety of industries reported that 77 percent extend credit to their customers.[23] Because credit sales are so prevalent, an assertive collection program is essential to managing a company's cash flow. A credit policy that is too lenient can destroy a business's cash flow, attracting nothing but slow-paying or "deadbeat" customers who never pay. On the other hand, a carefully designed policy can be a powerful selling tool, attracting customers and boosting cash flow. Entrepreneurs must remember that a sale does not count until they collect the cash from it! Transforming accounts receivable into cash is essential to staying in business.

FIGURE 12.5

Cash Flow Concerns

Source: American Express Corporation, 2005.

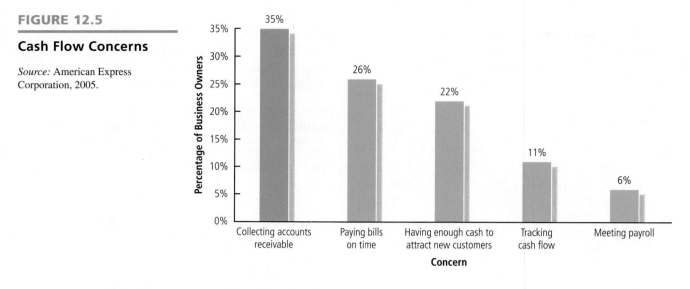

Parker LePla

When many of her public relations company's clients in the high-tech industry began to fail, Lynn Parker realized her business faced a serious threat. "We had several hundred thousand dollars in overdue accounts," she says. "We knew we were going to have to make collecting accounts receivable a priority." Parker implemented a flow-chart process for collecting her company's cash that prescribed the steps each employee should take, ranging from a simple e-mail from one of her account executives to turning the account over to a collection attorney. Her efforts paid off; in just six months, accounts past due for more than 90 days shrank from $450,000 to $45,000.[24]

How to Establish a Credit and Collection Policy The first step in establishing a workable credit policy is to screen customers carefully *before* granting them credit. Unfortunately, few small businesses conduct any kind of credit investigation before selling to a new customer. According to one survey, nearly 95 percent of small firms that sell on credit sell to *anyone* who wants to buy; most have no credit-checking procedure.[25]

HighTech Connect

Rene Siegel, president of HighTech Connect, a public relations firm that focuses on high-tech companies, recognizes the danger of performing services for companies that subsequently fail to pay. The chances of uncollectible accounts are especially high for HighTech Connect because the majority of its customers are risky high-tech start-ups. Before accepting a new client, Siegel invests the time to check out the company's credit rating, its capital base, its financial backers, and its reputation. In addition to a formal credit investigation, Siegel also relies on her extensive network of contacts in Silicon Valley to get the "inside scoop" on the companies wanting to hire HighTech Connect. Her screening diligence has paid off; since she initiated the process, only one customer has failed to pay HighTech Connect for its services, and that was a company that declared bankruptcy.[26]

A detailed credit application is the first line of defense against bad debt losses. Before selling to *any* customer on credit, business owners should have the customer complete a customized application designed to meet their companies' specific needs. After collecting enough information to assemble a credit profile, business owners should use it by checking the potential customer's credit references. The savings from lower bad debt expenses can more than offset the cost of using a credit reporting service such as TransUnion, Experian, Equifax, or Dun & Bradstreet (D&B). For entrepreneurs who sell to other business, D&B offers many useful services, including a Small Business Risk New Account Score, a tool for evaluating the credit risk of new businesses. The National Association of Credit Management (http://www.nacm.org) is another important source of credit information because it collects information on many small businesses that other reporting services ignore. The cost to check a potential customer's credit at reporting services such as these ranges from $15 to $85, a small price to pay when considering selling thousands of dollars worth of goods or services to a new customer. The Internet has made the job of credit checking much easier. Companies such as Dun & Bradstreet (http://www.dnb.com), Experian (http://www.experian.com), Equifax (http://www.equifax.com), TransUnion (http://www.transunion.com), Veritas Credit Corporation (http://www.veritas-usa.com), and KnowX (http://www.knowx.com) enable entrepreneurs to gather credit information on potential customers. Unfortunately, few small businesses take the time to conduct a credit check; in one study, just one-third of the businesses protected themselves by checking potential customers' credit.[27]

The next step involves establishing a firm written credit policy and letting every customer know in advance the company's credit terms. Industry practices often dictate credit terms (30 days is common), but a business does not have to abide by industry standards. A credit agreement must state clearly all the terms the business will enforce if the account goes bad—including interest, late charges, attorney's fees, and others. Failure to specify these terms in the contract means they *cannot* be added later after problems arise. When will you invoice? How soon is payment due: immediately, after 30 days, after 60 days? (According to a survey by the National Federation of Independent Businesses [NFIB], the most common term for small companies selling on credit is "net 30"— payment is due within 30 days of receiving the invoice.[28]) Will you add a late charge? If so, how much? (The NFIB poll reports that 65 percent of small business owners do *not* add late fees or charge interest on overdue balances.[29]) To maximize its cash flow, a small company's credit policies should be as tight as possible and within federal and state credit laws. According to the American Collectors Association, if a business is writing off more than five percent of sales as bad debts, the owner should tighten its credit and collection policy.[30]

The third step in an effective credit policy is to send invoices promptly because customers rarely pay *before* they receive their bills. The cornerstone of collecting accounts receivable on time is making sure you invoice your customers or send them their periodic billing statements promptly. "The sooner you mail your invoice, the sooner the check will be in the mail," says one entrepreneur. "In the manufacturing environment, get the invoice en route to the customer as soon as the shipment goes out the door," he advises. "Likewise, service industries with billable hours should keep track of hours daily or weekly and bill as often as the contract or agreement with the client permits."[31] Some businesses use **cycle billing,** in which a company bills a portion of its credit customers each day of the month to smooth out uneven cash receipts. Small business owners can take several steps to encourage prompt payment of invoices:

cycle billing
a method in which a company bills a portion of its credit customers each day of the month in order to smooth out uneven cash receipts.

- Ensure that all invoices are clear, accurate, and timely.
- State clearly a description of the goods or services purchased and an account number.
- Make sure that the prices and the language on invoices agree with the price quotations on purchase orders or contracts.
- Highlight the balance due and the terms of sale (e.g., "net 30") on all invoices. A study by Xerox Corporation found that highlighting with color the balance due section of invoices increased the speed of collection by 30 percent.[32]
- Include a telephone number and a contact person in your organization in case the customer has a question or a dispute.

When an account becomes overdue, a small business owner must take *immediate* action. The longer an account is past due, the lower is the probability of collecting it. As soon as an account becomes overdue, many business owners send a "second notice" letter requesting immediate payment. If that fails to produce results, the next step is a telephone call. When contacting a delinquent customer by phone, the goal is to get a commitment to pay the full amount of the bill by a specific date (*not* "soon" or "next week"). Following up with an e-mail or a letter that summarizes the telephone commitment also helps. If the customer still refuses to pay the bill, collection experts recommend the following:

- Sending a letter from the company's attorney.
- Turning the account over to a collection attorney.
- As a last resort, hiring a collection agency. (The Commercial Law League of America (http://www.clla.org/) can provide a list of reputable agencies.)

Although collection agencies and attorneys will take 25 to 50 percent of any accounts they collect, they are often worth the price. According to the American Collectors Association, only 5 percent of accounts more than 90 days delinquent will be paid voluntarily. When dealing with delinquent customers, business owners must be sure to abide by the provisions of the federal Fair Debt Collection Practices Act, which prohibits any kind of harassment when collecting debts (e.g., telephoning repeatedly, issuing threats of violence, telling third parties about the debt, or using abusive language). The primary rule when collecting past-due accounts is "*Never* lose your cool." Establishing a friendly but firm attitude that treats customers with respect is more likely to produce payment than hostile threats.

Table 12.6 outlines 10 collection blunders small business owners typically make and how to avoid them.

TABLE 12.6 Ten Collection Blunders and How to Avoid Them

Business owners often make mistakes when trying to collect the money their customers owe. Checking potential credit customers' credit records and creating a thorough sales contract that spells out exactly what happens if the account becomes past due can help to minimize collection problems. Sooner or later, however, even the best system will encounter late payers. What happens then? Business owners should avoid the following collection blunders.

Blunder 1

Delaying collection phone calls. Many entrepreneurs waste valuable time and resources sending four or five "past due" letters to delinquent customers, usually with limited effectiveness.

Instead

Once a bill becomes past due, call the customer within a week to verify that he or she received the bill and that it is accurate. Ask for payment.

Blunder 2

Failing to ask for payment in clear terms. To avoid angering a customer, some entrepreneurs ask meekly, "Do you think you could take care of this bill soon?"

Instead

Firmly, but professionally, ask for payment (the full amount) by a specific date.

Blunder 3

Sounding desperate. Some entrepreneurs show weakness by saying that they must have payment or they "can't meet payroll" or "can't pay bills." That gives the customer more leverage to negotiate additional discounts or time.

Instead

Ask for payment simply because the invoice is past due—without any other explanation. Don't apologize for your request; it's *your* money.

Blunder 4

Talking tough. Getting nasty with delinquent customers does not make them pay any faster and may be a violation of the Fair Debt Collections Practices Act.

Instead

Remain polite and professional when dealing with past-due customers, even if you think they don't deserve it. *Never* lose your temper. Don't ruin your reputation by being rude.

Blunder 5

Trying to find out the customer's problem. Some entrepreneurs think it is necessary to find out why a delinquent customer has not paid a bill.

TABLE 12.6 *Continued*

Instead

Don't waste time playing private investigator. Focus on the business at hand, collecting your money.

Blunder 6

Asking customers how much they can pay. When customers claim that they cannot pay the bill in full, inexperienced entrepreneurs ask, "Well, how much can you pay?" They don't realize that they have just turned control of the situation over to the delinquent customer.

Instead

Take charge of negotiations from the outset. Let the customer know that you expect full payment. If you cannot get full payment immediately, suggest a new deadline. Only as a last resort should you offer an extended-payment plan.

Blunder 7

Continuing to talk after you get a promise to pay. Some entrepreneurs blow the deal by not knowing when to stop talking. They keep interrogating a customer after they have a promise to pay.

Instead

Wrap up the conversation as soon as you have a commitment. Summarize the agreement, thank the customer, and end the conversation on a positive note.

Blunder 8

Calling without being prepared. Some entrepreneurs call customers without knowing exactly which invoices are past due and what amounts are involved. The effort is usually fruitless.

Instead

Have all account details in front of you when you call and be specific in your requests.

Blunder 9

Trusting your memory. Some entrepreneurs think they can remember previous collection calls, conversations, and agreements.

Instead

Keep accurate records of all calls and conversations. Take notes about each customer contact and resulting agreements.

Blunder 10

Letting your computer control your collection efforts. Inexperienced entrepreneurs tend to think that their computers can manage debt collection for them.

Instead

Recognize that a computer is a valuable tool in collecting accounts but that you are in control. "Past due" notices from a computer may collect some accounts, but your efforts will produce more results. Getting to know the people who handle the invoices at your customers' businesses can be a major advantage when collecting accounts.

Sources: Adapted from "Tips for Collecting Cash," *FSB,* May 2002, p. 72; Janine Latus Musick, "Collecting Payments Due," *Nation's Business,* January 1999, pp. 44–46; Bob Weinstein, "Collect Calls," *Entrepreneur,* August 1995, pp. 66–69; Elaine Pofeldt, "Collect Calls," *Success,* March 1998, pp. 22–24.

Other Techniques for Accelerating Accounts Receivable Small business owners can rely on a variety of other techniques to speed cash inflow from accounts receivable:

- Speed up orders by having customers e-mail or fax them to you.
- Send invoices when goods are shipped—not a day or a week later; consider faxing or e-mailing invoices to reduce in-transit time to a minimum. Most small business accounting software has features that allow users to e-mail the invoices they generate.
- Indicate in conspicuous print the invoice due date and any late payment penalties. (Check with an attorney to be sure all finance charges comply with state laws.)
- Restrict a customer's credit until past-due bills are paid.

- Deposit customer checks and credit card receipts *daily*.
- Identify the top 20 percent of your customers (by sales volume), create a separate file system for them, and monitor them closely. Twenty percent of the typical company's customers generate 80 percent of all accounts receivable.
- Ask customers to pay at least a portion of the purchase price up front. To preserve her company's cash flow, Jane Conner, owner of the Whitefish Gymnastics Club, requires her customers to pay for their 10-week exercise classes after the first session.[33]
- Watch for signs that a customer may be about to declare bankruptcy. If that happens, creditors typically collect only a small fraction, if any, of the debt owed.
- Consider using a bank's lockbox collection service (located near customers) to reduce mail time on collections. In a **lockbox** arrangement, customers send payments to a post office box the company's bank maintains. Several times each day, the bank collects payments and deposits them immediately in the company's account. The procedure sharply reduces processing and clearing times, especially if the lockboxes are located close to the firm's biggest customers' business addresses. The system can be expensive to operate, and it is most economical for companies with a high volume of large checks.
- Track the results of the company's collection efforts. Managers and key employees should receive a weekly report on the status of the company's outstanding accounts receivable.

lockbox

an arrangement in which customers send payments to a post office box that a company's bank maintains; several times a day, the bank collects payments and deposits them in the company's account.

Ransom Environmental

Although project managers at Ransom Environmental, an environmental consulting company in Newburyport, Massachusetts, viewed collecting accounts receivable as a necessary evil, CEO Steve Ransom decided his company had to make collections a priority to improve cash flow. Ransom began distributing a receivables status report at the company's weekly operations meetings. Given to managers, the report features a receivables-aging chart showing whose customers were behind on their payments and by how many days. Ransom Environmental quickly began to see an improvement in its collection patterns and in its cash flow. The company's average collection period has fallen from 75 days to 60 days, and faster collections have boosted cash flow, enabling Ransom to save between $1,000 and $2,000 a month in interest on its line of credit.[34]

security agreement

a contract in which a business selling an asset on credit gets a security interest in that asset (the collateral), protecting its legal rights in case the buyer fails to pay.

Another strategy that small companies, particularly those selling high-priced items, can use to protect the cash they have tied up in receivables is to couple a security agreement with a financing statement. This strategy falls under Article 9 of the Uniform Commercial Code (UCC), which governs a wide variety of business transactions, from the sale of goods to security interests. A **security agreement** is a contract in which a business selling an asset on credit gets a security interest in that asset (the collateral), protecting its legal rights in case the buyer fails to pay. To get the protection it seeks in the security agreement, the seller must file a financing statement called a UCC-1 form with the proper state or county office (a process the UCC calls "perfection"). The UCC-1 form gives notice to other creditors and to the general public that the seller holds a secured interest in the collateral named in the security agreement. The UCC-1 form must include the name, address, and signature of the buyer, a description of the collateral, and the name and address of the seller.

Suppose that Lanford Mechanical sells a piece of manufacturing machinery to Abbott Chemical Company for $64,000, accepting $12,000 in cash and retaining the $52,000 balance on account, payable over 24 months. As part of the sales contract (which also is governed by Article 2 of the UCC), Lanford gets Abbott to sign a security agreement giving Lanford a security interest in the machine. If Lanford files the financing statement (the UCC-1 form) with the secretary of state for a small fee, it has perfected its security interest in the machine. If Abbott fails to pay the account balance in full, Lanford can repossess the machine and sell it to satisfy the remaining balance. If Abbott were to declare bankruptcy, Lanford is not guaranteed payment, but its filing puts its claim to the machinery ahead of those of unsecured creditors. Lanford's degree of safety on this large credit sale is much higher with a security agreement and a properly filed financing statement.

Hands on ... How to

Control Your Company's Accounts Receivable

Mike Edwards, president of 5 Stones Group, a film production company based in Columbus, Ohio, should be pleased. The company's sales have reached their highest point to date and the company recently opened a second office in New York City and completed work on the highest profile project in its history—filming Lance Armstrong as he led the Tour of Hope, a charity bike ride.

Edwards, however, is not a happy man. 5 Stones Group is experiencing growing pains and the cash flow problems that accompany them. Because the jobs his business performs require Edwards to incur some rather sizeable expenses before they are completed, Edwards created a policy requiring clients to pay one-third of the fee up front, one-third at mid-project, and one-third on completion. Creating the policy was one thing; enforcing it has proved to be another matter for Edwards. Few of the company's clients abide by 5 Stones Group's payment policy. "Cash flow is critical," says Edwards. "If a client says that a payment will be made next Friday, you have to call next Friday. You have to continually track payments."

That job usually falls to Edwards' wife, Tiffany, who handles the company's finances. Collecting timely payments is a constant challenge. Clients often come up with creative reasons that they cannot pay their bills on time, sometimes quibbling over expenses or arguing about when the 30-day clock began ticking. Standing tough on the collection policy presents a dilemma for Edwards' young company: If they push the collection effort too hard, are they jeopardizing future jobs with their clients? "Our stance so far is that we want the relationship more than the [collection] terms," says Tiffany. We've given in." To avoid a cash crisis, Edwards has had to draw on 5 Stones Group's two lines of credit or charge some expenses to credit cards.

Research shows that 5 Stones Group is not alone in facing this problem. Small businesses report that their customers, particularly large companies, are stretching their accounts payable farther, paying invoices more slowly now than they were just a few years ago. When

faced with 30-day credit terms, it is not uncommon for large companies to delay their payments to 45 or even 60 days. The *Small Business Network Monitor*, a study of small businesses by American Express, confirms the challenge this presents for entrepreneurs. More than half of the small business owners surveyed say their companies experienced cash flow problems, and their primary concern is collecting accounts receivable. (Refer to Figure 12.4).

"If the money is coming in the front door at 100 miles per hour," explains Brian Hamilton, CEO of Sageworks, a financial consulting firm, "and going out the back door at 110 miles per hour, that's not a good thing. Businesses don't fail because they are unprofitable; they fail because they get crushed on the accounts receivable side." What steps can entrepreneurs take to avoid a cash crisis caused by slowly turning accounts receivable? The following steps can help:

- ***Increase your company's cash reserves.*** Smart business owners keep at least three months' worth of expenses on hand so that they aren't caught cash-short if receivables slow down more than expected or if sales suddenly drop.
- ***Boost your company's line of credit.*** Business owners can increase their lines of credit with their banks, but the key is to do so *before* you need the money. Be prepared to use your company's financial statements to prove to your banker why you need—and deserve—an increased line of credit.
- ***Monitor accounts receivable closely.*** Some small business owners generate daily summaries of their company's accounts receivable, always on the lookout for disturbing trends. Doing so enables them to spot slow payers who might become non-payers unless the company takes immediate action.
- ***Get to know the people responsible for paying invoices at your biggest customers' or clients' companies.*** Collections are easier if you know the right person to call.
- ***Take immediate action when an account becomes past due.*** Resist the tendency to simply sit back and wait for the customer to pay. If a customer has

not paid by the invoice due date, contact him or her immediately and ask for payment.

■ *Stick to your credit terms.* Define the credit terms with every client up front. If clients balk when it comes time for payment, remind them that they have a commitment to live up to the terms of the sales contract.

■ *Raise prices to cover the extra cost of late payments.* If clients refuse to pay on time, determine how much their slower payments cost your company, and raise your rates or your prices enough to cover the cost.

■ *Offer discounts to encourage early payment.* Cash discounts (such as "2/10, net 30," which means that you offer the client a two percent discount if he or she pays within 10 days; otherwise, the full invoice amount is due in 30 days) can reduce a small company's profit margin, but they also provide an incentive for clients to pay early. Remember: More companies fail for lack of cash than for lack of profit.

Source: Adapted from Amy Feldman, "The Cash-Flow Crunch," *Inc.*, December 2005, pp. 50–52.

Accounts Payable

The second element of the "big three" of cash management is accounts payable. The timing of payables is just as crucial to proper cash management as the timing of receivables, but the objective is exactly the opposite. Entrepreneurs should strive to stretch out payables as long as possible *without damaging their companies' credit rating.* Otherwise, suppliers may begin demanding prepayment or cash-on-delivery (C.O.D.) terms, which severely impair a company's cash flow, or they may stop doing business with it altogether. When one computer manufacturer ran into cash flow problems, it deferred payments to its suppliers for as long as 100 days (compared to an industry average of about 40 days). Because of the company's slow payments, many suppliers simply stopped selling to the computer maker.[35] One cash management consultant says, "Some companies pay too early and wind up forgoing the interest they could have earned on their cash. Others pay too late and either wind up with late penalties or being forced to buy on a C.O.D. basis, which really kills them."[36] It is perfectly acceptable for small business owners to regulate payments to their companies' advantage. Efficient cash managers set up a payment calendar each month that allows them to pay their bills on time and to take advantage of cash discounts for early payment.

Nancy Dunis, CEO of Dunis & Associates, a Portland, Oregon, marketing firm, recognizes the importance of controlling accounts payable. "Our payables must be functioning just right to keep our cash flow running smoothly," says Dunis. She has set up a simple five-point accounts payable system:[37]

1. *Set scheduling goals.* Dunis strives to pay her company's bills 45 days after receiving them and to collect all her receivables within 30 days. Even though "it doesn't always work that way," her goal is to make the most of her cash flow.

2. *Keep paperwork organized.* Dunis dates every invoice she receives and carefully files it according to her payment plan. "This helps us remember when to cut the check," she says, and "it helps us stagger our payments, over days or weeks," significantly improving the company's cash flow.

3. *Prioritize.* Dunis cannot stretch out all of her company's creditors for 45 days; some demand payment sooner. Those suppliers are at the top of the accounts payable list.

4. *Be consistent.* "Companies want consistent customers," says Dunis. "With a few exceptions," she explains, "most businesses will be happy to accept 45-day payments, so long as they know you'll always pay your full obligation at that point."

5. *Look for warning signs.* Dunis sees her accounts payable as an early warning system for cash flow problems. "The first indication I get that cash flow is in trouble is when I see I'm getting low on cash and could have trouble paying my bills according to my staggered filing system," she says.

Other signs that a business is heading for cash flow problems include difficulty making principal and interest payments on loans and incurring penalties for late payment of routine bills.

Business owners should verify all invoices before paying them. Some unscrupulous vendors will send out invoices for goods they never shipped or services they never rendered, knowing that many business owners will simply pay the bill without checking its authenticity. A common invoice scam aimed at small business owners involves bogus operators sending bills for ads in nonexistent printed or online "yellow pages" directories. In some cases, the directories actually do exist, but their distribution is so limited that ads in them are useless. One survey by the real Yellow Pages Publishers Association found that one-third of businesses had received bogus bills for yellow pages advertising.[38] To avoid falling victim to such scams, someone in the company—for instance, the accounts payable clerk—should have the responsibility of verifying *every* invoice received.

Generally, it is a good idea for owners to take advantage of cash discounts vendors offer. A cash discount (e.g., "2/10, net 30"—take a 2 percent discount if you pay the invoice within 10 days; otherwise, total payment is due in 30 days) offers a price reduction if the owner pays an invoice early. Failing to take advantage of this particular cash discount is the equivalent of borrowing at an interest rate of 36.7 percent! Therefore, if a business owner has enough cash on hand to pay the invoice on day 10, he or she should take advantage of the cash discount. If the business does not have enough cash on hand on day 10 but the owner can borrow it at an interest rate less than 36.7 percent, he or she should do so to take advantage of the cash discount. A clever cash manager also will negotiate the best possible credit terms with his suppliers. Almost all vendors grant their customers trade credit, and small business owners should take advantage of it. However, because trade credit is so easy to get, entrepreneurs must be careful not to overuse and abuse it, putting their businesses in a precarious financial position.

Favorable credit terms can make a tremendous difference in a company's cash flow. Table 12.7 shows the same most likely cash budget from Table 12.3 with one exception: instead of purchasing on C.O.D. terms as shown in Table 12.3, the owner has negotiated "net 30" payment terms (Table 12.7). Notice the drastic improvement in the company's cash flow resulting from improved credit terms.

If owners do find themselves financially strapped when payment to a vendor is due, they should avoid making empty promises that "the check is in the mail" or sending unsigned checks. Instead, they should openly discuss the situation with the vendor. Most vendors will work out payment terms for extended credit. One small business owner who was experiencing a cash crisis claims:

> One day things got so bad I just called up a supplier and said, "I need your stuff, but I'm going through a tough period and simply can't pay you right now." They said they wanted to keep me as a customer, and they asked if it was okay to bill me in three months. I was dumbfounded: *They didn't even charge me interest*.[39]

Small business owners also can improve their firms' cash flow by scheduling controllable cash disbursements so that they do not come due at the same time. For example, paying employees every two weeks (or every month) rather than every week reduces administrative costs and gives the business more time to use its cash. Owners of fledgling businesses may be able to conserve cash by hiring part-time employees or by using freelance workers rather than full-time, permanent workers. Scheduling insurance premiums monthly or quarterly rather than annually also can improve cash flows.

Wise use of business credit cards is another way to stretch the firm's cash balance. However, entrepreneurs should avoid cards that charge transaction fees. Credit cards differ in their interest-charging policies; many begin charging interest from the date of purchase, but some charge interest only from the invoice date. Increasingly, entrepreneurs are using low-interest credit cards to finance their business start-up costs. Although it is a risky practice (the low interest rates don't last forever), many entrepreneurs say that they cannot get start-up financing any other way.

TABLE 12.7 Cash Budget,* Most Likely Sales Forecast

	Jan.	Feb.	Mar.	Apr.
Cash Receipts:				
Sales	$150,000	$200,000	$200,000	$300,000
Credit Sales	112,500	150,000	150,000	225,000
Collections:				
60%—1st month after sale	$180,000	$67,500	$90,000	$90,000
30%—2nd month after sale	78,750	90,000	33,750	45,000
5%—3rd month after sale	11,250	13,125	15,000	5,625
Cash Sales	37,500	50,000	50,000	75,000
Interest	0	200	0	9
Total Cash Receipts	$307,500	$220,825	$188,750	$215,625
Cash Disbursements:				
Purchases*	$105,000	$140,000	$140,000	$210,000
Rent	2,000	2,000	2,000	2,000
Utilities	850	850	850	850
Interest	0	0	7,500	0
Tax Prepayment	0	0	50,000	0
Capital Addition	0	130,000	3	0
Miscellaneous	70	70	70	70
Wage/Salaries	30,000	40,000	45,000	50,000
Total Cash Disbursements*	$137,920	$312,920	$245,420	$262,920
End-of-Month Balance:				
Cash (beginning of month)*	$12,000	$181,580	$89,485	$32,815
+ Cash Receipts	307,500	220,825	188,750	215,625
− Cash Disbursements	137,920	312,920	245,420	262,920
Cash (end of month)*	181,580	89,485	32,815	(14,480)
Borrowing	0	0	0	24,480
Cash (end of month [after borrowing])*	$181,580	$89,485	$32,815	$10,000

*After negotiating net 30 trade credit terms

Inventory

Inventory is a significant investment for many small businesses and can create a severe strain on cash flow. The typical grocery store now stocks more than 49,000 items, three times as many as it did 20 years ago, and many other types of businesses are following this pattern.[40] Offering customers a wider variety of products is one way a business can outshine its competitors, but product proliferation increases the need for tight inventory control to avoid a cash crisis. Although inventory represents the largest capital investment for most small businesses, few owners use any formal methods for managing it. As a result, the typical small business not only has too much inventory, but also too much of the *wrong* kind of inventory! Because inventory is illiquid, it can quickly siphon off a company's pool of available cash. "Small companies need cash to grow," says one consultant. "They've got to be able to turn [cash] over quickly. That's difficult to do if a lot of money is tied up in excess inventory."[41] Surplus inventory yields a zero rate of return and unnecessarily ties up a company's cash. "The cost of carrying inventory is expensive," says one small business consultant. "A typical manufacturing company pays 25 percent to 30 percent of the value of the inventory for the cost of borrowed money, warehouse space, materials handling, staff, lift-truck expenses, and fixed costs. This shocks a lot of people.

Once they realize it, they look at inventory differently."[42] Marking down items that don't sell will keep inventory lean and allow it to turn over frequently. Even though volume discounts lower inventory costs, large purchases may tie up the company's valuable cash. Wise business owners avoid overbuying inventory, recognizing that excess inventory ties up valuable cash unproductively. In fact, only 20 percent of a typical business' inventory turns over quickly, so owners must watch constantly for stale items.[43] If a small business must pay suppliers within 30 days of receiving an inventory shipment and then the merchandise sits on the shelf for another 30 to 60 days (or more!), the pressure on its cash flow intensifies.

Carrying too little inventory is not the ideal solution to cash flow challenges because companies with excessive "stockouts" lose sales (and eventually customers if the problem persists). However, carrying too much inventory usually results in slow-moving inventory and a low inventory turnover ratio. Experienced business owners understand the importance of shedding slow-moving inventory during end-of-season sales, even if the price they get is below their normal markup.

Channeled Resources Inc.

Recognizing the high cost of holding inventory, Cindy Revenaugh, vice-president of sales at Channeled Resources, a company that sells recycled paper products, gives her sales force the power to sell slow-moving items at any price that is not below the company's cost. "We just want to move the stuff and get cash for it," says Revenaugh. "Even if they sell it at cost, it's better than letting it sit here."[44]

Carrying too much inventory increases the chances that a business will run out of cash. An entrepreneur's goal is to minimize the company's investment in inventory without sacrificing sales, selection, and customer satisfaction. "The cash that pays for goods is channeled into inventory," says one business writer, "where its flow is dead-ended until the inventory is sold and the cash is set free again. The cash flow trick is to commit just enough cash to inventory to meet demand."[45] Scheduling inventory deliveries at the latest possible date will prevent premature payment of invoices. Finally, given goods of comparable quality and price, an entrepreneur should purchase goods from the fastest supplier to keep inventory levels as low as possible. All of these tactics require entrepreneurs to manage their supply chains carefully and to treat their suppliers as partners in their businesses. To keep inventory churning rapidly through a small business requires creating a nimble, adaptive supply chain that responds to a company's changing needs.

Forever 21

At Forever 21, a retail clothing chain of more than 200 stores that targets teens to twenty-somethings with the latest fashions at very reasonable prices, managing inventory is a key ingredient in its strategy for success. CEO Don Chang and his wife, Jin, started from a single store in 1984 with the goal of attracting customers by constantly changing their inventory and offering the latest fashions much faster than their competitors. "Forever 21's inventory is fun, it's affordable, and it's always changing," says one industry analyst. Today, Forever 21 relies on a computerized point-of-sale system that constantly monitors which items are selling (and which ones are not) to keep its inventory fresh and turning fast. In addition, the company has integrated its global suppliers into a supply chain that responds quickly to fast-changing fashion trends. "Every week you'll see something new and different," says the company's CFO Larry Meyer. Forever 21 was one of the pioneers of "cheap chic," a retail philosophy that emphasizes "disposable fashion" over high quality; young women can purchase cutting-edge clothes at prices so low that they can afford to sell them to second-hand shops or donate them to charity after wearing them only a handful of times. The result is an inventory turnover ratio that is well above the industry average and stores that carry the latest fashions for a very short time before moving on to the next fashion trend. Forever 21 supplies its stores with small shipments of fresh merchandise several times a week, and customers purchase the items almost as fast.[46]

FIGURE 12.6

Coping with a Cash Crunch: Tactics Used by Small Businesses

Source: The Open Small Business Network 2005 Semi-Annual Monitor from American Express, March 28, 2005, http:www//home3.americanexpress.com/corp//pc/2005/osbn_sm1.asp.

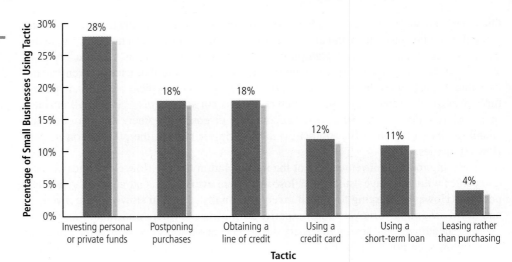

Monitoring the big three of cash management can help every business owner avoid a cash crisis while making the best use of available cash. According to one expert, maximizing cash flow involves "getting money from customers sooner; paying bills at the last moment possible; consolidating money in a single bank account; managing accounts payable, accounts receivable, and inventory more effectively; and squeezing every penny out of your daily business."[47]

Avoiding the Cash Crunch

LEARNING OBJECTIVES
5. Explain the techniques for avoiding a cash crunch in a small company.

Nearly every small business has the potential to improve its cash position with little or no investment. The key is to make an objective evaluation of the company's financial policies, searching for inefficiency in its cash flow. Young firms cannot afford to waste resources, especially one as vital as cash. By utilizing the following techniques, entrepreneurs can get maximum benefit from their companies' pool of available cash. Figure 12.6 shows the results of a recent survey of small business owners by American Express describing the techniques entrepreneurs use to address cash flow crunches.

Barter

bartering
the exchange of goods and services for other goods and services rather than for cash.

Bartering, the exchange of goods and services for other goods and services rather than for cash, is an effective way to conserve cash. An ancient concept, bartering has regained popularity in recent years. Today more than 500 barter exchanges operate across the United States, and they cater primarily to small and medium-sized businesses looking to conserve cash. More than 500,000 companies—most of them small—engage in more than $8.25 billion worth of barter each year.[48] Every day, entrepreneurs across the nation use bartering to buy much needed materials, services, equipment, and supplies—*without* using precious cash.

TradeMark Express

Chris DeMassa, founder of TradeMark Express, a 14-person trademark research and consulting company, relies on barter for as many of the products and services he purchases as possible. In the past, DeMassa has bartered for everything from basic business supplies to printing work. Bartering "makes better use of our resources and lowers our cost of doing business," says DeMassa.[49]

In addition to conserving cash, companies that use barter also have the opportunity to transform slow-moving inventory into much-needed products and services. Barter companies pay, on average, trade credits equal to three times the amount inventory liquidators would pay for the same merchandise.[50] Buying goods and services with barter also offers the benefit of a built-in discount. Although a company gets credit for the retail value of the goods or services it offers, the real cost to the company is less and depends on its gross profit margin. For instance, the owner of an Italian restaurant bartered $1,000 worth of meals for some new furniture, but his actual cost of the meals was only $680, given his gross profit margin of 32 percent. Business owners who barter also say that joining a barter exchange brings in customers who normally would not buy from them. For instance, Chris DeMassa estimates that 10 percent of his TradeMark Express's sales are generated through barter. "That's 10 percent that we wouldn't otherwise have," he observes.[51]

In a typical barter exchange, businesses accumulate trade credits when they offer goods or services through the exchange. Then, they can use their trade credits to purchase other goods and services from other members of the exchange. The typical exchange charges a $500 membership fee and a 10 percent transaction fee (5 percent from the buyer and 5 percent from the seller) on every deal. The exchange tracks the balance in each member's account and typically sends a monthly statement summarizing account activity.

Online barter exchanges have become extremely popular because of their convenience and the wide variety of items they list on their exchanges. Business owners can barter for advertising time and space, hotel stays, catering services, car rentals, airline tickets, office supplies, printing services, photography, carpet, cell phones, and many other products and services. Online barter exchanges usually charge lower membership and transaction fees than their offline counterparts. Before joining a barter exchange, business owners should investigate the fee structure, the selection and the prices of its goods and services, and its geographical coverage.

Trim Overhead Costs

High overhead expenses can strain a small firm's cash supply to the breaking point; simple cost-cutting measures can save big money. Frugal small business owners can trim their overhead in a number of ways.

Ask for Discounts and "Freebies" Another way entrepreneurs can conserve cash is to negotiate discounts on the purchases they do make and to make the use of free services whenever possible. For instance, rather than pay a high-priced consultant to assist him with his business plan, one entrepreneur opted instead to use the free services of his local Small Business Development Center (SBDC). The move not only improved the quality of his business plan, which enabled him to get the financing he needed to launch his business, but it also conserved valuable cash for the start-up.

When Dave Morgan launched Real Media, an Internet marketing company, he could muster only $40,000 to put into the new venture. Among other things, Morgan needed talented employees, but he knew that his $40,000 would not go very far toward attracting potential workers. He began recruiting potential employees and explained that he could not pay them salaries—at least at first. Of course, most withdrew their names, but two young people looking to build their résumés agreed to work at no pay for six months. In exchange, Morgan gave them titles as co-founders of the company and more responsibility than they would have gotten at a much larger company. His "cheapskate" strategy worked. After a year in business, Real Media had built a client base of 12 companies, and sales had climbed to $100,000. Five years later, Morgan sold Real Media, which had grown to more than 300 employees in 12 countries and sales of more than $30 million.[52]

Periodically Evaluate Expenses Business owners not only should attempt to keep their operating costs low, but they also should evaluate them periodically to make sure they have not gotten out of line. Comparing current expenses with past levels is helpful and so is comparing a company's expenses against industry standards. Useful resources for determining typical expenses in an industry include RMA's *Annual Statement Studies*, Dun & Bradstreet's *Industry Norms and Key Business Ratios*, and Prentice Hall's *Almanac of Business and Industrial Financial Ratios*.

Hi-Shear Technology

Linda Nespole, a manager at Hi-Shear Technology, an aerospace subcontractor, used this technique to cut thousands of dollars from her company's operating expenses each year. When Hi-Shear's cash flow was squeezed recently, Nespole began tracking some of the company's largest operating expenses, mostly utility bills, and discovered some unusually large increases. Basic repairs, preventive maintenance, and more efficient fixtures cut costs and generated enough savings to pay for themselves within just a few months. Nespole expanded her list and began charting company expenses and acting on trends she saw. The result: major cost savings in everything from telephone charges to retirement plan costs. Tracking and controlling expenses has become a priority for Hi-Shear's 125 employees, and the company's cash flow has never been better.[53]

When Practical, Lease Instead of Buy By leasing automobiles, computers, office equipment, machinery, and many other types of assets rather than buying them, an entrepreneur can conserve valuable cash. The value of these assets is not in *owning* them but in *using* them. Businesses can lease practically any kind of equipment—from office furniture and computers to construction equipment and manufacturing machinery. Leasing is a popular cash management strategy; according to a recent survey by the Equipment Leasing Association, 8 of 10 companies lease some or all of their equipment.[54] "These companies are long on ideas, short on capital, and in need of flexibility as they grow and change," says Suzanne Jackson of the Equipment Leasing Association of America. "They lease for efficiency and convenience."[55] For instance, to minimize its investment in technology that requires frequent updates, Forever 21 leases the point-of-sale system that helps drive its fast-turning inventory strategy.[56]

Although total lease payments typically are greater than those for a conventional loan, most leases offer 100 percent financing, which means that the owner avoids the large capital outlays required as down payments on most loans. (Sometimes a lease requires the first and last months' payments to be made up front.) Furthermore, leasing is an "off-the-balance-sheet" method of financing and requires no collateral. The equipment a company leases does not have to be depreciated because the small business does not actually own it. A lease is considered an operating expense on the income statement, not a liability on the balance sheet. Thus, leasing conserves a company's borrowing capacity. Because lease payments are fixed amounts paid over a particular time period, leasing allows business owners to forecast more accurately their cash flows. Lease agreements also are flexible. Leasing companies typically offer a variety of terms and allow businesses to stretch payments over a longer time period than those of a conventional loan. "There are so many ways to tailor a lease agreement to a company's individual equipment and financial needs that you might call it a personalized rental agreement," says the owner of a small construction firm.[57]

Leasing also protects a business against obsolescence, especially when it comes to equipment such as computer hardware and software, whose technological life is limited to perhaps just two or three years.

Delicato Family Vineyards

The Delicato family has been making fine wines in the foothills of California's Sierra Nevada Mountains for more than 80 years. This family-owned business uses more than 200 computers in its operation. Rather than purchase the computer equipment, the Delicato Family Vineyards leases it, a technique that has improved the company's cash flow.

For more than 80 years, the Delicato family has been creating fine wines from its winery in the foothills of California's Sierra Nevada Mountains; it was recently named the fastest-growing winery in California. In addition to marketing its own brands, Delicato Family Vineyards also serves as "the winemaker's winemaker," growing grapes and producing wine for some of California's most famous wineries. Although it remains a small, family-run business, Delicato Family Vineyards counts on technology to manage its production facilities and its growing operations, which span more than 6,000 acres of vineyards. "A lot of our operations here at Delicato are computer-based," says Michael Strohmaier, the company's director of information technology. Delicato Family Vineyards uses more than 200 computers in its operations—including the front office for taking and processing orders, the production department for aid in making the wine, and the sales force, which uses portable computers on sales calls. Initially, the company purchased its computer equipment, but keeping it up to date required a significant capital investment, which led Strohmaier to begin leasing computers. "Leasing helped us smooth out our budget," he says. "Now we have a more predictable budgeting process than we had previously, and that helps our cash flow management. [We also] have reduced our risk of getting caught with obsolete technology."[58]

Avoid Nonessential Outlays By forgoing costly ego indulgences like ostentatious office equipment, first-class travel, and flashy company cars, entrepreneurs can make the most efficient use of a company's cash. Before putting scarce cash into an asset, every business owner should put the decision to the acid test: "What will this purchase add to my company's ability to compete and to become more successful?" Making across-the-board spending cuts to conserve cash is dangerous, however, because the owner runs the risk of cutting expenditures that literally drive the business. One common mistake during business slowdowns is cutting marketing and advertising expenditures. Economic slowdowns present a prime opportunity for smart business owners to bring increased attention to their products and services and to gain market share if they hold the line on their marketing and advertising budgets as their competitors cut back. The secret to successful cost saving is cutting *nonessential* expenditures. "If the lifeblood of your company is marketing, cut it less," advises one advertising executive. "If it is customer service, that is the last thing you want to cut back on. Cut from areas that are not essential to business growth."[59]

Negotiate Fixed Loan Payments to Coincide with Your Company's Cash Flow Cycle Many banks allow businesses to structure loans so that they can skip specific payments when their cash flow ebbs to its lowest point. Negotiating such terms gives businesses the opportunity to customize their loan repayments to their cash flow cycles.

Ted Zoli, president of Torrington Industries, a construction materials supplier and contracting business, consistently uses "skipped payment loans" in his highly seasonal business. "Every time we buy a piece of construction machinery," he says, "we set it up so that we're making payments for eight or nine months, and then skipping three or four months during the winter."[60]

Torrington Industries

Buy Used or Reconditioned Equipment, Especially if it is "Behind-the-Scenes" Machinery One restaurateur saved thousands of dollars in the start-up phase of his business by buying used equipment from a restaurant equipment broker.

Hire Part-Time Employees and Freelance Specialists Whenever Possible Hiring part-time workers and freelancers rather than full-time employees saves on the cost of both salaries and benefits.

Outsource One way that many entrepreneurs use to conserve valuable cash is to outsource certain activities to businesses that specialize in performing them rather than hiring someone to do them in-house (or doing the activities themselves). In addition to saving cash, outsourcing enables entrepreneurs to focus on the most important aspects of running their businesses.

Debra Cohen, founder of Home Remedies of New York, a home improvement contract referral business, has just one employee in her very successful company: herself. Cohen focuses on sales, business development, and screening home improvement vendors and outsources almost every other aspect of her business, including Web site development and maintenance, graphic design, software development, financial record keeping, and others. "Stick to what you are good at and outsource everything else," she advises.[61]

Home Remedies of New York

Debra Cohen, founder of Home Remedies of New York, a home improvement referral company, focuses her efforts on those things that she does best: sales, business development, and screening vendors. To conserve cash, she outsources almost every other aspect of her business.

Control Employee Advances and Loans An entrepreneur should grant only those advances and loans that are necessary and should keep accurate records on payments and balances.

Establish an Internal Security and Control System Too many owners encourage employee theft by failing to establish a system of controls. Reconciling the bank statement monthly and requiring special approval for checks over a specific amount, say $1,000, will help to minimize losses. Separating record-keeping and check-writing responsibilities, rather than assigning them to a single employee, offers more protection.

Develop a System to Battle Check Fraud Bad checks and check fraud can wreak havoc on a small company's cash flow. On a typical day in the United States, consumers and businesses write two million checks that will be returned because of insufficient funds, a closed account, or some other problem. About 70 percent of all "bounced" checks occur because 9 of 10 customers fail to keep their checkbooks balanced; the remaining 30 percent of bad checks are the result of fraud. On a typical day in the United States, nearly 1.4 million checks are forged.[62] Simple techniques for minimizing losses from bad checks include requesting proper identification (preferably with a photograph) from customers, recording customers' telephone numbers, and training cashiers to watch for forged or counterfeit checks. Perhaps the most effective way to battle bad checks is to subscribe to an electronic check approval service. The service works at the cash register, and approval takes only a minute or less. The fee a small business pays to use the service depends on the volume of checks. For most small companies, charges amount to one to two percent of the cleared checks' value.

Change Your Shipping Terms Changing a company's shipping terms from "F.O.B. (free on board) buyer," in which the *seller* pays the cost of freight, to "F.O.B. seller," in which the *buyer* absorbs all shipping costs, can improve cash flow.

Start Selling Gift Cards

Prepaid gift cards can be a real boost to a small company's cash flow. Customers pay for the cards up front, but the typical recipient does not redeem the gift card until later, sometimes much later, giving the company the use of the cash during that time. Gift cards are appropriate for many businesses, especially those in the retail or service sectors.

Inspa Corporation

Colleen Stone, owner of Inspa Corporation, a fast-growing Seattle, Washington–based chain of day spas, uses gift cards to stretch her company's cash flow. Gift cards account for 25 percent of her company's sales, and Stone has discovered that many of the gift cards she sells are not redeemed for a year, giving her a source of interest-free cash in the interim. "We plow all that cash flow right back into opening new stores," says Stone.[63]

Switch to Zero-Based Budgeting Zero-based budgeting (ZBB) primarily is a shift in the philosophy of budgeting. Rather than build the current year budget on *increases* from the previous year's budget, ZBB starts from a budget of zero and evaluates the necessity of every item. "Start with zero and review all expenses, asking yourself whether each one is necessary," says one business consultant.[64]

Be on the Lookout for Employee Theft

Companies lose billions of dollars each year to employee theft. Because they often rely on informal procedures for managing cash (or no procedures at all) and often lack proper control procedures, small business owners are most likely to become victims of theft, embezzlement, and fraud by their employees. Experts estimate that employee theft cost small businesses $40 billion a year and that as much as 75 percent of all employee theft goes unnoticed.[65] Although any business can be a victim of employee theft, retailers are particularly vulnerable. Retailers lose 1.5 percent of the value of their merchandise to employee theft and shoplifting each year.[66] One source of the problem is the entrepreneur's attitude that "we're all family here; no one would steal from family." Although establishing a totalitarian police state and trusting no one is not conducive to a positive work environment, putting in place adequate financial control systems is essential. Separating key cash management duties among at least two employees such as writing checks and handling bank statements and conducting regular financial audits can be effective deterrents to employee theft.

You Be the Consultant

The Trusted Employee

Lloyd and Jim Graff, co-owners of Graff-Pinkert, a company in Oak Forest, Illinois, that buys and sells machines that make metal components, ran the family-owned business the way their father, who founded the company, had: on trust and a handshake. After all, they were still doing business with many of the same companies their father had done business with over the years. The Graffs extended that same level of trust to their family of 18 employees. If an employee needed money for a deposit on a home or for a family medical emergency, the Graffs would extend a loan—interest-free. Many employees and their families were friends outside of work and spent recreational time together.

That's why the Graffs were shocked and dismayed when they discovered that one of their workers, Patty Preston (not her real name), had been embezzling money from the business for more than four years. An 11-year employee and a mother of three children, Preston was a bookkeeper for Graff-Pinkert. Her illicit activities came to light while Preston was on vacation. Preston had neglected to deposit Jim Graff's last few payroll checks into his personal bank account. When he mentioned it in front of several workers, one of them grew concerned and revealed that she believed Preston had charged several Rugrats videotapes for her kids on the company's account at Home Depot. Another employee said that Preston also had purchased a storage shed for her home on a company account.

Jim immediately began to investigate the employees' allegations and discovered that they were true; Preston had been using company funds to purchase personal items. He contacted his brother, who was on vacation at the time. "I fired her for being a petty crook," Lloyd says. It didn't take long for the Graffs to discover that Preston's crime was anything but petty. To

finance a gambling habit and a luxurious lifestyle, she had embezzled more than $200,000 from Graff-Pinkert, a huge amount for a company whose annual sales were between $8 and $10 million. "Jim and I walked around punch-drunk as the enormity of the crime mounted up," recalls Lloyd. "It was a real blow to our confidence. The people who worked with her were horrified, even angrier than Jim and I. This was a co-worker they trusted. They felt violated."

Preston's duties included, among other things, writing checks and reconciling the company bank statement. Her embezzlement scheme was simple. She would write a check to a legitimate vendor or supplier and have one of the Graffs sign it. Then she would go to her typewriter and, using correction tape, change the name on the check, making it payable to her own credit card company. Because she also handled the bank statement, she could cover her tracks, and no one else saw what she was doing. Because they were focused on managing the company's rapid growth and because they saw their employees as part of an extended family, the Graffs never noticed the crime that was taking place right before their eyes. The small accounting firm they used, the same one their father had hired decades before, somehow never caught the embezzlement in their annual audits.

Graff-Pinkert had no fidelity insurance protecting them against employee theft, and they wanted to recover at least some of the money Preston had stolen. Because Preston had mailed fraudulent checks across state lines, she had committed a federal crime. The Graffs contacted the FBI and filed a lawsuit against Preston in federal court. In a settlement, Preston relinquished to Graff-Pinkert $72,000 she had accumulated in her profit-sharing plan. Because she had blown most of the money gambling in nearby casinos, Preston had few assets from which to make restitution to the company. At her sentencing, Preston said nothing, not even uttering an apology to the Graffs or to the handful of employees who showed up. The judge sentenced her to 24 months in a federal penitentiary and ordered her to continue to pay restitution to the company on her release. The Graffs receive checks for small amounts, sometimes just $25, irregularly from Preston, who now works as a hotel maid. Although they scrutinize their bank statements more carefully now, the Graffs business philosophy hasn't changed. "We're more skeptical but not cynical," says Lloyd. "We still approach it as a family business. If we couldn't run it that way, I'd hang it up."

1. Identify some of the factors that led Graff-Pinkert to become a victim of embezzlement. What impact does this crime have on a company's cash flow?
2. What recommendations would you make to the Graffs about protecting their business from embezzlement in the future?
3. Working with several of your classmates, use the resources of the Web to develop a list of steps entrepreneurs should take to prevent their businesses from becoming victims of employee theft and embezzlement.

Source: Adapted from John Grossmann, "A Thief Within," *Inc.*, May 2003, pp. 42–44.

Keep Your Business Plan Current

Before approaching any potential lender or investor, a business owner must prepare a solid business plan. Smart owners keep their plans up to date in case an unexpected cash crisis forces them to seek emergency financing. Revising the plan annually also forces the owner to focus on managing the business more effectively.

Invest Surplus Cash

Because of the uneven flow of receipts and disbursements, a company will often temporarily have more cash than it needs—for a week, month, a quarter, or even longer. When this happens, most small business owners simply ignore the surplus because they are not sure how soon they will need it. They believe that relatively small amounts of cash sitting around for just a few days or weeks are not worth investing. However, this is not the case. Small business owners who put surplus cash to work *immediately* rather than allowing it to sit idle soon discover that the yield adds up to a significant amount over time. This money can help ease the daily cash crunch during business troughs. "Your goal . . . should be to identify every dollar you don't need to pay today's bills and to keep that money invested to improve your cash flow," explains a consultant.[67]

However, when investing surplus cash, an entrepreneur's primary objective should *not* be to earn the highest yield (which usually carries with it high levels of risk); instead, the focus should be on the safety and the liquidity of the investments. Making high-risk investments with a company's cash cushion makes no sense and could jeopardize its future. The need to minimize risk and to have ready access to the cash restricts an entrepreneur's investment options to just a few, such as money market accounts, zero-balance accounts, and sweep accounts. A **money market account** is an interest-bearing account offered by a variety of financial institutions ranging from banks to mutual funds. Money market accounts pay interest while allowing depositors to write checks (most have minimum check amounts) without tying their money up for a specific period of time. After surviving a cash crisis shortly after launching their branding and communications company, Jaye Donaldson and her partner, Chester Makoski, now keep enough cash invested in a money market account to cover at least three to six months' of expenses.[68]

A **zero-balance account (ZBA)** is a checking account that technically never has any funds in it but is tied to a master account. The company keeps its money in the master account, where it earns interest, but it writes checks on the ZBA. At the end of the day, the bank pays all of the checks drawn on the ZBA; then it withdraws enough money from

money market account
an interest-bearing account that allows depositors to write checks without tying up their money for a specific period of time.

zero-balance account (ZBA)
a checking account that never has any funds in it. A company keeps its money in an interest-bearing master account tied to the ZBA; when a check is drawn on the ZBA, the bank withdraws enough money from the master account to cover it.

the master account to cover them. ZBAs allow a company to keep more cash working during the float period, the time between a check being issued and its being cashed. A **sweep account** automatically "sweeps" all funds in a company's checking account above a predetermined minimum into an interest-bearing account, enabling it to keep otherwise idle cash invested until it is needed to cover checks.

sweep account
a checking account that automatically sweeps all funds in a company's checking account above a predetermined minimum into an interest-bearing account.

Conclusion

Successful owners run their businesses "lean and mean." Trimming wasteful expenditures, investing surplus funds, and carefully planning and managing the company's cash flow enables them to compete effectively. The simple but effective techniques covered in this chapter can improve every small company's cash position. One business writer says:

> In the day-to-day course of running a company, other people's capital flows past an imaginative CEO as opportunity. By looking forward and keeping an analytical eye on your cash account as events unfold (remembering that if there's no real cash there when you need it, you're history), you can generate leverage as surely as if that capital were yours to keep.[69]

 ## Chapter Summary by Learning Objectives

1. Explain the importance of cash management to a small company's success.

Cash is the most important but least productive asset the small business has. The manager must maintain enough cash to meet the firm's normal requirements (plus a reserve for emergencies) without retaining excessively large, unproductive cash balances. Without adequate cash, a small business will fail.

2. Differentiate between cash and profits.

Cash and profits are *not* the same. More businesses fail for lack of cash than for lack of profits.

Profits, the difference between total revenue and total expenses, are an accounting concept. Cash flow represents the flow of actual cash (the only thing businesses can use to pay bills) through a business in a continuous cycle. A business can be earning a profit and be forced out of business because it runs out of cash.

3. Understand the five steps in creating a cash budget and use them to create one.

The cash budgeting procedure outlined in this chapter tracks the flow of cash through the business and enables the owner to project cash surpluses and cash deficits at specific intervals.

The five steps in creating a cash budget are as follows: determining an adequate minimum cash balance, forecasting sales, forecasting cash receipts, forecasting cash disbursements, and determining the end-of-month cash balance.

4. Describe fundamental principles involved in managing the "big three" of cash management: accounts receivable, accounts payable, and inventory.

Controlling accounts receivable requires business owners to establish clear, firm credit and collection policies and to screen customers *before* granting them credit. Sending invoices promptly and acting on past-due accounts quickly also improve cash flow. The goal is to collect cash from receivables as quickly as possible.

When managing accounts payable, a manager's goal is to stretch out payables as long as possible without damaging the company's credit rating. Other techniques include verifying invoices before paying them, taking advantage of cash discounts, and negotiating the best possible credit terms.

Inventory frequently causes cash headaches for small business managers. Excess inventory earns a zero rate of return and ties up a company's cash unnecessarily. Owners must watch for stale merchandise.

5. Explain the techniques for avoiding a cash crunch in a small company.

Trimming overhead costs by bartering, leasing assets, avoiding nonessential outlays, using zero-based budgeting, and implementing an internal control system boost a firm's cash flow position.

In addition, investing surplus cash maximizes the firm's earning power. The primary criteria for investing surplus cash are security and liquidity.

Discussion Questions

1. Why must entrepreneurs concentrate on effective cash flow management?
2. Explain the difference between cash and profit.
3. Outline the steps involved in developing a cash budget.
4. How can an entrepreneur launching a new business forecast sales?
5. What are the "big three" of cash management? What effect do they have on a company's cash flow?
6. Outline the basic principles of managing a small firm's receivables, payables, and inventory.
7. How can bartering improve a company's cash position?
8. What steps can entrepreneurs take to conserve the cash within their companies?
9. What should be a small business owner's primary concern when investing surplus cash?

Business Plan Pro

Business PlanPro

In addition to being a valuable planning tool, your cash flow statement can be a valuable tool with which to assess the future health and potential of your venture. As the chapter stated, cash is not profit, and there are aspects of understanding cash flow that are nonintuitive. We will review the cash flow that is in your plan and, based on this chapter, determine what you can learn from that cash flow statement and assess how financially solid your plan is based on your information to date.

Business Plan Exercises

On the Web

Go to http://www.prenhall.com/scarborough and look at the links associated with Chapter 12. The online resources listed there may offer additional information regarding the cash flow statement and the role it will play in your business plan.

In the Software

Review the information that you have regarding your sales forecast and the expense information you entered in your proforma profit and loss statement. Change any figures that your have now determined to be unrealistic, if necessary. Now, go to the Financial Statement section of your business plan and look at your Projected Cash Flow Statement. Do any of these months show a negative cash flow? If this is the case, based on your projections, you do not have an adequate cash cushion. The lowest, most negative amount indicates the minimal amount of additional cash your business needs. Make sure that your projections are realistic and that you have adequate cash to make it through this negative period. Advanced planning is your best opportunity to avoid bankruptcy. Conversely, are there months where your projections indicate an excess amount of cash? If so, explore options to use this cash to its best ability when that time comes.

Save any changes you have made in your plan. Let's work on the basis that this version of your plan represents your "most likely" outcome based on realistic expense and revenue projections. We are now going to do two "what-if" scenarios. Save this same file with the words "worst case" after the file name or some file name that will enable you to save all you work from before and create another version of your business plan. This will enable you to make changes in your plan, and we will assess what that does to your cash flow. For example, lower your revenues by 25 percent. What does that do to you cash flow? Now, increase your expenses by 25 percent. What impact does that have regarding the amount of cash you will need to get through the most negative cash flow months? If you are extending credit, increase that by 15 days, from 30 to 45 days, for example. What does your cash flow statement look like now? Make the changes that could paint a potentially negative picture for your venture and save the plan under the new "worst case" file name. Close that plan and open your original so we can start with your "most likely" scenario again.

Save your original under a "best case" file name. If you are planning to extend credit, decrease the number of collection days by seven. What does that do to your cash flow? Increase your revenues by 15 percent. Decrease your projected expenses by 15 percent. Working through these scenarios can help you to test and validate your numbers and prepare your for contingencies and options as your plan becomes a reality.

Building Your Business Plan

Review the data that affect your cash flow statement. Are there revisions you need to make based on your proforma cash flow statement? What are some of the most significant cash demands of your business? Is one due to cash tied up in inventory? Is one your payroll? Are rent or lease expenditures disproportionately high based on your projected revenues? Can you take steps to reduce or better control these expenditures as you build your revenue stream? Once you have answered these questions, again determine whether you have adequate cash for your venture, allowing for potential cost overrun or revenues below your projections.

Beyond the Classroom . . .

1. Interview several local small business owners about their cash management policies. Do they know how much cash their businesses have during the month? How do they track their cash flows? Do they use some type of cash budget? If not, ask whether you can help the owner develop one. Does the owner invest surplus cash? If so, where?

2. Volunteer to help a small business owner develop a cash budget for his or her company. What patterns do you detect? What recommendations can you make for improving the company's cash management system?

3. Contact the International Reciprocal Trade Association (http://www.irta.net/) and get a list of the barter exchanges in your state. Interview the manager of one of the exchanges and prepare a report on how barter exchanges work and how they benefit small businesses. Ask the manager to refer you to a small business owner who benefits from the barter exchange and interview him or her. How does the owner use the exchange? How much cash has bartering saved? What other benefits has the owner discovered?

4. Use the resources of the World Wide Web to research leasing options for small companies. The Equipment Leasing Association of America (http://www.elaonline.com/) and its Lease Assistant site (http://www.leaseassistant.org/) are good places to start. What advantages does leasing offer? Disadvantages? Identify and explain the various types of leases.

5. Contact a local small business owner who sells on credit. Is collecting accounts receivable on time a problem? What steps does the owner take to manage the company's accounts receivable? Do late payers strain the company's cash flow? How does the owner deal with customers who pay late?

13 | Sources of Financing: Debt and Equity

If you don't know who the fool
is in a deal, it's you.
—Michael Wolff

Learning Objectives

On completion of this chapter, you will be able to:

1 Explain the differences among the three types of capital small businesses require: fixed, working, and growth.
2 Describe the differences between equity capital and debt capital and the advantages and disadvantages of each.
3 Discuss the various sources of equity capital available to entrepreneurs.
4 Describe the process of "going public," as well as its advantages and disadvantages and the various simplified registrations and exemptions from registration available to small businesses wanting to sell securities to investors.
5 Describe the various sources of debt capital and the advantages and disadvantages of each.
6 Identify the various federal loan programs aimed at small businesses.
7 Describe the various loan programs available from the Small Business Administration.
8 Discuss valuable methods of financing growth and expansion internally.

Raising the money to launch a new business venture has always been a challenge for entrepreneurs. Capital markets rise and fall with the stock market, overall economic conditions, and investors' fortunes. These swells and troughs in the availability of capital make the search for financing look like a wild roller coaster ride. For instance, during the late 1990s, founders of dot-com companies were able to attract mountains of cash from private and professional investors, even if their businesses existed only on paper! Investors flocked to initial public offerings from practically any dot-com company. The market for capital became bipolar: easy-money times for dot-coms and tight-money times for "not-coms." Even established, profitable companies in "old economy" industries such as manufacturing, distribution, real estate, and brick-and-mortar retail could not raise the capital they needed to grow. Then, early in 2000, the dot-com bubble burst, and financing an Internet business also became extremely challenging.

Today, the challenge of attracting capital to start or to expand a business remains. Most entrepreneurs, especially those in less glamorous industries or those just starting out, face difficulty finding outside sources of financing. Many banks shy away from making loans to start-ups, and venture capitalists have become more risk averse, shifting their investments away from start-up companies to more-established businesses. Private investors have grown cautious, and making a public stock offering remains a viable option for only a handful of promising companies with good track records and fast-growth futures. The result has been a credit crunch for entrepreneurs looking for small to moderate amounts of start-up capital. Entrepreneurs and business owners needing between $100,000 and $3 million are especially hard hit because of the vacuum that exists at that level of financing.

In the face of this capital crunch, business's need for capital has never been greater. Experts estimate that the small business financing market exceeds $170 billion a year, yet that still is not enough to satisfy the capital appetites of entrepreneurs and their cash-hungry businesses.[1] When searching for the capital to launch their companies, entrepreneurs must remember the following "secrets" to successful financing:

- ■ *Choosing the right sources of capital for a business can be just as important as choosing the right form of ownership or the right location.* It is a decision that will influence a company for a lifetime, so entrepreneurs must weigh their options carefully before committing to a particular funding source. "It is important that companies in need of capital align themselves with sources that best fit their needs," says one financial consultant. "The success of a company often depends on the success of that relationship."[2]
- ■ *The money is out there; the key is knowing where to look.* Entrepreneurs must do their homework *before* they set out to raise money for their ventures. Understanding which sources of funding are best suited for the various stages of a company's growth and then taking the time to learn how those sources work is essential to success.
- ■ *Raising money takes time and effort.* Sometimes entrepreneurs are surprised at the energy and the time required to raise the capital needed to feed their cash-hungry, growing businesses. The process usually includes lots of promising leads, most of which turn out to be dead-ends. Meetings with and presentations to lots of potential investors and lenders can crowd out the time needed to manage a growing company. Entrepreneurs also discover that raising capital is an ongoing job. "The fund-raising game is a marathon, not a sprint," says Jerusha Stewart, founder of iSpiritus Soul Spa, a store selling personal growth and well-being products.[3]
- ■ *Creativity counts.* Although some traditional sources of funds now play a lesser role in small business finance than in the past, other sources—from large corporations and customers to international venture capitalists and state or local programs—are taking up the slack. To find the financing their businesses demand, entrepreneurs must use as much creativity in attracting financing as they did in generating the ideas for their products and services. For instance, after striking out with traditional sources of funding, EZConserve, a company that makes software that provides energy management tools for large PC networks, turned to the nonprofit group Northwest Energy Efficiency Alliance and received a sizeable grant as well as marketing assistance that fueled its growth.[4]

■ *The World Wide Web puts at entrepreneurs' fingertips vast resources of information that can lead to financing; use it.* The Web often offers entrepreneurs, especially those looking for relatively small amounts of money, the opportunity to discover sources of funds that they otherwise might miss. The Web site created for this book (http://www.prenhall.com/scarborough) provides links to many useful sites related to raising both start-up and growth capital. The Web also provides a low-cost, convenient way for entrepreneurs to get their business plans into potential investors' hands anywhere in the world. When searching for sources of capital, entrepreneurs must not overlook this valuable tool.

■ *Be thoroughly prepared before approaching potential lenders and investors.* In the hunt for capital, tracking down leads is tough enough; don't blow a potential deal. Be ready to present your business idea to potential lenders and investors in a clear, concise, convincing way. That, of course, requires a solid business plan and a well-rehearsed "elevator pitch"—one or two minutes on the nature of your business and the source of its competitive edge—capable of winning over potential investors and lenders.

■ *Entrepreneurs cannot overestimate the importance of making sure that the "chemistry" among themselves, their companies, and their funding sources is a good one.* Too many entrepreneurs get into financial deals because they needed the money to keep their businesses growing, only to discover that their plans do not match those of their financial partners.

Rather than rely primarily on a single source of funds as they have in the past, entrepreneurs must piece together capital from multiple sources, a method known as **layered financing.** They have discovered that raising capital successfully requires them to cast a wide net to capture the financing they need to launch their businesses.

layered financing
the technique of raising capital from multiple sources.

AgraQuest

Since launching AgraQuest, a company that makes a line of environmentally friendly agricultural biopesticides, Pamela Marrone has raised more than $60 million from a multitude of sources, providing a perfect illustration of the "patchwork" of start-up financing that has become so common. Marrone has negotiated eight different rounds of financing with more than 70 different investors, including friends, family members, major agricultural corporations, "angels" (private investors), and venture capital firms. "We've gotten money from everywhere," says Marrone. "We've raised a round of capital every year. AgraQuest now generates annual sales of more than $10 million and is growing fast, which provides the impetus for the constant search for cash. "A lot of entrepreneurs get indignant about the [fund-raising] process," says Marrone. "But you've got to put your ego aside and get the money in the door."[5]

This chapter will guide you through the myriad financing options available to entrepreneurs, focusing on both sources of equity (ownership) and debt (borrowed) financing.

Planning for Capital Needs

LEARNING OBJECTIVES
1. Explain the differences among the three types of capital small businesses require: fixed, working, and growth.

Becoming a successful entrepreneur requires one to become a skilled fund-raiser, a job that usually requires more time and energy than most business founders realize. In start-up companies, raising capital can easily consume as much as one-half of the entrepreneur's time and can take many months to complete. In addition, many entrepreneurs find it necessary to raise capital constantly to fuel the hefty capital appetites of their young, fast-growing companies. Most entrepreneurs seek less than $1 million (indeed, most need less than $100,000), which may be the toughest money to secure. Where to find this seed money depends, in part, on the nature of the proposed business and on the amount of money required. For example, the originator of a computer software firm would have different capital requirements than the founder of a coal mining operation. Although both entrepreneurs might approach some of the same types of lenders or investors, each would be more successful targeting specific sources of funds best suited to their particular financial needs.

Capital is any form of wealth employed to produce more wealth. It exists in many forms in a typical business, including cash, inventory, plant, and equipment. Entrepreneurs need three different types of capital, as follows.

capital
any form of wealth employed to produce more wealth.

Fixed Capital

Fixed capital is needed to purchase a company's permanent or fixed assets such as buildings, land, computers, and equipment. Money invested in these fixed assets tends to be frozen because it cannot be used for any other purpose. Typically, large sums of money are involved in purchasing fixed assets, and credit terms usually are lengthy. Lenders of fixed capital expect the assets purchased to improve the efficiency and, thus, the profitability of the business and to create improved cash flow that ensures repayment.

fixed capital
capital needed to purchase a company's permanent or fixed assets such as land, buildings, computers, and equipment.

Working Capital

Working capital represents a business's temporary funds; it is the capital used to support a company's normal short-term operations. Accountants define working capital as current assets minus current liabilities. The need for working capital arises because of the uneven flow of cash into and out of the business due to normal seasonal fluctuations (refer to Chapter 12). Credit sales, seasonal sales swings, or unforeseeable changes in demand will create fluctuations in *any* small company's cash flow. Working capital normally is used to buy inventory, pay bills, finance credit sales, pay wages and salaries, and take care of any unexpected emergencies. Lenders of working capital expect it to produce higher cash flows to ensure repayment at the end of the production/sales cycle.

working capital
capital needed to support a business's short-term operations; it represents a company's temporary funds.

Growth Capital

Growth capital, unlike working capital, is not related to the seasonal fluctuations of a small business. Instead, growth capital requirements surface when an existing business is expanding or changing its primary direction. For example, a small manufacturer of silicon chips for computers saw his business skyrocket in a short time period. With orders for chips rushing in, the growing business needed a sizable cash infusion to increase plant size, expand its sales and production workforce, and buy more equipment. During times of such rapid expansion, a growing company's capital requirements are similar to those of a business start-up. Like lenders of fixed capital, growth capital lenders expect the funds to improve a company's profitability and cash flow position, thus ensuring repayment.

growth capital
capital needed to finance a company's growth or its expansion in a new direction.

Although these three types of capital are interdependent, each has certain sources, characteristics, and effects on the business and its long-term growth that entrepreneurs must recognize.

"By God, gentlemen, I believe we've found it—the Fountain of Funding!"

Govworks.com

equity capital
capital that represents the personal investment of the owner (or owners) of a company; sometimes called risk capital.

TeleSym

debt capital
the financing that a small business owner has borrowed and must repay with interest

Equity Capital versus Debt Capital

Equity capital represents the personal investment of the owner (or owners) in a business and is sometimes called *risk capital* because these investors assume the primary risk of losing their funds if the business fails.

Govworks.com, an online provider of government services launched in 1999 by Kaleil Isaza Tuzman and Thomas Herman, grew quickly and within one year counted more than 200 employees on its payroll. Even though Tuzman and Herman had raised more than $60 million in start-up capital, the company had not reached the point at which it was generating positive cash flow when investors' affinity for Internet companies dried up. GovWorks.com, which was the subject of the film *Startup.com,* declared bankruptcy in late 2000, which meant that the founders and investors, which included private equity investors and venture capital firms, lost all of the money they had put into the company.[6]

If a venture succeeds, however, founders and investors share in the benefits, which can be quite substantial. The founders of and early investors in Yahoo, Sun Microsystems, Federal Express, Intel, and Microsoft became multimillionaires when the companies went public and their equity investments finally paid off. One early investor in Google, for example, put $100,000 into the start-up company that graduate students Sergey Brin and Larry Page started from their college dorm room; today, his equity investment is worth $100 million![7] To entrepreneurs, the primary advantage of equity capital is that it does not have to be repaid like a loan does. Equity investors are entitled to share in the company's earnings (if there are any) and usually to have a voice in the company's future direction.

The primary disadvantage of equity capital is that the entrepreneur must give up some—sometimes even *most*—of the ownership in the business to outsiders. Although 50 percent of something is better than 100 percent of nothing, giving up control of a company can be disconcerting and dangerous.

Karl Denninghoff and Raju Gulabani raised $18 million in venture capital for their software start-up TeleSym. In exchange for their investment, the venture capital firms took a controlling interest in the company as well as seats on TeleSym's board of directors (which is typical of most venture capital deals). Within three years, the board voted to fire both Denninghoff and Gulabani from the company they had co-founded. Fourteen months after their removal, TeleSym went out of business. According to one former employee, the move to fire the co-founders was "the kiss of death" for the TeleSym because no one else had as deep an understanding of the company's products as they did.[8]

Entrepreneurs are most likely to give up significant amounts of equity in their businesses in the start-up phase than in any other. To avoid having to give up majority control of their companies early on, entrepreneurs should strive to launch their companies with the smallest amount of money possible.

Debt capital is the financing that a small business owner has borrowed and must repay with interest. Very few entrepreneurs have adequate personal savings needed to finance the complete start-up costs of a small business; many of them must rely on some form of debt capital to launch their companies. Lenders of capital are more numerous than investors, although small business loans can be just as difficult (if not more difficult) to obtain. Although borrowed capital allows entrepreneurs to maintain complete ownership of their businesses, it must be carried as a liability on the balance sheet as well as be repaid with interest at some point in the future. In addition, because lenders consider small businesses to be greater risks than bigger corporate customers, they require higher interest rates on loans to small companies because of the risk–return tradeoff—the higher the risk, the greater is the return demanded. Most small firms pay the prime rate—the interest rate banks charge their most creditworthy customers—*plus* a few percentage points. Still, the cost of debt financing often is lower than that of equity financing. Because of the higher risks associated with providing equity capital to small companies, investors demand greater returns than lenders. In addition, unlike equity financing, debt financing does not require entrepreneurs to dilute their ownership interest in their companies. We now turn our attention to eight common sources of equity capital.

Sources of Equity Financing

Personal Savings

LEARNING OBJECTIVES
3. Discuss the various sources of equity capital available to entrepreneurs.

The *first* place entrepreneurs should look for start-up money is in their own pockets. It's the least expensive source of funds available. "The sooner you take outside money, the more ownership in your company you'll have to surrender," warns one small business expert.[9] Entrepreneurs apparently see the benefits of self-sufficiency; the most common source of equity funds used to start a small business is the entrepreneur's pool of personal savings.

Kiss My Face

In 1979, when Bob MacLeod and Stephen Byckiewicz launched Kiss My Face, a company that sold a line of soaps and shampoos, they could not persuade a bank to lend them any money, so they pooled all they had—just $10,000—and invested it in the business. Sales were thin in the early years, but they climbed steadily with the help of creative marketing and the strategic partnerships with larger companies that MacLeod and Byckiewicz forged. The entrepreneurs financed their company's growth with retained earnings and some debt but retained 100 percent ownership. Today, Kiss My Face is debt-free and tallies annual sales of more than $30 million. "We're very happy to have maintained complete control of our business," says MacLeod.[10]

Lenders and investors *expect* entrepreneurs to put their own money into a business start-up. If an entrepreneur is not willing to risk his or her own money, potential investors are not likely to risk their money in the business either. Furthermore, failing to put up sufficient capital of their own means that entrepreneurs must either borrow an excessive amount of capital or give up a significant portion of ownership to outsiders to fund the business properly. Excessive borrowing in the early days of a business puts intense pressure on its cash flow, and becoming a minority shareholder may dampen a founder's enthusiasm for making a business successful. Neither outcome presents a bright future for the company involved.

Friends and Family Members

Although most entrepreneurs look to their own bank accounts first to finance a business, few have sufficient resources to launch their businesses alone. After emptying their own pockets, where should entrepreneurs should turn for capital? The second place most entrepreneurs look is to friends and family members who might be willing to invest in a business venture. Because of their relationships with the founder, these people are most likely to invest. Often, they are more patient than other outside investors and are less meddlesome in a business's affairs than many other types of investors (but not always!).

CMB Sweets

In 2004, Carolina Braunschweig used her own money to launch CMB Sweets, a company that makes jams and jellies. Sales grew slowly, and the company's early life was marked by a series of financial struggles, which Braunschweig managed to work through. Before the company's second birthday, Braunschweig's father offered to invest $15,000 in CMB Sweets. Braunschweig accepted her father's offer, but the two agreed to treat the money as a loan rather than as an equity investment. Until she is able to pay back the loan (with interest), Braunschweig says she will treat her father as if he were a member of the company's board of directors. "I give him regular updates on sales volumes, on who has reordered, and on what new accounts [the sales] reps have landed," she says.[11]

Investments from family and friends are an excellent source of seed capital and can get a start-up far enough along to attract money from private investors or venture capital companies. Inherent dangers lurk in family business investments, however. Unrealistic expectations or misunderstood risks have destroyed many friendships and have ruined many family reunions. To avoid such problems, an entrepreneur must honestly present the investment opportunity and the nature of the risks involved to avoid alienating friends and family members if the business fails. Smart entrepreneurs treat family members and friends who invest in their companies in the same way they would treat business partners. Some investments in start-up companies return more than friends and family members ever could have imagined. In 1995, Mike and Jackie Bezos invested $300,000 into their son Jeff's start-up business, Amazon.com. Today, Mike and Jackie own six percent of Amazon.com's stock, and their shares are worth billions of dollars.[12] The accompanying "Hands on . . . How to" feature offers suggestions for structuring successful family or friendship financing deals.

Hands on ... How to

Structure Family and Friendship Financing Deals

Tapping family members and friends for start-up capital, whether in the form of equity or debt financing, is a popular method of financing business ideas. In a typical year, some 6 million individuals in the United States invest about $100 billion in entrepreneurial ventures. Unfortunately, these deals don't always work to the satisfaction of both parties. For instance, when actor Don Johnson needed seed capital to launch DJ Racing, a company that designs and races speedboats, he approached a wealthy Miami friend who made a $300,000 interest-free loan on nothing but a handshake. Within a year, a dispute arose over when Johnson was to pay back the loan. A lawsuit followed, which the two, now former friends settled out of court. The following suggestions can help entrepreneurs avoid needlessly destroying family relationships and friendships:

- *Consider the impact of the investment on everyone involved.* Will it work a hardship on anyone? Is the investor putting up the money because he or she wants to or because he or she feels obligated to? Can all parties afford the loan if the business folds? Lynn McPhee used $250,000 from family members to launch Xuny, a Web-based clothing store. "Our basic rule of thumb was, if [the investment is] going to strap someone, we won't take it," she says.

- *Keep the arrangement strictly business.* The parties should treat all loans and investments in a business-like manner, no matter how close the friendship or family relationship, to avoid problems down the line. "If the [family member] doesn't ask to go through a formal process, the risks for the business are significantly higher," says Tom Davidow, a family business consultant. If the transaction is a loan exceeding $10,000, it must carry a rate of interest at least as high as the market rate; otherwise the IRS may consider the loan a gift and penalize the lender.

- *Settle the details up front.* Before any money changes hands, both parties must agree on the details of the deal. How much money is involved? Is it a loan or an investment? How will the investor cash out? How will the loan be paid off? What happens if the business fails?

- *Never accept more than investors can afford to lose.* No matter how much capital you may need, accepting more than family members or friends can afford to lose is a recipe for disaster—and perhaps bankruptcy for the investors.

- *Create a written contract.* Don't make the mistake of closing a financial deal with just a handshake. The probability of misunderstandings skyrockets. Putting an agreement in writing demonstrates the parties' commitment to the deal and minimizes the chances of disputes from faulty memories and misunderstandings.

- ***Treat the money as "bridge financing."*** Although family and friends can help you to launch your business, it is unlikely that they can provide enough capital to sustain it over the long term. Sooner or later, you will need to establish a relationship with other sources of credit if your company is to survive and thrive. Consider money from family and friends as a bridge to take your company to the next level of financing.
- ***Develop a payment schedule that suits both the entrepreneur and the lender or investor.*** Although lenders and investors may want to get their money back as quickly as possible, a rapid repayment or cashout schedule can jeopardize a fledgling company's survival. Establish a realistic repayment plan that works for the parties without putting excessive strain on the young company's cash flow.
- ***Have an exit plan.*** Every deal should define exactly how investors will "cash out" their investments.

Derek Mercer called his favorite aunt, Delores Kessler, herself a successful entrepreneur, and asked her to look over a business plan for a software company he wanted to launch. Then he asked her to lend him $50,000 in start-up capital. Impressed by the quality of Mercer's business plan, Kessler agreed to lend the money on one condition: "It will be a business arrange-ment," she insisted, "with paperwork, not just a hug and off you go." With her business experience, Kessler convinced Mercer that $50,000 would not be sufficient start-up capital. Instead, she offered Mercer a $100,000 line of credit that he could draw on as needed in $10,000 increments at an interest rate tied to the prime rate. "It was crystal clear," recalls Mercer. "If I didn't make an interest payment, her assistant would call me."

Mercer launched Recruitmax Software Inc. and within a few years repaid the entire loan from his aunt. As the company grew and its capital requirements increased, Kessler helped her nephew establish contacts with potential investors and venture capitalists. Using those contacts, Mercer secured $17.3 million in venture capital and has built Recruitmax into a successful busi-ness with 230 employees and annual sales approaching $40 million. "I am just so proud of him," says Kessler of her nephew.

Source: Adapted from Paulette Thomas, "It's All Relative," *Wall Street Journal,* November 29, 2004, pp. RR4, R8; Andrea Coombes, "Retirees as Venture Capitalists," CBS.MarketWatch.com, November 2, 2003, http://netscape.marketwatch.com/news/story.asp?dist=feed&siteid=netscape&guid=/{E1267CD-32A4-4558-9F7E-40E4B7892D01}; Paul Kvinta, "Frogskins, Shekels, Bucks, Moolah, Cash, Simoleans, Dough, Dinero: Everybody Wants It. Your Business Needs It. Here's How to Get It," *Smart Business,* August 2000, pp. 74–89. Alex Markels, "A Little Help from Their Friends," *Wall Street Journal,* May 22, 1995, p. R10; Heather Chaplin, "Friends and Family," *Your Company,* September 1999, p. 26.

"Angels"

After dipping into their own pockets and convincing friends and relatives to invest in their business ventures, many entrepreneurs still find themselves short of the seed capital they need. Frequently, the next stop on the road to business financing is private investors. These **private investors ("angels")** are wealthy individuals, often entrepreneurs themselves, who invest in business start-ups in exchange for equity stakes in the companies. Angel investors have provided much-needed capital to entrepreneurs for many years. In 1938, when World War I flying ace Eddie Rickenbacker needed money to launch Eastern Airlines, millionaire Laurance Rockefeller provided it.[13] Alexander Graham Bell, inventor of the telephone, used angel capital to start Bell Telephone in 1877. More recently, compa-nies such as Google, Apple Computer, Starbucks, Kinko's, and the Body Shop relied on angel financing in their early years to finance growth. Today, angel capital is the largest source of external financing for companies in the seed and start-up phases.

In many cases, angels invest in businesses for more than purely economic reasons— for example, they have a personal interest or experience in a particular industry—and they are willing to put money into companies in the earliest stages long before venture capital firms and institutional investors jump in. Angel financing is ideal for companies that have outgrown the capacity of investments from friends and family but are still too small to attract the interest of venture capital companies. Angel financing is vital to the nation's small business sector because it fills this capital gap in which small companies need invest-ments ranging from $100,000 or less to perhaps $5 million. For instance, after raising the money to launch Amazon.com from family and friends, Jeff Bezos turned to angels for capital because venture capital firms were not interested in investing in a business start-up. Bezos attracted $1.2 million from a dozen angels before landing $8 million from venture capital firms a year later.[14]

Angels are a primary source of startup capital for companies in the embryonic stage through the growth stage, and their role in financing small businesses is significant. Research at the University of New Hampshire shows that nearly 230,000 angels invest $23 billion a year in 50,000 small companies, most of them in the start-up phase.[15] Because the angel market is so fragmented and, in many cases, built on anonymity, it is difficult to get a completely accurate estimate of its investment in business start-ups. Although they may disagree on the exact amount of angel investments, experts concur on one fact: angels are the largest single source of external equity capital for small businesses. Their investments in young companies exceed those of professional venture capitalists, providing more capital to 17 times as many small companies.

Angels fill a significant gap in the seed capital market. They are most likely to finance start-ups with capital requirements in the $10,000 to $2,000,000 range, well below the $3 million to $10 million minimum investments most professional venture capitalists prefer. Because a $1 million deal requires about as much of a venture capitalist's time to research and evaluate as a $10 million deal, venture capitalists tend to focus on big deals, where their returns are bigger. Angels also tolerate risk levels that would make venture capitalists shudder; as much as 80 percent of angel-backed companies fail.[16] One angel investor, a former executive at Oracle Corporation, says that of the 10 companies he has invested in, 7 flopped. Three of the start-ups, however, have produced 50-fold returns![17] Because of the inherent risks in start-up companies, many venture capitalists have shifted their investment portfolios away from start-ups toward more-established firms. That's why angel financing is so important: Angels often finance deals that no venture capitalist will consider.

The typical angel invests in companies at the seed or start-up growth stages and accepts 10 percent of the investment opportunities presented, makes an average of two investments every three years, and has invested an average of $80,000 of equity in 3.5 firms. Ninety percent say they are satisfied with their investment decisions.[18] When evaluating a proposal, angels look for a qualified management team and a business with a clearly defined niche, market potential, and competitive advantage. They also want to see market research that proves the existence of a sizable customer base.

Entrepreneurs in search of capital quickly learn that the real challenge lies in *finding* angels. Most angels have substantial business and financial experience, and many of them are entrepreneurs or former entrepreneurs. Because most angels frown on "cold calls" from entrepreneurs they don't know, locating them boils down to making the right contacts. Networking is the key. Asking friends, attorneys, bankers, stockbrokers, accountants, other business owners, and consultants for suggestions and introductions is a good way to start. Angels almost always invest their money locally, so entrepreneurs should look close to home for them—typically within a 50- to 100-mile radius. Angels also look for businesses they know something about, and most expect to invest their knowledge, experience, and energy as well as their money in a company. In fact, the advice and the network of contacts that angels bring to a deal can sometimes be as valuable as their money.

eSigma

When Troy Haaland and three co-workers left their jobs to launch eSigma, a company that offers Web-based business services, they recognized that although they had ample technical skill, they lacked managerial skill and business experience. Haaland and his co-founders approached two angel investors in the Chicago area and asked them not only to invest in the business, but also to help the entrepreneurs find the management talent they needed. The two angels invested $200,000 in eSigma and used their network of contacts to recruit a CEO for the company.[19]

Angels tend to invest in clusters as well. With the right approach, an entrepreneur can attract an angel who might share the deal with some of his or her cronies.

In 1995, Hans Severiens, a professional investor, created the Band of Angels, a group of about 150 angels (mostly Silicon Valley millionaires, many of whom are retired entrepreneurs) who meet monthly in Portola Valley, California, to listen to entrepreneurs pitch their business plans. The Band of Angels reviews about 30 proposals each month before inviting three entrepreneurs to make 20-minute presentations at their monthly meeting. Interested members often team up with one another to invest in the businesses they consider most promising. Over the years, the Band of Angels has invested a total of more than $117 million in promising young companies. The average investment is $700,000, which usually nets the angels between 15 percent and 25 percent of a company's stock. At one meeting, Craig McMullen, CEO of Cardiac Focus, a company that is developing a disposable vest to help doctors map patients' cardiac arrythmias without surgery, made a pitch for $2 million. Cardiac Focus needed the money to complete its management team, perform clinical trials, and file for approval from the Food and Drug Adminstration. Within weeks of the presentation, 14 members of the Band of Angels decided to invest, giving Cardiac Focus the capital it needed to reach the next phase of growth.[20]

Band of Angels

An important trend in angel investing is the formation of angel networks, organized groups of angels who pool their capital and make investment decisions much like venture capital companies do. Angel investing "is not what it used to be," says Bob Greene, cofounder of the investment company Oncore Capital. "It's getting more organized and more professional."[21] More than 200 angel networks now operate in the United States.[22] Taking a more sophisticated and formal approach than informal angel clusters, angel networks are more visible and make the task of locating angels much easier for entrepreneurs in search of capital.

When Albert Charpentier was looking for capital to launch Intellifit, a company that makes a booth that uses radio waves to scan shoppers' bodies in just 10 seconds to get the perfect fit in clothing, he approached Robin Hood Ventures, an angel network based in Philadelphia that typically invests up to $500,000 in a single round. Charpentier convinced Robin Hood Ventures to invest $200,000 in a first round of financing for Intellifit, which now has its body-scanning booths in more than a dozen retail clothing locations across the United States and England.[23]

Intellifit

Finding the capital to launch or expand their businesses is a struggle for many entrepreneurs. To finance the start-up of Intellifit, a company that makes a booth that uses radio waves to scan shoppers' bodies for the perfect fit in clothing, Albert Charpentier relied on financing from private investors ("angels").

The Internet has expanded greatly the ability of entrepreneurs in search of capital and angels in search of businesses to find one another. Dozens of angel networks have opened on the Web, many of which are members of the Angel Capital Association (http://www.angelcapitalassociation.org). The association reports that its average member group has 50 investors and invests $1.85 million in five small companies each year.[24] Another network, Active Capital (formerly called ACE-Net, the Access to Capital Electronic Network), is a Web-based listing service that provides a marketplace for entrepreneurs seeking between $250,000 and $5 million in capital and angels looking to invest in promising businesses. Since its inception in 1995, Active Capital has helped entrepreneurs raise more than $100 million.[25] Entrepreneurs pay a maximum of $1,000 a year to list information about their companies with Active Capital (http://www.activecapital.org), which potential angels can access at any time. One significant advantage to entrepreneurs who register their equity offerings with Active Capital is that the online registration exempts them from having to register their offerings separately with regulators in each state (which can cost anywhere from $10,000 to $50,000 per state). Small companies that raise capital through Active Capital do so by using one of the simplified registrations—often the Small Company Offering Registration (SCOR) or Regulation D, Rule 504—that we will cover later in this chapter.

Angels are an excellent source of "patient money," often willing to wait seven years or longer to cash out their investments. They earn their returns through the increased value of the business, not through dividends and interest. For example, more than 1,000 early investors in Microsoft Inc. are now multimillionaires. The $200,000 that Sun Microsystems co-founder Andy Bechtosheim invested in a small start-up named Google grew to be worth more than $300 million![26] Angels' return on investment targets tend to be lower than those of professional venture capitalists. Although venture capitalists shoot for 60 to 75 percent returns annually, angel investors usually settle for 20 to 50 percent (depending on the level of risk involved in the venture). Angel investors typically purchase 15 to 30 percent ownership in a small company, leaving the majority ownership to the company founder(s). They look for the same exit strategies that venture capital firms look for: either an initial public offering or a buyout by a larger company. The lesson: If an entrepreneur needs relatively small amounts of money to launch or to grow a company, angels are an excellent source.

Partners

As we saw in Chapter 4, entrepreneurs can take on partners to expand the capital foundation of a business.

CME Conference Video

When Lou Bucelli and Tim Crouse were searching for the money to launch CME Conference Video, a company that produces and distributes videotapes of educational conferences for physicians, they found an angel willing to put up $250,000 for 40 percent of the business. Unfortunately, their investor backed out when some of his real estate investments went bad, leaving the partners with commitments for several conferences but no cash to produce and distribute the videos. With little time to spare, Bucelli and Crouse decided to form a series of limited partnerships with people they knew, one for each videotape they would produce. Six limited partnerships produced $400,000 in financing, and the tapes generated $9.1 million in sales for the year. As the general partners, Bucelli and Crouse retained 80 percent of each partnership. The limited partners earned returns of up to 80 percent in just six months. Within two years, their company was so successful that venture capitalists started calling. To finance their next round of growth, Bucelli and Crouse sold 35 percent of their company to a venture capital firm for $1.3 million.[27]

Before entering into any partnership arrangement, however, entrepreneurs must consider the impact of giving up some personal control over operations and of sharing profits with others. Whenever entrepreneurs give up equity in their businesses (through whatever mechanism), they run the risk of losing control over it. As the founder's ownership in a company becomes increasingly diluted, the probability of losing control of its future direction and the entire decision-making process increases.

Rollerblades Inc.

At age 19, Scott Olson started a company that manufactured in-line skates—a company that he had big dreams for. Rollerblades Inc. grew quickly but soon ran into the problem that plagues so many fast-growing companies—insufficient cash flow. Through a series of unfortunate incidents, Olsen began selling shares of ownership in the company for the money he desperately needed to bring his innovative skate designs to market. Ultimately, investors ended up with 95 percent of the company, leaving Olson with the remaining scant 5 percent. Frustrated at not being able to determine the company's direction, Olson soon left to start another company. "It's tough to keep control," he says. "For every penny you get in the door, you have to give something up."[28]

Corporate Venture Capital

Large corporations have gotten into the business of financing small companies. Today, about 300 large corporations across the globe, including Motorola, Qualcomm, Intel, General Electric, Dow Chemical, Cisco Systems, UPS, Wal-Mart, and Johnson & Johnson, invest in fledgling companies, most often those in the product development and sales growth stages. Approximately 20 percent of all venture capital invested comes from corporations.[29] Young companies not only get a boost from the capital injections large companies give them, but they also stand to gain many other benefits from the relationship. The right corporate partner may share technical expertise, distribution channels, and marketing know-how and provide introductions to important customers and suppliers. Another intangible yet highly important advantage an investment from a large corporate partner gives a small company is credibility. Doors that otherwise would be closed to a small company magically open when the right corporation becomes a strategic partner.

When Chris Duggan, founder of Digital Orchid, a small company that provides ring tones and images for customizing cell phones, needed a first round of external capital to finance his company's fast growth, he turned to corporate venture capital. Just two years old, Digital Orchid already had built an impressive list of clients, including NASCAR and the National Hockey League. Duggan's first choice was the venture capital arm of wireless communications giant Qualcomm. "We were looking for something other than money," says Duggan. "We wanted someone who could provide a strategic fit. By aligning ourselves with Qualcomm, we'll have a better shot at deploying our products around the world."[30]

Digital Orchid

Foreign corporations such as Nestle S.A., the Swiss food giant, Japanese electronics companies Hitachi and Nokia, and Orange S.A., one of France's largest companies, are also interested in investing in small U.S. businesses. Often, these corporations are seeking strategic partnerships to gain access to new technology, new products, or access to lucrative U.S. markets. In return, the small companies they invest in benefit from the capital infusion as well as from their partners' international experience and connections. In other cases, small companies are turning to their customers for the resources they need to fuel their rapid growth. Recognizing how interwoven their success is with that of their suppliers, corporate giants such as AT&T, ChevronTexaco, and Ford now offer financial support to many of the small businesses they buy from.

Jeff Brown, CEO of RadioFrame Networks, found not only a customer in France's wireless technology giant Orange S.A., but also an investor. RadioFrame's technology improves the performance of wireless networks inside buildings, making it a perfect fit with Orange's primary business. Through its venture capital division, Orange invested $1.5 million in the 55-person company, giving it enough fuel to feed its growth.[31]

RadioFrame Networks

Venture Capital Companies

Venture capital companies are private, for-profit organizations that assemble pools of capital and then use them to purchase equity positions in young businesses they believe have high-growth and high-profit potential, producing annual returns of 300 to 500 percent within five to seven years. More than 1,300 venture capital firms operate across the United States today, investing billions of dollars (see Figure 13.1) in promising small companies in a wide variety of industries. *Pratt's Guide to Venture Capital Sources*, published by Venture Economics, is a valuable resource for entrepreneurs looking for venture capital. The guide, available in most libraries, includes contact information as well as investment preferences for hundreds of venture capital firms.

Colleges and universities have entered the venture capital business; more than 100 colleges across the nation now have venture funds designed to invest in promising businesses started by their students, alumni, and faculty.[32] Even the Central Intelligence Agency (CIA) has launched a venture capital firm called In-Q-Tel that invests in companies that are developing new technologies that could benefit it. One of In-Q-Tel's investments is in a company that is developing a three-dimensional Web browser that allows users to see "live" versions of the Web sites they visit.[33]

Venture capital firms, which provide about seven percent of all funding for private companies, have invested billions of dollars in high-potential small companies over the years, including such notable businesses as Google, Apple Computer, FedEx, Home Depot, Microsoft, Intel, Starbucks, and Genentech.[34] In many of these deals, several venture capital companies invested money, experience, and advice across several stages of

venture capital companies
private, for-profit organizations that purchase equity positions in young businesses they believe have high-growth and high-profit potential.

FIGURE 13.1

Venture Capital Funding

Source: Money Tree Survey,
PriceWaterhouseCoopers, 2006.

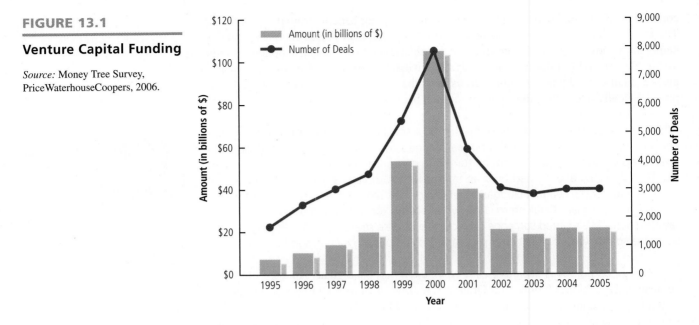

growth. Table 13.1 offers a humorous look at how venture capitalists decipher the language of sometimes overly optimistic entrepreneurs.

Policies and Investment Strategies   Venture capital firms usually establish stringent policies to implement their overall investment strategies.

INVESTMENT SIZE AND SCREENING   Most venture capital firms seek investments in the $3 million to $10 million range to justify the cost of investigating the large number of proposals they receive. The venture capital screening process is *extremely* rigorous. The typical venture capital company invests in less than one percent of the applications it receives. For example, the average venture capital firm screens about 1,200 proposals a year, but more than 90 percent are rejected immediately because they do not match the firm's investment criteria. The remaining 10 percent are investigated more thoroughly at a cost ranging from $2,000 to $3,000 per proposal. At this time, approximately 10 to 15 proposals will have passed the screening process, and these are subjected to comprehensive review. The venture capital firm will invest in 3 to 6 of these remaining proposals.

OWNERSHIP AND CONTROL   Most venture capitalists prefer to purchase ownership in a small business through common stock or convertible preferred stock. Typically, a venture capital company seeks to purchase 20 to 40 percent of a business, but in some cases, a venture capitalist may buy 70 percent or more of a company's stock, leaving its founders with a minority share of ownership.

Most venture capitalists prefer to let the founding team of managers employ its skills to operate a business *if* they are capable of managing its growth. However, it is quite common for venture capitalists to join the boards of directors of the companies they invest in or to send in new managers or a new management team to protect their investments.

*Jigsaw Data
Corporation*

Jim Fowler, founder of Jigsaw Data Corporation, a small company whose online service allows salespeople to trade business contacts online, discusses operating issues several times a week with the venture capitalists who invested in his company. El Dorado, the venture capital firm, has invested $2.5 million in Jigsaw so far. Fowler, a former Navy diver, has limited managerial experience and welcomes the advice. "Venture capitalists have to justify their investments, and they spend a lot more time on them [than before]," says Fowler.[35]

TABLE 13.1 Deciphering the Language of the Venture Capital Industry

By nature, entrepreneurs tend to be optimistic. When screening business plans, venture capitalists must make an allowance for entrepreneurial enthusiasm. Here's a dictionary of phrases commonly found in business plans and their accompanying venture capital translations.

Exploring an acquisition strategy—Our current products have no market.

We're on a clear P2P (pathway to profitability)—We're still years away from earning a profit.

Basically on plan—We're expecting a revenue shortfall of 25 percent.

Internet business model—Potential bigger fools have been identified.

A challenging year—Competitors are eating our lunch.

Considerably ahead of plan—Hit our plan in one of the last three months.

Company's underlying strength and resilience—We still lost money, but look how we cut our losses.

Core business—Our product line is obsolete.

Currently revising budget—The financial plan is in total chaos.

Cyclical industry—We posted a huge loss last year.

Entrepreneurial CEO—He is totally uncontrollable, bordering on maniacal.

Facing unprecedented economic, political, and structural shifts—It's a tough world out there, but we're coping the best we can.

Highly leverageable network—No longer works but has friends who do.

Ingredients are there—Given two years, we might find a workable strategy.

Investing heavily in R & D—We're trying desperately to catch the competition.

Limited downside—Things can't get much worse.

Long sales cycle—Yet to find a customer who likes the product enough to buy it.

Major opportunity—It's our last chance.

Niche strategy—A small-time player.

On a manufacturing learning curve—We can't make the product with positive margins.

Passive investor—She phones once a year to see whether we're still in business.

Positive results—Our losses was less than last year.

Repositioning the business—We've recently written off a multi-million-dollar investment.

Selective investment strategy—The board is spending more time on yachts than on planes.

Solid operating performance in a difficult year—Yes, we lost money and market share, but look how hard we tried.

Somewhat below plan—We expect a revenue shortfall of 75 percent.

Expenses were unexpectedly high—We grossly overestimated our profit margins.

Strategic investor—One who will pay a preposterous price for an equity share in the business.

Strongest fourth quarter ever—Don't quibble over the losses in the first three quarters.

Sufficient opportunity to market this product no longer exists—Nobody will buy the thing.

Too early to tell—Results to date have been grim.

A team of skilled, motivated, and dedicated people—We've laid off most of our staff, and those who are left should be glad they still have jobs.

Turnaround opportunity—It's a lost cause.

Unique—We have no more than six strong competitors.

Volume-sensitive—Our company has massive fixed costs.

Window of opportunity—Without more money fast, this company is dead.

Work closely with the management—We talk to them on the phone once a month.

A year in which we confronted challenges—At least we know the questions even if we haven't got the answers.

Sources: Adapted from Suzanne McGee, "A Devil's Dictionary of Financing," *Wall Street Journal,* June 12, 2000, p. C13; John F. Budd Jr., "Cracking the CEO's Code," *Wall Street Journal,* March 27, 1995, p. A20; "Venture-Speak Defined," *Teleconnect,* October 1990, p. 42; Cynthia E. Griffin, "Figuratively Speaking," *Entrepreneur,* August 1999, p. 26.

Sometimes venture investors step in and shake up the management teams in the companies in which they invest. "We change management in the companies we fund about 40 percent of the time," says Janet Effland, a partner in the venture capital firm Apax Partners.[36] In other words, entrepreneurs should *not* expect venture capitalists to be passive investors. Some serve only as financial and managerial advisors, but others take an active role managing the company—recruiting employees, providing sales leads, choosing attorneys and advertising agencies, and making daily decisions. The majority of these active venture capitalists say they are forced to step in because the existing management team lacks the talent and experience to achieve growth targets.

STAGE OF INVESTMENT Most venture capital firms invest in companies that are either in the early stages of development (called early-stage investing) or in the rapid-growth phase (called expansion-stage investing); very few invest in small companies that are in the start-up phase. Others specialize in acquisitions, providing the financing for managers and employees of a business to buy it out. About 98 percent of all venture capital goes to businesses in these stages, although a few venture capital firms are showing more interest in companies in the start-up phase because of the tremendous returns that are possible by investing then.[37] Most venture capital firms do not make just a single investment in a company. Instead, they invest in a company over time across several stages, where their investments often total $10 to $15 million.

INVESTMENT PREFERENCES The venture capital industry has undergone important changes over the last decade. Venture capital funds now are larger and more specialized. As the industry matures, venture capital funds increasingly are focusing their investments in niches—everything from low-calorie custards to the latest Web technology. Some will invest in almost any industry but prefer companies in particular stages, from start-up to expansion. Traditionally, however, only two percent of the companies receiving venture capital financing are in the start-up or seed stage, when entrepreneurs are forming a company or developing a product or service. Most of the start-up businesses that attract venture capital are technology companies—software, biotechnology, medical devices, and telecommunications.[38]

What Venture Capitalists Look For Small business owners must realize that it is very difficult for any small business, especially fledgling or struggling firms, to pass the intense screening process of a venture capital company and qualify for an investment. A sound business plan is essential to convincing venture capital firms to invest in a company. "Investors want to see proof that a concept works," says Geeta Vemuri, a principal in a venture capital firm.[39] Venture capital firms finance only about 3,000 deals in a typical year. Two factors make a deal attractive to venture capitalists: high returns and a convenient (and profitable) exit strategy. When evaluating potential investments, venture capitalists look for the following features.

COMPETENT MANAGEMENT The most important ingredient in the success of any business is the ability of the management team, and venture capitalists recognize this. To venture capitalists, the ideal management team has experience, managerial skills, commitment, and the ability to build teams. "If you don't have good management [in place], it's going to bite you," says Phil Soran, CEO of Compellent Technologies, a data storage company that has attracted venture capital successfully.[40]

COMPETITIVE EDGE Investors are searching for some factor that will enable a small business to set itself apart from its competitors. This distinctive competence may range from an innovative product or service that satisfies unmet customer needs to a unique marketing or R&D approach. It must be something with the potential to create a sustainable competitive edge, making the company a leader in its industry.

GROWTH INDUSTRY Hot industries attract profits—and venture capital. Most venture capital funds focus their searches for prospects in rapidly expanding fields because they believe the profit potential is greater in these areas. Venture capital firms are most

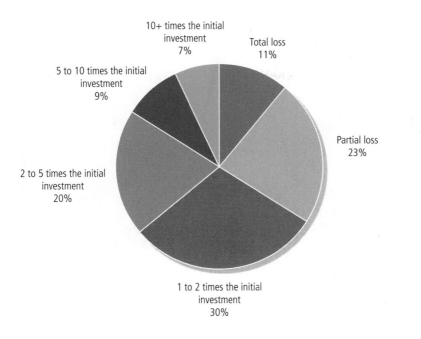

FIGURE 13.2

Average Returns on Venture Capital Investments

Source: Paul Keaton, "The Reality of Venture Capital," *Small Business Forum*, Arkansas Small Business Development Center, p. 8, http://asbdc.ualr.edu/bizfacts/501.asp ?print=Y,p.8.

interested in young companies that have enough growth potential to become at least $100 million businesses within three to five years. Venture capitalists know that most of the businesses they invest in will flop, so their winners have to be *big* winners (see Figure 13.2). One venture capital investor says, "If you want to get really good returns, your hits generally have to earn 10 times your investment in three to five years."[41]

VIABLE EXIT STRATEGY Venture capitalists not only look for promising companies with the ability to dominate a market, but they also want to see a plan for a feasible exit strategy, typically to be executed within three to five years. Venture capital firms realize the return on their investments when the companies they invest in either make an initial public offering or are acquired by or merged into another business. As the market for initial public offerings has softened, venture capitalists have had to be more patient in their exit strategies. Venture-backed companies that go public now take an average of 5.5 years from the time of their first venture capital investment to their stock offering, up from an average of less than three years in 1998.[42]

INTANGIBLE FACTORS Some other important factors considered in the screening process are not easily measured; they are the intuitive, intangible factors the venture capitalist detects by gut feeling. This feeling might be the result of the small firm's solid sense of direction, its strategic planning process, the chemistry of its management team, or a number of other factors.

Deborah Manchester, president of Zula USA LLC, a company that provides educational content for various media, recently raised more than $7 million in venture capital to finance the production of an educational television series based on a cast of characters she had created while recovering from foot surgery. Part of the company's appeal was the popularity the Zula characters had achieved among its target audience of young children and the endorsement parents and teachers gave the content. Manchester, who has extensive skills in the fields of child development and animation, used the capital to launch a television series called The Zula Patrol that airs on PBS.[43]

COMPANY Profile

Zula USA LLC

Despite its many benefits, venture capital is not suited for every entrepreneur. "[Venture capital] money comes at a price," warns one entrepreneur. "Before boarding a one-way money train, ask yourself if this is the best route for your business and personal desires, because investors are like department stores the day after Christmas—they expect a lot of returns in a short period of time."[44]

FIGURE 13.3

Initial Public Offerings (IPOs)

Source: Thomson Financial Securities Data.

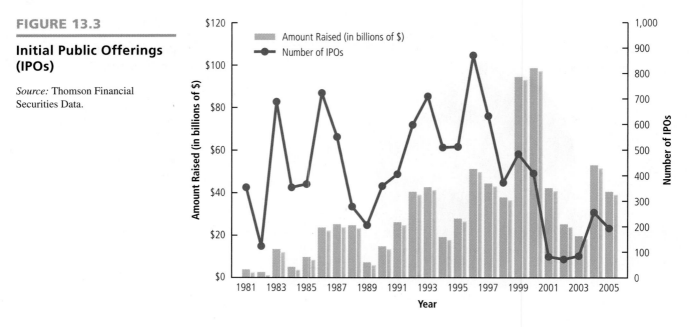

LEARNING OBJECTIVES
4. Describe the process of "going public" as well as its advantages and disadvantages and the various simplified registrations and exemptions from registration available to small businesses wanting to sell securities to investors.

initial public offering (IPO)
a method of raising equity capital in which a company sells shares of its stock to the general public for the first time.

Public Stock Sale ("Going Public")

In some cases, entrepreneurs can "go public" by selling shares of stock in their corporations to outside investors. In an **initial public offering (IPO),** a company raises capital by selling shares of its stock to the general public for the first time. A public offering is an effective method of raising large amounts of capital, but it can be an expensive and time-consuming process filled with regulatory nightmares. Once a company makes an initial public offering, *nothing* will ever be the same again. Managers must consider the impact of their decisions not only on the company and its employees, but also on its shareholders and the value of their stock.

Going public isn't for every business. In fact, most small companies do not meet the criteria for making a successful public stock offering. Over the last 20 years, an average of 440 companies per year have made initial public offerings of their stock, although the number of IPOs has fallen off significantly since 2000 (see Figure 13.3). Only about 20,000 companies in the United States—less than one percent of the total—are publicly held. Few companies with less than $20 million in annual sales manage to go public successfully. It is extremely difficult for a start-up company with no track record of success to raise money with a public offering. Instead, the investment bankers who underwrite public stock offerings typically look for established companies with the following characteristics:

- Consistently high growth rates.
- A strong record of earnings.
- Three to five years of audited financial statements that meet or exceed Securities and Exchange Commission (SEC) standards. After the Enron and WorldCom scandals, investors are demanding impeccable financial statements.
- A solid position in a rapidly growing industry. In 2000, the median age of companies making IPOs was 3 years; today, it is 15 years.[45]
- A sound management team with experience and a strong board of directors.

Entrepreneurs who are considering taking their companies public should first consider carefully the advantages and the disadvantages of an IPO. The advantages include the following.

Advantages

ABILITY TO RAISE LARGE AMOUNTS OF CAPITAL The biggest benefit of a public offering is the capital infusion the company receives. After going public, the corporation has the cash to fund R&D projects, expand plant and facilities, repay debt, or boost working capital balances without incurring the interest expense and the obligation to repay associated with debt financing. For instance, clothing retailer J. Crew recently made an IPO that raised $200 million, and Under Armour, the maker of high-performance athletic gear, raised $200 million in an S-1 filing. In one of the most publicized IPOs in recent history, Google sold 19.6 million shares at $85 per share, raising nearly $1.7 billion (before expenses) to fuel the company's growth.

IMPROVED CORPORATE IMAGE All of the media attention a company receives during the registration process makes it more visible. In addition, becoming a public company in some industries improves its prestige and enhances its competitive position, one of the most widely recognized intangible benefits of going public.

IMPROVED ACCESS TO FUTURE FINANCING Going public boosts a company's net worth and broadens its equity base. Its improved stature and financial strength make it easier for the firm to attract more capital—both debt and equity—and to grow.

ABILITY TO ATTRACT AND RETAIN KEY EMPLOYEES Public companies often use stock-based compensation plans to attract and retain quality employees. Stock options and bonuses are excellent methods for winning employees' loyalty and for instilling a healthy ownership attitude among them *if* the company's stock performs well in the market. Employee stock ownership plans (ESOPs) and stock purchase plans are popular recruiting and motivational tools in many small corporations, enabling them to hire top-flight talent they otherwise would not be able to afford.

USE OF STOCK FOR ACQUISITIONS A company whose stock is publicly traded can acquire other businesses by offering its own shares rather than cash. Acquiring other companies with shares of stock eliminates the need to incur additional debt.

LISTING ON A STOCK EXCHANGE Being listed on an organized stock exchange, even a small regional one, improves the marketability of a company's shares and enhances its image. Most publicly held companies' stocks do not qualify for listing on the nation's largest exchanges—the New York Stock Exchange (NYSE) and the American Stock Exchange (AMEX). However, the AMEX now has a market for small-company stocks, The Emerging Company Marketplace. Most small companies' stocks are traded on either the National Association of Securities Dealers Automated Quotation (NASDAQ) system's National Market System (NMS) and its emerging small-capitalization exchange or one of the nation's regional stock exchanges.

Despite these advantages, many factors can spoil a company's attempted IPO. In fact, only five percent of the companies that attempt to go public ever complete the process.[46] The disadvantages of going public include the following.

Disadvantages

DILUTION OF FOUNDER'S OWNERSHIP Whenever entrepreneurs sell stock to the public, they automatically dilute their ownership in their businesses. Most owners retain a majority interest in the business, but they may still run the risk of unfriendly takeovers years later after selling more stock.

LOSS OF CONTROL If enough shares are sold in a public offering, a founder risks losing control of the company. If a large block of shares falls into the hands of dissident stockholders, they could vote the existing management team (including the founder) out.

George Stathakis, owner of the highly successful chain of Stax's restaurants in Greenville, South Carolina, recalls investment bankers approaching him about taking his company public to fund its growth, but he refused them all. "The one thing you don't have when you go public is control," he says, "and that's something my partners and I just couldn't handle."[47]

Stax's

LOSS OF PRIVACY Taking their companies public can be a big ego boost for owners, but they must realize that their companies are no longer solely theirs. Information that was once private must be available for public scrutiny. The initial prospectus and the continuous reports filed with the SEC disclose a variety of information about the company and its operations—from financial data and raw material sources to legal matters and patents—to *anyone*, including competitors. Loss of privacy and loss of control are the most commonly cited as the reasons that CEOs choose not to attempt IPOs.[48]

REPORTING TO THE SEC Operating as a publicly held company is expensive, especially since Congress passed the Sarbanes-Oxley Act in 2002. The SEC traditionally has required publicly held companies to file periodic reports with it, which often requires a more powerful accounting system, a larger accounting staff, and greater use of attorneys and other professionals. Created in response to ethical fiascoes such as Enron and WorldCom, Sarbanes-Oxley was designed to improve the degree of internal control and the level of financial reporting by publicly held companies. Although many executives agree with the intent of the law, they contend that the cost of complying with it is overbearing. A study by Financial Executives International reports that the cost to public companies with $25 million to $99 million in annual revenues of complying with the most significant section of Sarbanes-Oxley averages $740,000 per year. The high cost of regulatory compliance dissuades many potential companies from going public.

Earth Fare

The owners of Earth Fare, a chain of organic supermarkets based in Asheville, North Carolina, recently hit $100 million in annual revenues and were considering making an IPO to finance the opening of a wave of new stores. However, after considering the cost of complying with Sarbanes-Oxley, they decided against the IPO. "The requirements to comply with [Sarbanes-Oxley] are so expensive, there's no way Earth Fare could have afforded it," says John Warner, chairman of the company's board of directors.[49]

Since Sarbanes-Oxley was passed, record numbers of public companies have decided to leave the public spotlight and "go private," reversing the initial public offering process and selling out to private investors. Kerzner International, a hotel group that went public in 2004, recently announced that a group of private investors was taking the company, which owns the Atlantis Resort in the Bahamas, private in a deal valued at $3.6 billion.[50]

FILING EXPENSES A public stock offering usually is an expensive way to generate funds for start-up or expansion. For the typical small company, the cost of a public offering is about 15 percent of the capital raised. On small offerings, costs can eat up as much as 40 percent of the capital raised, whereas on larger offerings, those above $25 million, only 10 to 12 percent will go to cover expenses. Once an offering exceeds $15 million, its relative issuing costs drop. The largest cost is the underwriter's commission, which is typically 7 percent of the proceeds on offerings less than $10 million and 13 percent on those over that amount.

ACCOUNTABILITY TO SHAREHOLDERS The capital that entrepreneurs manages is no longer just their own. Managers of publicly held firms are accountable to their companies' shareholders. Indeed, the law requires that they recognize and abide by a relationship built on trust. Profit and return on investment become the primary concerns for investors. If the stock price of a newly public company falls, shareholder lawsuits are inevitable. Investors whose shares decline in value often sue the company's managers for fraud and the failure to disclose the potential risks to which their investments expose them.

PRESSURE FOR SHORT-TERM PERFORMANCE In privately held companies, entrepreneurs are free to follow their strategies for success, even if those strategies take years to produce results. When a company goes public, however, entrepreneurs quickly learn that shareholders are impatient and expect results immediately. Founders are under constant pressure to produce growth in profits and in market share, which requires them to maintain a delicate balance between short-term results and long-term strategy.

DEMANDS ON TIME AND TIMING As impatient as they can be, entrepreneurs often find the time demands of an initial public offering frustrating and distracting. Managing the IPO takes time away from managing the company. Working on an IPO can consume as much as 75 percent of top managers' time. "You want to make sure you're not becoming a chief 'going public' officer as opposed to a chief executive officer," advises an investment banker.[51] When one company that produced sports entertainment software decided to go public, managers spent so much time focusing on the demands of the IPO that the company failed to get a new product to market in time for the Christmas season. Because it missed this crucial deadline, the company never recovered and went out of business.[52]

During this time, a company also runs the risk that the overall market for IPOs or for a particular industry may go sour. Factors beyond managers' control, such as declines in the stock market and potential investors' jitters, can quickly slam shut a company's "window of opportunity" for an IPO. For instance, when Nanosys, a pioneering company in nanotechnology, withdrew its initial public offering after receiving a lukewarm reception from potential investment bankers, several other nanotechnology companies postponed their planned IPOs.[53]

The Registration Process Taking a company public is a complicated, bureaucratic process that usually takes several months to complete. Many experts compare the IPO process to running a corporate marathon, and both the company and its management team must be in shape and up to the grueling task. The typical entrepreneur *cannot* take his or her company public alone. It requires a coordinated effort from a team of professionals, including company executives, an accountant, a securities attorney, a financial printer, and at least one underwriter. Table 13.2 shows a typical timetable for an IPO. The key steps in taking a company public include the following.

TABLE 13.2 Timetable for An Initial Public Offering

Time	Action
Week 1	Conduct organizational meeting with IPO team, including underwriter, attorneys, accountants, and others. Begin drafting registration statement.
Week 5	Distribute first draft of registration statement to IPO team and make revisions.
Week 6	Distribute second draft of registration statement and make revisions.
Week 7	Distribute third draft of registration statement and make revisions.
Week 8	File registration statement with the SEC. Begin preparing presentations for road show to attract other investment bankers to the syndicate. Comply with "blue sky" laws in states where offering will be sold.
Week 12	Receive comment letter on registration statement from SEC. Amend registration statement to satisfy SEC comments.
Week 13	File amended registration statement with SEC. Prepare and distribute preliminary offering prospectus (called a "red herring") to members of underwriting syndicate. Begin road show meetings.
Week 15	Receive approval for offering from SEC (unless further amendments are required). Issuing company and lead underwriter agree on final offering price. Prepare, file, and distribute final offering prospectus.
Week 16	Company and underwriter sign the final agreement. Underwriter issues stock, collects the proceeds from the sale, and delivers proceeds (less commission) to company.

Sources: Adapted from "Initial Public Offering," *Entrepreneur,* June 14, 2002, http://www.entrepreneur.com/article/0/4621,300892,00,html; PriceWaterhouseCoopers, "Going Public Timetable," http://www.pwcglobal.com/Extweb/industry.nsf/docid/2C9CA8A7F060404A85256AC5007A86B8#.

underwriter (or investment banker)
a financial company that serves two important roles: helping to prepare the registration statement for an issue and promoting the company's stock to potential investors.

CHOOSE THE UNDERWRITER The most important ingredient in making a successful IPO is selecting a capable **underwriter (or investment banker).** The underwriter serves two primary roles: helping to prepare the registration statement for the issue and promoting the company's stock to potential investors. The underwriter works with company managers as an advisor to prepare the registration statement that must be filed with the SEC, promotes the issue, prices the stock, and provides after-market support. Once the registration statement is finished, the underwriter's primary job is selling the company's stock through an underwriting syndicate of other investment bankers it develops. According to a study by Notre Dame professors Shane Corwin and Paul Schultz, the larger the syndicate that supports an IPO, the more likely it is that the company will obtain more favorable pricing and overall results from the offering.[54]

letter of intent
an agreement between the underwriter and the company about to go public that outlines the details of the deal.

NEGOTIATE A LETTER OF INTENT To begin an offering, the entrepreneur and the underwriter must negotiate a **letter of intent,** which outlines the details of the deal. The letter of intent covers a variety of important issues, including the type of underwriting, its size and price range, the underwriter's commission, and any warrants and options included. It almost always states that the underwriter is not bound to the offering until it is executed—usually the day before or the day of the offering. However, the letter usually creates a binding obligation for the company to pay any direct expenses the underwriter incurs relating to the offer.

registration statement
the document a company must file with the SEC that describes both the company and its stock offering and discloses information about the risk of investing.

PREPARE THE REGISTRATION STATEMENT After a company signs the letter of intent, the next task is to prepare the **registration statement** to be filed with the SEC. This document describes both the company and the stock offering and discloses information about the risks of investing. It includes information on the use of the proceeds, the company's history, its financial position, its capital structure, the risks it faces, its managers' experience, and *many* other details. The statement is extremely comprehensive and may take months to develop. To prepare the statement, entrepreneurs must rely on their team of professionals.

FILE WITH THE SEC When the statement is finished (with the exception of pricing the shares, proceeds, and commissions, which cannot be determined until just before the issue goes to market), the company officially files the statement with the SEC and awaits the review of the Division of Corporate Finance, a process that takes 30 to 45 days (or more). The Division sends notice of any deficiencies in the registration statement to the company's attorney in a comment letter. The company and its team of professionals must cure all of the deficiencies in the statement noted in the comment letter. Finally, the company files the revised registration statement, along with a pricing amendment (giving the price of the shares, the proceeds, and the commissions).

WAIT TO GO EFFECTIVE While waiting for the SEC's approval, the managers and the underwriters are busy. The underwriters are building a syndicate of other underwriters who will market the company's stock. (No stock sales can be made prior to the effective date of the offering, however.) The SEC also limits the publicity and information a company may release during this quiet period (which officially starts when the company reaches a preliminary agreement with the managing underwriter and ends 90 days after the effective date).

road show
a gathering of potential syndicate members sponsored by the managing underwriter for the purpose of promoting a company's initial public offering.

Securities laws do permit a **road show,** a gathering of potential syndicate members sponsored by the managing underwriter. Its purpose is to promote interest among potential underwriters in the IPO by featuring the company, its management, and the proposed deal. The managing underwriter and key company officials barnstorm major financial centers at a grueling pace.

Ometric Corporation

During the road show for Ometric Corporation, a South Carolina-based company that has developed the technology to provide real-time spectroscopy in a variety of industrial applications, CEO Walter Allessandrini made 140 presentations to potential syndicate members in both Europe and the United States in just two and a half weeks!

On the last day before the registration statement becomes effective, the company signs the formal underwriting agreement. The final settlement, or closing, takes place a few days after the effective date for the issue. At this meeting the underwriters receive their shares to sell and the company receives the proceeds of the offering.

Typically, the entire process of going public takes from 60 to 180 days, but it can take much longer if the issuing company is not properly prepared for the process.

MEET STATE REQUIREMENTS In addition to satisfying the SEC's requirements, a company also must meet the securities laws in all states in which the issue is sold. These state laws (or "blue-sky" laws) vary drastically from one state to another, and the company must comply with them.

Simplified Registrations and Exemptions

The IPO process just described (called an S-1 filing) requires maximum disclosure in the initial filing and discourages most small businesses from using it. Fortunately, the SEC allows several exemptions from this full-disclosure process for small businesses. Many small businesses that go public choose one of these simplified options the SEC has designed for small companies. The SEC has established the following simplified registration statements and exemptions from the registration process.

Regulation S-B Regulation S-B is a simplified registration process for small companies seeking to make initial or subsequent public offerings. Not only does this regulation simplify the initial filing requirements with the SEC, but it also reduces the ongoing disclosure and filings required of companies. Its primary goals are to open the doors to capital markets to smaller companies by cutting the paperwork and the costs of raising capital. Companies using the simplified registration process have two options: Form SB-1, a "transitional" registration statement for companies issuing less than $10 million worth of securities over a 12-month period, and Form SB-2, reserved for small companies seeking more than $10 million in a 12-month period.

To be eligible for the simplified registration process under Regulation S-B, a company must meet the following criteria:

- Be based in the United States or Canada.
- Have revenues of less than $25 million.
- Have outstanding publicly held stock worth no more than $25 million.
- Must not be an investment company.
- Must provide audited financial statements for two fiscal years.

The goal of Regulation S-B's simplified registration requirements is to enable smaller companies to go public without incurring the expense of a full-blown registration. Total costs for a Regulation S-B are approximately $35,000.

Regulation D (Rule 504): Small Company Offering Registration Created in the late 1980s, the Small Company Offering Registration (SCOR; also known as the Uniform Limited Offering Registration, ULOR) now is available in all 50 states and the District of Columbia. A little-known tool, SCOR is designed to make it easier and less expensive for small companies to sell their stock to the public by eliminating the requirement for registering the offering with the SEC. The whole process typically costs less than half of what a traditional public offering costs. Entrepreneurs using SCOR need an attorney and an accountant to help them with the issue, but many can get by without a securities lawyer, which can save tens of thousands of dollars. Some entrepreneurs even choose to market their companies' securities themselves (for example, to customers), saving the expense of hiring a broker. However, selling an issue is both time and energy consuming, and most SCOR experts recommend hiring a professional securities or brokerage firm to sell the company's shares. The SEC's objective in creating SCOR was to give small companies the same access to equity financing that large companies have via the stock market while bypassing many of the same costs and filing requirements.

The capital ceiling on a SCOR issue is $1 million (except in Texas, where there is no limit), and the price of each share must be at least $5. That means that a company can sell no more than 200,000 shares (making the stock less attractive to stock manipulators). A SCOR offering requires only minimal notification to the SEC. The company must file a standardized disclosure statement, the U-7, which consists of 50 fill-in-the-blank questions. The form, which asks for information such as how much money the company needs, what the money will be used for, what investors receive, how investors can sell their investments, and other pertinent questions, closely resembles a business plan, but also serves as a state securities offering registration, a disclosure document, and a prospectus. Entrepreneurs using SCOR may advertise their companies' offerings and can sell them directly to any investor, with no restrictions and no minimums. An entrepreneur can sell practically any kind of security through a SCOR, including common stock, preferred stock, convertible preferred stock, stock options, stock warrants, and others.

CorpHQ

Steve Crane and Art Aviles, Jr., co-founders of CorpHQ, a Web-portal that links small and home-based business owners in an online community, decided to bypass venture capital and relied on a SCOR offering to attract their first round of outside capital. The entrepreneurs believed that taking their company public not only would save them money, but also would create greater opportunities for future financing efforts, both of which have proved to be true. Early on, Crane and Aviles recognized the need to promote their newly public company, whose shares trade on the OTC Bulletin Board, in the investment community. "Our success as a public company depends not only on how well we do financially but also how well we market our company and our story to the financial markets," says Crane.[55]

A SCOR offering offers entrepreneurs needing equity financing several advantages:

- Access to a sizable pool of equity funds without the expense of full registration with the SEC. Companies often can complete a SCOR offering for less than $25,000.
- Few restrictions on the securities to be sold and on the investors to whom they can be sold.
- The ability to market the offering through advertisements to the public.
- New or start-up companies can qualify.
- No requirement of audited financial statements for offerings less than $500,000.
- Faster approval of the issue from regulatory agencies.
- The ability to make the offering in several states at once.

There are, of course, some *disadvantages* to using SCOR to raise needed funds:

- Partnerships cannot make SCOR offerings.
- A company can raise no more than $1 million in a 12-month period.
- An entrepreneur must register the offering in every state in which shares of stock will be sold to comply with their "blue sky" laws, although current regulations allow simultaneous registration in multiple states.
- The process can be time consuming, distracting an entrepreneur from the daily routine of running the company. A limited secondary market for the securities may limit investors' interest. Currently, SCOR shares must be traded through brokerage firms that make small markets in specific stocks. However, the Pacific Stock Exchange and the NASDAQ's electronic bulletin board recently began listing SCOR stocks, so the secondary market for them has broadened.

Regulation D (Rules 505 and 506): Private Placements Rules 505 and 506 of Regulation D, also known as the Private Placement Memorandum, are exemptions from federal registration requirements that give emerging companies the opportunity to sell stock through private placements without actually going public. In a private placement, a company sells its shares directly to private investors without having to register them with the SEC or incur the expenses of an IPO. Instead, a knowledgeable attorney simply draws up an investment agreement that meets state and federal requirements between the company and its private investors. Most companies offer private investors "book deals," proposals with terms the company determines made on a take-it-or-leave-it basis.

BioE

When Mike Haider, CEO of BioE, a biotech company in St. Paul, Minnesota, realized that his company needed growth capital, he turned once again to private placements because he had already raised more than $14 million for BioE from more than 200 individual investors in several small private placements. It took one year, hundreds of hours, and more than 100 presentations to potential investors, but Haider's persistence and patience paid off; he raised $8.5 million from 240 investors, mostly professional and business people from Minneapolis and St. Paul. The private placement cost BioE $600,000 in fees and expenses, far below what an IPO would have cost. Thanks to the capital infusion, BioE is on track to earn its first profit, and Haider could not be more pleased. "My full-time job is to ensure capital for this company," he says. "Just when you've finished raising money, it's time to start another round."[56]

A *Rule 505* offering has a higher capital ceiling than a SCOR offering ($5 million) in a 12-month period but imposes more restrictions (no more than 35 nonaccredited investors, no advertising of the offer, and more-stringent disclosure requirements).

Rule 506 imposes no ceiling on the amount that can be raised, but, like a Rule 505 offering, it limits the issue to 35 "nonaccredited" investors and prohibits advertising the offer to the public. There is no limit on the number of accredited investors, however. Rule 506 also requires detailed disclosure of relative information, but the extent depends on the dollar size of the offering.

These Regulation D rules minimize the expense and the time required to raise equity capital for small businesses. Fees for private placements typically range from 1 to 5 percent rather than the 7 to 13 percent underwriters normally charge for managing a public offering. Offerings made under Regulation D do impose limitations and demand certain disclosures, but they only require a company to file a simple form (Form D) with the SEC within 15 days of the first sale of stock. One drawback of private placements is that the SEC does not allow a company to advertise its stock offering, which means that entrepreneurs must develop a network of wealthy contacts if the placement is to succeed.

Section 4(6) Section 4(6) covers private placements and is similar to Regulation D, Rules 505 and 506. It does not require registration on offers up to $5 million if they are made only to accredited investors.

Intrastate Offerings (Rule 147) Rule 147 governs intrastate offerings, those sold only to investors in a single state by a company doing business in that state. To qualify, a company must be incorporated in the state, maintain its executive offices there, have 80 percent of its assets there, derive 80 percent of its revenues from the state, and use 80 percent of the offering proceeds for business in the state. There is no ceiling on the amount of the offering, but only residents of the state in which the issuing company operates can invest.

Ben & Jerry's Homemade

Years ago, Ben Cohen and Jerry Greenfield founded a small ice cream manufacturing business named after themselves that struck a chord with customers. Ben & Jerry's Homemade grew rapidly, and the founders needed $600,000 to build a new manufacturing plant in Vermont, where the company was based. They decided to "give the opportunity to our neighbors to grow with our company" by making an intrastate offering under Rule 147. Cohen and Greenfield registered their offering of 73,500 shares of stock with the Vermont Division of Banking and Insurance. Ben & Jerry's Homemade sold the entire offering (mostly to loyal customers) by placing ads in newspapers and stickers on ice cream containers that touted "Get a Scoop of the Action."[57]

Regulation A   Regulation A, although currently not used often, allows an exemption for offerings up to $5 million over a 12-month period. Regulation A imposes few restrictions, but it is more costly than the other types of exempted offerings, usually running between $80,000 and $120,000. The primary difference between a SCOR offering and a Regulation A offering is that a company must register its SCOR offering only in the states where it will sell its stock; in a Regulation A offering, the company also must file an offering statement with the SEC. Like a SCOR offering, a Regulation A offering requires only a simplified question-and-answer SEC filing and allows a company to sell its shares directly to investors.

Direct Stock Offerings   Many of the simplified registrations and exemptions just discussed give entrepreneurs the power to sidestep investment bankers and sell their companies' stock offerings directly to investors and, in the process, save themselves thousands of dollars in underwriting fees. By cutting out the underwriter's commission and many legal and most registration fees, entrepreneurs willing to handle the paperwork requirements and to market their own shares typically can make direct public offerings (DPOs) for 6 to 10 percent of the total amount of the issue, compared with 15 percent for a traditional stock offering.

Real Goods Trading Company

Real Goods Trading Company, a retailer of environmentally friendly products, was a pioneer of direct public offerings over the Web. In 1991, the company engineered a successful DPO that raised $1 million and followed with two more DPOs in later years that generated $3.6 million each. More than 5,000 of the company's loyal customers became investors. In fact, managers discovered that once customers became shareholders, they purchased nearly twice as much merchandise as customers who were not shareholders. Managers at Real Goods found that using the Web to reach potential investors was not only one of the best bargains, but also one of the most effective methods for selling its stock to the public.[58]

You Be the Consultant

Running on Empty

When 23-year-old Ross McDowell decided to open a retail store specializing in running shoes, he was quite comfortable making decisions about the kinds of shoes he would stock in the store's inventory, the décor of the retail space, and how to reach his potential customers. A competitive runner since the sixth grade, McDowell knew which shoes would sell best to his target audience, and he knew that he needed to round out his merchandise mix with hats, shirts, energy drinks and snacks, and other accessories. What he wasn't so sure about, however, was how to find the financing for his business. "I came from a middle class family and didn't have the money myself," he explains.

Gaining access to adequate capital is a challenge for many entrepreneurs but can be an especially vexing problem for those in the start-up phase, where risks are highest. Launching a business with too little capital is a

recipe for failure, as many entrepreneurs have learned. According to the SBA's Office of Advocacy, in one-third of small business bankruptcies, entrepreneurs cite financial problems as the cause of their companies' failure. Most entrepreneurs dig deep into their own pockets first before turning to friends and family members for the capital to launch their businesses. In many cases, however, these sources cannot provide sufficient capital to cover start-up costs. After emptying their own pockets and those of their friends and family members, where do entrepreneurs turn for the capital they need?

Before approaching any potential lender or investor, McDowell knew that he needed to put together a business plan that spelled out just how much money he would need to launch his store and how he planned to use it. "The most common pitfall is that everyone thinks sales will be bigger than they are and costs will be less than they are," says John Hammersley, director of loan programs for the SBA. McDowell researched the fixed expenses he could expect, including rent, utilities, and a salary for himself so he could pay his living expenses. Then he estimated how much it would take to equip the store, including items such as shelving, storage racks, cash registers, signs, and couches for customers to sit on. To make sure that he did not underestimate these costs, McDowell assumed that he would pay retail prices for everything. He also included wages for a part-time employee and advertising costs and came up with a total of $22,000.

With plans for the store's fixtures in place, McDowell needed to stock it with inventory. He decided to carry six different brands and, after meeting with sales representatives from all six companies, selected 25 popular styles of running shoes. Adding in the costs of the accessories such as shirts, shorts, hats, and other items brought the total cost estimate to $50,000.

McDowell estimated that his monthly operating expenses would be $6,500, but his business plan included strategies for reducing them by generating publicity for the new store and promoting it at running events and local schools. "You've got to be resourceful,"

he explains. McDowell's plan called for raising enough start-up capital for his shoe store to survive for three months without any revenue at all. McDowell managed to come up with 10 percent of the $72,000 start-up cost he estimates he will need to open the store. The question he faces now is where the remaining 90 percent will come from.

1. Describe the advantages and the disadvantages of both equity capital and debt capital for Ross McDowell.
2. Explain why the following funding sources would or would not be appropriate for McDowell: family and friends, angel investors, an initial public offering, a traditional bank loan, asset-based borrowing, or one of the many federal or SBA loans.
3. Work with a team of your classmates to brainstorm ways that Ross McDowell could attract the capital he needs for his businesses. What steps would you recommend he take before approaching the potential sources of funding you have identified?

Sources: Adapted from Gwendolyn Bounds, "The Great Money Hunt," *Wall Street Journal,* November 29, 2004, pp. R1, R4.

The World Wide Web is an easy-to-use avenue for direct public offerings and is one the fastest-growing sources of capital for small businesses. Much of the Web's appeal as a fund-raising tool stems from its ability to reach large numbers of prospective investors very quickly and at a low cost. "This is the only form of instantaneous international contact with an enormous population," says one Web expert. "You can put your prospectus out to the world."[59] Companies making direct stock offerings on the Web most often make them under either Regulation A or Regulation D. Direct public offerings work best for companies that have a single product or related product lines and a base of customers who are loyal to the company. In fact, the first company to make a successful DPO over the Internet was Spring Street Brewing, a microbrewery founded by Andy Klein. Klein raised $1.6 million in a Regulation A offering in 1996. Companies that make successful direct public offerings of their stock over the Web must meet the same standards that companies making stock offerings using more traditional methods. Experts caution Web-based fund seekers to make sure their electronic prospectuses meet SEC and state requirements.

Table 13.3 provides a summary of the major types of exemptions and simplified offerings. Of these, the limited offerings and private placements are most commonly used.

The Nature of Debt Financing

Debt financing involves the funds that the small business owner borrows and must repay with interest. Lenders of capital are more numerous than investors, although small business loans can be just as difficult (if not more difficult) to obtain. Although borrowed capital allows entrepreneurs to maintain complete ownership of their businesses, it must be carried as a liability on the balance sheet as well as be repaid with interest at some point in the future. In addition, because small businesses are considered to be greater risks than bigger corporate customers, they must pay higher interest rates because of the risk–return tradeoff—the higher the risk, the greater is the return demanded. Most small firms pay the **prime rate,** the interest rate banks charge their most creditworthy customers, *plus* two to

LEARNING OBJECTIVES
5. Describe the various sources of debt capital and the advantages and disadvantages of each.

prime rate
the interest rate banks charge their most credit-worthy customers.

TABLE 13.3 Simplified Registrations and Exemptions

Feature	Regulation D Rule 504 (SCOR)	Regulation D Rule 505	Regulation D Rule 506	Private Placements Section 4(6)	Intrastate Offerings	Regulation A	Form SB-1	Form SB-2
Ceiling on amount raised	$1 million in any 12-month period	$5 million in any 12-month period	None	$5 million	None	$5 million in any 12-month period	$10 million in any 12-month period	None
Limit on number of purchasers	No	No, if selling to accredited investors; maximum of 35 nonaccredited investors	No, if selling to accredited investors; maximum of 35 nonaccredited investors	No	No	No	No	No
Limitation on types of purchasers	Depends	Yes	Yes	Yes; all must be accredited	Yes; must be residents of the state in which the company is incorporated	No	No	No
General solicitation and advertising allowed	Yes, if the company sells to accredited investors; otherwise, no	No	No	No	Yes	Yes	Yes	Yes
Resale restrictions	Yes	Yes	Yes	Yes	Yes	No	No	No

Sources: Adapted from "IPO Alternatives: SEC Registration Exemptions," *Inc.*, November 1999, http://www.inc.com/articles/1999/11/15743.html; "Q&A: Small Business and the SEC," U.S. Securities and Exchange Commission, http://www.sec.gov/info/smallbus/qasbsec.htm; *Small Business: Efforts to Facilitate Equity Capital Formation,* A Report to the Chariman, Committee on Small Business, U.S. Senate, Government Accounting Office, Washington, DC, 2000, http://www.gao.gov/archive/2000/gg00190.pdf#search=%22simplified%20registrations%20 exemptions%20SB%22.

three percentage points. Still, the cost of debt financing often is lower than that of equity financing. Because of the higher risks associated with providing equity capital to small companies, investors demand greater returns than lenders. In addition, unlike equity financing, debt financing does not require an entrepreneur to dilute his or her ownership interest in the company.

Entrepreneurs seeking debt capital are quickly confronted with an astounding range of credit options varying greatly in complexity, availability, and flexibility. Not all of these sources of debt capital are equally favorable, however. By understanding the various sources of capital—both commercial and government lenders—and their characteristics, entrepreneurs can greatly increase the chances of obtaining a loan.

We now turn to the various sources of debt capital.

Commercial Banks

Commercial banks are the very heart of the financial market for small businesses, providing the greatest number and variety of loans to small companies. One study by the Small Business Administration found that commercial banks provide 64 percent of the credit available to small businesses, compared to 12.3 percent supplied by commercial finance companies, the next-most-prominent source of small business lending. The study also revealed that 67 percent of all small businesses that borrow from traditional sources get financing from banks.[60] For small business owners, banks are lenders of *first* resort. Most small business bank loans are for less than $100,000.[61]

Banks tend to be conservative in their lending practices and prefer to make loans to established small businesses rather than to high-risk start-ups. One expert estimates that only five to eight percent of business start-ups get bank financing.[62] Bankers want to see evidence of a company's successful track record before committing to a loan. They are concerned with a firm's operating past and will scrutinize its financial reports to project its position in the future. They are also want proof of the stability of the company's sales and about the ability of the product or service to generate adequate cash flows to ensure repayment of the loan. If they do make loans to a start-up venture, banks like to see sufficient cash flows to repay the loan, ample collateral to secure it, or a Small Business Administration (SBA) guarantee to insure it. Studies suggest that small community banks (those with less than $300 million in assets) are most likely to lend money to small businesses.[63] These small banks, which make up 90 percent of U.S. banking institutions, also are more likely than their larger counterparts to customize the terms of their loans to the particular needs of small businesses, offering, for example, flexible payment terms to match the seasonal pattern of a company's cash flow or interest-only payments until a piece of equipment begins generating revenue.

Mega Rentals

When Megan Decker, owner of Mega Rentals, a company that provides traffic control equipment for highway construction projects, had the opportunity to purchase a larger competitor, she went to her banker to discuss financing. Because her business is highly seasonal, incurring large cash outlays each spring and with major cash inflows not coming in until the fall (and virtually nonexistent in the Wisconsin winters), Decker requested loan repayment terms that matched her irregular cash flow patterns, and the bank agreed. "[The bank] tailored my revolving loans so that I'm paying the larger principal payments in November, when I actually have the money," says Decker. "It's a tremendous advantage for me as far as my cash flow is concerned."[64]

When evaluating a loan application, especially for a business start-up, banks focus on a company's capacity to create positive cash flow because they know that that's where the money to repay their loans will come from. The first question in most bankers' minds when reviewing an entrepreneur's business plan is "Can this business generate sufficient cash to repay the loan?" Even though they rely on collateral to secure their loans, the last thing banks want is for a borrower to default, forcing them to sell the collateral (often at "fire sale" prices) and use the proceeds to pay off the loan. *That's* why bankers stress cash flow when analyzing a loan request, especially for a business start-up. "Cash is more important than your mother," jokes one experienced borrower.[65]

Short-Term Loans Short-term loans, extended for less than one year, are the most common type of commercial loan banks make to small companies. These funds typically are used to replenish the working capital account to finance the purchase of more inventory, boost output, finance credit sales to customers, or take advantage of cash discounts. As a result, an entrepreneur repays the loan after converting inventory and receivables into cash. There are several types of short-term loans.

COMMERCIAL LOANS (OR "TRADITIONAL BANK LOANS") A basic short-term loan is the commercial bank's specialty. Business owners use commercial loans for a specific expenditure—to buy a particular piece of equipment or to make a specific purchase, and terms usually require repayment as a lump sum within three to six months. Two types of commercial loans exist: secured and unsecured. A secured loan is one in which the borrower's promise to repay is secured by giving the bank an interest in some asset (collateral). Although secured loans give banks a safety cushion in case the borrower defaults on the loan, they are much more expensive to administer and maintain. With an unsecured loan, the bank grants a loan to a business owner without requiring him or her to pledge any specific collateral to support the loan in case of default. Until a small business is able to prove its financial strength to the bank's satisfaction, it will probably not qualify for an unsecured commercial loan. For both secured and unsecured commercial loans, an entrepreneur is expected to repay the total amount of the loan at maturity. Sometimes the interest due on the loan is prepaid—deducted from the total amount borrowed.

line of credit

a short-term bank loan with a pre-set limit that provides working capital for day-to-day operations.

LINES OF CREDIT One of the most common requests entrepreneurs make of banks and commercial finance companies is to establish a commercial **line of credit,** a short-term loan with a pre-set limit that provides much-needed cash flow for day-to-day operations. With a commercial (or revolving) line of credit, a business owner can borrow up to the predetermined ceiling at any time during the year quickly and conveniently by writing himself or herself a loan. Banks set up lines of credit that are renewable for anywhere from 90 days to several years, and they usually limit the open line of credit to 40 to 50 percent of a firm's present working capital, although they will lend more for highly seasonal businesses. Bankers may require a company to rest its line of credit during the year, maintaining a zero balance, as proof that the line of credit is not a perpetual crutch. Like commercial loans, lines of credit can be secured or unsecured. A business typically pays a small handling fee (one to two percent of the maximum amount of credit) plus interest on the amount borrowed—usually prime plus three points or more.

The accompanying "Hands on . . . How to" feature describes the six most common reasons bankers reject small business loan applications and how to avoid them.

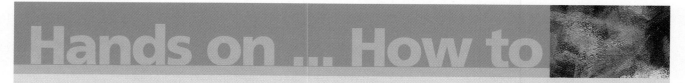

Get a Bank to Say "Yes" to Your Loan Application

Entrepreneurs often complain that bankers don't understand the financial needs they face when starting and operating their businesses. In many instances, however, business owners fail to help themselves when they apply for bank loans. Following are the six most common reasons bankers reject small business loan applications (and how you can avoid them).

Reason 1. "Our bank doesn't make small business loans." Cure: Before applying for a bank loan, research banks to find out which ones actively seek the type of loan you need. Some banks don't emphasize loans under $500,000, whereas others focus almost exclusively on small company loans. The Small Business Administration's reports *Micro-Business-Friendly Banks in the United States* and *Small Business Lending in the United States* are valuable resources for locating the banks in your area that are most likely to make small business loans. Small local banks tend to be the ones that are most receptive to small business loan requests.

Reason 2. "I don't know enough about you or your business." Cure: Develop a detailed business plan that explains what your company does (or will do) and describes how you will gain a competitive edge over your rivals. The plan should address your company's major competition, what it will take to succeed in the market, and how your business will gain a competitive advantage in the market. Also be prepared to supply business credit references and a personal credit history. Finally, make sure you have your "elevator pitch" honed; you should be able to describe your business, what it does, sells, or makes, and the source of its competitive edge in just one or two minutes.

Reason 3. "You haven't told me why you need the money." Cure: A solid business plan will explain how much money you need and how you plan to use it. Make sure your request is specific; avoid requests for loans "for working capital." Don't make the mistake of answering the question, "How much money do you need?" with "How much will you lend me?" A sound business plan always includes realistic financial forecasts that support your loan request. Remember: bankers want to make loans (after all, that's how they generate a profit), but they want to make loans only to those people they believe will repay them. Make sure your plan clearly shows how your company will be able to repay the bank loan.

Reason 4. "Your numbers don't support your loan request." Cure: Include a cash flow forecast in your business plan. Bankers analyze a company's balance sheet and income statement to judge the quality of its assets and its profitability, but they lend primarily on the basis of cash flow. They know that that's how you'll repay the loan. If adequate cash flow isn't available, don't expect a loan. Prove to the banker that you know what your company's cash flow is and how to manage it.

Reason 5. "You don't have enough collateral." Cure: Be prepared to pledge your company's assets—and perhaps your personal assets—as collateral for the loan. Bankers like to have the security of collateral before they make a loan. They also expect more than $1 in collateral for every $1 of money they lend. Banks typically lend 80 to 90 percent

of the value of real estate, 70 to 80 percent of the value of accounts receivable, and just 10 to 50 percent of the value of inventory pledged as collateral.

Reason 6. "Your business does not support the loan on its own." Cure: Be prepared to provide a personal guarantee on the loan. By doing so, you're telling the banker that if your business cannot repay the loan, you will. Many bankers see their small business clients and their companies as one and the same. Even if you choose a form of ownership that provides you with limited personal liability, most bankers will ask you to override that protection by personally guaranteeing the loan.

Ronald Reed launched Benchmark Mobility Inc., a home health-care equipment company, with just $1,800 of his own money. The business's rapid growth over the next few years outstripped Reed's ability to fund the company internally, and he had to turn to external sources of funding. "I was sitting on a couple hundred thousand dollars of business I couldn't do anything with because I had outgrown my personal credit," he says. Over the course of two years, Reed applied for business loans at 21 large banks but was turned down by all of them. "There were times when I wasn't sure I was going to meet payroll," he recalls. Frustrated by his lack of success, Reed turned to the Central Indiana Small Business Development Center, where a counselor referred him to a small local bank that ultimately approved a $250,000 line of credit. "That's a bank I never would have considered," says Reed. The lesson Reed learned? Shop around until you find just the right bank, one that fits your company's needs.

There's no magic to getting a bank to approve your loan request. The secret is preparing properly and building a solid business plan that enhances your credibility as a business owner with your banker. Use your plan to prove that you have what it takes to survive and thrive.

Sources: Adapted from Jim Melloan, "Do Not Say 'I Just Want the Money,'" *Inc.*, July 2005, p. 96; Anne Field, "Getting the Bank to Yes," *Success*, May 1999, pp. 67–71; J. Tol Broome, Jr., "How to Get A 'Yes' from Your Banker," *Nation's Business*, April 1996, p. 37; "Five Red Flags to Avoid When Applying for a Bank Loan," National Federation of Independent Businesses, June 18, 2002, http://www.nfib.com/object/3387621; "How a Start-up Small Business Can Maximize Chances for a Bank Loan," December 9, 2004, National Federation of Independent Businesses, http://www.nfib.com/object/IO_19179; Crystal Detamore-Rodman, "Just Your Size," *Entrepreneur*, April 2005, pp. 59–61.

FLOOR PLANNING Floor planning is a form of financing frequently employed by retailers of "big ticket items" that are easily distinguishable from one another (usually by serial number), such as automobiles, boats, and major appliances. For example, a commercial bank finances Auto City's purchase of its inventory of automobiles and maintains a security interest in each car in the order by holding its title as collateral. Auto City pays interest on the loan monthly and repays the principal as it sells the cars. The longer a floor-planned item sits in inventory, the more it costs the business owner in interest expense. Banks and other floor-planners often discourage retailers from using their money without authorization by performing spot checks to verify prompt repayment of the principal as items are sold.

Intermediate- and Long-Term Loans Banks primarily are lenders of short-term capital to small businesses, although they will make certain intermediate and long-term loans. Intermediate and long-term loans, which are normally secured by collateral, are extended for one year or longer and are normally used to increase fixed- and growth-capital balances. Small companies often face a greater challenge qualifying for intermediate- and long-term loans because of the increased risk to which they expose the bank. Commercial banks grant these loans for constructing a plant, purchasing real estate and equipment, expanding a business, and other long-term investments. Loan repayments are normally made monthly or quarterly. One of the most common types of intermediate-term loans is an installment loan, which banks make to small firms for purchasing equipment, facilities, real estate, and other fixed assets. When financing equipment, a bank usually lends the small business from 60 to 80 percent of the equipment's value in return for a security interest in the equipment. The loan's amortization schedule, which is based on a set number of monthly payments, typically coincides with the length of the equipment's usable life. In financing real estate (commercial mortgages), banks typically will lend up to 75 to 80 percent of the property's value and will allow a lengthier repayment schedule of 10 to 30 years.

term loan

a bank loan that imposes restrictions (covenants) on the business decisions an entrepreneur makes concerning the company's operations.

Another common type of loan banks make to small businesses is a **term loan.** Typically unsecured, banks grant these loans to businesses whose past operating history suggests a high probability of repayment. Some banks make only secured term loans, however. Term loans impose restrictions (called covenants) on the business decisions an entrepreneur makes concerning the company's operations. For instance, a term loan may set limits on owners' salaries, prohibit further borrowing without the bank's approval, or maintain certain financial ratios (recall the discussion of ratio analysis in Chapter 11). Entrepreneurs must understand all of the terms attached to term loans before accepting them.

Matching the amount and the purpose of a loan to the appropriate type and length of loan is important.

Keystone Protection Industries

When John Lawlor had the opportunity to acquire other businesses and fold them into Keystone Protection Industries, his $9 million commercial and industrial fire-protection company, he borrowed $900,000 on the company's revolving line of credit. When business slowed, however, Lawlor found it difficult to handle the interest rate on the line of credit and transferred the debt to a traditional fixed-rate long-term loan that was more suitable for handling the cost of the acquisitions, and the move improved his company's cash flow.[66]

Non-Bank Sources of Debt Capital

Although they are usually the first stop for entrepreneurs in search of debt capital, banks are not the only lending game in town. We now turn our attention to other sources of debt capital that entrepreneurs can tap to feed their cash-hungry companies.

Asset-Based Lenders Asset-based lenders, which are usually smaller commercial banks, commercial finance companies, or specialty lenders, allow small businesses to borrow money by pledging otherwise idle assets such as accounts receivable, inventory, or purchase orders as collateral. This form of financing works especially well for manufacturers, wholesalers, distributors, and other companies with significant stocks of inventory or accounts receivable. Even unprofitable companies whose financial statements could not convince loan officers to make traditional loans can get asset-based loans. These cash-poor but asset-rich companies can use normally unproductive assets—accounts receivable, inventory, fixtures, and purchase orders—to finance rapid growth and the cash crises that often accompany it.

Katalin Posztos, founder of Borneo Fitness International, a company that sells sporty, stylish activewear, faced a dilemma that confronts many entrepreneurs: Orders were pouring into her company, but she lacked the capital and the cash flow to fill them. Posztos tried to land a bank loan to finance the growth, but the four-year-old company's track record was not strong enough to convince bankers to lend any money. "We had a bunch of big orders and nowhere to go," recalls Posztos. That's when she turned to an asset-based lender, Capstone Business Credit. Using customer orders as collateral, Posztos borrowed enough capital to pay fabric suppliers and manufacturers to produce the garments she had designed. When she sold the clothing, Posztos took the accounts receivable that they generated and used them as collateral to borrow the money to launch a new upscale clothing line to complement the existing mass market line. Posztos's asset-based borrowing, which to date has cost $100,000 in interest and fees, has been "invaluable" she says; Borneo's sales have increased threefold to more than $8 million annually.[67]

Borneo Fitness International

Katalin Postzos and Shawn Boyer, co-founders of Borneo Fitness International (BFI) faced a dilemma: Orders for their company's stylish active wear were pouring in, but they lacked the capital to fill them. The entrepreneurs used asset-based financing to get the capital they needed, and BFI's sales increased three-fold.

Like banks, asset-based lenders consider in a company's cash flow, but they are more interested in the quality of the assets pledged as collateral. The amount a small business can borrow through asset-based lending depends on the **advance rate,** the percentage of an asset's value that a lender will lend. For example, a company pledging $100,000 of accounts receivable might negotiate a 70 percent advance rate and qualify for a $70,000 asset-based loan. Advance rates can vary dramatically depending on the quality of the assets pledged and the lender. Because inventory is an illiquid asset (i.e., hard to sell), the advance rate on inventory-based loans is quite low, usually 10 to 50 percent. A business pledging high-quality accounts receivable as collateral, however, may be able to negotiate up to an 85 percent advance rate. The most common types of asset-based financing are discounting accounts receivable and inventory financing.

advance rate
the percentage of an asset's value that a lender will lend.

DISCOUNTING ACCOUNTS RECEIVABLE The most common form of secured credit is accounts receivable financing. Under this arrangement, a small business pledges its accounts receivable as collateral; in return, the lender advances a loan against the value of approved accounts receivable. The amount of the loan tendered is not equal to the face value of the accounts receivable, however. Even though the bank screens the firm's accounts and accepts only qualified receivables, it makes an allowance for the risk involved because some will be written off as uncollectible. A small business usually can borrow an amount equal to 55 to 80 percent of its receivables, depending on their quality. Generally, lenders will not accept receivables that are past due.

INVENTORY FINANCING Here, a small business loan is secured by its inventory of raw materials, work in process, and finished goods. If an owner defaults on the loan, the lender can claim the pledged inventory, sell it, and use the proceeds to satisfy the loan (assuming the bank's claim is superior to the claims of other creditors). Because inventory usually is not a highly liquid asset and its value can be difficult to determine, lenders are willing to lend only a portion of its worth, usually no more than 50 percent of the inventory's value. Most asset-based lenders avoid inventory-only deals; they prefer to make loans backed by inventory *and* more secure accounts receivable. The key to qualifying for inventory financing is proving that a company has a plan or a process in place to ensure that the inventory securing the loan sells quickly.

National Direct

David Johnson, president of National Direct, a Toronto, Canada–based sports collectible business, needed $400,000 to finance a collection of pins licensed by World Wrestling Entertainment, but banks were not convinced that National Direct would turn over the inventory quickly. Johnson found the financing he needed through the Inventory Capital Group, a specialty inventory lender. After selling out the pin collection, Johnson then borrowed $1.2 million from Inventory Capital Group to introduce a commemorative pin collection aimed at Boston Red Sox fans. With the help of the inventory financing, National Direct's sales have more than doubled. "It has allowed us to make a large footprint in the market that a traditional bank would not have given us," says Johnson.[68]

Asset-based financing is a powerful tool, particularly for small companies that have significant sales opportunities but lack the track record to qualify for traditional bank loans. A small business that could obtain a $1 million line of credit with a bank would be able to borrow as much as $3 million by using accounts receivable as collateral. Asset-based borrowing is also an efficient method of borrowing because a small business owner has the money he or she needs when it is needed. In other words, the business pays only for the capital it actually needs and uses.

To ensure the quality of the assets supporting the loans they make, lenders must monitor borrowers' assets, making paperwork requirements on these loans intimidating, especially to first-time borrowers. In addition, asset-based loans are more expensive than traditional bank loans because of the cost of originating and maintaining them and the higher risk involved. Rates usually run from two to seven percentage points above the prime rate. Because of this rate differential, small business owners should not use asset-based loans for long-term financing; their goal should be to establish their credit through asset-based financing and then to move up to a line of credit.

Vendor Financing Many small companies borrow money from their vendors and suppliers in the form of trade credit. Because of its ready availability, trade credit is an extremely important source of financing to most entrepreneurs. When banks refuse to lend money to a start-up business because they see it as a high credit risk, an entrepreneur may be able to turn to trade credit for capital. Getting vendors to extend credit in the form of delayed payments (e.g., "net 30" credit terms) usually is much easier for small businesses than obtaining bank financing. Essentially, a company receiving trade credit from a supplier is getting a short-term, interest-free loan for the amount of the goods purchased.

It is no surprise that businesses receive three dollars of credit from suppliers for every two dollars they receive from banks as loans.[69] Vendors and suppliers often are willing to finance a small business's purchases of goods from 30 to 60 days (sometimes longer), interest-free.

FrogPad

Linda Marroquin, founder of FrogPad, a company that produces specialized computer keyboards and accessories, used vendor financing during the start-up phase of her company.

Linda Marroquin, CEO of FrogPad, a company that produces unique one-handed computer keyboards and other accessories, relied on vendor financing, negotiating payment terms that deferred more than $1 million in costs during the crucial start-up and product launch period. "With sales increasing 25 percent per month, vendor contributions have allowed us to sell product before we pay for it," says Marroquin. FrogPad's sales have surpassed $1 million annually and continue to grow rapidly.[70]

The key to maintaining trade credit as a source of funds is establishing a consistent and reliable payment history with every vendor.

Equipment Suppliers Most equipment vendors encourage business owners to purchase their equipment by offering to finance the purchase. This method of financing is similar to trade credit but with slightly different terms. Usually, equipment vendors offer reasonable credit terms with only a modest down payment, with the balance financed over the life of the equipment (often several years). In some cases, the vendor will repurchase equipment for salvage value at the end of its useful life and offer the business owner another credit agreement on new equipment. Some companies get equipment loans to lease rather than to purchase fixed assets. Start-up companies often use trade credit from equipment suppliers to purchase equipment and fixtures such as counters, display cases, refrigeration units, machinery, and the like. It pays to scrutinize vendors' credit terms, however; they may be less attractive than those of other lenders.

Commercial Finance Companies When denied bank loans, small business owners often look to commercial finance companies for the same types of loans. Commercial finance companies are second only to banks in making loans to small businesses, and, unlike their conservative counterparts, they are willing to tolerate more risk in their loan portfolios. Of course, their primary consideration is collecting their loans, but finance companies tend to rely more on obtaining a security interest in some type of collateral, given the higher-risk loans that make up their portfolios. Because commercial finance companies depend on collateral to recover most of their losses, they are able to make loans to small companies with very irregular cash flows or to those that are not yet profitable.

Approximately 150 large commercial finance companies, such as AT&T Small Business Lending, GE Capital Small Business Finance, and others, make a variety of loans to small companies, ranging from asset-based loans and business leases to construction and Small Business Administration loans. Dubbed "the Wal-Marts of finance," commercial finance companies usually offer many of the same credit options as commercial banks do. Because their loans are subject to more risks, finance companies charge a higher interest rate than commercial banks (usually prime plus at least two percent). Their most common methods of providing credit to small businesses are asset-based—accounts receivable financing and inventory loans. Rates on these loans vary but can be as high as 15 to 30 percent (including fees), depending on the risk a particular business presents and the quality of the assets involved. Because many of the loans they make are secured by collateral (usually the business equipment, vehicle, real estate, or inventory purchased with the loan), finance companies often impose more onerous reporting requirements, sometimes requiring weekly (or even daily) information on a small company's inventory levels or accounts receivable balances.

When Kevin Garlasco decided to move Princeton Laundry, his family's third-generation commercial laundry business, out of Manhattan to the Bronx to reduce operating costs, he knew he needed an infusion of working capital to stabilize the company. Even though Princeton Laundry had been serving the laundry needs of New York City hotels since 1918, its recent financial challenges caused every bank the Garlascos approached to refuse their loan applications. "We were falling [deeper] into a hole," recalls Kevin. Then the Garlascos turned to Business Alliance Capital, a commercial finance company, for help, and Business Alliance provided Princeton Laundry with a $600,000 revolving line of credit secured by accounts receivable. The line of credit has helped to turn Princeton Laundry around; its annual sales have grown 30 percent, climbing to more than $7 million. In addition, the reporting requirements that Business Alliance requires of Princeton Laundry have imposed a degree of discipline on the family members who manage the company. "Now we're running our business much more efficiently," says Kevin. Because Princeton Laundry's line of credit is secured by accounts receivable, making sure customers pay their bills on time is paramount. "I really have to keep control of my customers and keep them paying [on time]," he says.[71]

COMPANY Profile

Princeton Laundry

Savings and Loan Associations Savings and loan associations (S&Ls) specialize in loans for real property. In addition to their traditional role of providing mortgages for personal residences, savings and loan associations offer financing on commercial and industrial property. In the typical commercial or industrial loan, the S&L will lend up to

80 percent of the property's value with a repayment schedule of up to 30 years. Most S&Ls hesitate to lend money for buildings specially designed for a particular customer's needs. S&Ls expect the mortgage to be repaid from the company's future profits.

Stock Brokerage Houses Stockbrokers also make loans, and many of the loans they make to their customers carry lower interest rates than those from banks. These **margin loans** carry lower rates because the collateral supporting them—the stocks and bonds in the customer's portfolio—is of high quality and is highly liquid. Moreover, brokerage firms make it easy to borrow. Usually, brokers set up a line of credit for their customers when they open a brokerage account. To tap that line of credit, the customer simply writes a check or uses a debit card. Typically, there is no fixed repayment schedule for a margin loan; the debt can remain outstanding indefinitely as long as the market value of the borrower's portfolio of collateral meets minimum requirements. Aspiring entrepreneurs can borrow up to 50 percent of the value of their stock portfolios, up to 70 percent of their bond portfolios, and up to 90 percent of the value of their government securities. For example, one woman borrowed $60,000 to buy equipment for her New York health club, and a St. Louis doctor borrowed $1 million against his brokerage account to help finance a medical clinic.[72]

There is risk involved in using stocks and bonds as collateral on a loan. Brokers typically require a 30 percent cushion on margin loans. If the value of the borrower's portfolio drops, the broker can make a **margin (maintenance) call**—that is, the broker can call the loan in and require the borrower to provide more cash and securities as collateral. Recent swings in the stock market have translated into margin calls for many entrepreneurs, requiring them to repay a significant portion of their loan balances within a matter of days—or hours. If an account lacks adequate collateral, the broker can sell off the customer's portfolio to pay off the loan.

Over the last two decades, stockbrokers have been adding traditional loans to their line of small business financial services, but start-up companies rarely meet their stringent standards. For established companies, however, these loans can be an important source of funds.

Vertex Systems Inc.

Kevin Nikkhoo, founder of Vertex Systems Inc., a $10 million-a-year technology consulting firm, negotiated a small business loan from Morgan Stanley to finance the company's rapid growth. After negotiating with banks and other potential sources of funds, Nikkhoo decided to go with Morgan Stanley because they offered better terms and the potential to provide more funding as Vertex grew.[73]

Insurance Companies For many small businesses, life insurance companies can be an important source of business capital. Insurance companies offer two basic types of loans: policy loans and mortgage loans. **Policy loans** are extended on the basis of the amount of money paid through premiums into the insurance policy. It usually takes about two years for an insurance policy to accumulate enough cash surrender value to justify a loan against it. Once he or she accumulates cash value in a policy, an entrepreneur may borrow up to 95 percent of that value for any length of time. Interest is levied annually, but borrowers can defer repayment indefinitely. However, the amount of insurance coverage is reduced by the amount of the loan. Policy loans typically offer very favorable interest rates, often at or below prevailing loan rates at banks and other lending institutions. Only insurance policies that build cash value—that is, combine a savings plan with insurance coverage—offer the option of borrowing. These include whole life (permanent insurance), variable life, universal life, and many corporate-owned life insurance policies. Term life insurance, which offers only pure insurance coverage, has no borrowing capacity.

Insurance companies make **mortgage loans** on a long-term basis on real property worth a minimum of $500,000. They are based primarily on the value of the real property being purchased. The insurance company will extend a loan of up to 75 or 80 percent of the real estate's value and will allow a lengthy repayment schedule over 25 or 30 years so that payments do not strain the firm's cash flows excessively.

margin loans
loans from a stockbroker that use the the stocks and bonds in the borrower's portfolio as collateral.

margin (maintenance) call
occurs when the value of a borrower's portfolio drops and the broker calls the loan in, requiring the borrower to put up more cash and securities as collateral.

policy loan
a loan insurance companies make on the basis of the amount of money a customer has paid into a policy in the form of premiums.

mortgage loan
a loan insurance companies make on a long-term basis for real property worth at least $500,000.

Credit Unions Credit unions, nonprofit financial cooperatives that promote saving and provide loans to their members, are best known for making consumer and car loans. However, many are also willing to lend money to their members to launch businesses. More than 10,000 state- and federally-chartered credit unions with some 88 million members operate in the United States, and they make loans to their members totaling more than $172 billion a year, many of them for the purpose of starting a business.[74]

Credit unions don't make loans to just anyone; to qualify for a loan, an entrepreneur must be a member. Lending practices at credit unions are very much like those at banks, but they usually are willing to make smaller loans. Entrepreneurs around the globe are turning to credit unions to finance their businesses, sometimes borrowing tiny amounts of money.

Joseph Ogwal

When Joseph Ogwal, a refugee of war-torn Sudan, arrived in South Africa, he had nothing—literally. Ogwal, who has a degree in electronics engineering, wanted to start his own business to earn enough money to bring his family to South Africa, so he turned to the Cape Metropole South African Credit Co-operative (SACCO) for a small loan. With his $115 loan, Ogwal launched a consumer electronics repair business that already is earning a profit. With another loan from the credit union, he plans to expand his business, launching a training center for repair technicians.[75]

Bonds Bonds, which are corporate IOUs, have always been a popular source of debt financing for large companies. Few small business owners realize that they can also tap this valuable source of capital. Although the smallest businesses are not viable candidates for issuing bonds, a growing number of small companies are finding the funding they need through bonds when banks and other lenders say no. Because of the costs involved, issuing bonds usually is best suited for companies generating sales between $5 million and $30 million and have capital requirements between $1.5 million and $10 million. Although they can help small companies raise much-needed capital, bonds have certain disadvantages. The issuing company must follow the same regulations that govern businesses selling stock to public investors. Even if the bond issue is private, the company must register the offering and file periodic reports with the SEC.

Small manufacturers needing money for fixed assets have access to an attractive, relatively inexpensive source of funds in industrial development bonds (IDBs), which were created to give manufacturers access to capital at rates lower than they could get from traditional lenders. In 1999, Congress created the mini-bond program, which allows small companies to issue bonds through a streamlined application process and lower fees. Typically, the amount of money small companies issuing IDBs seek to raise is at least $1 million, but some small manufacturers have raised as little as $500,000 using IDBs. Even though the paperwork and legal costs associated with making an IDB issue can run up to two to three percent of the financing amount, IDBs remain a relative bargain for borrowing long-term money at a fixed interest rate.

Golterman & Sabo

After using bank loans for many years to finance his company's capital needs, Ned Golterman, co-owner of Golterman & Sabo, a small building materials company, decided to issue mini-bonds. Not only was Golterman able to avoid much of the complicated paperwork associated with a typical bond issue, but he also managed to get long-term financing for his company at a rate two percentage points below the best bank loan rate he could find and favorable repayment terms.[76]

Private Placements Earlier in this chapter, we saw how companies can raise capital by making private placements of their stock (equity). Private placements are also available for debt instruments. A private placement involves selling debt to one or a small number of investors, usually insurance companies or pension funds. Private placement debt is a hybrid between a conventional loan and a bond. At its heart, it is a bond, but its terms are tailored to the borrower's individual needs, as a loan would be.

Privately placed securities offer several advantages over standard bank loans. First, they usually carry fixed interest rates rather than the variable rates banks often charge.

credit union
a nonprofit financial cooperative that promotes saving and provides loans to its members.

Second, the maturity of private placements is longer than most bank loans: 15 years rather than 5. Private placements do not require hiring expensive investment bankers. Finally, because private investors can afford to take greater risks than banks, they are willing to finance deals for fledgling small companies.

Small Business Investment Companies Small business investment companies (SBICs), created in 1958 when Congress passed the Small Business Investment Act, are privately owned financial institutions that are licensed and regulated by the SBA. The 418 SBICs operating in the United States use a combination of private capital and federally guaranteed debt to provide long-term capital to small businesses. Most SBICs prefer later-round financing over funding raw start-ups. Because of changes in their financial structure made a few years ago, however, SBICs now are better equipped to invest in start-up companies. In fact, about 43 percent of SBIC investments go to companies that are no more than three years old.[77] Funding from SBICs helped launch companies such as Apple Computer, JetBlue Airways, Build-a-Bear Workshop, Federal Express, Staples, Sun Microsystems, and Callaway Golf.

Since 1958, SBICs have provided more than $46 billion in long-term debt and equity financing to some 100,000 small businesses, adding many thousands of jobs to the American economy.[78] SBICs must be capitalized privately with a minimum of $5 million, at which point they qualify for up to three dollars in long-term SBA loans for every dollar of private capital invested in small businesses. As a general rule, SBICs may provide financial assistance only to small businesses with a net worth of less than $18 million and average after-tax earnings of $6 million during its last two years. However, employment and total annual sales standards vary from industry to industry. SBICs are limited to a maximum investment or loan amount of 20 percent of their private capital to a single client.

SBICs provide both debt and equity financing to small businesses. Because of SBA regulations affecting the financing arrangements an SBIC can offer, most SBICs extend their investments as loans with an option to convert the debt instrument into an equity interest later. Most SBIC loans are in the much-needed range of $100,000 to $5 million, and the loan term is longer than most banks allow. The average SBIC loan is $664,200.[79] When they make equity investments, SBICs are prohibited from obtaining a controlling interest in the companies in which they invest (no more than 49 percent ownership). The average SBIC equity investment is $1.13 million, far below the average equity investment by venture capital firms of $12 million.[80] The most common forms of SBIC financing (in order of their frequency) are a loan with an option to buy stock, a convertible debenture, a straight loan, and preferred stock.

Outback Steakhouse

Outback Steakhouse, a highly successful restaurant chain based on an Australian theme, received early financing from an SBIC, Kitty Hawk Capital I, which allowed it to grow. In 1990, Outback had been in business less than three years when the SBIC decided to invest $151,000 to boost the company's working capital balance. That capital infusion gave Outback the financing it needed to get to the next level. The company made an initial public offering in 1991 and today generates sales of more than $2.5 billion a year.[81]

Outback Steakhouse, which now has locations around the globe, truly is a success story for the SBIC industry. Due to budget pressure at the federal level, however, the SBIC program now is fighting for survival.

Small Business Lending Companies Small business lending companies (SBLCs) make only intermediate- and long-term SBA-guaranteed loans. They specialize in loans that many banks would not consider and operate on a nationwide basis. Most SBLC loans have terms extending for at least 10 years. The maximum interest rate for loans of seven years or longer is 2.75 percent above the prime rate; for shorter-term loans, the ceiling is 2.25 percent above prime. Another feature of SBLC loans is the expertise the SBLC offers borrowing companies in critical areas. Corporations own most of the nation's SBLCs, giving them a solid capital base.

When Linda Black, who co-founded with her husband Clean Advantage, a company that makes a variety of cleaning products, began landing accounts with many of the nation's largest companies, she saw the need to expand her business. Black found the ideal location for her growing company in tiny Greer, South Carolina. The 55,000-square-foot building, formerly a toothpaste manufacturing operation, "was just perfect for us," says Black, who turned to an SBLC operated by non-bank lender CIT to finance the project. "We were able to offer Linda 90 percent financing with terms she could afford," says CIT loan office Mark Moreno. "We also [integrated] her working capital requirements into the same loan to give her a cushion to help with moving costs, setup, and other expenses," says Moreno.[82]

Clean Advantage

Federally Sponsored Programs

Federally sponsored lending programs have suffered from budget reductions in the last several years. Current trends suggest that the federal government is reducing its involvement in the lending business, but many programs are still quite active and some are actually growing.

LEARNING OBJECTIVES
6. Identify the various federal loan programs aimed at small businesses.

Economic Development Administration

The Economic Development Administration (EDA), a branch of the Commerce Department, offers loan guarantees to create new business and to expand existing businesses in areas with below-average income and high unemployment. Focusing on economically distressed communities, the EDA often works with local governments to finance long-term investment projects needed to stimulate economic growth and to create jobs by making loan guarantees. The EDA guarantees loans up to 80 percent of business loans between $750,000 and $10 million. Entrepreneurs apply for loans through private lenders, for whom an EDA loan guarantee significantly reduces the risk of lending. Start-up companies must supply 15 percent of the guaranteed amount in the form of equity, and established businesses must make equity investments of at least 15 percent of the guaranteed amount. Small businesses can use the loan proceeds for a variety of ways, from supplementing working capital and purchasing equipment to buying land and renovating buildings.

EDA business loans are designed to help replenish economically distressed areas by creating or expanding small businesses that provide employment opportunities in local communities. To qualify for a loan, a business must be located in a disadvantaged area, and its presence must directly benefit local residents. Some communities experiencing high unemployment or suffering from the effects of devastating natural disasters have received EDA Revolving Loan Fund Grants to create loan pools for local small businesses. For instance, the city of San Diego recently used matching funds from the EDA to make a $300,000 loan to Otay Auto Body Parts, a promising start-up company that sells after-market auto parts to both wholesalers and retailers. The small company used the loan to hire employees and to purchase inventory.[83]

Department of Housing and Urban Development

The Department of Housing and Urban Development (HUD) sponsors several loan programs to assist qualified entrepreneurs in raising needed capital. Community Development Block Grants (CDBGs) are extended to cities and counties that, in turn, lend or grant money to entrepreneurs to start small businesses that will strengthen the local economy. Grants are aimed at cities and towns in need of revitalization and economic stimulation. Some grants are used to construct buildings and plants to be leased to entrepreneurs, sometimes with an option to buy. Others are earmarked for revitalizing a crime-ridden area or making start-up loans to entrepreneurs or expansion loans to existing business owners. No ceilings or geographic limitations are placed on CDBG loans and grants, but projects must benefit low- and moderate-income families.

The city of Wichita, Kansas, and Cessna Aircraft Company used the loan guarantee provision of the CDBG program to purchase a large tract in a troubled neighborhood and to renovate it. They built the Cessna Learning Work Complex, which included a light assembly factory and a training/day care center for Cessna trainees from the local area. The renovation stimulated investments in the community, including a new bank, a library, a senior citizens center, and a housing complex.[84]

Cessna Aircraft Company and Wichita, Kansas

HUD also makes loan guarantees up to $5 million through its Section 108 provision of the Community Block Development Grant program. The agency has funded more than 1,200 projects since its inception in 1978. These loan guarantees allow a community to transform a portion of CDBG funds into federally guaranteed loans large enough to pursue economic revitalization projects that can lead to the renewal of entire town.

U.S. Department of Agriculture's Rural Business-Cooperative Service

The U.S. Department of Agriculture (USDA) provides financial assistance to certain small businesses through its Rural Business-Cooperative Service (RBS). The RBS program is open to all types of businesses (not just farms) and is designed to create nonfarm employment opportunities in rural areas—those with populations below 50,000 and not adjacent to a city where densities exceed 100 people per square mile. Entrepreneurs in many small towns, especially those with populations below 25,000, are eligible to apply for loans through the RBS program, which makes almost $900 million in loan guarantees each year.

The RBS does make a limited number of direct loans to small businesses, but the majority of its activity is in loan guarantees. Through its Business and Industry Guaranteed Loan Program, the RBS will guarantee as much as 80 percent of a commercial lender's loan up to $25 million (although actual guarantee amounts are almost always far less) for qualified applicants. Entrepreneurs apply for loans through private lenders, who view applicants with loan guarantees much more favorably than those without such guarantees. The RBS guarantee reduces a lender's risk dramatically because the guarantee means that the government agency would pay off the loan balance (up to the ceiling) if the entrepreneur defaults on the loan.

To make a loan guarantee, the RBS requires much of the same documentation as most banks and most other loan guarantee programs. Because of its emphasis on developing employment in rural areas, the RBS requires an environmental-impact statement describing the jobs created and the effect the business has on the area. The Rural-Business Cooperative Service also makes grants available to businesses and communities for the purpose of encouraging small business development and growth.

Small Business Innovation Research Program

Started as a pilot program by the National Science Foundation in the 1970s, the Small Business Innovation Research Program (SBIR) program has expanded to 11 federal agencies, ranging from NASA to the Department of Defense. These agencies award cash grants or long-term contracts to small companies wanting to initiate or to expand their research and development efforts. SBIR grants give innovative small companies the opportunity to attract early-stage capital investments *without* having to give up significant equity stakes or taking on burdensome levels of debt. The SBIR process involves three phases. Phase I grants, which determine the feasibility and commercial potential of a technology or product, last for up to 6 months and have a ceiling of $100,000. Phase II grants, designed to develop the concept into a specific technology or product, run for up to 24 months and have a ceiling of $750,000. Approximately 40 percent of all Phase II applicants receive funding. Phase III is the commercialization phase, in which the company pursues commercial applications of the research and development conducted in phases I and II and must use private or non-SBIR federal funding to bring a product to market.

Competition for SBIR funding is intense; only 12 percent of the small companies that apply receive funding. So far, more than 36,000 SBIR awards totaling in excess of $10 billion have gone to small companies, who traditionally have had difficulty competing with big corporations for federal R&D dollars. The government's dollars have been well invested. Nearly 40 percent of small businesses receiving second-phase SBIR awards have achieved commercial success with their products.[85]

PediSedate

Geoffrey Hart, a physician at Albert Einstein Memorial Center in Philadelphia, knew there had to be a better way to administer anesthesia to the frightened, injured children whom he treated in the emergency room. Many children panicked when members of the medical team approached them with the full-sized anesthesiology masks that covered their entire faces. Working with engineer David Chastain, Hart created the PediSedate, a child-sized headset with a swiveling snorkel that delivers the sedating medication and monitors the child's respiration. The earpieces connect to either a portable CD player or to a Nintendo Game Boy unit while simultaneously monitoring the oxygenation of the blood. To finance the cost of developing the PediSedate and bringing it to market, Hart and Chastain applied for and received both Phase I and a Phase II SBIR grants through the National Institutes of Health. "These grants made everything possible," says Chastain. "They enabled all of the product development and the clinical trial work [to receive approval from the FDA]."[86]

The Small Business Technology Transfer Program

The Small Business Technology Transfer Program (STTR) program complements the Small Business Innovation Research Program. Whereas the SBIR focuses on commercially promising ideas that originate in small businesses, the STTR uses companies to exploit the vast reservoir of commercially promising ideas that originate in universities, federally funded R&D centers, and nonprofit research institutions. Researchers at these institutions can join forces with small businesses and can spin off commercially promising ideas while remaining employed at their research institutions. Five federal agencies award grants of up to $500,000 in three phases to these research partnerships.

You Be the Consultant

Money Hunt

Always On Wireless

In 1988, when Rudy Prince launched his first business, JetFax, a software company that allowed users to send faxes over the Internet, he convinced several angel investors to put up $500,000 in start-up capital even though the company was little more than an idea on paper. Today Prince is looking for $1 million for his latest business venture, Always On Wireless, a company that markets the WiFlyer, a device that lets dial-up Internet subscribers connect to the Web wirelessly. This time, however, Prince and his partners have invested $200,000 of their own money in Always On and have a fully-developed product ready to go to market,

Prince has approached potential angel investors, but this time he is getting a different response: skepticism. "[Angels] are no longer relying as much on leaps of faith when it comes to investing," says Prince. He knows that angel investors typically expect to purchase 25 percent to 35 percent of a company's stock and to receive returns of 5 to 10 times their original investments.

Tympany Inc.

Chris Wasden, founder of Tympany, a Houston-based hearing diagnostics device company, worked for investment banker J.P. Morgan for nine years, and he knows

how the fund-raising business works. With his company up and running, Wasden is looking for $4.5 million to fuel Tympany's growth. Wasden's business plan projects third-year revenues of $6 million—if he can find the financing he needs. Wasden has spent nearly a year making more than 90 presentations to potential investors in the Houston area, but none of them have decided to invest in Tympany. Frustrated, Wasden wonders where to turn next.

Marian Heath Greeting Cards

Aaron Kushner, an entrepreneur whose family had been in the greeting card business for several years, has the opportunity to buy another company in the industry, Marian Heath Greeting Cards, from the daughter of the company's founder. Kushner and his business partner, Dan Steever, have a profitable business that is growing at a steady five percent a year, but they lack the $4 million they need to purchase Marian Heath. "We put together a small portion of the price with our own and friends' money, but we are going to need an equity partner," says Kushner. He admits, however, that it is extremely difficult to find "a good equity partner who isn't interested in controlling the entire company or flipping [selling] it in a short period of time."

1. Explain why the following funding sources would or would not be appropriate for Rudy Prince, John Acosta, and Aaron Kushner: family and friends, angel investors, venture capital, an initial public offering, a traditional bank loan, asset-based borrowing, or one of the many federal or SBA loans.

2. Rudy Prince knows that potential private investors in his company are looking to "cash out" their investments in five to seven years. Discuss the exit strategies that are available to Prince and his investors. What are the advantages and disadvantages of each one?

3. Work with a team of your classmates to brainstorm ways that Rudy Prince, John Acosta, and Aaron Kushner could attract the capital they need for their businesses. What steps would you recommend they take before they approach the potential sources of funding you have identified?

Source: Adapted from Paola Singer, "Capital Ideas," *Wall Street Journal,* May 8, 2006, pp. RR6, R12; David Worrell, "Common Cents," *Entrepreneur,* November 2004, pp. 72–74; Darren Dahl, "Earning Your Wings," *Inc.,* January 2005, pp. 40–42.

7. Describe the various loan programs available from the Small Business Administration.

Small Business Administration

The Small Business Administration (SBA) has several programs designed to help finance both start-up and existing small companies that cannot qualify for traditional loans because of their thin asset base and their high risk of failure. In its more than 50 years of operation, the SBA has helped nearly 20 million small businesses through a multitude of programs, enabling many of them to get the financing they need for start-up or for growth. The SBA's $45 billion loan portfolio makes it the single financial backer of small businesses in the nation.[87] To be eligible for SBA funds, a business must meet the SBA's criteria that define a small business. In addition, some types of businesses, such as those engaged in gambling, pyramid sales schemes, or real estate investment, among others, are ineligible for SBA loans.

The loan application process can take from three days to several months, depending on how well prepared the entrepreneur is and which bank is involved. To speed up processing times, the SBA has established a Certified Lender Program (CLP) and a Preferred Lender Program (PLP). Both are designed to encourage banks to become frequent SBA lenders. When a bank makes enough good loans to qualify as a certified lender, the SBA promises a fast turnaround time for the loan decision—typically 3 to 10 business days. About 850 lenders across the country are SBA certified lenders. When a bank becomes a preferred lender, it makes the final lending decision itself, subject to SBA review. In essence, the SBA delegates the application process, the lending decision, and other details to the preferred lender. The SBA guarantees up to 75 percent of PLP loans in case the borrower fails and defaults on the loan. The minimum PLP loan guarantee is $100,000, and the maximum is $500,000. About 500 lenders across the United States meet the SBA's preferred lender standards. Using certified or preferred lenders can reduce the processing time for an SBA loan considerably.

To further reduce the paperwork requirements involved in its loans, the SBA created the **Low Doc Loan Program** ("low documentation"), which allows small businesses to use a simple one-page application for all loan applications. Before the Low Doc Loan Program, a typical SBA loan application required an entrepreneur to complete at least 10 forms, and the SBA often took 45 to 90 days to make a decision about an application. Under the Low Doc Loan Program, response time is just three days.

Low Doc Loan Program
a program initiated by the SBA in an attempt to simplify and streamline the application process for small business loans.

To qualify for a Low Doc loan, a company must have average sales below $5 million during the previous three years and employ fewer than 100 people. Businesses can use Low Doc loans for working capital, machinery, equipment, and real estate. The SBA guarantees 85 percent of loans up to $100,000 and 75 percent of loans over that amount up to the loan ceiling of $150,000. Borrowers must be willing to provide a personal guarantee for repayment of the loan principal. Interest rates are prime plus 2.75 percent on loans of seven years or longer and prime plus 2.25 percent on loans of less than seven years. The average Low Doc loan is $79,500.

Richard Smith, owner of a whitewater rafting business, needed money to expand his 20-year-old company and to buy new equipment. Smith, however, was hesitant to approach the SBA because he wanted to avoid "myriads of paperwork." At his banker's urging, Smith decided to try the Low Doc Program, and within days of submitting his application, he received a $100,000 loan.[88]

Richard Smith

Another program designed to streamline the application process for SBA loan guarantees is the **SBA*Express* Program,** in which participating lenders use their own loan procedures and applications to make loans of up to $350,000 to small businesses. Because the SBA guarantees up to 50 percent of the loan, banks are often more willing to make smaller loans to entrepreneurs who might otherwise have difficulty meeting lenders' standards. Loan maturities on SBA*Express* loans typically are between five and ten years, but loan maturities for fixed assets can be up to 25 years. Currently, the SBA is planning to replace the Low Doc Program with the SBA*Express* Program. In fact, several SBA loan programs face potential elimination as Congress and the White House struggle with the federal budget.

SBA*Express* Program
an SBA program that allows participating lenders to use their own loan procedures to make SBA-guaranteed loans.

SBA Loan Programs

7(A) Loan Guaranty Program The SBA works with local lenders (both bank and non-bank) to offer a variety of loan programs all designed to help entrepreneurs who cannot get capital from traditional sources gain access to the financing they need to launch and grow their businesses. By far, the most popular SBA loan program is the **7(A) loan guaranty program** (see Figure 13.4). Private lenders extend these loans to small businesses, but the SBA guarantees them (85 percent of loans up to $150,000; 75 percent of loans above $150,000 up to the loan guarantee ceiling of $750,000). In other words, the SBA does not actually lend any money; it merely acts as an insurer, guaranteeing the lender this much repayment in case the small business borrower defaults on the loan. When they were just small companies, Callaway Golf, Outback Steakhouse, and Intel Corporation borrowed through the SBA's 7(A) loan program.

7(A) loan guaranty program
an SBA loan program in which loans made by private lenders to small businesses are guaranteed up to a ceiling by the SBA.

FIGURE 13.4

SBA 7(A) Guaranteed Loans

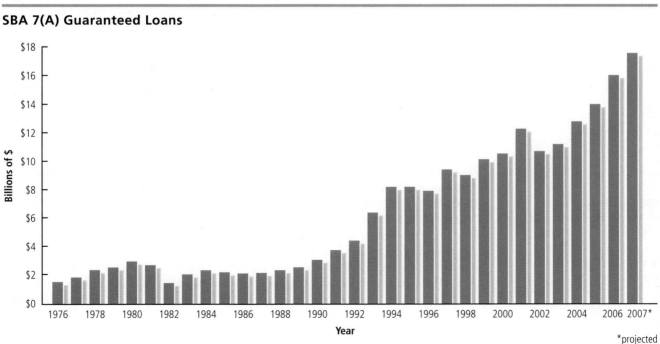

Source: U.S. Small Business Administration.

Because the SBA assumes most of the credit risk, lenders are more willing to consider riskier deals that they normally would refuse. Because of the SBA's guarantee, borrowers also have to come up with less collateral than with a traditional bank loan.

Lupita's Bakery and Fiesta Mexicana Family Restaurant

After working in the bakery business for 16 years, Abel Diaz used an SBA-guaranteed loan to open Lupita's Bakery in South Central Los Angeles. Given Diaz's modest collateral and the history of the area in which his bakery would operate (it had been the site of riots, violence, and other problems in the past), the SBA loan guarantee was essential for Diaz to qualify for a bank loan. Diaz's bakery was a success, and he soon opened bakeries in two more locations. Always on the lookout for business opportunities, Diaz saw the need for a restaurant and banquet facility in his community and once again applied for an SBA loan guarantee through a local bank, Banco Popular. Diaz now operates the highly successful Fiesta Mexicana Family Restaurant, and its adjoining banquet hall is booked almost every night of the week. "Abel Diaz has succeeded in both the bakery and the catering businesses and has created new jobs in a historically underserved area," says the SBA's Los Angeles District Director.[89]

Qualifying for an SBA loan guarantee requires cooperation among the entrepreneur, the participating lender, and the SBA. The participating lender determines the loan's terms and sets the interest rate within SBA limits. Contrary to popular belief, SBA-guaranteed loans do *not* carry special deals on interest rates. Typically, rates are negotiated with the participating lender, with a ceiling of prime plus 2.25 percent on loans of less than 7 years and prime plus 2.75 percent on loans of 7 to 25 years. Interest rates on loans of less than $25,000 can run up to prime plus 4.75 percent. The average interest rate on SBA-guaranteed loans is prime plus 2 percent (compared to prime plus 1 percent on conventional bank loans). The SBA also assesses a one-time guaranty fee of up to 3.75 percent for all loan guarantees.

The maximum loan available through the 7(A) guaranty program is $2,000,000, but the average loan amount is $154,000. The average duration of an SBA loan is 12 years—far longer than the average commercial small business loan. In fact, longer loan terms are a distinct advantage of SBA loans. At least half of all bank business loans are for less than one year. By contrast, SBA real estate loans can extend for up to 25 years (compared to just 10 to 15 years for a conventional loan), and working capital loans have maturities of seven years (compared with two to five years at most banks). These longer terms translate into lower payments, which are better suited for young, fast-growing, cash-strapped companies. In fact, the SBA's 7(A) loan program accounts for 40 percent of all long-term loans to the nation's 25 million small businesses. For instance, Craig Lindgren, owner of Boulder Exhibits, a company that designs and builds trade-show exhibits, recently borrowed $820,000 to purchase a 23,000-square-foot office and warehouse that he financed for 25 years with the help of the 7(A) program.[90]

The CAPLine Program In addition to its basic 7(A) loan guarantee program (through which the SBA makes about 84 percent of its loans), the SBA provides guarantees on small business loans for start-up, real estate, machinery and equipment, fixtures, working capital, exporting, and restructuring debt through several other methods. About two-thirds of all SBA's loan guarantees are for machinery and equipment or working capital. The **CAPLine Program** offers short-term capital to growing companies needing to finance seasonal build-ups in inventory or accounts receivable under five separate programs, each with maturities up to five years: seasonal line of credit (provides advances against inventory and accounts receivable to help businesses weather seasonal sales fluctuations), contract line of credit (finances the cost of direct labor and materials costs associated with performing contracts), builder's line of credit (helps small contractors and builders finance labor and materials costs), standard asset-based line of credit (an asset-based revolving line of credit for financing short-term needs), and small asset-based line of credit (an asset-based revolving line of credit up to $200,000). CAPLine is aimed at helping cash-hungry small businesses by giving them a credit line to draw on when they need it. These loans built

CAPLine Program

an SBA program that makes short-term capital loans to growing companies needing to finance seasonal buildups in inventory or accounts receivable.

around lines of credit are what small companies need most because they are so flexible, efficient, and, unfortunately, so hard for small businesses to get from traditional lenders.

Loans Involving International Trade For small businesses going global, the SBA has the **Export Working Capital (EWC) Program,** which is designed to provide working capital to small exporters. The SBA works in conjunction with the Export-Import Bank to administer this loan guarantee program. Applicants file a one-page loan application, and the response time normally is 10 days or less. The maximum loan is $2,000,000, and proceeds must be used to finance small business exports.

Paul Wilhelm landed a significant contract to export to Pakistan the diesel engine kits that his small company, PowerUp Inc., assembles. The only problem was that the start-up company lacked the working capital to fill the order, and because it had not yet established a track record, it did not qualify for a traditional loan. With the guidance of the Small Business Development Center at the University of Georgia, Wilhelm applied for a $125,000 SBA-guaranteed Export Working Capital loan and received approval within a week. "This export loan fit our business perfectly," says Wilhelm. "[It] was essential to the growth of our company, and we plan to use more of them in the future." After making the sale in Pakistan, PowerUp repaid the loan and shortly thereafter received approval on another Export Working Capital loan—this one for $1 million—to export engine parts to Pakistan.[91]

The **International Trade Program** is for small businesses that are engaging in international trade or are adversely affected by competition from imports. The SBA allows global entrepreneurs to combine loans from the Export Working Capital Program with those from International Trade Program for a maximum guarantee of $1,750,000. Loan maturities range from 1 to 25 years.

Section 504 Certified Development Company Program The SBA's Section 504 program is designed to encourage small businesses to expand their facilities and to create jobs. Section 504 loans provide long-term, fixed-asset financing to small companies to purchase land, buildings, or equipment. Three lenders play a role in every 504 loan: a bank, the SBA, and a **certified development company (CDC).** A CDC is a nonprofit organization licensed by the SBA and designed to promote economic growth in local communities. Some 270 CDCs operate across the United States. An entrepreneur generally is required to make a down payment of just 10 percent of the total project cost. The CDC puts up 40 percent at a long-term fixed rate, supported by an SBA loan guarantee in case the entrepreneur defaults. The bank provides long-term financing for the remaining 50 percent, also supported by an SBA guarantee. The major advantages of Section 504 loans are their fixed rates and terms, their 10- and 20-year maturities, and the low down payment required. The maximum loan amount is $1.5 million.

When he learned that Metalcraft Industries, a company that manufactures sheet metal and machine precision parts for the aerospace industry, was about to shut down and put out of work many residents of Cedar City, Utah, entrepreneur David Grant decided to take action. With the help of Mountain West Small Business Finance, a certified development company licensed by the SBA, Grant put together a financing package that allowed him and the company's management team to purchase the company and save it from the scrapheap. Today, Metalcraft Industries employs hundreds of people and has become one of Utah's most successful small businesses.[92]

As attractive as they are, 504 loans are not for every business owner. The SBA imposes several restrictions on 504 loans:

■ For every $35,000 the CDC loans, the project must create at least one new job or achieve a public policy goal such as rural development, expansion of exports, minority business development, and others.

Export Working Capital (EWC) Program
an SBA loan program that is designed to provide working capital to small exporters.

PowerUp Inc.

International Trade Program
an SBA loan program for small businesses that are engaging in international trade or are adversely affected by competition from imports.

certified development company (CDC)
a nonprofit organization licensed by the SBA and designed to promote growth in local communities by working with commercial banks and the SBA to make long-term loans to small businesses.

Metalcraft Industries

- Machinery and equipment financed must have a useful life of at least 10 years.
- The borrower must occupy at least two-thirds of a building constructed with the loan, or the borrower must occupy at least half of a building purchased or remodeled with the loan.
- The borrower must qualify as a small business under the SBA's definition and must not have a tangible net worth in excess of $7 million and not have an average net income in excess of $2.5 million after taxes for the preceding two years.

Because of strict equity requirements, existing small businesses usually find it easier to qualify for 504 loans than do startups.

Microloan Program About three-fourths of all entrepreneurs need less than $100,000 to launch their businesses. Indeed, most entrepreneurs require less than $50,000 to start their companies. Unfortunately, loans of that amount can be the most difficult to get. Lending these relatively small amounts to entrepreneurs starting businesses is the purpose of the SBA's **Microloan Program.** Called microloans because they range from just $100 to as much as $35,000, these loans have helped thousands of people take their first steps toward entrepreneurship. Banks typically shun loans in such small amounts because they consider them to be risky and unprofitable. In an attempt to fill the void in small loans to start-up companies, the SBA launched the microloan program in 1992. Since then entrepreneurs have borrowed more than $286 million, making the microloan program the largest source of funding for microenterprises. Today, more than 150 authorized lenders make SBA-backed microloans. The average size of a microloan is $13,000, with a maturity of three years (the maximum term is six years), and lenders' standards are less demanding than those on conventional loans. Nearly 40 percent of all microloans go to business start-ups.[93] All microloans are made through nonprofit intermediaries approved by the SBA.

Kimberly Arrington

Kimberly Arrington was a single mother of three struggling to make ends meet with the help of public assistance, but she had a dream of opening her own hair salon. With no capital of her own and a credit score no bank would consider, Arrington turned to the South Bronx Overall Economic Development Corporation (SoBRO) for help. Not only did SoBRO approve a microloan for Arrington, but the lender also helped her to hone her business skills with a management class. After just one year in business, Arrington's salon was profitable and had three employees.[94]

Although many consider the microloan program to be successful, political powers in Washington have earmarked it for elimination on several occasions.

Prequalification Loan Program The **Prequalification Loan Program** is designed to help disadvantaged entrepreneurs such as those in rural areas, minorities, women, the disabled, those with low incomes, veterans, and others to prepare loan applications and "prequalify" for SBA loan guarantees before approaching banks and lending institutions for business loans. Because lenders are much more likely to approve loans that the SBA has prequalified, these entrepreneurs have greater access to the capital they need. The maximum loan under this program is $250,000, and loan maturities range from 7 to 25 years. A local Small Business Development Center usually helps entrepreneurs prepare their loan applications at no charge.

Disaster Loans As their name implies, **disaster loans** are made to small businesses devastated by some kind of financial or physical loss. The maximum disaster loan usually is $1.5 million, but Congress often raises that ceiling when circumstances warrant. Disaster loans carry below-market interest rates, as low as four percent, and terms as long as 30 years. Loans for physical damage above $10,000 and financial damage of more than $5,000 require an entrepreneur to pledge some kind of collateral, usually a lien on the business property. The SBA has helped entrepreneurs whose businesses have been

Microloan Program
an SBA program that makes small loans, some as small as $100, to entrepreneurs.

Prequalification Loan Program
an SBA program designed to help disadvantaged entrepreneurs "prequalify" for SBA loan guarantees before approaching commercial lenders.

disaster loans
an SBA loan program that makes loans to small businesses devastated by some kind of financial or physical loss.

disrupted by a variety of disasters, ranging from hurricanes on the Southeastern coast and earthquakes on the West coast to floods and to tornadoes in the Midwest and the terrorist attacks of September 11, 2001.

In Louisiana alone, Hurricane Katrina shuttered more than 81,000 businesses, and many of them were unable to recover.

Tommy Andrade, owner of Tommy's Cuisine, an Italian-Creole restaurant in the Warehouse District in New Orleans, evacuated the day before Hurricane Katrina hit, hoping to return and reopen within a few days. Three months later, Andrade returned to a building and equipment that were almost completely destroyed. "My spirit was so damaged," he says. "Thinking of the employees and providing jobs to them is what gave me the strength to put things together and continue." With the help of a $350,000 SBA disaster loan, Andrade was able to rebuild his restaurant and reopen. He also took out another loan to repair a damaged apartment building he owned that provided housing for his employees. Customers soon returned, and the restaurant came to life again.[95]

Tommy's Cuisine

State and Local Loan Development Programs

Many states have created their own loan and economic development programs to provide funds for business start-ups and expansions. They have decided that their funds are better spent encouraging small business growth rather than "chasing smokestacks"—trying to entice large businesses to locate within their boundaries. These programs come in a wide variety of forms, but they all tend to focus on developing small businesses that create the greatest number of jobs and economic benefits. Although each state's approach to economic development is somewhat special, one common element is some kind of small business financing program: loans, loan guarantees, development grants, venture capital pools, and others. One approach many states have had success with is the use of **capital access programs (CAPs).** First introduced in Michigan in 1986, many states now offer CAPs that are designed to encourage lending institutions to make loans to businesses that do not qualify for traditional financing because of their higher risk. Under a CAP, a bank and a borrower each pay an upfront fee (a portion of the loan amount) into a loan-loss reserve fund at the participating bank, and the state matches this amount. The reserve fund, which normally ranges from 6 to 14 percent of the loan amount, acts as an insurance policy against the potential loss a bank might experience on a loan and frees the bank to make loans that it otherwise might refuse. One study of CAPs found that 55 percent of the entrepreneurs who received loans under a CAP would not have been granted loans without the backing of the program.[96]

capital access programs (CAPs)
a state lending program that encourages lending institutions to make loans to businesses that do not qualify for traditional financing because of their higher risk.

Even cities and small towns have joined in the effort to develop small businesses and help them grow. More than 7,500 communities across the United States operate **revolving loan funds (RLFs)** that combine private and public funds to make loans to small businesses, often at below-market interest rates. As money is repaid into the funds, it is loaned back out to other entrepreneurs. A study by the Corporation for Enterprise Development of RLFs in seven states found that the median RLF loan was $40,000 with a maturity of five years.[97]

revolving loan fund (RLF)
a program offered by communities that combine private and public funds to make loans to small businesses, often at below-market interest rates.

Brian Hale transformed his passion for snowmobiles, dirt bikes, and ATVs into a thriving business with the help of a loan from the Central Vermont Revolving Loan Fund. Hale's company, J.B. Motorsports and Salvage, repairs as well as refurbishes and sells these vehicles to customers looking for bargains. He used his loan to purchase an inventory of parts and to purchase a computer system to help him run the business more efficiently.[98]

J.B. Motorsports and Salvage

Internal Methods of Financing

Small business owners do not have to rely solely on financial institutions and government agencies for capital; their businesses have the capacity to generate capital. This type of financing, called **bootstrap financing,** is available to virtually every small business and

bootstrap financing
internal methods of financing a company's need for capital.

encompasses factoring, leasing rather than purchasing equipment, using credit cards, and managing the business frugally.

Factoring Accounts Receivable

Instead of carrying credit sales on its own books (some of which may never be collected), a small business can sell outright its accounts receivable to a factor. A **factor** buys a company's accounts receivable and pays for them in two parts. The first payment, which the factor makes immediately, is for 50 to 80 percent of the accounts' agreed-on (and usually discounted) value. The factor makes the second payment of 15 to 18 percent, which makes up the balance less the factor's service fees, when the original customer pays the invoice. Factoring is a more expensive type of financing than loans from either banks or commercial finance companies, but for businesses that cannot qualify for those loans, it may be the only choice.

Factoring deals are either *with recourse* or *without recourse*. Under deals arranged with recourse, a small business owner retains the responsibility for customers who fail to pay their accounts. The business owner must take back these uncollectible invoices. Under deals arranged without recourse, however, the owner is relieved of the responsibility for collecting them. If customers fail to pay their accounts, the factor bears the loss. Because the factoring company assumes the risk of collecting the accounts, it normally screens the firm's credit customers, accepts those judged to be creditworthy, and advances the small business owner a portion of the value of the accounts receivable. Factors discount anywhere from two to 40 percent of the face value of a company's accounts receivable, depending on a small company's:

- Customers' financial strength and credit ratings.
- Industry and its customers' industries because some industries have a reputation for slow payments.
- History and financial strength, especially in deals arranged with recourse.
- Credit policies.[99]

The discount rate on deals without recourse usually is higher than on those with recourse because of the higher level of risk they carry for the factor.

Although factoring is more expensive than traditional bank loans (a 2 percent discount from the face value of an invoice due in 30 days amounts to an annual interest rate of 24.5 percent), it is a source of quick cash and is ideally suited for fast-growing companies, especially start-ups that cannot qualify for bank loans. Small companies that sell to government agencies and large corporations, both famous for stretching out their payments for 60 to 90 days or more, also find factoring attractive because they collect the money from the sale (less the factor's discount) much faster.

Leasing

Leasing is another common bootstrap financing technique. Today, small businesses can lease virtually any kind of asset, from office space and telephones to computers and heavy equipment. By leasing expensive assets, the small business owner is able to use them without locking in valuable capital for an extended period of time. In other words, the manager can reduce the long-term capital requirements of the business by leasing equipment and facilities, and he or she is not investing his or her capital in depreciating assets. In addition, because no down payment is required and because the cost of the asset is spread over a longer time (lowering monthly payments), a company's cash flow improves.

Credit Cards

Unable to find financing elsewhere, many entrepreneurs launch their companies using the fastest and most convenient source of debt capital available: credit cards. A study by the Small Business Administration reports that other than personal savings, the most commonly used source of financing for startup ventures is credit cards (see Figure 13.5).[100] Putting business start-up costs on credit cards charging 21 percent or more in annual interest is expensive and risky, especially if sales fail to materialize as quickly as planned, but some entrepreneurs have no other choice.

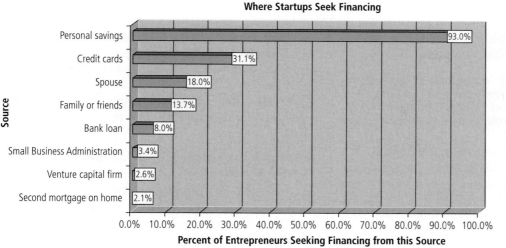

Where Startups Seek Financing

- Personal savings — 93.0%
- Credit cards — 31.1%
- Spouse — 18.0%
- Family or friends — 13.7%
- Bank loan — 8.0%
- Small Business Administration — 3.4%
- Venture capital firm — 2.6%
- Second mortgage on home — 2.1%

Source (y-axis)

0.0% 10.0% 20.0% 30.0% 40.0% 50.0% 60.0% 70.0% 80.0% 90.0% 100.0%

Percent of Entrepreneurs Seeking Financing from this Source

FIGURE 13.5

Where Do Small Businesses Get Their Financing? Percentage of Business Owners Who Used the Given Sources of Capital within the Last Year

Source: *Expected Costs of Startup Ventures,* Blade Consulting Group, Office of Advocacy, U.S. Small Business Administration, November 2003, pp. 23–24.

Mike and Susan Nikolich launched Tech Image Ltd., a technology public relations firm in Buffalo Grove, Illinois, with credit cards when they could not qualify for a bank loan. The 10 credit cards they used gave them access to $100,000 in credit; fortunately, they had to use only $10,000 of it before they convinced a commercial bank to grant the company a line of credit after three months of operation. "Those credit cards bailed me out at a time when banks wouldn't consider loaning me the money," says Nikolich. I'd do it again, and I'd do it the same way."[101]

COMPANY
Profile

Tech Images Ltd.

Chapter Summary by Learning Objectives

1. Explain the differences among the three types of capital small businesses require: fixed, working, and growth.

Capital is any form of wealth employed to produce more wealth. Three forms of capital are commonly identified: fixed capital, working capital, and growth capital.

Fixed capital is used to purchase a company's permanent or fixed assets; working capital represents the business's temporary funds and is used to support the business's normal short-term operations; growth capital requirements surface when an existing business is expanding or changing its primary direction.

2. Describe the differences between equity capital and debt capital and the advantages and disadvantages of each.

Equity financing represents the personal investment of the owner (or owners), and it offers the advantage of not having to be repaid with interest.

Debt capital is the financing that a small business owner has borrowed and must repay with interest. It does not require entrepreneurs to give up ownership in their companies.

3. Describe the various sources of equity capital available to entrepreneurs.

The most common source of financing a business is the owner's personal savings. After emptying their own pockets, the next place entrepreneurs turn for capital is family members and friends. Angels are private investors who not only invest their money in small companies, but they also offer valuable advice and counsel to them. Some business owners have success financing their companies by taking on limited partners as investors or by forming an alliance with a corporation, often a customer or a supplier. Venture capital companies are for-profit, professional investors looking for fast-growing companies in "hot" industries. When screening prospects, venture capital firms look for competent management, a competitive edge, a growth industry, and important intangibles that will make a business successful. Some owners choose to attract capital by taking their companies public, which requires registering the public offering with the SEC.

4. Describe the process of "going public," as well as its advantages and disadvantages and the various simplified registrations and exemptions from registration available to small businesses wanting to sell securities to investors.

Going public involves (1) choosing the underwriter, (2) negotiating a letter of intent, (3) preparing the registration statement, (4) filing file with the SEC, and (5) meeting state requirements.

Going public offers the advantages of raising large amounts of capital, improving access to future financing, improving corporate image, and gaining listing on a stock exchange. The disadvantages include dilution of the founder's ownership, loss of privacy, need to report to the SEC, filing expenses, and accountability to shareholders.

Rather than go through the complete registration process, some companies use one of the simplified registration options and exemptions available to small companies: Regulation S-B, Regulation D (Rule 504) Small Company Offering Registration (SCOR), Regulation D (Rule 505 and Rule 506) Private Placements, Section 4(6), Rule 147, Regulation A, direct stock offerings, and foreign stock markets.

5. Describe the various sources of debt capital and the advantages and disadvantages of each.

Commercial banks offer the greatest variety of loans, although they are conservative lenders. Typical short-term bank loans include commercial loans, lines of credit, discounting accounts receivable, inventory financing, and floor planning.

Trade credit is used extensively by small businesses as a source of financing. Vendors and suppliers commonly finance sales to businesses for 30, 60, or even 90 days.

Equipment suppliers offer small businesses financing similar to trade credit but with slightly different terms.

Commercial finance companies offer many of the same types of loans that banks do, but they are more risk oriented in their lending practices. They emphasize accounts receivable financing and inventory loans.

Savings and loan associations specialize in loans to purchase real property—commercial and industrial mortgages—for up to 30 years.

Stock-brokerage houses offer loans to prospective entrepreneurs at lower interest rates than banks because they have high-quality, liquid collateral—stocks and bonds in the borrower's portfolio.

Insurance companies provide financing through policy loans and mortgage loans. Policy loans are extended to the owner against the cash surrender value of insurance policies.

Mortgage loans are made for large amounts and are based on the value of the land being purchased.

Small business investment companies are privately owned companies licensed and regulated by the SBA that qualify for SBA loans to be invested in or loaned to small businesses.

Small business lending companies make only intermediate and long-term loans that are guaranteed by the SBA.

6. Identify the various federal loan programs aimed at small businesses.

The Economic Development Administration, a branch of the Commerce Department, makes loan guarantees to create and expand small businesses in economically depressed areas.

The Department of Housing and Urban Development extends grants (such as Community Development Block Grants) to cities that, in turn, lend and grant money to small businesses in an attempt to strengthen the local economy.

The Department of Agriculture's Rural Business-Cooperative Service loan program is designed to create nonfarm employment opportunities in rural areas through loans and loan guarantees.

The Small Business Innovation Research Program involves 11 federal agencies that award cash grants or long-term contracts to small companies wanting to initiate or to expand their research and development efforts.

The Small Business Technology Transfer Program allows researchers at universities, federally funded research and development centers, and nonprofit research institutions to join forces with small businesses and develop commercially promising ideas.

7. Describe the various loan programs available from the Small Business Administration.

Almost all SBA loan activity is in the form of loan guarantees rather than direct loans. Popular SBA programs include the Low Doc Program, the SBA Express Program, the 7(A) loan guaranty program, the CAPLine Program, the Export Working Capital Program, the Section 504 Certified Development Company Program, the Microloan Program, the Prequalification Loan Program, the Disaster Loan Program, and the 8(a) program.

Many state and local loan and development programs such as capital access programs and revolving loan funds complement those sponsored by federal agencies.

8. Discuss valuable methods of financing growth and expansion internally.

Small business owners may also look inside their firms for capital. By factoring accounts receivable, leasing equipment instead of buying it, and minimizing costs, owners can stretch their supplies of capital.

Discussion Questions

1. Why is it so difficult for most small business owners to raise the capital needed to start, operate, or expand their ventures?
2. What is capital? List and describe the three types of capital a small business needs for its operations.
3. Define equity financing. What advantage does it offer over debt financing?
4. What is the most common source of equity funds in a typical small business? If an owner lacks sufficient equity capital to invest in the firm, what options are available for raising it?
5. What guidelines should an entrepreneur follow if friends and relatives choose to invest in his or her business?
6. What is an "angel?" Assemble a brief profile of the typical private investor. How can entrepreneurs locate potential angels to invest in their businesses?
7. What advice would you offer an entrepreneur about to strike a deal with a private investor to avoid problems?
8. What types of businesses are most likely to attract venture capital? What investment criteria do venture capitalists use when screening potential businesses? How do these compare to the typical angel's criteria?
9. How do venture capital firms operate? Describe their procedure for screening investment proposals.
10. Summarize the major exemptions and simplified registrations available to small companies wanting to make public offerings of their stock.
11. What role do commercial banks play in providing debt financing to small businesses? Outline and briefly describe the major types of short-, intermediate-, and long-term loans commercial banks offer.
12. What is trade credit? How important is it as a source of debt financing to small firms?
13. What function do SBICs serve? How does an SBIC operate? What methods of financing do SBICs rely on most heavily?
14. Briefly describe the loan programs offered by the following:
    A. The Economic Development Administration.
    B. The Department of Housing and Urban Development.
    C. The Department of Agriculture.
    D. Local development companies.
15. Explain the purpose and the methods of operation of the Small Business Innovation Research Program and the Small Business Technology Transfer Program.
16. How can a firm employ bootstrap financing to stretch its current capital supply?
17. What is a factor? How does the typical factor operate? Explain the advantages and the disadvantages of using factors as a source of funding.

Business Plan Pro

 One of the most common reasons for creating a business plan is to secure funding. Your business plan can be an excellent communication tool for convincing lenders of the stability of your company and convey its potential earning power to investors. Think about the financial needs of your company. Do you need start-up funding to purchase equipment or for other reasons? Is your business going to need working capital based on your cash flow projections and needs? Does your business need additional financing for growth? If you have the need to raise capital for any purpose, your business plan can help you to clarify those needs and formulate a strategy for raising capital.

Business Plan Exercises
On the Web

If you need start-up or growth capital for your venture, visit http://www.prenhall.com/scarborough for Chapter 13 and review these financing options. Determine whether these sources may be of use as you explore financing opportunities. You will also find additional information regarding bootstrap and nontraditional funding.

Sample Plans

Review some sample plans and note the financial needs they expressed in the financial section of their plans. If you are creating a start-up plan, you may want to review the following sample plans:

- Elsewares Promotional
- Westbury Storage, Inc.
- Southeast Health Plans

If you are going to be searching for financing for an ongoing business, these plans may be of interest:

- Coach House Bed & Breakfast
- The Daily Perk
- Bioring SA (second-round financing)

These diverse plans present financial information in ways that may give you ideas on how to best communicate your financial needs. Use approaches that fit your plan as you consider what your audience will find enticing. Your lender will want to confirm that you are going to be able to make your payments on time, and investors will want to learn more about the growth and earning potential of your business. Leverage each aspect of the financial section—the break-even analysis, projected profit and loss, projected cash flow, projected balance sheet and business ratios—that you deem valuable for your financial audience.

In the Software

Open your business plan in Business Plan Pro and go to the Financial Plan section. You may want to begin this section by providing an overview of your financial situation and needs. You will then state your assumptions about your financial environment. Your assumptions will help to identify general facts on which you are basing your plan, such as anticipated economic conditions, current short-term and long-term interest rates, expected tax rates, personnel expenses, cash expenses, sales on credit, or any areas that you hope to develop and confirm through further research. Let the software lead you through this section.

You will then assess the type and amount of funding that you will need. Will this be short-term or long-term financing? Determine whether you are going to bring in capital through a loan or by taking on an investor. If you are adding investors, what percentage ownership will they now have? How does this effect your ownership position? What kind of control or influence will the investors have in the business? These questions will be important to address in this section of your business plan. Continue through the finance section, and discuss and review your numbers for your break-even point, projected profit and loss statement, and cash flow situation and make comments about your resulting balance sheet. This section will also enable you to review industry ratios as they compare to your anticipated business performance. Make certain this section clearly tells your financial story. Providing relevant information that will be meaningful to others who will review your plan for investment or loan purposes is critical.

Building Your Business Plan

One of the most valuable aspects of developing the financial section of your business plan is to assess the amount of financing needed, describe the use of these funds, and make certain that you can live with the financial consequences of these decisions. Keep in mind that potential lenders and investors will also be assessing the qualifications of your management team, the growth within your industry, your proposed exit strategy, and other factors as they assess the financial stability and potential of your venture. Your business plan can be an effective way to help you consider financing options and lead you through what you determine to be the most attractive options to pursue. This "financial road map" may allow you to analyze your funding options. Test each alternative against your plan to better assess its viability and fit with your venture's financial needs.

 Beyond the Classroom . . .

1. Interview several local business owners about how they financed their businesses. Where did their initial capital come from? Ask the following questions:
   A. How did you raise your starting capital? What percentage did you supply on your own?
   B. What percentage was debt capital and what percentage was equity capital?
   C. Which of the sources of funds described in this chapter do you use? Are they used to finance fixed, working, or growth capital needs?
   D. How much money did you need to launch your businesses? Where did subsequent capital come from? What advice do you offer others seeking capital?
2. Contact a local private investor and ask him or her to address your class. (You may have to search to locate one!) What kinds of businesses does this angel prefer to invest in? What screening criteria does he or she use? How are the deals typically structured?

3. Contact a local venture capitalist and ask him or her to address your class. What kinds of businesses does his or her company invest in? What screening criteria does the company use? How are deals typically structured?
4. Invite an investment banker or a financing expert from a local accounting firm to address your class about the process of taking a company public. What do they look for in a potential IPO candidate? What is the process, and how long does it usually take?
5. After a personal visit, prepare a short report on a nearby factor's operation. How is the value of the accounts receivable purchased determined? Who bears the loss on uncollected accounts?
6. Interview the administrator of a financial institution program offering a method of financing with which you are unfamiliar, and prepare a short report on its method of operation.
7. Contact your state's economic development board and prepare a report on the financial assistance programs it offers small businesses.

8. Go to the IPO section of the Web site for Hoover's (http://www.hoovers.com) and explore the details of a company that is involved in making an initial public offering. View some of the documents the company has filed with the SEC, especially the initial public offering filing. Prepare a brief report on the company. What is its business? Who are its major competitors? How fast is the industry growing? What risk factors has the company identified? How much money does it plan to raise in the IPO? What is the anticipated IPO stock price? How many shares of stock will the company sell in the IPO? Would you buy this company's stock? Explain your rationale.

14 | Choosing the Right Location and Layout

> A decision is the action an executive must take when he has information so incomplete that the answer does not suggest itself —Admiral Radford

> Facts are stubborn things, but statistics are more pliable. —Mark Twain

Learning Objectives

On completion of this chapter, you will be able to:

1. Explain the stages in the location decision: choosing the region, the state, the city, and the specific site.
2. Describe the location criteria for retail and service businesses.
3. Outline the location options for retail and service businesses.
4. Explain the site selection process for manufacturers.
5. Describe the criteria used to analyze the layout and design considerations of a building, including the Americans with Disabilities Act.
6. Explain the principles of effective layouts for retailers, service businesses, and manufacturers.

Location: A Source of Competitive Advantage

LEARNING OBJECTIVES
1. Explain the stages in the location decision: choosing the region, the state, the city, and the specific site.

Much like choosing a form of ownership and selecting particular sources of financing, the location decision has far-reaching and often long-lasting effects on a small company's future. Entrepreneurs who choose their locations wisely—with their customers' preferences and their companies' needs in mind—can establish an important competitive advantage over rivals who choose their locations haphazardly. Because the availability of qualified workers, tax rates, quality of infrastructure, traffic patterns, and many other factors vary from one site to another, the location decision is an important one that can influence the growth rate and the ultimate success of a company.

The location selection process is like an interactive computer game in which each decision opens the way to make another decision on the way to solving the puzzle. The answer to the puzzle, of course, is the best location for a business. At each step in the decision process entrepreneurs must analyze how well the characteristics of a particular location match the unique requirements of their businesses. Because of their significant impact on a company, location decisions can be difficult; however, as with the interactive computer game, there are many clues that guide entrepreneurs to the best decision.

The location decision process resembles a pyramid. The first level of the decision is the broadest, requiring an entrepreneur to select a particular region of the country. (We will address locating a business in a foreign country in Chapter 15, "Global Aspects of Entrepreneurship.") Then, an entrepreneur must choose the right state, then the right city, and, finally, the right site within the city. The "secret" to selecting the ideal location lies in knowing which factors are most important to a company's success and then finding a location that satisfies as many of them as possible, particularly those that are most critical. For instance, one of the most important location factors for high-tech companies is the availability of a skilled labor force, and their choice of location reflects this. If physically locating near customers is vital to a company's success, then an entrepreneur's goal is to find a site that makes it most convenient for her or his target customers to do business with the company.

Coastal Cotton

David Chang, owner of Coastal Cotton, a small retail chain specializing in casual cotton clothing, has seen his company grow from a single store in Hialeah, Florida, to 12 locations in outlet centers across the Southeast and in California. Because Coastal Cotton's primary target is bargain-hunting tourists, Chang chooses locations with high concentrations of those customers, including outlet malls ranging from Fort Arrowhead, California, to Myrtle Beach, South Carolina. "You have to know your customer base and be strategic about choosing sites," Chang explains.[1]

The characteristics that make for an ideal location often vary dramatically from one company to another due to the nature of their business. In the early twentieth century, companies looked for ready supplies of water, raw materials, or access to railroads; today, they are more likely to look for sites that are close to universities and offer high-speed Internet access and accessible airports. In fact, a recent study concluded that the factors that made an area most suitable for starting and growing small companies included access to dynamic universities, an ample supply of skilled workers, a nearby airport, a temperate climate, and a high quality of life.[2] The key to finding a suitable location is identifying the characteristics that can give a company a competitive edge and then searching for potential sites that meet those criteria.

Choosing the Region

The first step in selecting the best location is to focus at the regional level. Which region of the country has the characteristics necessary for a new business to succeed? Above all, the entrepreneur must always place the customer first in his or her mind when deciding on a location. As with the foregoing example, if your primary customers are bargain-hunting tourists, then the best locations will be where such people gather. Logic demands that the facts and figures should lead entrepreneurs to the best location for the specific type of business, not their personal preferences. Common requirements may include rapid growth in the population of a certain age group, rising disposable incomes, the existence of necessary infrastructure, a nonunion environment, and low costs. At the broadest level of the location decision, entrepreneurs usually determine which regions of the country are experiencing substantial growth. Every year many popular business publications prepare reports on the various regions of the nation—which ones are growing, which are stagnant, and which are declining. Studying shifts in population and industrial growth will give entrepreneurs an idea of where the action is—and isn't. Questions to consider include the following: How large is the population? How fast is it growing? What is the makeup of overall population? Which segments are growing fastest? Which segments are the slowest? What is the trend in the population's income, and is it increasing or decreasing? Are other businesses moving into the region, and if so, what kind of businesses are they? Generally, entrepreneurs want to avoid dying regions; such regions simply cannot support a broad base of potential customers. A small company's customers are the people, businesses, and industry in an area, and if it is to be successful, it must choose a location that is convenient to its customers.

One of the first stops entrepreneurs should make when conducting a regional evaluation is the U.S. Census Bureau. Excellent sources of basic demographic and population data include the *U.S. Statistical Abstract* and the *County and City Data Book*. The *U.S. Statistical Abstract* provides entrepreneurs looking for the right location with much helpful information, ranging from basic population characteristics and projections to poverty rates and energy consumption. Every state also publishes its own statistical abstract, which provides the same type of data for its own population. The *County and City Data Book* contains useful statistics on the populations of all of the nation's 3,141 counties and 12,175 cities with populations exceeding 2,500. In addition to the numerous publications it offers, the Census Bureau makes most of the information contained in its vast and valuable data banks available to entrepreneurs researching potential sites through its easy-to-use Web site (http://www.census.gov/). There, entrepreneurs can access for specific locations vital demographic information such as age, income, educational level, employment level, occupation, ancestry, commuting times, housing data (house value, number of rooms, mortgage or rent status, number of vehicles owned, and so on), and many other characteristics. Sorting through each report's 95 fields, entrepreneurs can prepare customized reports on the potential sites they are considering. These Web-based resources give entrepreneurs instant access to important site-location information that only a few years ago would have taken many hours of intense research to compile.

The Census Bureau's American FactFinder site (http://factfinder.census.gov) provides easily accessible demographic fact sheets and maps on nearly every community in the United States, including small towns. The Census Bureau's American Community Survey provides detailed information on the demographic and economic characteristics of areas with populations of at least 250,000 and of other selected areas with populations of at least 65,000. Both the American FactFinder and the American Community Survey allow entrepreneurs to produce easy-to-read, customizable maps of the information they generate in their searches.

The Herbal Remedy

When Scott Fiore was looking for a location for his natural pharmacy, The Herbal Remedy, he turned first to the demographic data from the U.S. Census Bureau. Not only did his analysis provide him with a picture of the potential customers in each area, but it also pointed him to Douglas County, Colorado, the fastest-growing county in the nation for the second year in a row. The profile that emerged from the demographic data for the county was one of young, affluent, well-educated residents, a perfect fit with Fiore's definition of his target customer. As he drove around the area, Fiore noticed that Douglas County and neighboring Arapaho County were "very sports-oriented, athletic places," which was also consistent with his target audience. More research led Fiore to the town of Littleton, which is conveniently located for customers in both counties but offers relatively low rental rates.[3]

The Population Reference Bureau (http://www.prb.org) provides a detailed breakdown of the most relevant data collected from the most recent census. The site also includes helpful articles that discuss the implications of the changing demographic and economic profile of the nation's population, such as the impact of aging baby boomers on business and the composition of the U.S. workforce. STAT-USA (http://www.statusa.gov) is a service of the U.S. Department of Commerce that offers both financial and economic data about the United States as well as trade data for the United States and for Europe. Here entrepreneurs can locate everything from the latest consumer price index and the number of housing starts to leads for global trading partners and tips on conducting business in practically any country in the world.

Other helpful resources merit mention as well. *Demographics USA* is a three-volume series covering the United States, its counties, and Zip Code areas. This useful publication provides market surveys on various segments of U.S. demographics, including purchasing power, retail sales by type of merchandise, employment and payroll data, and forecasts of economic conditions down to the county level. Entrepreneurs can use *Demographics USA* to analyze the level of competition in a particular area, assess the sales potential of a particular location, compare consumers' buying power across a dozen categories, and more. *Lifestyle Market Analyst*, an annual publication, matches population demographics with lifestyle interests. Section 1 gives demographics and lifestyle information by "Areas of Dominant Influence." Section 2 gives demographic and geographic information according to 57 lifestyle interests. Section 3 lists areas of dominant influence and lifestyles according to 42 demographic segments. It is wise to consult the introductory material on how to use this source. Entrepreneurs can use *Lifestyle Market Analyst* to determine, for example, how likely members of a particular market segment are to own a dog, collect antiques, play golf, own a vacation home, fly frequently, invest in stocks or bonds, or participate in a host of other activities.

Other sources of demographic data include Sales and Marketing Management's *Survey of Buying Power*, *Editor and Publisher Market Guide*, *The American Marketplace: Demographics and Spending Patterns*, Rand McNally's *Commercial Atlas and Marketing Guide*, and *Zip Code Atlas and Market Planner*. Sales and Marketing Management's *Survey of Buying Power*, published annually, provides statistics, rankings, and projections for every county and media market in the United States with demographics segmented by age, race, city, county, and state. This publication also includes current information on retail spending and forecasts for each category. The data are divided into 323 metro markets as defined by the Census Bureau and 210 media markets, which are television or broadcast markets defined by Nielsen Media Research. The *Survey* also includes several unique statistics. Effective buying income (EBI) is a measure of disposable income, and the buying power index (BPI), for which the *Survey* is best known, is a unique measure of spending power that takes population, EBI, and retail sales into account to determine a market's ability to buy goods and services.

The *Editor and Publisher Market Guide* is similar to the *Survey of Buying Power* but provides additional information on markets. The *Guide* includes detailed economic and demographic information, ranging from population and income statistics to information on climate and transportation networks for more than 1,600 key cities in both the United States and Canada.

The *American Marketplace: Demographics and Spending Patterns* provides useful demographic information in eight areas: education, health, income, labor force, living arrangements, population, race and ethnicity, and spending and wealth. Most of the tables in the book are derived from government statistics, but *The American Marketplace* also includes a discussion of the data in each table as well as a forecast of future trends. Many users say the primary advantage of *The American Marketplace* is its ease of use.

The *Commercial Atlas and Marketing Guide* reports on more than 123,000 places in the United States, many of which are not available through Census reports. It includes 11 economic indicators for every major geographic market; tables showing population trends, income, buying power, trade, and manufacturing activity; and large, cross-referenced maps. Its format makes it easy to collect large amounts of valuable data on any region in the country (and specific areas within a region).

The *Zip Code Atlas and Market Planner* is an extremely useful location and market-planning tool. It combines a breakdown of Zip Codes across the United States with maps featuring physical features such as mountains, rivers, and major highways. The *Atlas* provides demographic information on population, household income, and retail sales by industry for three-digit Zip Codes. The U.S. Census Bureau also offers the Zip Code Tabulation Areas (ZCTA) Web site (http://www.census.gov/geo/ZCTA/zcta.html), which organizes the wealth of census data by Zip Code. The database of 33,178 ZCTAs across the United States allows users to create tables and plot maps of census data by Zip Code.

The task of analyzing various potential locations—gathering and synthesizing data on a wide variety of demographic and geographic variables—is one ideally suited for a computer. In fact, a growing number of entrepreneurs are relying on geographic information systems (GIS), powerful software programs that combine map drawing with database management capability, to pinpoint the ideal location for their businesses. GIS packages allow users to search through virtually any database containing a wealth of information and plot the results on a map of the country, an individual state, a specific city, or even a single city block. The visual display highlights what otherwise would be indiscernible business trends. For instance, using GIS programs, entrepreneurs can plot their existing customer base on a map with various colors representing the different population densities. Then they can zoom in on those areas with the greatest concentration of customers, mapping a detailed view of Zip Code borders or even city streets. GIS street files originate in the U.S. Census Department's TIGER (Topographically Integrated Geographic Encoding Referencing) file, which contains map information broken down for every square foot of Metropolitan Statistical Areas (MSAs). TIGER files contain the name and location of every street in the country and detailed block statistics for the 345 largest urban areas. In essence, TIGER is a massive database of geographic features such as roads, railways, and political boundaries across the entire United States that, when linked with mapping programs and demographic databases, gives entrepreneurs incredible power to pinpoint existing and potential customers on easy-to-read digital maps.

The Small Business Administration's Small Business Development Center (SBDC) program also offers location analysis assistance to entrepreneurs. These centers, numbering more than 1,100 nationwide, provide training, counseling, research, and other specialized assistance to entrepreneurs and existing business owners on a wide variety of subjects—all at no charge. They are an important resource, especially for those entrepreneurs who may not have access to a computer. (To locate the SBA nearest you, contact the SBA office in your state or go to the SBA's home page at http://www.sba.gov/SBDC/).

For entrepreneurs interested in demographic and statistical profiles of international cities, Euromonitor International (http://www.euromonitor.com/) and the Organization for Economic Development and Cooperation (http://www.oecd.org) are excellent resources.

Once an entrepreneur has identified the best region of the country, the next step is to evaluate the individual states in that region.

Choosing the State

Every state has an economic development office working to recruit new businesses. Even though the publications produced by these offices will be biased in favor of locating in that state, they still are an excellent source of information and can help entrepreneurs to assess the business climate in each state. Some of the key issues to explore include the laws, regulations, and taxes that govern businesses and any incentives or investment credits the state may offer to businesses that locate there. For instance, Witt Everett recently relocated his box-printing business, Everett Graphics, from Oakland, California, to Evanston, Wyoming, lured, in part, by lower insurance and energy costs and incentives from Wyoming. The state offered Everett $3 million to build a 75,000-square-foot plant in Evanston, and his lease payments are credited toward the purchase of the building if the company creates 20 jobs with minimum after-tax salaries of $27,000.

Other factors entrepreneurs should consider when choosing a location include proximity to markets, proximity to raw materials, wage rates, quantity and quality of the labor supply, general business climate, tax rates, Internet access, and total operating costs.

Proximity to Markets Locating close to markets they plan to serve is extremely critical to manufacturers, especially when the cost of transformation of finished goods is high relative to their value. Locating near customers is necessary to remain competitive. Service firms often find that proximity to their clients is essential. If a business is involved in repairing equipment used in a specific industry, it should be located where that industry is concentrated. The more specialized a business, or the greater the relative cost of transporting the product to the customer, the more likely it is that proximity to the market will be of critical importance in the location decision. For instance, with its location in the center of the country and its ready access to a variety of transportation systems, St. Louis, Missouri, has become home to many companies' distribution centers. Not only do businesses in St. Louis benefit from a well-educated workforce, but they also can ship to customers anywhere in the country quickly and efficiently.

John Jansheski launched DenTek Oral Care, a company that makes oral care supplies, in Petaluma, California. However, he soon realized that that more than 80 percent of the company's shipments were going east of the Mississippi and that shipping products across the Rocky Mountains added three percentage points to the cost of DenTek's products. In 2001, Jansheski decided to relocate the company to Maryville, Tennessee. Although he has had to hire nearly all new workers (very few of the company's employees chose to make the move from California), Jansheski is confident the move has made his company more competitive. "It was the most important financial decision we've ever made," he says. "We're putting all of that money back into the company, and as a result, sales are twice what they were."[4]

COMPANY

Profile

DenTek Oral Care

Proximity to Needed Raw Materials If a business requires raw materials that are difficult or expensive to transport, it may need a location near the source of those raw materials. For instance, one producer of kitty litter chose a location on a major vein of kaolin, the highly absorbent clay from which kitty litter is made. Transporting the heavy, low-value material over long distances would be impractical—and unprofitable. In other situations in which bulk or weight is not a factor, locating manufacturing in close proximity to the suppliers can facilitate quick deliveries and reduce holding costs for inventories. The value of products and materials, their cost of transportation, and their unique function all interact to determine how close a business needs to be to its sources of supply.

Wage Rates Existing and anticipated wage rates will provide another measure for comparison among states. Wages can sometimes vary from one state or region to another, significantly affecting a company's cost of doing business. For instance, according to the Bureau of Labor Statistics, the average hourly compensation for workers (including wages and benefits) ranges from a low of $19.73 in the South to a high of $27.83 in the Northeast.[5] Wage rate differentials within geographic regions can be even more drastic. When reviewing wage rates, entrepreneurs must be sure to measure the wage rates for jobs that relate to their particular industries or companies. In addition to government surveys, local newspaper ads can give entrepreneurs an idea of the pay scale in an area. In addition, entrepreneurs can obtain the latest wage and salary surveys with an e-mail or a telephone call to the local chambers of commerce for cities in the region under consideration. Entrepreneurs should study not only prevailing wage rates but also *trends* in rates. How does the rate of increase in wage rates compare to those in other states? Another factor influencing wage rates is the level of union activity in a state. How much union-organizing activity has the state seen within the last two years? Is it increasing or decreasing? Which industries have unions targeted in the recent past?

Labor Supply Needs For many businesses, especially technology-driven companies, one of the most important characteristics of a potential location is the composition of the local workforce. Entrepreneurs must consider two factors when analyzing the labor supply in a potential location: the number of workers available in the area and their levels of education, training, adaptability, and experience.

Gateway Computers

When Gateway Computers' founder Ted Waite realized that attracting top managers and staying on top of the dynamic computer industry was difficult to do from the company's North Sioux City, South Dakota, headquarters, he moved the administrative hub to a suburb of San Diego, California, a hotbed of skilled workers and high-tech activity. Since moving Gateway's headquarters, Waite has filled nearly all of the top management posts with local talent. "It really came down to this being a great place to recruit people, with a quality of life [that is] unmatched," says Waite. Because operating costs in South Dakota are much lower than in California and because South Dakota has no state income tax, Gateway's production and support operations still are based in and around Sioux City.[6]

Of course, an entrepreneur wants to know how many qualified people are available in the area to do the work required in the business. However, unemployment and labor cost statistics can be misleading if a company needs people with specific qualifications. Some states have attempted to attract industry with the promise of cheap labor. Unfortunately, businesses locating there found exactly what the term implied—unskilled, low-wage labor that is ill suited for performing the work the companies needed.

Knowing the exact nature of the labor needed and preparing job descriptions and job specifications in advance will help a business owner to determine whether there is a good match with the available labor pool. Reviewing the major industries already operating in an area will provide clues about the characteristics of the local workforce as well. Checking with the high schools, colleges, and universities in the state to determine the number of graduates in relevant fields of study will provide an idea of the local supply of qualified workers. Again, as with wage and salary data, chambers of commerce and economic development agencies in the locations under study are almost always willing to go that extra mile to get you the information you need regarding the availability of employees of specific skills, knowledge, or training. Such planning will result in choosing a location with a steady source of quality labor.

Business Climate   What is the state's overall attitude toward your kind of business? Has it passed laws that impose restrictions on the way a company can operate? Does the state impose a corporate income tax? Is there an inventory tax? Are there "blue laws" that prohibit certain business activity on Sundays? Does the state offer small business support programs or financial assistance to entrepreneurs? Are you located in a rural area of the state that may offer special loan and promotion programs? These are just some of the issues an owner must compare on a state-by-state basis to determine the most suitable location.

Some states are more "small business friendly" than others. For instance, *Entrepreneur* magazine recently named Fort Worth/Arlington, Texas, one of the best locations for small businesses, citing its positive attitude toward growing and developing small companies as major assets. Many factors make Fort Worth (once known as Cowtown because of its stockyards) a desirable location, including its diversified economic base, a strong core of more than two dozen *Fortune* 500 companies, a significant population of private investors interested in investing in promising small companies, and several state and local government support systems offering entrepreneurial assistance and advice. The renaissance of the downtown business district is creating new opportunities for small businesses, and both the Dallas-Fort Worth International Airport and the Alliance Airport (a specialized commercial air facility) provide important pieces of business infrastructure.[7]

Tax Rates   Another important factor entrepreneurs must consider when screening states for potential locations is the tax burden they impose on businesses and individuals. Income taxes may be the most obvious tax states impose on both business and individual residents, but entrepreneurs also must evaluate the impact of payroll taxes, sales taxes, property taxes, inventory taxes, and specialized taxes on the cost of their operations. Currently, seven states impose no income tax on their residents, but state governments always impose taxes of some sort on businesses and individuals. In some cases, states offer special tax rates or are willing to negotiate fees in lieu of taxes for companies that will create jobs and stimulate the local economy.

After graduating from UCLA, Bruce Cowan, a native Californian, started Acclaim Electronics, an electronic chip and computer products distribution business in Carlsbad, California. Recently, however, Cowan decided to relocate his company to Las Vegas, Nevada, where taxes and regulatory costs are far lower. In fact, Nevada imposes no corporate, franchise, capital gains, or inventory taxes. Cowan says the move to Nevada has lowered Acclaim's annual operating costs by 40 percent.[8]

COMPANY Profile
Acclaim Electronics

Internet Access Speedy and reliable Internet access is an increasingly important factor in the location decision. Fast Internet access through cable, DSL, or T1 lines is essential for high-tech companies and those engaging in e-commerce. Even those companies that may not do business over the Web currently are finding it nearly certain that they will use the Web as a business tool. Companies that fall behind in high-tech communication will find themselves at a severe competitive disadvantage.

When Darryl Lyons, a third-generation rancher, began raising Angus cattle to sell from his ranch in Okmulgee, Oklahoma, he made all of his first-year sales of $140,000 to customers located within a 100-mile radius. Then Lyons began using the Web as a marketing tool, and sales climbed to $600,000. Now reaching customers across the globe, Lyons expects sales to reach more than $1.5 million. One problem Lyons faces in his remote location, however, is fast, reliable Internet service. Bad weather interrupts his telephone and Internet service about a dozen times a year, costing him an estimated $3,000 to $4,000 in lost sales each day it is out.[9]

COMPANY Profile
Darryl Lyons

Total Operating Costs When scouting a state in which to locate a company, an entrepreneur must consider the total cost of operating a business. For instance, a state may offer low utility rates, but its labor costs and tax rates may be among the highest in the nation. To select the ideal location, entrepreneurs must consider the impact of a state's total cost of operation on their business ventures. The state evaluation matrix in Table 14.1

TABLE 14.1 State Evaluation Matrix

			State Weighted Score (Weight × Score)		
Location Criterion	Weight	Score (Low = 1, High = 5)	State 1	State 2	State 3
Quality of labor force					
Wage rates					
Union activity					
Property/building costs					
Utility costs					
Transportation costs					
Tax burden					
Educational/training assistance					
Start-up incentives					
Raw material availability					
Quality of life					
Other					
Other					
		Total Score			

Assign to each location criterion a weight that reflects its relative importance to your company. Then score each state on a scale of 1 (low) to 5 (high). Calculate the weighted score (weight × score) for each state. Finally, add up the total weighted score for each state. The state with the highest total score is the best location for your business.

provides a handy tool designed to help entrepreneurs determine which states best suit the most important location criteria for their companies. This same matrix can be adapted to analyze individual cities as well. One recent study by consulting firm KPMG ranked 27 major cities in the United States according to the cost of operating a business in each one. Atlanta, Tampa, and Indianapolis were the three lowest-cost cities, and New York, San Jose, and Boston ranked as the three cities with the highest costs of doing business.[10]

The Neuron Farm LLC

When Mina Johnson-Glenberg launched The Neuron Farm LLC, a company that develops Web-based reading instructional applications, she decided to locate in Madison, Wisconsin, rather than in her home state of California. Because she needed skilled programmers and technology experts, Johnson-Glenberg initially thought that California would be the ideal location because of the high concentration of high-tech companies located there, especially in Silicon Valley. Intrigued by the low cost of operating a business in Madison, she discovered a large university and a ready supply of software talent and technologically savvy employees there. The city's high level of Internet usage, quality of life, and government programs designed to help entrepreneurs with grants and with assistance in building business plans made Madison all the more appealing to Johnson-Glenberg.[11]

Choosing the City

Population Trends Analyzing over time the lists of "best cities for business" compiled annually by many magazines reveals one consistent trend: Successful small companies in a city tend to track a city's population growth. In other words, more potential customers mean that a small business has a better chance of success.

Preferred Public Relations and Marketing

In 1999, when Michelle Tell and James Woodruff were working in Las Vegas hotels and casinos, they saw signs that the city was about to enter a growth spurt. They were right; more than 6,000 people a month move to Clark County, Nevada, home to Las Vegas. "We could see the growth that was going to take place, and we thought it would be a good time to start our own business," says Woodruff. Enticed by the city's rapid population growth, low tax rates, business-friendly environment, and reasonable cost of living, Tell and Woodruff launched Preferred Public Relations and Marketing, which has grown from a small home-based business into a 15-person company with annual revenues exceeding $1.5 million.[12]

Entrepreneurs should know more about the cities in which their businesses are located and than do the people who live there. By analyzing population and other demographic data, an entrepreneur can examine a city in detail, and the location decision becomes more than just an educated guess, or, worse, a shot in the dark. Studying the characteristics of a city's residents, including population size and density, growth trends, family size, age breakdowns, education, income levels, job categories, gender, religion, race, and nationality, gives an entrepreneur the facts she or he needs to make an informed location decision. In fact, using only basic census data, entrepreneurs can determine the value of the homes in an area, how many rooms they contain, how many bedrooms they contain, what percentage of the population own their homes, and how much residents' monthly rental or mortgage payments are. Imagine how useful such information would be to someone about to launch a bed and bath shop!

A company's location should match the market for its products or services, and assembling a demographic profile will tell an entrepreneur how well a particular site measures up to her or his target market's profile. For instance, an entrepreneur planning to open a fine art shop would likely want specific information on family income, size, age, and education. Such a shop would need to be in an area where people appreciate the product and have the discretionary income to purchase it.

Trends or shifts in population components may have more meaning than total population trends. For example, if a city's population is aging rapidly, its disposable income may be decreasing and the city may be gradually dying. On the other hand, a city may be experiencing rapid growth in the population of high-income, young professionals. For example, because it has one of the best telecommunications infrastructures in the world and offers low cost of doing business and ready access to venture capital, Atlanta, Georgia, is attracting droves of young people, many of them entrepreneurs. As a result, the city, in which the median age of inhabitants is 31.9 years, has seen an explosion of new businesses aimed at young people with rising incomes and hearty appetites for consumption.

The amount of available data on the population of any city or town is staggering. These statistics allow a potential business owner to compare a wide variety of cities or towns and to narrow the choices to those few that warrant further investigation. An analysis of these data makes it possible to screen out undesirable locations and to narrow the list of suitable locations to a few, but it does not make the final location decision for an entrepreneur. Entrepreneurs must see the potential locations on their "short list" firsthand. Only by personal investigation will an entrepreneur be able to add the intangible factor of intuition into the decision-making process. Spending time at a potential location will tell an entrepreneur not only how many people frequent it, but also what they are like, how long they stay, and what they buy. Walking or driving around the area will give an entrepreneur clues about the people who live and work there. What are their houses like? What kinds of cars do they drive? What stage of life are they in? Do they have children? Is the area on the rise, or is it past its prime?

When Tony Hard, owner of Planet Tan, a Dallas-based chain of tanning salons, scouts a new location for one of his company's outlets, he starts with basic demographic data, looking only at sites with at least 100,000 residents living within a three- to five-mile radius. Once he narrows the choices using the census data, Hard then visits the potential locations, where he looks at the conditions of the houses and nearby buildings, talks with the owners of existing businesses, looks for businesses that would complement his, and interviews local residents to judge their interest in patronizing his salons. If at least 30 percent of the potential customers he interviews say they would become customers, the site is a "go."[13]

Planet Tan

When evaluating cities as possible business locations, entrepreneurs should consider the following factors.

Competition For some retailers, it makes sense to locate near competitors because similar businesses located near one another may serve to increase traffic flow to both. This location strategy works well for products for which customers are most likely to comparison shop. For instance, in many cities, auto dealers locate next to one another in a "motor mile," trying to create a shopping magnet for customers. The convenience of being able to shop for dozens of brands of cars all within a few hundred yards of one another draws customers from a sizable trading area. Locating near competitors is a common strategy for restaurants as well.

When George Stathakis opened his sixth restaurant, Stax Omega, in Greenville, South Carolina, he chose a site at the intersection of an interstate highway and a busy road where several other popular restaurants were already operating. With years of experience in the restaurant business, Stathakis knows that a cluster of restaurants create business for one another. "I always liked the idea of locating my restaurants near competitors," he says.[14]

Stax Omega

Of course, this strategy has limits. Overcrowding of businesses of the same type in an area can create an undesirable impact on the profitability of all competing firms. Consider the nature of the businesses in the area. Do they offer the same-quality merchandise or comparable services? The products or services of a business may be superior to those that competitors currently offer, giving it a competitive edge.

Studying the size of the market for a product or service and the number of existing competitors will help an entrepreneur determine whether he or she can capture a sufficiently large market share to earn a profit. Again, census reports can be a valuable source of information. *County Business Patterns* gives a breakdown of businesses in manufacturing, wholesale, retail, and service categories and estimates companies' annual payrolls and number of employees broken down by county. *Zip Code Business Patterns* provides the same data as *County Business Patterns* except that it organizes the data by Zip Code. The *Economic Census*, which is produced for years that end in "2" and "7," gives an overview of the businesses in an area—their sales (or other measure of output), employment, payroll, and form of organization. It covers eight industry categories—including retail, wholesale, service, manufacturing, construction, and others—and gives statistics not only at the national level, but also by state, MSA, county, places with 2,500+ inhabitants, and Zip Code. The *Economic Census* is a useful tool for helping entrepreneurs determine whether the areas they are considering as a location are already saturated with competitors.

Clustering Some cities have characteristics that attract certain industries, and, as a result, companies tend to cluster there. **Clusters** are geographic concentrations of interconnected companies, specialized suppliers, and service providers that are present in a region.[15] According to Harvard professor Michael Porter, clusters are important because they allow companies in them to increase their productivity and to gain a competitive edge. For instance, with its highly trained, well-educated, and technologically literate workforce, Austin, Texas, has become a Mecca for high-tech companies. Home to Dell Computers and Hewlett-Packard, Austin offers many small technology companies exactly what they need to succeed.

Once a concentration of companies takes root in a city, other businesses in those industries tend to spring up there as well.

clusters

geographic concentrations of interconnected companies, specialized suppliers, and service providers that are present in a region.

Listen and Live Audio

For instance, New York City has long been the center of the advertising, fashion, finance, and publishing industries. That's why Alisa Weberman decided to move her audio book publishing company, Listen and Live Audio, from California to a location in New Jersey, not far from busy New York City. Being in close proximity to the publishing firms in New York City gave a huge boost to her company, which has since grown to six employees and generates annual revenues of $1 million. "The company really took off when we moved here," says Weberman, who chose the New Jersey location because of its lower operating costs and warehouse space availability.[16]

Compatibility with the Community One of the intangibles that can be determined only by a visit to an area is the degree of compatibility a business has with the surrounding community. In other words, a small company's image must fit in with the character of a town and the needs and wants of its residents. For example, Beverly Hills' ritzy Rodeo Drive or Palm Beach's Worth Avenue are home to shops that match the characteristics of the area's wealthy residents. Shops such as Cartier and Tiffany & Company and exclusive designer clothing stores abound, catering to the area's rich and famous residents.

Local Laws and Regulations Before settling on a city, an entrepreneur must consider the regulatory burden local government might impose. Government regulations affect many aspects of small business's operation, from acquiring business licenses and building permits to erecting business signs and dumping trash. Some cities are regulatory activists, creating so many rules that they discourage business creation; others take a more laissez-faire approach, imposing few restrictions on businesses.

zoning

a system that divides a city or county into small cells or districts to control the use of land, buildings, and sites.

Zoning laws can have a major impact on an entrepreneur's location decision. **Zoning** is a system that divides a city or county into small cells or districts to control the use of land, buildings, and sites. Its purpose is to contain similar activities in suitable locations. For instance, one section of a city may be zoned residential, whereas the primary retail district is zoned commercial and another is zoned industrial to house manufacturing operations. Before selecting a particular site within a city, entrepreneurs must explore local zoning laws to determine whether there are any ordinances that would place restrictions on

Beverly Hills' Rodeo Drive is home to many upscale retailers whose target customers match the profile of the area's residents.

business activity or that would prohibit establishing a business altogether. Zoning regulations may make a particular location out of bounds. In some cases, an entrepreneur may appeal to the local zoning commission to rezone a site or to grant a **variance** (a special exception to a zoning ordinance), but this is risky and could be devastating if the board disallows the variance. As the number of home-based businesses has increased in the last several years, more entrepreneurs have found themselves at odds with zoning commissions.

variance
a special exemption to a zoning ordinance.

Transportation Networks Business owners must investigate the quality of local transportation systems. Is an airport located nearby? Are flights available to the necessary cities, and are the schedules convenient? If a company needs access to a railroad spur, is one available in the city? How convenient is the area's access to major highways? What about travel distances to major customers? How long will it take to deliver shipments to them? Are the transportation rates reasonable? Where is the nearest seaport? In some situations, double or triple handling of merchandise and inventory causes transportation costs to skyrocket. For retailers, the availability of loading and unloading zones is an important feature of a suitable location. Some downtown locations suffer from a lack of sufficient space for carriers to unload deliveries of merchandise.

Police and Fire Protection Does the community in which you plan to locate offer adequate police and fire protection? If these services are not adequate and crime rates are high, the cost of the company's business insurance will reflect that.

Cost of Utilities and Public Services A location should be served by a governmental unit that provides water and sewer services, trash and garage collection, and other necessary utilities at a reasonable cost. The streets should be in good repair with adequate drainage. If the location is not within the jurisdiction of a municipality that provides these services, they will become a continuing cost to the business.

Quality of Life A final consideration when selecting a city is the quality of life it offers. For many entrepreneurs, quality of life is one of the key determinants of their choice of locale. Cities that offer comfortable weather, cultural events, colleges and universities, museums, outdoor activities, concerts, unique restaurants, and an interesting nightlife have become magnets for entrepreneurs looking to start companies. Over the last two decades, cities such as Austin, Boston, Seattle, San Francisco, Washington, Dallas, Minneapolis, and others have become incubators for creativity and entrepreneurship as educated young people drawn by the cities' quality of life have moved in.

Not only can a location in a city offering a high quality of life be attractive to an entrepreneur, but it can also make recruiting employees much easier.

Zefer Corporation

Matthew Burkley, CEO of Zefer Corporation, an Internet consulting firm, chose to locate his company's headquarters in an area in downtown Boston where high-tech companies are concentrated. As Zefer established offices across the country, managers chose locations where they could attract the most qualified workers—San Francisco's South of Market, Chicago's Bucktown, and lower Manhattan. Burkley discovered that the workers the company wants most are young people who want to live and work in neighborhoods filled with people like them and offering the shops, clubs, galleries, and restaurants they enjoy. "In today's labor market, you have to be where your team members want to be," says Burkley.[17]

Choosing the Site

The final step in the location selection process is choosing the actual site for the business. Again, facts will guide an entrepreneur to the best location decision. Every business has its own unique set of criteria for an ideal location. A manufacturer's prime consideration may be access to raw materials, suppliers, labor, transportation, and customers. Service firms need access to customers but generally can survive in lower-rent properties. A retailer's prime consideration is sufficient customer traffic. For example, an entrepreneur planning to launch a dry cleaning service should know that about 80 percent of the typical dry cleaner's customers live within a one-mile radius of the outlet and should choose a location accordingly.[18] The one element common to all three types of businesses is the need to locate where customers want to do business.

The site location decision draws on the most precise information available on the makeup of the area. Using the source of published statistics described earlier in this chapter, an entrepreneur can develop valuable insights regarding the characteristics of people and businesses in the immediate community.

Would you like to know how many people or families are living in your trading area, what type of jobs they have, how much money they make, their ages, the value of their homes, and their education level, as well as a variety of other useful information? Sometimes businesses pay large fees to firms and consultants for this market research information. However, this information is available free from public libraries and on the Web. Every decade, the U.S. government undertakes one of the most ambitious market research projects in the world, collecting incredibility detailed statistics on the nation's 298 million residents and compiling it into easy-to-read reports. The Census Bureau has divided the United States into 255 Metropolitan Statistical Areas. These are then subdivided into census tracts, which contain an average of four to five thousand people. These census tracts are subdivided into block statistics and are extremely useful for entrepreneurs considering sites in urban areas.

This mother lode of market research is available to entrepreneurs through some 1,300 state data centers across the country. Two reports entrepreneurs find especially useful when choosing locations are *Summary Population*, which provides a broad demographic look at an area, and *Housing Characteristics*, which offers a detailed breakdown of areas as small as city blocks. Nationally, the average block contains about 100 people. The data are available on the Web at the Census Bureau's Web site. Any entrepreneur with a computer can access this incredible wealth of data with just a few mouse clicks.

Location Criteria for Retail and Service Businesses

Few decisions are as important for retailers and service firms than the choice of a location. Because their success depends on a steady flow of customers, these businesses must locate their businesses with their target customers' convenience and preferences in mind. The following are important considerations.

Trade Area Size Every retail and service business should determine the extent of its **trading area,** the region from which a business can expect to draw customers over a reasonable time span. The primary variables that influence the scope of the trading area are the type and the size of the business. If a retail store specializes in a particular product line and offers a wide selection and knowledgeable sales people, it may draw customers from a great distance. In contrast, a convenience store with a general line of merchandise may have a small trading area because it is unlikely that customers would drive across town to purchase what is available within blocks of their homes or businesses. As a rule, the larger the store, the greater its selection, and the better its service, the broader is its trading area.

trading area
the region from which a business can expect to draw customers over a reasonable time span.

The typical movie theater draws its customers from an area of five to seven miles; however, the AMC Grand, a collection of 24 screens under one roof in Dallas, Texas, draws customers from as far as 25 miles away. This free-standing "megaplex" has expanded the normal theater trading area and attracts an amazing 3 million moviegoers a year even though it is not located near a shopping mall, as most theaters are. AMC Grand's attendance per screen averages 38 percent more than do AMC Entertainment's traditional theaters; its revenue per customer is 10 percent higher, and its profit margins are 12.5 percent higher.

COMPANY
Profile

AMC Grand

Twelve environmental factors that influence trading area size are as follows:

- Retail compatibility
- Degree of competition
- The index of retail saturation
- Reilly's Law of Retail Gravitation
- Transportation network
- Physical, racial, or emotional barriers
- Political barriers
- Customer traffic
- Adequate parking
- Reputation
- Room for expansion
- Visibility

Retail Compatibility Shoppers tend to be drawn to clusters of related businesses. That's one reason shopping malls and outlet shopping centers are popular destinations for

© Mike Baldwin / Cornered

© www.CartoonStock.com

retail compatibility
the benefits a company receives by locating near other businesses that sell complementary products and services or generate high volumes of traffic.

shoppers and, therefore, are attractive locations for retailers. The concentration of businesses pulls customers from a larger trading area than a single free-standing business does. **Retail compatibility** describes the benefits a company receives by locating near other businesses that sell complementary products and services or generate high volumes of foot traffic. Clever business owners choose their locations with an eye on the surrounding mix of businesses. For instance, grocery store operators prefer not to locate in shopping centers with movie theaters, offices, and fitness centers, all businesses whose customers occupy parking spaces for extended time periods. Drugstores, nail salons, and ice cream parlors have proved to be much better shopping center neighbors for grocers.

Restaurants have proved to be a particularly good match for many retail operations.

Talloni: A Shoe Salon

Michelle Goodman decided to open Talloni: A Shoe Salon in the central business district of Greer, South Carolina, when she learned that two new restaurants would be opening there. Goodman knew that the restaurants would generate customer traffic for her retail store, which is exactly what has happened. Goodman, who launched her store five months before the new restaurants opened, says that the two eateries have "definitely made a difference" in her shoe store's customer traffic and sales.[19]

Degree of Competition The size, location, and activity of competing businesses also influence the size of a company's trading area. If a business will be the first of its kind in a location, its trading area might be quite extensive. However, if the area already has 8 or 10 nearby stores that directly compete with a business, its trading area might be very small because the market is saturated with competitors. Market saturation is a problem for businesses in many industries, ranging from fast food restaurants to convenience stores. A study by the *Convenience Store News*, a trade publication of the convenience store industry, found that if the number of customers per convenience store in an area dropped below 3,000, the stores in that area suffered, and many were forced to close.

index of retail saturation
a measure of the potential sales per square foot of store space for a given product within a specific trading area; it is the ratio of a trading area's sales potential for a product or service to its sales capacity.

The Index of Retail Saturation One of the best measures of the level of saturation in an area is the index of retail saturation (IRS), which takes into account both the number of customers and the intensity of competition in a trading area. The **index of retail saturation** is a measure of the potential sales per square foot of store space for a given product within a specific trading area. It is the ratio of a trading area's sales potential for a particular product or service to its sales capacity:

$$IRS = (C \times RE)/RF$$

where   C = Number of customers in the trading area
RE = Retail expenditures = Average expenditure per person (in dollars) for the product in the trading area
RF = Retail facilities = Total square feet of selling space allocated to the product in the trading area

This computation is an important one for every retailer to make. Locating in an area already saturated with competitors results in dismal sales volume and often leads to failure.

To illustrate the index of retail saturation, suppose that an entrepreneur looking at two sites for a shoe store finds that he needs sales of $175 per square foot to be profitable. Site 1 has a trading area with 25,875 potential customers who spend an average of $42 on shoes annually; the only competitor in the trading area has 6,000 square feet of selling space. Site 2 has 27,750 potential customers spending an average of $43.50 on shoes annually; two competitors occupy 8,400 square feet of space. The calculations go as follows:

Site 1

$$IRS = (25,875 \times 42)/6,000$$
$$= \$181.12 \text{ sales potential per square foot}$$

Site 2

$$IRS = (27{,}750 \times 43.50)/8{,}400$$

$$= \$143.71 \text{ sales potential per square foot}$$

Although site 2 appears to be more favorable on the surface, the index shows that site 1 is preferable; site 2 fails to meet the minimum standard of $175 per square foot.

Reilly's Law of Retail Gravitation Reilly's Law of Retail Gravitation, a classic work in market analysis published in 1931 by William J. Reilly, uses the analogy of gravity to estimate the attractiveness of a particular business to potential customers. A business' ability to draw customers is directly related to the extent to which customers see it as a "destination" and is inversely related to the distance customers must travel to reach it. Reilly's model also provides a way to estimate the trade boundary between two market areas by calculating the "break point" between them. The break point between two primary market areas is the boundary between the two where customers become indifferent about shopping at one or the other location. The key factor in determining this point of indifference is the size of the communities. If two nearby cities have the same population sizes, then the break point lies halfway between them. The following is the equation for Reilly's Law[20]:

$$BP = \frac{d}{1 + \sqrt{\dfrac{P_b}{P_a}}}$$

where BP = Distance in miles from location A to the break point

       d = Distance in miles between locations A and B

     P_a = Population surrounding location A

     P_b = Population surrounding location B

For example, if city A and city B are 22 miles apart, and city A has a population of 22,500 and city B has a population of 42,900, the break point according to Reilly's law is

$$BP = \frac{22}{1 + \sqrt{\dfrac{42{,}900}{22{,}500}}} = 9.2 \text{ miles}$$

The outer edge of city A's trading area lies about 9 miles between city A and city B. Although only a rough estimate, this simple calculation using readily available data can be useful for screening potential locations.

Transportation Network The transportation networks are the highways, roads, and public service routes that presently exist or are planned. If customers find it inconvenient to get to a location, the store's trading area is reduced. Entrepreneurs should check to see whether the transportation system works smoothly and is free of barriers that might prevent customers from reaching their stores. Is it easy for customers traveling in the opposite direction to cross traffic? Do signs and traffic lights allow traffic to flow smoothly? When traffic flow is absolutely critical to the success of a business venture, make an extra effort to contact city government officials who are knowledgeable about transportation plans. Ask about future road construction projects that may be planned or under serious consideration. Such road construction could be either beneficial or disastrous.

Physical, Racial, or Emotional Barriers Trading area shape and size also are influenced by physical, racial, or emotional barriers that may exist. Physical barriers may be parks, rivers, lakes, or any other natural or people-made obstruction that hinders customer's access to the area. Locating on one side of a large park may reduce the number of customers that will drive around it to get to the store. If high-crime areas exist in any direction from the site, most of a company's potential customers will not travel through those neighborhoods to reach the business.

    In urban areas, new immigrants tend to cluster together, sharing a common culture and language. Some areas are defined by cultural barriers, where inhabitants are extremely loyal to the businesses in their neighborhoods. The "Little Havana" section of Miami and the "Chinatown" sections of San Francisco, New York, and Los Angeles are examples.

One of the most powerful emotional barriers affecting a location is fear. Businesses in areas where crime is a problem suffer because customers are not willing to travel into them. In South Central Los Angeles, an area once decimated by riots, only a handful of businesses have reopened to serve the local population. Business owners, afraid that the area's burned-out buildings and reputation for crime will dissuade customers from patronizing their businesses, have chosen locations in other parts of the city.

Political Barriers Political barriers are creations of law. County, city, or state boundaries—and the laws within those boundaries—are examples. State tax laws sometimes create conditions in which customers cross over to the next state to save money. For instance, North Carolina imposes a very low cigarette tax, and shops located near the state line do a brisk business in the product selling to customers from bordering states.

Other factors retailers should consider when evaluating potential sites include customer traffic, adequate parking, reputation, room for expansion, and visibility.

Customer Traffic Perhaps the most important screening criterion for a potential retail (and often for a service) location is the number of potential customers passing by the site during business hours. To be successful, a business must be able to generate sufficient sales to surpass its break-even point, and that requires an ample volume of customer traffic going past its doors. The key success factor for a convenience store is a high-volume location with easy accessibility. Entrepreneurs should know the traffic counts (pedestrian and/or auto) and traffic patterns at the sites they are considering as potential locations.

Piper's In the Park

Wanting to maximize customer traffic, Wendy Woods and Piper Lunsford decided to locate their restaurant, Piper's in the Park, in North Carolina's Research Triangle Park, one of the world's premier research parks and home to more than 48,000 employees. The restaurant, with annual revenues of more than $1 million, does a brisk business catering and serving meals to the employees who work in the nearby high-tech businesses.[21]

Adequate Parking If customers cannot find convenient and safe parking, they are not likely to stop in the area. Many downtown areas have lost customers because of inadequate parking. Although shopping malls average 5 parking spaces per 1,000 square feet of shopping space, many central business districts get by with 3.5 spaces per 1,000 square feet. Customers generally will not pay to park if parking is free at shopping centers or in front of competitive stores. Even when free parking is provided, some potential customers may not feel safe on the streets, especially after dark. Many large city downtown business districts become virtual ghost towns at the end of the business day. A location where traffic vanishes after 6 p.m. may not be as valuable as mall and shopping center locations that mark the beginning of the prime sales time at 6 p.m.

Reputation Like people, a site can have a bad reputation. In some cases, the reputation of the previous business will lower the value of the location. Sites where businesses have failed repeatedly create negative impressions in customers' minds; many people view the business as just another that soon will be gone. Sometimes previous failures are indicative of a fundamental problem with the location itself, but in other cases, the cause of the previous failure was not the choice of a poor location but a poorly managed business. When entrepreneurs decide to conduct business in a location that has housed pervious failures, it is essential that they make many highly visible changes to the site so that customers perceive the company as a "fresh start."

Underdog Coffee

The site in Portland, Oregon, that Allen Tackett had selected as the location for his coffee house had seen three businesses fail (including one coffee shop) within the last seven years. Tackett purchased the building and completely renovated it, giving his business, Underdog Coffee, a whole new look. A new, more visible backlit sign and a highly publicized grand opening drew customers to Underdog Coffee. Since launching the business in the original location, Tackett has opened a second location in Lebanon, Oregon, and is now accepting applications to franchise Underdog Coffee.[22]

Room for Expansion A location should be flexible enough to provide for expansion if success warrants it. Failure to consider this factor can result in a successful business being forced to open a second store when it would have been better to expand in its original location.

Planning for expansion is always a difficult issue with very real cost considerations. If the business is a success and expansion is warranted, does this location allow the facility to expand? Is the location under consideration able to be expanded or is it bounded by other businesses? Beginning with "extra" space for future expansion is very expensive. The business is incurring cost that may place an undue burden on profits. The issue of expansion always includes a dilemma. On one hand, having the needed space when growth occurs may mean that the business can stay at the same location. This allows the entrepreneur to avoid the cost and customer confusion created by moving the business to a new location. On the other hand, there are the up-front costs of having a location that is intentionally larger than is needed.

Visibility No matter what a small business sells and how well it serves customers' needs, it cannot survive without visibility. Highly visible locations simply make it easy for customers to make purchases. A site lacking visibility puts a company at a major disadvantage before it ever opens its doors for business.

You

Be the Consultant

Location Decisions

Every year, a host of business magazines, including *Entrepreneur*, *Fast Company*, *Forbes*, *Inc.*, and others, publish their lists of the best cities for starting a business. Each magazine establishes its own criteria, including population growth, regulatory burden, tax rates, rate of business formation, cost of living index, and others. Although the lists differ somewhat, many of the same cities appear on several lists. Use the Web (or locate a copy of the relevant issue of one of these magazines) to identify the most recent "best cities" listed. Use the lists and the sources of demographic data described in this chapter to help the following entrepreneurs determine which cities would be best for them as they face the location decision.

Vino con Vida. Sandra Gonzalez, 36, grew up in a family that made a living picking fruit throughout California. During the 10 years that she worked for the Wine Institute, a trade association in California, she noticed that few wine makers were

targeting Latino customers. Spotting an opportunity, she began planning to launch Vino con Vida ("Wine with Life"), a wine-education company that focuses on Latino customers and culture. She plans to partner with vintners and chefs to sponsor wine and food tastings, dinners, and winery tours that target Latino customers. Vino con Vida will educate Latino customers about wine and will educate the wine industry about Latinos and their unique culture and heritage.

Teriyaki Madness. Eric Garma, Rod Arreola, and Alan Arreola launched a teriyaki restaurant in their hometown of Seattle, Washington. Teriyaki Madness became profitable, but when it came time to expand, their research showed that the market in Seattle already was saturated with teriyaki restaurants. The entrepreneurs began to look at other cities to locate the next Teriyaki Madness. They see their restaurant as a fresh alternative to traditional fast food establishments. They are looking for a city that offers a fast-growing population and a supply of quality employees. In addition, they believe that it is important for the city to have a diverse population and a culture that embraces new concepts.

Motricity. Ryan Wuerch's Nashville-based software company, Motricity, recently acquired another, smaller software company in Raleigh, North Carolina. Shortly after the acquisition, Wuerch began making plans to move the headquarters of the newly acquired company to Nashville. Then his wife reminded him of the difficulty he experienced in finding top-notch high-tech employees in the Nashville area. After careful consideration, he decided that Nashville might not be the best location for Motricity after all. In addition to a supply of high-tech workers, Wuerch is looking for a city that fosters creativity and a high quality of life, factors he knows draw the employees he seeks to a city.

Pulse Fitness Center. Rita Hunter lives in upstate South Carolina and wants to open a full-service fitness center, preferably somewhere within the state's borders. In addition to targeting individuals

who want a wide range of exercise options, Hunter also plans to target businesses that want to offer physical fitness programs for their employees. She knows that a few large companies such as Gold's Gym dominate many markets and that other companies such as Curves target market niches (for example, busy women who want a quick, effective workout). She is looking for a location that offers a fast-growing population, a sizable population of young and middle-aged people, and a superior quality of life.

1. Use the "best cities" lists from some of the magazines mentioned previously and the sources of demographic data described in this chapter to help these entrepreneurs determine which cities would be best for them as they face the location decision.
2. What suggestions would you offer these entrepreneurs before they make the final location decisions for their companies?

Sources: Adapted from Jesse M. Cubbison, "Fitness Centers Get Quite a Workout Finding Locations," *GSA Business*, July 25, 2005, p. 17; Bill Breen, Michael A. Prospero, Jena McGregor, et al., "Fast Cities," *Fast Company*, November 2005, pp. 63–71; "On the Move," *Entrepreneur B.Y.O.B*, June 2004, pp. 98–99.

LEARNING OBJECTIVES
3. Outline the location options for retail and service businesses.

Location Options for Retail and Service Businesses

There are six basic areas where retail and service business owners can locate: the central business district (CBD); neighborhoods; shopping centers and malls; near competitors; outlying areas; and at home. According to the International Council of Shopping Centers, the average cost to lease space in a shopping center is about $15 per square foot. At a regional mall, rental rates run from $20 to $40 per square foot. In central business locations, the average cost is $43 per square foot (although rental rates can vary significantly in either direction of that average, depending on the city).[23] Of course, cost is just one factor a business owner must consider when choosing a location.

Central Business District

The central business district is the traditional center of town—the downtown concentration of businesses established early in the development of most towns and cities. Entrepreneurs derive several advantages from a downtown location. Because the business is centrally located, it attracts customers from the entire trading area of the city. In addition, a small business usually benefits from the customer traffic generated by the other stores in the district. However, locating in a CBD does have certain disadvantages. Many CBDs are characterized by intense competition, high rental rates, traffic congestion, and inadequate parking facilities.

Beginning in the 1950s, many cities saw their older downtown business districts begin to decay as residents moved to the suburbs and began shopping at newer, more convenient malls. Today, however, many of these CBDs are experiencing rebirth as cities restore them to their former splendor and shoppers return. Many customers find irresistible the charming atmosphere that traditional downtown districts offer with their rich mix of stores, their unique architecture and streetscapes, and their historic character. Cities have begun to reverse the urban decay of their downtown business districts through proactive revitalization programs designed to attract visitors and residents alike to cultural events by locating major theaters and museums in the downtown area. In addition, many cities are providing economic incentives to real estate developers to build apartment and condominium complexes in the heart of the downtown area. Vitality is returning as residents live and shop in the once nearly abandoned downtown areas. The "ghost-town" image is being replaced by both younger and older residents who love the convenience and excitement of life at the center of the city. One real estate developer experienced in Main Street locations says that his research shows that the best downtown streets for retailers are located in densely populated, affluent areas, are one-way, offer on-street parking, and are shaded by mature trees.[24]

Nello Gioia, owner of Ristorante Bergamo, an upscale Italian restaurant, took a chance on a downtown location on Main Street in Greenville, South Carolina, in 1985 when the city was just beginning an ambitious reclamation of its central business district. Unlike the busy, vibrant, highly desirable location Greenville's downtown is today, what Gioia saw then was a street spattered with offices, a few long-time resident businesses, and lots of shuttered and vacant stores. "The month before we opened, I got cold feet," recalls Gioia. "But I was up to my neck. I had to do it." Gioia had considered locating in a regional mall and a strip mall but decided that those locations were inconsistent with the image he wanted to create for his restaurant. "The one place that resembled where I came from [Bergamo, Italy] was downtown," says Gioia. Twenty years later, he is glad he took the chance on a downtown location; Greenville's central business district has become a well-known success story, and many other cities across the United States have used it as a model for reclaiming their downtowns.[25]

Ristorante Bergamo

Neighborhood Locations

Small businesses that locate near residential areas rely heavily on the local trading areas for business. Businesses that provide convenience as a major attraction for customers find that locating on a street or road just outside major residential areas provides the needed traffic counts essential for success. Gas stations and convenience stores seem to thrive in these high-traffic areas. One study of food stores found that the majority of the typical grocer's customers live within a five-mile radius. The primary advantages of a neighborhood location include relatively low operating costs and rents and close contact with customers.

Shopping Centers and Malls

Until the early twentieth century, central business districts were the primary shopping venues in the United States. As cars and transportation networks became more popular in the 1920s, shopping centers began popping up outside cities' central business districts. In October 1956, the nation's first shopping mall, Southdale, opened in the Minneapolis, Minnesota, suburb of Edina. Designed by Victor Gruen, the fully enclosed mall featured 72 shops anchored by two competing department stores (a radical concept at the time), a garden courtyard with a goldfish pond, an aviary, hanging plants, and artificial trees. With its multilevel layout and parking garage, Southdale was a huge success and forever changed the way Americans would shop.[26] Today shopping centers and malls have become a mainstay of the American landscape. Since 1970, the number of shopping malls and centers in the United States has climbed from 11,000 to more than 47,700, and they occupy 6.5 billion square feet of retail space.[27] Because many different types of stores operate under one roof, shopping malls give meaning to the term "one-stop shopping." In a typical month, more than 200 million adults visit malls or shopping centers, which generate $2 trillion in annual sales. There are eight types of shopping centers (see Table 14.2):

- ■ *Neighborhood shopping centers.* The typical neighborhood shopping center is relatively small, containing from 3 to 12 stores and serving a population of up to

Opened in 1956, Southdale was the first shopping mall in the United States. Its success changed the landscape of retail shopping and ushered in the era of one-stop shopping.

TABLE 14.2 Shopping Center Definitions

Type of Shopping Center	Concept	Square Feet (Including Anchors)	Acreage	Typical Anchor(s)		Anchor Ratio[a] (%)	Primary Trade Area[b] (miles)
				Number	Type		
Malls							
Regional center	General merchandise; fashion (mall, typically enclosed)	480,000–800,000	40–100	2 or more	Full-line department store; junior department store; mass merchant; discount department store; fashion apparel	50–70	5–15
Superregional center	Similar to regional center but has more variety and assortment	800,000+	68–120	3 or more	Full-line department store; junior department store; mass merchant; fashion apparel	50–70	5–25
Open-Air Centers							
Neighborhood center	Convenience	30,000–150,000	3–15	1 or more	Supermarket	30–50	3
Community center	General merchandise; convenience	100,000–350,000	10–40	2 or more	Discount department store; supermarket; drug; home improvement; large specialty/discount apparel	40–60	3–6
Lifestyle center	Upscale national chain specialty stores; dining and entertainment in outdoor setting	Typically 150,000–500,000 but can be smaller or larger	10–40	0–2	Not usually anchored in the traditional sense but may include book store; other large-format specialty retailers; multiplex cinema; small department store.	0–50	8–12
Power center	Category-dominant anchors; few small tenants	250,000–600,000	25–80	3 or more	Category killer; home improvement; discount department store; warehouse club; off-price	75–90	5–10
Theme/festival center	Leisure; tourist oriented; retail and service	80,000–250,000	5–20	N/A	Restaurants; entertainment	N/A	N/A
Outlet center	Manufacturers' outlet stores	50,000–400,000	10–50	N/A	Manufacturers' outlet stores	N/A	25–75

[a]The share of a center's total square footage that is attributable to its anchors.
[b]The area from which 60–80% of the center's sales originate.
Source: International Council of Shopping Centers, New York.

40,000 people who live within a 10-minute drive. The anchor store in these centers is usually a supermarket or a drugstore. Neighborhood shopping centers typically are straight-line strip malls with parking available in front and primarily serve the daily shopping needs of customers in the surrounding area.

■ *Community shopping centers.* A community shopping center contains from 12 to 50 stores and serves a population ranging from 40,000 to 150,000 people. The leading tenant often is a large department or variety store, a super drugstore, or a supermarket. Community shopping centers sell more clothing and other soft goods than do neighborhood shopping centers. Of the eight types of shopping centers, community shopping centers take on the greatest variety of shapes, designs, and tenants.

■ *Power centers.* A power center combines the drawing strength of a large regional mall with the convenience of a neighborhood shopping center. Anchored by several large specialty retailers such as warehouse clubs, discount department stores, or large specialty stores, these centers target older, wealthier baby boomers, who want selection and convenience. Anchor stores usually account for 80 percent of power center space, compared with 50 percent in the typical strip shopping center. Just as in a shopping mall, small businesses can benefit from the traffic generated by anchor stores, but they must choose their locations carefully so that they are not overshadowed by their larger neighbors.

■ *Theme or festival centers.* Festival shopping centers employ a unifying theme that individual stores display in their décor and sometimes in the merchandise they sell. Entertainment is a common theme for these shopping centers, which often target tourists. Many festival shopping centers are located in urban areas and are housed in older, sometimes historic, buildings that have been renovated to serve as shopping centers.

■ *Outlet centers.* As their name suggests, outlet centers feature manufacturers' and retailers' outlet stores selling name-brand goods at a discount. Unlike most other types of shopping centers, outlet centers typically have no anchor stores; the discounted merchandise they offer draws sufficient traffic. Most outlet centers are open-air and are laid out in strips or in clusters, creating small "villages" of shops.

■ *Lifestyle centers.* Typically located near affluent residential neighborhoods where their target customers live, lifestyle centers are designed to look less like shopping centers and malls and more like the busy streets in the central business districts that existed in towns and cities in their heyday. Occupied by many upscale national chain specialty stores such as Talbots, Coach, Sharper Image, and many others, these centers combine shopping convenience, and entertainment ranging from movie theaters and open-air concerts to art galleries and people-watching. "Lifestyle centers create a shopping-leisure destination that's an extension of customers' personal lifestyles," says one industry expert. The typical lifestyle center generates between $400 and $500 in sales per square foot compared to $330 in sales per square foot in traditional malls. Lifestyle centers are among the most popular types of shopping centers being built today; the first lifestyle center, The Shops of Saddle Creek, opened in Germantown, Tennessee, in 1987. Today 130 lifestyle centers operate across the United States.[28]

■ *Regional shopping malls.* The regional shopping mall serves a large trading area, usually from 5 to 15 miles or more in all directions. These enclosed malls contain from 50 to 100 stores and serve a population of 150,000 or more living within a 20- to 40-minute drive. The anchor is typically one or more major department stores, with smaller specialty stores occupying the spaces between the anchors. Clothing is one of the popular items sold in regional shopping malls.

■ *Superregional shopping malls.* A superregional mall is similar to a regional mall but is bigger, containing more anchor stores and a greater variety of shops selling deeper lines of merchandise. Its trade area stretches up to 25 or more miles out. Canada's West Edmonton Mall, the largest mall in North America, with more than 800 stores and 100 restaurants, is one of the most famous superregional malls in the world. In addition to its abundance of retail shops, the mall contains an ice skating rink, a waterpark, an amusement park, miniature golf courses, and a 21-screen movie complex.

Originally built on the foundation of major department stores, which serve as anchors and attract a significant volume of customer traffic, malls and shopping centers now are welcoming small businesses with their unique, sometimes quirky, product offerings, boutique atmospheres, and marketing approaches.

Talulah G

Meital Grantz, owner of Talulah G, a small retail clothing store that sells clothing lines from many of today's hottest designers, opened her first outlet in downtown Las Vegas, Nevada, in November 2001. A year later, Grantz moved the business to the Las Vegas Fashion Mall to benefit from the high customer traffic the mall generated. After moving into the mall, Grantz says daily sales climbed to $6,000 from $1,000. "Once we opened in the mall," she says, "the store took on a life of its own." Since then, she says, "we've been courted by malls all over America."[29]

When evaluating a mall or shopping center location, an entrepreneur should consider the following questions:

- Is there a good fit with other products and brands sold in the mall or center?
- Who are the other tenants? Which stores are the anchors that will bring people into the mall or center?
- Demographically, is the center a good fit for your products or services? What are its customer demographics? (See Figure 14.1.)
- How much foot traffic does the mall or center generate? How much traffic passes the specific site you are considering?
- How much vehicle traffic does the mall or center generate? Check its proximity to major population centers, the volume of tourists it draws, and the volume of drive-by freeway traffic. A mall or center that scores well on all three is more likely to be a winner.
- What is the mall's vacancy rate? What is the turnover rate of its tenants?
- How much is the rent and how is it calculated? Most mall tenants pay a base amount of rent plus a percentage of their sales.
- Is the mall or center successful? How many dollars in sales does it generate per square foot? Compare its record against industry averages. The New York-based International Council of Shopping Centers (http://www.icsc.org/) is a good source of industry information.

FIGURE 14.1

Shopping Mall Patterns

Source: International Council of Shopping Centers

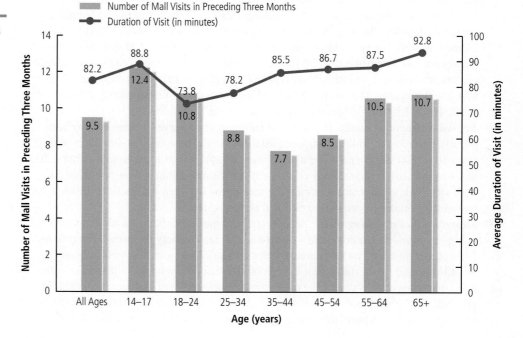

The Mall of America in Minneapolis, Minnesota, is the largest mall in the United States. With more than 500 stores, 50 restaurants, a theme park, an aquarium, a dinosaur museum, and many other features, the Mall of America is one of the nation's top tourist destinations.

A mall location is no longer a guarantee of success, however. Malls have been under pressure lately, and many weaker ones (known as "greyfields") have closed or have been redeveloped. The basic problem is an oversupply of mall space; there is 20 feet of mall retail space for every person in the United States! Another problem is that many malls are showing their age; 85 percent of the malls in the United States are more than 20 years old.[30] In addition, the demographic makeup of an area's shoppers often changes over time, creating a new socioeconomic customer base that may or may not be compatible with a small company's target customer profile. As a result, many malls have undergone extensive renovations to emphasize "entertailing," adding entertainment features to their existing retail space in an attempt to generate more traffic. For instance, in addition to its 520 retail shops and 60 restaurants, Minneapolis's Mall of America, the second largest mall in the United States (located only a few miles from Southdale, the nation's first mall), includes a seven-acre Camp Snoopy amusement park at its center, a 1.2 million-gallon aquarium, and a 14-screen movie complex.[31]

Near Competitors One of the most important factors in choosing a retail or service location is the compatibility of nearby stores with the retail or service customer. For example, stores selling high-priced goods find it advantageous to locate near competitors to facilitate comparison shopping. Locating near competitors might be a key factor for success in those businesses selling goods that customers shop for and compare on the basis of price, quality, color, and other factors.

Although some business owners avoid locations near direct competitors, others see locating near rivals as an advantage. For instance, restaurateurs know that successful restaurants attract other restaurants, which, in turn, attract more customers. Many cities have at least one "restaurant row," where restaurants cluster together; each restaurant is a source of customers to the others.

Locating near competitors has its limits, however. Clustering too many businesses of a single type into a small area ultimately will erode their sales once the market reaches the saturation point. When an area becomes saturated with competitors, the shops cannibalize sales from one another, making it difficult for any of them to be successful.

Outlying Areas Generally, it is not advisable for a small business to locate in a remote area because accessibility and traffic flow are vital to retail and service success, but there are exceptions. Some small firms have turned their remote locations into trademarks.

One small gun shop was able to use its extremely remote location to its advantage by incorporating this into its advertising to distinguish itself from its competitors. This location strategy is usually only effective if there are few comparable competitors. There must be a compelling reason for a potential customer to travel to an outlying area to shop.

An entrepreneur should consider the cost of a location (its rental or lease expense) in light of its visibility to potential customers. If a less expensive location is difficult to find and has a low traffic count, an entrepreneur will have to spend a disproportionate amount of money to advertise and promote the business as well as tell customers how to find it. Consequently, a superior and highly visible location may have a total lower cost if less advertising is needed. Many customers do not want to go exploring to find a business and, consequently, never bother to try.

Home-Based Businesses For more than 24 million people, home is where the business is, and their numbers are swelling. According to the Department of Commerce, home-based businesses represent the fastest-growing segment of the U.S. economy.[32] One recent study found that 52 percent of all small companies are home-based.[33] Although a home-based retail business usually is not ideal, locating a service business at home is quite popular. Many service companies do not have customers come to their places of business, so an expensive office location is unnecessary. For instance, customers typically contact plumbers or exterminators by telephone, and the work is performed in customers' homes.

Entrepreneurs locating their businesses at home reap several benefits. Perhaps the biggest benefit is the low cost of setting up the business. Most often, home-based entrepreneurs set up shop in a spare bedroom or basement, avoiding the cost of renting, leasing, or buying a building. With a few basic pieces of office equipment—computer, printer, fax machine, copier, telephone answering system, and scanner—a lone entrepreneur can perform just like a major corporation.

Home Remedies

After having difficulty locating reliable contractors for a home renovation project, Debra Cohen realized that other people faced the same problem and launched Home Remedies, a home-based contractor-referral business. The company screens home contractors specializing in various types of renovations and repairs and then refers them to homeowners. A stay-at-home mom living in Hewlett, New York, Cohen started Home Remedies with a $5,000 loan, a PC, and a refurbished fax machine. Business was so good that she repaid the business loan in just three months. Cohen works an average of 30 hours a week, and sales, which now exceed $100,000 a year, are growing rapidly.[34]

Choosing a home location has certain disadvantages, however. Interruptions are more frequent, the refrigerator is all too handy, work is always just a few steps away, and isolation can be a problem. Another difficulty facing some home-based entrepreneurs involves zoning laws. As their businesses grow and become more successful, entrepreneurs' neighbors often begin to complain about the increased traffic, noise, and disruptions from deliveries, employees, and customers who drive through their residential neighborhoods to conduct business. Many communities now face the challenge of passing updated zoning laws that reflect the reality of today's home-based businesses while protecting the interests of residential homeowners.

The Location Decision for Manufacturers

LEARNING OBJECTIVES
4. Explain the site selection process for manufacturers.

The criteria for the location decision for manufacturers are very different from those of retailers and service businesses; however, the decision can have just as much impact on the company's success. In some cases, a manufacturer has special needs that influence the choice of a location. For instance, when one manufacturer of photographic plates and film was searching for a location for a new plant, it had to limit its search to those sites with a large supply of available fresh water, a necessary part of its process. In other cases, the location decision is controlled by zoning ordinances. If a manufacturer's process creates offensive odors or excessive noise, it may be even further restricted in its choices.

Zoning maps show potential manufacturers the areas of the city or county set aside for industrial development. Most cities have developed industrial parks in cooperation with private industry. These industrial parks typically are equipped with sewage and electrical power sufficient for manufacturing. Many locations are not so equipped, and it can be extremely expensive for a small manufacturer to have such utilities brought to an existing site.

The type of transportation facilities required dictates the location of a plant in some cases. Some manufacturers may need to locate on a railroad siding, whereas others may only need reliable trucking service. If raw materials are purchased by the carload for economies of scale, the location must be convenient to a railroad siding. Bulk materials are sometimes shipped by barge and consequently require a facility convenient to a navigable river or lake. The added cost of using multiple shipping (e.g., rail-to-truck or barge-to-truck) can significantly increase shipping costs and make a location unfeasible for a manufacturer.

As fuel costs escalate, the cost of shipping finished products to customers also influences the location decision for many manufacturers. Dell Inc., the Round Rock, Texas–based maker of personal computers, recently built an assembly plant in Winston-Salem, North Carolina, citing the need to reduce shipping costs and to increase the speed of delivery to customers on the East Coast of the United States. As downward pressure on the prices of Dell's PCs continues due to intense competition in the industry, shipping costs were soaking up a larger percentage of its total revenue, prompting Dell to build the new plant.

In some cases the perishibility of the product dictates location. Vegetables and fruits must be canned in close proximity to the fields in which they are harvested. Fish must be processed and canned at the water's edge. The ideal location is determined by quick and easy access to the perishable products.

Foreign Trade Zones Foreign trade zones can be an attractive location for small manufacturers that engage in global trade and are looking to reduce or eliminate the tariffs, duties, and excise taxes they pay on the materials and parts they import and the goods they export. A **foreign trade zone** (see Figure 14.2) is a specially designated area in or near a United States customs port of entry that allows resident companies to import materials and components from foreign countries; assemble, process, manufacture, or package them; and then ship the finished product back out while either reducing or eliminating tariffs and duties. As far as tariffs and duties are concerned, a company located in a foreign trade zone is treated as if it is located outside the United States. For instance, a maker of speakers might import components from around the world and assemble them at its plant located in a foreign trade zone. The company would pay no duties on the components it imports or on the speakers it exports to other foreign

foreign trade zone
a specially designated area in or near a United States customs port of entry that allows resident companies to import materials and components from foreign countries; assemble, process, manufacture, or package them; and then ship the finished product back out while either reducing or eliminating tariffs and duties.

FIGURE 14.2

How a Foreign Trade Zone (FTZ) Works

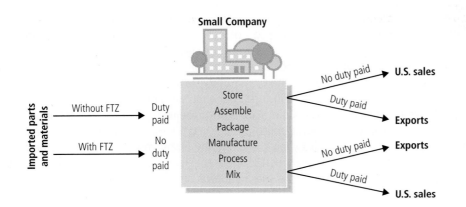

markets. The only duties the manufacturer would pay are on the speakers it sells in the United States.

Empowerment Zones Originally created to encourage companies to locate in economically blighted areas, **empowerment zones** offer businesses tax breaks on the investments they make within zone boundaries. Companies can get federal tax credits, grants, and loans for hiring workers living in empowerment zones and for investments they make in plant and equipment in the zones. Empowerment zones operate in both urban and rural areas, ranging from Los Angeles, California, to Sumter, South Carolina. Boston has a technology-oriented business incubator located within a federal empowerment zone called TechSpace, which provides high-potential start-up businesses with a full-service facility featuring completely integrated information technology and business services.

empowerment zone
an area designated as economically disadvantaged in which businesses get tax breaks on the investments they make within zone boundaries.

Business Incubators For many start-up companies, a business incubator may make the ideal initial location. A **business incubator** is an organization that combines low-cost, flexible rental space with a multitude of support services for its small business residents. The overwhelming reason for establishing an incubator is to enhance economic development by attracting new business ventures to an area, as well as to diversify the local economy. An incubator's goal is to nurture young companies during the volatile start-up period and to help them to survive until they are strong enough to go out on their own. Common sponsors of incubators include colleges or universities (25 percent), government entities (16 percent), economic development organizations (15 percent), and private investment groups (10 percent). Most incubators are "mixed-use," hosting a variety of start-up companies, followed by incubators that focus on technology companies.[35]

business incubator
an organization that combines low-cost, flexible rental space with a multitude of support services for its small business residents.

The shared resources that incubators typically provide their tenants include secretarial services, a telephone system, computers and software, fax machines, meeting facilities, and, sometimes, management consulting services and financing. Not only do these services save young companies money, but they also save them valuable time. Entrepreneurs can focus on getting their products and services to market faster than competitors rather than searching for the resources they need to build their companies. The typical incubator has entry requirements that prospective residents must meet. Incubators also have criteria that establish the conditions a business must maintain to remain in the facility as well as the expectations for "graduation" into the business community.

More than 1,000 incubators operate across the United States, up from just 12 in 1980. Perhaps the greatest advantage of choosing to locate a start-up company in an incubator is a greater chance for success; according to the National Business Incubation Association, graduates from incubators have a success rate of 87 percent. The average incubator houses 20 ongoing businesses employing 55 people.[36]

Action Publishing

Grady Busse, who co-founded Action Publishing, a company that produces academic day planners, calendars, and accessories, already knew the benefits that business incubators offered start-up companies because he had founded a successful small business in The Business Incubator Center in Grand Junction, Colorado, a decade before. Busse and his partners are convinced that if it had not been for the support, training, and resources of the incubator—from business training classes to office furniture and equipment—Action Publishing might not have survived. For instance, when the company's application for a loan from the state Community Development Block Grant funds stalled, Dean Didario, the incubator's loan fund manager, worked with Busse and state officials to resolve the problems, and Action Publishing received the much-needed loan. With the incubator's support, Action Publishing reached $1 million in sales in its first 10 months of operation. By its third year, the company employed 70 people and had annual revenues of $2.1 million. Now established and in need of additional space, Action Publishing has "graduated" from the incubator and occupies its own 15,000-square-foot facility.[37]

Increasingly, incubators no longer require small companies to locate physically within the incubator site, but they still provide business assistance to the small companies that join the incubator. These incubators connect entrepreneurs with a network of experts, consultants, and advisors and, in many cases, potential sources of financing.

Christie Stone, founder of Ticobeans, a New Orleans coffee distributor, joined Idea Village, a local incubator, but kept her warehouse space and office in their original location. Within a month of joining Idea Village, Stone had access to a team of accountants, lawyers, and advisors who helped her to implement and update her business plan. So far, she says she has paid just $3,000 for professional and consulting services that would have cost her more than $30,000 if she had not purchased them through the incubator. "We have been overwhelmed by what they have done for us," says Stone, who plans to use the incubator's network of contacts to raise $500,000 in capital to finance the company's expansion into other states.[38]

Ticobeans

Layout and Design Considerations

LEARNING OBJECTIVES
5. Describe the criteria used to analyze the layout and design considerations of a building, including the Americans with Disabilities Act.

Once an entrepreneur chooses the best location for the business, the next question deals with designing the proper layout for the building to maximize sales (retail) or productivity (manufacturing or service). **Layout** is the logical arrangement of the physical facilities in a business that contributes to efficient operations, increased productivity, and higher sales. Planning for the most effective and efficient layout in a business environment can produce dramatic improvements in a company's operating effectiveness and efficiency. An attractive, effective layout can help a company's recruiting efforts. One study conducted by the American Association of Interior Designers found that employees rated the look and feel of their workspaces as the third-most-important consideration (after salary and benefits) when deciding whether to accept or to quit a job.[39] The following factors have a significant impact on a building's layout and design.

layout
the logical arrangement of the physical facilities in a business that contributes to efficient operations, increased productivity, and higher sales.

Size A building must be large enough to accommodate a business's daily operations comfortably. If it is too small at the outset of operations, efficiency will suffer. There must be room enough for customers' movement, inventory, displays, storage, work areas, offices, and restrooms. Haphazard layouts undermine employee productivity and create organizational chaos. Too many small business owners start their operations in locations that are already overcrowded and lack the ability to be expanded. The result is that an owner is forced to make a costly move to a new location within the first few years of operation.

Lack of adequate room in the building may limit a company's growth. Most small businesses wait too long before moving into larger quarters, and they fail to plan their new space arrangements properly. To avoid this problem, experts recommend that new business owners plan their space requirements one to two years ahead and update the estimates every six months. When preparing the plan, entrepreneurs should include the expected growth in the number of employees, manufacturing, selling, or storage space requirements and the number and location of branches to be opened.

Construction and External Appearance Is the construction of the building sound? It pays to have an expert look it over before buying or leasing the property. Beyond the soundness of construction, does the building have attractive external and internal appearances? The physical appearance of the building provides customers with their first impression of a business. This is especially true in retail businesses. Many retailers provide the customer with a consistent building appearance as they add new units (e.g., fast food restaurants and motels). Is the building's appearance consistent with the entrepreneur's desired image for the business?

Small retailers must recognize the importance of creating the proper image for their stores and how their shops' layouts and physical facilities influence this image. A store's external appearance contributes significantly to establishing its identity among its target customers. In many ways a building's appearance sets the tone for what the customer can expect in the way of quality and service. The appearance should therefore reflect the business' "personality." Should the building project an exclusive image or an economical one? Is the atmosphere informal and relaxed or formal and business-like? Physical facilities send important messages to customers.

Communicating the right signals through layout and physical facilities is an important step in attracting a steady stream of customers. Retail consultant Paco Underhill advises merchants to "seduce" passersby with their storefronts. "The seduction process should start a minimum of 10 paces away," he says.[40]

Pacific Sunwear

When Pacific Sunwear, a surfing-oriented clothing company, redesigned its mall stores, managers opted for a unique curved entryway designed to remind shoppers of the "curl"—the tunnel that surfers see when they are inside a wave. Looking into the store, shoppers' eyes are drawn straight to the illuminated back wall, where shoes are displayed in a creative design.[41]

A store's window display can be a powerful selling tool if used properly. Often, a store's display window is an afterthought, and many business owners neglect to change their displays often enough. The following tips will help entrepreneurs create window displays that will sell:

- *Keep displays simple.* Simple, uncluttered, and creative arrangements of merchandise draw the most attention and have the greatest impact on potential customers.
- *Keep displays clean and current.* Dusty, dingy displays or designs that are outdated send a negative message to passersby.
- *Change displays frequently.* Customers do not want to see the same merchandise on display every time they enter a store. Experts recommend changing displays at least quarterly, but stores selling trendy items should change their displays twice a month.
- *Get expert help, if necessary.* Not every business owner has a knack for designing window displays. Their best bet is to hire a professional or to work with the design department at a local college or university.

Entrances All entrances to a business should invite customers in. Wide entryways and attractive merchandise displays that are set back from the doorway can draw customers into a business. A store's entrance should catch passing customers' attention and draw them inside. "That's where you want somebody to slam on the brakes and realize they're going someplace new," says retail consultant Paco Underhill.[42] Retailers with heavy traffic flows such as supermarkets or drugstores often install automatic doors to ensure a smooth traffic flow into and out of their stores. Retailers should remove any barriers that interfere with customers' easy access to the storefront. Broken sidewalks, sagging steps, mud puddles, and sticking or heavy doors not only create obstacles that might discourage potential customers, but they also create legal hazards for a business if they cause customers to be injured.

Americans with Disabilities Act (ADA)

a law that requires practically all businesses to make their facilities available to physically challenged customers and employees.

The Americans with Disabilities Act The **Americans with Disabilities Act (ADA)**, passed in July 1990, requires practically all businesses to make their facilities available to physically challenged customers and employees. In addition, the law requires businesses with 15 or more employees to accommodate physically challenged candidates in their hiring practices. Most states have similar laws, many of them more stringent than the ADA, that apply to smaller companies as well. The rules of the these state laws and the ADA's Title III are designed to ensure that mentally and physically challenged customers have equal access to a firm's goods or services. For instance, the act requires business owners to remove architectural and communication barriers when "readily achievable." The ADA allows flexibility in how a business achieves this equal access, however. For example, a restaurant could either provide menus in Braille or could offer to have a staff member read the menu to blind customers. A small dry cleaner might not be able to add a wheelchair ramp to its storefront without incurring significant expense, but the owner could comply with the ADA by offering curbside pickup and delivery services for disabled customers at no extra charge.

Although the law allows a good deal of flexibility in retrofitting existing structures, buildings that were occupied after January 25, 1993, must be designed to comply with all aspects of the law. For example, buildings with three stories or more must have elevators; an access ramp must be in place anywhere the floor level changes by more than one-half inch. In retail stores, checkouts aisles must be wide enough—at least 36 inches—to accommodate wheelchairs. Restaurants must have five percent of their tables accessible to wheelchair-bound patrons.

Complying with the ADA does not necessarily require businesses to spend large amounts of money. The Justice Department estimates that more than 20 percent of the cases customers have filed under Title III involved changes the business owners could have made at no cost, and another 60 percent would have cost less than $1,000.[43] In addition, companies with $1 million or less in annual sales or with 30 or fewer full-time employees that invest in making their locations more accessible to all qualify for a tax credit. The credit is 50 percent of their expenses between $250 and $10,500. Businesses that remove physical, structural, and transportation barriers for disabled employees and customers also qualify for a tax deduction of up to $15,000.

The ADA also prohibits any kind of employment discrimination against anyone with a physical or mental disability. A physically challenged person is considered to be "qualified" if he or she can perform the essential functions of the job. The employer must make "reasonable accommodation" for a physically challenged candidate or employee without causing "undue hardship" to the business.

The Americans with Disabilities Act has affected in a positive way how businesses deal with this segment of its customers and employees. The Department of Justice offers a technical assistance program that provides business owners with free information and technical assistance concerning the ADA. It also has an ADA Hotline that owners can call for information and publications on the ADA (800-514-0301).

Signs One of the lowest-cost and most effective methods of communicating with customers is a business sign. Signs tell potential customers what a business does, where it is, and what it is selling. The United States is a very mobile society, and a well-designed, well-placed sign can be a powerful tool for reaching potential customers.

A sign should be large enough for passersby to read it from a distance, taking into consideration the location and speed of surrounding traffic arteries. To be most effective, the message should be short, simple, and clear. A sign should be legible in both daylight and at night; proper illumination is a must. Contrasting colors and simple typefaces are best. The most common problems with business signs are that they are illegible, poorly designed, improperly located, poorly maintained, and have color schemes that are unattractive or are hard to read.

Before investing in a sign, an entrepreneur should investigate the local community's sign ordinance. In some cities and towns, local regulations impose restrictions on the size, location, height, and construction materials used in business signs.

Building Interiors Like exterior considerations, the functional aspects of building interiors are very important and require careful attention to detail. Designing a functional, efficient interior is not easy. Technology has changed drastically the way employees, customers, and the environment interact with one another, but smart entrepreneurs realize that they can influence the effectiveness of those interactions with well-designed layouts. The result can be a boost to a company's sales and profits. For instance, as their customers have changed, department stores and clothing retailers have modified the layouts of their stores. Because shoppers are busier than ever and want an efficient shopping experience (particularly for men), stores have moved away from the traditional departments (e.g., shoes, cosmetics, men's suits) and are organizing their merchandise by "lifestyle categories" such as sports, women's contemporary, men's business casual, and others.

These displays expose customers to merchandise that they otherwise might have missed and make it easier for them to, say, put together an entire outfit without having to roam from one department to another. Clothing retailer Gap recently began a makeover of its stores that has resulted in customers staying longer and spending more. Because men and women tend to shop differently, redesigned stores feature separate entrances for each. Women's sections are organized into lifestyle sections, and accessories are scattered throughout the store to encourage browsing. Because men prefer to shop more quickly, the men's side feature signage showing how to build the outfits on display, and individual items are neatly displayed and organized by size for efficiency.[44]

ergonomics

the science of adapting work and the work environment to complement employees' strengths and to suit customers' needs.

Piecing together an effective layout is not a haphazard process. **Ergonomics,** the science of adapting work and the work environment to complement employees' strengths and to suit customers' needs, is an integral part of a successful design. For example, chairs, desks, and table heights that allow people to work comfortably can help employees to perform their job faster and more easily. Design experts claim that improved lighting, better acoustics, and proper climate control benefit the company as well as employees. An ergonomically designed workplace can improve workers' productivity significantly and lower days lost due to injuries and accidents. Unfortunately, many businesses fail to incorporate ergonomic design principles into their layouts, and the result is costly. Every year, 1.8 million workers experience injuries related to repetitive motion or overexertion. The most frequent and most expensive workplace injuries are musculoskeletal disorders (MSDs), which cost U.S. businesses $20 billion in workers' compensation claims each year. According to Occupational Safety and Health Administration (OSHA), MSDs account for 34 percent of all lost-work-day injuries and illnesses and one-third of all workers compensation claims.[45] Workers who spend their days staring at computer monitors (a significant and growing proportion of the workforce) often are victims of MSDs.

The most common MSD is carpal tunnel syndrome (CTS), which occurs when repetitive motion causes swelling in the wrist that pinches the nerves in the arm and hand. Studies by the Bureau of Labor Statistics show that more than 42 percent of carpal tunnel syndrome cases require more than 30 days away from work.[46] The good news for employers, however, is that preventing injuries, accidents, and lost days does *not* require spending thousands of dollars on ergonomically correct solutions. Most of the solutions to MSDs are actually quite simple and inexpensive.

Sequins International

Sequins International, a maker of sequined fabrics and trimmings in Woodside, New York, uses adjustable chairs and machinery as well as automatic spooling devices to reducing workers' repetitive motions and taxing physical demands. These simple changes eliminated carpal tunnel syndrome and cut workers compensation costs to just $800, down from $98,000 five years before.[47]

Some solutions are decidedly low tech.

Designer Checks

When Designer Checks, a maker of custom checks based in Anniston, Alabama, consulted with an occupational therapist, owner Grady Burrow learned that one of the best ways to fight MSDs among its computer-dependent workforce is simply for workers to take frequent breaks and to move around. Department heads began scheduling regular exercise breaks designed to stretch employees' necks, shoulders, and hands. Before long, many managers began livening up their exercise breaks with music and dancing. Visitors to Designer Check's plant are likely to see managers and employees take to the production floor for a rousing rendition of the Macarena or the Hokey Pokey.[48]

When planning store, office, or plant layouts, business owners usually focus on minimizing costs. Although staying within a budget is important, minimizing injuries and enhancing employees' productivity with an effective layout should be the overriding issues. Many exhaustive studies have concluded that changes in office design have a direct

Pepper . . . and Salt
THE WALL STREET JOURNAL

From *The Wall Street Journal.
Permission, Cartoon Features
Syndicate.*

*"Clarence here will show you the way
to your new office."*

impact on workers' performance, job satisfaction, and ease of communication. In a reversal of the trend toward open offices separated by nothing more than cubicles, businesses are once again creating private offices in their workspaces. Many businesses embraced open designs, hoping that they would lead to greater interaction among workers. They have discovered, however, that most office workers need privacy and quiet surroundings to be productive. Michael Brill, an office space consultant, studied 11,000 workers to determine the factors that most affect their productivity and found that the ability to do distraction-free work topped the list.[49] Rather than encourage teamwork, open offices leave workers distracted, frustrated, and less productive—just like the characters in the Dilbert cartoon strip. "Open offices do lead to more unstructured communication, but those same offices can lead to problems of [employee] concentration," says Babson College's Tom Davenport, whose research shows that workplace design has a direct impact on white-collar workers' performances and productivity.[50]

Flyswat Inc., a company that develops customized tools and services for Internet browsing, designed the interior of their building to appeal to their 20-something, high-tech workforce. Co-founders John Rodkin, Leo Chang, and Raymond Crouse created a 150-square-foot indoor beach, complete with 3,000 pounds of sand, in their third-floor San Francisco office! Employees can scrunch the sand between their toes while gazing at banana trees, bird of paradise plants, tiki torches, and walls, floors, and ceilings painted to resemble grass and sky. "Why bother?" visitors ask. Because Flyswat employees often spend 60-plus hours a week there, the company founders want to give them a fun, enjoyable place to work. The company buys dinner for its workers four nights a week, maintains a fully stocked kitchen, and offers showers and a laundry room.[51]

**COMPANY
Profile**

Flyswat Inc.

On a more technical level, when evaluating an existing building's interior, an entrepreneur must be sure to determine the integrity of its structural components. Are the building's floors sufficiently strong to hold the business's equipment, inventories, and personnel? Strength is an especially critical factor for manufacturing firms that use heavy equipment. When multiple floors exist, are the upper floors anchored as solidly as the primary floor? Can inventory be moved safely and easily from one area of the plant to another? Is the floor space adequate for safe and efficient movement of goods and people? Consider the cost of maintaining the floors. Hardwood floors may be extremely attractive but require expensive and time-consuming maintenance. Carpeted floors may be extremely attractive in a retail business but may be totally impractical for a quality manufacturing firm. Entrepreneurs must consider the utility, durability, maintenance requirements, attractiveness, and, if important, effectiveness in reducing noise of carpet.

Like floors, walls and ceilings must be both functional and attractive. On the functional side, walls and ceilings should be fireproof and soundproof. Are the colors of walls and ceilings compatible, and do they create an attractive atmosphere for customers and employees? For instance, many high-tech companies use bright, bold colors in their designs because they appeal to their young employees. On the other hand, more-conservative companies such as accounting firms and law offices decorate with more subtle, subdued tones because they convey an image of trustworthiness and honesty. Upscale restaurants that want their patrons to linger over dinner use deep, luxurious tones and soft lighting to create the proper ambiance. Fast food restaurants, on the other hand, use strong, vibrant colors and bright lighting to encourage customers to get in and out quickly, ensuring the fast table turnover they require to be successful. In most cases, ceilings should be done in light colors to reflect the store's lighting.

For many businesses, a drive-through window adds another dimension to the concept of customer convenience and is a relatively inexpensive way to increase sales. Although drive-through windows are staples at fast food restaurants and banks, they can add value for customers in a surprising number of businesses.

Steel Supply Company

When Marshall Hoffman relocated his business, Steel Supply Company, to a building that had been used as a bank, the idea of using the drive-through window intrigued him. Looking for a way to improve customer service, Hoffman transformed the former bank lobby into his showroom floor and began advertising the convenience of buying steel at the drive-through window. Customers place their steel orders by telephone, pull up to the window, pay, and receive a ticket. The order goes by computer to a warehouse Hoffman built on the site. By the time the customer pulls up to the warehouse, the order is waiting. The window has been a hit with customers. Since moving into its new location, Steel Supply's sales have grown from $3.5 million to more than $6 million.[52]

Lighting and Scent Good lighting allows employees to work at maximum efficiency and comfort. Proper lighting is measured by what is ideal for the job being done. Proper lighting in a factory may be quite different from that required in an office or retail shop. Retailers often use creative lighting to attract customers to a specific display. Jewelry stores provide excellent examples of how lighting can be used to display merchandise effectively.

Lighting provides a good return on investment, given its overall impact on a business. Few people seek out businesses that are dimly lit because they convey an image of untrustworthiness. The use of natural light gives a business an open and cheerful look and actually can boost sales. A series of studies by energy research firm Heschong Mahone Group found that stores using natural light experience sales that are 40 percent higher than those of similar stores using fluorescent lighting.[53] In a retail environment, proper lighting should highlight featured products and encourage customers to stop and look at them.

Research shows that scents can have a powerful effect in retail stores. The Sense of Smell Institute reports that the average human being can recognize 10,000 different odors and can recall scents with 65 percent accuracy after one year, a much higher recall rate than visual stimuli produce. In one experiment, when Eric Spangenberg of Washington State University diffused a subtle scent of vanilla into the women's department of a store and rose maroc into the men's department, he discovered that sales nearly doubled; he also discovered that if he switched the scents, sales in both departments fell well below their normal average.[54] Many companies—from casinos to retail stores—are beginning to understand the power of using scent as a marketing tool. Almost every bakery uses a fan to push the smell of fresh-baked breads and sweets into pedestrian traffic lanes, tempting passersby to sample some of their delectable goodies. Appliance retailer H.H. Gregg has discovered that the faint smell of home cooking, such as apple pie or sugar cookies, boosted its in-store sales by 33 percent![55]

Where's My Cubicle?

Recently, Tim Jenkins, Darran Littlefield, and Jim Hodge, co-founders of consulting firm Point B, met with their newest employee. At most companies that would mean an orientation session that included a tour and introductions to the remainder of the staff before showing him to his cubicle. At Point B, however, it involved a lively conversation about the company over a cappuccino at a nearby Starbucks. In fact, Jenkins and Littlefield never have taken a new hire on a tour or showed one to his or her cubicle. That's because they don't have an office!

Despite generating $46 million in annual revenue, Point B has only virtual offices. Former employees of a large consulting firm, Jenkins, Littlefield, and Hodge grew tired of spending half their time in a stuffy office building and the other half on the road or in a client's office. When they launched Point B, they were determined not to force their employees into that same lifestyle. Today Point B has 223 employees working in Seattle, Denver, Phoenix, and Portland. Rather than hop on planes or into rental cars, as most consultants do, Point B employees work only for local clients and spend two to three days a week working from offices in their homes and the remaining time in their clients' offices.

The result is a very lean—and very inexpensive—organization. Unlike most consulting firms, Point B does not incur expensive rental rates or bourgeoning travel expenses, which enables them to offer clients lower prices and employees generous salary and benefit packages.

One key disadvantage of a virtual office, however, is the lack of opportunity to build a meaningful company culture among employees who do not share the same workspace. As efficient as telephone calls and e-mails are, they cannot substitute for face time with colleagues.

Therefore, the founders of Point B hold monthly social gatherings for all of their employees in each of its four markets. In addition, every quarter, employees gather together to review sales prospects and financial forecasts. Regular training sessions on topics ranging from ethics to sales techniques also get employees together, as do informal gatherings, for which the company pays.

Finding the right employees is an important piece of the puzzle for Point B, and Jenkins, Littlefield, and Hodge spend considerable time, energy, and resources to find and recruit candidates who can handle the autonomy and are self-motivated. Only four percent of applicants are hired at Point B, and those who are hired tend to stay. The company's employee turnover rate is just 10 percent, compared to an industry average of 20 percent. The co-founders of Point B enjoy the flexibility that their company's structure (or lack of it) gives them as much as their employees do. "Rather than building our lives around our business, we're building the business around our lives," says Jenkins.

1. What impact—both positive and negative—does a virtual office have on a small company and the people who work for it?
2. Develop a list of recommendations for small companies that use virtual offices or have significant numbers of employees engaged in telecommuting. Be sure to address selection practices, building a company culture, and communicating effectively as well as other relevant topics.
3. Would you want to work for a company such as Point B that has no physical office space? Explain.

Source: Adapted from Darren Dahl, "Office Optional," *Inc.*, December 2005, pp. 42–44.

Layout: Maximizing Revenues, Increasing Efficiency, or Reducing Costs

LEARNING OBJECTIVES
6. Explain the principles of effective layouts for retailers, service businesses, and manufacturers.

The ideal layout for a building depends on the type of business it houses and on the entrepreneur's strategy for gaining a competitive edge. Retailers design their layouts with the goal of maximizing sales revenue; manufacturers see layout as an opportunity to increase efficiency and productivity and to lower costs.

Layout for Retailers

Retail layout is the arrangement of merchandise in a store and its method of display. A retailer's success depends, in part, on a well-designed floor display. Retail expert Paco Underhill says "a store's interior architecture is fundamental to the customers' experience—the stage upon which a retail company functions."[56] A retail layout should pull customers into the store and make it easy for them to locate merchandise, compare price, quality, and features, and ultimately make a purchase. In addition, a floor plan should take customers past displays of other items that they may buy on impulse. Between 65 and 70 percent of all buying decisions are made once a customer enters a store, which means that the right layout can boost sales significantly. One study found that 68 percent of the items bought on major shopping trips (and 54 percent on smaller trips) were impulse purchases. Shoppers in this study were heavily influenced by in-store displays, especially those at the ends of aisles (called end-cap displays).[57]

Retailers have always recognized that some locations within a store are superior to others. Customer traffic patterns give the owner a clue to the best location for the highest-gross-margin items. Merchandise purchased on impulse and convenience goods should be located near the front of the store. Items people shop around for before buying and specialty goods will attract their own customers and should not be placed in prime space. Prime selling space should be restricted to products that carry the highest markups.

Layout in a retail store evolves from a clear understanding of customers' buying habits. If customers come into the store for specific products and have a tendency to walk directly to those items, placing complementary products in their path will boost sales. Observing customer behavior can help the owner to identify the "hot spots" where merchandise sells briskly and "cold spots" where it may sit indefinitely. By experimenting with factors such as traffic flow, lighting, aisle size, music type and audio levels, signs, and colors, an owner can discover the most productive store layout. For instance, one of the hot spots in a Barnes & Noble bookstore during the busy holiday season is the "Christmas table" at the front of the children's department. The table, which holds between 75 and 125 titles, draws lots of traffic, making it the most desired spot for a book aimed at children.[58]

Retailers have three basic layout patterns to choose from: the grid, the free form, and the boutique. The **grid layout** arranges displays in rectangular fashion so that aisles are parallel. It is a formal layout that controls the traffic flow through the store. Supermarkets and discount stores use the grid layout because it is well suited to self-service stores. This layout uses the available selling space most efficiently, creates a neat, organized environment, and facilitates shopping by standardizing the location of items. Figure 14.3 shows a typical grid layout.

Unlike the grid layout, the **free-form layout** is informal, using displays of various shapes and sizes. Its primary advantage is the relaxed, friendly shopping atmosphere it creates, which

grid layout
a formal arrangement of displays arranged in a rectangular fashion so that aisles are parallel.

free-form layout
an informal arrangement of displays of various shapes and sizes.

FIGURE 14.3

The Grid Layout

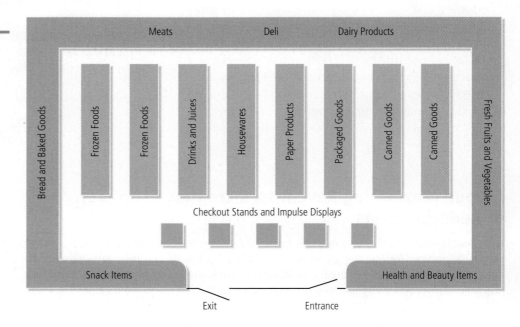

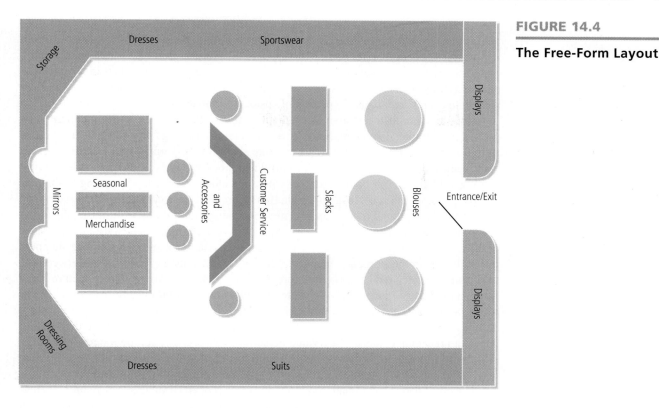

FIGURE 14.4

The Free-Form Layout

encourages customers to shop longer and increases the number of impulse purchases they make. Still, the free-form layout is not as efficient as the grid layout in using selling space, and it can create security problems if not properly planned. Figure 14.4 illustrates a free-form layout.

The **boutique layout** divides the store into a series of individual shopping areas, each with its own theme. It is like building a series of specialty shops into a single store. The boutique layout is more informal and can create a unique shopping environment for customers; small department stores sometimes use this layout (see Figure 14.5).

Whichever layout pattern they use, business owners should display merchandise as attractively as their budgets allow. Customers' eyes focus on displays, which tell them the type of merchandise the business sells. It is easier for customers to relate to one display than to a rack or shelf of merchandise. Open displays of merchandise can surround the focus display, creating an attractive selling area. Spacious aisles provide shoppers an open view of

boutique layout
an arrangement that divides a store into a series of individual shopping areas, each with its own theme.

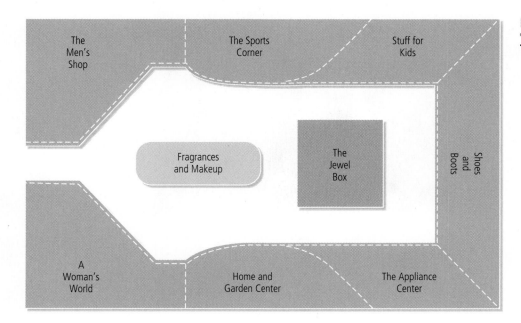

FIGURE 14.5

The Boutique Layout

merchandise and reduce the likelihood of shoplifting. One study found that shoppers, especially women, are reluctant to enter narrow aisles in a store. Narrow aisles force customers to jostle past one another (experts call this the "butt-brush factor"), which makes them extremely nervous. The same study also found that placing shopping baskets in several areas around a store can increase sales. Seventy-five percent of shoppers who pick up a basket buy something, compared to just 34 percent of customers who do not pick up a basket.[59]

Retailers can also boost sales by displaying together items that complement each other. For example, displaying ties near dress shirts or handbags next to shoes often leads to multiple sales. Placement of items on store shelves is important, too, and storeowners must keep their target customers in mind when stocking shelves. For example, putting hearing aid batteries on bottom shelves where the elderly have trouble getting to them or placing popular children's toys on top shelves where little ones cannot reach them can hurt sales. Even background music can be a merchandising tool if the type of music playing in a store matches the demographics of its target customers. Music can be a stimulant to sales because it has been proven to reduce resistance, warps the sense of time, allowing shoppers to stay longer in the store, and helps to produce a positive mental association between the music and the intended image of the store, something experts call audio architecture.[60]

Retailers must remember to separate the selling and nonselling areas of a store. Never waste prime selling space with nonselling functions (storage, office, dressing area, etc.). Although nonselling activities are necessary for a successful retail operation, they should not take precedence and occupy valuable selling space. Many retailers place their nonselling departments in the rear of the building, recognizing the value of each foot of space in a retail store and locating their most profitable items in the best selling areas.

Not every portion of a small store's interior space is of equal value in generating sales revenue. Certain areas contribute more to revenue than others. The value of store space depends on floor location in a multistory building, location with respect to aisles and walkways, and proximity to entrances. Space values decrease as distance from the main entry-level floor increases. Selling areas on the main level contribute a greater portion to sales than those on other floors in the building because they offer greater exposure to customers than either basement or higher-level locations. Therefore, main-level locations carry a greater share of rent than other levels.

Space values also depend on their position relative to the store entrance. Typically, the farther away an area is from the entrance, the lower is its value. Another consideration is that most shoppers turn to the right on entering a store and move around it counterclockwise.

FIGURE 14.6

Space Values for a Small Store

Source: *Retailing*, 6th ed., 1997 Prentice Hall.

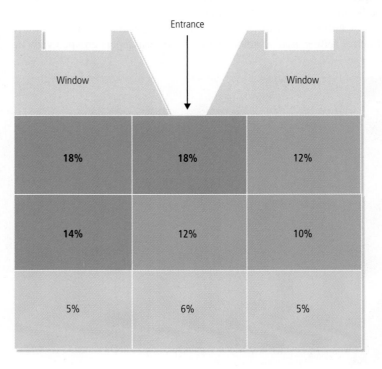

(This apparently is culturally determined; studies of shoppers in Australia and Great Britain find that they turn *left* on entering a store.) Finally, only about one-fourth of a store's customers will go more than halfway into the store. Based on these characteristics, Figure 14.6 illustrates space values for a typical small store.

Understanding the value of store space ensures proper placement of merchandise. The items placed in the high-rent areas of the store should generate adequate sales and contribute enough to profit to justify their high-value locations. The decline in value of store space from front to back of the shop is expressed in the 40-30-20-10 rule. This rule assigns 40 percent of a store's rental cost to the front quarter of the shop, 30 percent to the second quarter, 20 percent to the third quarter, and 10 percent to the final quarter. Similarly, each quarter of the store should contribute the same percentage of sales revenue.

For example, suppose that a small department store anticipates $720,000 in sales this year. Each quarter of the store should generate the following sales volume:

Front quarter	$720,000 × 0.40 = $288,000
Second quarter	$720,000 × 0.30 = $216,000
Third quarter	$720,000 × 0.20 = $144,000
Fourth quarter	$720,000 × 0.10 = $ 72,000
Total	$720,000

Hands on ... How to

Create the Ideal Layout Design

Although their lines of business could not be farther apart, both Dell Computer and Victoria's Secret understand the importance of creating the right layout for their businesses.

Dell Computer and Victoria's Secret couldn't be farther apart in their lines of business; one makes PCs, and the other sells lingerie. One thing both companies have in common, however, is that they recently faced the question of what makes for an effective layout. Dell recently built a new state-of-the-art assembly plant in Winston-Salem, North Carolina, one in which maximizing productivity and efficiency and minimizing costs were essential, given the fiercely competitive industry in which it competes. Victoria's Secret recently remodeled its stores, a move that was designed to boost sales and profits because, like Dell, the company faces tough competition in an industry filled with difficult challenges. What principles did they use in their new designs? Here is a glimpse into how Dell and Victoria's Secret created layouts for a new plant and remodeled stores in ways that have produced positive results for both companies.

Dell Computer

Dell Computer is well known for its core competencies in supply chain management and manufacturing processes. Dell's superior manufacturing efficiency enables the company to sell its made-to-order PCs for 10 to 20 percent less than its rivals. Although no one builds PCs more efficiently than Dell, downward pressure on PC prices has intensified and competition from rivals has escalated, which means that constantly improving efficiency and quality is paramount. At 750,000 square feet, Dell's new factory, called WS1, is twice the size of its Austin, Texas, facility. Based on 10 years of research, the factory is a modern marvel of lean manufacturing, efficiency, and ergonomics, capable of turning out a new PC every five seconds:

- **Heavy lifting.** Rather than allow workers to pack finished PCs into boxes for shipment, robots handle this task. Why? In the past, Dell saw too many of its workers injured by repetitively lifting hefty PCs into boxes. Robots also pluck computer chassis and put them on conveyer belts to minimize human handling.

- **Flexible manufacturing.** At Dell's older plants, assembly lines can produce only one type of computer without being shut down and retooled. WS1 employs a flexible manufacturing system that enables any assembly line to produce *any* of Dell's 40 different computer models one right after another without shutting down for retooling. "Other factories have a process-driven flow," explains designer Richard Komm. "WS1 is focused on one thing: How do we get it to the customer in the shortest amount of time." This one change has slashed Dell's factory downtime by 30 percent.

- **Teamwork.** Rather than have employees working alone at stations to build PCs, WS1 uses a "progressive build" concept in which three workers, each with a specific set of tasks, work in tandem to build a PC. The result: Employees learn their jobs faster, allowing Dell to reduce errors by as much as 30 percent.

- **Speed testing.** Working with each three-person progressive-build team is a tester whose job is to run a set of standard checks on every PC built to make sure that it is wired and assembled properly. If a machine passes this quick testing procedure, it moves on to a more extensive testing procedure farther down the line. If a machine fails the quick test, the employee notifies the team that made it so they can get the job right. "The faster you get feedback to the operator, the fewer the number of defects," explains Komm.

- **Lean inventory.** Every assembly line keeps a small supply of the most frequently used parts so that workers do not have to "run to the supermarket" (a nearby storage area) to build a PC. These storage areas are located in exactly the same place on every assembly line so that workers and supervisors can see in a glance which supplies are running low. Employees who serve as "parts runners" restock supplies frequently so that the lines never have to shut down for lack of parts.

Victoria's Secret

Victoria's Secret is well known for its live supermodel runway show featuring beauties such as Heidi Klum and Tyra Banks, but customers in the company's retail stores weren't getting what they expected. "Traditionally, our stores have had soft, feminine environments, but the ad campaigns were sexier," says Kathleen Baldwin, vice-president of store design. Walking into a Victoria's Secret retail store was more like taking a journey back into the Victorian era rather than embarking on an adventure into sexy, somewhat naughty, lingerie. The company decided that a major remake of its retail stores would boost customer traffic and sales and would encourage customers to linger for longer time periods. The goal was to create a more upscale image for Victoria's Secret in customers' minds. Here are some of the changes the company made:

- **An inviting "landing strip."** Victoria's Secret stores offer shoppers a spacious lobby that serves as a calming respite between the busy mall walkway or sidewalk and the bustling store interior. Although smaller stores don't have the room to offer this decompression zone, they are designed to be less "busy," containing more open space and fewer standing racks. Stores now feature more merchandise displays on the walls, where they will get plenty of notice.

■ *A central hub.* Previously, Victoria's Secret's cosmetics sections adjoined the retail stores but had separate entrances. The new layout places the cosmetics counter in the center of the store to act as a magnet, drawing customers in and inviting them to stay longer.

■ *A classier color scheme.* Victoria's Secret uses pink as its color "brand," but designers learned from the older stores that a little pink goes a long way. Originally designed to give the impression of a fantasy boudoir, the stores were bathed in Pepto-Bismol colors. The new layout features a simpler color scheme of cream and black with splashes of pink here and there to allow the colorful merchandise to pop out as customers browse.

■ *Bring the catalog to life.* Photos of supermodels in Victoria's Secret products now adorn store walls, and strategically placed slim television screens showing footage from past runway shows draw customers into areas of the store that normally are less traveled. Standard mannequins hardly do justice to many of the company's barely-there garments; therefore, designers purchased much more realistic wax-museum-type mannequins to display merchandise.

■ *A menu of choices.* Rather than cram lots of racks onto the showroom floor, creating a maze that shoppers had to navigate, the new layout features displays built directly into the walls of the store. Stocks of high-volume items such as bras and panties get prominent locations, and above them, grids of boxes contain molded plastic torsos that advertise underwear choices "almost like a bra and panty menu" according to Baldwin.

Sources: Adapted from Christopher Null, "Dude, You're Getting a Dell—Every Five Seconds," *Business 2.0*, December 2005, pp. 72–73; Monica Khemsurov, "Sexing up Victoria's Secret," *Business 2.0*, April 2004, pp. 54–55.

Layout for Manufacturers

Manufacturing layout decisions take into consideration the arrangement of departments, workstations, machines, and stock-holding points within a production facility. The general objective is to arrange these elements to ensure a smooth workflow (in a production facility) or a particular traffic pattern (in a service facility or organization).

Manufacturing facilities have come under increasing scrutiny as firms attempt to improve quality, decrease inventories, and increase productivity through facilities that are integrated, flexible, and controlled. Facility layout has a dramatic effect on product mix, product processing, and material handling, storage, and control, as well as production volume and quality.

Factors in Manufacturing Layout The ideal layout for a manufacturing operation depends on a number of factors, including the following:

■ *Type of product.* Product design and quality standards; whether the product is produced for inventory or for order; and the physical properties such as the size of materials and products, special handling requirements, susceptibility to damage, and perishibility.

■ *Type of production process.* Technology used; types of materials handled; means of providing a service; and processing requirements in terms of number of operations involved and amount of interaction between departments and work centers.

■ *Ergonomic considerations.* To ensure worker safety; to avoid unnecessary injuries and accidents; and to increase productivity.

■ *Economic considerations.*

■ *Space availability within the facility itself.*

Types of Manufacturing Layouts. Manufacturing layouts are categorized by either the workflow in a plant or by the production system's function. There are three basic types of layouts that manufacturers can use separately or in combination—product, process, and fixed position—and they are differentiated by their applicability to different conditions of manufacturing volume.

product (line) layout
an arrangement of workers and equipment according to the sequence of operations performed on a product.

PRODUCT LAYOUTS In a **product (line) layout,** a manufacturer arranges workers and equipment according to the sequence of operations performed on the product. Conceptually, the flow is an unbroken line from raw material input or customer arrival to finished goods or customer departure. This type of layout is applicable to rigid-flow, high-volume, continuous process or a mass-production operation, or when the service or product is highly standardized. Automobile assembly plants, paper mills, and oil refineries are examples of product layouts.

Product layouts offer the advantages of lower material handling costs; simplified tasks that can be done with low-cost, lower-skilled labor, reduced amounts of work-in-process inventory, and relatively simplified production control activities. All units are routed along the same fixed path, and scheduling consists primarily of setting a production rate.

Disadvantages of product layouts are their inflexibility, monotony of job tasks, high fixed investment in specialized equipment, and heavy interdependence of all operations. A breakdown in one machine or at one workstation can idle the entire line. This layout also requires business owners to duplicate many pieces of equipment in the manufacturing facility, which for a small firm can be cost-prohibitive.

process layout
an arrangement of workers and equipment according to the general function they perform, without any regard to any particular product or customer.

PROCESS LAYOUTS In a **process layout,** a manufacturer groups workers and equipment according to the general function they perform, without regard to any particular product or customer. Process layouts are appropriate when production runs are short, when demand shows considerable variation and the costs of holding finished goods inventory are high, or when the service or product is customized.

Process layouts have the advantages of being flexible for doing custom work and promoting job satisfaction by offering employees diverse and challenging tasks. Its disadvantages are the higher costs of materials handling, more-skilled labor, lower productivity, and more complex production control. Because the work flow is intermittent, each job must be individually routed through the system, scheduled at the various work centers, and have its status monitored.

fixed-position layout
an arrangement in which materials do not move down a production line but rather, because of their weight, size, or bulk, are assembled on the spot.

FIXED-POSITION LAYOUTS In **fixed-position layouts,** materials do not move down a line as in a production layout but rather, due to the weight, size, or bulk of the final product, are assembled in one spot. In other words, workers and equipment go to the material rather than having the material flow down a line to them. Aircraft assembly plants and shipyards typify this kind of layout.

FUNCTIONAL LAYOUTS Many layouts are designed with more than one objective or function in mind, and therefore combinations of the various layouts are common. For example, a supermarket, though primarily arranged on the basis of marketing, is partly a storage layout; a cafeteria represents a layout not only by marketing function but also by work flow (a food assembly line); and a factory may arrange its machinery in a process layout but perform assembly operations in a fixed sequence, as in a product layout.

Designing Layouts The starting point in layout design is determining how and in what sequence product parts or service tasks flow together. One of the most effective techniques is to create an overall picture of the manufacturing process using assembly charts and process flowcharts. Given the tasks and their sequence, plus knowledge of the volume of products to be produced or of customers to be served, an entrepreneur can analyze space and equipment needs to get an idea of the facility's capacity. When using a product or line layout, these demands take precedent, and manufacturers must arrange equipment and workstations to fit the production tasks and their sequence. With a process or functional layout, different products or customers with different needs place demands on the facility. Rather than having a single best flow, there may be one flow for each product or customer, and compromises in efficiency may be necessary. As a result, the layout for any one product or customer may not result in the achievement of optimal capacity but is flexible to serve the specific situation.

Analyzing Production Layouts Although there is no general procedure for analyzing the numerous interdependent factors that enter into layout design, specific layout problems lend themselves to detailed analysis. Two important criteria for selecting and designing a layout are worker effectiveness and material handling costs. A layout should improve job satisfaction and use workers at the highest skill level for which they are being paid. For instance, just as a machinist leaving his or her work station to secure needed tools is inefficient, so is an engineer spending half a working day delivering blueprints, a task a clerk could perform.

Manufacturers can lower materials handling costs by using layouts designed so that product flow is automated whenever possible and flow distances and times are minimized. The extent of automation depends on the level of technology and amount of capital available, as well as behavioral considerations of employees. Flow distances and times are usually minimized by locating sequential processing activities or interrelated departments in adjacent areas. The following features are important to a lean, efficient manufacturing layout:

1. Planned materials flow pattern
2. Straight-line layout where possible
3. Straight, clearly-marked aisles
4. Backtracking kept to a minimum
5. Related operations located close together
6. Minimum amount of in-process inventory on hand
7. Easy adjustment to changing conditions
8. Minimum materials handling distances
9. Minimum of manual handling of materials and products
10. Ergonomically designed work centers
11. Minimum distances between work stations and processes
12. No unnecessary re-handling of material
13. Minimum handling between operations
14. Minimum storage
15. Materials delivered to production employees just in time
16. Materials efficiently removed from the work area
17. Maximum visibility; maintain clear lines of sight to spot problems and improve safety
18. Orderly materials handling and storage
19. Good housekeeping; minimize clutter
20. Maximum flexibility
21. Maximum communication

Using the principles of lean manufacturing can improve efficiency and lower costs.

After second-generation business owner A.P. Merritt, Jr. studied the "5S" principles (Sort, Shine, Simplify, Standardize, and Sustain) that world-class auto maker Toyota uses in its lean manufacturing process, he became interested in applying the techniques to Merritt Tool, a 65-person company that manufactures parts for the aerospace industry. After studying and mapping the company's existing processes, teams of employees began looking for ways to streamline them to improve efficiency and to minimize waste. As employees throughout the company began to buy into the process, improvements became apparent. The results that Merritt Tool achieved by switching to a lean manufacturing process included a lower accident rate, higher quality, lower costs, faster customer deliveries, shorter setup times, fewer machine breakdowns, and higher employee satisfaction.[61]

Merritt Tool

Chapter Summary by Learning Objectives

1. Explain the stages in the location decision: choosing the region, the state, the city, and the specific site.

The location decision is one of the most important decisions an entrepreneur will make, given its long-term effects on the company. An entrepreneur should look at the choice as a series of increasingly narrow decisions: Which region of the country? Which state? Which city? Which site? Choosing the right location requires an entrepreneur to evaluate potential sites with target customers in mind. Demographic statistics are available from a wide variety of sources, but government agencies such as the Census Bureau have a wealth of detailed data that can guide an entrepreneur in the location decision.

2. Describe the location criteria for retail and service businesses.

For retailers, the location decision is especially crucial. Retailers must consider the size of the trade area, the volume of customer traffic, number of parking spots, availability of room for expansion, and the visibility of a site.

3. Outline the location options for retail and service businesses.

Retail and service businesses have six basic location options: central business districts (CBDs); neighborhoods; shopping centers and malls; near competitors; outlying areas; and at home.

4. Explain the site selection process for manufacturers.

A manufacturer's location decision is strongly influenced by local zoning ordinances. Some areas offer industrial parks designed specifically to attract manufacturers. Two crucial factors for most manufacturers are the reliability (and the cost of transporting) raw materials and the quality and quantity of available labor.

A foreign trade zone is a specially designated area in or near a U.S. customs port of entry that allows resident companies to import materials and components from foreign countries; assemble, process, manufacture, or package them; and then ship the finished product while either reducing or eliminating tariffs and duties.

Empowerment zones offer businesses tax breaks on the investments they make within zone boundaries.

Business incubators are locations that offer flexible, low-cost rental space to their tenants as well as business and consulting services. Their goal is to nurture small companies until they are ready to "graduate" into the business community. Many government agencies and universities offer incubator locations.

5. Describe the criteria used to analyze the layout and design considerations of a building, including the Americans with Disabilities Act.

When evaluating the suitability of a particular building, an entrepreneur should consider several factors: size (is it large enough to accommodate the business with some room for growth?); construction and external appearance (is the building structurally sound and does it create the right impression for the business?); entrances (are they inviting?); legal issues (does the building comply with the Americans with Disabilities Act?; if not, how much will it cost to bring it up to standard?); signs (are they legible, well-located, and easy to see?); interior (does the interior design contribute to our ability to make sales?; is it ergonomically designed?); and lights and fixtures (is the lighting adequate for the tasks workers will be performing?; what is the estimated cost of lighting?).

6. Explain the principles of effective layouts for retailers, service businesses, and manufacturers.

Layout for retail stores and service businesses depends on the owner's understanding of the customers' buying habits. Retailers have three basic layout options from which to choose: grid, free form, and boutique. Some areas of a retail store generate more sales per square foot and therefore are more valuable.

The goal of a manufacturer's layout is to create a smooth, efficient work flow. Three basic options exist: product layout, process layout, and fixed-position layout. Two key considerations are worker productivity and materials handling costs.

Discussion Questions

1. How do most small business owners choose a location? Is this wise?
2. What factors should a manager consider when evaluating a region in which to locate a business? Where are such data available?
3. Outline the factors important when selecting a state in which to locate a business.
4. What factors should a seafood processing plant, a beauty shop, and an exclusive jewelry store con-

sider in choosing a location? List factors for each type of business.

5. What intangible factors might enter into the entrepreneur's location decision?

6. What are zoning laws? How do they affect the location decision?

7. What is the trade area? What determines a small retailer's trade area?

8. Why is it important to discover more than just the number of passersby in a traffic count?

9. What types of information can the entrepreneur collect from Census data?

10. Why may a "cheap location" not be the "best location"?

11. What is a foreign trade zone? An empowerment zone? A business incubator? What advantages and disadvantages does each one of these offer a small business locating there?

12. Why is it costly for a small firm to choose a location that is too small?

13. What function does a small company's sign serve? What are the characteristics of an effective business sign?

14. Explain the Americans with Disabilities Act. Which businesses does it affect? What is its purpose?

15. What is ergonomics? Why should entrepreneurs utilize the principles of ergonomics in the design of their facilities?

16. Explain the statement, "Not every portion of a small store's interior space is of equal value in generating sales revenue." What areas are most valuable?

17. According to market research firm NPD Group, in 1985, women purchased 70 percent of all men's clothing; today, women buy just 34 percent of men's apparel. What implications does this have for modern store layouts?

18. What are some of the key features that are determine a good manufacturing layout?

Business Plan Pro

Analyzing the value of potential business site is critical. A retail or service-based company will ideally want a high-traffic location for optimal exposure. A manufacturing, repair, or storage business, for example, will need to address issues regarding the location's functionality. Selecting the wrong location places the business at a disadvantage before the other challenges of a managing a profitable business come into play. This chapter emphasizes that selecting the right location is critical to a retail venture or any business venture in which customers will benefit from face-to-face contact and the ability to view, touch, try, and ultimately purchase their products. The location also may have logistical characteristics that your business plan may need to address.

Business Plan Exercises
On the Web

The Web offers valuable information regarding location information. One resource mentioned earlier in the marketing chapter of the text is the PRIZM information from Claritas, Inc. (http://www.claritas.com/MyBestSegments). This information identifies the most common market segments in your Zip Code and may be a way to validate whether you location is in proximity to your target markets. PRIZM categorizes U.S. consumer markets based on demographic and customer segmentation profiling research data by Zip Code. A restaurant and retail business, for example, will find that having its location close to its target customers is a critical success factor. Additional information, such as traffic counts and other location attributes, will also be important to include in your business plan.

In the Software

Open your business plan and go to the Your Company section. Here is where you will describe your ideal, potential, or existing location. If you do have a location for your business, you may also want to mention it in your SWOT analysis. If your location possesses some of the positive attributes mentioned in the chapter, identify your location as a strength. If your location has negative characteristics, recognize it as a weakness and have your plan address how you will overcome the challenges your location presents. Your location may be so important to your business that you will also list it under the Keys to Success section. Remember to include the expense for your location—rent, lease, or mortgage payments—into the financial section of your plan.

Building Your Business Plan

Selecting your location is an important strategic business decision for most business ventures. Your business plan can help you to profile, describe, and ultimately decide on the most attractive business location available. Once you have secured a location, your plan can leverage that location's strongest attributes to optimize customer exposure, sales, and profits.

Beyond the Classroom . . .

1. Select a specific type of business you would like to go into one day and use Census data and Commerce Department reports from the World Wide Web or the local library to choose a specific site for the business in the local region. What location factors are critical to the success of this business? Would it be likely to succeed in your hometown?

2. Interview a sample of local small business owners. How did they decide on their particular locations? What are the positive and negative features of their existing locations?

3. Locate the most recent issue of either *Entrepreneur* or *Fortune* describing the "best cities for (small) business." (For *Entrepreneur*, it is usually the October issue, and for *Fortune*, it is normally an issue in November). Which cities are in the top 10? What factors did the magazine use to select these cities? Pick a city and explain what makes it an attractive destination for locating a business there.

4. Select a manufacturing operation, a wholesale business, or a retail store, and evaluate their layouts using the guidelines presented in this chapter. What changes would you recommend? Why? Does the layout contribute to a more effective operation?

5. Choose one of the businesses you studied in Exercise 4 and design an improved layout for the operation. How expensive would these alterations be?

6. Visit the Web site for the Census Bureau at http://www.census.gov/. Go to the Census data for your town and use them to discuss its suitability as a location for the following types of businesses:
   - A new motel with 25 units
   - bookstore
   - An exclusive women's clothing shop
   - A Mexican restaurant
   - A residential plumber
   - A day-care center
   - A high-quality stereo shop
   - A family hair care center

7. Use the resources on the World Wide Web or the local library to prepare a demographic profile of your hometown or city or of the town or city in which you attend college. Using the demographic profile as an analytical tool, what kinds of businesses do you think would be successful there? Unsuccessful? Explain. Use these same resources to prepare an analysis of the competition in the area.

15 | Global Aspects of Entrepreneurship

Learning Objectives

On completion of this chapter, you will be able to:

1 Explain why "going global" has become an integral part of many small companies' strategies.
2 Describe the principal strategies small businesses have for going global.
3 Explain how to build a thriving export program.
4 Discuss the major barriers to international trade and their impact on the global economy.
5 Describe the trade agreements that will have the greatest influence on foreign trade in the twenty-first century—WTO, NAFTA, and CAFTA.

Until recently, the world of international business was much like astronomy before Copernicus, who revolutionized the study of the planets and the stars with his theory of planetary motion. In the sixteenth century, the Copernican system replaced the Ptolemaic system, which held that the earth was the center of the universe with the sun and all the other planets revolving around it. The Copernican system, however, placed the sun at the center of the solar system with all of the planets revolving around it. Astronomy would never be the same.

In the same sense, business owners across the globe have been guilty of having Ptolemaic tunnel vision when it came to viewing international business opportunities. Like their pre-Copernican counterparts, owners saw an economy that revolved around the nations that served as their home bases. Market opportunities stopped at their homeland's borders. Global trade was only for giant corporations who had the money and the management talent to tap foreign markets and enough resources to survive if the venture flopped. This scenario no longer holds true in the twenty-first century.

Today the global marketplace is as much the territory of small upstart companies as it is that of giant multinational corporations. Powerful, affordable technology, the Internet, increased access to information on conducting global business, and the growing interdependence of the world's economies have made it easier for companies of all sizes to engage in international trade.

7DollarStuff.com

When Babson College sophomores Lin Miao and Blake Liguori decided to launch a company that sold posters and inexpensive wall decorations to dorm dwellers like themselves, they decided to go global from the outset. In addition to creating a Web site for their company, 7DollarStuff.com, the partners set up an e-Bay store for added exposure. Targeting young people in the United Kingdom, Miao and Liguori quickly learned a valuable lesson about international business: Product lines must be tailored to suit local customers' tastes and preferences. "Most of our U.S. products were art-related," explains Miao, "but we found that the UK customers are a pop [culture] community. They love music and movies more than U.S. customers." Miao and Liguori adapted the products they sold on their U.K. Web site to suit the movie, music, and pop-culture interests of that target market, and sales climbed quickly. Revenues for their company in its first full year of operation were $150,000.[1]

It is no longer a surprise to entrepreneurs that they face global competition in the marketplace. The new economic world order is the result of the interaction of many dynamic forces. Culture, politics, economics, and the basic social fabric of nations are evolving at unprecedented pace as change is facilitated by technology and challenged by global economic and competitive forces. These changes are redefining the dynamics of the industries on a global scale, forcing companies of all sizes to change the way they compete. As globalization transforms entire industries, even experienced business owners and managers must rethink the rules of competition on which they have relied for years. To thrive, they know they must develop new business models and new sources of competitive advantages. One recent survey by management consulting firm Bain and Company reports that 75 percent of global executives believe that they will have to revamp their core businesses to remain competitive, and 80 percent say that the speed of global business has made maintaining a competitive edge more difficult.[2]

Early-twenty-first century entrepreneurs recognize that the markets of today are small when compared to the market potential of tomorrow. The world market for goods and services continues to expand, fueled by a global economy that welcomes consumers with new wealth. Technology, which continues to become increasingly affordable and powerful, links trading partners, whether they are giant corporations or single individuals, with small businesses everywhere. One industry that is being transformed by wholesale changes in technology and global trends is movie making. Hollywood, California, remains (for now) the hub of movie-making activity, but significant segments of the business are being outsourced—often by small, independent studios—to workers in Canada, the United Kingdom, Australia, New Zealand, India, Malaysia, and others. "Everything in this globalized market is about finding the best place to get this done at lower costs," says Ralph Guggenheim, CEO of Alligator Planet, the small studio that produced the hit animated film *Toy Story* for Pixar in 1995.

When tiny Threshold Entertainment produced the animated film *Foodfight!*, company founder Larry Kasanoff and his colleagues developed, storyboarded, and scripted their idea in Santa Monica, California. When it came time to create the computer-generated animation, however, Threshold outsourced the job to teams of 100 animators in Europe, Australia, South Korea, and Los Angeles. Often, these animators worked on pieces of the film, coordinating their efforts into a finished film with the help of the Internet. "What do we care if [an animator] is in Van Nuys [California] or India?" asks Kasanoff.

Threshold Entertainment

The result of the globalization of the film industry has been higher-quality films produced at lower costs—often by small companies that did not even exist a decade ago. "The next Pixar isn't going to be in Emeryville," says Guggenheim. "It's going to be groups of people around the world linked together on the Web."[3]

The interdependence of nations is highlighted daily as billions of dollars in trade takes place with little or no national interference. In fact, the nationality of many products and the companies that make them have become blurred in the global economy. For instance, although Maytag is considered a U.S. company, most of its washers are made in factories located in Mexico. Similarly, U.S. customers who purchase a Camry from Japanese automaker Toyota are buying a car that was built in Kentucky. The top four makers of personal computers, three of whom are U.S.-based companies, outsource to suppliers 100 percent of the components that go into the PCs they make: Hard-disk drives (Japan, China, Singapore, and the United States), magnesium casings (China), LCD monitors and screens (South Korea, Taiwan, Japan, and China), and memory chips (South Korea, Taiwan, the United States, and Germany). Dell, the number one PC maker, purchases partly built laptop computers from contract manufacturers in the Far East and then completes final assembly in one of its own assembly plants in Ireland, Malaysia, China, or the United States. Finished computers then go to distribution centers in the United States, where they are packaged with other items and then shipped to customers.[4]

Entrepreneurs are discovering that the tools of global business are within their reach and that the benefits of conducting global business can be substantial. In fact, about two-thirds of the world's purchasing power lies outside of the borders of the United States. Randy Tofteland, CEO of SoftBrands, a Minneapolis-based company that sells software to the hospitality and manufacturing industries, is one entrepreneur who is tapping into the purchasing power of global markets. SoftBrands sells its software in 60 countries, and international sales account for nearly half of the company's $70 million in annual sales. "Trade is now seamless and global," says Tofteland, "and those who take advantage of it are going to be the long-term winners."[5]

"Grab some lederhosen, Sutfin. We're about to climb aboard the globalization bandwagon."

Why Go Global?

Failure to cultivate global markets can be a lethal mistake for modern businesses, whatever their size. A few decades ago, small companies needed to concern themselves mainly with competitors who were perhaps six blocks away; today, small companies face fierce competition from companies that may be six *time zones* away. As a result, entrepreneurs find themselves under greater pressure to expand into international markets and to build businesses without borders. It is not uncommon for entrepreneurs to purchase goods from overseas suppliers or to have the components they use in their products made in foreign countries and assembled in another country, and then to sell the finished products to customers in many countries.

Gayle Warwick Linens

Gayle Warwick, a designer of luxury linen sleepwear, home products, and lingerie, lives in London and purchases the organic, long-staple pima cotton that goes into her company's luxury garments in the American Southwest. She has the raw cotton spun and woven in Switzerland, finished in Italy, and embroidered in Vietnam.[6]

As the case of Gayle Warwick demonstrates, operating a successful business increasingly requires entrepreneurs to see their companies as global citizens rather than as companies based in a particular geographic region. For small companies around the world, going global is a matter of survival, not preference. To be successful, small companies must take their place in the world market.

Going global can put tremendous strain on a small company, but entrepreneurs who take the plunge into global business can reap the following benefits:

- *Offset sales declines in the domestic market.* Markets in foreign countries may be booming when those in the United States are sagging. In other words, a small company's export sales act as a counter-cyclical balance against flagging domestic sales.
- *Increase sales and profits.* Two forces are working in tandem to make global business increasingly attractive: income rising to levels at which potential sales are now possible, and the realization that 96 percent of the planet's population lives outside the United States.
- *Extend their products' life cycle.* Some companies have been able to take products that had reached the maturity stage of the product life cycle in the United States and sell them successfully in foreign markets.
- *Lower manufacturing costs.* In industries characterized by high levels of fixed costs, businesses that expand into global markets can lower their manufacturing costs by spreading those fixed costs over a larger number of units.
- *Lower the cost of their products.* Many companies find that purchasing goods or raw materials at the lowest cost requires them to shop the global marketplace.

Ruff Wear Inc.

As Patrick Kruse saw competition escalate for Ruff Wear, his company that makes dog booties and other canine products, he realized that he would have to cut his cost of production to remain competitive. He experimented with a Chinese factory and achieved lower costs for his company's products, but the quality was unacceptable. Kruse found the suppliers he needed in Vietnam, where he discovered companies that already were making products using processes that could be adapted quite easily to produce his line of dog products. Although the prices he pays for the items are somewhat higher than what he paid in China, the quality of the items he receives is much higher.[7]

- *Improve competitive position and enhance reputation.* Going up against some of the toughest competition in the world forces a company to hone its competitive skills.
- *Raise quality levels.* Customers in many global markets are much tougher to satisfy than those in the United States. One reason Japanese products have done so well worldwide is that Japanese companies must build products to satisfy their customers at home, who demand extremely high quality and are sticklers for detail. Businesses that compete in global markets learn very quickly how to boost their quality levels to world-class standards.

■ ***Become more customer-oriented.*** Delving into global markets teaches business owners about the unique tastes, customs, preferences, and habits of customers in many different cultures. Responding to these differences imbues businesses with a degree of sensitivity toward their customers, both domestic and foreign.

Success in a global economy requires being constantly innovative; staying nimble enough to use speed as a competitive weapon; maintaining a high level of quality and constantly improving it; being sensitive to foreign customers' unique requirements; adopting a more respectful attitude toward foreign habits and customs; hiring motivated, multilingual employees; and retaining a desire to learn constantly about global markets. In short, business owners must strive to become "insiders" rather than just "exporters."

As with any new venture, entrepreneurs must prepare for international sales. Before venturing into the global marketplace, entrepreneurs should ask themselves six questions:

1. Is there a profitable market in which our firm has the potential to be successful over the long run?
2. Do we have and are we willing to commit adequate resources of time, people, and capital to a global campaign?
3. Are we considering going global for the right reasons? Are domestic pressures forcing our company to seek global opportunities?
4. Do we understand the cultural differences, history, economics, value systems, opportunities, and risks of conducting business in the country (or countries) we are considering?
5. Is there a viable exit strategy for our company if conditions change or the new venture is not successful?
6. Can we afford *not* to go global?

Becoming a global entrepreneur does require a different mindset. To be successful, entrepreneurs must see their companies from a global perspective and must instill a global culture throughout their companies that permeates everything the business does. To these entrepreneurs and their companies, national boundaries are irrelevant; they see the world as a market opportunity. An absence of global thinking is one of the barriers that most often limit entrepreneurs' ability to move beyond the domestic market. Indeed, learning to *think globally* may be the first—and most challenging—obstacle an entrepreneur must overcome on the way to creating a truly global business. Global thinking is the ability to appreciate, understand, and respect the different beliefs, values, behavior, and business practices of companies and people in different cultures and countries. This requires entrepreneurs to do their homework to learn about the people, places, business techniques, potential customers, and culture of the countries in which they intend to do business. Several U.S. government agencies, including the Department of Commerce, offer vast amounts of information about all nations, including economic data that can be useful to entrepreneurs searching for market opportunities. Doing business globally presents extraordinary opportunities only to those who are prepared.

Build a Successful Global Company

When Mia Abbruzzese worked for athletic global shoemakers New Balance, Fila Sports, and Stride Rite, she became accustomed to traveling to Asia to visit the factories that turned out shoes. For 10 years, she traveled in business class and rode in limousines. Then she launched her own shoe company, Morgan & Milo, and although many of her destinations were the same, her style of travel changed dramatically. Now she buys coach airfare tickets on Orbitz and takes public buses and taxis to reach the Asian factories that make the line of children's shoes her company sells.

Abbruzzese used her experience at some of the world's largest shoe companies to realize her dream of owning her own international shoe business. With just three executives working from three different locations, an office loft in Boston that serves loosely as company headquarters, and connections to a Chinese shoe factory, Abbruzzese operates her small company on a global scale. Morgan & Milo creates children's shoe designs, has them manufactured to specifications in China, and sells them to retailers in the United States and Europe. Following are some of the lessons she has learned about operating a global small business.

Hit 'Em Where They Ain't

When asked about the secret to his batting titles, Hall of Fame baseball player Wee Willy Keeler, known as baseball's greatest place hitter, answered, "I hit 'em where they ain't." Abbruzzese took the same approach when building her international shoe company. She chose a niche—children's shoes—that she knew was being underserved by the major players in the shoe industry. "It's a great market no one is paying attention to," she says. Abbruzzese learned the benefits of pursuing "undiscovered" markets when she was at New Balance working on the walking shoe product line, which became the company's third biggest line. "I loved being in an overlooked category because people left you alone," she says.

Success in International Markets Depends on a Network of Connections

Because she had launched several shoe lines during her days in corporate America, Abbruzzese knew that success in the shoe business requires an extensive network of connections in all corners of the globe. Using her industry contacts, Abbruzzese found a Taiwanese investor who provided $595,000 in start-up capital for Morgan & Milo as well as enough working capital to cover the company's operating expenses until cash flow turns positive. The investor also introduced Abbruzzese to the owner of the factory in southern China that makes many of the shoes that Morgan & Milo designs. Two other contacts Abbruzzese relies on are industry veterans who have an extensive network of contacts in the shoe industry that have proved to be extremely valuable to her young company.

Rob Moyer, manager of outsourcing and development for Morgan & Milo, spends time in the Chinese factories that manufacture shoes for the company, making sure that they meet quality specifications and dealing with problems as they arise. Moyer also led Abbruzzese to Alan Paulenoff, another shoe industry veteran, who became Morgan and Milo's manager of sales and distribution. Paulenoff proved to be a major asset to Morgan and Milo because he had long-time relationships with key buyers at 40 retailers that sold children's shoes, including Macy's, Nordstrom, Rack Room, and others.

Organize for Speed

When she worked for the major shoe companies, Abbruzzese could not help but notice that the time it took from designing a shoe to getting it into retailer's stores was quite lengthy. One of the key competitive advantages of her small, faster, and more nimble company is *speed*. Morgan and Milo can go from shoe design to a finished product in just three or four months, compared to at least six months for a big shoe company, and retailers appreciate that. Manufacturing shoes in China and getting them into retail stores quickly, however, requires careful coordination across international borders, something that Morgan & Milo's organization is designed to do.

Invest in Technology

Operating a global company efficiently requires an investment in technology, and Abbruzzese has made that investment both in basics such as cell phones and e-mail and in sophisticated systems that track inventory, orders, and shipping schedules anywhere the world. With their investment in technology (which the company constantly updates), Abbruzzese and her team can track results and communicate with manufacturers in China or customers in Europe.

Look Bigger Than You Are

To build a successful global company, Abbruzzese understands that Morgan & Milo has to look bigger than it actually is. One way to accomplish that is to build a successful brand. "I couldn't just create shoes," she says. "I had to position them and create a story and feeling behind them." The logo and the polished, professional sales literature that Abbruzzese designed for Morgan & Milo go a long way toward creating the image of a big, successful company. "When competing in a global marketplace of shoe giants, you have to do all of the things that people don't expect from [a small company] operating out of a 1,000-square-foot office," she says.

Source: Adapted from Allessandra Bianchi, "Small & Global: The World As a Factory," *FSB*, June 2004, pp. 40–42.

FIGURE 15.1

Nine Strategies for Going Global

Strategies for Going Global

Small companies pursuing a global presence have nine principal strategies from which to choose: creating a presence on the Web, relying on trade intermediaries, outsourcing production, establishing joint ventures, engaging in foreign licensing arrangements, franchising, using counter-trading and bartering, exporting products or services, and establishing international locations (see Figure 15.1).

LEARNING OBJECTIVES
2. Describe the principal strategies small businesses have for going global.

Creating a Presence on the Web

Perhaps in our technology-rich global environment, the fastest, least expensive, and lowest-cost strategic option to creating a global business presence is creating a Web site. As you saw in Chapter 9 on e-commerce, the Web gives even the smallest businesses the ability to sell its goods and services all over the globe. By establishing a presence online, a local candy maker or a home-based luxury boat broker gains immediate access to customers around the world. With a well-designed Web site, an entrepreneur can extend its reach to customers anywhere in the world—and without breaking the budget. A company's Web site is available to anyone anywhere in the world and provides exposure 24 hours a day to its products or services seven days a week. For many small companies, the Web has become a tool that is as essential to doing business as the telephone and the fax machine.

Establishing a presence on the Web has become an important part of a company's strategy for reaching customers outside the United States. A study by Internet World Stats estimates the number of World Wide Web users to be 1.02 billion worldwide. Approximately 227 million of them live in the United States, leaving 795 million potential Web customers outside this country's borders.[8] Figure 15.2 shows global Internet usage by world region. eBay, another popular online channel for entrepreneurs, provides access to international shoppers; 49 percent of all registered eBay users live outside the United States.[9]

Before the advent of the Internet, small businesses usually took incremental steps toward becoming global businesses. They began selling locally, and then, after establishing a reputation, expanded regionally and perhaps nationally. Only after establishing themselves domestically did small businesses begin to think about selling their products or services internationally. The Web makes that business model obsolete because it provides small companies with a low-cost global distribution channel that they can utilize from the day they are launched.

That's the route that John Buckman took when he launched a company to sell the electronic music his wife, Jan Hanford, composed and recorded after her recording company lost interest in marketing her music. Although Buckman was an experienced entrepreneur (he was the founder of Lyris, an e-mail list-management company that generates $12 million in annual sales), he never had run a global business. However, both he and Hanford knew that the best markets for the electronic music his wife created and performed were not in

Magnatune.com

FIGURE 15.2

Internet Users by World Region

Source: Internet World Stats: Usage and Population Statistics, http://internetworldstats.com/stats.htm.

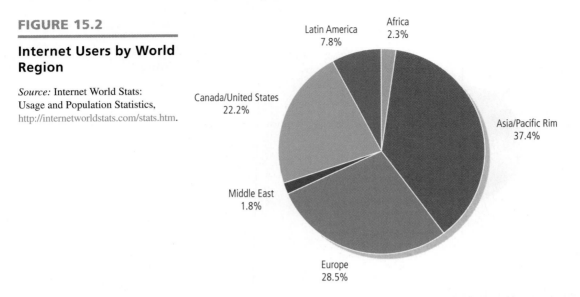

- Latin America 7.8%
- Africa 2.3%
- Canada/United States 22.2%
- Asia/Pacific Rim 37.4%
- Middle East 1.8%
- Europe 28.5%

the United States but in countries such as Israel, Singapore, and Mexico. The couple decided to launch Magnatune.com as a global online record label. Investing $1 million of their own money, Buckman and Hanford began building a Web site, making sure that its design did not look "too American" and appealed to the customers in the countries they were targeting. Buckman made sure that all prices appeared in local currencies and the site's content interfaced seamlessly with Google's translation service. After six months, the site was ready to go, and Buckman contacted 200 other electronic music artists about selling their songs on the Magnatune Web site. Twenty of them signed on, and before long, the site was getting lots of buzz among fans in music blogs and Webzines. Today, Magnatune has a global customer base of more than 10,000 people, about half of them from Europe, who purchase songs from more than 185 artists, including his wife, from around the world. Not only did Buckman recoup his $1 million investment in three years, but also Hanford sold more albums through Magnatune in six months than she had in the eight years with her previous record label.[10]

Ethics and Entrepreneurship

Counterfeit Goods on eBay: Whose Responsibility Are They?

Many U.S.-based companies engaged in international business face a threat from counterfeit goods produced by illicit manufacturers, many of which operate in foreign lands. Counterfeit goods seized in raids have ranged from helicopter components and DVDs to auto parts and birth control pills. (It is not uncommon for counterfeit DVDs of popular movies to be on sale in the streets in some foreign countries even before the genuine film hits the theaters.) Although the sale of phony goods has been taking place since long before the Internet, the Web has expanded the reach of counterfeit manufacturers and sellers. In fact, one site that constantly battles the sale of counterfeit designer and brand name goods is eBay, the global trading place, which has more than 150 million registered users.

The problem is so prevalent that many makers of designer and brand name merchandise have hired companies such as GenuOne, which uses proprietary software to scan eBay's Web site constantly, looking for items that are fake and violate trademark rights. GenuOne reports that it turns over some 10,000 trademark-infringing sales from eBay each month to its clients. Suspecting that eBay sellers were listing phony knockoffs of its jewelry for sale, upscale jeweler Tiffany secretly purchased several hundred items on eBay auctions from sellers all across the globe. Tiffany discovered that three of four items purchased were counterfeit! As a result, Tiffany filed a lawsuit against eBay, claiming that the e-commerce giant is facilitating the sale of counterfeit products on its site. The suit contends, in part, that "eBay charges hundreds of thousands of dollars in fees" for the sale of counterfeit goods and profits from fraudulent activity that is taking place on its site. The suit also claims that by facilitating the sale of fraudulent goods on its site, eBay is diminishing the value of the genuine items that Tiffany's produces and markets.

In an effort to combat fraudulent sales, eBay points to the "takedown notices" that it posts on its auction site. Once a manufacturer or retailer such as Tiffany notifies eBay that an item in one of its auctions is counterfeit, eBay removes the item from the auction and posts a takedown notice. These takedown notices were the result of an earlier lawsuit, *Hendrikson vs. eBay* (2001 U.S. Dist. LEXIS 14420), which eBay won when a court ruled that eBay was protected from copyright infringement claims by the Digital Millennium Copyright Act as long as the company removed the copyright-protected merchandise from its site once the authorized copyright holder notified eBay of the unauthorized merchandise. The ruling meant that eBay did not have to scour the millions of auctions that take place on its site to find counterfeit goods; that duty falls on the shoulders of the companies that make and sell the genuine items. Tiffany says that it has notified eBay of more than 19,000 bogus Tiffany items in its auctions, which eBay has taken down. "We are a marketplace," says eBay spokesperson Hani Durzi. "We are not a retailer; we don't own any of these products; we don't take possession of them. We can work with trademark owners to give them easy and efficient ways to alert [us] of specific sales, but there's no way we are to know that something violates trademark or intellectual property rights unless we are informed by the rights owner."

The latest lawsuit over the sale of counterfeit goods on eBay takes a different approach, claiming that eBay is guilty of trademark infringement (rather than copyright infringement as the earlier suit claimed), which is not covered by the Digital Millennium Copyright Act. The outcome of the case is significant. If eBay is found liable for trademark infringement, other manufacturers and retailers whose goods are counterfeited and sold on eBay also will file lawsuits. Laws in some foreign countries provide trademark holders with even greater protection than those in the United States; therefore, foreign companies will be watching the outcome of this case. If eBay loses the lawsuit, the ramifications could spell trouble for its business model.

1. Is it reasonable to expect eBay and other online auction sites to be responsible for its sellers' actions? Explain.
2. Should eBay be held responsible for verifying the authenticity of every item listed on its auction site? Explain.
3. Use the Internet to research the merits of the case against eBay, and then assume the role of the judge in the case. How would you rule? Explain your reasoning.

Sources: Adapted from Frank Fortunato, "eBay Knockoffs and Tiffany," *E-commerce Guide*, March 7, 2006, www.ecommerce-guide.com/article.php/3589751.

Trade Intermediaries

Another alternative for lower-cost and lower-risk entry into international markets is to use a trade intermediary. **Trade intermediaries** are domestic agencies that serve as distributors in foreign countries for domestic companies of all sizes. They rely on their networks of contacts, their extensive knowledge of local customs and markets, and their experience in international trade to market products effectively and efficiently all across the globe. These trade intermediaries serve as the export departments for small businesses, enabling the small companies to focus on what they do best and delegate

trade intermediaries
domestic agencies that serve as distributors in foreign countries for domestic companies of all sizes.

the responsibility for coordinating foreign sales efforts to the intermediaries. Although a broad array of trade intermediaries is available, the following are ideally suited for small businesses.

export management companies (EMCs)

merchant intermediaries that provide small businesses with a low-cost, efficient, off-site international marketing department.

Export Management Companies **Export management companies (EMCs)** are an important channel of foreign distribution for small companies just getting started in international trade or for those lacking the resources to assign their own people to foreign markets. Most EMCs are merchant intermediaries, working on a buy-and-sell arrangement with domestic small companies, taking title to the goods and then reselling them in foreign markets. They provide small businesses with a low-cost, efficient, independent international marketing and export department, offering services ranging from doing market research and giving advice on patent protection to arranging financing and handling shipping. More than 1,000 EMCs operate across the United States, and many of them specialize in particular industries, products, or product lines as well as in the foreign countries they target.

Johnson Level and Tool

William Johnson's Mequon, Wisconsin–based tool company, Johnson Level and Tool, already was selling its tools in four foreign markets when a representative from M&P Export Management, an export management company, approached him about representing Johnson's company in other foreign markets where this EMC had a presence. With the EMC's help, Johnson Level and Tool now sells its products in 40 international markets. After working with the EMC, company managers gained more experience in conducting international business and capitalized on other global opportunities. The company now has two manufacturing joint ventures with similar companies in Canada and Mexico.[11]

The greatest benefits EMCs offer small companies are ready access to global markets and an extensive knowledge base on foreign trade, both of which are vital for entrepreneurs who are inexperienced in conducting global business. In return for their services, EMCs usually earn an extra discount on the goods they buy from their clients or, if they operate on a commission rate, a higher commission than domestic distributors earn on what they sell. EMCs charge commission rates of about 10 percent on consumer goods and 15 percent on industrial products. Although EMCs rarely advertise their services, finding one is not difficult. The Federation of International Trade Associations (FITA) provides useful information for small companies about global business and trade intermediaries on its Web site (http://www.fita.org/emc.html), including a *Directory Export Management Companies*. Industry trade associations and publications and the U.S. Department of Commerce's Export Assistance Centers* also can help entrepreneurs to locate EMCs and other trade intermediaries.

export trading companies (ETCs)

businesses that buy and sell products in a number of countries and offer a wide variety of services to their clients.

Export Trading Companies Another tactic for getting into international markets with a minimum of cost and effort is through export trading companies. **Export trading companies (ETCs)** are businesses that buy and sell products in a number of countries, and they typically offer a wide range of services such as exporting, importing, shipping, storing, distributing, and others to their clients. Unlike EMCs, which tend to focus on exporting, ETCs usually perform both import and export trades across many countries' borders. Although EMCs usually create exclusive contracts with companies for a particular product line, ETCs often represent several companies selling the same product line. However, like EMCs, ETCs lower the risk of exporting for small businesses. Some of the largest ETCs in the world are based in the United States and Japan. In fact, many businesses that have navigated successfully Japan's complex system of distribution have done so with the help of ETCs.

*A searchable list of the Export Assistance Centers is available at the Export.gov Web site http://www.export.gov/comm_svc/eac.html.

The first rule of exporting: Realize that even the smallest companies and least experienced entrepreneurs have the potential to export.

In 1982, Congress passed the Export Trading Company Act to allow producers of similar products to form ETC cooperatives without the fear of violating antitrust laws. The goal was to encourage U.S. companies to export more goods by allowing businesses in the same industry to band together to form ETCs.

Manufacturer's Export Agents **Manufacturer's export agents (MEAs)** act as international sales representatives in a limited number of markets for various noncompeting domestic companies. Unlike the close, partnering relationship formed with most EMCs, the relationship between the MEA and a small company is a short-term one, and the MEA typically operates on a commission basis.

Export Merchants **Export merchants** are domestic wholesalers who do business in foreign markets. They buy goods from many domestic manufacturers and then market them in foreign markets. Unlike MEAs, export merchants often carry competing lines, which means they have little loyalty to suppliers. Most export merchants specialize in particular industries, such as office equipment, computers, industrial supplies, and others.

Resident Buying Offices Another approach to exporting is to sell to a **resident buying office,** a government-owned or privately owned operation of one country established in another country for the purpose of buying goods made there. Many foreign governments and businesses have set up buying offices in the United States. Selling to them is just like selling to domestic customers because the buying office handles all the details of exporting.

manufacturer's export agents (MEAs)
businesses that act as international sales representatives in a limited number of markets for noncompeting domestic companies.

export merchants
domestic wholesalers who do business in foreign markets.

resident buying offices
government-owned or privately owned operations of one country established in another country for the purpose of buying goods made there.

Foreign Distributors Some small businesses work through foreign distributors to reach international markets. Domestic small companies export their products to these distributors, who handle all of the marketing, distribution, and service functions in the foreign country.

In 1989, when Bill Weiller bought Purafil, a company that makes air filters, the business was on the verge of bankruptcy. "The [company] wasn't taking advantage of its international potential," says Weiller, who managed a European chemical operation before buying Purafil. Weiller quickly modernized the technology behind Purafil's air filtration products and expanded the product line into a broad range of industries. Today, Purafil provides more than 20,000 customized air filter installations around the world, including the Sistine Chapel in Rome and the Israel Museum, where the Dead Sea Scrolls are kept. Because the company is small (just 75 employees), Weiller did not have the budget to create a global sales force of his own. Instead, he sells internationally using a network of 140 foreign distributors. "Using sales reps who know the territory and culture helps us to be user-friendly and keep the local competitors out of the business," says David Nicholas, the company's chief operating officer.[12]

The Value of Using Trade Intermediaries Trade intermediaries such as these are becoming increasingly popular among businesses attempting to branch out into world markets because they make that transition much faster and easier. Most small business owners simply do not have the knowledge, resources, or confidence to go global alone. Intermediaries' global networks of buyers and sellers allow their small business customers to build their international sales much faster and with fewer hassles and mistakes. Entrepreneurs who are inexperienced in global sales and attempt to crack certain foreign markets quickly discover just how difficult the challenge can be. However, with their know-how, experience, and contacts, trade intermediaries can get small companies' products into foreign markets quickly and efficiently. The primary disadvantage of using trade intermediaries is that doing so requires entrepreneurs to surrender control over their foreign sales. Maintaining close contact with intermediaries and evaluating their performance regularly help to avoid major problems, however.

The key to establishing a successful relationship with a trade intermediary is conducting a thorough screening to determine which type of intermediary—and which one in particular—will best serve a small company's needs. Entrepreneurs should look for intermediaries that specialize in the products their companies sell and that have experience and established contacts in the countries they have targeted. An entrepreneur looking for an intermediary should compile a list of potential candidates using some of the sources listed in Table 15.1. After compiling a list of potential intermediaries, entrepreneurs should evaluate each one using the list of criteria to narrow the field to the most promising ones. Interviewing a principal from each intermediary on the final list should tell entrepreneurs which ones are best able to meet their companies' needs. Finally, before signing any agreement with a trade intermediary, it is wise to conduct thorough background and credit checks. Entrepreneurs with experience in global trade also suggest entering short-term agreements of about a year with new trade intermediaries to allow time to test their ability and willingness to live up to their promises. Many entrepreneurs begin their global business initiatives with trade intermediaries and then venture into international business on their own as their skill and comfort levels increase.

TABLE 15.1 Resources for Locating a Trade Intermediary

Trade intermediaries make doing business around the world much easier for small companies, but finding the right one can be a challenge. Fortunately, several government agencies offer a wealth of information to businesses interested in reaching into global markets with the help of trade intermediaries. Entrepreneurs looking for help in breaking into global markets should contact the International Trade Administration, the U.S. Commerce Department, and the Small Business Administration first to take advantage of the following services:

■ *Agent/Distributor Service (ADS).* Provides customized searches to locate interested and qualified foreign distributors for a product or service. (Search cost, $250 per country)

■ *Commercial Service International Contacts (CSIC) List.* Provides contact and product information for more than 82,000 foreign agents, distributors, and importers interested in doing business with U.S. companies.

■ *Country Directories of International Contacts (CDIC) List.* Provides the same kind of information as the CSIC List but is organized by country.

■ *Industry Sector Analyses (ISAs).* Offer in-depth reports on industries in foreign countries, including information on distribution practices, end-users, and top sales prospects.

■ *International Market Insights (IMIs).* Include reports on specific foreign market conditions, upcoming opportunities for U.S. companies, trade contacts, trade show schedules, and other information.

■ *Trade Opportunity Program (TOP).* Provides up-to-the-minute, prescreened sales leads around the world for U.S. businesses, including joint venture and licensing partners, direct sales leads, and representation offers.

■ *International Company Profiles (ICPs).* Commercial specialists investigate potential partners, agents, distributors, or customers for U.S. companies and issue profiles on them.

■ *Commercial News USA.* A government-published magazine that promotes U.S. companies' products and services to 259,000 business readers in 152 countries at a fraction of the cost of commercial advertising. Small companies can use *Commercial News USA* to reach new customers around the world for as little as $395.

■ *Gold Key Service.* For a small fee, business owners wanting to target a specific country can use the Department of Commerce's Gold Key Service, in which experienced trade professionals arrange meetings with prescreened contacts whose interests match theirs.

■ *Matchmaker Trade Delegations Program.* Helps small U.S. companies establish business relationships in major markets abroad by introducing them to the right contacts.

■ *Multi-State/Catalog Exhibition Program.* Working with state economic development offices, the Department of Commerce presents companies' product and sales literature to hundreds of interested business prospects in foreign countries.

■ *International Fair Certification Program.* Promotes U.S. companies' participation in foreign trade shows that represent the best marketing opportunities for them.

■ *National Trade Data Bank (NTDB).* Most of the information just listed is available from the NTDB, the U.S. government's most comprehensive database of world trade data. With the NTDB, small companies have access to information that only *Fortune* 500 companies could afford.

■ *Economic Bulletin Board (EBB).* Provides online trade leads and valuable market research on foreign countries compiled from a variety of federal agencies.

■ *U.S. Export Assistance Centers.* The Department of Commerce has established 19 export centers (SEACs) around the country to serve as one-stop shops for entrepreneurs needing export help (http://www.sba.gov/oit/export/useac.html).

■ *Trade Information Center.* Helps to locate federal export assistance, provides export assistance, and offers a 24-hour automated fax retrieval system that gives entrepreneurs free information on export promotion programs, regional market information, and international trade agreements. Call USA-TRADE.

■ *Office of International Trade.* The Small Business Administration provides a variety of export development assistance, how-to publications, and information on foreign markets.

■ *Export Hotline.* Provides no-cost trade information on more than 50 industries in 80 countries. Call (800) 872-9767.

■ *Export Opportunity Hotline.* Trade specialists have access to online databases and reports from government and private agencies concerning foreign markets. Call (202) 628-8389.

You
Be the Consultant

Where Do We Start?

Specialty Building Supplies is a small company with $6.4 million in annual sales that manufactures and sells a line of building supply products such as foundation vents, innovative insulation materials, and fireplace blowers to building supply stores in the northeastern United States. The eight-year-old company, founded by Tad Meyers, has won several awards for its unique and innovative products and has earned a solid reputation among its supply store customers and the builders and homeowners who ultimately buy its products. Before launching the company, Meyers had been a home builder. As he watched the price of home heating fuels climb dramatically over time, Meyers began to incorporate into the houses he built simple, inexpensive ways to help homeowners save energy. He began tinkering with existing products, looking for ways to improve them. The first product he designed (and the product that ultimately led him to launch Specialty Building Supplies) was an automatic foundation vent that was thermostatically controlled (no electricity needed). The vent would automatically open and close based on the outside temperature, keeping cold drafts from blowing under a house. Simple and inexpensive in its design, the Autovent was a big hit in newly constructed homes in the Northeast because it not only saved energy, but it also avoided a major headache for homeowners in cold climates: water pipes that would freeze and burst. Before long, Meyers stopped building houses and focused on selling the Autovent. Its success prompted him to add other products to the company's line.

Specialty's sales have been lackluster for more than a year now, primarily due to a slump in new home construction in its primary market. Tad Meyers recently met with the company's top marketing managers and sales-

people to talk about their options for getting Specialty's sales and profit growth back on track. "What about selling our products in international markets?" asked Dee Rada, the company's marketing manager. "I read an article just last week about small companies doing good business in other countries, and many of them were smaller than we are."

"Interesting idea," Meyers said, pondering the concept. "I've never really thought about selling anything overseas. In fact, other than my years in the military, I've never traveled overseas and don't know anything about doing business there."

"It's a big world out there. Where should we sell our products?" said Hal Milam, Specialty's sales manager. "How do we find out what the building codes are in foreign countries?" Would we have to modify our designs to meet foreign standards?"

"I don't know," shrugged Meyers. "Those are some good questions. . . ."

"How would we distribute our products?" asked Rada. "We have an established network of distributors here in the U.S., but how do we find foreign distributors?"

"I wonder if exporting is our only option," said Meyers. "There must be other ways to get into the global market besides exporting. What do you think? Where do we start?"

1. What advice would you offer Meyers and the other managers at Specialty Building Supplies about their prospects of "going global"?
2. How would you suggest these managers go about finding the answers to the questions they have posed? What other questions would you advise them to answer?
3. Outline the steps these managers should take to assemble an international marketing plan.

domestic joint venture
an alliance of two or more U.S. small companies for the purpose of exporting their goods and services abroad.

Joint Ventures

Joint ventures, both domestic and foreign, lower the risk of entering global markets for small businesses. They also give small companies more clout in foreign lands. In a **domestic joint venture,** two or more U.S. small businesses form an alliance for the purpose of exporting their goods and services. For export ventures, participating companies get antitrust immunity, allowing them to cooperate freely. The businesses share the responsibility and the costs of getting export licenses and permits, and they split the venture's profits. Establishing a joint venture with the right partner has become an essential part of maintaining a competitive position in global markets for a growing number of industries.

In a **foreign joint venture,** a domestic small business forms an alliance with a company in the target nation. The host partner brings to the joint venture valuable knowledge of the local market and its method of operation as well as of the customs and the tastes of local customers, making it much easier to conduct business in the foreign country. Sometimes foreign countries place certain limitations on joint ventures. Some nations require host companies to own at least 51 percent of the venture.

When Tony Raimondo took over as CEO of Behlen Manufacturing Company in a management buyout in 1984, one component of his strategy for turning around the promising but troubled company was to take the company's agricultural hardware products (grain bins, drying systems, and buildings) into new markets, including foreign markets. Throughout the 1980s and 1990s, Behlen, an employee-owned company, was exporting its products to a growing number of countries, including China. However, when he saw the company's sales in China diminished by companies selling knockoff copycat products, Raimondo decided to suspend exports there. Recognizing the potential for Behlen's products in China, Raimondo pursued a different global strategy: He established a joint venture with a company in Beijing to manufacture and sell Behlen's products in China. "For us to sustain market share [in China], we had to be on the inside," Raimondo says. Behlen now generates $10 million in foreign sales, about 10 percent of the company's annual revenue.[13]

foreign joint venture
an alliance between a U.S. small business and a company in the target nation.

Behlen Manufacturing Company

The most important ingredient in the recipe for a successful joint venture is choosing the right partner. A productive joint venture is much like a marriage, requiring commitment, communication, and understanding. In addition to picking the right partners, another key to creating a successful alliance is to establish common objectives. Defining *exactly* what each party in the joint venture hopes to accomplish at the outset will minimize the opportunity for misunderstandings and disagreements later. One important objective should be to use the joint venture as a learning experience, which requires a long-term view of the business relationship.

Often joint ventures fail because entrepreneurs failed to take the following steps:

■ Define at the outset important issues such as each party's contributions and responsibilities, the distribution of earnings, the expected life of the relationship, and the circumstances under which the parties can terminate the relationship.
■ Understand their partner's reasons and objectives for joining the venture.
■ Select a partner that shares their company's values and standards of conduct.
■ Spell out in writing exactly how the venture will work and where decision-making authority lies.
■ Select a partner whose skills are different from but compatible with those of their own company's.
■ Prepare a "prenuptial agreement" that spells out what will happen in case of a business "divorce."

Foreign Licensing

Rather than sell their products or services directly to customers overseas, some small companies enter foreign markets by licensing businesses in other nations to use their patents, trademarks, copyrights, technology, processes, or products. In return for licensing these assets, a small company collects royalties from the sales of its foreign licenses. Licensing is a relatively simple way for even the most inexperienced business owner to extend his or her reach into global markets. Licensing is ideal for companies whose value lies in its intellectual property, unique products or services, recognized name, or proprietary technology. Although many businesses consider licensing only their products to foreign companies, the licensing potential for intangibles such as processes technology, copyrights, and trademarks often is greater. Some entrepreneurs earn more money from licensing their know-how for product design, manufacturing, or quality control than they do from actually selling their finished goods in a highly competitive foreign market with which they are not familiar. Foreign licensing enables a small business to enter foreign markets quickly, easily, and with virtually no capital investment. Risks to the company include the potential loss of control over its manufacturing and marketing processes and creating a competitor if the licensee gains too much knowledge and control. Securing proper patent, trademark, and copyright protection beforehand can minimize those risks, however.

COMPANY Profile

Street Legend Ink

Mike Davis, Mark Davis, and Brandon Schultz, founders of Blokhedz, recently entered into a licensing agreement with International Enterprise to sell the Blokhedz comic book and related merchandise internationally.

Twins Mike and Mark Davis created the Blokhedz comic book characters for Street Legend Ink, a small animation company started in 2000 by Brandon Schultz, his father Michael, and two friends. Blokhedz is the story of Blak, an aspiring young rapper in Empire City who discovers that he has the supernatural power to control people with his rhymes. The Davis twins originally intended Blokhedz to be an animated film, but as they developed the storyboard for the film, they saw the potential for a comic book as well. Street Legend Ink recently entered into a licensing arrangement with International Enterprise to distribute the Blokhedz comic book internationally. "With our titles, we offer foreign markets a diverse collection of comics that have not been seen in their territories," says Tim Hegarty, International Enterprise's director of foreign licensing.[14]

International Franchising

Over the last several decades, a growing number of franchises have been attracted to international markets to boost sales and profits as the domestic market has become increasingly saturated with outlets and much tougher to wring growth from. Although international expansion is not a good idea for a new franchiser, it is an appropriate strategy for experienced franchisers. Both the cost and the complexity of franchising increase as the distance between the franchiser and its franchisees increases. In addition, complex legal and regulatory requirements and cultural differences make international franchising challenging for inexperienced franchisers. Franchisers that decide to expand internationally should take the following steps:

1. *Identify the country or countries that are best suited to the franchiser's business concept.* Factors to consider include a country's business climate, demographic profile, level of economic development, rate of economic growth, degree of legal protection, language and cultural barriers, and market potential. Franchisers making their first forays into global markets should consider focusing on a single nation or a small group of similar nations.
2. *Generate leads for potential franchisees.* Franchisers looking for prospective franchisees in foreign markets have many tools available to them, including international franchise trade shows, their own Web sites, trade missions, and brokers. Many franchisers have had success with trade missions such as those sponsored by trade groups such as the International Franchise Association or the U.S. Department of Commerce's Gold Key Program. These trade missions are designed to introduce franchisers to qualified franchise candidates in target countries. Others rely on brokers who have extensive business contacts in specific countries.
3. *Select quality candidates.* Just as in any franchise relationship, the real key to success is choosing the right franchisee. Because of the complexity and cost of international franchising, selecting quality franchisees is essential to success.

4. ***Structure the franchise deal.*** Franchisers can structure international franchise arrangements in a variety of ways, but three techniques are most popular—direct franchising, area development, and master franchising:

- Direct franchising, so common in domestic franchise deals, involves selling single-unit franchises to individual operators in foreign countries. Although dealing with individual franchisees makes it easier for the franchiser to maintain control, it also requires more of the franchiser's time and resources.
- Area development is similar to direct franchising, except that the franchiser allows the franchisee to develop multiple units in a particular territory, perhaps a province, a county, or even an entire nation. A successful area development strategy depends on a franchiser selecting and then supporting quality franchisees.
- Master franchising is the most popular strategy for companies entering international markets. Here, a franchiser grants an experienced master franchisee the right to sell outlets to sub-franchisees in a broad geographic area or an entire nation. Although master franchising simplifies a franchiser's expansion into global markets, it gives franchisers the least amount of control over their international franchisees. The U.S.-based home and business moving franchise Two Men and a Truck recently expanded into Ireland and the United Kingdom when it granted a master franchise to Dublin-based NDMG Holdings. NDMG Holdings plans to open 60 sub-franchises in the two countries within the next several years.[15]

Just as they do in the United States, franchisers in international markets sell virtually every kind of product or service imaginable—from fast food to child day care. In some cases, the products and services sold in international markets are identical to those sold in the United States. However, most franchisers have learned that adaptation is the key to making sure that their goods and services suit local tastes and customs. Traveling the world, one discovers that American fast food giants such as McDonalds and Domino's make significant modifications in their menu to remain attractive to the demands of local customers.

In addition to its 5,000 domestic outlets, Domino's Pizza operates more than 3,000 restaurants in 54 foreign countries, where local franchises offer pizza toppings that are quite different from traditional ones used in the United States, including squid (Japan), pickled ginger (India), tuna and sweet corn (England), green peas (Brazil), and reindeer sausage (Iceland), to cater to customers' palates. In Taiwan, the best-selling pizza is a seafood delight made with onions, peas, squid, shrimp, and crab toppings. Although the toppings used vary widely around the world, the dough, the sauce, and the cheese are standard in every Domino's location.[16] At McDonald's locations in India, Maharaja Macs made of chicken share the menu with Vegetable McNuggets, and in Japan, teriyaki burgers and a seafood burger made with fish and shrimp appear on the menu. McHuevos (a burger topped with a poached egg and mayonnaise) is a popular item in McDonald's in Uruguay. In China, McDonald's customers can enjoy seafood soup and sundaes made from red beans.[17]

COMPANY Profile

Domino's Pizza and McDonald's

Adapting their products and services to accommodate local tastes is one key to success for international franchises. The menu board in this New Delhi McDonald's advertises two sandwiches that McDonald's sells in India, the Maharaja Mac and the Vegetable Burger.

Although franchise outlets span the globe, Canada is the primary market for U.S. franchisers, with Japan and Europe following. These markets are most attractive to franchisers because they are similar to the U.S. market, with rising personal incomes, strong demand for consumer goods, growing service economies, and spreading urbanization. There is little doubt that franchising is becoming a two-way street and that globalization will continue to be a powerful force in the growth of the strategic marketing option. Entering early into promising markets and maintaining cultural sensitivity to local preferences are important to long-term success in international franchising.

Countertrading and Bartering

countertrade

a transaction in which a company selling goods in a foreign country agrees to promote investment and trade in that country.

A **countertrade** is a transaction in which a company selling goods in a foreign country agrees to promote investment and trade in that country. The goal of the transaction is to help offset the capital drain from the foreign country's purchases. As entrepreneurs enter more developing countries, they will need to develop skills at implementing this strategy. In some cases, small and medium-sized businesses find it advantageous to work together with large corporations who have experience in the implementation of this marketing strategy.

Countertrading does suffer numerous drawbacks. Countertrade transactions can be complicated, cumbersome, and time-consuming. They also increase the chances that a company will get stuck with merchandise that it cannot move. They can lead to unpleasant surprises concerning the quantity and quality of products required in the countertrade. Still, countertrading offers one major advantage: Sometimes it's the only way to make a sale.

Entrepreneurs must weigh the advantages against the disadvantages for their company before committing to a countertrade deal. Because of its complexity and the risks involved, countertrading is not the best choice for a novice entrepreneur looking to break into the global marketplace.

bartering

the exchange of goods and services for other goods and services.

Bartering, the exchange of goods and services for other goods and services, is another way of trading with countries lacking convertible currency. In a barter exchange, a company that manufactures electronics components might trade its products for the coffee that a business in a foreign country processes, which it then sells to a third company for cash. Barter transactions require finding a business with complementary needs, but they are much simpler than countertrade transactions.

Exporting

LEARNING OBJECTIVES
3. Explain how to build a thriving export program.

For many years, small businesses in the United States focused solely on the domestic market, never venturing beyond its borders. As global competition exerts pressure on domestic markets and trade agreements open foreign markets as never before, growing numbers of small companies are looking to exporting as a way of gaining or maintaining a competitive edge. Large companies continue to dominate exporting, however. Although small companies account for 97 percent of all U.S. businesses that export goods and services, they generate only 29 of the nation's export sales.[18] A recent study by the National Federation of Independent Businesses (NFIB) reports that just 13 percent of small business owners have generated foreign sales within the last three years and that most of their foreign sales simply are the result of taking orders from international customers. Only 12 percent of exporting small companies actively market their products and services in foreign markets regularly.[19]

The biggest barrier facing companies that have never exported is not knowing where or how to start. The U.S. Chamber of Commerce's Trade Roots initiative, an international trade leadership program that networks more than 3,000 local U.S. chambers of commerce, is a useful resource for entrepreneurs looking to launch into global business. The program provides information on the benefits and methods for its members who want to engage in international trade but aren't sure where to start. The U.S. Commercial Service's *Export Programs Guide* provides entrepreneurs with a comprehensive list of federal programs designed to help U.S. exporters. As another valuable source of information, the U.S. Export Assistance Centers (http://www.sba.gov/oit/export/useac.html) serve as single contact points for information on the multitude of federal export programs that are designed to help entrepreneurs who want to start exporting. Entrepreneurs who want to learn more about exporting should investigate *A Basic Guide to Exporting* (http://www.unzco.com/basicguide/), published by the Department of Commerce and Unz and Company. The U.S.

government export portal http:www.export.gov gives entrepreneurs access to valuable information about exporting in general (finance, shipping, documentation, and others) as well as details on individual nations (market research, trade agreements, statistics, and more). Learning more about exporting and realizing that it is within the realm of possibility for small companies—even *very* small companies—is the first, and often most difficult, step in breaking the psychological barrier to exporting. The next challenge is to create a sound export strategy:

Step 1. Recognize That Even the Tiniest Companies and Least Experienced Entrepreneurs Have the Potential to Export The size of the firm has nothing to do with the demand for its products. If the products meet the needs of global customers, there is a potential to export. Studies suggest that small companies that export grow markedly faster than those that do not.

After spotting ample sales opportunities for her company's products while on a trip to South Africa with a nonprofit organization, Ilene Robinson, president of Security Options, a small company in Detroit, Michigan, that sells products for securing office equipment, participated in a trade mission sponsored by the Commerce Department that was designed to promote exports to that nation. The trip paid big dividends for Robinson's small company. "We left Africa with five qualified partner proposals as a result of our trade mission meetings," she says. "Normally, it would have taken us several months to find these potential partners. Some of the contacts I met with are ready to move forward with us."[20]

Security Options

Step 2. Analyze Your Product or Service Is it special? It is new? Is it unique? Is it of high quality? Is it priced favorably because of lower costs or favorable exchange rates? In which countries would there be sufficient demand for it? In many foreign countries, products from the United States are in demand because they have an air of mystery about them. In some cases, entrepreneurs find that they must make slight modifications to their products to accommodate local tastes, customs, and preferences. For instance, when Joseph Zaritski, owner of an Australian juice company, began marketing his company's products in Russia, he met with limited success until he realized that package size was the problem. Willing customers simply could not afford to purchase the two-liter bottles in which the juice was packaged. Zaritski switched to one-liter bottles and saw sales climb by 80 percent within six months.[21]

Step 3. Analyze Your Commitment Are you willing to devote the time and energy to develop export markets? Does your company have the necessary resources? Patience is essential. Export start-ups can take from six to eight months (or longer), but entering foreign markets isn't as tough as most entrepreneurs think. Table 15.2 summarizes key issues managers must address in the export decision.

Step 4. Research Markets and Pick Your Target More than one-third of small business exporters sell to just one or two countries (see Figure 15.3). Before investing in a costly sales trip abroad, however, entrepreneurs should search the Web or make a trip to the local library or the nearest branch of the Department of Commerce. Exporters can choose from a multitude of guides, manuals, books, newsletters, videos, and other resources to help them research potential markets. Armed with research, entrepreneurs can avoid wasting a lot of time and money on markets with limited potential for their products and can concentrate on those with the greatest promise. Some of the most helpful tools for researching foreign markets are the Country and Industry Market Reports available at the U.S. government's export Web portal (http://www.export.gov/marketresearch.html), which provide detailed information on the economic, political, regulatory, and investment environment for countries ranging from Afghanistan to Zimbabwe. Research shows export entrepreneurs whether they need to modify their existing products and services to suit the tastes and preferences of their foreign target customers. Sometimes foreign customers' lifestyles, housing needs, body size, and cultures require exporters to make alterations in

TABLE 15.2 Management Issues in the Export Decision

I. Experience

1. With what countries has your company already conducted business (or from what countries have you received inquiries about your product or service)?
2. What product lines do foreign customers ask about most often?
3. Prepare a list of sale inquiries for each buyer by product and by country.
4. Is the trend of inquiries or sales increasing or decreasing?
5. Who are your primary domestic and foreign competitors?
6. What lessons has your company learned from past export experience?

II. Management and Personnel

1. Who will be responsible for the export entity's organization and staff? (Do you have an export "champion"?)
2. How much top management time
   a. should you allocate to exporting?
   b. can you afford to allocate to exporting?
3. What does management expect from its exporting efforts? What are your company's export goals and objectives?
4. What organization structure will your company require to ensure that it can service export sales properly? (Note the political implications, if any.)
5. Who will implement the plan?

III. Production Capacity

1. To what extent is your company using its existing production capacity? Is there any excess? If so, how much?
2. Will filling export orders hurt your company's ability to make and service domestic sales?
3. What will additional production for export markets cost your company?
4. Are there seasonal or cyclical fluctuations in your company's workload? When? Why?
5. Is there a minimum quantity foreign customers must order for a sale to be profitable?
6. To what extent would your company need to modify its products, packaging, and design specifically for its export targets? Is your product quality adequate for foreign customers?
7. What pricing structure will your company use? Will prices be competitive?
8. How will your company collect payment of its export sales?

IV. Financial Capacity

1. How much capital will your company need to begin exporting? Where will it come from?
2. How will you allocate the initial costs of your company's export effort?
3. Does your company have other expansion plans that would compete with an exporting effort?
4. By what date do you expect your company's export program to pay for itself?
5. How important is establishing a global presence to your company's future success?

Source: Adapted from U.S. Department of Commerce, *A Basic Guide to Exporting* (Washington, DC: Author, 1998), p. 3.

their product lines. Making just slight modifications to adapt products and services to local tastes can sometimes spell the difference between success and failure in the global market. Table 15.3 offers questions to guide entrepreneurs conducting export research.

Step 5. Develop a Distribution Strategy Should you use a trade intermediary or sell directly to foreign customers? As you learned earlier in this chapter, many small companies just entering international markets prefer to rely on trade intermediaries to break new ground. Relying on intermediaries often makes sense until an entrepreneur has the chance to gain experience in exporting and to learn the ground rules of selling in foreign lands.

Step 6. Find Your Customer According to a study by the National Federation of Independent Businesses, the most common problem among small business exporters is finding prospective customers (after all, establishing a network of business contacts takes

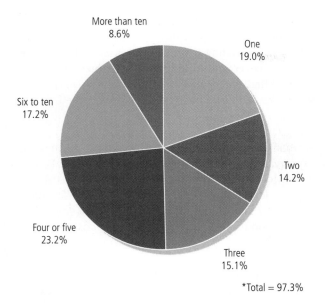

More than ten
8.6%

One
19.0%

Six to ten
17.2%

Two
14.2%

Four or five
23.2%

Three
15.1%

*Total = 97.3%

FIGURE 15.3

Small Business Exporting; Number of Countries to Which Small Exporters Sell

Source: National Federation of Independent Businesses, *National Small Business Poll: International Trade* (Washington, DC: Author, 2004), Volume 4, Issue 1, p. 3.

time and resources).[22] Small businesses can rely on a host of export specialists to help them track down foreign customers. The U.S. Department of Commerce and the International Trade Administration should be the first stops on any entrepreneur's agenda for going global. These agencies have the market research available for locating the best target markets for a particular company and specific customers in those markets. Industry Sector Analyses (ISAs), International Market Insights (IMIs), and Customized Market Analyses (CMAs) are just some of the reports and services global entrepreneurs find most useful. They also have knowledgeable staff specialists experienced in the details of global trade and in the intricacies of foreign cultures.

One of the most efficient and least expensive ways for entrepreneurs to locate potential customers for their companies' products and services is to participate in a trade mission.

TABLE 15.3 Questions to Guide International Market Research

- Is there an overseas market for your company's products or services?
- Are there specific target markets that look most promising?
- Which new markets abroad are most likely to open up or expand?
- How big is the market your company is targeting, and how fast is it growing?
- What are the major economic, political, legal, social, technological, and other environmental factors affecting this market?
- What are the demographic and cultural factors affecting this market (e.g., disposable income, occupation, age, gender, opinions, activities, interests, tastes, and values)?
- Who are your company's present and potential customers abroad?
- What are their needs and desires? What factors influence their buying decisions: price, credit terms, delivery terms, quality, brand name, and the like?
- How would they use your company's produce or service? What modifications, if any, would be necessary to sell to your target customers?
- Who are your primary competitors in the foreign market?
- How do competitors distribute, sell, and promote their products? What are their prices?
- What are the best channels of distribution for your product?
- What is the best way for your company to gain exposure in this market?
- Are there any barriers such as tariffs, quotas, duties, or regulations to selling your product in this market? Are there any incentives?
- Are there any potential licensing or joint venture partners already in this market?

Source: Adapted from U.S. Department of Commerce, *A Basic Guide to Exporting* (Washington, DC: Author, 1986), p. 11.

These missions usually are sponsored by either a federal or a state economic development agency or an industry trade association for the purpose of cultivating international trade by connecting domestic companies with potential trading partners overseas. A trade mission may focus on a particular industry or may cover several industries but target a particular country. "Trade missions are a great way to find quality buyers, partners, and agents in international markets," says Maria Cino, who has led many trade mission trips for the U.S. and Foreign Commercial Service.[23]

Global MED-NET

Chicago-based Global MED-NET, a small company that provides an emergency medical information storage and forwarding service, made its first export sale after CEO Patricia Schneider went on a trade mission trip to South Africa that was sponsored by the U.S. Commercial Service. The contacts Schneider made on the trip led to a $1 million order from Trauma Link, a South African company that is building a networked 911 emergency system. Schneider says that the trade mission trip was "a high-result, low-cost avenue to finding the best partner in South Africa."[24]

Step 7. Find Financing One of the biggest barriers to small business exports is lack of financing. Access to adequate financing is a crucial ingredient in a successful export program because the cost of generating foreign sales often is higher and collection cycles are longer than in domestic markets. The trouble is that bankers and other sources of capital don't always understand the intricacies of international sales and view financing them as excessively risky. In addition, among major industrialized nations, the U.S. government spends the least per capita to promote exports.

Several federal, state, and private programs are operating to fill this export financing void, however. Loan programs from the Small Business Administration include its Export Working Capital Program (90 percent loan guarantees up to $1,500,000), International Trade Loan Program (75 percent loan guarantees up to $1,250,000), and Export Express Program (75 percent loan guarantees up to $250,000). In addition, the Export-Import Bank (http://www.exim.gov), the Overseas Private Investment Corporation, and a variety of state-sponsored programs offer export-minded entrepreneurs both direct loans and loan guarantees. (Recall that the *Export Programs Guide* provides a list of the 20 government agencies that help companies to develop their export potential.) The Export-Import Bank (http://www.exim.gov), which has been financing the sale of U.S. exports for more than 70 years, provides small exporters with export credit insurance and loans through its working capital line of credit and a variety of pre-export loan programs. The Bankers Association for Foreign Trade (http://www.baft.org/jsps/) is an association of 150 banks around the world that matches exporters needing foreign trade financing with interested banks.

AquaTech International Corporation

With the help of Export-Import Bank guarantees on loans from PNC Financial Services, AquaTech International Corporation, maker of high-tech water purification equipment located in Canonsburg, Pennsylvania, was able to land several major export sales, including one $5 million contract with an Italian power company. AquaTech acquired $25 million in working capital loans to finance the international sales under the Export-Import Bank's Export Express program. "The exports supported by Ex-Im Bank make up roughly half of our business," says CEO Venkee Sharma. "Ex-Im Bank programs are critical to our small business export success. They allow us to go to the next level as an international business."[25]

Step 8. Ship Your Goods Export novices usually rely on international freight forwarders and custom-house agents—experienced specialists in overseas shipping—for help in navigating the bureaucratic morass of packaging requirements and paperwork demanded by customs. These specialists, also known as transport architects, are to exporters what travel agents are to travelers, and normally charge relatively small fees for a valuable service. They move shipments of all sizes to destinations all over the world efficiently, saving entrepreneurs many headaches. Shipping terms, always important for determining which party in a transaction pays the cost of shipping and bears the risk of loss or damage to the goods while they are in transit, take on heightened importance in

TABLE 15.4 Common International Shipping Terms and Their Meanings

Shipping Term Used	Seller's Responsibility	Buyer's Responsibility	Shipping Method
FOB ("free on board") seller	Deliver goods to carrier and provide export license and clean onboard receipt. Bear risk of loss until goods are delivered to carrier.	Pay shipping, freight, and insurance charges. Bear risk of loss while goods are in transit.	All
FOB ("free on board") buyer	Deliver goods to the buyer's place of business and provide export license and clean onboard receipt. Pay shipping, freight, and insurance charges. Bear risk of loss while goods are in transit.	Accept delivery of goods after documents are tendered.	All
FAS ("free along side")	Deliver goods alongside ship. Provide an "alongside" receipt.	Provide export license and proof of delivery of the goods to the carrier. Bear risk of loss once goods are delivered to the carrier.	Ship
CFR ("cost and freight")	Deliver goods to carrier, obtain export licenses, and pay export taxes. Provide buyer with clean bill of lading. Pay freight and shipping charges. Bear risk of loss until goods are delivered to buyer.	Pay insurance charges. Accept delivery of goods after documents are tendered.	Ship
CIF ("cost, insurance, and freight")	Same as CFR plus pay insurance charges and provide buyer with insurance policy.	Accept delivery of goods after documents are tendered.	Ship
CPT ("carriage paid to . . .")	Deliver goods to carrier, obtain export licenses, and pay export taxes. Provide buyer with clean transportation documents. Pay shipping and freight charges.	Pay insurance charges. Accept delivery of goods after documents are tendered.	All
CIP ("carriage and insurance paid to . . .")	Same as CPT plus pay insurance charges and provide buyer with insurance policy.	Accept delivery of goods after documents are tendered.	All
DDU ("delivered duty unpaid")	Obtain export license and pay import duty, pay insurance charges, and provide buyer documents for taking delivery.	Take delivery of goods and pay import duties.	All
DDP ("delivered duty paid")	Obtain export license, pay insurance charges, and provide buyer documents for taking delivery.	Take delivery of goods.	All

Source: Adapted from *Guide to the Finance of International Trade,* edited by Gordon Platt (HSBC Trade Services, Marine Midland Bank, and the *Journal of Commerce*). http://infoserv2.ita.doc.gov/efm/efm.nsf/503d177e3c6f0b48525675900112e24/6218a8703573b329852567590004c41f3/$FILE/Finance_.pdf/pp. 6-10.

international transactions. Table 15.4 explains the implications of some of the most common shipping terms used in international transactions.

Step 9. Collect Your Money Collecting foreign accounts can be more complex than collecting domestic ones, but by picking their customers carefully and checking their credit references closely, entrepreneurs can minimize bad-debt losses. Businesses engaging in international sales can use four primary payment methods (ranked from least risk to most risky): cash in advance, a letter of credit, a bank (or documentary) draft, and an open account. The safest method of selling to foreign customers is to collect cash in advance of the sale. This is the safest option for the seller because it eliminates the risk of collection problems and provides immediate cash flow. However, requiring cash payments up front may limit severely a small company's base of foreign customers.

FIGURE 15.4

How a Letter of Credit Works

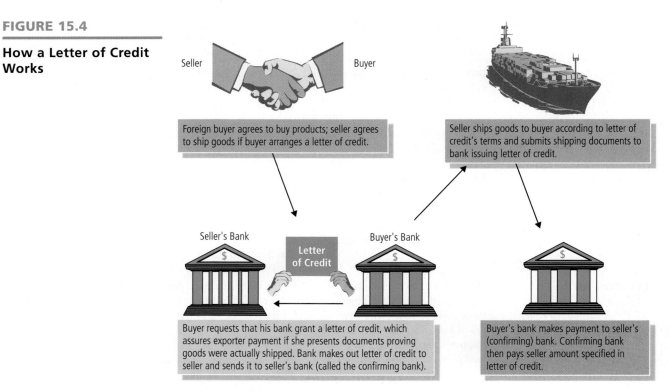

Seller   Buyer

Foreign buyer agrees to buy products; seller agrees to ship goods if buyer arranges a letter of credit.

Seller ships goods to buyer according to letter of credit's terms and submits shipping documents to bank issuing letter of credit.

Seller's Bank   **Letter of Credit**   Buyer's Bank

Buyer requests that his bank grant a letter of credit, which assures exporter payment if she presents documents proving goods were actually shipped. Bank makes out letter of credit to seller and sends it to seller's bank (called the confirming bank).

Buyer's bank makes payment to seller's (confirming) bank. Confirming bank then pays seller amount specified in letter of credit.

letter of credit

an agreement between an exporter's bank and the foreign buyer's bank that guarantees payment to the exporter for a specific shipment of goods.

bank draft

a document the seller draws on the buyer, requiring the buyer to pay the face amount either on sight or on a specified date.

A **letter of credit** is an agreement between an exporter's bank and the foreign buyer's bank that guarantees payment to the exporter for a specific shipment of goods. In essence, a letter of credit reduces the financial risk for the exporter by substituting a bank's creditworthiness for that of the purchaser (see Figure 15.4). A **bank draft** is a document the seller draws on the buyer, requiring the buyer to pay the face amount (the purchase price of the goods) either on sight (a sight draft) or on a specified date (a time draft) once the goods have been shipped. With either letters of credit or bank drafts, small exporters must be sure that all of the required documentation is present and accurate; otherwise, they may experience delays in the payments due to them from the buyer or the participating banks. Rather than use letters of credit or drafts, some exporters simply sell to foreign customers on open account. In other words, they ship the goods to a foreign customer without any guarantee of payment. This method is riskiest because collecting a delinquent account from a foreign customer is even more difficult than collecting past-due payments from a domestic customer. The parties involved in an international deal should agree in advance on an acceptable method of payment.

You
Be the Consultant

An Export Dilemma

After an extensive career in the fashion industry, Deirdre Quinn decided to launch Lafayette 148, a company that manufactures women's fine apparel. Recognizing that to be successful in the garment industry, the company had to be global in its scope from the outset, Quinn partnered with Shun Yen Siu, another veteran of the fashion industry, who grew up in Shantou, China. In the early days, Quinn and Siu proudly pointed out the "Made in New York" labels stitched inside their high-quality garments to their customers, including the upscale department store Saks

Fifth Avenue. By 2001, sales had climbed to $28 million, but Lafayette 148 was losing money because its production costs were too high. After the company's sales turned downward in the wake of the September 11 terrorist attacks in New York, Quinn and Siu knew that to become profitable, they would have to move production overseas and chose China as the home for their factory.

Siu returned to his hometown of Shantou, and within a few months he had acquired a 20,000-square-foot factory that could produce apparel for Lafayette 148 at a fraction of what it cost to manufacture it in New York. In its first full year of operation, the factory generated enough cost savings for Lafayette to break even on sales of $39 million. Because the factory was producing only 60 percent of Lafayette's garments, quotas—trade restrictions that limit the amount of goods that can be imported into the United States from foreign countries—were of little concern to Quinn and Siu.

That changed the next year, however, when Quinn and Siu raised the level of production in the Shantou factory to 95 percent of Lafayette's apparel, a move that would cut costs enough to allow the company to make a healthy profit. To do so required Quinn and Siu to develop a quota rights plan for Lafayette 148. Export quotas set strict limits on the quantity of foreign-made apparel that enters the United States, and manufacturers must obtain the rights to export certain amounts of apparel products into the United States. (A company trying to bring both silk blouses and cotton blouses into the United States may face different limits under the complex system of quotas.) Because demand for export rights often exceeds supply, companies trade export rights in the same way that investors trade stocks on Wall Street. When Quinn and Siu increased the production at their Chinese factory to 95 percent of the company's apparel, they had created an export rights plan, fully expecting to purchase the right to ship their entire production volume into the United States. They had

budgeted an average cost of $20 per garment for export rights for a total cost of several hundred thousand dollars. Unfortunately, Lafayette 148 did not have the cash available to purchase outright that much in export rights, and Quinn and Siu decided to buy export rights to the United States as orders from their customers came in. Their assumption was that prices for export rights would remain relatively stable.

Unfortunately for Quinn and Siu, demand for foreign apparel in the United States was much higher than anticipated, and by mid-summer, when they should have been shipping their garments from the Chinese factory, prices for export rights were more than double what they had budgeted and were still climbing. As a result, Quinn and Siu ended up with a warehouse full of women's fine apparel sitting in a warehouse in China with no way to export any of it to the United States. Every morning when Quinn arrived at her office at 148 Lafayette Street in New York, she checked the market prices for export rights. By August, they had hit $60 per garment, more than three times Lafayette's average cost of actually producing an article of clothing in its Chinese factory. Quinn and Siu realized that their export rights plan was completely useless and that the odds that Lafayette 148 would make a profit for the year were slipping away. Still, they needed to get their inventory from the warehouse in China exported to the United States so they could fill their customers' orders.

1. What justification for imposing quotas on imported goods do nations offer?
2. What costs do quotas impose on companies conducting global businesses? On customers?
3. What steps do you recommend that Quinn and Siu take to resolve their current export dilemma?
4. What steps do you recommend they take to avoid this problem in the future?

Source: Adapted from Catherine Curan, "Lafayette 148 Had High Hopes for Its New Chinese Factory," *Inc.*, December 2005, pp. 62–66.

Establishing International Locations

Once established in international markets, some small businesses set up permanent locations there. Establishing an office or a factory in a foreign land can require a substantial investment reaching beyond the budgets of many small companies. In addition, setting up an international office can be an incredibly frustrating experience in some countries where business infrastructure is in disrepair or is nonexistent. Getting a telephone line installed can take months in some places, and finding reliable equipment or shippers to transport goods to customers is nearly impossible. Securing necessary licenses and permits from bureaucrats often takes more than filing the necessary paperwork; in some nations, bureaucrats expect payments to "grease the wheels" of commerce. U.S. entrepreneurs consider payments to reduce the amount of red tape involved in an international transaction to be bribery, and many simply avoid doing business in countries where "grease payments" are standard procedure. In fact, the Foreign Corrupt Practice Act, passed in 1977, considers bribing foreign officials to be a criminal act. One study by the World Bank of "grease payments" for the purpose of minimizing the red tape imposed by foreign regulations concludes that the payments do not work; in fact, companies that actually used them experienced greater government scrutiny and red tape in their international transactions.[26] Finally, finding the right person to manage an international office is crucial to success; it also is a major challenge, especially for small businesses. Small companies usually have lean management staffs and cannot afford to send key people abroad without running the risk of losing their focus.

The major advantages to companies establishing international locations are lower production, marketing, and distribution costs as well as the ability to develop an intimate knowledge of local customers' preferences, tastes, and habits.

Leopard Forest Coffee Company

Robert Brown, owner of Leopard Forest Coffee Company, a small business located in Traveler's Rest, South Carolina, that roasts and distributes coffee, grew up in Zimbabwe. To ensure a steady supply of coffee beans and to keep the cost of the beans he buys low, Brown set up a coffee-growing operation on the 900-acre plantation he owns in Zimbabwe. He now imports 20 tons of coffee through the port city of Charleston, South Carolina, to his roasting plant in Traveler's Rest and sells it to retailers throughout the United States.[27]

Importing and Outsourcing

In addition to selling their goods in foreign markets, small companies also buy goods from distributors and manufacturers in foreign markets. In fact, the intensity of price competition in many industries—from textiles and handbags to industrial machinery and computers—means that more companies now shop the world market, looking for the lowest prices they can find. Because labor costs in countries such as China and India are far below those in other nations, businesses there offer goods and services at very low prices. Increasingly, these nations are home to well-educated, skilled workers that are paid far less than comparable workers in the United States or Western Europe. For instance, a computer programmer in the United States might earn $100,000 a year, but in India, a computer programmer doing the same work earns $20,000 a year or less. As a result, many companies either import goods or outsource work directly to manufacturers in countries where costs are far lower than they would be domestically.

This trend toward outsourcing to cut costs and remain competitive is prevalent among companies selling low-cost items as well as in those producing luxury goods. For many years, European makers of luxury clothing resisted outsourcing the production of anything other than their least expensive garments such as jeans and T-shirts to companies in Eastern Europe and Africa. Companies such as Giorgio Armani, Louis Vuitton, Gucci, Prada, Hugo Boss, and others retained the production of their high-end goods such as suits, shirts, blouses, and bags, which command premium prices at retail, in France and Italy. As a result of the pressure from labor costs and competition from lower-cost brands, these luxury retailers have begun outsourcing the production of some of their most exclusive lines to factories in developing nations. Giorgio Armani now produces 18 percent of its Armani Collezioni line, which includes wool trousers priced at $450 and silk jackets that sell for $1,500, in Eastern Europe. Suits that Hugo Boss sells at retail for $550 now are made in China, and Louis Vuitton now manufactures in China some of its denim-and-leather Macadam handbags that sell for $500.[28]

Genuine Scooter

Philip McCaleb had been running Scooterworks, a motor scooter-parts business for nine years, when he learned that Piaggio, the company that makes the classic Vespa scooter in Italy, was breaking off its manufacturing relationship with LML, a large scooter maker in India. Sensing an opportunity, McCaleb contacted LML about building a modified version of the classic Vespa scooter and then launched Genuine Scooter, a Chicago-based company to market the scooters. With an outsourcing contract in hand and just three

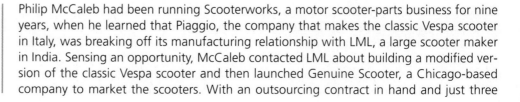

employees, McCaleb began selling his company's first scooter, a model called the Stella, for just $2,699, a price that was 37 percent lower than that of the Italian original. Genuine Scooter has since introduced two more models, the Buddy and the Black Cat, both of which are made in factories in Asia to keep costs low. Genuine Scooters generates annual sales of more than $5 million through a network of 65 dealers across the United States, and sales are growing rapidly as gasoline prices edge ever upward.[29]

Entrepreneurs who are considering importing goods and service or outsourcing their manufacturing to foreign countries should follow these steps:

■ *Make sure that importing or outsourcing is right for your business.* Even though foreign manufacturers often can provide items at significant cost savings, using them may not always be the best business decision. Entrepreneurs sometimes discover that achieving the lowest price may require a tradeoff of other important factors such as quality and speed of delivery. When Patrick Kruse, owner of Ruff Wear, the business that sells dog booties, began outsourcing many of his company's products to Chinese factories, he discovered that the quality of the goods was poor. "We actually had to refuse some shipments, which really hurt our business," he says.[30] In addition, some foreign manufacturers require sizable minimum orders, perhaps $200,000 or more, before they will produce a product.

■ *Establish a target cost for your product.* Before setting off on a global shopping spree, entrepreneurs first should determine exactly what they can afford to spend on manufacturing a product and make a profit on it. Given the low labor costs of many foreign manufacturers, products that are the most labor intensive make good candidates for outsourcing.

■ *Do your research before you leave home.* Investing time in basic research about the industry and potential suppliers in foreign lands is essential before setting foot on foreign soil. Useful resources are plentiful, and entrepreneurs should use them, including the Web, the Federation of International Trade Associations, industry trade associations, government agencies (for example, the U.S. Commercial Service's Gold Key Matching Service), and consultants.

■ *Be sensitive to cultural differences.* When making contacts, setting up business appointments, or calling on prospective manufacturers in foreign lands, make sure that you understand what is accepted business behavior and what is not. Again, this is where your research pays off; be sure to study the cultural nuances of doing business in the countries you will visit.

■ *Do your groundwork.* Once you locate potential manufacturers, contact them to set up appointments, and go visit them. Preliminary research is essential to finding reliable sources of supply, but "face time" with representatives from various companies allows entrepreneurs to judge the intangible factors that can make or break a relationship.

■ *Protect your company's intellectual property.* A common problem that many entrepreneurs have encountered with outsourcing is "knockoffs." Some foreign manufacturers see nothing wrong with agreeing to manufacture a product for a company and then selling their own "knockoff" version of it. Securing a nondisclosure agreement and a contract that prohibits such behavior helps, but experts say that securing a patent for the item in the source country itself (not just the United States) is a good idea.

■ *Select a manufacturer.* Using quality, speed of delivery, level of trust, degree of legal protection, cost, and other factors, select the manufacturer that can do the job for your company.

■ *Provide an exact model of the product you want manufactured.* Providing a manufacturer with an actual model of the item to be manufactured will save lots of time, mistakes, and problems. "It's always better to cost something from an actual item rather than an idea of an item," says Jennifer Adams, owner of a consulting firm that helps entrepreneurs to locate foreign manufacturers.[31]

■ *Stay in constant contact with the manufacturer and try to build a long-term relationship.* Communication is a key to building and maintaining a successful relationship with a foreign manufacturer. Weekly teleconferences, e-mails, and periodic visits are essential to making sure that your company gets the performance you expect from a foreign manufacturer.

Barriers to International Trade

LEARNING OBJECTIVES
4. Discuss the major barriers to international trade and their impact on the global economy.

Governments traditionally have used a variety of barriers to block free trade among nations in an attempt to protect businesses within their own borders. The benefit of protecting their own companies, however, comes at the expense of foreign businesses, which face limited access to global markets. Numerous trade barriers—domestic and international—restrict the freedom of businesses in global trading. Even with these barriers, international trade has grown to nearly $10.4 trillion.[32]

Domestic Barriers

Sometimes the biggest barriers potential exporters face are those right here at home. Three major domestic roadblocks are common: attitude, information, and financing. Perhaps the biggest barrier to small businesses exporting is the attitude that "My company is too small to export. That's just for big corporations." The first lesson of exporting is "Take nothing for granted about who can export and what you can and cannot export." The first step to building an export program is recognizing that the opportunity to export exists. Another reason entrepreneurs neglect international markets is a lack of information about how to get started. The keys to success in international markets are choosing the correct target market and designing the appropriate strategy to reach it. That requires access to information and research. Although a variety of government and private organizations make volumes of exporting and international marketing information available, many small business owners never use it. A successful global marketing strategy also recognizes that not all international markets are the same. Companies must be flexible, willing to make adjustments to their products and services, promotional campaigns, packaging, and sales techniques.

An additional obstacle is the inability of small firms to obtain adequate export financing. Financial institutions that serve smaller firms often are not experienced in financing international sales and are unwilling to accept the perceived higher levels of risk they create for the lender.

International Barriers

Domestic barriers aren't the only ones export-minded entrepreneurs must overcome. Trading nations also erect obstacles to free trade. Two types of international barriers are common: tariff and nontariff.

tariff
a tax, or duty, that a government imposes on goods and services imported into that country.

Tariff Barriers A **tariff** is a tax, or duty, that a government imposes on goods and services imported into that country. Imposing tariffs raises the price of the imported goods—making them less attractive to consumers—and protects the domestic makers of comparable product and services. Established in the United States in 1790 by Alexander Hamilton, the tariff system generated the majority of federal revenues for about 100 years. Currently, the *Harmonized Tariff Schedule*, which sets tariffs for products imported into the United States, includes 37,000 categories of goods. One-third of all products imported into the United States are subject to tariffs, but the average industrial U.S. tariff is two percent. Many developing nations impose tariffs that are as much as 12 times as high on imported goods.[33]

Nontariff Barriers Many nations have lowered the tariffs they impose on products and services brought into their borders, but they rely on other nontariff structures as protectionist trade barriers.

QUOTAS Rather than impose a direct tariff on certain imported products, nations often use quotas to protect their industries. A **quota** is a limit on the amount of a product imported into a country. Under the Agreement on Textiles and Clothing (ATC), many nations, including the United States, imposed quotas on the amount of clothing and textile products that could be imported from countries such as China, India, and Vietnam. On January 1, 2005, at the urging of the World Trade Organization, the United States eliminated the quotas on these items and the terminated the ATC. Textile imports to the United States and the European Union from China, in particular, soared by 40 percent, and within a year, both the United States and the European Union had renegotiated quotas (the agreements called them "safeguards") on half of the products China exported to these nations, including bras, bath towels, socks, wool suits, and many other items.[34]

quota
a limit on the amount of a product imported into a country.

EMBARGOES An **embargo** is a total ban on imports of certain products. The motivation for embargoes is not always economic, but it also can involve political differences, environmental disputes, terrorism, and other issues. For instance, the United States imposes embargoes on products from nations it considers to be adversarial, including Cuba, Iran, Iraq, and North Korea, among others. In other cases, embargoes originate from cultural differences. For instance, the United States imposes embargoes on any harp seal products from Norway under the Marine Mammal Protection Act. Norway, where seal products comprise a multi-million-dollar industry, has pushed for the elimination of the embargo, arguing that harp seals are not an endangered species.[35]

embargo
a total ban on imports of certain products into a country.

Dumping In an effort to grab market share quickly, some companies have been guilty of **dumping** products: selling large quantities of them at prices that are below cost in foreign countries. The United States has been a dumping ground for steel, televisions, shoes, and computer chips from other nations in the past. Under the U.S. Antidumping Act, a U.S. company filing a complaint must prove that the foreign company's prices are lower here than in the home country and that U.S. companies are directly harmed. Recently, the European Union claimed that Vietnam and China were dumping shoes in its member nations, charging prices that were below their cost of production. Faced with intense competition from the Far East, traditional European shoemakers were pressuring the European Union to raise the tariffs on imported shoes in an attempt to preserve their share of the home market.[36]

dumping
selling large quantities of goods at prices that are below cost in foreign countries in an effort to grab market share quickly.

Political Barriers

Entrepreneurs who go global quickly discover a labyrinth of political tangles. Although many U.S. business owners complain of excessive government regulation in the United States, they are often astounded by the complex web of governmental and legal regulations and barriers they encounter in foreign countries.

Companies doing business in politically risky lands face the very real dangers of government takeovers of private property; coups intended to overthrow ruling parties; kidnapping, bombings, and other violent acts against businesses and their employees; and other threatening events. Their investments of millions of dollars may evaporate overnight in the wake of a government coup or the passage of a law nationalizing an industry (giving control of an entire industry to the government).

Business Barriers

American companies doing business internationally quickly learn that business practices and regulations in foreign lands can be quite different from those in the United States. Simply duplicating the practices they have adopted (and have used successfully) in the domestic market and using them in foreign markets is not always a good idea. Perhaps the biggest shock comes in the area of human resources management, in which international managers discover that practices common in the United States, such as overtime and employee benefits, are restricted, disfavored, or forbidden in other cultures. Business owners new to international business sometimes are shocked at the wide range of labor costs they encounter and the accompanying wide range of skilled labor available. In some countries, what appear to be "bargain" labor rates turn out to be excessively high after accounting for the quality of the labor force and the benefits their governments mandate: from company-sponsored housing, meals, and clothing to profit-sharing and extended vacations. In many nations, labor unions are present in almost every company, yet they play a very different role than the unions in the United States. Although management–union relations are not as hostile as in the United States and strikes are not as common, unions can greatly complicate an international company's ability to compete effectively.

Cultural Barriers

The culture of a nation includes the beliefs, values, views, and mores that its inhabitants share. Differences in cultures among nations create another barrier to international trade. The diversity of languages, business philosophies, practices, and traditions make international trade more complex than selling to the business down the street. Consider the following examples:

- A U.S. entrepreneur, eager to expand into the European Union, arrives at the headquarters of his company's potential business partner in France. Confidently, he strides into the meeting room, enthusiastically pumps his host's hand, slaps him on the back, and says, "Tony, I've heard a great deal about you; please, call me Bill." Eager to explain the benefits of his product, he opens his briefcase and gets right down to business. The French executive politely excuses himself and leaves the room before negotiations ever begin, shocked by the American's rudeness and ill manners. Rudeness and ill manners? Yes—from the French executive's perspective.
- Another American business owner flies to Tokyo to close a deal with a Japanese executive. He is pleased when his host invites him to play a round of golf shortly after he arrives. He plays well and manages to win by a few strokes. The Japanese executive invites him to play again the next day, and again he wins by a few strokes. Invited to play another round the following day, the American asks, "But when are we going to start doing business?" His host, surprised by the question, says, "But we *have* been doing business."
- An American businesswoman in London is invited to a party hosted by an advertising agency. Unsure of her ability to navigate the streets and subways of London alone, she approaches a British colleague who is going to be driving to the party and asks him, "Could I get a ride with you?" After he turns bright red from embarrassment, he regains his composure and politely says, "Lucky for you I know what you meant." Unknowingly, the young woman had requested a sexual encounter with her colleague, not a lift to the party![37]
- An American businessman grows tired of trying to speak over the persistent chanting of a nearby group of Islamic men. Exasperated, he looks harshly at the group and said to his Muslim host, "Can't somebody shut those guys up?" Only then did he discover that "those guys" were Islamic priests chanting a call to prayer—and that he had just blown the deal he was trying to land.[38]
- An American goes to Malaysia to close a sizable contract. In an elaborate ceremony, he is introduced to a man he thinks is named "Roger." Throughout the negotiations, he calls the man "Rog" not realizing that his potential client was a "rajah," a title of nobility, not a name.[39]
- One company selling a razor aimed at women in Holland creates a television commercial showing a woman's leg and the product's name. Unfortunately, the ad proves to be completely ineffective because the product's name is slang for "homosexual," and Dutch viewers think the leg belongs to a transvestite.[40]

When American businesspeople enter international markets for the first time, they often are amazed at the differences in foreign cultures' habits and customs. In the first scenario just given, for instance, had the entrepreneur done his homework, he would have known that the French are very formal (backslapping is *definitely* taboo!) and do not typically use first names in business relationships (even among long-time colleagues). In the second scenario, a global manager would have known that the Japanese place a tremendous importance on developing personal relationships before committing to any business deals. Thus, he would have seen the golf games for what they really were: an integral part of building a business relationship.

Understanding and heeding these often subtle cultural differences is one of the most important keys to international business success. Conducting a business meeting with a foreign executive in the same manner as one with an American businessperson could doom the deal from the outset. Business customs and behaviors that are acceptable, even expected, in the United States may be taboo in others.

Entrepreneurs who fail to learn the differences in the habits and customs of the cultures in which they hope to do business are at a distinct disadvantage. The stories of business executives who unknowingly insulted their foreign counterparts are both lengthy, legendary, and a continuing reminder of the cost associated with a failure to prepare for dealing in a culture different from one's own.

Culture, customs, and the norms of behavior differ greatly among nations, and making the correct impression is extremely critical to building a long-term business relationship. Consider the following tips:

- In Great Britain, businesspeople consider it extremely important to conduct business "properly"—with formality and reserve. Boisterous behavior such as backslapping or overindulging in alcohol and ostentatious displays of wealth are considered ill mannered. The British do not respond to hard-sell tactics but do appreciate well-mannered executives. Politeness and impeccable manners are useful tools for conducting business successfully.
- Japanese executives conduct business much like the British, with an emphasis on formality, thoughtfulness, and respect. Don't expect to hear Japanese executives say "no," even during a negotiation; they don't want to offend or to appear confrontational. Instead of "no" the Japanese negotiator will say, "It is very difficult," "Let us think about that," or "Let us get back to you on that." Similarly, "yes" from a Japanese executive doesn't necessarily mean that. It could mean, "I understand," "I hear you," or "I don't understand what you mean, but I don't want to embarrass you."
- In India, a limp handshake and avoiding eye contact are not signs of weakness or dislike; they convey respect.[41]
- When doing business in Greece, U.S. executives must be thoughtful of their hand gestures; the hand-waving gesture that means "goodbye" in the United States is considered an insult in Greece.[42]
- In Japan and South Korea, exchanging business cards, known in Japan as *meishi*, is an important business function (unlike Great Britain, where exchanging business cards is less popular). A Western executive who accepts a Japanese companion's card and then slips it into his pocket or scribbles notes on it has committed a major blunder. Tradition there says a business card must be treated just as its owner would be—with respect. Travelers should present their own cards using both hands with the card positioned so the recipient can read it. (The flip side should be printed in Japanese, an expected courtesy).
- Greeting a Japanese executive properly includes a bow and a handshake—showing respect for both cultures. In many traditional Japanese businesses, exchanging gifts at the first meeting is appropriate. In addition, a love of golf (the Japanese are fanatics about the game) is a real plus for winning business in Japan.
- Entrepreneurs who are willing to engage in a hearty round of karaoke, a standard business practice in Taiwan, are likely to land more deals there. After a full day of business meetings, a group of Taiwanese businesspeople invited Pam Marrone, founder of AgraQuest, a biotechnology company that makes natural pest-management products, to participate in karaoke with them. "I ended up belting out—off-key— *My Way* by Frank Sinatra and closed the deal," she says.[43]
- Exercise caution when giving gifts in the Far East. Although gift giving is standard practice in Japan, businesspeople in other countries, such as Malaysia, may see a gift as a bribe. In many countries, gifts of flowers are considered inappropriate because they connote romantic attention. In South Korea, giving a clock as a gift is considered good luck, but in China, it is considered a bad omen.[44]

- Appearance and style are important to Italian businesspeople; they judge the polish and the expertise of the company's executives as well as the quality of its products and services. Italians expect presentations to be organized, clear, and exact. A stylish business wardrobe also is an asset in Italy. Physical contact is an accepted part of Italian society. Don't be surprised if an Italian businessperson uses a lingering handshake or touches you occasionally when doing business.

- In Mexico, making business appointments through a well-connected Mexican national will go a long way to assuring successful business deals. "People in Mexico do business with somebody they know, they like, or they're related to," says one expert. Because family and tradition are top priorities for Mexicans, entrepreneurs who discuss their family heritages and can talk knowledgeably about Mexican history are a step ahead. In business meeting, making extended eye contact is considered impolite.

- In China, entrepreneurs will need an ample dose of the "three Ps": patience, patience, patience. Nothing in China—especially business—happens fast, and entrepreneurs wanting to do business there must be persistent. In conversation and negotiations, periods of silence are common; they are a sign of politeness and contemplation. The Chinese view personal space much differently than Americans; in normal conversation, they will stand much closer to their partners.

- In the Pacific Rim, entrepreneurs must remember that each country has its own unique culture and business etiquette. Starting business relationships with customers in the Pacific Rim usually requires a third-party contact because Asian executives prefer to do business with people they know. In addition, building personal relationships is important. Many business deals take place over informal activities in this part of the world.

- American entrepreneurs doing business in the Pacific Rim should avoid hard-sell techniques, which are an immediate turnoff to Asian businesspeople. Harmony, patience, and consensus make good business companions in this region. It is also a good idea to minimize the importance of legal documents in negotiations. Although getting deals and trade agreements down in writing always is advisable, attempting to negotiate detailed contracts (as most American businesses tend to do) would insult most Asians, who base their deals on mutual trust and benefits.

You Be the Consultant

On to Japan...

"It's hard to believe how far we've come in just 14 months," said Tad Meyers, president of Specialty Building Supplies.

"That's true," chimed in Dee Rada, the company's marketing manager. "When we started this whole international business idea, we had no notion of how complicated and time-consuming it would be. We were total rookies! Which one of us would have thought we'd be trying to sell our products in Japan?"

"True. But now it looks like the big payoff is just around the corner," said Hal Milam, the company's sales manager.

As the three celebrated their success to date in taking their company into the exciting world of international business, each was proud of what they had accomplished and how much they had learned in just a short time. Yet, their excitement was tinged with anxiety because Meyers and Rada were about to travel abroad to meet with several potential distributors for the company's building supplies. In one week, they would be in Japan, negotiating deals with businesspeople they had never met before and whose native language neither spoke.

"I do know how to say 'Thank you' in Japanese," said Rada. "It's pronounced "Du-omo ah-ree-gha-toe.""

"You should probably find out how to say, 'Where's the bathroom?' and 'We're lost. Will you take us home?' in Japanese too," joked Milam.

"You know, we probably should find out as much as possible about how the Japanese do business," said Meyers. "I understand their way is very different from what we're used to."

"Such as . . .?" said Milam.

"You know . . . little things," said Rada. "I do know that they make a big deal out of exchanging business cards. They call it *meishi*. In fact, I've had cards printed for Tad and me with English on one side and Japanese on the other. When you take their cards, don't just stick them in your pocket or scribble notes on the backs of them. That's an insult."

"No kidding?" said Meyers. "I didn't know that . . .',

"I thought we'd take some gifts along to give to our guests," said Rada. "I've had them wrapped in pure white paper with these big red ribbons."

"What are you going to give them?" asked Milam.

"I had some nice golf shirts printed up with our logo, and then I had them add the U.S. and Japanese flags crossing one another."

"Cool! They ought to love that."

"We're taking along some brochures detailing our product line, emphasizing its unique nature and superb quality," said Rada. "I had them printed in Japanese just for this trip. Full-color, lots of pictures. They cost a few bucks, but I thought it would be a wise investment."

"We will be on a tight schedule while we're there," said Meyers. "We'll have to get right down to business, close the deal, and then get on to the next appointment. There won't be a lot of time for sightseeing or small talk. I hope we can have these deals done by the time we can back on the plane for home."

"I just hope they don't try to impress us with authentic Japanese meals while we're there," said Meyers. "I'm pretty much a 'meat-and-potatoes' kind of guy. I don't do sushi. But I hear that McDonald's has restaurants in Japan. I just hope there's one nearby!"

"Where's your sense of adventure?" teased Rada. "Remember: We can't afford to offend our guests. We need to be sensitive to their culture, habits, and tastes. I just hope we don't do something unintentional that upsets somebody. . . ."

1. Evaluate the preparations the Meyers and Rada have made for their upcoming trip to Japan.

2. Using the library and the World Wide Web as resources,* read about Japanese culture and Japanese business practices. Based on what you learn, would you advise them to change any of their plans? Explain.

*The Do's and Taboos of International Trade, Gestures: The Do's and Taboos of Body Language around the World, and Do's and Taboos around the World: A Guide to International Behavior, all by Roger Axtell, are excellent resources.

International Trade Agreements

LEARNING OBJECTIVES
5. Describe the trade agreements that will have the greatest influence on foreign trade in the twenty-first century— WTO, NAFTA, and CAFTA.

With the fundamental assumption that free trade among nations results in enhanced economic prosperity for all parties involved, the last 50 years have witnessed a gradual opening of trade among nations. Hundreds of agreements have been negotiated among nations in this period, with each contributing to free trade across the globe. Although completely free trade across international borders remains elusive, the following trade agreements have reduced some of the barriers to free trade that had stood for many years.

The World Trade Organization (WTO)

The World Trade Organization (WTO) was established in January 1995 and replaced the General Agreement of Tariffs and Trade (GATT), the first global tariff agreement, which was created in 1947 and designed to reduce tariffs among member nations. The WTO, currently with 149 member countries, is the only international organization that establishes rules for trade among nations. Its member countries represent more than 97 percent of all world trade. The rules and agreements of the WTO, called the multilateral trading system, are the result of negotiations among its members. The WTO actively implements the rules established by the Uruguay Round negotiations of GATT from 1986 to 1994 and continues to negotiate additional trade agreements. Through the agreements of the WTO, members commit themselves to nondiscriminatory trade practices. These agreements spell out the rights and obligations of each member country. Each member country receives guarantees that its exports will be treated fairly and consistently in other member countries' markets. The WTO's General Agreement on Trade in Services (GATS) addresses specific industries, including banking, insurance, telecommunications, and tourism. In addition, the WTO's intellectual property agreement, which covers patents, copyrights, and trademarks, defines rules for protecting ideas and creativity across borders.

In addition to the development of agreements among members, the WTO is involved in the resolution of trade disputes among members. The WTO system is designed to encourage dispute resolutions through consultation. If this approach fails, the WTO has a stage-by-stage procedure that can culminate in a ruling by a panel of experts.

NAFTA

free trade area
an association of countries that have agreed to eliminate trade barriers, both tariff and nontariff, among partner nations.

The North American Free Trade Agreement (NAFTA) created a free-trade area among Canada, Mexico, and the United States. A **free trade area** is an association of countries that have agreed to eliminate trade barriers, both tariff and nontariff, among partner nations. Under the provision of NAFTA, these barriers were eliminated for trade among the three countries, but each remained free to set its own tariffs on imports from nonmember nations.

NAFTA forged a unified United States-Canada-Mexico market of 431 million people with a total annual output of more than $13 trillion dollars in goods and services. This important trade agreement binds together the three nations on the North American continent into a single trading unit stretching from the Yukon to the Yucatan. Because Canada and the United States already had a free trade agreement in effect, the businesses that will benefit most from NAFTA are those already doing business, or those wanting to do business, with Mexico. NAFTA's provisions called for the reduction of tariffs to zero on most goods traded among these three nations by 2008. NAFTA's provisions have enhanced trade among the United States, Canada, and Mexico. It also has made that trade more profitable and less cumbersome for companies of all sizes and has opened new opportunities for many businesses. In NAFTA's first decade, trade among the three nations increased 173 percent; these countries now conduct nearly $2.2 trillion in trilateral trade each day.[45]

Among NAFTA's provisions are:

- **Tariff reductions.** Immediate reduction, then gradual phasing out, of most tariffs on goods traded among the three countries.
- **Elimination of nontariff barriers.** Most nontariff barriers to free trade are to be eliminated by 2008.
- **Simplified border processing.** Mexico, in particular, has opened its border and interior to U.S. truckers and simplified border processing.
- **Tougher health and safety standards.** Industrial standards involving worker health and safety are to become more stringent and more uniform.

Palermo's Villa

Palermo's Villa, a Milwaukee, Wisconsin–based, family-owned maker of frozen pizzas and pizza crusts that was founded in the 1930s by Jack Fallucca (affectionately known to his customers as Papa Palermo), began its expansion into Canada after NAFTA took effect. By promoting its quality products among Canadian grocers and food retailers, Palermo's Villa made the most of NAFTA's free trade provisions and has had to expand its plant capacity to keep up with demand for its products in the Canadian market.[46]

Central America Free Trade Agreement (CAFTA)

The Central America Free Trade Agreement (CAFTA) is to Central America what NAFTA is to North America. The agreement, which took effect on August 2, 2005, is designed to promote free trade among the United States and six Central American countries: Costa Rica, El Salvador, Guatemala, Honduras, Dominican Republic, and Nicaragua. U.S. exports to these six nations exceed $16 billion a year.[47] In addition to reducing tariffs among these nations, CAFTA protects U.S. companies' investments and intellectual property in the region, simplifies the export process for U.S. companies, and provides easier access to Central American markets. For instance, Paymaster Corporation, a small company in Elk Grove Village, Illinois, that makes check writing and signing machines, recently landed its first sale in Costa Rica as a result of CAFTA.[48]

Conclusion

To remain competitive, businesses must assume a global posture. Global effectiveness requires managers to be able to leverage workers' skills, company resources, and customer know-how across borders and throughout cultures across the world. Managers also must concentrate on maintaining competitive cost structures and a focus on the core of every business—the *customer!* Although there are no sure-fire rules for going global, small businesses that want to become successful international competitors should observe these guidelines:

- Make yourself at home in all three of the world's key markets: North America, Europe, and Asia. This triad of regions is forging a new world order in trade that will dominate global markets for years to come.
- Appeal to the similarities within the various regions in which you operate but recognize the differences in their specific cultures. Although the European Union is a single trading bloc composed of 25 countries, smart entrepreneurs know that each country has its own cultural uniqueness and do not treat them as a unified market. "Gone are the days when you could just roll out one product for the global market," says Hamad Malik, Middle East marketing director for the South Korean electronics company LG. LG has achieved tremendous success in the global market in a relatively short time by adapting its products to suit local customers' needs and preferences. For instance, in the Middle East, the company sells refrigerators with a special compartment for storing dates, a diet staple in that part of the world that spoils easily. In Korea, LG sells a refrigerator that isolates kimchi, a popular but smelly combination of fermented cabbage, garlic, and chili, from other foods. In India, where cricket is the national pastime, LG sells a television that includes a built-in cricket videogame.[49]
- Develop new products for the world market. Make sure your products and services measure up to world-class quality standards.
- Familiarize yourself with foreign customs and languages; constantly scan, clip, and build a file on other cultures: their lifestyles, values, customs, and business practices.
- Learn to understand your customers from the perspective of *their* culture, not your own. Bridge cultural gaps by adapting your business practices to suit their preferences and customs.
- "Glocalize." Make global decisions about products, markets, and management but allow local employees to make tactical decisions about packaging, advertising, and service.
- Recruit and retain multicultural workers who can give your company meaningful insight into the intricacies of global markets. Entrepreneurs with a truly global perspective identify, nurture, and utilize the talents and knowledge multicultural workers possess.
- Train employees to think globally, send them on international trips, and equip them with state-of-the-art communications technology.
- Hire local managers to staff foreign offices and branches.
- Do whatever seems best wherever it seems best, even if people at home lose jobs or responsibilities.
- Consider using partners and joint ventures to break into foreign markets you cannot penetrate on your own.

By its very nature, going global can be a frightening experience. Most entrepreneurs who have already made the jump, however, have found that the benefits outweigh the risks and that their companies are much stronger because of it.

Chapter Summary by Learning Objectives

1. Explain why "going global" has become an integral part of many small companies' strategies.

Companies that move into international business can reap many benefits, including offsetting sales declines in the domestic market, increasing sales and profits; extending their products' life cycles; lowering manufacturing costs; improving competitive position; raising quality levels; and becoming more customer oriented.

2. Describe the principal strategies small businesses have for going global.

Perhaps the simplest and least expensive way for a small business to begin conducting business globally is to establish a site on the World Wide Web. Companies wanting to sell goods on the Web should establish a secure ordering and payment system for online customers.

Trade intermediaries such as export management companies, export trading companies, manufacturer's export agents, export merchants, resident buying offices, and foreign distributors can serve as a small company's "export department."

In a domestic joint venture, two or more U.S. small companies form an alliance for the purpose of exporting their goods and services abroad. In a foreign joint venture, a domestic small business forms an alliance with a company in the target area.

Some small businesses enter foreign markets by licensing businesses in other nations to use their patents, trademarks, copyrights, technology, processes, or products.

Franchising has become a major industry for the United States. The International Franchise Association estimates that more than 20 percent of the nation's 4,000 franchisors have outlets in foreign countries.

Some countries lack a hard currency that is convertible into other currencies, so companies doing business there must rely on countertrading or bartering. A countertrade is a transaction in which a business selling goods in a foreign country agrees to promote investment and trade in that country. Bartering involves trading goods and services for other goods and services.

Although small companies account for 97 percent of the companies involved in exporting, they generate only 26 percent of the dollar value of the nation's exports. However, small companies, realizing the incredible profit potential it offers, are making exporting an ever-expanding part of their marketing plans.

Once established in international markets, some small businesses set up permanent locations there. Although they can be very expensive to establish and maintain, international locations give businesses the opportunity to stay in close contact with their international customers.

3. Explain how to build a thriving export program.

Building a successful export program takes patience and research. Steps include the following: Realize that even the tiniest firms have the potential to export; analyze your product or service; analyze your commitment to exporting; research markets and pick your target; develop a distribution strategy; find your customer; find financing; ship your goods; and collect your money.

4. Discuss the major barriers to international trade and their impact on the global economy.

Three domestic barriers to international trade are common: the attitude that "we're too small to export," lack of information on how to get started in global trade, and a lack of available financing.

International barriers include tariffs, quotas, embargoes, dumping, and political, business, and cultural barriers.

5. Describe the trade agreements that will have the greatest influence on foreign trade in the twenty-first century— WTO, NAFTA, and CAFTA.

The World Trade Organization (WTO) was established in 1995 to implement the rules established by the Uruguay Round negotiations of GATT from 1986 to 1994, and it continues to negotiate additional trade agreements. The WTO has 149 member nations and represents more than 97 percent of all global trade. The WTO is the governing body that resolves trade disputes among members.

The North American Free Trade Agreement (NAFTA) created a free trade area among Canada, Mexico, and the United States. The agreement created an association that knocked down trade barriers, both tariff and nontariff, among the partner nations.

The Central American Free Trade Agreement (CAFTA) created a free trade area among the United States and six nations in Central America: Costa Rica, El Salvador, Guatemala, Honduras, Dominican Republic, and Nicaragua. In addition to reducing tariffs among these nations, CAFTA protects U.S. companies' investments and intellectual property in the region, simplifies the export process for U.S. companies, and provides easier access to Central American markets.

Discussion Questions

1. Why must entrepreneurs learn to think globally?
2. What forces are driving small businesses into international markets?

3. What advantages does going global offer a small business owner? What are the potential risks?
4. Outline the eight strategies that small businesses can use to go global.

5. Describe the various types of trade intermediaries small business owners can use. What functions do they perform?
6. What is a domestic joint venture? What is a foreign joint venture? What advantages does taking on an international partner through a joint venture offer? What are the disadvantages?
7. What mistake are first-time exporters most likely to make? Outline the steps a small company should take to establish a successful export program.
8. What are the benefits of establishing international locations? What are the disadvantages?

9. Describe the barriers businesses face when trying to conduct business internationally. How can a small business owner overcome these obstacles?
10. What is a tariff? What is a quota? What impact do they have on international trade?
11. What impact have the WTO, NAFTA, and CAFTA trade agreements had on small companies that want to go global? What provisions are included in these trade agreements?
12. What advice would you offer to an entrepreneur interested in launching a global business effort?

Business Plan Pro

Business PlanPro Are there global opportunities that exist for your business? If so, include those as an "opportunity" into your SWOT analysis. Review the other sections that will benefit from incorporating these global plans into your business plan strategy. For example, you may need to address your global strategy in the marketing strategy and the Web site sections of your business plan. You may need to include additional expenses into the financial section of your business plan relating to your global strategy. If your global strategy influences risk, this is another factor to capture in your business plan.

Business Plan Exercises

On the Web

There are a number of Web resources that may assist with global strategies. You will find several of those links at the companion Web site http:www.prenhall.com/scarborough. One specific site that may helpful is a management portal for global strategy at http:www.themanager.org/ Knowledgebase/Strategy/Global.

In the Software

If you do plan to employ a global strategy, make certain that you have addressed that intent in your business plan. International activity of any kind may have implications for multiple sections of your business plan, including the product and services, market analysis, strategy, implementation, Web plans, management, and financial sections.

This is also an excellent time to review your entire plan, paying specific attention to the summary sections at the beginning of each major section. You may have used these areas for notes, but, at this time, review what you have written in the initial stage of each of these sections. Make certain that they provide a brief overview of what the section contains. Those sections include the following:

- Company
- Product and Services
- Market Analysis
- Strategy and Implementation
- Web Plan
- Management Plan
- Financial Plan

These initial introductory statements will add flow to your plan. You may also want to review each section to avoid redundancy and optimize the efficiency of your overall plan.

Building Your Business Plan

As you near the final stages of creating your business plan, have others review it. Do they understand the "story" your business plan is telling? Do they follow your rationale? Do they have questions that the plan should have addressed? Based on their comments, assess whether the plan was successful at communicating your message. If there are deficiencies, make those changes to avoid confusion.

Beyond the Classroom . . .

1. Go to lunch with a student from a foreign country. Discuss products and services that are most needed there. How does the business system there differ from ours? How much government regulation affects business? What cultural differences exist? What trade barriers has the government erected?
2. Review several current business publications and prepare a brief report on which nations seem to be

the most promising for U.S. entrepreneurs. What steps should a small business owner take to break into those markets? Which nations are the least promising? Why?
3. Select a nation that interests you and prepare a report on its business customs and practices. How are they different from those in the United States? How are they similar?

16 | Building a New Venture Team and Planning for the Next Generation

Leaders don't create followers; they create more leaders.
—Tom Peters

Big businesses can afford to hire managers and employees. Entrepreneurs need to hire missionaries. —Robert Kiyoaski

Learning Objectives

On completion of this chapter, you will be able to:

1 Explain the challenges involved in the entrepreneur's role as leader and what it takes to be a successful leader.
2 Describe the importance of hiring the right employees and how to avoid making hiring mistakes.
3 Explain how to create a company culture that encourages employee retention.
4 Describe the steps in developing a management succession plan for a growing business that will allow a smooth transition of leadership to the next generation.
5 Explain the exit strategies available to entrepreneurs.

Leadership in the New Economy

LEARNING OBJECTIVES
1. Explain the challenges involved in the entrepreneur's role as leader and what it takes to be a successful leader.

To be successful, an entrepreneur must assume a wide range of roles, tasks, and responsibilities, but none is more important than the role of leader. Some entrepreneurs are uncomfortable assuming this role, but they must learn to be effective leaders if their companies are to grow and reach their potential. **Leadership** is the process of influencing and inspiring others to work to achieve a common goal and then giving them the power and the freedom to achieve it. Without leadership ability, entrepreneurs—and their companies—never rise above mediocrity. Entrepreneurs can learn to be effective leaders, but the task requires dedication, discipline, and hard work. In the past, business owners often relied on an autocratic management style, one built on command and control. Today's workforce is more knowledgeable, has more options, and is more skilled and, as a result, expects a different, more sophisticated style of leadership. Companies that fail to provide that leadership are at risk of losing their best employees.

leadership
the process of influencing and inspiring others to work to achieve a common goal and then giving them the power and the freedom to achieve it.

The rapid pace of change in the new economy also is placing new demands on leaders. Technology is changing the ways in which people work, the ways in which the various parts of an organization operate and interconnect, and the ways in which competitors strive for market dominance. To remain in the game, companies must operate at this new speed of business, and that requires a new style of leadership. Leaders of small companies must gather information and make decisions with lightning-fast speed, and they must give workers the resources and the freedom to solve problems and exploit opportunities as they arise. Effective leaders now empower employees to act in the best interest of the business. In this way, leaders demonstrate trust in employees and respect for their ability to make decision. Many entrepreneurs have discovered that the old style of leadership has lost its effectiveness and that they must develop a new, more fluid and flexible style of leadership that better fits the needs of modern workers and competitive conditions.

Until recently, experts compared a leader's job to that of a symphony orchestra conductor. Like the symphony leader, an entrepreneur made sure that everyone in the company was playing the same score, coordinated individual efforts to produce a harmonious sound, and directed the orchestra members as they played. The conductor (entrepreneur) retained virtually all of the power and made all of the decisions about how the orchestra would play the music without any input from the musicians themselves. Today's successful entrepreneur, however, is more like the leader of a jazz band, which is known for its improvisation, innovation, creativity, and free-wheeling style. Max DePree, former CEO of Herman Miller, Inc., a highly successful office furniture manufacturer, explains the connection this way:

> Jazz band leaders must choose the music, find the right musicians, and perform—in public. However, the effect of the performance depends on so many things—the environment, the volunteers playing in the band, the need for everybody to perform as individuals and as a group, the absolute dependence of the leader on the members of the band, the need for the followers to play well . . . The leader of the jazz band has the beautiful opportunity to draw the best out of the other musicians. We have much to learn from jazz-band leaders, for jazz, like leadership, combines the unpredictability of the future with the gifts of individuals.[1]

Management and leadership are not the same; yet, both are essential to a company's success. Leadership without management is unbridled; management without leadership is uninspired. Leadership gets a small business going; management keeps it going. In other words, leaders are the architects of small businesses; managers are the builders. Some entrepreneurs are good managers yet are poor leaders; others are powerful leaders but are weak managers. The best bet for the latter is to hire people with solid management skills to help them to execute the vision they have for their companies. Stephen Covey, author of *Principle-Centered Leadership*, explains the difference between management and leadership in this way:

Leadership deals with people; management deals with things. You manage things; you lead people. Leadership deals with vision; management deals with logistics toward that vision. Leadership deals with doing the right things; management focuses on doing things right. Leadership deals with examining the paradigms on which you are operating; management operates within those paradigms. Leadership comes first, then management, but both are necessary.[2]

Leadership and management are intertwined; one without the other means that a small business is going nowhere. Leadership is especially important for companies in the growth phase, when entrepreneurs are hiring employees (often for the first time) and must keep the company and everyone in it focused on its mission as growth tests every seam in the organizational structure. At this stage, selling everyone in the company on the mission, goals, and objectives for which the leader is aiming is crucial to a business's survival and success.

Effective leaders exhibit certain behaviors. They:

- ■ *Create a set of values and beliefs for employees and passionately pursue them.* Values are the foundation on which a company's vision is built. Leaders should be like beacons in the night, constantly shining light on the principles, values, and beliefs on which they founded their companies. Whenever the opportunity presents itself, entrepreneurs must communicate with clarity the company's bedrock values and principles to employees and other stakeholders. Some entrepreneurs may not think that it is necessary to do so, but successful leaders know that they must hammer home the connection between their companies' values and its mission.
- ■ *Define and then constantly reinforce the vision they have for the company.* Effective leaders have a clear vision of where they want their companies to go, and they concentrate on communicating that vision to those around them. Unfortunately, this is one area in which employees say their leaders could do a better job. In a survey by Right Management Consultants, 30 percent of workers said that the area in which their leaders most needed improvement is engaging people in the company's vision and strategy. Clarity of purpose is essential to a successful organization because people want to be a part of something that is bigger than they are; however, the purpose must be more than merely achieving continuous quarterly profits.
- ■ *Respect and support their employees.* To gain the respect of their employees, leaders must first respect those who work for them. Successful leaders treat each employee with respect. They know that a loyal, dedicated work force is a company's most valuable resource, and they treat their employees that way.
- ■ *Set the example for their employees.* Leaders' words ring hollow if they fail to practice what they preach. Few signals are transmitted to workers faster than a leader who sells employees on one set of values and principles and then acts according to a different set. This behavior quickly undermines a leader's credibility among employees, who expect leaders to "walk their talk." That is why integrity is perhaps the most important determinant of a leader's effectiveness.
- ■ *Create a climate of trust in the organization.* Leaders who demonstrate integrity soon win the trust of their employees, an essential ingredient in the success of any organization. Honest, open communication and a consistent pattern of leaders doing what they say they will do serve to build trust in a business. Research suggests that building trust among employees is one of the most important tasks of leaders, wherever they may work. One extensive study across 62 nations found that trustworthy leaders were highly valued by employees in every culture studied.[3] Table 16.1 shows the results of a study that identified the top five "trust-building" and "trust-busting" actions leaders can take.
- ■ *Build credibility with their employees.* To be effective, leaders must have credibility with their employees, a sometimes challenging task for entrepreneurs, especially as

TABLE 16.1 **Trust-Building and Trust-Busting Behavior by Leaders**

Top Five Trust-Building Behaviors by Leaders

1. Communicate openly and honestly without distorting any information
2. Show confidence in staff abilities by treating them as skilled, competent associates
3. Listen to and value what others say, even though you may not agree with it
4. Keep promises and commitments
5. Practice what you preach

Top Five-Trust-Busting Behaviors by Leaders

1. Send mixed messages, making it impossible for employees to know where you stand
2. Act more concerned about your own welfare
3. Avoid taking responsibility for your actions
4. Jump to conclusions without checking the facts first
5. Hide information or lie

Source: "A Managers Guide to Trust," *CFO,* June 2006, p. 32.

their companies grow and they become insulated from the daily activities of their businesses. To combat the problem of losing touch with the problems their employees face as they do their jobs, many managers periodically return to the front line to serve customers. For instance, at Southwest Airlines, top managers spend one day each quarter loading baggage onto planes, checking passengers onto flights, serving as flight attendants, and other performing other front-line jobs. The CEO of a major hotel chain requires his executives to staff front-line jobs at least once a year.[4] The idea is that top managers will make better decisions about policies and procedures if they see firsthand the impact of those decisions on customers and front-line employees.

■ *Focus employees' efforts on challenging goals and keep them driving toward those goals.* When asked by a student intern to define leadership, one entrepreneur said, "Leadership is the ability to convince people to follow a path they have never taken before to a place they have never been—and upon finding it to be successful, to do it over and over again."[5]

■ *Provide the resources employees need to achieve their goals.* Effective leaders know that workers cannot do their jobs well unless they have the tools they need. They provide workers with not only the physical resources they need to excel, but also the necessary intangible resources such as training, coaching, and mentoring.

■ *Communicate with their employees.* Leaders recognize that helping workers to see the company's overarching goal is just one part of effective communication; encouraging employee feedback and then listening is just as vital. In other words, they know that communication is a two-way street. Open communication takes on even greater importance when a company faces a difficult or uncertain future.

■ *Value the diversity of their workers.* Smart business leaders recognize the value of their workers' varied skills, abilities, backgrounds, and interests. When channeled in the right direction, diversity can be a powerful weapon in achieving innovation and maintaining a competitive edge. Good leaders get to know their workers and to understand the diversity of their strengths. Especially important to young workers in the new economy is a leader's ability capacity for empathy, the ability to see things from another person's viewpoint.

■ *Celebrate their workers' successes.* Effective leaders recognize that workers want to be winners, and they do everything they can to encourage top performance among their people. The rewards they give are not always financial; in many cases, it may be as simple as a hand-written congratulatory note.

- ■ ***Are willing to take risks.*** Entrepreneurs know better than most that launching a business requires taking risks. They also understand that to remain competitive, they must constantly encourage risk taking in their companies. When employees try something innovative and it fails, they don't resort to punishment because they know that doing so would squelch creativity in the organization.
- ■ ***Encourage creativity among their workers.*** Rather than punish workers who take risks and fail, effective leaders are willing to accept failure as a natural part of innovation and creativity. They know that innovative behavior is the key to future success and do everything they can to encourage it among workers.
- ■ ***Maintain a sense of humor.*** One of the most important tools a leader can have is a sense of humor. Without it, work can become dull and unexciting for everyone.

Southwest Airlines

Former Southwest Airlines CEO Herb Kelleher is famous for creating a work environment where fun is the watchword. Kelleher, who appeared at one employee function on a Harley-Davidson motorcycle and at another dressed as Elvis Presley, encouraged employees to have fun at work. Flight attendants sometimes pop out of overhead bins as passengers board, or they tell jokes over the plane's public address system. Crews have been known to liven up the pre-flight safety demonstrations with song and dance routines. On Halloween, employees dress up in costumes and hand out cake to passengers. The culture of fun at Southwest Airlines has built an ésprit de corps that gives Southwest a unique advantage that competitors cannot match, and crown prince Herb Kelleher was its architect.[6]

- ■ ***Create an environment in which people have the motivation, the training, and the freedom to achieve the goals they have set.*** Leaders know that *their* success is determined by the success of their followers.
- ■ ***Become a catalyst for change.*** With market and competitive climates changing so rapidly, entrepreneurs must reinvent their companies constantly. Although leaders must cling to the values and principles that form the bedrock of their companies, they must be willing to change, sometimes radically, the policies, procedures, and processes within their businesses. If a company is headed in the wrong direction, the leader's job is to recognize that and to get the company moving in the right direction. "No leader knows enough about the future to make the optimal decision every time, but it's better to set a clear course today and tackle problems that arise tomorrow," says Andy Grove, former CEO of Intel, the computer chip maker.
- ■ ***Keep their eyes on the horizon.*** Effective leaders are never satisfied with what they and their employees accomplished yesterday. They know that yesterday's successes are not enough to sustain their companies indefinitely. They see the importance of building and maintaining sufficient momentum to carry their companies to the next level. "A leader's job is to rally people toward a better future," says Marcus Buckingham, who has spent nearly two decades studying effective leaders.[7]

Leading an organization, whatever its size, is one of the biggest challenges any entrepreneur faces. Yet, for an entrepreneur, leadership success is one of the key determinants of a company's success. Research suggests that there is no single "best" style of leadership; the style a leader uses depends, in part, on the situation at hand. Some situations are best suited for a participative leadership style, but in others, an authoritarian style actually may be best. Research by Daniel Goleman and others suggests that today's workers tend to respond more to adaptive, humble leaders who are results oriented and who take the time to cultivate other leaders in the organization.[8] Table 16.2 offers useful tips on how to become a successful leader.

TABLE 16.2 Tips for Becoming a Successful Leader in the New Economy

Leadership in the old days often meant that leaders had all of the answers and that employees were to follow them to the "promised land." Today, however, workers require a different style of leadership, one that involves more listening, empowering, delegating, and team building. The following tips can help you to become a more effective leader.

1. *Leaders are both confident and modest.* Being a leader is not about making yourself more powerful; it's about making the people around you more powerful.

2. *Leaders are authentic.* No one believes in a leader who fails to "walk the talk." Leadership requires integrity and sincerity. These characteristics are the building blocks of trust.

3. *Leaders are good listeners.* Successful leaders know that some of the best ideas come from the people who actually do a job every day, and these leaders are willing to listen to employees. The chief enemy of involving workers in decision making is grandiosity, the belief that the leader has all of the answers.

4. *Leaders are good at giving encouragement, and they are never satisfied.* Leaders constantly test their stamina and courage and those of the people in their organizations by raising the standards of performance. They are an organization's top cheerleaders when people succeed and are supportive when people fail.

5. *Leaders make unexpected connections.* Leaders arrange for interaction among people who otherwise might not get together. Then they listen for innovative ideas that result from those interactions and act on them.

6. *Leaders provide direction.* However, that does not mean that they have all of the answers, as the Wizard of Oz seemed to have. Modern leaders know how to ask probing, revealing questions of others that provide insight into the best course of action. Steve Miller, a manager at Royal Dutch Shell, says, "No leader can have all the answers. . . . The actual solutions about how best to meet the challenges of the moment have to be made by the people closest to the action. . . . The leader has to empower these front-line people, to challenge them, to provide them with the resources they need, and then hold them accountable."

7. *Leaders protect their people from danger and expose them to reality.* The surest way leaders can protect their organizations from danger is to keep everyone focused on the vision. Exposing people to reality means forcing the organization to face up to the need for change. Although many people are uncomfortable with and resistant to change, leaders know that their organizations must change or risk being left behind.

8. *Leaders create change and stand for values that don't change.* Although change is essential to an organization's survival, a leader must protect those values and principles that are central to the company's core. Losing these would cause the company to lose its identity. However, leaders must always watch for habits and assumptions that the company must change if it is to continue to prosper.

9. *Leaders lead by example.* Leaders recognize that they are always under the microscope and that workers are always interpreting leaders' actions. That is why leaders must live by the principles they espouse. Leaders use small gestures to send big messages.

10. *Leaders don't blame; they learn.* Leaders know that creativity and innovation carry with them the risk of failure. They also understand that creativity and innovation are essential to the organization's survival and *do not* punish people just because they tried and failed. Their attitude is: Try, fail, learn, and try again.

11. *Leaders look for and network with other leaders.* Successful leaders are *not* Lone Rangers. They look for allies and the opportunity to network with others so they can learn to become more effective leaders. Leaders build relationships.

12. *The job of the leader is to make more leaders.* In the past, the assumption was that an organization needed just one strong leader. Today, the organization with the most leaders usually wins. Your ultimate challenge is not just to become an effective leader, but also to create more leaders in your company.

Source: Adapted from "Make Yourself a Leader," *Fast Company*, June 1999, tear out booklet.

To be effective, a small business leader must perform many important tasks, including the following:

- Add the right employees to the entrepreneurial team and constantly improve their skills.
- Create a culture for retaining employees.
- Plan for "passing the torch" to the next generation of leadership.

Building an Entrepreneurial Team: Hiring the Right Employees

The decision to hire a new employee is an important one for every business, but its impact is magnified many times in a small company. Every new hire a business owner makes determines the heights to which the company can climb—or the depths to which it will plunge. "Bad hires" can poison a small company's culture. Unfortunately, hiring mistakes in business are all too common. In fact, a study reported in the *Harvard Business Review* concludes that 80 percent of employee turnover is caused by bad hiring decisions.[9] A study by Leadership IQ reports that 46 percent of newly hired employees will fail in their new jobs within 18 months and that only 19 percent will achieve unequivocal success. The study also revealed that the most common cause of failure was not a lack of technical skills for the job at hand but rather a lack of interpersonal skills.[10] The culprit in most cases? The company's selection and hiring process. Even the best training programs cannot overcome a flawed hiring decision.

As crucial as finding good employees is to a small company's future, it is no easy task. Today, rising demand for skilled knowledge workers and relatively low levels of unemployment have combined to create a hiring crisis for business owners. The severity of this labor shortage will worsen because of demographic trends. As baby boomers retire in increasing numbers, the pool of available workers will continue to dwindle. According to the Bureau of Labor Statistics, the labor force will grow by 1.1 percent a year from 2002 to 2012, compared to the 2.1 percent a year it grew between 1970 and 1995.[11] According to the National Commission for Employment Policy, the impact of these demographic changes will be a "skilled-worker gap" (in which the demand for skilled workers outstrips the supply) of 5.3 million employees in 2010 and 14 million in 2020.[12] As a result of the intense competition for quality workers among businesses, employers often feel pressured to hire someone, even if that person is not a good fit for the job. A study by Development Dimensions International (DDI) reports that 34 percent of hiring managers admit to making bad hiring decisions because they were under pressure to fill a job.[13] The result is the same: An expensive hiring mistake for the company.

Competition among businesses for quality workers is intense, and the battle for talent has taken on higher stakes, particularly for high-tech workers. "Tomorrow's world will be a world in which talent will redefine or demolish borders, and companies across the globe will have the ability to access this talent at any time or place, regardless of location," says one business writer.[14] Indeed, rapidly advancing technology and increasing globalization give companies of all sizes access to most of the same resources, including human resources, so that the balance of competitive power shifts to those companies with superior human resources. Entrepreneurs must approach the hiring process with a commitment to fill open positions with high-quality employees, even if it takes longer than expected.

Hiring mistakes are incredibly expensive, and no organization, especially small ones, can afford too many of them. The U.S. Department of Labor estimates that the cost of replacing a new employee who does not succeed is about one-third of that employee's potential first-year salary. This estimate factors in the amount a company must spend on recruiting, selecting, and training for the employee's replacement and the cost of lost productivity, but it does not count the cost of lost customers, low morale, and the negative impact a bad hire can have on a company.[15] Estimates that include these expenses place the cost of making a bad hire at two to two-and-a-half times the employee's potential first year salary.

Ethics and Entrepreneurship

The Ethics of Recruiting

The owners of Mindbridge Software, a Philadelphia-based intranet software company, are in a war for talent. Like many of their competitors in the tech world, they are looking for the best and brightest workers who display creativity and innovative thinking. The message they give to their recruiters is, "Don't break the law, and beyond that, pretty much anything goes." To lure the talent the company needs to grow, recruiters have waited outside the office of a struggling competitor and offered to buy lunch for employees as they left the building. On one occasion, when a prospective candidate Mindbridge really wanted balked, a recruiter watched to see which car he drove and then waited in the parking lot at the end of the day to talk with him. On another occasion, managers sent a recruiter to Boston with an airline ticket and told him not to come back without the prospect the company had been courting. Mindbridge recruited nearly half of its 80 employees using techniques such as these. "If we find someone who is a good fit, we'll do just about anything to get that person in the door," says Scott Testa, Mindbridge's chief operating officer. "If we don't do it, our competitors will."

Aggressive recruiting techniques have become so common that recruiters have developed their own jargon to describe them:

- Rustling: Calling a competitor's office and working the receptionist until you get transferred to an employee who fits the job you are seeking to fill.
- Poaching: Using aggressive and sometimes questionable tactics to hire away a rival's top talent.
- Lift-out: Recruiting an entire team of employees from a competitor in one fell swoop.
- On-boarding: Holding frequent follow-up meetings with a new hire to ensure that he or she is happy in the new position and to minimize the probability that a competitor will poach him or her.
- Peeling: Digging through another company's Web site to find its employee roster so that you can poach them.

- Ruse: Calling a competitor's office and misrepresenting yourself or playing dumb to convince the receptionist to connect you with a job prospect.

Chris Forman, CEO of AIRS, a training and consulting firm in Wilder, Vermont, is always looking for talented workers but refuses to use some of the recruiting tactics that companies rely on to recruit employees. Instead, Forman emphasizes to his 42 employees that *everyone* in the company is a recruiter. "It's not good enough to come to work, go to meetings, and do your job well," says Forman. "You need to be looking for talent." Employee referrals typically lead to about 200 interviews, from which AIRS hires about 10 people.

Many companies offer their employees financial incentives to recruit new hires. At NewsMarket, a fast-growing New York City-based Internet video company, employees can earn $2,000 for referring a candidate whom the company actually hires. Interviewers even ask job candidates for referrals. "We'll ask, 'Who are the top performers at your company besides you?'," says CEO Shoba Purushotaman.

Clew, a competitive intelligence company located in Boston, relies on perpetual job postings on key Internet sites and other places. The company even lists jobs that are not open and jobs that don't even exist yet. If someone applies for one of these jobs, the company tells him or her that the jobs are not currently open but asks them to stay in touch. Clew CEO David Carpe says that Clew recently was ready to hire for one of its perpetually listed jobs and drew from the list of applicants it had built from its listings. "We never had to outside that list," he says.

1. Legal experts say that poaching employees from other firms is not a violation of the law. Does obeying the law equate to ethical behavior? Explain.
2. Discuss the ethics of the recruiting techniques used by the companies described here.
3. Work with a team of your classmates to brainstorm other techniques that these companies might use to recruit the talent they need to grow.

Source: Adapted from Scott Wescott, "Scenes from the Talent Wars," *Inc.*, January 2006, pp. 29–31.

Avoiding Hiring Mistakes

Even though the importance of hiring decisions is magnified in small companies, small businesses are most likely to make hiring mistakes because they lack the human resources experts and the disciplined hiring procedures large companies have. In many small businesses, the hiring process is informal, and the results often are unpredictable. In the early days of a company, entrepreneurs rarely take the time to create job descriptions and specifications; instead, they usually hire people because they know or trust them rather than for their job or interpersonal skills. Then, as the company grows, business owners hire people to fit in around these existing employees, often creating a very unusual, inefficient organization structure built around jobs that are poorly planned and designed.

The following guidelines can help entrepreneurs to avoid making costly hiring mistakes as they build their team of employees.

Elevate Recruiting to a Strategic Position in the Company Assembling a quality work force begins with a sound recruiting effort. By investing time and money at this crucial phase of the staffing process, entrepreneurs can generate spectacular savings down the road by avoiding costly hiring mistakes. The recruiting process also is the starting point for building quality into a company. Recruiting is so important that many entrepreneurs choose to become actively involved in the process themselves. Truly aggressive entrepreneurs *never* stop recruiting because top-quality talent is hard to find.

Attracting a pool of qualified job candidates requires not only constant attention but also creativity, especially among smaller companies that often find it difficult to match the more generous offers large companies make. With a sound recruiting strategy and a willingness to look in new places, however, smaller companies *can* hire and retain high-caliber employees. The following techniques will help.

LOOK INSIDE THE COMPANY FIRST One of the best sources for top prospects is right inside the company itself. A promotion-from-within policy serves as an incentive for existing workers to upgrade their skills and to produce results. In addition, an entrepreneur already knows the employee's work habits, and the employee already understands the company's culture. At Sherwin-Williams, a maker of paints, more than 90 percent of managerial and professional positions are filled from within the company.[16]

ENCOURAGE EMPLOYEE REFERRALS To cope with the shortage of available talent, many companies are offering their employees (and others) bonuses for referring candidates who come to work and prove to be valuable employees. Employees serve as reliable screens because they do not want to jeopardize their reputations with their employer. Marsha Serlin, founder of United Scrap Metal (USM) in Chicago, Illinois, counts on her 115 workers for referrals when she needs to hire a new employee. One employee, Benito Rosales, who has worked for USM for 25 years, says that he has recruited about 30 of his relatives to work for the company.[17] To encourage employee referrals, many companies offer incentives for successful hires. Rewards companies offer to employees for successful referrals range from weekend getaways to cash. At Redback Network, a high-tech networking company, referral bonuses range from $2,500 to $10,000 (for especially hard-to-fill positions).[18]

MAKE EMPLOYMENT ADVERTISEMENTS STAND OUT Getting employment ads noticed in traditional media is becoming more difficult because they get lost in the swarm of ads from other companies.

Signal Corporation

Roger Mody, founder and former CEO of Signal Corporation, an information technology services provider, uses humor to make his employment ads stand out and to communicate the sense of fun in the company's culture. One ad ran a photo of Mody after a company pie-eating contest with the tag line "And you should see us on casual day."[19]

USE THE INTERNET AS A RECRUITING TOOL Although newspaper ads still top employers' list of job postings, many businesses are attracting candidates through other media, particularly the Internet. Posting job listings on career-oriented sites such as Monster.com, Hotjobs.com, and others not only expands a small company's reach far beyond an ad in a local newspaper, but it also is very inexpensive.

Darlene Chapin, recruiting manager at Cheetah Technologies, a computer network management company, says the Internet has proved to be the most effective recruiting tool she uses. Chapin emphasizes that the Internet is just one part of a comprehensive recruiting effort. Cheetah also uses ads in newspapers and technical publications, employee referrals, career fairs, college visits, and other methods to find employees.[20]

Cheetah Technologies

RECRUIT ON CAMPUS For many employers, college and university campuses remain an excellent source of workers, especially for entry-level positions. After screening résumés, a recruiter can interview a dozen or more high-potential students in just one day. On some campuses, competition for the best students is so intense that companies are going to extreme measures. For example, large sign-on bonuses for graduates in "hot" career fields are becoming more common.

FORGE RELATIONSHIPS WITH SCHOOLS AND OTHER SOURCES OF WORKERS Some employers have found that forging long-term relationships with schools and other institutions can provide a valuable source of workers. As colleges and universities begin to offer students more internship opportunities, a small business can gain greatly by hosting one or more students for a semester or for the summer. The company has an opportunity to observe the student's work habits and, if those habits are positive, sell the student on a permanent position on graduation.

RECRUIT "RETIRED" WORKERS By 2020, 20 percent of workers in the United States will have reached retirement age.[21] Many of these baby boomers plan to continue working after reaching retirement age to maintain their lifestyles, however, and small businesses are ready to hire them. With a lifetime of work experience and time on their hands and a strong work ethic, retired workers can be the ideal solution to many entrepreneurs' labor problems. One survey by CareerBuilder.com and America Online reports that 45 percent of hiring managers plan to recruit retirees from other companies or to encourage their own employees of retirement age to stay on.[22] Older employees also can be a valuable asset to small firms.

In 1992, managers at CVS Pharmacy, a chain of drug stores, saw the impact that demographic changes would have on their recruiting efforts and made a conscious decision to begin recruiting older workers, many of them retirees from other companies. In 1992, when CVS started the initiative, workers over 55 made up just 7 percent of its workforce; today, workers over 55 make up 16 percent of CVS's employees. "Without older workers, we wouldn't have a company," says Steve Wing, a top manager at CVS. "We have workers in their 70s and some in their 90s who are not just holding down entry-level jobs. Some [employers] use older workers just as greeters, but we employ them throughout the organization in all sorts of roles."[23]

CVS Pharmacy

CONSIDER USING OFFBEAT RECRUITING TECHNIQUES To attract the workers they need to support their growing businesses, some entrepreneurs have resorted to rather unconventional recruiting techniques such as the following:

- Sending young recruiters to mingle with college students on spring break.
- Having an airplane tow a banner over competitors' offices that reads, "Don't make a career mistake."
- Launching a monthly industry networking meeting for local workers at Internet companies.

■ Keeping a file of all of the workers mentioned in the "People on the Move" column in the business section of the local newspaper and then contacting them a year later to see if they are happy in their jobs.[24]

OFFER WHAT WORKERS WANT Adequate compensation and benefits are important considerations for job candidates, but other, less-tangible factors also weigh heavily in a prospect's decision to accept a job. Flexible work schedules and telecommuting that allow employees to balance the demands of work and life can attract quality workers to small companies. Many of the companies listed on *Fortune*'s "100 Best Companies to Work For" offer low-cost but valuable (from their employees' perspectives) perks such as take-home meals, personal concierge services that coordinate everything from dry cleaning to auto maintenance for employees, exercise facilities, and company movie outings.[25]

Take Two LLC

Teri Rogers, president of Take Two LLC, a film and video production company in Kansas City, Missouri, says her company's "family-first policy" that allows employees to adjust their work schedules to accommodate family obligations enables her to attract and retain quality employees. Rogers also periodically hires massage therapists, provides a daily breakfast and an afternoon snack, and gives a "spa day" to staffers who have worked hard to complete a special project.[26]

For young knowledge workers especially, a fun yet professionally challenging work environment can be as important as salary. Giving these workers challenging, rewarding assignments with a sense of purpose that is bigger than merely "making money for the company" is a powerful recruiting tool.

Create Practical Job Descriptions and Job Specifications Business owners must recognize that what they do *before* they ever start interviewing candidates for a position determines to a great extent how successful they will be at hiring winners. The first step is to perform a **job analysis,** the process by which a firm determines the duties and nature of the jobs to be filled and the skills and experience required of the people who are to fill them. Without a proper job analysis, a hiring decision is, at best, a coin toss. The first step in conducting a job analysis is to develop a **job description,** a written statement of the duties, responsibilities, reporting relationships, working conditions, and methods and techniques as well as materials and equipment used in a job. A results-oriented job description explains what a job entails and the duties the person filling it is expected to perform. A detailed job description includes a job title, job summary, duties to be performed, nature of supervision, job's relationship to others in the company, working conditions, definitions of job-specific terms, and general comments needed to clarify any of the foregoing.

Preparing job descriptions is a task most small business owners overlook; however, this may be one of the most important parts of the hiring process because it creates a blueprint for the job. It is important for a small company to define the tasks that need to be accomplished. Without this blueprint, a manager tends to hire the person with experience whom they like the best. Useful sources of information for writing job descriptions include the manager's knowledge of the job, the worker(s) currently holding the job, and the *Dictionary of Occupational Titles* (D.O.T), which is available at most libraries. *The Dictionary of Occupational Titles*, published by the Department of Labor, lists more than 20,000 job titles and descriptions and serves as a useful tool for getting a small business owner started when writing job descriptions. Internet searches also are a valuable tool for finding templates for writing job descriptions. There entrepreneurs can find templates and descriptions that they can easily modify to fit their companies' needs. Table 16.3 provides an example of the description drawn from the D.O.T. for an unusual job.

The second objective of a job analysis is to create a **job specification,** a written statement of the qualifications and characteristics needed for a job stated in terms such as education, skills, and experience. A job specification shows the small business manager what kind of person to recruit and establishes the standards an applicant must meet to be hired.

job analysis
the process by which a firm determines the duties and nature of the jobs to be filled and the skills and experience required of the people who are to fill them.

job description
a written statement of the duties, responsibilities, reporting relationships, working conditions, and methods and techniques as well as materials and equipment used in a job.

job specification
a written statement of the qualifications and characteristics needed for a job stated in terms such as education, skills, and experience.

TABLE 16.3 A Sample Job Description from the *Dictionary of Occupational Titles*

Code 413.687-010: *Worm Picker*—gathers worms to be used as fish bait: walks about grassy areas, such as gardens, parks, and golf courses, and picks up earthworms (commonly called dew worms and nightcrawlers). Sprinkles chlorinated water on lawn to cause worms to come to the surface and locates worms by use of lantern or flashlight. Counts worms, sorts them, and packs them into containers for shipment.

In essence, it is a written "success profile" of the ideal employee. Does the person have to be a good listener, empathetic, well organized, decisive, a "self-starter?" Should he or she have experience in Java or C++ programming? One of the best ways to develop this success profile is to study the top performers currently working for the company and to identify the characteristics that make them successful. Before hiring new sales representatives, sales managers at Blackboard, Inc., a Washington, D.C., company that sells software for the educational market, study their top sales producers to identify the characteristics they demonstrate in four areas—skills, experience, knowledge, and personality traits. Table 16.4 provides an example that links the tasks for a sales representative's job (drawn from job description) to the traits or characteristics an entrepreneur identified as necessary to succeed in that job. These traits become the foundation for writing the job specification.

Many business owners recruit employees without the help of either job descriptions or job specifications.

After making three serious hiring mistakes for one key position in his small software company, Brittenford Systems, Michael Mahoney realized that he had to rework his company's recruiting process. "The first step," he advises, "sounds absurdly basic, but I'll guarantee the majority of companies are not doing it: clearly defining the position." Only after Mahoney and his staff developed job descriptions and specifications did he advertise the job listing. Mahoney and his team eliminated 80 percent of the 250 applicants based on their résumés and the results of an employment test from PI Worldwide. Carefully designed telephone interviews culled another 15 percent of the applicants. The remaining candidates went through team interviews with Mahoney and his staff. Finally, Mahoney asked the two finalists for the job to write a one-page strategic plan for the company, which allowed Mahoney and his team to make their choice. The much-improved selection process worked; the new hire was a good fit for the company and within 90 days was producing significant results for Brittenford Systems.[27]

COMPANY Profile

Brittenford Systems

TABLE 16.4 Linking Tasks from a Job Description to the Traits Necessary to Perform a Job Successfully

Job Task	Trait or Characteristic
Generate and close new sales	"Outgoing"; persuasive; friendly
Make 15 "cold calls" per week	"Self-starter"; determined; optimistic; independent; confident
Analyze customers' needs and recommend proper equipment	Good listener; patient; empathetic
Counsel customers about options and features needed	Organized; polished speaker; "other oriented"
Prepare and explain financing methods	Honest; "numbers oriented"; comfortable with computers and spreadsheets
Retain existing customers	Customer oriented; relationship builder

One of the most important parts of the selection process is the interview. A common mistake business owners make is going into an interview unprepared.

Plan an Effective Interview Once an entrepreneur knows what to look for in a job candidate, he or she can develop a plan for conducting an informative job interview. Too often, business owners go into an interview unprepared, and as a result, they fail to get the information they need to judge the candidate's qualifications, qualities, and suitability for the job. A common symptom of failing to prepare for an interview is that the interviewer rather than the candidate does most of the talking. "It's the most common mistake made by interviewers," says one human resource manager.[28]

Conducting an effective interview requires an entrepreneur to know what he or she wants to get out of the interview in the first place and to develop a series of questions to extract that information. The following guidelines will help entrepreneurs to develop interview questions that will give them meaningful insight into an applicant's qualifications, personality, and character:

Develop a series of core questions and ask them of every candidate. To give the screening process more consistency, smart business owners rely on a set of relevant questions they ask in every interview. Of course, they also customize each interview using impromptu questions based on an individual candidate's responses.

Ask open-ended questions (including on-the-job "scenarios") rather than questions calling for "yes or no" answers. These types of questions are most effective because they encourage candidates to talk about their work experience in a way that will disclose the presence or the absence of the traits and characteristics that the business owner is seeking.

Create hypothetical situations candidates would be likely to encounter on the job and ask how they would handle them. Building the interview around these kinds of questions gives the owner a preview of the candidate's actual work habits and attitudes. Some companies take this idea a step farther and put candidates into a simulated work environment to see how they prioritize activities and handle mail, e-mail, and a host of "real-world" problems they are likely to encounter on the job, ranging from complaining customers to problematic employees. Known as **situational interviews,** their goal is to give interviewers keener insight into how candidates would perform in the work environment.

situational interview

an interview in which the interviewer gives candidates a typical job-related situation (e.g., a job simulation) to see how they respond to it.

Probe for specific examples in the candidate's past work experiences that demonstrate the necessary traits and characteristics. A common mistake interviewers make is failing to get a candidate to provide the detail they need to make an informed decision.

Ask candidates to describe a recent success and a recent failure and how they dealt with them. Smart entrepreneurs look for candidates who describe successes and failures with equal enthusiasm because they know that peak performers put as much into their failures as they do their successes and usually learn something valuable from their failures.

Arrange a "non-interview" setting that allows several employees to observe the candidate in an informal setting. Taking candidates on a plant tour, setting up a coffee break, or taking them to lunch gives more people a chance to judge a candidate's interpersonal skills and personality outside the formal interview process. These informal settings can be very revealing.

Before Jeffrey Swartz, CEO of Timberland, the popular shoe and boot maker, makes an offer to a candidate for a management position, he invites the candidate to participate in one of the company's community service projects. "In an interview, I'm sure you're more clever than I am," he says. "But on a service site, you will reveal who you [really] are."[29]

Timberland

Table 16.5 shows an example of some interview questions one business owner used to uncover the traits and characteristics he was seeking in a top-performing sales representative.

Conduct the Interview An effective interview contains three phases: breaking the ice, asking questions, and selling the candidate on the company.

BREAKING THE ICE In the opening phase of the interview, the manager's primary job is to diffuse the tension that exists because of the nervousness of both parties. Many skilled interviewers use the job description to explain the nature of the job and the company's

TABLE 16.5 Interview Questions for Candidates for a Sales Representative Position

Trait or Characteristic	Question
"Outgoing"; persuasive; friendly; "self-starter"; determined; optimistic; independent; confident	How do you persuade reluctant prospects to buy?
Good listener; patient; empathetic; organized; polished speaker; "other oriented"	What would you say to a fellow salesperson who was getting more than his share of rejections and was having difficulty getting appointments?
Honest; customer oriented, relationship builder	How do you feel when someone questions the truth of what you say?
	What do you do in such situations?
Other questions:	If you owned a company, why would you hire yourself?
	If you were head of your department, what would you do differently?
	How do you recognize the contributions of others in your department?
	If you weren't in sales, in what other job would you be?

culture to the applicant. Then they use "ice-breakers," questions about a hobby or special interest, to get the candidate to relax and begin talking.

ASKING QUESTIONS During the second phase of the interview, the employer asks the questions from the question bank to determine the applicant's suitability for the job. The interviewer's primary job at this point is to listen. Effective interviewers spend about twenty-five percent of the interview talking and about seventy-five percent listening. They also take notes during the interview to help them ask follow-up questions based on a candidate's comments and to evaluate a candidate after the interview is over. Experienced interviewers also pay close attention to a candidate's nonverbal clues, or body language, during the interview. They know that candidates may be able to say exactly what they want with their words, but that their body language does not lie.

Some of the most valuable interview questions are designed to gain insight into a candidate's creativity and capacity for abstract thinking. Known as **puzzle interviews,** their goal is to determine how candidates think by asking them offbeat questions such as, "How would you weigh a plane without using scales?", "How would you design Bill Gates's bathroom?" (a favorite at Microsoft), or "How do they make M&Ms?" The logic and creativity candidates use to derive an answer is much more important than the answer itself.

Entrepreneurs must be careful to make sure they avoid asking candidates illegal questions. At one time, interviewers could ask wide-ranging questions covering just about every area of an applicant's background. Today interviewing is a veritable minefield of legal liabilities waiting to explode in the unsuspecting interviewer's face. Although the Equal Employment Opportunity Commission (EEOC), the government agency responsible for enforcing employment laws, does not outlaw specific questions, it does recognize that some questions can result in employment discrimination. If a candidate files charges of employment discrimination against a company, the burden of proof shifts to the employer to prove that all pre-employment questions are job related and are nondiscriminatory. In addition, many states have passed laws that forbid the use of certain questions or screening tools in interviews. To avoid trouble, business owners should keep in mind why they are asking a particular question. The goal is to identify individuals who are qualified to do the job well. By steering clear of questions about subjects that are peripheral to the job itself, employers are less likely to ask questions that will land them in court. Wise business owners ask their attorneys to review their bank of questions before using them in an interview.

SELLING THE CANDIDATE ON THE COMPANY In the final phase of the interview, the employer tries to sell desirable candidates on the company. This phase begins by allowing the candidate to ask questions about the company, the job, or other issues. Again, experienced interviewers note the nature of these questions and the insights they give into the candidate's personality. This part of the interview offers the employer a prime opportunity to explain to the candidate why the company is an attractive place to work. Remember: The best candidates will have other offers, and it's up to you to make sure they leave the interview wanting to work for your company. Finally, before closing the interview, the employer should thank the candidate and tell him or her what happens next (for example, "We'll be contacting you about our decision within two weeks").

Table 16.6 provides a quiz for you to test your knowledge of the interview process, and Table 16.7 describes 10 interviewing mistakes small business owners should avoid.

Contact References and Conduct a Background Check Business owners should take the time to conduct a background check and contact a candidate's references. Background checks are inexpensive to perform, typically costing between $20 and $75, and identify red flags that allow a company to avoid making a hiring mistake. By performing a basic background check, employers can avoid candidates with criminal or other high-risk backgrounds.

---

puzzle interview

an interview that includes offbeat questions to determine how job candidates think and reason and to judge their capacity for creativity.

TABLE 16.6 What's Your IQ (Interviewing Quotient)?

Test your IQ—Interview Quotient—with the following true–false quiz.

T F   1. The best applicant is the one with the neatest appearance.

T F   2. You should study an applicant's application form or résumé before conducting an interview.

T F   3. It is your responsibility to maintain control over the progress of the interview.

T F   4. During the interview, you should do about 50 percent of the taking.

T F   5. You should avoid hiring applicants who have held more than four jobs in five years.

T F   6. To conduct a smoothly flowing interview, you should first put the applicant at ease.

T F   7. A good way to begin an interview is to challenge the applicant to prove that he or she can do the job.

T F   8. The best interview questions are those that will elicit "yes" or "no" responses.

T F   9. You can encourage applicants to elaborate on their answers by using silence or non-committal responses to their answers.

T F 10. In the interview, you should focus on the applicant's technical qualifications for the job and not his or her motivation, interpersonal skills, and attitudes.

T F 11. Nonverbal clues during an interview can be very revealing and are quite helpful when evaluating a candidate.

T F 12. You should provide the applicant with a complete job description prior to the interview.

T F 13. To make sure that you don't forget anything about a candidate, you should write down everything the applicant says during the interview.

T F 14. Most hiring managers make excellent interviewers.

T F 15. You should tell every applicant who is rejected exactly—and in great detail—why you rejected him or her.

T F 16. When making hiring decisions, your views alone are sufficient for determining which candidate is the best fit for a job.

T F 17. You should reject outright any candidate who displays nervousness because he or she would not be able to handle the stress of a job in your company.

T F 18. It is the interviewer's responsibility to describe the company's culture and values to each applicant.

Answers:

1. False. The old adage "Don't judge a book by its cover" applies in any interview. 2. True. Reviewing an application or résumé beforehand is an important part of planning and conducting an informative interview. 3. True. Your job is to control the flow of the interview so that it does not evolve into a meaningless conversation. 4. False. This is the most common mistake interviewers make. You should do about 25 percent of the talking. 5. False. Although job-hopping can be an indication that something is amiss, you should ask probing questions to determine the reasons for the job changes before drawing conclusions. 6. True. The purpose of the "ice-breaking" portion of the interview is to put the candidate at ease and to make the interview flow more smoothly. 7. False. Doing so only antagonizes the candidate and puts him or her on the defensive. 8. False. "Yes-No" questions make it easy for candidates to offer the "right" answers. Instead, open-ended, probing questions are much better at revealing meaningful information. 9. True. Silence can be an effective tool for an interviewer in an interview. Most candidates are not comfortable with silence and often step in to fill the vacuum with additional comments. 10. False. Although technical skills are important, research shows that when new employees fail in a job, the most common cause is a lack of interpersonal skills, not technical skills. 11. True. Although job candidates can control carefully the words they use, most cannot control their body language. Keen interviewers monitor candidates' nonverbal communications as well as their verbal communication. 12. False. Although it is a good idea to provide candidates with an overview of the job, giving them a complete job description beforehand is not. Having a complete job description allows candidates to plan and deliver the expected responses to an interviewer's questions and to hide behind the interview mask. 13. False. Writing down everything a candidate says is pointless and distracting for both the interviewer and the interviewee. However, interviewers should take notes during the interview and then write a summary of the candidate as soon as the interview is over. 14. False. Most hiring managers have received little or no training on conducting proper interviews. Everyone in the company who interviews needs training. 15. False. Explaining why you did not select a candidate is risky legally and invites an argument. A generic statement such as "We've decided to pursue others applicants whose qualifications and experience are aligned more closely with our needs" is much better. 16. False. Allowing other in the company to interview candidates not only increases the likelihood of making a good hire, but it also gives employees a sense of involvement in selecting their co-workers. 17. False. Almost every candidate is nervous in an interview situation; it's a natural reaction. 18. True. Candidates are looking for a good fit in a job as much as any company is, and understanding a company's culture is an important aspect of that fit.

Source: Adapted from Will Helminger, "The Hiring Manager's IQ (Interviewing Quotient) Test, Inc.," March 2005, http://www.inc.com/articles/ 2005/03/quiz.html.

TABLE 16.7 Ten Interviewing Mistakes

1. Succumbing to pressure to hire fast, which often arises as a result of failing to begin the search process far enough in advance. Plan ahead!

2. Falling victim to the halo effect, the tendency to attribute a host of positive attributes (e.g. intelligence, sense of humor, honesty, etc.) to a candidate based on one positive attribute (e.g. well spoken). This tendency is called the horn effect when it works in a negative fashion.

3. Asking leading or "canned" questions, those in which it is obvious to everyone involved, including the job applicant, what the "right" answer should be.

4. Talking too much. A common mistake inexperienced interviewers make is doing most of the talking while the candidate has to work hard just to become part of the conversation. Remember the 25/75 rule.

5. Failing to take notes during the interview. Jotting down key points, questions, and impressions as they occur will be of tremendous value when it's time to make a final decision about a particular candidate.

6. Accepting generalizations from a candidate. Effective interviewers probe for specific results and examples from candidates so they can verify applicants' qualifications and characteristics more objectively.

7. Asking questions that could lead to charges of discrimination and land the company in a nasty lawsuit. Keep questions job focused and consistent.

8. Failing to check a candidate's references. This routine procedure may uncover inconsistencies and falsehoods in the candidate's background. It can help small business owners avoid making a "bad hire" and lawsuits charging them with negligent hiring. Ask former employers, "Would you hire him or her again?"

9. Making snap judgments. A common tendency among novice interviewers is to make a decision about a candidate in the first few minutes of an interview and then to spend the rest of the interview justifying that decision.

10. Committing candidate-order error. Experienced interviewers know that the order in which they interview candidates can affect their evaluations of them. Most recent candidates tend to have the advantage. Be aware of this tendency.

Handyman Matters Franchising

Andy Bell, founder of Handyman Matters Franchising, a company that has more than 100 home repair franchises in 37 states, knows that performing background checks on applicants is essential in his business because his franchisees' workers go into customers' homes. "We took a random sample of 100 applicants, and [after a background check] only 30 of them were qualified to work in someone's home," he says, pointing out that some applicants had serious criminal offenses on their records.[30]

Although many business owners see checking references as a formality and pay little attention to it, others realize the need to protect themselves (and their customers) from hiring unscrupulous workers. Is it really necessary? Yes! According to the Society for Human Resource Management, more than half of candidates either exaggerated or falsified information about their previous employment on their résumés.[31] Checking references thoroughly can help employers to uncover false or exaggerated information. Rather than contacting only the references listed, experienced employers call applicants' previous employers and talk to their immediate supervisors to get a clear picture of the applicant's job performance, character, and work habits. After talking with the references a candidate for a top financial position his company had listed, one entrepreneur took the time to contact the applicant's previous employers. He soon discovered that the candidate had stolen money and misused company credit cards in a previous job. None of the references listed mentioned the incident.

Experienced small business owners understand that the hiring process provides them with one of the most valuable raw materials their companies count on for success—capable, hard-working people. They know that hiring an employee is not a single event but the beginning of a long-term relationship. Table 16.8 features some strange but true incidents that employers have encountered during the selection process.

TABLE 16.8 Strange but True!

If you read enough résumés, conduct enough interviews, and check enough references, sooner or later you will encounter something bizarre. Consider the following examples (all true).

- After having lunch with a job candidate, a business owner took the applicant to her office for more discussion. The discussion ended, however, when the applicant dozed off and began snoring.

- On his résumé, one candidate wrote, "It's best for employers if I not work with people." Another included the following note. "Please don't misconstrue my 14 jobs as job-hopping. I have never quit a job."

- An interviewer told a man applying for a clerical job to relax before taking a typing test. He flexed his fingers and then took off his shirt.

- An applicant at a warehouse proudly reviewed his prison record for the interviewer; adding that he had gotten much better: Rather than steal from his grandmother, he stole only from her friends and beat her up only if she refused to give him money.

- When asked about his personal interests, one candidate proudly replied, "Donating blood. Fourteen gallons so far!"

- At the end of an interview, the interviewer asked the candidate if he had any questions. His only question: "Is the office close enough so I can run home three times a day to Water Pik my teeth?"

- One candidate asked if he could bring his rabbit to work with him, adding that the rabbit was focused and reliable but that he himself had been fired before.

- When asked about why he had been fired from several jobs, one candidate said that his previous employers had conspired to place an evil curse on him.

- When asked what his ideal job would be, another candidate showed his lack of motivation by saying, "To lie in bed all day, eat chocolate, and get paid."

Recommendations from previous employers can sometimes be quite entertaining, too. The following are statements from managers about workers.

- "Works well when under constant supervision and cornered like a rat in a trap."

- "This young lady has delusions of adequacy."

- "A photographic memory but with the lens cover glued on."

- "If you were to give him a penny for his thoughts, you'd get change."

- "If you stand close enough to him, you can hear the ocean."

Source: "Hiring Horrors," *Your Company,* April 1999, p. 14: Mike B. Hall, "From Job Applicants," Joke-of-the-Day, www.jokeoftheday.com. December 8, 2000; Karen Axelon. "L-L-L-Losers!" *Business Start-Ups,* April 2000, p. 13.

You Be the Consultant

Who Moved My Workforce?

You would think that John Martell, CEO of Magnetech Industrial Services, a company that makes and repairs industrial magnets and motors, would be smiling all of the time. His company, now with eight locations, is thriving and generates annual sales of more than $25 million. Even though the manufacturing industry in the United States has seen better days, Magnetech has been growing steadily and now employs 170 skilled laborers, many of whom are industry veterans who have been with the company for many years.

Therein lies the greatest challenge facing Magnetech. Recently, as Martell was walking through the 25,000-square-foot factory at his South Bend, Indiana, headquarters, he realized that many of his employees would be retiring within the next decade, taking their knowledge, experience, and talent with them. Where, he wondered, would he find their replacements, the next generation of skilled workers? A quick analysis confirmed Martell's concerns. At least 80 percent of Magnetech's employees were in their 40s. "We have an issue," Martell realized.

The issue was central to Martell's plans for Magnetech. As other U.S.-based manufacturers were laying off workers and shifting their production offshore, Martell's plans called for growth and expansion in the United States. His goal was to push Magentech's sales to $100 million within two years, which would require him to triple the size of the company's workforce.

During the heyday of the United States' manufacturing era, finding and developing skilled manufacturing employees was simple. After graduating from high school, young people who demonstrated high levels of mechanical skills selected a trade and joined a union apprenticeship program to learn it. For the next several years, they worked alongside experienced workers, where they learned (literally) the tricks of the trade. As their skill levels and tenure with a company grew, so did their pay scales.

The world of manufacturing is a different place today, however. At the end of World War II, more than 35 percent of workers in the United States were members of a union; today, the percentage of union membership has dropped to just 12.5 percent of the workforce. As worker participation in unions has faded, so have union apprenticeship programs. Magnetech's need for skilled workers has never been higher, however. Technological innovations have made industrial machinery more sophisticated, and workers must constantly upgrade their skills to remain productive.

With no union apprentices available to hire, Martell has filled positions at Magnetech by using newspaper ads and word of mouth. He also has hired skilled workers away from competitors. The result is that some of the company's current workers know how to do their jobs well but do not understand how their jobs fit into the entire production process; they lack a vision of the "big picture."

1. What advice would you offer to Martell about recruiting the workers Magnetech will need to achieve its goals for growth?
2. What other advice can you offer to Martell about solving Magnetech's shortage of skilled labor?
3. What steps can Martell take to ensure that the company's more experienced workers teach new recruits the tricks of the trade?

Source: Adapted from Patrick J. Sauer, "Case Study: Magnetech," *Inc.*, January 2005, pp. 38–39.

LEARNING OBJECTIVES
3. Explain how to create a company culture that encourages employee retention.

culture
the distinctive, unwritten, informal code of conduct that governs an organization's behavior, attitudes, relationships, and style.

Creating an Organizational Culture That Encourages Employee Retention

Company Culture

A company's **culture** is the distinctive, unwritten, informal code of conduct that governs its behavior, attitudes, relationships, and style. It is the essence of "the way we do things around here." In many small companies, culture plays as important a part in gaining a competitive edge as strategy does. Culture has a powerful impact on the way people work together in a business, how they do their jobs, and how they treat their customers. Company culture manifests itself in many ways—from how workers dress and act to the language they use. For instance, at some companies, the unspoken dress code requires workers to wear suits and ties, but at other companies, employees routinely come to work in jeans and T-shirts. At the highly successful printing company Quad/Graphics, everyone—from the CEO to plant workers—wears the same uniform to emphasize the company's egalitarian culture and to remind employees that everyone is a "production worker."[32]

Although it is an intangible characteristic, a company's culture has a powerful influence on everyone the company touches, especially its employees. No two companies have the same culture.

Motive Communications

At Motive Communications, a software company in Austin, Texas, the company culture is strictly business and highly competitive. "We're not warm and fuzzy, there's not a lot of cheerleading, and we don't give back rubs on Fridays," says CEO Scott Harmon. To keep emotions out of the decision-making process, managers debate an issue and then wait a day before making the final decision. One employee says that in five years Harmon has sent her just three e-mails praising her work. "If you need lots of pats on the back, this is not the place for you," she says. This culture works for Motive Communications, however; the company is profitable and growing rapidly.[33]

Contrast the culture at Motive Communications to that at other companies, such as Burton Snowboards or Orvis, and the differences are readily apparent.

At Burton Snowboards, about one-fourth of employees bring their dogs to work on any given day. One employee says that some of his best ideas come to him when he is away from his desk, walking or playing with his dog. When associates at Orvis, a retailer of fine sporting equipment whose headquarters is in Manchester, Vermont, take their breaks, they can fly fish using free equipment on a 377-acre company-owned pond stocked with fish. "It helps align the associates with what we do and why we do it," says vice-president of human resources Mary Cheddie.[34]

Burton Snowboards and Orvis

Chelsea, a Weimaraner, looks on as her owner Cindy Brogan tends to business at Autodesk Inc., a software company in San Rafael, California. Autodesk welcomes employees to bring their dogs every working day, and up to 100 of the 800 employees take up the offer.

In many companies, the culture creates its own language.

At Disney, the corporate culture reflects the company's history in the entertainment business. Workers are not "employees"; they are "cast members." They don't merely go to work; they are either "on stage" (when in view of park visitors) or "backstage" (when not within site of park visitors). Disney's customers are "guests." When a cast member treats someone to lunch, it's "on the mouse." Anything negative—such as a cigarette butt on a walkway or an overflowing trashcan—is "a bad show," and when cast members go above and beyond to take care of guests' needs (as they often do), it is "a good show."

COMPANY Profile

Disney

Disney's culture is a key component in its customer service strategy.

An important ingredient in a company's culture is the performance objectives an entrepreneur sets and against which employees are measured. If entrepreneurs want integrity, respect, honesty, customer service, and other important values to be the foundation on which a positive culture can flourish, they must establish measures of success that reflect those core values. *Effective executives know that building a positive organizational culture has a direct, positive impact on the financial outcomes of an organization.* The intangible factors that comprise an organization's culture have an influence, either positive or negative, on the tangible outcomes of profitability, cash flow, return on equity, employee productivity, innovation, and cost control. An entrepreneur's job is to create a culture that has a positive influence on the company's tangible outcomes.

Pepper . . . and Salt
THE WALL STREET JOURNAL

As far as I know, Laidlaw, the customs of our corportate culture do not include hissy fits.

Sustaining a company's culture begins with the hiring process. Beyond the normal requirements of competitive pay and working conditions, the hiring process must focus on finding employees who share the values of the organization. The process is continuous. "Cultural change is a way to bring the organization together in the midst of change . . . it's an anchor," explains one CEO.[35]

Creating a culture that supports a company's strategy is no easy task, but entrepreneurs who have been most successful at it believe that having a set of overarching beliefs serves as a powerful guide for everyday action. Culture arises from an entrepreneur's consistent and relentless pursuit of a set of core values that everyone in the company can believe in. "Values outlive business models," says management guru Gary Hamel.[36]

Nurturing the right culture in a company can enhance a company's competitive position by improving its ability to attract and retain quality workers and by creating an environment in which workers can grow and develop. A company's culture must encourage exceptional performance and be compatible with the entrepreneur's values and beliefs. As a new generation of employees enters the workforce, companies are discovering that more relaxed, open cultures have an edge in attracting the best workers. These companies embrace nontraditional, fun cultures that incorporate concepts such as casual dress, team-based assignments, telecommuting, flexible work schedules, free meals, company outings, and many other unique options. Modern organizational culture relies on several principles that are fundamental to creating a productive, fun workplace.

Respect for Work and Life Balance Successful companies recognize that their employees have lives away from work. One study of Generation X workers found that those companies that people most wanted to work for erased the traditional barriers between home life and work life by making it easier for employees to deal with the pressures they face away from their jobs. These businesses offer flexible work schedules, part-time jobs, job sharing, telecommuting, sabbaticals, on-site day care, and dry cleaning.

Roger Greene, founder of Ipswitch Inc., a software company in Lexington, Massachusetts, has built his company on the concept of work–life balance. Company policy discourages employees from working late into the night or on weekends, and Greene recently actually increased the minimum vacation period for employees to five weeks a year. "Live life as it goes along and do neat things while you're working and enjoy every year of your life," he advises his employees. Ipswitch's rate of employee turnover is half the industry average.[37]

A Sense of Purpose As you learned in Chapter 3, one of the most important jobs an entrepreneur faces is defining the company's vision and then communicating it effectively to everyone the company touches. Effective companies use a strong sense of purpose to make employees feel connected to the company's mission. At motorcycle legend Harley-Davidson, employees are so in tune with the company's mission that some of them have tattooed the company's name on their bodies.

A Sense of Fun For some companies, the lines between work and play are blurred. The founders of these businesses see no reason for work and fun to be mutually exclusive. In fact, they believe that a workplace that creates a sense of fun makes it easier to recruit quality workers and encourages them to be more productive and more customer oriented. "Healthy and sustainable organizations focus on the fundamentals: quality, service, fiscal responsibility, leadership—but they didn't forget to add fun to that formula," says Leslie Yerkes, a consultant and author.[38]

At New Age Transportation, a small shipping and logistics company, an impromptu dance session has turned into an important part of the company's culture. Every day at 10 a.m. and 3 p.m., employees take a dance break, and CEO Carolyn Gable has been amazed at the impact it has had on employee morale and productivity. Before, says Gable, "Mike in truckload would never have had a conversation with Barbara in billing. Now they dance next to each other."[39]

Diversity Companies with appealing cultures not only accept cultural diversity in their workforces, but they also embrace it, actively seeking out workers with different backgrounds. Today businesses must recognize that a workforce that has a rich mix of cultural diversity gives the company more talent, skills, and abilities from which to draw. A study of the demographics of the United States quickly reveals a steady march toward an increasingly diverse population. In fact, demographic trends suggest that by 2050, African-Americans, Asians, Hispanics, and other non-white groups will comprise one-half of the U.S. population.[40] For companies to remain relevant in this environment, their workforces must reflect this diversity. Who is better equipped to deal with a diverse, multicultural customer base than a diverse, multicultural work force? Fred Kleisner, chairman and CEO of Wyndham International, a company that operates a chain of hotels, explains his approach to diversity: "I want diversity to be more than a corporate initiative. I want it to be a living part of our culture, a belief system and service philosophy that permeates each of our employees."[41]

Integrity Employees want to work for companies that stand for honesty and integrity. They do not want to check their own personal values systems at the door when they report to work. Indeed, many workers take pride in the fact that they work for companies that are ethical and socially responsible. They also expect a company to communicate with them openly and honestly about issues that matter to them.

Participative Management Today's workers do not respond well to the autocratic management styles of yesteryear. Company owners and managers must learn to trust and empower employees at all levels of the organization to make decisions and to take the actions they need to do their jobs well. As a company grows, managers must empower employees at all levels to act without direct supervision. For instance, at W.L. Gore, the manufacturer of Gore-Tex fabrics, the management style is so participative that there are no bosses, job titles, or organization charts.

Learning Environment Progressive companies encourage and support lifelong learning among their employees. They are willing to invest in their employees, improving their skills and helping them to reach their full potential. These companies are magnets for the best and the brightest young workers, who know that to stay at the top of their fields, they must always be learning.

Culinary managers at the Orlando, Florida–based restaurant chain Olive Garden, learn firsthand about the kind of food and restaurant experience top managers expect them to deliver to their customers. Several times a year, the company sends workers to the world-famous restaurant Riserva di Fizzano and its next-door neighbor, the Culinary Institute of Tuscany, in Italy to learn the finer points of food preparation, cooking, and customer service.[42]

Olive Garden

Managing Growth and a Changing Culture

As companies grow from start-up businesses into the growth phase and beyond, they often experience dramatic changes in their cultures. Procedures become more formal, operations grow more widespread, jobs take on more structure, communication becomes more difficult, and the company's personality begins to change. As more workers come on board, employees find it more difficult to know everyone in the company and what their jobs are. Unless entrepreneurs work hard to maintain their companies' unique cultures, they may wake up one day to find that they have sacrificed that culture—and the competitive edge that goes with it—in the name of growth.

Ironically, growth can sometimes be a small company's biggest enemy, causing a once successful business to spiral out of control into oblivion. The problem stems from the fact that the organizational structure (or lack of it!) and the style of management that makes an entrepreneurial start-up so successful often cannot support the business as it grows into adolescence and maturity. As a company grows, not only does its culture tend to change but so does its need for a management infrastructure capable of supporting that growth. Compounding the problem is the entrepreneur's tendency to see all growth as good. After all, who wouldn't want to be the founder of a small company whose rapid growth makes it destined to become the next rising star in the industry? Yet, achieving rapid growth and managing it are two distinct challenges. Entrepreneurs must be aware of the challenges rapid growth brings with it; otherwise they may find their companies crumbling around them as they reach warp speed.

In many cases, small companies achieve impressive growth because they bypass the traditional organizational structures, forego rigid policies and procedures, and maintain maximum flexibility. One study of business growth found that small companies have the edge over their larger rivals:

- Large companies' inability to react quickly is a major barrier to their growth. Small companies are naturally quick to respond.
- Rigid internal structures keep big companies from growing rapidly. Small companies typically bypass traditional structures.
- Large companies focus on expanding existing product and service lines, whereas small businesses concentrate more on creating new ones.
- Large companies are concerned with minimizing risks and defending their market share. Small companies are more willing to takes the risks necessary to conquer new markets.
- Large companies are reluctant to eradicate market research and technology that has worked in the past. Entrepreneurial companies have more of a "clean-slate" approach to research and technology.[43]

Growth, however, brings with it change: change in management style, organizational strategy, and methods of operations. Growth produces organizational complexity. In this period of transition, an entrepreneur's challenge is to walk a fine line between retaining the small-company traits that are the seeds of the business's success and incorporating the elements of the infrastructure essential to supporting and sustaining the company's growth.

Job Design Over the years, managers have learned that the job itself and the way it is designed is an important factor in a company's ability to attract and retain quality workers. In some companies, work is organized on the principle of **job simplification,** breaking the work down into its simplest form and standardizing each task, as in some assembly line operations. The scope of jobs organized in such a way is extremely narrow, resulting in impersonal, monotonous, and boring work that creates little challenge or motivation for workers. Job simplification invites workers to "check their brains at the door" and offers them little opportunity for excitement, enthusiasm, or pride in their work. The result can be apathetic, unmotivated workers who don't care about quality, customers, or costs.

To break this destructive cycle, some companies have redesigned workers' jobs. The following strategies are common: job enlargement, job rotation, job enrichment, flextime, job sharing, and flexplace.

Job enlargement (horizontal job loading) adds more tasks to a job to broaden its scope. For instance, rather than an employee simply mounting four screws in computers coming down an assembly line, a worker might assemble, install and test the entire motherboard (perhaps as part of a team). The idea is to make the job more varied and to allow employees to perform a more complete unit of work.

Job rotation involves cross-training employees so they can move from one job in the company to others, giving them a greater number and variety of tasks to perform. As employees learn other jobs within an organization, both their skills and their understanding of the company's purpose and processes rise. Cross-trained workers are more valuable because they give a company the flexibility to shift workers from low-demand jobs to those where they are most needed. As an incentive for workers to learn to perform other jobs within an operation, some companies offer skill-based pay, a system under which the more skills workers acquire, the more they earn.

---

job simplification
the type of job design that breaks work down into its simplest form and standardizes each task.

job enlargement (horizontal job loading)
the type of job design that adds more tasks to a job to broaden its scope.

job rotation
the type of job design that involves cross-training employees so they can move from one job in the company to others, giving them a greater number and variety of tasks to perform.

Job enrichment (vertical job loading) involves building motivators into a job by increasing the planning, decision-making, organizing, and controlling functions—traditionally managerial tasks—workers perform. The idea is to make every employee a manager—at least a manager of his or her own job.

To enrich employees' jobs, a business owner must build five core characteristics into them:

- *Skill variety* is the degree to which a job requires a variety of different skills, talents, and activities from the worker. Does the job require the worker to perform a variety of tasks that demand a variety of skills and abilities, or does it force him or her to perform the same task repeatedly?
- *Task identity* is the degree to which a job allows the worker to complete a whole or an identifiable piece of work. Does the employee build an entire piece of furniture (perhaps as part of a team) or does he or she merely attach four screws?
- *Task significance* is the degree to which a job substantially influences the lives or work of others—employees or final customers. Does the employee get to deal with customers, either internal or external? One effective way to establish task significance is to put employees in touch with customers so they can see how customers use the product or service they make.
- *Autonomy* is the degree to which a job gives a worker the freedom, independence, and discretion in planning and performing tasks. Does the employee make decisions affecting his or her work or must he or she rely on someone else (e.g., the owner, a manager, or a supervisor) to call the shots?
- *Feedback* is the degree to which a job gives the worker direct, timely information about the quality of his or her performance. Does the job give employees feedback about the quality of their work or does the product (and all information about it) simply disappear after it leaves the worker's station?

Flextime is an arrangement under which employees work a normal number of hours but have flexibility about when they start and stop work. Most flextime arrangements require employees to build their work schedules around a set of "core hours," such as 10 a.m. to 2 p.m., but give them the freedom to set their schedules outside of those core hours. For instance, one worker might choose to come in at 7 a.m. and leave at 3 p.m. to attend her son's soccer game and another may work from 11 a.m. to 7 p.m. Flextime not only raises worker morale, but it also makes it easier for companies to attract high-quality young workers who want rewarding careers without sacrificing their lifestyles. In addition, companies using flextime schedules often experience lower levels of tardiness, turnover, and absenteeism. Linda Field, founder of Field & Associates, a marketing and public relations firm in Houston, Texas, says that offering flextime helps her employees to keep their work and their lives in balance and gives her company access to a larger pool of more-qualified applicants.[44]

Flextime is becoming an increasingly popular job design strategy. A recent survey by the Society for Human Resource Management found that 57 percent of the nation's workers have flexible schedules, up from 52 percent in 1999.[45] The number of companies using flextime is likely to continue to grow as companies find recruiting capable, qualified full-time workers more difficult. Research shows that when considering job offers, candidates weigh heavily the flexibility of the work schedule companies offer.

Job sharing is a work arrangement in which two or more people share a single full-time job. For instance, two college students might share the same 40-hour-a-week job, one working mornings and the other working afternoons. Salary and benefits are prorated between the workers sharing a job. Because job sharing is a simple solution to the growing challenge of life-and-work balance, it will become more popular in the future. A recent study by the Society of Human Resource Management found that 37 percent of companies in the United States currently offer job sharing.[46] Companies already using it are finding it easier to recruit and retain qualified workers. "Employers get the combined strengths of two people, but they only have to pay for one," says one hotel sales manager, herself a job sharer.[47]

job enrichment (vertical job loading)
the type of job design that involves building motivators into a job by increasing the planning, decision making, organizing, and controlling functions workers perform.

flextime
an arrangement under which employees work a normal number of hours but have flexibility about when they start and stop work.

job sharing
a work arrangement in which two or more people share a single full-time job.

flexplace
a work arrangement in which employees work at a place other than the traditional office, such as a satellite branch closer to their homes or at home.

telecommuting
an arrangement under which employees working from their homes use modern communications equipment to hook up electronically to their workplaces.

Flexplace is a work arrangement in which employees work at a place other than the traditional office, such as a satellite branch closer to their homes or, in many cases, at home. Flexplace is an easy job design strategy for companies to use because of **telecommuting.** Using modern communication technology such as e-mail, voice mail, fax machines, and portable computers, employees have more flexibility in choosing where they work. Today, it is quite simple for workers to hook up electronically to their workplaces (and to all of the people and the information there) from practically anywhere on the planet. According to the Telework Advisory Group for WorldatWork, about 22 million Americans, nearly 10 percent of all working adults, telecommute at least once a week.[48] Telecommuting employees get the flexibility they seek, and they also benefit from reduced commuting times and expenses, not to mention a less expensive wardrobe (bathrobes and bunny slippers compared to business suits and wingtips). Companies reap many benefits as well, including improved employee morale, less absenteeism, lower turnover, and higher productivity. Studies show that telecommuting can reduce employee turnover by 20 percent and increase productivity between 15 and 20 percent.[49]

Almost half of full-time telecommuters work for small companies.[50]

Trillium Group

At Trillium Group, a Decatur, Georgia–based medical billing and collection company, 45 of 65 employees telecommute, but this work option is available only after employees prove themselves in an office setting. Trillium Group requires employees to work in-house full-time for the first 90 days before they become eligible for telecommuting, and those who do work from home must report to the office one day a week. Iris Feinberg, CEO of Trillium, says that success in telecommuting requires creating an agreement with employees that spells out specific work expectations and keeping lines of communication open. Supervisors visit employees who are telecommuting to ensure that employees' home work environments are organized to maximize safety, efficiency, and productivity. The Trillium Group has found that telecommuting has reduced employee turnover and increased the company's ability to recruit and retain quality workers. Feinberg says that "with the right people in place, the right system to accommodate work-at-home employees, and the right policies to manage them, telecommuting can strengthen staff members' ties to the company, even while they work from a distance."[51]

Before implementing telecommuting, entrepreneurs must address the following important issues:

- Does the nature of the work fit telecommuting? Obviously, some jobs are better suited for telecommuting than others.
- Have you selected the right employees for telecommuting? Telecommuting is not suitable for every job or for every worker. Experienced managers say that employees who handle it best are experienced workers who know their jobs well, are self-disciplined, and are good communicators.
- Can you monitor compliance with federal wage and hour laws for telecommuters? Generally, employers must keep the same employment records for telecommuters that they do for traditional office workers.
- Have you provided the necessary computer, communications, and ergonomically designed office equipment for employees to work offsite? Trying to "make do" with substandard equipment creates problems and frustration and undermines any telecommuting effort from the outset.
- Are you adequately insured? Employers should be sure that the telecommuting equipment employees use in their homes is covered under their insurance policies.
- Can you keep in touch? Telecommuting works well as long as long-distance employees stay in touch with headquarters.
- Have you created an equitable telecommuting policy that defines under what conditions telecommuting is acceptable? One danger of telecommuting is that it can create resentment among employees who remain office-bound.

A variation of telecommuting with which some companies are experimenting is **hoteling (hot desking),** in which employees who spend most of their time away from the office use the same office space at different times, just as travelers use the same hotel room on different days. For instance, consulting firms and other professional services companies are ideal candidates for hoteling. The concept, which often is used in conjunction with telecommuting, requires advance planning and coordination, but businesses that use it have been able to reduce the cost of leasing office space, sometimes by as much as 50 percent. Flexible office designs and furnishings allow workers to configure these "hot offices" (so-called because they usually turn over so quickly that the seats are still hot from the previous user) to suit their particular needs.

When Lou Hoffman, founder of a professional services firm in San Jose, California, realized that employees were using only 45 percent of the company's existing office space regularly, he implemented hoteling. One-third of the company's 65 employees began sharing office space on a rotating basis, and Hoffman added temporary workstations to handle the occasional overflows and schedule conflicts. Hoffman estimates that hoteling saved his company $130,000 in less than one year.[52]

Some companies that have tried hoteling have dropped it because of complaints from and confusion among employees and the difficulties of coordinating the program.

Rewards and Compensation

Another important aspect of creating a culture that attracts and retains quality workers is establishing a robust system of rewards and compensation. The rewards an employee gets from the job itself are intrinsic rewards, but managers have at their disposal a wide variety of extrinsic rewards (those outside the job itself) to attract, retain, and motivate workers. The key to using rewards to motivate involves tailoring them to the needs and characteristics of the workers. Entrepreneurs must base rewards and compensation on what is really important to their employees. For instance, to a technician making $25,000 a chance to earn a $3,000 performance bonus would most likely be a powerful motivator. To an executive earning $175,000 a year, it may not be.

One of the most popular rewards is money. Cash is an effective motivator—up to a point. Over the last 20 years, many companies have moved to **pay-for-performance compensation systems,** in which employees' pay depends upon how well they perform their jobs. In other words, extra productivity equals extra pay. By linking employees' compensation directly to the company's financial performance, a business owner increases the likelihood that workers will achieve performance targets that are in their best interest and in the company's best interest. Pay-for-performance systems work only when employees see a clear connection between their performance and their pay, however. That's where small businesses have an advantage over large businesses. Because they work for small companies, employees can see more clearly the impact their performances have on the company's profitability and ultimate success than their counterparts at large corporations.

To make sure that the salaries they pay are competitive, entrepreneurs can consult a variety of sources. The Bureau of Labor Statistics publishes the *Occupational Outlook Handbook,* which provides pay rates and job forecasts for hundreds of occupations. The Bureau of Labor Statistics' Web site (http://www.bls.gov/) contains wage and salary data by region. Other useful sources include the *American Wages and Salary Survey* published by Gale Research, the *American Almanac of Jobs and Salaries,* JobStar (http://www.jobstar.org/), and WageWeb (http://www.wageweb.com).

Money isn't the only motivator business owners have at their disposal, of course. In fact, money tends to be only a short-term motivator. In addition to the financial compensation they provide, most companies offer their employees a wide array of benefits, ranging from stock options and medical insurance to retirement plans and tuition reimbursement. **Stock options,** a plan under which the employees can purchase shares of a company's

hoteling (hot desking)
an arrangement in which employees who spend most of their time away from the office use the same office space at different times.

Hoffman Agency

pay-for-performance compensation system
a compensation system in which employees' pay depends on how well they perform their jobs.

stock options
a plan under which employees can purchase shares of a company's stock at a fixed price.

Cartoon Stock, Unit 2 lansdown
mews, bath, somerset BA1 5DY

"Aye, laddie, we do have an employee incentive program!"

stock at a fixed price, have become a popular benefit for employees, especially in the new economy. Stock options take on real value once the fair market price of a company's stock exceeds the exercise price, the price at which employees can purchase stock. (Note that if the fair market price of a stock never exceeds the exercise price, the stock option is useless.) When trying to attract and retain quality employees, many small companies rely on stock options to gain an edge over larger companies offering bigger salaries.

COMPANY
Profile

ExpenseWatch.com

Todd Palmieri, CEO of ExpenseWatch.com, a company that makes software to help companies track and control expenses, recently used stock options in his fast-growing company to recruit a new manager of operations. "We could not have recruited this person successfully—or possibly at all—without our stock option program," says Palmieri.[53]

Stock options produce a huge payoff for employees when companies succeed. Workers at highly successful companies such as Microsoft and Dell Computer have retired early as multimillionaires thanks to stock options.

In an economy in which they must compete aggressively for employees, entrepreneurs must recognize that compensation and benefits no longer follow a "one-size-fits-all" pattern. The diversity of today's workforce requires employers to be highly flexible and innovative with the compensation and benefits they provide. To attract and retain quality workers, creative entrepreneurs offer employees benefits designed to appeal to their employees' particular needs. This diversity has led to the popularity of "cafeteria" benefit plans, in which employers provide certain base benefits and then allocate a specific dollar amount for employees to select the benefits that suit their needs best. Beyond flexible benefits plans, many small companies are setting themselves apart from others by offering unique benefits, including the following[54]:

- Clothing retailer Eddie Bauer offers employees on-site massages to ease tension and to enhance creativity.
- Starbucks, a chain of coffee shops, provides its employees with a personal concierge service that handles employees' errands. Need to make reservations at a restaurant

and to order flowers for your friend's birthday celebration? The concierge will take care of it for you!

- Numerous Silicon Valley companies provide catered meals, on-site kitchens filled with fruit and snacks, and gymnasiums and athletic fields for employees. At Clif Bar, a 65-employee company that makes energy bars, employees on breaks can scale the 22-foot-high climbing wall located in the company gym. Clif Bar also hires trainers to conduct classes in aerobics, weightlifting, and other workouts on company time.

- At its San Jose, California, headquarters, Cisco Systems Inc. operates a child-care center for its employees' children, complete with Internet cameras so parents can connect to the Internet and check on their kids from work.

- One company that writes software for the insurance industry offers employees access to an ultramodern exercise facility 24 hours a day. Not only does the facility help recruit and retain workers, but the company's health insurance costs also have declined since it opened.

- Employees at Adobe Systems Inc. get a three-week paid sabbatical leave every five years to pursue some topic of interest to them.

- When workers at Gould Evans Goodman Associates, a Kansas City architectural firm, need a break, they can retreat to one of the company's "spent tents," camping tents set up in a corner complete with pillows, sleeping bags, soothing music, and alarm clocks (of course!).

Besides the wages, salaries, and attractive benefits they use as motivators, creative entrepreneurs have discovered that intangible incentives can be more important sources of employee motivation. After its initial impact, money loses its effectiveness; it does not have a lasting motivational effect (which for small businesses, with their limited resources, is a plus). Often for workers the most meaningful motivational factors are the simplest ones—praise, recognition, feedback, job security, promotions, and others—things that any small business, no matter how limited its budget, can do. When the economy is in a downturn, a business that can display its commitment to employees through a record of job security has a powerful tool with which to recruit good employees.

Praise is another simple yet powerful motivational tool. People enjoy getting praise, especially from a manager or business owner; it's just human nature. As Mark Twain said, "I can live for two months on a good compliment." Praise is an easy and inexpensive reward for employees producing extraordinary work. A short note to an employee for a job well done costs practically nothing, yet it can be a potent source of motivation. How often have you had an employer say "thank you" for a job you performed well?

At Voss Industries, an employee-owned small company that makes couplings for the aerospace industry, managers hold fervent employee celebrations when the company hits its performance targets for the year. The celebrations include lots of praise, recognition, and gifts. In addition to sharing in company profits, employees come away with gift certificates, weekend get-aways, and big-screen television sets—and a zealous fervor to achieve the next year's performance targets. "When you have a great year, you need to celebrate it," says sales manager David Kleinpeter.[55]

Voss Industries

One of the surest ways to destroy high performance is simply to fail to recognize it and the employees responsible for it. Failing to praise good work eventually conveys the message that an entrepreneur either does not care about exceptional performance or cannot distinguish between good work and poor work. In either case, through inaction, a business owner destroys employees' motivation to excel. A recent study conducted by Maritz Research reports that employees who left their jobs voluntarily said that a lack of recognition and praise, the absence of incentives, and dissatisfaction with the corporate culture were major factors (all three scored 5 on a scale of 1 to 5) in their decisions to leave.[56]

Because they lack the financial resources of bigger companies, small business owners must be more creative when it comes to giving rewards that motivate workers. In many

TABLE 16.9 Xvxry Pxrson is Important

One business owner let employees know how valuable they are with the following memo:

You Arx a Kxy Pxrson

Xvcn though my typxwritxr is an old modxl, it works vxry wxll—xxcxpt for onx kxy. You would not think that with all thx othxr kxys functioning propxrly, onx kxy not working would hardly bx noticxd; but just onx kxy out of whack sxxms to ruin thx wholx xffort.

You may say to yoursxlf—"Wxll, I'm only onx pxrson. No onx will noticx if I don't do my bxst." But it doxs makx a diffxrxncx to bx xffxctivx, an organization nxxds activx participation by xvxry onx to thx bxst of his or hxr ability

So thx nxxt timx you think you arx not important, rxmxmbxr my old typxwritxr. You arx a kxy pxrson.

Source: "You Arx a Kxy Pxrson," *Pasadena Weekly Journal of Business.* 155 S. EL Molino Avenue, Suite 101, Pasadena, California 91101.

cases, however, using rewards other than money gives small businesses an advantage because they usually have more impact on employee performance over time. Rewards do not have to be expensive to be effective.

Mackay Envelope Corporation

At Mackay Envelope Corporation, managers "go around and try to catch people in the act of doing something right," says owner Harvey Mackay. "Managers have a fistful of tickets to Vikings and Timberwolves games, to the opera and to Broadway shows, and we reward them right on the spot. We praise them in front of mother, God, and country!" he says.[57]

Entrepreneurs tend rely more on nonmonetary rewards such as praise, recognition, game tickets, dinners, letters of commendation, and others to create a work environment in which employees take pride in their work, enjoy it, are challenged by it, and get excited about it. In other words, the employees act like owners of the business. The goal is to let employees know that "every person is important" (see Table 16.9).

The accompanying "Hands on . . . How to" feature offers some useful tips on creating a culture that motivates employees to achieve higher levels of performance.

Create a Culture That Maximizes Employee Motivation

Ron Huston's computerized chip manufacturing business, Advanced Circuits, was stuck on a plateau. No matter how hard he tried, he could not push the Aurora, Colorado–based company's annual sales above the $26 million mark. Then Huston realized that he had 185 other people—his employees—who could help him to achieve the goals he had set; perhaps, he thought, they merely needed the proper motivation.

Huston already had a head start on many companies because he had been practicing open-book management, the practice of sharing a company's key financial and operating information with employees, since he founded Advanced Circuits in 1989. He posted on Advanced Circuits' intranet all of the company's critical numbers, the ones that drive sales and profits, and held monthly meetings with employees to review them.

Huston decided to tie financial incentives to improving the company's performance in key operational areas. Employees, who had always monitored the company's numbers on the intranet site, began watching them more closely, like exuberant baseball fans tracking the statistics and scores of their favorite team. Huston told his employees that if they could exceed the annual sales goal of $26 million by at least $1.2 million, he would reward them and their spouses with an all-expenses-paid three-day trip to Las Vegas. The incentive worked; employees surpassed the goal and achieved sales of $27.6 million, and Advanced Circuits, whose chips power Roomba robotic vacuum cleaners and the ball that drops in New York's Times Square to ring in the new year, has never looked back. Huston considers the $225,000 that it cost for the Las Vegas reward to be a good investment.

Smart entrepreneurs know that employee incentives and rewards can be powerful motivators. Not every small company can afford to offer as employee incentives trips to Las Vegas, but the good news is that providing meaningful motivators does not have to be expensive. How can entrepreneurs create a culture that maximizes employee motivation? The following tips will help.

Give employees the information they need to do their jobs well. Employees need timely information to maximize their job performance, and it's up to company owners to see that they get it. Ron Huston's open-book management methods give employees access to all of the company's operating and financial information, but even in companies that don't use open-book management, entrepreneurs must make sure that employees have access to the company's critical numbers (refer to Chapter 11).

Ask employees for their input and involve them in the decisions that affect their work. The people who perform a job every day are the real experts, so why not involve them in the decision-making process? At one small manufacturing operation, employees, not managers, made all of the decisions relating to the purchase of a $3 million piece of equipment. After all, they would be the ones using it.

Learn from employees what motivates them. Smart business owners know that motivating employees demands a variety of incentives ranging from money and trips to praise and recognition. The best way to find out what employees want is to get to know them and then ask them, something that small business owners can do much more easily than managers at large compa-

nies. When he started an incentive program, the owner of one small company assumed that his employees wanted money. He soon learned, however, that they valued time off much more than money and began rewarding employees with that.

Recognize employees for jobs well done and do it in front of others. A survey of 1,500 employees from a variety of work settings found that the most powerful motivator was recognition. Not only is it powerful, but it also doesn't cost anything. At G.S. Schwartz, a New York public relations company, employees who get stories about the company's clients into newspapers, magazines, radio, television, and other media ("hits" in PR lingo) are recognized through the company's "Hit of the Month" program. Managers devised the program with employees' help.

Let employees recognize each other. Peer recognition programs, in which employees recognize jobs well done by co-workers with a card or an e-mail, are gaining popularity. Because it comes from the people they work with every day, peer praise gives employees' self-esteem a boost. Companies that have instituted peer recognition programs report lower levels of employee turnover as well as higher level of engagement and motivation.

Write personal notes to employees whose performance is exceptional. A note from "the boss" recognizing an employee's good work is a great way to accelerate performance. These tangible points of recognition often make it to the home wall of fame—the refrigerator door!

Hold regular morale-building meetings. One advantage many small companies have over their larger counterparts is the ability to meet with all of their employees regularly. These meetings are ideal not only for communicating important information to employees, but also for getting feedback from them (listen!), recognizing outstanding individual performances, and celebrating company successes. At Oneupweb, a search engine marketing company in Leelanau, Michigan, CEO Lisa Wehr sponsors a barbeque lunch to recognize employee and company successes every other Friday. Although they may not be elaborate, team and company success celebrations build camaraderie and a sense of family.

Emphasize your company's commitment to long-term employment. Although no company can offer a blanket "no layoff" guarantee in this age, entrepreneurs who communicate a "lifetime employment without guarantees" attitude lay a solid foundation for motivating employees. When Diana Pohly's custom publishing company Pohly & Partners was hit hard by a recession, she and her management team had to cut $400,000 in operating expenses to remain profitable. Rather than lay off as many as 7 of the company's 39 employees, Pohly and her management team instead decided to "spread the pain," instituting pay cuts of 10 percent across all workers and an additional 5 percent for Pohly and other managers. The company avoided a crisis, remained profitable, and not only has since rescinded the pay cuts, but also has given employees merit pay bonuses. During the downturn, only two employees left, and those who remained pulled together as a cohesive team to keep costs under control.

Give employees the incentive to excel by offering them a profit-sharing plan or performance-based compensation. When employees have a sense of ownership in a company, they begin to *act* like owners. At Advanced Circuits, Ron Huston routinely gives employees monthly bonuses if they meet sales and productivity objectives and performance-based bonuses three times a year. In a typical year at Advanced Circuits, employees receive an additional 20 percent of their annual salaries as incentive-based bonuses.

Sources: Adapted from Ellyn Spragins, "The Best Bosses," *FSB*, October 2004, pp. 39–57; Patrick J. Sauer, "A Summer Fave Gets Saucy and Strategic," *Inc.*, July 2005, pp. 57–58; Shari Caudron, "The Top 20 Ways to Motivate Employees," *Industry Week*, April 3, 1995, pp. 12–18; Sheree R. Curry, "Losers," *Potentials*, November 2002, pp. 16–19; Erin White, "Praise from Peers Goes a Long Way," *Wall Street Journal*, December 19, 2005, p. B3.

LEARNING OBJECTIVES
4. Describe the steps in developing a management succession plan for a growing business that will allow a smooth transition of leadership to the next generation.

Management Succession: Passing the Torch of Leadership

More than 90 percent of all companies in the United States are family owned, and their contributions to the U.S. economy are significant. They create 64 percent of the nation's gross domestic product (GDP) and employ 62 percent of the private sector workforce. Not all family-owned businesses are small, however; one-third of the *Fortune* 500 companies are family businesses. Family firms also have created 80 percent of the U.S. economy's net new jobs over the last two decades.[58] Unfortunately, nearly 70 percent of first-generation businesses fail to survive into the second generation; of those that do survive, only 12 percent make it to the third generation, and just 3 percent make it to the fourth generation and beyond. The primary causes of family businesses' lack of continuity are inadequate estate planning, failure to create a management succession plan, and lack of funds to pay estate taxes.[59] In addition, sibling rivalries, fights over control of the business, and personality conflicts often lead to nasty battles that can tear families apart and destroy once-thriving businesses.

The best way to avoid deadly turf battles and conflicts is to develop a succession plan for the company. Although business founders inevitably want their businesses to survive them and almost 81 percent intend to pass them on to their children, they seldom support their intentions by a plan to accomplish that goal. About 25 percent of all family business owners do *not* have a formal management succession plan.[60] These owners dream of their businesses continuing in the family but take no significant steps to make their dreams a reality. In many situations the reason for failing to develop a succession plan is that the entrepreneur is unwilling to make tough, and potentially disruptive, family-oriented decisions that require selecting the successor. It is not unheard of that family feuds erupt over who is (and is not) selected as the successor in the family business. The average lifespan of a family-owned business is 24 years.[61]

The National Association of Stock Car Auto Racing (NASCAR), a business founded by "Big Bill" France in 1948, is one family business that has survived into the third generation of family ownership. Big Bill, who began promoting auto races on the sands of Daytona Beach (and who, with a group of race car

COMPANY

Profile

NASCAR

NASCAR has more than 75 million fans (42 percent of them are women) but remains a family run business. The average lifespan of a family-owned business is 24 years, but NASCAR is still going strong after nearly 60 years.

drivers, sketched out the organization's points system on a cocktail napkin), turned over the family business to his son, Bill Jr., in 1972. Bill Jr. set the family business on the fast track for growth, transforming it into one of the most popular spectator sports in the nation, second only to professional football. Big Bill's grandson, Brian, became CEO of NASCAR in 2003 and immediately began making changes to ensure the company's continued growth and expansion. Today NASCAR has 75 million fans, 40 million of whom spend at least eight hours a week watching, listening to, or reading about its races. NASCAR fans spend more than $2 billion a year on NASCAR-licensed products, and some 1,100 companies pay more than $1 billion a year to plaster their names on everything from race cars and caps to race tracks and T-shirts.[62]

Most of the family businesses in existence today were started after World War II, and their founders are ready to pass the torch of leadership on to the next generation. Experts estimate that between 1993 and 2013, $4.8 trillion in wealth will have been transferred from one generation to the next, much of it through family businesses.[63] For these companies to have a smooth transition from one generation to the next, they must develop management succession plans. Without a succession plan, family businesses face an increased risk of faltering or failing in the next generation. Family businesses with the greatest probability of surviving are the ones whose owners prepare a succession plan well before it is time to pass the torch of leadership to the next generation. Succession planning also allows business owners to minimize the impact of estate taxes on their businesses and on their successors' wealth as well.

Succession planning reduces the tension and stress created by these conflicts by gradually changing the guard. A well-developed succession plan is like the smooth, graceful exchange of a baton between runners in a relay race. The new runner still has maximum energy; the concluding runner has already spent her or his energy by running at maximum speed. The athletes never come to a stop to exchange the baton; instead, the handoff takes place on the move. The race is a skillful blend of the talents of all team members; the exchange of leadership is so smooth and powerful that the business never falters but accelerates, fueled by a new source of energy at each leg of the race.

How to Develop a Management Succession Plan

Creating a succession plan involves the following steps.

Step 1. Select the Successor There comes a time for even the most dedicated company founder to step down from the helm of the business and hand the reins over to the next generation. Entrepreneurs should never assume that their children want to take control of the business, however. Above all, they should not be afraid to ask, "Do you really want to take over the family business?" Too often, children in this situation tell Mom and Dad what they want to hear out of loyalty, pressure, or guilt. It is critical to remember at this juncture in the life of a business that children do not necessarily inherit their parents' entrepreneurial skills and interests. By leveling with the children about the business and their options regarding a family succession, the owner will know which potential heirs, if any, are willing to assume leadership of the business.

When naming a successor, merit is a better standard to use than birth order. When considering a successor, an entrepreneur should consider taking the following actions:

■ Make it clear to every family member involved that he or she is not required to join the business on a full-time basis. Family members' goals, ambitions, and talents should be foremost in their career decisions.

■ Do not assume that a successor must always come from within the family. Simply being born into a family does *not* guarantee that a person will make a good business leader.

■ Give family members the opportunity to work outside the business first to learn firsthand how others conduct business. Working for others will allow them to develop knowledge, confidence, and credibility before stepping back into the family business.

One of the worst mistakes entrepreneurs can make is to postpone naming a successor until just before they are ready to step down. The problem is especially acute when more than one family member works for the company and is interested in assuming leadership of it. Sometimes founders avoid naming successors because they don't want to hurt the family members who are not chosen to succeed them. However, both the business and the family will be better off if, after observing the family members as they work in the business, the founder picks a successor based on that person's skills and abilities.

Qualcomm

Qualcomm co-founder Irwin Jacobs made it clear that his oldest son, Paul, would be his successor as CEO of the highly successful wireless communications company when he stepped down. Even though Paul took over the CEO slot at just 42, he already had earned a Ph.D. in electrical engineering and had logged 18 years in the family business. Before assuming the role of CEO, the younger Jacobs had managed several divisions in the company and had played a vital role in developing some of Qualcomm's key technologies. "Growing up in the company . . . allowed me to get into very significant positions at a relatively young age," says Paul. "I have a lot of experience even though I'm not very old."[64]

Step 2. Create a Survival Kit for the Successor Once he or she identifies a successor, an entrepreneur should prepare a survival kit and then brief the future leader on its contents, which should include all of the company's critical documents (wills, trusts, insurance policies, financial statements, bank accounts, key contracts, corporate bylaws, and so forth). The founder should be sure that the successor reads and understands all of the relevant documents in the kit. Other important steps the owner should take to prepare the successor to take over leadership of the business include the following:

■ Create a strategic analysis for the future. Working with the successor, entrepreneurs should identify the primary opportunities and the challenges facing the company and the requirements for meeting them.

■ On a regular basis, share with the successor the entrepreneur's vision of the business' future direction, describing key factors that have led to its success and those that will bring future success.

■ Be open and listen to the successor's views and concerns.

■ Teach and learn at the same time.

■ Relate how the firm's key success factors have produced tangible results.

■ Tie the key success factors to performance and profitability.

■ Explain the strategies of the business and its key success factors.

■ Discuss the values and philosophy of the business and how they have inspired and influenced past actions.

■ Discuss the people in the business and their strengths and weaknesses.

■ Discuss the philosophy underlying the firm's compensation policy and explain why employees are paid what they are.

■ Make a list of the firm's most important customers and its key suppliers or vendors and review the history of all dealings with the parties on both lists.

- Discuss how to treat these key players to ensure the company's continued success and its smooth and error-free ownership transition.
- Develop a job description by taking an inventory of the activities involved in leading the company. This analysis can show successors those activities on which they should be spending most of their time.
- Document as much process knowledge—"how we do things and why"—as possible. After many years in their jobs, business owners are not even aware of their vast reservoirs of knowledge. For them, making decisions is a natural part of their business lives. They do it effortlessly because they have so much knowledge and experience. It is easy to forget that a successor will not have the benefit of those years of experience unless the founder communicates it.

Morry Stein, the head of Camp Echo Lake, a family-run youth camp, took the time to develop a successor's survival kit in case something happened to him. When he died tragically in an airplane crash, Stein's sons, Tony and George, and his wife were able to use the written instructions to help make the difficult transition. In the kit he left behind, Stein included the names of his most-trusted advisors, advice for handling different employees, where to find important company documents, and a touching pep talk for his family. The transition went smoothly not only because of the survival kit Stein had prepared, but also because he had taken the time to sit down regularly with both of his sons to discuss "the state of the camp," as he called it. "About ten years ago, we started having business meetings around the dining room table at my parents' house," explains Tony. "We talked about new program ideas, the future of camping, how we could raise tuition, when we would enter the business, what our strengths were, and what we liked to do."[65]

Camp Echo Lake

Step 3. Groom the Successor Typically, founders transfer their knowledge to their successors gradually over time. The discussions that set the stage for the transition of leadership are time consuming and require openness by both parties. In fact, grooming a successor is the founder's greatest teaching and development responsibility, and it takes time and deliberate effort. To create ability and confidence in a successor, a founder must be:

- Patient, realizing that the transfer of power is gradual and evolutionary and that the successor should earn responsibility and authority one step at a time until the final transfer of power takes place.
- Willing to accept that the successor will make mistakes.
- Skillful at using the successor's mistakes as a teaching tool.
- An effective communicator and an especially tolerant listener.
- Capable of establishing reasonable expectations for the successor's performance.
- Able to articulate the keys to the successor's successful performance.

Grooming a successor can begin at an early age simply by involving children in the family business and observing which ones have the greatest ability and interest in the company.

At age nine, Jay Alexander started going to work with his father at the family business, Alexander Machinery, a maker of textile and road construction equipment. At 11, Jay approached his father and asked for a job in the company, beginning a long succession of jobs over the next 12 years. "I've worked practically every job in the company," says Jay. "I've never worked anywhere else." When Jay's father, Bill, decided to step away from the business he founded, Jay was the natural choice as his successor, although Jay's sister also works for the company. "This business has come naturally to him" says Bill.[66]

Alexander Machinery

Step 4. Promote an Environment of Trust and Respect Another priceless gift a founder can leave a successor is an environment of trust and respect. Trust and respect on the part of the founder and others fuel the successor's desire to learn and excel and build the successor's confidence in making decisions. Developing a competent successor over a 5- to 10-year period is realistic. Empowering the successor by gradually delegating responsibilities creates an environment in which all parties can view objectively the growth and development of the successor. Customers, creditors, suppliers, and staff members can gradually develop confidence in the successor. The final transfer of power is not a dramatic, wrenching change but a smooth, coordinated passage. Founders must be careful at this stage to avoid the "meddling retiree syndrome" in which they continue to report for work after they have officially stepped down and take control of matters that are no longer their responsibility. Doing so undermines a successor's authority and credibility among workers quickly.

Step 5. Cope with the Financial Realities of Estate and Gift Taxes The final step in developing a workable management succession plan is structuring the transition to minimize the impact of estate, gift, and inheritance taxes on family members and the business. Entrepreneurs who fail to consider the impact of these taxes may force their heirs to sell a successful business just to pay the estate's tax bill. Recent tax legislation may reduce the impact of taxation on the continuity of family businesses. Currently, without proper estate planning, an entrepreneur's family members will incur a painful tax bite that can be as high as 45 percent when they inherit the business (see Table 16.10). Entrepreneurs should be actively engaged in estate planning at no later than age 45; those who start businesses early in their lives or whose businesses grow rapidly may need to begin as early as age 30. A variety of options exist that may prove to be helpful in reducing the estate tax liability. Each operates in a different fashion, but their objective remains the same: to remove a portion of business owners' assets from their estates so that when they die, those assets will not be subject to estate taxes. Many of these estate-planning tools need time to work their magic, so the key is to put them in place early on in the life of the business.

BUY-SELL AGREEMENT One of the most popular estate planning techniques is the buy/sell agreement. A **buy-sell agreement** is a contract that co-owners often rely on to

buy/sell agreement
a contract among co-owners of a business stating that each agrees to buy out the others in case of the death or disability of one.

TABLE 16.10 Changes in the Estate and Gift Taxes

After years of complaints from family business owners, Congress finally overhauled the often punishing structures of estate and gift taxes. The federal estate tax is actually interwoven with the gift tax, but under the modified law, the impact of the two taxes began differing in 2004. The estate tax is scheduled to be repealed in 2010, but under current provisions, it will reappear in 2011! The following table shows the exemptions and the minimum tax rates for the estate and gift taxes as they currently stand:

Year	Estate	Gift	Rate
2001	$675,000	$675,000	55%
2002	$1 million	$1 million	50%
2003	$1 million	$1 million	49%
2004	$1.5 million	$1 million	48%
2005	$1.5 million	$1 million	47%
2006	$2 million	$1 million	46%
2007	$2 million	$1 million	45%
2008	$2 million	$1 million	45%
2009	$3.5 million	$1 million	45%
2010	Tax repealed	$1 million	35% (gifts only)
2011 and after	$1 million	$1 million	55%

However, the federal laws governing estate taxes may change over the next few years, entrepreneurs whose businesses have been successful must not neglect estate planning. Even though the federal estate tax burden has eased somewhat (at least for a while), many states have *increased* their estate tax rates.

Sources: "Paris Hiltonomics," *Wall Street Journal,* April 14, 2005, p. A18; Tom Herman, "Estate Taxes Will Turn Sharply Lower on Jan. 1," *Wall Street Journal,* November 20, 2003, p. D2; Jeanne Lee, "Death and Estate Taxes," *FSB,* April 2004, p. 96.

ensure the continuity of a business. In a typical arrangement, the co-owners create a contract stating that each agrees to buy the others out in case of the death or disability of one. That way, the heirs of the deceased or disabled owner can "cash out" of the business while leaving control of the business in the hands of the remaining owners. The buy-sell agreement specifies a formula for determining the value of the business at the time the agreement is to be executed. One problem with buy-sell agreements is that the remaining co-owners may not have the cash available to buy out the disabled or deceased owner. To resolve this issue, many businesses purchase life and disability insurance for each of the owners in amounts large enough to cover the purchase price of their respective shares of the business.

Larry Jaffe and Bob Gross, co-owners of Jaffe and Gross, a successful jewelry store in Dayton, Ohio, failed to create a buy-sell agreement backed by insurance for their business. When Gross died suddenly of a heart attack, Jaffe did not have enough cash to purchase Gross's share of ownership in the business. "Bob just assumed that I'd be Larry's partner and the business would go on," says Gross's widow. However, Gross's heirs, who inherited his shares of the business, had no interest in operating the jewelry store, and without a buy-sell agreement or a succession plan in place, the 27-year-old company folded. Jaffe has since launched his own jewelry store, Jaffe's Jewelers, but admits that things would have been much easier had he and Gross taken the time to create a succession plan.[67]

Jaffe and Gross

LIFETIME GIFTING The owner of a successful business may transfer money to his or her children (or other recipients) from the estate throughout his or her life. Current federal tax regulations allow individuals to make gifts of $12,000 per year, per parent, per recipient that are exempt from federal gift taxes. Each child would be required to pay income taxes on the $12,000 gift he or she receives, but the children are usually in lower tax brackets than that of the giver. For instance, husband-and-wife business owners could give $1,440,000 worth of stock to their three children and their spouses over a period of 10 years without incurring any estate or gift taxes at all. To be an effective estate planning strategy, lifetime gifting requires time to work, which means that business owners must create a plan for using it early on.

SETTING UP A TRUST A **trust** is a contract between a grantor (the company founder) and a trustee (generally a bank officer or an attorney) in which the grantor gives to the trustee legal title to assets (e.g., stock in the company), which the trustee agrees to hold for the trust's beneficiaries (the founder's children). The beneficiaries can receive income from the trust, or they can receive the property in the trust, or both, at some specified time. Trusts can take a wide variety of forms, but two broad categories of trusts are available: revocable trusts and irrevocable trusts. A **revocable trust** is one that a grantor can change or revoke during his or her lifetime. Under present tax laws, however, the only trust that provides a tax benefit is an **irrevocable trust,** in which the grantor cannot require the trustee to return the assets held in trust. The value of the grantor's estate is lowered because the assets in an irrevocable trust are excluded from the value of the estate. However, an irrevocable trust places severe restrictions on the grantor's control of the property placed in the trust. Business owners use several types of irrevocable trusts to lower their estate tax liabilities:

trust
a contract between a grantor (the company founder) and a trustee in which the grantor gives the trustee legal title to assets (e.g. company stock), which the trustee holds for the trust's beneficiaries (e.g. the grantor's heirs).

revocable trust
a trust that a grantor can change or revoke during his or her lifetime.

irrevocable trust
a trust in which a grantor cannot require the trustee to return the assets held in trust.

- ■ **Bypass trust.** The most basic type of trust is the bypass trust, which allows business owners to put assets worth up to $2,000,000 (an amount that will increase each year by the amount of the estate exemption according to the schedule listed in Table 16.8) into a trust and to name their spouse as beneficiaries of the trust on their death. The spouse receives the income from the trust throughout his or her life, but the principal in the trust goes to the couple's heirs free of estate taxes on the spouse's death. A bypass trust is particularly useful for couples who plan their estates together. By leaving assets to one another in bypass trusts, they can make sure that their assets are taxed only once between them. However, entrepreneurs should work with experienced attorneys to create bypass trusts because the IRS requires that they contain certain precise language to be valid.

■ **Irrevocable life insurance trust (ILIT).** This type of trust allows business owners to keep the proceeds of a life insurance policy out of their estates and away from estate taxes, freeing up that money to pay the taxes on the remainder of their estates. To get the tax benefit, business owners must be sure that the business or the trust (rather than the owners themselves) owns the insurance policy. The primary disadvantage of an irrevocable life insurance trust is that if the owner dies within three years of establishing it, the insurance proceeds *do* become part of the estate and *are* subject to estate taxes. Because the trust is irrevocable, it cannot be amended or rescinded once it is established. Like most trusts, ILITs must meet stringent requirements to be valid, and entrepreneurs should use experienced attorneys to create them.

■ **Irrevocable asset trust.** An irrevocable asset trust is similar to a life insurance trust, except that it is designed to pass the assets (such as stock in a family business) in the parents' estate on to their children. The children do not have control of the assets while the parents are living, but they do receive the income from those assets. On the parents' death, the assets in the trust go to the children without being subjected to the estate tax.

■ **Grantor retained annuity trust (GRAT).** A grantor retained annuity trust (GRAT) is a special type of irrevocable trust and has become one of the most popular tools for entrepreneurs to transfer ownership of a business while maintaining control over it and minimizing estate taxes. Under a GRAT, an owner can put property (such as company stock) in an irrevocable trust for a maximum of 10 years. While the trust is in effect, the grantor retains the voting power and receives the interest income from the property in the trust. At the end of the trust (not to exceed 10 years), the property passes to the beneficiaries (heirs). The beneficiaries are required to pay a gift tax on the value of the assets placed in the GRAT. However, the IRS taxes GRAT gifts only according to their discounted present value because the heirs did not receive use of the property while it was in trust. The primary disadvantage of using a GRAT in estate planning is that if the grantor dies during the life of the GRAT, its assets pass back into the grantor's estate. These assets then become subject to the full estate tax.

Establishing a trust requires meeting many specific legal requirements and is not something business owners should do on their own. It is much better to work with experienced attorneys, accountants, and financial advisors to create them. Although the cost of establishing a trust can be high, the tax savings they generate are well worth the expense.

estate freeze
a strategy that minimizes estate taxes by creating two classes of stock for a business: preferred voting stock for the parents and nonvoting common stock for the children.

ESTATE FREEZE An **estate freeze** minimizes estate taxes by having family members create two classes of stock for the business: (1) preferred voting stock for the parents and (2) nonvoting common stock for the children. The value of the preferred stock is frozen, whereas the common stock reflects the anticipated increased market value of the business. Any appreciation in the value of the business after the transfer is not subject to estate taxes. However, the parent must pay gift taxes on the value of the common stock given to the children. The value of the common stock is the total value of the business less the value of the voting preferred stock retained by the parent. The parents also must accept taxable dividends at the market rate on the preferred stock they own.

family limited partnership (FLP)
a strategy that allows business-owning parents to transfer their company to their children (lowering their estate taxes) while still retaining control over it for themselves.

FAMILY LIMITED PARTNERSHIP Creating a **family limited partnership (FLP)** allows business-owning parents to transfer their company to their children (and lower their estate taxes) while still retaining control over it for themselves. To create a family limited partnership, the parents (or parent) sets up a partnership among themselves and their children. The parents retain the general partnership interest, which can be as low as one percent, and the children become the limited partners. As general partners, the parents control both the limited partnership and the family business. In other words, nothing in the way the company operates has to change. Over time, the parents can transfer company stock into the limited partnership, ultimately passing ownership of the company to their children.

One of the principal tax benefits of an FLP is that it allows discounts on the value of the shares of company stock the parents transfer into the limited partnership. Because a family business is closely held, shares of ownership in it, especially minority shares, are not as marketable as those of a publicly held company. As a result, company shares transferred into the limited partnership are discounted at 20 to 50 percent of their full market value, producing a large tax savings for everyone involved. The average discount is 40 percent, but that amount varies based on the industry and the individual company involved. An FLP is an ideal part of a succession plan "when there has been a buildup of substantial value in a business and the older generation has a substantial amount of liquidity," says one expert.[68]

Because of their ability to reduce estate and gift taxes, family limited partnerships became one of the most popular estate planning tools in recent years. However, a Tax Court ruling in 2005 against a Texas entrepreneur who, two months before he died, established an FLP that contained both business and personal assets cast a pall over the use of FLPs as estate-planning tools. Another case, however, calmed estate planners' fears and re-established the use of FLPs as legitimate estate-planning tools as long as entrepreneurs create them properly. The following tips will help entrepreneurs to establish an FLP that will withstand legal challenges:

- Establish a legitimate business reason other than avoiding estate taxes—such as transferring a business over time to the next generation of family members—for creating the FLP and document it on paper.
- Make sure all members of the FLP make contributions and take distributions according to a predetermined schedule. "Don't allow partners to use partnership funds to pay for personal expenses and do not time partnership distributions with personal needs for cash," says one attorney.[69]
- Do not allow members to put all of their personal assets (such as a house, automobiles, or personal property) into the FLP. Commingling personal and business assets in an FLP raises a red flag to the IRS.
- Expect an audit of the FLP. The IRS tends to scrutinize FLPs, so be prepared for a thorough audit.[70]

Developing a succession plan and preparing a successor require a wide variety of skills, some of which the business founder will not have. That's why it is important to bring into the process experts when necessary. Entrepreneurs often call on their attorneys, accountants, insurance agents, and financial planners to help them to build a succession plan that works best for their particular situations. Because the issues involved can be highly complex and charged with emotion, bringing in trusted advisors to help improves the quality of the process and provides an objective perspective.

Be the Consultant

Building Succession Plans

The Family Publisher

Years ago, Ted* started a company that today publishes three successful community newspapers. As he approaches retirement age, Ted says that he wants the business to remain in the family, but he refuses to discuss management succession issues with his three sons, all of whom work in the family business and would like to take it over when Ted retires. Rather than develop a management succession plan, Ted has included the company in his will, which means that his

*Names in this story have been changed.

wife and his three sons will inherit the business as equal owners.

Ted's son Frank and his brothers are concerned that by including the company in his will, Ted is creating the real possibility that estate taxes will create such a large financial burden that they will have to sell the business to pay the tax bill. With the business included in his estate, the value of Ted's estate is likely to exceed the exemption for the federal estate tax. Frank and his brothers also see the potential for a dispute over the roles they will assume in the business when their father does step down from the helm. What roles will they play in the family business? What about management control? Who will become CEO?

Frank and his brothers would like to get the benefit of their father's many years of experience in the newspaper business, but without a succession plan, any transfer of knowledge will be purely incidental.

The Plumber

At age 7, Roger Peugeot became an apprentice in the plumbing business his father started in 1950. After graduating from high school, Roger joined the family business full-time and then took it over when his father died suddenly 10 years later. The company now has $5 million in annual sales, 15 trucks, and 25 employees. At 60, Roger is approaching retirement age, and he wants to create a plan for transferring the business to his children that allows for a smooth transition of ownership and minimizes the impact of estate taxes. Roger and his wife already have set up bypass trusts so that after they are both gone, their estate will be taxed only once. Both of Roger's sons work in the family business. One is a master plumber, and the other is being groomed as a manager and hopes some day to become CEO.

1. What are the implications for these family businesses if their owners neglect to create management succession plans?
2. Outline the steps these owners should take to build management succession plans for their companies.
3. Describe the tools these business owners can use to minimize the impact of estate taxes on their family businesses.

Source: Adapted from James Lea, "Spirit Is Willing, But Lack of Succession Plan Is a Disaster," *BizJournals*, March 13, 2006, www.bizjournals.com/extraedge/consultants/family_business/2006/03/13/column235.html; Nadine Heintz, "How I Learned to Stop Worrying and Love the Death Tax," *Inc.*, August 2004, pp. 50–51.

LEARNING OBJECTIVES
5. Explain the exit strategies available to entrepreneurs.

Exit Strategies

Most family business founders want their companies to stay within their families, but in some cases, maintaining family control is not practical. Sometimes no one in the next generation of family members has an interest in managing the company or has the necessary skills and experience to handle the job. Under these circumstances, the founder must look outside the family for leadership if the company is to survive. Whatever the case, entrepreneurs must confront their mortality and plan for the future of their companies. Having a solid management succession plan in place well before retirement is near is absolutely critical to success. Entrepreneurs should examine their options once they decide it is time to step down from the businesses they have founded. Entrepreneurs who are planning to retire often use two strategies: sell to outsiders or sell to (nonfamily) insiders. We turn now to these two exit strategies.

Selling to Outsiders

As you learned in Chapter 7, selling a business to an outsider is no simple task. Done properly, it takes time, patience, and preparation to locate a suitable buyer, strike a deal, and make the transition. Advance preparation, maintaining accurate financial records, and timing are the keys to a successful sale. Too often, however, business owners, like some famous athletes, stay with the game too long until they and their businesses are well past their prime. They postpone selling until the last minute when they reach retirement age or when they face a business crisis. Such a "fire sale" approach rarely yields the maximum value for a business.

A straight sale may be best for those entrepreneurs who want to step down and turn the reins of the company over to someone else. However, selling a business outright is not an attractive exit strategy for those who want to stay on with the company or for those who want to surrender control of the company gradually rather than all at once.

When Paul and David Merage decided to sell their highly successful family business Chef America, their preference was to "cash out" and leave the business behind. The brothers, émigrés from Iran, launched Chef America in 1977 when they spotted three key trends that they believed would establish convenience foods as a market staple: more women joining the workforce, people eating more on the run, and people "grazing" rather than sitting down to the traditional three meals a day. After spending a great deal of money and effort on research and development, Chef America developed the predecessor to the company's hit product, the Hot Pocket, which achieved iconic status after being mentioned in an Austin Powers film. Chef America achieved market dominance in the frozen portable entrée category, making it one of the most profitable companies in the entire food industry. Recently, Swiss food giant Nestlé SA purchased Chef America for $2.6 billion.[71]

The financial terms of a sale also influence the selling price of the business and the number of potential bidders. Does the owner want "clean, cash only, 100 percent at closing" offers, or is the owner willing to finance a portion of the sale? The 100 percent, cash-only requirement dramatically reduces the number of potential buyers. On the other hand, the owner can exit the business free and clear and does not incur the risk that the buyer may fail to operate the business in a profitable fashion and not be able to complete the financial transition.

Selling to Insiders

When entrepreneurs have no family members to whom they can transfer ownership or who want to assume the responsibilities of running a company, selling the business to employees is often the preferred option. In most situations, the options available to owners are (1) sale for cash plus a note, (2) a leveraged buyout, and (3) an employee stock ownership plan (ESOP).

A Sale for Cash Plus a Note Whether entrepreneurs sell their businesses to insiders, outsiders, or family members, they often finance a portion of the sales price. The buyer pays the seller a lump-sum amount of cash up-front and the seller holds a promissory note for the remaining portion of the selling price, which the buyer pays off in installments. Because of its many creative financial options, this method of selling a business is popular with buyers. They can buy promising businesses without having to come up with the total purchase price all at one time. Sellers also appreciate the security and the tax implications of accepting payment over time. They receive a portion of the sale up-front and have the assurance of receiving a steady stream of income in the future. In addition, they can stretch their tax liabilities from the capital gains on the sale over time rather than having to pay them in a single year. In many cases, sellers' risks are lower because they may even retain a seat on the board of directors to ensure that the new owners are keeping the business on track.

When Jim and Lorraine Hudson decided to retire from the successful auto dealership they had operated for 26 years, they decided to sell the business to their daughter, Lynne, and her husband, Chad Millspaugh. The founding couple was confident in turning over the decision making to Lynne and Chad, but they needed help in structuring the sale so that it would give them the retirement income they sought but not put the new owners in a difficult financial position. Because the land the dealership occupied had become so valuable, they separated it from the business. They sold the dealership to the Millspaughs for $2 million, accepting a down payment and financing the balance. The Hudsons kept the real estate and will receive lease payments from it, providing them with a healthy retirement income.[72]

Leveraged Buyouts In a **leveraged buyout (LBO),** managers and/or employees borrow money from a financial institution and pay the owner the total agreed-on price at closing; then they use the cash generated from the company's operations to pay off the debt. The drawback of this technique is that it creates a highly leveraged business. Because of the high levels of debt they take on, the new management has very little room for error. Too many management mistakes or a slowing economy has led many highly leveraged businesses into bankruptcy.

leveraged buyout
an arrangement in which managers and/or employees borrow money from a financial institution and pay the owner the total agreed-on price at closing; then they use the cash generated from the company's operations to pay off the debt.

If properly structured, LBOs can be an attractive to both buyers and sellers. Because they get their money up-front, sellers do not incur the risk of loss if the buyers cannot keep the business operating successfully. The managers and employees who buy the company have a strong incentive to make sure the business succeeds because they own a piece of the action and some of their capital is at risk in the business. The result can be a highly motivated workforce that works hard and makes sure that the company operates efficiently.

**COMPANY
Profile**

*Springfield
Remanufacturing
Corporation*

In one of the most successful LBOs in recent years, Jack Stack and a team of managers and employees purchased an ailing subsidiary of International Harvester. The new company, Springfield Remanufacturing Corporation (SRC), which specializes in engine remanufacturing for automotive, trucking, agricultural, and construction industries, began with a debt to equity ratio that was astronomically high, but the team of motivated managers and employees turned the company around. Today SRC has more than 1,000 employees and $140 million in sales.[73]

**employee stock ownership
plan (ESOP)**

an arrangement in which employees and/or managers contribute a portion of their salaries and wages over time toward purchasing shares of a company's stock from the founder until they own the company outright.

Employee Stock Ownership Plans (ESOPs) Unlike LBOs, **employee stock ownership plans (ESOPs)** allow employees and/or managers (that is, the future owners) to purchase the business gradually, which frees up enough cash to finance the venture's future growth. With an ESOP, employees contribute a portion of their salaries and wages over time toward purchasing shares of the company's stock from the founder until they own the company outright. (In leveraged ESOPs, the ESOP borrows the money to buy the owner's stock up-front. Then, using employees' contributions, the ESOP repays the loan over time. Another advantage of a leveraged ESOP is that the principal and the interest the ESOP borrows to buy the business are tax deductible, which can save thousands or even millions of dollars in taxes.) Transferring ownership to employees through an ESOP is a long-term exit strategy that benefits everyone involved. The owner sells the business to the people he or she can trust the most—his or her managers and employees. The managers and employees buy a business they already know how to run successfully. In addition, because they own the company, the managers and employees have a huge incentive to see that it operates effectively and efficiently. One recent study of employee stock ownership plans in privately held companies found that the ESOPs increased sales, employment, and sales per employee by 2.4 percent a year.[74]

Chapter Summary by Learning Objectives

1. Explain the challenges involved in the entrepreneur's role as leader and what it takes to be a successful leader.

Leadership is the process of influencing and inspiring others to work to achieve a common goal and then giving them the power and the freedom to achieve it.

Management and leadership are not the same, yet both are essential to a small company's success. Leadership without management is unbridled; management without leadership is uninspired. Leadership gets a small business going; management keeps it going.

2. Describe the importance of hiring the right employees and how to avoid making hiring mistakes.

The decision to hire a new employee is an important one for every business, but its impact is magnified many times in a small company. Every new hire a business owner makes determines the heights to which the company can climb— or the depths to which it will plunge.

To avoid making hiring mistakes, entrepreneurs should develop meaningful job descriptions and job specifications, plan and conduct an effective interview, and check references before hiring any employee.

3. Explain how to create a company culture that encourages employee retention.

Company culture is the distinctive, unwritten code of conduct that governs the behavior, attitudes, relationships, and style of an organization. Culture arises from an entrepreneur's consistent and relentless pursuit of a set of core values that everyone in the company can believe in. Small companies' flexible structures can be a major competitive weapon.

Job-design techniques for enhancing employee motivation include job enlargement, job rotation, job enrichment, flextime, job sharing, and flexplace (which includes telecommuting).

Money is an important motivator for many workers, but not the only one. The key to using rewards such as recognition and praise and to motivate involves tailoring them to the needs and characteristics of the workers.

Giving employees timely, relevant feedback about their job performances through a performance appraisal system can also be a powerful motivator.

4. Describe the steps in developing a management succession plan for a growing business that will allow a smooth transition of leadership to the next generation.

As their companies grow, entrepreneurs must begin to plan for passing the leadership baton to the next generation well in advance. A succession plan is a crucial element in successfully transferring a company to the next generation.

Preparing a succession plan involves five steps: (1) Select the successor, (2) create a survival kit for the successor, (3) groom the successor, (4) promote an environment of trust and respect, and (5) cope with the financial realities of estate taxes.

5. Explain the exit strategies available to entrepreneurs.

Family business owners wanting to step down from their companies can sell to outsiders or to insiders. Common tools for selling to insiders (employees or managers) include sale for cash plus a note, leveraged buyouts (LBOs), and employee stock ownership plans (ESOPs).

Discussion Questions

1. What is leadership? What is the difference between leadership and management?
2. What behaviors do effective leaders exhibit?
3. Why is it so important for small companies to hire the right employees? What can small business owners do to avoid making hiring mistakes?
4. What is a job description? A job specification? What functions do they serve in the hiring process?
5. Outline the procedure for conducting an effective interview.
6. What is company culture? What role does it play in a small company's success? What threats does rapid growth pose for a company's culture?
7. Explain the differences among job simplification, job enlargement, job rotation, and job enrichment. What impact do these different job designs have on workers?

8. Is money the "best" motivator? How do pay-for-performance compensation systems work? What other rewards are available to small business managers to use as motivators? How effective are they?
9. Why is it so important for a small business owner to develop a management succession plan? Why is it so difficult for most business owners to develop such a plan? What are the steps that are involved in creating a succession plan?
10. Briefly describe the options a small business owner wanting to pass the family business on to the next generation can take to minimize the impact of estate taxes.

Business Plan Pro

 This chapter discusses the importance of people, their roles, and how they influence an organization. The Management section is where these issues are most often addressed in the business plan. This section of the plan captures the key information about your management team, both its strengths and weaknesses. The management section of the business plan also addresses other personnel issues for the venture.

Business Plan Exercises

Review the Management section of your business plan and make certain that it addresses the important management and personnel issues for your venture. Check to see that your plan includes the relevant concepts presented in this chapter and captures those thoughts. Think about the business culture your are hoping to build or alter. Assess the leadership abilities of your current management team. Are additional managers or other positions needed? Have you accounted for those new hires and the anticipated expenses associated with these additional employees? Does your plan address factors that will encourage retention of existing employees? Your plan may also benefit from succession planning or an exit strategy. Remember, you can add or modify topics of your choice within Business Plan Pro by right-clicking on the outline in the left-hand navigation of the page.

On the Web

Visit http://www.prenhall.com/scarborough and review the links that are presented under the Web Destinations tab. You will find resources that address leadership issues, interviewing techniques, employee incentive programs, succession planning, exit strategies, and other topics that you may find of value. These areas may offer additional insight for the human resource and managerial aspects of your business that you may choose to incorporate into your business plan.

In the Software

The chapters in this book have led you through all key aspects of creating a business plan. The final task you will complete, and one that many consider to be the most important section, is the executive summary. The executive summary is the first section presented, and your plan may be judged on its value and impact alone. Your executive summary should be no more than two pages—one is even better—and its intent is to capture the highlights of your plan. In addition to communicating important concepts and ideas about your plan, the executive summary should also include key financial numbers along with brief summaries of key sections. The conciseness of your executive summary will enable the reader to quickly grasp the essence of the plan for your business. This section should be compelling, enabling the reader to see your vision for the venture and motivate him or her to want to read the entire plan.

Sample Plans

Review an executive summary from a sample plan that you have found beneficial. You may also want to consider these options:

- Pegasus Sports
- Sagebrush Sam's
- Salvador's Inc.
- The Daily Perc

Identify attributes within other executive summaries that you find engaging.

Building Your Business Plan

Write your executive summary in Business Plan Pro. Remember, this section incorporates key highlights of information in the plan ahead. Show this executive summary to others and test its effectiveness in describing the most important ideas of your business plan.

 ## Beyond the Classroom . . .

1. Visit a local business that has experienced rapid growth in the last three years and ask the owner about the specific problems he or she had to face due to the organization's growth. How did the owner handle these problems? Looking back, what would he or she do differently?
2. Contact a local small business with at least 20 employees. Does the company have job descriptions and job specifications? What process does the owner use to hire a new employee? What questions does the owner typically ask candidates in an interview?
3. Ask the owner of a small manufacturing operation to give you a tour of his or her operation. During your tour, observe the way that jobs are organized. To what extent does the company use the following job design concepts: job simplification, job enlargement, job rotation, job enrichment, flextime, job sharing? Based on your observations, what recommendations would you make to the owner about the company's job design?
4. Contact five small business owners about their plans for passing their businesses on to the next generation. Do they intend to pass the business along to a family member? Do they have a management succession plan? When do they plan to name a successor? Have they developed a plan for minimizing the effects of estate taxes? How many more years do they plan to work before retiring?
5. Entrepreneurs say that they have learned much about leadership from the movies. "Films beg to be interpreted and discussed," says one leadership consultant, "and from those discussions business-people come up with principles for their own jobs." A recent survey of small-company CEOs by *Inc.* magazine[*] resulted in the following list of the best movies for leadership lessons: *Apollo 13* (1995), *The Bridge on the River Kwai* (1957), *Dead Poets Society* (1989), *Elizabeth* (1998), *Glengarry Glen Ross* (1992), *It's a Wonderful Life* (1946), *Norma Rae* (1979), *One Flew Over the Cuckoo's Nest* (1975), *Twelve Angry Men* (1957), and *Twelve O'Clock High* (1949). Rent one of these films and watch it with a group of your classmates. After viewing the movie, discuss the leadership lessons you learned from it and report the results to the other members of your class.

---

[*]Leigh Buchanan and Mike Hofman, "Everything I Know about Leadership, I Learned from the Movies," *Inc.*, March 2000, pp. 58–70.

Appendix

Josh Sudbury, Founder

Executive Summary

Total Health and Fitness is in the business of improving the community by promoting and providing the lifelong commitment to personal health and fitness that every American needs in a comfortable and convenient atmosphere.

This business is multifaceted, combining the health benefits of a calorie-conscious restaurant, dietary counseling, and personal fitness training. All three of these concepts will be located under one roof to maximize customer convenience and to allow for onsite cross-promotion. Many professionals living today's fast-paced American lifestyle end up neglecting their health because their busy schedules force them to work long hours and to give up healthy, home-cooked meals in favor of fast food or restaurant portions that are simply too large or too fatty. This lack of time also causes many working parents and business professionals to lose motivation and stray from their workout routines. This has led to an increasingly obese population, which has driven health care costs up for businesses and individuals and takes away from the everyday enjoyment of life.

The Total Health and Fitness concept will eliminate this time-loss problem. We will offer full dietary counseling to clients on a biweekly basis. These clients will receive from our licensed professional dieticians a full body-fat percentage analysis, sample meal plans, and sound advice on how to achieve their fitness goals. They can also purchase personal training from our professional personal trainers in our 4,000-square-foot fitness facility. After a good workout and some healthy eating tips, clients can walk next door and pick up a healthy, professionally prepared meal for themselves or even the entire family. This one-stop fitness shop will provide everything for the involved parent or busy professional who still wants to look good and feel great.

Total Health and Fitness will locate in the Cool Springs area of Williamson County, Tennessee. This area is the commercial and retail center for Brentwood and Franklin, two affluent suburbs just south of Nashville on Interstate 65. This area is perfect for a business such as this because it boasts a high median household income of more than $75,000. Furthermore, businesses in the fitness club industry can benefit greatly from a large population between the ages of 18 and 54 years. Brentwood and Franklin are both home to more than 30,000 people in that age bracket.

Customer service and quality nutritional and dietary advice will serve as the foundation of our marketing strategy. This business relies heavily on repeat customers, and the best way to retain customers is through expedient and accurate customer service. Our trainers and dieticians will be helpful, courteous, and informative. By keeping up to date

on the latest clinical studies and other fitness information through medical journals, Total Health and Fitness can succeed at staying on top of an ever-changing industry.

As an entrepreneur, I have had little experience. However, although this is my first start-up, I am able to draw on the experiences of my father and mother, who own their own business and have operated it successfully since 1984. My previous work experience includes working as a salesman for G.C.P., Inc. for the last two spring and summer seasons, as well as working as a night manager during high school in the shipping department of the same company. For this business, I am seeking debt financing in the amount of $130,000 for start-up costs and initial working capital. I will be investing $30,000 of my own money with the goal of remaining the sole owner and operator of Total Health and Fitness.

Vision

We seek to build a healthier community by giving people the opportunity to make the right fitness choices. We understand that maintaining a proper physical fitness regimen is difficult in today's fast-paced lifestyle. Total Health and Fitness combines fun and convenience with the benefits of staying healthy.

Mission Statement

Total Health and Fitness is in the business of promoting healthy choices among its community by offering the benefits of a first-class health and fitness club alongside an enjoyable restaurant that offers nothing but the most nutritious foods for its customers. Total Health and Fitness is in the business of improving the lives of its customers by saving them the time it takes to get to the gym, exercise, run home, and slave in the kitchen to prepare a healthy meal for their families. Total Health and Fitness combines convenience with health in an upbeat environment.

Company Values

We will operate on the basic principle of service to the customer above all else. Because we depend on our customers for business, we must ensure that they enjoy every aspect of each visit to our facility. As a health and fitness club, we must capitalize on every opportunity to keep up with the changing trends in the fitness industry by offering the best equipment and environment while avoiding the pitfalls of "burning out." We must continually renew ourselves in order to give the customers a new experience each time they return.

Competitive Advantage

This business is unique because it combines a health club with a healthy restaurant to bring about the utmost convenience for the on-the-go American. Our competitive advantage will be the convenience we offer. We must focus on selling the convenience of our products and services in order to differentiate ourselves from the competition.

Industry Profile and Overview

Industry Analysis

The fitness industry has been in full swing since the early 1980s. It is heavily marketed by influential members of society—from Hollywood to Capitol Hill. Since 1987 the percentage of Americans who are members of a health club has risen from 17 percent to 32.8 percent—a 90 percent increase in the percentage of memberships among the U.S. population. Almost one of every seven Americans older than five years is a member of some type of athletic or fitness center.[1]

Although the fitness industry caters to all ages, the main customer groups can be broken down into age and income, as shown in the following figure.[2]

Fitness Club Membership by Age

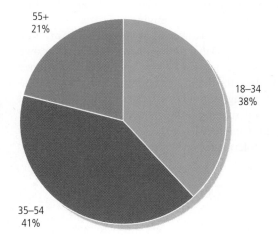

With the aging of the baby boomers, the growth rates of the top two age brackets from 1987 to 2000 were 143 and 350 percent, respectively. Ages 18 to 34 saw a miniscule growth rate in comparison at only 34 percent, whereas the under-18 group increased by 187 percent.[3]

Likewise, memberships by annual household income paint a familiar picture in that more than 46 percent of the health club members earn a household income of more than $75,000. Those ranging from incomes of $50,000 to $74,999 constituted 23 percent, and those with incomes from $25,000 to $49,999 claimed 20 percent of memberships nationwide.[4]

More women join health clubs than men, but only by 2 percent. Women also participate in more group-centered activities such as yoga classes and aerobics.[5]

Regulatory Restrictions

I have yet to discover any significant regulations placed on the Health and Fitness Industry. In fact, Congress introduced legislation favorable to health clubs nationwide as recently as last year. In May 2005, several legislators banded together to introduce legislation that would allow companies to get a tax break for giving employees health club memberships as a part of their benefits packages. Known as the Workforce Health Improvement Act (WHIP), it promoted physical fitness in the corporate world in order to trim down the ever-growing American public.[6]

Significant Trends

The industry has continued to increase its health club memberships over the last two decades. However, the latest trend in the fitness industry is circumventing the health club altogether. Online personal trainers have become all the rage and offer many advantages to the market Total Health and Fitness will pursue: the on-the-go parent/professional. By allowing individuals to get their workouts in their own homes and at their convenience, the World Wide Web has the potential to cut out the normal fitness club by giving people the personal training experience at home, without having to join a club or leave their homes. The primary drawback is the lack of a physical spotter who can assist the client with his or her form while exercising.[7]

In addition to on-site trainers, Total Health and Fitness has another important competitive edge over these online trainers because of our members' ability to have a healthy meal prepared for them while they exercise. Having this combination allows the customer to get in a workout and grab dinner for the family all in the same place and still get home in less time than it would take an online trainee to do the same exercises, shower, and prepare dinner for the family.

Growth Rate

Despite a lull in growth during the 1990s, the number of health, racquet, and sports clubs in America has increased from 6,211 total clubs in 1982 to 22,031 total clubs in 2003.

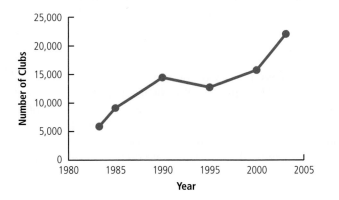

Fitness Industry Growth Trends

Source: IHRSA Lender's Guide, Second Edition

That represents a growth rate of 255 percent over the last 20 years and an average growth rate of nearly 13 percent per year. From 2000 to 2003, the total number of clubs jumped from 15,910 to 22,031, a total growth rate of 38 percent! This is clearly an industry on the rise.[8]

In 2003, there were more than 36.3 million health club memberships nationwide, 110 percent more than the 17.3 million in 1987. In addition, the number of "core members," those who use their memberships more than 100 times a year, has steadily grown as well, climbing from 5.3 million in 1987 to 14.6 million in 2003, a growth rate of 175 percent.[9] Not only is the industry growing overall, but members also are using their memberships more often.

Industry revenues also have grown steadily. From 1993 to 2002, total revenues increased from $6.5 million to $13.1 billion, an increase of more than 101 percent. Furthermore, revenues never decreased from one year to another during this time span, meaning that the industry has seen a trend of steady growth over the last decade. The average yearly increase in revenues over the industry for the last decade was 11.3 percent.

Key Success Factors in the Industry

Three key factors are crucial for building a successful health and fitness club.

1. ***Effective, specialized workout programs designed to target individual members.*** Both World Gym and Bally Total Fitness specifically cite effective personal training as tenets of their mission statements. Similarly, Curves lays claim to the most effective 30-minute workout in the industry, specifically designed for women.[10] Individualized exercise programs are a key component of Total Health and Fitness' strategy.

2. ***Membership in a community of people, not just a club.*** Successful chains in the exercise industry include in their advertisements that joining their club means joining a group of people all striving for the same goals: a better self-image through personal health and fitness. For instance, Curves makes direct connections with women by solidifying their claim to the "woman's health club" niche within the industry as a whole.

3. ***Real-world convenience.*** Although Bally Total Fitness and World Gym use their enormous size and multiple locations to help sign up members across the nation, Curves pushes the small investment of time it takes to complete their exercise regimen. By selling the idea of a "30-minute" workout, they cater to women who believe they are too busy and would waste money on a health club membership they wouldn't have the time to use.

Total Health and Fitness will focus on using these techniques within an already established community to achieve success. By offering specialized workout facilities and top-notch personal training, we can guarantee our customers that they will receive the most from their memberships. Furthermore, by offering the expediency of a restaurant on the grounds that prepares food in a manner congruent with a healthy lifestyle and the nutritional needs of the members and their families, Total Health and Fitness possesses a type of real-world convenience not found at other health clubs.

Outlook for the Future

The future outlook of the health and fitness industry is optimistic. The rate of obesity in the United States continues to climb. The rapid decline in the health of so many Americans (as illustrated in the accompanying table[11]) both raises the importance of a regular fitness regiment for all Americans and increases the number of potential clients for fitness facilities in the future. The ultimate goal is to bring about a decline in obesity rates through proper diet and regular exercise, both of which are offered at Total Health and Fitness.

Increase in Prevalence (%) of Overweight, Obesity, and Severe Obesity among U.S. Adults

	Overweight	Obesity	Severe Obesity
1999–2000	64.5	30.5	4.7
1988–1994	56.0	23.0	2.9
1976–1980	46.0	14.4	No data

Definitions: overweight, body mass index (BMI) ≥ 25; obesity, BMI ≥30; severe obesity, BMI ≥ 40.

Sources: Centers for Disease Control and Prevention, National Center for Health Statistics, *National Health and Nutrition Examination Survey. Health, United States,* 2002; K. M. Flegel, C. L. Ogden, M. D. Carroll, and C. L. Johnson, "Prevalence and trends in obesity among us adults 1999–2000," *JAMA,* 2002, Vol. 288, pp. 1723–1727; National Institutes of Health, National Heart, Lung, and Blood Institute, *Clinical Guidelines on the Identification, Evaluation and Treatment of Overweight and Obesity in Adults,* 1998.

Specifically, a range of states from Texas to West Virginia (which encompasses Tennessee) have an obesity rate of more than 25 percent.[12] Clearly, there is a need in the United States for more health and fitness facilities to facilitate the demand for weight loss programs and health initiatives.

Moreover, the industry's two largest client bases, young adults 18 to 34 years old and mature adults of age 55 years and over, are expected to grow rapidly in the near future, as the following chart indicates.[13]

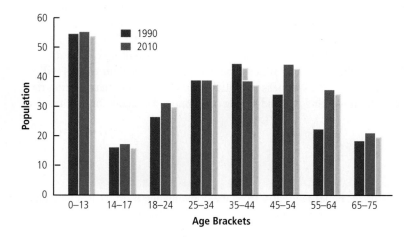

Projected U.S. Population Growth (millions)

Source: IHRSA 50 million member-ship members by 2010

The industry is expected to grow in step with the steady growth in these demographic sectors. Twenty-one-year-olds are the most likely to join a club; however, aging baby-boomers will increase the mature adult share of the market as they begin to pass 50. The increase in these population segments will produce increases in membership across the industry, especially for those companies that offer what these customers want in a fitness facility.

Business Strategy

Total Health and Fitness seeks to make itself a leader in the health club industry. We believe that we can garner a large share of the health club market in our target area by combining health food with the health club in a relaxed atmosphere.

Goals and Objectives

Goals Total Health and Fitness strives to become the family fitness specialist in the local community by providing customized, state-of-the-art exercise facilities and healthy dining opportunities for its members. We strive to offer the best, most practical real-world training in the industry to accommodate the lifestyle demands of our clients. We will offer first-class service at a reasonable price and avoid inconveniencing our clients by overselling memberships and overcrowding our facility. We will offer the best training in the market by finding the most capable trainers and paying them adequately.

In addition to personal training, Total Health and Fitness will offer weekly and monthly nutritional meal plans for clients who want extra assistance in sticking to a proper weight-balancing program. Clients will meet with our dieticians weekly for the first 6 weeks and monthly for the following 6 months to solidify a healthy meal plan that they can follow on their way to obtaining their desired body image. These clients will be able to conveniently purchase up to two of the meals on their meal plan a day at the in-house restaurant franchise.

To offer the healthiest and most nutritional foods to our clients, we must successfully recruit the right franchise for our restaurant. Restaurants such as T.G.I. Fridays, O'Charley's, Chili's, and Applebee's offer healthy menu items to attract a more health conscious customer. Total Health and Fitness will work with a franchise to create a full menu consisting only of healthier, better-balanced meals. The restaurant itself will operate independently of the fitness facility; however, the restaurant will sublease its space from Total Health and Fitness, and Total Health and Fitness will receive a percentage of all meals sold at the restaurant.

Objectives

1. Each trainer at Total Health and Fitness will serve at least 20 clients a week, allowing for a total membership of more than 120 clients.
2. Using the concept of personal training rather than faceless memberships, Total Health and Fitness will maintain a one-on-one relationship with its clients, ensuring that no matter how large the company gets, each client will feel like a member of an intimate family.
3. Total Health and Fitness dieticians will build a weekly diet for willing clients to follow that is based on their personal fitness goals. Offering this to our clients will allow them to reach their greatest fitness potential if they so choose, maximizing the benefit they receive from working out, and having our company to thank for their results.

SWOT Analysis

Strengths

- Total Health and Fitness benefits greatly from the convenience it offers its clients by incorporating the restaurant in its scheme. This limits the need for customers to count calories and analyze their food intake. This will be a major point of differentiation for Total Health and Fitness from other health clubs in the area.
- The size of the facility and membership will be limited to maintain a close relationship with our customers. This closeness will allow the owner and our staff to get feedback from our clients to learn about their personal fitness needs, ideas for improvement, suggestions, and complaints. Our goal is to maximize their enjoyment and the benefits they receive from their training experience.
- A personalized atmosphere allows women to exercise without feeling as though they are being watched and analyzed by other members, thus eliminating insecurities that take away from the potential of each workout. To achieve maximum individual concentration during workouts, Total Health and Fitness will introduce the home gym concept to our facility. By using individual rooms designed to feel like home gyms (equipped with adjustable dumbbell sets, benches, cardio machines, and video/audio systems), our customers can work out with a trainer or alone. Thus, they can receive the comforts of home, without the big investment.[14]

Weaknesses

- Total Health and Fitness will be competing with larger companies that have established names in the industry with proven track records and larger advertising budgets.
- The concept of combining a restaurant with a workout facility is new. Total Health and Fitness would be the first company to implement this strategy.
- The investment needed to start this company is significant.

Opportunities

- There is no other business that operates in the niche that Total Health and Fitness plans to occupy. We can use this establish a stronghold in the overall market.
- We have the opportunity to reach an upscale community and shape it in a healthier fashion. We plan to do our part by lowering the percentage of unhealthy and unfit members of the community.

Threats

- Larger rivals such as Gold's Gym and Bally's Total Fitness have deep pockets and may try to move into the market that Total Health and Fitness will establish.

Competitive Strategy

Total Health and Fitness seeks to use the differentiation approach to business strategy. We differentiate ourselves from our competitors by offering services that they do not or cannot offer. We will concentrate on customizing the health club experience to the needs of each person who chooses to become a member.

Competitor Analysis

By using the three key success factors in the health club industry identified earlier (specialized programs, community feel, convenience), we can analyze just how Total Health and Fitness stacks up against its competition.

Three direct competitors operate in the area and focus on personal fitness through training and a nutritional diet. Two larger companies, World Gym and Delta Clubs, operate facilities in the area. Chadwick's Personal Training, a smaller company, also has two locations near Franklin.

Chadwick's Personal Training is a local competitor operating in Franklin. This company offers personal training for its clients and their children. It has a small client base and it prides itself on the values it promotes through its fitness training and nutritional consulting.[15]

World Gym is a national chain that has various classes and amenities for the customers such as nutritional consulting. Their primary advantage is that they are open 24 hours a day, thus allowing their clients to choose the best workout time for their individual needs. They also offer day care facilities so that parents can work out without leaving their children at home.[16]

Delta Clubs offers four locations in the Nashville area, only one of which is located in our market area. Like World Gym, they offer day care, various fitness classes, and large facilities. They also offer a smoothie bar, which affords their clients healthy refreshments after a workout.

For all of their benefits, none of these businesses is targeting the market in the same way Total Health and Fitness will. Our company takes nutritional advice one step further: implementation. Our clients will also be afforded the individual attention of Chadwick's with the home-style accommodations that will make them feel comfortable while they enjoy their fitness experience. The following competitive profile matrix (and accompanying graph) summarizes the competitive positions of Total Health and Fitness and its primary competitors.

Competitive Profile Matrix for Brentwood/Franklin Market

Key Success Factor	Weight	Total Health and Fitness Score	Weighted Score	World Gym Score	Weighted Score	Delta Clubs Score	Weighted Score	Chadwick's Score	Weighted Score
Community Feel	0.20	4	0.8	3	0.6	3	0.6	4	0.8
Specialized Programs	0.15	3	0.45	4	0.6	4	0.6	2	0.3
Convenience	0.25	4	1	4	1	3	0.75	3	0.75
Nutrition	0.25	4	1	2	0.5	2	0.5	3	0.75
Perception	0.15	2	0.3	4	0.6	3	0.45	3	0.45
	1.00		**3.55**		**3.3**		**2.9**		**3.05**

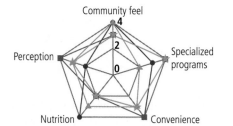

Total Health ■ World Gym ★ Delta Clubs ▲ Chadwick's

Competitive Profile Matrix Growth

Marketing Strategy

Target Market Total Health and Fitness will target professionals and parents on the go. The primary age bracket of our target audience is 18 to 54 years, although we will not hesitate to accommodate potential members above or below our target demographics. The industry profile cites the growth of the upper portion of the 18- to 54-year age bracket (34 to 54 years) as the second-fastest-growing age bracket in the industry, but the 18- to 34-year bracket remains the bedrock of our membership base.

Customers have the motivation to buy memberships at Total Health and Fitness because we will be the only health club in the area with nutritional counseling and a restaurant on-site that is focused on providing the right type of meals for its customers.

Web Site Total Health and Fitness will operate a Web site to offer clients and potential customers up-to-date information on deals and packages that the company will offer and the latest health and nutritional information. Our Web site will operate at the domain http://www.total-health-and-fitness.com. It is currently available for registration according to NetworkSolutions.com.

Pricing Clients of Total Health and Fitness will pay for their training in blocks of 8 or 12 visits. Those choosing to visit twice a week will pay for 8 workouts per month, and those choosing to visit three times a week will pay for 12 workouts per month. The 8-workout block costs $336 per month (at $42 per visit), and the 12-workout block costs $495 per month (at $41.25 per visit).

Clients who choose to have a nutritional food plan constructed for them to follow will be billed at a six-month sign-on fee of $400. For this fee, they will receive one meeting every two weeks with a registered dietician. At this meeting, clients will be weighed and measured and their progress will be assessed to determine their dietary and nutritional needs for the next training period. The following six months will be assessed at $100, and meetings with the dietician will be monthly. A total yearly package can be purchased for $800.

Market Analysis

The International Health, Racquet, and Sportsclub Association identifies target customers by age and income. A breakdown of how each group fits into our target market can be seen in the following tables and figures.

Club Membership by Age

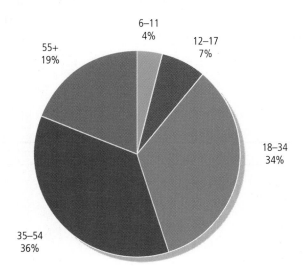

This table shows that majority of health club members are between 18 and 34 years, but a significant portion is in the 55-and-older category. Comparing this data to data compiled from the U.S. Census Bureau about the total number of potential clients in our targeted location of Brentwood/Franklin, Tennessee, reveals a good fit. The Brentwood/ Franklin area boasts a large number of residents who fall into these age groups. We estimate that there are more than 70,000 potential customers for Total Health and Fitness in our trade area.

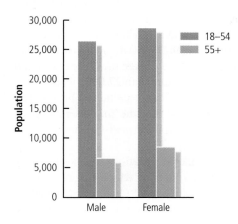

Population by Age and Sex for Brentwood/Franklin TN

Source: 2000 U.S. Census data

In addition, the median household income of the people who most frequently join health clubs is at least $50,000 per year, but the largest proportion comes from the income bracket above $75,000, as seen in the following table.

Once again, the population in the Brentwood/Franklin area compares favorably with the industry's profile of the typical fitness center customer. The area boasts relatively high incomes, with 50 percent of its median household incomes above the $75,000 mark. This market shows a high potential for establishing a solid customer base without having to resort to competing on the basis of low price.

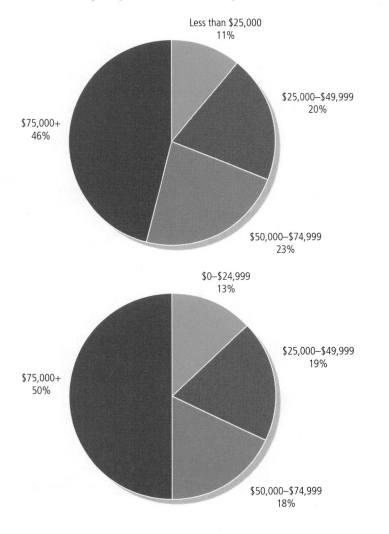

Club Membership by Annual Household Income

Household Income for Brentwood/Franklin TN

Advertising Total Health and Fitness will advertise in *The Tennessean* and its local satellite newspapers. Local newspapers are a perfect medium for us to use because they are regularly read by business professionals and more-mature customers, the markets on which our business is focused. *The Tennessean* has a total daily circulation of 173,304 and a total Sunday circulation of 241,017, all in the Nashville area. *Williamson A.M.*, a local newspaper distributed in the target market, reaches more than 23,000 homes each weekday and more than 30,000 homes on Sundays. Added to these numbers are the daily newsstand purchase figures, which push weekday publication sales to more than 27,000.[17]

Advertising rates in these publications are reasonable. Total Health and Fitness can place a 16-inch ad (the biggest size offered) in every edition for the first six months of business for just $624. To place an 8-inch ad in the paper for the next six months costs $336, making the total cost $960.

Other advertising will consist of radio ads on local talk radio stations such as the Steve Gill show, a popular conservative talk radio program, the host of which is a resident of Williamson County and a personal friend. The program airs on FM 99.7 and is owned by Cumulus Media. Steve and 99.7 FM have done many on-location promotions. These encourage the listeners to drop by and meet the on-air talent, and this brings them to the business. This is a marketing strategy I would pursue as part of our grand opening.

The station has more than 100,000 watts of power, boasting the largest listening audience in Tennessee. The listening audience is predominantly male and affluent, earning a median annual income of $75,000 a year. This station broadcasts directly to my target market and is a perfect fit for Total Health and Fitness. The most basic advertising plans for this radio station start at just a few hundred dollars. I will budget anywhere from $1,000 to $2,000 per month at start-up for advertising on FM 99.7.

Location and Layout

Total Health and Fitness will be located in a major shopping and commercial district between the cities of Brentwood and Franklin known as Cool Springs. Cool Springs is the retail hub of Williamson County and is home to various office complexes, retail shops, restaurants, and Cool Springs Galleria, a large and upscale shopping mall. These businesses serve the 93,000 people who live and work in the area. The area draws more than 11 million visitors annually and provides Franklin alone with more than $1 million a month in sales tax revenue.[18]

Source: www.mapquest.com

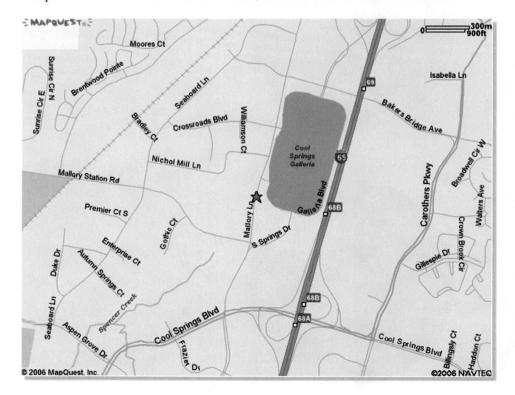

Total Health and Fitness will locate in the Cool Springs Center, located at 1945 Mallory Lane in Brentwood.[19] This location offers our business the benefits of a strip-mall style shopping center such as high consumer traffic. Currently there is more than 4,000 square feet available for lease. This space is divisible and can also be sublet, which will allow Total Health and Fitness to sublease a portion of its space to a restaurant franchise in order to offer our customers the added convenience that comprises our competitive advantage. The lease rate is $14 per square foot, which is considered to be a bargain in the Brentwood/Franklin market. I will seek a three-year lease with an additional three-year option.

The location of Total Health and Fitness is indicated on the accompanying map. The close proximity to Cool Springs Galleria, the large shopping mall, places Total Health and Fitness in a high-traffic retail area, conducive to walk-in traffic.

Description of Management Team

At the time of the company's inception, Josh Sudbury will serve as the Chief Executive Officer and President of Total Health and Fitness. I will be a graduate of Presbyterian College with a degree in History and a minor in Business Administration. I have had prior experience in business as a salesman for G.C.P., Inc., a concrete manufacturing company located in Gallatin, Tennessee. Prior to holding this position, I obtained management experience as the night shift manager for the same company's shipping department. I will also build on the business experiences of my father, who owns his own business, and has held numerous sales and management positions throughout his near 30-year career as an entrepreneur.

Because of the restaurant aspect of the business, I will need a better understanding of a profession in the health and nutrition industry. In order to do so, I will become a licensed Nutrition and Wellness Consultant. I can obtain these licenses from an accredited institution online for a total cost of $1,100.[20] Certification will require three months. To facilitate the nutritional planning, I will hire two Registered Dieticians in my first year of operation. To ensure the best possible service for my customers, I will offer dieticians an above-market wage of $45,000 per year.

I will initially hire five full-time trainers for my facility. These trainers will solicit and maintain their own clients. I will collect a fee for each training session for using of the Total Health and Fitness facility. This fee will be on a sliding scale, decreasing with the number of client sessions that each of the trainers performs in the previous month. The starting fee will be $15 and applies to trainers who complete 24 sessions or fewer a month. If the trainer completes between 25 and 35 sessions, the fee drops to $14 per session. Finally, if the trainer completes more than 35 sessions in a single month, the fee drops to $13. This plan gives trainers the incentive to increase the number of clients and the frequency of their visits, increasing revenues for Total Health and Fitness.

Company Structure

Total Health and Fitness will be organized as an S Corporation. This form of organization offers all the advantages of the corporation, such as continuity, easy transferability, and limited personal liability. The primary advantage of this form of organization is that its limited liability allows the owners and investors to avoid losing their personal assets should a member injure himself or herself in the facility and sue for damages. Over the course of the company's life, I will retain at least fifty-one percent ownership in Total Health and Fitness to maintain ultimate control over business decisions.

Financial Forecasts

The financial forecasts for Total Health and Fitness are located in Appendix A. Each projection contains an income statement compiled for the first year and cash flow statements that span three years and are projected monthly. There is a balance sheet for the fiscal year 2007 based on start-up costs and total investment projections. (Note: To conserve space, some of the financial projections were omitted.)

Loan Proposal

I will be investing $30,000 of my own money into Total Health and Fitness. These funds will be secured from the sale of my car through *Auto Trader* magazine. I will need a loan of $150,000 to cover my projected start-up costs. I have added roughly $25,000 to my loan in order to cover unexpected start-up costs and to have cash with which to operate on opening day.

Appendix A: Total Health and Fitness Layout

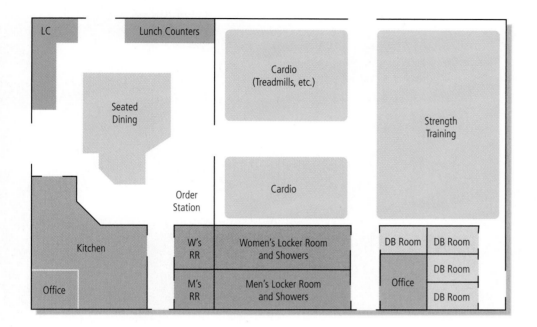

Appendix B: Financial Forecasts

Total Health and Fitness
Balance Sheet
January 2007

Assets		
<u>**Current Assets**</u>		
Cash and Equivalents	$	30,000
Inventory	$	882
Miscellaneous	$	2,000
Total Current Assets	**$**	**32,882**
<u>**Fixed Assets**</u>		
Equipment	$	87,500
Building	$	73,000
Intangibles	$	—
Signs	$	7,200
Computers and Other Noncurrent Assets	$	12,000
Total Fixed Assets	**$**	**179,700**
Total Assets	**$**	**212,582**
Liabilities		
<u>**Current Liabilities**</u>		
Notes Payable (Short Term)	$	—
Loan	$	21,839
Total Current Liabilities	**$**	**21,839**
<u>**Long-Term Liabilities**</u>		
Notes Payable	$	138,904
Total Liabilities	**$**	**160,743**
Owner's Equity	$	30,000
Total Liabilities and Owner's Equity	**$**	**212,582**

Total Health and Fitness
Cash Budget
Most Likely
January 2007–December 2007

	January	February	March	April	May	June	July	August
Cash Receipts:								
Sales								
Diet Counseling	$ 16,000	$ 14,000	$ 12,000	$ 11,200	$ 12,000	$ 12,800	$ 13,200	$ 12,250
Training Fees	$ 9,800	$ 8,960	$ 8,960	$ 10,500	$ 9,800	$ 9,800	$ 10,400	$ 9,800
Food Royalties	$ 665	$ 612	$ 612	$ 665	$ 665	$ 700	$ 624	$ 718
Sublease	$ 2,500	$ 2,500	$ 2,500	$ 2,500	$ 2,500	$ 2,500	$ 2,500	$ 2,500
Water/Sports Drinks	$ 100	$ 95	$ 90	$ 90	$ 100	$ 100	$ 100	$ 100
Total Cash Receipts	**$ 29,065**	**$ 26,167**	**$ 24,162**	**$ 24,955**	**$ 25,065**	**$ 25,900**	**$ 29,324**	**$ 25,368**
Cash Disbursements:								
Water/Sports Drinks	$ 75	$ 71	$ 68	$ 68	$ 75	$ 75	$ 75	$ 75
Rent	$ 4,667	$ 4,667	$ 4,667	$ 4,667	$ 4,667	$ 4,667	$ 4,667	$ 4,667
Utilities	$ 1,040	$ 1,040	$ 1,040	$ 1,040	$ 1,040	$ 1,040	$ 1,040	$ 1,040
Subscriptions	$ 40	$ 40	$ 40	$ 40	$ 40	$ 40	$ 40	$ 40
Trade Association	$ 950	$ —	$ —	$ —	$ —	$ —	$ —	$ —
Web Site	$ 400	$ 400	$ 400	$ 400	$ 400	$ 400	$ 400	$ 400
Loan Payment	$ 1,820	$ 1,820	$ 1,820	$ 1,820	$ 1,820	$ 1,820	$ 1,820	$ 1,820
Salaries	$ 11,979	$ 11,979	$ 11,979	$ 11,979	$ 11,979	$ 11,979	$ 11,979	$ 11,979
Office Supplies	$ 200	$ 200	$ 200	$ 200	$ 200	$ 200	$ 200	$ 200
Insurance Premiums	$ 1,500	$ —	$ —	$ —	$ —	$ —	$ 1,500	$ —
Tax Payment	$ —	$ —	$ —	$ 320	$ —	$ —	$ —	$ —
Maintenance	$ 150	$ 150	$ 150	$ 150	$ 150	$ 150	$ 150	$ 150
Cleaning Service	$ 200	$ 200	$ 200	$ 200	$ 200	$ 200	$ 200	$ 200
Computer Supplies	$ 75	$ 75	$ 75	$ 75	$ 75	$ 75	$ 75	$ 75
Advertising	$ 2,000	$ 2,000	$ 2,000	$ 2,000	$ 2,000	$ 1,500	$ 1,000	$ 1,000
Legal and Accounting Fees	$ 250	$ 250	$ 250	$ 250	$ 250	$ 250	$ 250	$ 250
Miscellaneous	$ 750	$ 750	$ 750	$ 750	$ 750	$ 750	$ 750	$ 750
Totals	**$ 26,096**	**$ 23,642**	**$ 23,639**	**$ 23,959**	**$ 23,646**	**$ 23,146**	**$ 24,146**	**$ 22,646**
End-of-Month Balance:								
Cash (beginning of month)	$ 25,000	$ 27,669	$ 30,494	$ 31,017	$ 32,013	$ 33,432	$ 36,186	$ 41,364
Cash Receipts	$ 29,065	$ 26,167	$ 24,162	$ 24,955	$ 25,085	$ 25,900	$ 29,324	$ 25,368
Cash Disbursements	$ 28,096	$ 23,642	$ 23,639	$ 23,959	$ 23,648	$ 23,146	$ 24,146	$ 22,646
Cash (end of month)	**$ 27,969**	**$ 30,494**	**$ 31,017**	**$ 32,013**	**$ 33,432**	**$ 36,186**	**$ 41,364**	**$ 44,086**
Borrowing								
Repayment								
Cash (end of month [after borrowing])	**$ 27,969**	**$ 30,494**	**$ 31,017**	**$ 32,013**	**$ 33,432**	**$ 36,186**	**$ 41,364**	**$ 44,086**

Total Health and Fitness
Cash Budget
Most Likely
January 2007–December 2007

	September	October	November	December
Cash Receipts:				
Sales				
Diet Counseling	$ 9,240	$ 9,700	$ 8,900	$ 8,900
Training Fees	$ 8,400	$ 7,840	$ 7,840	$ 7,000
Food Royalties	$ 780	$ 624	$ 624	$ 624
Sublease	$ 2,500	$ 2,500	$ 2,500	$ 2,500
Water/Sports Drinks	$ 90	$ 90	$ 80	$ 80
Total Cash Receipts	**$ 21,010**	**$ 20,754**	**$ 19,944**	**$ 19,104**
Cash Disbursements:				
Water/Sports Drinks	$ 68	$ 68	$ 60	$ 60
Rent	$ 4,667	$ 4,667	$ 4,667	$ 4,667
Utilities	$ 1,040	$ 1,040	$ 1,040	$ 1,040
Subscriptions	$ 40	$ 40	$ 40	$ 40
Trade Association	$ —	$ —	$ —	$ —
Web Site	$ 400	$ 400	$ 400	$ 400
Loan Payment	$ 1,820	$ 1,820	$ 1,820	$ 1,820
Salaries	$ 11,979	$ 11,979	$ 11,979	$ 11,979
Office Supplies	$ 200	$ 200	$ 200	$ 200
Insurance Premiums	$ —	$ —	$ —	$ —
Tax Payment	$ —	$ —	$ —	$ —
Maintenance	$ 150	$ 150	$ 150	$ 150
Cleaning Service	$ 200	$ 200	$ 200	$ 200
Computer Supplies	$ 75	$ 75	$ 75	$ 75
Advertising	$ 1,000	$ 1,000	$ 1,250	$ 2,000
Legal and Accounting Fees	$ 250	$ 250	$ 250	$ 250
Miscellaneous	$ 750	$ 750	$ 750	$ 750
Total	**$ 22,639**	**$ 22,639**	**$ 22,881**	**$ 23,631**
End-of-Month Balance:				
Cash (beginning of month)	$ 44,086	$ 42,458	$ 40,573	$ 37,636
Cash Receipts	$ 21,010	$ 20,754	$ 19,944	$ 19,104
Cash Disbursements	$ 22,639	$ 22,639	$ 22,881	$ 23,631
Cash (end of month)	**$ 42,458**	**$ 40,573**	**$ 37,636**	**$ 33,109**
Borrowing				
Repayment				
Cash (end of month [after borrowing])	**$ 42,458**	**$ 40,573**	**$ 37,636**	**$ 33,109**

Total Health and Fitness
Income Statement
Most Likely
January 2007–December 2007

Sales

Training	$	109,100		
Diet Counseling	$	140,190		
Food Royalties	$	7,913		
Water/Sports Drinks	$	1,115		
Sublease (2000 Sq ft)	$	30,000		
Net Sales Revenue	$	288,318		
CGS	$	836		
Gross Profit			$	**287,482**
Operating Expenses				
Lease			$	56,004
Advertising			$	18,750
Radio	$	14,750.		
Newspaper	$	4,000		
Trade Association			$	950
Insurance			$	3,000
Depreciation			$	6,750
Equipment Repairs/Maintenance			$	1,800
Salaries			$	143,750
Taxes and Benefits			$	35,958
Cleaning Service			$	2,400
Utilities			$	12,480
Heat and A/C	$	8,500		
Water	$	1,520		
Cable	$	300		
Telephone/Internet	$	2,160		
Loan w/Interest			$	21,839
Legal and Accounting			$	3,000
Miscellaneous			$	9,000
Total Operating Expenses			$	**315,680**
Net Income			$	**(28,199)**

Total Health and Fitness
Income Statement
Most Likely
January 2008–December 2008

Sales				
Training	$	127,000		
Diet Counseling	$	162,000		
Food Royalties	$	9,100		
Water/Sports Drinks	$	1,282		
Sublease (2000 Sq ft)	$	30,000		
Net Sales Revenue	$	329,382		
CGS	$	962		
Gross Profit			$	**328,421**
Operating Expenses				
Lease			$	56,004
Advertising			$	21,000
Radio	$	15,000		
Newspaper	$	6,000		
Trade Association			$	500
Insurance			$	3,000
Depreciation			$	6,750
Equipment Repairs/Maintenance			$	2,000
Salaries			$	150,000
Taxes and Benefits			$	37,500
Cleaning Service			$	2,400
Utilities			$	13,100
Heat and A/C	$	9,000		
Water	$	1,600		
Cable	$	300		
Telephone/Internet	$	2,200		
Loan w/Interest			$	21,839
Legal and Accounting			$	3,000
Miscellaneous			$	9,000
Total Operating Expenses			$	**326,093**
Net Income			**$**	**2,328**

CASE 1

Noah's Arf: Coming to the Dogs

When Kris Price sold her house and resigned from a successful 23-year career with Nike, Inc. to launch her own business, her friends and family thought she had lost her mind. Kris, however, saw things from a different perspective. After four years of hard work, research and planning, Kris realized her dream in June 2002 with the grand opening of her business, Noah's Arf (http://www.noahsarf.com). This full-service pet care facility located in Portland, Oregon, provides a safe, clean, and fun environment for pets. Customers can leave their pets at Noah's Arf, or they can hire the company to provide pet care in their own homes.

Kris spent a lot of time traveling as an exhibit manager for Nike and found it challenging to locate a good facility at which to leave her dog. With that, the idea for Noah's Arf was born. Kris began her research and visited dog day-care centers and dog washes throughout the country. Her research failed to find a business concept that offered all of the services she imagined for her venture. Her next step was to create a business plan.

Because Kris had never written a business plan before and did not consider herself to be a good writer, she decided to use *Business Plan Pro* to guide her. She says,

> I just kept at it and kept at it, and then went back and forth with the Small Business Administration (SBA) and took about a year getting my numbers right. The exercise of writing my business plan totally opened my eyes. I didn't know what was involved. *Business Plan Pro* asked questions that made me think about what was involved and made me do my research. There is no way I would have known all that without Business Plan Pro.

Kris scraped together $70,000 of her own money to invest, sold her house, and donated her car to the business. Armed with her business plan, Kris approached the SBA for a loan for $200,000. She says proudly,

> I lease this place. I wish I owned it. I have put a lot of money into the building considering it's not mine, but I had a vision of what I wanted it to look like and I don't think it would have worked if I had not put the money in. A lot of people said, "Don't you think you are getting in over your head? Why don't you try to launch one thing at a time?" I responded, "That's not the concept." A lot of people have day cares, and kitty condos and dog washes, but they don't have all in one. There is nothing else in Oregon like this.

The customers of Noah's Arf confirmed the vision Kris had. The company hit its break-even point within the first two months of operation. Within six months, Kris had a client base of 20 dogs that reside at Noah's Arf daily. The facility grew to a capacity of 40 day-care dogs with the ability to lodge 26 overnight stays, along with nine kitty condos. The company now employs two full-time and four part-time people and needs one more of each. "We are growing so fast I can't keep up with it. It's scaring me, it really is!" says Kris.

The busiest times for Noah's Arf are the holidays; in fact, most kitty condos and dog kennels are full over holidays such as Labor Day and Christmas. Kris has been busily promoting her in-home care service, and it has now reached capacity. The in-home care service requires Kris or an employee to visit a customer's house twice a day to check on animals, and, like the in-house experience, this service is also in the greatest demand around the holidays.

Initially, free publicity through local newspapers and neighborhood publications and newsletters brought in customers. In addition, Noah's Arf recently received the Multnomah Animal Control Facility Award and received a front-page write-up in *The Oregonian*, the premier newspaper for the Portland metropolitan area. Kris's choice of a location for Noah's Arf has helped sales because of a nearby dog park where potential customers take their dogs. Price hears that her business is "the talk of the dog park." To date, Noah's Arf has had to do very little advertising because most new customers hear about Noah's Arf by word of mouth.

When asked whether she will expand the current facility, Price says definitely not:

> I don't want it bigger because right now I know every dogs' name and after I walk them at night, kiss each of them, rub them down, give them a hug—I can still be very personal with them and that's the way I like it. If you get bigger, you lose track of all that. The next stage is to hire people and get them trained so that I can get out of the kennel and think more about the business side of things. I took my first day off in over a year last week, for my 50th birthday. I went to a spa, and I was a nervous wreck.

Looking ahead, Price plans to grow the business by opening similar facilities in other cities, and she has already scouted potential locations.

She says, laughing,

> I look back now and I can't even imagine I did it. Every day is like a Saturday now. I work probably 18 hours a day. I was up at 5 this morning. I work until 10 to 11 at night, and I love it. I am working on adrenalin now, that's all it is.

Exercises

1. What entrepreneurial qualities does Kris possess?
2. Review the initial plan for Noah's Arf at http:// www .bplans.com. What are the primary points of emphasis in this start-up business plan? How might this plan evolve as it

changes from a start-up plan to an ongoing business plan that will be used by the company?

3. Visit the Web site for Noah's Arf at http:// www.noahsarf.com. What recommendations do you have to improve this site?

4. What advertising and promotional strategies do you recommend for Noah's Arf?

5. What might you expect to be the most significant challenges for Kris in the future?

Source: Adapted from Sadie Dressekie, "Going to the Dogs" *Palo Alto Software*, May 20, 2006, http://www.paloalto.com/pr/viewrelease.cfm?r= NoahsArf .

CASE 2

Timbuk2: When Less Is More

Mark Dwight had big ambitions when he took over Timbuk2 (http://www.timbuk2.com). As a cycling enthusiast, Mark ran a design firm before doing corporate stints as head of product design and as a marketing executive at Cisco. He was between jobs when a friend mentioned that the San Francisco-based company Timbuk2 was for sale. Timbuk2 was founded in 1989 by a bike messenger who set out to create the ultimate delivery bag. The 1990s saw a cult-like following for the company among bike messengers and young urban professionals in the San Francisco Bay Area. By 2002, however, the company was nearly bankrupt. Along with eight private investors and a San Francisco-based venture capital firm, Mark bought the company with an eye toward growing the business.

Mark moved quickly to bring discipline to an organization that had known a loose "bike messenger" managerial style. Mark hired a controller and a product developer and then set about streamlining the manufacturing process. Within nine months, productivity doubled, and Mark re-introduced a messenger-style laptop bag offering more features at a lower price point. A part of this solution was outsourcing manufacturing to China, where costs were 30 percent lower.

The 45-year-old CEO had closed a deal that looked like a dream come true. Mark had been excited when the retail giant CompUSA had agreed to carry his product. Yet, just short four months later, with sales volumes booming, Mark realized he had made a mistake. The problem was one of financing.

Timbuk2 was feeling the squeeze of the slim profit margins on the deal with CompUSA and the constant pressure to meet the retailer's high-volume demand for the bags. CompUSA's smaller markups also meant that Timbuk2 had to bundle extra accessories with each bag to avoid undercutting the final sales price of Timbuk2's other retailers. With employees working overtime to prepare the bundles, Mark canceled the deal, pulled his company's bags from CompUSA shelves, and refocused the marketing channels of the business. All told, the deal resulted in a net loss of $50,000.

Mark knew that he needed to take a panoramic view of the company's strategy for long-term sustainability. Timbuk2 was no longer a niche business catering to bike messengers. Mark feared that the company would lose its uniqueness if he decided to distribute the company's products through mainstream retail stores rather than through small, independent distributors. He considered pursuing a path less traveled somewhere between the two extremes. With a goal of having a product that was synonymous with urban style rather than a bargain price, Mark modeled this new thinking after Coach, the maker of luxury leather handbags and other accessories, and its specialty brand approach to marketing. He also benchmarked other companies such as The Discovery Channel Store, Urban Outfitters, and Williams-Sonoma that successfully market their products through specialty retail channels.

Specialty stores possess some attributes of chain stores, but, unlike their big-box cousins, they attract customers who value brand and design over price when making purchase decisions. Stores following this retail strategy offer a deeper selection of merchandise, knowledgeable sales people, an innovative store environment, and higher prices (and profit margins), all which Mark saw as an excellent match for Timbuk2. This approach also enables smaller specialty retail stores to offer a defined market segment with distinctive items that emphasize "street cred" or brand cachet. These stores attract affluent customers who are less sensitive to price, and manufacturers supplying them experience higher margins in exchange for lower sales volumes compared to big-box channel alternatives.

Mark's first step in implementing this strategy was to approach Apple Computer's fledgling chain of retail stores about carrying Timbuk2's products. Apple agreed, and Timbuk2's $99 laptop bag, which appeared in July 2003, became an instant hit. The company's sales increased 130 percent as a result. That momentum fueled the creation of more than 30 new products, including iPod holsters, tote bags, and yoga-mat carriers. These items provided the backbone for expansion into new markets, and Mark now invests most of his time trying to expand Timbuk2's network of 1,200 specialty retailers. Timbuk2 is building elaborate point-of-purchase displays for its biggest accounts, including REI and EMS sporting goods stores. Its Marian handbag for women has been a hit at fashion boutiques. The diversified product lineup has given the company additional exposure, even in New York City, the hometown of rival bag manufacturer Manhattan Portage.

Mark thinks Timbuk2 still has plenty of growth potential. With talk of getting into footwear, Mark attributes his channel strategy as a primary reason for that optimism, and based on his experience, the place to go to buy your first pair of Timbuk2 shoes will not be a big-box store but a specialty store.

Exercises

1. Mark's goal was to grow the business. What risks was Mark taking with the decision to discontinue selling products through CompUSA?
2. What advantages does the specialty retail store distribution strategy offer Timbuk2? What risks does this strategy entail?
3. What role does pricing play in creating an image for a product or service? What pricing strategy do you recommend for Timbuk2? Explain.
4. Visit Timbuk2's Web site (http://www.timbuk2.com) and examine its product line. Work with a group of your classmates to brainstorm ideas for other products the company might consider offering. Explain the reasoning behind your choices.
5. What recommendations would you make to Mark to monitor his success and direct the company's strategy for the future?

Source: Adapted from Andrew Tilin, "Bagging the Right Customer" *Business 2.0*, May 2005, pp. 56–57.

CASE 3

Cloudveil: Dreams for Sale

Founding and running a business had been a tremendous experience for Stephen Sullivan. However, at this moment, he was worried. Cloudveil (http://www.cloudveil.com) is an outdoor sportswear company devoted to hard-core skiers and mountain climbers. It is the kind of place where the company would design a prototype garment one day and test it on the slopes the next. Despite revenues of about $5 million, the Jackson, Wyoming–based company was now strapped for cash and struggling to raise enough money to fuel production. One solution: Sell the business to a larger company that could offer the capital and infrastructure Cloudveil needed so desperately. However, selling out could mean squandering the brand credibility that Stephen and his partner and friend, Brian Cousins, had spent seven years building. That could result in the end of Cloudveil, and Stephen could not stomach the thought.

Stephen and Brian had independently moved to Jackson for its world-class skiing. The partners met while working in a local ski shop, and when not at work, they skied the slopes of the rugged Teton Mountains. The pair found that they had shared interests and shared a vision of designing their own line of outdoor apparel. The first tangible step toward that dream occurred when Stephen received a pair of ski pants from a friend returning from the French Alps. Stephen wore the lightweight pants on the slopes every day for one week. He found them to be the best he had ever worn—flexible, breathable, warm, and unlike any ski pants he had ever seen. He set up shop in his cabin and began designing ski apparel using the same soft-shell fabric. By early 1997, their dream became a reality, and Cloudveil's first line of outdoor ski apparel appeared in 13 retail stores nationwide later that fall.

Stephen and Brian focused on serving Jackson's hard-core backcountry skiing community. To get the word out about their company and its products, they sponsored ski competitions and rock-climbing festivals. Their grass-roots approach created awareness for Cloudveil and its product line and attracted a base of loyal customers. Cloudveil soon expanded its product line to include 150 products, and, with 15 employees, it generated $2 million in annual sales. From their cabin-based beginnings, Cloudveil was growing at an impressive pace, but that growth brought unexpected headaches.

The problems facing Stephen and Brian were typical for a growing business. Managing cash flow was a daily issue. Cloudveil's cash flow cycle—the time between manufacturing its products and collecting the cash from the sale—was a lengthy five to six months, which meant Cloudveil needed to find a way to finance the next season's production before collecting on the current one. Stephen began to spend less time on product development and invest more time addressing financial issues—such as dealing with complaints from unpaid designers. Realizing that the company needed managers with more business experience than they could supply, Stephen and

Brian brought on two partners, seasoned executives Jon Boris and Michael McGregor, who streamlined operations by automating Cloudveil's order fulfillment process.

Sales continued to climb, but cash flow remained a persistent problem. The partners knew they had to explore external financing options and began to consider making a deal with a venture capitalist or a private equity group. Cloudveil also began receiving calls from larger companies, would-be strategic buyers who wanted to purchase the company outright. Cloudveil needed more than just money, and, in many ways, selling the business was the easiest and most attractive option for the founders. To continue to grow, Cloudveil would require a significant investment in its infrastructure and to expand its brand. However, if the founders sold part or all of the company to outside investors, would Cloudveil be able to follow a long-term growth strategy under pressure from investors looking for big short-term returns? Stephen, who had been the company's creative force, feared that selling Cloudveil would result in the brand being diluted or, worse, completely neglected within a large company with multiple apparel lines. Stephen and the partners hesitantly agreed to meet with suitors and weigh their options.

Reality hit hard when Cloudveil's winter catalogs arrived at the Jackson warehouse. The 300,000 catalogs were expected to drive about one-third of the company's annual sales. They were ready to be mailed to potential customers, with only one problem: The company did not have enough cash on hand to pay the $56,000 in postage it would take to mail them! Brian and Stephen quickly scheduled a call with their new partners, Jon and Michael, to find a way to raise the needed capital. They agreed to not draw their salaries for four months until the catalog sales began to materialize. The management team made their decision just after Brian received an e-mail from Jim Reilly, senior vice president at Sports Brand International (SBI), a New York City apparel company that owns the Italian sportswear lines Fila and Ciesse. SBI expressed interest in acquiring Cloudveil. Brian called Reilly and liked what he heard. SBI was eager to capture a piece of the growing outdoor apparel market, and Cloudveil had the expertise and product line that SBI needed.

After a few meetings, all the partners except Stephen were convinced that SBI was a good fit for Cloudveil. Reilly's plan was to guide Cloudveil to $50 million in annual sales without cheapening the brand. Reilly assured them that SBI would not lower prices or degrade quality. Cloudveil would grow "without having to set foot in a Sports Authority," he said. Cloudveil, in turn, would create a new line of ski apparel for Fila, called Fila Mountain. Reilly pledged to keep the company in Jackson, which Brian, Jon, and Michael took as a sign that SBI understood what Cloudveil was all about.

Stephen was doubtful. Over the next few weeks, he spoke with Brian repeatedly to confirm they were doing the right thing. Each time Stephen called, Brian would rehash their reasoning, reminding Stephen that, unlike a venture capital firm or private equity group, SBI offered a global distribution system with a sophisticated supply chain. Stephen had invested a tremendous amount of sweat equity into the company and was finding it difficult to let go.

In December, Stephen agreed to the sale. The price was not disclosed under the terms of the sale. The four partners would call the shots for SBI's new division, Cloudveil Mountain Works. Stephen was SBI's new global brand vice president, and Brian assumed the position of division's president. Brian was to stay in regular contact with Reilly and to send quarterly reports to SBI's board. Cloudveil would remain in charge of its brand. Reilly's role would be to "play the traffic cop."

Soon, SBI's Fila and Ciesse lines were being produced at the same foreign factories as Cloudveil's products, giving Cloudveil additional leverage. SBI became one manufacturer's third-largest customer, and the higher production volumes it accounted for enabled Cloudveil to demand that more of the materials required for its products be stored at the factories, which significantly reduced turnaround time. Today, Cloudveil apparel is sold in 300 specialty stores in the United States and in Japan, Canada, England, Australia, Taiwan, and South Korea.

Stephen is pleased with the arrangement. He is spending more time in his "research laboratory"—the Teton Mountains. Brian is refocusing Cloudveil's strategy. "Some naysayers felt like we were selling out and that the brand would go to crap," says Brian. That has not happened, he insists. "We've been a Jackson company all along, and we're still a hometown brand."

Exercises

1. Discuss the reasons that a manufacturing company like Cloudveil might experience this type of cash flow problem. Is this a sign or poor management or is the nature of the business? What steps can a small company such as Cloudveil take to deal with a long cash flow cycle?

2. If Cloudveil continues to grow at a suitable pace, SBI is likely to continue its hands-off approach. If growth should slow and new product development costs exceed what SBI finds acceptable, what impact might this have on the initial arrangements with Cloudveil?

3. Did Brian and Stephen "sell out" by selling Cloudveil to SBI, or was this the best business decision under the circumstances? What other options did the founders have?

Source: Adapted from "Case Study: For Cash-Strapped Cloudveil, It Was a Very Hard Offer to Refuse," *Inc.,* August 2005, pp. 44–45.

CASE 4

WindVest Motorcycle Products: Down the Windy Road

WindVest, a small family business, has a unique product, one that is designed to keep the bugs out of your teeth. Motorcycle windshields were once big, awkward, and incredibly uncool. That changed when Norm Dober started manufacturing small, aerodynamic windscreens at a factory in Silicon Valley. This rigid piece of transparent plastic mounts to a motorcycle's handlebars with a crosspiece and two simple clamps. Despite its small size—just 14 to 18 inches high—the screen deflects wind and bugs from a much larger area around the driver. WindVest Motorcycle Products (http:www.wind vest.com) sells thousands of windscreens every year, has experienced an annual growth rate of 10% over the last six years, and generates $1.5 million in annual sales. Business is good.

The Dobers want their family business to continue to grow and to increase its profit margins. "I want to see WindVest on as many bikes in South Carolina as I do in California," declares Doug Dober, Norm's son, who handles the company's manufacturing and marketing. The company advertises in several biker publications and on four California radio stations. About one-third of all sales come through a handful of national distributors, which in turn sell the screen kits to retailers. WindVest sells another one-third of its products to retailers. The balance of WindVest sales are directly to bikers who purchase the kits at motorcycle shows, online, or by phone.

Geographically, the majority of the company's sales are in California, Arizona, Colorado, Texas, and Wisconsin. Without any real marketing effort, WindVest's sales also are strong in Florida. Domestically, Doug wants to reach new markets throughout the South and the Northeast. He is convinced that the best way to boost sales in new territories is to demonstrate the product at bike shows and rallies. That approach has worked well in California and other western states, but Doug has found he does not have the time to take his show across the country and manage the business. "There's a biker rally in New Hampshire that draws 300,000 people every year, and I can't get there," Doug laments. Some would argue that only a fraction of bikers at the New Hampshire will actually visit the WindVest booth and that Doug should concentrate on marketing where bikers live, not where they visit for a week. In fact, Doug has discovered that the company's success in Florida is the result of an enthusiastic distributor who has been promoting the WindVest to his customers. Doug is beginning to wonder whether the key to boosting sales might be cultivating more distributors like the one if Florida rather than attending bike shows. One potential strategy is to offer incentives to the salespeople who work for Windvest's distributors.

Manufacturing is also a growth-related issue. Doug would like to improve the company's manufacturing efficiency by restructuring its supply channel and finding suppliers closer to WindVest's headquarters in Campbell,

California. The parts WindVest purchases to make its windscreens are relatively expensive, particularly the molded plastic and the chrome-plated components. The Dobers realize that competitors might enter the market and sell low-cost versions of the WindVest, which would put pressure on their company to lower its costs and prices. The Dobers want better prices and service from their current suppliers but are not sure how to negotiate those arrangements. Like many small U.S. companies, they have a tendency to underestimate their negotiating power with suppliers. "I'm afraid of them telling me to get lost," says Doug. One factor in their favor is that U.S.-based auto-parts manufacturers are losing work to overseas suppliers, and these suppliers should be eager to keep a growing client such as WindVest. The good news is that WindVest has the potential to stay ahead of any future copycats by having the labor-intensive parts made in Mexico, where labor costs are a fraction of those in the United States. However, they wonder about the best way to find suppliers who have operations in Mexico.

This family-owned business does experience conflict. Norm Dober turned over most of the daily operations to Doug. However, Doug, who has worked at the company for seven years, is hesitant to delegate responsibilities. Doug is a self-confessed micromanager who takes on more tasks than he can handle. With 10 employees, Doug still handles all complaints and returns from customers, a complex and time-consuming task. Norm's wife, Marilyn, 63, keeps the books, assisted by her daughter, Tami, 38, who joined the company three years ago. She works with her mother in accounting, with a desire to take on more responsibility, such as handling receivables and collections. Marilyn worries that she will become irrelevant to the business if she delegates too much. The result: Family disputes often get heated.

The Dobers have share many common interests, including Harley-Davidson "hogs" equipped with WindVest windshields. Harley owners are a key component in the company's marketing mix. The business began exclusively marketing windshields designed for Harley-Davidson motorcycles. As the four major foreign manufacturers entered the American "cruiser bike" market in the 1990s, WindVest followed suit. "If it were not for the fact that we adapted and supported the foreign cruising motorcycles, we would not still be in business," says Doug. There are 348 authorized Harley-Davidson dealers located in 47 states (see accompanying table).

WindVest continues to look down the road to the future. With a constant focus on quality, the Dobers have restructured their management team in the areas of administration and manufacturing, are applying more effective internal communication techniques, and have learned the benefits of delegation. "As a result," says Doug, "margins are strong, profits are up, and we make fewer mistakes." With plans to enter the

Harley-Davidson Dealers

Number of Authorized Dealers by State

California	33
Pennsylvania	32
Ohio	30
Wisconsin	28
New York	27
Texas	21
Florida	21
North Carolina	18
New Jersey	13
Virginia	11
Tennessee	11
Indiana	11
Washington	9
Minnesota	8
Iowa	8
Illinois	8
Alabama	7
Oregon	6
New Hampshire	6
Maryland	6
Massachusetts	6
Michigan	6
Colorado	6
South Carolina	5
Oklahoma	5
Montana	5
Missouri	5
Louisiana	5
Georgia	5
West Virginia	4
South Dakota	4
New Mexico	4
North Dakota	4
Arizona	4
Wyoming	3
Utah	3
Nevada	3
Nebraska	3
Maine	3
Rhode Island	2
Mississippi	2
Kansas	2
Kentucky	2
Idaho	2
Delaware	2
Connecticut	2
Alaska	1
Arkansas	1

Source: Authorized Harley-Davidson Dealers, http://hogs4sale.com, June 4, 2006.

European market, the road to success for WindVest looks bright. "Go big or go home," states Doug.

Just be sure to keep the bugs out of you teeth as you travel.

Exercises

1. How might the Dobers address the management issues they face relating to control and delegation? What steps should they take to deal with the issues of running a family business?
2. What areas of WindVest's business plan are going to be the most important in the next two years?
3. What recommendations can you make to improve WindVest's domestic marketing strategy?
4. What challenges would you anticipate for WindVest as they enter the European market? What steps should the company take to enter this market?
5. Once you have decided on a strategy, brainstorm with others in your class to determine ways that WindVest can optimize the performance of its sales and distribution channels.

Sources: Personal communication with Doug Dober, June 8, 2006; Brian O'Reilly, "Against the Wind," *Fortune,* September 8, 2005, http://www.fortune.com/fortune/print.

Danielson Designs: Sign Me Up!

The story and the cast of characters sound like a melodrama. The first scene is set on the stage of a former coal mining boomtown of southern Colorado. The act opens on a historic Main Street with a backdrop of spectacular scenery, elegant Victorian architecture, cobblestone streets, and salt-of-the-earth townspeople. This is the idyllic American town where people envision growing up or settling down. Then the villains enter. As the community attempts to recover from years of economic depression and local businesses struggle to survive, Wal-Mart opens and devastates the last of the downtown businesses. Adding to the drama, gambling had become the saving hope for small-town America, and a few local real estate owners decided to call in the "slots and craps." When the dust cleared, residents had voted overwhelmingly to keep the city free from gambling. Was it destined to be another mining ghost town after all?

The next act pans in on what appears to be a Currier & Ives Christmas dinner. Annie and her husband, Mark, talk with his brother, Aaron, about how they can use their talents to help bolster the economic development of the community. Mark had run his own woodshop designing and building custom furniture, Annie had years of background in product development with a designer's eye, and Aaron had an MBA and a head for business. "How could we blend these into a mix that would provide employment opportunities for our community?" The Danielsons began to dream of a company that *might* make a difference in the economically depressed town they had come to call home.

Act three opens with 12 picture frames in stock, the details of the venture still sketchy, and the dream beginning to take shape. With their first trade show a success, the "family business" became a comic reality as four generations from both sides of the Danielson/Richardson tree scramble to fill orders that surpassed their wildest expectations. Mark and Aaron build frames in the woodshop, Annie and the grandmothers paint them at the kitchen table, and the grandpas scrounge boxes from the supermarket parking lot for the packing process, which they perform in the living room. This is all amidst the joyful hubbub of toddler cousins wandering about and great grandma baking zucchini bread for coffee breaks and wondering what all the excitement is about. The family members establish themselves as the heroes of the play as Danielson Designs (http:www.danielsondesigns.com) fights to save the distressed town of Trinidad, Colorado. Few would have predicted the magnitude of their success. Their story continues to this day with repeated encore performances.

Danielson Designs blossomed from family roots in this small, almost forgotten western community to become the country's premier manufacturer of hand-painted signs, wooden picture frames, and accessories. "What draws together every-thing we do is our unique aesthetic," according to Mark and Annie Danielson. This sense of Danielson style is "uptown country" and "traditional with a twist."

The product line is composed of unique vintage-style picture frames, home accessories, and signs, signs, everywhere some signs. With new product lines, no one anticipated the vigor with which signs would skyrocket to the top of their bestseller list. "It was shocking to witness the resonance generated by our 'Be careful how you address the Queen' sign," Mark said. Reassurance followed from the popularity of the slightly more nurturing, "Home is where your story begins." Annie's unique sense of design is the heart and soul of the company that bears her name. Her flair for interpreting traditional themes with sophistication and whimsy has propelled her company from its homegrown beginnings to her work being featured in *Country Living, Country Home, Romantic Home,* and other magazines.

Raising a family and growing a business in an innovation-driven industry has honed Annie's juggling skills. Both Annie and Mark and their family-partners Aaron and Helen made a commitment early in the game that they would not grow a company at the expense of their families. At times, they have settled for less business when more would have meant less time for family. Family is still at the heart of the matter. Annie's story is one of balance about giving expression to her God-given gifts of design and ambition while being faithful to her heart's desire to be a mother to her growing family. As the core business matured, Annie turned her sights to the retail world and opened Danielson Dry Goods in the heart of town. Featuring gifts, furniture, tabletops, and accessories, the renovated "Five 'n Dime" carries the unmistakable stamp of Annie's aesthetic sensibility.

"We felt we could do anything. It was a feeling of immortality, and we expanded into the areas of office furniture and home furnishings. We eventually realized that after shipping expenses, we were losing money hand over fist," Mark says. In addition, the high-end product line (with retail frames starting at $40) did not sell well, and then economic challenges hit with a vengeance. "The business was tanking," says Mark, pointing out that it could no longer support two families. "We could see the writing on the wall, and we needed to get into a more accessible price point if we are going to survive," he recalls. "The import market was beginning to go nuts, and competition was higher than ever." Mark and Annie bought out his brother and went back to their core business—affordable frames and signs. "We knew how to do it, and we could ship it UPS," Mark says with a laugh. In addition, they hesitantly implemented technology to replace their handcrafted operation, which meant that the operation required fewer employees. This allowed Mark and Annie to create customized signs in runs as small as 25 units. Today, customized signs sales account for 80% of their business and offer a layer of protection against foreign competitors that emulate their designs and keep pushing prices lower. When they purchased the business from Mark's brother, Mark and Annie thought that they might have to resort to downsizing the staff, then at 60, but their concerns proved to be unfounded. In fact, the work force since has grown to 70 people. When asked how Danielson Designs competes, Mark replies, "We are a design firm. They can copy what we did last year, but they don't know what we are designing now."

The Danielsons look back on those early days with wonder. The impact Danielson Designs has had on the family and the community they love has been life-changing. Those original 12 frames have evolved into thousands of designs. The handwritten, photocopied price list has become a beautiful full-color catalog and Web site. The old 900-square-foot shop has been replaced by 16,000 square feet of shop and offices. "What *really* gets us charged up is seeing our original dream come true," they say.

Moms have been able to paint frames out of their dining rooms and augment their family's income without leaving home. Young people find secure employment close to family and the town they have grown to love. Eyes light up as people develop talents they never knew they had. Laborers become apprentices and start gaining skills that propel them on their journey toward being master craftsmen. It's what makes business worthwhile.

The most significant challenge facing Danielson Design is the growing threat of global competition. Foreign manufacturers, particularly those from China, have entered the market and are producing similar products at a fraction of the price. Many of these products have strikingly similarities to Danielson's current lines. Offshore manufactures constantly scan the market, watch for the designs that sell best, duplicate them, and sell them at a fraction of the cost. "We just cannot compete with the cost of these foreign produced competitive products," laments Mark. "We are a design shop and we need to keep ahead of our competitors with innovative design work. That is our competitive edge." The question that remains is whether they can sustain it.

Exercises

1. Complete a SWOT analysis for Danielson Designs. Based on your analysis, what strategic recommendations can you make to the company?
2. Visit the Web site for Danielson Designs (http://www. danielsondesigns.com) and review the product and background information. What suggestions can you offer for improving the site?
3. What do you consider the greatest risks facing Danielson Designs in the immediate future?
4. How can the Danielsons maintain their company's competitive edge in the face of foreign competition?

Source: Personal communication with Mark Danielson, June 6, 2006; *Danielson Design*, www.danielsondesigns.com, May 20, 2006.

CASE 6

School Zone Publishing: Educating the Competition

Jonathan Hoffman scanned the shelves of the local Target store and saw his worst fears before him. His employee was right. The educational books and flash card products on the shelves appeared far too similar to those of his family's educational media company, School Zone. From the composition, look, and feel of these products, it was clear that they were knockoffs. He checked the package to find out the identity of his new competitor and found the name "Dogs in Hats." Dogs in Hats is a company recently founded by School Zone's former vice president of national sales and marketing, Peter Alfini. Jonathan suspected that Alfini had used School Zone's trademarked and copyrighted information and resources to launch this new line of competitive products. In addition, they were sitting on the shelf right next to his company's products in a retail chain that accounted for 10 percent of School Zone's total sales.

School Zone Publishing Company (http://http://www.schoolzone.com) began as The School Zone Learning Center in 1972. As a retail teachers' supply outlet, the company specialized in selling to teachers from its two stores in Grand Rapids, Michigan. By 1975, schools instituted changes in teaching methods in math and English, eliminating workbooks provided on a shared basis for home use. Parents soon experienced difficulty in finding educational material for use at home, and, capitalizing on the opportunity, School Zone began developing and selling products to parents. Today the company's product line has grown to include almost 200 educational books, flash cards, games, and other educational resources.

School Zone's directors of design and development, Dexter Peacock and Barb Peacock, began comparing their products with those from Dogs in Hats. They were looking for points of trademark and copyright infringement that had the potential to confuse School Zone's customers. In one instance, a School Zone capital "G" alphabet flashcard displayed a drawing of a girl with blonde pigtails, green bows, and a yellow shirt collar. The alphabet flashcard from Dogs in Hats was almost identical. The only significant difference was that the girl's hair color was brown. "Everything looked like ours," says Peacock. The designers were stunned by the similarities, and when they reported their findings to Jonathan, he was furious.

When Alfini resigned from School Zone after two years with the company, Jonathan was surprised. His departure hit even harder when Alfini hired two designers from School Zone to join the new venture he was launching, Dogs in Hats. Alfini contends that he started Dogs in Hats with his own ideas and resources and combined that with more than a decade of experience in educational publishing before joining School Zone. Jonathan suspected that Alfini had discovered School Zone's deal with Target while he was still working for School Zone.

Still, Jonathan thought that it was extremely suspicious that Dogs in Hats' products were so similar to School Zone's products and that Alfini also had struck a deal with Target.

This family-owned educational media company now had a problem. "We are nice people in a nice community. We aren't use to dealing with these kinds of issues," says Jonathan. He called an emergency meeting of School Zone Publishing's executive team, comprised of his mother, Joan, the company's president and co-founder, and his sister, Jennifer Dexter, the vice president of design and development, and his attorney. After reviewing Alfini's product line, all three came to the conclusion that Dogs in Hats had compromised School Zone's intellectual property. They decided to sue Dogs in Hats.

As time went on, the sales data from the summer season confirmed Jonathan's fear: Dogs in Hats was taking market share from School Zone. One six-week period after Dogs in Hats products were stocked at Target showed that School Zone sales of corresponding items dropped by 23%. Preparing the legal case became Jonathan's primary focus. Tension within the office increased when Jonathan suspected that a sales employee was leaking information to Alfini. With trust inside the company at an all-time low, Jonathan limited access to the copy room and closed the office after hours and on weekends. This was the only way he knew how to control the situation, but it was not the way he liked to manage the family business.

School Zone filed a complaint in federal district court in western Michigan listing 84 allegations against Dogs in Hats. The complaint sought payment for damages and attorneys' fees and demanded that Alfini destroy materials using School Zone's copyrighted and trademarked material. Dogs in Hats' answer to the complaint denied most of the allegations, conceding only that Alfini hired former employees of School Zone and that he in fact was present at School Zone's offices after resigning.

This began an extensive discovery process that lasted more than two years. As School Zone's legal filings and attorneys' fees approached $100,000, Hoffman and Dexter were begging Jonathan to drop the case. But Jonathan kept thinking about what his father would have done. Jim Peter had founded School Zone and died a few months before the Alfini conflict began. The company's attorneys warned that if School Zone did not defend its marks now, it would be more difficult to do so in the future. The case continued.

Three months later, a judge sent the parties into mediation. Western Michigan courts are famous for favoring alternative means of resolving disputes, but Jonathan faced the dilemma of whether to compromise and put the case in the past or to hold out for a potential victory in court.

Jonathan's family tried to convince him to attempt to settle out of court. They argued that a successful mediation would minimize expenses and avoid having to ask company clients, such as Target, to sit for depositions and to research records for relevant evidence. Jonathan chose to not take the path he initially felt his deceased father would have selected. Jonathan took another look at what this was doing to his family's company and agreed to mediation.

Dogs in Hats and School Zone agreed on a mediator, and Jonathan and Alfini found themselves sitting across the table from each other. They had not spoken in two years. The atmosphere of the mediation was professional, and, after eight hours of negotiations, Jonathan thought they were close to a deal. He left the meeting feeling surprisingly optimistic.

Meanwhile, School Zone's annual revenue had grown about 20%, surpassing $25 million, primarily because its interactive division was growing so rapidly. Jonathan hopes to reach a settlement, but if the two parties cannot, he has no qualms about battling it out in a courtroom before a judge. "Intellectual property is the lifeblood of my company," he says. "I'm trying to be logical. I sometimes worry this is about 8-year-old me, or my id, but I really do believe in justice."

After months of discussion, Jonathan and Alfini finally reached an out-of-court settlement. Although Jonathan is unable to discuss the details, he is happy that he can focus on his customers once again. He credits the case with providing perspective. Alfini is still in business, now living with his mother, and continues to have legal problems with disgruntled employees. "Some of the employees that left School Zone have been in contact with us and said how they now realize what a great company School Zone is" says Jonathan.

"I don't regret engaging in legal action" states Jonathan, "but this was an emotionally intense, pendulum-like experience that proved to be a distraction from the business." As far as offering advice to others, Jonathan suggests to assess the costs before going to court. "Know when to use the law and when not to. The cost may not be worth it."

Exercises

1. Did School Zone's hiring process play a role in this issue? What hiring recommendations can you offer School Zone to avoid this problem in the future?

2. Was it wise for Hoffman to protect his company's intellectual property the way he did? What consequences do small companies face if they fail to protect their intellectual property?

3. At what point should a company stop defending its intellectual property rights through the court system? Should entrepreneurs set thresholds based on time or expense, or is this a decision that cannot be determined by these types of parameters?

Sources: Personal communication with Jonathan Hoffman, June 6, 2006; Adapted from Lora Kolodny, "Case Study: Jonathan Hoffman Was Sure a Former Staffer Had Stolen His Company's Ideas," *Inc.*, September 2005, pp. 55–56.

CASE 7

Eminence Style: Running Away with It

Heather Antonelli's trip to India was an intentional diversion from the financial situation facing her company. The only thing on her mind, however, was that she had just defaulted on a $700,000 line of credit from Bank of America. Heather is the CEO of an Austin-based wholesale furniture company called Eminence Style. The company had experienced several months of declining sales, and she had just laid off 5 of her 11 employees and was facing business debt larger than she ever could have imagined. The question before her now was one that she had hoped to never face: Should she shut down her company and declare bankruptcy? Just a few years earlier, with sales approaching $3 million and growing, this dilemma was the farthest thing from her mind.

Heather founded Eminence Style with her mother, JoAnn, in Atlanta in 1996. They had self-funded the business, plowing the profits it generated back into the business. Annual sales grew slowly and steadily, and in 2001, Eminence Style had the opportunity to boost its sales significantly with one big order. A buyer from Sears ordered $2 million worth of Eminence Style's tables and armoires for the retailer's Great Indoors division. The problem was that Heather did not have the cash to pay her Hungarian factory to make the furniture to fill this large order, and, for the first time in the short history of the business, she began to shop for bank loans.

Heather found securing financing to be surprisingly easy. She received a $200,000 loan from the U.S. Small Business Administration (SBA), and, in the same week, Bank of America had agreed to provide the company a $700,000 line of credit. Heather also had managed to pull together $55,000 from her friends and her family. "It was like monopoly money," she recalls.

Eminence Style was on track to book $5.5 million in sales with profits projected to exceed $500,000. Things were looking good—until some of the variables began to change. First, the value of the dollar began to slip against the euro. Heather had paid the factory in Hungary a one-third deposit of $210,000 to fulfill the Sears order and had budgeted $420,000 to pay off the balance. However, the dollar continued to lose value and the balance due increased, topping out at $840,000. Heather managed to pay the manufacturer in full, but the falling exchange rate caused the company's profits to fall to $10,000, far below what she had projected. Initially, Heather considered this nothing more that a minor setback.

The next blow came in the following January. Her contact at Sears left, and his replacement was not interested in re-ordering from Eminence Style. Bank of America expected Antonelli to pay down her entire $700,000 of credit, now at its limit, in February. She pulled together $350,000 and persuaded her loan officer to give her more time, convinced she could turn things around. She had no idea what lie ahead.

The invasion of Chinese furniture manufacturers into the American market struck with a vengeance. Heather began losing customers to lower-priced Chinese rivals whose manufacturing costs were 50 percent less than those of her Hungarian factory. As she searched for a Chinese factory that met her standards, she raised prices by 30% to stay afloat. Heather also moved the company's headquarters to Austin, Texas, where her boyfriend lived, leaving her mother behind to run Eminence Style's show room in Atlanta. As Heather struggled to get the company back on track, her relationship with her mother was as stressed as those with her creditors.

In May of the following year, Bank of America called in the line of credit and gave Heather 60 days to pay off the remaining $350,000 the company owed. "I spent the summer doing the 'bank dance,'" she says. "It was horrible." When she returned from India, Heather reviewed her options. She put together projected profit and loss statements, budget forecasts, and sales predictions. It was clear that it would take a minimum of four years just to return the company to its break-even point. The business could no longer afford the employees and marketing necessary to generate substantial sales. The possibility of bankruptcy loomed larger.

Heather and her mother had personally guaranteed their loans. Chapter 13 bankruptcy would have allowed them to establish a plan to pay off the debt (at least in part), but closing the business and declaring Chapter 7 bankruptcy would end their legal obligations and free them from the debt entirely. However, they both were worried about the impact that defaulting on the loans would have on their lives. "I didn't want to feel like a failure," says Heather. JoAnn recalls that she had lots of questions about the possibility of declaring bankruptcy. "What would happen to our customers? Would I lose my home?" she says.

As Heather considered the ramifications of bankruptcy, she worried about her reputation, and JoAnn begged her daughter to keep the company open. The burden of the decision lay with Heather, who handled the company finances, and she knew she had to make a decision soon. Orders were backing up, and customers were calling. In addition, Congress had passed stricter bankruptcy laws that would require Heather to sign up for credit counseling and possibly to set up a repayment schedules instead of wiping the debt clean.

Exercises

1. What should Heather and JoAnn do? Explain.
2. Do you consider the problems that Eminence Style encountered to be the result of a difficult business environment or Heather's inabilities to properly anticipate, plan for, and deal with the financial issues of her company?
3. If Heather and her mother decide to close the business and declare bankruptcy, what options do they have under current bankruptcy laws? Which one would you recommend?
4. What steps could Heather and JoAnn have taken to avoid the problems that created this management dilemma?

Source: Adapted from Nadine Heintz, "Anatomy of a Business Decision Case Study: Her Line of Credit Was in Default," *Inc.*, December, 2005, pp. 59–60.

CASE 8

MTH Electric Trains: When Locomotives Collide

Mike Wolf, owner of MTH Trains, a manufacturer of model trains that he had started as a teenager, received a call from one of his hobby shop dealers. "Mike, we just got the Lionel C&O Alleghenys," the dealer said. "And, man, this thing looks just like yours." When he arrived, Mike picked up the $1,399.95 die-cast engine and stared at it in disbelief. Indeed, the details on the competitor's model train engine were uncharacteristically crisp and sharp. The small imperfections in the metal castings of the Lionel product that customers had learned to accept over the years were gone. Mike recognized the look and feel of the new product and realized that his company was now competing with a greatly improved product, one that looked suspiciously identical to his. Mike wasted no time responding.

MTH Electric Train's sales were approaching an all-time high of $60 million, and the company was closing in on Lionel Manufacturing's industry-leading position. Mike had narrowed the gap by offering innovative products and lower prices, but most important, his company made higher-quality trains. If his legendary competitor Lionel was able to match his quality, Mike feared that the sheer power of the nearly century-old brand would erode his company's competitive advantage. The Lionel brand struck a particularly strong note with middle-aged men for whom the name Lionel represented a return ticket to their childhood and who represented an important segment of both company's customer base.

Although model railroading presents an image of gentle, nostalgic innocence, this niche industry has always played rough. This rivalry began with the industry's legendary founder, Joshua Lionel Cowen, who founded Lionel Manufacturing in 1900 at the age of 23. Cowen aggressively battled his rivals of the day, A. C. Gilbert and the Ives Company, and built a reputation of being a fierce competitor. Cowen positioned model trains as the ultimate "feel-good father–son bonding hobby" as he ran off the tracks other train company competitors with an unrestrained style of advertising. By 1953, annual revenues had reached $32 million and Lionel had become the industry's icon. The 1960s, however, brought challenging times as Lionel introduced less expensive trains and relocated its production facilities to Mexico, which resulted in a disastrous decline in quality. These moves alienated Lionel's loyal, long-time customers and created an opportunity for small niche players to manufacture tin-plate reproductions of retired Lionel models.

One of those companies was Williams Reproductions, which Jerry Williams operated from his basement in Laurel, Maryland. Williams was a part-time railroading enthusiast, and paid neighborhood kids $1.50 an hour to assemble model engines and passenger and freight cars, which he then sold through hobby shops and train shows. Mike Wolf was 12 and among the first groups of boys who hammered rivets and

painted trim lines. Williams continued to enlist Mike's help, and, at the 1977 York, Pennsylvania, Train Show, the biggest on the railroading calendar, he put Mike in charge of the parts table. Williams told Mike he could keep 10 percent of all parts sales, and Mike knew he had found his life's calling when he went on to sell $150,000 of parts at the show.

With William's permission and support, Mike started Mike's Train House while still a teenager. His company was selling Williams's trains and parts by mail order from his bedroom, taking phone orders from the West Coast at night, processing credit card transactions, and maintaining a customer database on an early Apple computer. Mike was taking classes at a nearby college and developed a unique pick-up system with the local UPS driver. Mike parked a Ford Falcon in front of his house and used it as a mailbox. If he had a shipment ready to go out, Mike tied a red rag to the car's antenna as a signal, and the UPS driver stopped to pick it up. Mike's Train House, later renamed MTH Electric Trains (http://http://www.mth-railking.com), continued to grow, and MTH soon became Williams' largest distributor.

By the mid-1980s, Williams decided to sell off part of his business. Mike was his buyer of choice and at the age of 22 was one year younger than Joshua Lionel Cowen when he founded Lionel. The two entrepreneurs shared other traits. Both men stood five feet, five inches tall and had the same competitive, self-promoting, and audacious style. In 2002, *Classic Toy Trains* magazine named Wolf the most influential person in the industry in the previous 15 years.

Mike showed the Lionel engine in question to his top managers, all childhood friends and many of whom had worked in Jerry Williams's basement. The group backed Mike's decision to initiate an investigation at his design and manufacturing subcontractor's plant in South Korea, a company called Samhongsa. Like many manufacturers, MTH had reached a point at which the irresistible advantages of moving manufacturing overseas were evident. There had never been a reason for Mike to be concerned about his company's proprietary design drawings and tooling, but now he suspected that some of MTH's design secrets were leaking out to his number one competitor.

Fortunately, when he arrived in South Korea, Mike received prompt and diligent attention from both his Asian business partner and South Korean authorities. They discovered that a former designer of MTH trains at Samhongsa had left to become chief engineer at a rival company called Korea Brass. The former employee confessed to receiving stolen MTH designs on computer disks from accomplices at Samhongsa. A South Korean appellate court found Samhongsa's former designer and the top executive of Korea Brass guilty of trade-secret theft. The two perpetrators were paid to steal MTH's designs and use them to manufacture trains that Korea Brass then sold to Lionel. The link to Lionel was a U.S.-based Korea Brass sales agent named Yoo Chan Yang, who was in South Korea when the raid of Korea Brass' office took place. Korean agents seized Yang's computer and his hard drive containing e-mail correspondence with a high-level Lionel employee. This e-mail pointed to Lionel as a knowing recipient of the stolen designs and some of MTH's production schedules as well.

Although he had plenty of evidence, Mike knew that prosecuting Lionel in the United States would not be easy. First, the evidence trail began on the other side of the globe, and second, it would involve putting an American icon on trial. Nonetheless, Mike wanted Lionel brought to justice, and, ultimately, he wanted Lionel brought to its knees. Mike was fighting for the survival of his company and for a measure of revenge. Within months, Mike brought a civil action against Lionel, seeking $29 million in damages for misappropriation of trade secrets. The suit also named Korea Brass and Yoo Chan Yang as defendants.

The jury of a Detroit federal district court learned just how personal the dispute had become. MTH's counsel quoted e-mail correspondence from Korea Brass agent Yoo Chan Yang to former Lionel director of engineering Bob Grubba. One e-mail referred to MTH as "the dirty rat" and another stated, "By the time MTH realizes what is happening, the game should be over . . . we know exactly what the other camp is doing." Mike took the witness stand one week into the trial and knew that he was fortunate to be making his case to this jury. Most small businesses would not have made it this far in a civil theft-of-trade-secrets case against a much more established competitor with deeper pockets. At the time of the trial, Mike estimated his legal expenses would approach $4 million. He was able to continue only because his law firm felt confident enough of the outcome to work for a contingency fee.

To prove his case, Mike had to reveal much of his privately held company's information, which Mike found painful. He testified that MTH's profits fallen from $9.6 million to $6.2 in the three years since Lionels' product change. The same year Lionel competed with him model by model, profits fell to under $1 million, and by the following year, MTH lost $815,000. Two weeks after the trial started, the jury returned with a verdict form that included these questions:

- Was plaintiff the owner or co-owner of information that qualified as a trade secret?

- Did defendant Korea Brass and defendant Yang improperly acquire, disclose to Lionel, or use this information?

- Did defendant Lionel improperly acquire or use this information?

- Did improper use of this information cause injury to Mike's Train House's business?

The jury found the defendants guilty on all counts.

The court clerk came to the last two questions regarding damages and the award for MTH regarding past lost profits and future lost profits. For past lost profits: $11,978,887. For future profits: $13,794,518. In addition, the jury deemed that Lionel had unjustly enriched itself by $12,834,820 and Korea Brass and Yoo Chan Yang by $2,167,440 and that the defendants' actions were willful and malicious. All totaled, it added up to more than $40 million. Mike was relieved at the verdict and saw it as a victory.

It took U.S. District Judge John Corbett O'Meara nearly five months to issue his final ruling. The judge denied all of Lionel's post-trial motions, including an ongoing request that the verdict be dismissed for lack of evidence. The damages assessed by the jury and O'Meara stood, preventing Lionel from using its existing tooling or drawings to continue to manufacture the 20 engines that Lionel had created using MTH's stolen trade secrets.

Within weeks of the final court ruling, Lionel filed for protection under Chapter 11 of the U.S. Bankruptcy Code and issued a press release saying that "The MTH judgment alone has forced us to take this action." MTH is Lionel's largest unsecured creditor and will have a say in any reorganization plan for Lionel. There is a chance that Mike will come to own Lionel, or at least the rights to the Lionel trademark. However, there are other scenarios, some of which involve the loser of a devastating trade-secrets judgment outlasting the winner. Lionel is pressing for a reversal or downsizing of the jury verdict and could prevail on appeal.

From a high of 127 employees, MTH now employs 57. Mike has cut his salary from $195,000 to just $35,000 a year and has sold off much of his personal train collection. MTH's sales are off 50 percent from their peak just a few years ago. When asked if he would do it all again, Mike responds "yes" without hesitation. However, his answer to the question, "What's next for your company?" does not come as quickly.

Exercises

1. How would you assess the competitive environment in this niche industry? Is this the type of an environment that you would recommend entering?

2. Discuss the benefits and the risks of outsourcing the manufacturing of products to foreign countries.

3. What preventive measures might MTH have put in place to protect its designs and manufacturing processes when it outsourced production to the factory in South Korea?

4. If Mike had asked your advice when he first discovered that his company's trade secrets had been stolen, would you have suggested that he pursue the lawsuit against Lionel and the manufacturers in South Korea? Explain.

5. Brainstorm with others from your class regarding potential future strategies for MTH Electric Trains. What should Mike do with his company now?

Source: Adapted from John Grossmann, "Train Wreck," *Inc.*, February 2005, pp. 84–88.

CASE 9

TerraCycle: Garbage In, Garbage Out

As you walk the aisles of your favorite garden department, you may discover a unique type of plant food made by TerraCycle, a small company located in Trenton, New Jersey. The company's vermicompost tea fertilizer is a rich, organic brew made from the castings (the actual waste product) of red worms that are fed organic waste. Packaged in a yellow and green shrink-wrapped bottle made of recycled plastic and topped with unwanted extra spray devices from other manufacturers, TerraCycle may be the world's first commercial product made entirely from garbage. Even the shipping boxes are recycled, misprinted rejects from other companies. TerraCycle (http://www.terracycle.net) is sold through mass merchandisers, including Home Depot and Wal-Mart.

TerraCycle's flagship plant food was the top seller in its category after it debuted on HomeDepot.com. In a series of independent tests conducted at the Rutgers Eco-Complex in Bordentown, New Jersey, TerraCycle performed as well as or better than the products of its more established competitors, whose products are not organic. In addition, TerraCycle claims that its products never burn plants as other fertilizers might if they are not properly applied. The more you use, the healthier the plants become. It all adds up to a strong sales pitch. "We have an organic product that's both better and cheaper than the conventional product. What are people going to buy?" asks company founder Tom Szaky (pronounced zack-y). It is unusual for large-scale retailers to take a chance on a young, unproven company, especially one with a 24-year-old founder and CEO like Tom. One reason they are willing to do so is that TerraCycle retailers can earn gross margins two or three times those that they get from other companies' plant fertilizers.

Tom Szaky was born in Hungary, fled with his family to the Netherlands, and was raised in Canada. A high school plant project and a subsequent business plan competition led Tom and some friends to the creation of TerraCycle. The group had not solved the plant project problem they encountered when they all went off to college, Tom to Princeton University and his friends to McGill University in Montreal, but all three took the stalled plant project with them. It was there that one of the friends learned about fertilizing the plants with worm waste. He created a compost heap in a box in his kitchen, placed red worms in it, and started feeding them table scraps. By the time Tom came to visit during the fall of his freshman year, the plants his friend was experimenting with were thriving. Simultaneously, Tom had been searching for a business to enter in Princeton's annual business plan competition. If these worms could turn table scraps into a terrific fertilizer, he could only imagine what an army of worms could do! The theme of making money while recycling resonated with Tom, and when he returned to Princeton, Tom discovered that his friend Jon Beyer actually knew something about worms. Jon's father was an ecotoxicologist—a person who studies the effects of pollu-

tion on ecosystems. Tom and Jon thought the worm waste product was an excellent fit for Princeton's business plan competition. They came in fourth in the competition, missing out on any prize money, and kept working on the project.

After an unsuccessful experience with a "worm gin" that they had commissioned to be built for $20,000, the young entrepreneurs were on the verge of giving up. The process was labor intensive, and because working with the food source and the waste product itself was just plain disgusting, it was challenging to get others involved. They decided that they would liquidate their assets, sell the worm gin on eBay, and pay off their debts. However, a local AM talk radio station invited Tom and Jon to do a live interview. The disgruntled duo thought that it would be fitting way to conclude the experience. They went on WCTC-AM and told their story, and when they returned to Princeton, a message was waiting. A local entrepreneur, Suman Sinha, heard the interview and wanted to meet them. Tom and Jon showed him the worm gin and explained their initial hopes to expand. The meeting ended with Sinha writing a check for $2,000, enough to keep the fledgling company going. They expressed their gratitude and promised him one percent of the stock in return. With that, TerraCycle got a new lease on life. It was not the last extraordinary event to occur in the company's history.

Tom kept the company alive by entering and winning business plan contests. He had effectively, though not officially, dropped out of school, but Jon continued his studies. The two entered the Princeton business plan competition the following year and this time walked off with the first place prize of $5,000. In addition, Tom had won five other competitions, earning between $2,000 and $10,000 each, and the team expanded. The Carrot Capital Business Plan Challenge, an event sponsored by a prominent venture capital company, was next. This nationally promoted competition was extremely competitive because it offered the potential of $3 million in venture funding to be split among the top 10 contestants, including up to $1 million for the winner. Much to their surprise, Tom's team won the competition. On April 29, 2003, Tom rang the opening bell at NASDAQ and was interviewed on CNBC about his victory and the $1 million prize. There was just one catch. To receive the funding, the winner had to agree to Carrot Capital's terms. Carrot Capital was not interested in the three other entrepreneurs who had built the business with Tom. They only wanted Tom. The venture capitalists told Tom that he could become very wealthy just by telling his story and that they would take care the rest. "Well," said Tom, "if that's what you want, we don't have a deal." Leaving his million-dollar prize on the table, he walked out and returned to Princeton.

With only $500 in the bank, TerraCycle desperately needed capital, but there were no more business plan contests on the horizon. Tom and his colleagues had proved that there was money to be made in selling an organic vermicompost tea. One challenge they had yet to overcome, however, was to brew a tea with a significant shelf life of at least two years. As the team continued to work on that problem (which they eventually solved), they began to think about how to package the product. With their company's limited resources, they could not afford to buy new bottles and would have to settle for used ones. Tom found that the reclaimed bottles were generally one of four sizes but that all had the exact same cap size. Within each of the four size categories, the bottles had the same height and diameter. This meant that the recycled bottles could be run through a high-speed bottling machine. In addition, Tom realized that TerraCycle could make its liquid fertilizer entirely from recycled waste and sell it in reclaimed and recycled bottles packed in reclaimed or recycled boxes. With renewed vigor, Tom and his team set out to find financing for TerraCycle. Within five months, they had raised $1.2 million from private investors.

Tom has also been adept at generating attention through public relations efforts, landing articles about TerraCycle in *The New York Times, Inc., Time, BusinessWeek,* and *Real Simple*. In addition, stories about TerraCycle have appeared in dozens of newspapers and on several U.S. and Canadian television stations. Tom has managed to give the business the feel of an environmental crusade. TerraCycle's "Bottle Brigade" for example, has enlisted elementary schoolchildren and others to collect used soda bottles, which contributes five cents per bottle to the school, twice what TerraCycle pays recyclers. The solid waste is recycled, worthy organizations receive money, environmental consciousness is raised, the company gets the bottles it needs, and it all creates a compelling marketing message: TerraCycle is not just good for your plants—it's also good for your planet.

This theme has also proved to be an important recruiting factor for the small company, which cannot offer salaries and perks that are anywhere near those of larger companies. None of TerraCycle employees makes more than $30,000 a year, yet working at TerraCycle is an attractive option for many people because of its environmental mission and the financial rewards that are possible if the company reaches its potential. When TerraCycle placed an ad to fill 8 jobs, 150 people applied. Some employees took 85 percent pay cuts to join TerraCycle and receive stock options. Their decisions will pay off only if the company's financial performance is strong enough to make their stock options valuable.

Abundant labor and affordable real estate were two reasons TerraCycle decided to locate in out-of-the way Trenton, New Jersey. The company recently paid $275,000 for the 20,000-square-foot building that houses its production and bottling operation. Although Tom insists that he and his colleagues made the decision strictly for business reasons, it is apparent that TerraCycle is creating jobs in a community desperately in need of employment. All production takes place at the Trenton facility, and the permanent work force in the factory of only 12 people grows to 52 when the company hires temporary employees during peak production cycles.

Tom is doing all he can to grow TerraCycle. He is courting Kmart, Target, and Lowe's as customers and is lobbying for larger orders from Wal-Mart and Home Depot. Tom believes that focusing on large accounts is the right strategy for TerraCycle, but some experts disagree. With the help of these retail giants, Tom thinks TerraCycle can reach annual sales of $5 million, pay everyone a full salary, and earn a profit. Tom is also beginning to think that the time is right to bring in venture capitalists, which will supply much needed capital, impose financial discipline, and bring credibility to the company's valuation. For now, Tom is searching for another capital infusion of $1.6 million.

Tom's long-term vision is to take TerraCycle public or sell it to a larger company. He expects that to occur within the next five years. After all, who wouldn't want to invest in worms and garbage?

Exercises

1. What role does the company's public relations efforts play in TerraCycle's success? What factors make this company's story so attractive? What steps can other entrepreneurs take to generate PR for their companies?
2. Consider the steps the owners have taken to keep TerraCycle afloat. What entrepreneurial traits have Tom and his management team demonstrated in their actions?
3. What were the key considerations regarding the team's location decision for its manufacturing facility?
4. Do you agree with Tom's distribution strategy that focuses on large retail chains? What are the potential downsides to this strategy?
5. Where do you recommend that Tom look for the capital he needs to fuel TerraCycle's growth? What are the risks and the rewards of using venture capital to grow the company? What advantages and disadvantages do Tom, his team of managers, and the early angel investors face if TerraCycle goes public?

Source: Adapted from Bo Burlingham, "The Coolest Little Start-up in America," *Inc.*, July 2006, pages 78–83.

CASE 10

Technorati: "I've Been Googled!"

It was nearing midnight, and David was instant messaging with friends and employees. David knew that his fledgling business, the popular blog search engine Technorati, was about to go up against a new rival: Google. It was a competitor David had been anticipating since he launched Technorati in 2002.

When David founded Technorati, he knew that if blogging became as big as he anticipated, the Web giants eventually would notice. He had invested three years of time and effort to take advantage of Technorati's first-mover status and to build a competitive advantage for his company before the major players entered. That day finally arrived when Google Blog Search made its debut; David also knew that Yahoo and Microsoft had similar offerings on the way. If Technorati were to survive, David knew it would have to compete by using its superior technology. He had been pushing his programmers to refine Technorati's novel way of searching the growing number of weblogs. Despite the imposing presence of Google, David's instincts told him to ignore the new competition, focus on offering exactly what his audience wanted, and stick to the plan he had used to launch and manage Technorati.

History had shown that as Google added other new services, it did not eliminate its smaller rivals. For example, even though Google dominates the world of search engines, the search engine Ask Jeeves remains a viable business. Shopping.com survived Google's 2002 launch of Froogle and ultimately was purchased by eBay for $620 million in June 2005. Still, it was hard to imagine sitting back and doing nothing as one of the most powerful companies in the world invaded his company's turf. David had faith in the technology he had developed and did not believe that he should change his strategy now. Launching a major brand-building campaign to reinforce Technorati's image as the original blog search engine was not realistic because the company simply did not have the resources that effort would require. Plus, trying to outspend Google would be pointless. David also did not want to start looking for a buyer for Technorati. From his perspective, Google's approach to searching the Web would not live up to the unique expectations of bloggers. Google's famed PageRank algorithm indexes keywords and looks at the number of people linking to Web sites to establish optimal matches for each search. In other words, Google treats the Web like an enormous library, searching millions of pages and displaying the most relevant ones, regardless of how outdated they might be. David's view is that the blogosphere works more like a conversation than a library. Blog entries get stale quickly, and he made certain that the first page of Technorati search yielded items posted in the last 10 or 20 minutes.

A former Wall Street analyst, David developed his blog technology in early 2002 while working as chief technology officer at Sputnik, a wireless computer networking start-up he had co-founded. He created a blog in which he wrote about technology issues. Because he was curious to know who was reading it, he imbedded software code that would provide him with that information. At the time, most bloggers were techies like David or teenagers posting their diaries, but soon the blogging phenomenon began to reach new audiences. The traffic on David's Web site, which he named Technorati, was growing and even acquiring paying customers, including *The New York Times* and *Reuters*. Both publishers licensed the technology to track what bloggers were saying about their articles. David earned more validation for Technorati's concept when AOL wanted to collaborate with Technorati on its new blogging service, AOL Journals. David decided to exit Sputnik gracefully, signed a deal with AOL, and started raising angel capital. He devoted himself full-time to Technorati and its mantra: "Be of service."

David's instincts about the blogosphere proved correct, and Technorati has been scrambling to keep up with the blogging world's explosive growth. David raised $6.5 million in venture capital to fund the company's ability to serve the blogosphere, where more than 15 million blogs were being read by 30 million people. Soon, Technorati was performing millions of searches a day. The company was not yet profitable, but it was building a real business with a loyal following, using a Google-like business model. Revenues came from advertising, sponsorships, and syndication of its technology to other Web sites. Technorati had superior brand recognition over its competition, including Feedster, PubSub, and Bloglines, but going head to head with Google would be an entirely different game. Google's resources were at an entirely different level, dwarfing those of all other competitors.

David wondered what Google's blog strategy would be. Technorati was vulnerable on a number of strategic fronts, and keeping up with demand for blog searches was a constant challenge for the company. Searches on Technorati were taking longer and were increasingly generating error messages. Customer support was overwhelmed, with some queries taking as long as a week to answer. Bloggers were beginning to complain. What if Google's technology simply worked better than Technorati's and represented a new approach that David had not considered? Google certainly was experienced at handling huge volumes of Web searches quickly and efficiently.

When the prototype of Google's Blog Search went live, most of Technorati's work force was online, waiting. David spent about half-an-hour checking it out and then posted a welcome note to his new competitor on his blog, including some friendly trash-talking about all the things Technorati could do that Google could not, such as image finding. Much to his relief, there were no big surprises. Google Blog Search proved to be solid but simple. It experienced difficulties keeping up with the dymanic needs of the blogging world, and many search results it displayed were more than 24 hours old, which was not considered to be timely in the blogosphere. However,

Google delivered those results in less than half a second, compared with at least a full second for Technorati. It sounds minor, but in the world of Web search, it represented a significant difference.

Hitwise, a service that monitors Internet traffic, shows that Technorati's traffic growth is still greater than Google Blog Search. Technorati is tracking some 23.4 million blogs, adding some 70,000 more to the list every day, and getting 1.53 visitors for every 1 visitor to Google Blog Search. Still, to stay ahead, David knows he has to update Technorati's underlying software architecture.

David is certain that Google will continue to improve its blog search engine. His company also faces new competition from Yahoo, which rolled out a blog search function on its news page. He remains confident that Technorati will not lose its technological edge for some time. "What we're building is fundamentally difficult," David says. "If it were easy, everyone would be doing it." The larger question is whether Technorati represents a business concept with a sustainable competitive advantage.

Exercises

1. How would you characterize David's strategy based on the three strategic options presented in Chapter 3?
2. How would you assess the level of rivalry within this industry?
3. What are the ramifications of competing with a larger, more powerful competitor? What opportunities might exist?
4. How viable is Technorati's long-term competitive strategy again Google?
5. Is Technorati a business that should be for sale? Why or why not?

Source: Adapted from Michael Fitzgerald, "Going up against Google," *Inc.,* February, 2006, pp. 47–49.

CASE 11

Handmark: Hold the Phone

Handmark (http://www.handmark.com) had created a thriving business selling software for personal digital assistants and had captured 50 percent market share in its industry. Most vice-presidents of sales would be thrilled at that accomplishment, but Tom McKeon was not. Fewer people were buying PDAs, and for Handmark, the trend became a harsh reality with a single phone call. McKeon was talking to a senior buyer for Best Buy, Handmark's biggest retail partner. The Best Buy executive was calling to warn McKeon that over the next few months Best Buy was planning to radically decrease orders for both PDAs and associated software titles. "I got a sinking feeling in my stomach," McKeon says.

As difficult as it was to hear, the news was not completely unexpected. Research firms had been reporting on the "maturity" of the PDA market for some time, saying that the devices soon would be obsolete, replaced by so-called smart cell phones capable of both data and voice services. Revenue at Handmark had grown to $20 million as their popular titles enabled PDA users to play *Scrabble* or consult the *Oxford American Dictionary*. With only 20 employees in three offices, the company had become the dominant player in the market for PDA applications and enjoyed high-profile shelf space in retail chains such as Staples and CompUSA.

That dominant market share would be meaningless if PDAs wound up in the technology junk heap, and there were indications they may be there soon. In just one year, the worldwide PDA market had dipped 4.6%, according to the Gartner Group, compared with an 18% jump for mobile voice-and-data handsets. If Handmark was to survive, the company would have to quickly break into the market for mobile phone applications.

With that in mind, CEO Augie Grasis convened a series of emergency "wireless summits" to address the issue. The company's executives gathered every month in the United Airlines executive lounge at the Denver Airport, a point roughly equidistant from Handmark's offices in Dallas, Kansas City, and Silicon Valley, and attempted to map a strategy for breaking into the cell phone market. The barriers to entry were high, and Handmark had not established business relationships with mobile network operators. These entities acted as the guardians of the menus, or "decks," from which most mobile phone applications, such as ring tones and games, are downloaded and purchased. Handmark did have longstanding ties with some of the country's largest retailers, but relatively few customers were purchasing phone applications at these brick-and-mortar stores. The challenge was to convince customers to alter their purchasing behavior.

McKeon spoke with several retailers and knew that they were eager to begin carrying an all-in-one software and hardware bundle geared to neophyte smart-phone users. It was, as McKeon said, a "dream product." Not everyone at Handmark agreed, however. Handmark's engineers balked at the notion, and there were also many operational ramifications. Entering this market would require Handmark to provide expensive 24/7 customer support services. In addition, the competition from larger and wealthier companies such as Microsoft and Sony would be tough. The executives moved on to other options.

The other attribute retailers and wireless carriers both wanted were games customers could play on their phones. Teenagers were the market segment most likely to purchase mobile phone applications. This placed Handmark on familiar turf because half of its PDA revenues came from games. Cell-phone-based games could be made from recognizable brands, much like Handmark's PDA bestsellers, which included *Trivial Pursuit*, *Monopoly*, and *Tetris*. Unfortunately, the big names in the U.S. wireless market, such as Verizon, Cingular, AT&T, Sprint, and T-Mobile, were being pursued by game developers of all sizes. As a result of this demand, the cost of licensing games was increasing rapidly, and licensers such as Disney and Atari were selling the rights for their best characters and games to the highest bidders. It was a war Grasis knew the company could not afford to fight.

Grasis and Doug Edwards, Handmark's co-founder and vice president of marketing, came up with another idea. Handmark's educational and reference products, such as maps and dictionaries, were almost as popular among PDA users as were its games. Perhaps education and reference could become the company's competitive edge in the smart phone market.

Handmark executives contacted Rand McNally, one of the company's existing strategic partners, to negotiate licensing rights to make a cell phone version of its PDA Streetfinder software. Although Rand McNally was undergoing management changes and was not ready to commit to a new agreement, Chris Barnett, one of Rand McNally's licensing reps, was intrigued by Handmark's strategy. In a meeting with Handmark execs at the Consumer Electronics Show in Las Vegas, Handmark offered Grasis a job on the spot. "A lady [nearby] hit a huge jackpot on the slots when he accepted," Grasis says. "It was a fortuitous sign."

Within two months, Barnett got to work forging relationships with wireless carriers. Grasis, meanwhile, approached Kaplan, the New York City publisher of standardized test preparation guides. Over a series of meetings, Grasis made his case for a partnership: Kaplan was a brand the big retailers would want on their shelves, and Handmark was one of the only makers of mobile software the retailers trusted.

It took Handmark eight months and nearly half a million dollars to create Kaplan Test Prep Mobile Edition. Students—or their parents—could purchase the program, which consists of practice questions, study lists, and other tools, through Handmark's Web site, Amazon.com, Kaplan's Web site, or one of its 155 test centers nationwide. The programs are designed to run on any device, from traditional cell phones to feature phones and even palm devices, which have yet to vanish completely. Kaplan plans to make the product readily available wherever students need to have access to it, including big-box retailers.

Handmark, meanwhile, has inked deals with Sprint, Verizon, and Alltel to offer the product on their phone decks. The company already is rolling out other mobile phone products, including its Pocket Express wireless software service. Pocket Express offers consolidated news, financial information, weather, movie listings, maps, and other data to wireless phones and PDAs. Pocket Express runs on the Palm Treo, color BlackBerry, the Motorola Q, and other Windows mobile phones. Promotional strategies for Pocket Express include Handmark's Tour de France coverage with individual stage results, individual overall results, team stage results, team overall results, individual youth stage results, and other statistics. The software received accolades from the industry for its "user friendliness, configurability, and information selection" according to *PC Magazine,* and it won the Editors' Choice award. According to PC Magazine.com,

When you connect, you see a well-organized opening screen that gives access to news, sports, weather, movies, stocks, search, and more. Most sections let you browse among topics, and text fits nicely on our phone's screen. Cool extras include a dictionary, a TV guide, and white-page listings. Handmark also offers its similar On Demand service as a free add-on to Sprint's Power Vision service.

The question for Handmark remains: Will it be enough?

Exercises

1. What steps can small companies such as Handmark take to scan the market and the threats that it may present to avoid becoming obsolete?
2. How can technology-based companies keep up with rapidly changing markets, products, and competitors? Which is more important to success: strategy or resources?
3. What other options might Handmark pursue to promote its software? Work with a team of your classmates to generate some promotional ideas that may enable Handmark to connect with its key target markets.
4. How do the mission statements entrepreneurs create influence their view of an industry and their companies' place in it?

Source: Adapted from Lorra Kolodny, "The Problem: Handmark Had 50% of the Market for Software for PDAs. Unfortunately, Fewer People Are Buying PDAs," *Inc.,* November 2004, p. 50; "Handmark Pocket Express, PC Magazine, January 18, 2006, http://www.pcmag.com/article2/0,1895,1914059,00.asp.

Endnotes

Chapter 1

1. Robert W. Price, "Mastering Entrepreneurship," *Entrepreneurship*, 5th ed. (Dubuque, IA: McGraw-Hill, 2006), p. 1.
2. William J. Dennis, *Business Starts and Stops* (San Francisco: Wells Fargo; and Washington, DC: National Federation of Independent Businesses Education Foundation, 1999), p. 3.
3. Justin Martin, "Slump? What Slump?" *FSB*, December 2002/January 2003, pp. 62–67.
4. Howard H. Stevenson, "We Create Entrepreneurs," *Success*, September 1995, p. 51.
5. *Global Entrepreneurship Monitor 2004 Executive Report* (Babson Park, MA: Babson College; Kansas City, MO: Ewing Marion Kauffman Foundation; and London: London Business School, 2005), p. 12.
6. Ibid, pp. 12–30.
7. Benjamin Fulford, "Dressing for Kajuaru Fridays," *Forbes*, June 7, 2004, pp. 127–130.
8. David McClelland, *The Achieving Society* (Princeton, NJ: Van Nostrand, 1961), p. 16.
9. Rod Kurtz, "What It Takes," *Inc. 500*, Fall 2004, p. 120.
10. Evan T. Robbins, "E Is for Entrepreneurship," *Syllabus*, November 2002, p. 24.
11. *National Small Business Poll: Success, Satisfaction, and Growth* (Washington, DC: National Federation of Independent Businesses, 2002), p. 2.
12. Jeri Yoshida, "Groom to Grow," *Entrepreneur B.Y.O.B.*, December 2004, p. 108.
13. Gayle Sato Stodder, "Goodbye Mom & Pop," *Entrepreneur*, May 1999, p. 112.
14. Lea Goldman, "Machine Dreams," *Forbes*, May 27, 2002, pp. 149–150; Walter S. Mossberg, "A Vacuum That Even a Couch-Potato Could Love," *Wall Street Journal*, September 18, 2002, pp. D1, D12; iRobot Corporation, http://www.irobot.com/corp/default.asp.
15. *Global Entrepreneurship Monitor 2004 Executive Report* (Babson Park, MA: Babson College; Kansas City, MO: Ewing Marion Kauffman Foundation; and London: London Business School, 2005), p. 12.
16. Stephanie Clifford, "They Just Can't Stop Themselves," *Inc.*, March 2005, pp. 98–104.
17. Ibid, p. 104.
18. Gayle Sato Stodder, "Never Say Die," *Entrepreneur*, December 1990, p. 95.
19. George Gendron, "The Origin of the Entrepreneurial Species," *Inc.*, February 2000, p. 107.
20. "The History of Soaps and Detergents," *Inventors*, http://www.inventors.about.com/library/inventors/blsoap.htm.
21. John Heilemann, "Shawn Fanning's New Tune," *Business 2.0*, May 2005, pp. 38–41.
22. Bob Weinstein, "Success Secrets," *Business Start-Ups*, August 1995, p. 47.
23. John Case, "The Origins of Entrepreneurship," *Inc.*, June 1989, p. 52.
24. Richard Breeden, "Most Owners Are Content with Having a Business," *Wall Street Journal*, November 2, 2004, p. B6.
25. Cynthia Hodnett, "Young People Parlay Interests into Job," *Greenville News*, January 13, 2003, pp. 1E, 2E.
26. April Y. Pennington, "Garden State," *Entrepreneur*, April 2005, pp. 124–127.
27. Gayle Sato Stodder, "Are You Satisfied?" *Entrepreneur*, October 1999, p. 86.
28. David Armstrong and Brendan Coffey, "The Forbes 400," *Forbes*, September 30, 2002, pp. 99–124.
29. Tony Cook, "Secrets of the Millionaire Next Door," *Reader's Digest*, November 1997, p. 135.
30. Andy Serwer, "The Waltons: Inside America's Richest Family," *Fortune*, November 15, 2004, pp. 86–116.
31. William J. Dennis, *The Public Reviews Small Business* (Washington, DC: National Federation of Independent Businesses, 2005), pp. 11–12.
32. April Y. Pennington, "On the Rise," *Entrepreneur*, July 2005, p. 30.
33. Justin Martin, "Slump? What Slump?" *FSB*, December 2002/January 2003, p. 67.
34. Alison Overholt, "Entrepreneurs We Love: For Kicking Sand in the Face of Conventional Wisdom," *Inc.*, April 2005, p. 93; Lora Kolodny, "Work's a Beach: Companies where the Living Is Easy," *Inc.*, August 2004, pp. 56–60.
35. *NFIB Small Business Policy Guide* (Washington, DC: National Federation of Independent Businesses, 2003), p. 16.
36. Robert Johnson, "Owners Pressured to Work through Vacation Season," *Wall Street Journal*, July 27, 1999, p. B2.
37. Chantelle Ludski, "A Day in the Life: Entrepreneurship," mba.com, http://www.mba.com/ NR/exeres/4ECE6033-C16C-4DC4-816E-B04DEAA021A3,frameless.htm.
38. Stephanie Clifford and Rory Evans, "Romance: Love for the Workaholic," *Inc.*, February 2005, p. 53; April Y. Pennington, "Almost Famous," *Entrepreneur*, August 2005, p. 140.
39. Anne Fisher, "Is Your Business Taking Over Your Life?" *FSB*, November 2001, pp. 32–40.
40. Donna Fenn, "Time-Out," *Inc.*, July 2001, pp. 34–40.
41. William J. Dennis, *National Small Business Poll* (NFIB Foundation Series, Vol. 2, Issue 5) (Washington, DC: National Federation of Independent Businesses, 2002), p. 1.
42. Laura Koss-Feder, "Scratch a Niche," *Entrepreneur*, August 2005, pp. 92–96.
43. David Lidsky, "Tech Skeptic," *FSB*, January 24, 2003, http://www.fortune.com/fortune/smallbusiness/skeptic/0,15704,411307,00.html; Donna M McGuire, "Is Your Web Site Profitable?" *Small Business Information*, January 26, 2003, http://sbinformation.miningco.com/library/weekly/uc012603a.htm.
44. Patricia Fusco, "Internet Future Bright for Business," *Small Business Computing*, January 14, 2003, http://www.smallbusinesscomputing.com/biztools/article.php/1569091.
45. Devin Comiskey, "Studies Reveal Online Entrepreneurship Thriving," *E-Commerce Guide*, April 21, 2005, http://www.ecommerce-guide.com/news/trends/article.php/3499566; ShavingCream.com, http://www.shavingcream.com/.
46. "Opportunities in Exporting," Office of International Trade, U.S. Small Business Administration, http://www.sba.gov/OIT/txt/export/whyexport.html.

47. Jeff Bailey, "The Exporting Advantage," *Inc.*, August 2005, pp. 40–42.

48. "The Meaning of Generation X," JobCircle: Entrepreneurship, 2002, http://www.jobcircle.com/career/articles/3020.html.

49. Mark Jones, "Businesses Help Students Make Sense of Dollars," *GSA Business*, May 16, 2005, p. 15.

50. Colleen De Baise, "Women Business Owners Form Zenith," *Wall Street Journal*, June 1, 2005, p. B-5A; "Women-Owned Businesses in the United States, 2002: A Fact Sheet," Center for Women's Business Research, 2002, http://www.nfwbo.org/USStateFacts/US.pdf.

51. "Top Facts about Women-Owned Businesses," Center for Women's Business Research, 2005, http://www.nfwbo.org/topfacts.html.

52. Anne Fisher, "Why Women Rule," *FSB*, July/August 2004, pp. 47–52; Richard McGill Murphy, "The New Soccer Moms," *FSB*, July/August 2004, pp.20–23; Top Facts about Women-Owned Businesses," Center for Women's Business Research, 2005, http://www. nfwbo.org/topfacts.html.

53. Aliza Pilar Sherman, "Big Plans," *Entrepreneur*, February 2002, http://www.entrepreneur.com/article/0,4621,296515,00.html.

54. Alison Overholt, "25 Top Women Business Builders," *Fast Company*, May 2005, pp. 60–73.

55. Bridget Gonzales, *The Spirit of Entrepreneurship Thriving amongst Minority Groups*, (Washington, DC: Minority Business Development Agency, U.S. Department of Commerce, July 28, 2005), p. 1.

56. April Y. Pennington, "The Beat Goes On," *Entrepreneur*, July 2005, p. 38.

57. "Minority Share of U.S. Business Ownership Nears 15 Percent," SBA Number 02-02 ADVO, February 4, 2002, http://www.sba.gov/advo/press/02-02.html.

58. *Minorities in Business*, November 2001, U.S. Small Business Administration, Office of Advocacy (Washington, DC), http://www.sba.gov/advo/stats/min01.pdf.

59. "All Dolled Up," *Entrepreneur B.Y.O.B.*, July 2004, p. 106.

60. Nichole Torres, "From Part Time to Full Time," *Entrepreneur*, April 2002, http://www.entrepreneur.com/Your_Business/YB_SegArticle/0,4621,298297,-,00.html.

61. The *Small Business Economy 2004: A Report to the President* (Washington, DC: Small Business Administration Office of Advocacy, U.S. Government Printing Office, 2004), p. 2.

62. "Home Based Business Facts," National Black Business Trade Association, http://www.nbbta.org/homebiz.htm.

63. Joanne H. Pratt, *Home-Based Business: The Hidden Economy* (Small Business Research Summary, No. 194). (Washington, DC: U.S. Small Business Administration Office of Advocacy, March 2000), pp. 1–2.

64. Kristen Hampshire, "Behind the Music," *Entrepreneur*, June 2005, p. 49.

65. Chris Pentilla, "It's All Relative," *Entrepreneur*, March 2005, pp. 75–77; "Facts and Figures: Family Business in the U.S." *Family Business Magazine*, http://www.business.com/bdcframe.asp?ticker=&src=http%3A//rd.business.com/index.asp%3Fbdcz%3Di.l.l.ml.e%26bdcr%3D1%26bdcu%3Dhttp%253A//www.familybusinessmagazine.com/%26bdcs%3D0CD38920-C1E8-4FF8-B724-77BBCF2BA89F%26bdcf%3D0D92C0F3-4149-444B-938B-EFABD06FCD31%26

bdcp%3D%26partner%3Dbdc%26title%3DFamily%2520Business%2520magazine&back=http%3A//www.business.com/directory/media_and_entertainment/publishing/magazines/family_business_publishing/family_business_magazine/index.asp%3Dinc&path=/directory/media_and_entertainment/publishing/magazines/family_business_publishing/family_business_magazine; "Family Business Statistics," American Management Services, http://www.amserv.com/familystatistics.html.

66. Ibid.

67. Kathy Spencer-Mention, "All in the Family," *Greenville News*, November 3, 2002, pp. 1D, 12D.

68. Udayan Gupta, "And Business Makes Three: Couples Working Together," *Wall Street Journal*, February 26, 1990, p. B2.

69. Bob Weinstein, "For Better or Worse," *Your Company*, Spring 1992, pp. 28–31.

70. Echo M. Garrett, "And Business Makes Three," *Small Business Reports*, September 1993, pp. 27–31.

71. Marcus Green, "Couples Find Challenge, Pleasure Working Together," *Greenville News*, January 5, 2003, p. 1E.

72. Geoff Williams, "You're Fired!," *Entrepreneur*, July 2005, pp. 102–107.

73. Jeff Bailey, "Anger Can Power the Creation of New Companies," *Wall Street Journal*, June 4, 2002, p. B5.

74. *NFIB Small Business Policy Guide* (Washington, DC: NFIB Education Foundation, 2003), p. 21.

75. Tricia Tunstill, "Inspiration on the Menu," *FSB*, June 2004, p. 92.

76. *Small Business by the Numbers* (Washington, DC: U.S. Small Business Administration), 2004, http://www.sba.gov/advo/stats/sbfaq.pdf.

77. "Cognetics Corporate Quiz," Cognetics, Inc., http://www.cogonline.com/IndexL.htm; Garry Powers, "Wanted: More Small, Fast-Growing Firms," *Business & Economic Review*, April–June 1999, pp. 19–22.

78. Erskine Bowles, "Training Ground," *Entrepreneur*, March 1994, p. 168.

79. *Small Business by the Numbers* (Washington, DC: U.S. Small Business Administration), 2004, http://www.sba.gov/advo/stats/sbfaq.pdf.

80. Robert W. Price, "Mastering Entrepreneurship," *Entrepreneurship*, 5th ed. (Dubuque, IA: McGraw-Hill, 2006), p. 1; *NFIB Small Business Policy Guide* (Washington, DC: NFIB Education Foundation, 2003), p. 33.

81. *Small Business by the Numbers* (Washington, DC: U.S. Small Business Administration), 2004, http://www.sba.gov/advo/stats/sbfaq.pdf.

82. Bruce G. Posner, "Why Companies Fail," *Inc.*, June 1993, p. 102.

83. Rob Walker, "Starting over after Startup.com," *Fortune*, March 4, 2002, pp. 43–44.

84. Eugene Carlson, "Spreading Your Wings," *Wall Street Journal*, October 16, 1992, p. R2.

85. Daniel McGinn, "Why Size Matters," *Inc. 500*, Fall 2004, pp. 33–36.

86. Geoff Williams, "Pick Your Spot," *Entrepreneur B.Y.O.B.*, June 2002, pp. 102–109.

87. Michael Warsaw, "Great Comebacks," *Success*, July/August, 1995, p. 43.

88. Marc Gunther, "They All Want a Piece of Bill Gross," *Fortune*, November 11, 2002, p. 140.
89. Cliffors, "They Just Can't Stop Themselves," pp. 98–103.
90. Robert Huber, "Failure: The Seven Mistakes Entrepreneurs Make and How to Avoid Them," *Success*, March 1998, p. 60; "The Triangle," Integrity Publishing Company, http://www.integritypublishing.com/ex%20triangle%20web%20pages/xtri.execstaff.htm.
91. Tahl Raz, "60-Second Business Plan: Talking Trash," *Inc.*, November 1, 2002, http://www.inc.com/magazine/

20021101/24819.html; Marjorie Censer, "From the Ground Up: Student Entrepreneurs Create New Compost," *Daily Princetonian*, December 13, 2002, http://www.dailyprincetonian.com/archives/2002/12/13/news/6667.shtml.
92. G. David Doran, Michelle Prather, Elaine Teague, and Laura Tiffany, "Young Guns," *Business Start-Ups*, April 1999, pp. 28–35.
93. Barbara Carton, "Help Wanted," *Wall Street Journal*, May 22, 1995, p. R10.

Chapter 2

1. Siri Schubert, "From the Autobahn to Fifth Avenue," *Business 2.0*, August 2005, p. 42.
2. Small Serial Innovators: The Small Firm Contribution to Technical Change," CHI Research, U.S. Small Business Administration Office of Advocacy, No. 225, February 2003, http://www.sba.gov/advo/research/rs225.pdf.
3. "The Power of Innovation," *Inc.*, May 2001 (Special Issue: State of Small Business, 2001), p. 103; Leigh Buchanan, "Built to Invent," *Inc.*, August 2002, p. 53.
4. Warren Bennis, "Cultivating Creative Collaboration," *Industry Week*, August 18, 1997, p. 86.
5. "Polaroid, R.I.P.," *Fortune*, November 12, 2001, p. 44; Robert Epstein, "How To Get a Great Idea," *Reader's Digest*, December 1992, p. 103.
6. Roger von Oech, *A Whack on the Side of the Head* (New York: Warner Books, 1990), p. 108.
7. Siri Schubert, "Bound to Succeed," *Business 2.0*, April 2005, p. 50.
8. Michael Maiello, "They Almost Changed the World," *Forbes*, December 23, 2002, p. 217.
9. Peter Carbonara, "30 Great Small Business Ideas," *Your Company*, August/September 1998, pp. 32–58.
10. David H. Freedman, "Freeing Your Inner Think Tank, *Inc.*, May 2005, pp. 65–66.
11. Robert Fulghum, "Time to Sacrifice the Queen," *Reader's Digest*, August 1993, pp. 136–138.
12. Carla Goodman, "Sparking Your Imagination," *Entrepreneur*, September 1997, p. 32.
13. Ibid.
14. Ibid.
15. Joseph Rosenbloom, "The Lifetime Achiever," *Inc.*, September 2002, pp. 80–82.
16. Betty Edwards, *Drawing on the Right Side of the Brain* (Los Angeles: J. P. Tarcher, 1979), p. 32.
17. Roger von Oech, *A Whack on the Side of the Head* (New York: Warner Books, 1990), pp. 21–167; "Obstacles to Creativity," Creativity Web, http://www.ozemail.com.au/~caveman/Creative/Basics/obstacles.htm.
18. Sara J. Welch, "Walking on Water," *Successful Meetings*, October 2002, pp. 75–76.
19. Rob Wherry, "Planting Hope," *Forbes*, January 30, 2003, pp. 110–112.
20. Karen Axelton, "Imagine That," *Entrepreneur*, April 1998, p. 96; "Thomas Edison Biography," http://edison-ford-estate.com/ed_bio.htm.

21. Susan Warren, "Gel Used in Diapers Can Shield against Fires," *Wall Street Journal*, June 22, 2003, pp. B1, B3.
22. Mary Bellis, "Inventive Thinking Lesson Plans," About.com, http://inventors.about.com/library/lessons/bl_activity_11.htm; Mary Bellis, "Betty Nesmith Graham," About.com, http://inventors.about.com/library/inventors/blliquid_paper.htm.
23. Sally Fegley, "Painting the Town," *Entrepreneur*, July 1997, p. 14.
24. Joseph Schumpeter, "The Creative Response in Economic History," *Journal of Economic History*, November 1947, pp. 149–159.
25. *Bits & Pieces*, January 1994, p. 6.
26. "Make Your Company an Idea Factory," *FSB*, May/June 2000, p. 124.
27. Lee Gimpel, "I'm Stuck. Can You Pass the Play-Doh?" *Inc.*, August 2005, p. 68.
28. Robert Epstein, "How To Get a Great Idea," *Reader's Digest*, December 1992, p. 102.
29. Larry Olmstead, "Nonstop Innovation," *Inc.*, July 2005, p. 34.
30. Thea Singer and Lea Buchanan, "A Field Guide to Innovation," *Inc.*, August 2002, pp. 63–70.
31. "How Companies Turn Customers' Big Ideas into Innovations," *Strategy + Business*, January 12, 2005, http://www.strategy-business.com/media/file/sb_kw_01-12-05.pdf.
32. Alison Stein Wellner, "Proving You Have the Right Stuff," *Inc.*, July 2005, p. 28.
33. Thea Singer and Lea Buchanan, "A Field Guide to Innovation," *Inc.*, August 2002, pp. 63–70.
34. Lucas Conley, "Rise and Repeat," *Fast Company*, July 2005, pp. 76–77.
35. Stephanie Barlow, "Turn It On," *Entrepreneur*, May 1993, p, 52.
36. Mark Henricks, "Good Thinking," *Entrepreneur*, May 1996, p.70.
37. Harold Evans, "What Drives America's Great Innovators?" *Fortune*, October 18, 2004, pp. 84–86.
38. Kip Crosby, "Stumbling into the Future," *Forbes ASAP*, November 20, 2000, pp. 105–112; John Steele Gordon with Michael Maiello, "Pioneers Die Broke," *Forbes*, December 23, 2002, pp. 258–264.
39. Don Debelak, "Ideas Unlimited," *Business Start-Ups*, May 1999, pp. 57–58.

40. Siri Schubert, "Thinking Out of the Clamshell," *Business 2.0*, July 2005, p. 58.

41. Lucas Conley, "Rise and Repeat," *Fast Company*, July 2005, pp. 76–77.

42. Nina Sovich, "Look, Mom, I'm Rich," *FSB*, April 2004, p. 28;. "The Crayon Holder," By Kids, For Kids, http://kids.patentcafe.com/products/index.asp#2.

43. Geoff Williams, "Innovative Model," *Entrepreneur*, September 2002, p. 66.

44. Roy Rowan, "Those Hunches Are More Than Blind Faith," *Fortune*, April 23, 1979, p. 112.

45. Michael Waldholz, "A Hallucination Inspires a Vision For AIDS Drug," *Wall Street Journal*, September 29, 1993, pp. B1, B5.

46. Kate O'Sullivan, "Insect Inside," *Inc.*, November 15, 2001, p. 52.

47. Carla Goodman, "Sparking Your Imagination," *Entrepreneur*, September 1997, pp. 32–36.

48. Siri Schubert, "Folate Is Gr-r-reat!" *Business 2.0*, November 2004, p. 72.

49. Siri Schubert, "A Better Bounce," *Business 2.0*, March 2005, p. 58; Anne Goodwin Sides, "Glory Bound," *Popular Science*, July 2004, http://www.popsci.com/popsci/bown/2004/recreation/article/0,22221,768216,00.html.

50. Nick D'Alto, "Think Big," *Business Start-Ups*, January 2000, pp. 61–65.

51. Brian Nadel, "The Art of Innovation," Advertising Insert, *Fortune*, December 13, 2004, pp. S1–S22.

52. Janean Chun, "Theory of Creativity," *Entrepreneur*, p. 10.

53. Thea Singer, "Your Brain on Innovation," *Inc.*, September 2002, pp. 86–88.

54. Geoff Williams, "In Your Dreams," *Entrepreneur*, June 2005, p. 36.

55. Paul Bagne, "When to Follow a Hunch," *Reader's Digest*, May 1994, p. 77.

56. Susan Hansen, "The Action Hero," *Inc.*, September 2002, pp. 82–84.

57. "Ceiling Fan Leads to Physics Theory," *Laurens County Advertiser*, December 19, 1993, p. 4.

58. Thea Singer and Lea Buchanan, "Who? What? Where? Why? When? How?" *Inc.*, August 2002, p. 66.

59. Michael Waldholz, "A Hallucination Inspires a Vision For AIDS Drug," *Wall Street Journal*, September 29, 1993, p. B5.

60. Thea Singer and Leah Buchanan, "Seeing It Fresh," *Inc.*, August 2002, p. 68.

61. Robert Epstein, "How To Get a Great Idea," *Reader's Digest*, December 1992, p. 104.

62. Michael Waldholz, "A Hallucination Inspires a Vision For AIDS Drug," *Wall Street Journal*, September 29, 1993, p. B5.

63. Bridget Finn, "Brainstorming for Better Brainstorming," *Business 2.0*, April 2005, pp. 109–114.

64. Janean Chun, "Theory of Creativity," *Entrepreneur*, pp. 130–131.

65. Bridget Finn, "Brainstorming for Better Brainstorming," *Business 2.0*, April 2005, pp. 109–114.

66. Ed Brown, "A Day at Innovation U," *Fortune*, April 12, 1999, pp. 163–165.

67. The Hall of Science and Exploration, "Academy of Achievement: Linus Pauling, PhD," http://www.achievement.org/autodoc/page/pau0pro-1.

68. Alison Stein Wellner, "A Perfect Brainstorm," *Inc.*, October 2003, pp. 31–35.

69. Andy Raskin, "A Higher Plane of Problem-Solving," *Business 2.0*, June 2003, pp. 54–56; "TRIZ 40," Triz 40 Principles, http://www.triz40.com/aff_Principles.htm.

70. Andy Raskin, "A Higher Plane of Problem-Solving," *Business 2.0*, June 2003, p. 165.

71. Ibid.

72. StopFakes.gov/smallbusiness, U.S. Patent and Trademark Office, http://www.uspto.gov/smallbusiness/.

73. Anne Field, "How to Knock Out Knock Offs," Business Week, March 14, 2005, http://www.businessweek.com/@@7oPzcIQQnIwLqxsA/magazine/content/05_11/b3924446.htm.

74. "Snapshot," *Entrepreneur*, January 2003, p. 22.

75. Sara Schaefer Muñoz, "Patent No. 6,004,596: Peanut Butter and Jelly Sandwich," *Wall Street Journal*, April 5, 2005, pp. B1, B9; Malia Rulon, "Smucker Can't Patent PBJ, Court Says," *Greenville News*, April 9, 2005, pp. 18A, 21A.

76. "U.S. Patent Statistics," U.S. Patent and Trademark Office, http://www.uspto.gov/web/offices/ac/ido/oeip/taf/us_stat.pdf.

77. Michael S. Malone, "The Smother of Invention," *Forbes ASAP*, June 24, 2002, pp. 32–40.

78. Kris Frieswick, "License to Steal?" *CFO*, September 2001, pp. 89–91; Megan Barnett, "Patents Pending," *U.S. News & World Report*, June 10, 2002, pp. 33–34; Tomima Edmark, "On Guard," *Entrepreneur*, August 1997, pp. 92–94; Tomima Edmark, "On Guard," *Entrepreneur*, February 1997, pp.109–111.

79. Michael J. McCarthy, "Fake King Cobras Tee Off Maker of High End Clubs," *Wall Street Journal*, February 11, 1997, pp. A1, A8.

80. Michael B. Sapherstein, "The Registrability of the Harley-Davidson Roar: A Multimedia Analysis," http://www.bc.edu/bc_org/avp/law/st_org/iptf/articles/content/1998101101.html; Tomima Edmark, "How Much Is Too Much?" *Entrepreneur*, February 1998, pp. 93–95.

81. Paulette Thomas, "Case Study: Location Tops a Name in Restaurant Business," *Wall Street Journal*, March 16, 2004, p. B7.

82. Todd Spangler, "Zippo Snuffs Out Imitations," *The State*, February 25, 2003, pp.B1, B11.

83. Anne Field, "How to Knock Out Knock Offs," Business Week, March 14, 2005, http://www.businessweek.com/@@7oPzcIQQnIwLqxsA/magazine/content/05_11/b3924446.htm.

84. *Global Software Piracy Study* (Washington, DC: Business Software Alliance, May 2001), p. 1, http://www.bsa.org/resources/2001-05-21.55.pdf.

85. Anne Field, "How to Knock Out Knock Offs," Business Week, March 14, 2005, http://www.businessweek.com/@@7oPzcIQQnIwLqxsA/magazine/content/05_11/b3924446.htm.

Chapter 3

1. "AmEx's Ken Chenault Talks about Leadership, Integrity, and the Credit Card Business," *Leadership and Change, Knowledge @Wharton,* http://knowledge@wharton.upenn.edu/index/cfm?fa=printArticle&ID=1179.

2. Alvin Toffler, "Shocking Truths about the Future," *Journal of Business Strategy,* July/August 1996, p. 6.

3. Thomas A. Stewart, "You Think Your Company's So Smart? Prove It," *Fortune,* April 30, 2001, p. 188.

4. Jeffrey Pfeffer, "Dare to Be Different," Business 2.0, September 2004, p. 58; "Company Overview," Whole Foods Market, http://www.wholefoodsmarket.com/company/index.html.

5. Thomas A. Stewart, "Intellectual Capital: Ten Years Later, How Far We've Come," *Fortune,* May 28, 2001, p. 188.

6. Gary Hamel, "Innovation's New Math," *Fortune,* July 9, 2001, p. 130.

7. Verne Harnish, "The X Factor," *FSB,* December 2002/January 2003, pp. 81–84.

8. John Heilemann, "Showtime for Netflix," *Business 2.0,* March 2005, pp. 36–38; "Netflix Makes It Big in Hollywood," *Fortune,* June 13, 2005, p. 34; "About Netflix," Netflix, http://www.netflix.com/PressRoom?id=1005; "Netflix," *Wikipedia,* http://en.wikipedia.org/wiki/Netflix; Alan Cohen, "The Great Race," *FSB,* December 2002/January 2003, pp. 42–48; Brad Stone, "I Want a Movie! Now!" *Newsweek,* September 13, 2005, http://www.msnbc.com/id/5915470/site/newsweek; Jeffrey M. O'Brien, "The Netflix Effect," *Wired,* Issue 10.12, December 2002; "Wal-Mart, Netflix Agree on DVD Deal," *ZDNet,* http://news.zdnet.com/2100-9595_22-5713298.html.

9. Sean Doanhue, "Tom's of Mainstream," *Business 2.0,* December 2004, pp. 72–73; Melanie Wells, "Out of the Tube," *Forbes,* November 26, 2001, p. 200; "Tom's of Maine Common Good Report," http://www.tomsofmaine.com/downloads/pdf/common_good_report_2001.pdf; David Whitford, "Go West, Old Hippie," *FSB,* June 2004, pp. 30–31.

10. Ken Blanchard, "The New Bottom Line," *Entrepreneur,* February 1998, p. 127.

11. Mike Hoffman, "Archive," *Inc.,* April 2002, p. 132; "HP History and Facts," Hewlett Packard, http://www.hp.com/hpinfo/abouthp/histnfacts/.

12. Thomas A. Stewart, "Why Values Statements Don't Work," *Fortune,* June 10, 1996, p. 137.

13. Michael Barrier, "Back From the Brink," *Nation's Business,* September 1995, p. 21.

14. Richard Schneider, "Chain Reaction," *Guideposts,* April 2003, pp. 18–19; Chick-fil-A, http://www.chickfila.com/Company.asp.

15. Ellyn Spragins, "Unmasking Your Motivations," *FSB,* November 2002, p. 86; "Workplace 2000 Employee Insight Survey: A Report of Key Findings," MeaningfulWorkplace.com, http://www.meaningfulworkplace.com/survey/.

16. Ellyn Spragins, "Unmasking Your Motivations," *FSB,* November 2002, p. 86.

17. Chris Penttila, "Missed Mission," *Entrepreneur,* May 2002, pp.73–74.

18. "Mission Statement," Starbucks, http://www.starbucks.com/aboutus/environment.asp.

19. Susan Warren, "'Winglets' Help Planes Lift Off, Save Fuel," *Wall Street Journal,* February 4, 2005, pp. B1, B2.

20. Ed Welles, "Bulletproof Growth," *FSB,* March 2004, p. 45.

21. Jim Hopkins, "Big Businesses Can't Swallow These Little Fish," *USA Today,* March 27, 2002, p. 28-B.

22. Mark Jones, "Small Businesses Brace for National Competition," *GSA Business,* May 2, 2005, p. 15; Jenny Munro, "Changing Times," *Greenville News Business,* March 9, 2003, pp. 1, 8–9.

23. Michael M. Phillips, "Why Turkish Tailors Seem So Well-Suited to Work in Tennessee," *Wall Street Journal,* April 12, 2005, pp. A1, A7.

24. William J. Dennis, Jr., *National Small Business Poll: Competition* (Washington, DC: National Federation of Independent Businesses, 2003), Vol. 3, Issue 8, p. 1.

25. Jeffrey A. Trachtenberg, "Plot Twist: To Compete with Book Chains, Some Think Big," *Wall Street Journal,* August 24, 2004, pp. A1, A8; "About Jospeh-Beth," Joseph-Beth Booksellers, http://www.josephbeth.com/Default.aspx?tabindex=1&tabid=162&storeId=10.

26. Carolyn Z. Lawrence, "Know Your Competition," *Business Start-Ups,* April 1997, p. 51.

27. Beth Kwon, "Toolbox: Staying Competitive," *FSB,* December 2002/January 2003, p. 89.

28. Kirsten Osound, "Secret Agent Plan," *Entrepreneur,* June 2005, p. 98.

29. Brian Caulfield, "Know Your Enemy," *Business 2.0,* June 2004, pp. 89–90.

30. Shari Caudron, "I Spy, You Spy," *Industry Week,* October 3, 1994, p.36.

31. Stephen D. Solomon, "Spies Like You," FSB, June 2001, pp. 76–82.

32. Carolyn Z. Lawrence, "Know Your Competition," *Business Start-Ups,* April 1997, pp. 51–56.

33. Stephanie Gruner, "Spies Like Us," *Inc.,* August 1998, p. 45.

34. John DeVore, "Keeping Up with the Jones Co." *Small Business Computing,* October 1999, p. 26.

35. Erika Brown, "Analyze This," *Forbes,* April 1, 2002, pp. 96–98.

36. Laton McCartney, "Getting Smart about Knowledge Management," *Industry Week,* May 4, 1998, p. 30.

37. "Battling Brain Drain," *Sales & Marketing Management's Performance eNewsletter,* May 31, 2005, p. 1.

38. George Pór, "The Knowledge Ecology," *BizEd,* November/December 2001, p. 33.

39. Eric Schonfeld, "The World According to eBay," *Business 2.0,* January/February 2005, pp. 76–84.

40. Lewis Carroll, *Alice in Wonderland* (Mount Vernon, NY: Peter Pauper Press, 1937), pp. 78–79.

41. Rhonda Abrams, "Set Sights on One Big New Goal for '05," *Business,* October 10, 2004, p. 7; Mark Henricks, "In the BHAG," *Entrepreneur,* August 1999, pp. 65–67.

42. Joseph C. Picken and Gregory Dess, "The Seven Traps of Strategic Planning," *Inc.,* November 1996, p. 99.

43. David Whelan, "Easy Rider," *Forbes,* April 19, 2004, p. 94.

44. Michael E. Porter, *Competitive Strategy* (New York: Free Press, 1980), Chapter 2.

45. Shawn Tully, "Airlines: Why the Big Boys Won't Come Back," *Fortune,* June 14, 2004, pp. 101–104; Melanie Wells, "Lord of the Skies," *Forbes,* October 14, 2002, pp. 130–138; Barney Gimbel, "Southwest's New Flight Plan," *Fortune,* May 16, 2005, pp. 93–98; Donna Rosato, "The Plane Truth about Flying Cheap," *Money,* May 2004, pp. 83–86; David Whelan, "The Slipper Solution," *Forbes,* May 24, 2004, p. 64; Susan Carey, "Amid Jet Blue's Rapid Ascent, CEO Adopts Big Rivals' Traits," *Wall Street Journal,* August 25, 2005, pp. A1, A6.

46. Ann Zimmerman, "Behind the Dollar-Store Boom: A Nation of Bargain Hunters," *Wall Street Journal,* December 13, 2004, pp. A1, A10; Brendan Coffey, "Every Penny Counts," *Forbes,* September 30, 2002, pp. 68–70; Amber McDowell, "Discount Retailers Prosper amid Economic Instability," *Greenville News Business,* December 23, 2002, pp. 6, 13.

47. Susanna Hamner, "Lessons from a Retail Rebel," *Business 2.0,* June 2005, pp. 62–64.

48. Celia Farber, "Anice Hotel," *Inc.,* June 2002, pp. 88–90; Shelly Branch, "Havin' an Ice Team," *Fortune,* March 1, 1999, pp. 277–278; Eleena De Lisser, "The Hot New Travel Spot Is Freezing Cold," *Wall Street Journal,* October 16, 2002, pp. D1, D4; Ice Hotel, http://www.icehotel.com/.

49. Debra Phillips. "Leaders of the Pack," *Entrepreneur,* September 1996, p.127.

50. Mylene Mangalindan, "Web Retailers Try New Game," *Wall Street Journal,* December 2, 2004, pp. B1, B7.

51. Jena McGregor, "The Starbucks of Pharmacies?" *Fast Company,* April 2005, pp. 62–63.

52. Kathleen Conroy, Conroy Vyvyan, and Kathleen Phalen, "Breakfast Bar," *USA Weekend,* February 11–13, 2005, p. 8; April Y. Pennington, "Morning Glory," *Entrepreneur,* March 2005, p. 168; Matthew Maier, "A Store for Cereal (Seriously)," *Business 2.0,* October 2004, p. 42; Julia Boorstin, "Carb Appeal," *FSB,* October 2004, p. 28; "Snap, Crackle, Cash," *People,* November 22, 2004, p. 91.

53. Julie Schlosser, "Confetti Maker," *Fortune,* September 6, 2004, p. 52; "About the Fun Factory," Flutter Fetti Fun Factory, http://www.flutterfetti.com/company1.html.

54. Eilene Zimmerman, "Cellars Market," *FSB,* May 2004, pp. 82–83.

55. "Three Reasons Why Good Strategies Fail: Execution, Execution, . . ." *Strategic Management,* Knowledge@Wharton, University of Pennsylvania, http://knowledge.wharton.edu/index.cfm?fa=printArticle&ID=1252.

56. Joel Kurtzman, "Is Your Company off Course? Now You Can Find Out Why," *Fortune,* February 17, 1997, p. 128.

57. Michelle Bitoun, "Show Them the Data," *Trustee,* September 2002, p. 35.

58. Mark Henricks, "Who's Counting?" *Entrepreneur,* July 1998, pp. 70–73.

59. Robert S. Kaplan and David P. Norton, "The Balanced Scorecard—Measures That Drive Performance," *Harvard Business Review,* January–February 1992, pp. 71–79.

Chapter 4

1. Charles Fishman, "The Wal-Mart You Don't Know," *Fast Company*, December 2003, http://www.fastcompany.com/magazine/77/walmart.html.

2. Adam Lashinsky, "Where Dell Is Going Next," *Fortune*, October 18, 2004, pp. 115–120; Andy Serwer, "The Education of Michael Dell," *Fortune*, March 7, 2005, pp. 73–82.

3. Carla Goodman, "Can You Get There from Here?" *Entrepreneur*, December 1996, http://www.entrepreneur.com/article/0,4621,226677,00.html; "About Little Earth," Little Earth Productions, Inc., http://www.littlearth.com/pages05/about.shtml.

4. "The Home-Based Business Blog: Using eBay for Product Market Testing," Small Business Blog Center, http://www.allbusiness.com/blog/TheHomeBasedBusinessBlog/8180/003338.html?RSS=XXXX.

5. Karen J. Bannan, "Companies Save Time, Money with Online Surveys," *BtoBOnline.com*, June 6, 2003, http://www.btobonline.com/article.cms?articleId=11115.

6. Don Debelak, "Join Hands," *Entrepreneur*, September 2005, pp. 138–140.

7. Carla Goodman, "Can You Get There from Here?" *Entrepreneur*, December 1996, http://www.entrepreneur.com/article/0,4621,226677,00.html; "About Little Earth," Little Earth Productions, Inc., http://www.littlearth.com/pages05/about.shtml.

8. Jena McGregor, "The Art of Service: Intuit," *Fast Company*, October 2005, p. 53; Michael S. Hopkins, "America's 25 Most Fascinating Entrepreneurs: Scott Cook, Intuit," *Inc.*, April 2004, http://www.inc.com/magazine/20040401/25cook.html; "How Intuit Found Fame and Fortune and Beat Out Microsoft," Knowledge@Wharton, November 5, 2003, http://knowledge.wharton.upenn.edu/index.cfm?fa=viewArticle&id=869.

9. Don Debelak, "Join Hands," *Entrepreneur*, September 2005, pp. 138–140.

10. Michael Warsaw, "A Novel Plan," *Inc.*, October 1999, p. 21.

11. James Maguire, "Starting Your Own E-Business: Part 1," *Small Business Computing*, October 3, 2005, http://www.smallbusinesscomputing.com/emarketing/article.pho/35553126.

12. David Newton, "Model Behavior," *Entrepreneur*, March 2002, pp. 68–71.

13. Adam McCulloch, "Prefab with a View," *Business 2.0*, May 2005, p. 70.

14. Edward O. Welles, "Hell-Bent for Lather," *Inc.*, September 2001, http://www.inc.com/magazine/20010901/23308.html.

15. Jennifer Barr Kruger, "Marketing to the Future," *Photo Marketing Magazine*, September 2005, http://www.pmai.org/magazine/sept_2005_Youth.asp; "TRU Projects Teens Will Spend $169 Billion in 2004," Teenage

Research Institute, December 1, 2004, http://www. teenresearch.com/Prview.cfm?edit_id=287.

16. Jennifer Barr Kruger, "Marketing to the Future," *Photo Marketing Magazine*, September 2005, http://www. pmai.org/magazine/sept_2005_Youth.asp.

17. Mike Hughlett, "Target: Teens—Cell Phones Company Going after the Preteen Market," *Billings Gazette*, May 10, 2005, http://www.billingsgazette.com/index.php?display= rednews/2005/05/10/build/technology/20-teens.inc; "About Us," Firefly Mobile, http://www.fireflymobile.com/about/.

18. Don Debelak, "Molded in Your Image," *Entrepreneur*, August 2001, http://www.entrepreneur.com/article/ 0,4621,291290,00.html.

19. James Maguire, "Veteran E-Commerce Designer Finds Her Mojo," *Small Business Computing*, April 22, 2005, http://www.ecommerce-guide.com/article.php/3499766;

James Maguire, "Starting Your Own E-Business: Part 1" *Small Business Computing*, October 3, 2005, http://www.smallbusinesscomputing.com/emarketing/ article.pho/35553126.

20. Nicole L. Torres, "Sowing the Seeds," *Entrepreneur B.Y.O.B.*, May 2004, pp. 118–122.

21. Conversation with Charles Burke, CEO Burke Financial Associates.

22. "Raising Money," *Entrepreneur*, July 2005, p. 58.

23. Michael V. Copeland, "How to Make Your Business Plan the Perfect Pitch," *Business 2.0*, September 2005, p. 88.

24. Conversation with Charles Burke, CEO Burke Financial Associates.

25. Karen Axelton, "Good Plan, Stan," *Business Start-Ups*, March 2000, p. 17.

Chapter 5

1. Chris Harrison, "Form Is Everything," *E-Merging Business*, Fall–Winter 2000, pp. 194–199.

2. Jacquelyn Lynn, "Partnership Procedures," *Business Start-Ups*, June 1996, p. 73.

3. Amy Joyce, "Getting It Together," *Washington Post*, June 12, 2005, http://www.washingtonpost.com/wp-dyn/content/ article/2005/06/10/AR2005061001353.html.

4. Ibid.

5. Nichole L. Torres, "Buddy System," *Entrepreneur*, October 2005, p. 119.

6. Robert A. Mamis, "Partner Wars," *Inc.*, June 1994, http://www.inc.com/magazine/19940601/2956.html.

7. Michael Barrier, "Someone's in the Kitchen with Wolfgang," *Success*, September 2000, pp. 28–33; "Company Info," Wolfgang Puck, http://www.wolfgangpuck.com/company/.

8. "Investors FAQ," Sunoco Logistics, http://www.sunocologistics. com/investors/investors_faq.asp#2.

9. Chief Justice John Marshall, cited by Roger L. Miller and Gaylord A. Jentz, *Business Law Today* (St. Paul, MN: West Publishing Co., 1994), p. 632.

10. Paul J. Lim, "Google: Off and Running,: *U.S. News & World Report*, August 19, 2004, http://www.usnews.com/usnews/ biztech/buzz/archive/buzz040819.htm; Paul Shread, "Google IPO Investors Get a Break," Internet.com, August 19, 2004, http://www.internetnews.com/bus-news article.php/3397571.

11. Martha Doran, Nathan Oestreich, and Lena Rodriguez, "An Entrepreneur's Guide to the Selection of a Business Entity," Presented at the Western Decision Sciences Institute 31st Annual Meeting, Las Vegas, Nevada, April 2–5, 2002.

12. Caroline Bierbaum, Tiffany Wilson, Stephanie Fitch, and Adam Kemezis, "The Forbes 400," *Forbes*, October 10, 2005, p. 90.

Chapter 6

1. Megan Barnett, "Size up a Ready-Made Business," *U.S. News & World Report*, August 2, 2004, pp. 69–70.

2. Richard Gibson, "Franchise Fever," *Wall Street Journal*, December 15, 2003, pp. R1, R4.

3. National Economic Consulting Practice of PricewaterhouseCoopers, *Economic Impact of Franchised Businesses: A Study for the International Franchise Association* (New York: IFA Educational Foundation, 2004), p. 1.

4. Megan Barnett, "Size up a Ready-Made Business," *U.S. News & World Report*, August 2, 2004, p. 70.

5. Chieh Chieng, "Do You Want to Know a Secret?" *Entrepreneur*, January 1999, p. 174–178.

6. National Economic Consulting Practice of PricewaterhouseCoopers, *Economic Impact of Franchised Businesses: A Study for the International Franchise

Association* (New York: IFA Educational Foundation, 2004), p. 1.

7. Devlin Smith, "Can You Own a McDonald's Location?" *Entrepreneur*, March 26, 2001, http://www.entrepreneur. com/franzone/article/0,5847,288016,00.html.

8. "FAQ," Ben & Jerry's Homemade, Inc., http://www.benjerry. com/scoop_shops/franchise_info/faqs.cfm.

9. Anne Field, "Piping Hot Performance," *Success*, March 1999, pp. 76–80.

10. *The Profile of Franchising* (Washington, DC: FRANDATA Corp and the IFA Educational Foundation, 2000), p. 164.

11. Andrew A. Caffey, "Franchises That Offer Creative Financing," *Business Start-Ups*, September 1996, pp. 62–68.

12. April Y. Pennington, "The Right Stuff," *Entrepreneur*, September 2004, pp. 90–100.

13. Sara Wilson, "Major Dough," *Entrepreneur*, February 2004, pp. 96–98; "About Us," Z Pizza, http://www.zpizza.com/zpizza.php?page=about_story.

14. Tara Siegel Bernard, "The More the Merrier," *Wall Street Journal*, December 15, 2004, p. R6.

15. Glen Weisman, "The Choice Is Yours," Business Start-Ups, May 1997, pp. 24–30.

16. *The Profile of Franchising* (Washington, DC: FRANDATA Corp and the IFA Educational Foundation, 2000), p. 104.

17. *The Profile of Franchising*, (Washington, DC: FRANDATA Corp and the IFA Educational Foundation, 2000), p. 123.

18. Daniel Kruger, "You Want Data with That?" *Forbes*, March 29, 2004, pp. 58–59.

19. Julia Boorstin, "Delivering at Domino's Pizza," *Fortune*, February 7, 2005, p. 28.

20. "The Egg McMuffin," McDonald's Media Site, http://www.media.mcdonalds.com/secured/products/history/eggmcmuffin.html; "McDonald's Inventor Profiles," McDonald's Media Site, http://www.media.mcdonalds.com/secured/multi/people/inventors/; Gregory Matusky, "The Franchise Hall of Fame," *Inc.*, April 1994, pp. 86–89.

21. *The Profile of Franchising* (Washington, DC: FRANDATA Corp and the IFA Educational Foundation, 2000), p. 116.

22. Jeannie Ralston, "Before You Bet Your Buns," *Venture*, March 1988, p. 57.

23. Richard Gibson, "Franchise Fever," *Wall Street Journal*, December 15, 2003, p. R1.

24. Kelly K. Spors, "Not So Fast," *Wall Street Journal*, September 19, 2005, p. R11; Joshua Kurlantzick, "Serving Up Success," *Entrepreneur*, November 2003, http://www.entrepreneur.com/article/print/0,2361,311429,00.html; "Subway Restaurant News," Subway, http://www.subway.com/subwayroot/index.aspx.

25. Anne Fisher, "Risk Reward," *FSB*, December 2005/January 2006, p. 58.

26. Gregory Matusky, "What Every Business Can Learn from Franchising," *Inc.*, January 1994, p. 90.

27. Elaine Pofeldt, "Success Franchisee Satisfaction Survey," *Success*, April 1999, p. 59.

28. "State Settles Huge Franchise Fraud Case," Press Release, Office of New York State Attorney Eliot Spitzer, July 2, 2000, http://www.oag.state.ny.us/press/2000/jul/jul02a_00.html.

29. Anne Field, "Piping Hot Performance," *Success*, March 1999, pp. 76–80.

30. April Y. Pennington, "Would You Like a Franchise with That?" *Entrepreneur*, January 2005, pp. 120–127.

31. Steven J. Stark, "Have It Your Way," *Success*, April 1999, pp. 57–59.

32. Sara Wilson, "Coming of Age," *Entrepreneur B.Y.O.B.*, August 2004, pp. 84–87.

33. Joseph Wheeler, "The Multi-Unit Franchise Revolution," *Area Developer*, October 10, 2004, http://www.areadeveloper.us/archive.shtml.

34. Ibid.

35. "Bill Welter Creates Everybody's Favorite Place," *Area Developer*, August 10, 2004, http://www.areadeveloper.us/news_20040810.shtml.

36. Julie Bawden Davis, "The State of International Franchising," *Entrepreneur*, February 12, 2001, http://www.entrepreneur.com/article/0,4621,286607,00.html.

37. David J. Kaufmann, "The Big Bang: How Franchising Became an Economic Powerhouse the World Over," *Entrepreneur*, January 2004, http://www.entrepreneur.com/article/0,4621,312275,00.html.

38. Carlye Adler, "How China Eats a Sandwich," *Fortune*, March 21, 2005, pp. 210[B]–210[D].

39. Stat-USA, U.S. Foreign Commercial Service, "Franchising Industry in China," http://www.buyusainfo.net/docs/x_5566195.pdf.

40. Ibid.

41. Dale D. Buss, "New Dynamics for a New Era," *Nation's Business*, June 1999, p. 46.

42. Deborah Ball, "Dunkin' Donuts Plans to Open Shops Inside Wal-Mart Stores," *Wall Street Journal*, May 13, 2004, p. B7; Dan Morse, "Franchisees Test Water before Taking the Big Plunge," *Wall Street Journal*, May 11, 1999, p. B2.

43. Richard C. Hoffman and John F. Preble, "Convert to Compete: Competitive Advantage through Conversion Financing," *Journal of Small Business Management*, Vol. 41, No.2, April 2003, pp. 127–140.

44. Roberta Maynard, "Why Franchisers Are Looking Abroad," *Nation's Business*, October 1995, pp. 65–72.

45. Julia Boorstin, "Yum Isn't Chicken of China—or Atkins," *Fortune*, March 8, 2004, p. 50.

46. Gabrielle Solomon, "Co-Branding Alliances: Arranged Marriages Made by Marketers," *Fortune*, October 12, 1998, p. 188[N].

47. "Entrepreneur's 27th Annual Franchise 500," *Entrepreneur*, December, 2005. http://www.entrepreneur.com/franzone/rank/0,6584,12-12-F5-2006-0,00.html.

Chapter 7

1. Laura Rich, "Seller's Market," *Inc.*, May 2005, pp. 39–42.

2. Nichole Torres, "Fixer Upper," *Entrepreneur B.Y.O.B.*, November 2001, pp. 120–128; Ian Zack, "On the Rack," *Forbes*, March 5, 2001, http://www.forbes.com/forbes/2001/0305/152.html.

3. Abigail Tucker, "Artist Brings 'Star Wars' Mannequins to Real Life," *Greenville News*, February 27, 2005, p. 6E.

4. Joanne Gordon, "Suitable for Framing," *Forbes*, November 13, 2000, pp. 300–302.

5. Sara Harvey, "Legendary Clemson Bar to Get Facelift," *Greenville News*, August 31, 2003, pp. 1B, 7B.

6. Dimitra Kessenides, "Buyer Beware," *Inc.*, December 2004, pp. 48–49.

7. Crystal Detamore-Rodman, "An Acquired Taste," *Entrepreneur*, October 2004, pp. 62–64.

8. Luisa Kroll, "Gotcha: Pushing the Limits of Due Diligence," *Forbes*, October 30, 2000, pp. 186–187.

9. Richard Breeden, "Small Talk: Selling the Company," *Wall Street Journal*, April 6, 2004, p. B4.

10. Brandon Copple, "Food Fight," *FSB*, October 2004, pp. 95–96.

11. Nichole Torres, "Fixer Upper," *Entrepreneur B.Y.O.B.*, November 2001, p. 126.

12. Norm Brodsky, "What's Your Business Really Worth?" *Inc.*, April 2005, p. 55.

13. Richard Breeden, "Outsourcing Affects Owners' Plans to Sell Firms," *Wall Street Journal*, May 24, 2005, p. B7.

14. David Stires, "Founders to the Rescue!" *Fortune*, October 3, 2005, p. 28.

15. David Worrell, "Go for the Gold," *Entrepreneur*, October 2004, p. 70.

16. Samuel Fromartz, "Rising Empire," *FSB*, October 2001, pp. 73–77.

17. "Just Your Average Millionaire," *Kiplinger's*, June 2001, p. 124; Jayne J. Feld, "Do Bad Grades Mean Doom?" *The Princeton Review*, http://www.princetonreview.com/cte/articles/grads/badgrades.asp; Donna Winchester, "Pinellas' Upsized Ethics Class Heads for the Dome," *St. Petersburg Times*, September 24, 2003, http://www.sptimes.com/2003/09/24/Tampabay/Pinellas__upsized_eth.shtml.

18. Jill Andresky Fraser, "Putting Your Company on the Block", *Inc.*, April 2001, pp. 106–107.

19. David Worrell, "Go for the Gold," *Entrepreneur*, October 2004, pp. 75–76.

20. Peter Kafka, "In Focus," *Forbes*, November 15, 1999, p. 210.

21. Paulette Thomas, "Selling Your Business, Guarding Its Future," *Wall Street Journal*, August 16, 2005, p. B7.

22. Peter Collins, "Cashing Out and Maintaining Control," *Small Business Reports*, December 1989, p. 28.

23. Paul Kaihla, "Why China Wants to Scoop up Your Company," *Business 2.0*, June 2005, pp. 29–30; "State Aids Galesburg Company in Retaining Workers," Illinois Department of Commerce and Economic Opportunity, June 9, 2003, http://www.illinoisbiz.biz/dceo/Bureaus/Community_Development/News/PR_06092003.htm.

24. Kevin Kelly, "Look Under the Hood," *FSB*, October 2004, p. 35.

Chapter 8

1. Mark Henricks, "Soft Sell," *Entrepreneur*, September 1998, pp. 139–144; Neil DiBernado, "D&B Survey Finds the Smaller the Business, the Less Marketing Savvy," http://dnb.com/newsview/0898news1.htm.

2. Dale D. Buss, "The Little Guys Strike Back," *Nation's Business*, July 1996, p. 19.

3. Emily Fredrix, "Free Food Lures Men to Shopping," *Greenville News*, December 17, 2004, pp. 14A, 17A.

4. Howard Dana Shaw, "Customer Care Checklist," *In Business*, September/October, 1987, p. 28.

5. Georgia Flight, "Hipper Than Thou," *Business 2.0*, July 2005, p. 56. "Bibles," Zondervan Inc., http://www.zondervanbibles.com/home.asp.

6. Farnoosh Torabi, "Profiting by Targeting the Elite Buyer," *Money*, December 2003, p. 50.

7. Jamie Mejia and Gabriel Sama, "Media Players Say 'Si' to Latino Magazines," *Wall Street Journal*, May 15, 2002, p. B4.

8. Gisela M. Pedroza, "A Case of Amnasia," *Entrepreneur*, June 2002, pp. 22–24.

9. NPR's *Morning Edition*, January 5, 2000; "About Us," Divine, http://www.shop.edirectory.co.uk/divine/pages/editorial.asp?artid=296&cid=926.

10. "Wooing Women with Wine," *Business 2.0*, May 2005, p. 28; Melissa Korn, "Hey, Lady! Women and the Art of Product Development," *Fast Company*, October 2005, p. 40; "Red, White—or Light?" *Business Week*, April 1, 2005, http://www.businessweek.com/bwdaily/dnflash/apr2005/nf2005041_1795_db061.htm.

11. "Restaurant Spending," National Restaurant Association, http://www.restaurant.org/research/consumer/spending.cfm; Jimmy Boegle, "Fast Casual Redux," *Tucson Weekly*, December 25, 2003, http://www.tucsonweekly.com/gbase/chow/Content?oid=oid:52274; James M. Pethokoukis, "Bye-Bye Burgers," *U.S. News & World Report*, December 2, 2002, pp. 36–37.

12. Roberta Maynard, "New Directions in Marketing" *Nation's Business*, July 1995, p. 26.

13. Thomas Mucha, "What Works," *Business 2.0*, September 2005, pp. 47–49.

14. Josh Dean, "Dov Charney, Like It or Not," *Inc.*, September 2005, pp. 125–131.

15. Maureen Tkacik, "Hey Dude, This Sure Isn't the Gap," *Wall Street Journal*, February 12, 2002, pp. B1, B4.

16. Nancy L. Croft, "Smart Selling," *Nation's Business*, March 1988, pp. 51–52.

17. Al Cole, "Cinematic Chic," *Modern Maturity*, March–April 1998, p. 24.

18. Larry Selden and Geoffrey Colvin, "A Measure of Success," *Business 2.0*, November 2001, p. 59.

19. Stephen M. Silverman, "Retail Retold," *Inc. Technology*, Summer 1995, pp. 23–26.

20. Angela Garber Wolf, "Million-Dollar Questionnaire," *Small Business Computing*, January 2002, pp. 47–48.

21. Joseph Pereira, "Spying on the Sales Floor," *Wall Street Journal*, December 21, 2004, pp. B1, B4.

22. Marta Bright, Kristin Lahmeyer Drees, Carolin Kvitka, Aaron Lazenby, Katheryn Potterf, and Fred Sandsmark, "A Helping Hand," *Profit*, May 2004, p. 7.

23. Rachel Weingarten, "Fire That Client!" *Fortune*, June 27, 2005, p. 184[H].

24. Nick Wreden, "From Customer Satisfaction to Customer Loyalty," *Beyond Computing*, January/February 1999, pp. 12–14.

25. Charles Gerena, "Hey, a Little Service Here?" *Region Focus*, Summer 2004, p. 52.

26. Paul Hughes, "Service Savvy," *Business Start-Ups*, January 1996, p. 48.

27. Julie Johnson, "Inventor Has Vested Interest in New Idea," *Crain's Chicago Business*, September 2, 2002, p. 15; "ScotteVest," *Wall Street Journal*, January 15, 2003, pp. D1, D6; "Personal Tech Guide," *Forbes FYI*, October 10, 2005, p. 62.

28. Roberta Maynard, "Rich Niches," *Nation's Business*, November 1993, pp. 39–42.

29. Dale D. Buss, "Entertailing," *Nation's Business*, December 1997, pp. 18.

30. Tatiana Boncompagni, "Lady Walks into a Bar . . . and Gets Her Hair Done," *Wall Street Journal*, January 13, 2006, p. W8.

31. Dale D. Buss, "Entertailing," *Nation's Business*, December 1997, pp. 12–18.

32. Michael A. Prospero, "Leading Listener: Cabela's," *Fast Company*, October 2005, p. 53; Mike Schoby, "Jim and Dick Cabela," *Sports Afield*, April/May 2004, http://www.findarticles.com/p/articles/mi_qa3775/is_200404/ai_n9358147; Kevin Helliker, "Rare Retailer Scores by Targeting Men Who Hate to Shop," *Wall Street Journal*, December 17, 2002, pp. A1–A11.

33. Coeli Carr, "Don't Say It with Flowers," *FSB*, November 2005, pp. 93–94; "Quiplip Cards," Quiplip.com, http://www.quiplip.com/index.htm.

34. *Entrepreneur*, October 2001, p. 24.

35. James Maguire, "Business Remains Hot at Ice.com," *e-Commerce Guide*," May 23, 2005, www.e-commerceguide.com/solutions/advertising/article.php/3507011; Lin Grensing-Pophal, "Who Are You?" *Business Start-Ups*, September 1997, pp. 38–44.

36. Suzanne Hoppough, "Green Teeth," *Forbes*, October 17, 2005, p. 80; Cheryl Lu-Lien Tan, "Shopping Around: 'Green' Jeans," *Wall Street Journal*, October 13, 2005, p. D5.

37. "Marketing Definitions: Brand," BuildingBrands Inc., http://www.buildingbrands.com/definitions/02_brand_definition.shtml.

38. Mike Steere, "A Timeless Recipe for Success," *Business 2.0*, September 2003, pp. 47–49; "History," In-N-Out, http://www.in-n-out.com/; "Employment," In-N-Out, http://www.in-n-out.com/.

39. John Nardini, "Create a Blog to Boost Your Business," *Entrepreneur*, September 27, 2005, http://www.entrepreneur.com/article/0,4621,323598,00.html.

40. Ibid; Amanda C. Kooser, "Who Let the Blogs Out?" *Entrepreneur*, October 2002, http://www.entrepreneur.com/article/0,4621,303129,00.html.

41. Nardini, "Create a Blog to Boost Your Business," http://www.entrepreneur.com/article/0,4621,323598,00.html.

42. Aimee L. Stern, "How to Build Customer Loyalty," *Your Company*, Spring 1995, p.37.

43. "Deadly Game of Losing Customers," *In Business*, May 1988, p. 189.

44. Jerry Fisher, "The Secret's out," *Entrepreneur*, May 1998, pp. 112–119; Jim Campbell, "Good Customer Service Pays off," *UP*, November 1988, pp. 12–13.

45. "Keeping Customers for Life," *Communication Briefings*, September 1990, p. 3.

46. Adam Stone, "Retaining Customers Requires Constant Contact," *Small Business Computing*, January 11, 2005, http://www.smallbusinesscomputing.com/biztools/print.pho/3457221; Rahul Jacob, "Why Some Customers Are More Equal Than Others," *Fortune*, September 19, 1994, pp. 215–224.

47. Patricia Sellers, "Companies That Serve You Best," *Fortune*, May 31, 1993, p. 75.

48. Susan Hauser, "Out of Print? Not Walter Powell," *Wall Street Journal*, January 24, 2002, p. A16.

49. William A. Sherden, "The Tools of Retention," *Small Business Reports*, November 1994, pp. 43–47.

50. Richard Stone, "Retaining Customers Requires Constant Contact," *Small Business Computing*, January 11, 2005, http://www.smallbusinesscomputing.com/biztools/print.pho/3457221.

51. Staci Surrock, "Chico's Devotion to Real Women Wins Customer Loyalty," *Miami Herald*, January 16, 2006, http://www.miami.com/mld/miamiherald/business/13622717.htm; Katherine Hobson, "Chic—and Comfortable," *U.S. News & World Report*, May 13, 2002, p. 40.

52. "Ways & Means," *Reader's Digest*, January 1993, p. 56.

53. Thomas Mucha, "The Payoff for Trying Harder," *Business2.0*, July 2002, pp. 84–87.

54. Lucas Conley, "Customer-Centered Leader: Maxine Clark," *Fast Company*, October 2005, p. 54.

55. Emily Barker, "You Just Don't Get It," *Inc.*, November 2001, p. 120.

56. Faye Rice, "How to Deal with Tougher Customers," *Fortune*, December 3, 1990, pp. 39–40.

57. Mark Henricks, "Use It or Lose It," Entrepreneur, July 2004, p. 75; Sandra J. Ackerman, "Funding Matters: Encouraging Small Business Innovation," National Center for Research Resources, Winter 2005, http://www.ncrr.nih.gov/newspub/Winter05rpt/stories3.asp; "PediSedate," WHDH News 7 Boston, August 2, 2002, http://www.whdh.com/features/healthcast/H872/.

58. Rahul Jacob, "TQM: More Than a Dying Fad," *Fortune*, October 18, 1993, p. 67.

59. Rich Karlgaard, "Speaking of Hits," *Forbes*, December 8, 2003, p. 45.

60. Janie Magruder, "Tidy up Your Cleaning Regimen," *Greenville News*, May 3, 2003, pp. 1H, 5H.

61. Dave Zielinski, "Improving Service Doesn't Require a Big Investment," *Small Business Reports*, February 1991, p. 20.

62. Ibid.

63. A Little White Wedding Chapel, http://www.alittlewhitechapel.com/html/tunnel_of_love.html.

64. Emily Nelson, "Marketers Push Individual Portions and Families Bite," *Wall Street Journal*, July 23, 2002, pp. A1, A6.

65. Lucy McCauley, "Measure What Matters," *Fast Company*, May 1999, p. 100.

66. Gwendolyn Bounds, "Instant Christmas Spirit: Hire the Experts to Trim the Tree," *Wall Street Journal*, December 14, 2004, p. B1.

67. Michael Dell, "Thrive in a Sick Economy," *Business 2.0*, December 2002/January 2003, p. 88.

68. Bob Weinstein, "Bright Ideas," *Business Start-Ups*, August 1995, p. 57.

69. Alan Deutschman, "America's Fastest Risers," *Fortune*, October 7, 1991, p. 58.

70. Jeffrey Davis, "Growing for the Gold," *Business 2.0*, October 2005, p. 34.

71. Jeffrey Pfeffer, "The Face of Your Business," *Business 2.0*, December 2002/January 2003, p. 58.

72. "Two Strikes and You're Out . . . for Poor Customer Service," Amdocs Inc., June 15, 2004, http://www.amdocs.com/hotnews.asp?news_id=417.

73. "Hold That Price!" *Success*, May 1995, p. 25.

74. Brian L. Clark, "Interview: Pat Croce," *FSB*, November 2001, p. 44.

75. "Keeping Customers For Life," *Communication Briefings*, September 1990, p. 3.

76. Mark Henricks, "Satisfaction Guaranteed," *Entrepreneur*, May 1991, p. 122.

77. Scott McCormack, "Making Waves," *Forbes*, April 5, 1999, pp. 76–78.

78. Norm Brodsky, "Learning from JetBlue," *Inc.*, March 2004, pp. 59–60.

79. Ron Zemke and Dick Schaaf, "The Service Edge," *Small Business Reports*, July 1990, pp. 57–60.

80. Thomas A. Stewart, "After All You've Done for Your Customers, Why Are They Still NOT HAPPY?" *Fortune*, December 11, 1995, pp. 178–182.

81. Mark Henricks, "5 Best Customer Service Ideas," *Entrepreneur*, March 1999, p. 122.

82. Jennifer Vilaga, "Profitable Player: Kiehl's," *Fast Company*, October 2005, p. 55.

83. Brian Lee, "The 3 Cornerstones of Cultural Change," *CEO's Kickstart Retreat*, September 2005, pp. 1–5.

84. Anne Fisher, "A Happy Staff Equals Happy Customers," *Fortune*, July 12, 2004, p. 52.

85. Leonard L. Berry, "Customer Service Solutions," *Success*, July/August 1995, pp. 90–95.

86. Alice Dragoon, "Small Wonders," *CIO Magazine*, January 15, 2005, http://www.cio.com/archive/011505/et_article.html.

87. Ron Zemke and Dick Schaaf, "The Service Edge," *Small Business Reports*, July 1990, p. 60.

88. Desiree De Meyer, "Get to Market Faster," *Smart Business*, October 2001, pp. 62–65; Brian Dumaine, "How Managers Can Succeed through Speed," *Fortune*, February 13, 1989, pp. 54–59.

89. Geoff Williams, "Speed Freaks," *Entrepreneur*, September 1999, p. 120.

90. Jeran Wittenstein, "Fast Food," *Entrepreneur*, November 2005, pp. 132–133.

91. Mark Henricks, "Time Is Money," *Entrepreneur*, February 1993, p. 44.

92. Beth Batchelor, "Ready, Set, Build," *Information Week*, June 27, 2005, pp. 49–53.

93. Zina Moukheiber, "The World's Fastest Chemicals," *Forbes*, October 17, 2005, p. 63.

94. "Tech," *Entrepreneur*, May 2004, p. 46; Christopher Grosso, John McPherson, and Christiana Shi, "Retailing: What's Working Online," *McKinsey Quarterly*, Number 3, 2005, www.mckinseyquarterly.com/article_print.aspx?L2=20& L3=75&ar=163; David Miller, "Online Retail on Easy Street," *E-Commerce Guide*, January 26, 2006, http://www. ecommerce-guide.com/news/trends/print.php/3580126.

95. "Forward," *Entrepreneur*, July 2005, p. 37.

96. Christopher Saunders, "Survey Says: Get Your Business Online," *Small Business Computing*, http://www. smallbusinesscomputing.com/emarketing/print.php/3364331.

97. Ibid.

98. "Survey Shows Web Sites and Biz Growth Go Hand-in-Hand," *E-Commerce Guide*, October 18, 2005, http://www.ecommerce-guide.com/resources/ market_research/article.php/3557241.

99. Tara Siegel Bernard, "Building a Luxury Retail Business on the Web," *Wall Street Journal*, July 12, 2005, p. B4.

100. Stanley J. Winkelman, "Why Big-Name Stores Are Losing Out," *Fortune*, May 8, 1989, pp. 14–15.

101. Jonathan Eig, "For That Sweet Smell of Success, Some Try Scented Bowling Balls," *Wall Street Journal*, March 14, 2005, pp. A1, A13; Carrie Antlfinger, "Bowling Balls Come in Different Scents," *ABC News*, March 14, 2005, http://abcnews.go.com/US/wireStory?id=578880.

102. Jeannie Mandelker, "Crush Rivals by Launching Great Products," *Your Company*, October/November 1997, pp. 54–60.

103. "Silly Putty Stretches into Cyberspace for Its 50th Anniversary," Sillyputty.com, http://www.sillyputty.com/ campus_news/campus_news_Web.htm.

104. Jeannie Mandelker, "Crush Rivals by Launching Great Products," *Your Company*, October/November 1997, pp. 54–60; "Fast Break," *Success*, September 1998, p. 14.

105. Paul B. Brown, "The Eternal Second Act," *Inc.*, June 1988, pp. 119–120.

106. Paul B. Brown, "The Eternal Second Act," *Inc.*, June 1988, p. 120.

107. Kimberly L. McCall, "Bags to Riches," *Entrepreneur*, May 2005, p. 85.

108. Andy Raskin, "Why Retail Rocks," *Business 2.0*, June 2002, pp. 55–57.

109. Bob Weinstein, "Set in Stone," *Business Start-Ups*, October 1995, p. 27.

Chapter 9

1. JupiterResearch, "JupiterResearch Forecasts Online Retail Spending Will Reach $144 Billion in 2010, A CAGR of 12% from 2005" (New York: Author), February 6, 2006, p. 1.

2. Thomas Crampton, "10% of Population Has Shopped Online, Study Shows," *International Herald Tribune*, October 18, 2005, http://www.iht.com/articles/2005/10/18/ business/eshop.php.

3. Enid Burns, "Shoppers Shift to Online," ClickZ Network, November 16, 2005, http://www.clickz.com/stats/sectors/ retailing/article.php/3564781#table.

4. Heather Clancy, "E-Tail Therapy," *Entrepreneur*, January 2005, www.entrepreneur.com/article/0,4621,319052,00.html; Rieva Lesonsky, *Entrepreneur's Guide to Doing Business Online*, 2005, http://www.entrepreneur.com/downloads/ paypalbusinessonlineguide.pdf, p. 3; "Forward," *Entrepreneur*, July 2005, p. 37.

5. Pew Internet and American Life Project, *Internet: The Mainstreaming of Online Life* (Washington, DC: Author, 2005), p. 58.

6. Jerry Useem, "Our 10 Principles of the New Economy, Slightly Revised," *Business 2.0*, August/September 2001, p. 85.

7. JupiterResearch, "JupiterResearch Forecasts Online Retail Spending Will Reach $144 Billion in 2010, A CAGR of 12% from 2005" (New York: Author), February 6, 2006, p. 1.

8. Susan Kuchinskas, "Where Are We Now? A Decade of E-Commerce," *E-Commerce Guide*, www.ecommerceguide.com/news/trends/article.php/3426371.

9. Heather Clancy, "E-Tail Therapy," *Entrepreneur*, January 2005, www.entrepreneur.com/article/0,4621,319052,00.html; Rieva Lesonsky, *Entrepreneur's Guide to Doing Business Online*, 2005, http://www.entrepreneur.com/downloads/paypalbusinessonlineguide.pdf, p. 3.

10. James Maguire, "Lillian Vernon Redesign Tailors to User Preferences," *E-Commerce Guide*, April 15, 2005, www.ecommerce-guide.com/solutions/building/article.php/3498141.

11. Alaska Internet Marketing, "Marketing on the World Wide Web," http://www.alaskaoutdoors.com/Misc/info.html.

12. Jonathan Fahey, "Wheels of Fortune," *Forbes*, January 6, 2003, pp. 48–49.

13. Rieva Lesonsky, *Entrepreneur's Guide to Doing Business Online*, 2005, http://www.entrepreneur.com/downloads/paypalbusinessonlineguide.pdf, p. 3.

14. Maria Atanasov, "A Good Sign," *Smart Business*, February 2002, pp. 66–67.

15. Ana Rincon, "Internet a 'Springboard' for Small Business Growth," *Online Business*, December 7, 2005, http://onlinebusiness.about.com/b/a/225240.htm.

16. Melissa Campanelli, "Seal the Deal," *Entrepreneur*, June 2004, pp. 51–52.

17. Lynn Morrissey, "Helping Small Business Grow," *Forbes* insert, September 2, 2002.

18. Christopher Saunders, "Survey Says: Get Your Business Online," *Small Business Computing*, June 7, 2004, www.smallbusinesscomputing.com/emarketing/article.php/3364331.

19. Joanne H. Pratt, *E-Biz: Strategies for Small Business Success* (Washington, DC: U.S. Small Business Administration Office of Advocacy), October 2002, p. 13.

20. "e or Be Eaten," *Fortune*, November 8, 1999, p. 87.

21. Russ Banham, "Old Dogs, New Clicks," *CFO-IT*, Summer 2005, pp. 21–26.

22. Ibid.

23. Claire Tristram, "Many Happy Returns," *Small Business Computing*, May 1999, p. 73.

24. Ilana DeBare, "The Business of Blogging: Small Companies Promote Themselves through Web Logs," *SFGate*, May 5, 2005, http://www.sfgate.com/cgi-bin/article.cgi?file=/chronicle/archive/2005/05/05/BUG41CGI4K50.DTL&type=business.

25. Melissa Campanelli, "E-Business Busters," *Entrepreneur*, January 2000, pp. 46–50.

26. "Attracting Customers Online," eMarketer, December 2, 2005, http://www.imediaconnection.com/content/7445.asp.

27. "Privacy Worries Plague E-Biz," *Small Business Computing*, June 13, 2002, http://www.smallbusinesscomputing.com/emarketing/print.php/1365361.

28. "Survival of the Fastest," *Inc. Technology*, No. 4, 1999, p. 57.

29. Anne Stuart, "This Year's Model," *Inc.*, December 2002, p. 94; "Company Profile and History," http://www.edmunds.com/help/about/profile.html.

30. Steve Bennett and Stacey Miller, "The E-Commerce Plunge," *Small Business Computing*, February 2000, p. 50.

31. Brian Quinton, "Two Jakes with One Idea: E-Commerce," *Direct*, April 27, 2005, http://www.directmag.com/directtips/Two_Jakes_ecommerce/; Jennifer Schiff, "Two Jakes Furniture Swings in the Key of E-Commerce," *E-Commerce Guide*, March 7, 2005, http://www.ecommerce-guide.com/solutions/building/article.php/3488021; "About Us," Two Jakes, http://twojakes.com/about.cfm.

32. Tim Gray, "Online Shoppers Wary of Online Shopping," *E-Commerce Guide*, November 28, 2005, www.e-commerceguide.com/solutions/customer_relations/article.php/3566676.

33. Heather Clancy, "E-Tail Therapy," Entrepreneur, January 2005, www.entrepreneur.com/article/0,4621,319052,00.html; Melissa Campanelli, "Seal the Deal," *Entrepreneur*, June 2004, pp. 51–52; Alice Hill, "5 Reasons Customers Abandon Their Shopping Carts (and What You Can Do About It)," *Smart Business*, March 2001, pp. 80–84.

34. Laura Rush, "Fear of Abandonment," *Small Business Computing*, January 28, 2004, http://www.smallbusinesscomputing.com/emarketing/print.php/3304551.

35. James Maguire, "The 'Mystery Shopping' Report," *E-Commerce Guide*, February 21, 2006, www.e-commerceguide.com/solutions/customer_relations/article.php/3586441.

36. Emily Barker, Anne Marie Borrego, and Mike Hoffman, "I Was Seduced by the Web Economy," *Inc.*, February 2000, pp. 48–70.

37. "Technology," *Entrepreneur*, July 2005, p. 48.

38. Fred Vogelstein, "A Cold Bath for Dot-Com Fever," *U.S. News & World Report*, September 13, 1999, p. 37.

39. Can E-tailers Find Fulfillment with Drop Shipping?" *Inc.*, July 18, 2002, http://www.inc.com/articles/biz_online/do_biz_online/sell_online/24433.html.

40. Pui-Wing Tam and Mylene Mangalindan, "'Cyber Monday' Sales Strong, Web Sites Say," *Wall Street Journal*, November 29, 2005, pp. B1, B9; Mylene Mangalindan, "Web Retailer Spent Nearly a Year Laying Plans for the Holidays," *Wall Street Journal*, November 29, 2005, pp. B1, B9.

41. "Can E-tailers Find Fulfillment with Drop Shipping?" *Inc.*, July 18, 2002, http://www.inc.com/articles/biz_online/do_biz_online/sell_online/24433.html; "About Us," Spun.com, http://www.spun.com/help/aboutus.jsp.

42. Nigel F. Maynard, "Got Bulbs?" *Builder Online*, October 1, 2003, http://www.builderonline.com/Industry-news.asp?channelID=55&sectionID=13&articleID=17301; Bradley Cole, "Bright Idea Blossoms," *Chicago Post-Tribune*, November 14, 2003, http://www.lightingforthehome.com/pdf/post-tribune_111403.pdf; Karen M. Kroll, "Reach Out," *NFIB Business Toolbox*, July 29, 2003, http://www.nfib.com/object/3911233.html.

43. "B2B E-Commerce Headed for Trillions," Click-Z Stats, March 6, 2002, http://www.clickz.com/stats/sectors/b2b/article.php/10091_986661.

44. Robert McGarvey, "From: Business to: Business," *Entrepreneur*, June 2000, pp. 96–103; William J. Holstein, "Rewiring the 'Old Economy,'" *U.S. News & World Report*, April 10, 2000, pp. 38–40.

45. Robert McGarvey, "From: Business to: Business," *Entrepreneur*, June 2000, p. 98.

46. Bronwyn Fryer and Lee Smith, ".Com or Bust," *FSB*, December 1999/January 2000, p. 41.

47. Dana Dratch, "These E-Gardening Tips Will Help Your Web Site Grow from Sprout to Giant," *Bankrate.com*, February 29, 2000, http://www.bankrate.com/brm/news/biz/Ecommerce/20000117.asp.

48. Heidi Dawley, "Time-Wise, Internet Is Now TV's Equal," *Media Life*, February 1, 2006, http://medialifemagazine.com/artman/publish/article_2581.asp.

49. Eryn Brown, "9 Ways to Win on the Web," *Fortune*, May 24, 1999, p. 112.

50. Melissa Campanelli, "Dot.common Sense," *Entrepreneur*, May 2002, pp. 34–36; "Company Overview," Altrec.com, http://www.altrec.com/company/press/company.html.

51. Joanne H. Pratt, *E-Biz: Strategies for Small Business Success* (Washington, DC: U.S. Small Business Administration Office of Advocacy), October 2002, pp. 14, 28; dogbooties.com, http://www.dogbooties.com.

52. Heather Clancy, "E-Tail Therapy," Entrepreneur, January 2005, www.entrepreneur.com/article/0,4621,319052,00.html.

53. Melissa Campanelli, "Caught in the Web of Lies," Entrepreneur, January 2003, p. 37; fridgedoor.com, http://www.fridgedoor.com.

54. Geoff Williams, "Among Friends," *Entrepreneur*, June 2002, p. 30.

55. James Maguire, "Smart Marketing Helps Plus-Size Retailer Grow," *Small Business Computing*, September 7, 2005, www.smallbusinesscomputing.com/emarketing/article.php/3532441; "Junonia Named Top 50 Retail Web Site," Junonia, http://www.junonia.com/articles.htm.

56. Ralph F. Wilson, "The Five Mutable Laws of Web Marketing," *Web Marketing Today* (http://www.wilsonWeb.com/wmta/basic-principles.htm), April 1, 1999, pp. 1–7.

57. Péter Jascó, "Lonely Planet Online," *Gale Reference Reviews*, July 2005, http://reviews.gale.com/index.php/digital-reference-shelf/2005/07/lonely-planet-online/; "Lonely Planet 8th Most Powerful Brand in Asia-Pacific," *Scoop Independent News*, January 26, 2006, http://www.scoop.co.nz/stories/WO0601/S00363.htm; Lonely Planet, http://www.lonelyplanet.com/.

58. Sean Michael Kerner, "SMBs Reap E-Commerce Benefits," *Small Business Computing*, May 19, 2005, www.smallbusinesscomputing.com/emarketing/article.php/3506266.

59. John E. Dunn," Symantec: Spam Growth Slowing at Last," *InfoWorld*, January 12, 2005, http://www.infoworld.com/article/05/01/12/HNspamslowing_1.html.

60. James Maguire, "Smart Marketing Helps Plus-Size Retailer Grow," *Small Business Computing*, September 7, 2005, www.smallbusinesscomputing.com/emarketing/article.php/3532441.

61. Robert McGarvey, "Find Your Partner," *Entrepreneur*, February 2000, p. 74.

62. Robert McGarvey, "Irreconcilable Differences," *Entrepreneur*, February 2000, p. 75.

63. Ibid.

64. "World Internet Usage and Population Statistics," *Internet World Stats*, February 15, 2006, http://www.internetworldstats.com/stats.htm.

65. "The Top Ten Languages Used in the Web," *Internet World Stats*, February 15, 2006, http://www.internetworldstats.com/stats7.htm.

66. Melissa Campanelli, "Spanning the Globe," *Entrepreneur*, August 2000, http://www.entrepreneur.com/Your_Business/YB_PrintArticle/0,2361,277783,00.html.

67. "U.S. E-Commerce and Internet Business Statistics," Plunkett Research, August 17, 2005, www.plunkettresearch.com/technology/ecommerce_statistics_1.htm.

68. Joanna L. Krotz, "Rise to the Top of Search Results," *bCentral*, http://www.bcentral.com/articles/krotz/110.asp.

69. James Maguire, "MyWeddingFavors Shares Search Success Secrets," *E-Commerce Guide*, October 8, 2004, www.ecommerce-guide.com/solutions/advertising/article.php/3419121.

70. Ibid.

71. James Maguire, "Niche Target Market? Think Search!" *E-Commerce Guide*, August 6, 2004, http://www.ecommerce-guide.com/news/news/article.php/3391971.

72. Mylene Mangalindan, "Playing the Search-Engine Game," *Wall Street Journal*, June 16, 2003, pp. R1, R7.

73. "How to Get Customers to Come Back to Your Site," *Entrepreneur*, October 28, 2002, http://www.entrepreneur.com/article/o,4621,304098,00.html.

74. "Finding and Securing a Domain Name, " *Entrepreneur*, April 14, 2003, http://www.entrepreneur.com/Your_Business/YB_PrintArticle/0,2361,307741,00.html; Linda Formichelli, "The Domain Game," *Home Office Magazine*, January 2001, http://www.entrepreneur.com/Your_Business/YB_SegArticle/0,4621,285164,00.html.

75. Robert A. Mamis, "The Name Game," *Inc.'s The State of Small Business 2000*, pp. 141–144.

76. Alfred Gingold, "Click Here," *My Generation*, July–August 2001, p. 51.

77. Christopher Saunders, "How Do I: Attract and Keep Customers?" *E-Commerce Guide*, June 8, 2004, http://www.ecommerce-guide.com/news/article.php/3365551.

78. Karen J. Bannan, "*TapeInfo.com*," BtoB, September 12, 2005, http://www.btobonline.com/article.cms?articleId=25466.

79. Melissa Campanelli, "Holiday Bonus, *Entrepreneur*, September 2005, pp. 48-50.

80. Melissa Campanelli, "Good Incentive," *Entrepreneur*, August 2001, pp. 82-84.

81. Ibid.

82. Melissa Campanelli, "Spring Cleaning," *Entrepreneur*, April 2003, p. 44; Dan Blacharski, "Now Loading . . .", *Entrepreneur*, April 16, 2000, http://www.entrepreneur.com/Your_Business/YB_SegArticle/0,4621,271233,00.html.

83. Stavraka, "There's No Stopping E-Business. Are You Ready?" *Forbes*, December 13, 1999, Special Advertising Section.

84. James Maguire, "The 'Mystery Shopping' Report," *E-Commerce Guide*, February 21, 2006, www.e-commerce-guide.com/solutions/customer_relations/article.php/3586441.

85. Michele Marrinan, "The Shipping News," *Small Business Computing*, December 2001, pp. 47-48.

86. James Maguire, "Web Analytics: A User's Guide: Part 1," *E-commerce Guide*, October 4, 2004, www.e-commerceguide.com/solutions/customer_relations/article.php/3416791.

87. Jennifer Schiff, "Getting More Out of Your Web Site," *E-Commerce Guide*, November 29, 2005, www.ecommerce-guide.com/solutions/building/article.php/3567091.

88. *Pew Internet & American Life Project*, 2002, http://www.pewinternet.org/reports/reports.asp?Report=19& Section=ReportLevel1&Field=Level1ID&ID=43; Bob Tedeschi, "Privacy vs. Profits," *Smart Business*, October 2001, pp. 56–60.

89. Daniel Roth with Stephanie Mehta, "The Great Data Heist," *Fortune*, May 16, 2005, pp. 66–75.

90. Tim Gray, "310,000 Exposed by LexisNexis Data Breach," *Small Business Computing*, April 13, 2005, www.smallbusinesscomputing.com/news/article.php/3497386; "LexisNexis Data on 310,000 People Feared Stolen," *Reuters*, April 12, 2005, www.reuters.com/type=technologyNews&StoryID=8153492.

91. "Do You Know Where Your Identity Is? Personal Data Theft Eludes Easy Remedies," Knowledge@Wharton: Managing Technology, April 7, 2005, http://knowledge.Wharton.upenn.edu/index.cfm.Article&ID=1176.

92. "Press Release: Frequency and Effects of Virus Attacks Continue to Escalate, According to 10th Annual ICSA Virus Prevalence Survey," Cybertrust.com, April 5, 2005, http://www.cybertrust.com/pr_events/press_releases/2005/04/05/.

93. Melissa Campanelli, "A Wall of Fire," *Entrepreneur*, February 2000, pp. 48–49.

94. "Susan Kuchinskas, "Fraud Chewing E-Commerce Profits," November 11, 2005, *E-Commerce Guide*, November 11, 2005, www.ecommerce-guide.com/solutions/secure_pay/article.php/3563526.

95. Phebe Waterfield, "Building Blocks of Transparent Web Security: Server-Gated Cryptography," Yankee Group Research Inc., September 2005, p. 1.

96. Susan Greco, "The Fraud Bogeyman," *Inc.*, February 2001, pp. 103–104.

Chapter 10

1. Amy Cortese, "The Power of Optimal Pricing," *Business 2.0*, September 2002, pp. 68–70.

2. Ron Stodghill, "The Shipping News," *FSB*, December 2005/January 2006, p. 80.

3. Howard Scott, "The Tricky Art of Raising Prices," *Nation's Business*, February 1999, p. 32.

4. Joshua Levine, "Time is Money," *Forbes*, Sept. 18, 2000, pp. 178–185.

5. Matther Maier, "$100 Bottles of Beer on the Wall," *Business 2.0*, February 2006, p. 26.

6. Joann S. Lublin, "Fountain Pen Fashion: Try 5,072 Diamonds or Abe Lincoln's DNA," *Wall Street Journal*, August, 14, 2001, p. A1.

7. Geoff Williams, "Name Your Price," *Entrepreneur*, September 2005, p. 112.

8. Robert Shulman and Richard Miniter, "Discounting Is No Bargain," *Wall Street Journal*, December 7, 1998, p. A30.

9. William Echilkson, "The Return of Luxury," *Fortune*, October 17, 1994, p. 18.

10. Mark Henricks, "Stop on a Dime," *Entrepreneur*, January 2006, p. 27.

11. Christina Cheddar Berk, "Pricier Gourmet Sodas Grab Attention," *Wall Street Journal*, December 8, 2005, p. B3; "The Concept: Steaz Green Tea Soda," Healthy Beverage Company, http://www.steaz.com/the_concept/index.html.

12. Kathy Schultz, "Boutiques on a Budget," *Seattle Weekly*, September 22, 2004, http://www.seattleweekly.com/diversions/0438/040922_fashion_boutiques.php; Eric Engleman, "Fashion Maven: Funky Seattle Retailer Uses Unsold Clothing for Another Store," *Puget Sound Business Journal*, June 18, 2004, http://www.bizjournals.com/seattle/stories/2004/06/21/smallb1.html?page=2; Nichole L. Torres, "Choose Your Path," *Entrepreneur*, March 2005, http://www.entrepreneur.com/article/0,4621,319940,00.html.

13. Geoff Williams, "Name Your Price," *Entrepreneur*, September 2005, pp. 108–115.

14. Gayle Sato Stodder, "Paying the Price," *Entrepreneur*, October 1994, p. 54.

15. Alison Stein Wellner, "Boost Your Bottom Line by Taking the Guesswork Out of Pricing," *Inc.*, June 2005, p. 78.

16. Ibid, p. 80.

17. Norm Brodsky, "Dealing with Cost Hikes," *Inc.*, August 2005, p. 49.

18. Ibid.

19. Jacob Hale Russell, "The Great Green Way," *Wall Street Journal*, October 22–23, 2005, p. B3.

20. Matther Maier, "Finding Riches in a Mine of Credit Data," *Business 2.0*, October 2005, pp. 72–74.

21. Michael V. Marn, Eric V. Roegner, and Craig C. Zawada, "Pricing New Products," *The McKinsey Quarterly*, Number 3, 2003, p. 1.

22. Carolyn Z. Lawrence, "The Price is Right," *Business Start-Ups*, February 1996, p. 67.

23. Kemp Powers, "Game Theory," *FSB*, July/August 2004, pp. 93–94.

24. John Ewoldt, "Dollars and Sense: Kitchen in a Box," *Minneapolis-St. Paul Star Tribune*, August 29, 2005, http://www.startribune.com/104/story/57134.html; Alison Stein Wellner, "The New Science of Focus Groups," *American Demographics*, March 1, 2003, http://www.findarticles.com/p/articles/mi_m4021/is_2_25/ai_97818972#continue.

25. Suein Hang, "A Posh Ride for the Preschool Set," *Wall Street Journal*, November 11, 2004, pp. D1, D8.

26. Geoff Williams, "Name Your Price," *Entrepreneur*, September 2005, pp. 108–115.

27. Dayana Yochim, "Dump Your Duds," *The Motley Fool*, May 18, 2004, www.fool.com/news/commentary040518dy.htm.

28. Jathon Sapsford, "As Cash Fades, America Becomes a Plastic Nation," *Wall Street Journal*, July 23, 2004, pp. A1, A6.

29. "Top 10 Reasons to Start Accepting Credit Cards Today," *100 Best Merchant Accounts*, http://www.100best-merchant-accounts.com/articles1.html.

30. Debra D'Agostino, "In E-Commerce, Small Is the New Big," *CIO Insight*, January 6, 2006, www.cioinsight.com/

article2/0,1540,1917812,00.asp; "Fast Food and Cards," *CardWeb*, December 20, 2005, www.cardweb.com/cardtrak/news/2005/december/20a.html.

31. Gwendolyn Bounds and Robin Sidel, "Merchants Balk at Higher Fees for Credit Cards," *Wall Street Journal*, April 12, 2005, pp. B1, B8.

32. Robin Sidel, "Banks, Customers Adapt to Paperless Check Processing," *Wall Street Journal*, October 28, 2004, pp. B1, B3.

33. Bob Weinstein, "Getting Carded," *Entrepreneur*, September 1995, p. 76.

Chapter 11

1. Mike Hogan, "Stay in Touch," *Entrepreneur*, September 2005, pp. 44–46.

2. "Odds and Ends," *The Wall Street Journal,* July 25, 1990, p. Bl.

3. Richard G. P. MaMahon and Scott Holmes, "Small Business Financial Management Practices in North America: A Literature Review," *Journal of Small Business Management,* April 1991, p. 21.

4. Ellyn Spragins and Verne Harnish, "Size Doesn't Matter—Profits Do," *FSB*, March 2004, pp. 37–42.

5. Alison Stein Wellner, "Are You Paying Yourself Enough?" *Inc.*, November 2004, pp. 87–92.

6. William Bak, "The Numbers Game," *Entrepreneur,* April 1993, p. 54.

7. Diedrich Von Soosten, "The Roots of Financial Destruction," *Industry Week,* April 5, 1993, pp. 33–34.

8. Richard Maturi, "Take Your Pulse," *Business Start-Ups*, January 1996, p. 72.

9. G. Dean Palmer, "Marketing and Management Strategies of Small Rural Retailers in South-Side Virginia," Small Business Advancement National Center, University of Central Arkansas (Conway, Arkansas, 1995), http://www.sbaer.uca.edu/Research/1995/SSBIA/95swi052.txt.

10. Jill Andresky Fraser, "When Staffers Track Results," *Inc.,* October 1993, p. 42; Dan Callahan, "Everybody's An Accountant," *Business Ethics,* January/February 1994, p. 37.

11. "Debt Levels and Flows," Wikipedia, http://en.wikipedia.org/wiki/Debt_levels_and_flows#United_States_2.

12. Samuel Fromartz, "Escaping the Chains of Small Business Debt," *Forbes*, November 12, 2003, www.forbes.com/work/newswire/2003/11/12/rtr1144855.html.

13. William Bak, "The Numbers Game," *Entrepreneur,* April 1993, p. 57.

14. "Analyzing Creditworthiness," *Inc.,* November 1991, p. 196.

15. Ellyn Spragins and Verne Harnish, "Size Doesn't Matter—Profits Do," *FSB*, March 2004, pp. 37–42.

16. Mike Hogam "Stay in Touch," *Entrepreneur*, September 2005, pp. 44–46.

17. Scott Herhold, "Warning Sign," *Business 2.0,* August/September 2001, pp. 198–199.

18. Kayte Vanscoy, "Dead or Alive?" *Smart Business*, August 2001, p. 32.

19. David Worrell, "A Penchant for Profits," *Entrepreneur*, August 2005, p. 53.

20. Jon E. Hilsenrath, "Adventures in Cost Cutting," *Wall Street Journal*, May 10, 2004, pp. R1, R3.

21. Audrey Warren, "The Small Stuff," *Wall Street Journal*, May 10, 2004, p. R9.

22. Emily Barker, "Finance: Cheap Executive Officer," *Inc.*, April 1, 2002, pp. 114–116.

23. Ilan Mochari, "A Simple Little System," *Inc.,* October 1999, p. 87.

24. Bo Burlingham, "Inc. Query: Number Crunching," *Inc.*, February 1, 2002, http://www.inc.com/articles/finance/fin_manage/basic_fin_manage/23857.html.

25. Norm Brodsky, "The Magic Number," *Inc.*, September 2003, pp. 43–46.

26. Richard Breen, "Margins Melt as Cheese Burns Pizza Industry," *GSA Business*, January 24, 2005, pp. 1, 6.

27. John Case, "Critical Numbers in Action," *Inc.*, January 21, 2000, http://www.inc.com/articles/finance/fin_manage/forecast/15981.html.

28. Ibid.

29. William F. Doescher, "Taking Stock," *Entrepreneur,* November 1994, p. 64.

30. Ilan Mochari, "Significant Figures," *Inc.,* July 2000, p. 128.

31. Ibid.

32. Ilian Mochari, "Racking Out at the Mall," *FSB*, November 2005, p. 19; "Mall of America's Latest Store Is a Snooze," *USA Today*, September 20, 2005, www.usatoday.com/travel/destinations/2005-09-20-mall-nap_x.htm; "Catching Some Shut-Eye," *Sales & Marketing Management*, March 2006, www.salesandmarketing.com/smm/worklife/article_display.jsp?vnu_content_id=1002115801.

Chapter 12

1. Wendy Taylor and Marty Jerome, "Dead Men Talking," *Smart Business*, December 2001/January 2002, p. 19.

2. Amit Asaravala, "Salon's Got a Will to Survive," *Wired News*, March 11, 2005, http://www.wired.com/news/business/0,1367,62620,00.html; "Salon.com Still Kicking," *The Mercury News,* November 30, 2005, http://nl.newsbank.com/nl-search/we/Archives?s_site=mercurynews&p_multi=SJ|&p_product=SJ&p_theme=realcities&p_action=search&p_maxdocs=200&p_text_search-0=Salon.com&s_dispstring=Salon.com%20AND%20date(last%20180%20days)&p_field_date-0=YMD_date&p_params_date-0=date:B,E&p_text_date-0=-180qzD&p_perpage=10&p_

sort=YMD_date:D&xcal_useweights=no; "Salon.com to Charge Subscription Fee," *USA Today*, February 6, 2002, http://www.usatoday.com/tech/techinvestor/2001-03-21-salon.htm; Salon.com, *Wikipedia*, http://en.wikipedia.org/wiki/Salon.com; Verne Kopytoff, "Salon Warns It Is Nearly Out of Cash," *SFGate.com*, February 15, 2003, http://www.sfgate.com/cgi-bin/article.cgi?f=/c/a/2003/02/15/BU95644.DTL; Verne Kopytoff, "Salon Shares Suffer Another Blow," *SFGate.com*, November 22, 2002, http://www.sfgate.com/cgi-bin/article.cgi?f=/c/a/2002/11/22/BU79954.DTL&hw=Salon+com+delist&sn=002&sc=659; Dan Fost, "Salon.com Beats the Odds," *SFGate.com*, December 1, 2005, http://www.sfgate.com/cgi-bin/article.cgi?f=/c/a/2005/12/01/BUG3UFVRJ726.DTL&hw=Salon+com+delist&sn=001&sc=1000.

3. "Help! My Firm Is Hemorrhaging Cash," *Your Company*, April/May 1996, pp. 10–11.

4. National Federation of Independent Businesses, *National Small Business Poll: The Cash Flow Problem* (Washington, DC: Author, 2002), p. 2.

5. Jerry Useem, "The Icon That Almost Wasn't," *Inc: The State of Small Business 1998*, p. 142; "History," Ford Motor Company, http://www.ford.com/en/heritage/history/default.htm.

6. Daniel Kehrer, "Big Ideas for Your Small Business," *Changing Times*, November 1989, p. 58.

7. Douglas Bartholomew, "4 Common Financial Management Mistakes . . . And How To Avoid Them," *Your Company*, Fall 1991, p. 9.

8. Robert A. Mamis, "Money In, Money Out," *Inc.*, March 1993, p. 98.

9. Bartholomew, "4 Common Financial Management Mistakes . . . And How to Avoid Them," p. 9.

10. Phaedra Hise, "Paging for Cash Flow," *Inc.*, December 1995, p. 131.

11. Jenny Munro, "Halloween in July," *Business*, July 25, 2004, pp. 1, 6–7.

12. Gwendolyn Bounds, "Store's Sales Can Rest on a Moment," *Wall Street Journal*, January 3, 2006, p. A. 23.

13. Gwendolyn Bounds, "Preparing for the Big Bang," *Wall Street Journal*, June 29, 2004, pp. B1, B7.

14. Kortney Stringer, "Neither Anthrax nor the Economy Stops the Fruitcake," *Wall Street Journal*, December 19, 2001, pp. B1, B4; Dirk Smillie, "Signs of Life," *Forbes*, November 11, 2002, p. 160.

15. Bounds, "Store's Sales Can Rest on a Moment," p. A. 23.

16. National Federation of Independent Businesses, *National Small Business Poll: The Cash Flow Problem* (Washington, DC: Author, 2002), p. 1.

17. Amy Feldman, "The Cash-Flow Crunch," *Inc.*, December 2005, pp. 50–52.

18. Jill Andresky Fraser, "Monitoring Daily Cash Trends," *Inc.*, October 1992, p. 49.

19. William G. Shepherd, Jr., "Internal Financial Strategies," *Venture*, September 1985, p. 66.

20. David H. Bangs, *Financial Troubleshooting: An Action Plan for Money Management in the Small Business* (Dover, NH: Upstart Publishing Company, 1992), p. 61.

21. "Are You Ready for the Major Leagues?" *Inc.*, February 2001, p. 106.

22. "Cash Flow/Cash Flow Management," *Small Business Reporter*, No. 9, p. 5.

23. William Bak, "Make 'Em Pay," *Entrepreneur*, November 1992, p. 64.

24. Sean P. Melvin, "It's Payback Time," *Entrepreneur*, April 2002, pp. 67–68.

25. Richard G. P. McMahon and Scott Holmes, "Small Business Financial Management Practices in North America: A Literature Review," *Journal of Small Business Management*, April 1991, p. 21.

26. Ilan Mochari, "Collect from the Worst," *Inc.*, September 1999, p. 101.

27. "The Check Isn't in the Mail," *Small Business Reports*, October 1991, p. 6.

28. William J. Dennis, Jr., *National Small Business Poll: Getting Paid* (Washington, DC: National Federation of Independent Businesses, 2001), Volume 1, Issue 7, p. 11.

29. Ibid.

30. American Collectors Association, http://www.collector.com/; Howard Muson, "Collecting Overdue Accounts," *Your Company*, Spring 1993, p.4.

31. Richard J. Maturi, "Collection Dues and Don'ts," *Entrepreneur*, January 1992, p. 326.

32. Elaine Pofeldt, "Collect Calls," *Success*, March 1998, pp. 22–24.

33. Janine Latis Musick, "Collecting Payments Due," *Nation's Business*, January 1999, pp. 44–46.

34. Ilan Mochari, "Top Billing," *Inc.*, October 1999, p. 89.

35. Jim Carlton, "Tight Squeeze," *Wall Street Journal*, March 26, 1996, pp. A1, A6.

36. Jill Andresky Fraser, "A Confidence Game," *Inc.*, December 1989, p. 178.

37. Jill Andresky Fraser, "How to Get Paid," *Inc.*, March 1992, p. 105.

38. Eleena deLisser, "Yellow-Pages Con Artists Are Pushing Online Editions," *Wall Street Journal*, November 16, 1999, p. B2.

39. Shepherd, "Internal Financial Strategies," p. 68.

40. Mark Henricks, "No Long-Term Parking," *Entrepreneur*, January 2002, http://www.entrepreneur.com/article/0,4621,295660.html.

41. Stephanie Barlow, "Frozen Assets," *Entrepreneur*, September 1993, p. 53.

42. Roberta Maynard, "Can You Benefit from Barter?" *Nation's Business*, July 1994, p. 6.

43. "33 Ways to Increase Your Cash Flow and Manage Cash Balances," *The Business Owner*, February 1988, p. 8.

44. "301 Great Ideas for Selling Smarter," *Inc.*, January 1, 1998, p. 47.

45. Mamis, "Money In, Money Out," p. 102.

46. Pia Sarkar, "Disposable Chic," November 8, 2005, SFGate.com, http://www.sfgate.com/cgi-bin/article.cgi?f=/c/a/2005/11/08/BUGSOFKG9F1.DTL; Kimberly Pfaff, "Cheap Chic," *Retailing Today*, March 2002, http://www.icsc.org/srch/sct/sct0302/page35.php?region; "Forever 21 and IBM Fashion a One-Stop POS Solution with Just the Right Fit," Case Studies: IBM Global Financing, April 26, 2005, http://www-03.ibm.com/financing/pdf/us/igf5-a214.pdf.

47. Jeffrey Lant, "Cash Is King," *Small Business Reports*, May 1991, p. 49.

48. "Chris Pentilla, "Making the Trade," *Entrepreneur*, July 2005, pp. 84–85.

49. Ibid.

50. Melissa Campanelli, "Fair Trade," *Entrepreneur*, August 2001, pp. 33–35.

51. Pentilla, "Making the Trade," p. 84.

52. Stephanie Clifford, "Something for Nothing," *Inc.*, May 2005, pp. 54–56.

53. Ilan Mochari, "A Simple Little System," *Inc.*, October 1, 1999, p. 142.

54. "Choose Leasing: Leasing Benefits," Equipment Leasing Association, http://www.chooseleasing.org/Basics/BeneMean.htm.

55. Jill Amadio, "To Lease or Not to Lease?" *Entrepreneur*, February 1998, p. 133.

56. Pia Sarkar, "Disposable Chic," November 8, 2005, SFGate.com, http://www.sfgate.com/cgi-bin/article.cgi?f=/c/a/2005/11/08/BUGSOFKG9F1.DTL; Kimberly Pfaff, "Cheap Chic," *Retailing Today*, March 2002, http://www.icsc.org/srch/sct/sct0302/page35.php?region; "Forever 21 and IBM Fashion a One-Stop POS Solution with Just the Right Fit," Case Studies: IBM Global Financing, April 26, 2005, http://www-03.ibm.com/financing/pdf/us/igf5-a214.pdf.

57. Jack Wynn, "To Use But Not to Own," *Nation's Business*, January 1991, p. 38.

58. Jennifer Schiff, Buy versus Lease: What You Need to Know," *Small Business Computing*, July 28, 2005, http://www.smallbusinesscomputing.com/news/article.php/

59. 3523561; "Delicato Announces Successful New Long Term Financing," July 21, 2004, http://www.delicato.com/about/pressrelease/pdf/refi.pdf.

59. Roger Thompson, "Business Copes with the Recession," *Nation's Business*, January 1991, p. 20.

60. Bruce G. Posner, "Skipped-Payment Loans," *Inc.*, September 1992, p. 40.

61. Gerry Blackwell," Don't Hire, Outsource," *Small Business Computing*, July 5, 2005, http://www.smallbusinesscomputing.com/news/article.php/3512451.

62. "Check Fraud," Rutgers University, http://crimeprevention.rutgers.edu/crime/checkfraud/checkfraud.htm.

63. David Worrell, "It's in the Cards," *Entrepreneur*, April 2005, p. 57.

64. Thompson, "Business Copes with the Recession," p. 21.

65. Mary Paulsell, "The Problem of Employee Theft," Missouri Small Business Development Centers, October 10, 2002, http://www.missouribusiness.net/docs/problem_employee_theft.asp.

66. Julia Boorstin, "Alcohol Auditor," *Fortune*, June 27, 2005, p. 40.

67. Jill Andresky Fraser, "Better Cash Management," *Inc.*, May 1993, p. 42.

68. C. J. Prince, "Money to Burn?" *Entrepreneur*, July 2004, pp. 51–52.

69. Mamis, "Money In, Money Out," p. 103.

Chapter 13

1. Paul DeCeglie, "What about Me?" *Business Start-Ups*, June 2000, p. 45.

2. Udayan Gupta, "The Right Fit," *Wall Street Journal,* May 22, 1995, p. R8.

3. Aliza Pilar Sherman, "The Opposite Sex," *Entrepreneur*, September 2002, p. 36.

4. U. N. Umesh and Patrick Criteser, "Venture Capital's Foul Weather Friends," *Wall Street Journal*, January 14, 2003, p. B13; "Press Releases," Northwest Energy Efficiency Alliance, http://www.nwalliance.org/news/pressreleases.asp.

5. David Worrell, "Term Papers," *Entrepreneur*, March 2006, pp. 57–60.

6. Peter Loftus, "Lessons Learned Online Fuel a New Business," *Startup Journal: Wall Street Journal Center for Entrepreneurs*, September 3, 2002, http://www.startupjournal.com/runbusiness/failure/20020903-loftus.html.

7. Michael Brocks, "Advice for Your Business Owner Clients: Forget Landing Venture Capital," *American Institute of Certified Public Accountants*, April 6, 2006, http://www.aicpa.org/pubs/tpcpa/dec2004/advice.htm.

8. John Cook, "Recent Layoffs at Area Technology Companies," *Seattle Post-Intelligencer*, April 18, 2005, http://seattlepi.nwsource.com/venture/layoff.asp?id=739.

9. Elizabeth Fenner, "How to Raise the Cash You Need," *Money Guide*, Summer 1991, p. 45.

10. Jenny Wonderling, "The Art of Business," *Chronogram.com*, April 2002, http://www.chronogram.com/issue/2002/04/business1.htm; Carrie Coolidge, "The Bootstrap Brigade," *Forbes*, December 28, 1998, pp. 90–91.

11. Michael V. Copeland, "How to Find an Angel," *Business 2.0*, March 2006, p. 48.

12. Paul Kvinta, "Frogskins, Shekels, Bucks, Moolah, Cash, Simoleans, Dough, Dinero: Everybody Wants It. Your Business Needs It. Here's How to Get It," *Smart Business*, August 2000, pp. 74–89.

13. Joseph R. Bell, Kenneth M. Huggins, and Christine McClatchey, "Profiling the Angel Investor," presented at Small Business Institute Director's Association Conference, February 7, 2002, San Diego, California, p. 1; "Biography: Laurance Spelman Rockefeller," InfoPlease.com, http://www.infoplease.com/ipa/A0771997.html.

14. Pamela Sherrid, "Angels of Capitalism," *U.S. News & World Report*, October 13, 1997, pp. 43–45.

15. Jeffrey Sohl, "The Angel Investor Market in 2005," University of New Hampshire Center for Venture Research, http://www.unh.edu/cvr, 2005, p. 1; Copeland, "How to Find an Angel," *Business 2.0*, March 2006, p. 48.; Rhonda Abrams, "Pray for Angels' Help to Build Your Business," *Business*, April 10, 2005, p. 8.

16. Wendy Taylor and Marty Jerome, "Pray," Smart Business, July 2000, p. 45.

17. Silvia Sansoni, "Burned Angels," *Forbes*, April 19, 1999, pp. 182–185.

18. Jim Melloan, "Angels with Angels," *Inc.*, July 2005, pp. 93–104; Roger Barnes, "Touched by an Angel," *Black Enterprise*, June 2001, pp. 242–247; Susan Greco, "Get$$$Now.com," *Inc.*, September 1999, pp. 35–38; "Digging for Dollars," *Wall Street Journal*, February 24,

1989, p. R25; Quentin Hardy, "Where Angels Dare to Tread," *Forbes*, October 28, 2002, pp. 303–304.

19. Copeland, "How to Find an Angel," pp. 47–49.

20. "Vital Statistics," Band of Angels, http://www. bandangels.com/; Bonnie Azab Powell, "Angel Investors Fill Void Left by Risk Capital," *New York Times*, July 6, 2001, p. 28; Paul Kvinta, "Frogskins, Shekels, Bucks, Moolah, Cash, Simoleans, Dough, Dinero: Everybody Wants It. Your Business Needs It. Here's How to Get It," *Smart Business*, August 2000, pp. 74–89.

21. "Those High-Flying Angel Investors: VC Panel Talks UP Creative Financing for Startups," Innovation and Entrepreneurhship, *Knowledge@Wharton*, June 2, 2005, http://knowledge.wharton.upenn.edu/index.cfm/ArticleID= 1215.

22. Melloan, "Angels with Angels," pp. 93–104.

23. Copeland, "How to Find Your Angel," pp. 47–49; "About Us," Intellifit, http://www.intellifit.com/Intellifit/ AboutUs.aspx; "About Us," Robin Hood Ventures, http://www.robinhoodventures.com/aboutus.htm.

24. David Worrell, "Taking Flight," *Entrepreneur*, October 2004, p. 34.

25. David Worrell, "Guardian Angels," *Entrepreneur*, March 2005, pp. 58–60.

26. Lee Gomes, "The Angels Are Back, and This Time They Have a Trade Group," *Wall Street Journal*, April 11, 2005, p. B1.

27. Nancy Scarlato, "Money," *Business Start-Ups*, December 1995, pp. 50–51.

28. Mark Henricks, "Stand Your Ground," *Entrepreneur*, January 1993, p. 264.

29. Ernst & Young, *Corporate Venture Capital Report* (New York: Author, 2002), p. 3; Alistair Christopher, "Corporate Venture Capital: Moving to the Head of the Class," *Venture Capital Journal*, November 1, 2000, http://www.findarti- cles.com/cf_dls/m0ZAL/2000_Nov_1/66502342/print. jhtml.

30. Michelle Leder, "Come to Daddy," *Inc.*, May 2005, p. 48.

31. Mark Henricks, "Answering the Call," *Entrepreneur*, July 2002, pp. 19–21.

32. Arlyn Tobias Gajilan, "Big Money on Campus," *Your Company*, October 1999, p. 34.

33. Warren P. Strobel, "The Spy Who Funded Me (and My Start-Up)," *U.S. News & World Report*, July 17, 2000, pp. 38–39; Rick E. Yannuzzi, "In-Q-Tel: A New Partnership between the CIA and the Private Sector," *Defense Intelligence Journal*, Volume 9, Number 1, Winter 2000, pp. 25–38.

34. "Venture-Backed Companies Outperformed Peers in 10 Industries during U.S. Economic Downturn, New Study Shows," National Venture Capital Association, July 16, 2004, p. 1; Rebecca Buckman, "Baby Sitting for Start-Ups," *Wall Street Journal*, March 13, 2006, pp. B1, B3; "What Is Venture Capital?" *Venture Capital Journal*, 2001, pp. 32–36; Paul DeCeglie, "What about Me?" *Business Start-Ups*, June 2000, pp. 45–51.

35. Buckman, "Baby Sitting for Start-Ups," p. B1.

36. Janet Effland, "How to Bet on the Next Big Thing," *Business 2.0*, December 2002/January 2003, p. 90.

37. Singer, "Where the Money Is," pp. 52–55; National Venture Capital Association, http://www.nvca.org;

PriceWaterhouseCoopers MoneyTree Survey, http://www.pwcmoneytree.com/moneytree/index.jsp.

38. "Investments by Industry," PriceWaterhouseCoopers MoneyTree Survey, http://www.pwcmoneytree.com/mon- eytree/nav.jsp?page=industry.

39. Kate O'Sullivan, "Not-So-Easy Money, *CFO*, October 2005, p. 20.

40. Rebecca Buckman, "Baby Sitting for Start-Ups," *Wall Street Journal*, March 13, 2006, p. B3.

41. Stewart Alsop, "The Rules of Venture Capital," *Fortune*, April 15, 2002, p. 76.

42. Rebecca Buckman, "BabySitting for Start-Ups," *Wall Street Journal*, March 13, 2006, pp. B1, B3.

43. David Worrell, "Cracking the Code," *Entrepreneur*, December 2005, pp. 50–51; "History," Zula Patrol, http://www.thezulapatrol.com/zulapatrol/history.html.

44. Dave Pell, "What's Old Is New Again," *FSB*, July/August 2000, p. 122.

45. Jennifer Pellet, "Public Opinion," *Entrepreneur*, October 2002, pp. 76–81.

46. David R. Evanson, "Tales of Caution In Going Public," *Nation's Business*, June 1996, p. 58.

47. Francis B. Allgood, "Stathakis Keeps Stax's on Track, *GSA Business*, March 11, 2002, p. 3.

48. Roberta Maynard, "Are You Ready to Go Public?" *Nation's Business,* January 1995, pp. 30–32.

49. Tony Taylor, "A Going (Public) Concern," GSA Business, February 20, 2006, p. 15.

50. "Atlantis Owner, Kerzner International, to Go Private," *Meeting Industry Megasite*, March 22, 2006, p. 1.

51. Pellet, "Public Opinion," p. 79.

52. David R. Evanson and Art Beroff, "Synchronize Your Watches," *Entrepreneur*, November 1999, pp. 74–77.

53. Antonio Ragalado and Raymond Hennessey, "Nanosys Pulls IPO, Putting Nanotech Revolution on Hold," *Wall Street Journal*, August 5, 2004, pp, C1, C5.

54. "The More the Merrier," CFO, October 2005, p. 18.

55. David R. Evanson and Art Beroff, "It Ain't Over . . . ," *Entrepreneur*, December 1999, pp. 66–69; CorpHQ, http://www.corphq.com.

56. Jennifer Gill, "Just a Little Bit Public," Inc., August 2005, pp. 32–34.

57. Telephone interview with David Barash, Ben & Jerry's Homemade.

58. "About Us," Real Goods Trading Company, http://www.realgoods.com/about/history.cfm; "Real Goods Trading Company," Drew Field Direct Public Offering, http://www.dfdpo.com/clientsum5.htm.

59. Gianna Jacobson, "Find Your Fortune on the Internet," *Success,* November 1995, p. 50.

60. U.S. Small Business Administration, Office of Advocacy, *Micro-Business-Friendly Banks in the United States, 2001 Edition* (Washington, DC: Author, 2002), p. 2.

61. Keith Girard, "Small Business Borrowing Strong," *Daily News Digest*, December 6, 2005, http://www.allbusiness.com/ news/daily_news.asp?ID=11430#11431.

62. Karen Axelton, "Don't Bank on It," *Business Start-Ups*, May 1998, p. 116.

63. Cynthia E. Griffin, "Money in the Bank," *Entrepreneur*, July 2000, pp. 84–89; U.S. Small Business Administration, Office of Advocacy, *Micro-Business-Friendly Banks in the*

United States, 2001 Edition (Washington, DC: Author, 2002), p. 2.

64. Crystal Detamore Rodman, "Custom Deal," *Entrepreneur*, January 2006, pp. 55–58.

65. Daniel M. Clark, "Banks and Bankability," *Venture,* September 1989, p. 29.

66. Crystal Detamore-Rodman, "Fees of Danger," *Entrepreneur*, February 2005, pp. 50–52.

67. Catherine Curan, "In a Cash Crunch?" *Inc.*, March 2006, pp. 34–36.

68. Crystal Detamore Rodman, "Stock Exchange," *Entrepreneur*, June 2005, pp. 66–69.

69. "What Is Business Credit?" National Association of Credit Management, http://www.nacm.org/ aboutnacm/what.html; "Financing Small Business," *Small Business Reporter*, c3, p. 9.

70. David Worrell, "Leaping Into Action," *Entrepreneur*, May 2005, p. 57.

71. Crystal Detamore-Rodman, "Commercial Break," *Entrepreneur*, August 2004, pp. 50–51.

72. Scott McMurray, "Personal Loans from Brokers Offer Low Rates," *Wall Street Journal,* January 7, 1986, p. 31.

73. Crystal Detamore-Rodman, "Going for Broker," *Entrepreneur*, September 2002, pp. 52–54.

74. "Credit Union Statistics," Credit Union National Association, http://www.cuna.org/download/us_totals.pdf.

75. "Joseph Ogwal: Building a Stable Future for His Family," World Council of Credit Unions, http://www.woccu. org/cudev/microfinance/afr_splt.htm.

76. Sean P. Melvin, "Itsy-Bitsey Bonds," *Entrepreneur*, January 2002, pp. 78–82.

77. U.S. Small Business Administration, *SBIC Program Statistical Package*, (Washington, DC), 2003, http://www.sba.gov/INV/stat/table3.pdf.

78. National Association of Small Business Investment Companies, http://www.nasbic.org/.

79. U.S. Small Business Administration, *SBIC Program Statistical Package* (Washington, DC: Author, 2003), http://www.sba.gov/INV/tables/2001/stats/allsbic1.pdf.

80. U.S. Small Business Administration, *BIC Program Statistical Package* (Washington, DC: Author, 2003), http://www.sba.gov/INV/tables/2001/stats/allsbic4.pdf.

81. "Success Stories: Outback Steakhouse," National Association of Small Business Investment Companies, http://www.nasbic.com/success/stories/outback.cfm; "Company Statistics," Outback Steakhouse, http://www. corporate-ir.net/ireye/ir_site.zhtml?ticker=osi&script= 950&layout=11&item_id='ps=1*pg=2.

82. "CIT Helps a Miracle Company Clean up," *Lending Connections*, Volume 10, Issue 1, Fall 2002, pp. 1, 4; "The Downturn's Silver Lining for Small Business," *Small Business*, April 14, 2004, http://www.a1technology. com/blog/smallbiz/2004_04_12_smallbiz.htm.

83. Eric Symons, "City Loan Program Fuels Small Business Start-up," San Diego Economic Development Administration, May 2, 2006, pp. 1–2.

84. "Section 108 Case Studies," U.S. Department of Housing and Urban Development, http://www.hud.gov/offices/ cpd/communitydevelopment/programs/108/casestudies.cfm.

85. "Technology: SBIR/STTR," U.S. Small Business Administration, http://www.sba.gov/sbir/indexwhatwedo.html.

86. Sandra J. Ackerman, "Funding Matters: Encouraging Small Business Innovation," *NCCR Reporter*, Winter 2005, www.ncrr.nih.gov/newspub/Winter05rpt/stories3.asp.

87. "Overview and History of the SBA," U.S. Small Business Administration, http://www.sba.gov/aboutsba/history.html.

88. Laura M. Litvan, "Some Rest for the Paperwork Weary," *Nation's Business*, June 1994, pp. 38–40; Robert W. Casey, "Getting Down to Business," *Your Company*, Summer 1994, pp. 30–33.

89. "Small Business Administration," Office of Management and Budget, http://www.omb.gov.

90. Randy Myers, "Squeezing the SBA," *CFO*, November 2004, pp. 91–92.

91. Jim Hightower, "PowerUp Inc. Uses SBA Working Capital Loan to Finance Shipment to Pakistan Military," *Georgia Business Directory*, http://www.bizgeorgia.com/index2.php.

92. "Past Projects: Metalcraft Industries," Deseret CDC, http://www.deseretcdc.com/index.phtml?p=1-0; "About Us," Metalcraft Technologies, Inc., http://www.metalcraft.net/ about_us.htm.

93. *SBA Microloan Program: FY 2007*, Women Impacting Public Policy, http://www.wipp.org/news_details.asp? story_id=204&memberonly=False.

94. "Crossing the Bridge to Self-Employment Case Studies: National Credit Union Administration," Federal Deposit Insurance Corporation (no date), www.fdic.gov//con- sumers/microenterprise/ncuacase.html.

95. Riva Richmond, "SBA's Major Role in Gulf Coast Aid Continues," *Wall Street Journal*, April 18, 2006, p. B10.

96. Ziona Austrian and Zhongcai Zhang, "An Inventory and Assessment of Pollution Control and Prevention Financing Programs," Great Lakes Environmental Finance Center, Levin College of Urban Affairs, Cleveland State University, http://www.csuohio.edu/glefc/inventor.htm#sba.

97. Sharon Nelton, "Loans That Come Full Circle," *Nation's Business*, June 1999, pp. 35–36.

98. "Central Vermont Revolving Loan Fund," http://cvcac.org/Services/revolvingloan.htm.

99. Roberta Reynes, "A Big Factor in Expansion," *Nation's Business*, January 1999, pp. 31–32; Bruce J. Blechman, "The High Cost of Credit," *Entrepreneur,* January 1993, pp. 22–25.

100. Expected Costs of Startup Ventures, Blade Consulting Groups, Office of Advocacy, U.S. Small Business Administration, November 2003, pp. 23–24.

101. Nichole L. Torres, "Taking Credit," *Entrepreneur*, June 2005, p. 106.

Chapter 14

1. Roberta Maynard, "A Growing Outlet for Small Firms," *Nation's Business,* August 1996, pp. 45–48; "Guide to the Nation's Best Outlets," Outletbound.com, http://www.outletbound.com/cgi-bin/stores_by_name.cgi?StoreName=Coastal%20Cotton.

2. Mark Henricks, "Hot Spots," *Entrepreneur,* October 2005, pp. 68–74.

3. Michelle Prather, "Hit the Spot," *Business Start-Ups,* April 1999, p. 104.

4. David Worrell, "Move Over," *Entrepreneur*, September 2005, p. 55.

5. "Employee Costs per Hour," Bureau of Labor Statistics, http://stats.bls.gov/news.release/ecec.t07.htm.

6. Rob Swenson, "California Town Wins out over Return to South Dakota, *Argus Leader*, May 19, 2002, http://www.argusleader.com/specialsections/2002/gateway/Sundayarticle1.shtml; "Company Background," Gateway Computers, http://www.gateway.com/about/news_info/company_background.shtml; Tim W. Ferguson, "Sun, Fun, and Ph.D.s, Too," p. 222. *Forbes,* May 31, 1999, pp. 220–233.

7. Mark Henricks, "A Tale of 25 Cities," *Entrepreneur*, October 2000, pp. 86–94.

8. Chris Penttila, "State Your Case," *Entrepreneur*, March 2005, pp. 17–18.

9. Elaine Appleton, "E-Town, USA," *Inc. Technology*, 2000, Number 3, pp. 56–61.

10. Laura Demars, "A Georgia Peach Bests the Big Apple," *CFO,* May 2006, p. 24.

11. Henricks, "Hot Spots," pp. 68–74.

12. Henricks, "Hot Spots," pp. 68–74.

13. "Ask Inc.," *Inc.*, February 2005, p. 44.

14. Richard Breen, "Stax Omega Joins Pelham Party," *GSA Business*, December 27, 2004, pp. 5, 9.

15. "Clusters and Cluster Development," Institute for Strategy and Competitiveness, Harvard Business School, http://www.isc.hbs.edu/econ-clusters.htm.

16. Henricks, "Hot Spots," pp. 68–74.

17. Joel Kotkin, "Here Comes the Neighborhood," *Inc.,* July 2000, pp. 113–123.

18. Paulette Thomas, "Success Demands a Plan for the Future," *Wall Street Journal,* November 1, 2005, p. B6.

19. Richard Breen, "Downtown Greer Serves up More Businesses," *GSA Business,* February 21, 2005, p. 4.

20. Matt Rosenberg, About Reilly's Law of Retail Gravitation, About.com, http://geography.about.com/cs/citiesurbangeo/a/aa041403a.htm; G. I. Thrall and J. C. del Valle, "The Calculation of Retail Market Areas: The Reilly Model," *GeoInfoSystems* Volume 7, No. 4, 1997, pp. 46–49.

21. Judith Potwora, "Who's No. 1?" *Entrepreneur*, December 2004, p. 26; Doug Campbell, "High Tech Down South," *Region Focus,* September 2005, pp. 39–41.

22. Nichole L. Torres, "Cast off the Curse," *Entrepreneur,* December 2005, p. 118.

23. Maynard, "A Growing Outlet for Small Firms," pp. 45–48.

24. Mitchell Pacelle, "More Stores Spurn Malls for Village Square," *Wall Street Journal,* February 16, 1996, p. B1.

25. John C. Stevenson, "Downtown Fixture," *Business,* November 6, 2006, pp. 1, 8–9.

26. Paul Lukas, "Our Malls, Ourselves," *Fortune,* October 18, 2004, pp. 243–256.

27. "Industry Fun Facts," International Council of Shopping Centers, http://www.icsc.org/srch/about/impactofshoppingcenters/Did_You_Know.pdf.

28. "ICSC Shopping Center Definitions," International Council of Shopping Centers, www.icsc.org; Andrew Blum, "The Mall Goes Undercover," *Washington Post,* April 6, 2005, www.slate.com/id/2116246/; Parija Bhatnagar, "It's Not a Mall, It's a Lifestyle Center," *CNN/Money,* January 12, 2005, http://money.cnn.com/2005/01/11news/fortune500/retail_lifestylecenter.

29. Amy Chozick, "As Malls Think Small, Boutiques Get Their Big Chance," *Wall Street Journal,* June 24, 2005, pp. B1–B2.

30. Lukas, "Our Malls, Ourselves," p. 254.

31. "Industry Fun Facts," International Council of Shopping Centers, http://www.icsc.org/srch/about/impactofshoppingcenters/Did_You_Know.pdf.

32. Nichole L. Torres, "No Place Like Home," *Start-Ups,* September 2000, pp. 38–45; "Executive Overview," National Association of Home-Based Business's U.S.A. Home-Based Business Information Superhighway, http://www.usahomebusiness.com/homesite2.htm.

33. Joanne H. Pratt, "Home-Based Business: The Hidden Economy," *Small Business Research Summary,* No. 194, March 2000, U.S. Small Business Administration Office of Advocacy, http://www.sba.gov/ADVO/research/rs194.pdf.

34. Michelle Anton and Jennifer Basye Sander, "The Weekend Entrepreneur," *Entrepreneur,* March 2006, pp. 82–87.

35. Business Incubation FAQ," National Business Incubation Association, http://www.nbia.org/resource_center/bus_inc_facts/index.php.

36. "Business Incubation FAQ," National Business Incubation Association, http://www.nbia.org/resource_center/bus_inc_facts/index.php.

37. "2005 Outstanding Incubator Client: Action Publishing," National Business Incubation Association, December 7, 2005, http://www.nbia.org/awards_showcase/2005/client_action.php.

38. Darren Dahl, "Percolating Profits," *Inc.,* February 2005, pp. 38–40.

39. Marci McDonald, "The Latte Connections," *U.S. News & World Report,* March 20, 1999, pp. 63–66.

40. Laura Tiffany, "The Rules of . . . Retail," *Business Start-Ups,* December 1999, p. 106.

41. Georgia Flight, "Corporate Identity through Architecture," *Business 2.0,* November 2005, pp. 58–60.

42. Tiffany, "The Rules of . . . Retail," p. 106.

43. "Educational Kit," President's Committee on Employment of People with Disabilities, http://www50.pcepd.gov/pcepd/archives/pubs/ek99/wholedoc.htm#decisions.

44. Susanna Hamner, "Filling the Gap," *Business 2.0,* July 2005, p. 30; Matthew Maier, "The Department Store Rises Again," *Business 2.0,* August 2004, pp. 56–57; Ellen Byron, "Rethinking the Men's Department," *Wall Street Journal*, October 8–9, 2005, p. P9.

45. Proposal for an Ergonomics Program Standard," The Occupational Health and Safety Administration, http://www.osha-slc.gov/ergonomics-standard/ergo-faq.html.
46. Melissa J. Perenson, "Straighten Up," *Small Business Computing,* October 1999, pp. 77–80.
47. "Work Week," *Wall Street Journal,* November 16, 1999, p. A1.
48. Shane McLaughlin, "You Put Your Left Foot In," *Inc. Technology,* 1998, No. 2, p. 18.
49. Leigh Gallagher, "Get out of My Face," *Forbes,* October 18, 1999, pp. 105–106.
50. Linda Tischler, "Death to the Cubicle!" *Fast Company,* June 2005, pp, 29–30.
51. Laura Tiffany, "Personal Space," *Entrepreneur,* May 2000, p. 22; Brenda Moore, "We Don't Want to Know What People Wear to Work," *Wall Street Journal,* California Edition, September 29, 1999, p. CA2.
52. Heather Page, "Pedal to the Metal," *Entrepreneur,* August 1996, p. 15.
53. Jennifer Alsever, "Showing Products in a Better Light," *Business 2.0,* September 2005, p. 62.
54. Linda Tischler, "Smells Like a Brand Spirit," *Fast Company,* August 2005, pp. 52–59.
55. Tischler, "Smells Like a Brand Spirit," pp. 52–59.
56. Paul Keegan, "The Architect of Happy Customers," *Business 2.0,* August 2002, pp. 85–87.
57. "Business Bulletin," *Wall Street Journal,* April 15, 1999, p. A1.
58. Jeffrey A, Trachtenberg, "How a Children's Book Got a Christmas Break," *Wall Street Journal,* December 5, 2005, pp. B1, B5.
59. Kenneth Labich, "This Man Is Watching You," *Fortune,* July 19, 1999, pp. 131–134.
60. Colleen Bazdarich, "In the Buying Mood? Maybe It's the Muzak," *Business 2.0,* March 2002, p. 100.
61. Mark Albert, "This Shop Really Shines . . ." *Modern Machine Shop,* January 2004, http://www.findarticles.com/p/articles/ mi_m3101/is_8_76/ai_112862177.

Chapter 15

1. Nichole L. Torres, "Global Trade," *Entrepreneur*, February 2005, p. 120.
2. "Global Executives Brace for Change," *Sales & Marketing Management's Performance e-Newsletter*, January 10, 2005, p. 1.
3. Alan Deutschman, "Attack of the Baby Pixars," *Fast Company*, December 2005, pp. 61–65.
4. Jason Dean and Pui-Wing Tam, "The Laptop Trail," *Wall Street Journal*, June 9, 2005, pp. B1, B8.
5. Elizabeth Wasserman, "Happy Birthday, WTO?" *Inc.*, January 2005, pp. 21–23.
6. "Gayle Warwick Linens," *Forbes FYI*, October 2005, p. 24.
7. Mark Henricks, "The New China?" *Entrepreneur*, February, 2006, pp. 17–18.
8. "Internet Usage Statistics: The Big Picture," Internet World Stats, http://www.internetworldstats.com/stats.htm.
9. Frank Fortunato, "Going Global on eBay," *E-Commerce Guide*, December 6, 2004, www.ecommerce-guide.com/essentials/ebayt/article.php/3568976.
10. Darren Dahl, "Instantly International," *Inc.*, June 2005, p. 44.
11. Claudine Williams, "Searching for the Right Connection," Federation of International Trade Associations, www.fita.org/aotm/1000.html; "History," Johnson Level and Tool, http://www.johnsonlevel.com/history.html.
12. Julia Boorstin, "Small & Global: Exporting Cleaner Air," *FSB*, June 2004, pp. 42–44.
13. Wasserman, "Happy Birthday, WTO?" pp. 21–23.
14. Sufiya Abdur-Rahman, "Betting on 'Blak,'" *Black Enterprise*, April 2005, p. 43; "Hip Hop Comic Goes International," *Comic Book Bin*, July 22, 2005, http://comicbookbin.com/artman/exec/view.cgi/34/2070.
15. Mark Siebert, "Expanding Your Franchise Internationally," *Entrepreneur*, March 27, 2006, www.entrepreneur.com/article/0,4621,327040,00.html; Larry Weinberg, "Best Practices: Structuring an International Franchise Expansion," International Franchise Association, May 12, 2006, www.franchise.org/printarticle.asp?article=1444; "Two Men and a Truck Enter U.K. and Ireland," *Franchise International*, Second Quarter 2006, www.franchise-international.net/franchise/Two-Men-And-A-Truck-enter-UK-and-Ireland/1001?ck=1&s=279e12b7a1af70b89090ab0cdecc3c84.
16. "International Specialty Regional Toppings," Domino's, http://www.dominos.com/Public-EN/Site+Content/Secondary/Inside+Dominos/Pizza+Particulars/International+Speciality+Toppings/.
17. Geoffrey A. Fowler and Ramin Setoodeh, "Outsiders Get Smarter about China's Tastes," *Wall Street Journal*, August 4, 2004, pp. B1, B2; "McDonald's Menu Items," Wikipedia, http://en.wikipedia.org/wiki/McDonald's_menu_items.
18. Wasserman, "Happy Birthday, WTO?" pp. 21–23; C. J. Prince, "Foreign Affairs," *Entrepreneur*, March 2005, pp. 56–58.
19. National Federation of Independent Businesses, *NFIB National Small Business Poll: International Trade* (Washington, DC: Author, 2004), Volume 4, Issue 1, p. 1.
20. Erin Butler, "Making the Most of Trade Missions: Advice from Women Who've Been There (and Back)," *Export America*, April 2002, pp. 8–9.
21. Joseph Zaritski, "15 Tips to Start Successful Export Business," Australian Export Online: Export 61, http://www.export61.com/export-tutorials.asp?ttl=tips.
22. National Federation of Independent Businesses, *NFIB National Small Business Poll: International Trade* (Washington, DC: Author, 2004), Volume 4, Issue 1, p. 4.
23. Butler, "Making the Most of Trade Missions: Advice from Women Who've Been There (and Back)," p. 9.
24. Thelma Young, "Under Secretary of Commerce Phillip Bond Honors Chicago-Area Company for $1 Million Export Sale to South Africa," Technology Administration, June 18, 2003, http://www.technology.gov/PRel/p_pr030618.htm.
25. Marianna Ohe, "AquaTech International Wins Significant Export Contracts, Backed by PNC Working Capital Loan under Ex-Im Bank's New Fast Track Program," Export-Import

Bank, www.exim.gov/pressrelease.cfm/62EC206C-08B3-CDE0-CC9A88613EFDCFF4/.

26. Daniel Kaufmann and Shang-Jin Wei, "Does 'Grease Money' Speed up the Wheels of Commerce?" World Bank, http://www.worldbank.org/wbi/governance/pdf/grease.pdf.

27. Tony Taylor, "Small Businesses Find International Niche," *GSA Business*, May 29, 2006, p. 11; "About Us," Leopard Forest Coffee Company, http://www.leopardforestcoffee.com/about_us.htm.

28. Alessandra Galloni, Cecilie Rohwedder, and Teri Agins, "Breaking a Taboo, High Fashion Starts Making Goods Overseas," *Wall Street Journal*, September 27, 2005, pp. A1, A10.

29. Michael V. Copeland and Andrew Tilin, "Instant Companies: Get Someone to Build It," *Business 2.0*, June 2005, pp. 88–90; Tara Siegel Bernard, "Scooters' Popularity Offers a Chance for Growth," *Wall Street Journal*, September 20, 2005, p. B1.

30. Henricks, "The New China?" pp. 17–18.

31. Joshua Kurlantzick, "On Foreign Soil," *Entrepreneur*, June 2005, p. 92.

32. "Total Merchandise Trade," World Trade Organization, http://stat.wto.org/StatisticalProgram/WSDBViewData.aspx?Language=E.

33. Wasserman, "Happy Birthday, WTO?" pp. 21–23.

34. "Q & A: Chinese Clothes Exports to EU," BBC News, September 5, 2005, http://newsvote.bbc.co.uk/mpapps/pagetools/print/news.bbc.co.uk/1/hi/business/4194474.stm; Grant Nulle, "Bush Battles the Chinese Sock Threat," Ludwig von Mises Institute, December 29, 2005, http://www.mises.org/story/1986#.

35. Jaime Berkheimer, Stacey Cargile, Gabriel Richards, Erika Palsson, and Inbal Shem-Tov, "Issue Guide: Trade Embargoes, Seals, and More," University of California, Irvine, http://darwin.bio.uci.edu/~sustain/issueguides/Embargoes/index.html.

36. Juliane von Reppert-Bismarck, "Treading Softly in Shoe Spat," *Wall Street Journal*, January 10, 2006, p. A12.

37. Lawrence Van Gelder, "It Pays to Watch Words, Gestures While Abroad," *Greenville News*, April 7, 1996, p. 8E.

38. Sandy Asirvatham, "Old World Order," *Success*, October 1998, pp. 73–75.

39. Edward T. Hall, "The Silent Language of Overseas Business," *Harvard Business Review*, May–June 1960, pp. 5–14.

40. Christopher D. Lancette, "Hitting the Spot," *Entrepreneur*, September 1999, p. 40.

41. Scott McCartney, "Teaching Americans How to Behave Abroad," *Wall Street Journal*, April 11, 2006, pp. D1, D4.

42. Aliza Pilar Sherman, "Going Global," *Entrepreneur*, December 2004, p. 34.

43. Sherman, "Going Global," p. 34.

44. Sherman, "Going Global," p. 34.

45. "Trade Facts," Office of the United States Trade Representative, March 2006, http://www.ustr.gov/assets/Document_Library/Fact_Sheets/2006/asset_upload_file242_9156.pdf.

46. Joani Dong, "NAFTA Spells Success for Some Consumer-Oriented Products—with Some Reservations," *AgExporter*, January 2004, pp. 26–27; "History of Palermo's," Palermo's Villa, http://www.palermospizza.com/World/History.aspx.

47. Darren Dahl, "Son of NAFTA!" *Inc.*, July 2005, pp. 26–28.

48. "Benefits to Small and Medium-Sized Exporters," Export.gov, http://www.export.gov/fta/complete/CAFTA/SME_Ben.asp?dName=CAFTA.

49. Elizabeth Esfahani, "Thinking Locally, Succeeding Globally," *Business 2.0*, December 2005, pp. 96–98.

Chapter 16

1. Max DePree, *Leadership Jazz* (New York: Currency Doubleday 1992), pp. 8–9.

2. Francis Huffman, "Taking the Lead," *Entrepreneur*, November 1993, p. 101.

3. Edward Teach, "Suspicious Minds," *CFO*, June 2006, p. 31.

4. Ryan Underwood, "The CEO Next Door," *Fast Company*, September 2005, pp. 64–66; Jeffrey Pfeffer, "A Field Day for Executives," *Business 2.0*, December 2004, p. 88.

5. John Mariotti, "The Role of a Leader," *Industry Week*, February 1, 1999, p. 75.

6. Katrina Brooker, "Southwest Airlines: Can Anyone Replace Herb?" *Fortune*, April 17, 2000, http://www.fortune.com/fortune/fortune500/sou.html; "The Best of Herb Kelleher," *Your Company*, August/September 1999, pp. 60–70; Herb Kelleher, "A Culture of Commitment," *Leader to Leader*, No. 4, Spring 1997, http://www.drucker.org/leaderbooks/l2l/spring97/kelleher.html; Kathleen Melymuka, "Down-to-Earth Technology Helps Make Herb Kelleher's Southwest Airlines a Soaring Success," *Computerworld*, http://www.idg.net/crd_kelleher_10166.html.

7. Bill Breen, "The Clear Leader," *Fast Company*, March 2005, p. 66.

8. Dave Zielinski, "New Ways to Look at Leadership," *Presentations*, June 2005, pp. 26–33.

9. David Meyer, "Nine Recruiting and Selection Tips to Ensure Successful Hiring," About.com, http://humanresources.about.com/od/selectemployees/a/staff_selection_p.htm.

10. "Interpersonal Failure," *Inside Training Newsletter*, September 28, 2005, p. 1.

11. Michael W. Horrigan, "Employment Projections in 2012: Concepts and Context," *Monthly Labor Review*, February 2004, http://www.bls.gov/opub/mlr/2004/02/art1abs.htm.

12. Paula Kaihla, "The Coming Job Boom," *Business 2.0*, September 2003, pp. 97–104.

13. Jennifer Gilbert, "Choosing Wisely," *Sales & Marketing Management*, October 2004, p. 9.

14. Michael Friedenberg, "Prepare Our Children to Succeed or Lead," *Information Week*, April 2005, p. 74.

15. David Meyer, "Nine Recruiting and Selection Tips to Ensure Successful Hiring," About.com, http://humanresources.about.com/od/selectemployees/a/staff_selection_p.htm.

16. Geoff Colvin, "The 100 Best Companies to Work For," *Fortune*, January 20, 2006, p. 102.

17. Arlyn Tobias Gajilan, "Scrap Metal," *FSB*, December 2005/January 2006, pp. 95–96.

18. Karen Southwick, "To Survive: Hire Up," *Forbes ASAP*, April 3, 2000, pp. 117–118.

19. Christopher Caggiano, "Recruiting Secrets of the Smartest Companies Around," *Inc.*, October 1998, http://hiring.inc.com/inc/magazine/19981001/1008.html.

20. Christopher Caggiano, "The Truth about Internet Recruiting," *Inc.*, December 1999, p. 156.

21. Melissa Hennessy, "The Retirement Age," *CFO: Human Capital Issue*, 2006, pp. 43–45.

22. Richard Castellini, "Survey: More to See Pay Increase in 2006," CNN, January 4, 2006, http://www.cnn.com/2006/US/Careers/01/04/cb.aol.survey/index.html.

23. Joe Mullich, "They Don't Retire Them, They Hire Them," *Workforce Management*, December 2003, pp. 49–54.

24. Christopher Caggiano, "Recruiting Secrets," *Inc.*, October 1998, pp. 30–42.

25. Geoff Colvin, "The 100 Best Companies to Work For," *Fortune*, January 20, 2006, pp. 71–74.

26. Aliza Pilar Sherman, "Central Perks," *Entrepreneur*, September 2005, http://www.entrepreneur.com/article/print/0,2361,322834,00.html.

27. Michael Mahoney, "Perfect Match," *FSB*, April 2006, p. 100.

28. Ann Marsh, "Babbling Interviewer Disease," *Business 2.0*, March 2005, p. 54.

29. Kate Bonamici, "The Shoe-in," *Fortune*, January 20, 2006, p. 116.

30. Gwendolyn Bounds, "Handyman Etiquette: Stay Calm, Avert Eyes," *Wall Street Journal*, May 10, 2005, pp. B1, B4.

31. Jill Hecht Maxwell, "Of Resumes and Rap Sheets," *Inc. Technology 2000*, No. 2, p. 27.

32. Kate Bonamici, "Decoding the Dress Code," *Fortune*, January 11, 2006, pp. 130–131.

33. Joanne Gordon, "Management by Black Belt," *Forbes*, February 17, 2003, p. 54.

34. Jennifer Saranow, "Anybody Want to Take a Nap?" *Wall Street Journal*, January 24, 2005, p. R5.

35. Laurie Larson, "Changing Organizational Culture," *Trustee*, April, 2002, pp. 8–12.

36. Damon Darlin, "When Your Start-up Takes Off," *Business 2.0*, May 2005, p. 127.

37. Eleena De Lisser, "Start-up Attracts Staff with a Ban on Midnight Oil," *Wall Street Journal*, August 23, 2000, pp. B1, B6.

38. Nichole L. Torres, "Let the Good Times Roll," *Entrepreneur*, November 2004, p. 57.

39. Jess McCuan, "Mambo for Morale," *Inc.*, March 2005, p. 64.

40. "Fact Sheet: Diversity in the Workforce," Harvard University, 2006, http://www.uos.harvard.edu/diversity/fs_workforce.shtml.

41. Roy Harris, "The Illusion of Inclusion: Why Most Corporate Diversity Efforts Fail," *CFO*, May, 2001, p. 42.

42. "Training That's Easy to Swallow at the Olive Garden," *Inside Training Newsletter*, June 21, 2006, p. 1.

43. Anna Brady, "Small Is As Small Does," *Journal of Business Strategy*," January/February 1996, pp. 44–52.

44. Linda Field, "A Little Leeway Goes a Long Way," *Nation's Business*, November 1998, p. 6.

45. Adina Genn, "Nationwide Survey by Human Resources Group Finds More Employers Using Flextime," *Long Island Business News*, October 15, 2004, http://www.findarticles.com/p/articles/mi_qn4189/is_20041015/ai_n10171237.

46. Harriet Hagestad, "New Ways to Work: Telecommuting and Job Sharing," *Career Builder*, June 23, 2006, http://www.careerbuilder.com/JobSeeker/careerbytes/CBArticle.aspx?articleID=369&cbRecursionCnt=1&cbsid=49944662f7b64dc38639d9a3ef87dd18-204624985-R5-4.

47. Carol Kleiman, "Job Sharing Working Its Way into Mainstream," *Greenville News*, August 6, 2000, p. 3G.

48. "ITAC Press Release: Annual Survey Shows Americans Are Working from Many Different Locations Outside Their Employer's Office," International Telework Association and Council, October 4, 2005, http://www.workingfromanywhere.org/news/pr100405.htm.

49. Harriet Hagestad, "New Ways to Work: Telecommuting and Job Sharing," *Career Builder*, June 23, 1006, http://www.careerbuilder.com/JobSeeker/careerbytes/CBArticle.aspx?articleID=369&cbRecursionCnt=1&cbsid=49944662f7b64dc38639d9a3ef87dd18-204624985-R5-4; Peg Verone, "House Rules," *Success,* July 1998, pp. 22–24.

50. Lin Grensing-Pophal, *Telecommuting: Managing Off-Site Staff for Small Business* (Bellingham: WA: Self-Counsel Press), 2001, p. 9.

51. Gwen Moran, "It's 3:00 pm . . . Do You Know Where Your Telecommuters Are?" *Small Business Computing*, June 1, 2002, http://www.smallbusinesscomputing.com/biztools/print.php/685901.

52. Mark Henricks, "Musical Chairs," *Entrepreneur*, April 1999, pp. 77–79.

53. Tom Taulli, "Start-Ups and Stock Options," *Forbes*, May 16, 2006, http://www.forbes.com/2006/05/15/entrepreneurs-stockoption-google-cx_tt_0516taulli.html.

54. Jacquelyn Lynn, "Rub It In," *Entrepreneur*, September 1999, p. 46; Anne Fisher, "The 100 Best Companies to Work for in America," *Fortune*, January 12, 1998, pp. 69–70; Joann S. Lublin, "Climbing the Walls on Company Time," *Wall Street Journal*, December 1, 1998, pp. B1, B16; Pui-Wing Tam, "Silicon Valley Belatedly Boots up Programs to Ease Employees' Lives," *Wall Street Journal*, August 29, 2000, pp. B1, B14; Quentin Hardy, "Aloft in a Career without Fetters*," Wall Street Journal*, September 29, 1998, pp. B1, B14; Jerry Useem, "Welcome to the New Company Town," *Fortune*, January 10, 2000, pp. 62–70.

55. "Voss Celebrated a Great Year with an Employee Celebration That Included a Surprise Drawing for a Brand New Car," Company News, Voss Industries, http://www.vossind.com/carraffle.html.

56. "Full Recognition Tip," National Association for Employee Recognition, May 2005, http://www.recognition.org/displaycommon.cfm?an=1&subarticlenbr=77.

57. Scott Smith, "Mackay's Way," *Success*, September 2000, p. 16.

58. Ritch L. Sorenson, Keith H. Brigham, Thomas E. Holubik, and Robert L. Phillips, "Predictors of Longevity in Small Family Firms: An Exploratory Study," United States Association for Entrepreneurship and Small Business National Conference, Dallas, Texas, 2004; Facts and Figures," Family Firm Institute, http://www.ffi.org/genTemplate.asp?cid=186#us; Pat Curry, "Measured Steps," *Prosales,*

September 2002, http://www.findarticles.com/p/articles/mi_m0NTC/is_9_14/ai_100962585.

59. "Facts and Figures," Family Firm Institute, http://www.ffi.org/genTemplate.asp?cid=186#us; Pat Curry, "Measured Steps," *Prosales,* September 2002, http://www.findarticles.com/p/articles/mi_m0NTC/is_9_14/ai_100962585; Chris Pentilla, "It's All Relative," *Entrepreneur,* March 2005, pp. 75–77.

60. "Facts and Figures," Family Firm Institute, http://www.ffi.org/genTemplate.asp?cid=186#us; Pat Curry, "Measured Steps," *Prosales,* September 2002, http://www.findarticles.com/p/articles/mi_m0NTC/is_9_14/ai_100962585.

61. "Facts and Figures," Family Firm Institute, http://www.ffi.org/genTemplate.asp?cid=186#us; Pat Curry, "Measured Steps," *Prosales,* September 2002, http://www.findarticles.com/p/articles/mi_m0NTC/is_9_14/ai_100962585.

62. Brian O'Keefe and Julie Schlosser, America's Fastest Growing Sport," *Fortune,* September 5, 2005, pp. 48–64; John Heileman, "Dude, Where's My NASCAR?" *Business 2.0,* April 2005, pp. 32–34.

63. The Arthur Andersen/MassMutual American Family Business Survey, 1997, http://www.massmutual.com/fbn/index.htm.

64. Julie Schlosser, "The Son Rises at Qualcomm," *Fortune,* April 18, 2005, p. 45.

65. Patricia Schiff Estess, "Overnight Succession," *Entrepreneur,* February 1996, pp. 80–83.

66. Woody White, "Planning Eases Transfer of Control of Family Business," *Upstate Business,* October 8, 2000, p. 1.

67. H. G. Stern and Bob Vineyard, "Death of a Salesman (and His Business)," *Insureblog,* December 13, 21, 2005, http://insureblog.blogspot.com/2005/12/death-of-salesman-and-his-business.html; Tim Tresslar, "Jeweler Jaffe Returning to Downtown . . . Temporarily," *Dayton Business Journal,* June 9, 2006, http://dayton.bizjournals.com/dayton/stories/2006/06/12/tidbits1.html.

68. Joan Szabo, "Spreading the Wealth," *Entrepreneur,* July 1997, p. 63.

69. Gay Jervey, "Family Ties," *FSB,* March 2006, p. 60.

70. Gay Jervey, "Family Ties," *FSB,* March 2006, p. 60; Tom Herman, "Court Ruling Bolsters Estate Planning Tool," *Wall Street Journal,* May 27, 2004, p. D1.

71. Emily Nelson and Sarah Ellison, "Hot Pockets Started as Émigré Family Business," *Wall Street Journal,* May 8, 2002, p. B.4.

72. Lori Ioannou, "Keeping the Business All in the Family," *FSB,* November 2001, p. 75.

73. Springfield Remanufacturing Corporation, http://www.screman.com/index/htm.

74. "Largest Study Yet Shows ESOPs Improve Performance and Employee Benefits," National Center for Employee Ownership, http://www.nceo.org/library/esop_perf.html.

Appendix

1. John MacCarthy, et al., *IHRSA's Guide to the Health Club Industry. For Lenders and Investors,* 2nd ed.

2. Ibid., p. 4.

3. Ibid., p. 5.

4. Ibid., p. 5.

5. Ibid., p. 71.

6. Josephine Hearn, "Health Clubs Press for Membership Tax Breaks," *The Hill: The Executive,* 19 May 2005 and 23 February 2006, http://www.hillnews.com/thehill/export/TheHill/News/TheExecutive/051905_health.html.

7. Jim Bauer, "Online Personal Trainers: What Are Your Options?" http://www.askmen.com/sports/bodybuilding_100/146_fitness_tip.html

8. MacCarthy et al., p. 2.

9. MacCarthy et al., p. 1.

10. Bally Total Fitness Web site: https://onyx.ballyfitness.com/join/membership_prices/index.asp?mod=1&page=whybally&section_name=theballymission&source=whybally#video; World Gym Web site: http://www.yourworldgym.com/info/; Curves Web site: http://www.curves.com/.

11. http://www.obesity.org/subs/fastfacts/obesity_US.shtml.

12. Centers for Disease Control and Prevention, "Overweight and Obesity: Obesity Trends: US Obesity Trends 1985–2004," http://www.cdc.gov/nccdphp/dnpa/obesity/ trend/maps/.

13. MacCarthy et al., p. 20.

14. http://www.powerblock.com/homegyms.html.

15. Chadwick's Web site: www.chadwick'straining.com/index.htm.

16. World Gym Web site: www.worldgym.com.

17. "Williamson County Products," *The Tennessean,* http://www.tennessean.com/special/mediakit/WilliamsonProducts.pdf .

18. "Williamson County's Retail Profile," *Williamson Works,* http://www.williamsonworks.com/econindicators.htm.

19. Edwin B. Raskin Company Web site: http://www.raskinco.com/commercial.html.

20. American Fitness Professionals Association Web site: http://www.afpafitness.com/certified.htm.

Photo Credits

Chapter 1, page 11, Surf Diva, Inc.; page 11, Ariat International, Inc.; page 33, © David Turnley/CORBIS All Rights Reserved; page 33, © David Turnley/CORBIS All Rights Reserved.

Chapter 2, page 42, © Freitag; page 42, Freitag Lab. ag; page 50, AP Wide World Photos; page 51, Julie Jacobson/AP Wide World Photos; page 64, Courtesy SBI Enterprises, Inc./FLYBAR.

Chapter 3, page 86, Kimberly White/CORBIS–NY; page 109, Dennis Degnan/CORBIS–NY; page 111, © Cereality Cereal Bar & Cafe.

Chapter 4, page 127, Little Earth Productions, Inc.; page 128, © John Munson/Star Ledger/CORBIS; page 140, First Penthouse Limited.

Chapter 5, page 171, Steve Smith/Getty Images, Inc. – Taxi; page 173, Alan Levenson/CORBIS–NY; page 182, Tom & Dee Ann McCarthy/Corbis/Bettmann.

Chapter 6, page 193, © Taro Yamasaki/Time Life Pictures/
Getty Images, Inc.; page 198, Olivier Vidal/Getty Images, Inc—Liaison; page 209, Lon C. Dhiel/PhotoEdit Inc.

Chapter 7, page 225, Courtesy Clemson University News Services/Tiger News/David Kalk photo; page 250, Rose Prouser/Reuters Limited; page 258, Helen King/COR-BIS–NY.

Chapter 8, page 266, Courtesy Zondervan; page 301, PearlParadise.com; page 302, Peter Zuzga/AP Wide World Photos.

Chapter 9, page 326, Earth Treks, Inc.; page 328, Courtesy Dogbooties.com/Arrowhead Fabric; page 341, © Courtesy Sleepyheads.com.

Chapter 10, page 357, © Courtesy Steaz Green Tea; page 362, © Jeff Christensen/Reuters/Corbis; page 367, Alan Schein/ CORBIS–NY.

Chapter 11, page 392, © Courtesy of Smart Furniture, Inc.; page 402, SuperStock, Inc.; page 404, Richard Morell/CORBIS–NY.

Chapter 12, page 426, Michael Shay/Creative Eye/MIRA.com; page 454, Courtesy Delicato Family Vineyards; page 455, © Courtesy of Debra M. Cohen.

Chapter 13, page 471, Will Powers/AP Wide World Photos; page 493, Jeff Salter/Redux Pictures; page 494, Christopher Covatta.

Chapter 14, page 525, Robert Landau/CORBIS–NY; page 534, Guy Gillette/Getty Images/Time Life Pictures; page 537, © Owen Franken/CORBIS; page 551, Gerry Broome/AP Wide World Photos; page 551, Jennifer Graylock/AP Wide World Photos;

Chapter 15, page 569, Folio/Omni–Photo Communications, Inc.; page 570, Vatican Museums and Galleries, Vatican City, Italy/The Bridgeman Art Library; 574, Courtesy of Street Legends Ink; page 575, Douglas E. Curran/Getty Images, Inc.—Agence France Presse.

Chapter 16, page 608, Pearson Learning Photo Studio; page 615, George Nikitin/AP Wide World Photos; page 627, © Bettmann/CORBIS All Rights Reserved; page 627, Jonathan Ferrey/Getty Images.

Appendix, page 640, Ron Edmonds/AP Wide World Photos; page 641, BSIP/Phototake NYC; page 641, William Thomas Cain/Getty Images.

Name Index

Subject Index